1,000,000 Books

are available to read at

---◆---

www.ForgottenBooks.com

---◆---

Read online
Download PDF
Purchase in print

ISBN 978-0-265-03216-9
PIBN 10958114

1 MONTH OF
FREE
READING

at

www.ForgottenBooks.com

English
Français
Deutsche
Italiano
Español
Português

www.forgottenbooks.com

Mythology Photography **Fiction**
Fishing Christianity **Art** Cooking
Essays Buddhism Freemasonry
Medicine **Biology** Music **Ancient**
Egypt Evolution Carpentry Physics
Dance Geology **Mathematics** Fitness
Shakespeare **Folklore** Yoga Marketing
Confidence Immortality Biographies
Poetry **Psychology** Witchcraft
Electronics Chemistry History **Law**
Accounting **Philosophy** Anthropology
Alchemy Drama Quantum Mechanics
Atheism Sexual Health **Ancient History**
Entrepreneurship Languages Sport
Paleontology Needlework Islam
Metaphysics Investment Archaeology
Parenting Statistics Criminology
Motivational

ACT

APPROVED BY THE PEOPLE, NOVEMBER 8, 1932

(CHAPTER 310, ACTS OF 1932)

AND

ACTS AND RESOLVES

PASSED BY THE

General Court of Massachusetts

IN THE YEAR

1933

TOGETHER WITH

RETURNS OF VOTES UPON CONSTITUTIONAL AMENDMENT AND
QUESTIONS SUBMITTED TO VOTERS, TABLES SHOWING
CHANGES IN THE STATUTES, ETC.

PUBLISHED BY THE
SECRETARY OF THE COMMONWEALTH.

BOSTON
THE JORDAN & MORE PRESS
1933

CHAPTER 310.

The Commonwealth of Massachusetts

In the Year One Thousand Nine Hundred and Thirty-two.

AN ACT RELATIVE TO STATE AND PARTY PRIMARIES AND CONVENTIONS OF POLITICAL PARTIES. *Chap.*310

Be it enacted by the People, and by their authority:

SECTION 1. Section one of chapter fifty-two of the General Laws, as amended by section one of chapter twenty-five and chapter two hundred and ninety-five of the acts of nineteen hundred and twenty-seven, is hereby further amended by inserting, in the seventh line, after the word "the" the word: — party, — by striking out, in the tenth line, the word "committee" and inserting in place thereof the words: — state convention, — and by striking out, in the eleventh line, the words "the state" and inserting in place thereof the word: — said, — so as to read as follows: — *Section 1.* Each political party shall, in the manner herein provided, elect from among its enrolled members a state committee, the members of which shall hold office for two years from January first next following their election and until their successors shall have organized. Said committee shall consist of one member from each senatorial district, to be elected at the party primaries before each biennial state election by plurality vote of the members of his party in the district, and such number of members at large as may be fixed by the state convention, to be elected at said convention. *(margin: G. L. 52, § 1, etc., amended.)*

(margin: State committees. Election, terms, etc.)

The members of the state committee shall, in January following their election, meet and organize by the choice of a chairman, a secretary, a treasurer and such other officers as they may decide to elect. *(margin: Organization.)*

The secretary of the state committee shall, within ten days after such organization, file with the state secretary, and send to each city and town committee, a list of the members of the committee and of its officers. *(margin: Filing with state secretary, etc., of members, etc.)*

A vacancy in the office of chairman, secretary or treasurer of the committee or in the membership thereof shall be filled by the committee, and a statement of any such change shall be filed as in the case of the officers first chosen. *(margin: Vacancies, how filled.)* *(margin: Filing of statement of changes.)*

SECTION 2. Section two of said chapter fifty-two, as amended by section one of chapter one hundred and fourteen of the acts of nineteen hundred and twenty-five and by section two of chapter twenty-five of the acts of *(margin: G. L. 52, § 2, etc., amended.)*

nineteen hundred and twenty-seven, is hereby further amended by inserting, in the second line, after the word "the" the word: — party, — so as to read as follows: —

Ward and town committees, election, terms, etc.

Section 2. Each political party shall, in every ward and town, elect at the party primaries before each biennial state election from among the enrolled members of the party a committee to be called a ward or town committee, whose members shall hold office for two years from January first following their election and until their successors shall have organized, except as provided in section seven.

G. L. 52, § 9, etc., amended.

SECTION 3. Section nine of said chapter fifty-two, as amended by chapter one hundred of the acts of nineteen hundred and twenty-six, is hereby further amended by striking out, in the second and third lines, the words "delegates to the state convention, not less than one for each ward or town" and inserting in place thereof the words: — district delegates and the number of district alternate delegates, not less than one from each congressional district, and the number of delegates and alternate delegates at large, to the national convention, — and by striking out, in the eighth line, the word "August" and inserting in place thereof the word: — March, — so as to read as follows: — *Section 9.* The state committee shall fix the number of district delegates and the number of district alternate delegates, not less than one from each congressional district, and the number of delegates and alternate delegates at large, to the national convention. City and town committees shall fix the number of members of ward and town committees, not less than three for each ward or town. Notice of the number of delegates and members of committees to be elected shall be given by the state, city or town committee, as the case may be, to the state secretary on or before March first. In case a city or town committee fails to fix the number of the members of a ward or town committee and to give notice thereof as aforesaid to the state secretary, the number of members of such a ward or town committee to be elected shall not exceed ten.

Number of delegates to national convention.

Number of members of ward and town committees.

Notice to state secretary.

Maximum numerical membership of committees in certain cases.

G. L. 53, § 2, amended.

SECTION 4. Section two of chapter fifty-three of the General Laws is hereby amended by inserting, in the second line, after the word "provided" the words: — and except as provided by section fifty-four, — so as to read as follows: — *Section 2.* Except in the case of municipal nominations where city or town charters otherwise provide and except as provided in section fifty-four, candidates of political parties for all elective offices, except presidential elector, shall be nominated, and members of political committees and delegates to conventions shall be elected, in primaries or caucuses, and the nomination of any party other than a political party, in any district containing more than one ward or town, shall be made by a convention of delegates chosen by caucuses held under section one hundred and seventeen in the wards and towns of the district for which

Nominations, how made.

the nomination is to be made. All nominations and elections in primaries and caucuses shall be by direct plurality vote. No candidate shall be nominated, or political committee or convention delegate elected, in any other manner than is herein provided.

SECTION 5. Section twenty-eight of said chapter fifty-three, as amended by chapter ninety-six of the acts of nineteen hundred and twenty-six, is hereby further amended by striking out, in the fifth line, the word "presidential" and inserting in place thereof the word: — party, — so as to read as follows: — *Section 28.* State primaries shall be held on the seventh Tuesday preceding state elections, city primaries on the third Tuesday preceding city elections, town primaries on the second Tuesday preceding town elections, and party primaries on the last Tuesday in April; except that primaries before a special election shall be held on the second Tuesday preceding the special election. *(G. L. 53, § 28, etc., amended. Days and places of holding primaries.)*

Except in Boston, they shall be held wholly or partly by wards, precincts or towns, as the aldermen or selectmen may designate.

SECTION 6. Section thirty-two of said chapter fifty-three is hereby amended by striking out, in the second and fifth lines, the word "presidential" and inserting in place thereof the word: — party, — so as to read as follows: — *Section 32.* Ballots shall be prepared and provided, and the number thereof determined, in state and party primaries by the state secretary, in city and town primaries by the city or town clerk. No other ballots shall be received or counted, except that if ballots provided for a state or party primary are not delivered, or after delivery lost, destroyed or stolen, ballots similar as far as possible shall be provided by the city or town clerk and used at the primary. The number of ballots provided at a city or town primary shall not for any ward or town exceed one ballot of each party for each voter therein. No such ballots shall be printed in any printing establishment owned or managed by the city of Boston. *(G. L. 53, § 32, amended. Ballots for primaries, preparation and number.)*

SECTION 7. Section thirty-four of said chapter fifty-three, as amended by section one of chapter three hundred and two of the acts of nineteen hundred and twenty-three and section one of chapter three hundred and twelve of the acts of nineteen hundred and twenty-five, is hereby further amended by striking out said section and inserting in place thereof the following: — *Section 34.* At the top of each ballot shall be printed the words "Official ballot of the (here shall follow the party name)". On the back of each ballot when folded shall be printed the same words, followed by the number of the precinct and ward or the name of the town for which the ballot is prepared, the date of the primary and for state or party primaries a facsimile of the signature of the state secretary and for city or town primaries a facsimile of the signature of the city or town *(G. L. 53, § 34, etc., amended. Ballots, substance, arrangement and form.)*

clerk. Names of candidates for each elective office and for delegates to state conventions and for members of state committees shall be arranged alphabetically according to their surnames, except that names of candidates endorsed for nomination by a state convention shall be placed first and names of other candidates shall follow in alphabetical order.

Names of candidates for delegates to national conventions shall be arranged under separate headings, and in the following order, the names of candidates for delegates at large, alternate delegates at large, district delegates, and alternate district delegates. The names of candidates appearing in nomination papers containing nominations for all the places to be filled shall be placed first on said ballot, arranged in groups and in the same order as in the nomination papers. The names of candidates appearing in nomination papers containing nominations for less than all the places to be filled shall follow, alphabetically arranged. The ballot shall also contain a statement of the preference, if any, of each candidate for delegate as to a candidate for nomination for president, provided that such statement appears in his nomination papers; but no such statement of preference by any candidate for delegate shall appear upon the ballot unless such candidate for nomination for president files his written assent thereto with the state secretary on or before five o'clock in the afternoon of the last day for filing nomination papers. Such assent may be communicated by telegraph.

Names of candidates for ward or town committees and for delegates to national conventions shall be arranged in groups in such order as may be determined by lot, under the direction of the state secretary, who shall notify each state committee and give a representative of each such committee an opportunity to be present. When necessary, groups may be printed on the ballot in two or more columns.

Against the name of a candidate for an elective office, for a ward or town committee or for a member of a state committee shall be printed the street and number, if any, of his residence.

Against the name of a candidate for an elective office shall be printed the statement contained in the nomination paper placing him in nomination, or, if endorsed for nomination by a state convention, the statement, — "Endorsed for nomination by (name of political party) convention", — together with the eight word statement authorized by section forty-five.

No names shall be printed on a ballot other than those endorsed for nomination by state conventions and those presented on nomination papers. Immediately following the names of candidates, blank spaces equal to the number of persons to be chosen shall be provided for the insertion of other names.

The number of persons to be voted for for the different offices shall be stated on the ballot.

The form of ballots and the arrangement of printed matter thereon shall be in general the same as that of the official state ballots, except as otherwise provided in this chapter.

Section 8. Section thirty-five of said chapter fifty-three, as amended by section two of chapter three hundred and two of the acts of nineteen hundred and twenty-three and section two of chapter three hundred and twelve of the acts of nineteen hundred and twenty-five, is hereby further amended by striking out, in the fourth line, the word "state" and inserting in place thereof the word: — national, — so as to read as follows: — *Section 35.* A cross (X) marked against a name shall constitute a vote for the person so designated. A cross in the circle at the head of a group of candidates for a ward or town committee or for delegates to a national convention shall count as a vote for each candidate therein. A voter may vote for one or more candidates in any such group by marking a cross against the name of each such candidate, or he may insert another name and mark a cross against it. If he votes for more candidates than the number to be elected, his vote shall not be counted.

Section 9. Section forty-one of said chapter fifty-three is hereby amended by striking out said section and inserting in place thereof the following: —

PROVISIONS APPLYING TO STATE AND PARTY PRIMARIES.

Section 41. State primaries shall be held for the nomination of candidates of political parties for all offices to be filled at a state election, except presidential elector. Party primaries shall be held for the election of district members of state committees, members of ward and town committees, delegates to state conventions of political parties, and, in years in which presidential electors are to be elected, delegates and alternate delegates to the national conventions of political parties. Such nominations and elections shall be by direct plurality vote. Sections forty-two to fifty-three A, inclusive, shall apply to state and party primaries only.

Section 10. Section forty-two of said chapter fifty-three is hereby amended by striking out, in the fourth line, the word "August" and inserting in place thereof the word: — March, — so as to read as follows: — *Section 42.* In cities or towns where the aldermen or selectmen determine the question of holding primaries by wards, precincts, or groups of precincts, they shall give notice of their determination to the state secretary on or before March first; except that in case of primaries before special elections they shall give such notice at least fourteen days before the primaries.

Section 11. Section forty-three of said chapter fifty-three is hereby amended by striking out, in the first line,

Margin notes:
G. L. 53, § 35, etc., amended.
A cross to constitute a vote, etc.
G. L. 53, § 41, amended.
State and party primaries.
Sections applicable.
G. L. 53, § 42, amended.
Notice to state secretary that primaries will be held by wards, precincts, or groups of precincts.
G. L. 53, § 43, amended.

When polls shall be open.

the word "state" so as to read as follows: — *Section 43.* The polls at every primary shall be open during such hours, not less than nine in cities or two in towns, as may be designated by the aldermen in cities, and in towns by by-law or vote, or, in default of such by-law or vote, by the selectmen.

G. L. 53, § 44, etc., amended.

SECTION 12. Section forty-four of said chapter fifty-three, as amended by chapter one hundred and thirty-five of the acts of nineteen hundred and twenty-nine, is hereby further amended by striking out said section and inserting in place thereof the following: — *Section 44.* The nomina-

Nomination papers, number of signatures.

tion of candidates for nomination at state primaries shall be by nomination papers or by endorsement for nomination by state convention as provided in section fifty-four. The nomination of candidates for election at party primaries shall be by nomination papers only. In the case of offices to be filled by all the voters of the commonwealth nomination papers shall be signed in the aggregate by at least one thousand voters, not more than two hundred and fifty to be from any one county. Such papers for all other offices to be filled at a state election, and for members of committees and delegates to conventions, shall be signed by a number of voters equal in the aggregate to five voters for each ward or town in the district or county, but in no case shall more than two hundred and fifty be required.

G. L. 53, § 45, amended.

SECTION 13. Section forty-five of said chapter fifty-three is hereby amended by striking out, in the fifteenth line, the words "the state convention" and inserting in place thereof the word: — conventions, — so as to read

Same subject. Contents, qualifications of signers, acceptance, number of candidates.

as follows: — *Section 45.* Every nomination paper shall state, in addition to the name of the candidate, (1) his residence, with street and number thereof, if any, (2) the office for which he is nominated, (3) the political party whose nomination he seeks, and, except for candidates for ward and town committees and delegates to conventions the paper may state, in not more than eight words, the public offices which he holds or has held, and, if he is an elected incumbent of an office for which he seeks renomina-tion, that he is a candidate for such renomination.

Signatures shall be subject to section seven, and every voter may sign as many nomination papers for each office as there are persons to be nominated for or elected thereto, and no more.

A nomination paper shall be valid only in respect to a candidate whose written acceptance is thereon.

No nomination paper shall contain the name of more than one candidate, except in the case of delegates to conventions and members of ward and town committees.

G. L. 53, § 47, amended.

SECTION 14. Section forty-seven of said chapter fifty-three is hereby amended by striking out, in the second line,

Same subject. Preparation, etc.

the word "state", — so as to read as follows: — *Section 47.* Nomination papers for use in the nomination of candidates to be voted for at primaries shall be prepared, and on request furnished, by the state secretary.

SECTION 15. Section forty-eight of said chapter fifty-three is hereby amended by striking out, at the beginning of the second line, the word "state", — so as to read as follows: — *Section 48.* All nomination papers of candidates to be voted for at primaries shall be filed with the state secretary on or before the fifth Tuesday preceding the day of the primaries; except in the case of primaries before special elections, when nomination papers shall be filed on or before the second Tuesday preceding the day of the primaries. *G. L. 53, § 48, amended. Same subject. Last day for filing.*

SECTION 16. Section forty-nine of said chapter fifty-three is hereby amended by striking out said section and inserting in place thereof the following: — *Section 49.* If a person nominated to be voted for at a primary as a candidate for nomination for a public office or for election as a member of a political committee, dies before the day of the primary, or withdraws his name from nomination, or is found ineligible, and there is no other candidate of the same party for such nomination or election at such primary, the vacancy may be filled by the state committee, if the candidate is one to be voted for by all the voters of the commonwealth; and, in the case of candidates for nomination or election in a district, by the members of the ward and town committees in the wards and towns comprising the district. In case of the death, withdrawal or ineligibility of a candidate for delegate to a national convention, the vacancy may be filled in any manner which is clearly provided for on the nomination paper placing such candidate in nomination, before the signature of any voter is entered thereon, otherwise the remaining candidate or candidates nominated by the same nomination paper may fill the vacancy. Notice of the filling of such a vacancy shall be given by filing in the office of the state secretary, within the time provided by section fifty, a statement signed by the person or persons authorized to fill the vacancy, giving the name and residence of the candidate nominated, accompanied by his written acceptance. *G. L. 53, § 49, amended. Vacancies in case of death, withdrawal or ineligibility, how filled. Notice to state secretary.*

SECTION 17. Section fifty-one of said chapter fifty-three, as amended by chapter twenty-nine of the acts of nineteen hundred and twenty-five, is hereby further amended by striking out, in the fifth and sixth lines, the word "state", — so as to read as follows: — *Section 51.* The provisions of section one hundred and five of chapter fifty-four authorizing the opening of the ballot box at elections in towns, the taking therefrom of the ballots and counting thereof, prior to the closing of the polls, shall apply to primaries in towns. No ballots cast at a primary in cities shall be counted until the close of the polls. *G. L. 53, § 51, etc., amended. Counting of ballots.*

SECTION 18. Section fifty-two of said chapter fifty-three is hereby amended by striking out, in the first line, the word "state", by inserting, in the fourth line, after the word *G. L. 53, § 52, amended.*

"as" the words: — delegates to national and state conventions of political parties and as, — by inserting, in the eighth line, after the word "as" the words: — delegates to national and state conventions and as, — and by striking out, in the ninth and tenth lines, the words "delegates to state conventions and", — so as to read as follows: —

Canvass and returns of votes, etc. *Section 52.* Upon receipt of the records of votes cast at primaries the city or town clerk shall forthwith canvass the same and within four days after said primary make return of the votes for candidates for nomination for state offices, and for election as delegates to national and state conventions of political parties and as members of the state committee, to the state secretary, who shall forthwith canvass such returns, determine the results thereof, notify the successful candidates, and certify to the state committees the names of the persons nominated for state offices and elected as delegates to national and state conventions and as members of state committees. Said clerks shall determine the results of the vote for members of ward and town committees, issue proper certificates thereof to the successful candidates, and notify the chairmen of the city and town committees of the respective parties.

G. L. 53, § 53, amended.
Vacancies caused by ties or in delegations or committees, how filled. SECTION 19. Section fifty-three of said chapter fifty-three is hereby amended by striking out said section and inserting in place thereof the following: — *Section 53.* In case of a tie vote where the number of persons receiving equal votes exceeds the number of nominations available, there shall be deemed to be a vacancy. If the tie is between candidates for an office to be filled by all the voters of the commonwealth, the vacancy shall be filled by the state committee. If the tie is between candidates for nomination for any other office, the vacancy shall be filled by the members of the ward and town committees in the district for which the nomination is to be made. If there is a tie vote for delegates to a convention, such vacancy shall be filled by the delegates elected from the district, except that, if no delegate is elected, or if the delegates elected fail to make a choice within ten days, the vacancy shall be filled by the state committee. Notice of any action taken relative to filling such vacancy shall be given to the state secretary.

If there is a tie for members of a ward or town committee, the members elected shall fill the vacancy.

All vacancies caused by ties shall be filled only by the choice of one of the candidates receiving the tie vote.

G. L. 53, § 53A, amended.
Objections to nominations. SECTION 20. Section fifty-three A of said chapter fifty-three, being section three of chapter twenty-four of the acts of nineteen hundred and twenty-seven, is hereby amended by striking out, in the first line, the word "state" and by striking out, in the fifth and eighth lines, the word "such" and inserting in place thereof the word: — the, — so as to read as follows: — *Section 53A.* When nominations at the primaries are in apparent conformity with law, they

shall be valid unless written objections thereto are filed
with the state secretary within six days succeeding five
o'clock in the afternoon of the day of holding the primaries;
and such objections and all other questions relating thereto
shall be subject to section twelve, so far as applicable. A `Withdrawals of nominees.`
person nominated at the primaries may withdraw his name
from nomination by a request signed and duly acknowledged by him and filed with the state secretary within the
time prescribed in this section for filing objections to such
nominations.

SECTION 21. Section fifty-four of said chapter fifty-three `G. L. 53, § 54, amended.`
is hereby amended by striking out said section and inserting
in place thereof the following: —

PROVISIONS APPLYING TO PRE-PRIMARY CONVENTIONS.

Section 54. A political party shall, upon the call of its `Pre-primary conventions.`
state committee, but not later than June fifteenth, in a year
in which a biennial state election is held, hold a state convention for the purpose of adopting a platform, electing
such number of members at large of the state committee
as may be fixed by the convention, nominating presidential
electors and endorsing for nomination candidates for offices
to be filled by all the voters of the commonwealth, to be
voted for at the ensuing state primary, and for such other
purposes consistent with law as the convention may
determine. Such convention shall consist of the delegates
elected at the party primary as hereinbefore provided.
The number of delegates shall be one from each ward and
town and one additional for every fifteen hundred votes, or
major fraction thereof, above the first fifteen hundred
votes cast at the preceding biennial state election in such
ward or town for the political party candidate for governor.
In case of a vacancy occurring for any reason except a tie
vote such vacancy shall not be filled. Nothing herein
contained shall affect or diminish the operation of the
laws relating to state primaries contained in sections forty-
one to fifty-three A, inclusive.

SECTION 22. Said chapter fifty-three is hereby further `G. L. 53, new sections after § 54.`
amended by inserting, after section fifty-four, the two
following new sections: —

Section 54A. Every certificate of nomination of can- `Certificates of nomination of candidates endorsed by a state convention, contents.`
didates endorsed for nomination by a state convention
shall state that the nominee has been endorsed for nomination at such convention and shall include such facts as
are required by section eight. Such certificates shall be
signed, sworn to and filed as required by section five.

Each such candidate shall within ten days from the day `Written acceptance to be filed with state secretary.`
when the convention terminates file with the state secretary
his written acceptance of the nomination, otherwise his
name shall not be printed on the ballot as a candidate for
the office to which he was nominated, and he may add the
eight word statement authorized by section forty-five.
Such candidate may not withdraw such acceptance.

Section 54B. Delegates shall be seated in groups by senatorial districts. The convention shall be called to order by the chairman or acting chairman of the state committee, or in the absence of either then by a person designated in such manner as the rules of the party shall prescribe. The person who calls the convention to order shall preside until the election of a permanent chairman. He shall appoint a temporary secretary to receive the roll of the convention and a monitor from each group who shall receive the credentials of delegates and present them to the temporary secretary.

The convention shall not proceed to the election of a permanent chairman or transact any business until the time fixed for the opening thereof nor until a majority of the delegates named in the official roll shall be present. It shall then elect from among its delegates a permanent chairman and a permanent secretary, neither of whom shall be an officer of the state committee, and shall complete its organization. It shall make suitable rules for the conduct of its business, the order of which shall follow the purposes of the convention as stated in section fifty-four. The permanent secretary shall keep the records of the convention and transmit the same to the state secretary who shall retain them for a period of one year.

The permanent chairman and permanent secretary shall be chosen upon a call of the official roll. Committees of the convention shall be appointed by the convention, or by the permanent chairman, as the convention may order. When the vote of the convention is taken upon the election, nomination or endorsement for nomination of any candidate, the roll of the delegates shall be called and each delegate when his name is called shall arise in his place and announce his choice, except that when there is only one candidate to be voted for the roll need not be called, and except also that the monitor of a group, unless a member of the group objects, may announce the vote of such group.

SECTION 23. Said chapter fifty-three is hereby further amended by striking out sections sixty-five to seventy, inclusive, and the heading "PROVISIONS APPLYING TO PRESIDENTIAL PRIMARIES" preceding said section sixty-five.

OFFICE OF THE SECRETARY, BOSTON, November 30, 1932.

I hereby certify that the foregoing law entitled "An Act Relative to State and Party Primaries and Conventions of Political Parties" was approved by the People at the State Election held on November 8, 1932, pursuant to the provisions of Article XLVIII of the Amendments to the Constitution.

F. W. COOK,
Secretary of the Commonwealth.

ACTS AND RESOLVES

OF

MASSACHUSETTS

1933

☞ The General Court, which was chosen November 8, 1932, assembled on Wednesday, the fourth day of January, 1933, for its first annual session.

The oaths of office were taken and subscribed by His Excellency JOSEPH B. ELY and His Honor GASPAR G. BACON on Thursday, the fifth day of January, in the presence of the two Houses assembled in convention.

ACTS.

AN ACT REVIVING THE COLUMBIA COUNTER COMPANY.

Whereas, The deferred operation of this act would tend to defeat its purpose, therefore it is hereby declared to be an emergency law, necessary for the immediate preservation of the public convenience.

Be it enacted by the Senate and House of Representatives in General Court assembled, and by the authority of the same, as follows:

Emergency preamble.

The Columbia Counter Company, a corporation dissolved by chapter two hundred and seventy-three of the acts of nineteen hundred and twenty-eight, is hereby revived for a period of six months from the date of enactment hereof, with the same powers, duties and obligations as if said chapter had not been passed.

Columbia Counter Company revived.

Approved January 24, 1933.

AN ACT RELATIVE TO THE TAKING OF STRIPED BASS FROM THE WATERS OF PARKER RIVER AND ITS TRIBUTARIES WITHIN THE TOWNS OF NEWBURY, ROWLEY, GEORGETOWN AND GROVELAND, BY MEANS OF BOWED NETS.

Be it enacted, etc., as follows:

SECTION 1. Between the effective date of this act and April first next succeeding, and between December first of the current year and April first in the year nineteen hundred and thirty-four, the selectmen of the towns of Newbury, Rowley, Georgetown and Groveland may grant permits authorizing the taking of striped bass from the waters of Parker river and its tributaries within the limits of their respective towns, by means of bowed nets, under such regulations as they may deem advisable; provided, that the mesh of such a net shall not be less than three and one half inches, and that bass less than fifteen inches in length so taken shall be immediately returned alive to the water whence taken. Any person taking striped bass during said period from said waters by means of bowed nets shall not be subject to the provisions of section forty-nine of chapter one hundred and thirty-one of the General Laws if such bass are taken as authorized hereunder, otherwise he shall be subject to such provisions.

Taking of striped bass from waters of Parker river, etc., within certain towns, by means of bowed nets authorized during certain period.

Proviso.

SECTION 2. This act shall take effect upon its passage.

Approved February 3, 1933.

Chap. 3 An Act RELATIVE TO THE RENEWAL OF CERTAIN TEMPORARY REVENUE LOANS BY CITIES AND TOWNS.

Emergency
preamble.]

Whereas, The deferred operation of this act would, in part, defeat its purpose, therefore it is hereby declared to be an emergency law, necessary for the immediate preservation of the public convenience.

Be it enacted, etc., as follows:

1932, 303,
amended.

Chapter three hundred and three of the acts of nineteen hundred and thirty-two is hereby amended by striking out, in the seventh line, the word "or" and inserting in place thereof a comma, — and by inserting after the word "thirty-two" in the seventh and eighth lines the words: — or nineteen hundred and thirty-three, — so as to read as

Renewal of
certain tem-
porary revenue
loans by cities
and towns.

follows: — Any city or town, with the approval of the board specified in clause nine of section eight of chapter forty-four of the General Laws, may extend, for a period or periods not exceeding in the aggregate six months beyond the maximum term provided by law for an original revenue loan, any loan issued in anticipation of the revenue of the year nineteen hundred and thirty-one, nineteen hundred and thirty-two or nineteen hundred and thirty-three, and the approval as aforesaid of any such extension shall authorize the issue of renewal notes for the period or periods so approved, notwithstanding the provisions of said chapter forty-four. During the time that any such revenue loan, extended as aforesaid, remains outstanding, none of the receipts from the collection of taxes assessed by such city or town for the year against the revenue of which such loan was issued or for prior years shall be appropriated for any purpose without the approval of the board.

Approved February 3, 1933.

Chap. 4 An Act AUTHORIZING THE TOWN OF KINGSTON TO ACQUIRE GROUND WATER SOURCES OF SUPPLY AND RATIFYING CERTAIN ACTION TAKEN BY SAID TOWN IN RELATION THERETO.

Be it enacted, etc., as follows:

1885, 239, § 2,
amended.

SECTION 1. Section two of chapter two hundred and thirty-nine of the acts of eighteen hundred and eighty-five is hereby amended by inserting after the word "spring" in the third line the following: — , or of any ground water sources of supply by means of driven, artesian or other wells, — so as to read as follows: — *Section 2.* The said

Town of King-
ston may take
waters within
town limits.

town for the purposes aforesaid may take, by purchase or otherwise, and hold the waters of any pond, stream or spring, or of any ground water sources of supply by means of driven, artesian or other wells, within the limits of said town, and the water rights connected therewith, and also all lands, rights of way and easements necessary for hold-

ing and preserving such water, and for conveying the same
to any part of said town of Kingston; and may erect on
the land thus taken or held proper dams, buildings, fixtures
and other structures; and may make excavations, procure
and operate machinery, and provide such other means and
appliances as may be necessary for the establishment and
maintenance of complete and effective water works; and
may construct and lay down conduits, pipes and other
works, under or over any lands, water courses, railroads,
or public or private ways, and along any such way, in such
manner as not unnecessarily to obstruct the same; and
for the purpose of constructing, maintaining and repairing
such conduits, pipes and other works, and for all proper
purposes of this act, said town may dig up any such lands,
and, under the direction of the board of selectmen of the
town in which any such ways are situated, may enter upon
and dig up any such ways in such manner as to cause the
least hindrance to public travel on such ways.

SECTION 2. Said chapter two hundred and thirty- 1885, 239, new
nine is hereby further amended by inserting after section §2.
two the following new section: — *Section 2A.* No source Advice and
of water supply and no lands necessary for protecting and department of
preserving the quality of the water shall be taken under public health.
this act or used without first obtaining the advice and approval of the department of public health, and the location
of all dams, reservoirs and wells to be used as sources of
water supply under this act shall be subject to the approval
of said department.

SECTION 3. All action taken by the town of Kings- Certain action
ton in acquiring lands and taking water therefrom by validated and
means of driven, artesian or other wells, if otherwise valid, confirmed.
is hereby validated and confirmed to the same extent as
if section one of this act had then been in effect.

SECTION 4. This act shall take effect upon its passage.
Approved February 7, 1933.

AN ACT RELATIVE TO VALUATION OF CERTAIN SECURITIES *Chap.* 5
HELD BY INSURANCE COMPANIES OTHER THAN LIFE.

Whereas, The deferred operation of this act would tend Emergency
to defeat its purpose, therefore it is hereby declared to be preamble.
an emergency law, necessary for the immediate preservation of the public convenience.

Be it enacted, etc., as follows:

Section eleven of chapter one hundred and seventy- G. L. (Ter.
five of the General Laws, as appearing in the Tercentenary §11, amended.
Edition thereof, is hereby amended by striking out, in the
twenty-second line, the word "life", — so that the third
paragraph will read as follows: — He may value all bonds Valuation of
or other evidences of debt having a fixed term and rate ties held by
held by a company, if amply secured and not in default panies other
as to principal or interest, as follows: if purchased at than life.

.par, at the par value; if purchased above or below par, on the basis of the purchase price adjusted so as to bring the value to par at maturity and so as to yield meantime the effective rate of interest at which the purchase was made; *Provisos.* provided, that the purchase price shall in no case be taken at a higher figure than the actual market value when purchased; and provided, further, that the commissioner shall have full discretion in determining the method of calculating values according to the foregoing rule, and the values found by him in accordance with such method shall be final and binding; provided, also, that any such company may return such bonds or other evidences of debt at their market value or their book value, but in no event at an aggregate value exceeding the aggregate of the values calculated according to the foregoing rule.

Approved February 7, 1933.

Chap. 6 AN ACT RELATIVE TO THE RANK OF OFFICERS OF THE NATIONAL GUARD ON THE RETIRED LIST.

Be it enacted, etc., as follows:

G. L. (Ter. Ed.), 33, § 98, amended.

Rank of officers of the national guard on the retired list.

Section ninety-eight of chapter thirty-three of the General Laws, as appearing in the Tercentenary Edition thereof, is hereby amended by adding at the end thereof the following: —Nothing in this section shall authorize the placing of any officer on the retired list with a rank higher than that of major general. ˙ *Approved February 7, 1933.*

Chap. 7 AN ACT AUTHORIZING THE TOWN OF DANA TO USE, FOR MAINTENANCE PURPOSES OR IN REDUCTION OF THE TAX LEVY, CERTAIN MONEYS RECEIVED AS LAND DAMAGES FROM THE COMMONWEALTH.

Be it enacted, etc., as follows:

Town of Dana may use for certain purposes certain moneys received as land damages from state.

SECTION 1. The town of Dana is hereby authorized to use any moneys heretofore or hereafter received from the commonwealth as land damages under section twelve of chapter three hundred and twenty-one of the acts of nineteen hundred and twenty-seven, for maintenance purposes or in reduction of the tax levy, notwithstanding the provisions of section sixty-three of chapter forty-four of the

Proviso.

General Laws; provided, that not more than four thousand dollars shall be used as aforesaid in any one year.

SECTION 2. This act shall take effect upon its passage.
Approved February 9, 1933.

Chap. 8 AN ACT AUTHORIZING DOMESTIC CORPORATIONS TO CONTRIBUTE TO CERTAIN FUNDS FOR THE BETTERMENT OF SOCIAL AND ECONOMIC CONDITIONS.

Emergency preamble.

Whereas, The deferred operation of this act would tend to defeat its ῾purpose, therefore it is hereby declared to be an emergency law, necessary for the immediate preservation of the public convenience.

Be it enacted, etc., as follows:

SECTION 1. Every corporation organized under the laws of this commonwealth and doing business or operating therein may, by vote of its directors, or of its officers having the powers of directors, contribute such sum or sums of money as said directors or officers may determine to be reasonable to any general fund being raised by a relief committee or agency approved by the commissioner of public welfare, as evidenced by a writing filed in his office, and formed for the purpose of raising money to be used for the betterment of social and economic conditions in any community in which such corporation is doing business.

Domestic corporations may contribute to certain funds for the betterment of social and economic conditions.

SECTION 2. Nothing in this act shall be construed, either by reason of the limited period fixed therein or otherwise, as directly or indirectly restricting or otherwise affecting, except as therein provided, the rights and powers of corporations, as heretofore existing, with reference to payments of the nature above specified.

Construction of act.

SECTION 3. This act shall become inoperative at the expiration of one year from its effective date.

When inoperative.

Approved February 9, 1933.

AN ACT AUTHORIZING THE ONSET FIRE DISTRICT TO COLLECT GARBAGE AND OFFAL WITHIN SAID DISTRICT AND TO DISPOSE OF THE SAME.

Chap. 9

Be it enacted, etc., as follows:

SECTION 1. The Onset Fire District, in addition to the powers now vested in it by law, may collect garbage and offal within said district and dispose of the same, subject to the supervision of the board of health of the town of Wareham. For said purposes, the district may make contracts and raise and appropriate such sums as may be necessary.

The Onset Fire District may collect garbage and offal within said district and dispose of same.

SECTION 2. This act shall take effect upon its acceptance by a two thirds vote of the registered voters of said district present and voting thereon at the annual meeting to be held in the current year, or at any special meeting legally called for that purpose within two years after the passage of this act.   *Approved February 9, 1933.*

Effective upon acceptance.

AN ACT PROHIBITING UNLAWFUL INJURY TO OR INTERFERENCE WITH THE CARS OR TRACKS OF RAILWAY COMPANIES.

Chap. 10

Be it enacted, etc., as follows:

Section one hundred and three of chapter one hundred and fifty-nine of the General Laws, as appearing in the Tercentenary Edition thereof, is hereby amended by inserting after the word "signal" in the fifth line the words: — or whoever unlawfully and intentionally injures, molests, meddles or tampers with or destroys a track or car or any

G. L. (Ter. Ed.), 159, § 103, amended.

part, appliance or appurtenance thereof, of a railway company, or the mechanism or apparatus used in the operation of any such car, or whoever without right operates any such car or any mechanism or appliance thereof, — so as to read as follows: — *Section 103.* Whoever unlawfully and intentionally injures, molests or destroys any signal of a railroad corporation or railway company, or any line, wire, post or other structure or mechanism in connection with such signal, or prevents or in any way interferes with the proper working of such signal, or whoever unlawfully and intentionally injures, molests, meddles or tampers with or destroys a track or car or any part, appliance or appurtenance thereof, of a railway company, or the mechanism or apparatus used in the operation of any such car, or whoever without right operates any such car or any mechanism or appliance thereof, shall be punished by a fine of not more than five hundred dollars or by imprisonment for not more than two years, or both.

Approved February 9, 1933.

Injury to signals, or injury to or interference with cars or tracks of railway companies, prohibited.

Chap. 11 AN ACT RELATIVE TO THE VOTE REQUIRED TO CHANGE THE NAME OF A DOMESTIC MUTUAL INSURANCE COMPANY.

Be it enacted, etc., as follows:

G. L. (Ter. Ed.), 155, § 10, amended.

Section ten of chapter one hundred and fifty-five of the General Laws, as appearing in the Tercentenary Edition thereof, is hereby amended by inserting after the word "corporation" in the sixth and seventh lines the words: —, or, if such corporation without capital stock is a mutual insurance corporation, by two thirds of the votes of its policyholders cast at such a meeting, — so as to read as follows: — *Section 10.* A corporation, except one subject to chapter one hundred and fifty-six or chapters one hundred and sixty to one hundred and sixty-three, inclusive, may at a meeting duly called for the purpose, by vote of two thirds of each class of stock outstanding and entitled to vote, or, in case such corporation has no capital stock, by vote of two thirds of the persons legally qualified to vote in meetings of the corporation, or, if such corporation without capital stock is a mutual insurance corporation, by two thirds of the votes of its policyholders cast at such a meeting, or by a larger vote if its agreement of association or by-laws shall so require, change its name; provided, that no corporation subject to section twenty-six of chapter one hundred and eighty shall change its name until after approval of such change by the state secretary. Articles of amendment signed and sworn to by the president, treasurer and a majority of the directors or other officers having the powers of directors, shall within thirty days after such meeting be prepared, setting forth such amendment and the due adoption thereof. Such articles shall be submitted to the commissioner who shall examine them, and if he finds that they conform to the requirements of law, he

Change of name of certain corporations.

Proviso.

Articles of amendment, etc.

shall so certify and endorse his approval thereon. There-upon the state secretary shall direct the officers of the corporation to publish in such form as he may see fit, in a newspaper published in the county where the corporation has its principal office or place of business, notice of such change of name. When the state secretary is satisfied that such notice has been published as required by him, he shall, upon the payment of a fee of one dollar, grant a certificate of the name which the corporation shall bear, which name shall thereafter be its legal name, and he shall cause the articles of amendment to be filed in his office. In the case of corporations subject to chapter one hundred and seventy-five or one hundred and seventy-six, the approval of the commissioner of insurance shall be required before the commissioner of corporations and taxation approves the articles of amendment. No articles of amendment changing the name of any corporation shall take effect until they have been filed in the office of the state secretary as aforesaid. *Approved February 9, 1933.*

State secretary to direct publication, etc.

To grant certificate as to name of corporation, etc.

Approval of commissioner of insurance, when required.

Articles of amendment, when to take effect.

AN ACT AUTHORIZING THE DISSOLUTION OF THE TRUSTEES OF THE LEXINGTON MINISTERIAL FUND AND THE DISTRIBUTION OF ITS PROPERTY.

Chap. 12

Be it enacted, etc., as follows:

SECTION 1. The Trustees of the Lexington Ministerial Fund, incorporated by an act approved June sixteenth, eighteen hundred and seventeen, upon the acceptance of this act as hereinafter provided, is hereby authorized to dissolve and to convey, transfer and distribute all of the property of every nature held by it, or the proceeds thereof, to the following religious corporations and in the following proportions: One half of said property, to the First Congregational Society in Lexington, one quarter, to The First Baptist Church of Lexington, and one quarter to the Follen Church. Each such religious corporation shall hold the property so conveyed to it in perpetual trust, separate and apart from any other property, with full power to sell the whole or any part thereof from time to time and invest and reinvest the proceeds. The income from the property so held in trust shall be expended for the support of public worship.

The Trustees of the Lexington Ministerial Fund may dissolve, and may convey, transfer and distribute its property to certain religious corporations, etc.

SECTION 2. For the purposes of such distribution, The Trustees of the Lexington Ministerial Fund may convert into cash the whole or any part of the property held by it. The determination of the board of trustees of said The Trustees of the Lexington Ministerial Fund of the value of the property distributed in kind shall be final and conclusive.

May convert into cash whole or any part of property held by it, etc.

SECTION 3. Upon the completion of the transfer of said property, The Trustees of the Lexington Ministerial Fund shall file in the office of the state secretary and in the office of the commissioner of corporations and taxation a report

To file report of distribution upon completion of transfer of property, etc.

of such distribution, and thereupon said corporation shall be dissolved and terminated subject to the provisions of sections fifty-one, fifty-two and fifty-six of chapter one hundred and fifty-five of the General Laws.

Authority or right granted by act, limited, etc. SECTION 4. Whatever authority or right is granted or conferred by this act is hereby declared to be limited to such authority or right as the general court may constitutionally grant or confer, without prejudice to any proceeding that may be instituted in any court of competent jurisdiction to effect the purposes of this act.

Act not effective unless accepted, etc. SECTION 5. This act shall· not become effective unless within one year from the date of its passage, the First Congregational Society in Lexington, The First Baptist Church of Lexington and the Follen Church shall each at a meeting of its members, duly called and held, vote to accept this act and shall file in the office of the state secretary a certificate of such acceptance, and unless within such time the town of Lexington shall pass a vote assenting to the proceedings set forth in this act and shall cause a certificate of such vote to be filed with the state secretary.

Approved February 9, 1933.

Chap. 13 AN ACT ESTABLISHING IN THE TOWN OF WEBSTER REPRESENTATIVE TOWN GOVERNMENT BY LIMITED TOWN MEETINGS.

Be it enacted, etc., as follows:

Precinct voting, representative town meetings, etc., in town of Webster. SECTION 1. Upon the acceptance of this act by the town of Webster, as hereinafter provided, the selectmen shall forthwith divide the territory thereof into not less than five or more than ten voting precincts, each of which shall be plainly designated and shall contain not less than five hundred registered voters. All precincts shall contain approximately an equal number of registered voters.

Precincts, establishment, etc. The precincts shall be so established as to consist of compact and contiguous territory, to be bounded as far as possible by the center line of known streets and ways or by other well defined limits. Their boundaries shall be reviewed, and, if need be, wholly or partly revised by the selectmen in October, once in five years, or in October of any year when so directed by a vote of a representative town meeting.

Selectmen to report doings, etc. The selectmen shall, within twenty days after any establishment or revision of the precincts, file a report of their doings with the town clerk, the registrars of voters and the assessors, with a map or maps or description of the precincts and the names and residences of the registered voters therein. The selectmen shall also cause to be posted in the town hall a map or maps or description of the precincts as established or revised from time to time, with the names and residences of the registered voters therein. They shall also cause to be posted in at least one public place in each precinct a map or description of that precinct with the names and residences of the registered voters therein. The division of the town into voting precincts and any revision of such precincts shall take effect upon the date of the filing of the report thereof by the selectmen with the town clerk. Whenever the precincts are established or revised, the town clerk shall forthwith give written notice thereof to the state secretary, stating the number and designation of the precincts. Meetings of the registered voters of the several precincts for elections, for primaries, and for voting upon any question to be submitted to all the registered voters of the town, shall be held on the same day and at the same hour and at such place or places within the town as the selectmen shall in the warrant for such meeting direct. The provisions of the general laws relating to precinct voting at elections, so far as the same are not inconsistent with this act, shall apply to all elections and primaries in the town upon the establishment of voting precincts as hereinbefore provided.

Division into voting precincts, effective date.

Town clerk to give written notice to state secretary, etc.

Meetings of voters, when and where to be held.

Certain provisions of general laws to apply, etc.

SECTION 2. Other than the officers designated in section three as town meeting members at large, the representative town meeting membership shall in each precinct consist of the largest number divisible by three which will admit of a representation of all precincts by an equal number of members and which will not cause the total elected town meeting membership to exceed two hundred and fifty-two. The registered voters in every precinct shall, at a special election called for that purpose, to be held not sooner than thirty days after the establishment of precincts under this act, or at the first annual town election held after the establishment thereof, and at the first annual town election following any precinct revision where the number of precincts is changed, conformably to the laws relative to elections not inconsistent with this act, elect by ballot the number of registered voters in the precinct, other than the officers designated in section three as town meeting members at large, provided for in the first sentence of this section, to be town meeting members of the town. The first third in the order of votes received of members so elected shall serve three years, the second third in such order shall serve two years, and the remaining third in such order shall serve one year, from the day of the annual town meeting, or, in case such election is at a special meeting, from the next annual town meeting; in case of a tie vote affecting the division into thirds, as aforesaid, the members elected from the precinct shall by ballot determine the same; and thereafter, except as is otherwise provided herein, at each annual town election the registered voters of each precinct shall, in like manner, elect one third of the number of town meeting members to which that precinct is entitled for the term of three years, and shall at such election fill for the unexpired term or terms any vacancy or vacancies then existing in the number of town meeting members in their respective precincts. Upon every revision of the precincts where the number of

Representative town meeting membership, number, etc.

Town meeting members, election, terms, etc.

precincts is changed, the terms of office of all town meeting members from every precinct shall cease upon the election of their successors. The town clerk shall, after every election of town meeting members, forthwith notify each member by mail of his election.

SECTION 3. Any representative town meeting held under the provisions of this act, except as otherwise provided herein, shall be limited to the voters elected under section two, together with the following, designated as town meeting members at large; namely, any member of the general court of the commonwealth who is a resident of the town, the moderator, the town clerk, the selectmen, the town treasurer, the town counsel, the chairman of the trustees of the public library, the chairman of the planning board, the chairman of the school board, the chairman of the board of assessors, the chairman of the board of health, the chairman of the park commission, the chairman of the board of water commissioners, the chairman of the advisory board, the chairman of the sewer commission, the chairman of the highway commission, the tax collector and the chairman of the welfare board. The town clerk shall notify the town meeting members of the time and place at which representative town meetings are to be held, the notices to be sent by mail at least seven days before the meeting. The town meeting members, as aforesaid, shall be the judges of the election and qualifications of their members. One hundred town meeting members shall constitute a quorum for doing business; but a less number may organize temporarily and may adjourn from time to time. Notice of every adjourned representative town meeting shall be posted by the town clerk in five or more public places in the town, and he shall notify the members by mail of the adjournment at least twenty-four hours before the time of the adjourned representative town meeting. The notices shall state briefly the business to be acted upon at any meeting and shall include notice of any proposed reconsideration. All town meetings shall be public. The town meeting members as such shall receive no compensation. Subject to such conditions as may be determined from time to time by the representative town meeting, any voter of the town who is not a town meeting member may speak at any representative town meeting, but shall not vote. A town meeting member may resign by filing a written resignation with the town clerk, and such resignation shall take effect upon the date of such filing. No elected member whose official position entitles him to be a member at large shall act as a member at large during such times as he remains an elected member. A town meeting member who removes from the town shall cease to be a town meeting member and an elected town meeting member who removes from one precinct to another or is so removed by a revision of precincts shall not retain membership after the next annual election.

Section 4. Nomination of candidates for town meeting members to be elected under this act shall be made by nomination papers which shall bear no political designation, but to the name of a candidate for re-election there may be added the words "Candidate for Re-election". Nomination papers shall be signed by not less than ten registered voters of the precinct in which the candidate is nominated for office and filed with the town clerk at least ten days before the election. No nomination papers shall be valid in respect to any candidate unless his written acceptance is filed therewith. Nomination of candidates for town meeting members, how made. Acceptance of nomination.

Section 5. All articles in the warrant for every town meeting, so far as they relate to the election of the town moderator, town officers and town meeting members, and as herein provided, to referenda and all matters to be acted upon and determined by ballot, shall be so acted upon and determined by the registered voters of the town in their respective precincts. All other articles in the warrant for any town meeting, beginning with the annual town meeting in the year when said town meeting members are first elected, shall be acted upon and determined exclusively by town meeting members at a representative town meeting to be held at such time and place as shall be set forth by the selectmen in the warrant for the meeting, and subject to the referendum provided for by section eight. Warrant articles, how acted upon, etc.

Section 6. A moderator shall be elected by ballot at each annual town election, and shall serve as the moderator of all town meetings except as otherwise provided by law until his successor is elected and qualified. Nominations for moderator and his election shall be as in the case of other elective town officers, and any vacancy in such office may be filled by the town meeting members at a representative town meeting held for that purpose. If a moderator is absent, a moderator pro tempore may be elected by the town meeting members. Moderator, election, etc. Moderator pro tempore.

Section 7. In the event of any vacancy in the full number of elected town meeting members from any precinct the remaining elected members of the precinct may choose from among the registered voters thereof a successor to serve until the next annual town election. The town clerk may, and upon a petition therefor signed by not less than ten elected town meeting members from the precinct shall, call a special meeting for the purpose of filling such vacancy and shall mail a notice thereof to the remaining elected members from the precinct specifying the object and the time and place of such meeting which shall be held not less than four days after the mailing of such notice. At such meeting a majority of such members shall constitute a quorum and shall elect from their own number a chairman and a clerk. The election to fill such vacancy shall be by ballot and a majority of the votes cast shall be required for a choice. The clerk shall forthwith file with the town clerk a certificate of such election, to- Vacancies in full number of town meeting members, filling, etc. Calling of special meeting. Quorum. Choice by ballot. Certificate of election.

gether with a written acceptance by the member so elected, who shall thereupon be deemed elected and qualified as an elected town meeting member, subject to the provisions of section three respecting the election and qualifications of elected town meeting members.

Votes, when operative, etc. SECTION 8. No vote passed at any representative town meeting under any article in the warrant, except a vote to adjourn shall be operative until after the expiration of five days, exclusive of Sundays and holidays, from the dissolu-
Referendum. tion of the meeting. If within said five days a petition, signed by not less than five per cent of the registered voters of each precinct, containing their names and addresses as they appear on the list of registered voters, is filed with the selectmen requesting that the question or questions involved in such vote be submitted to the voters of the town at large, then the selectmen, within fourteen days after the filing of the petition, shall call a special meeting, which shall be held within ten days after the issuing of the call, for the purpose of presenting to the voters at large the question or questions so involved. The polls shall be opened at two o'clock in the afternoon and shall be closed not earlier than eight o'clock in the evening, and all votes upon any questions so submitted shall be taken by ballot, and the check list shall be used in the several precinct meetings in the same manner as in the election of town
Questions, how determined, etc. officers. The questions so submitted shall be determined by vote of the same proportion of voters at large voting thereon as would have been required by law of town meeting members had the question been finally determined at
Questions, how stated upon ballot, etc. a representative town meeting. The questions so submitted shall be stated upon the ballot in substantially the same language and form in which they were stated when presented to said representative town meeting by the moderator as appears from the records of the said meeting.
Votes operative if no petition, etc. If such petition is not filed within the said period of five days, the vote of the representative town meeting shall become operative upon the expiration of the said period.
Powers of town and its town meeting members, etc. SECTION 9. The town of Webster, after the acceptance of this act, shall have the capacity to act through and be bound by its said town meeting members who shall, when convened from time to time as herein provided, constitute representative town meetings; and the representative town meetings shall exercise exclusively, so far as will conform to the provisions of this act, all powers vested in the municipal corporation. Action in conformity with all provisions of law now or hereafter applicable to the transaction of town affairs in town meetings shall, when taken by any representative town meeting in accordance with the provisions of this act, have the same force and effect as if such action had been taken in a town meeting open to all the voters of the town as heretofore organized and conducted.
Rules. SECTION 10. The representative town meeting may

make such rules consistent with general law as may be considered necessary for conducting its meetings.

SECTION 11. The representative town meeting may appoint such committees of its members for investigation and report as it may consider necessary. *Committees for investigation.*

SECTION 12. All by-laws or parts of by-laws of the town inconsistent with the provisions of this act are hereby repealed. The provisions of chapter forty-four of the General Laws shall continue to apply in the town of Webster notwithstanding the provisions of this act. *Inconsistent by-laws repealed. G. L. 44 to continue to apply.*

SECTION 13. This act shall not abridge the right of the inhabitants of Webster to hold general meetings, as that right is secured to them by the constitution of this commonwealth; nor shall this act confer upon any representative town meeting in Webster the power finally to commit the town to any measure affecting its municipal existence or changing its government, without action thereon by the voters of the town at large, using the ballot and the check list therefor. *Certain rights not abridged, etc.*

SECTION 14. This act shall be submitted to the registered voters of the town of Webster at any annual town meeting. The vote shall be taken by ballot in accordance with the provisions of the General Laws, so far as the same shall be applicable, in answer to the question, which shall be placed upon the official ballot to be used for the election of town officers: "Shall an act passed by the General Court in the year nineteen hundred and thirty-three, entitled 'An Act establishing in the town of Webster representative town government by limited town meetings,' be accepted by this town?" *Submission to voters of town of Webster, etc.*

This act shall take effect upon its acceptance by a majority of the voters voting thereon. *Effective upon acceptance.*

SECTION 15. If this act is rejected by the registered voters of the town of Webster when submitted to said voters under section fourteen, it may again be submitted for acceptance in like manner from time to time to such voters at any annual town meeting in said town within three years thereafter, and, if accepted by a majority of the voters voting thereon at such a meeting, shall thereupon take effect.   *Approved February 9, 1933.* *Resubmission after rejection, etc.*

AN ACT AUTHORIZING THE ATLANTIC UNION COLLEGE TO GRANT THE DEGREE OF BACHELOR OF ARTS. *Chap. 14*

Be it enacted, etc., as follows:

Chapter ten of the acts of nineteen hundred and twenty-six is hereby amended by adding at the end thereof the words: — and of Bachelor of Arts, — so as to read as follows: — The Atlantic Union College, of Lancaster, is hereby authorized to grant to graduates of its four year college courses, qualified by scholarship and previous college entrance preparation, degrees of Bachelor of Religious Education and of Bachelor of Arts. *1926, 10, amended. Atlantic Union College may grant certain degrees.*

Approved February 9, 1933.

Chap. 15 An Act relative to the authority of the new england
CONSERVATORY OF MUSIC TO GRANT CERTAIN DEGREES.

Be it enacted, etc., as follows:

1925, 7, § 1,
amended.

Section 1. Section one of chapter seven of the acts of
nineteen hundred and twenty-five is hereby amended by
striking out all after the word "composition" in the seventh
line and inserting in place thereof the words: —, musical
research or supervision of school music, the degree of

New England
Conservatory
of Music may
grant degree of
Bachelor of
Music.

Bachelor of Music, — so as to read as follows: — *Section 1.*
The New England Conservatory of Music, a corporation
established by chapter one hundred and three of the acts
of eighteen hundred and seventy, is hereby authorized and
empowered to grant to students properly accredited and
recommended by the faculty council of said conservatory
upon their graduation from the collegiate department
thereof after completion of the four year course in applied
music, composition, musical research or supervision of
school music, the degree of Bachelor of Music.

May grant
degree of
Master of
Music.

Section 2. The said New England Conservatory of
Music is hereby authorized and empowered to grant to
students holding a bachelor's degree, who are properly
accredited and recommended by the faculty council of
said conservatory upon their completion of not less than
one year's post-graduate course in said conservatory in
applied music, composition, musical research, or supervision of school music, the degree of Master of Music.

Approved February 9, 1933.

Chap. 16 An Act relative to the time when the polls shall be
OPEN IN THE CITY OF SOMERVILLE FOR PRELIMINARY
MUNICIPAL ELECTIONS.

Be it enacted, etc., as follows:

1932, 281, § 1,
amended.

Chapter two hundred and eighty-one of the acts of
nineteen hundred and thirty-two is hereby amended by
striking out section one and inserting in place thereof the

Preliminary
municipal
elections in
city of
Somerville.

following: — *Section 1.* On the third Tuesday preceding
every regular or special municipal election in the city of
Somerville at which any elective municipal office is to be
filled, there shall be held, except as otherwise provided in
section ten, a preliminary election for the purpose of
nominating candidates therefor. The polls at every such

Polling hours.

election shall be open during such hours, not less than nine,

Certain laws
to apply.

as may be designated by the board of aldermen, and the
general laws relative to municipal elections shall apply
thereto, except as is otherwise specifically provided in
this act.   *Approved February 9, 1933.*

An Act relative to the appointment of certain departmental officers of the national guard. *Chap.* 17

Be it enacted, etc., as follows:

Section ninety of chapter thirty-three of the General Laws, as appearing in the Tercentenary Edition thereof, is hereby amended by striking out the last sentence of paragraph (k) and inserting in place thereof the following: — Departmental officers shall be appointed by the commander-in-chief from said list upon the recommendation of the chief of the department in which the appointment is to be made, provided that if such an officer is to be assigned or detailed to an organization the appointment shall be upon the recommendation of its commander.

G. L. (Ter. Ed.), 33, § 90, amended.

Appointment of departmental officers of the national guard. Proviso.

Approved February 9, 1933.

An Act extending the time within which the Furnace Village Water District shall commence to distribute water. *Chap.* 18

Be it enacted, etc., as follows:

Section 1. Section thirteen of chapter one hundred and forty-seven of the acts of nineteen hundred and thirty-one is hereby amended by striking out, in the last line, the word "two" and inserting in place thereof the word: — five, — so as to read as follows: — *Section 13.* For the purpose only of its acceptance, this act shall take effect upon its passage, and it shall take full effect upon its acceptance by a two thirds vote of the voters of said district present and voting thereon at a district meeting called, in accordance with the provisions of section eight, within four years after its passage; but it shall become void unless said district shall begin to distribute water to consumers within five years after its acceptance as aforesaid.

1931, 147, § 13, amended.

Time within which the Furnace Village Water District shall commence to distribute water, extended.

Section 2. This act shall take effect upon its passage.

Approved February 14, 1933.

An Act relative to improvement of brooks, streams and water courses in the town of Hingham. *Chap.* 19

Be it enacted, etc., as follows:

Section 1. The town of Hingham, for drainage purposes and for the purpose of protecting the public health, or either of said purposes, may, by its selectmen, from time to time improve brooks, streams and water courses, or any part thereof, within the limits of the town, by widening the same, removing obstructions in or over them, diverting the water, altering the courses or deepening the channels thereof, and may conduct any surface or ground water into the same, and may cover or pave any such channel or water course, or any part thereof, and may build retaining walls

Town of Hingham may improve brooks, streams and water courses within limits of town.

to support the banks of any such stream or water course, or any part thereof, within said town.

May take or acquire lands, rights of way, water rights, etc.

SECTION 2. For either or both of the purposes aforesaid, said town may take by eminent domain under chapter seventy-nine of the General Laws, or acquire by purchase or otherwise, lands, easements, rights of way, water rights and other property, on one or both sides of any such brook, stream or water course, or may in like manner take or otherwise acquire lands, easements, rights of way, water rights and other property to form new channels into which said water or any surface or ground water may be diverted,

May enter upon lands, etc.

within the limits of said town, and may enter into and upon any land or way, and may do thereon work necessary for any such improvement, and may construct upon any land taken or otherwise acquired under authority of this act such walks or ways as the town may determine that the public convenience and necessity require; and any person

Property damages, recovery.

who is injured in his property by any act of said town under the provisions of this act may recover from said town damages therefor under said chapter seventy-nine.

Assessment of betterments.

SECTION 3. If any limited and determinable area within said town receives benefit other than the general advantage to the community from any improvement made under authority of this act, under an order declaring the same to be done under the provisions of law authorizing the assessment of betterments, the selectmen shall, within two years after the completion of such improvement, determine the value of such benefit or advantage to the lands within such area, and assess upon each parcel thereof a proportionate share of the cost of such improvement, including therein all costs for the purchase and all damages for the taking of lands, easements, rights of way, water rights and other property in order to carry out such improvement, and all other sums expended under authority of this act, but not exceeding one half of such adjudged

G. L. 80, applicable.

benefit or advantage. The provisions of chapter eighty of the General Laws shall apply to such assessments and the collection thereof, except as otherwise herein provided.

Penalty for destruction of, or injury to, any drainage or sewerage work, etc.

SECTION 4. No person shall destroy or injure any drainage or sewerage work of said town, or without lawful authority pollute any natural water course in said town, or put or maintain any obstruction therein. Whoever violates any provision of this section shall be punished by a fine of not more than five hundred dollars or by imprisonment for not more than three months, or both.

SECTION 5. This act shall take effect upon its passage.
Approved February 14, 1933.

AN ACT RELATIVE TO IMPROVEMENT OF BROOKS, STREAMS AND WATER COURSES IN THE TOWN OF COHASSET.

Chap. 20

Be it enacted, etc., as follows:

SECTION 1. The town of Cohasset, for drainage purposes and for the purpose of protecting the public health, or either of said purposes, may, by its selectmen, from time to time improve brooks, streams and water courses, or any part thereof, within the limits of the town, by widening the same, removing obstructions in or over them, diverting the water, altering the courses or deepening the channels thereof, and may conduct any surface or ground water into the same, and may cover or pave any such channel or water course, or any part thereof, and may build retaining walls to support the banks of any such stream or water course, or any part thereof, within said town.

Town of Cohasset may improve brooks, streams and water courses within limits of town.

SECTION 2. For either or both of the purposes aforesaid, said town may take by eminent domain under chapter seventy-nine of the General Laws, or acquire by purchase or otherwise, lands, easements, rights of way, water rights and other property, on one or both sides of any such brook, stream or water course, or may in like manner take or otherwise acquire lands, easements, rights of way, water rights and other property to form new channels into which said water or any surface or ground water may be diverted, within the limits of said town, and may enter into and upon any land or way, and may do thereon work necessary for any such improvement, and may construct upon any land taken or otherwise acquired under authority of this act such walks or ways as the town may determine that the public convenience and necessity require; and any person who is injured in his property by any act of said town under the provisions of this act may recover from said town damages therefor under said chapter seventy-nine.

May take or acquire lands, rights of way, water rights, etc.

May enter upon lands, etc.

Property damages, recovery.

SECTION 3. If any limited and determinable area within said town receives benefit other than the general advantage to the community from any improvement made under authority of this act, under an order declaring the same to be done under the provisions of law authorizing the assessment of betterments, the selectmen shall, within two years after the completion of such improvement, determine the value of such benefit or advantage to the lands within such area, and assess upon each parcel thereof a proportionate share of the cost of such improvement, including therein all costs for the purchase and all damages for the taking of lands, easements, rights of way, water rights and other property in order to carry out such improvement, and all other sums expended under authority of this act, but not exceeding one half of such adjudged benefit or advantage. The provisions of chapter eighty of the General Laws shall apply to such assessments and the collection thereof, except as otherwise herein provided.

Assessment of betterments.

G. L. 80, applicable.

Penalty for
destruction
or injury of
any drainage
or sewerage
work, etc.

SECTION 4.   No person shall destroy or injure any drainage or sewerage work of said town, or without lawful authority pollute any natural water course in said town, or put or maintain any obstruction therein.   Whoever violates any provision of this section shall be punished by a fine of not more than five hundred dollars or by imprisonment for not more than three months, or both.

SECTION 5.   This act shall take effect upon its passage.

Approved February 14, 1933.

Chap. 21   AN ACT RELATIVE TO MARRIAGE CERTIFICATE FEES.

Emergency
preamble.

Whereas, The deferred operation of this act would tend to defeat its purpose, therefore it is hereby declared to be an emergency law, necessary for the immediate preservation of the public convenience.

Be it enacted, etc., as follows:

G. L. (Ter.
Ed.), 262,
§ 34,
amended.

Section thirty-four of chapter two hundred and sixty-two of the General Laws, as appearing in the Tercentenary Edition thereof, is hereby amended by striking out, in the fourth line, the words "one dollar" and inserting in place thereof the words: — two dollars, — so as to read as

Fees of town
clerks.

follows: — *Section 34.*   The fees of town clerks shall be as follows:

For entering notice of an intention of marriage and issuing the certificate thereof, and for entering the certificate of marriage which is filed by persons married out of the commonwealth, two dollars, which shall be paid at the time of such entry or filing.

For a certificate of a birth or death, twenty-five cents.

Approved February 14, 1933.

Chap. 22   AN ACT EMPOWERING THE UNITED HEBREW BENEVOLENT ASSOCIATION OF BOSTON TO TRANSFER ITS PROPERTY TO THE ASSOCIATED JEWISH PHILANTHROPIES, INC.

Be it enacted, etc., as follows:

United Hebrew
Benevolent
Association of
Boston may
transfer its
property to
the Associated
Jewish Philan-
thropies, Inc.

SECTION 1.   The United Hebrew Benevolent Association of Boston, incorporated under general law, is hereby empowered to transfer, assign, set over, and convey all funds and property held by it to the Associated Jewish Philanthropies, Inc., incorporated under general law, and the said Associated Jewish Philanthropies, Inc. is hereby empowered to receive the same and to hold, manage and dispose of all such funds and property charged with any trust, upon the same trusts, uses and purposes as if the same had continued to be held by the said United Hebrew Benevolent Association of Boston for the fulfillment of the charitable purposes of said corporation.

Power granted
to be exercised
only in con-
formity with
decree, etc.

SECTION 2.   The power hereby granted shall be exercised only in conformity with such a decree, if any, of the supreme judicial court, sitting in equity for the county of Suffolk,

as may be entered within one year after the passage of this
act.

SECTION 3. This act shall not take effect until it shall
have been accepted by the votes of the board of directors,
or the officers having the powers of directors, of each of said
corporations and copies of the respective votes of acceptance shall have been filed with the secretary of the commonwealth.   *Approved February 14, 1933.*

Effective upon
acceptance,
etc.

AN ACT RELATIVE TO GUARANTY CAPITAL OF CERTAIN
DOMESTIC MUTUAL INSURANCE COMPANIES.

Chap. 23

Be it enacted, etc., as follows:

SECTION 1. Chapter one hundred and seventy-five of
the General Laws, as appearing in the Tercentenary Edition thereof, is hereby amended by striking out section
seventy-nine and inserting in place thereof the following: —
Section 79. A mutual fire company may, at the time of its
formation or, if two thirds of the votes of its policyholders
cast at a meeting duly called for the purpose are recorded
in favor of such action, at any time after its formation,
establish a guaranty capital of not less than twenty-five
thousand nor more than two hundred thousand dollars,
divided into shares of a par value of one hundred dollars
each, to be invested as provided by this chapter for the
investment of the capital stock of domestic stock companies. Any such company may, at any time by a like
vote and with the written approval of the commissioner,
increase said guaranty capital to an amount not exceeding
two hundred thousand dollars. The holders of shares of
guaranty capital shall be entitled to a semi-annual dividend of not more than three and one half per cent on their
respective shares if the net profits or unused premiums,
left after all expenses, losses and liabilities then incurred,
with the reserve for reinsurance, are provided for, shall be
sufficient to pay the same. Shareholders and members of
such companies shall, except as otherwise provided herein,
be subject to the same provisions of law relative to their
right to vote as apply respectively to shareholders in stock
companies and policyholders in mutual fire companies.
The guaranty capital shall be applied to the payment of
losses only when the company has exhausted its assets,
exclusive of uncollected premiums; and when thus impaired, the directors may make good the whole or any
part of it by assessments upon the contingent funds of the
company at the date of such impairment. Such guaranty
capital shall be retired by the directors of the company at
par when the profits accumulated under section eighty
equal two per cent of its insurance in force; and such
guaranty capital may, upon the recording in favor of such
action of two thirds of the votes cast at a meeting duly
called for the purpose and with the written approval of the

G. L. (Ter.
Ed.), 175,
§ 79,
amended.

Guaranty capi-
tal of certain
domestic
mutual insur-
ance companies.

commissioner, be reduced or retired, if the net assets of the company above its reinsurance reserve and all other claims and obligations, exclusive of guaranty capital, for two years last preceding and including the date of its last annual statement under section twenty-five has been not less than twenty-five per cent of the amount of the guaranty capital. Due notice of any proposed action under this section on the part of the company shall be mailed to each policyholder of the company not less than thirty days before the meeting when such action is proposed to be taken, and shall also be advertised in two papers of general circulation, approved by the commissioner, not less than three times a week for a period of not less than four weeks before said meeting. No company with a guaranty capital which has ceased to do new business shall retire such capital or pay any dividends thereon, except from income from its investments, until it shall have performed or cancelled its policy obligations. The holders of the guaranty capital of a mutual fire company shall not be entitled in any event to share in the distribution of its assets beyond the amount of the par value of their shares and any dividends declared and payable thereon.

G. L. (Ter. Ed.), 175, § 90B, amended.

Certain restrictions as to issue of policies by certain mutual companies.

SECTION 2. Said chapter one hundred and seventy-five, as so appearing, is hereby further amended by striking out section ninety B and inserting in place thereof the following: — *Section 90B.* No policy shall be issued by a mutual company formed to transact business under the fourth clause of section forty-seven until it has established a fully paid up guaranty capital of not less than two hundred thousand dollars nor more than five hundred thousand dollars which shall be subject to the provisions of section seventy-nine, except as hereinafter and in section ninety-three D provided. Any such company may, subject to all the provisions of section seventy-nine relative to the increase of the guaranty capital of a domestic mutual fire company, increase said guaranty capital to an amount not exceeding five hundred thousand dollars. While a company is transacting business under said clause, the provisions of said section seventy-nine relative to the retirement of guaranty capital of a mutual fire company shall not apply, nor shall the provisions of said section relative to the reduction of guaranty capital authorize the reduction of its guaranty capital below two hundred thousand dollars.

Principals on certain bonds, etc., to be deemed members of company.

The principal on any bond or obligation executed by a mutual company as surety shall be deemed the member of the company under sections seventy-six, seventy-nine, eighty, eighty-one, eighty-three to eighty-five, inclusive, and ninety.   *Approved February 14, 1933.*

AN ACT PLACING THE OFFICE OF CHIEF OF POLICE OF THE
   TOWN OF MEDFIELD UNDER THE CIVIL SERVICE LAWS.

Chap. 24

Be it enacted, etc., as follows:

SECTION 1. The office of chief of police of the town of Medfield shall, upon the effective date of this act, become subject to the civil service laws and rules and regulations relating to the appointment and removal of police officers in towns, and the tenure of office of any incumbent thereof shall be unlimited, except that he may be removed in accordance with such laws and rules and regulations; provided, however, that Colman J. Hogan, the present incumbent of said office, may continue to serve as such without taking a civil service examination.

Office of chief of police of town of Medfield subject to civil service laws.

Proviso.

SECTION 2. This act shall be submitted to the voters of said town at the annual town meeting in the current year in the form of the following question, which shall be placed upon the official ballot to be used for the election of town officers at said meeting: "Shall an act passed by the General Court in the year nineteen hundred and thirty-three, entitled 'An Act placing the office of chief of police of the town of Medfield under the civil service laws', be accepted?" If a majority of the votes in answer to said question are in the affirmative, then this act shall thereupon take effect, but not otherwise.

Approved February 15, 1933.

Submission to voters, etc.

AN ACT PROHIBITING THE PRINTING OR PUBLICATION OF
   CERTAIN ADVERTISEMENTS FOR OR ON BEHALF OF UN-
   LICENSED INSURANCE COMPANIES AND FRATERNAL BENEFIT
   SOCIETIES.

Chap. 25

Whereas, The deferred operation of this act would tend to defeat its purpose, therefore it is hereby declared to be an emergency law, necessary for the immediate preservation of the public convenience.

Emergency preamble.

Be it enacted, etc., as follows:

SECTION 1. Chapter one hundred and seventy-five of the General Laws, as appearing in the Tercentenary Edition thereof, is hereby amended by inserting after section one hundred and sixty the following new section: — *Section 160A.* No person shall print or publish, or cause to be printed or published, in any newspaper, magazine, pamphlet or other periodical any advertisement for or on behalf of any foreign company or fraternal benefit society not licensed to transact business in this commonwealth, wherein such company or society solicits, or which is designed or intended to solicit or induce, residents of the commonwealth to take out policies of insurance, annuity or pure endowment contracts or benefit certificates issued or made by such company or society, or to act in any manner in the

G. L. (Ter. Ed.), 175, new section after § 160.

Printing or publication of certain advertisements for or on behalf of unlicensed insurance companies and fraternal benefit societies, prohibited.

solicitation of applications for, or to negotiate or act or aid in the negotiation of, such policies, contracts or certificates, or to collect premiums thereon, and no person shall transmit or publish any such advertisement for or on behalf of any such company or society from any radio broadcasting station located in the commonwealth. Violation of this section shall be punished by a fine of not less than fifty nor more than five hundred dollars. This section shall not apply to newspapers, magazines, pamphlets or other periodicals printed or published outside the commonwealth.

Penalty.

SECTION 2. Section five of chapter one hundred and seventy-six of the General Laws, as so appearing, is hereby amended by inserting after the word "sixteen" in the third line the words: —, one hundred and sixty A, — so as to read as follows: — *Section 5.* Societies shall be governed by this chapter, and shall be exempt from all other provisions of the insurance laws of the commonwealth except sections sixteen, one hundred and sixty A and one hundred and seventy-eight to one hundred and eighty, inclusive, of chapter one hundred and seventy-five, not only in governmental relations with the commonwealth, but for every other purpose; and no law hereafter enacted shall apply to them unless they are expressly designated therein.

G. L. (Ter. Ed.), 176, § 5, amended.

Laws applicable to fraternal societies.

Approved February 16, 1933.

Chap. 26 AN ACT REQUIRING CERTAIN MOTOR VEHICLES TRANSPORTING EXPLOSIVES OR INFLAMMABLES TO STOP AT RAILROAD CROSSINGS.

Emergency preamble.

Whereas, The deferred operation of this act would defeat its purpose to prevent without unnecessary delay collisions at railroad crossings between motor vehicles transporting explosives or inflammables and railroad trains, with consequent sacrifice of human life, therefore this act is hereby declared to be an emergency law, necessary for the immediate preservation of the public safety.

Be it enacted, etc., as follows:

SECTION 1. Section fifteen of chapter ninety of the General Laws, as amended by section five of chapter two hundred and seventy-one of the acts of nineteen hundred and thirty-two, is hereby further amended by inserting after the word "bus" in the sixth line the words: —, or any motor vehicle carrying explosive substances or inflammable liquids as a cargo, or part of a cargo, — so as to read as follows: — *Section 15.* Except as hereinafter otherwise provided, every person operating a motor vehicle, upon approaching a railroad crossing at grade, shall reduce the speed of the vehicle to a reasonable and proper rate, and shall proceed cautiously over the crossing. Every person operating a school bus, or any motor vehicle carrying explosive substances or inflammable liquids as a cargo,

G. L. (Ter. Ed.), 90, § 15, etc., amended.

Precautions at railroad crossings.

or part of a cargo, upon approaching a railroad crossing at grade, shall bring his vehicle to a full stop not more than seventy-five feet from the nearest track of said railroad, and shall not proceed to cross said railroad until he is satisfied that it is safe to do so. Whoever violates any provision of this section shall be punished by a fine of not less than ten nor more than fifty dollars.

SECTION 2. This act shall become operative on the expiration of thirty days from its passage.

When operative.

Approved February 16, 1933.

AN ACT AUTHORIZING THE CITY OF WORCESTER TO RECEIVE AND HOLD LAND AND STRUCTURES TO BE USED AS ATHLETIC FIELDS FOR PUBLIC SCHOOL ATHLETICS AND OTHER PURPOSES.

Chap. 27

Be it enacted, etc., as follows:

Chapter four hundred and seventy-one of the acts of nineteen hundred and twenty-two is hereby amended by striking out section one and inserting in place thereof the following: — *Section 1.* The city of Worcester may, by vote of the school committee and with the approval of the mayor, receive by deed of gift and hold in fee land, buildings and other structures in said city to be used as athletic fields for public school and other athletics and public events for which admission may be charged. The word "field", as hereinafter used, shall, if more than one such field is so acquired and used, import the plural.

1922, 471, § 1, amended.

City of Worcester may receive and hold land and structures to be used as athletic fields for public school athletics, etc.

Approved February 16, 1933.

AN ACT REGULATING THE ISSUE OF TEMPORARY LOANS BY CERTAIN COUNTIES.

Chap. 28

Be it enacted, etc., as follows:

Section thirty-seven of chapter thirty-five of the General Laws, as appearing in the Tercentenary Edition thereof, is hereby amended by striking out, in the fifth line, the words "with or without interest," and by striking out the fourth sentence and inserting in place thereof the following: — Such notes, if issued for less than one year, may be renewed from time to time; provided, that the period from the date of the original loan to the date of maturity of any refunding loan shall not be more than one year. Notes issued hereunder may be sold at such discount as the commissioners may deem proper, the discount to be treated as interest paid in advance, — so as to read as follows: — *Section 37.* County commissioners may borrow money in anticipation of, and to be repaid from, the county tax of the current year. If said tax has been granted, such loans shall not exceed its amount; otherwise they shall not exceed the amount of the previous annual tax. They may issue therefor county notes maturing within one year after the date when the debt for which they are issued was in-

G. L. (Ter. Ed.), 35, § 37, amended.

Issue of temporary loans by certain counties regulated.

Proviso.

curred. Such notes, if issued for less than one year, may be renewed from time to time; provided, that the period from the date of the original loan to the date of maturity of any refunding loan shall not be more than one year. Notes issued hereunder may be sold at such discount as the commissioners may deem proper, the discount to be treated as interest paid in advance. Such notes shall be signed by the treasurer, countersigned by a majority of the commissioners, and shall expressly be made payable from the taxes of the current year, but shall nevertheless be negotiable. Except as otherwise expressly provided by law, neither county commissioners nor county treasurers, except in Suffolk and Nantucket counties, may borrow money or negotiate loans upon the credit of the county. Notes may also be issued between January first and January tenth, in accordance with this section, in anticipation of assessments payable to the county by cities, towns or corporations, under statutory provisions and unpaid at the end of the preceding year, in cases in which the total cost of the project for which the assessment is levied was paid by the county in the first instance.

Approved February 16, 1933.

Chap. 29 AN ACT REGULATING THE USE OF UNEXPENDED PROCEEDS OF SERIAL BONDS AND NOTES ISSUED BY CERTAIN COUNTIES.

Be it enacted, etc., as follows:

G. L. (Ter. Ed.), 35, § 37A, amended.

Section thirty-seven A of chapter thirty-five of the General Laws, as appearing in the Tercentenary Edition thereof, is hereby amended by inserting after the word "loan" in the thirteenth line the following: —, and provided, further, that so much of such proceeds as has not been so applied at the expiration of two years from the completion of the project for which the loan was authorized shall become part of the next general unappropriated balance established under section twenty-nine or, if such loan was made on behalf of a district, shall be applied in reduction of assessments to be made upon it by the county,

County bonds and notes regulated.

— so as to read as follows: — *Section 37A.* Counties shall not issue any bonds or notes payable on demand, and they shall provide for the payment of all debts, except those incurred in anticipation of revenue or in anticipation of reimbursement from cities and towns, by such annual payments as will extinguish the same at maturity, and so that the first of such annual payments on account of any loan shall be made not later than one year after the date of the bond or note issued therefor, and so that the amount of such annual payment in any year on account of such debt, so far as issued, shall not be less than the amount of the

Use of proceeds, etc.

principal payable in any subsequent year. The proceeds of any sale of bonds or notes, except premiums, shall be used only for the purposes specified in the original authorization of the loan; provided, that unexpended amounts

Provisos.

may be applied to maturing annual payments of the same loan, and provided, further, that so much of such proceeds as has not been so applied at the expiration of two years from the completion of the project for which the loan was authorized shall become part of the next general unappropriated balance established under section twenty-nine or, if such loan was made on behalf of a district, shall be applied in reduction of assessments to be made upon it by the county. Any premium received upon such bonds or notes, less the cost of preparing, issuing and marketing them, shall be applied to the payment of the principal of the first bond or note to mature.

Approved February 16, 1933.

An Act relative to unlawful issue of policies in the Commonwealth by certain foreign insurance companies whose licenses have been revoked or suspended.

Chap. 30

Be it enacted, etc., as follows:

Section one hundred and fifty-six A of chapter one hundred and seventy-five of the General Laws, as appearing in the Tercentenary Edition thereof, is hereby amended by striking out, in the eighth line, the word "or" and inserting in place thereof the words: — and every foreign company, — so as to read as follows: — *Section 156A.* Every foreign company, other than a life company, whose capital stock or guaranty or deposit capital is reduced below the amounts required by section one hundred and fifty-one, one hundred and fifty-two or one hundred and fifty-five, or is impaired on the basis fixed by sections ten to twelve, inclusive, or whose net cash assets, computed on said basis, or whose contingent assets, required by said section one hundred and fifty-one or one hundred and fifty-two, become at any time from any cause less than the amounts required as aforesaid, and every foreign company whose license has been revoked or suspended as provided in section five, shall forthwith cease to issue policies and to make contracts of insurance in the commonwealth until such capital stock, guaranty or deposit capital or assets have been restored to the amounts required as aforesaid, or said license has been restored by the commissioner, as the case may be. Any company or any officer or agent thereof, issuing any policy or making any contract of insurance contrary to this section shall be punished by a fine of not less than one hundred nor more than one thousand dollars.

G. L. (Ter. Ed.), 175, § 156A, amended.

Certain foreign companies to cease transacting business, when.

Penalty.

Approved February 16, 1933.

Chap. 31 AN ACT RELATIVE TO PAYMENT OF PROCEEDS OF FIRE
INSURANCE POLICIES TO MORTGAGEES.

Be it enacted, etc., as follows:

G. L. (Ter.
Ed.), 175,
§ 97, amended.

Section ninety-seven of chapter one hundred and seventy-five of the General Laws, as appearing in the Tercentenary Edition thereof, is hereby amended by striking out, in the first line, the words "by an agreement with the insured or", — by striking out, in the second line, the words "taken out by" and inserting in place thereof the word: — insuring, — by striking out, in the third and fourth lines, the words "or for their benefit", — and by striking out, in the fifth line, the words "or agreement', — so as to read

Payment of
proceeds of
fire insurance
policies to
mortgagees.

as follows: — *Section 97*. If, by the terms of a fire insurance policy insuring a mortgagor, the whole or any part of the loss thereon is payable to mortgagees of the property, the company shall, upon satisfactory proof of the rights and title of the parties, in accordance with such terms, pay all mortgagees protected by such policy in the order of their priority of claim as their claim shall appear, not beyond the amount for which the company is liable, and such payment shall be to the extent thereof payment and satisfaction of the liability of the company under such policy.

Approved February 16, 1933.

Chap. 32 AN ACT AUTHORIZING THE CITY OF WORCESTER TO GRANT
CERTAIN EASEMENTS IN MYRTLE AND SOUTHBRIDGE
STREETS IN SAID CITY TO THE UNITED STATES OF AMERICA.

Be it enacted, etc., as follows:

City of
Worcester may
grant certain
easements to
United States
of America.

Upon petition therefor by the United States of America, and after seven days' notice inserted in at least two newspapers published in the city of Worcester and a public hearing thereon, the city council of said city may, by a two thirds vote of each branch thereof, with the approval of the mayor, grant to the petitioner easements to maintain areas for basement windows in Myrtle street and Southbridge street appurtenant to the post office in said city.

Approved February 16, 1933.

Chap. 33 AN ACT SUBJECTING THE DURANT, INCORPORATED, TO
FURTHER REGULATION BY THE DEPARTMENT OF PUBLIC
WELFARE.

Emergency
preamble.

Whereas, The deferred operation of this act would tend to defeat its purpose, therefore it is hereby declared to be an emergency law, necessary for the immediate preservation of the public convenience.

Be it enacted, etc., as follows:

The Durant, Incorporated, a Massachusetts corporation organized under general law, shall, in carrying out its corporate purposes, be subject to regulation by the department of public welfare with respect to the following: The Durant, Incorporated, subjected to further regulation by department of public welfare.

Use of property of the corporation, rental and other charges made by it, rate of return, and areas and methods of operation.

Such regulation by said department shall be in addition to that provided by general law with respect to corporations organized for charitable purposes.

Approved February 21, 1933.

AN ACT AUTHORIZING THE COUNTY OF DUKES COUNTY TO BORROW MONEY FOR THE PURPOSE OF CONTRIBUTING TO THE COST OF CONSTRUCTION OF A HIGHWAY IN THE TOWN OF OAK BLUFFS.

Chap. 34

Be it enacted, etc., as follows:

SECTION 1. For the purpose of contributing to the cost of the construction by the state department of public works of a highway in the town of Oak Bluffs, the county commissioners for the county of Dukes County may from time to time borrow upon the credit of the county such sums as may be necessary, not exceeding, in the aggregate, fifteen thousand dollars, and may issue bonds or notes of the county therefor, which shall bear on their face the words, Dukes County Highway Loan, Act of 1933. Each authorized issue shall constitute a separate loan, and such loans shall be payable in not more than five years from their dates. Such bonds or notes shall be signed by the treasurer of the county and countersigned by a majority of the county commissioners. The county may sell the said securities at public or private sale upon such terms and conditions as the county commissioners may deem proper, but not for less than their par value. Indebtedness incurred hereunder shall, except as herein provided, be subject to chapter thirty-five of the General Laws. County of Dukes County may borrow money for purpose of contributing to cost of construction of a highway in town of Oak Bluffs.

Dukes County Highway Loan, Act of 1933.

SECTION 2. The treasurer of said county, with the approval of the county commissioners, may issue temporary notes of the county, payable in not more than one year from their dates, in anticipation of the issue of serial bonds or notes under this act, but the time within which such serial bonds or notes shall become due and payable shall not, by reason of such temporary notes, be extended beyond the time fixed by this act. Any notes issued in anticipation of the serial bonds or notes shall be paid from the proceeds thereof. County treasurer may issue temporary notes, etc.

SECTION 3. This act shall take effect upon its acceptance during the current year by the county commissioners of said county, but not otherwise. Effective upon acceptance, etc.

Approved February 21, 1933.

Chap. 35 AN ACT AUTHORIZING THE PLACING OF THE WORDS "CANDIDATE FOR RE-ELECTION" ON NOMINATION PAPERS AND OFFICIAL BALLOTS FOR THE ELECTION OF OFFICERS IN TOWNS.

Emergency preamble.

Whereas, The deferred operation of this act would tend to defeat its purpose, therefore it is hereby declared to be an emergency law, necessary for the immediate preservation of the public convenience.

Be it enacted, etc., as follows:

G. L. (Ter. Ed.), 53, § 8, etc., amended.

SECTION 1. Chapter fifty-three of the General Laws, as amended in section eight by section four of chapter one hundred and thirty-five of the acts of nineteen hundred and thirty-two, is hereby further amended by striking out said section eight and inserting in place thereof the following:—

Certificates of nomination and nomination papers, contents, party designation.

Section 8. All certificates of nomination and nomination papers shall, in addition to the names of candidates, specify as to each, (1) his residence, with street and number, if any, (2) the office for which he is nominated, and (3), except as otherwise provided in this section and in city charters, the party or political principle which he represents, expressed in not more than three words. Certificates of nomination made by convention or caucus shall also state what provision, if any, was made for filling vacancies caused by the death, withdrawal or ineligibility of candidates. The surnames of the candidates for president and vice president of the United States shall be added to the party or political designation of the candidates for presidential electors. To the name of each candidate for alderman at large shall be added the number of the ward in which he resides. To the name of a candidate for a town office who is an incumbent thereof there may be added the words "Candidate for Re-election".

If a candidate is nominated otherwise than by a political party, the name of a political party shall not be used in his political designation. Certificates of nomination and nomination papers for town offices need not include a designation of the party or principle which the candidate represents.

G. L. (Ter. Ed.), 54, § 41, amended.

SECTION 2. Section forty-one of chapter fifty-four of the General Laws, as appearing in the Tercentenary Edition thereof, is hereby amended by inserting after the word "papers" in the twentieth line the following: — To the name of each candidate for a town office upon an official ballot who is an incumbent thereof shall be added the words "Candidate for Re-election", — so that the third

Election ballots to contain political designations of candidates, except, etc.

paragraph will read as follows: —To the name of each candidate for a state or city office, except city offices in cities where political designations are forbidden, shall be added in the same space his party or political designation or designations.

To contain words "Candidate for Re-election", when.

To the name of a candidate for a state or city office who is an elected incumbent thereof and who is one of two or more candidates therefor bearing the same name, there shall be added in the same space the words "Candidate for Re-election". To the name of each candidate for a town office upon an official ballot shall be added the designation of the party or principle which he represents, contained in the certificate of nomination or nomination papers. To the name of each candidate for a town office upon an official ballot who is an incumbent thereof shall be added the words "Candidate for Re-election". The town clerk shall add the words "Caucus Nominee" to the name of any candidate nominated for a town office by a caucus held under the provisions of sections one hundred and seventeen to one hundred and twenty, inclusive, of chapter fifty-three.

Approved February 23, 1933.

To contain party designations, etc., of candidates for town offices. Words "Candidate for Re-election" to be added, when. Words "Caucus Nominee" to be added, when.

AN ACT AUTHORIZING THE MORTGAGING OF A DECEDENT'S REAL ESTATE TO PAY THE WIDOW'S ALLOWANCE IF THE PERSONAL PROPERTY IS NOT SUFFICIENT.

Chap. 36

Be it enacted, etc., as follows:

Section two of chapter one hundred and ninety-six of the General Laws, as appearing in the Tercentenary Edition thereof, is hereby amended by inserting after the word "sold" in the tenth line and in the eleventh line, in each instance, the words: — or mortgaged, — and by inserting after the word "sale" in the twelfth line the words: — or mortgage, — so as to read as follows: — *Section 2.* Such parts of the personal property of a deceased person as the probate court, having regard to all the circumstances of the case, may allow as necessaries to his widow for herself and for his family under her care or, if there is no widow, to his minor children, not exceeding one hundred dollars to any child, and also such provisions and other articles as are necessary for the reasonable sustenance of his family, and the use of his house and of the furniture therein for six months next succeeding his death, shall not be taken as assets for the payment of debts, legacies or charges of administration. After exhausting the personal property, real property may be sold or mortgaged to provide the amount of allowance decreed, in the same manner as it is sold or mortgaged for the payment of debts, if a decree authorizing such sale or mortgage is made, upon the petition of any party in interest, within one year after the approval of the bond of the executor or administrator.

Approved February 23, 1933.

G. L. (Ter. Ed.), 196, § 2, amended. Allowance of necessaries to widow and children. Real estate may be sold or mortgaged to pay allowance if personal property is not sufficient.

AN ACT TO ENABLE THE TOWN OF MILTON TO REPAY IN PART CERTAIN SUMS PAID AS SEWER ASSESSMENTS.

Chap. 37

Be it enacted, etc., as follows:

SECTION 1. The town of Milton may repay, after determination by its board of sewer commissioners in accordance with the principles laid down by the supreme

Town of Milton may repay in part certain sums paid as sewer assessments.

judicial court in the recent case of Annie F. Mullen *v.*
Board of Sewer Commissioners of Milton, such parts of
amounts assessed under the authority of chapter three
hundred and four of the acts of eighteen hundred and
ninety-five, and any acts in amendment thereof and in
addition thereto, upon estates and owners in respect to
sewer construction in the calendar years of nineteen hundred
and twenty-seven to nineteen hundred and thirty-one,
inclusive, which have been paid, as would not have been assessed in case assessments upon said town on account of
the south metropolitan sewerage system had been excluded.

May borrow money, issue bonds, etc.

SECTION 2. For the purpose of providing funds to
carry out this act, said town may from time to time borrow
such sums as may be necessary, and may issue bonds or
notes therefor, which shall bear on their face the words,

Milton Sewer Assessment Loan, Act of 1933.

Milton Sewer Assessment Loan, Act of 1933. Such loans
shall be payable in not more than five years from their
dates. Indebtedness incurred under this act shall be
inside the statutory limit, and shall, except as provided
herein, be subject to chapter forty-four of the General
Laws, exclusive of the limitation contained in the first
paragraph of section seven thereof, as appearing in the
Tercentenary Edition of said General Laws.

Effective upon acceptance, etc.

SECTION 3. This act shall take full force and effect
upon its acceptance by said town at any meeting duly
called for the purpose; and said town may make appropriation and incur debt, as hereinbefore provided, at the same
meeting at which this act shall be accepted, due notice of
the purpose so to do having been given in the warrant for
said meeting.   *Approved February 23, 1933.*

Chap. 38 AN ACT AUTHORIZING THE TOWN OF COHASSET TO USE FOR
OTHER MUNICIPAL PURPOSES CERTAIN LAND ACQUIRED
FOR PARKING SPACE.

Be it enacted, etc., as follows:

Town of Cohasset may use for other municipal pur- poses certain land acquired for parking space.

SECTION 1. The town of Cohasset is hereby authorized
to use for the erection of a building to house highway
equipment and for other municipal purposes so much of the
following described real estate, acquired in the year nineteen hundred and twenty-eight for parking space purposes,
as the inhabitants of the town may from time to time determine in town meeting, — to wit: — a parcel of land containing sixteen thousand eight hundred and thirty-three
square feet and bounded generally as follows: southeasterly by James lane; southwesterly by land of the
New York, New Haven and Hartford Railroad Company;
northerly by other land of said railroad company; northeasterly by land of McGaw and Ruiter, as shown on a plan
filed with the selectmen and entitled "Plan of Proposed

parking space in the Town of Cohasset, Mass., Lewis W.
Perkins, C. E.'', dated February, 1928.

SECTION 2.   This act shall take effect upon its passage.
Approved February 24, 1933.

AN ACT VALIDATING THE PURCHASE BY THE TOWN OF *Chap. 39*
COHASSET, FOR CEMETERY PURPOSES, OF CERTAIN LAND
IN THE TOWN OF HINGHAM ADJOINING WOODSIDE CEME-
TERY.

Be it enacted, etc., as follows:

SECTION 1.   The action of the town of Cohasset whereby   The purchase
it purchased from Lucy F. Beale of Hingham, by deed   by town of
Cohasset, for
dated December twelfth, nineteen hundred and thirty,   cemetery pur-
and recorded in Plymouth County registry of deeds, book   poses, of certain land in
sixteen hundred and twenty-eight, page five hundred and   town of Hingham adjoining
sixty-five, a certain parcel of land in said Hingham, border-   Woodside
ing upon land used by said town of Cohasset as a cemetery   cemetery, validated.
and known as Woodside cemetery, is hereby validated and
confirmed; and said town of Cohasset may hold and use
said parcel as appurtenant to said cemetery, provided   Proviso.
no burials are made within the limits of said parcel.

SECTION 2.   This act shall take effect upon its passage.
Approved February 24, 1933.

AN ACT AUTHORIZING THE PROVIDENT INSTITUTION FOR *Chap. 40*
SAVINGS IN THE TOWN OF BOSTON TO MAKE FURTHER IN-
VESTMENTS IN THE PURCHASE AND IMPROVEMENT OF
REAL ESTATE IN THE CITY OF BOSTON TO BE USED FOR
THE TRANSACTION OF ITS BUSINESS.

Be it enacted, etc., as follows:

SECTION 1.   The Provident Institution for Savings   The Provident
in the Town of Boston, incorporated by an act passed in   Institution for
Savings in the
eighteen hundred and sixteen, may, subject to the approval   Town of
Boston may
of the commissioner of banks, invest in the purchase of   make further
real estate in the city of Boston to be used for the convenient   investments in
the purchase
transaction of its business, and in the erection and prepara-   and improvement of real
tion of a suitable building or buildings on land to be ac-   estate in city
quired hereunder, or in the alteration or renovation of any   of Boston, etc.
building located on said land or on land in said city now
owned by it, to be devoted in whole or in part to such use,
a sum not exceeding six hundred thousand dollars in addition to any sums which said bank has heretofore been
authorized to invest in land or buildings for such use, and
any sums received from any sale or taking of any part of
such land or buildings; provided, however, that nothing   Proviso.
contained herein shall be construed as authorizing a total
investment by said bank in real estate for such use exceeding in the aggregate the sum of one million six hundred
thousand dollars at any one time.

SECTION 2.   This act shall take effect upon its passage.
Approved February 24, 1933.

Chap. 41 AN ACT AUTHORIZING SAVINGS BANKS AND TRUST COM-
PANIES TO PURCHASE, LOAN UPON OR PARTICIPATE IN
LOANS UPON THE ASSETS OF CERTAIN CLOSED AND OTHER
BANKS.

Emergency
preamble.

Whereas, The deferred operation of this act would tend
to defeat its purpose to provide further relief to the depositors of closed banks in the present financial emergency,
therefore this act is hereby declared to be an emergency
law, necessary for the immediate preservation of the public
convenience.

Be it enacted, etc., as follows:

G. L. (Ter.
Ed.), 168, new
section at end
thereof.

SECTION 1. Chapter one hundred and sixty-eight of
the General Laws, as appearing in the Tercentenary
Edition thereof, is hereby amended by adding at the end

Savings banks
may purchase,
loan upon or
participate in
loans upon the
assets of cer-
tain closed and
other banks.

thereof the following new section: — *Section 56.* With
the approval of the commissioner, a savings bank may
advance or loan upon, or purchase, the whole or any part
of the assets of any other savings bank, or of the savings
department of any trust company, including savings
banks and trust companies now or hereafter in possession
of the commissioner under sections twenty-two to thirty-
six, inclusive, of chapter one hundred and sixty-seven, and
may participate in such an advance, loan or purchase with
one or more other savings banks or trust companies. The
savings bank making or participating in such an advance,
loan or purchase, for the purpose of effecting the same, may
assume and agree to pay the whole or any part of the deposit
and other liabilities of such other savings bank or savings
department. In the event of such approval by the commissioner, other provisions of law applicable to the investment of funds of savings banks and to the limitations upon

Conditions and
restrictions.

deposits therein shall not apply. The commissioner may
impose such conditions and restrictions as he may deem
necessary or advisable in respect to the deposit or other
liabilities assumed as hereinbefore provided, and in the
case of any new savings bank formed for the purpose of
purchasing any or all the assets and assuming any or all
the liabilities of any savings bank or savings department
of a trust company now or hereafter in his possession under
said sections he may impose such other and further conditions and restrictions concerning the business, investments
and operation of such new savings bank as he may deem
necessary or advisable. So much of section thirteen as
provides that no person shall hold an office in two savings
banks at the same time shall not prevent an officer or
trustee of any other savings bank from serving as an officer
or trustee of such new bank.

G. L. (Ter.
Ed.), 172, new
section after
§ 44.

SECTION 2. Chapter one hundred and seventy-two
of the General Laws, as so appearing, is hereby amended
by inserting after section forty-four the following new sec-

tion: — *Section 44A.* With the approval of the com- Trust companies may
missioner, a trust company, through its savings or com- purchase, loan
mercial department, may advance or loan upon, or pur- upon or participate in
chase, the whole or any part of the assets of any other trust loans upon the
company, including trust companies now or hereafter in assets of certain closed and
possession of the commissioner under sections twenty- other banks.
two to thirty-six, inclusive, of chapter one hundred and
sixty-seven, and may participate in such an advance, loan
or purchase with one or more other trust companies or
savings banks. The trust company making or participating in such advance, loan or purchase, for the purpose of
effecting the same, may, through its savings department,
assume and agree to pay the whole or any part of the
deposit and other liabilities of the savings department, and
may, through its commercial department, assume and
agree to pay the whole or any part of the deposit and other
liabilities of the commercial department, of such other
trust company. In the event of such approval by the
commissioner, other provisions of law applicable to the investment of funds of savings departments of trust companies shall not apply. The commissioner may impose Conditions and
such conditions and restrictions as he may deem necessary restrictions.
or advisable in respect to the deposit or other liabilities
assumed as hereinbefore provided, and in the case of any
new trust company formed for the purpose of purchasing
any or all of the assets and assuming any or all of the
liabilities of any trust company now or hereafter in his
possession under said sections, he may impose such other
and further conditions and restrictions concerning the
business, investments and operation of such new trust
company as he may deem necessary or advisable.

Section 3. Section sixty-one of said chapter one G. L. (Ter. Ed.), 172, § 61,
hundred and seventy-two, as so appearing, is hereby amended.
amended by inserting after the word "banks" in the fourth
line the following: —, subject, however, to section fifty-six
of chapter one hundred and sixty-eight, — so as to read as
follows: — *Section 61.* All such deposits shall be special Trust companies.
deposits and shall be placed in said savings department, and Investments of
all loans or investments thereof shall be made in accordance deposits in
with the law governing the investment of deposits in sav- savings department.
ings banks, subject, however, to section fifty-six of chapter
one hundred and sixty-eight. The investment committee
shall approve all loans and all purchases or sales of bonds,
stocks and notes made by or for the savings department,
and shall perform such other duties as the by-laws or board
of directors may prescribe. A record shall be made at
each meeting of the transactions of the committee and of
the names of those present. The committee may, by
vote or by a statement signed by a majority of its members,
approve changes of collateral security made by or for said
department, and the vote or statement, and the record
thereof, shall set forth all such changes.

Section 4. Section twenty-four of chapter one hundred G. L. (Ter. Ed.), 167, § 24, etc., amended.

and sixty-seven of the General Laws, as most recently amended by chapter two hundred and ninety-four of the acts of nineteen hundred and thirty-two, is hereby further amended by inserting after the word "sell" in the tenth line the following: — for cash or other consideration or as provided by section fifty-six of chapter one hundred and sixty-eight or section forty-four A of chapter one hundred and seventy-two, — so as to read as follows: — *Section 24.*

Authority of commissioner of banks in possession of property and business of certain banks.

Upon taking possession of the property and business of such bank, the commissioner may collect moneys due to the bank, and do all acts necessary to conserve its assets and business, and shall proceed to liquidate its affairs as hereinafter provided. He shall collect all debts due and claims belonging to it, and upon the order or decree of the supreme judicial court, or any justice thereof, may sell or compound all bad or doubtful debts, and on like order or decree may sell for cash or other consideration or as provided by section fifty-six of chapter one hundred and sixty-eight or section forty-four A of chapter one hundred and seventy-two, all, or any part of, the real and personal property of the bank on such terms as the court shall direct; and, in the name of such bank, may take a mortgage on such real property from a bona fide purchaser to secure the whole or a part of the purchase price, upon such terms and for such periods as the court shall direct. If, at any time

Enforcement of liability of stockholders of trust companies in possession.

after he has taken possession of the property and business of a trust company under section twenty-two, the commissioner deems it necessary to enforce the individual liability of stockholders therein, as described in the first sentence of section twenty-four of chapter one hundred and seventy-two, in order to pay the liabilities of such trust company, he may file a bill in equity, in the supreme judicial court for the county where the principal office of the trust company is located, against all persons who were stockholders therein at the time of such taking possession, to enforce such individual liability. The court may by its

Assessments by court.

decree assess upon the stockholders in such suit severally sums in proportion to the amounts of stock held by them respectively at the time of such taking possession; but no such stockholder shall be liable to pay a larger sum than the amount of the par value of the stock held by him at

Suits not to abate, etc.

the time of such taking possession. Such suit shall not abate by reason of the non-joinder of persons liable as respondents, unless the commissioner, after notice by plea or answer of their existence, unreasonably neglects to make them parties; nor shall it abate by reason of the death of a respondent, but his estate shall be liable in the hands of his executor or administrator, who may voluntarily appear, or who may be summoned by the commissioner to defend the suit.   *Approved February 24, 1933.*

An Act relative to certain provisions of law exempting proceeds of policies of life or endowment insurance from claims of creditors of persons effecting such insurance.

Chap. 42

Be it enacted, etc., as follows:

Chapter one hundred and seventy-six of the acts of nineteen hundred and twenty-eight is hereby amended by adding at the end thereof the following new section: — *Section 4.* This act shall apply to policies of life or endowment insurance issued or delivered in the commonwealth on or before July second, nineteen hundred and twenty-eight, as well as to those so issued or delivered after said date.   *Approved February 24, 1933.*

1928, 176, new section at end thereof.

Application of act.

An Act prohibiting riding upon the rear or on the side of street railway cars or motor buses without the consent of the persons in charge thereof.

Chap. 43

Be it enacted, etc., as follows:

Chapter eighty-five of the General Laws, as appearing in the Tercentenary Edition thereof, is hereby amended by inserting after section seventeen A the following new section: — *Section 17B.* Whoever rides upon the rear or side of any street railway car or motor bus without the consent of the person in charge thereof shall be punished by a fine of not more than twenty dollars.

Approved February 24, 1933.

G. L. (Ter. Ed.), 85, new section after § 17A.

Riding upon rear, etc., of street railway cars, etc., without consent of persons in charge thereof, prohibited.

An Act relative to discrimination against the treatment of gonorrhea or syphilis in certain hospitals.

Chap. 44

Be it enacted, etc., as follows:

Section one hundred and eighteen of chapter one hundred and eleven of the General Laws, as appearing in the Tercentenary Edition thereof, is hereby amended by striking out, in the second line, the words "venereal diseases in the out-patient department of" and inserting in place thereof the words: — gonorrhea or syphilis in, — and by inserting after the word "city" in the third line the words: — or town, — so as to read as follows: — *Section 118.* No discrimination shall be made against the treatment of gonorrhea or syphilis in any general hospital supported by taxation in any city or town where special hospitals, other than hospitals connected with penal institutions, are not provided for the treatment of such diseases at public expense; but any such hospital may establish a separate ward for their treatment.   *Approved February 24, 1933.*

G. L. (Ter. Ed.), 111, § 118, amended.

Discrimination against treatment of gonorrhea or syphilis in certain hospitals, when forbidden.

Chap. 45 AN ACT TO ERECT AND CONSTITUTE IN THE TOWN OF SOUTH HADLEY REPRESENTATIVE TOWN GOVERNMENT BY LIMITED TOWN MEETINGS.

Be it enacted, etc., as follows:

Representative town government by limited town meetings in town of South Hadley.

SECTION 1. There is hereby erected and constituted in the town of South Hadley the form of representative town government by limited town meetings hereinafter set forth.

Town meeting members, election, terms, etc.

SECTION 2. The voters of each precinct in the town of South Hadley shall, at the next ensuing annual town election held after the acceptance of this act, and conformably to the laws relative to elections not inconsistent with this act, elect by ballot from residents of the precinct town meeting members, other than the officers designated in section three of this act as town meeting members ex officiis, to the largest number which is divisible by three and which will not exceed two per cent of the number of registered voters in the precinct upon and including the first day of January next preceding said election. The first third in the order of votes received of members elected at such annual election in each precinct shall serve until the third succeeding annual election, the second third in the order of votes received at such election shall serve until the second succeeding annual election, and the remaining third in the order of votes received at such election shall serve until the first succeeding annual election; and thereafter except as herein provided, at each annual election the voters of each precinct in the town shall, in like manner, elect as town meeting members the largest number which will not exceed two thirds of one per cent of the number of registered voters in such precinct upon and including the first day of January next preceding such annual election, for the term of three years, and shall, at such election, fill for the unexpired term or terms any vacancies then existing in the number of town meeting members in the precinct.

Change of precincts, etc.

After the acceptance of this act, the boundaries of the precincts may from time to time be changed according to general law, but the precincts shall not number less than four. Upon every change of the precincts or of any precinct in the town, the terms of office of all town meeting members from every precinct which shall be in any way altered by such change, shall cease upon the election of their successors, and at the first ensuing annual town election there shall be a new election of town meeting members in every precinct so changed, as well as in any new precinct or precincts established, said election to be held in the manner hereinbefore prescribed for the first election under this act.

When terms of office of certain town meeting members shall cease, etc.

Tie vote.

In the case of a tie vote which affects the election of town meeting members in any precinct otherwise than as to term of office, the members elected from such precinct at the same election shall, by a majority vote, determine which of the voters receiving such tie vote shall serve as town meeting members from such precinct, and in case of a tie vote affecting the term of office of members elected, the members elected from such precinct at the same election other than those whose terms of office are affected by such tie vote, shall, by a majority vote, determine which member receiving such tie vote shall serve for the longer and which for the shorter term.

The town clerk shall, after every election of town meeting members, forthwith notify each member, by mail, of his election. *Notice to members elected.*

Section 3. The representative town meetings held under the provisions of this act, except as otherwise provided herein, shall be limited to the elected town meeting members together with the following, designated as town meeting members ex officiis, namely: any member of the general court of the commonwealth who is a registered voter of the town, the town moderator, the town clerk, the selectmen, the town treasurer, the town counsel if a registered voter of the town, the town collector of taxes, the chairman of the school committee, the chairman of the trustees of the public library, the chairman of the board of health, the chairman of the board of public welfare, the chairman of the park commissioners, the chairman of the municipal light commissioners, the tree warden, the chairman of the assessors of taxes, the finance committee, the chairman of the board of registrars of voters, the town accountant, and the chairman of any other board, commission or committee established in the town by authority of the general court. *Town meetings limited to elected town meeting members and certain designated town meeting members.*

The secretary or clerk of each of said boards, commissions and committees shall file with the town clerk a certificate of election of a chairman. *Certificate of election of chairman.*

Any elected town meeting member who becomes by appointment or election one of the officers designated as town meeting members, ex officiis, shall, upon such appointment or election, cease to be an elected town meeting member. The town clerk shall notify the town meeting members of the time and place at which representative town meetings are to be held, such notices to be sent by mail at least three days before any such meeting, but failure to comply with this provision shall not affect the legal force of any act of the meeting, and this provision shall be in addition to the warrant for such meeting duly published and served according to law. The representative town meeting shall have authority to determine the election and qualifications, as set forth in this act, of its members. A majority of the town meeting members shall constitute a quorum for doing business; but a less number may organize temporarily and may adjourn from time to time. All town meetings shall be held in public. Town meeting *When certain elected town meeting members shall cease to be such.* *Notice of town meetings.* *Town meeting members to determine election of members.* *Quorum.* *Meetings public.*

members shall receive no compensation as such. Subject to such conditions as may be determined from time to time by the representative town meeting, any voter of the town who is not a town meeting member may speak at any representative town meeting, but he shall not vote. An elected town meeting member may resign by filing a written resignation with the town clerk, and such resignation shall take effect on the date of such filing. An elected town meeting member who removes from the precinct from which he was elected shall cease to be a town meeting member.

SECTION 4. Nominations of candidates for town meeting members to be elected under this act shall be made by nomination papers which shall bear no political designation, but to the name of a candidate for re-election there may be added the words "Candidate for Re-election". Nomination papers shall be signed by not less than ten registered voters of the precinct in which the candidate is nominated for office and filed with the town clerk at least fifteen days before the election; provided, that an elected town meeting member may become a candidate for re-election by giving written notice thereof to the town clerk at least thirty days before the election.

SECTION 5. All articles in the warrant for every town meeting, so far as they relate to the election of the town moderator, town officers and town meeting members, and, as herein provided, to referenda and all matters to be acted upon and determined by ballot, shall be so acted upon and determined by the registered voters of the town in their respective precincts. All other articles in the warrant for any town meeting, beginning with the annual town meeting in the year when said town meeting members are first elected, shall be acted upon and determined exclusively by town meeting members at a representative town meeting to be held at such time and place as shall be set forth by the selectmen in the warrant for the meeting, and subject to the referendum provided for by section eight.

SECTION 6. The moderator shall continue to be elected by ballot in the same manner as is now provided. Any vacancy in the office shall be filled by the town meeting members at a meeting held for that purpose. If a moderator is absent a moderator pro tempore may be elected by the town meeting members.

SECTION 7. In the event of any vacancy in the full number of elected town meeting members from any precinct a majority of said members may choose from among the registered voters thereof a successor to serve until the next annual town election. The town clerk may, and upon a petition therefor signed by a majority of the elected town meeting members from the precinct shall, call a special meeting for the purpose of filling such vacancy and shall mail notice thereof to the remaining elected members from the precinct specifying the object and the time and place of such meeting which shall be held not less than four days after the mailing of such notice. At such meeting a majority of such members shall constitute a quorum and shall elect from their own number a chairman and a clerk. The election to fill such vacancy shall be by ballot and a majority of the votes cast shall be required for a choice. *Election by ballot.* The clerk shall forthwith file with the town clerk a certificate of such election, together with a written acceptance *Certificate of election.* by the member so elected, who shall thereupon be deemed elected and qualified as an elected town meeting member, subject to the provisions of section three respecting the election and qualifications of elected town meeting members.

SECTION 8. No article in the warrant shall at any *Warrant articles, disposition.* representative town meeting be finally disposed of by a vote to lay upon the table, to indefinitely postpone, or to take no action thereunder. No vote passed at any repre- *Votes, when effective.* sentative town meeting under any article in the warrant, except a vote to adjourn or a vote for the temporary borrowing of money in anticipation of revenue or a vote declared by a two thirds vote of the town meeting members present and voting thereon to be an emergency measure necessary for the immediate preservation of the peace, health, safety or convenience of the town, shall take effect until after the expiration of seven days, exclusive of Sundays and holidays, from the date of such vote. If, within *Referendum.* said seven days a petition, signed by not less than fifty registered voters from each precinct, the aggregate number of voters so signing being in no event less than five per cent of the number of registered voters of the town, containing the names and street addresses of the voters so signing as they appear on the list of registered voters, is filed with the selectmen asking that the question or questions involved in such vote be submitted to the voters of the town at large, then the selectmen within fourteen days of the filing of such petition shall call a special town meeting which shall be held within twenty-one days after notice of the call, for the sole purpose of presenting to the voters at large the question or questions so involved. All votes upon any questions submitted shall be taken by ballot, and the check lists shall be used in the several precincts in the same manner in which they are used in the election of town officers. The polls shall be opened at two o'clock *Opening and closing of polls, etc.* in the afternoon and shall be closed not earlier than eight o'clock in the evening and no ballots shall be removed or counted before the closing of the polls. The question or *Questions, how stated upon ballot, etc.* questions submitted to be voted upon at said town meeting shall be stated upon the ballot in substantially the same language and form in which they were stated when finally presented to said representative town meeting by the moderator as appears upon the records of said meeting, and such question or questions shall be determined by vote of the same proportion of the voters at large voting thereon as would have been required by law had the question been

Vote, when effective if no petition filed.

finally determined at a representative town meeting. If such petition be not filed within said period of seven days, the vote in the representative town meeting shall take effect upon the expiration of said period.

Powers of town and its town meeting members, etc.

SECTION 9. The town of South Hadley, after the acceptance of this act, shall have the capacity to act through and be bound by its said town meeting members who shall, when convened from time to time as herein provided, constitute representative town meetings; and the representative town meetings shall exercise exclusively so far as will conform to the provisions of this act, all powers vested in the municipal corporation. Action in conformity with all provisions of law now or hereafter applicable to the transaction of town affairs in town meetings shall, when taken by any representative town meeting in accordance with the provisions of this act, have the same force and effect as if such action had been taken in a town meeting open to all the voters of the town as heretofore organized and conducted.

Certain rights not abridged, etc.

SECTION 10. No right secured to the inhabitants of the town of South Hadley by the constitution of this commonwealth shall be abridged by this act; nor shall this act confer upon any representative town meeting the power to commit said town to any proposition affecting its municipal existence, or the form of its government without action thereon by the voters of said town at large using the ballot and check lists therefor.

Submission to voters of town of South Hadley, etc.

SECTION 11. This act shall be submitted to the registered voters of the town of South Hadley at any annual town meeting called within two years from the passage of this act. The vote shall be taken in precincts by ballot in accordance with the provisions of general law, so far as the same shall be applicable, in answer to the question, which shall be placed upon the official ballot to be used in the several precincts in said town at such election for the election of town officers: — "Shall an act passed by the general court in the year nineteen hundred and thirty-three, entitled 'An Act to erect and constitute in the town of South Hadley representative town government by limited town meetings', be accepted by this town?" If accepted by a majority of the voters voting thereon at any such annual meeting, this act shall thereupon take effect for all purposes incidental to the annual town election in said town in the year next ensuing, and shall take full effect beginning with said election.　　*Approved February 24, 1933.*

An Act authorizing savings and co-operative banks *Chap.* 46
to become members of the federal home loan bank
established for the district of new england.

Whereas, The deferred operation of this act would, in Emergency
part, defeat its purpose to afford relief in the existing finan- preamble.
cial emergency by making immediately available to sav-
ings and co-operative banks the assistance and co-operation
provided by the Federal Home Loan Bank Act, therefore
this act is hereby declared to be an emergency law, necessary for the immediate preservation of the public health,
safety and convenience.

Be it enacted, etc., as follows:

SECTION 1. Chapter one hundred and sixty-eight of the G. L. (Ter.
General Laws, as appearing in the Tercentenary Edition Ed.), 168, new
section after
thereof, is hereby amended by inserting after section two § 2.
the following new section: — *Section 2A.* Any such sav- Savings banks
ings bank may become a member of the Federal Home members of
Loan Bank established for the district of New England Federal Home
Loan Bank
under the provisions of an act of congress, approved July established for
district of
twenty-second, nineteen hundred and thirty-two, and New England.
known as the federal home loan bank act, or of any successor of said bank so established; and may, subject otherwise to the provisions of this chapter, subscribe to and invest
in such amounts of the stock of said home loan bank as
may be required by said act of congress to qualify such
savings bank for membership in said home loan bank.

SECTION 2. Chapter one hundred and seventy of the G. L. (Ter.
General Laws, as so appearing, is hereby amended by in- Ed.), 170, new
section after
serting after section forty-five the following new section:— § 45.
Section 45A. Any corporation subject to this chapter may Co-operative
become a member of the Federal Home Loan Bank estab- banks may become members
lished for the district of New England under the provisions of Federal
Home Loan
of an act of congress, approved July twenty-second, nine- Bank estab-
teen hundred and thirty-two, and known as the federal lished for district of
home loan bank act, or of any successor of said bank so New England.
established; and may, subject otherwise to the provisions
of this chapter, subscribe to and invest in such amounts
of the stock of said home loan bank as may be required
by said act of congress to qualify such corporation for
membership in said home loan bank.

Approved March 1, 1933.

An Act relative to certain lines, poles and other *Chap.* 47
equipment of the town of hingham and of the new
england telephone and telegraph company of
massachusetts, in the town of hingham.

Be it enacted, etc., as follows:

SECTION 1. All lines for the transmission of electricity, Certain lines,
for light, heat or power heretofore acquired or constructed poles and
other equip-
by the municipal lighting board of the town of Hingham, ment of town

of Hingham
and of The
New England
Telephone and
Telegraph
Company of
Massachu-
setts in said
town made
lawful, not-
withstanding,
etc.
and all lines for the transmission of intelligence by electricity heretofore acquired or constructed by The New
England Telephone and Telegraph Company of Massachusetts, upon, along, over or under the public ways and
places of said town, and the poles, piers, abutments, conduits and other fixtures necessary to sustain or protect the
wires of said lines, and in actual use on the effective date of
this act, are hereby made lawful notwithstanding the lack
of any valid locations therefor or any informality in the
proceedings relative to their location and erection; pro-
Proviso.
vided, that the said town of Hingham by its municipal
lighting board and said company shall, not later than the
first day of December in the current year, file with the
town clerk a map or maps showing in detail the location
and nature of the said lines, structures and fixtures in said
town; such map or maps to be recorded and kept with the
records of original locations for poles and wires in said
town.

SECTION 2.   This act shall take effect upon its passage.
Approved March 1, 1933.

Chap. 48   AN ACT PROVIDING THAT CERTAIN LANDS AND WATERS NOW
UNDER JURISDICTION OR CONTROL OF THE WATER AND
SEWER DEPARTMENT OF THE CITY OF MEDFORD BE TRANS-
FERRED TO THE JURISDICTION AND CONTROL OF THE PARK
DEPARTMENT OF SAID CITY.

Be it enacted, etc., as follows:

Certain lands
and waters in
city of Med-
ford to be
under control
of park de-
partment of
said city.
SECTION 1.   The lands and waters in that part of the
city of Medford within the area bounded by Forest street,
Elm street, Woodland road and the Stoneham line, now
under the control or jurisdiction of the water and sewer
department of the said city of Medford, shall hereafter be
under the control and jurisdiction of the park department
of the said city.

SECTION 2.   This act shall take effect upon its passage.
Approved March 1, 1933.

Chap. 49   AN ACT CREATING AN EMERGENCY FINANCE BOARD AND
DEFINING ITS POWERS AND DUTIES.

Emergency
preamble.
Whereas, The deferred operation of this act would defeat
its purpose, therefore it is hereby declared to be an emergency law, necessary for the immediate preservation of the
public convenience.

Be it enacted, etc., as follows:

Emergency
finance board,
membership,
terms.
SECTION 1.   There shall be in the department of the
state treasurer, subject to his control only to the extent of
his membership therein, an emergency finance board,
hereinafter called the board, consisting of the state treasurer
and the director of the division of accounts, ex officiis,
and three citizens of the commonwealth to be appointed
by the governor, with the advice and consent of the council,

who shall be designated in their initial appointments to
serve respectively for one, two and three years. The Chairman.
governor, with like advice and consent, shall, from time to
time, designate one of the members as chairman, may remove any appointive member, and shall fill any vacancy Vacancies.
in the appointive membership of the board for the unexpired term. Upon the expiration of the term of office of
an appointive member, his successor shall be appointed in
the manner aforesaid for three years. If the state treasurer Designation of certain tem-
or said director is unable by reason of absence or disability porary officers
to perform his duties as such member, said state treasurer, in certain cases.
or the commissioner of corporations and taxation, in the
case of said director, may, by a writing filed with the board,
designate an officer or employee in his department who
shall, without additional compensation therefor, perform
such duties during such absence or disability. The action
of a majority of the members shall constitute action of the
board; and whenever any action by the board is required
to be in writing, such writing shall be sufficient when signed
by a majority of the members. Each appointive member Compensation.
shall receive from the commonwealth as compensation the
sum of ten dollars for each day's attendance at board meetings; provided, that the total amount paid to any member Proviso.
for compensation as aforesaid shall not exceed five hundred
dollars in any one year. The commissioner of corporations Clerical assistance.
and taxation shall, upon request of the board, assign to it
such clerical assistance as it may need from the personnel
of the department of corporations and taxation, and any
expense incurred by said department by reason of such
assignment shall be deemed an expense of the board. The When exist-ence of board
existence of the board shall terminate and this act shall shall termi-
cease to be operative when, as determined by the governor, nate, etc.
the purposes of its establishment have been accomplished,
but not before the payment in full to the commonwealth of
all amounts borrowed by cities and towns under this act,
including interest.

SECTION 2. The treasurer of any city or town, if author- Board may grant its ap-
ized by a two thirds vote, as defined by section one of proval to peti-
chapter forty-four of the General Laws, and with the tion of a city or town to
approval of the mayor or the selectmen, may, on behalf borrow money
of such city or town, petition the board to approve of its from com-monwealth.
borrowing money from the commonwealth for ordinary
maintenance expenses, and the board may, if in its judgment the financial affairs of such city or town warrant,
grant its approval to the borrowing as aforesaid of specified
sums not at any time exceeding, in the aggregate, the total Aggregate amount.
amount represented by tax titles taken or purchased by
such city or town and held by it; provided, that such bor- Proviso.
rowing is made at any time or times prior to July first,
nineteen hundred and thirty-five. In case of such approval, Issue of notes, etc.
the treasurer of such city or town shall, without further
vote, issue notes, with interest at not less than four per
cent per annum, in the amount approved by the board, for

purposes of sale to the commonwealth only, and said notes, upon their tender to the state treasurer, shall forthwith be purchased by the commonwealth at the face value thereof. Such notes shall be payable in not more than one year, and may be renewed from time to time, if authorized by the board, but no renewal note shall be for a period of more than one year, and the maturity of any loan or renewal shall not be later than July first, nineteen hundred and thirty-six. Such notes shall be general obligations of the city or town issuing the same, notwithstanding the foregoing provisions. Indebtedness incurred by a city or town under authority of this act shall be outside its limit of indebtedness as fixed by chapter forty-four of the General Laws. The excess, if any, of the amount of interest payments received by the commonwealth on account of notes issued by cities and towns hereunder over the cost to the commonwealth for interest on money borrowed under section five, expenses of the board, including compensation paid to its appointive members, and expenses of administration of the funds provided by sections three and five shall be distributed to such cities and towns in November, nineteen hundred and thirty-nine, or earlier at the discretion of the board, in the proportion which the aggregate amounts payable by them on account of interest on such notes bear to the total amounts so payable by all cities and towns hereunder.

Distribution of excess of amount of interest payments received by commonwealth, etc.

SECTION 3. Until payment to the commonwealth of all principal and interest on account of any notes issued by a city or town hereunder and held by the commonwealth, all amounts received during any month by such city or town from the redemption or sale of land purchased or taken by it for non-payment of taxes, or from the assignment of any tax title held by it, shall, at the end of such month, be paid over to the state treasurer who shall receive and forthwith apply the same toward the payment of any note or notes issued hereunder by such city or town and then held by the commonwealth, and thereafter interest shall be payable only on the balance of such note or notes remaining unpaid.

Amounts received by city or town from assignment of any tax titles held by it, etc., to be paid monthly to state treasurer, until, etc.

SECTION 4. If a city or town fails to make any payment of principal or interest on any note issued by it hereunder, when due, the state treasurer shall have authority, not later than the issue of his warrant for its share of the state tax in any year, to issue his warrant requiring its assessors to include in the next annual tax levy the amount necessary to make such payment in full or to pay any instalment thereof as determined and certified to him by the board as hereinafter provided. If, in the opinion of the board, the financial affairs of any city or town failing or likely to fail to make payment as aforesaid warrant, the board may direct the assessment of the amount necessary to make such payment in full, in such number of annual instalments, not exceeding three, as may seem advisable; provided, that the amount of any instalment

Authority of state treasurer in case city or town fails to make payment when due.

Payment in instalments.

Proviso.

payable in any year shall not be less than the amount of any instalment payable in any subsequent year. Seasonably before the issue of the warrant of the state treasurer for the share of any city or town of the state tax in any year, the board shall determine and certify to the state treasurer the amount of such instalment required to be assessed upon any particular city or town in that year. The amount included under authority hereof in the state treasurer's warrant to the assessors of any city or town shall be collected and paid to him in the same manner and subject to the same penalties as state taxes, and if such amount is not duly paid as aforesaid by such city or town, the state treasurer shall have authority to withhold, from any sum due from the commonwealth to it and not previously pledged, the amount necessary to reimburse the commonwealth for such failure to pay.

SECTION 5. The state treasurer, with the approval of the governor and council, may borrow from time to time, on the credit of the commonwealth, such sums as may be necessary to provide funds for loans to municipalities as aforesaid, but not exceeding ten million dollars, and may issue and renew notes of the commonwealth therefor, bearing interest payable at such times and at such rate as shall be fixed by the state treasurer, with the approval of the governor and council. Such notes shall be issued for such maximum term of years as the governor may recommend to the general court in accordance with section three of Article LXII of the amendments to the constitution of the commonwealth, but such notes, whether original or renewal, shall be payable not later than November thirtieth, nineteen hundred and thirty-nine. All notes issued under this section shall be signed by the state treasurer, approved by the governor and countersigned by the comptroller. *State treasurer may issue and renew notes, etc.* *Term, etc.*

Approved March 1, 1933.

AN ACT FURTHER EXTENDING THE TIME DURING WHICH THE CITIES OF LYNN, PEABODY, SALEM AND BEVERLY AND THE TOWN OF DANVERS MAY TAKE WATER FROM THE IPSWICH RIVER FOR EMERGENCY PURPOSES. *Chap. 50*

Be it enacted, etc., as follows:

Section one of chapter one hundred and fifteen of the Special Acts of nineteen hundred and nineteen, as amended by section one of chapter sixty-six of the acts of nineteen hundred and twenty-two, by section one of chapter nineteen of the acts of nineteen hundred and twenty-five, by section one of chapter sixty-one of the acts of nineteen hundred and twenty-eight, and by section one of chapter thirty-one of the acts of nineteen hundred and thirty-one, is hereby further amended by striking out, in the twelfth and thirteenth lines the words "thirty-one, nineteen hundred and thirty-two and nineteen hundred and thirty-three" and inserting in place thereof the words: — thirty- *1919 (S), 115, § 1, etc., amended.*

three, nineteen hundred and thirty-four, nineteen hundred and thirty-five and nineteen hundred and thirty-six, — so as to read as follows: — *Section 1.* The cities of Lynn, Peabody, Salem and Beverly and the town of Danvers, authorized to take water from the Ipswich river or its tributaries during the months from December to May, inclusive, under the provisions of chapter five hundred and eight of the acts of nineteen hundred and one and chapters six hundred and ninety-eight, six hundred and ninety-nine and seven hundred of the acts of nineteen hundred and thirteen, are hereby further authorized, in case of emergency, to take water from said river or its tributaries during the months from June to November, inclusive, in the years nineteen hundred and thirty-three, nineteen hundred and thirty-four, nineteen hundred and thirty-five and nineteen hundred and thirty-six, or any of said years, in quantities not exceeding those which may be taken from December to May, inclusive, as set forth in said acts, whenever, in the opinion of the department of public health, the taking of water during the months aforesaid in the years mentioned, or any of them, is necessary to provide an adequate water supply for the cities and town herein mentioned, subject otherwise to the remaining provisions of said acts. *Approved March 1, 1933.*

Time during which the cities of Lynn, Peabody, Salem and Beverly and town of Danvers may take water from Ipswich river for emergency purposes, further extended.

Chap. 51 AN ACT REGULATING THE DISPLAY OF RED LIGHTS ON MOTOR VEHICLES AND REQUIRING CERTAIN MOTOR VEHICLES TO BE EQUIPPED WITH RED REFLECTORS VISIBLE FROM THE REAR.

Be it enacted, etc., as follows:

G. L. 90, § 7, etc., amended.

Section seven of chapter ninety of the General Laws, as most recently amended by section one of chapter one hundred and twenty-three of the acts of nineteen hundred and thirty-two, is hereby further amended by inserting after the word "number" in the fifty-second line the two following new sentences: — No motor vehicle so operated, except fire apparatus, shall display a red light in the direction toward which the vehicle is proceeding or facing. Every commercial motor vehicle or trailer having a carrying capacity of two tons or over shall, in addition to such rear light, be equipped with a red reflector, approved by the registrar, so placed at the rear of such vehicle as to reflect rays of light thrown upon such reflector from behind, — so as to read as follows: — *Section 7.* Every motor vehicle operated in or upon any way shall be provided with brakes adequate to control the movement of such vehicle and conforming to rules and regulations made by the registrar, and such brakes shall at all times be maintained in good working order. Every automobile shall be provided with at least two braking systems, each with a separate means of application, each operating directly or indirectly on at least two wheels and each of which shall suffice alone to stop

Brakes on motor vehicles.

said automobile within a proper distance as defined in said rules and regulations; provided, that if said systems are connected, combined or have any part in common, such systems shall be so constructed that a breaking of any one element thereof will not leave the automobile without brakes acting directly or indirectly on at least two wheels. One braking system shall be so constructed that it can be set to hold the automobile stationary. Every motor cycle shall be provided with at least one brake adequate to stop it within a proper distance as defined as aforesaid. Every motor vehicle so operated shall be provided with a muffler or other suitable device to prevent unnecessary noise and with a suitable bell, horn or other means of signalling, and with suitable lamps; and automobiles shall be provided with a lock, a key or other device to prevent such vehicle from being set in motion by unauthorized persons, or otherwise, contrary to the will of the owner or person in charge thereof. Every automobile operated during the period from one half an hour after sunset to one half an hour before sunrise shall display at least two white lights, or lights of yellow or amber tint, or, if parked within the limits of a way, one white light on the side of the automobile nearer the centre of the way, and every motor cycle so operated at least one white light, or light of yellow or amber tint, and every such motor cycle with a side-car attached, in addition, one such light on the front of the side-car, and every motor truck, trailer and commercial motor vehicle used solely as such, having a carrying capacity of three tons or over, in addition, a green light attached to the extreme left of the front of such vehicle, so attached and adjusted as to indicate the extreme left lateral extension of the vehicle or load, which shall in all cases aforesaid be visible not less than two hundred feet in the direction toward which the vehicle is proceeding or facing; and every such motor vehicle shall display at least one red light in the reverse direction; provided, that an automobile need display no light when parked within the limits of a way in a space in which unlighted parking is permitted by the rules or regulations of the board or officer having control of such way. Every automobile so operated shall have a rear light so placed as to show a red light from behind and a white light so arranged as to illuminate and not obscure the rear register number. No motor vehicle so operated, except fire apparatus, shall display a red light in the direction toward which the vehicle is proceeding or facing. Every commercial motor vehicle or trailer having a carrying capacity of two tons or over shall, in addition to such rear light, be equipped with a red reflector, approved by the registrar, so placed at the rear of such vehicle as to reflect rays of light thrown upon such reflector from behind. No headlamp or rear lamp shall be used on any motor vehicle so operated, and no device which obstructs, reflects or alters the beam of such headlamp shall be used in connection therewith, unless approved by the registrar. Application for the approval of a headlamp, or of a rear lamp, accompanied by a fee of fifty dollars, may be made to the registrar by any manufacturer thereof or dealer therein. Every automobile used for the carriage of passengers for hire, and every commercial motor vehicle or motor truck, so constructed, equipped or loaded that the person operating the same is prevented from having a constantly free and unobstructed view of the highway immediately in the rear, shall have attached to the vehicle a mirror or reflector so placed and adjusted as to afford the operator a clear, reflected view of the highway in the rear of the vehicle.

Mirrors or reflectors.

Approved March 1, 1933.

Chap. 52 AN ACT RELATIVE TO THE PLACING OF JAMES L. MOLLOY OF BOSTON ON THE RETIRED LIST OF COMMISSIONED OFFICERS OF THE MILITIA.

Be it enacted, etc., as follows:

The adjutant general may place James L. Molloy of Boston on retired list of commissioned officers of militia.

The adjutant general is hereby authorized and directed to place James L. Molloy of Boston upon the retired list of commissioned officers provided for the purpose by the provisions of section ninety-eight of chapter thirty-three of the General Laws, or corresponding provisions of earlier laws, with the rank of major, as of April twelfth, nineteen hundred and ten, notwithstanding that said Molloy did not serve as a commissioned officer for a sufficient period of time to satisfy the requirements of said provisions.

Approved March 1, 1933.

Chap. 53 AN ACT EMPOWERING THE LEOPOLD MORSE HOME FOR INFIRM HEBREWS AND ORPHANAGE TO TRANSFER ITS PROPERTY TO THE ASSOCIATED JEWISH PHILANTHROPIES, INC.

Be it enacted, etc., as follows:

Leopold Morse Home for Infirm Hebrews and Orphanage empowered to transfer its property to the Associated Jewish Philanthropies, Inc.

SECTION 1. The Leopold Morse Home for Infirm Hebrews and Orphanage, a corporation incorporated under general law under the name of the Boston Home for Aged and Infirm Hebrews and Orphanage, whose name was changed to its present name by chapter thirteen of the acts of eighteen hundred and ninety-four, is hereby empowered to transfer, assign, set over, and convey all funds and property held by it to the Associated Jewish Philanthropies, Inc., incorporated under general law, and the said Associated Jewish Philanthropies, Inc. is hereby empowered to receive the same and to hold, manage and dispose of all such funds and property charged with any trust, upon the same trusts, uses and purposes as if the same had continued to be held by the said Leopold Morse Home for Infirm Hebrews and Orphanage for the fulfillment of the charitable purposes of said corporation.

SECTION 2. The power hereby granted shall be exercised only in conformity with such a decree, if any, of the supreme judicial court, sitting in equity, for the county of Suffolk, as may be entered within one year after the passage of this act.

Power granted to be exercised only in conformity with decree, etc.

SECTION 3. This act shall not take effect until it shall have been accepted by the votes of the board of directors, or the officers having the powers of directors, of each of said corporations and copies of the respective votes of acceptance shall have been filed with the secretary of the commonwealth.   *Approved March 1, 1933.*

Effective upon acceptance, etc.

AN ACT AUTHORIZING THE REGISTRAR OF MOTOR VEHICLES TO SUSPEND THE REGISTRATION OF MOTOR VEHICLES OR TRAILERS DETERMINED TO BE UNSAFE.

Chap. 54

Be it enacted, etc., as follows:

Section two of chapter ninety of the General Laws, as most recently amended by chapter five of the acts of nineteen hundred and thirty-two, is hereby further amended by striking out the last paragraph, as printed in the Tercentenary Edition, and inserting in place thereof the following: — If the registrar shall determine at any time that, for any reason, a motor vehicle or trailer is unsafe or improperly equipped or otherwise unfit to be operated, he may refuse to register such motor vehicle or trailer or, if it is already registered, may suspend or revoke its registration. The horse power of every motor vehicle sought to be registered shall be determined by the commissioner of public works, and his determination shall be final and conclusive. The registration of every motor vehicle and trailer registered under this section shall expire at midnight on December thirty-first of each year.

G. L. 90, § 2, etc., amended.

Suspension of registration of motor vehicles or trailers determined to be unsafe.

Approved March 1, 1933.

AN ACT RELATIVE TO THE POWER OF THE LAND COURT TO ENFORCE ITS ORDERS AND DECREES AND RELATIVE TO SERVICE OF ITS PROCESSES.

Chap. 55

Be it enacted, etc., as follows:

Chapter one hundred and eighty-five of the General Laws, as appearing in the Tercentenary Edition thereof, is hereby amended by inserting after section twenty-five the following new section: — *Section 25A.* The court shall have like power and authority for enforcing orders, sentences and decrees made or pronounced in the exercise of any jurisdiction vested in it, and for punishing contempts of such orders, sentences and decrees and other contempts of its authority, as are vested for such or similar purposes in the supreme judicial or superior court in equity in relation to any suit in equity pending therein. Commitments for such contempts may be made to any jail in the commonwealth. Orders, precepts and processes issued by the court

G. L. (Ter. Ed.), 185, new section after § 25.

Power of land court to enforce its orders and decrees and relative to service of its processes.

may be served in Suffolk county by the officer in attendance upon the sessions of said court in said county, or in any county by any deputy sheriff to whom they are directed.

Approved March 1, 1933.

Chap. 56 AN ACT TO ENABLE THE MIDDLESEX COUNTY COMMISSIONERS TO ACQUIRE MORE LAND FOR THE PURPOSES OF THE MIDDLESEX COUNTY TRAINING SCHOOL AT CHELMSFORD IN SAID COUNTY.

Be it enacted, etc., as follows:

Middlesex county commissioners may acquire more land for purposes of Middlesex county training school at Chelmsford.

SECTION 1. The county commissioners of Middlesex county are hereby authorized to acquire by purchase, or by eminent domain under chapter seventy-nine of the General Laws, additional lands adjacent to the lands owned by the said county and used for the Middlesex county training school in the town of Chelmsford in said county, and, for said purpose, may expend out of any appropriation for the current year for the support of the said training school a sum not exceeding seven hundred and fifty dollars.

Effective upon acceptance, etc.

SECTION 2. This act shall take effect upon its acceptance during the current year by the county commissioners of said county, but not otherwise.

Approved March 1, 1933.

Chap. 57 AN ACT RELATIVE TO THE TIME FOR FILING AND CONTENTS OF STATEMENTS OF CANDIDATES FOR NOMINATION AT CITY PRIMARY ELECTIONS IN THE CITY OF EVERETT.

Be it enacted, etc., as follows:

1917 (S), 260, § 4, amended.

Section four of chapter two hundred and sixty of the Special Acts of nineteen hundred and seventeen is hereby amended by striking out, in the sixth and seventh lines, the words "at least ten days" and inserting in place thereof the words: — not later than four o'clock in the afternoon of the fourteenth day, — and by amending the statement of candidate included in said section by inserting after the word "Everett" in the second line of said statement the words: —, that on April first of the current year I resided at (number, if any) on (name of street) in the said city, — so as to read as follows: — *Section 4.* Any person

Names of candidates to appear upon primary ballot.

who is qualified to vote for a candidate for mayor, alderman, common councilman or member of the school committee, and who is a candidate for nomination for any of the said offices may have his name, as such candidate printed on the official ballots to be used at a city primary

Proviso.

election: *provided*, that he shall, not later than four o'clock in the afternoon of the fourteenth day prior to such city primary election, file with the city clerk a statement in writing of his candidacy in substantially the following form: —

STATEMENT OF CANDIDATE.

I, (   ), on oath declare that I reside at (number, if any) on (name of street), in the city of Everett, that on April first of the current year I resided at (number, if any) on (name of street) in the said city, that I am a voter therein qualified to vote for a candidate for the hereinafter mentioned office; that I am a candidate for nomination for the office of (mayor, alderman, common councilman or member of the school committee) for (state the term), to be voted for at the city primary election to be held on Tuesday, the   day of   , 19 , and I request that my name be printed as such candidate on the official ballots to be used at said city primary election. (Signed) *Form of statement of candidate.*

COMMONWEALTH OF MASSACHUSETTS.

Middlesex, ss.
Subscribed and sworn to on this   day of   , 19 , before me.
(Signed)

Justice of the Peace.
(Or Notary Public.)

Every such candidate shall at the same time file with the statement the petition of at least twenty-five voters of the city qualified to vote for a candidate for the said office. The petition shall be in substantially the following form: — *Petition to be filed.*

PETITION ACCOMPANYING STATEMENT OF CANDIDATE.

Whereas (name of candidate) is a candidate for nomination for the office of (mayor, alderman, common councilman or member of the school committee) for (state the term), we, the undersigned voters of the city of Everett, duly qualified to vote for a candidate for the said office, do hereby request that the name of said (name of candidate), as a candidate for nomination for said office, be printed on the official ballots to be used at the city primary election to be held on the   Tuesday of   , 19 .   We further state that we believe him to be of good moral character and qualified to perform the duties of the office. *Form of petition.*

Name of Voter.	Street number, if any.	Street.

No acceptance by a candidate for nomination named in the petition shall be necessary for its validity or for its filing, and the petition need not be sworn to. *Acceptance and oath unnecessary.*

Approved March 1, 1933.

Chap. 58 AN ACT RELATIVE TO TAX RETURNS OF BUSINESS AND MANU-
FACTURING CORPORATIONS.

Emergency
preamble.

Whereas, The deferred operation of this act would tend
to defeat its purpose, therefore it is hereby declared to be
an emergency law, necessary for the immediate preservation
of the public convenience.

Be it enacted, etc., as follows:

G. L. (Ter.
Ed.), 63, § 35,
amended.

Returns of
domestic
business
corporations.

SECTION 1. Chapter sixty-three of the General Laws,
as appearing in the Tercentenary Edition thereof, is hereby
amended by striking out section thirty-five and inserting
in place thereof the following: — *Section 35.* Every
domestic business corporation shall, on or before the tenth
day of April, make a return sworn to by its treasurer or
assistant treasurer, or in their absence or incapacity by any
other principal officer, in such form as the commissioner
prescribes, giving such information as the commissioner
requires for the determination of the tax imposed by this
chapter.

G. L. (Ter.
Ed.), 63, § 40,
amended.
Returns of
foreign corpo-
rations.

SECTION 2. Said chapter sixty-three, as so appearing,
is hereby further amended by striking out section forty
and inserting in place thereof the following: — *Section 40.*
Every foreign corporation shall make returns as provided
in sections thirty-five and thirty-six; and all provisions
of said sections shall apply to such corporations.

G. L. (Ter.
Ed.), 63, § 30,
amended.

SECTION 3. Section thirty of said chapter sixty-three,
as so appearing, is hereby amended by striking out, in the
fifty-first line, the words "when the return called for by
section thirty-five is due" and inserting in place thereof the
words: — of the year in which the tax is to be assessed, —

Value of cor-
porate excess in
certain cases,
how de-
termined.

so that the paragraph contained in lines forty-eight to
fifty-one, inclusive, will read as follows: — If by reason of
recent organization, or otherwise, the corporation is not
required to make to the commissioner a return of net income for a taxable year, the value of the corporate excess
shall be determined as of the first day of April of the year
in which the tax is to be assessed.

G. L. (Ter.
Ed.), 63, § 30,
amended.

SECTION 4. Said section thirty, as so appearing, is
hereby further amended by striking out, in the seventy-
third and seventy-fourth lines, the words "when the annual
return called for by section forty is due" and inserting in
place thereof the words: — of the year in which the tax is
to be assessed, — so that the paragraph contained in lines
seventy to seventy-four, inclusive, will read as follows: —

Value of cor-
porate excess
in certain
cases, how
determined.

If by reason of recent organization, or otherwise, the
corporation is not required to make to the commissioner a
return of net income for a taxable year, the value of the
corporate excess employed in this commonwealth shall be
determined as of the first day of April of the year in which
the tax is to be assessed.

Section 5. This act shall take effect as of January *Effective date.* first, nineteen hundred and thirty-three.

Approved March 2, 1933.

An Act authorizing the governor to proclaim the existence of a banking emergency and providing for the further protection of depositors in banks and the maintenance of the banking structure of the commonwealth.

Chap. 59

Whereas, The present financial crisis requires that this *Emergency* act be effective forthwith, therefore it is hereby declared *preamble.* to be an emergency law, necessary for the immediate preservation of the public safety and convenience.

Be it enacted, etc., as follows:

Section 1. Whenever it shall appear to the governor *Governor may* that the welfare of the commonwealth or any section or *proclaim the existence of a* territory thereof or the welfare and security of banking *banking emer-* institutions under the supervision of the commissioner of *gency, etc.* banks, in this act referred to as banks, or their depositors so require, he may proclaim that a banking emergency exists and that any bank or banks shall be subject to special regulation as hereinafter provided until the governor, by proclamation, declares the period of such banking emergency terminated. The governor may likewise declare such legal bank holidays as in his judgment such an emergency may require.

Section 2. During the period of any banking emer- *Authority of* gency so proclaimed, the commissioner of banks, hereinafter *commissioner of banks* called the commissioner, in addition to all other powers *during period* conferred upon him by law, shall have authority to order *of banking emergency.* any one or more banks to restrict all or any part of their business and to limit or postpone for any length of time the payment of any amount or proportion of the deposits in any of the departments thereof as he may deem necessary or expedient and may further regulate payments therefrom as to time and amount, as in his opinion the interest of the public or of such bank or banks or the depositors thereof may require, and any order or orders made by him here- under may be amended, changed, extended or revoked, in whole or in part, whenever in his judgment circumstances warrant or require. After the termination of any such banking emergency, any such order may be continued in effect as to any particular bank or banks as aforesaid if in the judgment of the commissioner circumstances warrant or require and the governor approves.

Section 3. The commissioner may by order authorize *New deposits* banks to receive new deposits, and such new deposits shall *to be segrega-* be special deposits and designated as new deposits, shall *ted from other* be segregated from all other deposits and may be invested *deposits, etc.* only in assets approved by the commissioner as being sufficiently liquid to be available when needed to meet any demands on account of such new deposits, which assets shall not be merged with other assets but shall be held in trust for the security and payment of such new deposits, except that income from such assets may to the extent authorized by the commissioner be used by the bank for other proper purposes of the institution; and the withdrawal of such new deposits shall not be subject in any respect to restriction or limitation under this act. The provisions of section fifty-four of chapter two hundred and sixty-six of the General Laws, as appearing in the Tercentenary Edition thereof, shall not apply in respect to the receipt of new deposits as aforesaid by any bank authorized by order to receive the same. The restrictions imposed in relation to new deposits so received by co-operative banks shall apply only to those received from the sale of shares of a new series, shares of any prior series and paid-up shares.

G. L. (Ter. Ed.), 266, § 54, not applicable.

Rules and regulations.

SECTION 4. Whenever the commissioner shall make any order hereunder, he may adopt such rules and regulations as he may deem proper for the protection of any bank or banks subject thereto or the depositors thereof, and any person violating any provision of such a rule or regulation shall be punished by a fine of not more than one thousand dollars or by imprisonment for not more than one year, or both.

Penalty.

Commissioner to place value on assets of bank in determining action to be taken under act, etc.

SECTION 5. In determining action to be taken under this act or under section twenty-two of chapter one hundred and sixty-seven of the General Laws, as appearing in the Tercentenary Edition thereof, the commissioner may place such fair value on the assets of any bank as in his discretion seems proper under the conditions prevailing and circumstances relating thereto.

Costs and expenses.

SECTION 6. Any costs and expenses incurred by the commissioner in the exercise of the powers given under this act may be assessed by him against the banks concerned and, when so assessed, shall be paid by such banks.

Invalidity of any provision of act not to affect other provisions, etc.

SECTION 7. If any provision of this act is held invalid by any court of final jurisdiction, no other provisions shall be affected by such decision but the same shall remain in full effect. The right to amend or repeal any provision of this act is hereby reserved by the general court.

Approved March 6, 1933.

Chap. 60 AN ACT AUTHORIZING THE TOWN OF CONCORD TO USE A CERTAIN LOAN BALANCE FOR LAYING AND RE-LAYING WATER MAINS.

Be it enacted, etc., as follows:

Town of Concord may use a certain loan balance for laying, etc., water mains.

SECTION 1. The town of Concord is hereby authorized to appropriate any balance of the water loan issued in nineteen hundred and thirty-two for laying and re-laying water mains of sixteen inches or more in diameter, for the

purpose of laying or re-laying water mains of not less than
six inches in diameter.

SECTION 2. This act shall take effect upon its passage.

Approved March 6, 1933.

AN ACT TO PROVIDE FOR THE ELECTION OF THE AUDITOR OF
ACCOUNTS OF THE CITY OF QUINCY BY THE CITY COUNCIL
OF SAID CITY.

Chap. 61

Be it enacted, etc., as follows:

SECTION 1. The auditor of accounts of the city of
Quincy shall, after the acceptance of this act, be elected
by the city council of said city to hold office for two years
and until the qualification of his successor, such action to
be effective without the approval of the mayor thereof,
notwithstanding any provisions to the contrary contained
in section fifty-two of chapter forty-three of the General
Laws.

The auditor of accounts of city of Quincy to be elected by city council, etc.

SECTION 2. An auditor of accounts of said city shall
be elected as provided in section one as soon as may be after
the acceptance of this act, and upon the qualification of
the auditor so elected the term of office of the then incumbent of said office shall cease.

When election shall be held, etc.

SECTION 3. This act shall be submitted for acceptance
to the registered voters of the city of Quincy at its city
election in the current year in the form of the following
question which shall be placed upon the official ballot to be
used at said election: "Shall an act passed by the general
court in the year nineteen hundred and thirty-three, entitled 'An Act to provide for the election of the auditor of
accounts of the city of Quincy by the city council of said
city', be accepted?" If a majority of the voters voting
thereon vote in the affirmative in answer to said question,
this act shall thereupon take effect, but not otherwise.

Submission to voters, etc.

Approved March 7, 1933.

AN ACT CHANGING THE NAME OF NICHOLS INC. TO NICHOLS
JUNIOR COLLEGE.

Chap. 62

Be it enacted, etc., as follows:

The name of Nichols Inc., a corporation incorporated
under general law January twenty-fifth, nineteen hundred
and thirty-two, is hereby changed to Nichols Junior College; and said corporation may use the designation of
"college" as aforesaid notwithstanding the provisions of
section eighty-nine of chapter two hundred and sixty-six
of the General Laws.   *Approved March 7, 1933.*

Name of Nichols Inc. changed to Nichols Junior College.

Chap. 63 AN ACT RELATIVE TO THE ACTION OF ASSESSORS AND COLLECTORS OF TAXES IN THE COLLECTION OF BETTERMENT ASSESSMENTS.

Be it enacted, etc., as follows:

G. L. (Ter. Ed.), 80, § 4, amended.

Collection of assessments.

SECTION 1. Chapter eighty of the General Laws, as appearing in the Tercentenary Edition thereof, is hereby amended by striking out section four and inserting in place thereof the following: — *Section 4.* Within a reasonable time after making the assessment the board shall certify to the assessors the list of assessments upon land in each town who shall forthwith commit such assessments with their warrant to the collector of taxes thereof, and he shall forthwith send notice in accordance, except as to the date of notice, with section three of chapter sixty, to the person designated under section one as the owner of each parcel assessed, and any demand for the payment of such assessment shall be made upon such person. Except as otherwise herein provided, the collector shall have the same powers and be subject to the same duties with respect to such assessments as in the case of the annual taxes upon real estate, and the law in regard to the collection of the annual taxes, to the sale of land for the non-payment thereof and to redemption therefrom shall apply to assessments made under this chapter, so far as the same are applicable; but the owner of land assessed shall not be personally liable for the assessment thereon. Every collector of taxes receiving a list and warrant from the assessors shall collect the assessment therein set forth, and at such times as the assessors shall direct shall pay over to the treasurer of the body politic on behalf of which the assessment was made the amounts collected by him.

G. L. (Ter. Ed.), 80, § 13, amended.

Apportionment.

SECTION 2. Section thirteen of said chapter eighty, as so appearing, is hereby amended by inserting after the word "unpaid" in the seventh line the words: — , as certified to them by the collector, — so as to read as follows: — *Section 13.* Assessments made under this chapter shall bear interest at the rate of six per cent per annum from the thirtieth day after the assessments have been committed to the collector. The assessors shall add each year to the annual tax assessed with respect to each parcel of land all assessments, constituting liens thereon, which have been committed to the collector prior to April second of such year and which have not been apportioned as hereinafter provided, remaining unpaid, as certified to them by the collector, when the valuation list is completed, with interest to the date when interest on taxes becomes due and payable. At any time before demand for payment by the collector and before the completion by the assessors of the valuation list for the year in which such assessments will first appear on the annual tax bill, the board of assessors may, and at the request of the owner of the land assessed shall, apportion all assessments made under this chapter into such number of equal portions, not exceeding ten, as is determined by said board or as is requested by the owner, as the case may be, but no one of such portions shall be less than five dollars. The assessors shall add one of said portions, with interest on the amount remaining unpaid from thirty days after the commitment of the original assessment to the collector to the date when interest on taxes becomes due and payable, to the first annual tax upon the land and shall add to the annual tax for each year thereafter one of said portions and one year's interest on the amount of the assessment remaining unpaid until all such portions shall have been so added; all assessments and apportioned parts thereof, and interest thereon as herein provided, which have been added to the annual tax on any parcel of land shall be included in the annual tax bill thereon. After an assessment or a portion thereof has been placed on the annual tax bill, the total amount of said bill shall be subject to interest under and in accordance with the provisions of section fifty-seven of chapter fifty-nine. The amount remaining unpaid of any assessment may be paid in full at any time notwithstanding a prior apportionment.   *Approved March 7, 1933.*

AN ACT RELATIVE TO THE MAINTENANCE OF PROPER TOILET FACILITIES IN INDUSTRIAL ESTABLISHMENTS.

Chap. 64

Be it enacted, etc., as follows:

Section one hundred and thirty-five of chapter one hundred and forty-nine of the General Laws, as appearing in the Tercentenary Edition thereof, is hereby amended by striking out, in the third and fourth lines, the words "for four weeks after the receipt of a written notice from an inspector" and inserting in place thereof the words: — after receiving notice from the department, — so as to read as follows: — *Section 135.* A criminal prosecution shall not be begun against a person for a violation of any provision of the two preceding sections unless he has, after receiving notice from the department of the changes necessary to comply with said sections, neglected to make such changes. A notice shall be sufficient under this section if given to one member of a firm, or to the clerk, cashier, secretary, agent or any other officer having charge of the business of a corporation, or to its attorney, or, in case of a foreign corporation, to the officer having charge of such factory or workshop; and such officer shall be personally liable for the amount of any fine if a judgment against the corporation is unsatisfied.

Approved March 7, 1933.

G. L. (Ter. Ed.), 149, § 135, amended.

Prosecutions for violation of two preceding sections relative to toilet facilities in industrial establishments.

Chap. 65 AN ACT RELATIVE TO THE SUPPORT AND REGULATION OF THE BUSINESS OF INSURANCE COMPANIES DURING THE PRESENT EMERGENCY.

Emergency preamble.

Whereas, The present abnormal disruption in the economic and financial processes in the commonwealth and elsewhere requires that this act be effective forthwith, therefore it is hereby declared to be an emergency law, necessary for the immediate preservation of the public safety and convenience.

Be it enacted, etc., as follows:

Authority of commissioner of insurance as to regulation of business of insurance companies during period of banking emergency.

SECTION 1. During the period of the banking emergency proclaimed by the governor on March sixth of the current year under section one of chapter fifty-nine of the acts of said year and during any further period for which it may be extended as hereinafter authorized with respect to insurers, and until such period or such period as extended as aforesaid is terminated under said section one or is terminated as hereinafter authorized with respect to insurers, the commissioner of insurance, hereinafter called the commissioner, in addition to all other powers conferred upon him by law, shall have authority to suspend, in whole or in part, the operation of any provision of the laws of the commonwealth relative to insurance, to order any one or more insurers to restrict all or any part of their business, to limit or postpone for any length of time the payment of any amounts payable under the terms of any of their policies of insurance or annuity or pure endowment contracts, and to make, rescind, alter and amend such rules and regulations governing the conduct of the business of any insurers as he may deem necessary or expedient to maintain sound methods of insurance and to safeguard the interests of holders of such policies and contracts or of beneficiaries thereunder and the interest of the public. He may issue such orders as he may find necessary or expedient to enforce such rules or regulations. He may at any time amend, extend or revoke, in whole or in part, any order made hereunder when in his judgment circumstances warrant or require. Authority is hereby given to the governor, by proclamation, to extend or terminate for the purposes of this act only, the banking emergency proclaimed under said section one, but without limiting or abridging any authority granted thereunder. After the termination of any such emergency or of its extension as aforesaid, any such rule, regulation or order may be continued in effect with respect to any particular insurer or insurers, if in the judgment of the commissioner circumstances warrant or require and the governor approves. The

Scope of word "insurer" or "insurers".

word "insurer" or "insurers", as used in this act, shall include all corporations, associations and societies to any extent subject to the supervision or control of the commissioner.

Section 2. Any violation of any order issued under Penalty.
this act, or of any provision of any rule or regulation made
by the commissioner pursuant thereto, shall be punished
by a fine of not more than one thousand dollars or by
imprisonment for not more than one year, or both.

Section 3. If any provision of this act is held invalid Invalidity of
by any court of final jurisdiction, no other provision shall of act not to
be affected by such decision, but the same shall remain in affect other
full effect.   *Approved March 9, 1933.* provisions.

An Act relative to the dissolution of business *Chap.* 66
    corporations in certain cases.

Whereas, The deferred operation of this act would tend Emergency
to defeat its purpose, therefore it is hereby declared to be preamble.
an emergency law, necessary for the immediate preservation of the public convenience.

Be it enacted, etc., as follows:

Section fifty of chapter one hundred and fifty-five of G. L. (Ter.
the General Laws, as appearing in the Tercentenary § 50, amended.
Edition thereof, is hereby amended by inserting after the
word "corporation" in the thirteenth line the words: —,
or if the votes of its stockholders are equally divided in the
election of directors, — so as to read as follows: — *Section* Dissolution of
50. A corporation which desires to close its affairs may, corporations.
unless otherwise provided in the agreement of association,
by the vote of a majority of its members if it has no capital
stock, otherwise by a vote of a majority of all its stock, or,
if two or more classes of stock have been issued, of a
majority of each class outstanding and entitled to vote,
authorize a petition for its dissolution to be filed in the
supreme judicial or superior court setting forth in substance
the grounds of the application, or such a petition may be so
filed by the holder or holders of not less than forty per cent
of the capital stock issued and outstanding and entitled to
vote of a corporation subject to chapter one hundred and
fifty-six, if the votes of its board of directors and of its
stockholders are equally divided on a question affecting
the general management of the affairs of the corporation,
or if the votes of its stockholders are equally divided in
the election of directors, and there appears to be no way
of reaching an agreement and breaking such deadlock;
and the court, after notice to parties interested and a hearing, may decree a dissolution of the corporation. A corporation so dissolved shall be held to be extinct in all
respects as if its corporate existence had expired by the
limitation of its charter.   *Approved March 9, 1933.*

Chap. 67 AN ACT RELATIVE TO THE SALE OF COMMERCIAL FERTILIZERS.

Be it enacted, etc., as follows:

G. L. (Ter.
Ed.), 94, § 1,
first par.
amended.

Definitions.

SECTION 1. Section one of chapter ninety-four of the General Laws, as appearing in the Tercentenary Edition thereof, is hereby amended by striking out the first paragraph and inserting in place thereof the following: — The following words as used in this section and the other sections of this chapter to which their definition is hereinafter respectively limited, unless the context otherwise requires, shall have the following meanings:

G. L. (Ter.
Ed.), 94, § 1,
certain defi-
nitions
amended.

SECTION 2. Said section one of said chapter ninety-four, as so appearing, is hereby further amended by striking out the paragraphs defining "Agricultural lime"; "Available Phosphoric acid"; "Brand"; "Commercial fertilizer"; "Copy" and "Fertilizer"; and inserting in their respective places the following new definitions: —

"Agricultural
lime".

"Agricultural lime", in sections two hundred and fifty to two hundred and sixty-one, inclusive, includes all the various forms of lime intended or sold for fertilizing purposes or for neutralizing soil acidity.

"Available
phosphoric
acid".

"Available phosphoric acid", in sections two hundred and fifty to two hundred and fifty-four, inclusive, and two hundred and fifty-six to two hundred and sixty-one, inclusive, the sum of the water-soluble and citrate-soluble phosphoric acid.

"Brand".

"Brand", in sections two hundred and twenty-five to two hundred and thirty-five, inclusive, and two hundred and fifty to two hundred and sixty-one, inclusive, any commercial feeding stuff or cattle feed, and any commercial fertilizer, respectively, distinctive by reason of name, trade mark or guaranteed analysis, or by any method of marking.

"Commercial
fertilizer".

"Commercial fertilizer", in sections two hundred and fifty to two hundred and sixty-one, inclusive, dried or partly dried manure, pulverized or ground, and each natural or artificial manure containing nitrogen, phosphoric acid, potash, calcium oxide or magnesium oxide, except the excrements and litter from domestic animals when sold in its natural state.

"Copy".

"Copy", in sections two hundred and twenty-five to two hundred and thirty-five, inclusive, and sections two hundred and fifty to two hundred and sixty-one, inclusive, any certified copy.

'Fertilizer'.

"Fertilizer", in sections two hundred and fifty to two hundred and sixty-one, inclusive, commercial fertilizer.

G. L. (Ter.
Ed.), 94, § 1,
new par.
added.

SECTION 3. Said section one of said chapter ninety-four, as so appearing, is hereby further amended by inserting after the paragraph defining "Fertilizer" the following new paragraph:—

'Fertilizer
grade".

"Fertilizer grade", in sections two hundred and fifty to two hundred and sixty-one, inclusive, shall apply only to fertilizer mixtures and shall represent only the minimum guarantee of its plant food expressed in round numbers and in the following order: — nitrogen, available phosphoric acid and water-soluble potash.

SECTION 4. Said section one of said chapter ninety-four, as so appearing, is hereby further amended by inserting after the paragraph defining "Food" the following new paragraph: —

G. L. (Ter. Ed.), 94, § 1, new par. added.

"Gypsum or land plaster", in sections two hundred and fifty to two hundred and sixty-one, inclusive, crude calcium sulphate and may contain twenty per cent of combined water.

"Gypsum or land plaster".

SECTION 5. Said section one of said chapter ninety-four, as so appearing, is hereby further amended by striking out the paragraph defining "Lime" and the paragraph defining "Magnesia".

G. L. (Ter. Ed.), 94, § 1, two paragraph stricken out.

SECTION 6. Said chapter ninety-four, as so appearing, is hereby further amended by striking out section two hundred and fifty and inserting in place thereof the following: — *Section 250.* No commercial fertilizer shall be sold or offered or exposed for sale without a plainly printed label accompanying it, displayed in the manner hereinafter set forth, and truly stating the following particulars:

G. L. (Ter. Ed.), 94, § 250, amended. Sale of commercial fertilizers regulated. Label, form and contents.

1. The number of pounds of the fertilizer sold or offered or exposed for sale.

2. The name, brand or trade mark, and, in the case of fertilizer mixtures, the fertilizer grade under which the fertilizer is sold, and, in the case of agricultural lime, its particular form.

3. The name and principal address of the manufacturer, importer or other person putting the fertilizer on the market in the commonwealth.

4. The minimum percentage of each of the following constituents which the fertilizer contains and which, in the case of fertilizer mixtures, shall be expressed in round numbers and in the following order: (a) nitrogen, (b) available phosphoric acid, (c) potash soluble in distilled water; except that when undissolved bone, untreated phosphate rock, tankage, pulverized natural manures, the ground seeds of plants, or wood ashes are sold unmixed with other substances, the minimum percentage of total phosphoric acid therein may be stated in place of the percentage of available phosphoric acid; and except that in the case of agricultural lime the label shall truly state the following: (a) minimum and maximum percentage of total calcium oxide, (b) minimum and maximum percentage of total magnesium oxide, (c) minimum percentage of calcium oxide and magnesium oxide combined as carbonates, (d) and, in the case of gypsum or land plaster, the minimum percentage of calcium oxide and of calcium sulphate.

5. If any part of the nitrogen contained in the fertilizer is derived from pulverized leather, hair, wool waste, peat,

garbage tankage, or from any inert material whatsoever, unless processed so that its nitrogen shall show a satisfactory activity by the methods of the Association of Official Agricultural Chemists of North America, the label shall truly state the specific materials from which such part of the nitrogen is derived.

G. L. (Ter. Ed.), 94, § 252, amended.

Certain provisions of label recognized as guaranteed analysis.

SECTION 7. Section two hundred and fifty-two of said chapter ninety-four, as so appearing, is hereby amended by striking out all after the word "fertilizer" in the fourth line, — so as to read as follows: — *Section 252.* The provisions of the printed label required under the two preceding sections relating to the constituents contained in any fertilizer shall be known and recognized as the guaranteed analysis of such fertilizer.

G. L. (Ter. Ed.), 94, § 254, amended.

Sale of commercial fertilizers regulated. Fees, etc.

SECTION 8. Section two hundred and fifty-four of said chapter ninety-four, as so appearing, is hereby amended by inserting after the word "fertilizer" in the ninth line the words: — , eight dollars for magnesium oxide when guaranteed in any such brand of fertilizer, — and by inserting after the word "lime" in said ninth line the words: — and gypsum, — so as to read as follows: — *Section 254.* No person shall sell or offer or expose for sale any commercial fertilizer until he has filed with the director a copy certified by him to be a true copy of the label required by section two hundred and fifty, excepting as to the item as to the number of pounds, for each brand of fertilizer to be sold, offered or exposed for sale and has paid to the said director an analysis fee for each brand aforesaid as follows: eight dollars for nitrogen, eight dollars for phosphoric acid, eight dollars for potash, contained or stated to be contained in any such brand of fertilizer, eight dollars for magnesium oxide when guaranteed in any such brand of fertilizer, and twelve dollars for each brand of agricultural lime and gypsum except gas house lime; nor unless he holds a valid and uncancelled certificate issued under section two hundred and fifty-six. Any person desiring in any year to sell or to offer or expose for sale any brand of commercial fertilizer in respect of which the requirements of this section as to the filing of a copy of the label thereof and the payment of the analysis fee therefor have not been complied with before January first of said year, may offer or expose for sale and sell the said brand upon filing a certified copy of the label thereof and paying the full analysis fee therefor. No person shall be obliged to file a copy of the label of, or to pay an analysis fee for, any brand of fertilizer for which a certified copy of the label has been filed and the analysis fee paid by the manufacturer or importer of such brand.

No person shall file with the director a false copy of the label of any fertilizer or brand of fertilizer.

G. L. (Ter. Ed.), 94, § 255, amended.

SECTION 9. Section two hundred and fifty-five of said chapter ninety-four, as so appearing, is hereby amended by inserting after the word "lime" in the twelfth line the words: — and gypsum, — so as to read as follows: — *Section 255.* In addition to the requirements of the preceding section, each person who sells or offers or exposes for sale any commercial fertilizer shall, on or before January first and July first in each year, file with the director a sworn statement in such form as he prescribes setting forth the number of net tons of fertilizer sold by him in the commonwealth during the preceding six months, stating in each case the number of tons of each brand sold, together with a permit allowing the director or his authorized deputy to examine the books of the person filing the statement, for the purpose of verifying the same, and shall thereupon pay to the director a fee of six cents a ton of two thousand pounds for the fertilizers so sold; except that no such statement, permit or fee shall be required in respect of agricultural lime and gypsum. The director or his authorized deputy may cancel the certificate for any brand of fertilizer in respect to which the requirements of this section have not been complied with. Whoever sells, offers or exposes for sale a fertilizer or brand of fertilizer without having filed the statement and permit and paid the fee required by this section shall be punished by a fine of not more than five hundred dollars. But no person shall be obliged to file a statement or permit, or to pay the fee required by this section, for any brand of fertilizer for which the statement and permit have been filed and for which the fee has been paid by the manufacturer or importer of such brand.

SECTION 10. Said chapter ninety-four, as so appearing, is hereby further amended by striking out section two hundred and fifty-six and inserting in place thereof the following: — *Section 256.* When the certified copy of the label of any brand of fertilizer has been filed, and the proper fees have been paid, the director shall issue a certificate to that effect; and the certificate shall authorize the sale, in compliance with sections two hundred and fifty to two hundred and sixty-one, inclusive, of the brand of fertilizer for which the certificate is issued, up to and including December thirty-first of the year for which it is issued. The said director or his authorized deputy may refuse to issue a certificate for any fertilizer or brand of fertilizer which does not contain at least one half of one per cent of nitrogen, or one half of one per cent of potash soluble in distilled water, or one per cent of phosphoric acid, or five per cent of calcium oxide, or five per cent of magnesium oxide, or which contains its potash, phosphoric acid, calcium or magnesium oxides in forms substantially insoluble by the methods of analysis for commercial fertilizers and agricultural lime products prescribed by the Association of Official Agricultural Chemists of North America, or which does not possess substantial properties as a fertilizer. The director or his authorized deputy may also refuse to issue a certificate for any fertilizer under a name,

Marginal notes:

Same subject. Statement, permit, fee.

G. L. (Ter. Ed.), 94, § 256, amended.

Certificate of filing of label etc.

Issue, etc.

brand or trade mark which is untrue in any particular, or which, in his opinion, would be misleading or deceptive in any particular, or would tend to mislead or deceive as to the constituents or properties of said fertilizer, and may refuse to issue more than one certificate for any fertilizer under the same name or brand, or to issue a certificate for any fertilizer under a name or brand to the use of which the person seeking it is not lawfully entitled. If a certificate is issued for any fertilizer and it is afterward discovered that the certificate itself, or the granting of it, or the manner of procuring it, was in any respect in violation of any provision of sections two hundred and fifty to two hundred and sixty-one, inclusive, the director or his authorized deputy may cancel the certificate. Whoever sells, offers or exposes for sale any fertilizer or brand of fertilizer for which no certificate has been issued by the director or his authorized deputy, or the certificate for which has been cancelled, shall be punished by a fine of not more than two hundred dollars.

SECTION 11. Said chapter ninety-four, as so appearing, is hereby further amended by striking out section two hundred and fifty-seven and inserting in place thereof the following: — *Section 257.* Each commercial fertilizer and brand of commercial fertilizer sold or offered or exposed for sale shall be subject to analysis by the director or by his duly designated deputy. The said director shall make or cause to be made in each year one or more analyses of each fertilizer and brand of fertilizer sold or offered or exposed for sale in the commonwealth, and shall collect the annual analysis fee provided for by section two hundred and fifty-four; and he, his inspectors and deputies, may enter upon any premises where any commercial fertilizer is sold or offered or exposed for sale to ascertain if sections two hundred and fifty to two hundred and sixty-one, inclusive, are complied with, and to take samples for analysis. The analysis of all fertilizers shall be made by the methods adopted by the Association of Official Agricultural Chemists of North America. The said director may publish or cause to be published in reports, bulletins, special circulars or otherwise, the results obtained by said analyses. Said publications shall also contain such additional information in relation to the character, composition, value and use of the fertilizers analyzed as the director sees fit to include. He may make or cause to be made for any person a free analysis of any commercial fertilizer or brand of commercial fertilizer sold or offered or exposed for sale in the commonwealth, but he shall not be obliged to make such free analysis, or to cause the same to be made, unless the samples therefor are taken and submitted in accordance with the rules and regulations which he prescribes. The results of any analysis made in accordance with the aforesaid sections, except a free analysis as aforesaid, shall be sent by the director to the person named in the printed label of the

Cancellation.

Penalty for sale, etc., if certificate not issued, etc.

G. L. (Ter. Ed.), 94, § 257, amended.

Annual analysis.

Publication of reports, etc.

Free analysis.

fertilizer analyzed at least fifteen days before any publication of such results.

SECTION 12. Said chapter ninety-four, as so appearing, is hereby further amended by striking out section two hundred and fifty-eight and inserting in place thereof the following: — *Section 258.* Each sample of commercial fertilizer taken for analysis shall be of not less than substantially two pounds in weight, and each sample shall be taken, whenever the circumstances conveniently permit, in the presence of the person selling or offering or exposing for sale the fertilizer sampled, or of a representative of such person. ·Broken packages shall not be sampled, and all samples shall be taken by means of a sampling tube so designed as to remove a core extending from the top to the bottom of the package, from substantially ten per cent of the fertilizer to be sampled, except that if fertilizer is sold or offered or exposed for sale in bulk ten single samples shall be taken from as many different portions of the lot. An unbroken package of fertilizer, not exceeding twenty-five pounds, may, upon tendering the market price, be taken for the purpose of analysis and the contents thereof shall constitute a suitable and legal sample for said purpose. All samples taken shall be thoroughly mixed and divided into two nearly equal samples, placed in suitable vessels, and marked and sealed. Both shall be retained by the director, but one shall be held intact by him for one year at the disposal of the person named in the label of the fertilizer sampled.

Approved March 13, 1933.

G. L. (Ter. Ed.), 94, § 258, amended.

Taking of samples for analysis regulated.

AN ACT RELATIVE TO THE CHARGES OF CERTAIN HOSPITALS FOR TREATING INJURED EMPLOYEES UNDER THE WORKMEN'S COMPENSATION LAW.

Chap. 68

Be it enacted, etc., as follows:

Section thirteen of chapter one hundred and fifty-two of the General Laws, as appearing in the Tercentenary Edition thereof, is hereby amended by adding at the end thereof the following new sentence: — Any hospital referred to in section seventy of chapter one hundred and eleven shall be precluded from recovering in any form of action any charges for services under this chapter in excess of the amount approved by the department.

Approved March 13, 1933.

G. L. (Ter. Ed.), 152, § 13, amended.

Charges of certain hospitals for treating injured employees under workmen's compensation law.

AN ACT PROVIDING FOR THE ADMISSION IN EVIDENCE OF A CERTIFICATE OF THE REGISTRAR OF MOTOR VEHICLES IN CERTAIN CASES.

Chap. 69

Be it enacted, etc., as follows:

Section twenty-three of chapter ninety of the General Laws, as appearing in the Tercentenary Edition thereof, is hereby amended by adding at the end thereof the following new paragraph: —

G. L. (Ter. Ed.), 90, § 23, amended.

Admission in evidence of a certificate of the registrar of motor vehicles in certain cases.

A certificate of the registrar or his authorized agent that a license or right to operate motor vehicles or a certificate of registration of a motor vehicle has not been restored or that the registrar has not issued a new license so to operate to the defendant or a new certificate of registration for a motor vehicle the registration whereof has been revoked, shall be admissible as evidence in any court of the commonwealth to prove the facts certified to therein, in any prosecution hereunder wherein such facts are material.

Approved March 13, 1933.

Chap. 70 AN ACT REQUIRING THE FILING WITH THE STATE SECRETARY OF CERTIFICATES OF APPOINTMENT OR ELECTION OF CLERKS AND ASSISTANT OR TEMPORARY CLERKS OF CITIES OR TOWNS AND GRANTING AUTHORITY TO SAID SECRETARY TO AUTHENTICATE ATTESTATIONS OF ANY SUCH OFFICER.

Be it enacted, etc., as follows:

G. L. (Ter. Ed.), 41, new section after § 19.

Filing with state secretary of certificates of appointment or election of clerks and assistant or temporary clerks of cities or towns.

SECTION 1. Chapter forty-one of the General Laws, as appearing in the Tercentenary Edition thereof, is hereby amended by inserting after section nineteen the following new section: — *Section 19A.* Upon the appointment or election of a clerk or an assistant or temporary clerk of a city or town, the officer making the appointment, otherwise the president of the city council of such city or the chairman of the board of selectmen of such town shall execute and file with the state secretary a certificate of such appointment or election, which shall specify the date thereof and the date of the expiration of the term of office, if any, otherwise that the tenure of office is unlimited, and which shall have appended thereto a statement signed by the person appointed or elected that he has entered upon the duties of such office. Upon presentation to the state secretary of a paper attested by any person as the holder of any such office, said secretary shall have authority to certify that such person is the holder thereof and attest to the genuineness of his signature.

Certification.

Filing of certificates as to present incumbents of office of city or town clerk, etc.

SECTION 2. As soon as may be after this act takes effect, like certificates in respect to the then incumbent of the office of city or town clerk and of the office of assistant city or town clerk shall be executed by the president of the city council or by the chairman of the board of selectmen and filed with the state secretary.

Approved March 13, 1933.

An Act relative to the connection by the town of Saugus of the main sewer or force main carrying the sewage of said town with the sewerage or sewage disposal system of the city of Lynn.

Chap. 71

Be it enacted, etc., as follows:

Section 1. Chapter ·two hundred and fifty-nine of the acts of nineteen hundred and twenty-nine is hereby amended by striking out section one and inserting in place thereof the following: — *Section 1.* The town of Saugus may connect ·its main sewer or force main with the west side intercepting sewer of the city of Lynn or with the sewage pumping station or the outfall sewer of said city; provided, that an agreement to this effect shall be made by said city and town acting through the board or officer having charge of the sewers in said city and the board of selectmen in said town or the board or officer having charge of sewers in said town in case the construction and operation of sewers in said town shall, subsequent to the effective date of this act, be delegated to such board or officer and approved by the mayor and city council of said city and by said town. The agreement shall state the terms and conditions upon which the said connection is to be made and shall be recorded by the city clerk in said city and the town clerk in said town in the records of their respective municipalities. The agreement shall provide for the payment by said town to said city of a stated sum at the time when the connection is made and also for a yearly payment toward the maintenance and/or operation of said pumping station and/or outfall works beginning in the year in which the connection is made. In case the main sewer or force main of said town should be connected with the west side intercepting sewer of said city, said town shall pay in addition a yearly rental for the use of said sewer beginning in the year in which the connection is made upon such terms as may be mutually agreed upon. Such payment by said town toward the maintenance and/or operation of the pumping station and/or outfall works of said city for the disposal of sewage of said town may be based upon the relative quantity of sewage contributed to said pumping station and/or outfall works by each municipality. The agreement shall also state the terms, conditions and regulations in accordance with which the sewage of said town may be discharged into the sewerage system of said city.

Section 2. Said chapter two hundred and fifty-nine is hereby amended by inserting after section one the following new section: — *Section 1A.* The city of Lynn shall set aside in a separate account the aforesaid stated sum paid by the town of Saugus as an entrance fee for the privilege of discharging the sewage of said town into the sewerage system of said city, and both the original sum

1929, 259, § 1, amended.

Town of Saugus may connect its main sewer or force main with west side intercepting sewer of city of Lynn, etc.

Proviso.

Terms and conditions of agreement, etc.

1929, 259, new section after § 1. Disposition of sum paid by town of Saugus, etc.

and the interest thereon shall be used solely for interest and principal payments on bonds already issued by said city for construction of its sewage pumping station and outfall works.   *Approved March 13, 1933.*

Chap. 72 AN ACT RELATIVE TO THE TRUSTEES OF THE LEANDER M. HASKINS HOSPITAL IN THE TOWN OF ROCKPORT.

Be it enacted, etc., as follows:

1920, 276, § 2, amended.

Trustees of the Leander M. Haskins Hospital in town of Rockport, election, terms, etc.

SECTION 1. Chapter two hundred and seventy-six of the acts of nineteen hundred and twenty is hereby amended by striking out section two and inserting in place thereof the following:—*Section 2.* The board of selectmen and the board of park commissioners of the town for the time being shall be trustees to manage said hospital, together with three other persons elected by said boards in joint convention for terms of three years. On the initial election of the said additional trustees, one shall be elected to serve for the term of one year, one for two years and one for three years and thereafter as their terms of office expire their successors shall be elected as above provided. If any vacancy occurs in the office of an elected trustee his successor shall be elected for the unexpired term. Upon the effective date of this act, the board of trustees as at present existing shall be abolished.

SECTION 2. This act shall take effect upon its passage.   *Approved March 14, 1933.*

Chap. 73 AN ACT ABOLISHING THE MASSACHUSETTS INDUSTRIAL AND DEVELOPMENT COMMISSION IN THE DEPARTMENT OF LABOR AND INDUSTRIES.

Be it enacted, etc., as follows:

Repeals.

Section nine A of chapter twenty-three of the General Laws, as amended by chapter ninety-nine of the acts of nineteen hundred and thirty-two, section nine B of said chapter twenty-three, as appearing in the Tercentenary Edition of the General Laws, and section nine C of said chapter twenty-three, as amended by chapter one hundred and eighty-seven of the acts of nineteen hundred and thirty-two, are hereby repealed.   *Approved March 14, 1933.*

Chap. 74 AN ACT TO ABOLISH THE DIVISION OF ORNITHOLOGY IN THE DEPARTMENT OF AGRICULTURE.

Be it enacted, etc., as follows:

G. L. (Ter. Ed.), 20, § 4, amended.

Department of agriculture, organization,

SECTION 1. Section four of chapter twenty of the General Laws, as appearing in the Tercentenary Edition thereof, is hereby amended by striking out, in the third line, the words ", a division of ornithology",— so as to read as follows:— *Section 4.* The commissioner shall organize the department in divisions, including a division of dairying

and animal husbandry, a division of plant pest control, directors and other employees.
a division of markets, a division of reclamation, soil survey
and fairs, and such other divisions as he may from time to
time determine, and shall assign to said divisions their
functions. The commissioner may appoint and remove
a director of each division to have charge of the work of
the division. The compensation of directors shall be
fixed by the commissioner, with the approval of the governor and council. The commissioner may also appoint an
inspector of apiaries and such other inspectors, investigators, scientific experts, clerks and other officers and assistants as the work of the department may require, and
may assign them to divisions, transfer and remove them.

SECTION 2. Section thirty-nine of chapter one hundred Repeal.
and twenty-eight of the General Laws, as so appearing, is
hereby repealed. *Approved March 14, 1933.*

AN ACT PROVIDING THAT THE HOLDER OF THE OFFICE OF
DIRECTOR OF THE DIVISION OF FORESTRY OF THE DEPART-
MENT OF CONSERVATION BE THE DIRECTOR OF THE DIVISION
OF PARKS IN SAID DEPARTMENT.

Be it enacted, etc., as follows:

SECTION 1. Chapter twenty-one of the General Laws, G. L. (Ter. Ed.), 21, § 3, amended.
as appearing in the Tercentenary Edition thereof, is
hereby amended by striking out section three and insert-
ing in place thereof the following: — *Section 3.* The com- Duties of commissioner of conservation.
missioner shall be the executive and administrative head of
the department. He shall be designated by the governor
as the director of the division of forestry, of fisheries and
game or of animal industry, but shall receive no salary as
such director. He shall supervise the work of all the divisions, and shall have charge of the administration and enforcement of all laws which it is the duty of the department to administer and enforce, and shall direct all inspections and investigations.

SECTION 2. Said chapter twenty-one, as so appearing, G. L. (Ter. Ed.), 21, § 11, amended.
is hereby amended by striking out section eleven and in-
serting in place thereof the following: — *Section 11.* The Director of division of forestry to be director of division of parks.
director of the division of forestry shall be ex officio the
director of the division of parks, but shall receive no additional compensation for performing the functions of the
latter office. Except as otherwise provided, the director Duties.
of the division of parks shall act for the commonwealth in
the care and management of parks and reservations owned
by the commonwealth outside of the metropolitan parks
district for purposes of recreation or conservation, and shall
perform such other similar duties as may be imposed upon
him by the commissioner in case the offices of commissioner
and director are held by different persons.

SECTION 3. Said chapter twenty-one, as so appearing, G. L. (Ter. Ed.), 21, § 12, amended.
is hereby further amended by striking out section twelve

Experts, clerical assistants, etc.

and inserting in place thereof the following: — *Section 12.* The director of the division of parks may appoint and remove such experts and clerical and other assistants as the work of said division may require, subject to the approval of the commissioner in case said offices of commissioner and director are held by different persons. The said director shall be allowed necessary traveling expenses for himself and his employees incurred in the discharge of the functions of said division.

Traveling expenses.

G. L. (Ter. Ed.), 132A, § 9, amended.

SECTION 4. Section nine of chapter one hundred and thirty-two A of the General Laws, as appearing in the Tercentenary Edition thereof, is hereby amended by striking out, in the second line, the word "director" and inserting in place thereof the word: — division, — so as to read as follows: — *Section 9.* The commissioner shall make an annual report of the acts of the division. ⸀

Annual report.

Approved March 14, 1933.

Chap. 76

AN ACT ABOLISHING THE DIVISION OF SMOKE INSPECTION IN THE DEPARTMENT OF PUBLIC UTILITIES AND RELATIVE TO THE ABATEMENT OF SMOKE IN THE CITY OF BOSTON AND VICINITY.

Be it enacted, etc., as follows:

Division of smoke inspection abolished.

Functions as to smoke inspection to be performed by commission of department of public utilities.

SECTION 1. Sections twelve C to twelve F, inclusive, of chapter twenty-five of the General Laws, as appearing in the Tercentenary Edition thereof, are hereby repealed, but, notwithstanding such repeal, all functions relative to smoke abatement, vested in the commission of the department of public utilities prior to the effective date of such repeal, whether or not delegated to the division of smoke inspection, shall be performed by said commission, but nothing in this section shall affect the abolition by section five of this act of the functions imposed by chapter four hundred and twelve of the acts of nineteen hundred and thirty upon said division.

G. L. (Ter. Ed.), 25, new section after § 9.

Smoke inspector, deputy inspectors, assistants, etc.

SECTION 2. Said chapter twenty-five, as so appearing, is hereby further amended by inserting after section nine the following new section: — *Section 9A.* For the performance of the department's duties relative to the administration and enforcement of chapter six hundred and fifty-one of the acts of nineteen hundred and ten, and acts in amendment thereof or in addition thereto, which have been vested in the commission by said chapter and acts, the commission may appoint a smoke inspector, and may employ such deputy inspectors, assistants and other employees as are required therefor.

G. L. (Ter. Ed.), 25, § 10, amended.

Commission to have control over officers and employees.

SECTION 3. Section ten of said chapter twenty-five, as so appearing, is hereby amended by striking out, in the second line, the word "three" and inserting in place thereof the word: — four, — so as to read as follows: — *Section 10.* The commission may assign to all officers and employees appointed or employed under the four preceding sections such duties as it shall from time to time deem advisable, but all acts of such officers and employees shall be done under the supervision and control of, and subject to revision by, the commission.

Section 4. Said chapter twenty-five, as so appearing, is hereby further amended by inserting after section ten the following new section: — *Section 10A.* The salaries of the smoke inspector and all deputy inspectors, assistants and employees employed under section nine A and the expenses incurred in the performance of the department's duties referred to in said section shall be apportioned annually by the state treasurer among the cities and towns comprising the district defined by said chapter six hundred and fifty-one, and acts in amendment thereof and in addition thereto, in proportion to their last annual taxable valuation, and the amount so apportioned shall be added to their proportion of the state tax. *G. L. (Ter. Ed.), 25, new section after § 10. Apportionment of cost among cities and towns comprising district defined by 1910, 651, etc.*

Section 5. Chapter four hundred and twelve of the acts of nineteen hundred and thirty is hereby repealed. *Repeal.*

Approved March 14, 1933.

An Act repealing the law requiring the psychiatric examination of certain prisoners in jails and houses of correction. *Chap. 77*

Be it enacted, etc., as follows:

Section 1. Section sixteen of chapter one hundred and twenty-seven of the General Laws, as appearing in the Tercentenary Edition thereof, is hereby amended by striking out the last sentence. *G. L. (Ter. Ed.), 127, § 16, amended.*

Section 2. Said chapter one hundred and twenty-seven, as so appearing, is hereby further amended by striking out section seventeen and inserting in place thereof the following: — *Section 17.* Specifications governing the manner and time of such physical examinations shall be promulgated by the department of public health. Said department shall prescribe the medical records to be kept, shall require such laboratory or other diagnostic aids to be used as in its judgment are expedient, and shall forward to the commissioner statements of the results of all such examinations, together with recommendations relative thereto. For the purpose of obtaining further information relative to such prisoners the commissioner may cause inquiry to be made of court physicians. and psychiatrists, probation officers and district attorneys, who have made examinations or investigations of such prisoners prior to conviction or who have prosecuted them, and such physicians, psychiatrists and probation officers shall furnish to the commissioner when requested all pertinent information in their possession. The commissioner may cause such further inquiry to be made relative to the offences committed by such prisoners and their past history and environment as he may deem *G. L. (Ter. Ed), 127, § 17, amended. Physical examinations of prisoners, specifications, statements, records.*

necessary. He shall cause records to be made of such examinations and investigations, and shall transmit copies thereof to the office of the board of probation, which shall cause the same to be filed with its office records.

SECTION 3. Section eighteen of said chapter one hundred and twenty-seven, as so appearing, is hereby amended by striking out, in the third and fourth lines, the words "or of the department of mental diseases", — so as to read as follows: — *Section 18.* Any officer named in section sixteen who neglects or refuses to comply with said section or who violates any rule or regulation of the department of public health made under section seventeen shall forfeit not more than fifty dollars.

SECTION 4. The division of examination of prisoners and all positions the incumbents of which are performing solely functions terminated by this act are hereby abolished.
Approved March 14, 1933.

Chap. 78 AN ACT DESIGNATING A PORTION OF THE NORTHERN ARTERY, SO CALLED, AS THE MONSIGNOR MCGRATH HIGHWAY.

Be it enacted, etc., as follows:

SECTION 1. So much of the Northern Artery, so called, as is located within the limits of the cities of Somerville and Cambridge shall be designated and known as the Monsignor McGrath Highway.

SECTION 2. This act shall take effect upon its passage.
Approved March 17, 1933.

Chap. 79 AN ACT RELATIVE TO THE ASSESSMENT OF A PORTION OF THE COST OF CERTAIN SEWERS IN THE TOWN OF NAHANT AND TO THE RECORDING OF CERTIFICATES OF SUCH ASSESSMENTS.

Be it enacted, etc., as follows:

SECTION 1. Section six of chapter two hundred and forty-one of the Special Acts of nineteen hundred and seventeen, as amended by chapter one hundred and sixty of the acts of nineteen hundred and twenty-three, is hereby further amended by striking out the second sentence, as appearing in said chapter one hundred and sixty, and inserting in place thereof the following: — In providing for the payment of the remaining portion of the cost of said system or systems the town may avail itself of any or all of the methods permitted by general laws, notwithstanding that certain of the public sewers authorized hereunder are not constructed in public ways, if the land to be assessed abuts upon any way and a public sewer is available to serve such land, and at the same meeting at which it determines the proportion of the cost which is to be borne by the town, it may by vote determine by which of such methods the remaining portion of said cost shall be provided for.

Section 2. Said chapter two hundred and forty-one is hereby further amended by inserting after section six the following new section: — *Section 6A.* The board of sewer commissioners shall within sixty days after the passage by it of an order determining the amounts of assessments as provided in section six, cause to be filed for record in the registry of deeds for the southern district of the county of Essex, a certificate or certificates setting forth the amounts assessed by its said order upon the owners of each and every estate so assessed within the area of said system, or systems, and also a plan showing the location of the sewers constructed within such area, a portion of the cost of which has been assessed by its said order.

1917 (S), 241, new section after § 6.
Recording of certificates of assessments.

Section 3. This act shall take effect upon its passage.

Approved March 17, 1933.

An Act relative to the time of filing annual returns of interests in certain ships and vessels as a basis of excise taxes thereon.

Chap. 80

Whereas, The deferred operation of this act would tend to defeat its purpose, therefore it is hereby declared to be an emergency law, necessary for the immediate preservation of the public convenience.

Emergency preamble.

Be it enacted, etc., as follows:

Section eight of chapter fifty-nine of the General Laws, as appearing in the Tercentenary Edition thereof, is hereby amended by striking out, in the fifth and sixth lines, the words "within thirty days after said date" and inserting in place thereof the words: — on or before July first following, — so as to read as follows: — *Section 8.* Individuals or partnerships owning an interest in any ship or vessel which has during the period of its business in the year preceding April first been engaged in interstate or foreign carrying trade or engaged exclusively in fishing and documented and carrying "papers" under the laws of the United States shall annually, on or before July first following, make a return on oath to the assessors of the town where such individuals reside or where such partnerships are taxable under clause seventh of section eighteen, respectively, setting forth the name of the ship or vessel, their interest therein, and the value of such 'interest. If the assessors are satisfied of the truth of the return they shall assess an excise tax of one third of one per cent upon such interest; and the person or partnership making such return shall be exempt from any tax upon said interest other than that assessed under this section.

G. L. (Ter. Ed.), 59, § 8, amended.

Interests in ships and vessels in interstate or foreign carrying trade or in fishing liable only to excise tax.

Approved March 17, 1933.

Chap. 81 AN ACT ESTABLISHING THE VOTING RIGHTS OF PERSONS HOLD-
ING ANNUITY OR PURE ENDOWMENT CONTRACTS AND
CERTAIN INSURANCE POLICIES ISSUED BY DOMESTIC LIFE
INSURANCE COMPANIES AND CLARIFYING CERTAIN LIMITA-
TIONS ON VOTING RIGHTS OF MEMBERS AND SHAREHOLDERS
OF SUCH COMPANIES.

Be it enacted, etc., as follows:

G. L. (Ter. Ed.), 175, § 94, first two paragraphs, amended.

    Section ninety-four of chapter one hundred and seventy-five of the General Laws, as appearing in the Tercentenary Edition thereof, is hereby amended by striking out the first two paragraphs and inserting in place thereof the following: —

Domestic mutual life companies.

Members.

    Except as provided in this section and in section one hundred and thirty-seven, every person insured under a policy of life or endowment insurance issued by a domestic mutual life company shall be a member thereof and entitled to one vote, and one vote additional for each five thousand dollars of insurance in excess of the first five thousand dollars, every person holding an annuity or pure endowment contract issued by any such company shall be, a member thereof and entitled to one vote and, in the case of an annuity contract, one vote additional for each one hundred and fifty dollars of annual annuity income in excess of the first one hundred and fifty dollars, and every person insured under any policy of insurance issued by any such company under clause sixth of section forty-seven

Annual meetings.

shall be a member thereof and entitled to one vote. Holders of such policies or contracts shall be notified of the annual meetings of the company by written notice, or by an imprint in the form prescribed by section seventy-six upon the filing back of its policies or contracts, or, in the case of policies upon which premiums are payable monthly or oftener, on some other prominent place on each policy, and also upon premium receipts or certificates of renewal.

Vote by proxies authorized.

    Members and shareholders may vote by proxies dated and executed within three months and returned and recorded on the books of the company seven days or more before the meeting at which they are to be used; but no member or shareholder of such a company shall, in person or by proxy, cast more than twenty votes, and no officer shall, himself or by another, ask for, receive, procure to be obtained or use a proxy vote. *Approved March 17, 1933.*

Chap. 82 AN ACT RELATIVE TO THE APPOINTMENT AND QUALIFICATION
OF DEPUTY COLLECTORS OF TAXES.

Be it enacted, etc., as follows:

G. L. (Ter. Ed.), 60, § 92, amended.

    SECTION 1. Chapter sixty of the General Laws, as appearing in the Tercentenary Edition thereof, is hereby amended by striking out section ninety-two and inserting in place thereof the following: — *Section 92.* Any officer authorized to collect taxes may appoint, subject to the approval of the commissioner, such deputies as such officer deems expedient. Any such deputy may be a woman. Such deputies shall give bond for the faithful performance of their duties in such sum and in such form, and subject to such conditions, as the commissioner may prescribe, and shall have all the powers of collectors.

SECTION 2. Chapter forty-one of the General Laws, as appearing in the Tercentenary Edition thereof, is hereby amended by striking out section thirty-seven and inserting in place thereof the following: — *Section 37.* A town treasurer, acting as collector of taxes, may, subject to the approval of the commissioner of corporations and taxation, appoint deputies, who shall give bond for the faithful performance of their duties in such sum and in such form, and subject to such conditions, as the said commissioner may prescribe; and such collector and deputies shall have all the powers of collectors of taxes. A treasurer acting as collector may issue his warrant to the sheriff of the county or his deputy, or to any constable of the town, directing them to distrain the property or take the body of any person delinquent in the payment of taxes, and may proceed in the same manner as collectors.

Approved March 17, 1933.

Deputy collectors of taxes, appointment.

Bond.

G. L. (Ter. Ed.), 41, § 37, amended.

Collection of taxes by treasurer.

AN ACT FURTHER REGULATING CERTIFICATES OF INSURANCE UNDER THE COMPULSORY MOTOR VEHICLE LIABILITY INSURANCE LAW, SO CALLED.

Chap. 83

Be it enacted, etc., as follows:

SECTION 1. Section thirty-four B of chapter ninety of the General Laws, as appearing in the Tercentenary Edition thereof, is hereby amended by striking out the second paragraph and inserting in place thereof the following: —

Such certificate of an insurance or surety company shall, except as hereinafter provided, be in a form prescribed by the commissioner of insurance, shall contain the recitals required by said section thirty-four A and, if at the time of the execution thereof the schedule of premium charges and classifications of risks for the year for which registration is sought have been fixed and established under section one hundred and thirteen B of chapter one hundred and seventy-five, shall state the rate at which and the classification under which the motor vehicle liability policy or bond referred to therein was issued or executed and the amount of the premium thereon and whether or not said premium is at the rate fixed and established as aforesaid, and each such certificate shall contain such other information as said commissioner may require. Such a certificate shall be executed in the name of the company by one of its officers, or by an insurance agent of the company licensed under chapter one hundred and seventy-five to solicit applica-

G. L. (Ter. Ed.), 90, § 34 B, second par., amended.

Certificates of insurance under the compulsory motor vehicle liability insurance law, regulated.

tions for and to negotiate motor vehicle liability policies or bonds or on his behalf by one of his agents or employees duly authorized by the company by a writing, in a form prescribed by said commissioner, filed in the office of said commissioner and not theretofore revoked by a writing filed as aforesaid, and no other person shall execute or issue such a certificate. A certificate executed on behalf of such licensed insurance agent shall also bear the signature of the person so executing it. Whoever issues or executes a certificate in a form other than that prescribed by said commissioner shall be punished by a fine of not less than fifty nor more than five hundred dollars.

G. L. (Ter. Ed.), 90, § 34B, fourth par., amended.

SECTION 2. Said section thirty-four B, as so appearing, is hereby further amended by striking out the fourth paragraph and inserting in place thereof the following: —

Same subject.

If such a certificate, whether or not conforming to the foregoing requirements of this section, is executed in the name of a company by a person hereinbefore specified, or is so executed by any other person in violation of this section under authorization of the company, and is filed with the registrar in connection with the registration of a motor vehicle, the company shall be estopped to deny the issue or validity of such certificate or that a motor vehicle liability policy or bond has in fact been issued or executed as set forth in such certificate.

Application of act.

SECTION 3. The provisions of this act shall not apply to certificates, as defined in section thirty-four A of chapter ninety of the General Laws, as appearing in the Tercentenary Edition thereof, issued in connection with registration of motor vehicles or trailers granted before September first of the current year.			*Approved March 17, 1933.*

Chap. 84 AN ACT AUTHORIZING THE TOWN OF PLYMOUTH, BY ITS BOARD OF HEALTH, TO OPERATE AND MAINTAIN A PIGGERY IN CONNECTION WITH THE DISPOSAL OF GARBAGE.

Be it enacted, etc., as follows:

Town of Plymouth may operate and maintain a piggery, etc.

SECTION 1. The town of Plymouth, by its board of health, may maintain and operate a piggery in connection with the disposal of garbage of the town, and sell the products of the piggery.

Effective upon acceptance, etc.

SECTION 2. This act shall take effect upon its acceptance by a majority of the legal voters of said town present and voting thereon at an annual town meeting.
			Approved March 17, 1933.

Chap. 85 AN ACT AUTHORIZING THE COUNTY COMMISSIONERS OF THE COUNTY OF PLYMOUTH TO LEASE TO THE TOWN OF PLYMOUTH CERTAIN PROPERTY.

Be it enacted, etc., as follows:

County commissioners of Plymouth county may

The county commissioners of the county of Plymouth, acting in the name and on behalf of said county, may from time to time lease to the town of Plymouth, for periods not exceeding five years each, the buildings now used by said county as a piggery, with such adjacent land and under such conditions as may be mutually agreed upon by the said parties, and the said town may, if authorized by vote at an annual town meeting, become party to such lease. *lease to town of Plymouth certain property.*

Approved March 17, 1933.

AN ACT PLACING THE OFFICE OF CHIEF OF THE FIRE DEPARTMENT OF THE CITY OF EVERETT UNDER THE CIVIL SERVICE LAWS. *Chap. 86*

Be it enacted, etc., as follows:

SECTION 1. The office of chief of the fire department of the city of Everett shall, upon the effective date of this act, become subject to the civil service laws and rules and regulations relating to permanent members of fire departments of cities, and the term of office of any incumbent thereof shall be unlimited, except that he may be removed in accordance with such laws and rules and regulations; provided, however, that James Evans, the present incumbent of said office, may continue to serve as such without taking a civil service examination. *Office of chief of fire department of city of Everett subject to civil service laws.*

SECTION 2. This act shall be submitted for acceptance to the registered voters of the city of Everett at its city election in the current year in the form of the following question which shall be placed upon the official ballot to be used at said election: "Shall an act passed by the general court in the year nineteen hundred and thirty-three, entitled 'An Act placing the office of chief of the fire department of the city of Everett under the civil service laws', be accepted?" If a majority of the voters voting thereon vote in the affirmative in answer to said question, this act shall thereupon take effect, but not otherwise. *Submission to voters, etc.*

Approved March 17, 1933.

AN ACT PROVIDING FOR THE FURTHER PROTECTION OF DEPOSITORS IN TRUST COMPANIES AND THE MAINTENANCE OF THE BANKING STRUCTURE OF THE COMMONWEALTH. *Chap. 87*

Whereas, The present banking emergency requires that this act be effective forthwith, therefore it is hereby declared to be an emergency law, necessary for the immediate preservation of the public safety and convenience. *Emergency preamble.*

Be it enacted, etc., as follows:

SECTION 1. Chapter one hundred and seventy-two of the General Laws is hereby amended by adding after section eighty-two, added by section one of chapter two hundred and ninety-five of the acts of nineteen hundred and thirty-two, under the caption, CONSERVATORSHIP, the following seven new sections: — *Section 83.* In addition to all other powers conferred upon him by law, the commissioner, whenever he shall deem it necessary in order to conserve the assets of any trust company for the benefit of *G. L. 172, seven new sections after § 82.* *Commissioner of banks may appoint a conservator for certain trust companies, etc.*

the depositors and creditors thereof, may, under his hand and official seal, appoint a conservator for such trust company, and require of such conservator such bond and security as the commissioner may deem proper.

A certificate of the appointment of such conservator shall forthwith be filed in the office of the commissioner. The conservator, with the approval of the commissioner,

may procure such expert assistance and advice as he considers necessary in the administration of the affairs of such trust company and with like approval may retain such of the officers and employees of such trust company as he deems necessary.

The conservator, under the direction and subject to the control of the commissioner, shall take possession forthwith of the property and business of such trust company and take such action as may be necessary to carry on its business and to conserve its assets, pending further disposition thereof, as provided by law.

Upon taking possession of the property and business of a trust company, the conservator shall forthwith give notice thereof to all persons holding or having possession of any assets of such trust company. No bank, trust company, association, firm or individual, knowing that a conservator has taken such possession, or having been notified thereof as aforesaid, shall have a lien or charge for any payment, advance or clearance thereafter made, or liability thereafter incurred, against any of the assets of the trust company of whose property and business the conservator shall have taken possession as aforesaid, except as otherwise provided in this and the six following sections.

During the time that such conservator remains in possession of such trust company, the rights of all parties with respect thereto shall, subject to the other provisions of this and the six following sections, be the same as if the commissioner had taken possession of such trust company.

Section 84. Such conservator, subject to such orders, rules and regulations as may be prescribed from time to time by the commissioner, may collect moneys due to the trust company, and do all acts necessary to continue its business or to conserve its assets. He shall collect all debts due and claims belonging to it, and with the approval of the commissioner, may sell or compound all bad or doubtful debts, and on like approval may sell all, or any part of, the real and personal property of the trust company on such terms as the commissioner shall approve; and, in the name of such trust company, may take a mortgage on such real property from a bona fide purchaser to secure the whole or a part of the purchase price, upon such terms and for such periods as the commissioner may approve.

To execute and perform the powers and duties conferred upon him, the conservator may, in the name of any such trust company prosecute and defend all suits and other legal proceedings and may, in the name of the trust company, execute, acknowledge and deliver all deeds, assignments, releases and other instruments necessary and proper to effectuate any sale of real or personal property or any compromise approved by the commissioner; and any deed or other instrument executed pursuant to the authority hereby given, shall be valid and effectual for all purposes to the same extent as though executed by the officers of the trust company by authority of its board of directors or of its stockholders. proceedings in name of trust company, etc.

Such conservators, and their assistants, shall be subject to all the penalties, and except as provided in sections eighty-three to eighty-nine, inclusive, to all other provisions of law, to which agents appointed by the commissioner for the purpose of liquidating the affairs of a bank are now or may hereafter be subject. Conservators, etc., to be subject to certain penalties and provisions of law.

Section 85. While a trust company is in the hands of such a conservator, the commissioner may require the conservator to set aside and make available for withdrawal by depositors and for payment to other creditors such amounts or proportions of their deposits or claims in any department thereof as the commissioner may deem necessary or expedient, and may by order authorize the conservator to receive new deposits, as provided in section three of chapter fifty-nine of the acts of nineteen hundred and thirty-three. Commissioner may require conservator to set aside certain amounts of deposits for withdrawal by depositors, etc.

Section 86. Whenever any trust company shall have resumed business with or without a reorganization, or whenever the commissioner shall have taken possession of its property or business as provided in section twenty-two of chapter one hundred and sixty-seven, the provisions of section three of chapter fifty-nine of the acts of nineteen hundred and thirty-three with respect to the segregation of new deposits received under section eighty-five shall no longer be effective and the deposits received thereunder shall be disposed of in such manner as the commissioner shall direct, unless the owner of any such deposit, within fifteen days after notice given by the conservator or the commissioner, in such manner as the commissioner shall prescribe, shall have withdrawn the same. When provisions as to segregation of new deposits shall no longer be effective, etc.

Section 87. The compensation of such conservator and of counsel, employees and assistants and all other expenses of such conservatorship, including costs and expenses incurred by the commissioner in relation to such trust company, shall be fixed by the commissioner and approved by the governor and council and paid out of the funds of such trust company; provided, however, that the compensation paid the conservator shall in no event be at a higher rate than the highest salary established in said trust company or at a rate in excess of one thousand dollars per month and that the total pay roll of the trust company at the time of the appointment Compensation of conservator, etc., to be fixed by commissioner, etc. Proviso.

of the conservator shall not be increased by reason of such compensation.

Commissioner may terminate the conservatorship in his discretion, etc.

Section 88. If the commissioner shall be satisfied that it may be safely done and that it would be in the public interest, he may, in his discretion, terminate the conservatorship and permit such trust company to resume business subject to such terms, conditions, restrictions or limitations as he may prescribe.

Certain power or authority not abridged, etc.

Section 89. Nothing contained in the six preceding sections shall, unless otherwise expressly provided therein, be deemed to abridge any power or authority to take possession of a trust company conferred upon the commissioner by chapter one hundred and sixty-seven or any power or authority conferred by any other provision of law.

Invalidity of any provision of act, etc., not to affect remainder of act, etc.

SECTION 2. If any provision of this act, or the application thereof to any person, firm, corporation or association or to any circumstances, is held invalid by any court of final jurisdiction, the remainder of this act, and the application of such provision to other persons or circumstances, shall not be affected thereby. The right to amend or to repeal this act or any provision thereof is hereby reserved by the general court. *Approved March 20, 1933.*

Chap. 88 AN ACT CHANGING THE TIME OF HOLDING CITY PRIMARIES IN THE CITY OF MEDFORD.

Be it enacted, etc., as follows:

1921, 140, § 2, amended.

Section two of chapter one hundred and forty of the acts of nineteen hundred and twenty-one is hereby amended by striking out, in the second and seventh lines, the word "second" and inserting in place thereof, in each instance, the word: — third, — so as to read as follows: — *Section 2.*

Date of city primary election, etc.

Except as otherwise provided herein, on the third Tuesday preceding every city election there shall be held a city primary election for the purpose of nominating candidates for elective offices. No special election shall be held until after the expiration of forty days from the calling of the special city primary election, which shall be held on the third Tuesday preceding such special election. At every

Aldermen to fix polling hours, etc.

city primary election the polls shall be kept open during such hours as shall be fixed by the board of aldermen and, except as otherwise provided in this act, every such city primary election shall be called by the same officers and held in the same manner as a regular city election, and polling places shall be designated, provided and furnished, official ballots, special ballots, ballot boxes, voting lists, specimen ballots, blank forms, apparatus and supplies shall be provided for every such city primary election of the same number and kind, and in the same manner and by the same officials as at a regular city election, and the same election officers shall officiate as at a regular city election.

(This bill, returned by the governor to the House of Representatives, the branch in which it originated, with his objections thereto, was passed by the House of Representatives, March 16, 1933, and, in concurrence, by the Senate, March 21, 1933, the objections of the governor notwithstanding, in the manner prescribed by the constitution; and thereby has "the force of a law".)

An Act making appropriations for the employment of additional persons as a measure of relief during the present unemployment emergency.

Chap. 89

Be it enacted, etc., as follows:

Section 1. To provide for the employment of additional labor and other personal services as a measure of relief during the present emergency caused by unemployment, the sums set forth in section two, for the several purposes and subject to the conditions therein specified, are hereby appropriated from the general fund or revenue of the commonwealth unless some other source of revenue is expressed, subject to the provisions of law regulating the disbursement of public funds and the approval thereof.

Appropriations for employment of additional persons as a measure of relief during the present unemployment emergency.

Section 2.

Item		
	Service of the Department of Conservation.	
A	For thinning trees and otherwise improving state forest lands owned by the commonwealth, a sum not exceeding seventy-five thousand dollars . .	$75,000 00

Department of Conservation.

	Service of the Department of Agriculture.	
B	For carrying out mosquito control projects in accordance with the provisions of chapter one hundred and twelve of the acts of nineteen hundred and thirty-one, except that no expenditures from the funds hereby appropriated shall be made in any city or town unless a petition from the mayor of the city or the selectmen of the town for the said work is received and approved by the state reclamation board, a sum not exceeding seventy-five thousand dollars, the same to be in addition to any amount heretofore appropriated for the purpose . .	75,000 00

Department of Agriculture.

	Service of the Department of Public Works.	
C	For removing abandoned hulks or wrecks lying along the waterfront of Boston harbor, a sum not exceeding fifty thousand dollars	50,000 00

Department of Public Works.

	Service of the Metropolitan District Commission.	
D	For cutting brush, clearing and other work in connection with the maintenance of park reservations, a sum not exceeding seventy-five thousand dollars, to be assessed upon the cities and towns of the metropolitan parks district in accordance with the method fixed by law, and to be expended under the direction and with the approval of the metropolitan district commission	75,000 00

Metropolitan District Commission.

Total		$275,000 00
General fund		$200,000 00
Metropolitan District fund		75,000 00
		$275,000 00

Not subject
to civil service
laws, etc.

SECTION 3. Persons employed for work authorized by section two shall not be subject to civil service laws or the rules and regulations made thereunder.

SECTION 4. This act shall take effect upon its passage.

Approved March 23, 1933.

Chap. 90 AN ACT AUTHORIZING THE NEW ENGLAND CONFERENCE OF THE EVANGELICAL CHURCH, INC. TO MAKE CONTRACTS TO PAY ANNUITIES AND VALIDATING CERTAIN CONTRACTS ALREADY MADE BY SAID CORPORATION.

Be it enacted, etc., as follows:

The New
England
Conference of
the Evangeli-
cal Church, Inc.
may make
contracts to
pay annui-
ties.

SECTION 1. The New England Conference of the Evangelical Church, Inc., a corporation established by law in this commonwealth, may, in consideration of the receipt of funds to be devoted to the purposes for which it is incorporated, bind itself to pay fixed yearly sums in one or more payments each year to such person or persons as may be agreed upon, for a term of years or for the life of such person or persons.

Certain con-
tracts already
made, vali-
dated.

SECTION 2. Any such contracts made by said corporation prior to the effective date of this act, in so far as they are illegal for want of authority to make the same, are hereby validated.   *Approved March 23, 1933.*

Chap. 91 AN ACT PLACING THE OFFICE OF CHIEF ENGINEER OF THE FIRE DEPARTMENT OF THE CITY OF SOMERVILLE UNDER THE CIVIL SERVICE LAWS.

Be it enacted, etc., as follows:

Office of chief
engineer of
the fire de-
partment of
the city of
Somerville
subject to
civil service
laws.

SECTION 1. The office of chief engineer of the fire department of the city of Somerville shall, upon the effective date of this act, become subject to the civil service laws and rules and regulations relating to permanent members· of fire departments of cities, and the term of office of any incumbent thereof shall be unlimited, except that he may be removed in accordance with such laws and rules and regulations; provided that the person holding said office on said date shall continue in office on the same tenure as theretofore.

Submission
to voters, etc.

SECTION 2. This act shall be submitted for acceptance to the registered voters of the city of Somerville at its city election in the current year in the form of the following question which shall be placed upon the official ballot to be used at said election: "Shall an act passed by the general court in the year nineteen hundred and thirty-three, entitled 'An Act placing the office of chief engineer of the fire department of the city of Somerville under the civil service laws', be accepted?" If a majority of the voters voting thereon vote in the affirmative in answer to said question, this act shall thereupon take effect, but not otherwise.

Approved March 23, 1933.

An Act providing a penalty for fraudulently pro- *Chap.* 92
CURING FOOD OR BEVERAGE FROM COMMON VICTUALLERS.

Be it enacted, etc., as follows:

Chapter one hundred and forty of the General Laws, as G. L. (Ter. Ed.), 140, § 12, etc., amended.
amended in section twelve by chapter eighty-six of
the acts of nineteen hundred and thirty-two, is hereby
further amended by striking out said section twelve and
inserting in place thereof the following: — *Section 12.* Penalty for fraudulently procuring accommodations at an inn, lodging house or boarding house, etc., and for fraudulently procuring food or beverage from common victuallers.
Whoever puts up at an inn, lodging house or boarding house
and, without having an express agreement for credit,
procures food, entertainment or accommodation without
paying therefor, and with intent to cheat or defraud the
owner or keeper thereof; or, with such intent, obtains
credit at an inn, lodging house or boarding house for such
food, entertainment or accommodation by means of any
false show of baggage or effects brought thereto; or, with
such intent, removes or causes to be removed any baggage
or effects from an inn, lodging house or boarding house while
a lien exists thereon for the proper charges due from him
for fare and board furnished therein, shall be punished
by a fine of not more than two hundred dollars or by imprisonment for not more than one year; and whoever,
without having an express agreement for credit, procures
food or beverage from a common victualler without paying
therefor and with intent to cheat or defraud shall be punished by a fine of not more than fifty dollars or by imprisonment for not more than three months. The words "lodg- "Lodging house" defined.
ing house", as used herein, shall mean a lodging house as
defined in section twenty-two.

Approved March 23, 1933.

An Act relative to the issue of licenses and certifi- *Chap.* 93
CATES OF PUBLIC CONVENIENCE AND NECESSITY FOR
SIGHT-SEEING AUTOMOBILES CARRYING PERSONS IN OR
FROM THE CITY OF BOSTON.

Be it enacted, etc., as follows:

Section 1. Section two of chapter three hundred and 1931, 399, § 2, amended.
ninety-nine of the acts of nineteen hundred and thirty-one
is hereby amended by inserting after the word "is" in the
third .line the word: — first, — and by inserting after the
word "unless" in the fourth line the word: — thereafter, —
so as to read as follows: — *Section 2.* It shall be un- Operation of sight-seeing automobiles regulated.
lawful for a person or a corporation to offer or furnish
service by a sight-seeing automobile in or from the city of
Boston unless said automobile is first licensed hereunder
and unless thereafter a certificate of public convenience
and necessity is obtained as hereinafter provided, and it
shall be unlawful for a person to operate such an automobile
as driver in or from said city unless he is licensed so to do
as hereinafter provided.

1931, 399, § 5, amended.

SECTION 2.   Section five of said chapter three hundred and ninety-nine is hereby amended by striking out, in the third line, the word "first", — so as to read as follows: —

Certificate of public convenience and necessity, etc.

Section 5.   No person or corporation shall offer or furnish service by sight-seeing automobiles in or from the city of Boston unless said person or corporation has obtained from the department of public utilities a certificate declaring that public convenience and necessity require such opera-

Public hearing.

tion.   Said department may, after public hearing, issue or refuse to issue such a certificate and may attach to the exercise of the privilege conferred by said certificate such

Terms and conditions.

terms and conditions as to operation and fares as the said department may deem that public convenience and neces-

Suspension or revocation.

sity require.   Said department may, after notice and hearing, suspend or revoke any such certificate for cause or alter or amend any terms or conditions attached to the

Rules, orders and regulations.

exercise of the privilege conferred thereby.   Said department may make suitable and reasonable rules, orders and regulations governing the operation and fares of sight-seeing automobiles carrying persons in or from the city of Boston, and may revise, alter, amend and annul the same;

Proviso.

provided, that such rules, orders and regulations shall not be inconsistent with those lawfully established by the board of street commissioners of the city of Boston, by the Boston traffic commission, by the board of park commissioners of said city, or by said police commissioner.

Approved March 23, 1933.

Chap. 94 AN ACT AUTHORIZING CERTAIN OFFICERS TO DIRECT THE WEIGHING OF MATERIAL FOR ROAD CONSTRUCTION AND CERTAIN OTHER ARTICLES.

Be it enacted, etc., as follows:

G. L. (Ter. Ed.), 94, new section after § 249F.

SECTION 1.   Chapter ninety-four of the General Laws, as appearing in the Tercentenary Edition thereof, is hereby amended by inserting after section two hundred and forty-nine F under the caption "MATERIAL FOR ROAD CONSTRUC-

Director of standards, inspectors and sealers may direct material for road construction to be weighed.

TION", the following new section: — *Section 249G.*   The director of standards or any inspector of standards in any town, or a sealer of weights and measures within his town, wherein any quantity of material for road construction in the course of delivery is found may direct the person in charge of the material to convey the same without delay or charge to scales designated by such director, inspector or sealer, who shall there determine the quantity of the material and its weight together with the tare weight, and shall direct said person to return to such scales immediately after unloading the material; and upon such return the director, inspector or sealer shall determine the tare weight. The scales designated by the director, inspector or sealer as aforesaid may be the public scales of the town or any other scales therein which may have been duly tested and sealed, and shall be such scales as in his judgment are most convenient.

SECTION 2. Said chapter ninety-four, as so appearing, is hereby further amended by striking out section two hundred and forty-five and inserting in place thereof the following: — *Section 245.* The director of standards or any inspector of standards in any town, or a sealer of weights and measures within his town, wherein any quantity of coke, charcoal or coal in the course of delivery is found may direct the person in charge of the goods to convey the same without delay or charge to scales designated by such director, inspector or sealer, who shall there determine the quantity of the goods, and, if they are not in baskets or bags as required by section two hundred and forty-one, shall determine their weight together with the tare weight, and shall direct said person to return to such scales immediately after unloading the goods; and upon such return, the director, inspector or sealer shall determine the tare weight. The scales designated by the director, inspector or sealer as aforesaid may be the public scales of the town or any other scales therein which have been duly tested and sealed, and shall be such scales as in his judgment are most convenient.   *Approved March 23, 1933.*

G. L. (Ter. Ed.), 94, § 245, amended.

Director of standards, inspectors and sealers may direct coke, charcoal or coal to be weighed.

AN ACT RELATIVE TO CERTAIN BORROWINGS BY THE CITY OF WORCESTER FOR THE PURPOSES OF STREET CONSTRUCTION, PERMANENT PAVING AND SIDEWALK CONSTRUCTION IN SAID CITY.

Chap. 95

Be it enacted, etc., as follows:

SECTION 1. Section one of chapter sixty-nine of the acts of nineteen hundred and thirty-one is hereby amended by striking out, in the third and thirteenth lines, the word "two" and inserting in place thereof, in each instance, the word: — three, — so as to read as follows: — *Section 1.* For the purposes of street construction and permanent paving in the city of Worcester, said city may borrow, from time to time within a period of three years from the passage of this act, such sums as may be necessary, not exceeding, in the aggregate, one million two hundred and fifty thousand dollars, and may issue bonds or notes therefor, which shall bear on their face the words, Worcester Street Improvement Loan, Act of 1931. Each authorized issue for the purposes aforesaid shall constitute a separate loan, and such loans shall be payable in not more than ten years from their dates. For the purpose of sidewalk construction of brick, stone, or concrete in the said city, said city may borrow, from time to time within a period of three years from the passage of this act, such sums as may be necessary, not exceeding, in the aggregate, two hundred and fifty thousand dollars, and may issue bonds or notes therefor, which shall bear on their face the words, Worcester Sidewalk Construction Loan, Act of 1931. Each authorized

1931, 69, § 1, amended.

City of Worcester, loans for street construction and permanent paving.

Loans for sidewalk construction.

issue for such sidewalk construction shall constitute a separate loan, and such loans shall be payable in not more than five years from their dates. No loan shall be authorized under this act unless a sum equal to an amount not less than ten per cent of the loan so authorized is voted for the same purpose to be provided from taxes or other sources of revenue of the year when authorized. Indebtedness incurred under this act shall be in excess of the amount authorized by chapter two hundred and eleven of the Special Acts of nineteen hundred and sixteen, as amended by chapter one hundred and thirty-eight of the acts of nineteen hundred and twenty, but shall, except as provided herein, be subject to chapter forty-four of the General Laws.

Certain borrowings authorized.

SECTION 2. So much of the amount authorized by said section one of said chapter sixty-nine for sidewalk construction as remained unborrowed on the first day of January of the current year may be borrowed either for the purpose of street construction and permanent paving in said city or of sidewalk construction therein, or in part for each such purpose, subject nevertheless to the provisions of said section one, as amended hereby, applicable to a borrowing for that purpose.

SECTION 3. This act shall take effect upon its passage.
Approved March 23, 1933.

Chap. 96 AN ACT EXEMPTING ORDERS FOR PAYMENT OF LABOR OR TRADE UNION OR CRAFT DUES OR OBLIGATIONS FROM THE OPERATION OF THE LAWS REGULATING ASSIGNMENTS OF WAGES.

Be it enacted, etc., as follows:

G. L. (Ter. Ed.), 154, new section at end thereof.

Chapter one hundred and fifty-four of the General Laws, as appearing in the Tercentenary Edition thereof, is hereby amended by adding at the end thereof the following new

Chapter not to apply to trade union, etc., dues.

section: — *Section 8.* None of the foregoing sections of this chapter shall be applicable to or control or prohibit the deduction of labor or trade union or craft dues or obligations from wages of an employee by an employer in accordance with a written request made by the individual employee. *Approved March 23, 1933.*

Chap. 97 AN ACT CHANGING THE ALCOHOLIC CONTENT OF CERTAIN BEVERAGES UNDER THE LAWS OF THE COMMONWEALTH IN ORDER TO RENDER THE MANUFACTURE AND PREPARATION OF SUCH BEVERAGES PERMISSIBLE UNDER FEDERAL LAW.

Emergency preambles.

Whereas, The sole and exclusive purpose of this act is to enable the manufacture and the preparation within the commonwealth, in conformity with the requirements of federal law, of certain alcoholic beverages the sale whereof has been made lawful by act of Congress approved March twenty-second in the current year; and

Whereas, In order that the people of the commonwealth may take full advantage of the provisions of said act of Congress upon its becoming effective and upon the passage of further legislation by the general court permitting the sale within the commonwealth of such beverages, this act is hereby declared to be an emergency law, necessary for the immediate preservation of the public convenience.

Be it enacted, etc., as follows:

SECTION 1. Section one of chapter one hundred and thirty-eight of the General Laws, as appearing in the Tercentenary Edition thereof, is hereby amended by striking out, in the fifth and sixth lines, the words "two and three fourths per cent of alcohol by weight at sixty degrees Fahrenheit" and inserting in place thereof the words: — three and two tenths per cent of alcohol by weight, — so that the paragraph contained in the fourth to seventh lines, inclusive, will read as follows: — G. L. (Ter. Ed.), 138, § 1, amended.

"Certain non-intoxicating beverages", all beverages containing not less than one half of one per cent and not more than three and two tenths per cent of alcohol by weight. Such beverages shall be deemed not to be intoxicating liquor. "Certain non-intoxicating beverages" defined.

SECTION 2. Section three of said chapter one hundred and thirty-eight, as so appearing, is hereby amended by striking out, in the first and second lines, the words "two and three quarters per cent of alcohol by weight at sixty degrees Fahrenheit" and inserting in place thereof the words: — three and two tenths per cent of alcohol by weight, — so as to read as follows: — *Section 3.* Any beverage containing more than three and two tenths per cent of alcohol by weight, and distilled spirits, shall be deemed to be intoxicating liquor within the meaning of this chapter. G. L. (Ter. Ed.), 138, § 3, amended. Definition of intoxicating liquor.

SECTION 3. The provisions of this act are hereby declared to be limited to the authorization of the manufacture and preparation of beverages of an alcoholic content not exceeding three and two tenths per cent by weight, and no provision of law relative to the sale, keeping and exposing for sale and transportation of intoxicating or non-intoxicating beverages shall be affected by this act. Limitation of provisions of act.

Approved March 23, 1933.

AN ACT AUTHORIZING THE TOWN OF WESTON TO USE A CERTAIN LOAN BALANCE FOR LAYING AND RE-LAYING WATER MAINS. *Chap.* 98

Be it enacted, etc., as follows:

SECTION 1. The town of Weston is hereby authorized to appropriate any balance of the water loan issued in nineteen hundred and thirty-one for the acquisition of land, the construction of a standpipe and the installation of driven wells, for the purpose of laying and re-laying water mains of not less than six inches in diameter.

SECTION 2.   This act shall take effect upon its passage.

Approved March 27, 1933.

Chap. 99 AN ACT PROVIDING FOR ADVANCE PAYMENTS ON ACCOUNT OF TAXES FOR THE YEARS NINETEEN HUNDRED AND THIRTY-THREE AND NINETEEN HUNDRED AND THIRTY-FOUR IN CERTAIN CITIES AND TOWNS.

Emergency preamble.

Whereas, The deferred operation of this act would tend to defeat its purpose, therefore it is hereby declared to be an emergency law, necessary for the immediate preservation of the public convenience.

Be it enacted, etc., as follows:

Advance payments of taxes on real estate in certain cities and towns authorized.

SECTION 1.   The owner or person in possession of real estate assessable in any city or town for the taxes of the current year shall, upon application to the assessors, or any one of them, in such city or town, be given a certificate in such form as the commissioner of corporations and taxation, hereinafter called the commissioner, may prescribe, of the amount of the tax assessed upon such real estate for the preceding year.   If such real estate was part of a larger parcel which has been divided by sale, mortgage, upon a petition for partition or otherwise since April first of said preceding year, the assessors shall apportion the tax on such larger parcel for said year and specify in such certificate the amount of the tax applicable to the real estate to which the application relates.   The holder of such a certificate shall, at any time and from time to time prior to September first in the current year, be entitled to pay to the collector of taxes of such city or town an amount or amounts not exceeding in the aggregate ninety per cent of the amount of the tax as set forth in the certificate; provided, that no instalment of less than ten per cent of the amount of the tax as aforesaid or in any event less than five dollars shall so be received.   The collector shall, upon receiving the first payment, take up and retain the said certificate and shall give in exchange therefor, and for each additional payment received under this section, a receipt in such form as the commissioner may prescribe.   The collector shall, within a period of seven days of the receipt of any payment hereunder, transmit the same to the city or town treasurer, and render to the city or town auditor or accountant, or corresponding official, a statement of the date and amount thereof and such other facts as may be prescribed by the commissioner.

Interest to be allowed on advance payments of taxes on real estate.

SECTION 2.   Payments made under section one shall be treated as advance payments on account of the tax assessed or to be assessed for the current year on the real estate to which they relate and the collector shall credit ' on the tax list for said year committed to him by the assessors and on the tax bill for such real estate the amount of each such payment. Persons making any payment to the collector hereunder shall be allowed interest thereon at such rate, not exceeding six per cent per annum as may be fixed in a city by its treasurer with the approval of the mayor or in a town by its treasurer with the approval of the selectmen, for the period beginning with the date of such payment and ending with the date when the tax for said year becomes due and payable. Errors in such credits shall be adjusted by the collector upon application filed with him by the person assessed within thirty days of the receipt of the tax bill.

SECTION 3. Any person who was assessed in the preceding year a tax with respect to his personal estate may in like manner pay to the collector of the city or town in which such tax was assessed an amount or amounts not exceeding in the aggregate ninety per cent of such tax, as advance payments on account of any tax assessed or to be assessed therein in the current year with respect to his personal estate, and the provisions of the two preceding sections shall, so far as apt, apply to payments so made. *Advance payments of taxes on personal estate authorized.*

SECTION 4. The payment of a portion of a tax under this act shall not preclude the person making the payment from applying for and receiving an abatement of the taxes assessed upon him, in accordance with chapter fifty-nine of the General Laws; and if it is finally determined that the amount which he has paid is in excess of the tax properly assessable upon him, the excess, with interest at the rate of six per cent per annum from the date of payment, shall be refunded to him. *Payment of portion of tax not to affect abatements.*

SECTION 5. This act shall be operative with respect to taxes assessed or to be assessed for the current year in any city upon its acceptance, during said year and prior to July first, by vote of the city council thereof, approved by the mayor, and in any town upon its acceptance as aforesaid by the selectmen; and it shall be operative with respect to the taxes assessed or to be assessed for the year nineteen hundred and thirty-four in any city or town upon its acceptance, during the year nineteen hundred and thirty-four and prior to July first, in the manner aforesaid, and in construing this act in its application to any city or town accepting it as aforesaid during the year nineteen hundred and thirty-four, the words "current year" shall mean the year nineteen hundred and thirty-four and the words "preceding year" shall mean the year nineteen hundred and thirty-three. *Acceptance of act.*   *Approved March 28, 1933.*

*Chap.*100 AN ACT GRANTING DISCRETIONARY POWER TO PROBATE COURTS IN THE ISSUING OF NEW LETTERS OF ADMINISTRATION ON ESTATES WHICH ARE IN PROCESS OF SETTLEMENT BY PUBLIC ADMINISTRATORS.

Emergency preamble.

Whereas, The deferred operation of this act would tend to defeat its purpose, therefore it is hereby declared to be an emergency law, necessary for the immediate preservation of the public convenience.

Be it enacted, etc., as follows:

G. L. (Ter. Ed.), 194, § 7, amended.

Powers of public administrators to cease upon the granting of letters of administration to another person.

Chapter one hundred and ninety-four of the General Laws, as appearing in the Tercentenary Edition thereof, is hereby amended by striking out section seven and inserting in place thereof the following: — *Section 7.* If, after the granting of letters of administration to a public administrator and before the final settlement of the estate, the husband, widow or an heir of the deceased, in writing, claims the right of administration or requests the appointment of some other suitable person to the trust, the probate court may, in its discretion, grant letters of administration accordingly, or if, after the granting of such letters to a public administrator, a will of the deceased is proved and allowed, said court shall grant letters testamentary or letters of administration with the will annexed. When the person to whom such letters are granted gives the bond required by law the powers of the public administrator over the estate shall cease.   *Approved March 29, 1933.*

*Chap.*101 AN ACT RELATIVE TO THE APPROVAL OF THE FORM OF SURVIVORSHIP ANNUITY CONTRACTS AND EXEMPTING SUCH CONTRACTS FROM CERTAIN PROVISIONS OF LAW RELATIVE TO POLICIES OF LIFE INSURANCE.

Be it enacted, etc., as follows:

G. L. (Ter. Ed.), 175, § 132, amended.

SECTION 1. Section one hundred and thirty-two of chapter one hundred and seventy-five of the General Laws, as appearing in the Tercentenary Edition thereof, is hereby amended by striking out the first paragraph and inserting in place thereof the following: —

Life, annuity, etc., policies, approval of.

No policy of life or endowment insurance and no annuity, survivorship annuity or pure endowment contract shall be issued or delivered in the commonwealth until a copy of the form thereof has been on file for thirty days with the commissioner, unless before the expiration of said thirty days he shall have approved the form of the policy or contract in writing; nor if the commissioner notifies the company in writing, within said thirty days, that in his opinion the form of the policy or contract does not comply with the laws of the commonwealth, specifying his reasons therefor, provided that such action of the commissioner shall be subject to review by the supreme judicial court; nor shall any such policy or contract, except policies of industrial insurance, on which the premiums are payable monthly or oftener, and except annuity or pure endowment contracts, whether or not they embody an agreement to refund to the estate of the holder upon his death or to a specified payee any sum not exceeding the premiums paid thereon with compound interest, and except survivorship annuity contracts, be so issued or delivered unless it contains in substance the following:

SECTION 2. Section one hundred and forty of said chapter one hundred and seventy-five, as so appearing, is hereby amended by striking out the first sentence of the third paragraph and inserting in place thereof the following: — This section shall not apply to annuity, survivorship annuity or pure endowment contracts, nor to any domestic stock life company issuing only non-participating policies, — so that said third paragraph will read as follows: — *G. L. (Ter. Ed.), 175, § 140, amended.*

This section shall not apply to annuity, survivorship annuity or pure endowment contracts, nor to any domestic stock life company issuing only non-participating policies. A foreign life company which does not provide in every participating policy hereafter issued or delivered in the commonwealth that the proportion of the surplus accruing upon said policy shall be ascertained and distributed annually and not otherwise, except as hereinafter provided, either by payment in cash of the amount apportioned to a policy, or by its application to the payment of premiums or to the purchase of paid-up additions, or for the accumulation of the amounts from time to time apportioned, said accumulations to be subject to withdrawal by the policyholder, shall not be permitted to do new business within the commonwealth. *Annual dividends, etc., provisions of section not to apply to certain contracts of insurance.*

SECTION 3. Section one hundred and forty-four of said chapter one hundred and seventy-five, as so appearing, is hereby amended by striking out the last paragraph and inserting in place thereof the following: — *G. L. (Ter. Ed.), 175, § 144, amended.*

This section shall not apply to annuity or pure endowment contracts with or without return of premiums, or of premiums and interest, whether simple or compound, or to survivorship annuity contracts or survivorship insurance policies, and, in the case of a policy providing for both insurance and an annuity, shall apply only to that part of the policy providing for insurance; but every such policy providing for a deferred annuity on the life of the insured only shall, unless paid for by a single premium, provide that, in the event of the non-payment of any premium after three full years' premiums shall have been paid, the annuity shall automatically become converted into a paid-up annuity for such proportion of the original annuity as the number of completed years' premiums paid bears to the total number of premiums required under the policy. *Provisions of section relative to cash surrender value, etc., not to apply to certain contracts.* *Approved March 29, 1933.*

Chap.102 AN ACT PROVIDING FOR THE ABOLISHING OF THE INDEPEND-
ENT INDUSTRIAL SHOEMAKING SCHOOL IN THE CITY OF
LYNN.

Be it enacted, etc., as follows:

Independent
Industrial
Shoemaking
School
abolished.

SECTION 1. The Independent Industrial Shoemaking
School, established in the city of Lynn under chapter one
hundred and seventy-four of the Special Acts of nineteen hundred and sixteen, is hereby abolished.

G. L. (Ter.
Ed.), 74, § 11,
amended.

SECTION 2. Section eleven of chapter seventy-four of
the General Laws, as appearing in the Tercentenary
Edition thereof, is hereby amended by striking out, in the
second line, the words "cities of Lynn and" and inserting
in place thereof the words: — city of, — so as to read as

State reim-
bursement.

follows: — *Section 11.* The counties of Bristol, Essex
and Norfolk, and the city of Northampton shall, so long
as their respective schools are approved, be reimbursed by
the commonwealth as are towns under section nine.

G. L. (Ter.
Ed.), 74, § 23,
repealed.

SECTION 3. Section twenty-three of said chapter
seventy-four, as so appearing, is hereby repealed.

Acceptance
of act.

SECTION 4. This act shall be submitted for acceptance
to the registered voters of the city of Lynn at its city
election in the current year in the form of the following
question which shall be placed upon the official ballot to
be used at said election: "Shall the Independent Industrial
Shoemaking School in the city of Lynn be abolished?" If
a majority of the voters voting thereon vote in the affirmative in answer to said question, this act shall thereupon take effect, but not otherwise.
Approved March 29, 1933.

Chap.103 AN ACT RELATIVE TO THE PAYMENT OF PENSIONS TO FIRE-
MEN IN CERTAIN CITIES.

Be it enacted, etc., as follows:

G. L. (Ter.
Ed.), 32, § 81,
amended.

Section eighty-one of chapter thirty-two of the General
Laws, as appearing in the Tercentenary Edition thereof,
is hereby amended by inserting after the word "payable"
in the second line the words: — weekly or, — so as to read

Amount of
pension pay-
able to
firemen in cer-
tain cities.

as follows: — *Section 81.* Any permanent member of a
fire department retired under the preceding section shall
receive an annual pension, payable weekly or monthly,
equal to one half of the annual salary or other compensation
received by him at his retirement. The pension of any call
or substitute call fireman retired under said section shall
be the same as that of a permanent member of the first
grade of the same department in which he served, or, if
there be no grades, his compensation shall be that of a
permanent member of the department performing duties
like those which he performed. *Approved March 29, 1933.*

AN ACT RELATIVE TO THE TERMS OF CERTAIN NOTES TO BE *Chap.*104
ISSUED BY THE COMMONWEALTH.

Be it enacted, etc., as follows:

The terms of the notes which the state treasurer is authorized to issue under chapter forty-nine of the acts of the current year, creating an emergency finance board and defining its powers and duties, shall be for periods of years ending not later than November thirtieth, nineteen hundred and thirty-nine, as recommended by the governor in a message to the general court dated March twenty-seventh, nineteen hundred and thirty-three, in pursuance of section three of Article LXII of the amendments to the constitution.   *Approved March 30, 1933.*

AN ACT REDUCING THE SALARY OR OTHER COMPENSATION *Chap.*105
OF STATE OFFICERS AND EMPLOYEES.

Whereas, The deferred operation of this act would defeat its purpose, which is primarily to afford immediate relief to the taxpayers of the commonwealth, therefore it is hereby declared to be an emergency law, necessary for the immediate preservation of the public convenience. Emergency preamble.

Be it enacted, etc., as follows:

SECTION 1. The salary of each official and employee in the service of the commonwealth, whose salary is fixed in accordance with the standard rates of salary incorporated in the rules and regulations governing the classification of personal service as prepared by the division of personnel and standardization of the commission on administration and finance and approved by the governor and council, and the salary of each official and employee whose salary is fixed by or subject to the approval of the governor and council or governor in accordance with a schedule of standard rates of salary adopted by the governor and council or governor, is hereby reduced, if it is fifty-two hundred and fifty dollars or under, by an amount equivalent to one and one half steps in the salary range established for the grade or position which he occupies, and, if it is in excess of fifty-two hundred and fifty dollars, by an amount equivalent to two steps in the salary range established for the grade or position which he occupies, said step, in either case, to be the same as the standard increment heretofore used by said division, the governor and council or the governor as the basis for increases in salary for the particular grade or position. Reduction of salaries of state officials and employees.

The said division is hereby directed to revise said schedules of salary ranges to conform to the provisions hereof.

SECTION 2. The yearly rate of salary of each official and employee in the service of the commonwealth whose salary is established otherwise than as set forth in the Rate of salary reduction.

preceding section shall be reduced, if it is fifty-two hundred and fifty dollars or under, by an amount equal to ten per cent thereof, and, if it is in excess of fifty-two hundred and fifty dollars, by an amount equal to fifteen per cent thereof; provided, that the salary of each member of the general court shall be reduced by an amount equal to ten per cent thereof. The provisions of this act shall not apply to scrubwomen.

Act to apply to certain institutions receiving contributions from the commonwealth.

After the effective date of this act, no further payment to any institution which receives from the commonwealth contributions in excess of one hundred thousand dollars annually shall be made by the commonwealth on account of any such contribution unless and until there has been filed with the comptroller a certificate by the trustees of such institution and by said division that the salary of each officer and employee of such institution has been reduced in like manner and amount as provided by this section in the case of salaries of officials and employees in the service of the commonwealth other than members of the general court.

"Salary" defined.

SECTION 3. The word "salary", as used in sections one and two, shall include all compensation from the commonwealth, however payable and whether or not for full time, and in the case of an official or employee whose salary is paid in part from funds of the state treasury and in part from federal, county, municipal or other funds shall mean that part payable from funds of the state treasury.

Enforcement of provisions of act.

SECTION 4. The said division, the comptroller and the state treasurer are hereby directed to enforce the provisions of sections one and two. Nothing in said sections shall be construed to limit the respective powers of said division and officers as now defined by law.

Period of operation of act.

SECTION 5. The reduction in salaries provided for by this act shall be effective only for the period beginning April first in the current year and ending November thirtieth, nineteen hundred and thirty-four, except that the reduction in salaries of the members of the general court shall be effective as of the first Wednesday in January of the current year and shall continue only until the end of the legislative year of nineteen hundred and thirty-four.

Act not to affect certain pension, etc., allowances.

SECTION 6. No reduction in salary or compensation made by this act shall affect the amount payable, under chapter thirty-two of the General Laws or any other provision of law, to any officer or employee by way of pension, annuity or retirement allowance or the amount of any annuity contribution payable by any member of the state retirement system. *Approved April 3, 1933.*

An Act placing the office of chief of the fire department of the town of Weymouth under the civil service laws. *Chap.*106

Be it enacted, etc., as follows:

SECTION 1. The office of chief of the fire department of the town of Weymouth shall, upon the effective date of this act, become subject to the civil service laws and rules and regulations relating to the permanent members of the fire departments of towns, and the tenure of office of any incumbent thereof shall be unlimited, except that he may be removed in accordance with such laws and rules and regulations; but the person holding said office on said effective date may continue to serve as such without taking a civil service examination.

SECTION 2. This act shall take effect upon its passage.

Approved April 3, 1933.

An Act relating to the conditions of admission of foreign mutual surety companies. *Chap.*107

Be it enacted, etc., as follows:

SECTION 1. Section one hundred and fifty-one of chapter one hundred and seventy-five of the General Laws, as appearing in the Tercentenary Edition thereof, is hereby amended by striking out all after the word "dollars" in the twenty-sixth line down to and including the word "dollars" in the thirty-first line, and inserting in place thereof the following: — ; or (b), if it proposes to transact business under the fourth clause of said section forty-seven, a fully paid-up guaranty capital, established in accordance with the laws of its home state, unimpaired on the basis fixed by sections ten to twelve, inclusive, of not less than two hundred thousand dollars and net cash assets, so computed, exclusive of said guaranty capital, of not less than one hundred thousand dollars, or, if the company has net cash assets, so computed, of not less than two million dollars, in lieu of such a guaranty capital, a guaranty fund, unimpaired as aforesaid, of not less than two hundred thousand nor more than five hundred thousand dollars, satisfactory to the commissioner, if such fund is legally established under the laws of its home state, — by inserting after the word "capital" in the fifty-seventh line the words: — or the guaranty fund, — and by striking out, in the sixtieth and sixty-first lines, the words "such capital" and inserting in place thereof the words: — any such capital, guaranty fund, — so that clause second will read as follows: — Second, It has satisfied the commissioner that (1) it is fully and legally organized under the laws of its state or government to do the business it proposes to transact; that (2) it has, if a stock company, other than a life company, a fully paid-up capital, exclusive of stockholders'

G. L. (Ter. Ed.), 175, § 151, amended.

Certain conditions of admission of foreign insurance companies.

Certain
conditions of
admission of
foreign insur-
ance com-
panies.

obligations of any description, unimpaired on the basis
fixed by sections ten to twelve, inclusive, of an amount
not less than is required by sections forty-eight and fifty-
one of domestic stock companies transacting the same
classes of business; that (3), it has, if a mutual company,
other than a life company, and (a), if it proposes to transact business under any one of the clauses of section forty-
seven, except the fourth, sixth, eleventh, fourteenth or
fifteenth, or under the first and eighth clauses thereof,
net cash assets computed on the basis fixed by sections
ten to twelve, inclusive, at least equal to the amount of
capital required by sections forty-eight and fifty-one of
a domestic stock company transacting the same classes
of business, or net cash assets, so computed, of not less
than fifty thousand dollars and contingent assets of not less
than three hundred thousand dollars, or net cash assets,
so computed, of not less than seventy-five thousand dollars
and contingent assets of not less than one hundred and fifty
thousand dollars; or (b), if it proposes to transact business
under the fourth clause of said section forty-seven, a fully
paid-up guaranty capital, established in accordance with
the laws of its home state, unimpaired on the basis fixed
by sections ten to twelve, inclusive, of not less than two
hundred thousand dollars and net cash assets, so computed,
exclusive of said guaranty capital, of not less than one
hundred thousand dollars, or, if the company has net cash
assets, so computed, of not less than two million dollars,
in lieu of such a guaranty capital, a guaranty fund, unimpaired as aforesaid, of not less than two hundred thousand nor more than five hundred thousand dollars, satisfactory to the commissioner, if such fund is legally established under the laws of its home state; or (c), if it proposes
to transact business under the sixth clause of said section
forty-seven, net cash assets, so computed, of not less than
two hundred thousand dollars, or net cash assets, so computed, of not less than one hundred thousand dollars and
contingent assets of not less than four hundred thousand
dollars; or (d), if it proposes to transact business under the
first and second, or under the first, second and eighth
clauses of said section forty-seven, net cash assets, so
computed, at least equal to the amount of capital required
by said sections forty-eight and fifty-one of a domestic
stock company transacting the same classes of business,
or net cash assets, so computed, of not less than two hundred
thousand dollars and contingent assets of not less than
four hundred thousand dollars, or (e), if it proposes to
transact business under the first and third, the third and
eighth, or the first, third and eighth clauses of said section
forty-seven, net cash assets computed on the basis fixed
by sections ten to twelve, inclusive, of not less than three
hundred thousand dollars, or net cash assets, so computed,
of not less than one hundred and fifty thousand dollars
and contingent assets of not less than three hundred

thousand dollars; or (*f*), if it proposes to transact business under any two or more of the fourth, fifth, sixth, seventh, eighth, ninth, tenth, twelfth and thirteenth clauses of said section forty-seven, net cash assets, computed as aforesaid, at least equal to the amount of capital required by said sections forty-eight and fifty-one of a domestic stock company transacting the same classes of business, or net cash assets, computed as aforesaid, of not less than seventy-five thousand dollars, and contingent assets of not less than one hundred and fifty thousand dollars, for each clause under which it proposes to transact business, in addition, in any case, to the guaranty capital or the guaranty fund and net cash assets required by (*b*) hereof if it proposes to transact business under said fourth clause, and in addition to the net cash or net cash and contingent assets required by (*c*) hereof if it proposes to transact business under said sixth clause; that (4) any such capital, guaranty fund and assets, other than contingent, are well invested and available for the payment of losses in the commonwealth, that the company is in a sound financial condition and that its business policies, methods and management are sound and proper; and (5) that it insures in a single risk wherever located an amount no larger than one tenth of its net assets except as provided in section twenty-one.

SECTION 2. Section five of said chapter one hundred and seventy-five, as so appearing, is hereby amended by inserting after the word "capital" the second time it occurs in the tenth line, and in the twelfth line, respectively, the words: — or guaranty fund, — by striking out, in the fifteenth line, the words "section one hundred and sixty-three" and inserting in place thereof the words: — this chapter, — and by striking out, in the thirty-seventh to the fortieth lines, inclusive, the words: — "Such company or its agents shall not make any contracts, or issue any policies, of insurance in the commonwealth after such revocation or suspension is effective nor until its license is restored by the commissioner.", — so as to read as follows: — *Section 5.* If the commissioner is satisfied, upon examination or other evidence submitted to him, that any foreign company is insolvent or is in an unsound financial condition, or that its business policies or methods are unsound or improper, or that its condition or management is such as to render its further transaction of business hazardous to the public or its policyholders, or that it is transacting business fraudulently, or that its officers or agents have refused to submit to an examination under section four or to perform any legal obligation relative thereto or that the amount of its funds, net cash or contingent assets is deficient or that its capital stock or deposit or guaranty capital or guaranty fund is impaired, as set forth in section twenty-three A, or that such capital stock, deposit or guaranty capital or guaranty fund has been reduced below the amount required by section one hundred and fifty-one, he shall revoke the license issued to said company under section one hundred and fifty-one and the licenses issued to all of its agents under this chapter; or, if he is satisfied, as aforesaid, that any foreign company has violated any provision of law or has failed to comply with its charter, he may revoke such licenses or suspend them for a period not exceeding the unexpired terms thereof. He shall give written notice to the company specifying the date on which such revocation or suspension shall be effective, the term of any such suspension and the ground for such revocation or suspension; provided, that if the ground for revocation or suspension is that the company has violated any provision of law or has failed to comply with its charter, the effective date of such revocation or suspension shall be not less than ten days from the date of issue of said notice, and the particulars of such violation or failure to comply with its charter shall be specified in said notice. Such notice may be served by registered mail, sent postage prepaid, addressed to the company at its last home office address or, in the case of a company described in section one hundred and fifty-five, to its resident manager in the United States at his last address, appearing on the records of the commissioner. An affidavit of the commissioner, in such form as he may prescribe, or of anyone authorized by him to give such notice, appended to a copy thereof, that such notice has been mailed as aforesaid shall be prima facie evidence that such notice has been duly given. He shall also cause notice of such revocation or suspension to be published in such manner as he may deem necessary for the protection of the public. A company aggrieved by a revocation or suspension of its license hereunder, may within ten days from the effective date of such revocation or suspension file a petition in the supreme judicial court for the county of Suffolk for a review of such action of the commissioner. The court shall summarily hear and determine the question whether the ground for revocation or suspension specified in the notice of the commissioner exists and may make any appropriate order or decree. If the order or decree is adverse to the petitioning company it may within ten days therefrom appeal to the full court; and in case of such an appeal the revocation or suspension of the license of the said company shall continue in full force until the final determination of the question by the full court, unless vacated by the commissioner during the pendency of such appeal.

Petitions for review.

G. L. (Ter. Ed.), 175, § 6, amended.

Section 3. Section six of said chapter one hundred and seventy-five, as so appearing, is hereby amended by inserting before the word "is" in the twenty-sixth line the words: — or its guaranty fund under section ninety C, — so that the first paragraph will read as follows: — If it appears to the commissioner that the capital of a domestic

Certain domestic insurance com-

stock company other than a life company is impaired to the extent of one quarter or more on the basis fixed by sections ten to twelve, inclusive, but that the company can with safety to the public and its policyholders be permitted to continue to transact business, he shall notify the company in writing that its capital is legally subject to be made good as provided in section sixty-nine. If such a company other than a life company shall not within three months after receiving such notice satisfy the commissioner that it has fully made good its capital or reduced it as provided in section seventy-one, or, if he is satisfied that any domestic company is insolvent or in an unsound financial condition, or that its business policies or methods are unsound or improper, or that its condition or management is such as to render its further transaction of business hazardous to the public or to its policyholders or creditors, or that it is transacting business fraudulently or that it or its officers or agents have refused to submit to an examination under section four or seventy-three, or that it has attempted or is attempting to compromise with its creditors on the ground that it is financially unable to pay its claims in full, or that, when its assets are less than its liabilities, inclusive of unearned premiums but exclusive of capital, if any, it has attempted or is attempting to the disadvantage of policyholders who have sustained losses to prefer or, has preferred, by reinsurance, policyholders who have sustained no losses, he shall, or, if he is satisfied that any domestic company has exceeded its powers or has violated any provision of law, or that the amount of its funds, insurance in force or premiums or number of risks is deficient or that its guaranty capital under section ninety B or its guaranty fund under section ninety C is impaired, as set forth in sections twenty-three, seventy-four, ninety-three D and one hundred and sixteen, he may, apply to the supreme judicial court for an injunction restraining it in whole or in part from further proceeding with its business. The court may issue a temporary injunction forthwith and may after a full hearing make the injunction permanent and may appoint one or more receivers to take possession of the property and effects of the company and to settle its affairs, subject to such rules and orders as the court may prescribe.

Approved April 3, 1933.

panies to make good impaired capital.

AN ACT EXTENDING THE PERIOD OF PUBLIC CONTROL AND MANAGEMENT OF THE EASTERN MASSACHUSETTS STREET RAILWAY COMPANY.   *Chap.*108

Be it enacted, etc., as follows:

SECTION 1. Upon the termination on the fifteenth day of January, nineteen hundred and thirty-four, of the five year period of the management and control by trustees of the Eastern Massachusetts Street Railway Company,

Extension of public control of Eastern Massachusetts Street Railway Com-

hereinafter called the company, under the provisions of
chapter two hundred and ninety-eight of the acts of nineteen hundred and twenty-eight, the public management
and control of the company by trustees shall be extended,
subject to the provisions of said chapter two hundred and
ninety-eight and of this act, for a period of five years from
said date. Except as hereinafter otherwise expressly
provided, the provisions of said chapter two hundred and
ninety-eight shall remain in full force and effect for such
further period of five years.

SECTION 2. Upon the filing with the state secretary of
a certified copy of the vote of acceptance provided for in
section four hereof, trustees shall be appointed and confirmed as provided in section two of said chapter two
hundred and ninety-eight, with the powers, duties and
responsibilities set forth in said chapter, for terms of five
years from the fifteenth day of January, nineteen hundred
and thirty-four. If upon said date trustees have not been
appointed and confirmed as aforesaid, the trustees who shall
hold office on the fourteenth day of said January, under
the provisions of said chapter two hundred and ninety-
eight, shall be trustees under the provisions of this act
until trustees shall have been appointed and confirmed
under the provisions hereof. The trustees appointed or
existing under the provisions of this act shall, on said
fifteenth day of January, nineteen hundred and thirty-four,
assume the management and control of the company and,
subject to the provisions of said chapter two hundred and
ninety-eight and of this act, shall continue to exercise said
management and control during said period of five years.

SECTION 3. For the purposes of this act, the words
"extended period specified in section one", as used in section
five of said chapter two hundred and ninety-eight, shall
include the period of extension granted by this act; the
words "expiration of the five year period of management
and operation by trustees as herein provided", as used in
section eleven of said chapter, shall mean the expiration
of the period of extension granted by this act; and the
words "close of the period of management and control by
trustees as provided for by the special act", as used in
section nine of said chapter two hundred and ninety-eight,
shall mean the close of the period of extension granted
by said chapter two hundred and ninety-eight.

SECTION 4. This act shall take effect as of January
fifteenth, nineteen hundred and thirty-four, except for
the purpose of its acceptance as hereinafter provided and
for the purpose of appointing trustees hereunder, upon its
acceptance by the company given by a vote of the holders
of not less than a majority of all the stock of the company
at a meeting held for the purpose, a copy of which vote,
certified by the clerk of the company, shall be filed with the
state secretary; provided, however, that this act shall
become void unless such a certified copy of said vote of

acceptance shall be so filed on or before November first, nineteen hundred and thirty-three.

Approved April 3, 1933.

An Act relative to the braking equipment of certain small tractors designed for use elsewhere than on public ways. *Chap.*109

Be it enacted, etc., as follows:

Section seven of chapter ninety of the General Laws, as most recently amended by chapter fifty-one of the acts of the current year, is hereby further amended by adding at the end of the second sentence the words: — ; and provided, further, that a tractor having a draw-bar pull rating of ten horse power or less and capable of a maximum speed of not more than eighteen miles an hour and designed specially for use elsewhere than on the traveled part of ways may be operated thereon if equipped with a single braking system which shall suffice to stop such tractor within a proper distance as aforesaid, — so that said second sentence will read as follows: — Every automobile shall be provided with at least two braking systems, each with a separate means of application, each operating directly or indirectly on at least two wheels and each of which shall suffice alone to stop said automobile within a proper distance as defined in said rules and regulations; provided, that if said systems are connected, combined or have any part in common, such systems shall be so constructed that a breaking of any one element thereof will not leave the automobile without brakes acting directly or indirectly on at least two wheels; and provided, further, that a tractor having a draw-bar pull rating of ten horse power or less and capable of a maximum speed of not more than eighteen miles an hour and designed specially for use elsewhere than on the traveled part of ways may be operated thereon if equipped with a single braking system which shall suffice to stop such tractor within a proper distance as aforesaid. *Approved April 5, 1933.*

G. L. (Ter. Ed.), 90, § 7, etc., amended.

Certain tractors may be equipped with a single braking system.

An Act further penalizing certain employers who fail to keep, or unlawfully refuse to permit the inspection or examination of, certain registers and records under the minimum wage law, so called. *Chap.*110

Be it enacted, etc., as follows:

Section eight of chapter one hundred and fifty-one of the General Laws, as appearing in the Tercentenary Edition thereof, is hereby amended by striking out, in the thirteenth and fourteenth lines the words "not less than five nor more than fifty" and inserting in place thereof the words: — three hundred, — and by striking out, in the eighteenth line, the words "superior court" and inserting in place thereof the word: — courts, — so as to

G. L. (Ter. Ed.), 151, § 8, amended.

Register of
women and
minors to
be kept by
employers.
read as follows: — *Section 8.* Every employer of women
and minors shall keep a register of the names, addresses
and occupations of all women and minors employed by
him, together with a record of the amount paid each week
to each woman and minor, and if the commission shall so
require, shall also keep for a specified period, not exceeding
six months, a record of the hours worked by such employees,
and shall, on request of the commission or of the department of labor and industries, permit the commission or
any of its members or agents, or the department or any
duly accredited agent thereof, to inspect the said register
and to examine such parts of the books and records of
employers as relate to the wages paid to women and
minors, and the hours worked by such employees. Any
employer failing to keep a register or records as herein
provided, or refusing to permit their inspection or examination, shall be punished by a fine of three hundred
dollars. The commission may also subpœna witnesses,
administer oaths and take testimony, and require the
production of books and documents. Such witnesses
shall be summoned in the same manner and be paid by
the commonwealth the same fees as witnesses before the
courts.   *Approved April 5, 1933.*

---

*Chap.*111 AN ACT TO MODIFY THE REQUIREMENTS FOR THE LEGALITY
OF CERTAIN RAILROAD BONDS FOR INVESTMENT FOR
SAVINGS BANKS, INSTITUTIONS FOR SAVINGS AND TRUST
COMPANIES IN THEIR SAVINGS DEPARTMENTS.

Emergency
preamble.
Whereas, The deferred operation of this act would tend
to defeat its purpose, therefore it is hereby declared to be
an emergency law, necessary for the immediate preservation of the public convenience.

Be it enacted, etc., as follows:

Certain rail-
road bonds
legal invest-
ment for sav-
ings banks.
Wherever in clauses third and sixteenth of section fifty-
four of chapter one hundred and sixty-eight of the General
Laws a number of fiscal years is mentioned, the fiscal years
beginning in the years nineteen hundred and thirty-one
and nineteen hundred and thirty-two shall be excluded
from the count if the inclusion of such years or either of
them would render the security of any railroad ineligible
for investment, and all railroad securities which were
eligible for investment by savings banks on January first,
nineteen hundred and thirty-one, or have become eligible
for such investment since that date or shall hereafter, prior
to April first, nineteen hundred and thirty-four, become
eligible for such investment, shall continue to be eligible
for such investment until April first, nineteen hundred and
thirty-four; provided, however, that the securities of a
railroad company which has defaulted during the year
nineteen hundred and thirty-one or which shall have defaulted prior to April first, nineteen hundred and thirty-

four, in the payment of matured principal or interest or any of its mortgage or funded indebtedness shall not be eligible for such investment. *Approved April 5, 1933.*

An Act facilitating the reorganization of certain trust companies and empowering certain holders of deposits in certain national banking associations to take in substitution therefor preferred stock in such associations.

*Chap.*112

Whereas, The present banking emergency requires that this act be effective forthwith, therefore it is hereby declared to be an emergency law, necessary for the immediate preservation of the public safety and convenience.

Emergency preamble.

Be it enacted, etc., as follows:

Section 1. Whenever in the opinion of the commissioner of banks, hereinafter called the commissioner, any trust company, organized under general or special laws, requires reorganization and a plan for reorganization hereunder has been approved by him as fair and equitable to all depositors, creditors and shareholders thereof and as being in the public interest, such plan may be carried out under and subject to the provisions of this act, but nothing herein shall preclude a reorganization in any other manner authorized by law. Any plan so approved shall become effective upon such approval, except that if it involves a reduction of amounts due depositors and other creditors it shall become effective as provided in section two.

Reorganization plan of trust companies, approval of commissioner of banks.

Section 2. The commissioner, in his discretion, may cause the fair value of the assets of any such trust company to be ascertained and thereafter determine what, if any, reduction of the deposit account or other claim of each depositor or creditor must be made in order to restore the trust company to a solvent condition and to provide for a capital structure in such amount or proportion as the commissioner deems advisable, and he may, in his discretion, approve a plan of reorganization involving such a reduction, if such plan meets the conditions required for approval under section one. The commissioner shall cause at least five days notice of such plan to be given, in such manner as he may require, to each depositor and other creditor of the trust company who shall not have previously assented in writing thereto except those having claims which are proposed to be paid in full or to be retained as liabilities at their full amounts, of the amount or percentage of reduction as so determined. After depositors and other creditors of the trust company representing at least two thirds in amount of the total deposit and other liabilities in its commercial department and in its savings department, respectively, as shown by the books of the trust company, except liabilities of depositors and creditors

Commissioner to determine fair value of assets.

Reduction of deposit accounts or other claims.

Consent of depositors, creditors and stockholders required.

constituting claims as aforesaid, and holders of at least a majority of the stock of the trust company outstanding and entitled to vote shall have assented in writing to the plan, the supreme judicial court for the county where the principal office of the trust company is located, on petition of the commissioner and after notice to the trust company, may authorize or order a reduction of the deposit account or other claim of each depositor or creditor in the respective departments in such trust company in accordance with the plan of reorganization, so as to divide the loss equitably among the depositors and other creditors in the respective departments aforesaid; provided, that notwithstanding the fact that the holders of a majority of the stock of the trust company outstanding and entitled to vote shall not have assented to the plan approved, the court may authorize or order a reduction as aforesaid, and may make such further order with respect to such stock or the holders thereof as justice and equity may require. The approved plan of reorganization as affected by the decree of the court shall become effective upon the entry of such decree.

Proviso.

Depositors, creditors and stockholders bound by plan.

SECTION 3. In any reorganization of a trust company the plan for which shall have become effective as provided herein, all depositors, creditors and stockholders thereof, whether or not they shall have assented to such plan, shall be fully and in all respects subject to and bound by the provisions of such plan, and claims of all depositors, creditors and stockholders shall be treated as if they had assented to such plan. The valuation placed upon the assets of the trust company by the commissioner shall be final and conclusive upon all depositors, creditors and stockholders and all other persons.

Carrying out of reorganization plan.

SECTION 4. When any plan of reorganization becomes effective, all books, records and assets of the trust company as reorganized shall be disposed of in accordance with such plan and the affairs thereof shall be conducted in accordance with law and subject to the conditions, restrictions and limitations which may have been prescribed by the commissioner.

Enforcement of stockholders' liability after appointment of conservator.

SECTION 5. At any time after a conservator shall have been appointed for any trust company as provided in section eighty-three of chapter one hundred and seventy-two of the General Laws, the commissioner may enforce the individual liability of stockholders therein, as described in the first sentence of section twenty-four of said chapter one hundred and seventy-two, in the manner and subject to the provisions set forth in section twenty-four of chapter one hundred and sixty-seven of the General Laws, and upon order or decree of the supreme judicial court for the county where the principal office of the trust company is located may compromise or compound the individual statutory liability of any or all of the stockholders of such trust company, including those who may have subscribed to stock or otherwise furnished funds to assist in a reorganization hereunder, in an amount or amounts approved by the commissioner. In the event of resumption of business by a trust company as provided in section twenty-three of said chapter one hundred and sixty-seven or section eighty-eight of said chapter one hundred and seventy-two, the commissioner may retain the right to enforce in behalf and for the benefit of the trust company the individual liability of its stockholders who shall not have assisted in a reorganization hereunder or whose liability shall not have been compromised or compounded as hereinbefore provided, and may enforce such liability in the manner and subject to the provisions set forth in said section twenty-four of said chapter one hundred and sixty-seven; and the expense of the enforcement thereof shall be paid from the funds of the trust company, and any sums collected by the commissioner as a result thereof shall be paid into the trust company.

SECTION 6. Any trust company reorganizing under this act or resuming business under section twenty-three of chapter one hundred and sixty-seven of the General Laws or section eighty-eight of chapter one hundred and seventy-two of the General Laws, with the approval of the commissioner and if authorized by vote of stockholders owning a majority of the shares of stock thereof outstanding and entitled to vote, at a meeting duly called for the purpose, may issue participating certificates, and preferred stock of a par value of not less than ten dollars per share, in such amount or amounts and in such classes, for cash or such other good and valuable consideration and subject to such provisions, preferences, voting powers, restrictions or qualifications as shall be approved by the commissioner, and such a trust company may make such amendments in its agreement of association or articles of organization, if any, as may be necessary for any such purpose; but in the case of any newly organized trust company which has not yet issued capital stock, the requirement of vote of stockholders shall not apply but in such case a vote of a majority of the incorporators shall be required. Any or all classes of such preferred stock or certificates provided for herein may be set up upon the books of such trust company in such manner and in such amounts as the commissioner may approve. *Reorganized trust company may issue participating certificates and preferred stock.*

SECTION 7. (a) The holders of such preferred stock or certificates shall be entitled to such earned dividends or interest thereon as the commissioner shall approve, not in excess of six per cent per annum. The holders of any and all classes of such preferred stock or of such certificates shall not be held individually responsible as such holders for any contracts, debts or engagements of such trust company and shall not be liable for assessment to restore impairments in the capital of such trust company as now provided by law with reference to holders of capital stock. The words "common stock" or "capital stock", as used in *Preferred stock or certificate holders entitled to dividends.* *Certain terms defined.*

this act, shall not include preferred stock or certificates issued under this act.

Dividends on common stock regulated.

(b) No dividends shall be declared or paid on common stock until the dividends or interest payable on such preferred stock and certificates as herein provided shall have been paid in full, and if such trust company is placed in voluntary liquidation, or a conservator is appointed therefor, or the commissioner shall take possession thereof, no payments shall be made to the holders of the common stock until the holders of all classes of preferred stock or such certificates are paid in full together with any declared dividends or interest due thereon in accordance with the provisions of this act.

Commissioner of corporations and taxation to prescribe rules and regulations.

(c) To carry out the provisions of this act, the commissioner of corporations and taxation from time to time may prescribe such rules and regulations, relating to the filing of said articles of amendment and other instruments, as he may deem necessary or desirable, and may fix the fee for such filing.

Certain persons and corporations authorized to acquire preferred stock or certificates.

SECTION 8. Any bank as defined in section one of chapter one hundred and sixty-seven of the General Laws with the approval of the commissioner, or the commonwealth or any political sub-division thereof, or any charitable or religious institution or organization, or any person or corporation acting as fiduciary, in addition to all other powers conferred upon them by law, may substitute or exchange in whole or in part for the equivalent of par value of preferred stock or certificates as herein provided of any such trust company, their deposits therein, and for the equivalent of par value of preferred stock of a national banking association in the hands of a conservator or receiver, their deposits therein. It shall be lawful for any bank, as so defined, with the approval of the commissioner, to acquire, hold and dispose of preferred stock and certificates as herein provided to the extent of the aggregate par value of any common stock of any such trust company owned by such bank.

Stockholders or directors' meetings authorized.

SECTION 9. During the time that a trust company is in the hands of a conservator appointed under section eighty-three of chapter one hundred and seventy-two of the General Laws, or in the possession of the commissioner under section twenty-two of chapter one hundred and sixty-seven of the General Laws, the commissioner may, in his discretion, authorize meetings of the stockholders or directors thereof to be held for such purposes as he may approve.

Trust companies may avail themselves of benefits of federal act.

SECTION 10. Any trust company which is or hereafter may become a stockholder in a federal reserve bank within the federal reserve district where such trust company is situated under the United States "Federal Reserve Act" approved December twenty-third, nineteen hundred and thirteen, or any acts in amendment thereof, and while such trust company continues as a member bank, is hereby authorized to exercise such power and do any and all things necessary to avail itself of the benefits of the act of congress of March ninth, nineteen hundred and thirty-three entitled "An Act to Provide Relief in the Existing National Emergency in Banking, and for Other Purposes" and any acts in amendment thereof, and any other acts of congress granting powers to or conferring benefits on such member banks now or hereafter passed, without otherwise limiting or impairing in any way the authority conferred upon the commissioner under the laws of the commonwealth.

SECTION 11. The supreme judicial court, or any justice thereof, shall have jurisdiction in equity to enforce the provisions of this act and to act upon all applications and in all proceedings thereunder. *Enforcement of act.*

SECTION 12. If any provision of this act, or the application thereof to any person, firm, corporation or association or to any circumstances, is held invalid by any court of final jurisdiction, the remainder of this act, and the application of such provision to other persons or circumstances, shall not be affected thereby. The right to amend or to repeal this act or any provision thereof is hereby reserved by the general court. *Invalidity of any provision of act not to affect rest of act.*

SECTION 13. After the expiration of two years from the effective date hereof, no reorganization shall be commenced nor any preferred stock issued under this act. *Duration of act.*

Approved April 6, 1933.

AN ACT RELATIVE TO LOAN ORDERS FOR TEMPORARY LOANS IN THE CITY OF BOSTON.   *Chap.*113

Be it enacted, etc., as follows:

SECTION 1. Section two of chapter four hundred and eighty-six of the acts of nineteen hundred and nine is hereby amended by inserting after the word "first" in the twenty-fourth line the words: — , except that in the case of loan orders for temporary loans in anticipation of taxes the second of said readings and votes may be had not less than twenty-four hours after the first, — so as to read as follows: — *Section 2.* The mayor from time to time may make to the city council in the form of an ordinance or loan order filed with the city clerk such recommendations other than for school purposes as he may deem to be for the welfare of the city. The city council shall consider each ordinance or loan order presented by the mayor and shall either adopt or reject the same within sixty days after the date when it is filed as aforesaid. If the said ordinance or loan order is not rejected within said sixty days it shall be in force as if adopted by the city council unless previously withdrawn by the mayor. Nothing herein shall prevent the mayor from again presenting an ordinance or loan order which has been rejected or withdrawn. The city council may originate an ordinance or loan order and may reduce or reject any item in any loan and, subject to the approval of the mayor, may amend an ordinance. All sales of land *1909, 486, § 2, amended.* *Mayor of Boston may make recommendations, except for school purposes.*

other than school lands, all appropriations for the purchase of land other than for school purposes, and all loans voted by the city council shall require a vote of two thirds of all the members of the city council; and shall be passed only after two separate readings and by two separate votes, the second of said readings and votes to be had not less than fourteen days after the first, except that in the case of loan orders for temporary loans in anticipation of taxes the second of said readings and votes may be had not less than twenty-four hours after the first. No amendment increasing the amount of land to be sold or the amount to be paid for the purchase of land, or the amount of loans, or altering the disposition of purchase money or of the proceeds of loans shall be made at the time of the second reading and vote.

SECTION 2. This act shall take effect upon its passage.
Approved April 6, 1933.

Loan orders for temporary loans.

---

*Chap.*114 AN ACT RELATIVE TO THE NOTICE REQUIRED TO BE GIVEN TO COUNTIES, CITIES, TOWNS AND CERTAIN PERSONS IN CASE OF DEFECTS IN PUBLIC WAYS AND ELSEWHERE.

Be it enacted, etc., as follows:

SECTION 1. Chapter eighty-four of the General Laws, as appearing in the Tercentenary Edition thereof, is hereby amended by striking out section eighteen and inserting in place thereof the following: — *Section 18.* A person so injured shall, within ten days thereafter, if such defect or want of repair is caused by or consists in part of snow or ice, or both, and in all other cases, within thirty days thereafter, give to the county, city, town or person by law obliged to keep said way in repair, notice of the name and place of residence of the person injured, and the time, place and cause of said injury or damage; and if the said county, city, town or person does not pay the amount thereof, he may recover the same in an action of tort if brought within two years after the date of such injury or damage. Such notice shall not be invalid or insufficient solely by reason of any inaccuracy in stating the name or place of residence of the person injured, or the time, place or cause of the injury, if it is shown that there was no intention to mislead and that the party entitled to notice was not in fact misled thereby. The words "place of residence of the person injured", as used in this and the two following sections, shall include the street and number, if any, of his residence as well as the name of the city or town thereof.

SECTION 2. Section nineteen of said chapter eighty-four, as so appearing, is hereby amended by inserting after the word "the" the last time it appears in the sixteenth line the words: — name and place of residence of the person injured and the, — so as to read as follows: — *Section 19.* Such notice shall be in writing, signed by the person injured or by some one in his behalf, and may be given, in the case

G. L. (Ter. Ed.), 84, § 18, amended.

Notice of injury caused by defect in highway, etc.

"Place of residence" defined.

G. L. (Ter. Ed.), 84, § 19, amended.

Service of notice.

of a county, to one of the county commissioners or the county treasurer; in the case of a city, to the mayor, the city clerk or treasurer; in the case of a town, to one of the selectmen or to the town clerk or treasurer. If the person injured dies within the time required for giving the notice, his executor or administrator may give such notice within thirty days after his appointment. If by reason of physical or mental incapacity it is impossible for the person injured to give the notice within the time required, he may give it within ten days after such incapacity has been removed, and if he dies within said ten days his executor or administrator may give the notice within thirty days after his appointment. Any form of written communication signed by the person so injured, or by some person in his behalf, or by his executor or administrator, or by some person in behalf of such executor or administrator, which contains the information that the person was so injured, giving the name and place of residence of the person injured and the time, place and cause of the injury or damage, shall be considered a sufficient notice.

SECTION 3. Said chapter eighty-four, as so appearing, is hereby further amended by striking out section twenty and inserting in place thereof the following: — *Section 20.* A defendant shall not avail himself in defence of any omission to state in such notice the name or place of residence of the person injured, or the time, place or cause of the injury or damage, unless, within five days after receipt of a notice, given within the time required by law and by an authorized person referring to the injuries sustained and claiming damages therefor, the person receiving such notice, or some person in his behalf, notifies in writing the person injured, his executor or administrator, or the person giving or serving such notice in his behalf, that his notice is insufficient and requests forthwith a written notice in compliance with law; provided, that if the notice does not contain either the place of residence of the person injured or the place of residence or business address of the person giving or serving the notice on behalf of the person so injured, such notice of insufficiency shall not be required, and the defendant may avail himself in defence of any omission or defect in the notice. If the person authorized to give such notice, within five days after the receipt of such request, gives a written notice complying with the law as to the name and place of residence of the person injured, and the time, place and cause of the injury or damage, such notice shall have the effect of the original notice, and shall be considered a part thereof.

Approved April 6, 1933.

G. L. (Ter. Ed.), 84, § 20, amended. Correction of defective notice.

*Chap.*115 AN ACT TO ENABLE ASSISTANT SUPERINTENDENTS AND STEWARDS OF STATE HOSPITALS TO APPROVE ACCOUNTS IN CERTAIN CASES.

Be it enacted, etc., as follows:

G. L. (Ter. Ed.), 123, § 32, amended.

Supervision of accounts of state hospitals.

Chapter one hundred and twenty-three of the General Laws, as appearing in the Tercentenary Edition thereof, is hereby amended by striking out section thirty-two and inserting in place thereof the following: — *Section 32.* All accounts for the maintenance of each of the state hospitals shall be approved by the superintendent thereof or in his absence by the assistant superintendent, or in the absence of the superintendent and of the assistant superintendent by the steward, or, if the trustees so vote, by said trustees or by the chairman or some member designated by him, and shall be filed with the comptroller, and shall be paid by the commonwealth. Full copies of the pay rolls and bills shall be kept at each hospital.

Approved April 6, 1933.

*Chap.*116 AN ACT RELATIVE TO THE SALE OF MEAT AND MEAT PRODUCTS CONTAINING CERTAIN PRESERVATIVES.

Be it enacted, etc., as follows:

G. L. (Ter. Ed.), 94, new section after § 153.

Sulphur dioxide not to be added to meat or meat products.

Chapter ninety-four of the General Laws, as appearing in the Tercentenary Edition thereof, is hereby amended by inserting after section one hundred and fifty-three the following new section: — *Section 153A.* Whoever himself or by his agent sells or offers for sale any meat or meat product to which has been added any sulphur dioxide or compound thereof shall be punished by a fine of not less than fifteen nor more than one hundred dollars.

Approved April 6, 1933.

*Chap.*117 AN ACT TO PREVENT ADVERTISEMENTS TENDING TO DISCRIMINATE AGAINST PERSONS OF ANY RELIGIOUS SECT, CREED, CLASS, DENOMINATION OR NATIONALITY BY PLACES OF PUBLIC ACCOMMODATION, RESORT OR AMUSEMENT.

Be it enacted, etc., as follows:

G. L. (Ter. Ed.), 272, new section after § 92.

Advertisements tending to discrimination on account of race, color or religion, prohibited.

Chapter two hundred and seventy-two of the General Laws, as appearing in the Tercentenary Edition thereof, is hereby amended by inserting after section ninety-two the following new section: — *Section 92A.* No owner, lessee, proprietor, manager, superintendent, agent or employee of any place of public accommodation, resort or amusement shall, directly or indirectly, by himself or another, publish, issue, circulate, distribute or display, or cause to be published, issued, circulated, distributed or displayed, in any way, any advertisement, circular, folder, book, pamphlet, written, or painted or printed notice or sign, of any kind or description, intended to discriminate against or actually discriminating against persons of any religious sect, creed, class, race, color, denomination or nationality, in the full enjoyment of the accommodations, advantages, facilities or privileges offered to the general public by such places of public accommodation, resort or amusement; provided, that nothing herein contained shall be construed to prohibit the mailing to any person of a private communication in writing, in response to his specific written inquiry.

A place of public accommodation, resort or amusement within the meaning hereof shall be defined as and shall be deemed to include any inn, whether conducted for the entertainment, housing or lodging of transient guests, or for the benefit, use or accommodation of those seeking health, recreation or rest, any restaurant, eating-house, public conveyance on land or water or in the air, bathhouse, barber shop, theatre and music hall. *Place of public accommodation, etc., to include inn.*

Any person who shall violate any provision of this section, or who shall aid in or incite, cause or bring about, in whole or in part, such a violation shall be punished by a fine of not more than one hundred dollars, or by imprisonment for not more than thirty days, or both. *Penalty.*

Approved April 6, 1933.

AN ACT PROHIBITING THE TAKING OF CERTAIN HERRING OR ALEWIVES FROM THE WATERS OF PLYMOUTH HARBOR, KINGSTON BAY, DUXBURY BAY AND CERTAIN WATERS OF PLYMOUTH BAY. *Chap.118*

Be it enacted, etc., as follows:

Chapter one hundred and thirty of the General Laws, as appearing in the Tercentenary Edition thereof, is hereby amended by inserting after section forty-eight the following new section: — *Section 48A.* Whoever takes any herring or alewives less than four inches in length from the waters of Plymouth harbor, Kingston bay, Duxbury bay or from that part of the waters of Plymouth bay lying westerly of an imaginary line drawn from the northeasterly extremity of Rocky Point to Gurnet Light, shall be punished by a fine of not less than five nor more than fifty dollars. *G. L. (Ter. Ed.), 130, new section after § 48. Taking of herring in certain waters of Plymouth harbor, Plymouth, Kingston and Duxbury bays, regulated.*

Approved April 6, 1933.

AN ACT RELATIVE TO SERVICE BY REGISTERED MAIL OF NOTICES OF CANCELLATION OF MOTOR VEHICLE LIABILITY POLICIES OR BONDS BY THE COMPANIES ISSUING OR EXECUTING THEM AND TO APPEALS FROM SUCH CANCELLATIONS. *Chap.119*

Be it enacted, etc., as follows:

SECTION 1. Section one hundred and thirteen A of chapter one hundred and seventy-five of the General Laws, as appearing in the Tercentenary Edition thereof, is hereby amended by inserting after the word "That" in the nine- *G. L. (Ter. Ed.), 175, § 113A, amended.*

teenth line the following: — , except as otherwise provided
in section one hundred and thirteen D, — by inserting after
the word "and" in the twenty-sixth line the following: —
that notice of cancellation sent by the company to the
insured, by registered mail, postage prepaid, with a return
receipt of the addressee requested, addressed to him at his
residence or business address stated in the policy shall be a
sufficient notice and that an affidavit of any officer, agent
or employee of the company, duly authorized for the purpose, that he has so sent such notice addressed as aforesaid
shall be prima facie evidence of the sending thereof as
aforesaid; together with a provision, — and also by striking out, in the thirty-fifth line, the word "receiving" and
inserting in place thereof the words: — the sending of, —
so that provision numbered (2) will read as follows: —

Sufficiency of
notice of can-
cellation of
motor vehicle
liability
policies or
bonds.

(2) That, except as otherwise provided in section one
hundred and thirteen D, no cancellation of the policy,
whether by the company or by the insured, shall be valid
unless written notice thereof is given by the party proposing
cancellation to the other party and, except when the intended effective date thereof is the date of expiration of
the registration of the motor vehicle or trailer covered by
the policy, to the registrar of motor vehicles in such form
as the department of public works may prescribe, at least
fifteen days in each case prior to the intended effective
date thereof, which date shall be expressed in said notice,
and that notice of cancellation sent by the company to the
insured, by registered mail, postage prepaid, with a return
receipt of the addressee requested, addressed to him at his
residence or business address stated in the policy shall be a
sufficient notice and that an affidavit of any officer, agent
or employee of the company, duly authorized for the purpose, that he has so sent such notice addressed as aforesaid
shall be prima facie evidence of the sending thereof as
aforesaid; together with a provision that, in the event of a
cancellation by the insured, he shall, if he has paid the
premium on the policy to the company, or to its agent
who issued the policy, or to the duly licensed insurance
broker, if any, by whom the policy was negotiated, be
entitled to receive a return premium after deducting the
customary monthly short rates for the time the policy
shall have been in force, or in the event of cancellation by
the company, the insured shall, if he has paid the premium
as aforesaid, be entitled to receive a return premium calculated on a pro rata basis; provided, that if the insured after
the sending of a notice of cancellation by the company
files a new certificate under section thirty-four H of said
chapter ninety prior to the intended effective date of such
cancellation, the filing of said certificate shall operate to
terminate the policy on the date of said filing, and the
return premium, if any, payable to the insured shall be
computed as of the date of said filing, instead of the intended effective date of cancellation expressed in the notice

thereof; and provided further, that if the final effective date of a cancellation by the company is fixed by an order of the board of appeal on motor vehicle liability policies and bonds or of the superior court, or a justice thereof, as provided in section one hundred and thirteen D, the return premium, if any, payable to the insured shall be computed as of such final effective date.

SECTION 2. Section one hundred and thirteen D of said chapter one hundred and seventy-five, as so appearing, is hereby amended by striking out the first paragraph and inserting in place thereof the following: —

G. L. (Ter. Ed.), 175, § 113D, amended.

Any person aggrieved by the issue by any company, or an agent thereof on its behalf, of a written notice purporting to cancel a motor vehicle liability policy or bond, both as defined in section thirty-four A of chapter ninety, or by the refusal of any company, or an agent thereof on its behalf, to issue such a policy or to execute such a bond as surety, may, at any time prior to the intended effective date of cancellation expressed in such notice, or within ten days after such a refusal, file a written complaint with the commissioner, unless he has secured a certificate, as defined in said section thirty-four A, from another company. The complaint shall be in such form and contain such information, including the address of the complainant, as the commissioner may prescribe. The complaint, if it relates to the issue of a notice of cancellation, shall specify the registration number of the motor vehicle or trailer covered by the policy or bond and the said intended effective date of cancellation or, if it relates to a refusal as aforesaid, the date thereof. The board of appeal on motor vehicle liability policies and bonds, hereinafter called the board, may allow such complaint to be amended.

Proceedings on complaints relative to cancellations or refusal of companies to issue policies or bonds.

SECTION 3. Said section one hundred and thirteen D, as so appearing, is hereby further amended by adding at the end thereof the following new paragraph: —

G. L. (Ter. Ed.), 175, § 113D, amended.

Any person aggrieved by the cancellation of such a policy or bond may file a written complaint with the commissioner within ten days thereafter, unless he has secured a certificate, as defined in section thirty-four A of chapter ninety, from another company. Such complaint, and all proceedings, findings and orders thereon, appeals therefrom and decrees on such appeals shall, except as hereinafter provided, be subject to all the foregoing provisions of this section which are applicable in case a person is aggrieved by the issue of a notice of cancellation. The filing of such a complaint shall not affect the operation of the cancellation. The commissioner shall not transmit an attested copy of such a complaint to the registrar of motor vehicles. If the board finds in favor of the complainant on such a complaint, the order shall, unless the policy or bond will sooner expire, effect the reinstatement of the policy or bond on a date to be specified in such order which shall not be earlier than the date on which the written

Same subject. Appeal to commissioner of insurance.

memorandum of the finding and order is filed in the office
of the commissioner, and the policy or bond shall again be in
full force and effect from the date so specified, but not
beyond its date of expiration in any case, pending the decree
of the superior court or a justice thereof if the company
takes an appeal from such a finding and order. Such a
decree reversing a finding and order of the board in favor
of the company on such a complaint shall order that the
policy or bond be reinstated, and such a decree reversing
a finding and order in favor of the complainant shall order
that the policy or bond be cancelled; and such a decree of
reinstatement or cancellation shall, unless the policy or bond
has expired or will sooner expire, specify a date not earlier
than five days from the entry thereof, upon which the reinstatement or cancellation shall be effective.

G. L. (Ter. Ed.), 90, § 34H, amended. SECTION 4. Section thirty-four H of chapter ninety
of the General Laws, as appearing in the Tercentenary
Edition thereof, is hereby amended by inserting after the
word "seventy-five" in the sixteenth line the words: —
that he is aggrieved by the issue of such notice, — by
striking out, in the nineteenth line, the word "thereunder"
and inserting in place thereof the words: — from such
order, — and by inserting after the word "appeal" in the
twenty-first line the following: —, or as specified in such
a decree ordering a cancellation of such a policy or bond
after its reinstatement by said board of appeal, — so that
the first paragraph will read as follows: —

Revocation of registration upon cancella-tion of policy or bond, etc. Exceptions. In the event that the registrar receives written notice,
in conformity with section one hundred and thirteen A of
chapter one hundred and seventy-five, from the owner of a
motor vehicle cancelling the motor vehicle liability policy
or bond covering the same, he shall revoke the registration
of such motor vehicle on the effective date of the cancellation as specified in such notice unless not later than two
days prior to such effective date the registrar shall have
received a new certificate covering the same motor vehicle.
The registrar shall, forthwith upon receiving written notice
in conformity with said section one hundred and thirteen A
from an insurance or surety company purporting to cancel
such a policy or bond issued or executed by it, give written
notice to the owner of the motor vehicle covered by said
policy or bond that the registration thereof will be revoked
as of the final effective date of the cancellation as specified
in the notice given by such company in case the owner does
not file a complaint under section one hundred and thirteen
D of said chapter one hundred and seventy-five that he is
aggrieved by the issue of such notice, or as specified in an
order of the board of appeal on motor vehicle liability
policies and bonds affirming such cancellation under said
section one hundred and thirteen D in case the owner does
not claim an appeal from such order, or as specified in a
decree of the superior court or a justice thereof affirming
such cancellation on 'uch appeal, or as specified in such a

decree ordering a cancellation of such a policy or bond after its reinstatement by said board of appeal, unless not later than two days prior to such effective date as finally specified the registrar shall have received a new certificate covering the same motor vehicle.

SECTION 5.   Said section thirty-four H, as so appearing, is hereby further amended by inserting after the third paragraph the following new paragraph: — G. L. (Ter. Ed.), 90, § 34H, amended.

The registrar shall, upon receipt of an attested copy of a finding and order of said board of appeal, or of a decree of the superior court or a justice thereof, ordering the reinstatement of a motor vehicle liability policy or bond, forthwith rescind the revocation of the registration of the motor vehicle covered thereby. Revocation of registration of motor vehicle to be rescinded in certain cases.

SECTION 6.   The provisions of this act shall not apply with respect to motor vehicle liability policies and bonds, both as defined in section thirty-four A of chapter ninety of the General Laws, as appearing in the Tercentenary Edition thereof, issued or executed in connection with the registration of motor vehicles or trailers under said chapter ninety for operation during any part of the current year. Act not to apply during current year.

Approved April 6, 1933.

An Act authorizing and regulating the manufacture, transportation and sale of wines and malt beverages. *Chap.*120

Whereas, The deferred operation of this act would in part defeat its purpose to enable the people of the commonwealth to take immediate advantage of certain legislation by congress amending the laws enacted to enforce the eighteenth amendment to the constitution of the United States, therefore this act is hereby declared to be an emergency law, necessary for the immediate preservation of the public health and convenience. Emergency preamble.

Be it enacted, etc., as follows:

SECTION 1.   Section seventeen of chapter six of the General Laws, as most recently amended by section one of chapter three hundred and five of the acts of nineteen hundred and thirty-two, is hereby further amended by inserting after the word "board" in the seventh line the words: — , the alcoholic beverages control commission, — so as to read as follows: — *Section 17.* The armory commissioners, the art commission, the commission on administration and finance, the commissioner of state aid and pensions, the commissioners on uniform state laws, the public bequest commission, the state ballot law commission, the board of trustees of the Soldiers' Home in Massachusetts, the milk regulation board, the alcoholic beverages control commission and the trustees of the state library shall serve under the governor and council, and shall be G. L. (Ter. Ed.), 6, § 17, etc., amended.

Alcoholic beverages control commission to serve under governor and council.

subject to such supervision as the governor and council deem necessary or proper.

SECTION 2. Said chapter six, as appearing in the Tercentenary Edition thereof, is hereby amended by adding at the end thereof the following three new sections: —

Section 43. There shall be a commission to be known as the alcoholic beverages control commission, to consist of three members, to be appointed by the governor, with the advice and consent of the council. Not more than two of such members shall be members of the same political party. Said members shall be designated in their initial appointments to serve for one, two and three years, respectively. The governor shall designate one of the members as chairman. Upon the expiration of the term of office of a member, his successor shall be appointed in the manner aforesaid for three years. The chairman shall receive a salary not to exceed five thousand dollars and each other member shall receive a salary not to exceed four thousand dollars. The governor may, with like advice and consent, remove any such member and fill any vacancy for the remainder of the unexpired term.

Section 44. The commission shall have general supervision of the conduct of the business of manufacturing, importing, exporting, storing, transporting and selling wines and malt beverages and also of the quality and purity thereof.

The commission shall submit to the governor and to the general court as soon as may be after the end of each state fiscal year a full report of its action and of the conduct and condition of traffic in alcoholic beverages during such year, together with recommendations for such legislation as it deems necessary or desirable for the better regulation and control of such traffic and for the promotion of temperance in the use of such beverages. The members shall receive their necessary traveling and other expenses incurred while in the performance of their official duties.

Section 45. The commission may appoint and remove, and fix the compensation of, a secretary, with the approval of the governor and council. It may expend for such clerical and other assistance as may be necessary for the performance of its duties such amounts as may be appropriated. Each member of the commission, and each of its employees having access to moneys received by it, shall give to the state treasurer a bond for the faithful performance of his duties in a penal sum and with sureties approved by the governor and council.

DEFINITIONS.

SECTION 3. In this act, unless the context otherwise requires, the following words shall have the following meanings: —

"Commission", the alcoholic beverages control commission established under section forty-three of chapter six of the General Laws.

"Alcoholic beverages", any liquid intended for human consumption as a beverage and containing one half of one per cent or more of alcohol by volume.

"Wines", all fermented alcoholic beverages made from fruits, flowers, herbs or vegetables, other than cider made from apples, and containing not more than three and two tenths per cent of alcohol by weight.

"Malt beverages", all alcoholic beverages manufactured or produced by the process of brewing or fermentation of malt, with or without cereal grains or fermentable sugars, or of hops, and containing not more than three and two tenths per cent of alcohol by weight.

"Hotel", a building or part of a building owned or leased and operated by a person holding a duly issued and valid license as an innholder, under the provisions of chapter one hundred and forty of the General Laws and provided with adequate and sanitary kitchen and dining room equipment and capacity for preparing, cooking and serving suitable food for its guests, including travelers and strangers and its other patrons and customers, and in addition meeting and complying with all the requirements imposed upon innholders under said chapter one hundred and forty.

"Restaurant", space, in a suitable building, leased or rented or owned by a person holding a duly issued and valid license as a common victualer under the provisions of said chapter one hundred and forty, and provided with adequate and sanitary kitchen and dining room equipment and capacity for preparing, cooking and serving suitable food for strangers, travelers and other patrons and customers, and in addition meeting and complying with all the requirements imposed upon common victualers under said chapter one hundred and forty.

"Club", a corporation organized or chartered for any purpose described in section two of chapter one hundred and eighty of the General Laws, whether under federal or state law, including any body or association lawfully operating under a charter granted by a parent body so organized or chartered, and including also any organization or unit mentioned in clause twelfth of section five of chapter forty of the General Laws, owning, hiring, or leasing a building, or space in a building, of such extent and character as may be suitable and adequate for the reasonable and comfortable use and accommodation of its members; provided, that such club files with the local licensing authorities and the commission annually within the first ten days of February in each year a list of the names and residences of its officers; and provided, further, that its affairs and management are conducted by a board of directors, executive committee, or similar body chosen by the members at its annual meeting, and that no member or any officer, agent or employee of the club is paid, or directly

Certain words
as used in act,
defined. or indirectly receives in the form of salary or other compensation, any profits from the disposition or sale of alcoholic beverages to the members of the club or its guests introduced by members beyond the amount of such salary as may be fixed and voted annually within two months after January first in each year by the members or by its directors or other governing body and as reported by the club to the local licensing authorities and the commission within three months after such January first, and as shall in the judgment of the local licensing authorities and the commission be reasonable and proper compensation for the services of such member, officer, agent, or employee.

"Local licensing authorities", the licensing boards and commissions established in any city or town under special statute or city charter, or under section four of chapter one hundred and thirty-eight of the General Laws, or corresponding provisions of earlier laws, or, in a city having no such board or commission, a board appointed by the mayor without confirmation by the aldermen and in accordance with the provisions of said section four, or, in default of such appointment, the aldermen, or, in a town having no such board or commission, the selectmen. In any city having a licensing board established under said section four or corresponding provisions of earlier laws, section seven of said chapter one hundred and thirty-eight shall be applicable to such board during such time as licenses are authorized to be issued therein under this act.

"Licensing authorities", the commission or the local licensing authorities, or both, as the case may be.

SALE OF WINES AND MALT BEVERAGES TO BE DRUNK ON
THE PREMISES.

Licenses to
sell certain
wines and
malt beverages
to be drunk
on the premises
to be issued to
common
victualers.

SECTION 4. Any common victualer duly licensed under chapter one hundred and forty of the General Laws to conduct a restaurant in any city or town wherein the granting of licenses to sell wines and malt beverages is authorized under this act, and any innholder duly licensed under said chapter to conduct a hotel in any such city or town, may be licensed by the local licensing authorities to sell, between such hours as the local licensing authorities may from time to time fix, either generally, or specially for each licensee, to travelers, strangers and other patrons and customers not under twenty-one years of age, wines and malt beverages to be served and drunk only in the dining room or dining rooms of the restaurant or hotel, and in such other public rooms or areas of a hotel as the local licensing authorities may in the case of any hotel licensee deem reasonable and proper, and approve in writing. No person, firm, corporation, association or other combination of persons, directly or indirectly, or through any agent, employee, stockholder, officer or other person, or any subsidiary whatsoever, doing business under the provision already defined as a restaurant, shall be granted more than one license in any city or town. Such sales may also be made by licensed innholders to registered guests occupying private rooms in their hotels, respectively.

During such time as the sale of wines and malt beverages is authorized in any city or town under this act, the au-. thority to grant licenses to innholders and common victualers therein shall be vested in the local licensing authorities. Local licensing authorities to grant licenses.

Any club in any city or town wherein the granting of licenses to sell wines and malt beverages is authorized under this act may be licensed by the local licensing authorities to sell such wines and malt beverages to its own members only, and also, subject to regulations made by the local licensing authorities, to guests introduced by members, and to no others. Club licenses.

The local licensing authorities may determine in the first instance, when originally issuing and upon each annual renewal of licenses under this section, the amount of the license fee, in no case less than twenty-five nor more than five hundred dollars, except as hereinafter provided, to be paid by each licensee. respectively. Before issuing a license to any applicant therefor under this section, or before a renewal of such license, the local licensing authorities shall cause an examination to be made of the premises of the applicant to determine that such premises comply in all respects with the appropriate definition of section three and that the applicant is not less than twenty-one years of age and a person of good character in the city or town in which he seeks a license hereunder. Whenever in the opinion of the local licensing authorities any applicant fails to establish to their satisfaction his compliance with the above requirements, or any other reasonable requirements which they may from time to time make with respect to licenses under this section or the conduct of his business by any licensee hereunder, or fails to maintain such compliance, the local licensing authorities may refuse to issue or to renew or, if already issued, may, after hearing or opportunity therefor suspend, revoke or cancel any license to such applicant. In case of suspension, revocation or cancellation of a license, no abatement or refund of any part of the fee paid therefor shall be made. License fee. Suspension, etc., of license.

Section 5. A railroad corporation operating any line of railroad within the commonwealth may sell, in any dining car or club car of a train after leaving and before reaching the terminal stops of such train, wines and malt beverages to be drunk in such cars, if the commission sees fit to issue a license to such railroad corporation, the license fee for which shall be not less than twenty-five dollars for each car to which it applies. The commission may also issue licenses to sell wines and malt beverages to the owner or operator of any passenger vessel operating Railroad and steamboat licenses.

out of any port of the commonwealth, under such regulations as the commission may prescribe as to the portions of the vessel in which the same may be sold to be drunk while the vessel is under way. The annual license fee for each vessel shall be determined by the commission as it shall deem proper in view of the size and capacity of the vessel, the nature and frequency of its trips, and other features of its business deemed by the commission to be pertinent. No sale shall be made on any train before starting from or after arriving at a terminal station or upon a passenger vessel while tied up in any port of the commonwealth. No other license shall be required for the sales hereinbefore in this section authorized. Whenever in the opinion of the commission any applicant fails to establish to its satisfaction his compliance with the above requirements, or any other reasonable requirements which it may from time to time make with respect to licenses under this section or the conduct of his business by any licensee hereunder, or fails to maintain such compliance, it may refuse to issue or to renew or, if already issued, may after hearing or opportunity therefor suspend, revoke or

Suspension, etc., of license. cancel any license to such applicant. In case of suspension, revocation or cancellation of a license, no abatement or refund of any part of the fee paid therefor shall be made.

Licenses to certain amusement places. In a city or town wherein the granting of licenses to sell wines and malt beverages is authorized under this act, special licenses for the sale thereof may be issued by the local licensing authorities to the responsible manager of any course of concerts conducted by a corporation organized under section two of chapter one hundred and eighty of the General Laws, or corresponding provisions of earlier laws, or under special law, and furnishing at such concerts light refreshments, at tables only, in the building in which such concerts are given, and to the responsible manager of any banquet or public dinner given or served in any building or dining room if the place where such banquet or public dinner is given is not one in which the sale of such wines and malt beverages is already licensed to be

Special license for picnics, etc. made. The local licensing authorities may also grant to any responsible organization or individual conducting a picnic, barbecue, moonlight excursion, field day or outing of any kind in any city or town wherein the sale of wines or malt beverages is authorized under this act a special license to sell or dispense the same to persons in attendance

Fee. thereon or participating therein. The fees for such special licenses shall be fixed from time to time by the local licensing authorities and need not be uniform.

Penalties. Any person holding a license to sell malt beverages and wine to be drunk on the premises, who shall allow any adulteration on said premises of malt beverages or wines so as to increase their alcoholic content, shall be punished by a fine of not less than two hundred nor more than five hundred dollars, and such license shall be suspended for a period of not less than six months. Any person selling alcohol or intoxicating beverages containing more than three and two tenths per cent of alcohol by weight on premises of a person licensed to sell malt beverages and wines, or any person selling alcohol or alcoholic beverages of the same alcoholic content for the purpose of so adulterating malt beverages or wines intended to be drunk on premises of a person so licensed, or any person so adulterating or causing to be adulterated malt beverages or wines on premises of a person so licensed, shall be punished by a fine of not less than two hundred dollars, or by imprisonment for not less than six months, or both.

SALES OF WINES AND MALT BEVERAGES NOT TO BE DRUNK ON THE PREMISES.

SECTION 6. The local licensing authorities in any city or town wherein the granting of such licenses is authorized under this act may grant a license to any suitable applicant, approved by the commission, to sell at retail, in bottles or other containers, wines and malt beverages not to be drunk on the premises. Each license shall describe the premises to which it applies, and not more than one location shall be included in any license. One such license may be granted in any such city or town for each population unit of one thousand and for each additional fraction thereof up to but not exceeding a population of ten thousand, one additional license for each population unit of two thousand and for each additional major fraction thereof above a population of ten thousand up to but not exceeding a population of fifty thousand, and one additional license for each population unit of five thousand and for each additional major fraction thereof above a population of fifty thousand; provided, that one such license may be granted in any such town irrespective of population. No person, firm, corporation, association, or other combination of persons, directly or indirectly, or through any agent, employee, stockholder, officer or other person or any subsidiary whatsoever, shall be granted, in the aggregate, more than three such licenses in the commonwealth, or be granted more than one such license in any city or town. Any sale of wines or malt beverages shall be conclusively presumed to have been made in the store wherein the order was received from the customer. The license fee shall be not less than twenty-five nor, except as hereinafter provided, more than five hundred dollars for the shop or other place of business designated in the license, the amount being fixed and subject to change from year to year by the local licensing authorities as they shall deem just and proper in view of the location of the licensee's place of business, his probable volume of sales, or of his actual volume of sales in the previous year. The local licensing authorities may prescribe the hours within which the sale of wines and

Retail license to sell certain wines and malt beverages not to be drunk on the premises.

Population unit.

License fee.

malt beverages may be made by licensees under this
section and, if the hours so prescribed ·extend in their
judgment beyond the usual closing time of establishments
engaged in the same general kind of business in the same
city or town as the licensee, the local licensing authorities
may prescribe that no sales of goods, other than wines and
malt beverages, shall be made by the licensee during such
extended period.

Wholesale
license.

SECTION 7. The commission may license any suitable
applicant to sell at wholesale to other licensees in any city
or town in which the sale is authorized under this act,
and to transport and deliver to such licensees, wines and
malt beverages manufactured by any licensed manufacturer under the provisions of section eight.

Fee.

The license fee for each wholesaler of wines or malt
beverages shall be such sum, not less than two hundred
and fifty nor more than one thousand dollars, as under the
circumstances of the licensee's probable volume of sales
under this section the commission shall deem just and
proper.

MANUFACTURE OF WINES AND MALT BEVERAGES.

Manufacturer's
license.

SECTION 8. The commission may issue to individuals,
and to partnerships composed solely of individuals, who
are both citizens and residents of the commonwealth, and
to corporations organized under the laws of this commonwealth, licenses to manufacture wines or malt beverages.
The commission may issue to any corporation organized
under the laws of any other state and now engaged in the
manufacture of wines or malt beverages, and all of the
factories of which are located within the commonwealth, a
license for a period of three months from the passage of
this act, to manufacture wines and malt beverages, and
such foreign corporation shall, for such period, have the
right to manufacture and sell wines and malt beverages to
the same extent as domestic corporations so licensed.

Sales by
manufacturers
regulated.

Manufacturers of wines or malt beverages may sell the
same to any licensee holding a valid license granted by the
licensing authorities for the sale within the commonwealth
in accordance with the provisions of this act, and may also
sell wines or malt beverages for export from this commonwealth into any state where the sale of the same is not by
law prohibited, and into any foreign country. All wines
and malt beverages sold by any manufacturer thereof shall
be sold and delivered only in bottles filled and sealed by
such manufacturer upon his own premises, and in such
manner, and under such conditions, and with such labels
or other marks to identify the manufacturer, as the commission shall from time to time prescribe by regulations;
provided, that sales of wines and malt beverages may be
made in kegs, casks or barrels to holders of wholesale
licenses; and provided, further, that sales of wines and
malt beverages may be made in kegs, casks or barrels by

any manufacturer or holder of a wholesale license to any common victualer, innholder or club, licensed by the local licensing authorities to sell wines and malt beverages to be drunk on the premises, if the nature and extent of the restaurant, hotel or club business of such licensee is, in the judgment of the commission, such as to justify the sale by such licensee of wines and malt beverages by draft under such conditions as the commission may from time to time by regulation prescribe.

Every licensed manufacturer of any wines or malt beverages shall keep such records in such detail and affording such information as the commission may from time to time prescribe, and shall file with the commission, whenever and as often as it may require, duplicates or copies of such records, and the commission shall at all times, through its designated officers or agents, have access to all books, records and other documents of every licensed manufacturer relating to the business which he is licensed hereunder to conduct. *Record to be kept by manufacturer.*

The license fee for each manufacturer of wines or malt beverages shall be such sum, not less than five hundred nor more than twenty-five hundred dollars, as under the circumstances of the licensee's probable volume of sales under this section, the capacity of his plant and the location thereof, the commission shall deem just and proper. *Fee.*

Section 9. The commission may authorize any suitable applicant to sell, and may issue to such applicant a foreign manufacturer's agency license for the sale of, wines or malt beverages bought from, and shipped into the commonwealth by, a manufacturer of wines or malt beverages located in any other state or in a foreign country and may authorize the receipt of such shipments to be made in casks, barrels, kegs or other containers as well as in bottles, in either case bearing such seals or other evidences of the identity and origin of the contents as the commission may prescribe. Such holders of foreign manufacturers' agency licenses may bottle any wines or malt beverages so received by them in bulk, but such bottling and the sealing and labelling of the bottles shall be done only upon such premises and under such conditions as the commission shall approve. Any such holder of a foreign manufacturer's agency license shall, subject to the approval of the commission, be entitled to resell, transport and deliver such imported wines or malt beverages in the same manner and to the same licensees and subject to the same conditions and license fees as apply to licensees for the manufacture within the commonwealth of wines or malt beverages under the provisions of section eight. In order to ensure the necessary control of traffic in wines and malt beverages for the preservation of the public peace and order, the shipment of such wines and malt beverages into the commonwealth, except as provided in this section, is hereby prohibited. *Foreign manufacturer's agency license.*

ADDITIONAL FEES FOR PRIVILEGE OF MANUFACTURING AND
SELLING, OR IMPORTING AND SELLING, WINES AND MALT
BEVERAGES.

Manufacturers
and holders of
foreign manu-
facturer's
license to pay
additional fees.

SECTION 10. Every manufacturer of wines or malt
beverages and every holder of a foreign manufacturer's
agency license for the sale thereof shall, in addition to the
license fees elsewhere provided in this act, be liable for
and pay to the commonwealth, for the privilege enjoyed
by him as such manufacturer or foreign manufacturer's
agency, the sum of one dollar for each and every barrel of
thirty-one gallons of wine or malt beverages sold within
the commonwealth by such manufacturer or foreign manufacturer's agency, respectively, or a proportionate amount
where any other form of container is used. Every person
subject to this section shall keep a true and accurate account of all wines and malt beverages sold by him and shall
make a return thereof to the commission within ten days
after the last day of each month, covering his sales during
such month, and shall at the time of such return make
payment to the commission of the amount due under this
section for such sales in such month. The commission is
hereby authorized to prescribe rules and regulations governing the method of keeping accounts, making returns
and paying the additional fees provided for in this section.

Commission to
issue rules
and regula-
tions.

TRANSPORTATION.

Transportation
of certain
wines and
malt beverages,
regulated.

SECTION 11. Any resident of the commonwealth may,
but only for his own use and that of his family and guests,
transport wines and malt beverages, without any license
or permit. Retail licensees for the sale of wines and malt
beverages not to be drunk on the premises and manufacturers of wines or malt beverages and all others holding
licenses issued by the commission for the sale of wines and
malt beverages may transport and deliver anywhere in the
commonwealth wines and malt beverages ordered from and
sold by them, in vehicles operated under the control of
themselves or of their employees or agents; provided, that
the owner of every such vehicle shall have obtained for
such vehicle from the commission a vehicle permit for the
transportation of wines and malt beverages. The fee for
such vehicle permits shall be one dollar each, and the permits shall be valid for one year from their respective dates
unless earlier canceled or revoked by the commission.
Every person operating such a vehicle when engaged in
such transportation or delivery shall carry the vehicle
permit for the vehicle operated by him and shall, upon
demand of any constable, policeman, member of the state
police, or any employee of the commission or of the registry
of motor vehicles, produce such permit for inspection, and
failure to produce such permit shall constitute prima facie
evidence of unlawful transportation and shall in the discretion of the commission be sufficient cause for the revocation or cancellation of such permit.

SECTION 12. Except as provided in the preceding section, wines and malt beverages may be transported within the commonwealth only by a railroad or steamboat corporation, or an individual or corporation regularly and lawfully conducting a general express or trucking business, and in each case holding a transportation permit in full force and effect issued by the commission and valid for one year unless earlier canceled or revoked; provided, that any such individual or company now doing business in the commonwealth shall be considered to be licensed for a period of thirty days after the passage of this act. The fee for each transportation permit shall be twenty-five dollars and shall cover all rolling stock and vehicles of such permittee.

Transportation by railroads, etc.

LICENSES FOR THE MANUFACTURE AND SALE, AND PERMITS FOR THE TRANSPORTATION AND DELIVERY OF, WINES AND MALT BEVERAGES.

SECTION 13. The terms "licenses" and "permits", wherever employed as substantives in this act, are used in their technical sense of a license or permit revocable at pleasure and without any assignment of reasons therefor by the licensor, the commonwealth, acting through the same officers or agents and under the same delegated authority, as authorized the issue of such licenses. The provisions for the issue of licenses and permits hereunder imply no intention to create rights generally for persons to engage or continue in the transaction of the business authorized by the licenses or permits respectively, but are enacted with a view only to meet the reasonable demand of the public for pure wines and malt beverages and, to that end, to provide, in the opinion of the local licensing authorities, an adequate number of places at which the public may obtain, in the manner and for the kind of use indicated, the different sorts of wines and malt beverages for the sale of which provision is made.

Terms "licenses" and "permits" defined.

No such licensee or permittee shall have any vested or monetary right in the continuance of his license or permit. Whenever it appears by sale of premises in connection with which a license has been issued, by probate or bankruptcy proceedings, or otherwise, that such license has acquired any monetary value in excess of the license fee, the licensing authorities may increase the amount of the license fee correspondingly, notwithstanding any maximum limitation herein upon fees for that class of licenses, or may take other action deemed by them appropriate to divest the license of such monetary value or to make such value inure to the benefit of the city or town instead of the licensee or his estate or his assigns.

License fee may be increased in certain cases.

Whenever it shall appear to the local licensing authorities that the nature of the business, or of the equipment and service, of any hotel, restaurant or club no longer satisfies the definition thereof contained in this act, or that the

Cancellation of licenses issued to hotels, etc.

same has become primarily and chiefly a place for the sale and consumption of wines or malt beverages, and that it is without genuine and substantial patronage for its supposed principal purpose of providing food or food and lodging, or that wines or malt beverages are being or have been sold and served therein over, and drunk by customers standing at, a bar or counter except counters equipped with stools for the use of patrons, instead of at tables in the dining or other rooms and quarters as contemplated by or authorized under the provisions of this act, it shall be the duty of the local licensing authorities forthwith to cancel the license of such hotel, restaurant or club. All licenses and permits, unless otherwise in this act provided, shall be for the term of one year from their respective dates of issue, subject, however, to cancellation or revocation within such term; but the licensing authorities may, for convenience, provide that all licenses and permits of any one class shall expire upon the same date, as specified by the licensing authorities, and in any such case the said authorities may provide for the payment of the appropriate proportional part of any license fees issued in that class. The licensing authorities may, however, when first issuing licenses under this act, provide that they shall be temporary only for such less period than one year as the licensing authorities may determine in order to enable said authorities to make such further and more complete investigation of the fitness of applicants to whom such temporary licenses are issued, as to the premises in which the licensee's business is to be conducted, and for any other purposes deemed by the licensing authorities material. Such temporary licenses to be issued by the local licensing authorities shall become effective on such date, not earlier than April seventh in the current year, as the local licensing authorities shall designate, but any such temporary licenses granted for the sale of wines and malt beverages not to be drunk on the premises shall lapse and become void ninety days after their respective dates unless in the meantime duly approved by the commission.

Any manufacturer holding a federal permit to manufacture wines or malt beverages may sell, for a period not exceeding thirty days after the passage of this act, without a license as otherwise required in this act, wines or malt beverages; provided, that when the commission issues a license to such manufacturer said license shall take effect as of the seventh day of April in the current year or as of the date of the passage of this act, if said date of passage is subsequent to said seventh day of April.

Term of licenses.

Temporary licenses.

Sales by certain manufacturers without a license permitted for thirty day period. Proviso.

REGULATIONS.

Commission to make regulations.

SECTION 14. The commission may, with the approval of the governor and council, make regulations not inconsistent with the provisions of this act for clarifying, carrying out, enforcing and preventing violation of, all and any of its provisions, and also for inspection of the premises and method of carrying on the business of any licensee, for insuring the purity, and penalizing the adulteration or in any way changing the quality or content, of any wine or malt beverage, and for the proper and orderly conduct of the licensed business; and every such regulation, when so approved, shall be printed in full in one issue of some newspaper of general circulation published on the same day in each of the cities of Boston, New Bedford, Lowell, Worcester, Springfield and Pittsfield, and copies of such regulations shall be furnished to each licensee. From and after the date of such publication, any such regulation made and approved as aforesaid shall have the force and effect of law until the following March first, and, if approved by the general court, but not otherwise, shall continue to have such force and effect until it is set aside by a final decree of a court of competent jurisdiction or is amended or annulled by the commission.

The commission shall, at least annually on or before December thirty-first of each calendar year, publish in a convenient pamphlet form all regulations then in force, and shall furnish copies of such pamphlets to every licensee authorized under the provisions of this act to sell wines and malt beverages. *Regulations to be published.*

SECTION 15. It shall be unlawful for any licensee to sell wines or malt beverages not to be drunk on the premises, or any proprietor of a restaurant or of a hotel or any club duly licensed to sell wines or malt beverages to be drunk on the premises, to lend or borrow money, or receive credit, directly or indirectly, to or from any manufacturer of wines or malt beverages, or to or from any member of the family of such a manufacturer, or to or from any stockholder in a corporation manufacturing such wines and malt beverages, and for any such manufacturer, or any member of the family of such manufacturer, or any stockholder in a corporation manufacturing such wines or malt beverages, to lend money or otherwise extend credit, except in the usual course of business and for a period not exceeding sixty days, directly or indirectly, to any such licensee; or to acquire, retain or own, directly or indirectly, any interest in the business of any such licensee or in the premises occupied by any such licensee in the conduct of the licensed business, or in any equipment, property or furnishings used on such premises, or for any person, firm, corporation or association to acquire, own or retain, directly or indirectly, any such interest while such person, firm, corporation or association also owns or holds or controls a majority interest, as partner, stockholder, trustee, or in any other manner or capacity, in the business or plant of any manufacturer, wholesaler of wines or malt beverages or the holder of a foreign manufacturer's agency license. The violation of any of the above provisions of *Extension of credit to licensees by manufacturers, regulated.*

this section shall be sufficient cause for the revocation of the licenses of all licensees involved in such violation.

ALIENS.

Licenses not to be issued to aliens.

SECTION 16. No license for the sale of wines and malt beverages shall be issued to any person who is not, at the time of his application therefor, a citizen of the United States, or to any agent of any such person, or to any corporation a majority of whose stockholders are in fact aliens, and no person not such a citizen shall be appointed as manager or other principal representative of any licensee; provided, that any alien, who has applied for and received his first naturalization papers and who satisfies the licensing authorities of his bona fide intention to apply for and take out his final papers, may in the discretion of the licensing authorities be given a license which shall not continue or be renewed beyond the date when such final papers are obtainable by the applicant unless he applies for and takes out the same.

Manager, etc., of corporation required to be a citizen.

No corporation, organized under the laws of the commonwealth or of any other state or foreign country, shall be given a license to sell in any manner any wines or malt beverages unless such corporation shall have first appointed, in such manner as the licensing authorities by regulation prescribe, as manager or other principal representative, a citizen of the United States, and shall have vested in him by properly authorized and executed written delegation as full authority and control of the premises, described in the license of such corporation, and of the conduct of all business therein relative to wines and malt beverages as the licensee itself could in any way have and exercise if it were a natural person resident in the commonwealth, nor unless such manager or representative is, with respect to his character, satisfactory to the licensing authorities.

Act not to impair treaty rights.

No provision of this act shall impair any right growing out of any treaty to which the United States is a party.

Certain fees to be used for old age assistance.

SECTION 17. All fees received by the commission under this act shall be paid into the treasury of the commonwealth and used for reimbursing, after the expenses of the commission have been paid, cities and towns for assistance given by them to aged citizens under the provisions of chapter one hundred and eighteen A of the General Laws, in the manner provided by section three of said chapter, and all such fees received by local licensing authorities shall be paid monthly into the treasuries of their respective cities and towns.

Cities and towns to vote to grant licenses at state election.

SECTION 18. The state secretary shall cause to be placed on the official ballot used in the cities and towns at each biennial state election the following question: — "Shall licenses be granted in this city (or town) for the sale therein of wines and malt beverages?"

If a majority of the votes cast in a city or town in answer to the question are in the affirmative, such city or town shall be taken to have authorized, for the two calendar years next succeeding, the sale in such city or town, of wines and malt beverages, subject to the provisions of federal law and of this act. Act to be operative for two years if accepted in any city or town.

SECTION 19. Prior to January first, nineteen hundred and thirty-five, and pending the taking, in any manner authorized under this act, of the vote in any city or town on the question of granting licenses for the sale therein of wines and malt beverages, the granting of such licenses and the sale of wines and malt beverages under this act shall be authorized therein upon the filing with the city or town clerk of an order to that effect by the mayor of such city or the selectmen of such town, but not otherwise. If a vote on such question is not earlier taken in any city or town, such vote shall be taken therein at any special state election held prior to the next biennial state election, for whatever purpose called, or at the next municipal election, if any occurs prior to May first, nineteen hundred and thirty-four, for whatever purpose called. If no vote on such question has been earlier taken in any city or town, the city council or the selectmen thereof may, and the selectmen of any town, within thirty days after the filing with the town clerk of a petition signed by registered voters therein equal in number to at least one per cent of the whole number of registered voters therein, and conforming to the provisions of section thirty-eight of chapter forty-three of the General Laws with respect to initiative petitions, shall, call a special election therein for the purpose of submitting such question, to be held not later than May first, nineteen hundred and thirty-four. Any vote on such question taken under this section shall have the same legal effect, for the period ending on December thirty-first, nineteen hundred and thirty-four, as a vote at a biennial state election under section eighteen. Acceptance of act by cities and towns prior to state election in year 1934.

SECTION 20. No licensee for the sale of wines and malt beverages not to be drunk on the premises shall sell, transport or deliver any such wines or malt beverages on Sundays, legal holidays or on any day on which a state or municipal election or primary is held in the city or town wherein the licensed premises are situated, nor shall there be sold in any restaurant any such wines or malt beverages during polling hours on any day on which such an election or primary is held in the city or town in which such restaurant is conducted. Sales by certain licensees on Sundays, etc., prohibited.

SECTION 21. Whoever being licensed under this act employs any person under twenty-one in the direct handling or selling of wines or malt beverages or whoever makes a sale of wines or malt beverages to any person under twenty-one shall be punished by a fine of not less than fifty dollars or by imprisonment for not less than three months, or both. Employment of minors prohibited.

Rules or regu-
lations of
metropolitan
district com-
mission not to
restrict sales
in certain cases.

SECTION 21A. No rule or regulation made by the metropolitan district commission for the government and use of the reservations or boulevards under its care shall prohibit or restrict the sale of wines or malt beverages in any building or place outside the limits of said reservations or boulevards if a license for such sale has been granted hereunder.

Analysis of
wines and
malt beverages
by depart-
ment of public
health.

SECTION 22. The analyst or assistant analyst of the department of public health shall upon request make, free of charge, an analysis of all wines and malt beverages sent to it by the licensing authorities or by police officers or other officers authorized by law to make seizures of wines and malt beverages, if the department is satisfied that the analysis requested is to be used in connection with the enforcement of the laws of the commonwealth. The said department shall return to such police or other officers, as soon as may be, a certificate, signed by the analyst or assistant analyst making such analysis, of the percentage of alcohol by weight which such samples of wines or malt beverages contain. Such certificate shall be prima facie evidence of the composition and quality of the wines or malt beverages to which it relates, and the court may take judicial notice of the signature of the analyst or the assistant analyst, and of the fact that he is such.

Certificate of
analysis.

SECTION 23. A certificate shall accompany each sample of wines or malt beverages sent for analysis by an officer to the department of public health stating by whom the wines or malt beverages were seized, the date of the seizure and the name and residence of the officer who seized said wines or malt beverages. Said department shall note upon said certificate the date of the receipt and the analysis of said wines or malt beverages and the percentage of the alcohol, as required by the preceding section. Said certificate shall be in the following form:

ss.   CITY OF   (OR TOWN OF)   19 .
To the Department of Public Health.

SIRS: — I send you herewith a sample of   taken from wine or malt beverages seized by me   (date)   19 .
Ascertain the percentage of alcohol it contains, by weight, and return to me a certificate herewith upon the annexed form.

Constable of
Police Officer of

COMMONWEALTH OF MASSACHUSETTS.

DEPARTMENT OF PUBLIC HEALTH,
BOSTON,   19 .

This is to certify that the   received by this Department with the above statement and analyzed by me contains   per cent of alcohol, by weight

Received   19 .
Analysis made   19 .

DEPARTMENT OF PUBLIC HEALTH.
By ....
Analyst.

Section 24. The state secretary shall provide and cause officers to be supplied with a suitable number of the forms prescribed by the preceding section. The certificate of the department of public health, given substantially in the form hereinbefore set forth, shall be admitted as evidence on trials for the forfeiture of wines and malt beverages as to the composition and quality of the wines and malt beverages to which it relates. State secretary to provide forms.

Section 25. No person shall tamper with samples of wines or malt beverages taken as provided in section fifty-one or alter the statements made upon the forms or certificates aforesaid. Tampering with samples, etc.

Section 26. Any court or trial justice may cause wines and malt beverages which have been seized under this act to be analyzed by a competent chemist, and the reasonable expense thereof, including a fee of not more than five dollars for each analysis, shall be taxed, allowed and paid like other expenses in criminal cases. Analysis by order of court.

Section 27. The delivery of wines or malt beverages in or from a building, booth, stand or other place, except a private dwelling house, or in or from a private dwelling house if any part thereof or its dependencies is used as an inn, eating house or shop of any kind, or other place of common resort, such delivery in either case being to a person not a resident therein, shall be prima facie evidence that such delivery is a sale. "Delivery" prima facie evidence of sale in certain cases.

Section 28. If two persons of full age make complaint to a district court or trial justice that they have reason to believe and do believe that wines or malt beverages, described in the complaint, are kept or deposited by a person named therein in a store, shop, warehouse, building, vehicle, steamboat, vessel or place, and are intended for sale contrary to law, such court or justice, if it appears that there is probable cause to believe said complaint to be true, shall issue a search warrant to a sheriff, deputy sheriff, city marshal, chief of police, deputy chief of police, deputy marshal, police officer or constable, commanding him to search the premises in which it is alleged that such wines or malt beverages are deposited, and to seize such wines or malt beverages, the vessels in which they are contained and all implements of sale and furniture used or kept and provided to be used in the illegal keeping or sale of such wines or malt beverages, and securely keep the same until final action thereon, and return the warrant with his doings thereon, as soon as may be, to a district court or trial justice having jurisdiction in the place in which such wines or malt beverages are alleged to be kept or deposited. Search warrants, issue of.

Section 29. A warrant shall not be issued for the search of a dwelling house, if no tavern, store, grocery, eating house or place of common resort is kept therein, or of any club, unless one of the complainants makes oath that he has evidence that such wines or malt beverages have been sold therein or taken therefrom for the purpose of being Search of dwelling houses and clubs regulated.

sold by the occupant, or by his consent or permission, contrary to law, within one month next before making such complaint, and are then kept therein for sale contrary to law by the person complained against. Such complainant shall state the facts and circumstances which constitute such evidence, and such allegations shall be recited in the complaint and warrant.

Complaint to designate building to be searched.

SECTION 30. The complaint shall particularly designate the building, structure and place to be searched, the wines or malt beverages to be seized, the person by whom they are owned, kept or possessed and intended for sale, and shall allege the intent of such person to sell the same contrary to law. The warrant shall allege that probable cause has been shown for the issuing thereof; and the place to be searched, the wines or malt beverages to be seized, and the person believed to be the owner, possessor, or keeper of such wines or malt beverages, intending to sell the same contrary to law, shall be designated therein with the same particularity as in the complaint and the complainants shall be summoned to appear as witnesses.

Duties of officer acting under search warrant.

SECTION 31. The officer to whom the warrant is committed shall search the premises and seize the wines or malt beverages described in the warrant, the casks or other vessels in which it is contained, and all implements of sale and furniture used or kept and provided to be used in the illegal keeping or sale of such wines or malt beverages, if they are found in or upon said premises, and shall convey the same to some place of security, where he shall keep the wines or malt beverages and vessels until final action is had thereon.

Penalty for search without warrant.

SECTION 32. A sheriff, deputy sheriff, city marshal, chief of police, deputy chief of police, deputy or assistant marshal, police officer or constable who, without a search warrant duly committed to him, searches for or seizes wines or malt beverages in a dwelling shall be punished by a fine of not less than five nor more than fifty dollars.

Notice of trial to determine ownership of wines, etc., seized.

SECTION 33. The court or trial justice before whom the warrant is returned shall, within twenty-four hours after the seizure thereunder of the wines or malt beverages and the vessels containing them, issue a notice, under seal, and signed by the justice or the clerk of said court, or by the trial justice, commanding the person complained against as the keeper of the wines or malt beverages seized and all other persons who claim any interest therein or in the casks or vessels containing the same to appear before said court or trial justice, at a time and place therein named, to answer to said complaint and show cause why such wines or malt beverages and the vessels containing them should not be forfeited.

Contents of notice.

SECTION 34. The notice shall contain a description of the number and kind of vessels, the quantity and kind of wines or malt beverages seized, as nearly as may be, and shall state when and where they were seized. It shall, not less than fourteen days before the time appointed for the trial, be served by a sheriff, deputy sheriff, constable or police officer upon the person charged with being the keeper thereof by leaving an attested copy thereof with him personally or at his usual place of abode, if he is an inhabitant of the commonwealth, and by posting an attested copy on the building in which the wines or malt beverages were seized, if they were found in a building; otherwise in a public place in the city or town in which the wines or malt beverages were seized.

SECTION 35. If, at the time appointed for trial, said notice has not been duly served, or other sufficient cause appears, the trial may be postponed to some other day and place, and such further notice issued as shall supply any defect in the previous notice; and time and opportunity for trial and defence shall be given to persons interested. *Postponement of trial.*

SECTION 36. At the time and place designated in the notice, the person complained against, or any person claiming an interest in the wines or malt beverages and vessel seized, or any part thereof, may appear and make his claim verbally or in writing, and a record of his appearance and claim shall be made, and he shall be admitted as a party to the trial. Whether a claim as aforesaid is made or not, the court or trial justice shall proceed to try, hear and determine the allegations of such complaint, and whether said wines or malt beverages and vessels, or any part thereof, are forfeited. If it appears that the wines or malt beverages, or any part thereof, were at the time of making the complaint owned or kept by the person alleged therein for the purpose of being sold in violation of law, the court or trial justice shall render judgment that such and so much of the wines and malt beverages so seized as were so unlawfully kept, and the vessels in which they are contained, shall, except as hereinafter provided, be forfeited to the commonwealth. If a motor vehicle is seized under the provisions of this act and is held to be a container or implement of sale of wines or malt beverages contrary to law, the court or trial justice shall, unless good cause to the contrary is shown, order a sale of such motor vehicle by public auction and the officer making the sale, after deducting the expense of keeping the motor vehicle, the fee for the seizure and the cost of the sale, shall pay all liens, according to their priorities, which are established, by intervention or otherwise, at said trial or in other proceedings brought for said purpose, as being bona fide and as having been created without the lienor having any notice that such motor vehicle was being used or was to be used as a container or implement of sale of wines or malt beverages contrary to law. The balance, if any, of the proceeds of the sale shall be forfeited to the commonwealth and shall be paid by said officer into its treasury. All liens against any motor vehicle sold under the provisions of *Forfeiture of wines, etc., seized on warrant.*

this section shall be transferred from said motor vehicle to the proceeds of its sale.

Disposition of forfeited wines, etc.

SECTION 37. Any wines or malt beverages and vessels so forfeited shall, by authority of the written order of the court or trial justice, be forwarded to the commissioner of public safety, who upon receipt of the same shall notify said court or justice thereof. If, in the judgment of the commissioner, it is for the best interests of the commonwealth that such wines or malt beverages and vessels be destroyed, he shall destroy or cause the destruction of such wines or malt beverages and vessels, but if, in his judgment it is for the best interests of the commonwealth to sell the same, he shall cause the same to be sold, or he may deliver such wines or malt beverages to any department or agency of the commonwealth for medical, mechanical or scientific uses; provided, that such sale or delivery shall be in accordance with and subject to such federal laws and regulations as may be applicable. The proceeds of such sales shall be paid into the treasury of the commonwealth. The officer who serves said order of the court or justice shall be allowed therefor fifty cents, but shall not be entitled to receive any traveling fees or mileage on account of the service thereof.

Wines, etc., not forfeited to be returned.

SECTION 38. If it is not proved on the trial that all or part of the wines or malt beverages seized was kept or deposited for sale contrary to law, the court or trial justice shall issue a written order to the officer having the same in custody to return so much thereof as was not proved to be so kept or deposited and the vessels in which it is contained, to the place as nearly as may be from which it was taken, or to deliver it to the person entitled to receive it. After executing such order, the officer shall return it to the court or trial justice with his doings endorsed thereon.

Forfeiture of furniture, etc.

SECTION 39. All implements of sale and furniture seized under sections twenty-eight and thirty-one shall be forfeited and disposed of in the manner provided for the forfeiture and disposition of wines and malt beverages; but the court or trial justice may, if it is deemed to be for the interest of the commonwealth, order the destruction or sale of said property by any officer qualified to serve criminal process and the proceeds of a sale thereof shall be paid over to the county; and said officer shall make return of the order for such destruction or sale and his doings thereon to the court or justice issuing the same. The

Motor vehicles.

provisions of this section shall not apply to a motor vehicle if seized and held to be an implement of sale as aforesaid, but the disposition of such a motor vehicle shall be governed by the provisions of section thirty-six.

Costs.

SECTION 40. If no person appears and is admitted as a party as aforesaid, or if judgment is rendered in favor of all the claimants who appear, the cost of the proceedings shall be paid as in other criminal cases. If only one party appearing fails to sustain his claim, he shall pay all the costs except the expense of seizing and keeping the wines and malt beverages, and an execution shall be issued against him therefor. If judgment is rendered against two or more claimants of distinct interest in the wines and malt beverages, the costs shall, according to the discretion of the court or trial justice, be apportioned among such parties, and executions shall be issued against them severally. If such execution is not forthwith paid, the defendant therein named shall be committed to jail, and shall not be discharged therefrom until he has paid the same and the costs of commitment, or until he has been imprisoned thirty days.

SECTION 41. A claimant whose claim is not allowed as aforesaid, and the person complained against, shall each have the same right of appeal to the superior court as if he had been convicted of crime; but before his appeal is allowed he shall recognize to the commonwealth in the sum of two hundred dollars, with sufficient surety or sureties, to prosecute his appeal to the superior court and to abide the sentence of the court thereon. Upon such appeal, any question of fact shall be tried by a jury. On the judgment of the court after verdict, whether a forfeiture of the whole or any part of the wines or malt beverages and vessels seized, or otherwise, similar proceedings shall be had as are directed in the five preceding sections. *Appeal.*

SECTION 42. A mayor, alderman, selectman, deputy sheriff, chief of police, deputy chief of police, city marshal, deputy or assistant marshal, police officer or constable, in his city or town, or, in the county of Dukes or Nantucket, the sheriff anywhere within his county, may without a warrant arrest any person whom he finds in the act of illegally manufacturing or selling, transporting, distributing or delivering wines or malt beverages, and seize the wines or malt beverages, vessels and implements of sale in the possession of such person, and detain them until warrants can be procured against such person, and for the seizure of said wines or malt beverages, vessels and implements, under this act. Such officers shall enforce or cause to be enforced the penalties provided by law against every person who is guilty of a violation of any law relative to the sale of wines or malt beverages of which they can obtain reasonable proof. *Arrest without warrant in certain cases.*

SECTION 43. A complaint or indictment for the violation of any provision of law relative to wines or malt beverages shall not, unless the purposes of justice require such disposition, be placed on file or disposed of except by trial and judgment according to the regular course of criminal proceedings. It shall be otherwise disposed of only upon motion in writing stating specifically the reasons therefor and verified by affidavit if facts are relied on. If the court or magistrate certifies in writing that he is satisfied that the cause relied on exists and that the interests of public *Disposition of prosecution regulated.*

justice require the allowance thereof, such motion shall be allowed and said certificate shall be filed in the case.

SECTION 44. Upon the conviction of a holder of a license or permit under this act of the violation of any law relative to the business he is licensed or permitted to pursue, the court in which or the magistrate before whom he has been convicted shall send to the authorities which issued the license or permit a certificate under seal, showing the time and place of such conviction.

SECTION 45. Upon the conviction of a person of the illegal keeping or sale of wines or malt beverages, the court or magistrate by whom he has been convicted shall issue and cause to be served upon the owner of the building, or agent of such owner in charge of the building, used for such illegal keeping or sale, if he resides within the commonwealth and is not the person so convicted, a written notice that the tenant of said building has been convicted as aforesaid; and a return thereof shall be made to the court or magistrate issuing it. Such notice, so served, shall be deemed to be due and sufficient notice under section twenty of chapter one hundred and thirty-nine of the General Laws.

SECTION 46. The forms heretofore in use may continue to be used in prosecutions under this act, and if substantially followed shall be deemed sufficient to fully and plainly, substantially and formally describe the several offences in each of them set forth, and to authorize the lawful doings of the officers acting by virtue of the warrants issued in substantial conformity therewith; but this section shall not exclude the use of other suitable forms.

SECTION 47. All wines and malt beverages which are kept for sale contrary to law and the implements and vessels actually used in selling and keeping the same are declared to be common nuisances.

SECTION 48. All buildings or places used by clubs for the purpose of selling, distributing or dispensing wines or malt beverages to their members or others shall be deemed common nuisances unless duly licensed under this act. Whoever keeps or maintains, or assists in keeping or maintaining, such a common nuisance shall be punished by a fine of not less than fifty nor more than one hundred dollars and by imprisonment for not less than three nor more than twelve months.

SECTION 49. No person shall manufacture, sell, or expose, or keep for sale, or transport, wines or malt beverages, except as authorized in this act.

SECTION 50. A violation by any person of any provision of this act for which a specific penalty is not provided or a violation by a licensee of any provision of his license or of any regulation made under authority of this act shall be punished by a fine of not less than fifty nor more than five hundred dollars or by imprisonment for not less than one nor more than six months.

Licensing authorities to be notified of conviction.
Owner of building to be notified of conviction.
Forms for prosecution.
Wines, etc., illegally kept, etc., common nuisances.
Clubs used for selling wines, etc., common nuisances.
Penalty.
Illegal sale, etc., of wines, etc., prohibited.
Penalty.

SECTION 51. The licensing authorities or their agents may at any time enter upon the premises of a person who is licensed by them under this act to ascertain the manner in which such person conducts his business and to preserve order. Such licensing authorities or their agents may at any time take samples for analysis from any wines or malt beverages kept on such premises, and the vessel or vessels containing such samples shall be sealed on the premises by the seal of the vendor, and shall remain so sealed until presented to the state department of public health for analysis and duplicate samples shall be left with the dealer. *Licensing authorities may enter premises.*

SECTION 52. The local licensing authorities after notice to the licensee and reasonable opportunity for him to be heard by them, may declare his license forfeited, or may suspend his license for such period of time as they may deem proper, upon satisfactory proof that he has violated or permitted a violation of any condition thereof, or any law of the commonwealth. If the license is declared to have been forfeited, the licensee shall be disqualified to receive a license for one year after the expiration of the term of the license so forfeited, and if he is the owner of the premises described in such forfeited license, no license shall be issued to be exercised on said premises for the residue of the term thereof. *Forfeiture or suspension of license.*

SECTION 53. Section two of chapter one hundred and thirty-eight of the General Laws, as appearing in the Tercentenary Edition thereof, shall not apply to selling or exposing or keeping for sale wines or malt beverages in accordance with the provisions of this act. *Certain provisions of general laws not to apply.*

SECTION 54. In respect to their constitutionality, all the provisions of this act are hereby declared to be separable. *Constitutionality.*

SECTION 55. Any applicant for a license who is aggrieved by the action of the local licensing authorities in refusing to grant the same or any one who is aggrieved by the action of such authorities in suspending, canceling, revoking or declaring forfeited the same, may appeal therefrom to the commission within such time as the commission may by regulation prescribe, and the decision of the commission shall be final; but pending a decision on the appeal, the action of the local licensing authorities shall have the same force and effect as if the appeal had not been taken. Upon the petition of twenty-five taxpayers of the city or town in which a license has been granted by such authorities or upon its own initiative, the commission may investigate the granting of such license and may, after a hearing, revoke or modify such license if, in its opinion, circumstances warrant. *Appeal to commission from decision of local authorities.*

Approved April 7, 1933.

*Chap.*121 AN ACT RELATIVE TO SALARY REDUCTIONS IN THE CITY OF
BOSTON AND THE COUNTY OF SUFFOLK.

Be it enacted, etc., as follows:

Certain provisions of general law not to affect salary reductions in Boston.

SECTION 1. Neither the provisions of chapter thirty-one of the General Laws as amended nor any civil service rule or regulation shall apply to any reductions made pursuant to the provisions of this act in the salary of any person holding office or employment classified under the civil service rules in the city of Boston or county of Suffolk when such reduction in salary applies equally or uniformly to all persons of the same grade or classification.

1875, 241, § 5, amended.

SECTION 2. Section five of chapter two hundred and forty-one of the acts of eighteen hundred and seventy-five is hereby amended by adding at the end thereof the following new sentence: — The school committee may during the school year which commenced on September first, nineteen hundred and thirty-two, and which ends on August thirty-first, nineteen hundred and thirty-three, reduce the salaries of teachers and other officials and employees of the school department, provided that such reduction in salaries applies uniformly to all persons of the same grade or classification and receiving the same

Reduction of salaries of school teachers, etc.

salary, — so as to read as follows: — *Section 5.* The school committee shall have the supervision and direction of the public schools, and shall exercise the powers and perform the duties in relation to the care and management of schools which are now exercised and performed by the school committee of said city, except so far as they may be changed or modified by this act, and shall have the powers and discharge the duties which may hereafter be imposed by law upon the school committees of cities and towns. They may elect teachers, and may discharge those now in office, as well as those hereafter elected. They shall appoint janitors for the school-houses, fix their compensation, designate their duties, and may discharge them at pleasure. They may fix the compensation of the teachers, but the salaries established at the commencement of each school year shall not be increased during such year. The school committee may during the school year which commenced on September first, nineteen hundred and thirty-two, and which ends on August thirty-first, nineteen hundred and thirty-three, reduce the salaries of teachers and other officials and employees of the school department, provided that such reduction in salaries applies uniformly to all persons of the same grade or classification and receiving the same salary.

Reduction of salaries by executive order.

SECTION 3. During the calendar year nineteen hundred and thirty-three the mayor of Boston may by executive order reduce for the period beginning with the date of the passage of this act and ending December thirty-first, nineteen hundred and thirty-three, the salary of every office and position, the salary of which is paid from the treasury of the city of Boston in whole or in part, and whether such salary is fixed by statute, city ordinance or otherwise, and whether or not such office or position is subject to civil service or classified under the civil service rules or under the county classification plan, except the members of the city council and its employees, the officers and employees of the police department, the school department, the department of school buildings, the licensing board, the finance commission and the Boston Port Authority, and provided that such reduction applies uniformly and equally to all persons thereby affected receiving the same amount or rate of salary, and provided that the salary of no person shall be reduced by a greater percentage than that of a person receiving a larger salary. The mayor shall give written notice of any such general reduction in such salary to the police commissioner, the school committee, the board of commissioners of school buildings, the superintendent of construction thereof, the city council, the licensing board, the finance commission and the Boston Port Authority. If within ten days of the delivery of such notice the officer, committee, board or other body so notified does not reduce the salary of each office and position under the control or the jurisdiction of said officer, committee, board or other body upon the same uniform basis and for the same period of time as the reduction put into effect by the mayor, the mayor forthwith by executive order, in the same manner and with the same authority as hereinbefore provided, and upon the same basis, shall effect reductions in the salary of each office and position of the departments, boards and other bodies so notified, wherever such reductions have not theretofore been made pursuant to this section and after the delivery of such notice. Such reductions shall be in force from the effective date of the reductions specified in the executive order first made by the mayor. All necessary authority to effect such temporary reductions is hereby granted to the mayor, to the city council, and to such other officers, committees, boards, or bodies as may effect reductions pursuant to this section, including, without limiting the generality of the foregoing, the authority to reduce salaries fixed by statute, by any rule or vote of the school committee, by ordinance, or otherwise, and the salaries of persons subject to civil service. The mayor taking office on January first, nineteen hundred and thirty-four, may by executive order continue in effect for the calendar year nineteen hundred and thirty-four the reductions made pursuant to the provisions of this section. During the period in which any reduction in salary hereunder is effective, no further reduction therein shall be made.

SECTION 4. The words "salary" or "salaries" as used in this act shall include all wages and compensation how- "Salary" defined.

ever payable and whether or not for full time, and in the case of an official or employee whose salary is payable in part from funds of the treasury of the city of Boston and in part from state or other funds, shall mean that part payable from the funds of the city treasury.

Reductions in salaries not to affect certain pensions and annuities.

SECTION 5. No reduction in salary or compensation made under the provisions of this act shall affect the amount payable, under chapter thirty-two of the General Laws or any other provision of law, to any officer or employee of said county or city as a pension or annuity under any noncontributory pension law.

Prior reductions and contributions ratified.

SECTION 6. All action heretofore taken by said city of Boston or any of the officials thereof in making deductions from salaries of officers and employees paid from the treasury of the city of Boston as contributions to public welfare is hereby ratified and confirmed and shall have the same force and effect as if they were reductions made under the provisions of this act.

Suspension of operation of acts, etc.

SECTION 7. All acts, parts of acts, rules and regulations, and ordinances inconsistent with this act are hereby suspended during the period of its operation.

Scrubwomen excepted from provisions of act.

SECTION 7A. Any woman employed by the city of Boston or the county of Suffolk as a scrubwoman, shall not be subject to any provisions of this act.

SECTION 8. This act shall take effect upon its passage.

Approved April 11, 1933.

---

*Chap.*122 AN ACT RELATIVE TO THE TAKING OR KILLING OF WATER-FOWL AND OTHER MIGRATORY BIRDS IN CERTAIN CASES.

Emergency preamble.

Whereas, The deferred operation of this act would in part defeat its purpose, therefore it is hereby declared to be an emergency law, necessary for the immediate preservation of the public convenience.

Be it enacted, etc., as follows:

G. L. (Ter. Ed.), 131, new section after § 87.

Chapter one hundred and thirty-one of the General Laws, as appearing in the Tercentenary Edition thereof, is hereby amended by inserting after section eighty-seven the following new section: — *Section 87A.* Whenever, in the opinion of the director, any species of waterfowl or other migratory bird subject to federal regulation becomes a menace to the marine fisheries of the commonwealth or becomes a nuisance with respect to property along or near the shores thereof. he may authorize any person in writing to take or kill such birds during any period when such taking or killing is otherwise unlawful, subject to such regulations as he may prescribe; provided, that such rules and regulations shall at all times conform to the federal laws and regulations relative thereto.

Taking, etc., of certain birds causing nuisances, authorized.

Proviso.

Approved April 12, 1933.

An Act authorizing the city of newburyport to pay *Chap.123*
A CERTAIN CLAIM LEGALLY UNENFORCEABLE BY REASON
OF ITS FAILURE TO COMPLY WITH CERTAIN PROVISIONS
OF ITS CHARTER.

Be it enacted, etc., as follows:

SECTION 1. The city of Newburyport is hereby authorized to expend a sum of money, not exceeding three hundred and forty-eight dollars and eighty-five cents, in the payment and discharge of a certain claim of The Martin W. Dugan Company for material furnished for the construction of a fence enclosing the Highland Cemetery in said city, said claim being unenforceable against said city by reason of its failure to comply with the provisions of its charter as appearing in section twenty-eight of chapter forty-three of the General Laws, as appearing in the Tercentenary Edition thereof.

SECTION 2. This act shall take effect upon its acceptance, during the current year, by vote of the city council of said city, subject to the provisions of its charter, but not otherwise.   *Approved April 12, 1933.*

An Act prohibiting the sale as pure milk of the com- *Chap.124*
BINATION OF MILK FAT WITH MILK, CREAM OR SKIMMED
MILK, WHETHER OR NOT CONDENSED, EVAPORATED, CON-
CENTRATED, POWDERED, DRIED OR DESICCATED.

Be it enacted, etc., as follows:

Section seventeen A of chapter ninety-four of the General Laws, as appearing in the Tercentenary Edition thereof, is hereby amended by inserting after the word "fat" in the twelfth line the following: — No person himself or by his servant or agent shall sell, exchange or 'deliver, or have in his possession with intent to sell, exchange or deliver, or expose, or offer for sale or exchange, as pure milk, any milk, cream, or skimmed milk in any of the aforesaid forms to which has been added or with which has been blended or compounded any milk fat, — so as to read as follows: — *Section 17A.* No person himself or by his servant or agent shall, for the purposes of sale or exchange, add any fat or oil other than milk fat to, or blend or compound the same with, any milk, cream or skimmed milk, whether or not condensed, evaporated, concentrated, powdered, dried or desiccated, so that the resulting product is in imitation or semblance of milk, cream or skimmed milk whether or not condensed, evaporated, concentrated, powdered, dried or desiccated, nor shall any person himself or by his servant or agent sell, exchange or deliver, or have in possession with intent to sell, exchange or deliver, or expose or offer for sale or exchange, any milk, cream or skimmed milk in any of the aforesaid forms to which

G. L. (Ter. Ed.), 94, § 17A, amended.

Combination of certain fats and oils with milk, etc., penalized.

has been so added or with which has been so blended or
compounded any fat or oil other than milk fat. No
person himself or by his servant or agent shall sell, exchange or deliver, or have in his possession with intent
to sell, exchange or deliver, or expose, or offer for sale or
exchange, as pure milk, any milk, cream, or skimmed milk
in any of the aforesaid forms to which has been added or
with which has been blended or compounded any milk
fat. Whoever violates any provision of this section shall
be punished by the penalties prescribed by section twenty-
four.   *Approved April 12, 1933.*

*Chap.*125 AN ACT RELATIVE TO THE POWERS OF THE ASSOCIATED
JEWISH PHILANTHROPIES, INC.

Be it enacted, etc., as follows:

SECTION 1. The Associated Jewish Philanthropies,
Inc., a corporation organized under General Laws, may
at meetings duly called for the purpose adopt by-laws
regulating the custody, investment and management of
the whole or any part of its funds or property heretofore
or hereafter received by it by gift, bequest, or devise, to
be devoted by said corporation to the purposes for which
it is or may be incorporated, and may provide that any
or all of such by-laws shall not be subject to amendment
so as to affect the custody, management or investment
of such property or the application of the income or proceeds
thereof; provided, however, that such by-laws shall not
affect, change or limit the purposes to which such property
is directed to be devoted by the testator or donor of such
property.

SECTION 2. An addition to or change of the purposes
of said corporation shall not affect the application of any
gift, devise or bequest made to said corporation prior to
the making of such addition or change, or of the proceeds
of such gift, devise or bequest, if by the terms of any by-
law theretofore adopted by said corporation, the application
of such gift, devise or bequest is limited to the purpose
for which said corporation was organized at the time of
the receipt of such gift, devise or bequest.
                                   Approved April 12, 1933.

*Chap.*126 AN ACT INCREASING THE FEE FOR REGISTRATION AS A
PHARMACIST BY RECIPROCITY WITH OTHER STATES.

Be it enacted, etc., as follows:

Section twenty-four of chapter one hundred and twelve
of the General Laws, as amended by chapter two hundred
and twenty-seven of the acts of nineteen hundred and
thirty-two, is hereby further amended by striking out, in
the twenty-second line, the word "ten" and inserting in
place thereof the word: — twenty-five, — so as to read as

follows: — *Section 24.* A person who desires to do business as a pharmacist shall, upon payment of five dollars to the board of registration in pharmacy, herein and in sections twenty-five to forty-two, inclusive, called the board, be entitled to examination, and, if found qualified, shall be registered as a pharmacist, and shall receive a certificate signed by the president and secretary of the board. Any person failing to pass such examination shall upon request be re-examined, after the expiration of three months, at any regular meeting of the board, upon payment of five dollars. The board may grant certificates of registration as assistants after examination upon the terms above named, but such certificates shall not allow the holder thereof to carry on the business of pharmacy. The board may grant certificates of registration to such persons as shall furnish with their applications satisfactory proof that they have been registered by examination in some other state; provided, that such other state shall require a degree of competency equal to that required of applicants in this commonwealth. Every such applicant for registration as a registered pharmacist shall pay to the secretary of the board twenty-five dollars at the time of filing his application. No such certificate shall be granted until the person applying therefor shall have signified his intention of acting under the same in this commonwealth. No certificate shall be granted under this section unless the applicant shall have submitted evidence satisfactory to the board that he is a citizen of the United States.

Approved April 18, 1933.

Examination of pharmacists for registration.

Certificates.

Reciprocity certificates.

Proviso.

An Act relative to the furnishing of blanks for use in giving notice of intention of marriage.

*Chap.*127

Be it enacted, etc., as follows:

Section twenty of chapter two hundred and seven of the General Laws, as appearing in the Tercentenary Edition thereof, is hereby amended by striking out, in the second line the word "him" and inserting in place thereof the words: — the state secretary, — and by striking out, in the fourth line, the word "him" and inserting in place thereof the words: — such clerk or registrar, — so as to read as follows: — *Section 20.* The clerk or registrar shall require written notice of intention of marriage, on blanks furnished by the state secretary, containing such information as is required by law and also a statement of absence of any legal impediment to the marriage, to be given such clerk or registrar under oath, by both of the parties to such intended marriage if both dwell in his town, or, if the parties dwell in different towns within the state, or if one dwells outside the state, by the party dwelling in his town, or, if both dwell outside the state, by both such parties; provided, that if a registered physician makes affidavit to the

G. L. (Ter. Ed.), 207, § 20, amended.

Notice of intention of marriage to be in writing on blank forms to be furnished by state secretary.

satisfaction of the clerk or registrar that a party so required is unable, by reason of illness, to appear, such notice may be given on behalf of such party, by his or her parent or legal guardian, or, in case there is no parent or legal guardian competent to act, by the physician certifying to the illness, or by the other party irrespective of such other party's residence. The oath to such notice shall be to the truth of all the statements contained therein whereof the party subscribing the same could have knowledge, and may be given before the clerk or registrar or before a regularly employed clerk in his office designated by him in writing and made a matter of record in the office. No fee shall be charged for administering such oath. In towns having an assistant clerk or registrar, he may administer the oath.   *Approved April 18, 1933.*

*Chap.*128 AN ACT FURTHER REGULATING THE APPOINTMENT OF CONSTABLES.

Be it enacted, etc., as follows:

G. L. (Ter. Ed.), 41, new section after § 91A.

Constables, appointment of, regulated.
Chapter forty-one of the General Laws, as appearing in the Tercentenary Edition thereof, is hereby amended by inserting after section ninety-one A the following new section: — *Section 91B.* Constables shall not be appointed by mayors or selectmen under section ninety-one or ninety-one A except as hereinafter provided. A person desiring to be appointed as aforesaid shall make a written application therefor to the appointing authority stating his reasons for desiring such appointment and such information as may be reasonably required by said authority relative to his fitness for said office. Such application shall also contain a statement as to the moral character of the applicant signed by at least five reputable citizens of the city or town of his residence, one of whom shall be an attorney-at-law. The appointing authority shall also investigate the reputation and character of every applicant and his fitness for said office. The chief of police or other official having charge of the police shall upon request give the appointing authority all possible assistance in making such investigation. The office of constable shall be filled only by appointment of an applicant hereunder who is found by the appointing authority, after investigation as aforesaid, to be a person of good repute and character and qualified to hold said office.
        Approved April 18, 1933.

*Chap.*129 AN ACT RELATIVE TO THE USE AND MANAGEMENT OF REAL ESTATE OF A DECEDENT BY HIS EXECUTOR OR ADMINISTRATOR FOR THE PURPOSE OF THE PAYMENT OF DEBTS FROM THE RENTS THEREOF.

Be it enacted, etc., as follows:

G. L. (Ter. Ed.), 202, new section after § 4.
Chapter two hundred and two of the General Laws is hereby amended by inserting after section four, as appear-

ing in the Tercentenary Edition thereof, the following new
section: — *Section 4A.* If the personal property of a deceased person appears to be insufficient to pay his debts,
the probate court may, subject to the rights of the widow
under section one of chapter one hundred and ninety-six,
after notice, authorize the executor or administrator to
take charge of the real property of the deceased or any part
thereof and collect the rents thereof for such period of time
as the court deems proper, and, during such period, to make
necessary repairs and do all other things which it may
consider needful for the preservation of such real property
and as a charge on the interest of the decedent therein;
provided, that if any person interested in the estate shall
give bond as provided in section thirteen, no such authorization shall be given. The balance, if any, of said rents,
subject to rights of dower or curtesy, and the rights of the
widow and minor children of the decedent under section
two of chapter one hundred and ninety-six, shall be assets
in the hands of the executor or administrator for the payment of debts in like manner as are the proceeds of real
property sold for the payment of debts. An order giving
authority to the executor or administrator as aforesaid
shall have effect, notwithstanding an appeal therefrom,
until it is otherwise ordered by a justice of the supreme
judicial court.   *Approved April 18, 1933.*

Executor, etc., may take charge of real estate of deceased and collect the rents thereof, if personal property is insufficient to pay debts.

An Act extending the time for appeals from the   *Chap.*130
refusal of assessors to abate taxes.

Be it enacted, etc., as follows:

SECTION 1. Section sixty-four of chapter fifty-nine of
the General Laws, as appearing in the Tercentenary Edition thereof, is hereby amended by striking out, in the
second line, the word "thirty" and inserting in place thereof
the word: — sixty, — so that the first paragraph will read
as follows: — A person aggrieved by the refusal of assessors
to abate a tax may, within sixty days after receiving the
notice provided in the preceding section, appeal therefrom
by filing a complaint with the clerk of the county commissioners, or of the board authorized to hear and determine
such complaints, for the county where the property taxed
lies, and if on hearing the board finds that the property
has been overrated, it shall make a reasonable abatement
and an order as to costs. If the list of personal property
required to be brought in to the assessors was not brought
in within the time specified in the notice required by section twenty-nine, no tax upon personal property shall be
abated unless the appellate board finds good cause for this
delay or unless the assessors have so found as provided in
section sixty-one. A tax or assessment upon real estate
may be abated whether or not a list of property was brought
in within the time specified by the notice required by sec-

G. L. (Ter. Ed.), 59, § 64, amended.

Appeal to county commissioners from refusal of assessors to abate tax.

tion twenty-nine; provided, that the application for an abatement of such a tax or assessment included a sufficient description of the particular real estate as to which an abatement is requested.

G. L. (Ter.
Ed.), 59, § 65,
amended.

SECTION 2. Section sixty-five of said chapter fifty-nine, as so appearing, is hereby amended by striking out, in the fourth line, the word "thirty" and inserting in place thereof

Appeal to
board of tax
appeals.

the word: — sixty, — so as to read as follows: — *Section 65.* A person aggrieved as aforesaid may, instead of pursuing the remedy provided in section sixty-four, but subject to the same conditions, appeal to the board of tax appeals by filing a petition with such board within sixty days of the giving of the notice required by section sixty-three. Such appeal shall be heard and determined by said board in the manner provided by chapter fifty-eight A. The board may enter such order as justice may require in the manner provided in the preceding section with respect to complaints removed from the county commissioners.

Approved April 18, 1933.

Chap.131 AN ACT AUTHORIZING THE SUPREME COUNCIL OF THE ROYAL ARCANUM, A FRATERNAL BENEFIT SOCIETY, TO ERECT AND MAINTAIN A HOME FOR AGED AND INDIGENT MEMBERS AND THE WIDOWS AND ORPHANS OF MEMBERS.

Be it enacted, etc., as follows:

The Supreme Council of the Royal Arcanum, a fraternal benefit society incorporated under general law, is hereby authorized, subject to such terms and conditions as the commissioner of insurance may impose and with his written approval, to erect, equip, operate and maintain, within or without the commonwealth, a home for its aged and indigent members and the widows and orphans of its members, and for the aforesaid purpose it may acquire or purchase and hold real estate, notwithstanding any provisions of chapter one hundred and seventy-six of the General Laws to the contrary. The cost of erecting, equipping, operating and maintaining such home shall be defrayed by a special building fund to be raised and maintained in such manner as the said society may provide in its constitution and by-laws.

Failure of any member of said society to contribute by the payment of dues or assessments to the said special building fund shall not affect or prejudice his rights as a member of said society, anything in its constitution or by-laws to the contrary notwithstanding.

Approved April 18, 1933.

AN ACT PROVIDING FOR A CONVENTION TO ACT UPON A *Chap.*132
PROPOSED AMENDMENT TO THE CONSTITUTION OF THE
UNITED STATES RELATIVE TO THE REPEAL OF THE EIGHT-
EENTH AMENDMENT.

Whereas, In order that immediate action may be taken   Emergency
hereunder, if deemed urgent by the governor and council,   preamble.
this act is hereby declared to be an emergency law, necessary
for the immediate preservation of the public convenience.

Be it enacted, etc., as follows:

SECTION 1. For the purpose of acting upon an amend-   Convention to
ment to the constitution of the United States proposed by a   act on repeal
of eighteenth
joint resolution of congress, whereof a certified copy has   amendment.
been transmitted by the department of state under date
of February twenty-first, nineteen hundred and thirty-
three, to his excellency the governor of the commonwealth,
with the request that the same be submitted to a convention
for such action as may be had, there shall meet in the
state house in Boston a convention of delegates, elected as
hereinafter provided. The convention shall be held at
such time following the election of such delegates as the
governor may determine.

SECTION 2. The number of delegates to the convention   Delegates to
shall be forty-five, and each district established under   the convention,
number and
section one of chapter fifty-seven of the General Laws, as   election
appearing in the Tercentenary Edition thereof, for the   thereof.
purpose of electing representatives in the congress of the
United States, shall elect three delegates, all of whom shall
be residents of the district. Voters participating in such
election shall have the qualifications prescribed by law of
voters for state officers. The election of such delegates
in the several districts shall occur at the biennial state
election in the year nineteen hundred and thirty-four, or
at a special state election, as the governor and council may   Special state
order; and full power and authority are hereby vested in   election.
the governor and council to order such special election and
to appoint the time for holding the same. A special
election hereunder shall be held wholly or partly by wards,
precincts or towns, as the election commissioners in Boston
and the aldermen in other cities and selectmen in towns
may designate, and they shall give notice of their determination to the state secretary on or before the sixth Tuesday
preceding the day set for the election. In wards or towns
where voting at elections is commonly by precincts, the
election commissioners and city and town clerks shall
designate which of the election officers shall serve, in case
such election is held in larger units.

SECTION 3. As soon as may be after the date of the   Caucus to
election of delegates hereunder has been determined as   nominate
candidates for
provided in section two, the governor, lieutenant governor,   election as
councillors, state secretary, state treasurer, attorney general   delegates.

and state auditor shall, on the call of the governor, meet in caucus in the state house for the purpose of nominating candidates to be voted for in the several districts at such election. The caucus may adopt rules for its procedure and may adjourn from time to time. The governor and state secretary shall respectively serve as its president and clerk. The caucus shall nominate by a majority vote a group of three candidates from each district favoring ratification of the proposed amendment and a group of three candidates from each district opposing such ratification, as evidenced by signed statements of their respective positions on the question of ratification filed with the clerk of the caucus. A return of the proceedings of the caucus and of its nominees, grouped in accordance with their position in relation to the ratification of the proposed amendment, shall be filed in the office of the state secretary, certified by the president and clerk of the caucus, not later than the fifth Tuesday preceding the day of the election. In case of any vacancy occurring in the list of nominees in any district, the remaining nominees from the same district and in the same group shall, if the time is sufficient therefor, fill the same.

Designations appearing on official ballot.
SECTION 4. The provisions of law relative to ballots used in the election of state officers shall apply, so far as applicable, and except as otherwise provided herein, to ballots used in the election of delegates under this act. The names of the persons nominated for each district under section three shall appear on the ballots to be used therein, arranged alphabetically by their surnames in groups as nominated, one group under the designation: — "Delegates Favoring Ratification (For Repeal)" and the other group under the designation: — "Delegates Opposed to Ratification (Against Repeal)." To the name of each candidate shall be added the name of the street, with street number, if any, and the name of the city or town, where he resides. The relative positions of the two groups on the ballot shall be determined by the state secretary by lot. Directly preceding the aforesaid designations shall appear the following general heading: — "Election of Delegates to a Constitutional Convention called to Ratify or Reject the Following Amendment to the Constitution of the United States, proposed by Joint Resolution of Congress." Then shall follow the text of the proposed amendment. No designation, save as aforesaid, shall appear in connection with any name appearing on the ballot. No name of any candidate, except of nominees under section three, shall be printed on the ballot, but three blank spaces shall be left in which the voter may insert the name of any legal voter of the district not printed on the ballot for whom he desires to vote.

Provisions of election laws to apply.
SECTION 5. All laws governing the election of state officers, including the canvassing, recount and return of votes therefor and the determination of the results of the

voting, shall, so far as applicable and except as otherwise provided in this act, apply to the election of delegates under this act. No ballots cast at the election of delegates under this act shall be counted until the close of the polls. The time within which copies of records of votes cast under this act shall be transmitted to the state secretary, as provided in section one hundred and twelve of chapter fifty-four of the General Laws, shall be seven days.

SECTION 6. The state secretary shall, as soon as the results of the election have been finally determined, notify the successful candidates of their election and shall summon them to meet in convention in the state house at such time as shall have been designated for the convening thereof. The governor shall call the convention to order and shall preside thereover until a president is chosen. The state secretary shall call the roll of the delegates and act as clerk of the convention until a clerk is chosen. The delegates shall be judges of the returns and elections of the members of the convention. The convention shall proceed to organize by the choice of a president, clerk and such other officers as it may determine, and by establishing rules for its procedure. Twenty-three delegates shall constitute a quorum. Upon the completion of its organization, the convention shall take into consideration the advisability and propriety of ratifying or rejecting the amendment to the constitution submitted as aforesaid and shall vote to ratify or reject the same. The convention shall be provided by the superintendent of buildings, at the expense of the commonwealth, with suitable quarters and facilities for exercising its functions. The members shall receive no compensation for their services, but shall each be entitled to receive the sum of ten cents for every mile of ordinary traveling distance from his place of abode to the place of sitting of the convention. The convention shall, subject to the approval of the governor and council, provide for such other necessary expenses of its session as it shall deem expedient. The governor, with the advice and consent of the council, is hereby authorized to draw his warrant on the treasury for any of the foregoing expenses.

SECTION 7. If the convention ratifies such proposed amendment to the constitution of the United States by a majority of its members present and voting, the president of the convention shall thereupon transmit to the governor duly authenticated certificates of the action of the convention, in triplicate, and thereupon the governor shall transmit to the secretary of state of the United States one of said triplicates, duly authenticated by the state secretary under the great seal of the commonwealth. Another of said triplicates, authenticated in like manner, shall be deposited by the state secretary in the state archives.

Approved April 20, 1933.

State secretary to notify successful candidates.

Convention, calling of, proceedings.

Ratification of amendment, notice to be sent to governor, etc.

Chap.133 AN ACT PROVIDING FOR BIENNIAL MUNICIPAL ELECTIONS IN THE CITY OF SALEM.

Be it enacted, etc., as follows:

Biennial municipal elections in Salem.

SECTION 1. Beginning with the year nineteen hundred and thirty-five, municipal elections in the city of Salem, for the choice of mayor, members of the city council and members of the school committee shall be held biennially on the Tuesday next following the first Monday in December in each odd-numbered year. No municipal election shall be held in said city in the year nineteen hundred and thirty-four.

Mayor and city councillors, election, term.

SECTION 2. At the biennial municipal election to be held in said city in nineteen hundred and thirty-five and at every biennial municipal election thereafter, the mayor and all members of the city council shall be elected to serve for two years from the first Monday in January following their election and until their successors are qualified. The members of the city council elected by and from the various wards of said city at the municipal election held in the year nineteen hundred and thirty-two, shall continue to hold office until the qualification of their successors who shall be elected at the municipal election in the year nineteen hundred and thirty-five.

Inauguration.

SECTION 3. On the first Monday in January following a regular municipal election, or on the day following when said first Monday is a holiday, at ten o'clock in the forenoon, the mayor-elect and the councillors-elect shall meet and be sworn to the faithful discharge of their duties. The oath shall be administered as provided in section seventeen of chapter forty-three of the General Laws, as appearing in the Tercentenary Edition thereof.

School committee.

SECTION 4. Members of the school committee of the said city, except members elected to fill vacancies, if any, elected in the year nineteen hundred and thirty-one shall continue to hold office until the qualification of their successors who shall be elected at the biennial municipal election in the year nineteen hundred and thirty-five. Members of said school committee to be elected in the year nineteen hundred and thirty-three shall be elected to serve for four years from the first Monday in January following their election and until their successors are qualified. At the biennial municipal election in the year nineteen hundred and thirty-five there shall be elected four members of the school committee, one to serve for two years and three to serve for four years from the first Monday in January following their election and until their successors are qualified, and thereafter at every biennial municipal election three members of the school committee shall be elected to serve for four years from the first Monday in January following their election and until their successors are qualified. Vacancies in the school committee shall be filled as provided in section thirty-six of chapter forty-three of the General Laws, as appearing in the Tercentenary Edition thereof.

SECTION 5. This act shall be submitted to the voters of the city of Salem at the annual city election in the current year in the form of the following question which shall be printed on the official ballot to be used at said election: — "Shall an act passed by the general court in the year nineteen hundred and thirty-three, entitled 'An Act providing for biennial municipal elections in the city of Salem', be accepted?" If a majority of the voters voting thereon vote in the affirmative in answer to said question, then this act shall take full effect in said city; otherwise it shall be of no effect and the officers elected at said election shall respectively hold office for the terms now provided by law. *Approved April 20, 1933.*

Acceptance of act.

An Act regulating the granting of certain permits to be at liberty from the state prison. **_Chap._134**

Be it enacted, etc., as follows:

SECTION 1. Chapter one hundred and twenty-seven of the General Laws is hereby amended by striking out section one hundred and thirty-three, as appearing in the Tercentenary Edition thereof, and inserting in place thereof the following: — *Section 133*. The board of parole may, at its discretion, grant to a prisoner sentenced to the state prison for a crime committed on or after January first, eighteen hundred and ninety-six, at any time after the expiration of his minimum term of sentence, a permit to be at liberty therefrom during the unexpired portion of the maximum term of his sentence, upon such terms and conditions as it shall prescribe. If the prisoner is held in the prison upon two or more sentences, he may receive such permit after he has served a term equal to the aggregate of the minimum terms of the several sentences, and in such case he shall be subject to all the provisions of this section until the expiration of a term equal to the aggregate of the maximum terms of said sentences.

G. L. (Ter. Ed.), 127, § 133, amended.

Permits to certain prisoners to be at liberty from state prison.

SECTION 2. Notwithstanding the passage of this act, the provisions of said section one hundred and thirty-three, as in effect immediately prior to the effective date of this act, shall continue in force for the benefit of any prisoner sentenced prior to said date who is or may be entitled under said provisions to be granted a permit to be at liberty. *Approved April 20, 1933.*

Chap.135 AN ACT RELATIVE TO THE DATE OF INAUGURAL OF THE CITY
GOVERNMENT OF THE CITY OF EVERETT.

Be it enacted, etc., as follows:

1892, 355, § 11,
amended.

Inauguration
of city govern-
ment of
Everett.

Chapter three hundred and fifty-five of the acts of eighteen hundred and ninety-two is hereby amended by striking out section eleven and inserting in place thereof the following: — *Section 11.* The mayor elect and the members elect of the city council shall, on the first Monday in the January succeeding their election, except when said first Monday falls on a legal holiday, in which event on the following day, at twelve o'clock, noon, assemble together and be sworn to the faithful discharge of their duties. The oath may be administered to the mayor by the city clerk, or by a judge of a court, or by a justice of the peace, and the oath may be administered to the members of the city council by the mayor, or by the city clerk, or by a justice of the peace. In case of the absence of the mayor elect on said day, or if a mayor shall be subsequently elected, the oath of office may at any time thereafter be administered to him in the presence of the city council; and at any time after said day the oath of office may be administered in the presence of either branch of the city council to a member of such branch who was absent thereon or who shall be subsequently elected. A certificate that such oath has been taken by the mayor shall be entered in the journal of both branches of the city council, and in the journal of each branch shall be entered a certificate that the oath has been so taken by the members of that branch.

Approved April 20, 1933.

Chap.136 AN ACT RELATIVE TO THE HOLDING OF PROFESSIONAL SPORTS AND GAMES, SO CALLED, ON THE LORD'S DAY IN CELTIC PARK IN THE HYDE PARK DISTRICT OF THE CITY OF BOSTON.

Be it enacted, etc., as follows:

SECTION 1. So much of the provisions of section twenty-two of chapter one hundred and thirty-six of the General Laws, as appearing in the Tercentenary Edition thereof, as provides that "no sport or game shall be permitted in a place, other than a public playground or park, within one thousand feet of any regular place of worship" shall not apply in case of Celtic park, so called, in the Hyde Park district of the city of Boston.

SECTION 2. This act shall take effect upon its passage.

Approved April 20, 1933.

An ACT RELATIVE TO PREFERENCE UNDER THE CIVIL SERVICE *Chap.137*
LAWS OF HOLDERS OF CONGRESSIONAL MEDALS OF HONOR.

Whereas, The deferred operation of this act would in Emergency
part defeat its purpose, therefore it is hereby declared to be preamble.
an emergency law, necessary for the immediate preservation
of the public convenience.

Be it enacted, etc., as follows:

Chapter thirty-one of the General Laws, as most recently G. L. (Ter.
amended in section twenty-one by chapter eighty-nine Ed.), 31, § 21,
of the acts of nineteen hundred and thirty-two, is hereby etc., amended.
further amended by striking out said section twenty-one
and inserting in place thereof the following: — *Section 21.* Veteran's
The word "veteran", as used in this chapter, shall mean preference
(1) any person who has served in the army, navy or marine service law.
corps of the United States in time of war or insurrection Veteran
and whose last discharge or release from active duty therein defined.
was an honorable one, regardless of any prior discharge or
release therefrom, or (2) any person who has distinguished
himself by gallant or heroic conduct while serving in the
army, navy or marine corps of the United States and has
received a decoration designated as the congressional medal
of honor from the president of the United States or the
secretary of war, or from a person designated by the president or the said secretary to act as the personal representative of the president or said secretary for the presentation of
such decoration, and is recorded in the files of the war
department or the navy department of the United States
as having received such decoration; provided, that the Provisos.
person claiming to be a veteran under this section was a
citizen of the commonwealth at the time of his induction
into such service or has resided in the commonwealth for
five consecutive years next prior to the date of filing application with the commissioner under this chapter; and
provided, further, that any such person who at the time of
entering said service had declared his intention to become a
subject or citizen of the United States and withdrew such
intention under the provisions of the act of congress approved July ninth, nineteen hundred and eighteen, and
any person designated as a conscientious objector upon his
discharge, shall not be deemed a "veteran" within the
meaning of this chapter.   *Approved April 20, 1933.*

An ACT AUTHORIZING THE CITY OF BOSTON TO COMPENSATE *Chap.138*
CERTAIN PERSONS FOR DAMAGE TO THEIR PROPERTY BY
THE EXPLOSION OF DYNAMITE USED IN CONNECTION WITH
SEWER CONSTRUCTION.

Be it enacted, etc., as follows:

SECTION 1. For the purpose of discharging a moral
obligation, the city of Boston may pay to the owners of

property, located in the West Roxbury district of said city, which was damaged on June thirtieth, nineteen hundred and thirty-two by the explosion of dynamite used in connection with sewer construction, in compensation for such damage, such sums, not exceeding in the aggregate fifteen thousand dollars, as may have been mutually agreed upon, prior to the effective date of this act, by the legal department of said city and said owners, and as may be determined by said legal department and approved by the mayor in the case of property with respect to which the amount of damages has not been so agreed upon prior to said effective date.

SECTION 2. This act shall take effect upon its acceptance during the current year by vote of the city council of said city, subject to the provisions of its charter, but not otherwise.   *Approved April 20, 1933.*

---

*Chap.*139 AN ACT RELATIVE TO THE POLICE FORCE OF THE CITY OF CAMBRIDGE.

Be it enacted, etc., as follows:

The reserve police force of the city of Cambridge, established under authority of sections twenty-six to twenty-eight, inclusive, of chapter one hundred and eight of the Revised Laws, is hereby abolished, without prejudice to the right of said city hereafter to accept any then existing provisions of law providing for the establishment of such a force. All members of said reserve police force who on the effective date of this act have served as such for six months or more shall upon said date become members of the regular police force of said city.   *Approved April 20, 1933.*

---

*Chap.*140 AN ACT AUTHORIZING THE COMMERCIAL TRAVELLERS' EASTERN ACCIDENT ASSOCIATION OF BOSTON TO CHANGE ITS NAME.

Emergency preamble.

Whereas, The deferred operation of this act would cause unnecessary inconvenience and delay, therefore it is hereby declared to be an emergency law, necessary for the immediate preservation of the public convenience.

Be it enacted, etc., as follows:

The Commercial Travellers' Eastern Accident Association, of Boston, a fraternal benefit society organized under general law, by vote of its directors, with the approval of the commissioner of insurance and subject in all other respects to section ten of chapter one hundred and fifty-five of the General Laws, as most recently amended by chapter eleven of the acts of the current year, may change its name to Eastern Commercial Travelers Accident Association or a similar name.   *Approved April 26, 1933.*

An Act authorizing the commercial travellers' boston benefit association (incorporated), of boston, to change its name. *Chap.*141

Whereas, The deferred operation of this act would cause unnecessary inconvenience and delay, therefore it is hereby declared to be an emergency law, necessary for the immediate preservation of the public convenience. *Emergency preamble.*

Be it enacted, etc., as follows:

The Commercial Travellers' Boston Benefit Association (Incorporated), of Boston, a fraternal benefit society organized under general law, by vote of its directors, with the approval of the commissioner of insurance and subject in all other respects to section ten of chapter one hundred and fifty-five of the General Laws, as most recently amended by chapter eleven of the acts of the current year, may change its name to Eastern Commercial Travelers Health Association or a similar name.   *Approved April 26, 1933.*

An Act relative to crop loans to farmers by the united states of america. *Chap.*142

Whereas, The deferred operation of this act would in part defeat its purpose to enable Massachusetts farmers to take advantage of certain federal aid, therefore this act is hereby declared to be an emergency law, necessary for the immediate preservation of the public convenience. *Emergency preamble.*

Be it enacted, etc., as follows:

During the period of three years from the effective date of this act, mortgages executed by farmers on crops growing or to be grown on land within the commonwealth owned by them to secure loans from the United States of America whereof the proceeds are to be used for the purchase of seed, fertilizer and materials for crop production, or any of them, shall be deemed to be mortgages of personal property; provided, that such mortgages shall, within thirty days from the date written in the mortgage, be recorded on the records of the city or town where the mortgagor resides when the mortgage is made, and on the records of the city or town where he then principally transacts his business. *Crop loans to farmers by federal government.*
        Approved April 26, 1933.

An Act relative to the sale by the new england power company of its properties, franchises and works in the state of vermont. *Chap.*143

Be it enacted, etc., as follows:

New England Power Company, a Massachusetts corporation subject to chapter one hundred and sixty-four of the General Laws, is hereby authorized to sell, transfer and convey its Vermont properties, franchises and works for cash and/or securities and on such terms and conditions as shall be approved by vote of at least two thirds of all its stock outstanding and entitled to vote and as shall be approved by the Massachusetts department of public utilities as consistent with the public interest.

Approved April 26, 1933.

---

*Chap.*144 AN ACT REVISING THE LAWS RELATIVE TO CO-OPERATIVE BANKS.

Emergency preamble.

Whereas, The deferred operation of this act would tend to defeat its purpose, which includes the protection of members of co-operative banks by further limitations upon withdrawals, the protection of home owners who find it difficult to carry their co-operative bank loans by making further provisions for the reduction and suspension of payments under loans, the further protection of home owners by enabling co-operative banks to borrow from the Federal Home Loan Bank for the purpose of making real estate loans, and the further protection of members and home owners by providing for the consolidation of co-operative banks, therefore it is hereby declared to be an emergency law, necessary for the immediate preservation of the public convenience.

Be it enacted, etc., as follows:

G. L., 170, etc., amended.

The General Laws are hereby amended by striking out chapter one hundred and seventy, as amended, and inserting in place thereof the following:

CHAPTER 170.

CO-OPERATIVE BANKS.

DEFINITIONS.

Section 1. The following words as used in this chapter, unless the context otherwise requires, shall have the following meanings:

"Commissioner", the commissioner of banks.

"Corporation" or "bank", a co-operative bank incorporated as such in this commonwealth.

INCORPORATION.
Agreement of Association.

Section 2. Twenty or more persons who associate themselves by a written agreement to form a co-operative bank for the purpose of accumulating the savings of its members and loaning such accumulations to them may, upon compliance with sections two, three, four and five, become a corporation with all the powers and privileges and subject to all the duties, restrictions and liabilities set forth in all general laws relating to such corporations. Said agreement shall set forth that the subscribers thereto associate themselves with the intention of forming a corporation to transact business within the commonwealth, and shall specify:

First. The name by which the corporation shall be known, the words "co-operative bank" to form a part thereof.

Second. The purpose for which it is to be formed.

Third. The town where its business is to be transacted.

Each associate shall subscribe to the articles his name, residence and post office address.

Notice and Hearing.

Section 3. The subscribers to said agreement shall give notice to the board of bank incorporation of their intention to form a co-operative bank, and shall apply to said board for a certificate that public convenience and advantage will be promoted by the establishment thereof. Said board may grant such certificate, which shall be deemed revoked if the applicants therefor do not become incorporated and begin business within six months after its date of issue. Upon receipt of such application, said board shall furnish the subscribers a form of notice, specifying the names of the proposed incorporators and the name and location of the proposed co-operative bank and assigning a date and place for a public hearing on the application. The subscribers shall publish the notice at least once a week for three successive weeks, in one or more newspapers designated by said board, and published in the town where it is desired to establish the bank, or, if there is no newspaper in such town, in the town where a newspaper is published, which is nearest to the location of the bank. If said board refuses to issue such certificate, no further proceedings shall be had, but the application may be renewed after one year from the date of the refusal, in which case notice of a public hearing thereon shall be published as herein provided.

First Meeting.

Section 4. The first meeting of the subscribers to the agreement of association shall be called by a notice signed either by that subscriber to the agreement who is designated therein for the purpose, or by a majority of the subscribers; and the notice shall state the time, place and purpose of the meeting. A copy of the notice shall, seven days at least before the day appointed for the meeting, be given to each subscriber, or left at his residence or usual place of business, or deposited in the post office, postage prepaid, and addressed to him at his residence or usual place of business, and another copy thereof and an affidavit by one of the signers that the notice has been duly served shall be recorded with the records of the corporation. If all the incorporators shall in writing, endorsed upon the agreement of association, waive such notice and fix the time and place of the meeting, no notice shall be required. The subscribers to the agreement of association shall hold the franchise until the organization has been completed. At the first meeting, or at any adjournment thereof, the incorporators shall organize by the choice by ballot of a temporary clerk, by the adoption of by-laws and by the election, in such manner as the by-laws may determine, of a president, a clerk of the corporation, a treasurer, a board of not less than five directors, and such other officers as the by-laws may prescribe. All the officers so elected shall be sworn to the faithful performance of their duties. The temporary clerk shall make and attest a record of the proceedings until the clerk has been chosen and sworn, including a record of the choice and qualification of the clerk.

Articles and Certificate of Incorporation.

Section 5. The president and a majority of the directors who are elected at the first meeting shall make, sign and make oath to, articles in duplicate setting forth:

(a) A true copy of the agreement of association, the names of the subscribers thereto, and the name, residence and post office address of each of the officers of the corporation.

(b) The date of the first meeting and the successive adjournments thereof, if any.

One duplicate original of the articles so signed and sworn to shall be submitted to said board, and the other, together with the records of the proposed corporation, to the commissioner of corporations and taxation, who shall examine the same and may require such amendment thereof or such additional information as he considers necessary. If he finds that the articles conform to the three preceding sections, and that sections three and six have been complied with, he shall so certify and endorse his approval thereon. Thereupon the articles shall be filed in the office of the state secretary, who upon receipt of five dollars shall issue a certificate of incorporation in the following form:

COMMONWEALTH OF MASSACHUSETTS.

Be it known that whereas (the names of the subscribers to the agreement of association) have associated themselves with the intention of forming a corporation under the name of (the name of the corporation), for the purpose (the purpose declared in the agreement of association), and have complied with the provisions of the statutes of this commonwealth in such case made and provided, as appears from the articles of organization of said corporation, duly approved by the commissioner of corporations and taxation and recorded in this office: Now, therefore, I (the name of the state secretary), secretary of the commonwealth of Massachusetts, do hereby certify that said (the names of the subscribers to the agreement of association), their associates and successors, are legally organized and established as, and are hereby made, an existing corporation under the name of (name of the corporation), with the powers, rights and privileges, and subject to the limitations, duties and restrictions, which by law appertain thereto.

Witness my official signature hereunto subscribed, and the great seal of the commonwealth of Massachusetts hereunto affixed, this   day of   in the year (the date of the filing of the articles of organization).

The state secretary shall sign the certificate of incorporation and cause the great seal of the commonwealth to be affixed thereto, and such certificate shall have the force and effect of a special charter. The existence of every such corporation which is not created by special law shall begin upon the filing of the articles of organization in the office of the state secretary, who shall also cause a record of the certificate of incorporation to be made, and such certificate or such record, or a certified copy thereof, shall be conclusive evidence of the existence of the corporation.

By-Laws.

Section 6. The shareholders of every such corporation shall make and adopt the necessary by-laws consistent with law for the government of its affairs. Copies of all by-laws and changes or additions thereto shall be filed with the commissioner immediately upon their adoption. All such by-laws, changes and additions shall be approved by the commissioner before becoming effective.

The by-laws shall provide for and determine —

(a) The time for holding the annual meeting of the shareholders and the monthly meetings of the board of directors, and for the receipt of moneys.

(b) The manner of calling either regular or special meetings.

(c) The number necessary to constitute a quorum at all meetings.

(d) The qualifications of electors.

(e) The number, title and duties of officers and standing committees, their terms of office and the manner of their election or appointment.

(f) The care and custody of money, securities and property of the bank.

(g) The method of loaning the funds of the bank.

(h) The proportion of profits, if any, to be reserved upon voluntary withdrawals.

(i) The time within which satisfactory security for real estate loans shall be offered.

(j) Whether partial payments of less than fifty dollars may be received upon loans.

(k) The rate of fines to be charged upon delinquent payments.

(l) The manner of transferring shares and the fee therefor.

(m) The manner in which and conditions under which the by-laws may be amended.

MANAGEMENT.

Officers, Election, etc.

Section 7. The business and affairs of every such corporation shall be managed by a board of not less than five directors to be elected by the shareholders. Directors may be elected for terms of not less than one nor more than three years, and, in case the term is more than one year, they shall be divided into classes and an equal number, as nearly as may be, elected each year. All vacancies in the board or in any office may be filled by the board of directors for the unexpired term. The directors may employ such additional assistance as they may deem necessary and determine the compensation therefor. Each officer and director when appointed or elected shall take an oath that he will faithfully and impartially discharge the duties devolving upon him, and the fact that the oath has been taken shall be entered in the records of the corporation; and if a person appointed or elected does not, within thirty days thereafter, take the oath, his office shall thereupon become vacant. The clerk of the corporation shall be chosen by the shareholders, and the president, vice president, treasurer, assistant treasurer, if any, and other officers whose election is not otherwise herein expressly provided for, shall be chosen by the board of directors. No shareholder shall be entitled to more than one vote at any meeting, and no shareholder shall vote by proxy. All officers shall be elected by ballot, shall be shareholders when nominated, and shall continue to hold their offices until their successors shall have been chosen and shall have assumed their duties, and no such corporation shall expire from neglect to elect officers at the time prescribed in its by-laws. If an officer ceases to be a shareholder, his office shall thereupon become vacant. If a director fails both to attend the regular meetings of the board and to perform any of the duties devolving upon him as such director for six consecutive months, his office may be declared by the board at the next regular meeting to be vacant. A record of any vacancy shall be entered upon the books of the corporation, and a transcript of such record shall be sent by mail to the person whose office has been made vacant. The records of all meetings of the corporation and board of directors shall be read by the president or a director, other than the clerk, designated by the president.

Security Committee.

Section 8. At the first meeting of the board of directors after the annual meeting for the election of officers, the board shall elect from its own number a security committee of at least three members, who shall examine real estate offered as security for loans and report thereon as required by section twenty-six, and shall perform such other duties as may be required of them by law.

The personal examination of any parcel of real estate by the security committee may be omitted by special vote of the board of directors.

No member of the security committee shall make an official report upon property offered as security for a loan in which he has a personal interest.

Duties of Treasurer. Bonds.

Section 9. The treasurer shall keep the accounts and have charge of all books and papers necessary therefor, and dispose of and secure the safe-keeping of all money, securities and property of the corporation, in the manner designated by the by-laws, and the treasurer, and all other permanent employees having access at all times to the cash or negotiable securities, shall give to the corporation bonds for the faithful performance of their respective duties in such amounts as the board of directors may require, in accordance with section twenty-four of chapter one hundred and sixty-eight relative to savings banks, except that the giving of schedule or blanket bonds shall be permitted only in the discretion of the commissioner.

Assistant Treasurer.

Section 10. Such corporation may provide in its by-laws for an assistant treasurer if the commissioner approves and, if it has assets in excess of five million dollars, for such additional number of assistant treasurers as the commissioner approves. An assistant treasurer may perform all the duties of the treasurer.

Meetings, Place of Business.

Section 11. The board of directors shall hold stated monthly meetings at any place in the town where the bank is located, and its usual business shall be transacted at its office only, which shall be in the town named in its agreement of association; but moneys due the bank may be collected by the treasurer, or other person duly empowered by the directors, upon such days and in such other places as may be designated by vote of the board of directors and approved by the commissioner, and the bank may advertise these branches in such manner as the commissioner may prescribe.

CAPITAL.
Issue of Shares.

Section 12. The capital to be accumulated shall be unlimited and shall be divided into shares of the ultimate value of two hundred dollars each. The shares may be issued in quarterly, half yearly or yearly series, in such amounts and at such times as the board of directors may determine. Shares of a prior series may be issued after a new series, subject to the approval of the board of directors. Paid-up shares may be issued, subject to the approval of the board of directors, each share to have a value of two hundred dollars, which shall be paid by the purchaser when the shares are issued, together with interest from the last distribution of profits at a rate fixed by the directors, but not in excess of the rate distributed to unmatured shares. The total value of paid-up shares outstanding at any one time shall not exceed ten per cent of the assets of the corporation.

Payment of Dues.

Section 13. On or before the regular monthly meeting for the receipt of moneys, as fixed by the by-laws, every shareholder shall pay to the corporation, as a contribution to its capital, one dollar as dues upon each unmatured share held by him until it is withdrawn, forfeited, suspended, retired or matured. Payment of dues on each series shall begin with its issue.

Shares Issued to Minors or Fiduciaries.

Section 14. Shares may be issued to and held by minors, by corporations and by fiduciaries, including a trustee in bankruptcy or receiver, if he is duly authorized to receive and hold such shares by an order or decree of the court by which he was appointed. Shares held by a minor may, in the discretion of the directors, be withdrawn, as provided in section seventeen, by the minor or by his parent or guardian, and in either case payments made on such withdrawals shall be valid. A minor under the age of eighteen shall not have the right to vote upon shares held by him in his own name. If shares are held in trust, the name and residence of the beneficiary shall be disclosed and the account shall be kept in the name of the holder as trustee for such person. If no other notice of the existence and terms of the trust has been given in writing to the corporation, such shares may, upon the death of the trustee, be withdrawn by the person named as beneficiary or by his legal representatives. Persons holding shares in any capacity as provided in this section, whether or not originally issued to them in such capacity, shall have the legal authority to transfer, pledge, assign or withdraw said shares subject to the provisions of law and the by-laws of the corporation. Except as otherwise provided in this chapter and in chapter one hundred and fifty-five, title to shares shall devolve and pass in the same manner as title to other personal property.

Joint Accounts.

Section 15. Shares may be issued to and held in the name of two or more persons as joint tenants, or in the name of two or more persons or the survivor or survivors of them, or in the name of husband and wife as tenants by the entirety. Payment to any of the persons so holding shares, while all of them are living, shall discharge the liability to all, and in the event of the death of any one of them the corporation shall be liable only to the survivor or survivors of them, and a payment to any of the survivors shall discharge the liability of the corporation to all survivors. Shares may be issued and held by two or more persons as tenants in common. Any one of the holders of shares held jointly, by survivorship, by the entirety or in common, who is not also entitled to vote as an individual shareholder or otherwise, may vote as the representative of all such holders at any meeting of the shareholders; but if more than one holder of shares so held attempts to vote as the representative of all, none of such holders shall be permitted to vote.

Issue and Holding of Shares Limited.

Section 16. Except as otherwise provided in this section, no person shall hold more than forty unmatured, ten matured and ten paid-up shares in any one bank at the same time, and the number of shares which may be held at the same time in any joint account provided for in section fifteen shall not exceed eighty unmatured shares, twenty matured and twenty paid-up shares. Either party to such a joint account may also hold shares in his individual name, but the total amount of such shares held by him, both jointly and individually, in such corporation at the same time shall not exceed eighty unmatured shares, twenty matured shares and twenty paid-up shares. Shares issued to and held by more than one fiduciary in the same estate shall not be considered as a joint account under this chapter. Any person, however, who has received shares in a co-operative bank by inheritance or devise under a will, or by execution of a power of attorney contained in any mortgage by the foreclosure thereof, may continue to hold such shares notwithstanding that the total number of his shares thereby becomes greater than the limits provided in this section.

There shall be no limit to the number of shares that may be issued to qualify for a co-operative bank mortgage, upon property purchased from the corporation.

Withdrawal of Shares.

Section 17. A shareholder, upon giving thirty days' written notice to the treasurer of his intention so to do, may withdraw unmatured shares not pledged for real estate loans, and, upon giving ninety days' written notice to the treasurer of his intention so to do, may withdraw matured or paid-up shares, but the treasurer may waive such notice, in his discretion, under such restrictions as may be imposed by the board of directors. Such shareholder shall be paid the balance remaining after deducting from the amount then standing to the credit of the shares all fines, any other charges legally incurred, and such part of the profits credited thereto as the by-laws may prescribe. All withdrawals shall be paid in the order of the expiration of the notices thereof. The directors may at any time order that not more than one half of the then cash on hand and in banks and one half of the funds received thereafter until such order is rescinded shall be applicable to the demands of withdrawing shareholders, and such limitations shall be effective until the rescission of such vote, except as otherwise provided in section twenty-one. Whenever there is an unusual demand for the withdrawal of shares, the board of directors, with the approval of the commissioner, or the commissioner, in his discretion, may order that the right of any withdrawing shareholder, or the holder of shares which have reached maturity, to payment of the withdrawal value of his shares shall be limited to not in excess of twenty per cent of the value of said shares, or four hundred dollars, at any one time. Said sums shall be paid in order upon the expiration of the notice or the date of shares reaching maturity and in rotation. While the foregoing order is in effect no loans from the funds of the corporation shall be made except loans on its shares, nor shall dividends be paid in cash to the holders of matured and paid-up shares on which notice of withdrawal has been filed. Said dividends shall be credited to the account of the holder and shall be distributed as prescribed in the order of limitation of payments.

No loans shall be made, secured by the value of the shares of the borrower, in excess of the limitations applying to withdrawals under this section, while any restrictions as to withdrawals are in force.

Suspension of Shares.

Section 18. The shares of a non-borrower who continues in arrears more than six months shall, at the option of the directors, if he fails to pay the arrears within thirty days after notice, be declared suspended, and the withdrawal value of the shares at the time of suspension shall be ascertained, and after deducting all fines and other legal charges the balance remaining shall be transferred to an account to be designated as the "suspended shares account", to the credit of the defaulting shareholder, who shall be entitled, upon thirty days' notice, to receive out of the funds appropriated for the payment of withdrawals the balance so transferred without interest from the time of the transfer, all defaulting shareholders being entitled to receive their balances so transferred in the order of the expiration of the notices thereof. All shares suspended shall cease to participate in any profits accruing after the adjustment and valuation of shares last preceding said suspension.

Retirement of Shares.

Section 19. The directors may retire the unpledged shares of any series after four years from the date of their issue, by enforcing the withdrawal of the same in the following manner: the treasurer shall seasonably send to every shareholder in the series in which the shares are to be retired a notice in the following form, and the shares shall be retired in accordance with its provisions:

The board of directors have voted to retire on the day of , 19 , shares in series No. , in which you are a shareholder.

Should you desire to have your shares, or any number of them, retired and to receive the full value thereof, you will please notify the treasurer in writing on or before , 19 .

If the shares voluntarily offered exceed the number desired, the shares to be retired will be determined by lot from those offered.

If the number so offered is less than the number desired, the number offered shall be retired and the balance determined by lot from the remaining shares in the series.

The shareholders whose shares are retired shall be paid the full value thereof, less all fines and any other charges legally incurred. Shares pledged for share loans shall be treated as unpledged shares. Wherever shares are retired between the dates of adjustment of profits, interest shall be paid upon the full value of the shares from the date of the preceding adjustment to the date of retirement, at the rate at which profits were distributed at said preceding adjustment.

The directors may, under rules made by them, retire matured or paid-up shares at any time and in such order and manner as they may provide.

The commissioner, whenever he deems it necessary for the welfare of the shareholders in any such corporation, may order the retirement of matured and paid-up shares or of unmatured shares in any series after four years from the date of issue, and the board of directors shall, in the manner hereinbefore provided, comply with the order of the commissioner.

Maturity of Shares.

Section 20. Whenever shares of a given series reach a value of two hundred dollars, either by the payment of dues, the addition of a regular dividend or the addition of interest as hereinafter provided, they shall be deemed matured and all payments of dues thereon shall cease, and the owner of each unpledged share shall be paid out of the funds of the corporation the matured value thereof, subject to all other provisions of this chapter. For the purpose of determining the maturity of shares between the dates of adjustment of profits, there shall be added to the value of the shares interest for all full months from the date of the preceding adjustment to the date when the addition thereof will mature the shares. The interest to be added shall be at the same rate at which profits were distributed at the last preceding adjustment; but before the payment of matured shares all arrears and fines shall be deducted. If the shareholder shall so elect, and at the option of the directors, there may be issued to the holder thereof a certificate for any number of shares that have matured, not exceeding ten, and such shares shall continue as matured shares in said corporation, subject to be withdrawn or retired as provided in sections seventeen and nineteen. In the event of the dissolution and winding up of such corporation, by process of law or otherwise, any member holding matured or paid-up shares of such corporation shall not thereby be entitled to any preference over any holder of unmatured shares, and all shares, whether matured, paid-up or unmatured, shall be held and treated as belonging to one general class of liability.

Payment of Deferred Withdrawals and Maturities.

Section 21. Whenever a notice of withdrawal of either unmatured, matured or paid-up shares has been filed, or shares have reached maturity and no certificate thereof has been issued under section twenty, and there has been no payment made thereon under section seventeen for a period of six months from the date when payment thereof is due, all the receipts of the bank from any source whatever shall, after the payment of the legitimate expenses of conducting business and the payment of such dividends as may be allowed by the commissioner, be applied to the payment of such withdrawals and maturities of shares; and the commissioner shall direct the method of disbursing the funds of the bank. This section shall not apply to a bank which may become subject to sections twenty-two to thirty-six, inclusive, of chapter one hundred and sixty-seven.

Payment of Shares of Deceased Shareholder.

Section 22. Upon the death of any shareholder, the value of the shares standing in his name shall be paid to his legal representatives; provided, that if the value thereof does not exceed two hundred dollars, and there has been no demand for payment thereof by a duly appointed executor or administrator, payment may be made, in the discretion of the president and treasurer of the corporation, after the expiration of thirty days from the death of such shareholder, to the husband, widow or next of kin of such deceased, upon presentation of a copy of the death certificate and the surrender of the pass book or certificate evidencing the shares, and such payment shall be a full discharge of all obligations of the corporation in respect to such shares.

LOANS AND INVESTMENTS.
Method of Loaning Funds.

Section 23. The funds accumulated, after due allowance for all necessary expenses and the payment of shares, may, at each stated monthly meeting, be loaned to qualified applicants at a rate of interest not less than five per cent per annum, payable in monthly instalments upon the amount loaned, except as otherwise provided in section twenty-eight.

Limitation of Loans.

Section 24. Any person whose application is accepted shall be entitled, upon giving proper security, to receive a real estate loan of not exceeding two hundred dollars for each unpledged share held by him, or a share loan within the limitations hereinafter provided.

Loans and Investment of Funds.

Section 25. The directors may invest funds in any of the securities named in the second clause of section fifty-four of chapter one hundred and sixty-eight, or in the stock or obligations of the Federal Home Loan Bank referred to in section fifty-six of this chapter, or of any successor of said bank, or may loan such funds upon first mortgages on real estate situated in this commonwealth or upon the shares of the corporation, subject to the provisions of sections twenty-six to twenty-nine, inclusive, at a rate fixed by the board of directors. The corporation may loan such funds to other co-operative banks, and may make loans to the holders of unpledged unmatured, matured and paid-up shares of other co-operative banks, on such terms and at such rate of interest as may be fixed by the board of directors.

Applications for Loans on Real Estate.

Section 26. No loan shall be made upon real estate unless a written application is made therefor, showing the date, name of applicant, amount of loan desired, description of property offered and other information deemed necessary. A written report thereon shall be made by at least two members of the security committee, signed by them, approving the security offered and certifying to the value of the property according to their best judgment. The application and report shall be filed and preserved with all other papers relating to the loan.

Loans on Real Estate.

Section 27. For every loan made upon real estate a note shall be given, accompanied by a transfer and pledge of the requisite number of shares standing in the name of the borrower, and secured by a mortgage of real estate situated in the commonwealth, the title to which is in the name of the borrower and which is unencumbered by any mortgage or lien other than municipal liens or such as may be held by the corporation making the loan. No loan upon one parcel of real estate shall exceed eight thousand dollars, and no loan shall exceed eighty per cent of the value of the mortgaged property, if improved real estate, nor more than fifty per cent of such value, if vacant land, as certified by the security committee. The shares so pledged shall be held by the corporation as collateral security for the performance of the conditions of the note and mortgage. The note and mortgage shall recite the number of shares and the series to which the shares belong and the amount of money advanced thereon, and shall be conditioned upon the payment at or before the stated meetings of the corporation of the monthly dues on said shares, and the interest upon the loan, with all fines on payments in arrears, until said shares reached their matured value or until said loan is otherwise cancelled and discharged. If the borrower fails to offer security satisfactory to the directors within the time prescribed by the by-laws, his right to the loan shall be forfeited and he may be charged with one month's interest at the determined rate, and with such part of the expenses incurred as may be determined by the board of directors; and the money appropriated for such loan may subsequently be reloaned.

Conversion of Loans on Real Estate.

Section 28. Whenever the full value of all shares originally and subsequently pledged to secure any loan on improved real estate made and secured as aforesaid, after deducting all fines and other charges legally incurred respecting said shares, shall equal or exceed twenty-five per cent of the original amount of the note evidencing such loan, but not earlier than four years after the date of said note, such loan may, at the option of the owner of such shares and with the approval of the directors, be converted into a demand or time loan bearing interest at a determined rate payable monthly or quarterly, and evidenced by a new note secured by a first mortgage in common form upon said real estate; provided, that upon application of the shareholder for such conversion, a report approving the security for such converted loan and a certification of the value of the real estate securing the same shall be made in the manner provided by section twenty-six for original co-operative bank loans, and that said loan when so converted will not exceed sixty per cent of the value of the real estate securing the same, as certified as aforesaid, and said shareholder shall subscribe for such number of shares in the current series and, until the discharge of such converted loan, shall hold such number of shares as the treasurer may determine.

In the event of the conversion as aforesaid of a co-operative bank mortgage into a common form mortgage, the full value of the shares pledged to secure the co-operative bank mortgage, after deducting all fines and any other charges legally incurred and such sum as will leave the unpaid balance a multiple of fifty dollars, shall be credited to the owner thereof, the co-operative bank mortgage discharged and the shares pledged to secure the same surrendered and cancelled.

No loan or mortgage shall so be converted as to render the total amount of such converted loans held by such corporation in excess of fifteen per cent of the aggregate amount of loans secured by mortgages of real estate held by such corporation. Every parcel of real estate mortgaged to secure a converted loan shall be revalued at intervals of not more than three years so long as it is so mortgaged, by at least two members of the security committee of the corporation, who shall certify in writing according to their best judgment the value of the real estate so mortgaged. Such reports shall be filed and preserved with the records of the corporation. If, at the time of any such revaluation, the amount outstanding on such a converted loan is in excess of sixty per cent of the value of the real estate mortgaged to secure the same, a reduction in the amount of such loan shall be required, as promptly as may be practicable, sufficient to bring its amount within sixty per cent of the said value; provided, that no such reduction shall be required prior to the maturity of the loan.

Loans on Shares.

Section 29. Loans may be made upon unmatured, matured or paid-up shares which are not already pledged, except as provided in section seventeen, to an amount not exceeding ninety per cent of their withdrawal value at the time of the loan, and for every such loan a note shall be given, accompanied by a transfer and pledge of the shares borrowed upon as collateral for the loan.

Loans upon shares held in the names of two or more persons, except fiduciaries and persons holding as tenants in common, may be made to one or more of the owners thereof, and a note signed by such owner or owners shall be deemed a valid pledge of the shares in said account and sufficient evidence of the debt created thereby, notwithstanding that said note is not signed by all or any other owner thereof.

No loans shall be made on shares held in trust unless power so to borrow is contained in the instrument creating the trust or given by a decree of the probate court having jurisdiction.

Interest Payments.

Section 30. A borrowing shareholder shall, in addition to the dues on his shares, pay interest monthly on his loan, at the determined rate, or as provided in section thirty-one, until his shares reach their matured value, or until the loan has been repaid. Interest may be computed from the date on which the money is advanced; and when the said matured value is reached, the shares shall be cancelled, the loan discharged, and the balance, if any, due upon the shares shall be paid to the member.

Agreement for Reduction of Interest.

Section 31. If at any time the board of directors, by a two thirds vote of all the directors, elect to reduce the rate of interest on any outstanding real estate loans, a new mortgage shall not be required, but a written agreement for the reduction of said rate of interest, signed by the borrowing shareholder and the treasurer of the bank, shall be valid and shall not otherwise affect or impair the existing mortgage, and thereafter the shareholder shall make the monthly payments on the loan in accordance with the terms of said agreement.

Repayment of Loans.

Section 32. A loan may be repaid by the owner or owners of the equity of redemption at any time, whereupon the account shall be charged with the full amount of the loan, all monthly instalments of interest and fines in arrears and any other legal charges. Credit shall be given for the withdrawal value of the shares pledged and transferred as security, the pass book shall be surrendered to the corporation, and the balance shall be received by the corporation in full satisfaction of said loan. In all settlements made between stated meetings for the receipt of money loan interest shall be charged as of the date of the stated meeting next succeeding such settlement. Such owner or owners desiring to retain his shares and membership must repay his loan without claiming credit for his shares.

Partial payment of loans shall be received in amounts of fifty dollars or a multiple thereof, or in such less amount as may be fixed by the by-laws. For each two hundred dollars so repaid upon a real estate loan, upon request of the shareholder one share of stock shall be released from pledge.

Reduction of Loans.

Section 33. With the approval of the board of directors, any shares pledged for a real estate loan may, at the request of the owner thereof, be cancelled, whereupon there shall be endorsed on the mortgage note as a credit upon the amount of the loan the full value of such shares, less all monthly instalments of interest and fines in arrears, unpaid taxes at the option of the directors, any other legal charges and such sum as will leave the amount of the loan a multiple of fifty dollars. Such cancellation and credit may be made even if the amount of the loan will not thereby be reduced as to principal. Thereupon new shares in the current series shall be issued to the shareholder in the proportion of one share to each two hundred dollars of the loan then remaining unpaid. The new shares issued shall be transferred and pledged to the bank as security for the amount of the loan remaining unpaid, and the fact thereof shall be endorsed upon or attached to the note in the following form:

, 19 .

The value of the shares herein pledged, less deductions authorized by section thirty-three of chapter one hundred and seventy of the General Laws, as amended, amounting to $, has this day been applied as a credit upon this note, leaving a balance due and unpaid of $, to secure which   shares of series   have been issued, and are hereby transferred and pledged.

For value received, I or we promise to pay to said corporation or its order   dollars at or before its monthly meeting on the   day of each month hereafter, being the amount of the monthly dues on the shares hereby substituted, and of the monthly interest upon said balance of $, together with all fines chargeable by the by-laws of said corporation upon arrears of such payments until said substituted shares shall reach maturity, or otherwise sooner pay to said corporation or its order the said balance of $, with interest and fines as aforesaid.

Witness,

(Signature)

Approved

Treasurer.

Neither the note evidencing the loan nor the mortgage securing the same shall be prejudiced by the application of the value and the change of shares, notwithstanding the fact that a provision for such application and change was not originally made in the note or mortgage, and both note and mortgage shall continue to be held by the bank as good and sufficient security for the balance remaining unpaid.

After the application of the value as a credit, the amount of the loan shall forthwith be reduced to an equal extent, and the owner shall thereafter be liable for only the reduced amount and any arrearages or penalties occasioned by his own default.

No action under this section shall affect the rights of the holder, other than the corporation granting the accommodation, of any mortgage recorded prior to June first, nineteen hundred and thirty-three, unless the written assent of such holder shall be obtained, nor shall any such action affect the rights of an original borrower whose note is dated prior to said date, unless his written assent shall be obtained.

Suspension of Payments.

Section 34. For the accommodation of any owner of shares pledged for a real estate loan who is actually engaged in the military or naval service of the United States, or who is the wife or a dependent member of the family of a person so engaged, or for the accommodation of any owner of shares so pledged who is otherwise temporarily unable to make payments to such a corporation on account of his loan because of unemployment or other emergency, the directors may cause to be endorsed on the mortgage note, as a credit upon the amount of the loan, the full value of the shares pledged to secure the same, less all monthly instalments of interest and fines in arrears, unpaid taxes at the option of the directors, any other legal charges and such sum as will leave the amount of the loan a multiple of fifty dollars, and thereupon such shares shall be cancelled and further payments and fines waived. Such credit and cancellation may be made even if the amount of the loan will not thereby be reduced as to principal. The amount of the loan remaining due as aforesaid shall be payable as provided in section thirty-five with interest payable monthly at the rate existing at the time of suspension and subject to such fine as may be prescribed by the by-laws of the corporation for default by shareholders in payment of interest and to foreclosure or other remedy provided by law, in case of default; provided, that the person seeking such accommodation, or any person in his behalf, shall sign a written request therefor, stating his reasons and agreeing in consideration thereof to abide fully by the terms of this section and section thirty-five and also all requirements of the directors, who shall be the sole judges of the necessity of the accommodation and the time when such accommodation shall be terminated; and provided, further, that no suspension of payments as aforesaid for any cause other than that the accommodated person is engaged in the military or naval service of the United States or is the wife or a dependent member of the family of a person so engaged shall extend for a period longer than two years.

Neither the note evidencing the loan nor the mortgage

securing the same shall be prejudiced by the application of
the value of the shares provided for in this section or the
pledging of new shares provided for in section thirty-five,
notwithstanding the fact that a provision for such application and pledging was not originally made in the note or
mortgage, and both note and mortgage shall continue to be
held by the corporation as good and sufficient security for
the balance remaining unpaid.

Resumption of Suspended Payments.

Section 35.   The person thus accommodated, or his successors in title, may at any time, and shall upon the request
of the directors at any time after the expiration of said
military or naval service or after the period of accommodation granted under section thirty-four for temporary inability to make the required payments has been terminated
as therein provided, or after the vesting in either case of the
mortgaged estate in a person other than the person accommodated, subscribe to and pledge as security for the balance due on the loan one new share in the current series
issued by the corporation for each two hundred dollars or
fraction thereof of said balance.   Failure to subscribe to
and pledge such shares, when so requested, or to make
payments thereon in accordance with law or the by-laws
of the corporation, shall render said balance immediately
due and payable, and payment thereof may be enforced
against the security by foreclosure proceedings or by any
other remedy provided by law for the collection of debts.
The fact of the pledging of new shares shall be endorsed
upon or attached to the note in the following form:

, 19 .

The value of the shares formerly pledged herein, less deductions authorized by section thirty-four of chapter one hundred
and seventy of the General Laws, as amended, amounting to
$, has been applied on the   day of
as a credit upon this note, leaving a balance due and unpaid of
$, to secure which   shares of series   have
been issued, and are hereby transferred and pledged.   For value
received, I or we promise to pay to said corporation or to its
order   dollars at or before its monthly meeting on the
          day of each month hereafter, being the amount of
the monthly dues on the shares hereby substituted, and of the
monthly interest upon said balance of $, together with all
fines chargeable by the by-laws of said corporation upon arrears
of such payments, until said substituted shares shall reach maturity, or otherwise sooner to pay to said corporation or its order
the said balance of $, with interest and fines as afore-
said.

Witness,

(Signature)

Approved

Treasurer.

No action under this section shall affect the rights of the
holder, other than the corporation granting the accommodation, of any mortgage recorded prior to June first, nine-

teen hundred and thirty-three, unless the written assent of
such holder shall be obtained, nor shall any such action
affect the rights of an original borrower whose note is dated
prior to said date, unless his written assent shall be obtained.

Recovery of Loan.

Section 36. If the owner of shares pledged for a real
estate loan is in arrears for dues, interest or fines for four
monthly payments or commits any breach of the conditions
of a mortgage, the directors may, after twenty-one days'
notice, mailed to the last known address of the shareholder,
declare the shares forfeited if the arrears then remain
unpaid, or such breach continues. The account of the
shareholder shall then be debited with the arrears of interest
and fines to the date of forfeiture, and the shares shall be
credited upon the loan at their withdrawal value. The
balance of the account shall immediately become due and
payable, and may, and after six months shall, be enforced
against the security, and be recovered, together with interest thereon, as all debts are recovered at law. If the shares
of a shareholder are in arrears at the maturity of the series,
his account shall be charged with the amount of the loan
and all arrears at the date of maturity, and shall be credited
with the value of the shares; the balance of the account
shall immediately become due and payable, and may, and
after six months shall, be enforced against the security, and
be recovered, together with interest thereon, as all debts
are recovered at law.

In the event of the transfer or pledge of shares in any
class to the corporation as collateral security for a loan, or
as collateral security for the performance of the conditions
of a mortgage, or if said shares held as collateral are sold or
forfeited for the non-performance of the conditions of said
loan, or if said mortgage is foreclosed for breach of the conditions thereof, the treasurer of the corporation shall have
full authority to transfer or assign all the shares pledged for
the purposes set forth in said pledge or mortgage to the corporation or purchaser at said sale or foreclosure.

Real Estate Acquired.   Common Form Mortgages.

Section 37. Any such corporation may purchase at
public or private sale real estate upon which it may have a
mortgage, judgment, lien or other encumbrance, or in
which it may have an interest, and may sell, convey or lease
the real estate acquired by it, and on the sale thereof may
take a mortgage thereon in common form or in co-operative
bank form, or mortgages in both forms, to secure the payment of the purchase price or a part thereof. All real estate
shall be sold within five years after the acquisition of title
thereto; but the commissioner may, on petition of the
security committee of the corporation and for cause, grant
additional time for the sale of the same.

Assignment of Loans to Insurance Companies.

Section 38. Any such corporation may insert in its form of real estate mortgage a clause providing that in case of any loss by fire on the mortgaged property in respect to which the fire insurance companies shall deny liability as to the insured, the corporation may at its option assign the debt and note for which the mortgage was given, and also the mortgage, to the insurance companies, upon payment to the corporation by such companies of the amount due upon the mortgage loan at the time of the fire, together with the unpaid interest, and fines, if any, accrued thereon at the date of the assignment, less the value of the forfeited shares as hereinafter provided, whereupon the note and mortgage shall forthwith become a note and mortgage for such total balance due, payable upon demand with interest semi-annually at the same rate as therein stated, the first payment of interest to be due six months after the date of the assignment, and any shares of the corporation pledged as security for the note and mortgage loan shall be forfeited by the corporation immediately before the execution and delivery to the insurance companies of such assignment, and the withdrawal value of shares so forfeited shall, at the time of the assignment, be credited as a part payment on said mortgage loan, the balance thereof being the balance of the loan due at the time of the assignment to the insurance companies as aforesaid. Any mortgage note taken under this section shall contain proper reference thereto.

Investment in Real Estate used as Place of Business.

Section 39. Any such corporation may, with the approval of the commissioner, invest a sum not exceeding its surplus and guaranty fund accounts in the purchase of a suitable site and the erection or preparation of a suitable building for the convenient transaction of its business, but in no case exceeding five per cent of its dues capital or one hundred thousand dollars. Any such corporation may, with the approval of the commissioner, expend a sum not exceeding one per cent of its dues capital for alterations in any building leased by it for the transaction of its business, but in no case exceeding its surplus and guaranty fund accounts.

May Borrow Money.

Section 40. Such corporation may by a vote of at least three fifths of all its directors, with the consent of the commissioner, borrow from any source to meet withdrawals and to make loans on shares of the corporation.

Such corporation may by a similar vote, with the consent of the commissioner, borrow from the Federal Home Loan Bank referred to in section fifty-six, to make real estate loans, the proceeds of which are to be used for the purpose of repairing or remodeling, to refinance existing mortgages,

for new home construction owned by or built for a bona fide
home owner occupant, and to make real estate loans on
homes already constructed and owned and occupied or to
be occupied by the borrower.

As security for a loan made under this section, the corporation may assign and pledge its real estate notes and
mortgages and any other securities.   Every such loan shall
constitute a debt which shall be satisfied, in case of liquidation of the affairs of the corporation, before any distribution
of its assets to its shareholders.

GENERAL PROVISIONS.

Fines.

Section 41.   A shareholder making default in the payment of his monthly dues and interest shall be charged such
a fine, not exceeding two per cent a month on each dollar in
arrears, as may be fixed by the by-laws, but in no case in
excess of the fine imposed on monthly payments six months
in arrears.   No fine shall be imposed upon a fine in arrears.

No shareholder whose shares are withdrawn, forfeited,
suspended or retired shall be charged with fines upon such
shares in excess of the profits distributed thereto, and if no
profits shall have been distributed to such shares, no fines
shall be charged thereon.   This section shall not prevent
the owner or owners from being charged with fines according
to law upon interest in arrears.

Transfer of Shares.   Fee.

Section 42.   Any such corporation may charge a fee for
the transfer of shares, not exceeding twenty-five cents.
Shares, whether matured, unmatured or paid-up, may be
transferred only on the books of the corporation, in such
manner as its by-laws may provide.

Bank or Officers not to take Certain Fees, etc.   Penalty.

Section 43.   No such corporation, and no person acting in
its behalf, shall ask for, take or receive a fee, brokerage, commission, gift or other consideration for or on account of a
loan made by or on behalf of such corporation, other than
appears on the face of the note or contract by which the
loan purports to be made; but this section shall not apply
to a reasonable charge for services in the examination of
property and titles, and for the preparation and recording
of conveyances to the corporation as security for its loans.
Whoever violates any provision of this section shall be
punished by a fine of not less than one hundred nor more
than one thousand dollars.

Distribution of Earnings.

Section 44.   The board of directors shall distribute to the
shares existing at the time of distribution the net profits,
less such an amount as is required by law to be transferred

to the guaranty fund, and less such an amount as may be transferred to the surplus under existing provisions of law. Such distribution shall be made annually, semi-annually or quarterly before the close of business on each day when a new series of shares is issued. Net profits shall be distributed to the various shares existing at the time of such distribution in proportion to their value at that time, and shall be computed upon the basis of a single share fully paid to the date of the distribution.

At each distribution of net profits on unmatured shares there shall also be distributed profits on outstanding matured and paid-up shares at a rate per cent fixed by the directors, not to exceed five per cent per annum, except as provided in section forty-six, but in no case to exceed the rate credited to unmatured shares. Net profits distributed on outstanding matured and paid-up shares shall be credited to the owner thereof and shall be payable on demand at any time thereafter, out of the funds of such corporation, and upon such profits not withdrawn no interest shall accrue or be distributed.

No profits shall be distributed to shareholders in excess of five per cent per annum, unless at such distribution period there shall have been reserved and credited to the guaranty fund the maximum per cent of the net profits under section forty-five, or so much thereof as is necessary to increase said fund to ten per cent of the total liabilities of the corporation. Subject to the provisions of the preceding sentence, there may be appropriated from the surplus account an amount sufficient to declare a dividend at a rate not in excess of that of the last preceding dividend, but the total of any such appropriations during any twelve months shall not exceed the amount credited to the surplus account during the same period.

The board of directors shall cause to be recorded in the minutes of its meeting the distribution of all profits and all amounts charged or credited to the guaranty fund or surplus.

Losses shall be charged to the guaranty fund or surplus immediately after their occurrence.

Guaranty Fund.

Section 45. At each distribution of profits the board of directors shall reserve as a guaranty fund not less than one nor more than five per cent of the net profits accrued since the last preceding adjustment, until such fund amounts to ten per cent of its total liabilities, and the fund shall thereafter be maintained and held, and shall at all times be available to meet losses in the business of the corporation from depreciation of its securities or otherwise. The board of directors may at any time, by vote duly recorded, transfer to the guaranty fund such part of the surplus account as they deem wise.

Surplus Account.

Section 46. At each distribution of profits not more than one per cent of the net profits accrued since the last preceding adjustment shall be credited to the surplus account, unless there shall have been reserved and credited to the guaranty fund the maximum per cent of the net profits under the preceding section. Any such corporation may hold in its surplus account such sum as the board of directors may, from time to time, deem wise; but whenever the guaranty fund and surplus account together exceed ten and one fourth per cent of its total liabilities, the board of directors shall declare an extra dividend, provided such dividend does not reduce the guaranty fund and surplus account together to less than ten per cent of the total liabilities.

Reserve Required.

Section 47. Every such corporation shall establish and at all times maintain, as a reserve to meet withdrawals of shares and applications for share loans, an amount equal to not less than three per cent of its total resources. Such reserve shall consist of any or all of the following: (*a*) cash on hand; (*b*) balances payable on demand due from any trust company incorporated in this commonwealth or national banking association having its principal place of business within this commonwealth; (*c*) bonds of the United States; (*d*) bonds and notes of this commonwealth or (*e*) deposits in The Co-operative Central Bank in accordance with chapter forty-five of the acts of nineteen hundred and thirty-two. If at any time the reserve of any such corporation falls below the amount herein required, such corporation shall not make any real estate loans, except additional loans and reloans upon property already mortgaged to such corporation, until such reserve shall have been fully restored.

General Accounts.

Section 48. The general accounts of every such corporation shall be kept by double entry, and the treasurer shall, at least monthly, make a trial balance of such accounts, to be recorded in a book provided for that purpose. All money received from each shareholder shall be received by persons designated by the directors, and entered in a pass book provided for the use of, and to be held by, the shareholder. The pass book shall be plainly marked with the name and address of the shareholder, the number of shares held by him and the number or designation and date of issue of each series or issue to which said shares, respectively, belong. All payments from the funds of every such corporation shall be made by the treasurer or such other officer or officers as the by-laws may provide, and the record of such payments shall show the date, name of payee, amount, purpose for which made, and the signature of the payee acknowledging receipt of the funds.

Annual Reports.

Section 49. Every such corporation shall annually, within thirty days after its regular meeting day for the receipt of moneys in October, make to the commissioner, in such form as he prescribes, a report, signed and sworn to by the treasurer of the corporation, showing accurately the condition thereof at close of business on that day. The president and three or more directors shall certify and make oath that the report is correct, according to their best knowledge and belief. If a report is defective or appears to be erroneous, the commissioner shall notify the corporation to amend the same within fifteen days. A corporation neglecting to make the report required by this section on or before the time named therein, or to amend the same within fifteen days, if notified by the commissioner to do so, shall forfeit five dollars for each day during which such neglect continues.

Consolidation of Banks.

Section 50. At any time prior to June first, nineteen hundred and thirty-five, any two or more such corporations may consolidate into a single corporation, upon such terms as shall have been agreed upon by vote of two thirds of the board of directors of each corporation and as shall have been approved in writing by the commissioner, provided such action is approved at a special meeting of the shareholders of each corporation called for that purpose, by a vote of at least two thirds of those shareholders present, qualified to vote, and voting. Notice of such special meeting, setting forth the terms agreed upon, shall be sent by the clerk of each corporation to each shareholder thereof by mail, postage prepaid, at least thirty days before the date of the meeting. Notice of the meeting shall also be advertised three times in one or more newspapers published in each town in which the main office of any of said corporations is situated, and if there be no such newspaper, then in a newspaper published in the county where the town is situated, the last publication to be at least one day before the meeting. A certificate under the hands of the presidents and clerks of all such corporations, setting forth that each of said corporations has complied with all the requirements of this section, shall be submitted to the commissioner, who, if he shall approve such consolidation, shall endorse his approval upon such certificate, and thereupon such consolidation shall become effective. Upon consolidation of any such corporation with another, as herein provided:

(1) The corporate existence of all but one of the consolidating corporations shall be discontinued and consolidated into that of the remaining corporation, which shall continue. All and singular the rights, privileges and fran-

chises of each discontinuing corporation and its right, title
and interest to all property of whatever kind, whether real,
personal or mixed, and things in action, and every right,
privilege, interest or asset of conceivable value or benefit
then existing which would inure to it under an unconsoli-
dated existence, shall be deemed fully and finally, and without any right of reversion, transferred to or vested in the
continuing corporation, without further act or deed, and
such continuing corporation shall have and hold the same
in its own right as fully as the same was possessed and held
by the discontinuing corporation from which it was, by
operation of the provisions hereof, transferred.

(2) A discontinuing corporation's rights, obligations and
relations to any person, member, creditor, trustee or beneficiary of any trust, as of the effective date of the consolidation, shall remain unimpaired, and the continuing corporation shall, by the consolidation, succeed to all such relations,
obligations and liabilities, as though it had itself assumed
the relation or incurred the obligation or liability; and its
liabilities and obligations to creditors existing for any cause
whatsoever shall not be impaired by the consolidation; nor
shall any obligation or liability of any member in any such
corporation, continuing or discontinuing, which is party to
the consolidation, be affected by any such consolidation,
but such obligations and liabilities shall continue as fully
and to the same extent as the same existed before the
consolidation.

(3) A pending action or other judicial proceeding to
which any of the consolidating corporations is a party shall
not be deemed to have abated or to have discontinued by
reason of the consolidation, but may be prosecuted to final
judgment, order or decree in the same manner as if the consolidation had not been made; or the continuing corporation may be substituted as a party to any such action or
proceeding to which the discontinuing corporation was a
party, and any judgment, order or decree may be rendered
for or against the continuing corporation that might have
been rendered for or against such discontinuing corporation
if consolidation had not occurred.

(4) After such consolidation, a foreclosure of a mortgage
begun by any of the discontinuing corporations may be
completed by the continuing corporation, and publication
begun by the discontinuing corporation may be continued
in the name of the discontinuing corporation. Any certificate of possession, affidavit of sale or foreclosure deed relative to such foreclosure shall be executed by the proper
officers in behalf of whichever of such corporations actually
took possession or made the sale, but any such instrument
executed in behalf of the continuing corporation shall recite that it is the successor of the discontinuing corporation
which commenced the foreclosure.

A new name, or the name of any of the consolidating corporations may be adopted as the name of the continuing

corporation at the special meetings called as herein provided, and it shall become the name of the continuing corporation upon the approval of the consolidation, without further action under the laws of the commonwealth as to change or adoption of a new name on the part of the continuing corporation.

The commissioner shall determine the value of the shares in each discontinuing corporation, after agreement between the directors of the consolidating corporations.

Reduction of Liability.

Section 51. Whenever it has been determined, upon investigation by the commissioner, that the losses of any co-operative bank resulting from a depreciation in the value of its assets or otherwise, exceed its guaranty fund and surplus accounts, so that the estimated value of its assets is less than the total amount due to shareholders, he may order a suspension of dividends or a reduction of its liability to its shareholders in such manner as to distribute the loss equitably among the shareholders. If, thereafter, such a bank shall realize from such assets a greater amount than was fixed in the order of reduction, such assets shall be divided among the then remaining shareholders whose credits were so reduced, but to the extent of such reduction only and any balance of said excess remaining shall be transferred to the surplus account.

Set-off or Recoupment of Shares.

Section 52. In the event that legal proceedings have been commenced to restrain such corporation from doing its actual business, or if the commissioner has taken possession of the corporation as provided in section twenty-two of chapter one hundred and sixty-seven, or if such corporation has commenced to dissolve voluntarily as provided by law, a person or persons, in any capacity authorized to hold shares, indebted to such a corporation for a real estate or other debt, may have set off, at their withdrawal value, less any amount paid by the bank to discharge any default in the terms and conditions of said mortgage, the shares pledged to secure the same, and during the pendency thereof, the rights of the persons entitled to such set-offs shall be determined as of the time of the commencement of such proceeding, and shall exist whether the indebtedness is t en due or payable, or becomes due and payable at a later date.

Shares shall not be so set off or recouped by any such person unless held and owned by him on the date of the commencement of such proceedings, or of possession so taken.

Powers and Duties of Commissioner of Banks.

Section 53. The commissioner shall have the same duties and powers in respect to every such corporation which he has in respect to savings banks. In the examination of every co-operative bank inquiry shall be made as to the nature and resources of the corporation in general, the methods of conducting and managing its affairs, the actions of its officers, the investment of its funds, and whether the administration of its affairs is in compliance with its by-laws and with statutory requirements. At each visitation, a thorough examination and audit shall be made of the books, securities, cash, assets, liabilities, income and expenditures, including a trial balance of the shareholders' ledgers, for the period elapsed since the preceding examination. The person in charge of the examination shall render to the commissioner a report of his findings, in such form as the commissioner prescribes, and a copy thereof shall be rendered to the board of directors within ten days after the original has been submitted to the commissioner, together with a notice of the amount of the fee to be paid as provided in the following section, which shall be due and payable within thirty days after the date of the notice. Upon the failure of any such corporation to pay the required fee within the time prescribed herein, the commissioner shall report the facts to the attorney general, who shall immediately bring an action to recover the fee. The commissioner shall annually make a report to the general court of such facts and statements relative to such corporations, and in such form, as he considers that the public interest requires. The officers of every such corporation shall answer truly all inquiries made, and shall make all returns required, by the commissioner.

Fees for Examination and Audit.

Section 54. To defray the expenses of the examination and audit provided for by the preceding section, every such corporation so examined and audited shall, upon notice from the commissioner, pay to him as a fee therefor the actual cost of such examination and audit, not including any portion of the overhead expense of the division of banks and loan agencies. Immediately after the close of the fiscal year of the commonwealth, that part of the overhead expense of the division which shall be determined by the commissioner to be attributable to the supervision of such corporations shall be assessed upon and paid by each such corporation in the proportion that its total assets bear to the aggregate total assets of all co-operative banks as shown by their annual reports at the close of business on their respective regular meeting days for the receipt of money in October; provided, that an assessment upon any such corporation, together with the fee payable as aforesaid for the actual cost of its examination and audit, shall not exceed twenty cents per one thousand dollars of assets as shown by its statement of condition on the date of such examination and audit. For the purpose of this section, traveling and hotel expense shall be included in the overhead expense of the aforesaid division.

May become Members of Certain Leagues.

Section 55. Any such corporation may, by vote of a majority of its directors, become a member of a league or leagues organized for the purpose of protecting and promoting the interests of co-operative banks, and may pay to such league or leagues its proportionate share of the expenses thereof, together with such contribution to the purposes of the league or leagues as may, in the opinion of the directors of such corporation, be reasonable and necessary.

May become Member of Federal Home Loan Bank.

Section 56. Any corporation subject to this chapter may become a member of the Federal Home Loan Bank established for the district of New England under the provisions of an act of congress, approved July twenty-second, nineteen hundred and thirty-two, and known as the federal home loan bank act, or of any successor of said bank so established; and may, subject otherwise to the provisions of this chapter, subscribe to and invest in such amounts of the stock of said home loan bank as may be required by said act of congress to qualify such corporation for membership in said home loan bank.

Co-operative Banking to be Done only under this Chapter. Exception. Penalty.

Section 57. No person and no association or corporation, except as provided in section fifty-eight, shall transact in this commonwealth the business of accumulating the savings of its members and loaning to them such accumulations in the manner of a co-operative bank, unless incorporated in this commonwealth for such purpose. Whoever violates any provision of this section shall be punished by a fine of not more than one thousand dollars, and the supreme judicial or the superior court shall have jurisdiction in equity to enforce this section.

Foreign Corporations.

Section 58. This chapter shall not prevent a corporation organized under the laws of any other state for the purpose of accumulating the savings of its members and loaning to them such accumulations in the manner of a co-operative bank, substantially as provided in this chapter, from loaning money upon mortgages of real estate located within this commonwealth.   *Approved April 27, 1933.*

An Act revising certain provisions of law relative to cancellation of motor vehicle liability policies and bonds.   *Chap.*145

Be it enacted, etc., as follows:

Section 1. Section one hundred and thirteen A of chapter one hundred and seventy-five of the General Laws, as most recently amended by section one of chapter one hun-   G. L. (Ter. Ed.), 175, § 113A, etc., amended.

dred and nineteen of the acts of the current year, is hereby further amended by striking out the provision therein numbered (2) and inserting in place thereof the following: —

Compulsory motor vehicle liability policies, contents.

(2) That, except as otherwise provided in provision (2) A and in section one hundred and thirteen D, no cancellation of the policy, whether by the company or by the insured, shall be valid unless written notice thereof is given by the

Cancellation.

party proposing cancellation to the other party and to the registrar of motor vehicles in such form as the department of public works may prescribe, at least fifteen days in each case prior to the intended effective date thereof, which date shall be expressed in said notice, and that notice of cancellation sent by the company to the insured, by registered mail, postage prepaid, with a return receipt of the addressee requested, addressed to him at his residence or business address stated in the policy shall be a sufficient notice and that an affidavit of any officer, agent or employee of the company, duly authorized for the purpose, that he has so sent such notice addressed as aforesaid shall be prima facie evidence of the sending thereof as aforesaid; together with a provision that, in the event of a cancellation by the insured, he shall, if he has paid the premium on the policy to the company, or to its agent who issued the policy, or to the duly licensed insurance broker, if any, by whom the policy was negotiated, be entitled to receive a return premium after deducting the customary monthly short rates for the time the policy shall have been in force, or in the event of cancellation by the company, the insured shall, if he has paid the premium as aforesaid, be entitled to receive a return premium calculated on a pro rata basis; provided, that if the insured after the sending of a notice of cancellation by the company, which is also duly filed with the registrar of motor vehicles, or after giving such a notice to the company and the said registrar, files a new certificate under section thirty-four H of chapter ninety prior to the intended effective date of such cancellation, the filing of said certificate shall operate to terminate the policy on the date of said filing, and the return premium, if any, payable to the insured shall be computed as of the date of said filing, instead of the intended effective date of cancellation expressed in the notice thereof; and provided further, that if the final effective date of a cancellation by the company is fixed by an order of the board of appeal on motor vehicle liability policies and bonds or of the superior court, or a justice thereof, as provided in section one hundred and thirteen D, the return premium, if any, payable to the insured shall be computed as of such final effective date.

G. L. (Ter. Ed.), 175, § 113A, etc., amended.

SECTION 2. Said section one hundred and thirteen A, as so amended, is hereby further amended by inserting after provision numbered (2), the following new provision: —

Compulsory motor vehicle liability policy, termination of.

(2) A. That the policy shall terminate upon a sale or transfer by the owner thereof of the motor vehicle or trailer covered thereby, or upon his surrender to the registrar of motor

vehicles of the registration plates issued to him by said
registrar under chapter ninety with a written statement, in
such form as the said registrar may require, that they are
surrendered to cancel the registration of such motor vehicle
or trailer and the policy, and that upon a termination of the
policy as aforesaid, the insured shall, if he has paid the
premium on the policy as provided in provision (2), be entitled to receive a return premium computed as in the case
of a cancellation of the policy by the insured under said
provision (2).

SECTION 3. The provisions of this act shall not apply to
motor vehicle liability policies and bonds, both as defined in
section thirty-four A of chapter ninety of the General Laws,
issued or executed in connection with the registration of
motor vehicles or trailers for operation during the current
year or any part thereof.   *Approved April 27, 1933.*

Act not to
apply to certain
policies, etc.,
during current
year.

AN ACT RELATIVE TO CERTAIN ORDERS OF THE BOARD OF
APPEAL ON MOTOR VEHICLE LIABILITY POLICIES AND
BONDS AND DECREES OF THE SUPERIOR COURT ON APPEAL
THEREFROM.

*Chap.*146

Be it enacted, etc., as follows:

SECTION 1. Section one hundred and thirteen D of
chapter one hundred and seventy-five of the General Laws,
as most recently amended by sections two and three of chapter one hundred and nineteen of the acts of the current year,
is hereby further amended by striking out the fourth paragraph and inserting in place thereof the following: — A
complaint may allege that a cancellation is invalid, or improper and unreasonable, or both, or that a refusal to issue
or execute such a policy or bond is improper and unreasonable. The board shall after due hearing forthwith make a
finding in respect to the issue or issues raised by the complaint, and it may also, in any case, make a finding as to
whether or not the complainant is a proper and suitable person to whom to issue such a policy or on behalf of whom to
execute such a bond as surety. The board shall in all cases
enter, in such form as it may prescribe, an appropriate order.
If the board finds in favor of the company in the case of
such a cancellation, the order shall, unless the policy or
bond has expired, affirm the cancellation and specify the
date, which shall be ten days from the date of the filing of a
memorandum of the finding and order in the office of the
commissioner as hereinafter provided, on which the cancellation shall be effective; but, if the policy or bond will
expire on or before the termination of a period of ten days
from said date of filing, the order shall specify a date prior
to such expiration, or the board may dispense with such a
specification.

SECTION 2. Said section one hundred and thirteen D,
as so amended, is hereby further amended by striking out

G. L. (Ter.
Ed.), 175,
§ 113D, etc.,
amended.

Compulsory
motor vehicle
liability
policies.
Hearings be-
fore board of
appeal.

G. L. (Ter.
Ed.), 175,
§ 113D, etc.,
amended.

Appeals to
court on pro-
ceedings on
complaints
relative to
cancellations
or refusal of
companies to
issue policies.

the sixth paragraph and inserting in place thereof the following: — Any person or company aggrieved by any finding or order of the board, other than a finding that the complainant is or is not a suitable and proper person to whom to issue such a policy or on behalf of whom to execute such a bond as surety, may, within ten days after the filing of the memorandum thereof in the office of the commissioner, unless the policy or bond has expired or will expire prior to the expiration of said period, and any person or company aggrieved by any finding of the board that a complainant is or is not a suitable and proper person as aforesaid may, in any case, within said period, appeal therefrom to the superior court or any justice thereof, in any county. The appellant shall file with his appeal a duly certified copy of the complaint and of the finding and order thereon, and, if the appeal is taken from a finding and order of the board in respect to a cancellation, the clerk of the court shall forthwith upon the filing of such an appeal, give written notice of the filing thereof to said registrar. The court or justice shall, after such notice to the parties as it or he deems reasonable, give a summary hearing on such appeal and shall have jurisdiction in equity to review all questions of fact and law, and to affirm or reverse such finding or order and may make any appropriate decree. The court or justice may allow such complaint, finding or order to be amended. The decision of the court or justice shall be final. If the court or justice finds in favor of the company in the case of such a cancellation, the decree shall, unless the policy or bond has expired, affirm the cancellation and specify a date not earlier than five days from the entry thereof, on which the cancellation shall become effective; but, if the policy or bond will expire on or before the termination of a period of five days from such entry, the decree shall specify a date prior to such expiration, or the court or justice may dispense with such a specification. The clerk shall, within two days after the entry thereof, send an attested copy of the decree to each of the parties and the commissioner and, in the case of a decree rendered upon an appeal in respect to the cancellation of such a policy or bond, to said registrar, or his office. The court or justice may make such order as to costs as it or he deems equitable. The superior court may make reasonable rules to secure prompt hearings on such appeals and a speedy disposition thereof.

Act not to
apply during
current year to
certain motor
vehicles.

SECTION 3. The provisions of this act shall not apply with respect to motor vehicle liability policies or bonds, both as defined in section thirty-four A of chapter ninety of the General Laws, as appearing in the Tercentenary Edition thereof, issued or executed in connection with the registration of motor vehicles or trailers under said chapter for operation during any part of the current year.

Approved April 27, 1933.

An Act providing for notice of appeals to the county commissioners from refusals to abate betterment assessments.

Chap.147

Be it enacted, etc., as follows:

Chapter eighty of the General Laws is hereby amended by striking out section ten, as appearing in the Tercentenary Edition thereof, and inserting in place thereof the following: — *Section 10.* A person who is aggrieved by the refusal of a board of officers of a city, town or district to abate an assessment may, instead of pursuing the remedy provided by section seven, appeal within the time limited therein to the county commissioners of the county in which the land assessed is situated. The person so appealing shall, within ten days after the filing of said appeal, give written notice thereof to such city, town or district. Such notice may be given by mailing a copy of the appeal by registered mail, postage prepaid, to the board which made the assessment or to the clerk of such city, town or district. The county commissioners shall hear the parties, and shall have the same powers and duties with respect to the abatement of such assessment as the board by which it was assessed, and may make an order as to costs. The decision of the county commissioners shall be final.

Approved April 27, 1933.

G. L. (Ter. Ed.), 80, § 10, amended.

Appeals to county commissioners from refusal to abate betterment assessments.

An Act dissolving certain corporations.

Chap.148

Whereas, It is necessary that certain delinquent and other corporations be dissolved in the current year, therefore this act is hereby declared to be an emergency law, necessary for the immediate preservation of the public convenience.

Emergency preamble.

Be it enacted, etc., as follows:

SECTION 1. Such of the following named corporations as are not already legally dissolved are hereby dissolved, subject to the provisions of sections fifty-one, fifty-two and fifty-six of chapter one hundred and fifty-five of the General Laws: —

Certain corporations dissolved.

A. A. Phillips Company, A. Altshuler Mdsg. Co., Inc., A & G Grocery Company, Inc., The, A & V Auto Repair Shop, Inc., A. Bartington, Inc., A. Bon Marche of New Bedford, Inc., A. Burlingame Company, A. C. Fisher Co., A. C. Purrington & Co. Inc., A. Deschenes Company, A. Eastwood Co., A. F. Powers Company, A. J. Raymond Co., A. L. Braley, Incorporated, A. L. Fink Inc., A. L. Liquidating Company, A. L. Wells, Inc., A. L. White & Company, Inc., A. P. Soucy Inc., A. S. Manzi, Inc., A. T. Corporation, A. W. Peterson and Company, Incorporated, Academy Garage and Service Station, Inc., Ace Advertising Service, Inc., Ace Shoe Co., The, Acme Bottling Company, Inc., Acme Drug & Chemical Co., Acme Manufacturing Co.,

Inc., Acme Storage Warehouse Co., Activity Frocks, Inc., Acushnet Mills Corporation, Adams, Blake & Bonney, Inc., Adams House, Limited, The, Adell Mfg. Co., Inc., The, Adhesive Products Company, Adrian VanLeeuwen, Inc., Advance Fibre Process Company, Advisory Committee on Advertising, Inc., Aetna Realty Company, Affiliated Stores, Inc., The, Agawam Amusement Corporation, Ajax Golf Game Company, Inc., Aker Lumber Company, The, Al. A. Rosenbush Company, Alabam, Inc., The, Albert E. Knudsen, Inc., Albert Neckwear Company, Albert Your Hairdresser, Inc., Albion Florist, Inc., Alcra Corporation, Aldis Owen Hall Foundation - - University & College of Liberal Arts, Incorporated, Alfred Self & Co. Inc., Alfred T. Pitman Co., Inc., Algonquin Leather Company, Alhambra Theatre Co., All In One Soap Company, Inc., Allen & Allen, Inc., Allen & Woodworth Company, Allied Business Builders, Inc., Allied Construction Co., Inc., Allied Specialty Leather Co., Allston Plumbing Co., Inc., Allston Public Market, Inc., Alton Realty Co., Inc., Alvita Food Products Inc., American Agricultural Chemical Company of Massachusetts, The, American Banner & Novelty Co., American Battery and Equipment Co., American Brick Company, American Coal Company, American Electrical Company, American Fireside League, Incorporated, American Fish Machinery Company, American International Engineering Associates Incorporated, American Motor Equipment Company, American Motors, Incorporated, American Pastry Products Corporation, American Realty Corporation, American Rug Mills, Inc., American Sailplane Company, American Sapphire Blue Swine Registry Inc., American Steel Boat Corporation, Amesbury Building Corporation, The, Anderson & Caskin Co. Inc., Anderson and Nelson Company, Anderson Cadillac LaSalle Company, Andover Homes Inc., Andren-Myerson Co., Anmuth & Gilbert, Inc., Ansel Fineberg Company, Apex Co-operative Tailors & Cleansers Association, Apple Tree Diners, Inc., Appleton Pharmacy, Inc., Aqua Rubber Company, Archdeacon & Sullivan, Inc., Arlington Amusement Company, Arlington Market, Inc., Arlington Motor Corporation, Arlington National Corporation, Arlington Street Garage Inc., Arlington Yellow Cab Company, Arnold's Inc., Arthur F. Hickey Shoe Co. Inc., Arthur's Incorporated, Artistic Metal Letter Co., Asbestos Textile Company, The, Aspinwall Apartments, Inc., Aspirin Seltzer Corporation, Associated Orchestra Service, Inc., Associated Sales Company, Associated Theatres, Inc., Assured's Insurance Adjustment Bureau, Inc., Astor Lunch Company, Athens News Store Inc., Atherton Corporation, Atlantic Cement Products Corporation, Atlantic Finance Corporation, Atlantic Herring Co., Atlantic Malt Co., Inc., Atlantic Markets, Incorporated, Atlantic Pressed Steel Company, Inc., Atlas Suit Case Company, Inc., Attleboro Amusement Co., Attleboro Paint & Hardware Co. Inc., Auburndale Conservatories, Inc., Austin St. Garage Inc.,

Austin-Sutherland Lumber Co., Inc., The, Auto-Hydro- Certain corporations dissolved.
Craft, Inc., Auto List Publishing Co., Auto-Manual Shut-
Off Incorporated, Auto Owners Service Association, Inc.,
Auto Tire Exchange Inc., Automatic Floor Waxing Ma-
chine Corporation, Automatic Stoker Corporation, Auto-
mobile Service Company, Automotive Consulting Service
Corp., Avon Amusement Company Inc.

B. A. Cook & Company Incorporated, B. A. Dargo Co.,
B & B Sandwich Shoppe, Inc., B. & S. Shoe, Inc., B.-G. and
S. Company, B. H. Lippin Co. Incorporated, B. S. Canner
Co., Babcock Realty Corporation, Bacheller-Bean Com-
pany, Baer Yorra Shoe Company, Bain-Roberts Company,
Baker Market Co., Inc., Bancroft Woolen Yarn Company,
Bank and Office Equipment Engineers, Inc., Barbecue Inn,
Inc., Bargain Bazaar, Inc., The, Barger Furniture Co.,
Barney's Lunch Inc., Barnstable County Motors, Inc., Bar-
rett Builders' Supply Company, Inc., Barry's Garage Inc.,
Barton Shoe Co., Inc., Baskin & Kessler, Incorporated,
Batchelder Manufacturing Company, Bates Brothers Com-
pany, Battery Containers, Incorporated, Bay Grove Motor
Company, Bay State Amusement Co., Inc., Bay State De-
velopment Corporation, Bay State Engraving Company,
Inc., Bay State Florist Supply Co., Bay State Flying Serv-
ice, Inc., Bay State Insulating & Refrigerating Co., Inc.,
Bay State Insurance Agency Corporation, Bay State
Premium Company, Bay State Wiping Materials, Inc., Bay
State Woolen Waste Company, Beacon Body Company,
Beacon Cafeteria, Inc., Beacon Fast Freight Corporation,
Beacon Hill Taxi Corporation, Beautiful Novelty Shop, Inc.,
The, Beaver Construction Company, Beck Hall, Inc.,
Becker Fur Importers, Inc., Begeka Company, Belle Vue
Mills, Belmarsh Drug Co., The, Belmont Builders Supply
Co. Inc., Belmont Motor Mart, Inc., Belvidere Manage-
ment Corporation, Bemis Heater, Incorporated, Ben C.
Goulston Shoe Company, Ben Rosenblum, Inc., Bent and
Bush Company, The, Berger Textile Products Co., Berkeley
Associates, Inc., Berkeley Clothes, Inc., Berkshire Electric
Company, Berkshire Farmers Exchange, Inc., Berkshire
Mercantile Agency, Inc., Berkshire Mercantile of Green-
field, Inc., Berkshire Mercantile of Holyoke, Inc., Berkshire
Mercantile of Pittsfield, Inc., Berkshire Mercantile of
Worcester, Inc., Berkshire Vinegar Company, Berle Prod-
ucts Company, The, Berman-Haskell Shoe and Leather
Company, Bernard's Inc., Bernner & Co. Inc., Berry's Golf
Club Inc., Betty Louise Book Shops Corporation, Big Store,
Inc., The, Big Three Sportwear Company, Billy's Dew Drop
Inn, Inc., Bilt-Rite Oil Burner Inc., Blackstone Produce,
Inc., Blackstone-Sussman Company, Blake Process Ma-
chine Company, Inc., Blanchard Linotype School Inc.,
Bland's Auto Exchange Inc., Bleyle's, Inc., Bloomberg
Bros. Co., Bloomfield & Betten Company, Inc., Blotner
Realty Company, Blount Engineering Company, Blue
Cross Sanitary Process Company, Blue Plate, Inc., The,

Blue Ribbon Lunch, Inc., Bluebeard's Castle Inc., Bluebell, Inc., The, Board Realty Co., Bobby's Dress Shops Inc., Bogen & Tenenbaum, Inc., Bon Ton Furniture Co., Inc., Boothby Company, Bostock Shoe Co. Inc., Boston and New York Transportation Co., Inc., Boston Auto Fabrics Company, Boston Auto Top Co., Boston Beef & Provision Company, Boston Branch Grocery, Inc., Boston Cafeteria Inc., Boston Chair Co. Inc., Boston Chocolate Co., Boston Cornice & Metal Works, Inc., Boston Flour Company, Inc., Boston Gear Works Sales Co., Boston Linotypers' Supply Company, Incorporated, Boston Match Company, Boston Metallic Bed Company, Inc., Boston Mortgage Bond Company, Boston Office Furniture Exchange, Incorporated, Boston Realty Corporation, Boston Retail Drygoods Co., Inc., Boston Sellers Kitchens, Inc., Boston Stores News, Inc., Boston Transit Mixers Inc., Boston Tye Form Company Inc., Boston Utilities Company, Inc., Boston Vapor Heating Co., Bosworth & Beal Inc., Bosworth Mills, Inc., The, Boulevard Hotel Caterers Inc., Bourne Market Co. Inc., Bourne Natural Gas Co., Brackett Heel Company, Brad Swift, Incorporated, Bradford Hat Company, The, Bradken Corporation, Bradley, MacRae Co. Inc., Bradley Stuc-O-Tint Company, Inc., Breen Publicity Service, Inc., Briar Dale Farm, Inc., Bridge-Golf Company, Brighton Investment Co. Inc., Briscoe Corporation, Bristol Amusement Co., Bristol County Sales Company, Bristol Furniture Company, Inc., Bristol Manufacturing Corporation, Bristol Real Estate Corp., Bristol Spa, Inc., Broadmore Restaurant, Inc., The, Broadway Indoor Golf Course Inc., Broadway Plumbing & Heating Co., Inc., Broadway Vulcanizing and Tire Co., Inc., Brookford Grocery, Inc., Brookline Avenue Indoor Golf Course, Inc., Brookline Development Company, Brookline Electric Co., Brookline Importing Company, Brooklyn Ash Removal Company of Massachusetts, Brophy Counter Company, Brouillet Products, Inc., Browning-Drake Radio Corporation, Brunswick-Balke-Collender Company of Massachusetts, The, Bryant G. Smith & Sons Company, Bryce & Company, Inc., Buckman Tanning Company, Buerkel-Gaston, Inc., Bur-Beck Sales Co., Burgess Construction Company, Burns Fecht Bicknell Co., Burr & Gillen Motor Co. Inc., Burton & Rogers Manufacturing Company, Burton H. Wiggin Company, Butler Hill Company, Inc., Buyers' Service Weekly Inc., Buzzell's Inc. of Lynn, Buzzell's of New England Inc., Byrnes Motor Co.

C. A. Boyce & Co. Inc., C. A. Phillips Co., Inc., C. & E. Motor Transportation Co. Inc., C & F Corporation, C. & V. Electrical Co., C. & W. Hudson Essex Sales Inc., C. B. Gummo Incorporated, C. B. Reed & Company, Inc., C. B. Roberts Engineering Company, C. G. Gilman Wagon Co., C. H. Graves & Sons Inc., C. M. Neily Co., C. Malaguti Bakery, Inc., C. Wesley Fraser, Inc., Caldwell & Atwood Rubber Products, Inc., California Shows, Inc.,

Callahan-Faunce Corporation, Cambridge Masons Supply
Company, Camp Tekoa, Inc:, Canton Theatre Company,
Cap Realty Co. Inc., Cape Cod Cleaners Inc., Cape Cod
Country Club, Inc., Cape Cod Investment Company, Cape
Cod Oyster Farms Co., Cape Cod Police Protective Asso-
ciation, Inc., Cape Cod Properties Inc., Cape Cod Publish-
ing Company, The, Cape Cod Sand & Cement Co., Cape
Inc., Capital Acceptance and Mortgage Corporation, Capi-
tal Garage Company Inc., Capitol Amusement Co. of Law-
rence, Inc., Capitol Pharmaceuticals, Inc., Cardarelli &
Holmes, Inc., Carl G. Peschel & Son, Inc., Carlisle-Ayer
Company, Carlmace Company, Carolina Engineering Con-
struction Company, Carolina Plantation, Inc., Cartwright
& Hurley, Inc., Cecil M. Pelton, Inc., Cellilli & Rock, Inc.,
Center Baking Company Inc., Center Market, Inc., Central
Autogenous Welding and Manufacturing Company, Central
Cafe, Inc., Central Hotels Corporation, The, Central Light
& Power Company, Central Tombar Golf Course, Inc.,
Central Warehouse & Distributing Corporation of New
England, Centre Building Corporation, Centurion, Inc.,
Century Motors of New Bedford, Inc., Chamber of Com-
merce Dining Rooms, Inc., Champion Garment Co.,
Chandler and Farquhar Company, Chandler Manufactur-
ing Company, Change-Over Heel Company, Chapel Mills
Manufacturing Company, Charles A. Baldwin Company,
Chas. E. Howe Co., Chas. E. Howe Insurance Inc., Charles
Hall, Incorporated, Charles J. Murphy Company, Charles
M. Bestick Incorporated, Charles Q. Sherman, Inc., Charles
S. Wigglesworth Incorporated, Charles V. Daiger Company,
Inc., Charles Wing Company, The, Charlton Printing Com-
pany, Chase & Bowen, Inc., Chase Auto Supply, Inc.,
Chase Disc Camera Corporation, Chase Sales & Service Inc.,
Chatfield Manufacturing Corporation, The, Chatham
Phenix Corporation of Massachusetts, Chauncy-Bedford
Buildings, Incorporated, Chaves Shoe Company, Cheer-
ful Chat, Inc., Chelsea Distributing Corporation, Chemical
& Dye Corporation of New England, Cheshire Cider
& Vinegar Company, Chester I. Campbell Organization
Inc., The, Chestnut Hill Avenue Apartments, Inc., The,
Chicopee Falls Stock Company, Chicopee Realty Trust,
Inc., Chicopee Transportation Company, Inc., Chilten
Restaurant, Inc., Chiswick Pharmacy, Inc., Christy's, Inc.,
Cigamat Company of New England, Cities Engineering
Company, Citrus Juice Company, City Cleansers & Dyers,
Inc., City Service Hotels Corporation, City Title Com-
pany, Claire Mae Shoppe Inc., Clean-Art Laundry Com-
pany, Clean Town Inc., Clearfield Fuel and Ice Company,
Inc., Clemence Company, Clement Realty Corp., Clemson
Knife Company, Clothes Shop, Inc., The, Coal Carburetor
Sales Co. of Worcester, Coal Carburetor Sales of Lowell,
Inc., Coca Cola Bottling Corporation, Cochrane Company,
The, Codman Square Auto Renting Co. Inc., Cogan Furni-
ture, Inc., Collier Gas Heating Corporation, Colonial Cab

Company, Colonial Curtain Company, Colonial Holding
Corp., Colonial Inc., Colonial Marble & Tile Co., Colonial
Marble Company, Inc., Colonial Meat Market, Inc.,
Colonial Sandwich Shoppe Inc., Colonial Shoe Co., Inc.,
Colony Food Stores Associates of New England, Incor-
porated, Colpak Dress Corporation, Colrain Manufactur-
ing Company, Columbia Chevrolet, Inc., Columbia Fuel
Oil Corporation, Columbia Shoe Co., Inc., Columbia Wood
Heel Co., Columbus Garage, Inc., Columbus Press, Inc.,
Columbus Realty Corporation, Combo Manufacturing
Company, Commercial Finance Corporation, Commercial
Laundry Company, Commercial Wool Stock Co., Commer-
cial Writing Service, Inc., Commonwealth Apartments Co.,
Commonwealth Avenue Pharmacy Inc., Commonwealth
Company, The, Commonwealth Contracting Co. Inc.,
Commonwealth Drug & Chemical Co., Commonwealth
Golf Courses, Inc., Commonwealth Mortgage & Loan Co.,
Inc., Commonwealth Motor Sales Co., Inc., Common-
wealth Thread Company, Inc., Community Garage, Inc.,
Community Newspapers, Incorporated, Community Serv-
ice Corporation, Conee Ornamental Iron Works, Inc., Con-
necting Rod & Armature Exchange, Inc., Connor Auto-
motive Service, Inc., Consolidated Airways, Inc., The, Con-
solidated Ice & Fuel Dealers Association Inc., Consolidated
Manufacturing Company, Consolidated Mortgage and
Investment Corporation, Consolidated Radio Inc., Con-
struction & Realty Corporation, Consumers' Supply
Company, Continental Worsted Mills, Inc., Conz-Brault
Company, Cooley Brothers Company, The, Coolidge Cor-
ner Realty Co. Inc., Coolidge Piano Company, Coolidge
Realty Co. Inc., Cooper & Brush Cotton Co., Co-operative
Trading Co., Inc., Copley Players Inc., Copley Producing
Company, Inc., The, Cordis Mills, Corey Hill Golf Club,
Inc., Cornhill Cigar Manufacturing Company, Inc., Corn-
hill Corporation, Cortex Company, Cosmic Corporation,
Cosmic Foods Inc., Cotter & Moran Inc., Cotton & Gould,
Inc., Country Craft Dress Company, Countryside Spas Inc.,
County Construction Co., Inc., Court Clothing Company,
Coward Auto Supply Company, Cradock Finance, Incor-
porated, Crane's Inc., Craneway Diaphram Co., Inc.,
Creative Reading, Inc., Credit Protective Bureau Inc.,
Creditors Protective League of New England, Inc., Creed-
Kellogg Company, The, Crescent Tanning Company, Crim-
son Delicatessen, Inc., Crispy Baking Company, Inc., The,
Crocker Garage Company, Cross and Roberts, Inc., Cross
Motor Co., Crystal Merchandising Corporation, Inc.,
Crystal Spring Bleaching and Dyeing Company, Cumber-
land Oil Company, Cundari Construction Company, Cur-
tain-Craft Co., Inc., The, Curtain Shop, Inc., The, Curtis &
Swift Inc., Cut Price Auto Supply Company of New
Bedford.

D. & D. Clothing Co. Inc., D. B. Wesson, Inc., D. Eddy
and Sons Company, D. F. Sullivan, Inc., D. H. Craig Com-

pany Incorporated, D. J. Khoury & Company, Inc., D. L. Page, Inc., The, D. M. Dillon Steam Boiler Works, D. R. Emerson Company, Dacey and Tibbetts, Inc., Dairymaid Creameries, Inc., Dalton-Jackson Black Fox Company, Daly's Golden Rule Shoe Co., Daly's Golden Rule Shoe, Inc., Dame and Sons, Inc., Dane Machine Company, Incorporated, Daniel Finberg & Son, Inc., Darling Holding Corporation, David, Berman Company, Incorporated, David S. Sher, Incorporated, David Siegel, Solomon I. Fein, Hyman Schwartz, Associated Dentists, Inc., David Weinstein, Inc., David's Inc. of Brockton, Davis Bros., Inc., The, Davis Ice Cream Company, De Dutch Amusement, Inc., De Haven Attractions, Incorporated, DeLuxe Dining Car Co., DeMott Estates, Incorporated, Deacon & Son, Inc., Dealers Construction Company of Boston, Incorporated, Deci Realty and Investment Corporation, Dedham Motor Mart, Inc., Delmark Shoe Company, Dependable Fuel Company, Desiccated Foods of Florida, Inc., Devonshire Corporation, The, Devonshire Securities Corporation, Diamond Brothers, Inc., Diamond Laboratories Inc., Dillon Boat Works, Inc., Direct Sales & Finance Co., Distributors --Incorporated, Diverse Investments Trust, Inc., Dodge Brothers, Inc., Dodson Plumbing Co. Inc., Doherty & Stickney Steam and Sprinkler Corporation, Dome Realty Co., Donn D. Sargent Co., Inc., Donnelly Valve Sales Corporation, Dorchester Knight & Whippet Corporation, Dover Process Label & Printing Co., Dover Smoker Lunch, Inc. (1931), Dow Leather Finish Co., Downes Motor Co. Inc., Drake Lunch Company, Drake's Cafeteria, Inc., Drucker School, Inc., The, Dry Stencil Sales Corporation, Duchesse Salted Nut Company, Dudley Bootery, Inc., Dudley Wood Works Co., DunWhit Bowling Greens, Inc., Duraflex Company of New England Inc., The.

E. A. Allen Company, E. and A. M. Fullerton Inc., E. C. Atwater Company, E. Dedham Street Stables, Inc., E. F. Dakin Company, The, E. G. Higgins Co., E. J. Leland Company, The, E. L. Fitzhenry Company, E. M. Low Company, E. P. Boggs Company, E. R. Nash Leather Company, Incorporated, E. Swenson & Son, Inc., Eager Transportation Co., Eager's Commercial Garage, Inc., Eagle Motor Freight Service, Inc., Eagle Motor Tours, Inc., Eagleston Shop, Inc., Earl Ward Company, The, East Boston & Lynn Finance Corporation, East Boston Lumber Company, East Braintree Drug Co., Inc., East Coast Hotel Company, East India Kip Corp., Eastern Amusement Company, Eastern Automotive Products Company, Eastern Fabrics Corp., Eastern Flour Mills, Inc., Eastern Holding & Developing Co. Inc., Eastern Motors Corporation, Eastern Novelty Company, Inc., Eastern Realty Corporation of Worcester, Eastern Service Marine Company, Eastern Service Refrigerator Company, Eastern States Aircraft Corporation, Eastern Tire and Rubber Co. Inc., The, Economy Hat Works Incorporated, Edmund L. Reddy Plumbing Co.,

Certain corporations dissolved.

Inc., Educational Arts Building Incorporated, The, Edward F. Miner Building Company, Edward Wilson Inc., Edwin Clapp Stores of Detroit, Inc., The, Edwin S. Parker Co., Elaclaire, Inc., Electric Boat Company of Massachusetts, Electric Chain Company of Massachusetts, Electric Investors Inc., Electric Machine and Instrument Company, Electric Rug Washing Co., Electrical Household Utilities, Inc., Electrical Manufacturing Corporation, Electro-Heat Corporation, Electro Weld Company, The, Electrolight Manufacturing Company, 1140 Commonwealth Avenue Inc., Elgin Shoe Company, Elias Howe Company, Eliot Mills, Inc., Eliot Realty Company, Elliott-Lindabury Corporation, Elmwood Pharmacy, Inc., Embassy Market Co., Emergency Pumping Co., Empire Fashion Shop Inc., Empire Spice Co., Empire Woolen Co., Inc., Engel-Cone Shoe Company, Engineering Sales Corporation, Enwright Lunch Corporation, Epstein-Douglas Co. Inc., Equitable Commercial Company, The, Essex County Realty Co., Inc., Essex Rug Company, Eteenpäin Co-operative Society, European Securities Corporation, Evans Construction Company, Evans Friction Cone Company, Even-Wear Shoe Co., Everett Ice Cream Company.

F. A. Gallagher, Inc., F. A. Nichols Chair Company, F. & W. Realty Trust, Inc., F. D. Rankins Co., Inc., F. E. Nelson Company, F. H. Van Blarcom, Inc., F. I. Rabidou Iron Co., F. J. Van Etten Company, F. M. Fielder Corporation, The, F. S. Brightman Company, F. V. Chaney, Inc., F. W. Hampshire Corporation, F. W. Montgomery, Inc., F. X. Horan, Inc., Faburnat Realty Corp., Factory Exchange, Inc., The, Fair Sex Shoe Company, Inc., Fairburn-Piper Motor Car Company, Inc., Fall River Dye Works, Inc., Fall River Tube Company, Famous Shoe Shops Inc., Farber Shoe Company, Inc., Fashion Millinery Co., Inc., Fashion Shoe Co., Inc., Faunce & Spinney, Incorporated, Federal Clothing Company, Federal Hardware and Supply Co., Federal Lunch, Inc., Federal Realty Company, Federal Soda Fountain Co., Fein Brothers, Inc., Fellows Box Company, Fenway Laundry Co., Ferguson Company, Fibre Corporation, The, Fibreboard Company, Fidelity Discount Corporation, Fields Corner Sales Company, Fifield-Robbins Company, Incorporated, Fifth Oakland Syndicate, Incorporated, Financial Service Plan, Inc., Fine's Fashion Shop, Inc., Finn's Labor Agency, Inc., Fire Prevention Bureau Inc., The, First Mortgage Investment Corporation, First National Chain Filling Stations, Inc., First National Clothiers Inc., First National Insurance Agency, Inc., First National Parlor Furniture Co., Inc., First National Underwriting Corporation of New England, Fischer & Loomis, Inc., Fisher Florist Corporation, Fisher, Inc., Fisheries Equipment Corporation, Fisher's, Inc., Fitchburg Foundry Company, Fitchburg Mfg. Co., Fitchburg Motor Dispatch, Inc., Fitchburg Motor Mart, Inc., Fitchburg Needlecraft Co., Fitzsimmons Leather Corp., Flagg Chemical Corporation, Fleming Machine Company, Flex-or-crete Incorpo- rated, Flint Drug Company, Inc., Florida Pasco Land Company, Florida Syndicate, Incorporated, The, Flower Growers Exchange, Inc., Foldit Corporation, The, Foley & Donovan, Inc., Foley Company, The, Folger Hotel Corporation, The, Follett & Kinney Machine Co. Inc., Forbes and Murray, Inc., Foster Dry Goods Co., Inc., Foster's, Inc., Four Hundred Eighty Boylston Street, Inc., Four Seas Company, The, Foursome Amusement Corporation, Fowler Oil Co., Inc., Foxcroft Realty Corporation, Framingham Construction & Supply Co., Framingham Duntile Company, Inc., Framingham Wood Heel Co., Inc., Frank Costa Company, Frank Ford Company, Frank Losordo Co., Inc., Frank Pratt Tire Company, Inc., Franklin Automatic Heating Inc., Franklin Co-operative Farmers' Ass'n, Franklin Engineering Company, Franklin Field Motor Mart, Inc., Franklin Kane Company, Franklin Leather Co., Franklin Newton Motor Co., Franklin Park Theatre, Inc., Franklin Supply Company, Inc., Franklin Theatre Corporation, Fraser Company, The, Fred M. Foley Company, Freddie's System of Bakeries, Inc., Freefuel Sales Company of Mass., Freeley Bros. Inc., Freeman Motors, Inc. (1930), French Motor Trucking Co., Friendly Merchants Association, Inc., Fritsystem, Inc., The, Frost Boston & Providence Despatch, Inc., Frostonian Sales Company, Fuller Brook Farm, Incorporated, Fuller Furniture Company, Fuller Motor Sales Company, Fullmore Garage, Inc., Furbush & Company, Incorporated.

G & R Investment Company, G. F. H. Corporation, The, G. H. Mansfield & Co., Inc., G. H. T. Brown & Company Incorporated, G. L. Grant, Inc., G. M. Smith Optical Company, G. P. & R. E. Hatch Co., G. P. Wilman Company, G. S. Inc., G. W. Dobbins Company Inc., G. W. J. Murphy Company, Gaffney Sales Corporation, The, Gallozzi & Company, Inc., Gallup Tire Company Inc., Garden City Taxi Company, Garden Furniture Company, Gardner Flying Club, Incorporated, Gardner Furniture Company, The, Gardner General Foundry, Inc., Gardner Loan Association, Inc., Gardner Motor Car Company, Gardner Shoe Co., Inc., Gas Equipment Corporation, Gaynor's Lunch, Inc., General Bankers Corporation, General Fibre Corporation, General Heating Equipment Company, General Investment Company, General Lacquer Corporation, General Management Corporation, General Manufacturing Corporation, General Reed & Rattan Company, Inc., General Shoe Findings Company, Inc., The, General Sports, Inc., General Spray Painting Company, The, General Television Corporation, Geo. A. Fletcher & Co. Inc., George Baker & Sons, Inc., George C. Torngren, Incorporated, George D. Baker Company, George E. Soar Company, George H. Carter Company, George H. Loud & Sons, Inc., George Howard and Sons Company, George Liberman Barber Supply Co., Inc., George Nelson Brown, Incorporated, George

P. Cox Last Company, George W. Harvey Company, George W. Nixon, Inc., George W. O'Brien Inc., George W. Thompson Co., Georgetown Shoe Company, Gerard Inns, Inc., Gershaw Hardware Co., Inc., Ginsberg Junk Company, Inc., Glatky Furniture Company, Incorporated, Glenn's Spa, Inc., Globe Phone M'f'g. Co., Glover & Company, Inc., Glue Liquidation Corporation, Gnome Recreation Laboratories, Inc., Goetting Realty Company, Golden Costume Company, Goldman and Waite Incorporated, Goldsmith Shoe Company, Golson Shoe Company, Goodenough and Mayo Company, Goodnow Shoe Company, The, Gown Shop, Inc., The, Graceful Frocks, Inc., Graham & Cameron, Inc., Granite Block Waiting Room Inc., Granite City Construction Corp., Grant & Company, Inc., Great Northern Finance and Investment Corporation, Green Dry Goods Company, Green Mountain Ranch & Stores Co., Green River Malt Co. of Mass., Green Rooms, Incorporated, The, Greenfield Home Development Company, Greenfield Petroleum Company, Inc., Greenlay Construction Co. Inc., Gregoire Laboratory & Drug Company, The, Grey's Incorporated, Grossman's Inc., Guy-Lawrence Construction Co., Guy P. Hale Company, Inc.

H. C. Folger Company, H. E. Holbrook Company (1911), H. E. Smith & Son, Inc., H. H. Sullivan, Inc., H. M. Kinports Company, H. N. Desmarais Company, H. S. Connor, Inc., H. S. White Hardware Co. Inc., H. T. Lindsay Co., Inc., H. T. West Company, H. W. Bassett, Inc., H. W. Doane Co., H. W. Northridge Co., Inc., H. W. Sperry, Inc., H. W. Thomas Furniture Company, Haines Square Pharmacy, Inc., Halfer Marbleizing Company, The, Hall Paint & Hardware Company, Hall Projector Company, Inc., Hall Troy Company, Hambly's Specialty Co., Hamilton Perkins Co., Hamlin Securities Corporation, Hampden Upholstering Works, Inc., Hancock Realty Corp., Handy Chair & Table Co., Handy Lunch Inc. of West Springfield, Hanscom Hardware Co., Harlans Company, The, Harney Shoe Co., Harold Clothing Company, Harper Conservatory of Music, Inc., Harper XL Products Corporation, Harris Theatre Corporation, Harrison Supply Company, Inc., Harry Cohen & Sons, Inc., Harry Katz Company, Harry Raymond, Inc., Harry's Lunch Company, Harry's Men's Shop, Inc., Harrysaul Bedding Co., Inc., Hart Leonard Co. Inc., Hartley Clock Company, Hartmann Bros. Leather Co., Hartwell Export Corporation, Harvard Drive-Yourself, Inc., Harvard Golf Course Company, Incorporated, Harwich Sporting Club Inc., Harwin Corporation, Haseltine & Company, Incorporated, Haskell Motor Company, Hastings Creek Dredge Company, Hatters Hat Box Co. Inc., Hawley Folsom Company, Health Disk Company of America, Health Products Corporation of America, Hearns Pharmacy Incorporated, Heating, Engineering & Manufacturing Company, Helios Battery Co. Inc., Henry James & Son, Inc., Henry L. Kincaide & Co., Inc., Henry, The Hatter, Inc., Henry

Thomas Company, Inc., Herbert C. Veno Co., Hiawatha
Hotel, Inc., Hibbard Electric Company, Highland Grocery,
Inc., Hill Lumber Company, Hillcrest Development Co.,
Hillsboro Camp, Inc., Hillside Coffee Shoppe, Inc., Hilma
Shoppe, Inc., The, Hirschen Furniture Company, Inc.,
Hitchcock Furniture Company, The, Hitchings-Stephens
Corporation, Hobart and Farrell Company, Hodges & Need-
ham Company, Incorporated, Holders, Incorporated, Hol-
land Laundry, Inc., The, Holland Market, Inc., Holland
Tulip Bulb Farms Co., Holland's Far East Tea, Coffee and
Cocoa Company, Hollis Street Theatre Corporation, Holly-
wood Inn of Boston, Inc., Holmes, Luce Company, Holyoke
Surgical Hospital, Inc., Home Builders Counselors, Inc.,
The, Home Builders' Supply Company, Home Sales Com-
pany, Hooper Printing Company, Hoover's Highland
Garage, Inc., Horace S. Lowell, Incorporated, Horté Lab-
oratories, Inc. (1928), Horté Laboratories, Inc., The (1930),
Horton Corporation, Hotel and Inn Co. of Pemberton,
Hotel DeWitt Company, Hotel Paramount Company, Inc.,
Houghton & Dutton Company, Howard Investment Co.,
Hoyt Wood Heel Corp., Hub Construction Co., The, Hub
Dry Goods Co., Hub Haberdashers, Inc., The, Hub Lamp
Manufacturing Company, Hub Moulding Co., Hub Pro-
vision Company, Inc., The, Hudnut Company, The, Hud-
son Theatre Inc., Hunt Stone-Tile Co., Hyde Engineering
Company, Hyde Park Alleys, Inc., Hydro Sales Company
Inc., Hytex Dresses, Inc.

I. Ligham Co., Inc., I. Millman, Inc., I. Wolper Com-
pany, Iceberg Manufacturing Co., Ideal Dresses, Inc., Ideal
Furniture Company, Improved Cushion Shoe Co., Improved Specialties Company, Independent Bottling Company, Inc., Independent Junk Company, Independent
Laundry, Inc., Indian Lake Driving Club, Industrial Appraisal Company, Industrial Associates, Inc., Industrial
Counsellors, Inc., Industrial Engineering Group, Inc.,
Industrial Manufacturing Co., Industrial Pipe and Supply
Co., Initial Electric & Manufacturing Co., Inman Square
Amusement Company, Institute of Current Literature Incorporated, Insurance Underwriters, Inc., Internal Combustion Atomizers Company, International Commerce Corporation, International Metal Products Company, International Shoe Polish, Inc., International Truck Corpora-
tion of Worcester, The, Investment Trust of North America
Incorporated, Invisible Window Screen Inc., Ipswich Baking Company, Incorporated, Iroquois, Inc., The, Irving J.
Lyon Company, Isaac Prouty & Co. Incorporated, Isabella
Silver Black Fox Ranches, Incorporated, It, Inc., Italian
Groceries Corporation, Italian Union Co-Operative Association of Mansfield, Incorporated.

J. A. Boyer Company, J. A. Moran Co. Inc., J. A. Parker,
Inc., J. B. Simas Company, The, J. D. Daley Company,
J. E. Farnsworth Co., Inc., J. Farrell & Co., Inc., J. Heslor
& Co. Inc., J. I. Williams Book Company, J. J. Moore, Inc.,

Certain
corporations
dissolved.
J. L. Bertsch Company, J. Lipsitz Company, J. M. Archambault Shoe Co., J. M. Devlin Co. Inc., J. Margolis, Inc., J. Murray Walker & Company, Inc., J. Roy Hiltz, Inc., J. T. Warder & Co., Inc., J. W. Moulton & Son, Inc., J. W. Stone & Co. Inc., Jack Spratt, Inc., Jack Stone Auto Company, Inc., Jackson and Chapman Inc., Jackson Realty Corporation, Jackson Shoe Company, Jamaica Publishing Company, James Barrett Manufacturing Company, James C. Williams Extract Company, James J. Shannon Co., James L. Donovan, Inc., James R. Cooper Company, Inc., James Wilkins, Inc., Jannini's Chemical Co. Inc., Jaze Inc., Jeanne, Inc., Jeremiah Williams & Company, Inc., Jinny Ricky Laboratories, Inc., Joanne Dress Shoppe, Inc., John A. Sheehan, Inc., John Adam Dagyr, Inc., John Alden, Inc., John E. Agnew and Son Company, John E. Swanson, Inc., John F. Gould Co., Inc., John F. Meldon Co., John J. Boland Co., Inc., John J. Grothe Company Inc., John J. Ryan Shoe Company, John Livor, Inc., John P. Manos Incorporated, John Richardson Company, John Shaw & Co., Inc., John T. Kilcourse Company, John V. Wilson Co., John Venezia Company, John W. Bartlett Co., Inc., Johnson-Meloy, Incorporated, Jones & Hewitt Optical Co. Inc., Jones & Polson, Inc., Jones-Dexter Corporation, Joseph Blatt, Inc., Joseph Ladies' Hairdresser Inc., Joseph Ryack Coat Front Co. Inc., Josiah Pearce & Sons, Inc., Jud's Motor Transportation Co., Inc., Just Right Hardwood Golf Tee Company.

K-M Express Company, Inc., K. R. Charlton Inc., Kaden Bros., Inc., Kakas Bros., Inc., Kalo Paper Company, Inc., Kane Co., The, Kapo Products Company, Inc., Katharine Gibbs School, Inc. (1917), Keith C. Brown & Co., Inc., Kel-Bur Products Company, Incorporated, The, Keldox Metals, Inc., Kelly and Jones Co., The, Kendall Print, Inc., The, Kenmore Da-Nite Golf, Inc., Kennedy Engineering Co., Kennedy Marine Basin, Inc., Kenney's Bakery & Delicatessen Company, Keramic Tile & Marble Works, Inc., Keystone Engineering Corporation, Kilby Realty Company, Kilby Street Corporation, Kildew of New England, Inc., Killory-Moriarty Shoe Co., Kimball Orchards, Inc., Kimber-Marling, Inc., King Philip Mills, Kingsley's, Inc., Kingston Realty Co. Inc., Kirk & Klesper, Inc., Kirkley's, Inc., Kirstein Tanning Co., Klaff, Inc., Klauer Bros. Inc., Knickerbocker Music Co., Knollwood Inc., Kollen's Delicatessen and Bakery, Incorporated, Korola Company, Kringle Company.

L. & K. Mfg. Co., Inc., L. & L. Department Stores, Inc., L. & M. Motor Sales Company, L. F. Abbott Company, The, L. Kaplan Co., Inc., L. M. Brock & Co., Inc., L. V. B. Tension Company, L. W. Anthony Co., La Due-Mann Inc., LaMode Company, La Salle Cleansers and Dyers, Inc., Labor Construction Corporation of America, Ladew-Jones Co., Lafayette Corporation, Lafayette Ice Company, Lafayette Shoe Co., Lake Erie-Anakin Company of New

England, Lake Quinsigamond Amusement Company, Lake Realty Corporation, Lake Shore Amusement Co., Inc., Lakewood Construction Company, Laminated Materials Company, Lancaster Mills, Landers and Hall, Inc., Landlords' Inn Company (1927), Landlords' Inn Company, Inc. (1929), Lane & Frost, Inc., Lane Tube Corporation, Langer-Lippman Shoe Co., The, Langley-Wharton Co., Inc., Lansing Sales Company, Laskey-Lesley Co., Lavacote, Incorporated, Lawrence Braiding Machine Co., Inc., Lawrence Credit Service Collection Exchange, Inc., Lea Gordon & Company, Inc., Lead Mine Ice Company, Leatherbee Company, Legal Collection Guarantee Association, Inc., Lenox Cabin Inc., Lenox Visiting Nurse Association, Inc., Leo Kabatznick, Inc., Leominister Glass and Mirror Corporation, Leominster Oil Burner Corporation, Leominster Steam Laundry Company, Incorporated, Leonard and Hamilton Foundry Company, Levaggi's, Inc., Lewis A. Crossett Company, Lexington Gardens, Inc., Lexington Hardware and Supply Company, Lincoln Hill Poultry Farm, Inc., Lincoln Street Realty Co., Lincolnsfield Mills Incorporated, Lindsay, Inc., Linehan Corset Company, Linscott-Tyler-Wilson Company, Lithuanian Importing Company, Little Dorothy Dresses, Inc., Litvack Shoe Co., Locatelli-Sullivan Company, Lock-Em-All Mfg. Co., Locomobile Company of Massachusetts, Inc., Loeffler's Victoria Garage, Inc., Lomac Company, The, London Fashion Clothiers, Ltd., Longwood Towers Corporation, Loring Coes & Co. Incorporated, Lorraine Analytical Service, Incorporated, Lothian Court Apartments, Inc., Lougee-Swanson Inc., Louie's Tea and Candy, Inc., Louis B. Schiller Co., Louis Goldberg Co., Louis S. Silvey, Inc., Louise B. Van Everen, Inc., Lowell Amusement Company, Lowell Miniature Golf Company, Inc., The, Lowell Plastering Company, Lowell Radio Company, Ludden's Paint Store, Inc., Luigi, Inc., Lumen, Incorporated, Lumsden Brothers Company, Lunt-Jillson Co., The, Lunt-Moss Corporation, Lyman Snow, Inc., Lynn Baseball Club Inc., Lynn Beach Garage, Inc., Lynn-Franklin Company, Lynn Lace and Braid Company, Lyons Electric Refrigerator Company, Lyons Haberdashery, Inc., Lyonwood, Inc., Lysander Kemp & Sons Corporation.

M. Barry Shoe Co. Inc., M. Croman & Co., Inc., M. F. Cahill Co., M. Gannino, Inc., M. H. Corash Co., Inc., M. H. Loonie Construction Co., Inc., M. J. Lynch, Inc., M. J. Taylor and Company, Inc., M. L. Howard Piano Company, M. L. Quinn Incorporated, M. Mishel & Co., Inc., M. S. L. Clothing Company, M. Zaff Bag and Burlap Company, MacDonald and Blank, Inc., MacGown Gown Shop, Inc., MacRobert Shoe Co., Mac-Val Inc., Mac Work ·Clothes, Inc., Macallister Co. Inc., Macdonald & Sons Inc., Macdonald, Goss Company, Inc., Mack Electric Corporation, Madden & Somerset Co., Madden Pharmacy, Inc., Magann's Garage, Inc., Magazine & Book Corporation, The, Magnus Drug Co., Main Hardware & Furniture Company, Main Realty Corporation, Majestic Hotel Company, Malcolm Shoe Corp., Malden Auditorium Company, Malden Bedding Co., Inc., Malden Holding Company, Malden Products Company, Malden Times Publishing Co., Malloy Lunch Inc., Manchester Ice Company, Manhattan Food Stores Company, Mann Brothers Company, Mann Novelty Co., Inc., Many-Use Oil Corporation, The, Maple Wood Heel Company, Marine Engine & Repair Inc., Marine Steam Motors Corporation, Marshall Bakeries, Inc., Marston's Hash Co., Inc., Martha's, Inc., Martha's Vineyard Nash, Inc., Mason Auto Service Inc., Mass-Bay Corporation, Massachusetts Air Ferries, Inc., Massachusetts Bay Company, Massachusetts Incorporation Company, Massachusetts Land Company, Massachusetts Lumber & Box Company, Massod Manufacturing Company, Inc., Mathews Candy Company Inc., Mattapan Delivery Company, Inc., May Boston Oil Burner Corporation, Mayfair Manor, Incorporated, Mayfair Products Company, Mayfair Realty Co., Inc., Mayflower, Inc., The, Mayflower Laundries, Inc., The, Mayflower Meat Market Inc., Mayflower Publishers, Inc., The, Mayflower Rubber Works Company, Maynard Drug Company, The, Maynard Equipment Company, Inc., Mayo Corporation, The, Maywood Realty Company, Mazze-Sharff, Incorporated, McAdams Auto Supply Co., Inc., McBride's Union Market, Inc., McConnel Motors, Inc., McGilvray Inc., McGrath Tag Stringer Company, McHeffey Express Company, McIntire-Sawyer Glass Co. Inc., McKee-Dodge Employment Corporation, McLaughlin & Company, Inc., McMichael, & Co., Inc., McNally Building Company, Mead-Carter-Gifford Corporation, Meade Rubber Sales Company, Mechanical Leather Specialties Mfg. Co., Medical Products Sales Company, Melba Shoe Co., Meleney Ventilating Company, The, Melrose Miniature Golf Inc., Melrose Motor Sales Incorporated, Mercantile Investment Corp., Merchants & Manufacturers Finance Company, Merchants Guardian Company, Inc., Merchants' Motor Lines Inc., Merchants Publishing Company, Incorporated, Merit Shoe Co. of Lynn, Factory B, Merrimac Construction Company Inc., Merrimack Hosiery, Inc., Merrimack Wood Heel Company, Inc., Messenger & Fox, Inc., Metropolitan Amusement Agency, Inc., Metropolitan Camp Goods Company, Metropolitan Garment Company, Metropolitan Sand & Gravel Company, Inc., Mica Mines Corporation, Middlesex Cash Market, Inc., Middlesex Garage of Boston, Incorporated, Middlesex Knitting Company, Mignon Candy and Restaurant Inc., Miller Bros. Pickle Co., Miller Trolley Shoe Company, Miller's Cafeteria Inc., Miller's Dye House, Inc., Millett Corporation, Millett-Woodbury Company, Milliken Molded Products Co., Milton Construction and Engineering Corporation, Milton Shoe Company, Miniature Heel Machine Company, Minit Foods of Massachusetts, Inc., Minot Fisheries Inc., Miss Holland, Incorporated,

Miss Sullivan, Inc., Missouri-Kansas Farms Company, Mittineague Coal Company, The, Model Comb Company, Model Novelty Corporation, Model Shoe Company, Inc., Model Shoe Stores, Inc., Modern Shoe Co. Inc. of Haverhill, Mohawk Confectionery Company, Inc., The, Mohawk Motor Company, Morandi-Proctor Company, Morris & Company, S. A., Incorporated, Morris Dress Co. Inc., Morris Katz, Incorporated, Morry Rogers, Inc., Morse Hardware Company, Inc., Morse, of Lynn, Inc., Mortgage and Equity Investment Company, The, Mortgage-Certificate Trust Inc., The, Mortgage Guaranty Company, Morton Drug Company, Morton Furniture Co., Morton Hardware Company, Inc., Morton Kosher Meat Market, Inc., Morton Theatre, Inc., Morton Trucks Inc., Motor Equipment Company of Milford, Motor Mart Garage Corporation, Mount Auburn Motor Mart, Inc., Mount Holyoke Spring Water Company, Mountain Mill Company, Mrs. Sherburne, Inc., Muddy Pond Cranberry Company, Municipal Producers of Holyoke, Inc., Munmohani, Inc., Murphy Express Company, Murray, Slade and Kent Company, Murray's Inc., Mutual Finance Corporation, Mutual Industrial Service of Cambridge, Inc., Mutual State, Inc., Mydans-Curley, Inc., Mystic Jewelry Company, Inc., Mystic Knitting Company, Inc., Mystic Mica Company.

N & H Department Store Inc., N. E. Miniature Golf, Inc., N. V. A. Smoker Lunch, Inc., N. Ward Company, Inc., Nantucket Motor Sales Co., Narroweave, Inc., Nash Sales Corp., Nash's Inc., Nashua Shoe Manufacturing Co., Nason Construction Co., Inc., Nathan Goldsmith, Inc., Natick Tag & Label Corporation, Nation Wide Publicity Corporation, National All-Teed Golf Corporation, National Brake Service Incorporated of N. E., National Electrical Instrument Company, National High Pressure Hose Co., National Moving Company, Inc., National Printers Supply Company, National Real Estate Bureau, Inc., National Sales Corporation, National Seaseald Fillets, Inc., National Shoe Co. of Haverhill, National Transportation Co., National Upholstered Furniture Co., Natrado, Incorporated, Needham Miniature Golf Club, Inc., Neff and Morse, Incorporated, Nehi Bottling Co., Inc., Nelson D. White & Sons, Inc., Nelson Motor Company, Nelson, Russell Inc., Nepsco, Incorporated, Neptron Corporation, Nestlé's Milk Products, Inc., Netherland Butter and Egg Company, Netoco North Attleboro Theatre, Inc., Neverbreak Heel Manufacturing Co., New Acme Plating Co., New Bedford Spinning Company, New Bedford Tom Thumb Golf Course, Inc., New City Hotel Company, New Energy Manufacturing Company, New England Broadcasting System Incorporated, New England Catalin Company, New England Consolidated Corporation, New England Construction Company, The, New England Diners Inc., New England Engineering Corporation, New England Express Exchange, Inc., New England Machine Exchange, Inc., New England Maintenance

Certain corporations dissolved.

Company, Inc., New England Minerals, Inc., New England
Paper Company, Inc., New England Picture Departments,
Inc., New England Power Construction Company, New
England Public Relations, Inc., New England Rags & Junk
Company, New England Realty Company, New England
Rock Excavating Company, New England Sail Plane Com-
pany, New England Specialties Combustion Co., New Eng-
land Traders Association, Inc., New England Trans-At-
lantic Line Inc., New England Tunnel Co., New Shore
Gardens, Inc., New Star Manufacturing Co., New York
Stores, Inc., New York Wearing Apparel, Inc., Newbert
Color Corporation, Newbury Associates, Inc., Newbury-
port Theatres, Inc., Newhall & Blevins Inc., Newman Shoe
Company (1929), Newton Box Company, Newton Con-
tracting Company, Newton Garage & Automobile Company, Newton Roofing Company, Newton Stables Inc.,.
Newton Tombar Golf Course, Inc., Niagara Realty Corpora-
tion, Nicholas Sannella & Son Inc., Nichols Confectionery
Company, Noble and Brown, Inc., Nonotuck Garage Com-
pany, Norcross-Cameron Company (1904), Norfolk Securi-
ties Company, Norman R. Adams, Inc., Norris Company,
Inc., The, Norris-Redfield Co., North Atlantic Investment
Trusts, Incorporated, North Dighton Stove Company,
North Natick Realty, Inc., North Plymouth Coal Com-
pany, North Reading Wagon Co., North Shore Chevrolet,
Inc., North Shore Market Co., North Shore Tile Company,
Northampton Indoor Golf Academy, Inc., Northern Air-
lines, Incorporated, Northern Waste Company, Northside
School Inc., Norton Tire Stores, Inc., Norwood Central
Motors, Inc., Norwood Spray Company, Noseworthy-
DeCosta, Inc., Novelty Furniture Shoppe, Inc., The,
Novelty Rug Mills Incorporated, Novelty Shoe Co. of Bing-
hamton, N. Y., Noyes Outlet Company, Nutting's Marble-
head Yachts, Inc.
Oak Hill Village Bus Service Co., Oakes Manufacturing
Company, Oakhurst Company, Ocean Realty Corporation,
Oil Burner Engineering Corporation, The, Oko Zinc & Lead
Company, Old Colony Airways Corporation, Old Colony
Automobile Company, Old Colony Silver Black Fox Com-
pany Inc., Old Scotch Remedies, Ltd., Old South Engraving
Company, Old South Sandwich Shop Inc., Olmstead Cor-
poration, Onset Cafeteria, Inc., Opera House Incorporated,
Oppenheim Clothing Co., Inc., Orr Hardware Company,
Otis Allen & Son Company, Ovington Sales Company, Ox-
ford-Eustis Realty Company, Oxford Motors, Inc., Oxford
Woolen Company, Oxidite Manufacturing Company.
P & S Laundry Inc., P. & S. Pharmacy Inc., P. & W. Sales
Corporation, P. C. Athas & Co., Inc., P. F. Shea Incor-
porated, P. J. Griffin Construction Co., P. W. L. Flying
Service, Inc., Package Confectionery Company, Package
Confectionery Company, Inc., Packard Paint & Varnish
Co. Inc., Padichah Cigarette Co., Page Securities Corpora-
tion, Paine-Hoban, Inc., Palace Amusement Company,

Palace Florists, Inc., Palmer Cloak & Suit Co., Inc., Palmer
Concrete Products Co., Paramount Cab Co. of Boston, Inc.,
Paramount Foods Incorporated, Paramount Petroleum
Company, Inc., Paramount Petticoat Company, Paramount
Products Corporation, Paris Store Company of Fitchburg,
Parisian Perfume Shoppes Incorporated, Park Electrical
Company, Park Lunch, Inc., Parker Furniture Co., Inc.,
Parker Hill Realty Co. Inc., Parker Jewelry Co., Parker
Mills, Parkerson Corporation, Parkman-Wasgatt Company,
Inc., Patrick J. Sullivan, Inc., Paxtons Inc., Payne-Bates,
Inc., Pedomusclar Clinics Incorporated, Peerless Dress
Company, Inc., The, Peg & Paul, Inc., Pemaquid Mills,
Peninsular Storage and Warehouse Company, Pennacchio
& Russo Co., People's Educational and Amusement Associa-
tion, Inc., The, Peoples Mercantile Company, The, Pepler
Weaving Company, Pepperell Spring Water Company, Inc.,
Perkins Co., The, Perryville Woolen Mills, Inc., Peter
Vezina & Co. Inc., Petrie Studios Inc., Pettengill Wood Heel
Company, Phenix Plate Company, The, Philip's Market,
Inc., Phillips Novelty Shoe Store, Inc., Phillips Rubber Co.
Inc., The, Phoenix Shoe Mfg. Co., Phoenix Shoe Mfg. Cor-
poration, Phonograph Publishing Company, The, Pictorial
Educator Publishing Company, Pierce Davis Corporation,
Pilgrim Engraving Co., Pilgrim Park, Inc., Pilgrim Steel &
Wrecking Co., Pillowcraft Co., Inc., Pine Grove Filling Sta-
tion, Inc., Pioneer Realty Company Incorporated, The,
Pioneer Rubber Company, Pioneer Service Association,
Inc., Pioneer Slip Cover Co., Inc., Pittsfield Co-operative
Coal Company, Pittsfield Eastern Oil Burner Company,
Plate Realty Company, Play-O-Lite Company, Plaza
Theatre, Inc., Plum Island Beach Company, Plymouth
Amusement Co., Plymouth Theatre Co., Pocasset Miniature
Golf, Inc., Point Breeze Corporation, Pontoosuc Woolen
Manufacturing Company, Poole Printing Company, Pope
Company Inc., The, Poponesset Land Company, Porter
Manufacturing Company, Porter Theatre Company, Portu-
guese Real Estate Improvement Company, Postal Realty
Company, Inc., Power Products, Inc., Preble Box Toe Co.,
Premier Fox Farms, Inc., Premier Investment Company,
Premier Oil Co., Premier Upholstering Co., Prescott Realty
Company, Press of James Kent Eaton (a corporation), The,
Price Millinery Corporation, Price Shoe Company, Pride
Transport Co., Prime Dress Manufacturing Company,
Prince Reenforced Rubber Company, Prize Shoe Co. Inc.,
The, Professional Realty Company, Inc., Progress Corpora-
tion, Progressive Bulb Farms Incorporated, Progressive
Coal Company, Inc., Progressive Investors Inc., Prospect
Construction Company, Inc., Prouty Furniture Company,
Inc., Prudential Company, The, Public Lunch & Delicates-
sen Co., Inc., Public Motor Sales Co., Pura-Tex Co. Inc.,
The, Pure Food Lunch Company, Pure White Refined Oil
Company, Inc., Puritan Confectionery Co., Puritan Gro-
cery Stores, Inc., Puritan Pharmacy, Inc., Puritan Real

Estate Trust, Inc., Pushpull Valve Cap Company, Pynchon Realty Co.

Quality Appliance Dealers, Inc., Quality Paint & Hardware Store, Inc., Quality Shop, Inc., Quality Upholstering Company, Quashnet Company, Queen Quality Undergarment Co. Inc., Quincy Amusement Corporation, Quincy Automobile Company, Inc., Quincy Drug Company, Inc., Quincy Mortgage & Acceptance Corp., Quincy Pump Co.

R. & S. Footwear Co., R. Davis Department Store Co., R. F. Sheeran & Co., Inc., R. H. Ducey Co., R. J. Warren Company, R. M. Rubin Co. Inc., R. N. Ellis Incorporated, R. V. C. Construction Company of Newton Inc., Radio Advertising Inc., Radio Markets, Inc., Radio Sales Corporation, Radium Springs, Inc., The, Rainbow Extension Corporation, Rainbow Shoe Co., Ramsdell Tool & Manufacturing Co., Raphel Dress Mfg. Co. Inc., The, Ray Cotton Company, Ray Detective Agency and Merchants Secret Service Incorporated, Ray Dress Shops, Inc., Ray Furniture Co., Raydon Manufacturing Company, Raymond Kimball & Sons, Inc., Rayner Manufacturing Company, Re-Bo Products Company, Reading Dairy Company, Real Estate News, Inc., Realty Corporation of Cambridge, The, Reardon Boiler Company, Red Riding Hood Stores, Inc., Red Wing Flying Service, Inc., Redden Resilient Wheel Company, Redgate Bros. Inc., Regal Baking Corporation, Regal Corset Company, Regent Garage Company, Reisig Hair Felt Co., Inc., Reliable Garment Co., Inc., Renard Cocoanut Grove, Inc., Reponens' Service System, Inc., Republic Fuel, Inc., Restaurant Momart, Inc., Revere Ark Company, Revere Automobile Co. Inc., Revere Building, Inc., Revere Hardware Company, Revirwen Investment and Securities Company, Richards-McKoan Company, Richardson Roofing Company, The, Rico Ignition Company, Riggs & Company, Incorporated, Rite-Way Golf, Inc., Rite-Way Stores, Inc., Riverside Gardens, Incorporated, Riverside Leather Co., Inc., Road Building Service, Inc., Robbins & Norris, Inc., Robbins-Clarke Coal Company, Robert Leonard Company, Robert W. Powers Company, Robert Wise, Inc., Roberts Battery Service Company, Robinson Auto Repair Company, Inc., Rockport Granite Company, Rockrimmon Oil Company, Rogers Incorporated, Rogers Trucking Company, Rogosa Realty Corporation, Rolland Stores Corporation, Rollins Dress Co. Inc., Roope, Folkins, & Hamilton Roofing Co., Rose Gift & Novelty Co., Inc., Rose Manufacturing Co., Inc., Roseloom Manufacturing Co., Ross Jewelry Company, Inc., Rossman Electric Supply Co., Rotosales Manufacturing Company, Roxbury Auto Renting Co., Roy-Art Company, Roy J. Foster & Company, Inc., Roy Manufacturing Company, Royal Blue Line Co. of New York, Royal Cafeteria, Inc., Royal Cloak & Suit Co., Royal Coat Co. Inc., Royal Comb Company, Royal Film Exchange, Inc., Royal Furniture Corporation of Boston, Royal Metal-Clad Door Company, Inc., Royal Motors, Inc., Royal Paper Box Company, Certain corporations dissolved. Royal Restaurant Corporation, Royal-Sills Company, Inc., Royal Specialty Shops Inc., Royall Holding Corporation, Rubber Mills Outlet Corp., Rubin Cramer Co., Inc., Rudser Operating Company, Ruggles Street Garage, Inc., Ryan-Hamilburg Motor Co., Ryan-Rogers Shoe Company, Rylan Motor Company.

S. A. Meagher Company, S. & L. Transportation Co. Inc., S & S Enterprises, Inc., S & W Company, Inc., S. B. & H. Company, S. Barrile Manufacturing Co., S. C. Donovan Company, Inc., S. C. Lowe Supply Company, S. E. Aaron Company, S. E. Bentley Company, The, S. H. Appleman Co., S. J. Farber Shoe Co., S. Landow Company, of Springfield, The, S. R. Hazelton Manufacturing Co., The, S. Servetnick Inc., S. Shapiro Company, S. Silk Co. Inc., S. Slotnick, Inc., S. Sodekson Company, S. V. L. Manufacturing Company, Saben Lock Nut Co., Inc., Sadie Kelly's Spa Inc., Safety Truck Chain Company, Inc., The, St. Regis Hotel and Restaurant Co., Sal-Mo Company, The, Salem Street Realty Co., Sales Analyst Inc., Sally's, Inc., Sam's Clothes Shop, Inc., Samuel H. White Company, Inc., Samuel Wasserman Co., Sanborn Construction Co., Inc., Sanborn Motors Inc., Sanford Tire Corporation, Sarnoff-Irving Hat Stores Company, Satin Electric Corp., Saugus Excavating Co., Inc., The, Saugus Theatre, Inc., Savo Baking Company, Inc., Savoy Products, Inc., Savoy Sand Company, Sawyer's Market, Inc., Sayli's Parisian Beauty Salon, Inc., Sayvoyl Corporation of New England, The, Scanlan-Wilson Furniture Company, Scheinfeldt, Inc., Sch. Governor Fuller, Inc., Schumaker-Santry Company, Scott & Blake, Incorporated, Searing & Company, Inc., Seaver Kosher Meat & Poultry Markets, Inc., Second Oakland Syndicate, Incorporated, Securities Trust Corporation, Security Building and Development Company, Security Construction Company, Security Investment Company, Security Mortgage Association Inc., The, Security, Realty & Mortgage Co., Security Share Co., Segerson Bros., Incorporated, Service Excavating Co., Service, Inc., Service Supply Co., Inc., Sharon Box Company, Sharon Real Estate Company, Shawmut Petroleum Company, Shawmut Securities Corporation, Shawmut Shoe Company, Inc., Shawsheen River Farm, Inc., Sheep, Inc., Sheinfield-Nollman Inc., Shellcrest Stock Farm Company, Shepard Motors, Inc., Sherman Bros. Shoe Co., Sherman Power Construction Company, Shipbuilding and Motor Equipment, Ltd., Shopping Guide of Worcester, Inc., Shopping Guide Operating Co., Inc., Shops of Irregulars, Inc., The, Shorey-Dunham, Inc., Shove Mills, Shwom Realty Company, Inc., Sibley Nash Co., Inc., Sibulkin & Sons Shoe Co., Sidney F. Hooper Realty Company, Sief Supply Co., Silhouette Dining Room Inc., The, Silver's Bakery, Inc., Simpson Furniture Company, Six Little Tailors, Inc. of Boston, 1654 Corporation, Skiff's Incorporated, Slater-Hale Company, Slyde On Co., Smith & Dove Manufacturing Company, Smith Corporation, The, Smith Heating Co., Smith Mills, Smith Tablet Company, Inc., The, Snyder Sales Company, Inc., Somerset Textile Company, Somerville Motor Sales Co., Soulliere Motor Co., South Bellingham Realty Co., South Boston Construction Co., South Boston Motor Mart, Inc., South Deerfield Farmers Exchange, Inc., South Huntington Avenue Garage Inc., South Lawrence Amusement Co., Inc., South Shore Construction Co. Inc., Southbridge Theatre Operating Company, Southgate Machinery Co., Soutter, Gooch & Holbrook, Inc., Spack Associates, Inc., The, Spafford Company, Incorporated, The, Speak-O-Phone Co., Inc. of Massachusetts, Specialty Sales Corporation, Spencer Court Realty Company, Spofford Machine Co. Inc., Sport-O-Gram Newspaper Publishing Co. Inc., The, Sports Development Corporation, Sportsmen's Club of Greater Boston, Inc., The, Spring-O-Pedic Company, Springfield Brick Inc., Springfield Cadillac, Inc., Springfield Kelvinator Sales, Inc., Springfield Tire Service Co., Inc., Springfield Trust Associates, Inc., Springfield Yellow Cab Company, Stafford Corporation, The, Stanco Tile Co. of Boston, The, Standard Candy Company, Standard Construction and Realty Company, Inc., The, Standard Stores, Incorporated, Standard Supply Company, Incorporated, The, Standard Tanning Company, Stanleys' Furniture, Inc., Star Machine Co., Inc., Star Wood Heel Co., State Motor Co., Inc., State Theatre Club Inc., The, Statistical Bureau, Incorporated, The, SteCo Inc., Steelex Company, Stephen J. Tobin, Inc., Step-in-all Manufacturing Company, Inc., Sterling Chemical Co., Sterling Cloak Co., Inc., Sterling Worsted Company, The, Sterns Lumber Company, Stetson Shops Incorporated, Stevens Bread Company, Stevens Market, Inc., Stewart Clothes Shop, Inc., Stockbridge Pharmacy, Inc., Ston-Craf Co., The, Stone & Andrew Company, Stone & Webster Construction Company, Stone Machine Company, Stony Brook Carbonizing Company, Stout, Scanlan Company, Stow Golf and Country Club, Inc., Strandway Motors, Inc., Strogoff's, Inc., Stuart-Chevrolet Company, Studebaker Sales Company of Rhode Island, Style Dress Shop, Inc., The, Style Garment Shop, Inc., The, Suburban Motor Car Co., Inc., Suffolk Engraving & Electrotyping Co., Sugden Company, The, Sumner Hardware Co., SunShine, Incorporated, Sunkist Fruit Stores of Worcester Inc., Superior Cloak Co., Inc., Superior Coal Combustion Company, Inc., Superior Oil Burner Manufacturing Co., Inc., Superior Tailors Inc., Supreme Garment Mfg. Co. Inc., Sure Lube Products Incorporated, Surety Underwriters Corporation, Surfside Motors, Inc., Swaine Iron Works, Inc., Swan-Russell Company, Swan's Island Fisheries, Inc., Swartz Bros. Inc., Swartz Drug Company, Sweet-Hot of New England, Inc., Sydney L. Curry Inc.

T. Berman Company, T. C. Brooks Company, T. J.

McMahon Co., T. P. Lancaster Company, The, Tabor Certain corporations dissolved. Furniture Co., The, Talbot Laundry Co., Talbot-Quincy, Inc., Tancar Oil Company, Tarlow-Jones Shoe Company Inc., The, Tate Manufacturing Company, Taunton Rubber Company, Tax Digest, Inc., Taxi Inc., of Cambridge, Taxi Service Company, Taylor-Adams Co.,Inc.,Taylor-Rousseau Inc., Ted's Mens Shops, Inc., Temple & Company, Inc., Temple Shops, Inc., The, Ten Associates Inc., Tenney & Company, Inc., Tenser Radio Corporation, Terminal Electric Supply Co., Terminal Gas & Supply Company, Testa, Landino and Scurto Engineering Co. Inc., Theatrical Corporation, The, Thermo Coal Heating Co., Inc., Thimia's Spa, Inc., Thos. F. Kelley Company Inc., Thomas Leyland & Co. Inc., Thomas R. Flynn Inc., Thompson Box Company, Thorndike Realty Corporation, 325 Washington Street Corp., Three Millers Lowell Company, Thrift Coal Company, Inc., Tierney's Flower Shoppe Inc., Tobias Furniture Co., Todd, Inc., Toddman Stores, Inc., Tolman-Fox Corporation, Tom Talbot's Weymouth Corporation, Tom Thumb Golf Club, Inc., Tomkinson Plumbing & Heating Co., Toppan Boat and Engine Company, Torrey-Warren Furniture Manufacturing Company, Touraine Shoe Corporation, Tower Motor Co., Townleigh Holding Corporation, Traffic Tire Service Co., Trans-Pecos Oil & Gas Co., Tredrite Mat Company, Tremont Indoor Golf Courses, Inc., Tremont Investment Company, Tri-Sigma Corporation, The, Trimont Laundry, Inc., Triple City Rug Company, Troy Long Wharf Co. Inc., Tufts Motor Company, Inc., Turn Stile Process, Inc., Turner Corporation, The, Turnpike Golf, Incorporated, 20 Exchange Street, Inc., Twill Products Company, Two Forty Worthington Co., 224 Commonwealth Avenue, Inc., Two Town Taxi Inc., Tydee Company.

U. S. Brick & Tile Co., Underwear Syndicate Company, Underwrap Company, The, Union Cotton Manufacturing Company, Union Fire Insurance Agency (Incorporated), Union Shoe Mart, Inc., Unique Theatre Company of Boston, United Buyers' League, Inc., United Clothing Co., United Concrete Products Corporation, United Co-operative Society of Gardner, United Dealers Corporation, United Distributing System, Inc., United Electric Apparatus Company, United Garage Company, Inc., United Investors, Inc., United Persian Rug Importers, Inc., United States Air Lines (Corporation), United States Automobile Association Inc., United States Investment Company, United States Marble Works, Inc., United States Producing Co. Inc., United Tea and Coffee Company, Inc., United Textile Warehouse Company, United Wheel & Rim Company, United Wood Heel Co., Inc., Universal Armature Corporation, Universal Candy and Chocolate Machinery Company, Inc., Universal Coal Company, Universal Grinding Machine Company, Universal Keyless Lock Company, Universal Medical Fund Company, Universal Safety Tread

Company, University Apartments Inc., Uphams Corner
Indoor Golf Course Inc., Utilities Investors, Inc., Utilities
Management Corporation, Utility Service Corporation.

Vacation Training Camp, Inc., Valley Textiles Co., Inc.,
Van I. Bennett Inc., Vanadium Wire Company, Incor-
porated, Vassara Fruit Co., Inc., Vaughn-Upton Company,
Vendamuse Corporation, Vendomatic Corporation, The,
Venture Inn, Inc., Vi-Tone Food Products, Inc., Victory
Amusement Co., Victory Tenants Corporation, Vinson's,
Inc., Virgin-Doucette Co., Viscoloid Company, Inc., The,
Vizzini's Loan Association, Inc., Vogue Dress Co., Von
Sotta System, Inc., Vose Construction Company, Vosine
Company, The, Voye Electric Supply Co.

W. A. Fuller & Son Inc., W. A. Lieson Company, W. A.
Norton Company, W. A. Shea, Inc., W. A. Webster Lum-
ber Co., W. B. Pratt Inc., W. D. Byron & Sons Leather
Company, W. E. Maynard, Incorporated, W. E. Putnam
Company, W. G. Shaw Furniture Co. Inc., W. H. Bennett
Co., W. H. Brayton Co., W. H. Morton Co. Inc., W. H.
Sharp Co-operative Shoe Company, W. H. Virgie Company,
The, W. J. Spinney, Inc., W. L. White Motor Co., W. M.
Brown, Inc., W. M. Hall Company, W. N. Gleason Com-
pany, The, Wacco Supply Company, Wachusett Orchards,
Inc., Wachusett Realty Company, Inc., Wakefield Rattan
Company, Walker Clothes, Inc., Walker-Indian Company,
Wallace Nutting, Incorporated, Walsh & Brown Company,
Walsh Drug Company, Walsh Specialty Shop Inc., The,
Walter Baker & Company, Limited (1895), Walter J.
Moran, Inc., Walters, Inc., Waltham Auto Exchange, Inc.,
Waltham Bleachery and Dye Works, The, Waltham
Building Corporation, Waltham Doughnut Corporation,
Waltzer of Revere Beach, Incorporated, Wampanoag Mills,
Warren Hide & Leather Co., Warren Hotel Company, War-
ren Soap Manufacturing Company, Warren T. Simpson
Company, Washington and Devonshire Realty Company
Inc., Washington Clothing Co. Inc., Washington (District
of Columbia) Investment Trust, Inc., Wass Motor Sales,
(Inc.), Waterloo Textile Corporation, Watt-Negus Auto-
matic Train Control Company of United States, Way-
bright Manufacturing Co., Webb Steamship Company,
Weber Bros., Inc., Webster Coal Company, Incorporated,
Webster-McHatton Lumber Co., Weir-Jackson Company,
Welburn Cadillac Company, Welch Paint & Glass Co.,
Wellesley Excavating Company, Inc., Wellesley Hills
Exchange, Inc., Wellings Coal Co., Wellington-Pierce Com-
pany, Wellman's Inc., Wentworth Hotel Company, West
Boylston Manufacturing Company, The, West End Real
Estate Corporation, West India Fruit Company, West
Stockbridge and Hudson Marble and Lime Company,
Westerly Granite Co., Inc., Western Associates, Inc., The,
Western Counties Finance Corporation, Western Fruit &
Produce Company, Westfield Tire and Rubber Company,
Inc., Westwood Laboratories Co., Wetmore-Savage Air-

craft Corp., White & Company, Inc., White Construction Company, Inc., White House Laundry Corporation, White Motor Tours, Inc., Whitman Patching Machine Co. Inc., Whittemore-Woodbury Company, Whittier & Whitney Inc., Wickham and Roe Company, Wiig, Inc., Wilbraham Sales and Service, Inc., Wilder & Ballou Co., Wilgel Company, Inc., Willard M. Pettey, Incorporated, Wm. Anderson Co., Wm. C. Codman & Son, Inc., William Cashman & Sons, Inc., William F. Baird Company, William F. Bennett Co., Inc., The, William F. Hennessey & Sons, Incorporated, William F. Kerrigan Company, William F. O'Brien, Inc., William G. Barker Company, William H. Bassett Co. of Stoughton, William J. Sullivan Company, William Karp Tire Company, William L. Fletcher, Inc., William Rocklin, Inc., Williamstown Farmers Exchange, Inc., Willowcraft Shops, Inc., Wilmur Motors, Inc., Wilson Furniture Manufacturing Company, Inc., Wilson Refrigeration and Sales Corporation, Winchester Furniture Company, Winchester Realty Company, Windsor Cafeteria, Inc., Winter Garden Golf Courses, Inc., Winthrop Motor Sales, Inc., Winthrop Textile Corporation, Wiswell the Druggist, Inc., Withers, Inc., Wolcott Square Pharmacy, Inc., Wolfe Leather Co., Wollaston Associates, Inc., Wonder Laundries, Inc., Wonderly's, Inc., Wood & Wood, Incorporated, Wood-Crafters, Inc., The, Woodbourne Apartments, Inc., Woodcock Taxi Inc., Woodruff, Keefe and Rogal, Inc., Woodward School, The, Wooleather Manufacturing Co., Worcester Apron Co. Inc., Worcester Auto Company, Incorporated, Worcester Auto Livery, Inc., Worcester Credit Grantors Association, Inc., Worcester Fire Extinguisher Company, Worcester Grill Inc., Worcester Mortgage Corporation, Worcester Motor Company, Inc., Worcester Olympia Company, Worcester Rubber Company, Worcester Silk Mills Corporation, Worcester Tire Corporation, Worden-Hotz Company, Wright & Wright, Incorporated.

Y-D Service Garage of Worcester, Inc., Y-D Supplies Company, Yale Shoe Co., Inc., Yun Ho Co., Inc.

Zeena Gabelnick, Inc., Zola Dress Co., The, Zoll Leather Company.

Charitable and Other Corporations.

Ashby Silver Fox Club, Inc., Associated Hebrew Schools of Greater Boston, Inc.

Bay State Mutual Fire Insurance Company (1919), Brackett Charitable Trust, Incorporated, The, Brookline Service Club, Inc.

Colonial of Salem, The.

Delta Tau Delta Club of Boston.

Federal Disability Corporation, Fisher Ames Club of Dedham, The, Fraternal Building Association of Everett, Incorporated, The.

Glover Home and Hospital, The.

Certain
corporations
dissolved.

Haskins, Inc., Hingham Village Improvement Society, Incorporated.

Ladies Benevolent Circle of Clarendon Street Baptist Church.

Mutual Help Association of the People of Monaster: The Birthday of Virgin Mary, The.

New Bedford Female Reform and Relief Association, Norwegian Mission Home.

Omicron Club, Inc.

Second Baptist Society in Haverhill, Somerville Playgrounds Association, Stores Mutual Protective Association of Boston, Inc.

Western Hampshire Farmers' Exchange, Inc., The.

PUBLIC SERVICE CORPORATIONS.

Hampshire Electric Company, Humarock Beach Water Company.

Medway and Dedham Street Railway Company, Mill River Electric Light Company.

Ware Electric Company.

Pending suits
not affected,
etc.

SECTION 2. Nothing in this act shall be construed to affect any suit now pending by or against any corporation mentioned herein, or any suit now pending or hereafter brought for any liability now existing against the stockholders or officers of any such corporation, or to revive any charter previously annulled or any corporation previously dissolved, or to make valid any defective organization of any of the supposed corporations mentioned herein.

Suits upon
choses in
action, how
brought, etc.

SECTION 3. Suits upon choses in action arising out of contracts sold or assigned by any corporation dissolved by this act may be brought or prosecuted in the name of the purchaser or assignee. The fact of sale or assignment and of purchase by the plaintiff shall be set forth in the writ or other process; and the defendant may avail himself of any matter of defence of which he might have availed himself in a suit upon a claim by the corporation, had it not been dissolved by this act.

Obligation to
file tax
returns, etc.

SECTION 4. Nothing in this act shall be construed to relieve the last person who was the treasurer or assistant treasurer, or, in their absence or incapacity, who was any other principal officer of each of the corporations named in this act, from the obligation to make a tax return as of April first following the date of dissolution as required by chapter sixty-three of the General Laws. The tax liability of each of the corporations named in this act shall be determined in accordance with the existing laws of this commonwealth.

Effective
date of act.

SECTION 5. This act shall be operative as of March thirty-first in the current year.

Approved April 28, 1933.

AN ACT RELATIVE TO THE DISPOSITION OF RECEIPTS FROM THE BOARD OF REGISTRATION OF BARBERS.

*Chap.*149

Whereas, The deferred operation of this act would tend to defeat its purpose, therefore it is hereby declared to be an emergency law, necessary for the immediate preservation of the public convenience.

Emergency preamble.

Be it enacted, etc., as follows:

SECTION 1. Section forty of chapter thirteen of the General Laws, as appearing in the Tercentenary Edition thereof, is hereby amended by striking out, in the ninth and tenth lines, the following ", and the premium therefor shall be paid from the funds in the state treasury to the use of the board", — so as to read as follows: — *Section 40.* The board shall hold regular meetings at the state house on the first Tuesdays of January, May and October in each year, and such additional meetings at such times and places as it may determine. At the regular meeting in January it shall annually organize by the choice of a chairman and a secretary, who shall be members of the board. Before entering upon the discharge of the duties of his office, the secretary shall give to the state treasurer a bond, with such sureties as shall be approved by the governor and council, conditioned upon the faithful discharge of his duties. Such bond, with the approval of the board and with the oath of office endorsed thereon, shall be filed in the office of the state secretary. The board shall have a common seal, and the members thereof may administer oaths.

G. L. (Ter. Ed.), 13, § 40, amended.

Board of registration of barbers. Meetings, organization, etc.

SECTION 2. Section eighty-seven O of chapter one hundred and twelve of the General Laws, as so appearing, is hereby amended by striking out all after the word "treasurer" in the third line, — so as to read as follows:—*Section 87O.* Fees referred to in sections eighty-seven F to eighty-seven R, inclusive, shall be paid in advance to the secretary of the board, who shall pay them monthly to the state treasurer.

G. L. (Ter. Ed.), 112, § 87O, amended.

Disposition of fees.

SECTION 3. All receipts from the board of registration of barbers heretofore paid into the treasury and held as a special fund under said section eighty-seven O are hereby transferred to the general fund of the commonwealth.

Transfer of certain fees heretofore paid.

Approved April 28, 1933.

AN ACT AUTHORIZING THE LICENSED OPERATION ON THE LORD'S DAY OF CERTAIN AMUSEMENT ENTERPRISES AT AMUSEMENT PARKS AND BEACH RESORTS.

*Chap.*150

Whereas, The deferred operation of this act would tend to defeat its purpose, therefore it is hereby declared to be an emergency law, necessary for the immediate preservation of the public convenience.

Emergency preamble.

Be it enacted, etc., as follows:

G. L. (Ter.
Ed.), 136, § 2,
amended.

SECTION 1. Section two of chapter one hundred and thirty-six of the General Laws, as appearing in the Tercentenary Edition thereof, is hereby amended by inserting after the word "to" in the tenth line the words: — amusement enterprises lawfully conducted under section four A

Being present
at or taking
part in certain
entertainments
on Lord's day
regulated.

or to, — so as to read as follows: — *Section 2.* Whoever on the Lord's day is present at a game, sport, play or public diversion, except a concert of sacred music, a public entertainment duly licensed as provided in section four or a free open air concert given by a town, or by license of the mayor or the selectmen, upon a common or public park, street or square, or except a game of golf conducted on an open air golf course other than a miniature golf course, so called, shall be punished by a fine of not more than five dollars. Whoever on the Lord's day takes part in any game, sport, play or public diversion, except as aforesaid, shall be punished by a fine of not more than fifty dollars. This and the following section shall not apply to amusement enterprises lawfully conducted under section four A or to sports or games conducted in accordance with sections twenty-one to twenty-five, inclusive, in any city or town which accepts said sections or in accordance with sections twenty-six to thirty-two, inclusive, in any city or town in which said sections twenty-six to thirty-two are then in force.

G. L. (Ter.
Ed.), 136, new
section after
§ 4.
Licenses to
keep open
bowling alleys,
etc., on the
Lord's day.

SECTION 2. Said chapter one hundred and thirty-six is hereby amended by inserting after section four, as so appearing, the following new section: — *Section 4A.* The mayor of a city or the selectmen of a town, upon written application therefor, and upon such terms and conditions as they may prescribe, may grant licenses for the maintenance and operation upon the Lord's day at amusement parks or beach resorts, so called, in such city or town, of any enterprise hereinafter described, for admission to which or for the use of which a payment of money or other valuable consideration may or may not be charged, namely: — Bowling alleys; shooting galleries restricted to the firing therein of rifles, revolvers or pistols using cartridges not larger than twenty-two calibre; photographic galleries or studios in which pictures are made and sold; games approved by the state department of public safety; and such amusement rides, so called, riding devices or other amusement devices as may lawfully be operated therein on secular days. Any licensee hereunder may distribute premiums or prizes in connection with any game or device lawfully maintained and operated by him under authority hereof.

G. L. (Ter.
Ed.), 136. § 6,
etc., amended.

SECTION 3. Section six of said chapter one hundred and thirty-six, as most recently amended by chapter ninety-six of the acts of nineteen hundred and thirty-two, is hereby further amended by adding at the end thereof the following new paragraph: —

Nor shall it prohibit the conduct of any enterprise lawfully conducted under section four A.

Section 4. Section seventeen of said chapter one hundred and thirty-six, as so appearing, is hereby amended by adding at the end thereof the following sentence: — This section shall not apply to the discharge of firearms in any shooting gallery licensed under section four A, and subject to the restrictions therein imposed.

Approved April 28, 1933.

Regulating the keeping open of certain amusement places.
G. L. (Ter. Ed.), 136, § 17, amended.
Discharge of firearms on Lord's day regulated.

An Act increasing the amount of local taxes exempt from penalty interest.

*Chap.*151

Be it enacted, etc., as follows:

Section 1. Section fifty-seven of chapter fifty-nine of the General Laws, as appearing in the Tercentenary Edition thereof, is hereby amended by striking out, in the twelfth line, the word "two" and inserting in place thereof the word: — three, — so as to read as follows: — *Section 57.* Taxes shall be payable in every city, town and district in which the same are assessed, and bills for the same shall be sent out, not later than October fifteenth of each year, unless by ordinance, by-law or vote of the city, town or district, an earlier date of payment is fixed. On all taxes remaining unpaid after the expiration of seventeen days from said October fifteenth, or after such longer time as may be fixed by any city, town or district which fixes an earlier date for payment, but not exceeding thirty days from such earlier date, interest shall be paid at the following rates computed from the date on which the taxes become payable: at the rate of six per cent per annum on all taxes and, by way of penalty, at the additional rate of two per cent per annum on the amount of all taxes in excess of three hundred dollars assessed to any taxpayer, in any one city or town, if such taxes remain unpaid after the expiration of three months from the date on which they became payable, but if, in any case, the tax bill is sent out later than the day prescribed, interest shall be computed only from the expiration of such seventeen days or said longer time. In no case shall interest be added to taxes paid prior to the expiration of seventeen days from the date when they are payable, nor shall any city or town so fix an earlier date of payment and longer time within which taxes may be paid without interest as would permit the payment of any taxes without interest after November first of the year in which they are due. Bills for taxes assessed under section seventy-five shall be sent out not later than December twenty-sixth, and such taxes shall be payable not later than December thirty-first. If they remain unpaid after that date, interest shall be paid at the rates above specified, computed from December thirty-first until the day of payment, but if, in any case, the tax bill is sent out later than December twenty-sixth, said taxes shall be payable not later than ten days from the day upon

G. L. (Ter. Ed.), 59, § 57, amended.
Date for payment of taxes. Interest.

which said bill is sent out, and interest shall be computed from the fifteenth day following the date when the tax becomes due. In all cases where interest is payable it shall be added to and become a part of the tax.

Application of act. SECTION 2. This act shall apply only to taxes assessed in the current year and thereafter.

Approved April 28, 1933.

---

*Chap.*152 AN ACT RELATIVE TO THE PRACTICE OF MEDICINE BY HOSPITAL INTERNES OR MEDICAL OFFICERS.

Be it enacted, etc., as follows:

G. L. (Ter. Ed.), 112, § 9, amended.

Limited registration of hospital internes, etc.

Chapter one hundred and twelve of the General Laws is hereby amended by striking out section nine, as appearing in the Tercentenary Edition thereof, and inserting in place thereof the following: — *Section 9.* An applicant for limited registration under this section who shall furnish the board with satisfactory proof that he is twenty-one or over and of good moral character, that he has creditably completed not less than three and one half years of study in a legally chartered medical school having the power to grant degrees in medicine, and that he has been appointed an interne or medical officer in a hospital or other institution maintained by the commonwealth, or by a county or municipality thereof, or in a hospital incorporated under the laws of the commonwealth may, upon the payment of five dollars, be registered by the board as a hospital medical officer for such time as it may prescribe; but such limited registration shall entitle the said applicant to practice medicine only in the hospital or other institution designated on his certificate of limited registration, or outside such hospital or other institution for the treatment, under the supervision of one of its medical officers who is a duly registered physician, of persons accepted by it as patients, and in either case under regulations established by such hospital or other institution. Limited registration under this section may be revoked at any time by the board.

Approved April 28, 1933.

---

*Chap.*153 AN ACT GRANTING TO THE JEWISH WAR VETERANS OF THE UNITED STATES CERTAIN PRIVILEGES GRANTED TO OTHER WAR VETERANS' ORGANIZATIONS.

Be it enacted, etc., as follows:

G. L. (Ter. Ed.), 33, § 60, amended.

Unauthorized drilling with firearms, etc., forbidden, etc.

SECTION 1. Section sixty of chapter thirty-three of the General Laws, as appearing in the Tercentenary Edition thereof, is hereby amended by inserting after the word "States" in the twenty-eighth line the words: — , and of the Jewish War Veterans of the United States, — so as to read as follows: — *Section 60.* No body of men, except the volunteer militia, the troops of the United States and the Ancient and Honorable Artillery Company of Boston, except as provided in the following section, shall maintain an armory, or associate together at any time as a company or organization, for drill or parade with firearms, or so drill or parade; nor shall any town raise or appropriate money toward arming, equipping, uniforming, supporting or providing drill rooms or armories for any such body of men; provided, that associations wholly composed of soldiers honorably discharged from the service of the United States may parade in public with arms, upon the reception of any regiment or company of soldiers returning from said service, and for escort duty at the burial of deceased soldiers, with the written permission of the aldermen of the city or selectmen of the town where they desire to parade; that students in educational institutions where military science is a prescribed part of the course of instruction may, with the consent of the governor, drill and parade with firearms in public, under the superintendence of their teachers; that members of schools for military instruction conducted with the approval of the governor, may drill and parade with firearms in public, under the supervision of their instructors; that foreign troops whose admission to the United States has been consented to by the United States government may, with the consent of the governor, drill and parade with firearms in public; and any body of men may, with the consent of the governor, drill and parade in public with any harmless imitation of firearms approved by the adjutant general; that regularly organized posts of the Grand Army of the Republic, and of The American Legion, and regularly organized camps of the United Spanish War Veterans and regularly organized posts of the Veterans of Foreign Wars of the United States, and of the Jewish War Veterans of the United States, and regularly organized detachments of the Marine Corps League may drill and parade with firearms in public, under the supervision of their duly authorized officers; that the Kearsarge Association of Naval Veterans, Inc., may at any time parade in public their color guards of not more than twelve men armed with firearms, that the Society of Colonial Wars in the Commonwealth of Massachusetts, the Order of the Founders and Patriots of America, the Massachusetts Society of the Sons of the American Revolution, the Society of the Sons of the Revolution in the Commonwealth of Massachusetts, the Society of the War of 1812 in the Commonwealth of Massachusetts, and regularly organized branches of any of said societies may at any time parade in public their uniformed color guards of ten men with firearms; that regularly organized camps of the Sons of Veterans may at any time parade in public their color guards of ten men with firearms; and that any organization heretofore authorized by law may parade with side-arms; and any veteran association composed wholly of past members of the militia of the commonwealth may maintain an armory for the use of the organizations of the militia to which its members belonged;

provided, that such drill or parade is not in contravention of the laws of the United States.

G. L. (Ter. Ed.), 40, § 5, cl. (12), etc., amended.

Section 2. Clause (12) of section five of chapter forty of the General Laws, as amended by section three of chapter one hundred and fourteen of the acts of nineteen hundred and thirty-two, is hereby further amended by striking out, in the nineteenth line, the word "and" and inserting in place thereof a comma, — and by inserting after the word "States" in the twentieth line the words: — and the Jewish War Veterans of the United States, — so as to read as fol-

Towns may appropriate money for monuments, etc.

lows: — (12) For erecting headstones or other monuments at the graves of persons who served in the war of the revolution, the war of eighteen hundred and twelve, the Seminole war, the Mexican war, the war of the rebellion or the Indian wars or who served in the military or naval service of the United States in the Spanish American war or in the World war; for acquiring land by purchase or by eminent domain under chapter seventy-nine, purchasing, erecting, equipping or dedicating buildings, or constructing or dedicating other suitable memorials, for the purpose of properly commemorating the services and sacrifices of persons who served as aforesaid; for the decoration of the graves, monuments or other memorials of soldiers, sailors and marines who served in the army, navy or marine corps of the United States in time of war or insurrection and the proper observance of Memorial Day and other patriotic holidays under the auspices of the local posts of the Grand Army of the Republic, United Spanish War Veterans, The American Legion, the Veterans of Foreign Wars of the United States and the Jewish War Veterans of the United States and under the auspices of the Kearsarge Association of Naval Veterans, Inc. and of local garrisons of the Army and Navy Union of the United States of America and of local chapters of the Massachusetts Society of the Sons of the American Revolution and of local detachments of the Marine Corps League, and of a local camp of the Sons of Union Veterans of the Civil War or a local tent of The Daughters of Union Veterans of the Civil War in the case of a town in which there is no post of the Grand Army of the Republic; or for keeping in repair graves, monuments or other memorials erected to the memory of such persons or of its firemen and policemen who died from injuries received in the performance of their duties in the fire or police service or for decorating the graves of such firemen and policemen or for other memorial observances in their honor. Money appropriated in honor of such firemen may be paid over to, and expended for such purposes by, any veteran firemen's association or similar organization.

G. L. (Ter. Ed.), 264, § 5, etc., amended.

Section 3. Section five of chapter two hundred and sixty-four of the General Laws, as amended by chapter two hundred and ninety-eight of the acts of nineteen hundred and thirty-two, is hereby further amended by inserting after the word "States" in the twenty-second line the words:

— , or to a post or department of the Jewish War Veterans of the United States, — so as to read as follows: — *Section 5.* Whoever publicly mutilates, tramples upon, defaces or treats contemptuously the flag of the United States or of Massachusetts, whether such flag is public or private property, or whoever displays such flag or any representation thereof upon which are words, figures, advertisements or designs, or whoever exposes to public view, manufactures, sells, exposes for sale, gives away or has in possession for sale or to give away or for use for any purpose, any article or substance, being an article of merchandise or a receptacle of merchandise or articles upon which is attached, through a wrapping or otherwise, engraved or printed in any manner, a representation of the United States flag, or whoever uses any representation of the arms or the great seal of the commonwealth for any advertising or commercial purpose, shall be punished by a fine of not less than ten nor more than one hundred dollars or by imprisonment for not more than one year, or both; but a flag belonging to an organization of veterans of the civil war, to a camp of the United Spanish War Veterans, to a post or department of The American Legion, or to a post or department of the Veterans of Foreign Wars of the United States, or to a post or department of the Jewish War Veterans of the United States, or belonging to or used in the service of the United States or the commonwealth, may have the names of battles and the name and number of the organization to which such flag belongs inscribed thereon. Words, figures, advertisements or designs attached to, or directly or indirectly connected with, the flag or any representation thereof in such manner that the flag or its representation is used to attract attention to or advertise such words, figures, advertisements or designs, shall for the purposes of this section be deemed to be upon the flag. For the purposes of this section, a flag shall be deemed to continue to belong to any organization of veterans hereinbefore specified, although such organization has ceased to exist, during such time as it remains in the lawful ownership or custody of any other of the aforesaid organizations or of the commonwealth or of any political subdivision thereof, or of any patriotic or historical society incorporated under the laws of the commonwealth or determined by the adjutant general to be a proper custodian thereof.   *Approved April 28, 1933.*

Penalty for misuse of flag, etc.

AN ACT TO PROTECT CERTAIN BIRDS NOT NOW PROTECTED BY STATUTE.

Chap.154

Be it enacted, etc., as follows:

Chapter one hundred and thirty-one of the General Laws is hereby amended by striking out section seventy-seven, as appearing in the Tercentenary Edition thereof, and inserting in place thereof the following: — *Section 77.* Whoever, except as provided in section eighty-four, eighty-five,

G. L. (Ter. Ed.), 131, § 77, amended.
Penalty for killing wild birds.

Exceptions.

eighty-seven or ninety, hunts or has in his possession a wild or undomesticated bird except an English sparrow, crow blackbird, crow, jay, starling, sharp-shinned hawk, cooper's hawk, goshawk or great horned owl, or wilfully destroys, disturbs or takes a nest or eggs of any wild or undomesticated bird, except such as are not protected by this section, shall be punished by a fine of not less than twenty nor more than fifty dollars for each bird taken, killed or had in possession or for each nest or egg disturbed, destroyed or taken; but any person may kill or attempt to kill any wild bird which he has reasonable cause to believe has damaged or is about to damage any property, including domesticated animals, poultry and game on game-rearing farms or preserves or on state owned game reservations, and a person who has a certificate from the director that he is engaged in the scientific study of ornithology or is collecting in the interests of a scientific institution may at any season take or kill, or take the nests or eggs of, a wild or undomesticated bird, except woodcock, ruffed grouse and quail. This section shall not authorize a person to enter upon private grounds without the consent of the owner thereof for the purpose of taking nests or eggs or killing birds. It shall be unlawful for any city, town or county or any private organization to offer or pay bounties for the killing or taking of any hawk or owl.   *Approved April 28, 1933.*

*Chap.*155 AN ACT PROVIDING FOR BIENNIAL MUNICIPAL ELECTIONS IN THE CITY OF MALDEN.

Be it enacted, etc., as follows:

Biennial municipal elections in city of Malden.

SECTION 1. Beginning with the year nineteen hundred and thirty-three, municipal elections in the city of Malden for the choice of mayor, aldermen, common councilmen and members of the school committee shall be held biennially on the second Tuesday in December in each odd-numbered year.

Mayor, aldermen, etc., terms.

SECTION 2. Beginning with the biennial municipal election to be held in the year nineteen hundred and thirty-three, the mayor, aldermen and common councilmen of said city shall be elected for terms of two years from the first Monday in January following their election and until their successors are qualified.

School committee.

SECTION 3. At the biennial municipal election to be held in the year nineteen hundred and thirty-three and at every biennial municipal election thereafter, all members of the school committee to be elected shall be elected to serve for four years each and until their successors are qualified. The members of said committee elected in the year nineteen hundred and thirty-one shall continue to hold office until the qualification of their successors who shall be elected at the biennial municipal election in the year nineteen hundred and thirty-five, and the members of said committee elected in the year nineteen hundred and thirty-two shall continue to hold office until the qualification of their successors who shall be elected at the biennial municipal election in the year nineteen hundred and thirty-seven. If a vacancy occurs in the school committee by failure to elect, or otherwise, the city council and the remaining members of the school committee shall meet in joint convention and elect a suitable person to fill the vacancy until the first Monday in January following the next regular municipal election; and, if there would be a vacancy on said first Monday, it shall be filled at such regular municipal election for the balance of the unexpired term.

SECTION 4. So much of chapter one hundred and sixty-nine of the acts of eighteen hundred and eighty-one, and acts in amendment thereof and in addition thereto, as is inconsistent with this act, is hereby repealed. 1881, 169, etc., in part, repealed.

SECTION 5. This act shall be submitted for acceptance to the qualified voters of said city at the annual city election in the current year in the form of the following question, which shall be placed upon the official ballot to be used at said election: — "Shall an act passed by the general court in the current year, entitled 'An Act providing for biennial municipal elections in the city of Malden' be accepted?" If a majority of the votes cast on said question are in the affirmative, this act shall thereupon take full effect; otherwise it shall be of no effect and the officers elected at said election shall respectively hold office for the terms now provided by law. *Approved April 28, 1933.* Acceptance of act.

AN ACT AUTHORIZING THE METROPOLITAN DISTRICT COMMISSION TO APPOINT WILLIAM P. CROWE AS A PERMANENT POLICE OFFICER. *Chap.*156

Be it enacted, etc., as follows:

SECTION 1. The metropolitan district commission may, when a vacancy occurs in its police force or when the personnel of said force is increased or a new position is established therein, appoint as a permanent member of said police force William P. Crowe, who was temporarily injured in the performance of his duty as a call officer employed by said commission under chapter ninety-two of the General Laws; provided, that a physician selected by said commission certifies to it that he has examined said Crowe and finds him physically fit to serve as such police officer. If said Crowe is appointed as aforesaid his retirement allowance under section seventy of chapter thirty-two of the General Laws shall cease.

SECTION 2. This act shall take effect upon its passage. *Approved May 3, 1933.*

Chap.157 AN ACT PROVIDING THAT FAILURE OF A BOARD OF OFFICERS TO TAKE ACTION UPON A PETITION FOR ABATEMENT OF A BETTERMENT ASSESSMENT SHALL, FOR THE PURPOSES OF APPEAL, BE EQUIVALENT TO REFUSAL TO ABATE THE ASSESSMENT.

Be it enacted, etc., as follows:

G. L. (Ter. Ed.), 80, new section after § 10.

Appeal upon failure of board to act on petition for abatement of betterment assessment.

SECTION 1. Chapter eighty of the General Laws is hereby amended by inserting after section ten, as appearing in the Tercentenary Edition thereof, the following new section: — *Section 10A.* If the board with which a petition for the abatement of an assessment has been duly filed in accordance with the provisions of section five fails to act upon said petition within four months of the date of the filing of such petition, the petition shall be deemed to be denied, and the petitioner shall have the right within sixty days after the expiration of said four months to appeal as if the board had in fact denied the said petition;

Proviso.

provided, that if the assessment has been paid, no appeal shall be taken after the expiration of ten months from the time of payment.

G. L. (Ter. Ed.), 80, § 5, amended.

Petition for abatement.

SECTION 2. Section five of said chapter eighty, as so appearing, is hereby amended by striking out, in the fourth and fifth lines, the words "within sixty days after such filing", — so as to read as follows: — *Section 5.* The owner of any real estate upon which betterments have been assessed may, within six months after notice of such assessment has been sent out by the collector, file with the board a petition for an abatement thereof, and the board shall grant such abatement as may be necessary to make such assessment conform to section one. Such petition may be filed with the clerk or secretary of the board, or delivered by mail or otherwise at their office. The board shall within ten days after their decision upon the petition give written notice thereof to the petitioner. If an assessment is abated by the board the assessment so determined shall stand as the assessment upon the land, and if it has not been paid shall be collected in the same manner as the original assessment. If the assessment has been paid, the person by whom it was paid shall be reimbursed by the body politic on behalf of which it was assessed to the amount of the abatement allowed, with interest at the rate of six per cent per annum from the time of payment.

Application of act to pending petitions.

Proviso.

SECTION 3. This act shall apply to petitions for abatement pending when it takes effect; provided, that the time within which any petitioner in such a petition shall have the right to take an appeal under this act shall not be less than sixty days from the effective date thereof.

Approved May 3, 1933.

AN ACT AUTHORIZING THE IMMEDIATE REDUCTION OF SAL- *Chap.*158
ARIES OR REMUNERATION ATTACHED TO CERTAIN OFFICES
IN THE CITY OF WOBURN.

Be it enacted, etc., as follows:

SECTION 1.   Section twenty of chapter one hundred and   1897, 172,
seventy-two of the acts of eighteen hundred and ninety-   § 20, etc.,
seven, as amended by chapter one hundred and eighty-two   amended.
of the Special Acts of nineteen hundred and seventeen,
is hereby further amended by striking out, in the fifth line,
the word "changing" and inserting in place thereof the
word: — increasing, — so as to read as follows: — *Section
20.*   The city council shall establish by ordinance the sal-   Power of city
aries or remuneration of the offices created by this act, in   council of the
                                                                city of
case the same are not fixed herein, and of such other offices   Woburn to
as may hereafter be created; and no ordinance of the city   regulate
                                                             salaries of
council increasing any such salary or remuneration shall   municipal
receive its final passage by the city council after the last   officers.
day of September, and no such ordinance shall take effect
until the municipal year succeeding that in which the ordinance is passed.   Every such proposed ordinance shall be
published once in full in at least one newspaper of the city,
and in any additional manner that may be provided by
ordinance, at least ten days before its final passage.   Such
salaries shall be in full for all services rendered the city by
the incumbents of the respective offices in the discharge of
the duties thereof.

SECTION 2.   This act shall take effect upon its acceptance   Acceptance
by the city council of said city, with the approval of the   of act.
mayor.   *Approved May 3, 1933.*

AN ACT ESTABLISHING AN APPROPRIATION LIMIT FOR THE   *Chap.*159
CITY OF BOSTON.

Be it enacted, etc., as follows:

SECTION 1.   The city of Boston may, by vote of the city   Appropriation
council, with the approval of the mayor, in the manner   limit for city
                                                          of Boston.
specified in section three of chapter four hundred and
eighty-six of the acts of nineteen hundred and nine, make
appropriations for municipal purposes, other than purposes heretofore excluded from the statutory tax limit, for
the financial year ending December thirty-first, nineteen
hundred and thirty-three, from moneys raised or to be
raised by taxation during said year or received or to be
received or available or to become available during said
year from any other source than trust funds, loans made
under authority of any statute in effect prior to January
first of the current year, or income from the water income
division of the department of public works, the printing
department and the City Record, not exceeding the sum of
thirty-six million seven hundred and fifty thousand dol-

lars; provided, that said maximum amount of appropriations may be exceeded for such emergency appropriations as may be approved by a board composed of the attorney general, the state treasurer and the director of the division of accounts, from the proceeds of loans which said city is hereby authorized to make for said purpose, outside its limit of indebtedness, with the approval of said board.

Certain expenditures, etc., authorized in anticipation of appropriations. SECTION 2. Expenditures may be made and liabilities may be incurred by said city under section six of chapter two hundred and sixty-six of the acts of eighteen hundred and eighty-five, as amended by section one of chapter three hundred and twenty of the acts of eighteen hundred and eighty-nine, in anticipation of appropriations therefor in the current year, to an amount not exceeding for each department one half the entire amount appropriated for the department during the preceding year, any provision of said section six, as so amended, to the contrary notwithstanding.

SECTION 3. This act shall take effect upon its passage.

Approved May 3, 1933.

---

*Chap.*160 AN ACT RELATIVE TO PUBLIC BATH HOUSES IN THE TOWN OF MANCHESTER.

Be it enacted, etc., as follows:

SECTION 1. The town of Manchester may accept the provisions of section twelve of chapter forty of the General Laws, as appearing in the Tercentenary Edition thereof, at a special meeting of said town duly called for the purpose and held prior to July first of the current year, by a two thirds vote at such meeting, and upon such acceptance the provisions of said section shall be effective in said town to the same extent as if said section had been accepted at an annual meeting of the town.

SECTION 2. This act shall take effect upon its passage.

Approved May 5, 1933.

---

*Chap.*161 AN ACT AUTHORIZING THE USE OF THE SAME BALLOT AT CERTAIN SPECIAL STATE ELECTIONS HELD ON THE SAME DAY.

Emergency preamble.

Whereas, The deferred operation of this act would defeat its purpose, therefore it is hereby declared to be an emergency law, necessary for the immediate preservation of the public convenience.

Be it enacted, etc., as follows:

Authorizing placing of names of certain candidates on ballot at special state election.

The names of the candidates, with their proper political designations and all other data authorized or required by law to be placed on the official ballot for use in any senatorial or representative district wherein a special election is ordered to be held for the filling of a vacancy in either branch of the general court on the same date as the special state election ordered by the governor and council under chapter one hundred and thirty-two of the acts of the current year, may be placed on the ballot to be used in such district at such special state election, any provision of said chapter one hundred and thirty-two to the contrary notwithstanding.   *Approved May 5, 1933.*

AN ACT REDUCING THE PER DIEM COMPENSATION OF GRAND AND TRAVERSE JURORS.   *Chap.*162

Whereas, The deferred operation of this act would prevent the several counties from saving a substantial amount of money, therefore this act is hereby declared to be an emergency law, necessary for the immediate preservation of the public convenience.   Emergency preamble.

Be it enacted, etc., as follows:

Section twenty-five of chapter two hundred and sixty-two of the General Laws, as appearing in the Tercentenary Edition thereof, is hereby amended by striking out, in the second line, the word "seven" and inserting in place thereof the word: — six, — and by striking out, in the third line, the word "six" and inserting in place thereof the word: — five, — so as to read as follows: — *Section 25.* The compensation of traverse jurors impanelled to try cases of murder in the first degree shall be six dollars, and that of all other traverse jurors and of grand jurors five dollars, for each day's service. All jurors shall receive for each day of actual attendance five cents a mile for travel out and home. If the expense of a juror who attends court, necessarily and actually incurred for transportation out and home once in each day, exceeds the amount of the said allowance for travel, he shall be allowed the amount of such expense in lieu of the said travel allowance. If a grand or traverse juror is required to be in attendance for five or more consecutive days he shall receive his fees not later than the end of every fifth day of such attendance.   G. L. (Ter. Ed.), 262, § 25, amended.
                    Jurors' fees, etc.

                    Approved May 5, 1933.

AN ACT RELATIVE TO THE BONDING OF CERTAIN OFFICERS AND EMPLOYEES OF CREDIT UNIONS, TO THEIR RESERVES AND TO THE MAKING OF LOANS BY THEM.   *Chap.*163

Be it enacted, etc., as follows:

SECTION 1. Section fifteen of chapter one hundred and seventy-one of the General Laws, as appearing in the Tercentenary Edition thereof, is hereby amended by striking out the last sentence and also by adding at the end thereof the following new paragraph: —   G. L. (Ter. Ed.), 171, § 15, amended.

The treasurer and all other officers and employees of a credit union having access to the cash or negotiable securities in its possession shall each give a bond to the directors in such amount and with such surety or sureties and conditions as the commissioner may prescribe, and shall file with   Treasurer, etc., of credit unions to give bond.

him an attested copy thereof, with a certificate of its custodian that the original is in his possession, and the provisions of section twenty-four of chapter one hundred and sixty-eight relative to bonds of officers of savings banks shall apply to bonds given hereunder. The treasurer, and any other officers and employees required to give bond, may be included in one or more blanket or schedule bonds; provided, that such bonds are approved by the commissioner as to the amounts and conditions thereof and as to the sureties thereon.

G. L. (Ter. Ed.), 171, § 21, amended.

SECTION 2. Section twenty-one of said chapter one hundred and seventy-one, as so appearing, is hereby amended by inserting after the word "commonwealth" in the tenth line the words: —, or, to the extent authorized by section three of chapter two hundred and sixteen of the acts of nineteen hundred and thirty-two, in the shares of Central Credit Union Fund, Inc., — and by inserting after the word "provided" in the fifteenth and sixteenth lines the following: —, or in the shares of Central Credit Union Fund, Inc., provided that such bonds, notes or shares are the absolute property and under the control of such credit union, — so as to read as follows: — *Section 21.* The capital, deposits and surplus of a credit union shall be invested in loans to members, with approval of the credit committee, as provided in the following section, and also when so required herein, of the board of directors; and any capital, deposits or surplus funds in excess of the amount for which loans shall be approved by the credit committee and the board of directors, may be deposited in savings banks or trust companies incorporated under the laws of this commonwealth, or in national banks located therein, or invested in any bonds or bankers' acceptances which are at the time of their purchase legal investments for savings banks in this commonwealth, or, to the extent authorized by section three of chapter two hundred and sixteen of the acts of nineteen hundred and thirty-two, in the shares of Central Credit Union Fund, Inc., or in the shares of co-operative banks incorporated in this commonwealth. At least five per cent of the total assets of a credit union shall be carried as cash on hand or as balances due from banks and trust companies, or invested in the bonds or notes of the United States, or of any state, or subdivision thereof, which are legal investments for savings banks as above provided, or in the shares of Central Credit Union Fund, Inc., provided that such bonds, notes or shares are the absolute property and under the control of such credit union. Whenever the aforesaid ratio falls below five per cent, no further loans shall be made until the ratio as herein provided has been re-established. Investments, other than personal loans, shall be made only with the approval of the board of directors.

Investment of funds.

G. L. (Ter. Ed.), 171, § 24, amended.

SECTION 3. Section twenty-four of said chapter one hundred and seventy-one, as so appearing, is hereby

amended by adding at the end of subdivision (A) thereof
the following new paragraph: —

The amount of a loan under paragraph 2, 3, 5 or 6 se- Loans
cured by an unendorsed note of the borrower may, in the regulated.
discretion of the credit committee, exceed by not more than
one hundred dollars the amount warranted, in their opinion,
by the value of the collateral offered as security for the loan;
but the total amount of any such loan shall not exceed the
amount stated in the paragraph under which the loan is
made.   *Approved May 5, 1933.*

AN ACT RELATIVE TO PROCEEDINGS FOR THE SALE OR   *Chap.*164
TAKING OF PROPERTY FOR NON-PAYMENT OF TAXES AND
RELATED PROCEEDINGS.

Be it enacted, etc., as follows:

SECTION 1. Section one of chapter sixty of the General G. L. (Ter.
Laws, as appearing in the Tercentenary Edition thereof, is Ed.), 60, § 1,
hereby amended by striking out the third paragraph and amended.
inserting in place thereof the following: —

"Publication", as applied to any notice, advertisement or Term
other instrument, the publication of which is required by "publication"
law, shall mean the act of printing it once in a newspaper defined.
published in the town, if any, otherwise in the county,
where the land or other property to which the notice or
other instrument relates is situated. The publication shall
be made at least fourteen days prior to the date stated for
the occurrence of the event to which the publication relates.

SECTION 2. Said chapter sixty is hereby further amended G. L. (Ter.
by striking out section forty-two, as so appearing, and Ed.), 60, § 42,
inserting in place thereof the following: —*Section 42.* The Notice to be
collector shall, fourteen days before the sale, post a notice posted.
similar to that required by section forty in two or more
convenient and public places.

SECTION 3. Said chapter sixty is hereby further amended G. L. (Ter.
by striking out section fifty-three, as so appearing, and Ed.), 60, § 53,
inserting in place thereof the following: — *Section 53.* If Taking for
a tax on land is not paid within fourteen days after demand taxes.
therefor and remains unpaid at the date of taking, the
collector may take such land for the town, first giving
fourteen days' notice of his intention to exercise such Notice.
power of taking, which notice may be served in the manner
required by law for the service of subpoenas on witnesses
in civil cases or may be published, and shall conform to
the requirements of section forty. He shall also, fourteen
days before the taking, post a notice so conforming in two
or more convenient and public places.

                                        Approved May 5, 1933.

𝕮𝖍𝖊 𝕮𝖔𝖒𝖒𝖔𝖓𝖜𝖊𝖆𝖑𝖙𝖍 𝖔𝖋 𝕸𝖆𝖘𝖘𝖆𝖈𝖍𝖚𝖘𝖊𝖙𝖙𝖘

EXECUTIVE DEPARTMENT,
BOSTON, MAY 16, 1933.

HONORABLE FREDERIC W. COOK
Secretary of the Commonwealth
State House
SIR:

Governor's declaration making chapter 164 of the acts of the current year an emergency law.

I, Joseph B. Ely, by virtue of and in accordance with the provisions of the Forty-eighth Amendment to the Constitution, "The Referendum II, Emergency Measures", do declare that in my opinion the immediate preservation of the public peace, health, safety and convenience requires that the law passed on the fifth day of May, in the year nineteen hundred and thirty-three, entitled, "An Act relative to Proceedings for the Sale or Taking of Property for Non-Payment of Taxes and Related Proceedings", should take effect forthwith, that it is an emergency law, and that the facts constituting the emergency are as follows:

Because its delayed operation will result in serious expense and hardship to the citizens and communities whom it is intended that this law shall benefit.

Very truly yours,
JOSEPH B. ELY.

Office of the Secretary, Boston, May 17, 1933.

I hereby certify that the accompanying statement was filed in this office by His Excellency the Governor of the Commonwealth of Massachusetts at three o'clock, P.M., on the above date, and in accordance with Article Forty-eight of the Amendments to the Constitution said chapter takes effect forthwith, being chapter one hundred and sixty-four, acts of nineteen hundred and thirty-three.

F. W. COOK,
Secretary of the Commonwealth.

Chap.165 AN ACT ENLARGING THE CLASS OF PERSONS ENTITLED TO APPLY FOR ABATEMENT OF LOCAL TAXES AND TO PURSUE OTHER REMEDIES IN RELATION THERETO.

Be it enacted, etc., as follows:

G. L. (Ter. Ed.), 59, § 59, amended.

SECTION 1. Section fifty-nine of chapter fifty-nine of the General Laws, as appearing in the Tercentenary Edition thereof, is hereby amended by adding at the end thereof the following: — If a person other than the person to whom a tax on real estate is assessed is the owner thereof, or has an interest therein, or is in possession thereof, and pays the tax, he may thereafter prosecute in his own name

Abatements. Persons entitled to apply therefor.

any application, appeal or action provided by law for the abatement or recovery of such tax, which after the payment thereof shall be deemed for the purposes of such application, appeal or action, to have been assessed to the person so paying the same.

SECTION 2. Section sixty-one of said chapter fifty-nine, as so appearing, is hereby amended by striking out the last sentence and inserting in place thereof the following: — A person applying for an abatement of a tax on real estate may have an abatement although no list of the owner's estate was brought in as required by the said notice; provided, that in any application for an abatement of such a tax the applicant shall include a sufficient description in writing of the particular real estate as to which an abatement is requested.   *Approved May 5, 1933.*

G. L. (Ter. Ed.), 59, § 61, amended.

Conditions of abatement.

Proviso.

AN ACT AUTHORIZING THE USE WITHOUT CHARGE OF ARMORIES FOR DRILL PURPOSES BY CERTAIN ORGANIZATIONS OF WAR VETERANS.

*Chap.*166

Be it enacted, etc., as follows:

Subsection (a) of section forty-eight of chapter thirty-three of the General Laws, as most recently amended by chapter one hundred and sixty-one of the acts of nineteen hundred and thirty-two, is hereby further amended by inserting after the word "by" in the ninth line the words: — drill teams, — so as to read as follows: — (a) Armories provided for the militia shall be used by the militia for the military purposes or purposes incidental thereto designated by the commander-in-chief. Any armory, when not in use for military purposes, may be used, without charge and subject only to rules and regulations promulgated by the military custodian of such armory and approved by the governor and council, for social activities or athletics by military units stationed in such armory, or for drill purposes by drill teams, bands or drum corps composed of members of organizations of war veterans. No non-military use of an armory under this section shall be permitted which interferes with its military use, but such non-military use shall not be deemed to interfere with military use if all unit commanders affected can conveniently and without detriment to the service utilize the armory for the usual military purposes at other than the usual time or in other than the usual manner.   *Approved May 5, 1933.*

G. L. (Ter. Ed.), 33, § 48, subsect. (a), etc., amended.

Use of armories regulated.

AN ACT RELATIVE TO APPEALS UPON CERTAIN MATTERS CONCERNING TAXATION.

*Chap.*167

Be it enacted, etc., as follows:

SECTION 1. Section sixty-five of chapter fifty-nine of the General Laws, as most recently amended by section two of chapter one hundred and thirty of the acts of the current

G. L. (Ter. Ed.), 59, § 65, etc., amended.

year, is hereby further amended by striking out, in the sixth line, the words "of the giving of" and inserting in place thereof the words: — after receiving, — so as to read

as follows: — *Section 65.* A person aggrieved as aforesaid may, instead of pursuing the remedy provided in section sixty-four, but subject to the same conditions, appeal to the board of tax appeals by filing a petition with such board within sixty days after receiving the notice required by section sixty-three. Such appeal shall be heard and determined by said board in the manner provided by chapter fifty-eight A. The board may enter such order as justice may require in the manner provided in the preceding section with respect to complaints removed from the county commissioners.

Section 2. Section thirty-six of chapter sixty-two of the General Laws, as appearing in the Tercentenary Edition thereof, is hereby amended by inserting after the word "after" in the third line the word: — receiving, — so

as to read as follows: — *Section 36.* If any person who has failed to file a return, or has filed an incorrect or insufficient return, and has been notified by the commissioner of his delinquency, refuses or neglects within twenty days after receiving such notice to file a proper return, or if any person files a fraudulent return, the commissioner shall determine the income of such person, taxable under this chapter, according to his best information and belief, and assess the same at not more than double the amount so determined.

Section 3. Section seventy-one of chapter sixty-three of the General Laws, as so appearing, is hereby amended by inserting after the word "after" in the fourth line the words: — the date of, — so as to read as follows: — *Section 71.* Except as otherwise provided, any party ag-

grieved by any decision of the commissioner upon any matter arising under this chapter from which an appeal is given, may appeal to the board of tax appeals within thirty days after the date of notice of his decision. Any overpayment of tax determined by decision of said board of tax appeals shall be reimbursed by the commonwealth with interest at the rate of six per cent per annum from the time of payment. Taxes, excises, costs or expenses of any kind assessed upon any corporation, company or association, except a municipal corporation, under the provisions of this chapter or corresponding provisions of earlier laws, which are unpaid and are uncollectable, may be abated by the board of tax appeals on the recommendation of the attorney general and commissioner at any time after the expiration of five years from the date when the same became payable.

Section 4. Chapter fifty-eight A of the General Laws, as amended in section six by section ten of chapter one hundred and eighty of the acts of nineteen hundred and thirty-two, is hereby further amended by striking out said section six and inserting in place thereof the following: —

Section 6. The board shall have jurisdiction to decide appeals under the provisions of section forty-two E of chapter forty; sections eleven, fourteen and twenty-five of chapter fifty-eight; of clauses seventeenth and twenty-second of section five of chapter fifty-nine; of sections seven, thirty-nine, sixty-four, sixty-five, seventy-three and eighty-one of said chapter fifty-nine; of section two of chapter sixty A; of section forty-five of chapter sixty-two; of sections two, five, eighteen A, twenty-eight, fifty-one, sixty and seventy-one of chapter sixty-three; of section six of chapter sixty-four; of sections five and ten of chapter sixty-four A; of sections twenty-five and twenty-six of chapter sixty-five; of section four of chapter sixty-five A; and under any other provision of law wherein such jurisdiction is or may be expressly conferred. Except as otherwise provided by law, no appeal to the board shall stay the collection of any tax or excise. Whenever the commissioner of corporations and taxation, in this chapter called the commissioner, or a board of assessors, before whom or which an application in writing for the abatement of a tax is or shall be pending, fails to act upon said application, except with the written consent of the applicant, prior to the expiration of four months from the date of filing of such application, it shall then be deemed to be denied, and the taxpayer shall have the right, at any time within ninety days thereafter, to take any appeal from such denial to which he may be entitled by law, in the same manner as though the commissioner or board of assessors had in fact refused to grant the abatement applied for.

SECTION 5. The provisions of section four shall apply to all applications for abatement pending when they take effect; provided, that the time within which any taxpayer shall have the right to take an appeal thereunder shall not be less than ninety days from the effective date thereof.

Approved May 5, 1933.

Board of tax appeals, jurisdiction.

Certain provisions of act to apply to pending applications for abatement.

AN ACT RELATIVE TO PROCEEDINGS BY COLLECTORS OF TAXES IN RESPECT TO DEMANDS AND TO FORMS FOR USE IN THE COLLECTION OF LOCAL TAXES.

Chap.168

Be it enacted, etc., as follows:

SECTION 1. Chapter sixty of the General Laws is hereby amended by striking out section sixteen, as appearing in the Tercentenary Edition thereof, and inserting in place thereof the following: — *Section 16.* The collector shall, before selling the land of a resident, or non-resident, or distraining the goods of any person, or arresting him for his tax, serve on him a statement of the amount thereof with a demand for its payment. If two or more parcels of land are assessed in the name of a resident, or non-resident, the statement of the aggregate amount of the taxes thereon may be made in one demand. Such demand may also include taxes due

G. L. (Ter. Ed.), 60, § 16, amended.

Proceedings by collectors of taxes prior to sale, etc.

Demand.

on account of tangible personal property and any motor vehicle excise tax. If the heirs of a deceased person, co-partners or two or more persons are jointly assessed, service need be made on only one of them. Such demand for the tax upon land may be made upon the person occupying the same on April first of the year in which the tax is assessed. No demand need be made on a mortgagee, unless he has given notice under section thirty-eight, in which case no demand need be made on the owner or occupant. Demand shall be made by the collector by mailing the same to the last or usual place of business or abode, or to the address best known to him, and failure to receive the same shall not invalidate a tax or any proceedings for the enforcement or collection of the same.

G. L. (Ter. Ed.), 60, § 5, amended.
Collectors to collect poll taxes.

Section 2. Said chapter sixty is hereby further amended by striking out section five, as so appearing, and inserting in place thereof the following: — *Section 5.* A collector of taxes receiving from the assessors a list and warrant under the preceding section shall forthwith proceed to collect the poll taxes from the persons entered on such list. Poll taxes shall be due and payable at the expiration of thirty days from the date upon which the notice under section three was issued by the collector. At the expiration of said thirty days the collector may issue a demand for payment or may include a statement of the amount due in a demand issued under section sixteen. All laws relating to the collection of taxes, to the duties and powers of collectors, to money collected as taxes, interest, charges and fees, to the accounting for and turning over of money so collected, and to the crediting thereof to the collector, shall apply to the collection of poll taxes from the persons whose names appear on such lists.

G. L. (Ter. Ed.), 60, § 105, amended.
Forms.

Section 3. Said chapter sixty is hereby further amended by striking out section one hundred and five, as so appearing, and the schedule of forms thereto annexed, and inserting in place thereof the following: — *Section 105.* Forms to be used in proceedings for the collection of taxes under this chapter and of all assessments which the collector is authorized or required by law to collect shall be as prescribed by the commissioner.

Demand may include statement of old age assistance tax.

Section 4. A collector of taxes may include in a demand issued under the provisions of said section sixteen a statement of any old age assistance tax assessed under section one of chapter three hundred and ninety-eight of the acts of nineteen hundred and thirty-one or any amendment thereof. *Approved May 5, 1933.*

AN ACT RELATIVE TO TRANSFERS OF DEFECTIVE DELIN- *Chap.*169
QUENTS AND DRUG ADDICTS FROM ONE INSTITUTION TO
ANOTHER UNDER THE DEPARTMENT OF CORRECTION.

Be it enacted, etc., as follows:

Chapter one hundred and twenty-seven of the General G. L. (Ter.
Laws is hereby amended by inserting after section one section after
hundred and eleven, as appearing in the Tercentenary § 111.
Edition thereof, the following new section: — *Section 111A.* Removal of
He may remove any person committed to a department for linquents, etc.,
defective delinquents or for drug addicts established at any from one in-
institution under the department of correction under sec- another.
tion one hundred and seventeen of chapter one hundred and
twenty-three, from such department to a like department
at any other institution under the department of correction.
Approved May 5, 1933.

AN ACT RELATIVE TO THE AUTHORITY OF STATE DEPART- *Chap.*170
MENTS, COMMISSIONS OR BOARDS TO PROCURE QUARTERS
OR OCCUPY PREMISES OUTSIDE THE STATE HOUSE OR OTHER
BUILDING OWNED BY THE COMMONWEALTH AND TO THE
EXECUTION OF LEASES THEREFOR.

Whereas, The deferred operation of this act would tend Emergency
to defeat its purpose, therefore it is hereby declared to be preamble.
an emergency law, necessary for the immediate preservation
of the public convenience.

Be it enacted, etc., as follows:

Chapter eight of the General Laws is hereby amended by G. L. (Ter.
striking out section ten A, as appearing in the Tercentenary amended.
Edition thereof, and inserting in place thereof the following: — *Section 10A.* The executive or administrative head Leasing by
of any state department, commission or board, after an ments, etc., of
appropriation has been made for the payment of rent for the premises out-
then current fiscal year, may, subject to the approval of the ings owned by
superintendent of buildings and of the governor and coun- common-
cil, procure quarters or occupy premises outside of the state approval.
house or other building owned by the commonwealth, and,
subject to like approval, may, in the name and behalf of the
commonwealth, execute a lease or leases of any such quarters or premises for a term or terms not exceeding five years
each.   *Approved May 9, 1933.*

AN ACT RELATIVE TO THE EDUCATIONAL QUALIFICATIONS OF *Chap.*171
APPLICANTS FOR REGISTRATION AS QUALIFIED PHYSICIANS.

Whereas, The deferred operation of this act would tend Emergency
to defeat its purpose, therefore it is hereby declared to be preamble.
an emergency law, necessary for the immediate preservation of the public convenience.

Be it enacted, etc., as follows:

G. L. (Ter. Ed.), 112, § 2, amended.

SECTION 1. Section two of chapter one hundred and twelve of the General Laws, as appearing in the Tercentenary Edition thereof, is hereby amended by striking out the second sentence and inserting in place thereof the following: — Each applicant who shall furnish the board with satisfactory proof that he is twenty-one or over and of good moral character, that he possesses the educational qualifications required for graduation from a public high school, that he has attended four years of instruction of not less than thirty-two school weeks in each year in one or more legally chartered medical schools and that he has received the degree of doctor of medicine, or its equivalent, from a legally chartered medical school having the power to confer degrees in medicine shall, upon payment of twenty-five dollars, be examined, and, if found qualified by the board, be registered as a qualified physician and entitled to a certificate in testimony thereof, signed by the chairman and secretary.

Educational requirements for registration as qualified physicians.

Present law to apply in certain cases.

SECTION 2. The provisions of said section two as existing immediately prior to the effective date of this act shall continue to govern as to the eligibility of any applicant for registration as a qualified physician, who was on March tenth, nineteen hundred and seventeen, a matriculant of any legally chartered medical school having power to confer degrees in medicine, notwithstanding the passage of this act. *Approved May 9, 1933.*

Chap.172 AN ACT PROVIDING FOR ADDITIONAL STATE AID IN THE EXTERMINATION OF STARFISH IN THE WATERS OF BUZZARD'S BAY, VINEYARD SOUND, NANTUCKET SOUND AND IN CERTAIN OTHER WATERS.

Emergency preamble.

Whereas, The deferred operation of this act would tend to defeat its purpose, therefore it is hereby declared to be an emergency law, necessary for the immediate preservation of the public convenience.

Be it enacted, etc., as follows:

Extermination of starfish in Buzzard's Bay, etc.

The division of fisheries and game of the department of conservation may expend such sums, not exceeding in the aggregate, fifteen thousand dollars, as may hereafter be appropriated therefor, in addition to the unexpended balance of the amount appropriated by item two hundred and eighty-two b of chapter three hundred and seven of the acts of nineteen hundred and thirty-two, and subject to the same conditions and restrictions as are imposed by chapter two hundred and forty-four of the acts of nineteen hundred and thirty-two, for the purpose of exterminating starfish in the waters of Buzzard's Bay, Vineyard Sound, Nantucket Sound or in any other waters wherein such extermination may be deemed desirable by said division, in co-operation with municipalities whose territory extends into such waters.   *Approved May 9, 1933.*

AN ACT RELATIVE TO THE BOARD OF PUBLIC WELFARE OF THE CITY OF SPRINGFIELD.

*Chap.*173

Be it enacted, etc., as follows:

SECTION 1. Section eight of chapter ninety-four of the acts of eighteen hundred and fifty-two is hereby amended by striking out, in the third and fourth lines of the second paragraph, the words ", three persons to be overseers of the poor", — so that said paragraph will read as follows: —

1852, 94, § 8, amended.

The city council shall, annually, as soon after their organization as may be convenient, elect by joint ballot, in convention, three assessors, a collector of taxes, and a chief engineer and as many assistants not exceeding twelve as they may by vote determine, and fix their compensations, and the compensations of the city clerk, city treasurer, and school committee. They shall also, in such manner as they shall determine by any by-law, appoint, or elect, all other subordinate officers not herein otherwise directed for the ensuing year, and define their duties and fix their compensations in cases where the same are not defined and fixed by the laws of the commonwealth. All sittings of the mayor and aldermen, and of the common council, shall be public, when they are not engaged in executive business.

Election of certain municipal officers in the city of Springfield.

SECTION 2. Section eleven of said chapter ninety-four is hereby amended by striking out the first paragraph.

1852, 94, § 11, amended.

SECTION 3. Chapter one hundred and twenty-six of the acts of eighteen hundred and seventy-three is hereby amended by striking out section three and inserting in place thereof the following: — *Section 3.* There shall be a board of public welfare consisting of five citizens of the city of Springfield, one of whom shall annually, within sixty days after the organization of the city council, be appointed by the mayor, with the approval of the city council by concurrent vote, for five years from the first day of April next following. Not more than three members of said board shall be members of the same political party. No person shall be appointed a member of said board unless he shall have been a resident of said city for at least three years next prior to his appointment, and no member of the city council or person who holds any political office for which he receives compensation shall be a member of said board. The mayor may, with the approval of the city council by concurrent vote, remove for cause any member of said board. Vacancies by reason of resignation, removal from the city, removal from office, membership in the city council or holding of political office for which compensation is received shall be filled for the unexpired term by the mayor, with the approval of the city council by concurrent vote.

1873, 126, § 3, amended.

Board of public welfare, appointment, term, removal.

Said board shall have all the rights and powers and perform all the duties conferred and imposed upon it by law or ordinance. Said board may make rules for the government of its procedure, and shall choose one of its members to be chairman for such term as it may prescribe.

1878, 97, repealed. SECTION 4. Chapter ninety-seven of the acts of eighteen hundred and seventy-eight is hereby repealed.

Present board to continue in office. SECTION 5. The present members of the board of public welfare of the city of Springfield shall continue to hold office until the expiration of their respective terms of office, and the mayor shall, within two months from the effective date of this act, with the approval of the city council by concurrent vote, appoint the two additional members of said board provided for under section three of this act, qualified as provided therein, one of whom shall be appointed for four years and one for five years, from April first in the current year.

SECTION 6. This act shall take effect upon its passage.

Approved May 9, 1933.

*Chap.*174 AN ACT MAKING APPROPRIATIONS FOR THE MAINTENANCE OF DEPARTMENTS, BOARDS, COMMISSIONS, INSTITUTIONS AND CERTAIN ACTIVITIES OF THE COMMONWEALTH, FOR INTEREST, SINKING FUND AND SERIAL BOND REQUIREMENTS, AND FOR CERTAIN PERMANENT IMPROVEMENTS.

Be it enacted, etc., as follows:

Appropriations for maintenance of state departments, etc., for interest, sinking fund and bond requirements, and for certain improvements. SECTION 1. To provide for the maintenance of the several departments, boards, commissions and institutions, of sundry other services, and for certain permanent improvements, and to meet certain requirements of law, the sums set forth in section two as reduced under authority of section three hereof, for the several purposes and subject to the conditions specified in said section two, are hereby appropriated from the general fund or revenue of the commonwealth, unless some other source of revenue is expressed, subject to the provisions of law regulating the disbursement of public funds and the approval thereof, for the fiscal year ending November thirtieth, nineteen hundred and thirty-three, or for such other period as may be specified.

SECTION 2.

Service of the Legislative Department.

Item		
1	For the compensation of senators, a sum not exceeding seventy-three thousand eight hundred dollars	$73,800 00
2	For the compensation for travel of senators, a sum not exceeding fifty-eight hundred dollars . .	5,800 00
3	For the compensation of representatives, a sum not exceeding four hundred thirty-three thousand eight hundred dollars	433,800 00
4	For the compensation for travel of representatives, a sum not exceeding thirty-six thousand three hundred dollars	36,300 00
5	For the salaries of the clerk of the senate and the clerk of the house of representatives, a sum not exceeding ninety-six hundred dollars . . .	9,600 00

Item
6 For the salaries of the assistant clerk of the senate and the assistant clerk of the house of representatives, a sum not exceeding sixty-seven hundred and twenty dollars $6,720 00
7 For such additional clerical assistance to, and with the approval of the clerk of the house of representatives, as may be necessary for the proper despatch of public business, a sum not exceeding thirty-eight hundred and forty dollars . . 3,840 00
8 For such additional clerical assistance to, and with the approval of the clerk of the senate, as may be necessary for the proper despatch of public business, a sum not exceeding fourteen hundred and forty dollars 1,440 00
9 For the salary of the sergeant-at-arms, a sum not exceeding thirty-eight hundred and forty dollars . 3,840 00
10 For clerical assistance, office of the sergeant-at-arms, a sum not exceeding five thousand and ninety-six dollars 5,096 00
11 For the compensation for travel of doorkeepers, assistant doorkeepers, general court officers, pages and other employees of the sergeant-at-arms, authorized by law to receive the same, a sum not exceeding sixty-five hundred and ninety-four dollars 6,594 00
12 For the salaries of the doorkeepers of the senate and house of representatives, and the postmaster, with the approval of the sergeant-at-arms, a sum not exceeding seventy-six hundred and eighty dollars 7,680 00
13 For the salaries of assistant doorkeepers to the senate and house of representatives and of general court officers, with the approval of the sergeant-at-arms, a sum not exceeding forty-eight thousand five hundred and seventy-six dollars . . . 48,576 00
14 For compensation of the pages of the senate and house of representatives, with the approval of the sergeant-at-arms, a sum not exceeding eighty-seven hundred and thirty-six dollars . . . 8,736 00
15 For the salaries of clerks employed in the legislative document room, a sum not exceeding fifty-four hundred and seventy-two dollars . . . 5,472 00
16 For certain other persons employed by the sergeant-at-arms, in and about the chambers and rooms of the legislative department, a sum not exceeding three thousand and twenty-four dollars . . 3,024 00
17 For the salaries of the chaplains of the senate and house of representatives, a sum not exceeding fourteen hundred and forty dollars . . 1,440 00
18 For personal services of the counsel to the senate and assistants, a sum not exceeding fifteen thousand and forty-eight dollars 15,048 00
19 For personal services of the counsel to the house of representatives and assistants, a sum not exceeding fifteen thousand one hundred and ninety-two dollars 15,192 00
20 For clerical and other assistance of the senate committee on rules, a sum not exceeding thirty-eight hundred and forty dollars . . . 3,840 00
21 For clerical and other assistance of the house committee on rules, a sum not exceeding thirty-eight hundred and forty dollars . . . 3,840 00
22 For traveling and such other expenses of the committees of the present general court as may be authorized by order of either branch of the general court, a sum not exceeding four thousand dollars 4,000 00

Item
23 For expenses of advertising hearings of the committees of the present general court, including
expenses of preparing and mailing advertisements
to the various newspapers, with the approval of
the comptroller of the commonwealth, a sum not
exceeding one hundred dollars   . $100 00
24 For printing, binding and paper ordered by the senate and house of representatives, or by concurrent
order of the two branches, with the approval of
the clerks of the respective branches, a sum not
exceeding fifty thousand dollars   .   .   .   50,000 00
25 For printing the manual of the general court, with
the approval of the clerks of the two branches, a
sum not exceeding five thousand dollars   .   .   5,000 00
26 For expenses in connection with the publication of
the bulletin of committee hearings and of the
daily list, and for the expense of printing a cumulative index to the acts and resolves of the current
year, with the approval of the joint committee on
rules, a sum not exceeding fifteen thousand six
hundred dollars 15,600 00
27 For stationery for the senate, purchased by and with
the approval of the clerk, a sum not exceeding five
hundred dollars 500 00
28 For office and other expenses of the committee on
rules on the part of the senate, a sum not exceeding three hundred dollars 300 00
29 For office expenses of the counsel to the senate, a
sum not exceeding five hundred dollars   .   .   500 00
30 For stationery for the house of representatives, purchased by and with the approval of the clerk, a
sum not exceeding eight hundred dollars   .   .   800 00
31 For office and other expenses of the committee on
rules on the part of the house, a sum not exceeding
two hundred dollars 200 00
32 For office expenses of the counsel to the house of representatives, a sum not exceeding five hundred
dollars 500 00
33 For contingent expenses of the senate and house of
representatives, and necessary expenses in and
about the state house, with the approval of the
sergeant-at-arms, a sum not exceeding fourteen
thousand eight hundred dollars   .   .   .   14,800 00
34 For the purchase of outline sketches of members of
the senate and house of representatives, a sum not
exceeding sixteen hundred dollars   .   .   .   1,600 00
34a For reprinting the latest edition of the state house
guide book, a sum not exceeding five hundred
dollars 500 00
34b For the payment of witness fees to persons summoned to appear before committees of the general
court, and for expenses incidental to summoning
them, with the approval of the sergeant-at-arms,
a sum not exceeding two hundred dollars   .   .   200 00
34c For expenses of the revision and rearrangement of
the general statutes of the commonwealth, as
authorized by chapter fifty-eight of the resolves
of nineteen hundred and thirty and by chapters
sixty-seven and sixty-eight of the resolves of
nineteen hundred and thirty-one, including preparation of the index, a sum not exceeding nine
thousand dollars, the same to be in addition to
any amount heretofore appropriated for the
purpose 9,000 00
                                                      _____
        Total $803,278 00

Service of the Judicial Department.

Item

Supreme Judicial Court, as follows:
35 For the salaries of the chief justice and of the six associate justices, a sum not exceeding ninety-three thousand seven hundred and twenty dollars $93,720 00
36 For traveling allowance and expenses, a sum not exceeding forty-five hundred dollars . . 4,500 00
37 For the salary of the clerk for the commonwealth, a sum not exceeding sixty-one hundred and fifty-four dollars 6,154 00
38 For clerical assistance to the clerk, a sum not exceeding seventeen hundred and twenty-eight dollars . 1,728 00
39 For law clerks, stenographers and other clerical assistance for the justices, a sum not exceeding twenty-three thousand and forty dollars . . 23,040 00
40 For office supplies, services and equipment of the supreme judicial court, a sum not exceeding forty-five hundred dollars 4,500 00
41 For the salaries of the officers and messengers, a sum not exceeding twenty-nine hundred and twenty dollars 2,920 00
42 For the commonwealth's part of the salary of the clerk for the county of Suffolk, a sum not exceeding fourteen hundred and forty dollars . . 1,440 00

Reporter of Decisions:
43 For the salary of the reporter of decisions, a sum not exceeding fifty-six hundred and eighty dollars . 5,680 00
44 For clerk hire and office supplies, services and equipment, a sum not exceeding ninety-eight hundred and twenty dollars 9,820 00

Pensions:
45 For the pensions of retired court officers, a sum not exceeding two hundred dollars 200 00

Total $153,702 00

Superior Court, as follows:
46 For the salaries of the chief justice and of the thirty-one associate justices, a sum not exceeding three hundred sixty-four thousand four hundred and sixty-seven dollars $364,467 00
47 For traveling allowance and expenses, a sum not exceeding nineteen thousand five hundred dollars 19,500 00
48 For the salary of the assistant clerk, Suffolk county, a sum not exceeding nine hundred and sixty dollars 960 00
49 For clerical work, inspection of records and doings of persons authorized to admit to bail, for an executive clerk to the chief justice, and for certain other expenses incident to the work of the court, a sum not exceeding ten thousand three hundred and twenty dollars 10,320 00
50 For pensions of retired justices, a sum not exceeding twelve thousand dollars 12,000 00

Total $407,247 00

Justices of District Courts:
51 For compensation of justices of district courts while sitting in the superior court, a sum not exceeding twenty-four thousand one hundred and ninety-two dollars $24,192 00
52 For expenses of justices of district courts while sitting in the superior court, a sum not exceeding thirty-two hundred and forty dollars . . 3,240 00

Item

53   For reimbursing certain counties for compensation
of certain special justices for services in holding
sessions of district courts in place of the justice,
while sitting in the superior court, a sum not
exceeding sixty-five hundred dollars .   .   . $6,500 00

      Total $33,932 00

Judicial Council:

54   For expenses of the judicial council, as authorized by
section thirty-four C of chapter two hundred and
twenty-one of the General Laws, as appearing in
the Tercentenary Edition thereof, a sum not
exceeding fifteen hundred dollars   .   . $1,500 00

55   For compensation of the secretary of the judicial
council, as authorized by said section thirty-four
C of said chapter two hundred and twenty-one,
a sum not exceeding thirty-three hundred and
sixty dollars 3,360 00

      Total $4,860 00

Administrative Committee of District Courts:

56   For compensation and expenses of the administrative committee of district courts, a sum not exceeding seventeen hundred and sixty dollars   . $1,760 00

Probate and Insolvency Courts, as follows:

57   For the salaries of judges of probate of the several
counties, a sum not exceeding one hundred five
thousand nine hundred and forty-seven dollars . $105,947 00

58   For pensions of retired judges, a sum not exceeding
sixty-three hundred and seventy-five dollars   .   6,375 00

59   For the compensation of judges of probate when
acting outside their own counties for other judges
of probate, a sum not exceeding thirteen thousand four hundred and forty dollars .   .   13,440 00

60   For expenses of judges of probate when acting outside their own counties for other judges of probate, as authorized by section forty of chapter
two hundred and seventeen of the General Laws,
as appearing in the Tercentenary Edition thereof,
a sum not exceeding nine hundred dollars .   .   900 00

61   For the salaries of registers of the several counties, a
sum not exceeding sixty thousand four hundred
and forty-three dollars 60,443 00

62   For the salaries of assistant registers, a sum not exceeding sixty-nine thousand seven hundred and
ninety dollars 69,790 00

      Total $256,895 00

Administrative Committee of Probate Courts:

63   For expenses of the administrative committee of
probate courts, a sum not exceeding five hundred
dollars $500 00

For clerical assistance to Registers of the several
counties, as follows:

64   Barnstable, a sum not exceeding twenty-one hundred and sixteen dollars   .   .   . $2,116 00

65   Berkshire, a sum not exceeding forty-one hundred
and eighty dollars 4,180 00

66   Bristol, a sum not exceeding thirteen thousand nine
hundred dollars 13,900 00

67   Dukes county, a sum not exceeding six hundred
dollars 600 00

Item
68 Essex, a sum not exceeding fifteen thousand eight
    hundred and twenty dollars $15,820 00
69 Franklin, a sum not exceeding ten hundred and
    forty dollars 1,040 00
70 Hampden, a sum not exceeding ninety-six hundred
    and twenty dollars 9,620 00
71 Hampshire, a sum not exceeding sixteen hundred
    and forty dollars 1,640 00
72 Middlesex, a sum not exceeding forty-four thousand
    seven hundred and twenty dollars . . . 44,720 00
73 Norfolk, a sum not exceeding eleven thousand six
    hundred and fifteen dollars . . . 11,615 00
74 Plymouth, a sum not exceeding forty-three hundred
    and thirty-four dollars 4,334 00
75 Suffolk, a sum not exceeding fifty-nine thousand
    two hundred and forty dollars . . . 59,240 00
76 Worcester, a sum not exceeding fourteen thousand
    three hundred and twenty dollars . . . 14,320 00

       Total $183,145 00

District Attorneys, as follows:
77 For the salaries of the district attorney and assist-
    ants for the Suffolk district, a sum not exceeding
    fifty-seven thousand three hundred and seven
    dollars $57,307 00
78 For the salaries of the district attorney and assist-
    ants for the northern district, a sum not exceed-
    ing twenty-two thousand nine hundred and forty-
    seven dollars 22,947 00
79 For the salaries of the district attorney and assist-
    ants for the eastern district, a sum not exceeding
    fourteen thousand three hundred and twenty
    dollars 14,320 00
80 For the salaries of the district attorney, deputy dis-
    trict attorney and assistants for the southeastern
    district, a sum not exceeding fourteen thousand
    eight hundred and ninety-six dollars . . . 14,896 00
81 For the salaries of the district attorney and assist-
    ants for the southern district, a sum not exceeding
    ninety-nine hundred and eighty-four dollars . 9,984 00
82 For the salaries of the district attorney and assist-
    ants for the middle district, a sum not exceeding
    fourteen thousand three hundred and twenty
    dollars 14,320 00
83 For the salaries of the district attorney and assist-
    ants for the western district, a sum not exceeding
    eight thousand and sixty-four dollars . . 8,064 00
84 For the salary of the district attorney for the north-
    western district, a sum not exceeding twenty-
    eight hundred and eighty dollars . . . 2,880 00
85 For traveling expenses necessarily incurred by the
    district attorneys, except in the Suffolk district,
    for the present and previous years, a sum not ex-
    ceeding nine thousand dollars 9,000 00

       Total $153,718 00

Service of the Land Court.
86 For the salaries of the judge, associate judges, the
    recorder and court officer, a sum not exceeding
    forty thousand nine hundred and fifty-four
    dollars $40,954 00
87 For engineering, clerical and other personal serv-
    ices, a sum not exceeding thirty-seven thousand
    nine hundred and forty dollars 37,940 00

Item
88 For personal services in the examination of titles, for publishing and serving citations and other services, traveling expenses, supplies and office equipment, and for the preparation of sectional plans showing registered land, a sum not exceeding sixteen thousand dollars $16,000 00

    Total $94,894 00

Service of the Board of Probation.

89 For personal services of the commissioner, clerks and stenographers, a sum not exceeding fifty thousand one hundred and thirty dollars . . . $50,130 00
90 For services other than personal, including printing the annual report, traveling expenses, rent, office supplies and equipment, a sum not exceeding eleven thousand four hundred dollars . . 11,400 00

    Total $61,530 00

Service of the Board of Bar Examiners.

91 For personal services of the members of the board, a sum not exceeding ten thousand five hundred and sixty dollars $10,560 00
92 For other services, including printing the annual report, traveling expenses, office supplies and equipment, a sum not exceeding eighty-eight hundred and sixty dollars . . . 8,860 00

    Total $19,420 00

Service of the Executive Department.

93 For the salary of the governor, a sum not exceeding ninety-four hundred and sixty-seven dollars . $9,467 00
94 For the salary of the lieutenant governor, a sum not exceeding thirty-eight hundred and forty dollars . 3,840 00
95 For the salaries of the eight councillors, a sum not exceeding seventy-six hundred and eighty dollars . 7,680 00
96 For the salaries of officers and employees of the department, a sum not exceeding thirty-four thousand one hundred dollars . . . 34,100 00
97 For certain personal services for the lieutenant governor and council, a sum not exceeding twenty-two hundred and five dollars . . . 2,205 00
98 For travel and expenses of the lieutenant governor and council from and to their homes, a sum not exceeding one thousand dollars . . 1,000 00
99 For postage, printing, office and other contingent expenses, including travel of the governor, a sum not exceeding fifteen thousand dollars . . 15,000 00
100 For postage, printing, stationery, traveling and contingent expenses of the governor and council, a sum not exceeding twenty-five hundred dollars 2,500 00
101 For expenses incurred in the arrest of fugitives from justice, a sum not exceeding one thousand dollars . 1,000 00
102 For payment of extraordinary expenses and for transfers made to cover deficiencies, with the approval of the governor and council, a sum not exceeding one hundred thousand dollars . . 100,000 00
103 For the purchase of an automobile for the governor, a sum not exceeding three thousand dollars . 3,000 00
104 For certain maintenance expenses of the governor's automobile, a sum not exceeding two thousand dollars 2,000 00

    Total $181,792 00

Service of the Adjutant General.

Item
105 For the salary of the adjutant general, a sum not exceeding thirty-nine hundred and thirty-six dollars $3,936 00
106 For personal services of office assistants, including services for the preparation of records of Massachusetts soldiers and sailors, a sum not exceeding thirty-two thousand two hundred and forty dollars 32,240 00
107 For services other than personal, printing the annual report, and for necessary office supplies and expenses, a sum not exceeding fifty-five hundred dollars 5,500 00
108 For expenses of the national guard convention and for expenses not otherwise provided for in connection with military matters and accounts, a sum not exceeding eight thousand dollars . . 8,000 00

Total $49,676 00

Service of the Militia.

109 For allowances to companies and other administrative units, a sum not exceeding one hundred fifty-six thousand dollars $156,000 00
110 For certain allowances for national guard officers, as authorized by paragraph (d) of section one hundred and forty-five of chapter thirty-three of the General Laws, as appearing in the Tercentenary Edition thereof, a sum not exceeding twenty-four thousand dollars 24,000 00
111 For pay and transportation of certain boards, a sum not exceeding two thousand dollars . . 2,000 00
112 For pay and expenses of certain camps of instruction, a sum not exceeding four thousand dollars . 4,000 00
113 For pay and transportation in making inspections and surveys, and for escort duty, a sum not exceeding four thousand dollars . . . 4,000 00
114 For transportation of officers and non-commissioned officers for attendance at military meetings, a sum not exceeding four thousand dollars . 4,000 00
115 For transportation to and from regimental and battalion drills, a sum not exceeding fifteen hundred dollars 1,500 00
116 For transportation when appearing for examination, a sum not exceeding two hundred dollars . 200 00
117 For expenses of rifle practice, a sum not exceeding eleven thousand dollars 11,000 00
118 For compensation, transportation and expenses in the preparation for camp duty maneuvers, a sum not exceeding twenty-five thousand dollars . 25,000 00
119 (This item consolidated with Item 139.)
120 For compensation for special and miscellaneous duty, a sum not exceeding eleven thousand seven hundred and fifty dollars . . . 11,750 00
121 For compensation for accidents and injuries sustained in the performance of military duty, a sum not exceeding seven thousand dollars . 7,000 00
122 To cover certain small claims for damages to private property arising from military maneuvers, a sum not exceeding six hundred dollars . . 600 00
123 For expenses of maintaining an aero squadron, a sum not exceeding four thousand dollars . 4,000 00
124 For premiums on bonds for officers, a sum not exceeding fifteen hundred dollars . . . 1,500 00

Item
125 For instruction in military authority, organization
     and administration, and in the elements of mili-
     tary art, a sum not exceeding eleven thousand
     dollars $11,000 00
126 For expenses of operation of the twenty-sixth divi-
     sion, a sum not exceeding forty-five hundred dol-
     lars 4,500 00
127 For clerical and other expenses for the office of the
     property and disbursing officer, a sum not exceed-
     ing ten thousand two hundred and sixty dollars .   10,260 00

          Total $282,310 00

Service of Special Military Expenses.

128 For the expense of furnishing certificates of honor
     for service on the Mexican border, as authorized
     by law, a sum not exceeding twenty-five dollars . $25 00
129 For expense of testimonials to soldiers and sailors of
     the world war, to be expended under the direction
     of the adjutant general, a sum not exceeding five
     hundred dollars 500 00

          Total $525 00

Service of the State Quartermaster.

130 For personal services of the state quartermaster,
     superintendent of armories, superintendent of
     arsenal and certain other employees of the state
     quartermaster, a sum not exceeding twenty-three
     thousand six hundred dollars $23,600 00
131 For expert assistance, the employment of which may
     be exempt from civil service rules, in the disburse-
     ment of certain money to the officers and enlisted
     men of the militia for compensation and allow-
     ances, a sum not exceeding eleven hundred and
     sixty dollars 1,160 00
132 For the salaries of armorers and assistant armorers
     of first class armories, and superintendent of
     armories, a sum not exceeding one hundred thirty-
     six thousand one hundred and seventy-four dol-
     lars 136,174 00
133 For certain incidental military expenses of the
     quartermaster's department, a sum not exceeding
     seven hundred dollars 700 00
134 For office and general supplies and equipment, a
     sum not exceeding ninety-eight hundred dollars .   9,800 00
135 For the care and maintenance of the camp ground
     and buildings at Framingham, a sum not exceed-
     ing nine hundred dollars 900 00
136 For the maintenance of armories of the first class,
     including the purchase of certain furniture, a sum
     not exceeding one hundred forty-four thousand
     eight hundred dollars 144,800 00
137 For reimbursement for rent and maintenance of
     armories of the second and third classes, a sum not
     exceeding sixty-three hundred dollars   .   .   6,300 00
138 For allowances for a mechanic for each battery of
     field artillery, a sum not exceeding seventeen
     thousand six hundred dollars 17,600 00
139 For maintenance of horses, for rental of stables, in-
     cluding water and certain other incidental services
     for the housing of horses and mules, and for main-
     taining, operating and repairing certain trucks, a
     sum not exceeding thirty-nine thousand five hun-
     dred dollars; provided, that the sum appropri-

Item

ated by this item is hereby made available for such expenditures, including the purchase of land and buildings, as may be necessary for housing, repairing and maintaining any federal property that may be assigned by the war department of the United States $39,500 00

140 (This item consolidated with Item 139.)

141 For expense of maintaining and operating the Camp Curtis Guild rifle range, a sum not exceeding twenty thousand eight hundred and twenty-seven dollars 20,827 00

Total $401,361 00

Service of the State Surgeon.

142 For personal services of the state surgeon, and regular assistants, a sum not exceeding sixty-eight hundred dollars $6,800 00

143 For services other than personal, and for necessary medical and office supplies and equipment, a sum not exceeding twenty-five hundred dollars . 2,500 00

144 For the examination of recruits, a sum not exceeding ninety-five hundred dollars 9,500 00

Total $18,800 00

Service of the State Judge Advocate.

145 For compensation of the state judge advocate, as provided by law, a sum not exceeding fourteen hundred and forty dollars $1,440 00

Service of the Commission on Administration and Finance.

146 For personal services of the commissioners, a sum not exceeding twenty-five thousand and eighty-seven dollars $25,087 00

147 For personal services of assistants and employees, a sum not exceeding one hundred seventy thousand four hundred and ninety dollars . . . 170,490 00

148 For other expenses incidental to the duties of the commission, a sum not exceeding eighteen thousand dollars 18,000 00

Total $213,577 00

Purchase of paper:

149 For the purchase of paper used in the execution of the contracts for state printing, other than legislative, with the approval of the commission on administration and finance, a sum not exceeding thirty-eight thousand dollars $38,000 00

Service of the Armory Commissioners.

150 For compensation of members, a sum not exceeding two thousand two hundred and eight dollars . $2,208 00

151 For office, incidental, and traveling expenses, a sum not exceeding one hundred dollars . . . 100 00

Total $2,308 00

Service of the Commissioner of State Aid and Pensions.

152 For personal services of the commissioner and deputies, a sum not exceeding ten thousand six hundred and eighty dollars $10,680 00

153 For personal services of agents, clerks, stenographers and other assistants, a sum not exceeding twenty-seven thousand one hundred and fifty-two dollars 27,152 00

Item

154   For services other than personal, including printing the annual report, traveling expenses of the commissioner and his employees, and necessary office supplies and equipment, a sum not exceeding forty-seven hundred and sixty dollars . . **$4,760 00**

         Total **$42,592 00**

For Expenses on Account of Wars.

155   For reimbursing cities and towns for money paid on account of state and military aid to Massachusetts soldiers and their families, the sum of four hundred eighteen thousand dollars, the same to be paid on or before the fifteenth day of November in the current year, in accordance with the provisions of existing laws relative to state and military aid **$418,000 00**

156   For certain care of veterans of the civil war and their wives and widows, as authorized by section twenty-five of chapter one hundred and fifteen of the General Laws, as appearing in the Tercentenary Edition thereof, a sum not exceeding fifty thousand dollars 50,000 00

157   For expenses of printing certain volumes of records of Massachusetts soldiers in the civil war, a sum not exceeding six thousand dollars, the same to be in addition to any unexpended balance of an appropriation made for the purpose in the previous year 6,000 00

         Total **$474,000 00**

Service of the Massachusetts Soldiers' Home.

158   For the maintenance of the Soldiers' Home in Massachusetts, with the approval of the trustees thereof, a sum not exceeding one hundred ninety-three thousand two hundred and forty dollars, the same to be in addition to certain receipts from the United States government. Payments from the state treasury under this item shall be made only upon vouchers filed with the comptroller in accordance with the procedure prescribed under section eighteen of chapter twenty-nine of the General Laws, as appearing in the Tercentenary Edition thereof **$193,240 00**

Service of the Art Commission.

159   For expenses of the commission, a sum not exceeding two hundred dollars **$200 00**

Service of the Commissioners on Uniform State Laws.

160   For expenses of the commissioners, a sum not exceeding six hundred dollars **$600 00**

Service of the Alcoholic Beverages Control Commission.

160a   For the administrative expenses of the alcoholic beverages control commission, including salaries of the commissioners and their employees, and for all contingent expenses required for the administration of chapter one hundred and twenty of the acts of the current year, including rent of offices, travel, and office and incidental expenses, a sum not exceeding twenty-five thousand dollars, which shall be payable from fees collected under said chapter one hundred and twenty . .   **$25,000 00**

Service of the State Library.

Item

161 For personal services of the librarian, a sum not
     exceeding fifty-five hundred dollars   .   .   . $5,500 00
162 For personal services of the regular library assist-
     ants, temporary clerical assistance, and for serv-
     ices for cataloguing, a sum not exceeding thirty-
     eight thousand four hundred dollars .   .   .   38,400 00
163 For services other than personal, including printing
     the annual report, office supplies and equipment,
     and incidental traveling expenses, a sum not
     exceeding fifteen hundred dollars   .   .   .   1,500 00
164 For books and other publications and things needed
     for the library, and the necessary binding and re-
     binding incidental thereto, a sum not exceeding
     nine thousand dollars 9,000 00

              Total $54,400 00

Service of the Superintendent of Buildings.

165 For personal services of the superintendent and
     office assistants, a sum not exceeding ten thousand
     one hundred dollars $10,100 00
166 For personal services of engineers, assistant engi-
     neers, firemen and helpers in the engineer's de-
     partment, a sum not exceeding fifty-seven
     thousand four hundred and fourteen dollars   .   57,414 00
167 For personal services of state house guards and
     assistant state house guards, a sum not exceeding
     forty-two thousand three hundred and twenty
     dollars 42,320 00
168 For personal services of janitors, a sum not exceed-
     ing twenty-four thousand nine hundred dollars   .   24,900 00
169 For other personal services incidental to the care and
     maintenance of the state house, a sum not exceed-
     ing sixty-eight thousand two hundred and forty
     dollars .· 68,240 00
170 For personal services of the central mailing room, a
     sum not exceeding forty-eight hundred dollars   .   4,800 00

              Total $207,774 00

Other Annual Expenses:

171 For contingent, office and other expenses of the
     superintendent, a sum not exceeding two hundred
     and fifty dollars $250 00
172 For telephone service in the building and expenses
     in connection therewith, a sum not exceeding
     forty-three thousand dollars 43,000 00
173 For services, supplies and equipment necessary to
     furnish heat, light and power, a sum not exceeding
     thirty-seven thousand dollars 37,000 00
174 For other services, supplies and equipment neces-
     sary for the maintenance and care of the state
     house and grounds, including repairs of furniture
     and equipment, a sum not exceeding twenty-eight
     thousand dollars 28,000 00
175 For office and other expenses of the central mailing
     room, a sum not exceeding one hundred dollars   .   100 00

              Total $108,350 00

For the Maintenance of Old State House.

176 For the contribution of the commonwealth toward
     the maintenance of the old provincial state house,
     the sum of fifteen hundred dollars   .   .   . $1,500 00

Special Committee.

Item
177 For expenses of the advisory committee for the
town of Mashpee, as authorized by chapter two
hundred and twenty-three of the acts of nineteen
hundred and thirty-two, a sum not exceeding five
hundred dollars $500 00

Service of the Secretary of the Commonwealth.

178 For the salary of the secretary, a sum not exceeding
sixty-six hundred and twenty-seven dollars . $6,627 00
179 For the salaries of officers and employees holding
positions established by law, and other personal
services, a sum not exceeding one hundred eight
thousand one hundred and forty dollars . . 108,140 00
180 For services other than personal, traveling expenses,
office supplies and equipment, for the arrangement and preservation of state records and papers,
and for advertising the purpose of sections
twenty-eight A to twenty-eight D of chapter six
of the General Laws, as appearing in the Tercentenary Edition thereof, a sum not exceeding
nineteen thousand five hundred dollars . . 19,500 00
181 For postage and expressage on public documents,
and for mailing copies of bills and resolves to certain state, city and town officials, a sum not exceeding thirty-five hundred dollars . . . 3,500 00
182 For printing registration books, blanks and indices,
a sum not exceeding one thousand dollars . . 1,000 00
183 For the purchase of certain supplies and equipment,
and for other things necessary in connection with
the reproduction of the manuscript collection
designated "Massachusetts Archives", a sum
not exceeding nineteen hundred dollars . . 1,900 00
184 For the purchase and distribution of copies of certain journals of the house of representatives of
Massachusetts Bay from seventeen hundred and
fifteen to seventeen hundred and eighty, inclusive, as authorized by chapter four hundred and
thirteen of the acts of nineteen hundred and
twenty, a sum not exceeding seven hundred and
fifty dollars 750 00
185 For the purchase of ink for public records of the
commonwealth, a sum not exceeding nine hundred dollars 900 00
186 For traveling expenses of the supervisor of public
records, a sum not exceeding seven hundred dollars . . . . 700 00.

Total . . . . $143,017 00.

Indexing vital statistics:
187 For the preparation of certain indexes of births, mar-
riages and deaths, a sum not exceeding nine thousand dollars $9,000 00

For printing laws, etc.:
188 For printing and distribution of the pamphlet edition of the acts and resolves of the present year, a
sum not exceeding forty-three hundred and fifty
dollars $4,350 00
189 For printing and binding the blue book edition of
the acts and resolves of the present year, a sum
not exceeding six thousand dollars . . . 6,000 00
190 For the printing of reports of decisions of the
supreme judicial court, a sum not exceeding
thirty-one thousand eight hundred dollars, the

Item

same to be in addition to any unexpended balance of an appropriation made for the purpose in the previous year $31,800 00

191 For printing and binding public documents, a sum not exceeding twenty-five hundred dollars . . 2,500 00

Total $44,650 00

For matters relating to elections:

192 For personal and other services in preparing for primary elections, and for the expenses of preparing, printing and distributing ballots for primary and other elections, a sum not exceeding twenty-seven thousand dollars $27,000 00

193 For the printing of blanks for town officers, election laws and blanks and instructions on all matters relating to elections, a sum not exceeding fifteen hundred dollars 1,500 00

194 For furnishing cities and towns with ballot boxes, and for repairs to the same; for the purchase of apparatus to be used at polling places in the canvass and counting of votes; and for providing certain registration facilities, a sum not exceeding five hundred dollars 500 00

Total $29,000 00

Medical Examiners' Fees:

195 For medical examiners' fees, as provided by law, a sum not exceeding one thousand dollars . . $1,000 00

Service of the Treasurer and Receiver-General.

196 For the salary of the treasurer and receiver-general, a sum not exceeding fifty-six hundred and eighty dollars $5,680 00

197 For salaries of officers and employees holding positions established by law and additional clerical and other assistance, a sum not exceeding fifty-five thousand nine hundred dollars 55,900 00

198 For services other than personal, traveling expenses, office supplies and equipment, a sum not exceeding fifteen thousand five hundred dollars . . 15,500 00

Total $77,080 00

Commissioners on Firemen's Relief:

199 For relief disbursed, with the approval of the commissioners on firemen's relief, subject to the provisions of law, a sum not exceeding seventeen thousand five hundred dollars $17,500 00

200 For expenses of administration by the commissioners on firemen's relief, a sum not exceeding five hundred dollars 500 00

Total $18,000 00

Payments to Soldiers:

201 For expenses of administering certain laws relating to payments in recognition of military service in the world war, a sum not exceeding twenty-seven hundred and twenty dollars, to be paid from the receipts from taxes levied under authority of chapters two hundred and eighty-three and three hundred and forty-two of the General Acts of nineteen hundred and nineteen . . . $2,720 00

Item
202 For making payments to soldiers in recognition
of service during the world war, as provided by
law, a sum not exceeding ten thousand dollars, to
be paid from receipts from taxes levied as specified in item two hundred and one   .   .   . $10,000 00
203 For payments to soldiers and sailors in the volunteer
service of the United States during the Spanish-
American war, and to certain of their dependents,
as authorized by section one of chapter five hundred and sixty-one of the acts of eighteen hundred
and ninety-eight, as amended by section one of
chapter four hundred and seventy-one of the acts
of eighteen hundred and ninety-nine, a sum not
exceeding two hundred dollars 200 00

Total $12,920 00

State Board of Retirement:
204 For personal services in the administrative office of
the state board of retirement, a sum not exceeding
ten thousand one hundred and eighty dollars   . $10,180 00
205 For services other than personal, printing the annual report, and for office supplies and equipment,
a sum not exceeding fifty-three hundred dollars .   5,300 00
206 For requirements of annuity funds and pensions for
employees retired from the state service under
authority of law, a sum not exceeding two hundred ten thousand dollars 210,000 00

Total $225,480 00

Board of Tax Appeals:
207 For personal services of the members of the board
and employees, a sum not exceeding thirty-seven
thousand one hundred and fifty-four dollars   . $37,154 00
208 For services other than personal, traveling expenses, office supplies and equipment, and rent, a
sum not exceeding sixteen thousand dollars   .   16,000 00

Total $53,154 00

Service of the Emergency Finance Board.
208a For the administrative expenses of the emergency
finance board, authorized by chapter forty-nine
of the acts of the current year, a sum not exceeding four thousand dollars. The state comptroller
is hereby directed to certify for payment, expenses
authorized by this appropriation, from the receipts from notes issued under said chapter, the
same to be in anticipation of a refund to said
receipts from the excess interest account provided in section two of said chapter, and to make
the necessary adjustments between the said receipts account and excess interest account before
any distribution of said excess is made to the
cities and towns entitled thereto   .   .   . $4,000 00

Requirements for Extinguishing the State Debt.
209 For sinking fund requirements and for certain serial
bonds maturing during the present year, the sum
of one million six hundred seventy-one thousand
three hundred ninety-nine dollars and fifty cents,
payable from the following accounts and funds in
the following amounts: — from the surplus of
sinking fund revenue, four hundred twenty thou-

Item

sand dollars; from the Highway Fund, two hundred four thousand six hundred forty-nine dollars and fifty cents; and the remainder from the General Fund $1,671,399 50

209a To meet one fourth of the expenditures authorized by sections one and two of chapter one hundred and twenty-two of the acts of nineteen hundred and thirty-one, and already in the main incurred, which is the proportionate part intended to be ultimately met by the commonwealth during the current fiscal year, thereby reducing by the sum hereby appropriated the amount that may be borrowed under section three of said chapter, without otherwise affecting the authority to borrow under said section three the remainder of the amount authorized to be borrowed thereunder, the sum of two million one hundred and twenty-five thousand dollars, the same to be paid from the Highway Fund $2,125,000 00

Interest on the Public Debt.

210 For the payment of interest on the direct debt of the commonwealth, a sum not exceeding eight hundred sixty-nine thousand dollars, of which sum two hundred thirty-nine thousand dollars shall be paid from the Highway Fund . . . $869,000 00

Service of the Auditor of the Commonwealth.

211 For the salary of the auditor, a sum not exceeding fifty-six hundred and eighty dollars . . . $5,680 00

212 For personal services of deputies and other assistants, a sum not exceeding forty-eight thousand one hundred dollars 48,100 00

213 For services other than personal, traveling expenses, office supplies and equipment, a sum not exceeding fifty-seven hundred and seventy-five dollars . 5,775 00

Total $59,555 00

Service of the Attorney General's Department.

214 For the salary of the attorney general, a sum not exceeding seventy-five hundred and seventy-four dollars $7,574 00

215 For the compensation of assistants in his office, and for such other legal and personal services as may be required, a sum not exceeding seventy-eight thousand four hundred and thirty-four dollars . 78,434 00

216 For services other than personal, traveling expenses, office supplies and equipment, a sum not exceeding six thousand dollars 6,000 00

217 For the settlement of certain small claims, as authorized by section three A of chapter twelve of the General Laws, as appearing in the Tercentenary Edition thereof, a sum not exceeding five thousand dollars 5,000 00

218 For the settlement of certain claims, as provided by law, on account of damages by cars owned by the commonwealth and operated by state employees, a sum not exceeding four thousand dollars . 4,000 00

Total $101,008 00

Service of the Department of Agriculture.

219 For the salary of the commissioner, a sum not exceeding fifty-six hundred and eighty dollars . $5,680 00

Item

220 For personal services of clerks and stenographers, a sum not exceeding nineteen thousand five hundred and forty dollars $19,540 00

221 For traveling expenses of the commissioner, a sum not exceeding nine hundred dollars . . . 900 00

222 For services other than personal, printing the annual report, office supplies and equipment, and printing and furnishing trespass posters, a sum not exceeding seven thousand dollars . . . 7,000 00

223 For compensation and expenses of members of the advisory board, a sum not exceeding seventeen hundred and forty-four dollars 1,744 00

224 For services and expenses of apiary inspection, a sum not exceeding two thousand dollars . . 2,000 00

Division of Dairying and Animal Husbandry:

225 For personal services, a sum not exceeding thirteen thousand nine hundred and twenty dollars . 13,920 00

226 For other expenses, including the enforcement of the dairy laws of the commonwealth, a sum not exceeding sixty-nine hundred and fifty dollars . 6,950 00

227 For administering the law relative to the inspection of barns and dairies by the department of agriculture, a sum not exceeding twenty-two thousand dollars 22,000 00

Division of Plant Pest Control:

228 For personal services, a sum not exceeding ten thousand eight hundred and fifty dollars . . 10,850 00

229 For other expenses, a sum not exceeding forty-six hundred dollars 4,600 00

Division of Ornithology:

230 For personal services for the period ending May thirty-first of the current year, upon which date all functions of this division shall cease, a sum not exceeding sixteen hundred and fifty dollars . 1,650 00

231 For other expenses, a sum not exceeding two hundred dollars 200 00

Division of Markets:

232 For personal services, a sum not exceeding nineteen thousand three hundred and twenty dollars . 19,320 00

233 For other expenses, a sum not exceeding forty-five hundred and twenty-five dollars . . . 4,525 00

Division of Reclamation, Soil Survey and Fairs:

234 For personal services, a sum not exceeding eleven thousand four hundred dollars 11,400 00

235 For travel and other expenses, a sum not exceeding sixty-three hundred and twenty-five dollars . 6,325 00

236 For state prizes and agricultural exhibits, a sum not exceeding thirty thousand dollars, the same to be in addition to any amount heretofore appropriated for this purpose, and any unexpended balance remaining at the end of the current fiscal year may be used in the succeeding year 30,000 00

Specials:

237 For work in protecting the pine trees of the commonwealth from white pine blister rust, and for payments of claims on account of currant and gooseberry bushes destroyed in the work of suppressing white pine blister rust, a sum not exceeding nine thousand dollars 9,000 00

Item
238 For quarantine and other expenses in connection
     with the work of suppression of the European corn-
     borer, so called, a sum not exceeding five thousand
     dollars, the same to be in addition to any amount
     heretofore appropriated for the purpose   .   . $5,000 00
239 For quarantine and other expenses in connection
     with the work of suppression of the Japanese
     beetle, so called, a sum not exceeding thirty-four
     hundred dollars 3,400 00
240 For the cost of work of inspecting certain orchards
     of the commonwealth to provide for effective
     apple pest control, a sum not exceeding thirty-
     eight hundred dollars 3,800 00

                Total $189,804 00

                Service of State Reclamation Board.
241 For expenses of the board, a sum not exceeding
     ninety-one hundred and forty dollars   .   . $9,140 00
     Special:
242 For the maintenance and construction of drainage
     ditches, as authorized by chapter three hundred
     and fifteen of the acts of nineteen hundred and
     thirty-one, a sum not exceeding twenty-four thou-
     sand three hundred dollars, the same to be
     assessed upon certain towns as required by law .   24,300 00

                Total $33,440 00

                Service of the Department of Conservation.
     Administration:
243 For the salary of the commissioner, a sum not ex-
     ceeding fifty-six hundred and eighty dollars   . $5,680 00
244 For traveling expenses of the commissioner, a sum
     not exceeding one hundred dollars   .   .   .   100 00
245 For telephone service and certain other office charges
     of the department, a sum not exceeding twenty-
     six hundred and forty dollars 2,640 00
246 For personal services of a telephone operator and
     office boy, a sum not exceeding eighteen hundred
     and thirty dollars 1,830 00

                Total $10,250 00
     Division of Forestry:
247 For personal services of office assistants, a sum not
     exceeding ninety-eight hundred and eighty dol-
     lars $9,880 00
248 For services other than personal, including printing
     the annual report, and for traveling expenses, nec-
     essary office supplies and equipment, and rent, a
     sum not exceeding sixty-five hundred dollars   .   6,500 00
249 For the salaries and expenses of foresters and for
     necessary labor, supplies and equipment in main-
     taining forest tree nurseries, a sum not exceeding
     twelve thousand and seventy dollars   .   .   12,070 00
250 For the reforesting of land, as authorized by section
     ten of chapter one hundred and thirty-two of the
     General Laws, as appearing in the Tercentenary
     Edition thereof, a sum not exceeding five hundred
     dollars 500 00
251 For aiding towns in the purchase of equipment for
     extinguishing forest fires and for making pro-
     tective belts or zones as a defence against forest
     fires, for the present and previous years, a sum not
     exceeding seven hundred and fifty dollars .   .   750 00

Item

252 For the personal services of the state fire warden and his assistants, and for other services, including traveling expenses of the state fire warden and his assistants, necessary supplies and equipment and materials used in new construction in the forest fire prevention service, a sum not exceeding forty-six thousand seven hundred and fifteen dollars, the same to be in addition to any funds allotted to Massachusetts by the federal authorities . . $46,715 00

253 For the suppression of the gypsy and brown tail moths, and for expenses incidental thereto, a sum not exceeding forty-five thousand dollars, the same to be in addition to any amount heretofore appropriated for the purpose, and any unexpended balance remaining at the end of the current fiscal year may be used in the succeeding year . . 45,000 00

254 For the planting and maintenance of state forests, a sum not exceeding eighteen thousand seven hundred and sixty dollars 18,760 00

255 For the development of state forests, including the cost of maintenance of such nurseries as may be necessary for the growing of seedlings for the planting of state forests, as authorized by sections thirty to thirty-six, inclusive, of chapter one hundred and thirty-two of the General Laws, as appearing in the Tercentenary Edition thereof, a sum not exceeding one hundred twenty-five thousand and fifty dollars, the same to be in addition to any amount heretofore appropriated for this purpose, and any unexpended balance remaining at the end of the current fiscal year may be used in the succeeding year 125,050 00

256 For the maintenance of the Standish monument reservation, a sum not exceeding nineteen hundred dollars 1,900 00

257 For the maintenance of Mount Grace state forest, a sum not exceeding four hundred dollars . . 400 00

258 For reimbursement to certain towns, as authorized by section twenty-four of chapter forty-eight of the General Laws, as appearing in the Tercentenary Edition thereof, a sum not exceeding three hundred dollars 300 00

259 For the expenses of forest fire patrol, as authorized by section twenty-eight A of said chapter forty-eight, as so appearing, a sum not exceeding twenty-nine hundred and twenty dollars . . 2,920 00

Total $270,745 00

Division of Parks:

260 For personal services for the period ending May thirty-first of the current year, upon which date all functions of this division as then constituted shall cease, a sum not exceeding twenty-nine hundred and seventy-five dollars . . . $2,975 00

261 For other administrative expenses of the director of the division of parks, as authorized by chapter three hundred and ninety-one of the acts of nineteen hundred and thirty-one, a sum not exceeding sixteen hundred dollars 1,600 00

Total $4,575 00

Division of Fisheries and Game:

262 For the salary of the director, a sum not exceeding forty-three hundred and twenty dollars . . $4,320 00

Item
263 For personal services of office assistants, a sum not exceeding fourteen thousand four hundred and forty dollars $14,440 00
264 For services other than personal, including printing the annual report, traveling expenses and necessary office supplies and equipment, and rent, a sum not exceeding eleven thousand two hundred dollars 11,200 00
265 For expenses of exhibitions and other measures to increase the interest of the public in the protection and propagation of fish and game, a sum not exceeding one thousand dollars 1,000 00

Enforcement of laws:
266 For personal services of fish and game wardens, a sum not exceeding seventy thousand three hundred and twenty dollars 70,320 00
267 For traveling expenses of fish and game wardens, and for other expenses necessary for the enforcement of the laws, a sum not exceeding thirty-two thousand nine hundred and twenty-five dollars . 32,925 00

Biological work:
268 For personal services to carry on biological work, a sum not exceeding ninety-two hundred and eighty dollars 9,280 00
269 For traveling and other expenses of the biologist and his assistants, a sum not exceeding twenty-four hundred dollars 2,400 00

Propagation of game birds, etc.:
270 For the maintenance of game farms and fish hatcheries, and for the propagation of game birds and animals and food fish, a sum not exceeding one hundred eight thousand eight hundred and forty dollars 108,840 00

Damages by wild deer and wild moose:
271 For the payment of damages caused by wild deer and wild moose, for the present year and previous years, as provided by law, a sum not exceeding fifty-seven hundred dollars 5,700 00

Supervision of public fishing and hunting grounds:
272 For personal services, a sum not exceeding eleven hundred and forty dollars 1,140 00
273 For other expenses, a sum not exceeding fifteen hundred dollars 1,500 00

Special:
274 For improvements and additions at fish hatcheries and game farms, a sum not exceeding ninety-seven hundred dollars, the same to be in addition to any amount heretofore appropriated for the purpose . 9,700 00

Protection of wild life:
275 For expenses incurred in the protection of certain wild life, a sum not exceeding fifteen hundred and sixty dollars 1,560 00

Marine fisheries:
276 For personal services for regulating the sale and cold storage of fresh food fish, a sum not exceeding thirteen thousand and twenty dollars . . 13,020 00
277 For other expenses of regulating the sale and cold storage of fresh food fish, a sum not exceeding thirty-two hundred and seventy-five dollars . 3,275 00

Item

State Supervisor of Marine Fisheries:
278 For personal services of the state supervisor of marine fisheries and his assistants, a sum not exceeding eighty-two hundred and eighty dollars . $8,280 00
279 For office and other expenses of the state supervisor of marine fisheries, a sum not exceeding thirty-nine hundred and seventy-five dollars . . 3,975 00

Enforcement of shellfish and other marine fishery laws:
280 For personal services for the enforcement of laws relative to shellfish and other marine fisheries, a sum not exceeding seventeen thousand eight hundred and ninety dollars 17,890 00
281 For other expenses for the enforcement of laws relative to shellfish and other marine fisheries, a sum not exceeding eleven thousand three hundred and seventy-five dollars 11,375 00
282 For expenses of purchasing lobsters, subject to the conditions imposed by chapter two hundred and sixty-three of the acts of nineteen hundred and twenty-eight, a sum not exceeding ninety-five hundred dollars 9,500 00

Total $341,640 00

Bounty on seals:
283 For bounties on seals, a sum not exceeding six hundred and seventy-five dollars . . . $675 00

Division of Animal Industry:
284 For the salary of the director, a sum not exceeding thirty-eight hundred and forty dollars . . $3,840 00
285 For personal services of clerks and stenographers, a sum not exceeding twenty-three thousand five hundred and forty dollars 23,540 00
286 For services other than personal, including printing the annual report, traveling expenses of the director, office supplies and equipment, and rent, a sum not exceeding fourteen thousand four hundred dollars 14,400 00
287 For personal services of veterinarians and agents engaged in the work of extermination of contagious diseases among domestic animals, a sum not exceeding eighty-seven thousand six hundred dollars 87,600 00
288 For traveling expenses of veterinarians and agents, including the cost of any motor vehicles purchased for their use, a sum not exceeding twenty-eight thousand six hundred and fifty dollars . 28,650 00
289 For reimbursement of owners of horses killed during the present and previous years, travel, when allowed, of inspectors of animals, incidental expenses of killing and burial, quarantine and emergency services, and for laboratory and veterinary supplies and equipment, a sum not exceeding sixty-five hundred dollars 6,500 00
290 For reimbursement of owners of tubercular cattle killed, as authorized by section twelve A of chapter one hundred and twenty-nine of the General Laws, as appearing in the Tercentenary Edition thereof, and in accordance with certain provisions of law and agreements made under authority of section thirty-three of said chapter one hundred and twenty-nine, as so appearing, during the present and previous year, a sum not exceeding five hundred thousand dollars, the same to be in addition to any amount heretofore appropriated for the

Item

purpose, and any unexpended balance remaining
at the end of the current fiscal year may be used
in the succeeding year $500,000 00

Total $664,530 00

Reimbursement of towns for inspectors of animals:
291 For the reimbursement of certain towns for compensation paid to inspectors of animals, a sum not
exceeding fifty-five hundred dollars . . . $5,500 00

Service of the Department of Banking and Insurance.

Division of Banks:
292 For the salary of the commissioner, a sum not exceeding fifty-six hundred and eighty dollars . $5,680 00
293 For services of deputy, directors, examiners and
assistants, clerks, stenographers and experts, a
sum not exceeding two hundred ninety-one thousand nine hundred and twenty dollars . . 291,920 00
294 For services other than personal, printing the annual
report, traveling expenses, office supplies and
equipment, a sum not exceeding sixty-two thousand two hundred and seventy-five dollars . 62,275 00

Total $359,875 00

Supervisor of Loan Agencies:
295 For personal services of supervisor and assistants, a
sum not exceeding twelve thousand three hundred
dollars $12,300 00
296 For services other than personal, printing the annual report, office supplies and equipment, a sum
not exceeding fifteen hundred and forty-five dollars 1,545 00

Total $13,845 00

Division of Insurance:
297 For the salary of the commissioner, a sum not exceeding fifty-six hundred and eighty dollars . $5,680 00
298 For other personal services of the division, including
expenses of the board of appeal and certain other
costs of supervising motor vehicle liability insurance, a sum not exceeding one hundred eighty-two
thousand one hundred and eighty dollars, of which
sum not more than thirty-five thousand dollars
may be charged to the Highway Fund . . 182,180 00
299 For other services, including printing the annual
report, traveling expenses and necessary office
supplies and equipment, a sum not exceeding
thirty-seven thousand three hundred and seventy-
five dollars 37,375 00

Total $225,235 00

Division of Savings Bank Life Insurance:
300 For personal services of officers and employees, a
sum not exceeding thirty thousand three hundred
and twenty dollars $30,320 00
301 For publicity, including traveling expenses of one
person, a sum not exceeding nineteen hundred
dollars 1,900 00
302 For services other than personal, printing the annual
report, traveling expenses, rent, office supplies and
equipment, a sum not exceeding ten thousand four
hundred dollars 10,400 00

Item
303 For encouraging and promoting old age annuities
     and the organization of mutual benefit associa-
     tions among the employees of industrial plants in
     the commonwealth, a sum not exceeding twenty-
     nine hundred and seventy dollars .   .   . $2,970 00

        Total $45,590 00

Service of the Department of Corporations and Taxation.

Corporation and Tax Divisions:
304 For the salary of the commissioner, a sum not ex-
     ceeding seventy-one hundred dollars   . $7,100 00
305 For the salaries of certain positions filled by the com-
     missioner, with the approval of the governor and
     council, and for additional clerical and other
     assistance, a sum not exceeding two hundred
     twenty thousand and sixty dollars, of which sum
     not more than fifty thousand dollars may be
     charged to the Highway Fund to cover the esti-
     mated cost of collection of the gasoline tax, so
     called 220,060 00
306 (This item consolidated with Item 307.)
307 For other services, necessary office supplies and
     equipment, travel, and for printing the annual
     report, other publications and valuation books, a
     sum not exceeding forty-three thousand one hun-
     dred and fifty dollars 43,150 00

        Total $270,310 00

Income Tax Division (the three following appro-
     priations are to be made from the receipts from
     the income tax):
308 For personal services of the director, assistant direc-
     tor, assessors, deputy assessors, clerks, stenograph-
     ers and other necessary assistants, a sum not ex-
     ceeding four hundred seventeen thousand nine
     hundred and thirty-four dollars   .   .   . $417,934 00
309 (This item consolidated with Item 310.)
310 For services other than personal, and for traveling
     expenses, office supplies and equipment, a sum not
     exceeding one hundred thirty-eight thousand five
     hundred and fifty dollars 138,550 00

        Total $556,484 00

Division of Accounts:
311 For personal services, a sum not exceeding seventy-
     seven thousand six hundred dollars .   .   . $77,600 00
312 For other expenses, a sum not exceeding eleven
     thousand four hundred and fifty dollars   .   11,450 00
313 For the administrative expenses required under the
     provisions of chapter four hundred of the acts of
     nineteen hundred and thirty, a sum not exceeding
     seventy-seven hundred and sixty dollars   .   7,760 00
314 For services and expenses of auditing and installing
     systems of municipal accounts, the cost of which
     is to be assessed upon the municipalities for which
     the work is done, a sum not exceeding one hundred
     sixty thousand seven hundred and seventy-four
     dollars 160,774 00
315 For the expenses of certain books, forms and other
     material, which may be sold to cities and towns
     requiring the same for maintaining their system of

Item

accounts, a sum not exceeding eighteen thousand
dollars $18,000 00

Total $275,584 00

Reimbursement for loss of taxes:
316 For reimbursing cities and towns for loss of taxes on
land used for state institutions and certain other
state activities, as certified by the commissioner
of corporations and taxation for the fiscal year
ending November thirtieth, nineteen hundred and
thirty-three, a sum not exceeding one hundred
twenty-six thousand two hundred dollars . . $126,200 00

Service of the Department of Education.
317 For the salary of the commissioner, a sum not exceeding eighty-five hundred and twenty dollars . $8,520 00
318 For personal services of officers, agents, clerks,
stenographers and other assistants, but not including those employed in university extension
work, a sum not exceeding ninety-five thousand
five hundred and twenty dollars . . . 95,520 00
319 For traveling expenses of members of the advisory
board and of agents and employees when required
to travel in discharge of their duties, a sum not
exceeding fifty-seven hundred dollars . . 5,700 00
320 For services other than personal, necessary office
supplies, and for printing the annual report and
bulletins as provided by law, a sum not exceeding
ninety-five hundred dollars 9,500 00
321 For expenses incidental to furnishing school committees with rules for testing the sight and hearing
of pupils, a sum not exceeding one hundred and
fifty dollars 150 00
322 For printing school registers and other school blanks
for cities and towns, a sum not exceeding fourteen
hundred dollars 1,400 00
323 For assisting small towns in providing themselves
with school superintendents, as provided by law,
a sum not exceeding one hundred one thousand
five hundred dollars 101,500 00
324 For the reimbursement of certain towns for the payment of tuition of pupils attending high schools
outside the towns in which they reside, as provided
by law, a sum not exceeding two hundred six
thousand dollars 206,000 00
325 For the reimbursement of certain towns for the
transportation of pupils attending high schools
outside the towns in which they reside, as provided by law, a sum not exceeding one hundred
seventy-five thousand dollars 175,000 00
326 For the reimbursement of certain cities and towns
for a part of the expense of maintaining agricultural and industrial vocational schools, as provided by law, a sum not exceeding one million five
hundred six thousand one hundred two dollars and
eighty-two cents 1,506,102 82
327 For the expense of promotion of vocational rehabilitation in co-operation with the federal government, including rent, with the approval of the
department of education, a sum not exceeding
fourteen thousand two hundred and fifty-five
dollars 14,255 00
328 For aid to certain persons receiving instruction in
the courses for vocational rehabilitation, as au-

Item

thorized by section twenty-two B of chapter
seventy-four of the General Laws, as appearing in
the Tercentenary Edition thereof, a sum not
exceeding twenty-five hundred dollars . . $2,500 00

329 For the education of deaf and blind pupils of the
commonwealth, as provided by section twenty-
six of chapter sixty-nine of the General Laws, as
appearing in the Tercentenary Edition thereof, a
sum not exceeding four hundred thirty-six thousand dollars 436,000 00

330 For expenses of holding teachers' institutes, a sum
not exceeding two thousand dollars . .   2,000 00

331 For aid to certain pupils in state teachers' colleges,
under the direction of the department of educa-
tion, a sum not exceeding four thousand dollars .   4,000 00

332 For the training of teachers for vocational schools,
to comply with the requirements of federal authorities under the provisions of the Smith-Hughes
act, so called, a sum not exceeding twenty-eight
thousand seven hundred and ninety dollars .   28,790 00

333 For assistance to the children of certain soldiers, for
the present and previous years, as authorized by
chapter two hundred and sixty-three of the acts of
nineteen hundred and thirty, a sum not exceeding
sixty-nine hundred dollars 6,900 00

Total $2,603,837 82

English-speaking Classes for Adults:

334 For personal services of administration, a sum not
exceeding ten thousand nine hundred dollars . $10,900 00

335 For other expenses of administration, a sum not
exceeding twenty-six hundred dollars . .   2,600 00

336 For reimbursement of certain cities and towns, a
sum not exceeding one hundred ten thousand
dollars 110,000 00

Total $123,500 00

University Extension Courses:

337 For personal services, a sum not exceeding one hundred twenty-seven thousand five hundred and
twenty dollars $127,520 00

338 For other expenses, a sum not exceeding thirty-four
thousand three hundred and fifty dollars . .   34,350 00

Total $161,870 00

Division of Immigration and Americanization:

339 For personal services, a sum not exceeding thirty-
three thousand two hundred and sixty-four dollars $33,264 00

340 For other expenses, a sum not exceeding fifty-one
hundred and thirty-six dollars . . .   5,136 00

Total $38,400 00

Division of Public Libraries:

341 For personal services of regular agents and office
assistants, a sum not exceeding ten thousand four
hundred and twenty dollars $10,420 00

342 For other services, including printing the annual
report, traveling expenses, necessary office supplies and expenses incidental to the aiding of
public libraries, a sum not exceeding ten thousand
dollars 10,000 00

Total $20,420 00

Item

Division of the Blind:

343 For general administration, furnishing information, industrial and educational aid, and for carrying out certain provisions of the laws establishing said division, a sum not exceeding forty-two thousand three hundred and ten dollars $42,310 00

344 For the maintenance of local shops, a sum not exceeding fifty-nine thousand six hundred and forty dollars 59,640 00

345 For maintenance of Woolson House industries, so called, to be expended under the authority of said division, a sum not exceeding twenty-seven thousand eight hundred and forty dollars . . 27,840 00

346 For the maintenance of certain industries for men, to be expended under the authority of said division, a sum not exceeding one hundred thirteen thousand seven hundred and twenty dollars . 113,720 00

347 For instruction of the adult blind in their homes, a sum not exceeding sixteen thousand eight hundred and twenty dollars 16,820 00

348 For expenses of providing sight-saving classes, with the approval of the division of the blind, a sum not exceeding twenty thousand one hundred dollars . 20,100 00

349 For aiding the adult blind, subject to the conditions provided by law, a sum not exceeding one hundred seventy-one thousand dollars . . 171,000 00

Total $451,430 00

Teachers' Retirement Board:

350 For personal services of employees, a sum not exceeding eleven thousand four hundred and eighty dollars $11,480 00

351 For services other than personal, including printing the annual report, traveling expenses, office supplies and equipment, and rent, a sum not exceeding thirty-nine hundred dollars . . 3,900 00

352 For payment of pensions to retired teachers, a sum not exceeding eight hundred seventy-four thousand dollars 874,000 00

353 For reimbursement of certain cities and towns for pensions to retired teachers, a sum not exceeding two hundred thirty-four thousand eight hundred nineteen dollars and fifty cents . . 234,819 50

354 For payment into the annuity fund for the period of the year nineteen hundred and thirty-two, in accordance with certain actuarial figures, a sum not exceeding fifteen thousand nine hundred and ninety-seven dollars 15,997 00

Total $1,140,196 50

Massachusetts Nautical School:

355 For personal services of the secretary and office assistants, a sum not exceeding forty-five hundred and forty dollars $4,540 00

356 For services other than regular clerical services, including printing the annual report, rent, office supplies and equipment, a sum not exceeding twenty-two hundred and seventy-five dollars . 2,275 00

357 For the maintenance of the school and ship, a sum not exceeding seventy-eight thousand two hundred and forty-five dollars 78,245 00

Total $85,060 00

Item

State Teachers' Colleges and Massachusetts School of Art:

358　For the maintenance of the several state teachers' colleges and the Massachusetts School of Art, with the approval of the commissioner of education, a sum not exceeding one million four thousand nine hundred and fifty dollars　.　　$1,004,950 00

359　For maintenance of boarding halls at the several state teachers' colleges, with the approval of the commissioner of education, a sum not exceeding one hundred eighty-eight thousand four hundred and fifty dollars　.　.　.　.　.　.　188,450 00

373　For grading and surfacing the playfield at the Worcester state teachers' college, a sum not exceeding one thousand dollars and the unexpended balance of any appropriation heretofore made for the purpose　.　.　.　.　.　.　.　1,000 00

　　　Total.　.　.　.　.　.　.　$1,194,400 00

Textile Schools:

375　For the maintenance of the Bradford Durfee textile school of Fall River, with the approval of the commissioner of education and the trustees, a sum not exceeding fifty-eight thousand seven hundred and fifty dollars, of which sum ten thousand dollars is to be contributed by the city of Fall River, and the city of Fall River is hereby authorized to raise by taxation the said sum of ten thousand dollars　.　.　.　.　.　.　$58,750 00

376　For the maintenance of the Lowell textile institute, with the approval of the commissioner of education and the trustees, a sum not exceeding one hundred fifty-seven thousand six hundred dollars, of which sum ten thousand dollars is to be contributed by the city of Lowell, and the city of Lowell is hereby authorized to raise by taxation the said sum of ten thousand dollars　.　157,600 00

377　For the maintenance of the New Bedford textile school, with the approval of the commissioner of education and the trustees, a sum not exceeding fifty-eight thousand seven hundred dollars, of which sum ten thousand dollars is to be contributed by the city of New Bedford, and the city of New Bedford is hereby authorized to raise by taxation the said sum of ten thousand dollars　.　58,700 00

　　　Total.　.　.　.　.　.　.　$275,050 00

Massachusetts State College:

378　For maintenance and current expenses of the Massachusetts state college, with the approval of the trustees, a sum not exceeding nine hundred thirty-six thousand two hundred and sixty dollars　.　$936,260 00

379　For an emergency fund to meet the needs of harvesting big crops or other unforeseen conditions, which clearly indicate that additional revenue will be produced to equal the expenditure, a sum not exceeding twenty-five hundred dollars, provided, however, that this appropriation be available only after approval of particular projects covered by it has been obtained from the governor and council　.　.　.　.　.　.　.　2,500 00

379a　For aid to certain students, with the approval of the trustees, a sum not exceeding twenty-five hundred dollars　.　.　.　.　.　.　.　2,500 00

Item
380 For expense of renewing and improving certain
     steam lines, a sum not exceeding twenty-five
     thousand dollars $25,000 00

          Total $966,260 00

Service of the Department of Civil Service and Registration.
     Administration:
381 For personal services of telephone operator for the
     department, a sum not exceeding twelve hundred
     and twenty dollars $1,220 00

     Division of Civil Service:
382 For the salaries of the commissioner and associate
     commissioners, a sum not exceeding eighty-six
     hundred and forty dollars $8,640 00
383 For other personal services of the division, a sum not
     exceeding one hundred twenty-one thousand seven
     hundred and twenty dollars 121,720 00
384 For other services and for printing the annual report,
     and for office supplies and equipment necessary
     for the administration of the civil service law, a
     sum not exceeding thirty-two thousand two hun-
     dred and fifty dollars 32,250 00

          Total $162,610 00

     Division of Registration:
385 For the salary of the director, a sum not exceeding
     seventeen hundred and twenty-eight dollars . $1,728 00
386 For clerical and certain other personal services of the
     division, a sum not exceeding thirty-six thousand
     seven hundred and eighty dollars . . .   36,780 00
387 For services of the division other than personal,
     printing the annual reports, office supplies and
     equipment, except as otherwise provided, a sum
     not exceeding twelve thousand dollars . .   12,000 00

          Total $50,508 00

     Board of Registration in Medicine:
388 For personal services of the members of the board, a
     sum not exceeding forty-one hundred and twenty-
     eight dollars $4,128 00
389 For personal services of members of the board and
     examiners for the registration of chiropodists, a
     sum not exceeding five hundred and seventy-six
     dollars 576 00
390 For traveling expenses, a sum not exceeding four
     hundred dollars 400 00

          Total $5,104 00

     Board of Dental Examiners:
391 For personal services of the members of the board, a
     sum not exceeding thirty-six hundred and forty-
     eight dollars $3,648 00
392 For traveling expenses, a sum not exceeding five
     hundred dollars 500 00
393 For travel and other expenses necessary in providing
     for the enforcement of law relative to the registra-
     tion of dentists, a sum not exceeding two thousand
     dollars 2,000 00

          Total $6,148 00

Item

Board of Registration in Pharmacy:
394 For personal services of members of the board, a sum not exceeding forty-one hundred and twenty-eight dollars $4,128 00
395 For personal services of agent, a sum not exceeding twenty-three hundred and eighty dollars . .   2,380 00
396 For traveling expenses, a sum not exceeding thirty-five hundred dollars 3,500 00

     Total $10,008 00

Board of Registration of Nurses:
397 For personal services of members of the board, a sum not exceeding two thousand and sixteen dollars . $2,016 00
398 For traveling expenses, a sum not exceeding four hundred and fifty dollars 450 00

     Total $2,466 00

Board of Registration in Embalming:
399 For personal services of members of the board, a sum not exceeding two hundred and eighty-eight dollars $288 00
400 For traveling expenses, a sum not exceeding three hundred dollars 300 00
401 For the dissemination of useful knowledge among and for the benefit of licensed embalmers, a sum not exceeding five hundred dollars . . .   500 00

     Total $1,088 00

Board of Registration in Optometry:
402 For personal services of members of the board, a sum not exceeding eighteen hundred and twenty-four dollars $1,824 00
403 For traveling expenses, a sum not exceeding five hundred dollars 500 00

     Total $2,324 00

Board of Registration in Veterinary Medicine:
404 For personal services of the members of the board, a sum not exceeding five hundred and seventy-six dollars $576 00
405 For other services, printing the annual report, traveling expenses, office supplies and equipment, a sum not exceeding three hundred dollars . .   300 00

     Total $876 00

State Examiners of Electricians:
406 For traveling expenses, a sum not exceeding thirty-four hundred and fifty dollars $3,450 00

Board of Registration of Public Accountants:
407 For personal services of members of the board, a sum not exceeding six hundred and forty-nine dollars $649 00
408 For expenses of examinations, including the preparation and marking of papers, and for other expenses, a sum not exceeding eighteen hundred and eighty dollars 1,880 00

     Total $2,529 00

State Examiners of Plumbers:
409 For personal services of the members of the board, a sum not exceeding one thousand and fifty-six dollars $1,056 00

Item
410 For traveling expenses, a sum not exceeding eleven
       hundred dollars $1,100 00

       Total $2,156 00

Board of Registration of Barbers:
411 For personal services of the members of the board
       and assistants, a sum not exceeding sixteen thou-
       sand and eighty dollars $16,080 00
412 For travel and other necessary expenses, a sum not
       exceeding seventy-five hundred dollars . . 7,500 00

       Total $23,580 00

Service of the Department of Industrial Accidents.
413 For personal services of members of the board, a sum
       not exceeding forty thousand two hundred and
       thirty-four dollars $40,234 00
414 For personal services of secretaries, medical ad-
       viser, inspectors, clerks and office assistants, a
       sum not exceeding one hundred twenty-six thou-
       sand seven hundred dollars 126,700 00
415 For expenses of impartial examinations, a sum not
       exceeding twenty-eight thousand five hundred
       dollars 28,500 00
416 For traveling expenses, a sum not exceeding eighty-
       two hundred and fifty dollars 8,250 00
417 For other services, printing the annual report, nec-
       essary office supplies and equipment, a sum not
       exceeding eleven thousand two hundred dollars . 11,200 00

       Total $214,884 00

Service of the Department of Labor and Industries.
418 For the salaries of the commissioner, assistant and
       associate commissioners, a sum not exceeding
       nineteen thousand five hundred and eighty dollars $19,580 00
419 For clerical and other assistance to the commissioner,
       a sum not exceeding sixty-nine hundred and forty
       dollars 6,940 00
420 For personal services for the inspectional service and
       for traveling expenses of the commissioner, assist-
       ant commissioner, associate commissioners and
       inspectors of labor, and for services other than
       personal, printing the annual report, rent of dis-
       trict offices, and office supplies and equipment for
       the inspectional service, a sum not exceeding one
       hundred forty-nine thousand three hundred and
       sixty dollars, which sum includes the services of an
       expert in the reduction of occupational diseases;
       provided, that said expert shall not be subject to
       civil service laws or the rules and regulations
       made thereunder 149,360 00
421 For personal services for the statistical service and
       for services other than personal, printing report
       and publications, traveling expenses and office
       supplies and equipment for the statistical service,
       a sum not exceeding fifty-eight thousand nine
       hundred and sixty dollars 58,960 00
422 For clerical and other personal services for the opera-
       tion of free employment offices, a sum not exceed-
       ing fifty-seven thousand and sixty dollars . . 57,060 00
423 For personal services for the division on necessaries
       of life, a sum not exceeding six thousand and
       thirty dollars 6,030 00

Item
424 For clerical and other assistance for the board of conciliation and arbitration, a sum not exceeding fourteen thousand seven hundred and twenty dollars $14,720 00
425 For personal services of investigators, clerks and stenographers for the minimum wage service, a sum not exceeding fourteen thousand six hundred and eighty dollars 14,680 00
426 For compensation and expenses of wage boards, a sum not exceeding fifteen hundred dollars . . 1,500 00
427 For personal services for the division of standards, a sum not exceeding twenty-nine thousand nine hundred and twenty dollars . . . 29,920 00
430 For rent, necessary office supplies and equipment for the free employment offices, a sum not exceeding eleven thousand three hundred and seventy-five dollars 11,375 00
431 For services other than personal, traveling expenses, office supplies and equipment for the division on necessaries of life, a sum not exceeding one thousand dollars 1,000 00
432 For other services, printing, traveling expenses and office supplies and equipment for the board of conciliation and arbitration, a sum not exceeding thirty-six hundred and twenty-five dollars . . 3,625 00
433 For services other than personal, printing, traveling expenses and office supplies and equipment for minimum wage service, a sum not exceeding forty-two hundred and twenty-five dollars . . 4,225 00
434 For other services, printing, traveling expenses and office supplies and equipment for the division of standards, a sum not exceeding sixteen thousand eight hundred and seventy-five dollars . . 16,875 00

Total $395,850 00

Massachusetts Industrial and Development Commission:
435 For personal services, including the employment of experts for services authorized under section nine B of chapter twenty-three of the General Laws, as appearing in the Tercentenary Edition thereof, for the period ending May thirty-first of the current year, upon which date all functions of this commission shall cease, a sum not exceeding forty-eight hundred and fifty dollars . . . $4,850 00
436 For other services and expenses, including office supplies and travel, a sum not exceeding fifteen hundred dollars 1,500 00

Total $6,350 00

Service of the Department of Mental Diseases.
437 For the salary of the commissioner, a sum not exceeding ninety-four hundred and sixty-seven dollars $9,467 00
438 For personal services of officers and employees, a sum not exceeding one hundred seventeen thousand five hundred dollars 117,500 00
439 For transportation and medical examination of state charges under its charge for the present year and previous years, a sum not exceeding fourteen thousand dollars 14,000 00
440 For the support of state charges boarded in families under its charge, or temporarily absent under its authority, for the present year and previous years, a sum not exceeding three thousand dollars . 3,000 00

Item
441 For the support of state charges in the Hospital Cottages for Children, a sum not exceeding fifteen thousand six hundred dollars $15,600 00
442 For other services, including printing the annual report, traveling expenses and office supplies and equipment, a sum not exceeding seventeen thousand nine hundred dollars 17,900 00

Total $177,467 00

Division of Mental Hygiene:
443 For the expenses of investigating the nature, causes and results of mental diseases and defects and the publication of the results thereof; and of what further preventive or other measures might be taken and what further expenditures for investigation might be made which would give promise of decreasing the number of persons afflicted with mental diseases or defects; and for making a survey of the feeble-minded within the commonwealth and an estimate of the number requiring hospital or custodial care or training such as the institutions for the feeble-minded are especially equipped to give, a sum not exceeding eighty-seven thousand two hundred and eighty dollars, the same to be in addition to any amount heretofore appropriated for the purpose . . . $87,280 00

Psychiatric examinations:
444 For services and expenses of psychiatric examinations of prisoners for the period ending May thirty-first of the current year, upon which date all functions provided for by this item shall cease, a sum not exceeding thirty thousand dollars . $30,000 00

For the maintenance of and for certain improvements at the following institutions under the control of the Department of Mental Diseases:
445 Boston psychopathic hospital, a sum not exceeding two hundred twelve thousand four hundred and fifty dollars $212,450 00
446 Boston state hospital, a sum not exceeding seven hundred thirty-six thousand two hundred and fifty dollars 736,250 00
447 Danvers state hospital, a sum not exceeding six hundred thirty-five thousand eight hundred and fifty dollars 635,850 00
448 Foxborough state hospital, a sum not exceeding three hundred sixty-four thousand nine hundred dollars 364,900 00
449 For expenses of boiler settings and other improvements in the boiler room at the Foxborough state hospital, a sum not exceeding three thousand dollars 3,000 00
450 Gardner state colony, a sum not exceeding four hundred nineteen thousand seven hundred dollars . 419,700 00
451 Grafton state hospital, a sum not exceeding four hundred sixty-three thousand three hundred dollars 463,300 00
452 Medfield state hospital, a sum not exceeding five hundred thirty-seven thousand eight hundred and fifty dollars 537,850 00
453 Metropolitan state hospital, a sum not exceeding three hundred fifty-two thousand three hundred dollars 352,300 00

Item
454 Northampton state hospital, a sum not exceeding
four hundred forty-three thousand three hundred
and fifty dollars $443,350 00
455 Taunton state hospital, a sum not exceeding four
hundred sixty-five thousand six hundred dollars . 465,600 00
456 Westborough state hospital, a sum not exceeding
four hundred sixty-six thousand dollars . . 466,000 00
457 For the expense of purchasing and installing electric
refrigeration units at the Westborough state hospital, a sum not exceeding nine thousand dollars . 9,000 00
458 Worcester state hospital, a sum not exceeding seven
hundred eighteen thousand one hundred and fifty
dollars 718,150 00
459 Monson state hospital, a sum not exceeding four
hundred thirty-nine thousand five hundred and
fifty dollars 439,550 00
460 Belchertown state school, a sum not exceeding three
hundred seventy-six thousand one hundred dollars 376,100 00
461 Walter E. Fernald state school, a sum not exceeding
five hundred forty-one thousand one hundred
dollars 541,100 00
462 Wrentham state school, a sum not exceeding four
hundred forty-eight thousand nine hundred and
fifty dollars 448,950 00

Total $7,633,400 00

Service of the Department of Correction.
463 For the salary of the commissioner, a sum not exceeding fifty-six hundred and eighty dollars . $5,680 00
464 For personal services of deputies, members of the
board of parole and advisory board of pardons,
agents, clerks and stenographers, a sum not exceeding seventy-seven thousand seven hundred
and eighty dollars 77,780 00
465 For services other than personal, including printing
the annual report, necessary office supplies and
equipment, a sum not exceeding seven thousand
dollars 7,000 00
466 For traveling expenses of officers and employees of
the department when required to travel in the discharge of their duties, a sum not exceeding ten
thousand one hundred dollars 10,100 00
467 For the removal of prisoners, to and from state
institutions, a sum not exceeding sixty-one hundred dollars 6,100 00
468 For assistance to discharged prisoners, a sum not
exceeding seven hundred dollars . . . 700 00
469 For the expense of the service of what is known as
the central index, a sum not exceeding one thousand dollars 1,000 00

Total $108,360 00

Division of Research for the Prevention of Crime:
470 For expenses of the division hereby authorized, a
sum not exceeding seventeen thousand four hundred dollars; provided, that the persons employed hereunder shall not be subject to civil service laws or the rules and regulations made thereunder $17,400 00
For the maintenance of and for certain improvements at the following institutions under the
control of the Department of Correction:
471 State farm, a sum not exceeding six hundred four
thousand seven hundred and forty dollars . . $604,740 00

Item
472 For the cost of an engineering study relative to generating or supplying electric power to the state farm, a sum not exceeding two thousand dollars . $2,000 00
473 For the cost of installing water mains for fire protection at the state farm, a sum not exceeding fourteen thousand four hundred dollars .   .   .   14,400 00
474 (This item omitted.)
475 State prison, a sum not exceeding three hundred sixty-four thousand eight hundred and fifty dollars, including twenty-nine dollars to reimburse Edward Loring, an employee at the prison, for injuries received and clothing destroyed in the performance of his duty 364,850 00
476 Massachusetts reformatory, a sum not exceeding three hundred ninety-six thousand three hundred and fifty dollars 396,350 00
477 Prison camp and hospital, a sum not exceeding fifty-three thousand two hundred and fifty dollars   .   53,250 00
478 Reformatory for women, a sum not exceeding one hundred sixty-two thousand eight hundred and twenty dollars 162,820 00
479 For the town of Framingham, according to a contract for sewage disposal at the reformatory for women, the sum of six hundred dollars   .   .   600 00
480 State prison colony, a sum not exceeding two hundred sixty-four thousand nine hundred dollars   .   264,900 00
480a For the construction and furnishing of a dormitory unit at the state prison colony, a sum not exceeding one hundred forty thousand dollars. In anticipation of the completion of this dormitory, the commissioner of correction, upon the receipt of such sum of money as represents a fair reimbursement of the commonwealth for the damages for condemnation of property, is hereby authorized to convey the land and buildings located at the prison camp and hospital in the town of Rutland to the metropolitan district water supply commission 140,000 00
481 For the construction of a cow barn and dairy unit at the state prison colony, a sum not exceeding thirty-five thousand dollars 35,000 00

Total $2,038,910 00

Service of the Department of Public Welfare.
Administration:
482 For the salary of the commissioner, a sum not exceeding sixty-six hundred and twenty-seven dollars $6,627 00
483 For personal services of officers and employees and supervision of homesteads and planning boards, a sum not exceeding forty-two thousand six hundred and eighty dollars 42,680 00
484 For services other than personal, printing the annual report, traveling expenses, including expenses of auxiliary visitors, office supplies and expenses, and contingent expenses for the supervision of homesteads and planning boards, a sum not exceeding fifty-seven hundred dollars 5,700 00

Total $55,007 00

Division of Aid and Relief:
485 For personal services of officers and employees, a sum not exceeding one hundred seventy-six thousand and eighty dollars; provided, that the em-

Item

ployment of persons authorized under item I of
chapter sixty-nine of the acts of nineteen hundred
and thirty-two may be continued, and shall not be
subject to civil service laws or the rules and regulations made thereunder $176,080 00

486 For services other than personal, including traveling
expenses and office supplies and equipment, a sum
not exceeding thirty-one thousand nine hundred
dollars 31,900 00

The following items are for reimbursement of
cities and towns for expenses of the present
year and previous years, and are to be in addition to any unexpended balances of appropriations made for the purpose in the previous year:

487 For the payment of suitable aid to mothers with
dependent children, a sum not exceeding one
million one hundred thousand dollars . . 1,100,000 00

488 For the burial by cities and towns of indigent persons
who have no legal settlement, a sum not exceeding nine thousand dollars 9,000 00

489 For expenses in connection with smallpox and other
diseases dangerous to the public health, a sum not
exceeding one hundred twenty-nine thousand
dollars 129,000 00

490 For the support of sick indigent persons who have
no legal settlement, a sum not exceeding one hundred nineteen thousand dollars . . . 119,000 00

491 For temporary aid given to indigent persons with no
legal settlement, and to shipwrecked seamen by
cities and towns, and for the transportation of
indigent persons under the charge of the department, a sum not exceeding three million eight
hundred and twenty-five thousand dollars . . 3,825,000 00

Old age assistance:

492 For personal services required for the administration of old age assistance provided by chapter one
hundred and eighteen A of the General Laws, as
amended by section three of chapter two hundred
and fifty-nine of the acts of nineteen hundred and
thirty-two, a sum not exceeding eighty-one thousand five hundred and twenty dollars . . 81,520 00

493 For other expenses, including rent, travel, office supplies and other necessary expenses, required for
the administration of old age assistance provided
by said chapter one hundred and eighteen A, a sum
not exceeding twenty-three thousand seven hundred dollars 23,700 00

Total $5,495,200 00

Division of Child Guardianship:

494 For personal services of officers and employees, a
sum not exceeding one hundred ninety-nine thousand seven hundred dollars . . . $199,700 00

495 For services other than personal, office supplies and
equipment, a sum not exceeding forty-four hundred dollars 4,400 00

496 For tuition in the public schools, including transportation to and from school, of children boarded
by the department, for the present and previous
years, a sum not exceeding three hundred thousand
dollars 300,000 00

Item
497 For the care and maintenance of children, for the present and previous years, a sum not exceeding one million two hundred seventy-eight thousand six hundred dollars $1,278,600 00

Total $1,782,700 00

Division of Juvenile Training, Trustees of Massachusetts Training Schools:
498 For services of the secretary and certain other persons employed in the executive office, a sum not exceeding fourteen thousand and forty dollars . $14,040 00
499 For services other than personal, including printing the annual report, traveling and other expenses of the members of the board and employees, office supplies and equipment, a sum not exceeding thirty-four hundred dollars 3,400 00

Boys' Parole:
500 For personal services of agents in the division for boys paroled and boarded in families, a sum not exceeding thirty-eight thousand four hundred and sixty dollars 38,460 00
501 For services other than personal, including traveling expenses of the agents and boys, and necessary office supplies and equipment, a sum not exceeding twenty-one thousand dollars 21,000 00
502 For board, clothing, medical and other expenses incidental to the care of boys, a sum not exceeding twenty-seven thousand dollars 27,000 00

Girls' Parole:
503 For personal services of agents in the division for girls paroled from the industrial school for girls, a sum not exceeding thirty-one thousand six hundred and twenty dollars 31,620 00
504 For traveling expenses of said agents for girls paroled, for board, medical and other care of girls, and for services other than personal, office supplies and equipment, a sum not exceeding eighteen thousand three hundred dollars 18,300 00

Tuition of children:
505 For reimbursement of cities and towns for tuition of children attending the public schools, a sum not exceeding eighty-five hundred dollars . . 8,500 00

Total $162,320 00

For the maintenance of and for certain improvements at the institutions under the control of the trustees of the Massachusetts training schools, with the approval of said trustees, as follows:
506 Industrial school for boys, a sum not exceeding one hundred forty-five thousand seven hundred dollars $145,700 00
507 Industrial school for girls, a sum not exceeding one hundred thirty-one thousand seven hundred and fifty dollars 131,750 00
508 Lyman school for boys, a sum not exceeding two hundred eight thousand two hundred dollars . 208,200 00

Total $485,650 00

Massachusetts Hospital School:
509 For the maintenance of the Massachusetts hospital school, to be expended with the approval of the

Item

trustees thereof, a sum not exceeding one hundred seventy-five thousand six hundred and sixty dollars $175,660 00

State Infirmary:

510 For the maintenance of the state infirmary, to be expended with the approval of the trustees thereof, a sum not exceeding nine hundred thirty-six thousand seven hundred dollars . . . $936,700 00

511 For expense of retubing and repairing certain boilers, a sum not exceeding four thousand dollars, the same to be in addition to any unexpended balance of an appropriation heretofore made for the purpose 4,000 00

511a For construction of new filter beds, a sum not exceeding twenty thousand dollars . . . 20,000 00

Total $960,700 00

Service of the Department of Public Health.

Administration:

512 For the salary of the commissioner, a sum not exceeding seventy-one hundred dollars . . . $7,100 00

513 For personal services of the health council and office assistants, a sum not exceeding eighteen thousand five hundred and forty dollars 18,540 00

514 For services other than personal, including printing the annual report, traveling expenses, office supplies and equipment, a sum not exceeding eleven thousand and twenty-five dollars . . . 11,025 00

Service of Adult Hygiene (cancer):

515 For personal services of the division, including cancer clinics, a sum not exceeding forty-two thousand seven hundred dollars 42,700 00

516 For other expenses of the division, including cancer clinics, a sum not exceeding thirty-three thousand and fifty dollars 33,050 00

Service of Child Hygiene:

517 For personal services of the director and assistants, a sum not exceeding thirty-three thousand five hundred dollars 33,500 00

518 For services other than personal, traveling expenses, office supplies and equipment, a sum not exceeding fourteen thousand four hundred dollars . 14,400 00

Service of Maternal and Child Hygiene:

519 For personal services for extending the activities of the division in the protection of mothers and conservation of the welfare of children, a sum not exceeding twenty-one thousand eight hundred and fifty dollars 21,850 00

520 For other expenses for extending the activities of the division in the protection of mothers and conservation of the welfare of children, a sum not exceeding ninety-two hundred dollars . . 9,200 00

Division of Communicable Diseases:

521 For personal services of the director, district health officers and their assistants, epidemiologists, bacteriologist and assistants in the diagnostic laboratory, a sum not exceeding seventy thousand two hundred and forty dollars. 70,240 00

Item

522 For services other than personal, traveling expenses, laboratory, office and other necessary supplies, including the purchase of animals and equipment, and rent of certain offices, a sum not exceeding fifteen thousand and seventy-five dollars . . $15,075 00

Venereal Diseases:

523 For personal services for the control of venereal diseases, a sum not exceeding thirteen thousand and eighty dollars 13,080 00

524 For services other than personal, traveling expenses, office supplies and equipment, a sum not exceeding twenty-eight thousand dollars 28,000 00

Wassermann Laboratory:

525 For personal services of the Wassermann laboratory, a sum not exceeding sixteen thousand two hundred dollars 16,200 00

526 For expenses of the Wassermann laboratory, a sum not exceeding five thousand dollars . . . 5,000 00

Antitoxin and Vaccine Laboratories:

527 For personal services in the investigation and production of antitoxin and vaccine lymph and other specific material for protective inoculation and diagnosis of treatment, a sum not exceeding sixty-eight thousand four hundred and twenty dollars 68,420 00

528 For other services, supplies, materials and equipment necessary for the production of antitoxin and other materials as enumerated above, a sum not exceeding thirty-four thousand five hundred dollars 34,500 00

Inspection of Food and Drugs:

529 For personal services of the director, analysts, inspectors and other assistants, a sum not exceeding forty-nine thousand seven hundred and forty dollars 49,740 00

530 For other services, including traveling expenses, supplies, materials and equipment, a sum not exceeding eleven thousand and fifty dollars . . 11,050 00

Shellfish Enforcement Law:

531 For personal services for administering the law relative to shellfish, a sum not exceeding eighteen hundred and forty dollars 1,840 00

532 For other expenses for administering the law relative to shellfish, a sum not exceeding one thousand dollars 1,000 00

Water Supply and Disposal of Sewage, Engineering Division:

533 For personal services of the director, engineers, clerks and other assistants, a sum not exceeding sixty-four thousand eight hundred and forty dollars . 64,840 00

534 For other services, including traveling expenses, supplies, materials and equipment, a sum not exceeding seventeen thousand one hundred and fifty dollars 17,150 00

Water Supply and Disposal of Sewage, Division of Laboratories:

535 For personal services of laboratory director, chemists, clerks and other assistants, a sum not exceeding forty-one thousand and twenty dollars . 41,020 00

Item
536 For other services, including traveling expenses, sup-
       plies, materials and equipment, a sum not exceed-
       ing seventy-two hundred dollars   .   .   . $7,200 00

              Total $635,720 00

     Division of Tuberculosis:
537 For personal services of the director, stenographers,
       clerks and other assistants, a sum not exceeding
       thirty-four thousand five hundred and forty dol-
       lars $34,540 00
538 For services other than personal, including printing
       the annual report, traveling expenses and office
       supplies and equipment, a sum not exceeding
       fifty-three hundred and fifty dollars .   .   .   5,350 00
539 To cover the payment of certain subsidies for the
       maintenance of hospitals for tubercular patients,
       a sum not exceeding four hundred five thousand
       dollars 405,000 00
540 For personal services for certain children's clinics for
       tuberculosis, a sum not exceeding fifty-five thou-
       sand five hundred dollars. 55,500 00
541 For other services for certain children's clinics for
       tuberculosis, a sum not exceeding thirty-one thou-
       sand two hundred dollars 31,200 00

              Total $531,590 00

     For the maintenance of and for certain improve-
       ments at the sanatoria, as follows:
542 Lakeville state sanatorium, a sum not exceeding two
       hundred fifty-eight thousand nine hundred and
       fifty dollars $258,950 00
543 North Reading state sanatorium, a sum not exceed-
       ing two hundred nineteen thousand six hundred
       and fifty dollars 219,650 00
544 Rutland state sanatorium, a sum not exceeding two
       hundred eighty-one thousand one hundred and
       fifty dollars 281,150 00
545 Westfield state sanatorium, a sum not exceeding two
       hundred twenty-eight thousand nine hundred and
       sixty-five dollars 228,965 00

              Total $988,715 00

     Pondville Cancer Hospital:
546 For maintenance of the Pondville cancer hospital,
       including care of radium, a sum not exceeding two
       hundred thirty thousand two hundred and fifty
       dollars $230,250 00

              Service of the Department of Public Safety.

     Administration:
547 For the salary of the commissioner, a sum not ex-
       ceeding fifty-six hundred and eighty dollars   . $5,680 00
548 For personal services of clerks and stenographers, a
       sum not exceeding eighty thousand four hundred
       and eighty dollars 80,480 00
549 For contingent expenses, including printing the an-
       nual report, rent of district offices, supplies and
       equipment, and all other things necessary for the
       investigation of fires and moving picture licenses,
       as required by law, and for expenses of administer-
       ing the law regulating the sale and resale of tickets
       to theatres and other places of public amusement

Item

by the department of public safety, a sum not exceeding fifty thousand dollars . . . $50,000 00

Division of State Police:
550 For the salaries of officers, including detectives, a sum not exceeding four hundred seven thousand six hundred dollars, of which sum not more than one hundred and forty thousand dollars may be charged to the Highway Fund 407,600 00
551 For personal services of civilian employees, a sum not exceeding sixty-three thousand five hundred and fifty dollars 63,550 00
552 For other necessary expenses of the uniformed division, including traveling expenses of detectives, a sum not exceeding three hundred fifty thousand dollars, of which sum not more than one hundred fifty-six thousand nine hundred dollars may be charged to the Highway Fund 350,000 00
553 For maintenance and operation of the police steamer, a sum not exceeding forty-five hundred and fifty-four dollars 4,554 00
554 For personal services, rent, supplies and equipment necessary in the enforcement of provisions of law relative to explosives and inflammable fluids and compounds, a sum not exceeding thirteen thousand six hundred and forty dollars . . . 13,640 00

Division of Inspections:
555 For the salary of the chief of inspections, a sum not exceeding thirty-eight hundred and forty dollars 3,840 00
556 For the salaries of officers for the building inspection service, a sum not exceeding fifty-two thousand eight hundred and sixty dollars . . . 52,860 00
557 For traveling expenses of officers for the building inspection service, a sum not exceeding eleven thousand one hundred and sixty dollars . . 11,160 00
558 For the salaries of officers for the boiler inspection service, a sum not exceeding sixty-four thousand five hundred and twenty dollars . . . 64,520 00
559 For traveling expenses of officers for the boiler inspection service, a sum not exceeding sixteen thousand seven hundred dollars . . . 16,700 00
560 For services, supplies and equipment necessary for investigations and inspections by the division, a sum not exceeding nine hundred dollars . . 900 00

Board of Elevator Regulations:
561 For expenses of the board, a sum not exceeding one hundred and forty dollars 140 00

Board of Boiler Rules:
562 For personal services and other expenses of members of the board, including necessary traveling expenses, office supplies and equipment, a sum not exceeding five hundred dollars . . . 500 00
563 (This item consolidated with Item 562.)

Total $1,126,124 00

Fire Prevention Service:
564 For the salary of the state fire marshal, a sum not exceeding thirty-eight hundred and forty dollars $3,840 00
565 For personal services of fire inspectors and others, a sum not exceeding thirty-nine thousand six hundred and five dollars 39,605 00

Item
566   For traveling expenses of fire inspectors, a sum not exceeding thirteen thousand seven hundred dollars $13,700 00
567   For other services, office rent and necessary office supplies and equipment, a sum not exceeding forty-three hundred and fifty dollars   .   .   4,350 00

Total $61,495 00

State Boxing Commission:
568   For compensation and clerical assistance for the state boxing commission, a sum not exceeding thirteen thousand six hundred and twenty dollars   .   . $13,620 00
569   For other expenses of the commission, a sum not exceeding twelve thousand dollars   .   .   12,000 00

Total $25,620 00

Service of the Department of Public Works.

The appropriations made in the following three items are to be paid two thirds from the Highway Fund and one third from the Port of Boston receipts:
570   For the salaries of the commissioner and the associate commissioners, a sum not exceeding eighteen thousand four hundred and sixty dollars   . $18,460 00
571   For personal services of clerks and assistants to the commissioner, a sum not exceeding eighty-seven hundred and fifty dollars .   .   .   8,750 00
572   For traveling expenses of the commissioners, a sum not exceeding seventeen hundred and forty dollars   1,740 00

Total $28,950 00

Functions of the department relating to highways (the following appropriations, except as otherwise provided, are made from the Highway Fund):
573   For the personal services of the chief engineer, engineers and office assistants, including certain clerks and stenographers, a sum not exceeding eighty-nine thousand three hundred and twenty dollars $89,320 00
574   For services other than personal, including printing pamphlet of laws and the annual report, and necessary office supplies and equipment, a sum not exceeding ten thousand three hundred dollars   .   10,300 00
575   For the suppression of gypsy and brown tail moths on state highways, a sum not exceeding twelve thousand dollars 12,000 00
576   For the construction and repair of town and county ways, a sum not exceeding two million six hundred thousand dollars   .   .   .   2,600,000 00
577   For aiding towns in the repair and improvement of public ways, a sum not exceeding nine hundred ninety thousand dollars   .   .   .   990,000 00
578   For the maintenance and repair of state highways, including care of snow on highways, expenses of traffic signs and lights, and payment of damages caused by defects in state highways, with the approval of the attorney general; for care and repair of road-building machinery; and for the purchase and improvement of a nursery for roadside planting, a sum not exceeding two million seven hundred ten thousand dollars   .   .   2,710,000 00
578a   For the maintenance and operation of the new public works building, a sum not exceeding forty thousand dollars 40,000 00

Item
579 For the purpose of enabling the department of public works to secure federal aid for the construction of highways, a sum not exceeding five hundred twenty-five thousand dollars, and in addition there is hereby transferred the sum of seven hundred twenty-five thousand dollars from the appropriation previously made for the elimination of grade crossings $525,000 00

580 For administering the law relative to advertising signs near highways, a sum not exceeding fourteen thousand seven hundred and twenty dollars, to be paid from the General Fund 14,720 00

Registration of Motor Vehicles:
581 For personal services, a sum not exceeding nine hundred thirty thousand two hundred dollars, of which sum ten thousand dollars may be charged to the General Fund, and the remainder shall be paid from the Highway Fund 930,200 00

582 For services other than personal, including traveling expenses, purchase of necessary supplies and materials, including cartage and storage of the same, and for work incidental to the registration and licensing of owners and operators of motor vehicles, a sum not exceeding five hundred forty-three thousand five hundred and fifty dollars, to be paid from the Highway Fund 543,550 00

583 For printing and other expenses necessary in connection with publicity for certain safety work, a sum not exceeding one thousand dollars, to be paid from the Highway Fund 1,000 00

Total $8,466,090 00

Specials:
584 (This item omitted.)
585 For certain highway improvements in the city of Revere, as authorized by chapter four hundred and forty-five of the acts of nineteen hundred and thirty-one, as amended by chapter two hundred and fifty-eight of the acts of nineteen hundred and thirty-two, a sum not exceeding five hundred and fifty thousand dollars, to be paid from the Highway Fund and to be in addition to the unexpended balance of any appropriation heretofore made for the purpose and to be in anticipation of a further appropriation in nineteen hundred and thirty-three sufficient to complete the work authorized by said chapters. The department of public works is hereby authorized to make contracts and incur expenses within the total sum of one million three hundred fifty-five thousand dollars authorized by said chapters $550,000 00

586 There is hereby added to the sum appropriated in nineteen hundred and thirty-two for land damages and other expenses incidental to the laying out of a state highway extending from Alewife Brook parkway in the city of Cambridge through said city and certain towns, including Concord, as authorized by chapter three hundred and two of the acts of nineteen hundred and thirty-two, a sum not exceeding one hundred thirty thousand dollars, to be paid from the Highway Fund . 130,000 00

Total $680,000 00

[Item]

Functions of the department relating to waterways and public lands:

587   For personal services of the chief engineer and assistants, a sum not exceeding fifty thousand six hundred dollars $50,600 00

588   For services other than personal, including printing pamphlet of laws and the annual report, and for necessary office and engineering supplies and equipment, a sum not exceeding seventeen hundred dollars 1,700 00

589   For the care and maintenance of the province lands and of the lands acquired and structures erected by the Provincetown tercentenary commission, a sum not exceeding forty-seven hundred dollars .   4,700 00

590   For the maintenance of structures, and for repairing damages along the coast line or river banks of the commonwealth, and for the removal of wrecks and other obstructions from tide waters and great ponds, a sum not exceeding twenty-two thousand five hundred dollars 22,500 00

591   For the improvement, development and protection of rivers and harbors, tide waters and foreshores within the commonwealth, as authorized by section eleven of chapter ninety-one of the General Laws, as appearing in the Tercentenary Edition thereof, and of great ponds, a sum not exceeding twenty-five thousand dollars, and any unexpended balance of the appropriation remaining at the end of the current fiscal year may be expended in the succeeding fiscal year for the same purposes; provided, that all expenditures made for the protection of shores shall be upon condition that at least fifty per cent of the cost is covered by contributions from municipalities or other organizations and individuals, and that in the case of dredging channels for harbor improvements at least twenty-five per cent of the cost shall be so covered; and further provided that the department of public works may expend a sum not exceeding eight thousand dollars of the total appropriation for dredging near the state pier at New Bedford without any restriction as to contributions . .   25,000 00

592   For re-establishing and permanently marking certain triangulation points and sections, as required by order of the land court in accordance with section thirty-three of chapter ninety-one of the General Laws, as appearing in the Tercentenary Edition thereof, a sum not exceeding one thousand dollars 1,000 00

593   For expenses of surveying certain town boundaries, by the department of public works, a sum not exceeding five hundred dollars . . .   500 00

594   For the operation and maintenance of the New Bedford state pier, a sum not exceeding ten thousand dollars 10,000 00

595   For the compensation of dumping inspectors, a sum not exceeding one thousand dollars . .   1,000 00

596   For continuing the work in gauging the flow of water in the streams of the commonwealth, a sum not exceeding four thousand dollars . .   4,000 00

597   For the maintenance and repair of certain property in the town of Plymouth, a sum not exceeding thirty-eight hundred dollars 3,800 00

Item

The unexpended balance of the appropriation made by item six hundred and thirty-eight of chapter two hundred and forty-five of the acts of nineteen hundred and thirty-one for certain work in the Taunton river, authorized by chapter four hundred and five of the acts of nineteen hundred and thirty, is hereby reappropriated.

598 For the operation and maintenance of the Cape Cod Canal pier, a sum not exceeding thirty-five hundred dollars $3,500 00

598a For the erection of buildings on the Cape Cod Canal pier, a sum not exceeding twelve thousand five hundred dollars 12,500 00

Total $140,800 00

Functions of the department relating to Port of Boston (the following items are to be paid from the Port of Boston receipts):

599 For the supervision and operation of common-wealth pier five, including the salaries or other compensation of employees, and for the repair and replacement of equipment and other property, a sum not exceeding one hundred nine thousand six hundred dollars $109,600 00

600 For the maintenance of pier one, at East Boston, a sum not exceeding seventy-seven hundred and eighty dollars 7,780 00

601 For the maintenance and improvement of common-wealth property under the control of the department in connection with its functions relating to waterways and public lands, a sum not exceeding ninety-eight thousand two hundred dollars . 98,200 00

602 For dredging channels and filling flats, a sum not exceeding fifty-five thousand dollars, the same to be in addition to any unexpended balance of the appropriation made for the purpose in the previous year 55,000 00

Total $270,580 00

Service of the Department of Public Utilities.

603 For personal services of the commissioners, a sum not exceeding thirty-four thousand and eighty dollars, of which sum one half shall be assessed upon the gas and electric companies in accordance with existing provisions of law . . . $34,080 00

604 For personal services of secretaries, employees of the accounting department, engineering department and rate and tariff department, a sum not exceeding thirty-one thousand one hundred and forty dollars, of which sum fifteen thousand five hundred and seventy dollars shall be assessed upon the gas and electric companies in accordance with existing provisions of law 31,140 00

605 For personal services of the inspection department, a sum not exceeding forty-one thousand four hundred and fifty dollars 41,450 00

606 For personal services of clerks, messengers and office assistants, a sum not exceeding twelve thousand two hundred and eighty dollars, of which sum one half shall be assessed upon the gas and electric companies in accordance with existing provisions of law 12,280 00

Item

607   For personal services of the telephone and telegraph division, a sum not exceeding thirteen thousand three hundred and thirty dollars .   .   . $13,330 00

608   For stenographic reports of hearings, a sum not exceeding twenty-five hundred dollars .   .   .   2,500 00

609   For traveling expenses of the commissioners and employees, a sum not exceeding forty-nine hundred and twenty-five dollars .   .   .   4,925 00

610   For services other than personal, printing the annual report, office supplies and equipment, a sum not exceeding three thousand dollars .   .   .   3,000 00

611   For stenographic reports of evidence at inquests held in cases of death by accident on or about railroads, a sum not exceeding twenty-five hundred dollars   2,500 00

Total $145,205 00

The following items are to be assessed upon the gas and electric companies:

612   For personal services of the division of inspection of gas and gas meters, a sum not exceeding twenty thousand nine hundred dollars .   .   . $20,900 00

613   For expenses of the division of inspection of gas and gas meters, including office rent, traveling and other necessary expenses of inspection, a sum not exceeding four thousand dollars .   .   4,000 00

614   For other services, printing the annual report, for rent of offices and for necessary office supplies and equipment, a sum not exceeding forty-three hundred and fifty dollars .   .   .   4,350 00

615   For the examination and tests of electric meters, a sum not exceeding two hundred and fifty dollars   250 00

Total $29,500 00

Special Investigations:

616   For personal services and expenses of special investigations, including legal assistants as needed, a sum not exceeding ten thousand dollars, of which such sum as shall be expended in the investigation of gas and electric companies shall be assessed upon gas and electric companies in accordance with existing provisions of law .   .   . $10,000 00

Division of Smoke Inspection:

The following items are to be assessed upon the cities and towns comprising the district defined by chapter six hundred and fifty-one of the acts of nineteen hundred and ten, and acts in amendment thereof or in addition thereto:

617   For personal services of the division for the period ending May thirty-first of the current year, upon which date all functions of this division shall cease, a sum not exceeding eighteen thousand two hundred and forty dollars .   .   . $18,240 00

618   For other services, printing the annual report, rent of offices, travel, and necessary office supplies and equipment, a sum not exceeding seven thousand dollars 7,000 00

618a   For services and expenses in connection with the abatement of smoke in Boston and vicinity, under the direction and with the approval of the department of public utilities, a sum not exceeding sixty-five hundred dollars .   .   .   6,500 00

Total $31,740 00

Item

Sale of Securities:

619   For personal services in administering the law relative to the sale of securities, a sum not exceeding
thirty-three thousand eight hundred and forty
dollars $33,840 00

620   For expenses other than personal in administering
the law relative to the sale of securities, a sum not
exceeding eighty-three hundred and seventy-five
dollars 8,375 00

Total $42,215 00

Miscellaneous.

621   For the maintenance of Bunker Hill monument and
the property adjacent, to be expended by the
metropolitan district commission, a sum not exceeding eleven thousand dollars   .   .   . $11,000 00

The following items are to be paid from the Highway Fund, with the approval of the Metropolitan District Commission:

622   For maintenance of boulevards and parkways, a sum
not exceeding five hundred forty-six thousand and
forty dollars 546,040 00

623   For resurfacing of boulevards and parkways, a sum
not exceeding one hundred thousand dollars   .   100,000 00

624   For maintenance of Wellington bridge, a sum not
exceeding forty-nine hundred and fifty-four dollars 4,954 00

Total $661,994 00

Unclassified Accounts and Claims.

625   For the compensation of veterans of the civil war
formerly in the service of the commonwealth, now
retired, a sum not exceeding seventy-eight hundred dollars $7,800 00

626   For the compensation of any veteran who may be
retired by the governor under the provisions of
sections fifty-six to fifty-nine, inclusive, of chapter
thirty-two of the General Laws, as appearing in the
Tercentenary Edition thereof, a sum not exceeding twenty-three thousand dollars   .   .   .   23,000 00

627   For the compensation of certain prison officers and
instructors formerly in the service of the commonwealth, now retired, a sum not exceeding fifty-two
thousand dollars 52,000 00

628   For the compensation of state police officers formerly
in the service of the commonwealth, and now
retired, a sum not exceeding thirty-five hundred
and forty dollars 3,540 00

629   For the compensation of certain women formerly
employed in cleaning the state house, and now
retired, a sum not exceeding nine hundred dollars   900 00

Total $87,240 00

For certain other aid:

630   For the compensation of certain public employees
for injuries sustained in the course of their employment, as provided by section sixty-nine of chapter
one hundred and fifty-two of the General Laws, as
appearing in the Tercentenary Edition thereof, a
sum not exceeding sixty thousand dollars, of
which sum not more than twenty thousand dollars
may be charged to the Highway Fund   .   . $60,000 00

Item

631 For the payment of certain annuities and pensions
     of soldiers and others under the provisions of cer-
     tain acts and resolves, a sum not exceeding
     forty-five hundred and ninety-six dollars .   . $4,596 00

              Total $64,596 00

632 For reimbursing officials for premiums paid for pro-
     curing sureties on their bonds, as provided by
     existing laws, a sum not exceeding one hundred
     fifty dollars $150 00
633 For payment of any claims, as authorized by section
     eighty-nine of chapter thirty-two of the General
     Laws, as appearing in the Tercentenary Edition
     thereof, for allowances to the families of members
     of the department of public safety doing police
     duty killed or fatally injured in the discharge of
     their duties, a sum not exceeding two thousand
     dollars 2,000 00
634 For small items of expenditure for which no appro-
     priations have been made, and for cases in which
     appropriations have been exhausted or have re-
     verted to the treasury in previous years, a sum
     not exceeding five hundred dollars   .   .   500 00
635 For reimbursement of persons for funds previously
     deposited in the treasury of the commonwealth on
     account of unclaimed savings bank deposits, a sum
     not exceeding five hundred dollars   .   .   500 00
636 For the heirs-at-law or next of kin of John Kou-
     kourakis, as authorized by chapter twenty-eight
     of the resolves of nineteen hundred and twenty-
     nine, a sum not exceeding seven hundred sixty-
     nine dollars and sixty-five cents, payment of
     which shall be certified by the comptroller of the
     commonwealth only upon the filing by the attor-
     ney general of satisfactory releases or other evi-
     dence that the payment is accepted in full com-
     pensation on the part of the commonwealth in
     respect thereto 769 65

              Total $3,919 65

DEFICIENCIES.

For deficiencies in certain appropriations of previous years, in certain items, as follows:

Judicial Department.

Probate and Insolvency Courts:
For the compensation of judges of probate when acting outside their own counties for other judges of
probate, the sum of forty-seven hundred and fifty-
five dollars $4,755 00
For expenses of judges of probate when acting outside their own counties for other judges of probate,
as authorized by section forty of chapter two hundred and seventeen of the General Laws, as
appearing in the Tercentenary Edition thereof,
the sum of one hundred twenty-six dollars and
thirty-two cents 126 32

Land Court.

For personal services in the examination of titles, for
publishing and serving citations and other services,
traveling expenses, supplies and office equipment,
and for the preparation of sectional plans showing
registered land, the sum of fifty dollars   .   .   50 00

Militia.

Item

For transportation of officers and non-commissioned officers for attendance at military meetings, the sum of four hundred six dollars and sixty-four cents $406 64

State Quartermaster.

For the maintenance of armories of the first class, including the purchase of certain furniture, the sum of sixty-six dollars and fifty-eight cents .   66 58

Secretary of the Commonwealth.

For printing laws, etc.:
For printing and distribution of the pamphlet edition of the acts and resolves of the year nineteen hundred and thirty-two, the sum of forty dollars and ninety-four cents 40 94

Department of Agriculture.

Division of Dairying and Animal Husbandry:
For other expenses, including the enforcement of the dairy laws of the commonwealth, the sum of forty dollars and fifty-eight cents 40 58

Department of Conservation.

Division of Animal Industry:
For reimbursement of certain towns for compensation paid to inspectors of animals, the sum of two hundred seventy-nine dollars and fifty-six cents .   279 56
For traveling expenses of veterinarians and agents, including the cost of any motor vehicles purchased for their use, the sum of sixty-six dollars and twenty-five cents 66 25

Division of Forestry:
For aiding towns in the purchase of equipment for extinguishing forest fires and for making protective belts or zones as a defence against forest fires, for the present and previous years, the sum of three hundred sixty-one dollars and twenty-six cents .   361 26

Department of Education.

For the education of deaf and blind pupils of the commonwealth, as provided by section twenty-six of chapter sixty-nine of the General Laws, the sum of twenty-one hundred seventy-five dollars and twenty-five cents 2,175 25
For the reimbursement of certain towns for the payment of tuition of pupils attending high schools outside the towns in which they reside, as provided by law, the sum of sixteen thousand four hundred fifty-seven dollars and sixty-nine cents .   16,457 69
For the reimbursement of certain towns for the transportation of pupils attending high schools outside the towns in which they reside, as provided by law, the sum of twenty-five thousand six hundred seventy-seven dollars and thirty-one cents .   25,677 31
For assisting small towns in providing themselves with school superintendents, as provided by law, the sum of twenty-two hundred thirty-two dollars and twenty-six cents 2,232 26

Division of the Blind:
For expenses of providing sight-saving classes, with the approval of the division of the blind, the sum of five hundred seventy-five dollars .   .   .   575 00

Department of Civil Service and Registration.

Division of Registration:
For services of the division other than personal,
printing the annual reports, office supplies and
equipment, except as otherwise provided, the sum
of three hundred eighteen dollars and ten cents . $318 10

Department of Correction.

For traveling expenses of officers and employees of
the department when required to travel in the discharge of their duties, the sum of two hundred
forty-four dollars and twenty-eight cents .   .   244 28

State Prison:
For expenses of fire prevention work at the state
prison, the sum of six hundred twenty-one dollars
and twenty-eight cents 621 28

Department of Public Welfare.

Division of Juvenile Training, Trustees of Massachusetts Training Schools:
For reimbursement of cities and towns for tuition of
children attending the public schools, the sum of
one hundred thirty-two dollars and eighty-one
cents 132 81

Department of Public Works.

Functions of the department relating to highways:
For administering the law relative to advertising
signs near highways, the sum of fifteen dollars and
eighty-two cents, to be paid from the General
Fund 15 82
For the construction and repair of town and
county ways, the sum of sixty dollars and eighty-
one cents, to be paid from the Highway Fund .   60 81
For the maintenance and repair of state highways,
including care of snow on highways, expenses of
traffic signs and lights, and payment of damages
caused by defects in state highways, with the approval of the attorney general; for care and repair
of road-building machinery; and for the purchase
and improvement of a nursery for roadside planting, the sum of forty dollars and sixty-four cents,
to be paid from the Highway Fund .   .   .   40 64
For the purpose of enabling the department of public
works to secure federal aid for the construction of
highways, the sum of three dollars, to be paid
from the Highway Fund 3 00

Registration of Motor Vehicles:
For services other than personal, including traveling
expenses, purchase of necessary supplies and materials, including cartage and storage of the same,
and for work incidental to the registration and
licensing of owners and operators of motor vehicles, the sum of three dollars and eight cents, to be
paid from the Highway Fund 3 08

Functions of the department relating to waterways and public lands:
For the supervision and operation of commonwealth
pier five, including the salaries or other compensation of employees, and for the repair and replacement of equipment and other property, the
sum of seventy-eight dollars and ninety-five cents,
to be paid from the Port of Boston receipts .   78 95

Item

For dredging channels and filling flats, the sum of six hundred seventy-seven dollars and two cents, to be paid from the Port of Boston receipts . $677 02

Unclassified Accounts and Claims.

For payment of any claims, as authorized by section eighty-nine of chapter thirty-two of the General Laws, as appearing in the Tercentenary Edition thereof, for allowances to the families of members of the department of public safety doing police duty killed or fatally injured in the discharge of their duties, the sum of three hundred thirty dollars and sixty-two cents 330 62

Total $55,837 05

Metropolitan District Commission.

The following items are to be assessed upon the several districts in accordance with the methods fixed by law, unless otherwise provided, and to be expended under the direction and with the approval of the metropolitan district commission:

637 For maintenance of the Charles River basin, a sum not exceeding one hundred ninety-eight thousand seven hundred and forty-six dollars . . . $198,746 00

638 For maintenance of park reservations, a sum not exceeding eight hundred sixty-one thousand six hundred dollars, including a deficiency amounting to ten dollars 861,600 00

639 For the expense of holding band concerts, a sum not exceeding twenty thousand dollars . . 20,000 00

640 For services and expenses of the division of metropolitan planning, as authorized by chapter three hundred and ninety-nine of the acts of nineteen hundred and twenty-three, a sum not exceeding eight thousand dollars 8,000 00

641 For maintenance of the Nantasket Beach reservation, a sum not exceeding eighty-four thousand three hundred dollars 84,300 00

642 For maintenance of Wellington bridge, a sum not exceeding fourteen thousand eight hundred and sixty-two dollars, the same to be in addition to the amount appropriated in item six hundred and twenty-four 14,862 00

643 For the maintenance and operation of a system of sewage disposal for the north metropolitan sewerage district, a sum not exceeding three hundred forty-six thousand six hundred and forty-five dollars 346,645 00

644 For the maintenance and operation of a system of sewage disposal for the south metropolitan sewerage district, a sum not exceeding two hundred thirty-two thousand five hundred and ten dollars 232,510 00

645 For the maintenance and operation of the metropolitan water system, a sum not exceeding eight hundred fifty-one thousand eight hundred and eighty dollars, including retirement of soldiers under the provisions of the General Laws . . 851,880 00

646 For the construction of additions and improvements to certain supply and distribution mains, as a part of the cost of maintenance of the metropolitan water system, a sum not exceeding two hundred fifty thousand dollars, the same to be in addition to any unexpended balance of an appropriation made for the purpose in the previous year . . 250,000 00

Item
647 For the purchase and installation of additional
      pumping equipment, as a part of the cost of main-
      tenance of the metropolitan water system, a sum
      not exceeding fifty thousand dollars, the same to
      be in addition to any unexpended balance of an
      appropriation made for the purpose in the previous
      year $50,000 00

           Total $2,918,543 00

      General and Highway Funds   .   .   . $54,790,181 52
      Metropolitan District Commission   .   .   2,918,543 00

Modification
of amounts of
certain appro-
priation items
to accomplish
salary re-
ductions.

SECTION 3.   Each sum expressed by section two to be
available in whole or in part for personal services is hereby
reduced by such amount as will make available for salaries
and compensation so much only as is required for such
salaries and compensation as reduced by chapter one hundred and five of the acts of the current year, entitled "An
Act reducing the Salary or other Compensation of State
Officers and Employees."   The state comptroller, in setting
up such items for personal services on the appropriation
ledger in his bureau, shall take as the amounts appropriated therefor by this act the said sums as reduced as aforesaid, and he shall forthwith notify each officer having
charge of any office, department or undertaking which
receives such an appropriation for personal services of the
amount thereof as so set up.   The division of personnel and
standardization shall furnish, upon the request of the state
comptroller, all necessary assistance in carrying out the
provisions of this section.

Expenditures
in excess of
appropriations
regulated.

SECTION 4.   No expenditures in excess of appropriations
provided for under this act shall be incurred by any department or institution, except in cases of emergency, and then
only upon the prior written approval of the governor and
council.

Appropriations
for mainte-
nance of certain
institutions to
include allow-
ances.

SECTION 5.   The sums appropriated for maintenance of
certain institutions include allowances for the purchase of
coal to April first, nineteen hundred and thirty-four, and
balance representing these sums may be carried forward
at the end of the fiscal year.

Expenditures
for public
buildings
regulated.

SECTION 6.   No payment shall be made or obligation
incurred under authority of any special appropriation made
by this act for construction of public buildings or other
improvements at state institutions until plans and specifications have been approved by the governor, unless otherwise provided by such rules and regulations as the governor
may make.

Copies of act
to be sent to
department
heads.

SECTION 7.   The budget commissioner is hereby directed
to send a copy of sections four, six and eight of this act to
each departmental, divisional and institutional head
immediately following the passage of this act.

Allowances
for board, etc.,
regulated.

SECTION 8.   No expenses incurred on and after the date
of the passage of this act for mid-day meals by state em-

ployees, other than those who receive as part of their compensation a non-cash allowance in the form of full or complete boarding and housing, and those employees who are stationed beyond commuting distance from their homes for a period of more than twenty-four hours, shall be allowed by the commonwealth.

SECTION 9.   This act shall take effect upon its passage.

Approved May 9, 1933.

AN ACT RELATIVE TO THE ANNUAL REPORT OF COUNTY TREASURERS.

*Chap.*175

Be it enacted, etc., as follows:

SECTION 1.   Section twenty-five of chapter thirty-five of the General Laws, as appearing in the Tercentenary Edition thereof, is hereby amended by striking out all after the word "contain" in the fifth line down to and including the word "also" in the seventh line, — so as to read as follows: — *Section 25.* Immediately after January tenth, the county treasurer shall annually prepare a report of the county receipts and expenditures for the preceding year, stated separately under the heads prescribed by the director of accounts for keeping the treasurer's books.   Such statement shall contain a table setting forth the appropriation made by the general court for each specific object, the amount expended therefrom, the unexpended balance thereof, and any excess of payments over said appropriation.

G. L. (Ter. Ed.), 35, § 25, amended.

Annual report of county treasurers.

SECTION 2.   Section twenty-seven of said chapter thirty-five, as so appearing, is hereby amended by striking out, in the second and third lines, the words "in number sufficient to furnish a copy for every three hundred inhabitants of the county", and by striking out all after the word "county" in the fifth line down to and including the word "inhabitants" in the seventh line, — so as to read as follows: — *Section 27.* The county treasurer shall cause such report to be printed and bound with his own report, and shall send a copy to the state library, to the director of accounts, and to the mayor of each city and the selectmen of each town in the county.   He shall, at the close of each year, advertise in not more than three newspapers published in the same or an adjoining county an account of the county receipts and expenditures arranged under distinct heads, and a specific statement of the county debts, the purposes for which incurred and their dates of maturity.

G. L. (Ter. Ed.), 35, § 27, amended.

Publication and distribution of annual reports.

Approved May 9, 1933.

AN ACT RELATIVE TO THE LAYING OUT OF STATE HIGHWAYS ACROSS LOCATIONS OF RAILROAD CORPORATIONS.

*Chap.*176

Be it enacted, etc., as follows:

Chapter one hundred and sixty of the General Laws is hereby amended by striking out section one hundred and four, as appearing in the Tercentenary Edition thereof, and

G. L. (Ter. Ed.), 160, § 104, amended.

When a high-
way may be
laid out across
a railroad. inserting in place thereof the following: — *Section 104.* A
public way may be laid out across a railroad previously
constructed, if the county commissioners, or the department of public works in the case of a state highway,
adjudge that public necessity and convenience so require;
and in such case, after notice to the railroad corporation
and a hearing of all parties interested, said commissioners
or department, or a city or town by authority of the county
commissioners granted upon petition of its board of aldermen or selectmen, may thus lay out a way across a railroad,
in such manner as not to injure or obstruct the railroad,
and otherwise in conformity with sections ninety-seven and
ninety-eight. A public way shall not be permitted to cross
at a level with the railroad unless it is determined by the
department of public works, in the case of a state highway,
or the county commissioners, in the case of any other public
way, after notice to all persons interested and a hearing,
that public necessity so requires, and the department of
public utilities consents thereto in writing. A copy of the
proceedings of the department of public works in laying out
a state highway under this section, including a copy of the
plan of so much of said way as lies within the location of the
railroad, shall be filed in the office of the county commissioners of the county where such way is located.

Approved May 9, 1933.

Chap.177 AN ACT VALIDATING CERTAIN ACTS OF THE DEPARTMENT OF
PUBLIC WORKS IN LAYING OUT AND CONSTRUCTING A STATE
HIGHWAY ACROSS THE LOCATION OF THE BOSTON AND
ALBANY RAILROAD COMPANY IN WORCESTER.

Be it enacted, etc., as follows:

The order of the department of public works dated
November third, nineteen hundred and thirty-one, laying
out a state highway in the city of Worcester across the
location of the Boston and Albany Railroad Company at a
point about six hundred feet northerly of Grafton street at
station 2101 + 38.93 of the base line of the location of said
railroad, said station being identical with station 114 +
62.00 of the base line of the location of said state highway
as appearing on a plan entitled "The Commonwealth of
Massachusetts, Plan of Road in the city of Worcester,
Worcester County, Laid out as a State Highway by the
Department of Public Works November 3, 1931, Scale 40
feet to the inch, A. W. Dean, Chief Engineer," and also
the construction of said state highway across the said railroad location by means of an underpass sixty-four feet in
width and its approaches, are hereby validated, ratified and
confirmed in so far as either such layout or construction
may be invalid by reason of any want of authority of said
department; and all rights of owners of property, or their
lessees, with reference to claims for damages on account

of said layout and/or construction are hereby declared not
to be affected by any such want of authority; and the time
within which said owners, or their lessees, may petition the
superior court for assessment of damages on account of said
layout and/or construction is hereby extended for one year
from the effective date of this act.

Approved May 9, 1933.

AN ACT ESTABLISHING IN THE TOWN OF EASTHAMPTON *Chap.*178
REPRESENTATIVE TOWN GOVERNMENT BY LIMITED TOWN
MEETINGS.

Be it enacted, etc., as follows:

SECTION 1. There is hereby established in the town of Representative
Easthampton the form of representative town government town govern-
by limited town meetings hereinafter set forth. ment in Easthampton.

SECTION 2. Upon the acceptance of this act by the town Establishment
of Easthampton as hereinafter provided, the selectmen of voting
shall forthwith divide the territory thereof into voting precincts.
precincts, each of which shall be plainly designated and
shall contain not less than four hundred registered voters.
The precincts shall be so established as to consist of compact and contiguous territory to be bounded, as far as possible, by the center line of known streets and ways or by
other well-defined limits. Their boundaries shall be reviewed, and, if need be, wholly or partly revised, by the
selectmen in December, once in five years, or in December
of any year when so directed by a vote of a representative
town meeting held not later than November twentieth of
that year.

The selectmen shall, within ten days after any estab- Report of
lishment or revision of the precincts, file a report of their selectmen
doings with the town clerk, the registrars of voters and the lishment, etc.,
assessors, with a map or maps or description of the pre- of voting precincts and the names and residences of the registered cincts.
voters therein. The selectmen shall also cause to be posted
in the town hall a map or maps or description of the precincts as established or revised from time to time, with the
names and residences of the registered voters therein; and
they shall also cause to be posted in at least one public
place in each precinct a map or description of that precinct,
with the names and residences of the registered voters
therein. The division of the town into voting precincts
and any revision of such precincts shall take effect upon the
date of the filing of the report thereof by the selectmen with
the town clerk. Whenever the precincts are established
or revised, the town clerk shall forthwith give written
notice thereof to the state secretary, stating the number
and designation of the precincts. Meetings of the registered voters of the several precincts, for elections, for
primaries, and for voting upon any question to be submitted
to all the registered voters of the town, shall be held on the

same day and at the same hour and at such place or places within the town as the selectmen shall in the warrant for such meeting direct. The provisions of chapters fifty to fifty-six, inclusive, of the General Laws relating to precinct voting at elections, so far as the same are not inconsistent with this act, shall apply to all elections and primaries in the town upon the establishment of voting precincts as hereinbefore provided.

Elected town meeting members, election, terms, etc.

SECTION 3. Other than the officers designated in section four and in the by-laws of the town as town meeting members at large, the representative town meeting membership shall in each precinct consist of the largest number divisible by three, and which will not exceed four per cent of the registered voters in the precinct, and which will cause the total membership to be as nearly one hundred and eighty as may be. The registered voters in every precinct shall, at the first annual town election held after the establishment of such precinct, and the registered voters of any precinct affected by any revision of precincts at the first annual town election following such revision, conformably to the laws relative to elections not inconsistent with this act, elect by ballot the number of registered voters in the precinct, other than the officers designated in section four and in the by-laws as town meeting members at large, provided for in the first sentence of this section, to be town meeting members of the town. The first third, in the order of votes received, of members so elected shall serve three years, the second third in such order shall serve two years, and the remaining third in such order shall serve one year, from the day of the annual town meeting; in case of a tie vote affecting the division into thirds, as aforesaid, the members elected from the precinct shall by ballot determine the same; and thereafter, except as is otherwise provided herein, at each annual town election the registered voters of each precinct shall, in like manner, elect, for the term of three years, one third of the number of elected town meeting members to which such precinct is entitled, and shall at such election fill for the unexpired term or terms any vacancy or vacancies then existing in the number of elected town meeting members in such precinct. The terms of office of all elected town meeting members from every precinct revised as aforesaid shall cease upon the election as hereinbefore provided of their successors. The town clerk shall, after every election of town meeting members, forthwith notify each such member by mail of his election.

Town meeting members at large.

SECTION 4. Any representative town meeting held under the provisions of this act, except as otherwise provided herein, shall be limited to the town meeting members elected under section three, together with the following town meeting members at large, namely: any member of the general court of the commonwealth from the town, the moderator, the town clerk, the members of the board of selectmen, the town treasurer, the town counsel, the chairman of the school committee, the chairman of the finance committee, the chairman of the board of assessors, the chairman of the board of public works, and such other town meeting members at large as may be provided for by the by-laws of the town, and authority to adopt such by-laws is hereby conferred.

The town clerk shall notify the town meeting members of the time and place at which representative town meetings are to be held, the notices to be sent by mail at least seven days before the meeting. The town meeting members, as aforesaid, shall be the judges of the election and qualifications of their members. A majority of the town meeting members shall constitute a quorum for doing business; but a less number may organize temporarily and may adjourn from time to time, but no town meeting shall adjourn over the date of an election of town meeting members. All town meetings shall be public. The town meeting members as such shall receive no compensation. Subject to such conditions as may be determined from time to time by the members of the representative town meeting, any registered voter of the town who is not a town meeting member may speak at any representative town meeting, but shall not vote. A town meeting member may resign by filing a written resignation with the town clerk, and such resignation shall take effect on the date of such filing. No elected member whose official position entitles him to be a member at large shall act as a member at large during such time as he remains an elected member. A town meeting member who removes from the town shall cease to be a town meeting member, and a town meeting member who removes from the precinct from which he was elected to another precinct may serve only until the next annual town meeting. *Notice of meetings.*

Resignation of town meeting member.

Section 5. Nomination of candidates for town meeting members to be elected under this act shall be made by nomination papers, which shall bear no political designation, but to the name of a candidate for re-election there may be added the words "Candidate for Re-election." Nomination papers shall be signed by not less than ten voters of the precinct in which the candidate resides, and shall be filed with the town clerk at least ten days before the election. No nomination papers shall be valid in respect to any candidate whose written acceptance is not thereon or attached thereto when filed. *Nomination of candidates for town meeting members.*

Section 6. The articles in the warrant for every town meeting, so far as they relate to the election of the moderator, town officers and town meeting members, and as herein provided, to referenda, and all matters to be acted upon and determined by ballot, shall be so acted upon and determined by the registered voters of the town in their respective precincts. All other articles in the warrant for any town meeting shall be acted upon and determined exclusively by town meeting members at a meeting to be held at such time and place as shall be set forth by the selectmen in the war- *Articles in town warrant, how acted upon.*

rant for the meeting, subject to the referendum provided
for by section nine.

Moderator,
election, etc.
SECTION 7. A moderator shall be elected by ballot at
each annual town meeting, and shall serve as moderator of
all town meetings, except as otherwise provided by law,
until a successor is elected and qualified. Nominations
for and election of a moderator shall be as in the case of
other elective town officers, and any vacancy in the office
may be filled by the town meeting members at a meeting
held for that purpose. If a moderator is absent, a moderator pro tempore may be elected by the town meeting
members.

Vacancies,
how filled.
SECTION 8. Any vacancy in the full number of town
meeting members from any precinct, whether arising from
a failure of the registered voters thereof to elect, or from any
other cause, may be filled, until the next annual election,
by the remaining members of the precinct from among the
registered voters thereof. Upon petition therefor, signed
by not less than ten town meeting members from the precinct, notice of any vacancy shall promptly be given by
the town clerk to the remaining members from the precinct in which the vacancy or vacancies exist, and he shall
call a special meeting of such members for the purpose of
filling such vacancy or vacancies. He shall cause to be
mailed to every such member, not less than five days before
the time set for the meeting, a notice specifying the object,
time and place of the meeting. At the said meeting a
majority of the members from such precinct shall constitute a quorum, and they shall elect from their own number
a chairman and a clerk. The choice to fill any vacancy
shall be by ballot, and a majority of the votes cast shall be
required for a choice. The chairman and clerk shall count
the ballots and shall make a certificate of the choice and
forthwith file the same with the town clerk, together with
a written acceptance by the member or members so chosen,
who shall thereupon be deemed elected and qualified as a
town meeting member or members, subject to the right of
all the town meeting members to judge of the election and
qualifications of the members as set forth in section four.

Certain votes
of town
meeting subject
to referendum.
SECTION 9. A vote passed at any representative town
meeting authorizing the expenditure of twenty thousand
dollars or more as a special appropriation, or establishing
a new board or office or abolishing an old board or office or
merging two or more boards or offices, or fixing the term of
office of town officers, where such term is optional, or increasing or reducing the number of members of a board, or
adopting a new by-law, or amending an existing by-law,
shall not be operative until after five days, exclusive of Sundays and holidays, from the dissolution of the meeting.
If, within said five days, a petition, signed by not less than
five per cent of the registered voters of the town containing
their names and addresses as they appear on the list of
registered voters, is filed with the selectmen asking that the

question or questions involved in such a vote be submitted to the registered voters of the town at large, then the selectmen, after the expiration of five days, shall call a special meeting which shall be held within fourteen days after the issuing of the call, for the sole purpose of presenting to the registered voters at large the question or questions so involved. The polls shall be opened at two o'clock in the afternoon and shall be closed not earlier than eight o'clock in the evening, and all votes upon any questions so submitted shall be taken by ballot, and the check list shall be used in the several precinct meetings in the same manner as in the election of town officers. The questions so submitted shall be determined by a majority vote of the registered voters of the town voting thereon, but no action of the representative town meeting shall be reversed unless at least twenty per cent of the registered voters shall so vote. Each question so submitted shall be in the form of the following question, which shall be placed upon the official ballot: — "Shall the town vote to approve the action of the representative town meeting whereby it was voted (brief description of the substance of the vote)?" If such petition is not filed within said period of five days, the vote of the representative town meeting shall become operative and effective upon the expiration of said period.

SECTION 10. The town, after the acceptance of this act, shall have the capacity to act through and to be bound by its town meeting members, who shall, when convened from time to time as herein provided, constitute representative town meetings; and the representative town meetings shall exercise exclusively, so far as will conform to the provisions of this act, all powers vested in the municipal corporation. Action in conformity with all provisions of law now or hereafter applicable to the transaction of town affairs in town meeting, shall, when taken by any representative town meeting in accordance with the provisions of this act, have the same force and effect as if such action had been taken in a town meeting open to all the voters of the town as organized and conducted before the establishment in said town of representative town meeting government. *Town to act through its town meeting.*

SECTION 11. This act shall not abridge the right of the inhabitants of the town to hold general meetings, as secured to them by the constitution of this commonwealth; nor shall this chapter confer upon any representative town meeting in said town the power finally to commit the town to any measure affecting its municipal existence or substantially changing its form of government without action thereon by the voters of the town at large, using the ballot and the check list therefor. *Right of inhabitants of town to hold meetings not abridged.*

SECTION 12. This act shall be submitted to the registered voters of the town of Easthampton for acceptance at its annual town election in the year nineteen hundred and thirty-four. The vote shall be taken by ballot in accordance with the provisions of the general laws, so far as the *Submission of act to voters for acceptance.*

same shall be applicable, in answer to the question, which shall be placed upon the official ballot to be used in said town at said election: "Shall an act passed by the general court in the year nineteen hundred and thirty-three, entitled 'An Act establishing in the town of Easthampton representative town government by limited town meetings' be accepted by this town?" If accepted by a majority of the voters voting thereon, this act shall thereupon take effect for all purposes incidental to the annual town election in said town in the year nineteen hundred and thirty-five, and shall take full effect beginning with said election.

Resubmission
of act after
rejection. SECTION 13. If this act is rejected by the registered voters of the town of Easthampton when submitted to said voters under section twelve, it may be submitted for acceptance in like manner, to such voters at any annual town election in said town not later than the annual town election in the year nineteen hundred and thirty-seven, and, if accepted by a majority of the voters voting thereon at such an election, shall thereupon take effect for all purposes incidental to the next annual town election in said town, and shall take full effect beginning with said election.

Approved May 9, 1933.

---

*Chap.*179 AN ACT AUTHORIZING THE DEPARTMENT OF PUBLIC WORKS TO DREDGE AND FURTHER PROTECT THE HARBOR IN THE TOWN OF GOSNOLD.

Be it enacted, etc., as follows:

SECTION 1. The department of public works is hereby authorized and directed to dredge and enlarge the harbor in the town of Gosnold in such location and to such depth as it may deem necessary, and further to protect the same.

SECTION 2. For the purpose aforesaid, the department may expend a sum not exceeding ten thousand dollars from the appropriation made by item number five hundred and ninety-one of the general appropriation act of the current year; provided, that an amount equal to at least ten per cent of the amount to be expended hereunder is contributed by persons and/or political subdivisions of the commonwealth; and provided, further, that no part of said sum shall be available or expended until said town of Gosnold, in the manner provided by section twenty-nine of chapter ninety-one of the General Laws, has assumed liability for damages that may be incurred hereunder.

Approved May 9, 1933.

An Act providing for the establishment of a right of way for public access to lake marguerite, also known as simon pond, in the town of sandisfield.

Chap.180

Be it enacted, etc., as follows:

Section 1. The county commissioners of Berkshire county are hereby authorized and directed to lay out a right of way in the town of Sandisfield to Lake Marguerite, also known as Simon pond, in said town for public access to said lake, in accordance with plans therefor approved by the department of public works and showing the location and dimensions of such right of way. If it is necessary to acquire land for the purpose of laying out such right of way the commissioners shall at the time such right of way is laid out take such land by eminent domain under chapter seventy-nine of the General Laws. Any person sustaining damages in his property by the laying out of such right of way, or by specific repairs or improvements thereon, shall be entitled to recover the same under said chapter seventy-nine; provided, that the right to damages, if any, shall vest upon the recording of an order of taking by the commissioners and that no entry or possession for the purpose of constructing a public way on land so taken shall be required for the purpose of validating such taking or for the payment of damages by reason thereof.

Right of way to Lake Marguerite in town of Sandisfield, layout authorized.

Section 2. The selectmen of the town of Sandisfield from time to time may make specific repairs on or improve such way to such extent as they may deem necessary, but the county of Berkshire, or any town therein, shall not be required to keep such right of way in repair nor shall they be liable for injury sustained by persons traveling thereon; provided, that sufficient notice to warn the public is posted where such way enters upon or unites with an existing public way.

Improvement of right of way by town authorized.

Section 3. All expenses incurred by the commissioners in connection with such right of way shall be borne by the county of Berkshire, or by such towns therein and in such proportion, as the commissioners may determine.

Section 4. Said right of way shall not be discontinued or abandoned unless authorized by the general court.

Section 5. Nothing in this act shall be construed to abridge or limit the powers of the department of public health or of any local board of health under general or special law.

Section 6. This act shall take effect upon its passage.

(This bill, returned by the governor to the House of Representatives, the branch in which it originated, with his objections thereto, was passed by the House of Representatives, May 9, 1933, and, in concurrence, by the Senate, May 10, 1933, the objections of the governor notwithstanding, in the manner prescribed by the constitution; and thereby has "the force of a law".)

Chap.181 AN ACT AUTHORIZING LOCAL BOARDS OF PUBLIC WELFARE
TO AID NEEDY PERSONS IN THE CULTIVATION OF VEGETABLE
GARDENS.

Emergency
preamble.

Whereas, The deferred operation of this act would tend
to defeat its purpose, therefore it is hereby declared to be
an emergency law, necessary for the immediate preservation
of the public convenience.

Be it enacted, etc., as follows:

G. L. (Ter.
Ed.), 117, new
section after
§ 2.

Seeds, plants,
etc., to be
furnished
certain
persons.

Chapter one hundred and seventeen of the General Laws,
as appearing in the Tercentenary Edition thereof, is hereby
amended by inserting after section two the following new
section: — *Section 2A.* The board of public welfare may,
subject to such conditions and terms as it may prescribe,
furnish any such poor and indigent person applying therefor with seeds, plants, fertilizer and tools to cultivate
vegetable gardens of their own. *Approved May 11, 1933.*

Chap.182 AN ACT AUTHORIZING THE COUNTY OF FRANKLIN TO FUND A
TEMPORARY LOAN ISSUED FOR THE CONSTRUCTION OF THE
COURT HOUSE IN GREENFIELD.

Be it enacted, etc., as follows:

County of
Franklin.
Funding of
court house
loan.

SECTION 1. For the purpose of funding the Franklin
County Court House Anticipation Loan, Act of 1931,
issued under the provisions of section four of chapter four
hundred and forty-nine of the acts of nineteen hundred and
thirty-one, the treasurer of Franklin county, with the approval of the county commissioners, may borrow on the
credit of the county a sum not exceeding fifty thousand
dollars, and may issue bonds or notes of the county therefor, which shall bear on their face the words, Franklin
County Court House Funding Loan, Act of 1933. Such
loan shall be payable in not more than ten years from its
date. Such bonds or notes shall be signed by the treasurer
of said county and countersigned by a majority of the
county commissioners. The county may sell said securities
at public or private sale upon such terms and conditions as
the county commissioners may deem proper, but not for
less than their par value. Indebtedness incurred under
this act shall, except as herein provided, be subject to
chapter thirty-five of the General Laws.

SECTION 2. The proceeds of the loan issued under
authority of section one shall be applied to the payment of
an outstanding loan issued under authority of said section
four, and known as the "Franklin County Court House
Anticipation Loan, Act of 1931".

SECTION 3. The proceeds of the sale of the old court
house building and site as provided in said section four, so
far as necessary, shall be applied to the payment of the loan
authorized in section one of this act, and any balance from

the proceeds of said sale shall be applied to the payment of indebtedness authorized under section three of said chapter four hundred and forty-nine; provided, that not more than ten thousand dollars of the debt maturing in any one year shall be paid from said balance.

Section 4.   This act shall take effect upon its passage.
Approved May 12, 1933.

An Act relative to registration fees for certain publicly owned motor vehicles. *Chap.*183

Whereas, The deferred operation of this act would tend to defeat its purpose, therefore it is hereby declared to be an emergency law, necessary for the immediate preservation of the public convenience. Emergency preamble.

Be it enacted, etc., as follows:

Section 1.   Section thirty-three of chapter ninety of the General Laws, as most recently amended by section one of chapter two hundred and forty-nine of the acts of nineteen hundred and thirty-two, is hereby further amended by striking out, in the first line of the fourth paragraph, as appearing in said section one of said chapter two hundred and forty-nine, the words "motor vehicle" and inserting in place thereof the word: — automobile, — so that said paragraph will read as follows: — For the registration of every automobile and trailer owned by the commonwealth or any political subdivision thereof and used solely for official business, not exempt from the payment of fees as hereinbefore provided, two dollars. G. L. (Ter. Ed.), 90, § 33, etc., amended.

Registration fees for certain publicly owned motor vehicles.

Section 2.   This act shall be operative as of January first in the current year.   *Approved May 12, 1933.* When operative.

An Act repealing the provisions of the charter of the city of Melrose which require the annual publication of a particular account of the receipts and expenditures of said city and a schedule of all city property and of the city debt. *Chap.*184

Be it enacted, etc., as follows:

Section 1.   Section nineteen of chapter one hundred and sixty-two of the acts of eighteen hundred and ninety-nine is hereby amended by striking out the fourth sentence.

Section 2.   This act shall take effect upon its passage.
Approved May 12, 1933.

An Act relative to the publication of by-laws in towns. *Chap.*185

Whereas, The deferred operation of this act would tend to defeat its purpose it is hereby declared to be an emergency law necessary for the immediate preservation of the public convenience. Emergency preamble.

Be it enacted, etc., as follows:

G. L. (Ter. Ed.), 40, § 32, amended.

Publication of by-laws in towns.

SECTION 1. Chapter forty of the General Laws is hereby amended by striking out section thirty-two, as appearing in the Tercentenary Edition thereof, and inserting in place thereof the following: — *Section 32.* Before a by-law takes effect it shall be approved by the attorney general and shall be published in a town bulletin or pamphlet, copies of which shall be posted in at least five public places in the town; and if the town be divided into precincts copies shall be posted in one or more public places in each precinct of the town; or, instead of such publishing in a town bulletin or pamphlet and such posting, shall be published at least three times in one or more newspapers, if any, published in the town, otherwise in one or more newspapers published in the county. The requirements of publishing in a town bulletin or pamphlet and posting, or publishing in one or more newspapers, as above, may be dispensed with if notice of the by-law be given by delivering a copy thereof at every occupied dwelling or apartment in the town, and affidavits of the persons delivering the said copies, filed with the town clerk, shall be conclusive evidence of proper notice hereunder.

Provisions of act not to affect existing by-laws.

SECTION 2. Nothing in this act shall affect any town by-law in force on the effective date of this act.

Approved May 12, 1933.

---

*Chap.*186 AN ACT REDUCING THE SALARIES OR OTHER COMPENSATION OF COUNTY OFFICERS AND EMPLOYEES, EXCEPT IN THE COUNTY OF SUFFOLK.

Emergency preamble.

Whereas, The deferred operation of this act would cause substantial inconvenience, therefore it is hereby declared to be an emergency law, necessary for the immediate preservation of the public convenience.

Be it enacted, etc., as follows:

Reduction of salaries of certain county officers, etc., except in Suffolk county, authorized.

SECTION 1. The salary of each official or employee in the service of each county of the commonwealth, except Suffolk, whose salary is payable from the treasury of one or more counties, or from funds administered by and through county officials, and whose salary is fixed in accordance with the compensation schedules adopted by the county personnel board, is hereby reduced, if it is fifty-two hundred and fifty dollars or under, by an amount equivalent to one and one half steps in the salary range established for the grade or position which he occupies, and, if it is in excess of fifty-two hundred and fifty dollars, by an amount equivalent to two steps in the salary range established for the grade or position which he occupies, said step, in either case, to be the same as the standard increment heretofore used by said board as the basis for increases in salary for the particular grade or position; provided, that in any grade or position in the service of any such county, determined by the county personnel board to be identical with or substantially equal to a grade or position in the service of the commonwealth, the reduction hereunder shall be the same as that made with respect to such latter grade or position; and provided, further, that the salary or compensation of any official or employee of any such county now receiving less than the minimum rate provided for his grade or position in the classification schedule of June first, nineteen hundred and thirty-one, shall not be reduced hereunder to an amount less than that to which it would be reduced if he were receiving the minimum rate of his grade or position.

SECTION 2. The salary of each official and employee in the service of each county, except Suffolk, including judges, clerks, assistant clerks, probation officers and other officials and employees of the municipal and district courts, whose salary is paid from the treasury of one or more counties or from funds administered by and through county officials, and whose salary is established otherwise than as set forth in the preceding section, shall be reduced, if it is fifty-two hundred and fifty dollars or under, by an amount equal to ten per cent thereof, and, if it is in excess of fifty-two hundred and fifty dollars, by an amount equal to fifteen per cent thereof; provided, that the salary or compensation of any official or employee of any such county now receiving less than the rate provided for his grade or position in the classification schedule of June first, nineteen hundred and thirty-one shall not be reduced hereunder to an amount less than that to which it would be reduced if he were receiving the minimum rate of his grade or position. The provisions of this act shall not apply to scrubwomen. *Reduction of salaries of certain county officers, etc., employed by more than one county.*

SECTION 3. The word "salary", as used in sections one and two, shall include all compensation from the county, however payable and whether or not for full time. *"Salary" defined.*

SECTION 4. The county personnel board, and the county commissioners for their respective counties, are hereby directed to enforce the provisions of sections one and two. Nothing in said sections shall be construed to limit the respective powers of said board and officers as now defined by law. *County personnel board, etc., to enforce provisions of act.*

SECTION 5. The reduction in salaries provided for by this act shall be effective only for the period beginning May first in the current year and ending December thirty-first, nineteen hundred and thirty-four. *Effective date of reductions.*

SECTION 6. No reduction in salary or compensation made by this act shall affect the amount payable, under chapter thirty-two of the General Laws or any other provision of law, to any officer or employee by way of pension, annuity or retirement allowance or the amount of any annuity contribution payable by any member of any county retirement system.   *Approved May 12, 1933.* *Not to affect pensions, etc.*

*Chap.*187 AN ACT RELATIVE TO THE EXPENSES OF SNOW AND ICE RE-
MOVAL FROM STATE HIGHWAYS.

Be it enacted, etc., as follows:

G. L. (Ter.
Ed.), 81, § 19,
amended.

Towns to have
police jurisdic-
tion over state
highways.

Removal of
snow from
state high-
ways.

SECTION 1. Section nineteen of chapter eighty-one of
the General Laws, as appearing in the Tercentenary Edition thereof, is hereby amended by striking out the last four
sentences, so as to read as follows: — *Section 19.* A town
shall have police jurisdiction over all state highways within
its limits. It shall forthwith give written notice to the
department or its employees of any defect or want of repair
in such highways; but it may make necessary temporary
repairs of a state highway without the approval of the
department.

The department shall at the expense of the commonwealth keep such state highways or parts thereof as it may
select sufficiently clear of snow and ice to be reasonably safe
for travel; and the town in which any such state highway
or part thereof lies shall forthwith give written notice to the
department or its employees of any failure to keep such
highway or part thereof clear of ice and snow as aforesaid.

SECTION 2. No assessments for or on account of any
work done under said section nineteen during the fiscal
year ending November thirtieth, nineteen hundred and
thirty-two shall be made upon the several cities and towns
of the commonwealth.   *Approved May 12, 1933.*

*Chap.*188 AN ACT RELATIVE TO THE PRIVILEGES OF NON-RESIDENTS
TO OPERATE MOTOR VEHICLES IN THIS COMMONWEALTH
WITHOUT MASSACHUSETTS REGISTRATION.

Be it enacted, etc., as follows:

G. L. (Ter.
Ed.), 90, § 3,
amended.

Reciprocal
privileges to
non-residents
to operate
motor vehicles.

Section three of chapter ninety of the General Laws, as
appearing in the Tercentenary Edition thereof, is hereby
amended by striking out the first sentence and inserting in
place thereof the following: — Subject to the provisions of
section three A and except as otherwise provided in section
ten, a motor vehicle or trailer owned by a non-resident who
has complied with the laws relative to motor vehicles and
trailers, and the registration and operation thereof, of the
state or country of registration, may be operated on the ways
of this commonwealth without registration under this
chapter, to the extent, as to length of time of operation and
otherwise, that, as finally determined by the registrar, the
state or country of registration grants substantially similar
privileges in the case of motor vehicles and trailers duly
registered under the laws and owned by residents of this
commonwealth; provided, that no motor vehicle or trailer
shall be so operated beyond a period of thirty days after
either the date of entry of the vehicle in any one year or the
acquisition by such non-resident of a regular place of abode

or business within the commonwealth, except during such time as the owner thereof maintains in full force a policy of liability insurance providing indemnity for or protection to him, and to any person responsible for the operation of such motor vehicle or trailer with his express or implied consent, against loss by reason of the liability to pay damages to others for bodily injuries, including death at any time resulting therefrom, caused by such motor vehicle or trailer, at least to the amount or limits required in a motor vehicle liability policy as defined in section thirty-four A, nor unless the owner or operator of such motor vehicle or trailer, while operating the same during such additional time, has on his person or in the vehicle in some easily accessible place a permit issued by the registrar which then authorizes the operation of such vehicle without registration under this chapter.   *Approved May 12, 1933.*

An Act authorizing the county of Norfolk to reimburse the clerk of the district court of East Norfolk for money stolen from the clerk's office of said court.   *Chap.*189

Be it enacted, etc., as follows:

The county of Norfolk may pay to Lawrence W. Lyons, clerk of the district court of East Norfolk, the sum of three hundred and forty-five dollars and forty-eight cents, to reimburse him for money stolen from the clerk's office of said court on June twenty-fifth, nineteen hundred and thirty-two.   *Approved May 12, 1933.*

An Act relative to the loss of trust company certificates of deposit or co-operative bank share certificates.   *Chap.*190

Be it enacted, etc., as follows:

Section twenty of chapter one hundred and sixty-seven of the General Laws, as appearing in the Tercentenary Edition thereof, is hereby amended by adding at the end thereof the following new sentence: — The provisions of this section shall apply to trust company certificates of deposit and to matured and paid-up share certificates of co-operative banks, — so as to read as follows: — *Section 20.* When a pass book issued by a savings bank, a co-operative bank or the savings department of a trust company has been lost, stolen or destroyed, the person in whose name it was issued or his legal representative, may make written application to such bank, for payment of the amount of the deposit represented by said book or for the issuance of a duplicate book therefor. Thereupon with the written consent of the bank, he may give, or authorize the bank at his expense to give, public notice of such application by advertising the same at least once a week for three successive weeks in a news-

G. L. (Ter. Ed.), 167, § 20, amended.

Advertising lost pass books, etc.

paper published in or nearest to the town where such bank is situated. If such book shall not be presented to said bank within thirty days after the date of the first advertisement, as aforesaid, the bank shall, upon proof that such notice has been given, pay the amount due on said book or issue a duplicate book therefor; and upon such payment or delivery of a new book, all liability of the bank on account of the original book shall cease. The provisions of this section shall apply to trust company certificates of deposit and to matured and paid-up share certificates of co-operative banks.   *Approved May 12, 1933.*

---

*Chap.*191 An Act relative to notice by the registrar of motor vehicles of the revocation or suspension of any registration of motor vehicles or of any license to operate the same and of the suspension of any right to operate such vehicles.

Be it enacted, etc., as follows:

G. L. (Ter. Ed.), 90, § 22, amended.
Notice of revocation or suspension of registration of motor vehicles or of licenses to operate same for offences under motor vehicle laws, etc.

Section twenty-two of chapter ninety of the General Laws, as appearing in the Tercentenary Edition thereof, is hereby amended by adding thereto the following: — Upon the suspension or revocation of any license or registration the registrar shall forthwith send written notice thereof to the licensee or registrant as the case may be. Such notice mailed by the registrar or any person authorized by him to the last address as appearing on the registrar's records shall be deemed a sufficient notice and a certificate of the registrar, or of any person so authorized, that such notice has been mailed in accordance with this section shall be deemed prima facie evidence thereof and shall be admissible in any court of the commonwealth as to the facts contained therein.

Upon the suspension of the right to operate a motor vehicle without a license of any person, the registrar shall forthwith send written notice thereof to such person and such notice mailed by the registrar or any person authorized by him to such person, to his last and usual place of abode shall be deemed a sufficient notice and a certificate as described in the preceding paragraph shall be likewise deemed prima facie evidence and shall be admissible in like manner in any court of the commonwealth.
          Approved May 12, 1933.

---

*Chap.*192 An Act abolishing the open season on deer in Barnstable County and further regulating the hunting of deer.

Be it enacted, etc., as follows:

G. L. (Ter. Ed.), 131, § 104, amended.

Section 1. Chapter one hundred and thirty-one of the General Laws is hereby amended by striking out section one hundred and four, as appearing in the Tercentenary Edition thereof, and inserting in place thereof the following: —

Section 104. Whoever constructs, erects, sets, repairs or tends any snare for the purpose of catching or killing any mammal, or takes a mammal by such means or by the aid or use of any motor vehicle or artificial light except as authorized herein, shall be punished by a fine of not less than fifty nor more than two hundred dollars. The construction, erection, setting, repairing or tending of any snare by any person shall be prima facie evidence of a violation by him of this section. Nothing in this section shall be construed to prohibit the hunting of raccoons or skunks or any unprotected mammal in a lawful manner with artificial light, provided no motor vehicle is used therefor. Upon application to the director by the owner or occupant of land, the director may grant to him a permit authorizing him, a member of his family, or a person permanently employed by him, if authorized by him so to do, for such period during the close season for deer, not exceeding ninety days, as may be specified in the permit, to set or use a torch light or jack light on such land for the purpose of taking, injuring or killing any deer thereon which he has reasonable cause to believe has damaged or is about to damage crops or fruit trees thereon; and in the event of the taking, injuring or killing of a deer as aforesaid, the person by whom or under whose direction the deer was taken, injured or killed shall, within twenty-four hours thereafter, send to the director a written report, signed by him, of the facts relative to the said taking, injuring or killing.

Use of snares, etc., in killing mammals, penalized. Exception.

SECTION 2. Said chapter one hundred and thirty-one, as amended in section one hundred and nine by chapter two hundred and sixty-four of the acts of nineteen hundred and thirty-two, is hereby further amended by striking out said section and inserting in place thereof the following: — *Section 109.* Subject to the restrictions and provisions hereinafter contained, any person duly authorized to hunt in the commonwealth may hunt a deer, by the use of a shotgun or bow and arrow, in all counties except Nantucket and Barnstable, between one half hour before sunrise and one half hour after sunset of each day beginning with the first Monday in December and ending with the following Saturday, and in any or all of the counties of Berkshire, Franklin, Hampden and Hampshire, if the additional hunting period hereinafter specified is authorized in such county or counties by the director, as evidenced by an order filed in his office and advertised in a newspaper or newspapers published in such county or counties not less than ten days prior to the first Monday in December, between one half hour before sunrise and one half hour after sunset of each day, beginning with the second Monday in December and ending with the following Saturday. No person shall, except as provided in the preceding section, kill more than one deer. No deer shall be hunted on land posted in accordance with section one hundred and twenty-three, or on land under control of the metropolitan district commission, or in any state reser-

G. L. (Ter. Ed.), 131, § 109, etc., amended.

Open season for deer.

Open season abolished in Barnstable county.

vation subject to section one hundred and fourteen except as provided therein. No person shall make, set or use any trap, torch light or jack light, salt lick or other device for the purpose of ensnaring, enticing, taking, injuring or killing a deer. No person shall use or carry on his person an arrow adapted for hunting purposes unless it is plainly marked with his name and permanent address. Whoever wounds or kills a deer shall, within forty-eight hours thereafter, send to the director a written report, signed by him, of the facts relative to the wounding or killing. Whoever violates any provision of this section shall be punished by a fine of not less than fifty nor more than one hundred dollars.

Penalty.

G. L. (Ter. Ed.), 131, § 112, amended.

SECTION 3. Said chapter one hundred and thirty-one is hereby further amended by striking out section one hundred and twelve, as so appearing, and inserting in place thereof the following: — *Section 112.* No person shall in any county except Nantucket or Barnstable between one half hour before sunrise on the first Monday in December and one half hour after sunset on the following Saturday, or, in Berkshire, Franklin, Hampshire or Hampden county, between one half hour before sunrise on the second Monday in December and one half hour after sunset on the following Saturday, if such additional period for hunting deer is authorized in such county under section one hundred and nine, hunt a bird or mammal with a rifle, revolver or pistol or by the aid of a dog, or have in his possession, or under his control, in any wood or field, a rifle, revolver or pistol, or a dog adapted to the hunting or pursuing of birds or mammals, or, while in pursuit of birds or mammals, have in his possession, or under his control, on any highway, any such firearm or dog.   *Approved May 12, 1933.*

Hunting of birds or mammals with firearms, or by aid of dog, regulated.

---

*Chap.*193 AN ACT FURTHER REGULATING HOURS OF LABOR OF WOMEN AND CHILDREN EMPLOYED IN MANUFACTURE OF LEATHER.

Be it enacted, etc., as follows:

G. L. (Ter. Ed.), 149, § 59, amended.

SECTION 1. Section fifty-nine of chapter one hundred and forty-nine of the General Laws, as appearing in the Tercentenary Edition thereof, is hereby amended by inserting after the word "goods" in the fourth line the words: — or leather, — so as to read as follows: — *Section 59.* No person, and no agent or officer of a person, shall employ a woman over twenty-one in any capacity for the purpose of manufacturing before six o'clock in the morning or after ten o'clock in the evening, or in the manufacture of textile goods or leather after six o'clock in the evening. Whoever violates any provision of this section shall be punished by a fine of not less than twenty nor more than fifty dollars.

Night labor for women regulated.

Penalty.

G. L. (Ter. Ed.), 149, § 66, amended.

SECTION 2. Section sixty-six of said chapter one hundred and forty-nine, as so appearing, is hereby amended by inserting after the word "goods" in the fifth line the words:

— or leather, — so as to read as follows: — *Section 66.* No person shall employ a boy under eighteen or a girl under twenty-one or permit such a boy or girl to work in, about or in connection with any establishment or occupation named in section sixty before five o'clock in the morning or after ten o'clock in the evening, or in the manufacture of textile goods or leather after six o'clock in the evening; provided, that girls under twenty-one may be employed as operators in regular service telephone exchanges until, but not after, eleven o'clock in the evening.

Approved May 12, 1933.

Hours of labor of boys under eighteen and girls under twenty-one, regulated.

An Act continuing and extending the existing preference in the classified labor service to persons with dependents.

Chap.194

Whereas, The deferred operation of this act would tend to defeat its purpose, therefore it is hereby declared to be an emergency law, necessary for the immediate preservation of the public convenience.

Emergency preamble.

Be it enacted, etc., as follows:

Chapter three hundred and sixteen of the acts of nineteen hundred and thirty-one, as amended by chapter one hundred and eighty-three of the acts of nineteen hundred and thirty-two, is hereby further amended by striking out, in the second line, the word "thirty-three" and inserting in place thereof the word: — thirty-four, — so as to read as follows: — Until May fifteenth in the year nineteen hundred and thirty-four, the commissioner of civil service, on receipt of a requisition from the head of any department, board or commission of the commonwealth or of a city or town for temporary laborers in the classified labor service, shall, in certifying eligible applicants for positions in said service, give preference to persons so eligible who have one or more persons dependent upon them for support; provided, that in giving such preference veterans having such dependents shall be preferred over other persons so eligible for employment and having such dependents. Employment under this act shall not be continued beyond the period named in the requisition, which period shall not exceed three months. No re-employment or further employment shall be allowed at the end of such period, except by consent of the commissioner.

1931, 316, etc., amended.

Preference to persons with dependents in labor service.

Approved May 16, 1933.

An Act providing for the inclusion of interest in the assessment of additional taxes upon certain corporations.

Chap.195

Whereas, The deferred operation of this act would tend to defeat its purpose, therefore it is hereby declared to be an emergency law, necessary for the immediate preservation of the public convenience.

Emergency preamble.

Be it enacted, etc., as follows:

G. L. (Ter.
Ed.), 63, § 45,
amended.

SECTION 1.   Section forty-five of chapter sixty-three of the General Laws, as appearing in the Tercentenary Edition thereof, is hereby amended by inserting after the word "same" in the fifth line the words: —, with interest at six per cent from October twentieth of said year, — so as to

Assessment
of additional
taxes on
certain cor-
porations.

read as follows: — *Section 45.*   If the commissioner discovers from the verification of a return, or otherwise, that the full amount of any tax due under sections thirty to fifty-one, inclusive, has not been assessed, he may, at any time within two years after September first of the year in which such assessment should have been made, assess the same, with interest at six per cent from October twentieth of said year, first giving notice to the corporation to be assessed of his intention; and a representative of the corporation shall thereupon have an opportunity, within ten days after such notification, to confer with the commissioner as to the proposed assessment.   After the expiration of ten days from the notification the commissioner shall assess the amount of the tax remaining due to the commonwealth, and shall give notice to the corporation so assessed.   Any tax so assessed shall be payable to the commissioner fourteen days after the date of the notice.

Effective
date, etc.

SECTION 2.   This act shall take effect as of January first, nineteen hundred and thirty-three, and shall apply to taxes assessed in the year nineteen hundred and thirty-three and thereafter.   *Approved May 16, 1933.*

---

*Chap.*196   AN ACT ABOLISHING THE AGE LIMITATION OF FOURTEEN YEARS FOR ALTERNATIVE CRIMINAL PROCEEDINGS WITHIN THE JUVENILE AGE.

Be it enacted, etc., as follows:

G. L. (Ter.
Ed.), 119,
§ 74, amended.

SECTION 1.   Section seventy-four of chapter one hundred and nineteen of the General Laws, as appearing in the Tercentenary Edition thereof, is hereby amended by striking out, in the second line, the word "fourteen" and inserting in place thereof the word: — seventeen, — so as to read

Criminal pro-
ceedings
against
children be-
tween seven
and seventeen.

as follows: — *Section 74.*   Criminal proceedings shall not be begun against any child between seven and seventeen years of age, except for offences punishable by death or imprisonment for life, unless proceedings against him as a delinquent child have been begun and dismissed as required by section sixty-one.

G. L. (Ter.
Ed.), 119,
§ 75, amended.

SECTION 2.   Section seventy-five of said chapter one hundred and nineteen, as so appearing, is hereby amended by striking out, in the second line, the word "fourteen" and inserting in place thereof the word: — seventeen, — and by striking out, in the third and fourth lines, the words "or against any child between fourteen and seventeen years

Complaint
and warrant.

of age", — so as to read as follows: — *Section 75.*   Upon complaint against any child between seven and seventeen years of age against whom proceedings have been begun and dismissed as required by section sixty-one for any offence not punishable by death or imprisonment for life, such court or trial justice shall examine, on oath, the complainant and the witnesses produced by him, shall reduce the complaint to writing and cause it to be subscribed by the complainant, and may issue a warrant reciting the substance of the accusation and requiring the officer to whom it is directed forthwith to take the person accused and bring him before said court or trial justice, to be dealt with according to law, and to summon such witnesses as shall be named therein to appear and give evidence on the examination. The provisions of section fifty-five shall apply to proceedings under this section except that the summons shall require the person summoned to show cause why the child should not be committed to the Lyman school or an industrial school.   *Approved May 16, 1933.*

An Act relieving cities and towns of the metropolitan parks district of financial obligation in relation to the maintenance of boulevards.   *Chap.197*

Be it enacted, etc., as follows:

SECTION 1. Chapter ninety-two of the General Laws is hereby amended by striking out section fifty-six, as appearing in the Tercentenary Edition thereof, and inserting in place thereof the following: — *Section 56.* The proportion in which each town of the metropolitan parks district, including Cohasset with respect to the maintenance of Nantasket beach reservation only, shall annually pay money into the treasury of the commonwealth to meet the cost of maintenance of said reservation and the Charles river basin and any deficiency in the amounts previously paid in, as found by said treasurer, shall be based upon the respective taxable valuations of the property of said towns. The cost of maintenance of boulevards shall be annually appropriated by the general court from the Highway Fund. *G. L. (Ter. Ed.), 92, § 56, amended. Apportionment of maintenance of Nantasket beach reservation and Charles river basin.*

SECTION 2. Section fifty-seven of said chapter ninety-two, as so appearing, is hereby amended by striking out, in the sixth line, the words "and boulevards", — so as to read as follows: — *Section 57.* The commission shall annually, in accordance with the provisions of the three preceding sections, determine the proportion in which each of the towns of said district shall annually pay money into the treasury of the commonwealth to meet the interest, sinking fund and serial or other bond requirements and the cost of maintenance of reservations, and shall transmit the determination of the commission to the state treasurer. *G. L. (Ter. Ed.), 92, § 57, amended. Commission to make apportionments.*

SECTION 3. Section thirty-four of chapter ninety of the General Laws, as so appearing, is hereby amended by striking out, in the forty-sixth line, the words "the commonwealth's share of".   *Approved May 16, 1933.* *G. L. (Ter. Ed.), 90, §34, amended.*

*Chap.*198 AN ACT RELATIVE TO THE EXEMPTION FROM LOCAL TAXA-
TION OF INSTITUTIONS FOR THE TREATMENT OF MENTAL
DISORDERS.

Be it enacted, etc., as follows:

G. L. (Ter. Ed.), 59, § 5, amended.

SECTION 1.   Subsection (c) of clause Third of section five of chapter fifty-nine of the General Laws, as appearing in the Tercentenary Edition thereof, is hereby amended by striking out, in the third and fourth lines of said subsection, the words "or for the treatment of mental or nervous diseases" and inserting in place thereof the following: —, or principally for the treatment of mental diseases or mental disorders, — so that said subsection will read as follows: —

Property used for care of persons suffering from mental disorders not exempt from taxation in certain cases.

(c) Real or personal property of such an institution or corporation, occupied or used wholly or partly as or for an insane asylum, insane hospital, or institution for the insane, or principally for the treatment of mental diseases or mental disorders, shall not be exempt unless at least one fourth of all property so occupied or used, wholly or partly, on the basis of valuation thereof, and one fourth of the income of all trust and other funds and property held for the benefit of such asylum, hospital or institution and not actually occupied or used by it for such purposes, is used and expended entirely for the treatment, board, lodging or other direct benefit of indigent insane persons, or indigent persons in need of treatment for mental diseases, as resident patients, without any charge therefor to such persons either directly or indirectly, except that such a benevolent or charitable institution or corporation conducting an insane asylum, insane hospital or institution for the insane to which persons adjudged insane by due process of law may be committed shall be exempt from taxation on personal property and buildings so occupied or used, but shall be subject to taxation on the fair cash value of the land owned by it and used for the purposes of such asylum, hospital or institution.

Effective date.

SECTION 2.   This act shall take effect as of April first, nineteen hundred and thirty-two.

Approved May 16, 1933.

*Chap.*199 AN ACT RELATIVE TO THE ASSIGNMENT OF QUARTERS IN THE
STATE HOUSE FOR THE USE OF THE VETERANS OF INDIAN
WARS.

Be it enacted, etc., as follows:

G. L. (Ter. Ed.), 8, § 17, etc., amended.

SECTION 1.   Section seventeen of chapter eight of the General Laws, as most recently amended by section one of chapter one hundred and eighty-eight of the acts of nineteen hundred and thirty-two, is hereby further amended by striking out, in the seventh line, the word "and" and inserting a comma, and by inserting after the word "States" in the eighth line the words: — and of the Veterans of Indian Wars, — so as to read as follows: — *Section 17.* There shall be set apart and suitably furnished a room or rooms in the state house for the use of the Grand Army of the Republic of the department of Massachusetts, the Massachusetts department of The American Legion, of the United Spanish War Veterans, of the Disabled American Veterans of the World War, of the Veterans of Foreign Wars of the United States and of the Veterans of Indian Wars, respectively, such room or rooms to be under the charge of the state commanders of the respective departments, subject to this chapter. The headquarters thus established for the first named department shall be used for storing its supplies and property, relics and mementos of the war of the rebellion and for arranging and preserving a history of persons, who served in the army, navy or marine corps during such war in organizations of the commonwealth, or of citizens of the commonwealth who served in the regular army, navy or marine corps of the United States, which said department may collect or desire to preserve. The headquarters thus established for each of the other departments shall be used for storing and preserving the records and other property of the department and relics and mementos of the World war and Spanish war.

Rooms in state house for use of war veteran organizations.

SECTION 2. Section eighteen of said chapter eight, as most recently amended by section two of said chapter one hundred and eighty-eight, is hereby further amended by striking out, in the sixth line, the word "and" and inserting in place thereof a comma, and by inserting after the word "States' in the seventh line the words: — and of the Veterans of the Indian Wars, — so as to read as follows: — *Section 18.* The histories, relics and mementos of the Grand Army of the Republic of the department of Massachusetts and the records of the Massachusetts department of the United Spanish War Veterans, of The American Legion, of the Disabled American Veterans of the World War, of the Veterans of Foreign Wars of the United States and of the Veterans of the Indian Wars shall be accessible at all times, under suitable rules and regulations, to members of the respective departments and to others engaged in collecting historical information. Whenever any such department ceases to exist, its records, papers, relics and other effects shall become the property of the commonwealth.

G. L. (Ter. Ed.), 8, § 18, etc., amended.

Records, etc., of such organizations.

Approved May 16, 1933.

AN ACT AUTHORIZING THE INVESTMENT OF MUNICIPAL TRUST FUNDS IN SHARES OF CO-OPERATIVE BANKS.

Be it enacted, etc., as follows:

Section fifty-four of chapter forty-four of the General Laws, as appearing in the Tercentenary Edition thereof, is hereby amended by inserting after the word "towns", in the fourth line, the words: — in shares of co-operative

G. L. (Ter. Ed.), 44, § 54 amended.

banks, or, — so as to read as follows: — *Section 54.* Trust
funds, including cemetery perpetual care funds, unless
otherwise provided or directed by the donor thereof, shall
be placed at interest in savings banks, trust companies
incorporated under the laws of the commonwealth, or
national banks, or invested by cities and towns in shares of
co-operative banks, or in securities which are legal investments for savings banks. This section shall not apply to
Boston.   *Approved May 16, 1933.*

*Chap.*201 AN ACT PROVIDING FOR THE FURNISHING WITHOUT CHARGE
OF COPIES OF CRIMINAL RECORDS BY CLERKS OF COURTS TO
DISTRICT ATTORNEYS AND CERTAIN POLICE OFFICERS.

Be it enacted, etc., as follows:

Section five of chapter two hundred and sixty-two of the
General Laws, as appearing in the Tercentenary Edition
thereof, is hereby amended by adding at the end thereof the
following: — ; provided, that clerks shall, upon the request of the chief police officer of any city or town, or of
any district attorney within the commonwealth, furnish
without charge to such chief police officer or district attorney certified copies of criminal records in their custody, —
so as to read as follows: — *Section 5.* When clerks cause
copies to be printed which they are required to furnish, they
shall make no charge for such printed copies in excess of the
amount actually paid for the printing thereof. They may
require the estimated cost of said printing to be paid in
advance, and they shall supervise the printing and correct
the proofs without charge. All written copies, including
such as are prepared for printing, shall be charged for at the
rate of twenty cents a page; provided, that clerks shall,
upon the request of the chief police officer of any city or
town, or of any district attorney within the commonwealth, furnish without charge to such chief police officer
or district attorney certified copies of criminal records in
their custody.   *Approved May 16, 1933.*

*Chap.*202 AN ACT REQUIRING THE FILING WITH THE DEPARTMENT OF
PUBLIC UTILITIES OF CERTAIN CONTRACTS OF GAS, ELECTRIC
AND WATER COMPANIES.

Be it enacted, etc., as follows:

SECTION 1. Chapter one hundred and sixty-four of the
General Laws is hereby amended by inserting after section
eighty-five, as appearing in the Tercentenary Edition
thereof, the following new section: — *Section 85A.* A gas
or electric company that has, prior to the effective date of
this section, entered into or shall thereafter enter into any
contract with an affiliated company as defined in section
eighty-five, for the payment of any fees, salaries, commis-

sions or percentages for services of any kind furnished or rendered, or to be furnished or rendered, to such gas or electric company shall file with the department within ten days after said effective date a copy of any such existing contract and any extension or modification thereof, if in writing, or, if not in writing, a statement of all the terms thereof, and within ten days after the execution of any such contract, or of any extension or modification of any such contract whether or not existing on said effective date, a copy thereof, if in writing, or, if not in writing, a statement setting forth all the terms thereof.   A gas or electric company failing to file a copy or statement as required herein shall forfeit five dollars for each day during which such failure continues.   All such forfeitures may be recovered by an information in equity brought in the supreme judicial court by the attorney general, at the relation of the department, and when so recovered shall be paid to the commonwealth.

SECTION 2.   Chapter one hundred and sixty-five of the General Laws is hereby amended by inserting after section four, as so appearing, the following new section: — *Section 4A.*   A water company that has, prior to the effective date of this section, entered into or shall thereafter enter into any contract with an affiliated company as herein defined, for the payment of any fees, salaries, commissions or percentages for services of any kind furnished or rendered, or to be furnished or rendered, to such water company shall file with the department within ten days after said effective date a copy of any such existing contract and any extension or modification thereof, if in writing, or, if not in writing, a statement of all the terms thereof, and within ten days after the execution of any such contract, or of any extension or modification of any such contract whether or not existing on said effective date, a copy thereof, if in writing, or, if not in writing, a statement setting forth all the terms thereof. The words "affiliated company", as appearing in this section, shall be defined as in section eighty-five of chapter one hundred and sixty-four except that, in construing the definition in said section eighty-five for the purposes hereof, the words "a company subject to this chapter" shall mean a company as defined in section one of this chapter.   A water company failing to file a copy or statement as required herein shall forfeit five dollars for each day during which such failure continues.   All such forfeitures may be recovered by an information in equity brought in the supreme judicial court by the attorney general, at the relation of the department, and when so recovered shall be paid to the commonwealth.   *Approved May 16, 1933.*

G. L. (Ter. Ed.), 165, new section after § 4.
Certain contracts of water companies with affiliated companies to be filed with department of public utilities.

Chap.203 An Act relative to the use, setting and maintenance of certain traps or other devices for the capture of fur-bearing animals.

Be it enacted, etc., as follows:

G. L. (Ter.
Ed.), 131,
§ 105A,
amended.

Use of traps,
etc., for cap-
ture of certain
mammals,
regulated.

Penalty.

Chapter one hundred and thirty-one of the General Laws is hereby amended by striking out section one hundred and five A, as appearing in the Tercentenary Edition thereof, and inserting in place thereof the following: — *Section 105A.* Whoever uses, sets or maintains any trap or other device for the capture of fur-bearing animals which is likely to cause continued suffering to an animal caught therein, and which is not designed to kill such animal at once or take it alive unhurt, shall be fined fifty dollars; but this section shall not apply to traps or other devices for protection of property if set or maintained on land by the owner or tenant thereof, or, if authorized by such owner or tenant, by any member of his family or person employed by him.   *Approved May 16, 1933.*

Chap.204 An Act relative to the use of buildings and premises and the occupancy of lots in the city of Boston.

Be it enacted, etc., as follows:

1924, 488, § 3,
etc., amended.

SECTION 1. Paragraph (*a*) under paragraph (8) of section three of chapter four hundred and eighty-eight of the acts of nineteen hundred and twenty-four, as amended by section one of chapter one hundred and forty-three of the acts of nineteen hundred and thirty-two, is hereby further amended by striking out all after the word "vehicle" in the third line, as appearing in said section one, and inserting in place thereof the following: —, provided that such a garage, except a building exempted from being licensed as a garage by section fourteen of chapter one hundred and forty-eight of the General Laws, is licensed as provided in paragraph (9), — so as to read as follows: —

Use of build-
ings in Boston
in single
residence
districts.

(*a*) A garage or parking of automobiles, except garage space for or parking of not more than three automobiles, of which not more than one may be a commercial vehicle, provided that such a garage, except a building exempted from being licensed as a garage by section fourteen of chapter one hundred and forty-eight of the General Laws, is licensed as provided in paragraph (9).

1924, 488, § 3,
etc., amended.

SECTION 2. Said paragraph (8) of said section three is hereby further amended by striking out paragraph (*c*) thereunder and inserting in place thereof the following paragraph: —

Signs, etc.,
exception.

(*c*) Signs except those pertaining to the lease, sale or use of the lot or building on which placed, and not exceeding a total area of eight square feet, and except further that on a lot occupied by a dwelling there shall not be more than one such sign, pertaining to the use thereof or bearing the name or occupation, or both, of an occupant, for each

3,

and eighty of the acts of nineteen hundred and thirty-one, is hereby further amended by striking out said paragraph and inserting in place thereof the following: —

Set-back: On lots abutting on one side of a street between Set-back. two intersecting streets in a sixty-five foot general residence district, and in any adjacent forty foot or thirty-five foot single or general residence district, no building shall hereafter be erected or altered to be nearer the street line than the average set-back of existing buildings within such limits, subject to the following provisions:

SECTION 5. Section sixteen of said chapter four hundred and eighty-eight, as amended, is hereby further amended by striking out paragraph (12), as amended by section five of chapter two hundred and twenty of the acts of nineteen hundred and twenty-seven, and inserting in place thereof the following: — 1924, 488, § 16, etc., amended.

(12) On a lot occupied by a dwelling, a one story building of accessory use thereto and not more than fifteen feet high measured to the mean height of the gable may be located in and occupy not more than thirty per cent of the rear yard of such dwelling. The area occupied by such a building of accessory use shall not be included as occupied area in computing the percentage of lot occupancy. An accessory building for automobiles may be attached to the side of a dwelling; provided, that all open spaces for said dwelling shall be measured from the outside walls of the accessory building. Bulk district regulations. One story buildings.

SECTION 6. Said section sixteen of said chapter four hundred and eighty-eight, as amended, is hereby further amended by adding after paragraph (14), inserted by section five of said chapter one hundred and eighty, the following new paragraph: — 1924, 488, § 16, etc., amended.

(15) On a corner lot the entrance to the dwelling shall not be determinative of the front of the structure, but the front may be taken on either street. Structure on corner lots.

Approved May 18, 1933.

*Chap.*203 AN ACT RELATIVE TO THE USE, SETTING AND MAINTENANCE

G. I
Ed.,
§ 10
ame

Use
etc.,
ture
man
regu

Pen

Chapter 203, Acts of 1933.
Referendum petition filed June 6, 1933.
See page 728.

or tenant thereof, or, if authorized by such owner or tenant, by any member of his family or person employed by him.   *Approved May 16, 1933.*

*Chap.*204 AN ACT RELATIVE TO THE USE OF BUILDINGS AND PREMISES AND THE OCCUPANCY OF LOTS IN THE CITY OF BOSTON.

Be it enacted, etc., as follows:

1924, 488, § 3, etc., amended.

SECTION 1. Paragraph (*a*) under paragraph (8) of section three of chapter four hundred and eighty-eight of the acts of nineteen hundred and twenty-four, as amended by section one of chapter one hundred and forty-three of the acts of nineteen hundred and thirty-two, is hereby further amended by striking out all after the word "vehicle" in the third line, as appearing in said section one, and inserting in place thereof the following: —, provided that such a garage, except a building exempted from being licensed as a garage by section fourteen of chapter one hundred and forty-eight of the General Laws, is licensed as provided in paragraph (9), — so as to read as follows: —

Use of buildings in Boston in single residence districts.

(*a*) A garage or parking of automobiles, except garage space for or parking of not more than three automobiles, of which not more than one may be a commercial vehicle, provided that such a garage, except a building exempted from being licensed as a garage by section fourteen of chapter one hundred and forty-eight of the General Laws, is licensed as provided in paragraph (9).

1924, 488, § 3, etc., amended.

SECTION 2. Said paragraph (8) of said section three is hereby further amended by striking out paragraph (*c*) thereunder and inserting in place thereof the following paragraph: —

Signs, etc., exception.

(*c*) Signs except those pertaining to the lease, sale or use of the lot or building on which placed, and not exceeding a total area of eight square feet, and except further that on a lot occupied by a dwelling there shall not be more than one such sign, pertaining to the use thereof or bearing the name or occupation, or both, of an occupant, for each family housed and no such sign shall exceed one square foot in area.

SECTION 3. Section four of said chapter four hundred and eighty-eight is hereby amended by striking out paragraph (5) and inserting in place thereof the following: — 1924, 488, § 4, amended.

(5) Accessory uses customarily incident to any of the above uses. The term "accessory use" shall be construed as in section three, except that said term as used in this section shall, elsewhere than in a thirty-five foot district, include a garage in the basement or cellar, or both, of a building. General residence districts.

SECTION 4. Section thirteen of said chapter four hundred and eighty-eight, as amended in the fourth paragraph, entitled *"Set-back"*, by section four of chapter one hundred and eighty of the acts of nineteen hundred and thirty-one, is hereby further amended by striking out said paragraph and inserting in place thereof the following: — 1924, 488, § 13, etc., amended.

Set-back: On lots abutting on one side of a street between two intersecting streets in a sixty-five foot general residence district, and in any adjacent forty foot or thirty-five foot single or general residence district, no building shall hereafter be erected or altered to be nearer the street line than the average set-back of existing buildings within such limits, subject to the following provisions: Set-back.

SECTION 5. Section sixteen of said chapter four hundred and eighty-eight, as amended, is hereby further amended by striking out paragraph (12), as amended by section five of chapter two hundred and twenty of the acts of nineteen hundred and twenty-seven, and inserting in place thereof the following: — 1924, 488, § 16, etc., amended.

(12) On a lot occupied by a dwelling, a one story building of accessory use thereto and not more than fifteen feet high measured to the mean height of the gable may be located in and occupy not more than thirty per cent of the rear yard of such dwelling. The area occupied by such a building of accessory use shall not be included as occupied area in computing the percentage of lot occupancy. An accessory building for automobiles may be attached to the side of a dwelling; provided, that all open spaces for said dwelling shall be measured from the outside walls of the accessory building. Bulk district regulations. One story buildings.

SECTION 6. Said section sixteen of said chapter four hundred and eighty-eight, as amended, is hereby further amended by adding after paragraph (14), inserted by section five of said chapter one hundred and eighty, the following new paragraph: — 1924, 488, § 16, etc., amended.

(15) On a corner lot the entrance to the dwelling shall not be determinative of the front of the structure, but the front may be taken on either street. Structure on corner lots.

Approved May 18, 1933.

Chap.205 AN ACT AUTHORIZING THE PURCHASE BY THE ARMORY COM-
MISSIONERS OF CERTAIN PROPERTY IN THE TOWN OF
NATICK FOR MILITARY PURPOSES.

Be it enacted, etc., as follows:

Armory
commissioners
authorized to
purchase from
the Dennison
Manufactur-
ing Company
certain land in
town of
Natick.

SECTION 1. The armory commissioners, on behalf of
the commonwealth, are hereby authorized, with the approval of the governor and council, to acquire by purchase
from the Dennison Manufacturing Company, a Massachusetts corporation incorporated under general law, at an expense not to exceed one hundred thousand dollars, exclusive of interest charges hereinafter provided, for the purpose of housing, and providing proper facilities for the
repair of, certain motor apparatus and other property
owned and/or issued to and used by the military forces of
the commonwealth, the land with buildings situated thereon
in the town of Natick and bounded and described as follows, to wit: Westerly by Speen street fourteen hundred
eighty-six and twenty-one hundredths feet; southerly by
land now or formerly of the Boston & Albany Railroad
Company, fourteen hundred seventy-eight and seven one
hundredths feet; easterly, three hundred three and seventy-
four one hundredths feet; and northeasterly, sixteen hundred fifty-eight and fifty-three one hundredths feet by land
now or formerly of the commonwealth; and northerly by
land now or formerly of Rufus B. Morse et al., four hundred
thirty-one and fifteen one hundredths feet. The conveyance of said premises shall be subject to certain easements and rights appurtenant thereto, all as set forth in the
original certificate of title, numbered twenty-seven thousand six hundred and twenty-four, of the land court.

Said sum of one hundred thousand dollars shall be paid
as follows: — Eight thousand dollars on the date of the
delivery to the armory commissioners of the deed of conveyance of said premises, twenty-three thousand dollars,
together with accrued interest from said date, at the rate
of three and one half per cent per annum, on ninety-two
thousand dollars, during the month of December, nineteen
hundred and thirty-three; twenty-three thousand dollars,
together with accrued interest at the same rate on sixty-
nine thousand dollars since the date of the last interest
payment, during the month of December, nineteen hundred and thirty-four; twenty-three thousand dollars, together with accrued interest at the same rate on forty-six
thousand dollars since the date of the last interest payment, during the month of December, nineteen hundred
and thirty-five; twenty-three thousand dollars, together
with accrued interest on said amount at the same rate
since the date of the last interest payment, during the
month of December, nineteen hundred and thirty-six.

Every contract, agreement or instrument of conveyance
entered into under authority hereof shall be approved, as
to form, by the attorney general.

SECTION 2. Acceptance of this act by said Dennison Manufacturing Company, as evidenced by a vote of its board of directors filed in the office of the state secretary, shall constitute a contract between said company and the commonwealth, binding upon said company, by which it agrees to convey said property, and to accept payment therefor, as hereinbefore provided. The provisions of section twenty-seven of chapter twenty-nine of the General Laws shall not be applicable to any contract or agreement entered into by the armory commissioners under authority of this act. *Acceptance of act by company.*

SECTION 3. Upon the acquisition of said property by the armory commissioners as aforesaid the provisions of sections thirteen to seventeen, inclusive, of chapter fifty-eight of the General Laws shall apply to said property to the same extent as if it were a state military camp ground, except that for the purpose of reimbursing the town of Natick under said provisions for loss of taxes on said property in the years nineteen hundred and thirty-four and nineteen hundred and thirty-five, the word "land" as used in said sections shall include such buildings and structures on the land so acquired as were located thereon at the time of its acquisition hereunder. *Reimbursement of town for loss of taxes.*

SECTION 4. The commonwealth shall reimburse said Dennison Manufacturing Company the amount of taxes on the property to be conveyed hereunder assessed to and paid by said company in the year nineteen hundred and thirty-three.

SECTION 5. This act shall take full effect upon its acceptance, on or before July thirty-first in the current year and in the manner hereinbefore set forth, by said Dennison Manufacturing Company; otherwise it shall be of no effect.   *Approved May 18, 1933.*

AN ACT ENABLING THE TOWN OF WINCHESTER TO CONVEY A PORTION OF A PUBLIC PLAYGROUND. *Chap.206*

Be it enacted, etc., as follows:

SECTION 1. The town of Winchester, by its board of park commissioners, may transfer and convey to The New Hope Baptist Church of Winchester, a corporation organized under general law, approximately twenty-three hundred and thirty-nine square feet of land abutting the church lot of said corporation, heretofore acquired by said town and now held for public playground purposes and no longer needed for public use, in consideration of the granting by said corporation of an easement of public way or the release by it of all damages sustained by the laying out of a way, for public use, extending from Cross street over the northwesterly portion of said church lot to said playground.

SECTION 2. This act shall take effect upon its passage.   *Approved May 24, 1933.*

Chap.207 AN ACT PROVIDING FOR THE LIGHTING OF THE OVERPASS FOR VEHICULAR TRAFFIC, AND ITS CONNECTIONS, AT THE JUNCTION OF THE REVERE BEACH PARKWAY AND BROADWAY IN THE CITY OF REVERE AND THE IMPROVING OF THE AREAS ADJOINING SAID OVERPASS.

Be it enacted, etc., as follows:

SECTION 1. The metropolitan district commission is hereby authorized and directed to improve the areas adjoining the overpass for vehicular traffic at the junction of the Revere Beach parkway and Broadway in the city of Revere by such grading, loaming, seeding and planting as it may deem necessary or desirable, and to install and maintain a system of street lighting on said overpass and the connections therewith. For said purposes said commission may expend not exceeding seventy-five hundred dollars out of the appropriation made by item six hundred and twenty-two of the general appropriation act of the current year, and all expense incurred after the current year in maintaining said lighting system shall be paid from the annual appropriation for the maintenance of boulevards and parkways.

SECTION 2. This act shall take effect upon its passage.
Approved May 24, 1933.

Chap.208 AN ACT AUTHORIZING THE TOWN OF FAIRHAVEN TO HOLD A SPECIAL TOWN ELECTION FOR THE FILLING OF CERTAIN VACANCIES SIMULTANEOUSLY WITH THE SPECIAL STATE ELECTION TO BE HELD ON JUNE THIRTEENTH IN THE CURRENT YEAR.

Be it enacted, etc., as follows:

SECTION 1. For the purpose of filling a vacancy in its board of selectmen, its board of public welfare and its planning board, for the unexpired terms, the town of Fairhaven is hereby authorized to hold a special town election on June thirteenth in the current year simultaneously with the special state election to be held on said date and at the same polling places; but separate ballots, ballot boxes, check lists and election officers shall be used for the election of said town officers and otherwise said special town election shall be held and conducted in the same manner as an annual town meeting.

SECTION 2. This act shall take effect upon its passage.
Approved May 24, 1933.

AN ACT RELATIVE TO THE WATER SUPPLY OF THE TOWN OF *Chap.*209
MILTON.

Be it enacted, etc., as follows:

SECTION 1. Chapter three hundred and seven of the acts of nineteen hundred and two is hereby amended by striking out section six and inserting in place thereof the following: — *Section 6.* Said town may, for the purposes provided by this act, issue from time to time bonds, notes or scrip as provided by chapter forty-four of the General Laws, as from time to time amended. Such bonds, notes or scrip shall be in serial form, shall bear on their face the words Town of Milton Water Loan, shall be signed, made payable and bear interest, and be used and disposed of by said town, all as provided in said chapter, as so amended.

SECTION 2. Sections seven and eight of said chapter three hundred and seven are hereby repealed.

SECTION 3. Said chapter three hundred and seven is hereby further amended by striking out section thirteen and inserting in place thereof the following: — *Section 13.* The prices or rates for the use of water in said town shall be determined in each year in accordance with section twenty-seven of chapter ninety-two of the General Laws, as from time to time amended. And said town may adopt such by-laws, and authorize the water commissioners to adopt such rules and regulations, not inconsistent with statutory provisions, as may be convenient or proper for regulating all minor matters of business routine.

SECTION 4. Said chapter three hundred and seven is hereby further amended by adding at the end thereof the following new section: — *Section 18.* Any surplus realized by the water department of said town from the rates and charges, may, from time to time, be disposed of or applied, either in the discharge of obligations of the town in connection with its water department, or for the extension or replacements of its works, as the town may determine.

Approved May 24, 1933.

AN ACT AUTHORIZING THE CONVEYANCE TO THE UNITED *Chap.*210
STATES OF AMERICA OF A TRACT OF LAND IN PETERSBURG, VIRGINIA, AND THE MASSACHUSETTS MILITARY MONUMENT LOCATED THEREON.

Be it enacted, etc., as follows:

For the purpose of transferring to the United States of America for incorporation in the Petersburg National Military Park, which is being established under an act of congress approved July third, nineteen hundred and twenty-six, a certain tract of land owned by the commonwealth in Petersburg, Virginia, upon which stands the Massachusetts military monument erected under the pro-

visions of chapter seventy-two of the resolves of nineteen
hundred and ten, the governor and council are hereby
authorized, on behalf of the commonwealth, to convey to
the United States of America said tract of land and military
monument, with the provision that the grantee shall maintain the property so conveyed without expense to the
commonwealth.   *Approved May 24, 1933.*

Chap.211 AN ACT AUTHORIZING THE SELECTMEN OF THE TOWN OF
DEDHAM TO EXERCISE THE POWERS OF CEMETERY COM-
MISSIONERS, SEWER COMMISSIONERS, PARK COMMISSION-
ERS, GYPSY MOTH SUPERINTENDENT AND TREE WARDEN IN
SAID TOWN.

Be it enacted, etc., as follows:

Powers and
duties of
certain officers
and boards
of the town of
Dedham to be
vested in the
selectmen.

SECTION 1.   The board of selectmen of the town of Dedham, as constituted from time to time, from and after the
annual town election in the year nineteen hundred and
thirty-four, in addition to any powers and duties vested in
them immediately prior to the effective date of this act,
shall have and exercise, under the designation of selectmen,
all the powers and duties vested immediately prior to said
election and from time to time by general or special law or
by town by-law in the following boards and officers in said
town, to wit: — cemetery commissioners, sewer commissioners, park commissioners, gypsy moth superintendent
and tree warden; and such boards and offices shall thereupon be abolished.   No contracts or liabilities then in force
shall be affected by such abolition, but the selectmen shall
in all respects be the lawful successor of the boards and
offices so abolished.

Commissioner
of public
works, ap-
pointment,
powers and
duties.

SECTION 2.   As soon as practicable after the effective date
of this act, the selectmen shall appoint for a term expiring
on April first, nineteen hundred and thirty-five, and fix the
compensation of, a commissioner of public works, who shall
administer, under the supervision and direction of the
selectmen, as departments of the town, the boards and
offices whose powers and duties are transferred to them
under section one.   He shall also be superintendent of
streets and shall have charge of street lighting.   In nineteen hundred and thirty-five and thereafter the selectmen
shall annually in March appoint such a commissioner for a
term of one year beginning on April first following, and fix
his compensation.   Said commissioner shall be responsible
to the selectmen for the efficient administration of all departments within the scope of his duty.   He shall be
specially fitted by education, training and experience to
perform the duties of said office, shall be appointed without
regard to his political belief and, when appointed, may or
may not be a resident of the town or of the commonwealth.
During his tenure he shall hold no elective or other appointive office, nor shall he be engaged in any other business

or occupation. The selectmen by a majority vote may at any time remove him for cause, after a hearing or an opportunity therefor; provided, that a written statement setting forth specific reasons for such removal is filed with the town clerk and a copy thereof delivered to or sent by registered mail to said commissioner. Such action of the selectmen shall be final.

SECTION 3. The commissioner of public works shall be the administrative head of all the departments placed in his charge as aforesaid. His powers and duties, in addition to those otherwise conferred or imposed upon him, shall include the following: — Commissioner of public works to be head of certain departments.

(a) To organize, continue or discontinue, from time to time, such departments or subdivisions thereof, not inconsistent with the provisions of this act, as the selectmen may by vote determine.

(b) To appoint upon merit and fitness alone, and, subject to the limitations hereinafter contained, to remove, all superintendents or chiefs of the said departments and all subordinate officers and employees therein; and to fix the salaries and wages of all subordinates and employees therein. No superintendent or chief of a department shall be removed by the commissioner of public works unless at least five days prior to such removal a written statement setting forth specific reasons for such removal is delivered, or sent by registered mail, to him.

(c) To attend all regular meetings of the selectmen when requested by them so to do, and to recommend to the selectmen for adoption such measures requiring action by them or by the town as he may deem necessary or expedient.

(d) To keep full and complete records of his office, and to render to the selectmen, as often as may be required by them, a full report of all operations under his control during the period reported on; and annually, or oftener if required by the selectmen, to make for publication a synopsis of all his reports.

(e) To keep the selectmen fully advised as to the needs of the town within the scope of his duties, and to furnish the selectmen, on or before the thirty-first day of December of each year, a detailed list of the appropriations required during the next ensuing fiscal year for the proper conduct of all departments of the town under his control.

SECTION 4. This act shall be submitted to the registered voters of the town of Dedham for acceptance at its annual town election in the year nineteen hundred and thirty-four, in the form of the following question, which shall be placed on the official ballot used in the election of town officers at said election: "Shall an act passed by the general court in the year nineteen hundred and thirty-three, entitled 'An Act authorizing the Selectmen of the Town of Dedham to exercise the Powers of Cemetery Commissioners, Sewer Commissioners, Park Commissioners, Gypsy Moth Super- Acceptance of act.

intendent and Tree Warden in said Town', be accepted?''
If a majority of the votes cast in answer to said question
are in the affirmative this act shall take effect forthwith;
otherwise it shall not take effect.

Approved May 24, 1933.

Chap.212 AN ACT AUTHORIZING THE CONVEYANCE TO THE TOWN OF
SHEFFIELD, BY THE TRUSTEES OF PUBLIC RESERVATIONS,
OF PINE KNOLL RESERVATION IN SAID TOWN.

Be it enacted, etc., as follows:

SECTION 1. The trustees of public reservations, incorporated by chapter three hundred and fifty-two of the acts
of eighteen hundred and ninety-one, are hereby authorized
to convey to the town of Sheffield four certain tracts or parcels of land lying in said town and known as the Pine Knoll
reservation, said tracts and parcels being more particularly
described in a deed of Mary E. Dewey and others, dated
November twentieth, nineteen hundred and two, recorded
in Berkshire county registry of deeds, southern district,
book one hundred and eighty-eight, page two hundred and
sixty-five, conveying the same. to said trustees. Said
tracts and parcels are to be conveyed to said town on condition that the same be held, managed and maintained by
said town as a public park or reservation under chapter
forty-five of the General Laws, as appearing in the Tercentenary Edition thereof, and the said town is hereby authorized to acquire, hold, manage and maintain said tracts and
parcels for the purposes and in the manner aforesaid.

SECTION 2. This act shall take effect upon its passage;
but the authority conferred thereby is hereby declared to be
limited to such authority as the general court is competent to
grant.   *Approved May 24, 1933.*

Chap.213 AN ACT RELATIVE TO THE SETTLEMENT OF CERTAIN EM-
PLOYEES OF STATE AND COUNTY TUBERCULOSIS HOSPITALS
AND SANATORIA.

Be it enacted, etc., as follows:

G. L. (Ter.
Ed.), 116, § 2,
amended.

Settlement not
acquired while
receiving pub-
lic relief.

Exceptions.

Chapter one hundred and sixteen of the General Laws is
hereby amended by striking out section two, as appearing
in the Tercentenary Edition thereof, and inserting in place
thereof the following: — *Section 2.* No person shall acquire
a settlement, or be in the process of acquiring a settlement,
while receiving public relief other than aid or relief received
under chapter one hundred and fifteen, unless, within two
years after receiving such relief, he tenders reimbursement
of the cost thereof to the commonwealth or to the town
furnishing it. No former patient of a state or county tuberculosis sanatorium or hospital, who is employed in such an
institution, shall lose or gain a settlement or be in the process of losing or gaining a settlement while so employed.

Approved May 24, 1933.

AN ACT ESTABLISHING SPECIAL FOX-HUNTING LICENSES FOR NON-RESIDENT MEMBERS AND GUESTS OF CLUBS OR ASSOCIATIONS CONDUCTING FOX HUNTS IN THE COMMONWEALTH.

*Chap.*214

Be it enacted, etc., as follows:

SECTION 1. Section five of chapter one hundred and thirty-one of the General Laws, as most recently amended by section one of chapter two hundred and seventy-two of the acts of nineteen hundred and thirty-two, is hereby further amended by inserting after the word "license" in the tenth line the words: —, or a special fox-hunting license issued under section eight A, — and by striking out, in the eleventh line, the word "three" and inserting in place thereof the word: — four, — so as to read as follows: — *Section 5.* Except as provided in section ninety-one, ninety-two, ninety-six, ninety-nine or one hundred and eight, no person shall hunt any bird or mammal, and no person, unless he is under fifteen years of age, shall fish, except as hereinafter provided, in any of the inland waters of the commonwealth, and no person shall use, set, tend or maintain any trap, or take or attempt to take any mammal by means thereof, without first having obtained a sporting, hunting, fishing or trapping license, or a special fox-hunting license issued under section eight A, as the case may be, authorizing him so to do, as provided in the four following sections; provided, that nothing in sections five to twelve, inclusive, shall be construed as affecting in any way the general laws relating to trespass, or as authorizing the hunting, or the possession of, birds or mammals, contrary to law, or the taking of fish, or the possession thereof, contrary to law. But said last mentioned sections shall not prohibit any person who is a legal resident of the commonwealth or any member of his immediate family, residing on land owned or leased by him, from hunting or trapping on such land or from fishing in any inland waters bordered by such land; provided, that he is or they are actually domiciled thereon, and that the land is used exclusively for agricultural purposes, and not for club, shooting or fishing purposes; and provided, further, that the burden of proof shall rest upon the person claiming such exemptions to show that he is entitled thereto.

SECTION 2. Said chapter one hundred and thirty-one is hereby further amended by inserting after section eight, as appearing in the Tercentenary Edition thereof, the following new section: — *Section 8A.* A non-resident member or non-resident invited guest of a club or association conducting fox hunts within the commonwealth may procure a special fox-hunting license authorizing him, for periods not exceeding, in the aggregate, six days within any calendar year and during regular fox hunts conducted by such club or association, to hunt foxes only. No such

G. L. (Ter. Ed.), 131, § 5, etc., amended.

Licensing of hunters, trappers and fishermen regulated. Fox-hunting licenses.

G. L. (Ter. Ed.), 131, new section after § 8.

Special fox-hunting licenses.

license shall be valid unless, not less than fifteen days prior to the holding of any such fox hunt, the club or association conducting the same files with the director its non-resident membership list. The fee for every such license shall be two dollars. Licenses under this section shall be issued by the director, or by a city or town clerk specially designated therefor by him, in the form prescribed upon blanks furnished by the division, and shall bear the data required by section six which shall be furnished to such director or clerk by the applicant. The provisions of said section six relative to the transfer or loan of a license issued thereunder and relative to the carrying on the person of such a license and its production for examination shall apply in the case of a license issued under this section. Whoever for the purpose of procuring a license under this section for himself or another falsely makes any representation or statement required by this section or said section six shall be punished by a fine of not less than ten nor more than fifty dollars, or by imprisonment for not more than one month, or both. Each licensee under this section shall, within ten days after the close of each hunt in which he participates, report in writing to the director the number of foxes taken or killed by him at such hunt and, not later than December thirty-first of the year of issue, shall return his license to the director with an endorsement thereon stating the total number of foxes taken or killed by him under authority thereof and specifying the dates on which he hunted thereunder. No license hereunder shall be granted to a minor.

G. L. (Ter. Ed.), 131, §12, etc., amended.

SECTION 3. Said chapter one hundred and thirty-one is hereby further amended by striking out section twelve, as most recently amended by section five of said chapter two hundred and seventy-two, and inserting in place thereof the

Non-resident licensees entitled to carry from state fish, etc., legally taken.

following: — *Section 12.* Except as prohibited or limited by federal legislation or regulation, any person who holds a sporting, hunting, fishing, trapping or special fox-hunting license issued to him as a non-resident may carry from the commonwealth such fish, birds or mammals as have been legally taken within the commonwealth.

Approved May 24, 1933.

Chap.215 AN ACT RELATIVE TO THE PREPARATION OF A TOPOGRAPHICAL SURVEY AND MAP OF THE COMMONWEALTH.

Emergency preamble.

Whereas, The deferred operation of this act would tend to defeat one of its purposes which is to provide unemployment relief, therefore it is hereby declared to be an emergency law, necessary for the immediate preservation of the public convenience.

Be it enacted, etc., as follows:

Preparation of certain maps, etc.,

The department of public works is hereby authorized to confer from time to time with the director or a representative of the United States geological survey and to co-operate with said survey in the preparation of a contour topographical survey and map of this commonwealth. Said department may arrange with said director or representative concerning all details of the work to be carried out on the part of the commonwealth. Said department is hereby authorized to receive contributions from individuals, associations, corporations or others, toward meeting the commonwealth's portion of the cost of the work herein provided for. Said contributions shall be deposited with the state treasurer and shall be available for meeting said portion of the cost of the work, without appropriation by the general court. Subject in any fiscal year hereafter to appropriation, said department may expend to meet said portion of the cost of the work such sums, in addition to available proceeds of such contributions, as will make the total expenditure of the commonwealth equal to the amount expended for said work by the United States of America, but in no event shall the total expenditure of the commonwealth, including contributions as aforesaid, exceed fifty thousand dollars in any one year. Expenditures incurred in the current fiscal year by said department under authority hereof, except in so far as paid from the proceeds of such contributions, shall be paid from item numbered five hundred and seventy-eight of the general appropriation act of the current year.   *Approved May 26, 1933.* — by department of public works.

AN ACT FURTHER REGULATING THE NUMBER OF LICENSES THAT MAY BE ISSUED FOR THE SALE AT RETAIL OF WINES AND MALT BEVERAGES NOT TO BE DRUNK ON THE PREMISES. — *Chap.*216.

Whereas, The deferred operation of this act would tend to defeat its purpose, therefore it is hereby declared to be an emergency law, necessary for the immediate preservation of the public convenience. — Emergency preamble.

Be it enacted, etc., as follows:

Section six of chapter one hundred and twenty of the acts of the current year is hereby amended by striking out the third sentence and inserting in place thereof the following: — In each ward of any such city, in each voting precinct of any such town having a population in excess of forty thousand, in each other such town as a whole, one such license may be granted for each population unit of one thousand and for each additional fraction thereof up to but not exceeding a population of ten thousand, one additional license for each population unit of two thousand and for each additional fraction thereof above a population of ten thousand up to but not exceeding a population of fifty thousand, and one additional license for each population unit of five thousand and for each additional fraction thereof above a population of fifty thousand; provided, that one such license may be granted in any such — 1933, 120, § 6, amended. Number of licenses for sale at retail of wines, etc., regulated.

town irrespective of population, and provided, further, that in any such city or town which has an increased resident population during the summer months, the local licensing authorities may make an estimate prior to June first in any year of such temporary resident population as of July tenth following, and one such license, to be effective from June first to October first only, may be granted for each unit of one thousand, or additional fraction thereof, of such population as so estimated. Any license granted in excess of any provision of this section shall be void.

Approved May 26, 1933.

---

*Chap.*217 An Act to provide for the improvement of the dike across the mouth of Herring River in the town of Wellfleet and the Herring River and its tributaries.

Emergency preamble.

Whereas, The deferred operation of this act would tend to defeat its purpose, therefore it is hereby declared to be an emergency law, necessary for the immediate preservation of the public convenience.

Be it enacted, etc., as follows:

For the purpose of providing better drainage above the dike across the mouth of Herring river in the town of Wellfleet, the department of public works is hereby authorized and directed, in consultation with the state reclamation board, to make such changes as appear to be necessary in the said dike and its appurtenances and to dredge or clear all obstructions in the channels above the said dike. For the purpose of this act the department may expend such sums not exceeding ten thousand dollars as may be appropriated. One half of the expenditures authorized under this act shall be assessed by the state treasurer on the towns within the county of Barnstable in proportion to their valuations as additions to their respective quotas of the state tax next to be assessed. *Approved May 26, 1933.*

---

*Chap.*218 An Act authorizing the town of Arlington to convey a portion of the Ethel L. Wellington playground.

Be it enacted, etc., as follows:

Section 1. The town of Arlington is hereby authorized to convey the following portion of the Ethel L. Wellington playground located on Grove street in said town: Beginning at the northeasterly corner of said playground, said point being about one hundred seventeen and sixty-two hundredths feet southerly from the southerly line of Dudley street, thence running westerly by land of Gerardo Riccardi one hundred thirty-three and eighty-eight hundredths feet, thence running easterly to a point on Grove street thirteen and five tenths feet southerly of the point of beginning, and thence running northerly to point of beginning.

SECTION 2. This act shall take effect upon its passage.
Approved May 26, 1933.

AN ACT RELATIVE TO ELIGIBILITY FOR OLD AGE ASSISTANCE. *Chap.219*

Whereas, The deferred operation of this act would tend to defeat its purpose, therefore it is hereby declared to be an emergency law, necessary for the immediate preservation of the public convenience.

Be it enacted, etc., as follows:

Section one of chapter one hundred and eighteen A of the General Laws, as appearing in the Tercentenary Edition thereof, is hereby amended by striking out, in the fourth line, the words "arrival at such age" and inserting in place thereof the words: — the date of application for such assistance, — so as to read as follows: — *Section 1.* Adequate assistance to deserving citizens in need of relief and support seventy years of age or over who shall have resided in the commonwealth not less than twenty years immediately preceding the date of application for such assistance, subject to such reasonable exceptions as to continuity of residence as the department of public welfare, in this chapter called the department, may determine by rules hereinafter authorized, shall be granted under the supervision of the department. Such assistance shall, wherever practicable, be given to the aged person in his own home or in lodgings or in a boarding home, and it shall be sufficient to provide such suitable and dignified care. No person receiving assistance hereunder shall be deemed to be a pauper by reason thereof. *Approved May 26, 1933.*

G. L. (Ter. Ed.), 118A, § 1, amended.

Department of public welfare to supervise rendering of assistance to aged citizens. Eligibility for such assistance.

AN ACT TO PROVIDE FOR THE MORE EFFECTIVE ENFORCEMENT OF DECREES OF THE MINIMUM WAGE COMMISSION. *Chap.220*

Be it enacted, etc., as follows:

SECTION 1. Chapter one hundred and fifty-one of the General Laws is hereby amended by inserting after section eleven the following four new sections: — *Section 11A.* If the commission shall at any time find, after investigation, that an employer engaged in manufacturing continues to violate any such decree, after his name has been published under section eleven, it may order such employer to cause to be affixed to every article thereafter manufactured in the course of such violation or to its container, or both, a tag, stamp, label or other device in such form, color and type as the commission may prescribe, stating the fact that such article is manufactured in whole or in part by the labor of women and minors in violation of a decree of the commission. Within ten days after the issuance of such an order to any employer he may file with

G. L. (Ter. Ed.), 151, four new sections after § 11. Enforcement of decrees of minimum wage commission relative to manufacturers.

the commission his objections thereto in writing. The commission shall, within ten days after such filing, suspend, amend, revoke or reaffirm such order. Refusal or failure to comply with an order of the commission issued under this section and in full force and effect shall be punished by imprisonment for not more than thirty days or by a fine of not more than five hundred dollars, or both.

Enforcement in respect to retailers. *Section 11B.* The commission may insert in any order issued under section eleven A, a provision that a dealer selling at retail within the commonwealth any article to which, or to the container of which, is attached a tag, stamp, label or other device in pursuance of such an order shall keep conspicuously posted on his premises in such place, form, type and manner as the commission may prescribe, a notice that articles are for sale on said premises manufactured in whole or in part by the labor of women or minors in violation of a decree of the commission. A dealer failing to comply with such a provision shall be subject to the penalties prescribed in section eleven A.

Penalty for removing, etc., tag, labels, etc. *Section 11C.* Whoever knowingly and wilfully defaces, removes or destroys a tag, stamp, label or other device attached to an article or its container in pursuance of an order of the commission issued under section eleven A, or a notice posted as required in section eleven B, shall be subject to the penalties prescribed in section eleven A. The department of labor and industries shall enforce this and the two preceding sections.

Rescinding of orders, when. *Section 11D.* The commission may on its own initiative or at the request of an employer rescind any order issued under section eleven A, if after an investigation it determines such employer is complying with its decree.

Provisions of act limited. SECTION 2. No order shall be issued by the minimum wage commission under section eleven A of chapter one hundred and fifty-one of the General Laws, inserted by section one of this act, affecting any employer in respect to wages paid by him in any occupation for which it has established a minimum wage by decree rendered prior to the effective date of this act, unless and until, in a proceeding conducted as provided in section five of said chapter one hundred and fifty-one, it shall have reinvestigated said wage and affirmed, modified or rescinded the same.

Approved May 26, 1933.

---

*Chap.*221 AN ACT ABOLISHING THE REQUIREMENT THAT EXECUTORS AND ADMINISTRATORS GIVE NOTICE OF THEIR APPOINTMENT.

Be it enacted, etc., as follows:

G. L. (Ter. Ed.), 195, §§ 1 to 4, repealed. SECTION 1. Sections one to four, inclusive, of chapter one hundred and ninety-five of the General Laws, as appearing in the Tercentenary Edition thereof, are hereby repealed.

Section 2. Section eight of said chapter one hundred and ninety-five, as so appearing, is hereby amended by striking out, in the twelfth and thirteenth lines, the words "and also the notice of appointment of such executor or administrator", — so as to read as follows: — *Section 8.* An executor or administrator who is appointed in, but resides out of, the commonwealth shall not enter upon the duties of his trust nor be entitled to receive his letter of appointment until he shall, by a writing filed in the registry of probate for the county where he is appointed, have appointed an agent residing in the commonwealth, and, by such writing, shall have agreed that the service of any legal process against him as such executor or administrator, or that the service of any such process against him in his individual capacity in any action founded upon or arising out of any of his acts or omissions as such executor or administrator, shall, if made on said agent, have like effect as if made on him personally within the commonwealth, and such service shall have such effect. Said writing shall state the name and address of the agent. An executor or administrator who, after his appointment, removes from, and resides without, the commonwealth shall so appoint a like agent.

G. L. (Ter. Ed.), 195, § 8, amended.

Agent of non-resident executor or administrator.

Section 3. Section two of chapter one hundred and ninety-seven of the General Laws, as so appearing, is hereby amended by striking out, in the first and second lines the words "who has given due notice of his appointment does not within six months thereafter" and inserting in place thereof the words: — does not within six months after the approval of his bond, — so as to read as follows: — *Section 2.* If an executor or administrator does not within six months after the approval of his bond have notice of demands against the estate of the deceased sufficient to warrant him to represent such estate to be insolvent, he may, after the expiration of said six months, pay the debts due from the estate and shall not be personally liable to any creditor in consequence of such payments made before notice of such creditor's demand; and if such executor or administrator is in doubt as to the validity of any debt which, if valid, he would have a right to pay under this section, he may, with the approval of the probate court, after notice to all persons interested, pay such debt or so much thereof as the court may authorize.

G. L. (Ter. Ed.), 197, § 2, amended.

Payment of debts by executors, etc.

Section 4. Section nine of said chapter one hundred and ninety-seven, as so appearing, is hereby amended by striking out, in the second line, the following ", after having given due notice of his appointment," — so as to read as follows: — *Section 9.* Except as provided in this chapter, an executor or administrator shall not be held to answer to an action by a creditor of the deceased which is not commenced within one year from the time of his giving bond for the performance of his trust, or to such an action which is commenced but not entered within said year

G. L. (Ter. Ed.), 197, § 9, amended.

Time within which creditors shall bring actions.

unless before the expiration thereof the writ in such action
has been served by delivery in hand upon such executor
or administrator or service thereof accepted by him or a
notice stating the name of the estate, the name and address
of the creditor, the amount of the claim and the court in
which the action has been brought has been filed in the
proper registry of probate. An executor, administrator
or administrator de bonis non shall not be held to answer
to an action by a creditor of the deceased which is commenced but not entered within any other or additional
period of limitation for bringing such action provided by or
under this chapter unless before the expiration of such
period the writ in such action has been served by delivery
in hand upon him or service thereof accepted by him or a
notice as aforesaid has been filed in the proper registry of
probate. The probate court may allow creditors further
time for bringing actions, not exceeding two years from the
time of the giving of his official bond by such executor or
administrator, provided that application for such further
time be made before the expiration of one year from the
time of the approval of the bond.

G. L. (Ter.
Ed.), 202,
§ 20, amended.

SECTION 5. Chapter two hundred and two of the
General Laws is hereby amended by striking out section twenty, as appearing in the Tercentenary Edition
thereof, and inserting in place thereof the following: —

Time within
which real
estate is liable
to be sold for
payment of
debts.

Section 20. No interest in the real estate of a deceased
person conveyed absolutely or in mortgage for value and
in good faith by an instrument duly recorded shall be
liable to be taken on execution, or sold under any judicial
proceeding for payment of his debts, costs of court, or
claims against his estate, except claims for taxes, municipal
assessments or succession taxes, legacies or other charges
created by will of the deceased, or the expenses or charges
of administration, after the expiration of one year from the
time of such executor or administrator giving bond for the
performance of his trust, unless in pursuance of a license
to sell granted in consequence of an order for the retention
of assets passed under the provisions of section thirteen of
chapter one hundred and ninety-seven upon a petition
filed within said year or before said conveyance or mortgage
is recorded, or unless in pursuance of a license to sell
granted upon a petition filed in the registry of probate
within said year, or unless for the satisfaction in whole or in
part of a claim of which notice has been filed in the registry
of probate within said year, stating substantially the
name and address of the claimant, the nature and amount of
the claim and the court, if any, in which proceedings are
pending to determine or enforce the same. Said notice
shall be filed with the other proceedings in the case and
entered upon the docket under the name of the estate of
the deceased.

G. L. (Ter.
Ed.), 204,
§ 26, amended.

SECTION 6. Section twenty-six of chapter two hundred
and four of the General Laws, as so appearing, is hereby

amended by striking out, in the third and fourth lines, the words "notice of an appointment or", — so as to read as follows: — *Section 26.* If an executor, administrator, guardian, conservator, trustee, receiver, commissioner or other fiduciary officer appointed by the probate court, or a person employed by him to give notice of sale of real estate, has failed to file an affidavit of such notice in the probate court and such affidavit cannot be obtained, the court may, upon petition of any person interested in real estate the title to which may be affected thereby, stating the particular failure complained of and averring that the affidavit cannot be obtained, order notice by publication to creditors of, and others interested in, the estate in the settlement of which the failure complained of occurred. If, upon return of such notice and after hearing, the court is satisfied that such notice was in fact given, it may make a decree to that effect. *Failure of proof of notice of sale, how remedied.*

SECTION 7. Section five of chapter two hundred and twenty-eight of the General Laws, as so appearing, is hereby amended by striking out all after the word "bond" in the fourth line, — so as to read as follows: — *Section 5.* Such citation shall be returnable at such time as the court may order and shall be served fourteen days at least before the return day; but it shall not issue after the expiration of one year from the time such executor or administrator has given bond. *G. L. (Ter. Ed.), 228, § 5 amended.* *Citation.*

SECTION 8. This act shall become effective on the first day of October in the current year and shall apply only with respect to executors and administrators whose bonds shall have been approved after said date. *Effective date, etc.*

Approved May 26, 1933.

AN ACT RELATIVE TO CERTAIN RETIREMENT ALLOWANCES PAYABLE TO CERTAIN EMPLOYEES OF THE CITY OF SOMER-VILLE. *Chap.222*

Be it enacted, etc., as follows:

SECTION 1. Subsection two of section six of chapter one hundred and eighty-four of the acts of nineteen hundred and thirty is hereby amended by striking out paragraph (c) and the following paragraph and inserting in place thereof the following: — *1930, 184, § 6, amended.*

(c) If he has a prior service certificate in full force and effect an additional pension which is the actuarial equivalent of twice the pension which would have been payable on account of the accumulated deductions which would have resulted from contributions made during the period of his creditable prior service rendered both before and after age sixty had the system then been in operation. *Conditions for retirement allowance, etc. Additional pension.*

(d) The total pension of any member payable under the provisions of this section shall not, however, exceed one half of his average annual regular compensation during *Total pension.*

the five years immediately preceding his retirement, nor shall the total pension of any member, who has fifteen or more years of total creditable service be less than an amount which, added to his annuity, shall make his total retirement allowance equal to four hundred and eighty dollars per annum.

1930, 184, § 9,
amended.

SECTION 2. Section nine of said chapter one hundred and eighty-four is hereby amended by striking out paragraph (2) and inserting in place thereof the following: —

Reduction of
pensions in
certain cases.

(2) Should such physician or physicians report and certify to the retirement board that such disability beneficiary is engaged or able to engage in a gainful occupation, and should the retirement board find that his earnings, if he is so engaged, are less than the final regular compensation at which he was retired, but more than the difference between said final regular compensation and his retirement allowance, then the amount of his pension shall be reduced to an amount which, together with his annuity and his earnings, shall equal the amount of his final regular compensation. Should his earnings be later changed, the amount of his pension may be further modified; provided, that the new pension shall not exceed the amount of the pension originally granted nor shall it exceed an amount which, when added to the amount earned by the beneficiary together with his annuity, equals the amount of his final regular compensation. With the approval of the head of any department in which a vacancy exists, in the same employment in which such beneficiary was employed by the city at the time of his retirement, or in a similar employment, said board may order such beneficiary to return and be restored to active service in the employment of the city in such department. If such beneficiary refuses so to return, said board may revoke or suspend his pension. If a beneficiary is so restored to active service at a compensation less than his final regular compensation, but greater than the difference between the amount of his final regular compensation and his retirement allowance, then the amount of his pension shall be reduced to an amount which, when added to his annuity and the compensation at which he is so restored, shall equal the amount of the final regular compensation at which he was retired. Should his compensation be later changed, the amount of his pension may be modified as hereinbefore provided. Such a beneficiary restored to active service at a compensation less than his final regular compensation shall not become an active member of the retirement system, and upon eventual retirement shall receive the same retirement allowance which he was receiving prior to his restoration to active service. The requirements of chapter thirty-one of the General Laws and rules adopted thereunder, relative to an original appointment or to reinstatement, shall not apply to restoration under this section to active service in an office or position subject to said chapter; but the

head of the department to service in which the beneficiary is restored shall notify the commissioner of civil service of such restoration, and the person restored shall thereafter have all rights under said chapter thirty-one which he would have had if he had been continuously employed in the active service of the city from the time of his original appointment.

Section 3. Said section nine is hereby further amended by adding thereto the following new paragraph: — *1930, 184, § 9, amended.*

(4) Upon application by a beneficiary whose pension has been revoked or suspended under paragraph (2), the retirement board shall cause him to be again examined by a physician or physicians under paragraph (1). If such physician or physicians report and certify to said board that such beneficiary is no longer engaged or able to engage in any gainful occupation or employment, his pension may, by order of said board, be restored to him. *Re-examination after suspension, etc., of pension.*

Section 4. Section fifteen of said chapter one hundred and eighty-four is hereby amended by striking out paragraph (4) and inserting in place thereof the following: — *1930, 184, § 15, amended.*

(4) The Pension Reserve Fund shall be the fund from which shall be paid the pensions to members not entitled to credit for prior service and benefits in lieu thereof. Should such a beneficiary, retired on account of disability, be restored to active service with a compensation which causes his pension to cease under paragraph (2) or (3) of section nine, the pension reserve thereon shall be transferred from the Pension Reserve Fund to the Pension Accumulation Fund. Should the pension of a disability beneficiary be reduced under said paragraph (2), the amount of the annual reduction in his pension shall be paid annually into the Pension Accumulation Fund during the period of such reduction. *Pension reserve fund.*

Section 5. This act shall take effect upon its acceptance during the current year by vote of the city council of said city, subject to the provisions of its charter. *Acceptance of act.*

Approved May 26, 1933.

An Act providing retirement allowances based on annuity and pension contributions for employees of the city of Everett. *Chap.223*

Be it enacted, etc., as follows:

PURPOSE OF THE ACT.

Section 1. The purpose of this act is to improve the efficiency of the public service of the city of Everett, hereinafter called the city, by the retirement of disabled or superannuated employees.

DEFINITIONS.

Section 2. The following words and phrases as used in this act, unless a different meaning is plainly required by the context, shall have the following meanings: —

(1) "Retirement system", the arrangement provided in this act for the retirement of, and payment of retirement allowances to, employees as defined in paragraph (2) of this section.

(2) "Employee", any person who is regularly employed in the service of, and whose salary or compensation is paid by, the city, except employees who hold office by popular election, who are not members at the time of their election, and teachers in the public schools as defined by section six of chapter thirty-two of the General Laws. In all cases of doubt the retirement board shall decide who is an employee within the meaning of this act.

(3) "Member", any employee included in the retirement system as provided in section four of this act.

(4) "Retirement board", the board provided in section fourteen of this act to administer the retirement system.

(5) "Service", service as an employee as described in paragraph (2) of this section and paid for by the city of Everett.

(6) "Prior service', service rendered prior to the date the retirement system becomes first operative, for which credit is allowable under the provisions of section five of this act.

(7) "Membership service", service as an employee rendered since last becoming a member.

(8) "Creditable service", "prior service" plus "membership service", for which credit is allowable as provided in section five of this act.

(9) "Beneficiary", any person in receipt of a pension, an annuity, a retirement allowance or other benefit as provided by this act.

(10) "Regular interest", interest at four per centum per annum compounded annually; provided, that if the actual net interest earned on the reserves of the retirement system be less than four per centum, the rate may be reduced to not less than three per centum per annum after the retirement board has given the members ninety days' notice of a proposed reduction in rate; and provided, further, that such reduction shall not affect any payments or credits made prior to the date of the change in rate.

(11) "Accumulated deductions", the sum of all the amounts deducted from the compensation of a member and standing to his credit in the annuity savings fund, together with regular interest thereon.

(12) "Annuity", annual payments for life derived from the accumulated deductions of a member. All annuities shall be paid in monthly instalments.

(13) "Pension", annual payments for life derived from contributions made by the city. All pensions shall be paid in monthly instalments.

(14) "Retirement allowance", the sum of the "annuity" and the "pension".

(15) "Regular compensation", the annual compensa-

tion determined by the head of the department for the individual service of each employee in that department and the compensation determined by duly constituted authority for appointed officers of the city, exclusive of bonus or overtime payments.

(16) "Annuity reserve", the present value of all payments to be made on account of any annuity or benefit in lieu of any annuity computed upon the basis of such mortality tables as shall be adopted by the retirement board and regular interest.

(17) "Pension reserve", the present value of all payments to be made on account of any pension or benefit in lieu of any pension computed upon the basis of such mortality tables as shall be adopted by the retirement board and regular interest.

(18) "Actuarial equivalent", a benefit of equal value when computed upon the basis of such mortality tables as shall be approved by the retirement board and regular interest.

NAME AND DATE SYSTEM IS FIRST OPERATIVE.

SECTION 3. A retirement system is hereby established and placed under the management of the retirement board for the purpose of providing retirement allowances under the provisions of this act for employees of, or employees paid by, the city. The retirement system so created shall have the powers and privileges of a corporation and shall be known as the "Everett Retirement System", and by such name all of its business shall be transacted, all of its funds invested, all warrants for money drawn and payments made, and all of its cash and securities and other property held. The retirement system so created shall begin operation upon the first day of January, nineteen hundred and thirty-five.

MEMBERSHIP.

SECTION 4. (1) The membership of the retirement system shall be constituted as follows: —

(a) All persons who become employees and, except as otherwise provided in the last sentence of subsection (2) of section nine, all employees who enter or re-enter the service of the city on or after the date the retirement system becomes operative may become members of the retirement system on their own application, and all such employees who shall complete one year of service thereafter and disability beneficiaries restored to active service to whom the provisions of subsection (3) of said section nine apply shall become members of the retirement system, and after becoming members as above provided shall receive no pension or retirement allowance from any other pension or retirement system supported wholly or in part by the city, nor shall they be required to make contributions to any other pension or retirement system of the city, anything to the contrary in this or any other special or general law notwithstanding.

(b) All persons who are employees on the date when this retirement system becomes operative and who are not then covered by any other pension or retirement law of the commonwealth shall become members as of the first day this retirement system becomes operative, unless on or before a date not more than sixty days thereafter, to be set by the retirement board, any such employee shall file with the retirement board on a form prescribed by the board a notice of his election not to be covered in the membership of the system and a duly executed waiver of all present and prospective benefits which would otherwise inure to him on account of his participation in the retirement system.

(c) An employee who is covered by any other pension or retirement law of the commonwealth, including a special law accepted by, and applicable to employees of, the city on the date when this retirement system becomes operative shall not be considered to have become a member of this retirement system unless said employee shall then or thereafter make written application to join this system and shall therein waive and renounce all benefits of any other pension or retirement system supported wholly by the city, but no such employee shall receive credit for prior service unless he make such application for membership within one year from the date this retirement system becomes operative.

(2) An employee whose membership in the retirement system is contingent on his own election and who elects not to become a member may thereafter apply for and be admitted to membership; but no such employee shall receive prior service credit unless he becomes a member within one year from the date this retirement system becomes operative.

(3) The retirement board may deny the right to become members to any class of officials appointed for fixed terms, or to any class of part-time employees, or it may, in its discretion, make optional with persons in any such class their individual entrance into membership.

(4) It shall be the duty of the head of each department to submit to the retirement board a statement showing the name, title, compensation, duties, date of birth and length of service of each member of his department, and such information regarding other employees therein as the retirement board may require. The retirement board shall then place each member in one of the following groups:—

Group 1. — General employees, including clerical, administrative and technical workers, laborers, mechanics and all others not otherwise classified;   ·

Group 2. — Members of the police department and the fire department of the city;

Or in any other group of not less than two hundred and fifty persons which may be hereafter recommended by the actuary on the basis of service and mortality experience, and approved by the retirement board to cover all or part of any group or groups previously created or any additional classes of employees. When the duties of a member so require, the retirement board may reclassify him in and transfer him to another group.

(5) Should any member in any period of six consecutive years after last becoming a member be absent from service more than five years, or should any member withdraw his accumulated deductions or become a beneficiary hereunder or die, he shall thereupon cease to be a member.

CREDITABLE SERVICE.

SECTION 5. (1) Under such rules and regulations as the retirement board shall adopt, each person becoming a member within one year from the date he first becomes eligible to membership who was in service at the time the system became operative, or who re-entered the service within five years after rendering service prior to the time the system became operative shall file a detailed statement of all service as an employee rendered by him prior to the day on which the system first became operative for which he claims credit, and of such facts as the retirement board may require for the proper operation of the system.

(2) The retirement board shall fix and determine by appropriate rules and regulations how much service in any year is equivalent to a year of service, but in no case shall more than one year of service be creditable for all service in one calendar year, nor shall the retirement board allow credit as service for any period of more than one month's duration during which the employee was absent without pay.

(3) Subject to the above restrictions and to such other rules and regulations as the retirement board may adopt, the retirement board shall verify, as soon as practicable after the filing of such statements of service, the service therein claimed, and shall certify as creditable all or such part of the service claimed as may be allowable.

In lieu of a determination of the actual compensation of the member that was received during such period of prior service, the retirement board shall use for the purposes of this act the compensation rates which, if they had progressed in accordance with the rates of salary increase shown in the tables as prescribed in paragraph (10) of section fourteen of this act, would have resulted in the same average salary of the member for the five years immediately preceding the date this system became operative as the records show the member actually received.

(4) Upon verification of the statements of service the retirement board shall issue prior service certificates certifying to each member entitled to credit for prior service the length of service rendered prior to the date the retirement system first became operative, with which he is

credited on the basis of his statement of service. So long as membership continues a prior service certificate shall for retirement purposes be final and conclusive as to such service; provided, that any member may, within one year from the date of issuance or modification of such certificate, request the retirement board to modify or correct his prior service certificate.

When membership ceases such prior service certificates shall become void. Should the employee again become a member, such employee shall enter the system as an employee not entitled to prior service credit except as provided in subsection three of section nine.

(5) Creditable service at retirement shall consist of the membership service rendered by the member since he last became a member and also, if he has a prior service certificate which is in full force and effect, the amount of the service certified on his prior service certificate.

SERVICE RETIREMENT.

Conditions for Allowance.

SECTION 6. (1) Any member in service who shall have attained age sixty shall, either upon his own written application or that of the head of his department, be retired for superannuation not less than thirty nor more than ninety days after the filing of such application. A member whose retirement is applied for by the head of his department shall be entitled to a notice of such application and to a hearing before the retirement board, provided he requests such hearing in writing within ten days of the receipt of such notice; and unless the retirement board finds on hearing, that the member is able to properly perform his duties and files a copy of its findings with the head of his department, the retirement shall become effective thirty days from the time of the filing of such finding.

Any member in service who shall have attained age seventy shall be retired for superannuation not less than thirty nor more than ninety days after attaining such age, or after this system becomes operative, if such age was attained prior thereto.

Amount of Allowance.

(2) Upon retirement for superannuation a member of the retirement system shall receive a retirement allowance consisting of —

(a) An annuity which shall be the actuarial equivalent of his accumulated deductions at the time of his retirement, and

(b) A pension equal to the annuity allowable at age sixty, computed on the basis of contributions made prior to the attainment of age sixty, and

(c) If he has a prior service certificate in full force and effect an additional pension which is the actuarial equivalent of twice the pension which would have been payable under paragraph (b) above, on account of the accumulated deductions which would have resulted from contributions made during the period of his creditable prior service had the system then been in operation.

The total pension of any member payable under the provisions of this section shall not, however, exceed one half of his average annual regular compensation during the five years immediately preceding his retirement, nor shall the total pension of any member who has fifteen or more years of total creditable service be less than an amount which, added to his annuity, shall make his total retirement allowance equal to four hundred and eighty dollars per annum.

ORDINARY DISABILITY RETIREMENT.

Conditions for Allowance.

SECTION 7. (1) Upon the application of a member in service or of the head of his department, any member who has had twenty or more years of creditable service may be retired by the retirement board, not less than thirty and not more than ninety days next following the date of filing such application, on an ordinary disability retirement allowance; provided, that the city physician, after a medical examination of such member, shall certify that such member is mentally or physically incapacitated for the further performance of duty, that such incapacity is likely to be permanent and that such member should be retired.

Amount of Allowance.

(2) Upon retirement for ordinary disability a member shall receive a service retirement allowance if he has attained age sixty; otherwise he shall receive an ordinary disability retirement allowance consisting of —

(a) An annuity which shall be the actuarial equivalent of his accumulated deductions at the time of his retirement, and

(b) A pension of ninety per centum of the pension that would have been provided by the city for the member had he remained without further change of compensation in the service of the city until he reached age sixty and then retired.

ACCIDENTAL DISABILITY RETIREMENT.

Conditions for Allowance.

SECTION 8. (1) Upon application of a member in service, or of the head of his department, any member who has been totally and permanently incapacitated for duty as the natural and proximate result of an accident occurring in the performance and within the scope of his duty at some definite time and place, without wilful negligence on his part, shall be retired not less than thirty nor

more than ninety days following the date of filing of such
application; provided, that the city physician, after an
examination of such member, shall report that said member
is physically or mentally incapacitated for the further
performance of duty, that such incapacity is likely to be
permanent, and that said member should be retired, and
the retirement board shall concur in such report and find
that the physical or mental incapacity is the natural and
proximate result of such an accident and that such disability
is not the result of wilful negligence on the part of said
member and that said member should be retired.

Amount of Allowance.

(2) Upon retirement for accidental disability a member
shall receive a service retirement allowance if he has attained age sixty; otherwise he shall receive an accidental
disability retirement allowance consisting of —

(a) An annuity which shall be the actuarial equivalent
of his accumulated deductions at the time of his retirement,
and

(b) A pension equal to one half of the average rate of
his regular annual compensation for the year immediately
preceding the date of the accident.

RE-EXAMINATION OF BENEFICIARIES RETIRED ON ACCOUNT OF DISABILITY.

SECTION 9. (1) Once each year during the first five
years following retirement of a member on a disability
retirement allowance, and once in every three-year period
thereafter, the retirement board may, and upon his application shall, require any disability beneficiary who has not
yet attained age sixty to undergo a medical examination
by the city physician or a physician or physicians designated by the retirement board and approved by the mayor,
such examination to be made at the place of residence
of said beneficiary or other place mutually agreed upon.
Should any disability beneficiary who has not yet attained
the age of sixty refuse to submit to at least one medical
examination in any such period of one or three years, as
the case may be, his allowance may be discontinued until
his withdrawal of such refusal, and should his refusal continue for a year, all his rights in and to his pension shall be
revoked by the retirement board.

(2) Should such physician or physicians report and
certify to the retirement board that such disability beneficiary is engaged in or is able to engage in a gainful occupation paying more than the difference between his retirement allowance and his final regular compensation, and
should the retirement board concur in such report, then,
the amount of his pension shall be reduced to an amount
which, together with his annuity and the amount earnable
by him, shall equal the amount of his final regular compensation. Should his earning capacity be later changed,

the amount of his pension may be further modified; provided, that the new pension shall not exceed the amount of the pension originally granted nor shall it exceed an amount, which, when added to the amount earnable by the beneficiary together with his annuity, equals the amount of his final regular compensation. A beneficiary restored to active service at a salary less than the final regular compensation upon the basis of which he was retired shall not become a member of the retirement system.

(3) Should a disability beneficiary be restored to active service at a compensation not less than his final regular compensation, his retirement allowance shall cease, he shall again become a member of the retirement system, and he shall contribute thereafter at the same rate he paid prior to disability. Any prior service certificate on the basis of which his service was computed at the time of his retirement shall be restored to full force and effect, and in addition upon his subsequent retirement he shall be credited with all his service as a member.

RETURN OF ACCUMULATED DEDUCTIONS.

SECTION 10. (1) Within sixty days after the filing with the retirement board of a request therefor, any member who shall have ceased to be an employee by resignation or discharge or for any reason other than death or retirement shall be paid the amount of his accumulated deductions.

(2) Should a member die while an employee, his accumulated deductions shall be paid to his legal representative; provided, that if the sum so due does not exceed three hundred dollars, and there has been no demand therefor by a duly appointed executor or administrator, payment may be made, after the expiration of three months from the date of death of such member, to the persons appearing, in the judgment of the retirement board, to be entitled thereto, and such payment shall be a bar to recovery by any other person.

ACCIDENTAL DEATH BENEFIT.

SECTION 11. If, upon receipt by the retirement board of proper proofs of the death of a member, the retirement board shall decide that such death was the natural and proximate result of an accident occurring not more than one year prior to the date of death at some definite time and place while the member was in actual performance and within the scope of his duty, and not the result of wilful negligence on his part, and if the deceased member is survived by any of the dependents enumerated below, there shall be paid, in addition to accumulated deductions under subsection (2) of section ten, an accidental death benefit consisting of a pension equal to one half the average regular annual compensation received by the deceased member for the year preceding the date of the accident, said pension to be paid —

(a) To the surviving husband or wife of the deceased member so long as he or she lives and remains unmarried; or

(b) If there be no surviving husband or wife or if the surviving husband or wife dies or remarries before every child of such deceased member shall have attained the age of eighteen years, then to his child or children under such age, divided in such manner as the retirement board in its discretion shall determine to continue as a joint and survivor pension until every such child dies or attains the age of eighteen years; or

(c) If there be no husband or wife or child under the age of eighteen years surviving such deceased member, then to either his or her dependent father or dependent mother, as the retirement board in its discretion shall determine, to continue for life or until remarriage.

OPTIONAL BENEFITS.

SECTION 12. Subject to the provisions that no optional selection shall be effective in case a beneficiary dies within thirty days after retirement, and that such a beneficiary shall be considered as an active member at the time of death, until the first payment on account of any retirement allowance is made, the member, or if he be an incompetent then his wife, or if he have no wife, his conservator or guardian, may elect to convert the retirement allowance otherwise provided for in this system into a lesser retirement allowance of equivalent actuarial value payable throughout his life, with the provision that —

Option 1. — If he die before he has received in payments of his annuity the present value of his annuity as it was at the time of his retirement, the balance shall be paid to his legal representative or to such person having an insurable interest in his life as he, or if he be an incompetent then his wife, or if he have no wife, his conservator or guardian, shall have nominated by written designation duly acknowledged and filed with the retirement board; or

Option 2. — Upon his death, his lesser retirement allowance shall be continued throughout the life of and paid to such person having an insurable interest in his life as he, or if he be an incompetent then his wife, or if he have no wife, his conservator or guardian, shall have nominated by written designation duly acknowledged and filed with the retirement board at the time of his retirement; or

Option 3. — Upon his death, one half his lesser retirement allowance shall be continued throughout the life of and paid to such person having an insurable interest in his life as he, or if he be an incompetent then his wife, or if he have no wife, his conservator or guardian, shall have nominated by written designation, duly acknowledged and filed with the retirement board at the time of his retirement.

COMPENSATION BENEFITS OFFSET.

SECTION 13. Any amounts paid or payable by the city under the provisions of the workmen's compensation law to a member or to the dependents of a member on account of death or disability shall be offset against and payable in lieu of any benefits payable out of funds provided by the city under the provisions of this act on account of the death or disability of a member. If the value of the total commuted benefits under the workmen's compensation law is less than the reserve on the pension otherwise payable under this act, the value of such commuted payments shall be deducted from such pension reserve and such benefits as may be provided by the pension reserve so reduced shall be payable under the provisions of this act.

ADMINISTRATION.

SECTION 14. (1) The management of the retirement system is hereby vested in a retirement board, the membership of which shall be constituted as follows: —

(a) The auditor of the city for the time being,

(b) One person to be appointed by the mayor of the city, subjected to confirmation by the board of aldermen, who shall serve for a term of three years commencing on the date when the retirement system becomes first operative and until the qualification of his successor, and

(c) One person who shall be a member of the retirement system and who shall be appointed by the mayor of the city subject to such confirmation, to serve for a term of one year commencing on the date when the retirement system becomes first operative and until the qualification of his successor.

(2) As the terms of the appointed members expire, their successors shall be appointed for terms of three years each and until the qualification of their successors. On a vacancy occurring in the appointed membership of the retirement board, for any cause other than the expiration of a term of office, a successor to the person whose place has become vacant shall be appointed for the unexpired term in the same manner as above provided.

(3) The members of the retirement board shall be reimbursed from the expense fund for any expense or loss of salary or wages which they may incur through service on the retirement board.

(4) The retirement board shall elect from its membership a chairman, and shall by a majority vote of all its members appoint a secretary, who may be, but need not be, one of its members. It shall engage such actuarial and other service as shall be required to transact the business of the retirement system. The funds to meet the costs of administering the retirement system shall be derived from appropriations of the city from the annual tax levy. The retirement board shall submit an estimate of

such costs to the mayor not later than January first of each year. Such amount as shall be required in the first year of operation to defray the expenses of the establishment and maintenance of the retirement system shall be appropriated by the city council.

(5) The retirement board shall keep in convenient form such data as shall be necessary for actuarial valuations of the various funds of the retirement system and for checking the experience of the system.

(6) The retirement board shall keep a record of all of its proceedings, which shall be open to public inspection. It shall publish annually a report showing the fiscal transactions of the retirement system for the preceding municipal year, the amount of accumulated cash and securities of the system, and the last balance sheet showing the financial condition of the system by means of actuarial valuation of the assets and liabilities thereof. The board shall submit said report to the mayor and shall furnish copies thereof to the city clerk for distribution.

Legal Adviser.

(7) The city solicitor of the city shall be the legal adviser of the retirement board.

Medical Examinations.

(8) The city physician of the city shall arrange for and pass upon all medical examinations required under the provisions of this act, shall investigate all essential statements and certificates by or in behalf of a member in connection with an application for disability retirement, and shall report in writing to the retirement board his conclusions and recommendations upon all the matters referred to him. If required, other physicians may be employed by the retirement board to report on special cases.

Duties of Actuary.

(9) The retirement board shall designate an actuary who shall be the technical adviser of the retirement board on matters regarding the operation of the funds created by the provisions of this act, and shall perform such other duties as are required in connection therewith.

(10) Immediately after the establishment of the retirement system the actuary shall make such investigation of the mortality, service and compensation experience of the members of the system as he shall recommend and the retirement board shall authorize, and on the basis of such investigation he shall recommend for adoption by the retirement board such tables and such rates as are required by section fifteen. The retirement board shall adopt tables and certify rates, and as soon as practicable thereafter the actuary shall make a valuation, based on such tables and rates, of the assets and liabilities of the funds created by this act.

(11) Three years after the system becomes operative, and at least once in each five-year period thereafter, the actuary shall make an actuarial investigation into the mortality, service and compensation experience of the members and beneficiaries of the retirement system, and shall make a valuation of the assets and liabilities of the funds thereof, and taking into account the result of such investigation and valuation the retirement board shall —

(a) Adopt for the retirement system such mortality, service and other tables as shall be deemed necessary; and

(b) Certify the rates of contribution payable by the city on account of new entrants.

(12) On the basis of such tables as the retirement board shall from time to time adopt, the actuary shall make an annual valuation of the assets and liabilities of the reserve funds of the system created by this act.

METHOD OF FINANCING.

SECTION 15. All of the assets of the retirement system shall be credited, according to the purpose for which they are held, to one of the following five funds, namely, the Annuity Savings Fund, the Annuity Reserve Fund, the Pension Accumulation Fund, the Pension Reserve Fund, or the Expense Fund.

Annuity Savings Fund.

(1) (a) The Annuity Savings Fund shall be the fund to which shall be paid the deductions from the compensation of members. The treasurer of the city shall withhold four per centum of the regular compensation due on each pay day to all employees who are members of this retirement system. The various amounts so withheld shall be transferred immediately thereafter to the retirement system and credited to the accounts of the respective members so contributing, and shall be paid into and become a part of said Annuity Savings Fund.

(b) In determining the amount earnable by a member in a payroll period, the retirement board may consider the rate of annual compensation payable to such member on the first day of the payroll period as continuing throughout such payroll period, and it may omit deduction from compensation for any period less than a full payroll period if an employee was not a member on the first day of the payroll period.

(c) The deductions provided for herein shall be made notwithstanding that the minimum compensation provided for by law for any member shall be reduced thereby. Every member shall be deemed to consent and agree to the deductions provided for herein and shall receipt for his full salary or compensation, and the payment of his full salary or compensation less the deductions provided for hereunder shall be considered a full and complete discharge and acquittance of all claims and demands whatsoever for the services rendered by such person during the period covered by such payment, except as to the benefits provided under this act.

(d) In addition to the contributions deducted from compensation as hereinbefore provided, subject to the approval of the retirement board, any member may redeposit in the Annuity Savings Fund by a single payment or by an increased rate of contribution an amount equal to the total amount which he previously withdrew therefrom, as provided in this act, or any part thereof; or any member may deposit therein by a single payment or by an increased rate of contribution an amount computed to be sufficient to purchase an additional annuity, which, together with his prospective retirement allowance, will provide for him a total retirement allowance of not to exceed one half of his salary at age sixty. Such additional amounts so deposited shall be treated as a part of his accumulated deductions, except in the event of his retirement, when they shall' not be used to increase the pension payable, and shall be treated as excess contributions returnable to the member in cash or in providing an excess annuity of equivalent actuarial value. The accumulated deductions of a member withdrawn by him or paid to his estate or to his designated beneficiary in event of his death as provided in this act shall be paid from the Annuity Savings Fund. Upon the retirement of a member his accumulated deductions shall be transferred from the Annuity Savings Fund to the Annuity Reserve Fund.

Annuity Reserve Fund.

(2) The Annuity Reserve Fund shall be the fund from which shall be paid all annuities and all benefits in lieu of annuities, payable as provided in this act. Should a beneficiary, retired on account of disability, be restored to active service with a compensation not less than his regular compensation at the time of his last retirement, his annuity reserve shall be transferred from the Annuity Reserve Fund to the Annuity Savings Fund, and credited to his individual account therein.

Pension Accumulation Fund.

(3) (a) The Pension Accumulation Fund shall be the fund into which shall be accumulated all reserves for the payment of all pensions and other benefits payable from contributions made by the city, and from which shall be paid all pensions and other benefits on account of members with prior service credit. Contributions to and payments from the Pension Accumulation Fund shall be made as follows: —

(b) On account of each member there shall be paid annually into the Pension Accumulation Fund by the said city, for the preceding fiscal year, a certain percentage of the regular compensation of each member, to be known as the "normal contribution", and an additional percentage of his regular compensation to be known as the "accrued liability contribution." The rates per centum of such contributions shall be fixed on the basis of the liabilities of the retirement system as shown by actuarial valuation. Until the first valuation the normal contribution shall be one and eighty-nine hundredths per centum, and the accrued liability contribution shall be two and fifty-four hundredths per centum, of the regular annual compensation of all members.

(c) On the basis of regular interest and of such mortality and other tables as shall be adopted by the retirement board, the actuary engaged by the board to make each valuation required by this act during the period over which the accrued liability contribution is payable, immediately after making such valuation, shall determine the uniform and constant percentage of the regular compensation of the average new entrant, which if contributed on the basis of compensation of such new entrant throughout his entire period of active service is computed to be sufficient to provide for the payment of any pension payable on his account. The rate per centum so determined shall be known as the "normal contribution" rate. After the accrued liability contribution has ceased to be payable, the normal contribution rate shall be the rate per centum of the regular compensation of all members obtained by deducting from the total liabilities of the Pension Accumulation Fund the amount of the funds in hand to the credit of that fund and dividing the remainder by one per centum of the present value of the prospective future salaries of all members as computed on the basis of the mortality and service tables adopted by the retirement board and regular interest. The normal rate of contribution shall be determined by the actuary after each valuation.

(d) Immediately succeeding the first valuation, the actuary engaged by the retirement board shall compute the rate per centum of the total regular compensation of all members which is equivalent to four per centum of the amount of the total pension liability on account of all members and beneficiaries which is not dischargeable by the aforesaid normal contribution made on account of such members during the remainder of their active service. The rate per centum originally so determined shall be known as the "accrued liability contribution rate."

(e) The total amount payable in each year to the Pension Accumulation Fund shall be not less than the sum of the rates per centum known as the normal contribution rate and the accrued liability contribution rate of the total compensation earnable by all members during the preceding year; provided, that the amount of each annual accrued liability contribution shall be at least three per centum greater than the preceding annual accrued liability payment, and that the aggregate payments of the city shall be sufficient when combined with the amount in the fund to provide the pensions and other benefits payable out of the fund during the year then current.

(*f*) The accrued liability contribution shall be discontinued as soon as the accumulated reserve in the Pension Accumulation Fund shall equal the present value, as actuarially computed and approved by the retirement board, of the total liability of such fund less the present value, computed on the basis of the normal contribution rate then in force, of the prospective normal contributions to be received on account of persons who are at that time members.

(*g*) All pensions, and benefits in lieu thereof, with the exception of those payable on account of members who receive no prior service allowance, payable from contributions of the city, shall be paid from the Pension Accumulation Fund.

(*h*) Upon the retirement of a member not entitled to credit for prior service, an amount equal to his pension reserve shall be transferred from the Pension Accumulation Fund to the Pension Reserve Fund.

Pension Reserve Fund.

(4) The Pension Reserve Fund shall be the fund from which shall be paid the pensions to members not entitled to credit for prior service and benefits in lieu thereof. Should such a beneficiary, retired on account of disability, be restored to active service with a compensation not less than his average regular compensation for the year preceding his last retirement, the pension reserve thereon shall be transferred from the Pension Reserve Fund to the Pension Accumulation Fund. Should the pension of a disability beneficiary be reduced as a result of an increase in his earning capacity, the amount of the annual reduction in his pension shall be paid annually into the Pension Accumulation Fund during the period of such reduction.

Expense Fund.

(5) The Expense Fund shall be the fund to which shall be credited all money appropriated by the city to pay the administration expenses of the retirement system, and from which shall be paid all the expenses necessary in connection with the administration and operation of the system.

Appropriations.

(6) (*a*) On or before the first day of December in each year the retirement board shall certify to the mayor the amount of the appropriation necessary to pay to the various funds of the retirement system the amounts payable by the city as enumerated in this act for the year beginning on the first day of January of the succeeding year, and items

of appropriation, providing such amounts shall be included in the budget.

(b) To cover the requirements of the system for the period prior to the date when the first regular appropriation is due, as provided by paragraph (a) of this subsection, such amounts as shall be necessary to cover the needs of the system shall be paid into the Pension Accumulation Fund and the Expense Fund by special appropriations to the system.

MANAGEMENT OF FUNDS.

Section 16. (1) The retirement board may invest the funds of the retirement system in such securities as are approved from time to time by the commissioner of insurance for the investment of the funds of life insurance companies under the laws of the commonwealth.

(2) The retirement board shall annually allow regular interest on the average balance for the preceding year to the credit of the various funds from the interest and dividends earned from investments. Any excess earnings over the amount so credited shall be used for reducing the amount of contributions required of the city during the ensuing year. Any deficiency shall be paid by the city during the ensuing year.

(3) The treasurer of the city shall be custodian of the several funds. All payments from said funds shall be made by him only upon vouchers signed by two persons designated by the retirement board. A duly attested copy of a resolution of the retirement board designating such persons and bearing upon its face specimen signatures of such persons shall be filed with the treasurer as his authority for making payments upon such vouchers. No voucher shall be drawn unless it shall have been previously authorized by resolution of the retirement board.

(4) For the purpose of meeting disbursements for pensions, annuities and other payments an amount of money, not exceeding ten per centum of the total amount in the several funds of the retirement system, may be kept on deposit in one or more banks or trust companies organized under the laws of the commonwealth or of the United States; provided, that the sum on deposit in any one bank or trust company shall not exceed ten per centum of the paid-up capital and surplus thereof.

(5) The retirement board may, in its discretion, transfer to or from the Pension Accumulation Fund the amount of any surplus or deficit which may develop in the reserves creditable to the Annuity Reserve Fund or the Pension Reserve Fund, as shown by actuarial valuations.

(6) Except as otherwise provided herein, no member and no employee of the retirement board shall have any direct interest in the gains or profits of any investment made by the retirement board, nor as such receive any pay or emolument for his services. No member or employee of the

board shall, directly or indirectly, for himself or as an agent, in any manner use any of the securities or other assets of the retirement board, except to make such current and necessary payments as are authorized by the retirement board; nor shall any member or employee of the retirement board become an endorser or surety or in any manner obligor for moneys loaned by or borrowed from the retirement system.

(7) Each member of the retirement board, and the treasurer of the city in his capacity as custodian of the several funds, shall severally give bond for the faithful performance of his duties in a sum and with sureties or surety approved by the city council.

EXEMPTION OF FUNDS FROM TAXATION AND EXECUTION.

SECTION 17. The pensions, annuities and retirement allowances and the accumulated deductions and the cash and securities in the funds created by this act are hereby exempted from any state, county or municipal tax of this commonwealth, and shall not be subject to execution or attachment by trustee process or otherwise, in law or in equity, or under any process whatsoever, and shall be non-assignable except as specifically provided in this act.

RECEIPT OF BOTH RETIREMENT ALLOWANCE AND SALARY FORBIDDEN.

SECTION 18. No beneficiary of the retirement system shall be paid for any service, except service as a juror and such service as he may be called upon to perform in the police or fire department in a time of public emergency, rendered by him to the city after the date of the first payment of any retirement allowance hereunder, except as provided in section nine of this act, and except as further provided in this section.

Notwithstanding the above provision, a beneficiary may be employed, for periods of not exceeding one year at a time, with the approval of the mayor and board of aldermen, and may receive compensation from the city for the services so rendered; provided, that the annual rate of compensation paid, together with the regular retirement allowance received, shall not exceed the regular compensation of the said beneficiary at the time of retirement.

RIGHT OF APPEAL.

SECTION 19. The supreme judicial court shall have jurisdiction in equity upon the petition of the retirement board or any interested party or upon the petition of not less than ten taxable inhabitants of the city to compel the observance and restrain any violation of this act and
e rules and regulations authorized or established thereunder.

TENURE UNAFFECTED.

Section 20. Nothing contained in this act shall affect the right or power of the city or other duly constituted authority in regard to demotion, transfer, suspension or discharge of any employee.

INCONSISTENT ACTS.

Section 21. Any of the provisions of sections forty-four, forty-five, seventy-seven, eighty and eighty-three of chapter thirty-two of the General Laws, as amended, which may be inconsistent herewith, and any other acts or parts of acts inconsistent herewith, shall, on and after the effective date of this act, apply only to such employees of the city as are, on said effective date, entitled to the benefits thereof. Nothing herein contained shall be construed as affecting the provisions of sections forty-nine to sixty, inclusive, or of section ninety-two of chapter thirty-two of the General Laws as amended.

Section 22. On or before September first, in the current year, the question of the approval of the provisions of this act shall be finally voted upon by the city council of the city of Everett, and, whether or not said provisions are approved by such vote, they shall be submitted for acceptance to the qualified voters of said city at the biennial municipal election to be held in the current year, in the form of the following question, which shall be printed upon the official ballot to be used in said city at said election: — "Shall an act passed by the General Court in the year 1933, entitled 'An act providing retirement allowances based on annuity and pension contributions for employees of the City of Everett', be accepted?" If a majority of the voters voting thereon vote in the affirmative in answer to this question this act shall thereupon take full effect; otherwise it shall not take effect.

Approved May 26, 1933.

An Act authorizing the trial in juvenile sessions of certain proceedings against parents.

Chap.224

Be it enacted, etc., as follows:

Section two of chapter two hundred and seventy-three of the General Laws, as appearing in the Tercentenary Edition thereof, is hereby amended by adding at the end thereof the following: — Such a proceeding, if founded upon the same allegations as a proceeding under sections forty-two to forty-seven, inclusive, of chapter one hundred and nineteen may be heard and disposed of in the juvenile session of the court, — so as to read as follows: — *Section 2.* Proceedings under the preceding section shall be begun, if in the superior court, in the county in which is situated the place where the husband and wife last lived together or where the husband or wife or parent of the child is liv-

G. L. (Ter. Ed.), 273, § 2, amended.

Jurisdiction and venue of certain cases pertaining to divorce, etc., and to neglected children.

ing, and, if begun in a district court or before a trial justice, in the court or before the trial justice having such place within its or his judicial district. Such a proceeding, if founded upon the same allegations as a proceeding under sections forty-two to forty-seven, inclusive, of chapter one hundred and nineteen may be heard and disposed of in the juvenile session of the court.

Approved May 26, 1933.

*Chap.*225 AN ACT RELATIVE TO THE APPLICATION OF THE ONE DAY'S REST IN SEVEN LAW TO WATCHMEN AND EMPLOYEES MAINTAINING FIRES.

Be it enacted, etc., as follows:

G. L. (Ter. Ed.), 149, § 50, amended.

Application of one day's rest in seven law to watchmen, etc.

Chapter one hundred and forty-nine of the General Laws is hereby amended by striking out section fifty, as appearing in the Tercentenary Edition thereof, and inserting in place thereof the following: — *Section 50.* Sections forty-seven and forty-eight shall not apply to (*a*) janitors; (*b*) employees whose duties include no work on Sunday other than (1) setting sponges in bakeries, (2) caring for live animals, (3) caring for machinery; (*c*) employees engaged in the preparation, printing, publication, sale or delivery of newspapers; (*d*) farm or personal service; (*e*) any labor called for by an emergency that could not reasonably have been anticipated; nor shall said sections apply to persons maintaining fires in establishments wherein no boiler having a pressure capacity exceeding fifteen pounds is operated or to watchmen in such establishments.

Approved May 26, 1933.

*Chap.*226 AN ACT RELATING TO SEWER ASSESSMENTS IN THE TOWN OF DANVERS.

Be it enacted, etc., as follows:

SECTION 1. The share of the cost of construction of the system of sewage disposal of the South Essex Sewerage District paid by the town of Danvers under chapter three hundred and thirty-nine of the acts of nineteen hundred and twenty-five, as amended, shall be included by said town as an item in determining the total cost of the system of sewerage and sewage disposal in said town constructed under chapter two hundred and twenty-nine of the Special Acts of nineteen hundred and sixteen, for the purpose of assessing estates benefited thereby under authority of said chapter two hundred and twenty-nine.

SECTION 2. This act shall take effect upon its acceptance by a majority of the town meeting members of the town of Danvers present and voting thereon at an annual or special town meeting of said town, subject, however, to referendum under the provisions of section eight of chapter two hundred and ninety-four of the acts of nineteen hundred and thirty.

Approved May 26, 1933.

An Act authorizing the department of public works to expend certain sums for the completion of the pier on the cape cod canal. *Chap.227*

Be it enacted, etc., as follows:

The department of public works is hereby authorized to expend the appropriation made by item five hundred and ninety-eight A of chapter one hundred and seventy-four of the acts of the current year, in addition to any sum or sums heretofore authorized, for the completion of the pier on the Cape Cod canal, authorized by chapter four hundred and forty-one of the acts of nineteen hundred and thirty-one.   *Approved May 26, 1933.*

An Act to prevent fraud and misrepresentation in the sale of gasoline, lubricating oils and other motor fuels, and to prevent adulteration thereof. *Chap.228*

Be it enacted, etc., as follows:

Chapter ninety-four of the General Laws is hereby amended by inserting after section two hundred and ninety-five, as appearing in the Tercentenary Edition thereof, the following new section under the heading "Petroleum Products": — *Section 295A.* Whoever, himself or by his servant or agent, sells or offers to sell, from any tank or other container or from any pump or other distributing device, any gasoline, lubricating oil or other motor fuel other than the product indicated by the name, trade name, trade mark, symbol, sign or other distinguishing mark of the manufacturer or distributor of said product, if any, appearing on said container or distributing device, or adulterates any of said products offered for sale under such distinguishing mark of the manufacturer or distributor of said product or substitutes therefor any other gasoline, lubricating oil, motor fuel or petroleum product, shall be punished by a fine of not more than two hundred dollars or by imprisonment for not more than one year. *Approved May 26, 1933.*

G. L. (Ter. Ed.), 94, new section after § 295.

Sale of gasoline, etc., from pumps, etc., regulated. Penalty.

An Act authorizing the department of correction to acquire an additional water supply for the bridgewater state farm. *Chap.229*

Be it enacted, etc., as follows:

For the purpose of supplying the Bridgewater state farm with pure water for domestic and other purposes, the department of correction, on behalf of the commonwealth, may, with the approval of the governor and council, take by eminent domain under chapter seventy-nine of the General Laws, or acquire by gift, purchase or otherwise, the waters of any pond or stream, or of any ground water sources of supply, by means of driven, artesian or other wells, within the limits of the town of Bridgewater not already appropriated for purposes of a public water supply, and the water rights connected with any such water sources; and may so take, or acquire by gift, purchase or otherwise, and hold, all lands, rights of way and easements necessary for collecting, storing, holding, purifying and preserving the purity of such water and for conveying the same to any part of the lands of the Bridgewater state farm.   For the purposes of this act, the said department of correction may purchase water from the town of Bridgewater, any adjoining municipality, or from any individual or corporation therein, at such price as may be mutually agreed upon by said department and the vendor and approved by the governor and council, and the said municipalities are hereby authorized to sell water to said department.   No source of water supply and no lands necessary for preserving the quality of the water shall be taken or used under this act without first obtaining the advice and approval of the department of public health, and the location of all dams, reservoirs and wells to be used as sources of water supply under this act shall be subject to the approval of said department.   *Approved May 26, 1933.*

---

*Chap.*230   AN ACT AUTHORIZING THE PURCHASE OF ADDITIONAL LAND
FOR THE MOUNT EVERETT STATE RESERVATION.

Be it enacted, etc., as follows:

Subject to appropriation, the Mount Everett reservation commission is hereby authorized to purchase, at the expense of the commonwealth, not exceeding one hundred and fifty-two acres of land owned by Celeste May, located southerly of and adjacent to the Mount Everett state reservation, at a cost not exceeding twelve hundred dollars.

Approved May 26, 1933.

---

*Chap.*231   AN ACT AMENDING THE CHARTER OF THE CITY OF PITTSFIELD.

Be it enacted, etc., as follows:

1932, 280, § 10, amended.

SECTION 1.   Section ten of chapter two hundred and eighty of the acts of nineteen hundred and thirty-two is hereby amended by striking out the first paragraph and inserting in place thereof the following: —

Who may be candidates for municipal office in city of Pittsfield.

Any person who is qualified to vote for a candidate for any elective municipal office and who is a candidate for nomination thereto, shall be entitled to have his name as such candidate printed on the official ballot to be used at a preliminary election; provided, that at least ten days prior to such preliminary election he shall file with the city clerk a statement in writing of his candidacy, and with it the petition of at least fifty voters, qualified to vote for a candidate for the said office, if the nomination is to be made from the voters of a ward, and of at least three hundred voters so qualified if the nomination is to be made at large, whose signatures on said petition are certified as hereinafter provided. Said petition shall be submitted to the registrars of voters on or before five o'clock in the afternoon of the second Wednesday preceding the day on which such preliminary election is to be held, and the registrars shall certify thereon the number of signatures thereon which are names of voters in said city qualified to sign the same. The registrars need not certify a greater number of names than are required to make a nomination, increased by one fifth thereof. Said statement and petition shall be in substantially the following form: —

SECTION 2. Section twenty-six of said chapter two hundred and eighty is hereby amended by striking out the fifth paragraph and inserting in place thereof the following: — 1932, 280, § 26, amended.

The commissioner of public welfare shall perform the duties and have the powers heretofore imposed and conferred upon the superintendent of public welfare and the duties and powers imposed and conferred upon the board of public welfare and such other similar duties as may be prescribed by ordinance. Commissioner of public welfare, powers and duties.

SECTION 3. Said chapter two hundred and eighty is hereby further amended by inserting after section thirty the following new section: — *Section 30A.* The civil service laws shall not apply to the appointment of the mayor's secretaries or of the stenographers, clerks, telephone operators and messengers connected with his office, and the mayor may remove such appointees without a hearing and without making a statement of the cause of their removal. 1932, 280, new section after § 30. Civil service laws not to apply to certain appointees in mayor's office.

SECTION 4. Section thirty-seven of said chapter two hundred and eighty is hereby amended by striking out the third paragraph and inserting in place thereof the following: — 1932, 280, § 37, amended.

Said committee shall annually elect one of its number as chairman to serve in the absence of the mayor, shall annually appoint one of its number to attend the meetings of the city council and shall annually appoint one of its number as secretary, who shall be under its direction and control. Said committee shall elect teachers and a superintendent of schools annually, except as provided by section forty-one of chapter seventy-one of the General Laws, and may dismiss or suspend such teachers and superintendent, subject to section forty-two of said chapter seventy-one. Such superintendent shall not be elected from the membership of said committee. Said committee may, under chapter thirty-one of the General Laws, appoint, suspend or remove such subordinate officers and assistants, including janitors of school buildings, as it may deem necessary for the proper discharge of its duties. The committee shall fix the salaries of such secretary and Chairman of school committee.

Election of superintendent, teachers, etc.

superintendent and may remove such secretary for sufficient cause.

SECTION 5. Section one of this act shall take effect for the nomination and election of municipal officers in the current year and sections two, three and four thereof shall take effect upon the organization of the city government on the first Monday in January, nineteen hundred and thirty-four.   *Approved May 26, 1933.*

---

*Chap.*232 AN ACT ABOLISHING THE COMMISSIONERS OF PUBLIC WORKS IN THE TOWN OF FRAMINGHAM AND VESTING THE POWERS OF SAID COMMISSIONERS IN THE BOARD OF SELECTMEN.

Be it enacted, etc., as follows:

SECTION 1. Chapter seven hundred and one of the acts of nineteen hundred and fourteen is hereby repealed.

SECTION 2. From and after the date when this act becomes fully effective as hereinafter provided, the board of selectmen of the town of Framingham, in addition to any and all powers vested in them on said date, shall be vested with all of the powers and duties heretofore conferred by law upon and exercised by the commissioners of public works, including the powers and duties of water commissioners, sewer committee and highway surveyors. No contracts or liabilities existing at the time of the acceptance of this act shall be affected thereby, but the selectmen shall be the lawful successors of said commissioners of public works in respect to all matters relating to the construction, care and maintenance of highways, bridges, drains and sidewalks, and in all other respects and for all purposes whatsoever.

SECTION 3. This act shall be submitted for acceptance to the legal voters of said town, present and voting thereon, by ballot in their respective precincts at the annual town election in the year nineteen hundred and thirty-four. At such election there shall be placed upon the ballot the following question: — "Shall an Act passed by the General Court in the year nineteen hundred and thirty-three, entitled 'An Act Abolishing the Commissioners of Public Works in the Town of Framingham and vesting the Powers of Said Commissioners in the Board of Selectmen', be accepted?" If a majority of the votes cast in answer to said question are in the affirmative this act shall become fully effective beginning with and for the purposes of the annual town election in the year nineteen hundred and thirty-five; but if the result of such vote is otherwise, this act shall be void.   *Approved May 26, 1933.*

AN ACT RELATIVE TO EXPENDITURES BY THE DEPARTMENT
OF EDUCATION DURING THE CURRENT YEAR IN AIDING
STUDENTS IN STATE TEACHERS COLLEGES.

Be it enacted, etc., as follows:

Subject to appropriation, the department of education
may, during the current year, expend under section five of
chapter seventy-three of the General Laws, as amended by
section fifteen of chapter one hundred and twenty-seven
of the acts of nineteen hundred and thirty-two, not more
than six thousand dollars in aiding students in state teachers
colleges, including the Massachusetts school of art, notwithstanding and in lieu of the limitation of amount of
such expenditures contained in said section five.

Approved May 26, 1933.

AN ACT PROVIDING FOR THE COLLECTION BY THE COM-
MISSIONER OF CORPORATIONS AND TAXATION OF THE
EXCISE PAYABLE TO THE COMMONWEALTH FOR THE
PRIVILEGE OF MANUFACTURING AND SELLING OR IMPORT-
ING AND SELLING WINES AND MALT BEVERAGES.

Whereas, The deferred operation of this act would tend to
defeat its purpose, therefore it is hereby declared to be an
emergency law, necessary for the immediate preservation
of the public convenience.

Emergency preamble.

Be it enacted, etc., as follows:

SECTION 1. Chapter one hundred and twenty of the acts
of the current year is hereby amended by striking out section ten and inserting in place thereof the following: —
Section 10. Every manufacturer of wines or malt beverages
and every holder of a foreign manufacturer's agency license
for the sale thereof shall, in addition to the license fees
elsewhere provided in this act, be liable for and pay to the
commonwealth as an excise, for the privilege enjoyed by
him as such manufacturer or foreign manufacturer's agency,
the sum of one dollar for each and every barrel of thirty-
one gallons of wine or malt beverages sold within the
commonwealth by such manufacturer or foreign manufacturer's agency, respectively, or a proportionate amount
where any other form of container is used. Every person
subject to this section shall keep a true and accurate account of all wines and malt beverages sold by him and shall
make a return thereof to the commissioner of corporations
and taxation, hereinafter called the commissioner, within
ten days after the last day of each month, covering his
sales during such month, and shall at the time of such
return make payment to the commissioner of the amount
due under this section for such sales in such month. The
commissioner is hereby authorized to prescribe rules and
regulations governing the method of keeping accounts,

1933, 120, § 10, amended.

Excise on manufacture, etc., of beer and malt beverages, collection of.

making returns and paying the excise provided for in this section. Such rules and regulations may provide for the waiver of payment of the excise in respect to any wines or malt beverages if it appears that an excise has already been paid under the provisions of this section in respect thereto.

Sums due to the commonwealth under this section may be recovered by the attorney general in an action brought in the name of the commissioner. The commission may suspend the license of a person subject to this section, at the suggestion of the commissioner, for failure to pay such sums when due. The commissioner shall have the same powers and remedies with respect to the collection of said sums as he has with respect to the collection of income taxes under chapter sixty-two of the General Laws.

1933, 120, § 17, amended.

Receipts under act to be used to reimburse cities and towns.

SECTION 2. Said chapter one hundred and twenty is hereby further amended by striking out section seventeen and inserting in place thereof the following: — *Section 17.* All moneys received by the commission and by the commissioner of corporations and taxation under this act shall be paid into the treasury of the commonwealth and, after the expenses of the commission have been paid, used for reimbursing cities and towns for assistance given by them to aged citizens under the provisions of chapter one hundred and eighteen A of the General Laws, in the manner provided by section three of said chapter, and all moneys so received by local licensing authorities shall be paid monthly into the treasuries of their respective cities and towns.

Approved May 31, 1933.

Chap.235 AN ACT RELATIVE TO PURCHASE OF BONDS OF THE BOSTON ELEVATED RAILWAY COMPANY BY THE BOSTON METROPOLITAN DISTRICT.

Whereas, The deferred operation of this act would, in part, defeat its purpose to provide funds to meet certain bonds at maturity, therefore this act is hereby declared to be an emergency law, necessary for the immediate preservation of the public safety and convenience.

Be it enacted, etc., as follows:

SECTION 1. The trustees of the Boston metropolitan district, hereinafter called the district, in the name and on behalf of the district, may from time to time, prior to May first, nineteen hundred and thirty-four, if they deem it in the interest of the district so to do, at the request of the board of trustees of the Boston Elevated Railway Company, purchase bonds of the Boston Elevated Railway Company, hereinafter called the company, hereafter issued or reissued under the authority of section eighteen of chapter three hundred and thirty-three of the acts of nineteen hundred and thirty-one for the purposes of paying or refunding bonds, coupon notes or other evidences of indebtedness of the company payable at periods of more than one year from the date thereof, to an amount not exceeding five. million ninety-eight thousand dollars, and shall, in the case of each such purchase, procure the funds necessary therefor by the issue of notes or bonds of the district under and in the manner provided in section ten of chapter three hundred and eighty-three of the acts of nineteen hundred and twenty-nine and section two of chapter one hundred and forty-seven of the acts of nineteen hundred and thirty-two, and the provisions of said sections shall apply thereto in the same manner and to the same extent as if such notes or bonds of the district were specifically authorized in said chapter three hundred and eighty-three; provided, that any notes or bonds of the district issued under authority of this act shall be for such terms not exceeding three years from the date thereof, and shall bear interest payable semi-annually at such rates, as said trustees of the district, subject to the approval of the department of public utilities, shall from time to time determine.   All amounts received by the district from interest upon each bond issue of the company so purchased shall be applied in payment of interest upon the notes or bonds of the district issued hereunder to provide funds for the purchase of such bond issue of the company; and all amounts received by the district in payment of each such bond issue of the company shall be applied in payment of the principal of the notes or bonds of the district issued hereunder to provide funds for the purchase of such bond issue of the company.

SECTION 2.   Each bond issue of the company so purchased shall be payable not later than three years from the date thereof, and shall bear interest payable semi-annually at the same rate as the notes or bonds of the district issued to provide funds for the purchase of such bond issue of the company.   In the event that said notes or bonds of the district are sold at a discount below par, the bond issue of the company purchased with the proceeds thereof shall be purchased by the district at the same discount below par. Said bonds of the company, both as to income and principal, are hereby made exempt from all taxes levied under authority of the commonwealth while held by the district and shall contain a recital to such effect.   Said bonds of the company shall not be disposed of by the district without authority of the general court.   The proceeds of said bonds of the company shall be used by it only for the purposes hereinbefore set forth.

SECTION 3.   The company shall reimburse the district, at the request of the trustees thereof, for all expenses incidental to the authorization, preparation, issue, registration and payment of interest and principal of the aforesaid notes and bonds of the district. *Approved May 31, 1933.*

Chap.236 AN ACT REQUIRING THE FILING OF ANNUAL RETURNS BY CERTAIN INCORPORATED CLUBS AND OTHER CORPORATIONS.

Emergency preamble.

Whereas, The deferred operation of this act would tend to defeat its purpose, therefore it is hereby declared to be an emergency law, necessary for the immediate preservation of the public convenience.

Be it enacted, etc., as follows:

G. L. (Ter. Ed.), 180, new section after § 26.

Certain incorporated clubs, etc., to file annual returns.

SECTION 1. Chapter one hundred and eighty of the General Laws is hereby amended by inserting after section twenty-six, as appearing in the Tercentenary Edition thereof, the following new section: — *Section 26A.* Every corporation heretofore or hereafter organized under general or special law for any purpose mentioned in section twenty-six shall annually, on or before November first, prepare and submit to the state secretary a certificate which shall be signed and sworn to by its president and treasurer, or its presiding and financial officers having the powers of president and treasurer, and a majority of its directors, or officers having the powers of directors, stating: —

1. The name of the corporation.
2. The location (with street address) of its principal office or headquarters.
3. The date of its last preceding annual meeting.
4. The names and addresses of all the officers and directors, or officers having the powers of directors, of the corporation, and the date at which the term of office of each expires.

The state secretary shall examine such certificate, and if he finds that it conforms to the requirements of this chapter he shall, upon payment of a fee of two dollars, file the same in his office.

Failure by such a corporation for two successive years to submit such a certificate shall be sufficient cause for the revocation of its charter by the state secretary.

This section shall not apply to literary, benevolent, charitable, scientific or religious corporations whose real or personal property is exempt from taxation.

Returns for current year.

SECTION 2. Every corporation subject to the provisions of section one shall prepare and submit the certificate required thereby within four months after the effective date of this act. Failure by such a corporation to comply with this section shall be sufficient cause for the revocation of its charter by the state secretary. The filing of a certificate under this section shall be deemed a compliance with section one for the current year by the corporation filing the same.

Approved May 31, 1933.

AN ACT EXTENDING THE EQUITY JURISDICTION OF THE *Chap.237*
PROBATE COURTS TO THE ENFORCEMENT OF FOREIGN
JUDGMENTS FOR SUPPORT.

Be it enacted, etc., as follows:

SECTION 1. Section six of chapter two hundred and G. L. (Ter.
fifteen of the General Laws, as appearing in the Tercen- Ed.), 215,
                                                          § 6, amended.
tenary Edition thereof, is hereby amended by striking out
the last sentence and inserting in place thereof the following: — They shall also have jurisdiction in equity to enforce foreign judgments for support of a wife or of a wife
and minor children against a husband who is a resident or
inhabitant of this commonwealth, upon petition of the wife
filed in the county of which the husband is a resident or
inhabitant.   Jurisdiction under this section may be exercised upon petition according to the usual procedure in
probate courts, — so as to read as follows: — *Section 6.*
Probate courts shall have jurisdiction in equity, concurrent Equity juris-
                                                              diction of
with the supreme judicial and superior courts, of all cases   probate
and matters relative to the administration of the estates of courts.
deceased persons, to wills, including questions arising under
section twenty of chapter one hundred and ninety-one, to
trusts created by will or other written instrument and, in
cases involving in any way the estate of a deceased person
or the property of any absentee whereof a receiver has been
appointed under chapter two hundred or the property of a
person under guardianship or conservatorship, to trusts
created by parol or constructive or resulting trusts, of all
matters relative to guardianship and conservatorship and
of all other matters of which they now have or may hereafter be given jurisdiction.   They shall also have jurisdiction in equity to enforce foreign judgments for support of a
wife or of a wife and minor children against a husband who
is a resident or inhabitant of this commonwealth, upon
petition of the wife filed in the county of which the husband
is a resident or inhabitant.   Jurisdiction under this section
may be exercised upon petition according to the usual
procedure in probate courts.

SECTION 2.   This act shall take effect upon its passage.
Approved June 6, 1933.

AN ACT AUTHORIZING THE METROPOLITAN DISTRICT COM- *Chap.238*
MISSION TO APPOINT FRED L. JOHNSON AS A PERMANENT
POLICE OFFICER.

Be it enacted, etc., as follows:

SECTION 1.   The metropolitan district commission may,
when a vacancy occurs in its police force or when the personnel of said force is increased or a new position is established therein, appoint as a permanent member of said
police force Fred L. Johnson, who was temporarily injured
in the performance of his duty as a call officer employed

by said commission under chapter ninety-two of the General Laws, and was thereby prevented from retaining his standing on the civil service list for appointment on the police force of the city of Lynn; provided, that a physician selected by said commission certifies to it that he has examined said Johnson and finds him physically fit to serve as such police officer. The time during which said Johnson has served as said call officer shall, upon his appointment hereunder, be deemed a part of his period of service as a permanent officer.

SECTION 2. This act shall take effect upon its passage.
Approved June 6, 1933.

---

*Chap.*239 AN ACT RELATIVE TO THE UNIFORM OF MEMBERS OF THE STATE POLICE.

Emergency preamble.

Whereas, The deferred operation of this act would in part defeat its purposes, therefore,it is hereby declared to be an emergency law, necessary for the immediate preservation of the public safety and convenience.

Be it enacted, etc., as follows:

G. L. (Ter. Ed.), 22, new section after § 9B.

Uniforms for state police.

Chapter twenty-two of the General Laws is hereby amended by inserting after section nine B, as appearing in the Tercentenary Edition thereof, the following new section: — *Section 9C.* The commissioner may prescribe by rules and regulations a standard form or forms of uniform to be worn by members of the division of state police. A uniform or any distinctive part thereof so prescribed shall be worn only by members of said division entitled thereto under said rules and regulations. Violation of this section shall be punished by a fine of not less than ten nor more than one hundred dollars. *Approved June 6, 1933.*

---

*Chap.*240 AN ACT GIVING PREFERENCE TO CERTAIN FORMER EMPLOYEES IN THE LABOR SERVICE OF THE CITY OF NEW BEDFORD FOR RE-EMPLOYMENT THEREIN.

Be it enacted, etc., as follows:

SECTION 1. Thomas A. Sylvia and other former employees in the labor service of the city of New Bedford, who were removed therefrom in the year nineteen hundred and thirty by order of the division of civil service, by reason of the fact that certain classification requirements under the civil service law were not complied with, shall, if duly registered as applicants for employment in the labor service of said city, be given preference for re-employment therein.

SECTION 2. This act shall take effect upon its passage.
Approved June 6, 1933.

AN ACT GIVING PREFERENCE TO JAMES L. BRESNAHAN IN *Chap.*241
THE LABOR SERVICE OF THE CITY OF CAMBRIDGE FOR
RE-EMPLOYMENT THEREIN.

Be it enacted, etc., as follows:

SECTION 1.   James L. Bresnahan, a former employee in
the labor service of the city of Cambridge, who was removed therefrom in the year nineteen hundred and twenty-
eight by order of the division of civil service, by reason of
the fact that certain classification requirements under the
civil service law were not complied with, shall, if duly
registered as an applicant for employment in the labor
service of said city, be given preference for re-employment
therein.

SECTION 2.   This act shall take effect upon its passage.
Approved June 6, 1933.

AN ACT CONFIRMING THE LAYING OUT OF PUBLIC WAYS IN *Chap.*242
THE TOWN AND CITY OF LEOMINSTER.

Be it enacted, etc., as follows:

SECTION 1.   The location and laying out of all highways
and other ways laid out since May twenty-second, nineteen
hundred and fourteen by any municipal authority of the
town and city of Leominster are hereby legalized and
confirmed, notwithstanding any failure to file a copy of
the order of taking or a description and plan of the way for
record in the registry of deeds for the county or district in
which the land lies, as is required by section three of chapter
seventy-nine of the General Laws or other applicable
provisions of law.

SECTION 2.   This act shall take effect upon its passage,
but shall not affect any suit or other proceedings at law now
pending.   *Approved June 6, 1933.*

AN ACT RELATIVE TO ACCUMULATED LIABILITY CONTRIBU- *Chap.*243
TIONS FOR THE BOSTON RETIREMENT SYSTEM.

Be it enacted, etc., as follows:

SECTION 1.   Section six of chapter five hundred and
twenty-one of the acts of nineteen hundred and twenty-two,
as amended by section one of chapter two hundred and
fifty-one of the acts of nineteen hundred and twenty-four,
is hereby further amended by striking out the fifth paragraph and inserting in place thereof the following: —

On and after January first, nineteen hundred and thirty-
three, the accumulated liability contribution shall be
computed as a constant percentage of the total pay roll of
all members and shall be sufficient to provide during the
thirty year period immediately following the year nineteen
hundred and thirty-two for all pensions to be paid on
account of members who are entitled to credit for prior

service which are not provided by the normal contributions made on their account, and the funds in hand on the thirty-first day of December, nineteen hundred and thirty-two, which have been accumulated on their account. The accumulated liability contributions shall be at least equal to regular interest on the amount of the accumulated liability and shall be at least three per cent greater in amount each year than the amount for the preceding year. After the year nineteen hundred and thirty-six, the accumulated liability contributions shall be at least equal to regular interest on the accumulated liability plus one per centum of the accumulated liability as it existed on the thirty-first day of December, nineteen hundred and thirty-two. The accumulated liability contributions shall be discontinued as soon as the accumulated liability has been liquidated.

SECTION 2.   This act shall take effect upon its passage.
Approved June 6, 1933.

*Chap.*244 AN ACT REQUIRING THE ISSUE OF ORDERS OF NOTICE TO RESPONDENTS IN PETITIONS TO VACATE JUDGMENT.

Be it enacted, etc., as follows:

G. L. (Ter. Ed.), 250, § 16, amended.
SECTION 1.   Section sixteen of chapter two hundred and fifty of the General Laws, as appearing in the Tercentenary Edition thereof, is hereby amended by striking out, in the first line, the words "may thereupon" and inserting in place thereof the words: — , before vacating a judgment on such a petition, shall, — so as to read as follows: —

Vacating judgment. Order of notice and supersedeas.
Section 16.   The court, before vacating a judgment on such a petition, shall order notice thereof returnable at such time and to be served in such manner as it may direct, and may issue a stay or supersedeas of an execution issued on such judgment and an order for a return thereof with a certificate of the proceedings thereon. Upon the hearing of such petition, the court may vacate such judgment, and dispose of the case as if the judgment had not been entered.

When operative.
SECTION 2.   This act shall become operative September first in the current year.   *Approved June 6, 1933.*

*Chap.*245 AN ACT PROVIDING FOR THE APPLICATION OF CERTAIN LAWS AFFECTING VETERANS AND THEIR ORGANIZATIONS TO THE DISABLED AMERICAN VETERANS OF THE WORLD WAR.

Be it enacted, etc., as follows:

G. L. (Ter. Ed.), 5, § 9, amended.
SECTION 1.   Section nine of chapter five of the General Laws, as appearing in the Tercentenary Edition thereof, is hereby amended by inserting after the word "Legion" in the fourth line the words: — , Disabled American Veterans of the World War, — and by inserting after the word "Legion" in the seventeenth line the words: — , one copy of the volume relating to the Disabled American Veterans of the World War to each chapter of the Disabled American

Veterans of the World War, — so as to read as follows: —
Section 9. The state secretary shall annually procure copies of the proceedings of the annual encampments of the departments of Massachusetts, Grand Army of the Republic, United Spanish War Veterans, The American Legion, Disabled American Veterans of the World War and Veterans of Foreign Wars of the United States, held in that year, with the general and special orders, circulars and other papers forming parts thereof, and shall cause the same to be kept as parts of the records of the commonwealth. He shall annually cause copies thereof, including in the case of those relating to the Grand Army of the Republic the portraits of the department officers and staff and of the executive committee of the national encampment, to be printed and bound; and shall cause one printed and bound copy of each to be sent to each town library in the commonwealth. He shall also send one copy of each volume relating to the Grand Army of the Republic to each Grand Army post, one copy of the volume relating to the United Spanish War Veterans to each camp of Spanish War Veterans, one copy of the volume relating to The American Legion to each post of The American Legion, one copy of the volume relating to the Disabled American Veterans of the World War to each chapter of the Disabled American Veterans of the World War, and one copy of the volume relating to the Veterans of Foreign Wars to each post of the Veterans of Foreign Wars of the United States, in the commonwealth. He shall cause the other copies of each to be distributed in the same manner as the annual report of the state secretary.

Preservation, etc., of copies of proceedings of Massachusetts department of Disabled American Veterans of the World War and of other war veterans' organizations.

SECTION 2. Clause (12) of section five of chapter forty of the General Laws, as most recently amended by section two of chapter one hundred and fifty-three of the acts of the current year, is hereby further amended by inserting after the word "States" in the twentieth line the words: — , under the auspices of the local chapters of the Disabled American Veterans of the World War, — so as to read as follows: — (12) For erecting headstones or other monuments at the graves of persons who served in the war of the revolution, the war of eighteen hundred and twelve, the Seminole war, the Mexican war, the war of the rebellion or the Indian wars or who served in the military or naval service of the United States in the Spanish American war or in the World war; for acquiring land by purchase or by eminent domain under chapter seventy-nine, purchasing, erecting, equipping or dedicating buildings, or constructing or dedicating other suitable memorials, for the purpose of properly commemorating the services and sacrifices of persons who served as aforesaid; for the decoration of the graves, monuments or other memorials of soldiers, sailors and marines who served in the army, navy or marine corps of the United States in time of war or insurrection and the proper observance of Memorial Day and other patriotic

G. L. (Ter. Ed.), 40, § 5, etc., amended.

Towns, etc., may appropriate money for veterans' monuments, etc.

holidays under the auspices of the local posts of the Grand Army of the Republic, United Spanish War Veterans, The American Legion, the Veterans of Foreign Wars of the United States and the Jewish War Veterans of the United States, under the auspices of the local chapters of the Disabled American Veterans of the World War and under the auspices of the Kearsarge Association of Naval Veterans, Inc. and of local garrisons of the Army and Navy Union of the United States of America and of local chapters of the Massachusetts Society of the Sons of the American Revolution and of local detachments of the Marine Corps League, and of a local camp of the Sons of Union Veterans of the Civil War or a local tent of The Daughters of Union Veterans of the Civil War in the case of a town in which there is no post of the Grand Army of the Republic; or for keeping in repair graves, monuments or other memorials erected to the memory of such persons or of its firemen and policemen who died from injuries received in the performance of their duties in the fire or police service or for decorating the graves of such firemen and policemen or for other memorial observances in their honor. Money appropriated in honor of such firemen may be paid over to, and expended for such purposes by, any veteran firemen's association or similar organization.

G. L. (Ter. Ed.), 40, § 9, amended.

SECTION 3. Section nine of chapter forty of the General Laws, as appearing in the Tercentenary Edition thereof, is hereby amended by inserting after the word "States" in the third line the words: — and for a chapter or chapters of the Disabled American Veterans of the World War, — and by inserting after the word "posts" in the fifth line, the words: — , or chapter or chapters, — so as to read as follows: — *Section 9.* A city or town may for the purpose of

Towns, etc., may lease parts of armories for war veterans' posts.

providing suitable headquarters for a post or posts of The American Legion and of the Veterans of Foreign Wars of the United States and for a chapter or chapters of the Disabled American Veterans of the World War, lease for a period not exceeding five years buildings or parts of buildings which shall be under the direction and control of such post or posts, or chapter or chapters, subject to regulations made in cities by the mayor with the approval of the council and in towns by vote of the town, and for said purposes a town with a valuation of less than five million dollars may annually appropriate not more than one thousand dollars; a town with a valuation of five million dollars but not more than twenty million dollars may annually appropriate not more than fifteen hundred dollars; a town with a valuation of twenty million dollars but not more than seventy-five million dollars may annually appropriate not more than two thousand dollars; a town with a valuation of seventy-five million dollars but not more than one hundred fifty million dollars may annually appropriate not more than twenty-five hundred dollars; and a town with a valuation of one hundred fifty million dollars or more may annually appropriate twenty-five hundred dollars for each one hundred fifty million dollars of valuation, or fraction thereof. The city council of a city may, by a two thirds vote, appropriate money for armories for the use of the state militia, for the celebration of holidays, for the purpose of providing or defraying the expenses of suitable quarters for posts of the Grand Army of the Republic, including the heating and lighting of such quarters, and for other like public purposes to an amount not exceeding in any one year one fiftieth of one per cent of its valuation for such year.

SECTION 4. Section seventy of chapter two hundred and sixty-six of the General Laws, as appearing in the Tercentenary Edition thereof, is hereby amended by inserting after the word "States" in the eighth line the words: —, the Disabled American Veterans of the World War, — so as to read as follows: — *Section 70.* Whoever, not being a member of the Military Order of the Loyal Legion of the United States, the Grand Army of the Republic, the Sons of Veterans, the Woman's Relief Corps, the Union Veterans' Union, the Union Veteran Legion, the Military and Naval Order of the Spanish-American War, the United Spanish War Veterans, the American Officers of the Great War, the Veterans of Foreign Wars of the United States, the Military Order of Foreign Wars of the United States, the Disabled American Veterans of the World War or the American Legion, wilfully wears or uses the insignia, distinctive ribbons or membership rosette or button thereof for the purpose of representing that he is a member thereof shall be punished by a fine of not more than twenty dollars or by imprisonment for not more than one month, or both.

Approved June 6, 1933.

G. L. (Ter. Ed.), 266, § 70, amended.

Penalty for unlawful use of insignia of war veterans' organizations.

AN ACT RELATIVE TO THE WAIVER OF JURY TRIALS IN CERTAIN CRIMINAL CASES INVOLVING DEFENDANTS PROSECUTED UNDER SEPARATE INDICTMENTS OR COMPLAINTS.

*Chap.*246

Be it enacted, etc., as follows:

SECTION 1. Section six of chapter two hundred and sixty-three of the General Laws, as appearing in the Tercentenary Edition thereof, is hereby amended by striking out the comma after the word "more" in the thirteenth line and inserting in place thereof the words: — charged with offenses growing out of the same single chain of circumstances or events whether prosecuted under the same or different indictments or complaints, — so as to read as follows: — *Section 6.* A person indicted for a crime shall not be convicted thereof except by confessing his guilt in open court, by admitting the truth of the charge against him by his plea or demurrer or by the verdict of a jury accepted and recorded by the court or, in any criminal case other than a capital case, by judgment of the court rendered as hereinafter provided. Any defendant in the

G. L. (Ter. Ed.), 263, § 6, amended.

Waiver of right to trial by jury in certain criminal cases.

superior court in a criminal case other than a capital case, whether begun by indictment or upon complaint, may, if he shall so elect, when called upon to plead, or later and before a jury has been impanelled to try him upon such indictment or complaint, waive his right to trial by jury by signing a written waiver thereof and filing the same with the clerk of the court, whereupon he shall be tried by the court instead of by a jury, but not, however, unless all the defendants, if there are two or more charged with offenses growing out of the same single chain of circumstances or events whether prosecuted under the same or different indictments or complaints shall have exercised such election before a jury has been impanelled to try any of the defendants; and in every such case the court shall have jurisdiction to hear and try such cause and render judgment and sentence thereon.

Effective date. SECTION 2. This act shall become effective on October first of the current year. *Approved June 6, 1933.*

---

*Chap.*247 AN ACT RELATIVE TO THE JOINT TRIAL IN THE SUPERIOR COURT OF ACTIONS INVOLVING THE SAME SUBJECT MATTER.

Be it enacted, etc., as follows:

G. L. (Ter. Ed.), 231, new section after § 84.

Pleading and practice. Joint trial of actions in superior court.

SECTION 1. Chapter two hundred and thirty-one of the General Laws is hereby amended by inserting after section eighty-four, as appearing in the Tercentenary Edition thereof, the following new section: — *Section 84A.* If two or more actions to recover damages or indebtedness arising out of the same accident, event or transaction are pending in the superior court, whether in the same or in different counties, the court or any justice thereof may order that some or all of them be tried together in such county as he may designate. This section shall not limit existing powers of the courts or justices thereof relative to the consolidation or joint trial of causes.

Effective date. SECTION 2. This act shall take effect on October first in the current year. *Approved June 6, 1933.*

---

*Chap.*248 AN ACT RELATIVE TO THE TIME OF TAKING EFFECT OF CERTAIN VOTES PASSED AT REPRESENTATIVE TOWN MEETINGS IN THE TOWN OF SAUGUS FOR THE PURPOSES OF REFERENDUM.

Be it enacted, etc., as follows:

Section eight of chapter fifty-five of the acts of nineteen hundred and twenty-eight is hereby amended by striking out, in the fifth, sixth and twenty-ninth lines, the word "five" and inserting in place thereof, in each instance, the word: — ten, — and by striking out, in the sixth line, the words "dissolution of the meeting" and inserting in place thereof the words: — close of the session of the meeting at which said vote was passed, — so as to read as follows: — *Section 8.* No vote, except a vote to adjourn or authorizing the borrowing of money in anticipation of the receipt of taxes for the current year, passed at any representative town meeting shall be operative until after the expiration of ten days, exclusive of Sundays and holidays, from the close of the session of the meeting at which said vote was passed. If within said ten days, a petition, signed by not less than three hundred registered voters of the town, containing their names and addresses as they appear on the list of registered voters, is filed with the selectmen asking that the question or questions involved in such vote be submitted to the registered voters of the town at large, then the selectmen, after the expiration of five days, shall forthwith call a special meeting for the sole purpose of presenting to the registered voters at large the question or questions so involved. The polls shall be opened at twelve o'clock noon and shall be closed not earlier than eight o'clock in the evening and all votes upon any questions so submitted shall be taken by ballot, and the check list shall be used in the several precinct meetings in the same manner as in the election of town officers. The questions so submitted shall be determined by vote of the same proportion of voters at large voting thereon as would have been required by law of the town meeting members had the question been finally determined at a representative town meeting. The questions so submitted shall be stated upon the ballot in substantially the same language and form in which they were stated when presented to said representative town meeting by the moderator, and as appears from the records of said meeting. If such petition is not filed within the said period of ten days, the vote of the representative town meeting shall become operative and effective upon the expiration of said period.

Approved June 6, 1933.

AN ACT SUBJECTING THE OFFICE OF COMMISSIONER OF SOLDIERS' RELIEF AND STATE AND MILITARY AID OF THE CITY OF SOMERVILLE TO THE CIVIL SERVICE LAWS.

*Chap.*249

Be it enacted, etc., as follows:

SECTION 1. The office of commissioner of soldiers' relief and state and military aid of the city of Somerville shall, upon the effective date of this act, become subject to the civil service laws and rules and regulations, and the term of office of any incumbent thereof shall be unlimited, except that he may be removed in accordance with such laws and rules and regulations, but the person holding said office on said effective date may continue therein without taking a civil service examination.

SECTION 2. This act shall take effect upon its acceptance during the current year by vote of the board of aldermen of said city, subject to the provisions of its charter.

Approved June 6, 1933.

*Chap.*250 An Act authorizing the town of clinton to refund certain taxes erroneously assessed upon and collected from james w. and margaret casson.

Be it enacted, etc., as follows:

The town of Clinton is hereby authorized to refund to James W. and Margaret Casson of said Clinton, the sum of one hundred and ninety-four dollars and forty-six cents, the same being the amount which has heretofore been collected by said town from said Cassons as taxes upon certain real estate in said town, which through mistake was erroneously assumed by the assessors of said town to have been the property of said Cassons.

Approved June 6, 1933.

*Chap.*251 An Act relative to the procedure required for the placing underground of certain transmission lines.

Emergency preamble.

Whereas, The deferred operation of this act would tend to defeat its purpose, therefore it is hereby declared to be an emergency law, necessary for the immediate preservation of the public convenience.

Be it enacted, etc., as follows:

G. L. (Ter. Ed.), 166, § 22A, amended.

Procedure relative to the placing underground of transmission lines.

Chapter one hundred and sixty-six of the General Laws is hereby amended by striking out section twenty-two A, inserted by chapter two hundred and sixty-six of the acts of nineteen hundred and thirty-two, and inserting in place thereof the following: — *Section 22A.* Whenever in a city or town the officer or board duly authorized to grant locations for underground conduits proposes, under authority of special law or in pursuance of an agreement between the owner of overhead lines used for the transmission of electricity or intelligence and the city or town, to order or give permission for the removal and placing underground of such lines, such officer or board shall hold a public hearing on such proposal after notice as provided in the first paragraph of section twenty-two. Within ten days after such hearing such officer or board shall file his or its decision with the city or town clerk. Any owner of real estate abutting upon that part of the way under which the lines are to be placed, or any owner of such lines, aggrieved by such decision may, within thirty days after its filing as aforesaid, appeal therefrom to the department of public utilities and the department, after notice and hearing of all parties interested, may by order, which shall be final, affirm, modify or annul such decision.   *Approved June 10, 1933.*

An Act relative to the taking of clams and other shellfish at wollaston beach in the city of quincy. *Chap.252*

Be it enacted, etc., as follows:

No permit or other authorization from the metropolitan district commission shall be required for taking clams or other shellfish during the months of November, December, January, February and March from any part of the flats within the Quincy Shore reservation under the control of said commission in the city of Quincy which is not then declared by the department of public health to be a contaminated area.   *Approved June 10, 1933.*

An Act increasing the powers of the commissioner of agriculture in the enforcement of certain laws concerning the protection and sale of milk. *Chap.253*

Be it enacted, etc., as follows:

Chapter ninety-four of the General Laws is hereby amended by striking out sections twenty-nine A, thirty and thirty-one, as appearing in the Tercentenary Edition thereof, and inserting in place thereof the following sections: — *Section 29A.* The director shall, after reasonable notice and a hearing, and with the approval of the governor and council, prescribe, and may from time to time in like manner modify or amend, rules and regulations to govern the methods and frequency of making tests for determining the composition or milk-fat content of milk or cream as a basis for payment in buying or selling. The director or the commissioner of agriculture, their inspectors and deputies, may enter upon premises where tests of milk or cream are made to determine whether rules and regulations made hereunder are being observed. G. L. (Ter. Ed.), 94, §§ 29A, 30 and 31, amended. Milk-fat content of milk or cream; rules, etc., governing tests for determining.

Section 30. The director shall enforce sections twenty-five to thirty-one, inclusive, and the rules and regulations made thereunder, and may prosecute or cause to be prosecuted any person violating any provision of said sections or of said rules and regulations, and the commissioner of agriculture or his designated assistant shall have concurrent authority with the director in prosecuting or causing to be prosecuted any person violating any provision of the rules and regulations established under section twenty-nine A. Sections twenty-five to thirty, inclusive, and the rules and regulations made thereunder, shall not affect any person using any centrifugal or other machine or test to determine the composition or milk-fat content of milk or cream if such use or test is made for the information of such person only, and not for purposes of inspection or as a basis for payment in buying or selling. Commissioner of agriculture, assistant and director of Massachusetts agricultural experiment station to enforce certain sections.

Section 31. Whoever hinders or obstructs the director or the commissioner of agriculture, or any inspector or Penalty for interfering with commis-

sioner, etc., and
for violation of
certain
sections.

deputy of either said director or said commissioner, in the discharge of any authority or duty imposed upon him by any provision of sections twenty-five to thirty, inclusive, whoever violates any provision of said sections, and whoever knowingly violates any provision of the rules and regulations made thereunder, shall be punished by a fine of not less than fifteen nor more than fifty dollars.

Approved June 10, 1933.

*Chap.*254 AN ACT RELATIVE TO THE DATE OF ASSESSMENT OF TAXES, TO THE PAYMENT THEREOF AND TO THE LISTING OF RESIDENTS.

Be it enacted, etc., as follows:

G. L. (Ter.
Ed.), 33, § 6,
amended.

Assessors'
report of
persons
liable to en-
rolment in
military
service.

SECTION 1. Chapter thirty-three of the General Laws is hereby amended by striking out section six, as appearing in the Tercentenary Edition thereof, and inserting in place thereof the following: — *Section 6.* Assessors shall annually, in January, February or March, make a report of the number of persons living within their respective limits liable to enrolment, and shall place a certified copy thereof in the hands of the clerks of their respective towns, who shall place it on file with the records of such town, and annually, in March, April or May, transmit reports of the number of such persons to the adjutant general.

G. L. (Ter.
Ed.), 40, § 17,
amended.

Assessments
for street
sprinkling.

SECTION 2. Section seventeen of chapter forty of the General Laws, as so appearing, is hereby amended by striking out, in the twelfth line, the word "April" and inserting in place thereof the word: — January, — so as to read as follows: — *Section 17.* If a city determines that the public ways or any portion thereof shall be sprinkled in whole or in part at the expense of the abutters, such expense for a municipal year, and the proportion thereof to be borne by abutters, and the rate to be assessed upon each linear foot of frontage upon such ways, shall be estimated and determined by the board of aldermen and assessed upon the estates abutting on such ways in proportion to the number of linear feet of each estate upon such ways or portion thereof sprinkled. The amount of such assessments upon each estate shall be determined by said board, or, if said board so designates, by the board of public works, board of street commissioners, superintendent of streets or other officer; and such board or officer shall, as soon as may be after the first day of January, cause a list of such ways or portions thereof to be made, specifying each estate and the number of linear feet thereof abutting thereon, the amount per linear foot, and the amount on each estate of such assessment, and certify and commit said list to the assessors of taxes. In a town such assessment shall be made by the assessors.

G. L. (Ter.
Ed.), 51, § 2,
amended.

SECTION 3. Section two of chapter fifty-one of the General Laws, as so appearing, is hereby amended by striking out, in the third line, the word "April" and insert-

ing in place thereof the word: — January, — so as to read
as follows: — *Section 2.* If the name of a female who is
duly registered as a voter is changed by marriage or by
decree of court, her right to vote in her former name shall
continue until January first next following.

Vote by woman whose name has been changed.

SECTION 4. Section three of said chapter fifty-one, as
so appearing, is hereby amended by striking out, in the
third and fourth lines, the word "April" and inserting in
place thereof, in each instance, the word: — January, —
so as to read as follows: — *Section 3.* A person qualified
to vote in a city or town divided into wards or voting precincts shall be registered and may vote in the ward or voting
precinct in which he resided on January first preceding the
election, or, if he became an inhabitant of such city or town
after said January first, in the ward or voting precinct in
which he first became a resident.

G. L. (Ter. Ed.), 51, § 3, amended.

Place of registration and voting.

SECTION 5. Section four of said chapter fifty-one, as so
appearing, is hereby amended by striking out, in the second
and third lines, the words "April or May" and inserting in
place thereof the words: — January, February or March, —
and by striking out, in the fifth, sixth and twenty-first
lines, the word "April" and inserting in place thereof, in
each instance, the word: — January, — so as to read as
follows: — *Section 4.* Except as otherwise provided by
law, the assessors, assistant assessors, or one or more of
them, shall annually, in January, February or March, visit
every building in their respective cities and towns and, after
diligent inquiry, shall make true lists containing, as nearly
as they can ascertain, the name, age, occupation, and residence on January first in the current year, and the residence
on January first in the preceding year, of every male person
twenty years of age or older, residing in their respective
cities and towns, liable to be assessed for a poll tax, and of
soldiers and sailors exempted from the payment of a poll
tax under section five of chapter fifty-nine; and, except in
cities and towns having listing boards, shall also make true
lists containing the same facts relative to every woman
twenty years of age or older residing in their respective
cities and towns.

G. L. (Ter. Ed.), 51, § 4, amended.

Assessors to make lists of persons liable to a poll tax and of women voters.

Any inmate of the soldiers' home in Chelsea shall have
the same right as any other resident of that city to be
assessed and to vote therein.

The assessors shall, upon the personal application of an
assessed or listed person for the correction of any error in
their original lists, and whenever informed of any such
error, make due investigation, and, upon proof thereof,
correct the same on their books. When informed of the
omission of the name of a person who is averred to have
lived in the city or town on January first in the current
year, and to have been assessed, or listed as provided in
this section, there in the preceding year, they shall make
due investigation, and, upon proof thereof, add the name
to their books, and, except in cities and towns having

listing boards, give immediate notice thereof to the registrars of voters. They shall preserve for two years all applications, certificates and affidavits received by them under this section.

G. L. (Ter. Ed.), 51, § 7, amended.

SECTION 6. Section seven of said chapter fifty-one, as so appearing, is hereby amended by striking out, in the seventh and eighth lines, the word "April" and inserting in place thereof, in each instance, the word: — January, —

Form and contents of street lists.

so as to read as follows: — *Section 7.* Except in cities and towns having listing boards, the assessors shall name or designate in such street lists all buildings used as residences, in their order on the street where they are located, by giving the number or other definite description of each building so that it can be readily identified, and shall place opposite to or under each number or other description of a building the name, age and occupation of every person residing therein on January first of the current year who is listed under section four, and his residence on January first of the preceding year.

G. L. (Ter. Ed.,) 51, § 8, amended.

SECTION 7. Section eight of said chapter fifty-one, as so appearing, is hereby amended by striking out, in the second line, the word "April" and inserting in place thereof the word: — January, — so as to read as follows: — *Section 8.* If a male resident in a city or town, except in one having

Assessment of persons not previously assessed.

a listing board, on January first was not assessed for a poll tax, or if an exempted soldier or sailor or a woman in such a city or town was not listed under section four, such person shall, in order to establish his right to be assessed or listed, present to the assessors before the close of registration a sworn statement that he was on said day a resident of such city or town, and a sworn list of his polls and estate. If the assessors are satisfied that such statement is true, they shall assess or list him, as the case may be, and give him a certificate thereof.

G. L. (Ter. Ed.), 51, § 9, amended.

SECTION 8. Section nine of said chapter fifty-one, as so appearing, is hereby amended by striking out, in the second and eighth lines, the word "April" and inserting in place thereof, in each instance, the word: — January, — so as to

Certain persons desiring to be registered to present statement to assessors, etc.

read as follows: — *Section 9.* A person who becomes a resident of a city or town, except one having a listing board, after January first and desires to be registered as a voter shall present to the assessors a sworn statement that he became a resident therein at least six months preceding the election at which he claims the right to vote. If the assessors are satisfied that such statement is true, they shall give him a certificate that he became a resident therein as aforesaid, and shall forthwith notify the registrars of voters of the city or town, if in the commonwealth, where such person resided on January first, that they have given such certificate.

G. L. (Ter. Ed.), 51, new section after § 14A.

SECTION 9. Said chapter fifty-one, as so appearing, is hereby further amended by inserting after section fourteen A the following new section: — *Section 14B.* In

cities and towns in which the listing of residents for the
purposes of determining their liability to be assessed a poll
tax and of determining their right to vote is governed by
special law, and in cities and towns which have accepted
section fourteen A, the provisions of this chapter relative to
assessors and assistant assessors shall apply to the officers
performing like duties in such cities and towns. In case
any such provision of this chapter contains a date for the
performance of an official act by a board of assessors,
assessor or assistant assessor, which act by special law is to
be performed in any city or town by a listing board or by
an officer other than an assessor or assistant assessor, the
date for the performance of such act fixed by this chapter
shall prevail over the date fixed therefor by such special law,
in case of difference. Where, in any special law, April first
is stated as the date as of which the legal residence of any
person shall be determined, such residence shall be determined as of January first instead of April first.

Inconsistent provisions of special laws superseded.

SECTION 10. Section thirty-two of said chapter fifty-
one, as so appearing, is hereby amended by striking out,
in the sixth line, the word "March" and inserting in place
thereof the word: — December, — so as to read as follows:
— *Section 32.* Registrars shall seasonably post or publish
notices stating the places and hours for holding all sessions,
including the final sessions preceding any election, and also
stating that after ten o'clock in the evening of the last day
fixed for registration they will not, until after the next election, add any name to the registers except the names of
voters examined as to their qualifications between the
December thirty-first preceding and the close of registration.

G. L. (Ter. Ed.), 51, § 32, amended.

Notices of sessions for registration, etc.

SECTION 11. Section thirty-four of said chapter fifty-
one, as so appearing, is hereby amended by striking out, in
the ninth line the word "March" and inserting in place
thereof the word: — December, — so as to read as follows:
—*Section 34.* After ten o'clock in the evening of a day on
which registration is to cease, the registrars shall not register any person as a voter until after the next primary or
election, except that they shall furnish, or cause to be
furnished, to each person waiting in line at said hour of
ten o'clock for the purpose of being registered a card or slip
of identification bearing such person's name and shall, before registration ceases, register such person if found
qualified. The registrars may, however, enter or correct
on the registers the names of persons whose qualifications
as voters have been examined between December thirty-
first preceding and the close of registration.

G. L. (Ter. Ed.), 51, § 34, amended.

Not to enter names on registers after close of regis- tration, except, etc.

SECTION 12. Section thirty-six of said chapter fifty-one,
as so appearing, is hereby amended by striking out, in the
sixth line, and in the form set forth at the end of said section,
the word "April" and inserting in place thereof, in each
instance, the word: — January, — so as to read as follows:
— *Section 36.* They shall keep in general registers, records
of all persons registered as qualified to vote in the city or

G. L. (Ter. Ed.), 51, § 36, amended.

Records to be kept in general register.

town. They shall enter therein the name of every such voter written in full, or instead thereof the surname and first Christian name or that name by which he is generally known, written in full, and the initial of every other name which he may have, and also his age, place of birth and residence on January first preceding or at the time of becoming an inhabitant of the city or town after said day, the date of his registration and his residence at such date, his occupation and the place thereof, the name and location of the court which has issued to him letters of naturalization and the date thereof, if he is a naturalized citizen, and any other particulars necessary to identify him fully. Except in Boston, the general registers shall have uniform headings in substantially the following form, and blank books suitable for the purpose shall be provided at cost by the state secretary to registrars applying therefor:

When Registered.	Name.	Signature of Applicant.	Residence January 1, or Subsequent Date.	Age.	Place of Birth.	Occupation.	Place of Occupation.	Minutes of Naturalization, Court issuing Letters and Date of Naturalization.	Residence at Date of Registration.	Remarks.

G. L. (Ter. Ed.), 51, § 37, amended.

SECTION 13. Section thirty-seven of said chapter fifty-one, as so appearing, is hereby amended by striking out, in the third line, the words "said day" and inserting in place thereof the words: — January first, — and by striking out, in the fifth and eleventh lines, the word "April" and inserting in place thereof, in each instance, the word: —

Annual register, entries, arrangement, etc. Exception.

January, — so as to read as follows: — *Section 37.* The registrars, after April first, shall prepare an annual register containing the names of all qualified voters in their city or town for the current year, beginning with January first. Such names shall be arranged in alphabetical order, and, opposite to the name of each voter, his residence on January first preceding or on any subsequent day when he became an inhabitant of the city or town. The registrars shall enter in the annual register every name contained in the lists transmitted to them by the assessors under section five, which they can identify as that of a person whose name was borne on the voting list of the city or town at the last preceding election or town meeting, giving the residence of each such person on January first, which, in the case of a person assessed a poll tax, shall be the place at which he was so assessed. They shall make all inquiries and investigations necessary to identify such person, and they shall not enter in the annual register the name of a person objected to by any registrar until such person has been duly notified and given an opportunity to be heard. They shall forthwith enter in the annual register the name of every person whose qualifications as a voter have been determined by them in the current year and whose name has accordingly been entered in the general register. They shall, on or before the first Monday of August in each year, send notice in writing to each voter of the preceding year whose name has not been entered in the annual register of the current year that the name of such voter has not been so entered, such notice to be sent by first class mail enclosed in an envelope bearing the proper address to which the same may be returned in case of non-delivery, and the registrars shall prepare a list of the names of voters not so entered, which shall be open to public inspection in their principal office, or shall be posted by copy in the places where copies of voting lists are required to be posted under section fifty-seven of chapter fifty-one. This section shall not apply to cities and towns having listing boards.

SECTION 14. Section forty-three of said chapter fifty-one, as so appearing, is hereby amended by striking out, in the fifth line, the word "April" and inserting in place thereof the word: — January, — so as to read as follows: — *Section 43.* Every male applicant for registration, except in cities and towns having listing boards, whose name has not been transmitted to the registrars as provided in section five, shall present a tax bill or notice from the collector of taxes, or a certificate from the assessors showing that he was assessed as a resident of the city or town on January first preceding, or a certificate that he became a resident therein at least six months preceding the election at which he claims the right to vote, and the same shall be prima facie evidence of his residence.

G. L. (Ter. Ed.), 51, § 43, amended.

Male applicant to present tax bill or certificate.

SECTION 15. Section fifty-five of said chapter fifty-one, as so appearing, is hereby amended by striking out, in the fourth line, the word "April" and inserting in place thereof the word: — January, — so as to read as follows: — *Section 55.* Registrars shall, from the names entered in the annual register of voters, prepare voting lists for use at elections. In such voting lists they shall place the names of all voters entered on the annual register, and no others, and opposite to the name of each his residence on January first preceding or at the time of his becoming an inhabitant of such place after said day. They may enter the names of women voters in separate columns or lists. In cities, they shall prepare such voting lists by wards, and if a ward or a town is divided into voting precincts, they shall prepare the same by precincts, in alphabetical order, or by streets. Names shall be added thereto or taken therefrom as persons are found to be qualified or not qualified to vote.

G. L. (Ter. Ed.), 51, § 55, amended.

Voting lists, contents, arrangement, etc.

SECTION 16. Section seven of chapter fifty-three of the General Laws, as so appearing, is hereby amended by strik-

G. L. (Ter. Ed.), 53, § 7, amended.

Nomination
papers, form,
qualifications
of signers.

ing out, in the second line, the word "April" and inserting in place thereof the word: — January, — so as to read as follows: — *Section 7.* Every voter signing a nomination paper shall sign in person, with his name as registered, and shall state his residence on January first preceding, and the place where he is then living, with the street and number, if any; but any voter who is prevented by physical disability from writing or who had the right to vote on May first, eighteen hundred and fifty-seven, may authorize some person to write his name and residence in his presence; and every voter may sign as many nomination papers for each office as there are persons to be elected thereto, and no more. Every nomination paper of a candidate for a state office and, except where otherwise provided by law, of a candidate for a city or town office shall be submitted, on or before five o'clock in the afternoon of the Friday preceding the day on which it must be filed, to the registrars of the city or town where the signers appear to be voters. In each case the registrars shall check each name to be certified by them on the nomination paper and shall forthwith certify thereon the number of signatures so checked which are names of voters both in the city or town and in the district or division for which the nomination is made, and only names so checked shall be deemed to be names of qualified voters for the purposes of nomination. The registrars need not certify a greater number of names than are required to make a nomination, increased by one fifth thereof. Names not certified in the first instance shall not thereafter be certified on the same nomination papers. The state secretary shall not be required to receive nomination papers for a candidate after receiving such papers containing a sufficient number of certified names to make a nomination, increased by one fifth thereof.

G. L. (Ter.
Ed.), 54,
§ 135,
amended.

SECTION 17. Section one hundred and thirty-five of chapter fifty-four of the General Laws, as so appearing, is hereby amended by striking out, in the fifth line, the word "April" and inserting in place thereof the word: — January, — so that the first paragraph of said section will read as follows: —

Local or state-
wide recount,
how and by
whom con-
ducted, notice
of result,
etc.

If, on or before five o'clock in the afternoon on the third day following an election in a ward of a city or in a town, ten or more voters of such ward or town, except Boston, and in Boston fifty or more voters of a ward, shall sign in person, adding thereto their respective residences on the preceding January first, and cause to be filed with the city or town clerk a statement sworn to by one of the subscribers that they have reason to believe and do believe that the records, or copies of records, made by the election officers of certain precincts in such ward or town, or in case of a town not voting by precincts, by the election officers of such town, are erroneous, specifying wherein they deem them to be in error and that they believe a recount of the ballots cast in such precincts or town will

affect the election of one or more candidates voted for at
such election, specifying the candidates, or will affect the
decision of a question voted upon at such election, specifying the question, the city or town clerk shall forthwith
transmit such statement and the envelope containing the
ballots, sealed, to the registrars of voters, who shall, without unnecessary delay, but not before the last hour for
filing requests for recounts as aforesaid, open the envelopes,
recount the ballots and determine the questions raised;
but upon a recount of votes for town officers in a town
where the selectmen are members of the board of registrars
of voters, the recount shall be made by the moderator,
who shall have all the powers and perform all the duties
conferred or imposed by this section upon registrars of
voters.

SECTION 18. Section two of chapter fifty-eight of the
General Laws, as so appearing, is hereby amended by
striking out, in the first line, the word "April" and inserting in place thereof the word: — January, — and by inserting after the word "fifty-nine", in the third line, the
words: — , sixty A, — so as to read as follows: — *Section 2.*
The commissioner shall annually, on or before January first,
forward to each board of assessors a list of all corporations
known to him to be liable on said day to taxation under
chapters fifty-nine, sixty A and sixty-three, with such
other information as in his judgment will assist them in the
assessment of taxes.

G. L. (Ter. Ed.), 58, § 2, amended.

Commissioner of corporations and taxation to forward to assessors lists of corporations, etc.

SECTION 19. Section three of said chapter fifty-eight,
as so appearing, is hereby amended by striking out, in the
first line, the words "before April" and inserting in place
thereof the words: — about January, — so as to read as
follows: — *Section 3.* The commissioner shall annually,
on or about January first, furnish to each board of assessors
all the information relating to the assessment, valuation
and ownership of property taxable in their town that has
come into possession of his department, particularly under
chapter sixty-five. He shall give to said assessors any
further instruction and supervision as to their duties needed
to secure uniform assessment and just taxation, and to
equalize the valuation of property for purposes of state,
county and local taxation.

G. L. (Ter. Ed.), 58, § 3, amended.

Information relative to property and instruction to assessors, etc.

SECTION 20. Section thirteen of said chapter fifty-
eight, as so appearing, is hereby amended by striking out,
in the first line, the word "twenty-five" and inserting in
place thereof the word: — thirty-five, — and by striking
out, in the second, third, sixth and eighth lines, the word
"April" and inserting in place thereof, in each instance, the
word: — January, — so as to read as follows: — *Section 13.*
In nineteen hundred and thirty-five and in every fifth
year thereafter the commissioner shall between January
first and June first determine as of January first the fair
cash value of all land in every town owned by the commonwealth and used for the purposes of a public institution, a

G. L. (Ter. Ed.), 58, § 13, amended.

Valuation of certain state and county lands every five years.

fish hatchery, game preserve or wild life sanctuary, a state military camp ground or a state forest; and he shall between January first and June first in the year nineteen hundred and twenty-five and in every fifth year thereafter, determine as of January first the fair cash value of all land in every town held by county commissioners for hospital purposes under sections seventy-eight to ninety, inclusive, of chapter one hundred and eleven. This determination shall be in such detail as to lots, subdivisions or acreage as the commissioner may deem necessary, and to assist him in making it he may require oral or written information from any officer or agent of the commonwealth or of any county or town therein and from any other inhabitant thereof, and may require such information to be on oath. Such officers, agents and persons, so far as able, shall furnish the commissioner with the required information in such form as he may indicate, within fifteen days after being so requested by him.

G. L. (Ter. Ed.), 58, § 15, amended.

SECTION 21. Section fifteen of said chapter fifty-eight, as so appearing, is hereby amended by striking out the word "April" in the fourteenth and fifteenth lines and inserting in place thereof the word: — January, — and by striking out in the sixteenth line the word "May" and inserting in place thereof the word: — February, — so that said section will read as follows: — *Section 15.* The valuation determined under the two preceding sections shall be in effect for the purposes of sections seventeen and seventeen A during the year in which such valuation is made and the four succeeding years, and until another valuation is made under sections thirteen and fourteen, except that whenever land is acquired by the commonwealth or by county commissioners for the purposes set forth in section thirteen the commissioner shall adopt the assessed valuation of said land made in the year last preceding such acquisition, and such assessed valuation shall be the valuation of the land for the purposes of sections seventeen and seventeen A, until a new valuation is made by the commissioner or by the board of tax appeals under section thirteen or fourteen; provided, that as to land used for a state forest such assessed valuation shall be reduced by deducting therefrom the value of all forest products removed from such land between January first on which it was last assessed and January first in the year for which the reimbursement is to be made, the amount thereof to be certified annually before February first to the commissioner by the state forester.

Effect of determination of value of certain state, etc., lands.

G. L. (Ter. Ed.), 58, § 21, amended.

SECTION 22. Section twenty-one of said chapter fifty-eight, as so appearing, is hereby amended by striking out, in the eighth line, the word "April" and inserting in place thereof the word: — January, — so as to read as follows: — *Section 21.* Such proportion of the tax paid by each corporation, company or association under sections fifty-three to sixty, inclusive, of chapter sixty-three, except railroad, street railway, electric railroad, telephone, telegraph, gas,

Distribution of certain corporate franchise taxes.

electric light, gas and electric light and water companies, as corresponds to the proportion of its stock owned by persons residing in this commonwealth, shall be distributed, credited and paid to the several towns in which, from the returns or other evidence, it appears that such persons resided on January first preceding, according to the number of shares so held in such towns respectively. If stock is held by a fiduciary, the beneficiary shall be regarded as the shareholder for the purpose of distribution under this section, and if a town is a shareholder, the distribution shall be the same as if the stock were owned by a resident thereof.

SECTION 23. Section twenty-four of said chapter fifty-eight, as so appearing, is hereby amended by striking out, in the thirteenth line, the word "April" and inserting in place thereof the word: — January, — so as to read as follows: — *Section 24.* The corporate franchise tax paid by gas, electric light, gas and electric light and water companies shall be distributed, credited and paid to towns of the commonwealth or shall be retained by the commonwealth in the manner following: Such part of said tax paid by each of said corporations as is paid on account of shares of its stock owned by non-residents of Massachusetts shall be retained by the commonwealth. The remainder of such tax shall be distributed, credited and paid to the town of the commonwealth where the business of the corporation is carried on; and if any such corporation carries on its business in more than one such town, this part of the tax paid by it shall be distributed, credited and paid to such towns in proportion to the value of the works, structures, real estate, machinery, poles, underground conduits, wires and pipes of the corporation in each of them on January first, as determined from the returns or in any other manner.

G. L. (Ter. Ed.), 58, § 24, amended.

Distribution of franchise tax of gas, electric and water companies.

SECTION 24. Section twenty-six of said chapter fifty-eight, as so appearing, is hereby amended by striking out, in the sixth and eleventh lines, the word "April" and inserting in place thereof, in each instance, the word: — January, — so as to read as follows: — *Section 26.* A guardian who holds, or whose ward holds, shares of stock in any corporation the tax on whose shares is distributed in whole or in part according to the residence of the shareholder, including banks located in the commonwealth liable to taxation, and an executor, administrator, trustee or other person who holds in trust any such stock, shall annually, between January first and tenth, return under oath to the commissioner the names and residences, on the first day of that month, of themselves and of all such wards or other persons to whom any part of the income from such stock is payable, the number of shares of stock so held and the name and location of the corporation.

G. L. (Ter. Ed.), 58, § 26, amended.

Guardians, executors, administrators, trustees, etc., to make returns of certain stock held.

A partnership shall annually, between January first and tenth, make a like return, stating the amount of such stock owned by the firm, the names and residences of all the

partners and the proportional interest or ownership of
each partner in said stock.

If a guardian, executor, administrator, trustee or partnership neglects to make the returns required by this section
on or before April tenth of each year, the commissioner
shall give notice by mail, postage prepaid, to such fiduciary
or partnership of such default. If such fiduciary or
partnership omits to file said return within thirty days
after such notice of default has been given, he or it shall
forfeit to the commonwealth not less than five nor more
than ten dollars for each day for fifteen days after the expiration of said thirty days, and not less than ten nor more
than two hundred dollars for each day thereafter during
which such default continues, or any other sum, not greater
than the maximum forfeiture, which the court may deem
just and equitable. Such forfeiture may be recovered as
provided in chapter sixty-three.

G. L. (Ter.
Ed.), 59, § 6,
amended.

SECTION 25. Section six of chapter fifty-nine of the
General Laws, as so appearing, is hereby amended by
striking out, in the fifth line, the words "in September"
and inserting in place thereof the words: — on July first, —

Land held by
city or town,
etc., in another,
for water
supply, etc.
Valuation.

so as to read as follows: — *Section 6.* Property held by a
city, town or district, including the metropolitan water
district, in another city or town for the purpose of a water
supply, the protection of its sources, or of sewage disposal,
if yielding no rent, shall not be liable to taxation therein;
but the city, town or district so holding it shall, annually
on July first, pay to the city or town where it lies an amount
equal to that which such city or town would receive for
taxes upon the average of the assessed values of the land,
which shall not include buildings or other structures except
in the case of land taken for the purpose of protecting the
sources of an existing water supply, for the three years last
preceding the acquisition thereof, the valuation for each
year being reduced by all abatements thereon. Any part
of such land or buildings from which any revenue in the
nature of rent is received shall be subject to taxation.

If such land is part of a larger tract which has been
assessed as a whole, its assessed valuation in any year shall
be taken to be that proportional part of the valuation of the
whole tract which the value of the land so acquired, exclusive of buildings, bore in that year to the value of the
entire estate.

G. L. (Ter.
Ed.), 59, § 8,
etc., amended.

SECTION 26. Section eight of said chapter fifty-nine, as
amended by chapter eighty of the acts of nineteen hundred
and thirty-three, is hereby further amended by striking out,
in the fourth line, the word "April" and inserting in place
thereof the word: — January, — and by striking out, in the
seventh line, the word "July" and inserting in place thereof

Interests in
ships and
vessels in
interstate or

the word: — April, — so as to read as follows: — *Section 8.*
Individuals or partnerships owning an interest in any ship
or vessel which has during the period of its business in the
year preceding January first been engaged in interstate or

foreign carrying trade or engaged exclusively in fishing and documented and carrying "papers" under the laws of the United States shall annually, on or before April first following, make a return on oath to the assessors of the town where such individuals reside or where such partnerships are taxable under clause seventh of section eighteen, respectively, setting forth the name of the ship or vessel, their interest therein, and the value of such interest. If the assessors are satisfied of the truth of the return they shall assess an excise tax of one third of one per cent upon such interest; and the person or partnership making such return shall be exempt from any tax upon said interest other than that assessed under this section.

foreign carrying trade or in fishing liable only to excise.

SECTION 27. Section nine of said chapter fifty-nine, as appearing in the Tercentenary Edition thereof, is hereby amended by striking out, in the second line, the word "April" and inserting in place thereof the word: — January, — so as to read as follows: — *Section 9.* The poll tax shall be assessed upon each person liable thereto in the town of which he is an inhabitant on January first in each year, except in cases otherwise provided for by law. The poll tax of minors liable to taxation shall be assessed to, and in the place of the residence of, the parents or guardians having control of the persons of such minors; but if a minor has no parent or guardian within the commonwealth, he shall be personally taxed for his poll, as if he were of full age. The poll tax of every other person under guardianship shall be assessed to his guardian in the place where the guardian is taxed for his own poll. In a city each inhabitant liable to assessment shall be assessed in the ward where he dwells; but no tax shall be invalid by reason of a mistake of the assessors in ascertaining the ward where a person should be assessed.

G. L. (Ter. Ed.), 59, § 9, amended.

Poll tax, where assessed.

SECTION 28. Section ten of said chapter fifty-nine, as so appearing, is hereby amended by striking out, in the first line, the word "April" and inserting in place thereof the word: — January, — so as to read as follows: — *Section 10.* A person liable to a poll tax, who is in a town on January first, and who, when inquired of by the assessors thereof, refuses to state his legal residence, shall for the purpose of taxation be deemed an inhabitant thereof. If he designates another town as his legal residence, said assessors shall notify the assessors of such other town, who shall thereupon tax him as an inhabitant thereof; but he shall not be exempt from the payment of a tax legally assessed upon him in his legal domicile.

G. L. (Ter. Ed.), 59, § 10, amended.

Determination of legal residence for poll tax.

SECTION 29. Section eleven of said chapter fifty-nine, as so appearing, is hereby amended by striking out, in the third and fifth lines, the word "April" and inserting in place thereof, in each instance, the word: — January, — so as to read as follows: — *Section 11.* Taxes on real estate shall be assessed, in the town where it lies, to the person who is either the owner or in possession thereof on January first,

G. L. (Ter. Ed.), 59, § 11, amended.

Land, where and to whom assessed.

and the person appearing of record, in the records of the county, or of the district, if such county is divided into districts, where the estate lies, as owner on January first, even though deceased, shall be held to be the true owner thereof, and so shall the person so appearing of record under a tax deed not invalid on its face. Real estate held by a religious society as a ministerial fund shall be assessed to its treasurer in the town where the land lies. Buildings erected on land leased by the commonwealth under section twenty-six of chapter seventy-five shall be assessed to the lessees, or their assignees, at the value of said buildings. Except as provided in the three following sections, mortgagors of real estate shall for the purpose of taxation be deemed the owners until the mortgagee takes possession, after which the mortgagee shall be deemed the owner.

G. L. (Ter. Ed.), 59, § 18, amended.
SECTION 30. Section eighteen of said chapter fifty-nine, as so appearing, is hereby amended by striking out, in the third, ninth and twenty-second lines, the word "April" and inserting in place thereof, in each instance, the word: — January, — so that the opening paragraph and paragraph First and Second of said section will read as follows: —
Personal estate, where and to whom assessed.
Section 18. All taxable personal estate within or without the commonwealth shall be assessed to the owner in the town where he is an inhabitant on January first, except as provided in chapter sixty-three and in the following clauses of this section:

First, All tangible personal property, including that of persons not inhabitants of the commonwealth, except ships and vessels used in or designed for use in carrying trade or commercial fishing, shall, unless exempted by section five, be taxed to the owner in the town where it is situated on January first.

Second, Machinery employed in any branch of manufacture or in supplying or distributing water, including machines used or operated under a stipulation providing for the payment of a royalty or compensation in the nature of a royalty for the privilege of using or operating the same, and all tangible personal property within the commonwealth leased for profit, or, in the case of domestic business and foreign corporations as defined in section thirty of chapter sixty-three and domestic manufacturing corporations as defined in section thirty-eight C of said chapter and foreign manufacturing corporations as defined in section forty-two B of said chapter, machinery used in the conduct of their business, shall be assessed where such machinery or tangible personal property is situated to the owner or any person having possession of the same on January first.

G. L. (Ter. Ed.), 59, § 19, amended.
SECTION 31. Section nineteen of said chapter fifty-nine, as so appearing, is hereby amended by striking out, in the third line, the word "April" and inserting in place thereof the word: — January, — so as to read as follows: — *Section*
Mortgaged, etc., personal property, who deemed owner.
19. Personal property mortgaged or pledged shall for the

purpose of taxation be deemed the property of the party in possession thereof on January first.

SECTION 32. Said chapter fifty-nine is hereby further amended by striking out section twenty, as so appearing, and inserting in place thereof the following: — *Section 20.* When a state tax is to be assessed, or an assessment is required to reimburse the commonwealth under section forty-one of chapter forty-four for expenses incurred under sections thirty-five to forty, inclusive, of said chapter, the state treasurer shall send by mail to the assessors of the several towns his warrants for the assessment thereof, in such amounts as may be estimated by the commissioner.

G. L. (Ter. Ed.), 59, § 20, amended. State treasurer to send warrants.

SECTION 33. Said chapter fifty-nine is hereby further amended by striking out section twenty-one, as so appearing, and inserting in place thereof the following: — *Section 21.* The assessors shall assess state taxes, including all lawful assessments by the commonwealth for which they receive warrants under the preceding section and county taxes duly certified to them, or they may assess such state and county taxes as estimated in advance by the commissioner. They shall also assess town taxes voted by their respective towns and all taxes duly voted and certified by fire, water, light and improvement districts therein. Such district taxes shall be subject to the law relative to the assessment and collection of town taxes, so far as applicable. Except as otherwise provided, all taxes shall be assessed as of January first.

G. L. (Ter. Ed.), 59, § 21, amended. Duty of assessors.

SECTION 34. Section twenty-nine of said chapter fifty-nine, as so appearing, is hereby amended by striking out the last three sentences and inserting in place thereof the following: — It shall also require all persons, except corporations making returns to the commissioner of insurance as required by section thirty-eight of chapter one hundred and seventy-six, to bring in to the assessors before a date therein specified, which shall not be later than March first following, unless the assessors for cause shown extend the time to April first, true lists, similarly itemized, of all real and personal estate held by them respectively for literary, temperance, benevolent, charitable or scientific purposes on January first preceding, or at the election of any such corporation on the last day of its fiscal year last preceding said January first, and to state the amount of receipts and expenditures for said purposes during the year last preceding said days. The assessors may require from any person claiming under the seventeenth, eighteenth, twenty-second or twenty-third clause of section five an exemption from taxation, a full list of all such person's taxable property, both real and personal.

G. L. (Ter. Ed.), 59, § 29, amended. Notices and lists.

SECTION 35. Section thirty-three of said chapter fifty-nine, as so appearing, is hereby amended by striking out, in the fifth line, the word "April" and inserting in place thereof the word: — January, — so as to read as follows: —

G. L. (Ter. Ed.), 59, § 33, amended.

Storage ware-
houses to give
certain in-
formation to
assessors.

Section 33. All persons engaged in the business of storing or keeping merchandise in storage warehouses shall, within ten days after a request therefor by the assessors of the town where said property is so stored or kept, permit said assessors to copy from their records a list of the names and addresses of all persons who appear, on January first in such year, to have any such property stored or kept in any such warehouse; but such persons shall not be required to furnish lists of persons having property stored in warehouses which is composed of imported goods in original packages and owned by the importer, or of goods that have been received for export trade. Failure to comply with this section shall be punished by a fine of not more than five hundred dollars or by imprisonment for not more than ninety days.

G. L. (Ter.
Ed.), 59, § 39,
amended.

SECTION 36. Section thirty-nine of said chapter fifty-nine, as so appearing, is hereby amended by striking out, in the seventh line, the word "June" and inserting in place thereof the word: — March, — so as to read as follows: —

Valuation of
machinery,
poles, wires,
etc.

Section 39. The valuation at which the machinery, poles, wires and underground conduits, wires and pipes of all telephone and telegraph companies shall be assessed by the assessors of the respective towns where such property is subject to taxation shall be determined annually by the commissioner, subject to appeal to the board of tax appeals, as hereinafter provided, and shall by him be certified to the assessors on or before March fifteenth. A board of assessors aggrieved by a valuation made by the commissioner under this section may, within ten days after notice of his valuation, apply to said board of tax appeals. Said board shall hear and decide the subject matter of such appeal and give notice of its decision to the commissioner and to the assessors; and its decision as to the valuation of the property shall be final and conclusive, except as provided in section seventy-three, relative to abatements. The assessors shall, in the manner provided by law, assess the machinery, poles, wires and underground conduits, wires and pipes of all telephone and telegraph companies as certified and at the value determined by the commissioner or by the board of tax appeals, and such assessment by a board of assessors shall be deemed to be a full compliance with the oath of office of each assessor and a full performance of his official duty with relation to the assessment of such property, except as provided in the following section.

G. L. (Ter.
Ed.), 59, § 41,
amended.

SECTION 37. Section forty-one of said chapter fifty-nine, as so appearing, is hereby amended by striking out, in the fourth line, the word "June" and inserting in place thereof the word: — March, — and by striking out, in the ninth line, the word "April" and inserting in place thereof the word: — January, — so as to read as follows: —

Telephone and
telegraph com-
panies to make
returns, etc.

Section 41. Every telephone or telegraph company owning any property required to be valued by the commissioner under section thirty-nine shall annually, on or before a date determined by the commissioner but in no case later than March first, make a return to the commissioner signed and sworn to by its treasurer. This return shall be in the form and detail prescribed by the commissioner and shall contain all information which he shall consider necessary to enable him to make the valuations required by section thirty-nine, and shall relate, so far as is possible, to the situation of the company and its property on January first of the year when made. Property returned to the commissioner as herein provided need not be included in the list required to be filed by a telephone or telegraph company under section twenty-nine.

SECTION 38. Section forty-five of said chapter fifty-nine, as so appearing, is hereby amended by striking out, in the second line, the word "April" and inserting in place thereof the word: — January, — so as to read as follows: — *Section 45.* The commissioner shall provide each city and town, on or before January first annually, suitable books for the use of the assessors in the assessment of taxes, which shall contain blank columns, with uniform headings for a valuation list, and blank tables for aggregates, in the following form or in such other form as the commissioner shall from time to time determine; provided, that in lieu of the valuation list provided for in this section and the preceding two sections, the assessors of any city or town may, with the assent of the commissioner, prepare a valuation list upon books furnished by the city or town and in such form as the commissioner shall approve, and that, for the separate listing of poll taxes under section four of chapter sixty, such portion of the books furnished by the commissioner as he shall determine may contain only the first three columns of said form. *G. L. (Ter. Ed.), 59, § 45, amended.*

Commissioner to furnish books to assessors.

SECTION 39. Said chapter fifty-nine, as so appearing, is hereby further amended by striking out in the form appended to section forty-five the word "April" wherever it appears and inserting in place thereof the word: — January. *G. L. (Ter. Ed.), 59, § 45, form, amended.*

SECTION 40. Section forty-seven of said chapter fifty-nine, as so appearing, is hereby amended by striking out, in the third line, the word "October" and inserting in place thereof the word: — July, — so as to read as follows: — *Section 47.* The assessors shall fill up the table of aggregates by an enumeration of the necessary items included in the lists of valuation and assessments, and shall annually, on or before July first, deposit in the office of the commissioner an attested copy of the same. *G. L. (Ter. Ed.), 59, § 47, amended.*

Assessors to prepare table of aggregates, etc.

SECTION 41. Section forty-nine of said chapter fifty-nine, as so appearing, is hereby amended by striking out, in the second line, the word "October" and inserting in place thereof the word: — July, — so as to read as follows: — *Section 49.* The assessors, except those of Boston, on or before July first, nineteen hundred and twenty-two, and in *G. L. (Ter. Ed.), 59, § 49, amended.*

Assessors to deposit copies of valuation

books
with commis-
sioner.

every third year thereafter, shall deposit in the office of the commissioner, in books to be by him provided for the purpose, a copy of the assessors' valuation books of those years, to be by them certified under oath. This shall not excuse, in such years, the filing of a separate copy of the table of aggregates under section forty-seven.

G. L. (Ter.
Ed.), 59, § 57,
etc., amended.

Date for
payment of
taxes.

Interest.

SECTION 42. Said chapter fifty-nine is hereby further amended by striking out section fifty-seven, as amended by section one of chapter one hundred and fifty-one of the acts of nineteen hundred and thirty-three, and inserting in place thereof the following: — *Section 57*. Taxes shall be payable in every city, town and district in which the same are assessed, in two equal instalments, on July first and on October first of each year, and bills for the same shall be sent out not later than June fourteenth of each year. On all taxes remaining unpaid after November first of the year in which they are payable, interest shall be paid at the following rates, computed from October first of such year: at the rate of six per cent per annum on all taxes, and, by way of penalty, at the additional rate of two per cent per annum on the amount of all taxes in excess of three hundred dollars assessed to any taxpayer, in any one city or town, if such taxes remain unpaid after December thirty-first of the year in which they are payable. Bills for taxes assessed under section seventy-five shall be sent out not later than December twenty-sixth, and such taxes shall be payable not later than December thirty-first. If they remain unpaid after that date, interest shall be paid at the rates above specified, computed from December thirty-first until the day of payment, but if, in any case, the tax bill is sent out later than December twenty-sixth, said taxes shall be payable not later than ten days from the day upon which said bill is sent out, and interest shall be computed from the fifteenth day following the date when the tax becomes due. In all cases where interest is payable it shall be added to and become a part of the tax.

G. L. (Ter.
Ed.), 59, § 59,
etc., amended.

Abatements.

SECTION 43. Said chapter fifty-nine, as amended in section fifty-nine by section one of chapter one hundred and sixty-five of the acts of nineteen hundred and thirty-three, is hereby further amended by striking out said section fifty-nine and inserting in place thereof the following: — *Section 59*. A person aggrieved by the taxes assessed upon him may, on or before December first of the year to which the tax relates, apply to the assessors for an abatement thereof; and if they find him taxed at more than his just proportion, or upon an assessment of any of his property in excess of its fair cash value, they shall make a reasonable abatement. A person aggrieved by a tax assessed upon him under section seventy-five or reassessed upon him under section seventy-seven may apply for such abatement at any time within six months after notice of such assessment or reassessment is sent to him. A tenant of real estate paying rent therefor and under obligation to pay more than one half of the taxes thereon may apply for such abatement. If a person other than the person to whom a tax on real estate is assessed is the owner thereof, or has an interest therein, or is in possession thereof, and pays the tax, he may thereafter prosecute in his own name any application, appeal or action provided by law for the abatement or recovery of such tax, which after the payment thereof shall be deemed for the purposes of such application, appeal or action, to have been assessed to the person so paying the same.

SECTION 44. Section seventy-three of said chapter fifty-nine, as so appearing, is hereby amended by striking out, in the third line, the words "within one year after April" and inserting in place thereof the words: — on or before December, — so as to read as follows: — *Section 73.* Any company aggrieved by the taxes assessed on it relating to any property valued in accordance with section thirty-nine may, on or before December first of the year to which the tax relates, apply to the commissioner for an abatement thereof; and if the commissioner finds that the company is taxed at more than its just proportion, or upon an assessment of any of its said property in excess of its fair cash value, he shall make a reasonable abatement. No company which has not duly filed the return required by section forty-one shall have an abatement unless it shall furnish to the commissioner a reasonable excuse for the delay, or unless such tax exceeds by more than fifty per cent the amount of the tax which would have been assessed on such property if the return had been seasonably filed, and in such case only the excess over such fifty per cent shall be abated. Whenever any application for abatement hereunder is made, the commissioner shall give notice thereof to the assessors of the town in which is located any of the property with reference to which an abatement of the tax is asked for, and such assessors may appear before the commissioner and be heard by him with relation to the subject of the abatement. The commissioner shall, within ten days after his decision on an application for abatement hereunder, give written notice thereof to the applicant and to the assessors. A company aggrieved by the refusal of the commissioner to abate a tax hereunder may prosecute an appeal from his decision in the manner and to the tribunals provided for a person aggrieved by the refusal of assessors to abate a tax, and all laws relating to such an appeal from a refusal of assessors to abate a tax shall apply in proceedings hereunder.

SECTION 45. Section seventy-four of said chapter fifty-nine, as so appearing, is hereby amended by striking out, in the tenth line, the word "April" and inserting in place thereof the word: — January, — so as to read as follows: — *Section 74.* Whenever an abatement is finally made to any corporation taxable under chapter sixty-three upon any tax assessed by the assessors of any town, upon or in respect

Margin notes:

G. L. (Ter. Ed.), 59, § 73, amended.

Telephone or telegraph companies may apply for abatement of commissioner's valuation of property taxable locally, etc.

G. L. (Ter. Ed.), 59, § 74, amended.

Commissioner to be notified of abatement of local taxes

to corporations
liable to fran-
chise tax.

of works, structures, real estate, motor vehicles, machinery, poles, underground conduits, wires and pipes, the
assessors, commissioners or court granting such abatement
shall forthwith notify the commissioner thereof, and shall
state in such notice what sum was determined by such
assessors, commissioners or court to have been the full and
fair cash value of such works, structures, real estate, machinery, poles, underground conduits, wires and pipes on the
first day of January on which the tax so abated was originally assessed or to have been the proper value of any such
motor vehicle owned by such corporation and assessed
under chapter sixty A.

G. L. (Ter.
Ed.), 59, § 83,
amended.

SECTION 46. Section eighty-three of said chapter fifty-
nine, as so appearing, is hereby amended by striking out,
in the second line, the word "July" and inserting in place
thereof the word: — April, — and by striking out, in the
eighth line, the word "April" and inserting in place thereof
the word: — January, — so as to read as follows: —

Returns by
assessors of
names of cer-
tain corpora-
tions and as-
sessed value of
certain cor-
porate property
and motor
vehicles.

Section 83. Assessors shall annually, on or before the first
Monday of April, return to the commissioner the names of
all domestic and foreign corporations, except banks of
issue and deposit, having a capital stock divided into
shares, organized for the purposes of business or profit and
established in their respective towns or owning real estate
therein, and a detailed statement of the works, structures,
real estate, machinery, poles, underground conduits, wires
and pipes owned by each of said corporations and situated
in such town, with the value thereof, on January first
preceding, and the amount at which the same is assessed
in said town for the then current year. The assessors shall
at the same time return to the commissioner a detailed
statement of all motor vehicles owned by each such corporation and the amount at which each such vehicle is
assessed under chapter sixty A for said year. An assessor
neglecting to comply with this section shall be punished by
a fine of one hundred dollars.

Penalty.

G. L. (Ter.
Ed.), 59, § 84,
amended.

SECTION 47. Section eighty-four of said chapter fifty-
nine, as so appearing, is hereby amended by striking out,
in the second line, the word "April" and inserting in place
thereof the word: — January, — so as to read as follows: —

Assessors to
state cause of
diminished
valuations.

Section 84. If the assessors of a town ascertain that the
aggregate valuation thereof has been diminished since
January first of the preceding year, they shall return with
the table of aggregates, or with the books, which they are
required by sections forty-seven, forty-eight and forty-
nine to deposit in the office of the commissioner, a statement, on oath, of the causes which in their opinion have
produced such diminution.

G. L. (Ter.
Ed.), 59, § 85,
amended.

SECTION 48. Section eighty-five of said chapter fifty-
nine, as so appearing, is hereby amended by striking out,
in the first line, the word "September" and inserting in
place thereof the word: — July, — so as to read as follows:

Returns by as-
sessors to com-
missioner of

— *Section 85.* Assessors shall annually, on or before July

first, make a return to the commissioner, in such form as *certain ex-*
he may prescribe, of the value of property exempted from *empted prop-erty.*
taxation under clauses twenty-second and twenty-third of
section five, together with the amount of taxes which would
have been assessed on such property but for said exemption.

SECTION 49. Section eighty-six of said chapter fifty- *G. L. (Ter.*
nine, as so appearing, is hereby amended by striking out, *Ed.), 59, § 86, amended.*
in the first line, the word "October" and inserting in place
thereof the word: — July, — so as to read as follows: —
Section 86. Assessors shall annually, on or before July first, *Assessors to*
forward to the commissioner a statement showing the whole *make returns of exempted*
amount of exempted property entered upon the valuation *property, etc.*
lists of their respective towns in accordance with section
fifty-one, and the amount in each class, and stating separately the aggregate amount belonging to each class em-
braced in clause third of section five, and shall also forward
such lists and statements required by section twenty-nine
relative to real and personal property exempt from taxation under said clause as have been received by them.

SECTION 50. Chapter sixty of the General Laws is *G. L. (Ter.*
hereby amended by striking out section three, as so appear- *Ed.), 60, § 3, amended.*
ing, and inserting in place thereof the following: — *Section* *Tax bills and*
3. The collector shall forthwith, after receiving a tax list *notices, dates, etc.*
and warrant, send notice to each person assessed, resident
or non-resident, of the amount of his tax; if mailed, it shall
be postpaid and directed to the town where the assessed
person resided on January first of the year in which the tax
was assessed, and, if he resides in a city, it shall, if possible,
be directed to the street and number of his residence. If
he is assessed for a poll tax only, the notice shall be sent
on or about June fourteenth of the year in which the tax
is assessed. An omission to send the notice shall not affect
the validity either of a tax or of the proceedings for its
collection. All tax bills or notices issued pursuant to this
section shall be dated January first of the year to which the
tax relates. The tax notice and bill shall state that all
checks, drafts or money orders shall be made payable to or
to the order of the city, town or district and not to or to the
order of any officer, board or commission.

SECTION 51. Section sixteen of said chapter sixty, as *G. L. (Ter.*
amended by section one of chapter one hundred and sixty- *Ed.), 60, § 16, etc., amended.*
eight of the acts of nineteen hundred and thirty-three, is
hereby further amended by striking out, in the fourteenth
line, the word "April" and inserting in place thereof the
word: — January, — so as to read as follows: — *Section 16.* *Demand.*
The collector shall, before selling the land of a resident, or
non-resident, or distraining the goods of any person, or
arresting him for his tax, serve on him a statement of the
amount thereof with a demand for its payment. If two
or more parcels of land are assessed in the name of a resident,
or non-resident, the statement of the aggregate amount of
the taxes thereon may be made in one demand. Such
demand may also include taxes due on account of tangible

personal property and any motor vehicle excise tax. If the heirs of a deceased person, co-partners or two or more persons are jointly assessed, service need be made on only one of them. Such demand for the tax upon land may be made upon the person occupying the same on January first of the year in which the tax is assessed. No demand need be made on a mortgagee, unless he has given notice under section thirty-eight, in which case no demand need be made on the owner or occupant. Demand shall be made by the collector by mailing the same to the last or usual place of business or abode, or to the address best known to him, and failure to receive the same shall not invalidate a tax or any proceedings for the enforcement or collection of the same.

G. L. (Ter. Ed.), 60, § 22, amended.
Partial payment of tax.
SECTION 52. Said chapter sixty is hereby further amended by striking out section twenty-two, as so appearing, and inserting in place thereof the following: — *Section 22.* After the delivery of a tax, including assessments for betterments or other purposes but not including a poll tax, to a collector for collection, the owner of the estate or person assessed or a person in behalf of said owner or person may, if the tax or assessments are upon real estate, at any time and from time to time up to the date when advertisements may be prepared for the sale of the same, and if it is a personal tax, at any time and from time to time up to the date when a warrant or other process may be issued for the enforcement and collection thereof, tender to the collector a partial payment of the tax not less than ten per cent of the total tax but in no event less in amount than ten dollars, which shall be received, receipted for and applied toward the payment of the tax. The acceptance of any partial payment in accordance with this section shall not invalidate any demand made for a tax, prior to the acceptance of such partial payment; provided that the amount stated in the demand was the amount due at the date when the demand was made. If in any court it shall be determined that the tax is more than the amount so paid, judgment shall be entered for such excess and interest upon the amount thereof to the date of the judgment, and on the amount paid to the date of payment, with costs if otherwise recoverable. The part payment authorized by this section shall not affect a right of tender, lien or other provision of law for the recovery of the amount of such tax, or interest or costs thereon, remaining due, but if the part payment is more than the tax, as finally determined, the excess, without interest, shall be repaid to the person who paid it.

G. L. (Ter. Ed.), 60, § 37, amended.
SECTION 53. Section thirty-seven of said chapter sixty, as so appearing, is hereby amended by striking out, in the third line, the word "April" and inserting in place thereof the word: — January.

G. L. (Ter. Ed.), 60, § 38, amended.
SECTION 54. Section thirty-eight of said chapter sixty, as so appearing, is hereby amended by striking out, in the

second line, the word "September" and inserting in place thereof the word: — July, — so as to read as follows: —
Section 38. If a mortgagee of land situated in the place of his residence, before July first of the year in which the tax is assessed, gives written notice to the collector that he holds a mortgage on land, with a description of the land, the demand for payment shall be made on the mortgagee instead of the mortgagor.

Mortgagee may give notice requiring demand to be made on him.

SECTION 55. Section fifty-one of said chapter sixty, as so appearing, is hereby amended by striking out, in the sixth and eleventh lines, the word "April" and inserting in place thereof, in each instance, the word: — January, — so as to read as follows: — *Section 51.* If unimproved and unoccupied land does not exceed four thousand square feet in area, or is laid out in lots or parcels no one of which exceeds such area, and the taxes unpaid for any one year do not exceed fifty cents on such land, or on any such lot or parcel thereof, the collector may give notice of the sale by publication of an advertisement stating the name of the owner of record of each lot on January first of the year of assessment, the tax due thereon and the number of such lot on a street, way or plan, without further description thereof. The collector may convey in one deed to the same purchaser or convey to the town any number of the lots so advertised and sold, and said deed shall state the name of said owner of record of each lot conveyed therein, on January first of said year, the amount of the taxes and costs due for each lot, and the number on the street, way or plan of each lot respectively, and need contain no further description of the lot, owner or amount due. The cost of the sale shall be apportioned equally among all the lots sold, and the cost of the deed shall be apportioned equally among all the lots conveyed thereby.

G. L. (Ter. Ed.), 60, § 51, amended.

Sale together of several parcels of small value, etc.

SECTION 56. Section fifty-nine of said chapter sixty is hereby amended by striking out, in the second line, the word "January" and inserting in place thereof the word: — October, — so as to read as follows: — *Section 59.* If a tax on land is assessed to a mortgagor and mortgagee separately, any part thereof remaining unpaid on October first following its assessment may be paid by either party. If a mortgagee pays a tax, interest or costs thereon which by law or by the terms of the mortgage was payable by the mortgagor, the amount so paid shall be added to the mortgage debt. If it is by law or by the terms of the mortgage payable by the mortgagee, and is paid by the mortgagor, the amount so paid shall be deducted from the mortgage debt unless the parties have, in writing, otherwise agreed.

G. L. (Ter. Ed.), 60, § 59, amended.

Mortgagor or mortgagee may pay tax.

SECTION 57. Section three of chapter sixty-one of the General Laws, as so appearing, is hereby amended by striking out, in the fourteenth line, the word "May" and inserting in place thereof the word: — February, — and by striking out, in the sixteenth line, the words "April first" and inserting in place thereof the words: — December

G. L. (Ter. Ed.), 61, § 3, amended.

Taxation of forest products and forest lands, etc.

thirty-first, — so as to read as follows: — *Section 3.* The standing growth on classified forest land shall not be taxed, but the owner of such land, except as hereinafter provided, shall pay a products tax of six per cent of the stumpage value upon all wood or timber cut therefrom, and one tenth of such taxes collected by the town shall be paid to the state treasurer. Trees standing on such land shall not be included in the town valuation in apportioning the state or county tax among the towns. But an owner of classified forest land may annually cut, free of tax, wood or timber from such land, not exceeding twenty-five dollars in stumpage value; provided, that such wood or timber is for his own use or for that of a tenant of said land only. Buildings or other structures standing on classified forest land shall be taxed as real estate with the land on which they stand. Classified forest land shall be subject to special assessments and betterment assessments. The owner shall make a sworn return to the assessors before February first in each year of the amount of all wood and timber cut from such land during the year ending on the preceding December thirty-first.

G. L. (Ter. Ed.), 63, § 3, amended.

SECTION 58. Section three of chapter sixty-three of the General Laws, as so appearing, is hereby amended by striking out, in the first, second and sixteenth lines, the word "April" and inserting in place thereof, in each instance, the word: — January, — so as to read as follows: —

Annual returns of banks, etc.

Section 3. Every bank shall within the first ten days of January make a return as of January first, sworn to by its cashier or by its treasurer, or in their absence or incapacity by any other principal officer, in such form as the commissioner prescribes, giving: —

(*a*) A copy of such parts as the commissioner may designate of the federal return or returns for the year by the income of which the tax is to be measured, provided that if any bank shall have participated in filing a consolidated return of income to the federal government, it shall file with the commissioner a statement of net income in such form as he may prescribe, showing its gross income and deductions in accordance with the law and regulations governing the usual federal returns of corporations not so participating; and such additional information as he may require to determine the net income as defined in section one.

(*b*) The name of each shareholder with his residence and the number of shares belonging to him at the close of the business day last preceding January first as the same then appeared on the books of said bank.

Whenever the time for filing the federal return has been extended, the commissioner may extend the time for filing the return required under this section.

G. L. (Ter. Ed.), 63, § 5, amended.

SECTION 59. Section five of said chapter sixty-three, as so appearing, is hereby amended by striking out, in the seventh line, the word "April" and inserting in place thereof

the word: — January, — so as to read as follows: —
Section 5. Such proportion of the tax paid by each bank
under the foregoing sections, after deducting any refund
and any interest or costs paid on account thereof, as corresponds to the proportion of its stock owned by persons
residing in this commonwealth shall be determined by the
commissioner and be distributed, credited and paid to the
several towns in which from returns or other evidence it
appears that such persons resided on January first preceding, according to the number of shares so held in such towns
respectively, and the remainder of such tax shall be retained by the commonwealth. The commissioner shall
forthwith upon such determination give written notice by
mail or at their office to the assessors of each town thereby
affected of the aggregate amount so charged against and
credited to it; and they may within ten days after notice
of such determination appeal therefrom to the board of tax
appeals. *(Distribution of tax. Appeals.)*

SECTION 60. Section fifty-three of said chapter sixty-
three, as so appearing, is hereby amended by striking out,
in the twelfth line, the word "April" and inserting in place
thereof the word: — January, — so that the first paragraph
thereof will read as follows: — Every corporation organized
under general or special laws of the commonwealth for
purposes of business or profit, having a capital stock
divided into shares, except banks otherwise taxable under
this chapter, except insurance companies with capital stock
and mutual insurance companies with a guaranty capital
or permanent fund whose premiums are otherwise taxable
under this chapter, and except corporations taxable under
sections thirty to fifty-one, inclusive, in addition to all
returns required by its charter, and in addition to all returns otherwise required under this chapter, shall annually,
between April first and tenth, make a return to the commissioner, on oath of its treasurer, stating the name and
place of business of the corporation, and setting forth as of
January first of the year in which the return is made: *(G. L. (Ter. Ed.), 63, § 53, amended. Taxation of corporate franchises. Annual returns to commissioner.)*

SECTION 61. Section fifty-four of said chapter sixty-
three, as so appearing, is hereby amended by striking out,
in the tenth line, the word "March" and inserting in place
thereof the word: — December, — so that the paragraph
included in lines nine to seventeen, inclusive, will read as
follows: — Street railway and electric railroad corporations
shall also state the length of track operated by them in
each town on December thirty-first preceding the return,
to be determined by measuring as single track the total
length of all tracks operated by them, including sidings
and turnouts, and including tracks owned by them, those
which they lease and those over which they have trackage
rights only, and the amount of dividends paid on their
capital stock during the year ending on September thirtieth
preceding the return, and during each year from the organi-
zation of the company. *(G. L. (Ter. Ed.), 63, § 54, amended. Additional information required of certain corporations, etc.)*

G. L. (Ter. Ed.), 80, § 1, amended.

SECTION 62. Section one of chapter eighty of the General Laws, as so appearing, is hereby amended by striking out, in the fourteenth line, the word "April" and inserting in place thereof the word: — January, — so as to read as follows: — *Section 1.* Whenever a limited and determinable area receives benefit or advantage, other than the general advantage to the community, from a public improvement made by or in accordance with the formal vote or order of a board of officers of the commonwealth or of a county, city, town or district, and such order states that betterments are to be assessed for the improvement, such board shall within six months after the completion of the improvement determine the value of such benefit or advantage to the land within such area and assess upon each parcel thereof a proportionate share of the cost of such improvement, and shall include in such cost all damages awarded therefor under chapter seventy-nine; but no such assessment shall exceed the amount of such adjudged benefit or advantage. The board shall in the order of assessment designate as the owner of each parcel the person who was liable to assessment therefor on the preceding January first under the provisions of chapter fifty-nine.

Assessment of cost of public improvements.

G. L. (Ter. Ed.), 80, § 13, etc., amended.

SECTION 63. Section thirteen of said chapter eighty, as amended by section two of chapter sixty-three of the acts of nineteen hundred and thirty-three, is hereby further amended by striking out, in the seventh line, the word "April" and inserting in place thereof the word: — January, — so as to read as follows: — *Section 13.* Assessments made under this chapter shall bear interest at the rate of six per cent per annum from the thirtieth day after the assessments have been committed to the collector. The assessors shall add each year to the annual tax assessed with respect to each parcel of land all assessments, constituting liens thereon, which have been committed to the collector prior to January second of such year and which have not been apportioned as hereinafter provided, remaining unpaid, as certified to them by the collector, when the valuation list is completed, with interest to the date when interest on taxes becomes due and payable. At any time before demand for payment by the collector and before the completion by the assessors of the valuation list for the year in which such assessments will first appear on the annual tax bill, the board of assessors may, and at the request of the owner of the land assessed shall, apportion all assessments made under this chapter into such number of equal portions, not exceeding ten, as is determined by said board or as is requested by the owner, as the case may be, but no one of such portions shall be less than five dollars. The assessors shall add one of said portions, with interest on the amount remaining unpaid from thirty days after the commitment of the original assessment to the collector to the date when interest on taxes becomes due and payable, to the first annual tax upon the land and shall add to

Apportionment.

the annual tax for each year thereafter one of said portions and one year's interest on the amount of the assessment remaining unpaid until all such portions shall have been so added; all assessments and apportioned parts thereof, and interest thereon as herein provided, which have been added to the annual tax on any parcel of land shall be included in the annual tax bill thereon. After an assessment or a portion thereof has been placed on the annual tax bill, the total amount of said bill shall be subject to interest under and in accordance with the provisions of section fifty-seven of chapter fifty-nine. The amount remaining unpaid of any assessment may be paid in full at any time notwithstanding a prior apportionment.

SECTION 64. Section five of chapter one hundred and one of the General Laws, as so appearing, is hereby amended by striking out, in the twenty-first line, the word "April" and inserting in place thereof the word: — January, — so as to read as follows: — *Section 5*. Every transient vendor, before making any sales of goods, wares or merchandise in a town, shall make application to the aldermen or selectmen or other board authorized to issue such licenses and, unless the fee therefor is fixed as hereinafter provided, shall file with them a true statement, under oath, of the average quantity and value of the stock of goods, wares and merchandise kept or intended to be kept or exposed by him for sale. Said board shall submit such statement to the assessors of the town, who, after such examination and inquiry as they deem necessary, shall determine such average quantity and value, and shall forthwith transmit a certificate thereof to said board. Thereupon the board shall authorize the town clerk, upon the payment by the applicant of a fee equal to the taxes assessable in said town under the last preceding tax levy therein upon an amount of property of the same valuation, to issue to him a license authorizing the sale of such goods, wares and merchandise within the town. The board may, however, authorize the issue of such license without the filing of said statement as aforesaid, upon the payment of a license fee fixed by it. Upon payment of such fee, said town clerk shall thereupon issue such license, which shall remain in force so long as the licensee shall continuously keep and expose for sale in such town such stock of goods, wares or merchandise, but not later than the first day of January following its date. Upon such payment and proof of payment of all other license fees, if any, chargeable upon local sales, such town clerk shall record the state license of such transient vendor in full, shall endorse thereon "local license fees paid" and shall affix thereto his official signature and the date of such endorsement.

SECTION 65. Wherever in any section of said General Laws, as amended by this act, reference is made to the residence of any person on January first of the preceding year and said preceding year is the year nineteen hundred

Marginal notes:

G. L. (Ter. Ed.), 101, § 5, amended.

Transient vendors, etc. Local license. Application, fee, etc.

Meaning of word "residence" as used in this act.

and thirty-four, such reference shall relate to April first, instead of January first.

Effective date.   SECTION 66. This act shall take effect on December thirty-first, nineteen hundred and thirty-four.

Approved June 10, 1933.

*Chap.*255 AN ACT RELATIVE TO REPORTS TO APPELLATE DIVISIONS OF DISTRICT COURTS.

Be it enacted, etc., as follows:

G. L. (Ter. Ed.), 231, § 108, amended.

SECTION 1. Section one hundred and eight of chapter two hundred and thirty-one of the General Laws, as appearing in the Tercentenary Edition thereof, is hereby amended by striking out the second sentence in the third paragraph thereof and inserting in place thereof the following: —

Appellate divisions of district courts. Reports.

The request for such a report shall be filed with the clerk of any district court within five days after notice of the finding or decision and, when the objection is to the admission or exclusion of evidence, the claim for a report shall also be made known at the time of the ruling and shall be reduced to writing in a summary manner and filed with the clerk, in the municipal court of the city of Boston, within two days, and in any other district court, within five days, after the making of such ruling. A draft report filed within the period required for a request for a report under this section shall be deemed to include a request for a report.

Effective date.   SECTION 2. This act shall take effect on the first day of October in the current year.

Approved June 10, 1933.

*Chap.*256 AN ACT RELATIVE TO THE DISPOSITION OF MONEYS REPRESENTED BY CERTAIN BANK BOOKS BELONGING TO FORMER PATIENTS OF CERTAIN STATE HOSPITALS.

Be it enacted, etc., as follows:

G. L. (Ter. Ed.), 123, new section after § 39B.

Chapter one hundred and twenty-three of the General Laws is hereby amended by inserting after section thirty-nine B, inserted therein by chapter two hundred and four of the acts of nineteen hundred and thirty-two, the following new section: — *Section 39C.* Any bank book belonging to a patient who has been discharged or has escaped from any state hospital, which shall have been in the custody of the superintendent of such hospital and remained unclaimed for more than two years and represents a deposit in a savings bank or trust company within the commonwealth may be presented by the department to such bank accompanied by the written request of the department for payment to it of so much of such deposit as is equivalent to the amount due the commonwealth for the support of such patient, and such bank shall thereupon pay to the department the amount so requested. *Approved June 10, 1933.*

Disposition of certain unclaimed funds of patients in state hospitals.

AN ACT RELATIVE TO COMPENSATION FOR SPECIFIC INJURIES *Chap.257*
TO FINGERS UNDER THE WORKMEN'S COMPENSATION LAW.

Be it enacted, etc., as follows:

Section thirty-six of chapter one hundred and fifty-two of the General Laws, as appearing in the Tercentenary Edition thereof, is hereby amended by striking out paragraph (*j*) and inserting in place thereof the following: — G. L. (Ter. Ed.), 152, § 36, amended.

(*j*) For the loss by severance of two phalanges of each of two fingers of the same hand which for the purposes hereof may include the thumb of the left or minor hand but not the thumb or index finger of the right or major hand, or of each of two or more toes of the same foot, two thirds of the average weekly wages of the injured person, but not more than ten dollars nor less than four dollars a week for a period of twenty-five weeks, for each hand or foot so injured, and any compensation payable under this paragraph shall be in addition to any compensation payable under paragraphs (*g*), (*h*), (*i*), and (*k*), or any of them, subject, however, to the limitation contained in said paragraph (*k*).   *Approved June 10, 1933.* Payments under workmen's compensation law for certain injuries.

AN ACT RELATIVE TO THE CONTROL AND USE OF THE WATERS *Chap.258*
OF PLUG POND IN THE CITY OF HAVERHILL.

Be it enacted, etc., as follows:

SECTION 1. The powers and duties granted to and imposed upon the city of Haverhill by chapter three hundred and forty-eight of the acts of eighteen hundred and ninety-one, and by chapter four hundred and seventeen of the acts of eighteen hundred and ninety-two as amended by chapter four hundred and thirty-three of the acts of eighteen hundred and ninety-six, and amendments thereto, insofar as such powers and duties relate to the use of the waters of Plug pond, sometimes called Lake Saltonstall, shall be exercised by the municipal council of said city and land owned by said city within the water shed of said pond shall be maintained, improved and controlled by said municipal council in such manner as they shall deem for the best interests of the said city.

SECTION 2. Said municipal council may temporarily abandon the use of the waters of said pond for a source of public water supply, if in its judgment said waters are not necessary therefor, and said council shall, in such event and during the time of such abandonment, maintain said waters for use by the public for bathing, boating and other recreational purposes.

SECTION 3. During such time as the waters of said pond shall be maintained by the municipal council for the uses specified in section one or two, the said municipal council shall adequately police and supervise the same.

SECTION 4. This act shall take effect upon its acceptance during the current year by vote of the municipal council of said city, subject to the provisions of its charter.

Approved June 10, 1933.

---

*Chap.*259 AN ACT RELATIVE TO THE CONSTRUCTION AND OPERATION OF A SYSTEM OF SEWERS AND SEWAGE DISPOSAL BY THE TOWN OF SAUGUS.

Be it enacted, etc., as follows:

1929, 350, § 1, amended.

Town of Saugus, sewage disposal.

SECTION 1. Chapter three hundred and fifty of the acts of nineteen hundred and twenty-nine is hereby amended by striking out section one and inserting in place thereof the following: — *Section 1.* The town of Saugus may lay out, construct, maintain and operate a system or systems of main drains and common sewers, and a system of sewage disposal, for a part or the whole of its territory, with such connections and other works as may be required for a system of sewage disposal, and may construct such sewers or drains over and under land or tidewater in said town and in the city of Lynn as may be necessary to conduct the sewage to the filter beds, treatment works and/or to the outfall sewer of the city of Lynn, and, for the purpose of providing better surface or other drainage, may make, lay and maintain such drains as it deems best. And for the purposes aforesaid, the town may, within its limits, and in the city of Lynn, make and maintain sub-drains. Before any sewers and/or sub-drains are laid within the confines of the city of Lynn upon any public way, street or other land under the control of the city of Lynn, the location, construction and placement thereof shall be approved by the board having charge of the same in the city of Lynn and by the city council and mayor thereof.

1929, 350, § 4, amended.

May take land, etc., by eminent domain.

SECTION 2. Said chapter three hundred and fifty is hereby further amended by striking out section four and inserting in place thereof the following: — *Section 4.* Said board of sewer commissioners, acting for and on behalf of said town, may take by eminent domain under chapter seventy-nine of the General Laws, or acquire by purchase or otherwise, any lands, water rights, rights of way or easements, public or private, in said town, and in the city of Lynn, necessary for accomplishing any purpose mentioned in this act, and may in said town and in the city of Lynn construct and maintain such main drains and sewers and/or sub-drains under or over any land, bridge, water course, railroad, railway, private way, boulevard or other public way, or within the location of any railroad, and may enter upon and dig up any private land, private way, public way or railroad location, for the purpose of laying such drains and sewers and/or sub-drains, and of maintaining and repairing the same, and may do any other thing proper or necessary for the purposes of this act; provided, that they shall not take in fee any land of a railroad corporation, and that they shall not enter upon or construct any drain or sewer within the location of any railroad corporation except at such time and in such manner as they may agree upon with such corporation, or, in case of failure to agree, as may be approved by the department of public utilities. Such work as may be done hereunder within the confines of the city of Lynn shall be done so as not to cause any unnecessary obstruction or hindrance to public travel. No way in said city of Lynn shall be dug up except with the consent of the state department of public works, in the case of a state highway, or in the case of other public ways with the consent of the authority having charge of public ways in the city of Lynn. Furthermore, any such ways so dug up in the city of Lynn shall be restored to the satisfaction of said state department of public works, if a state highway, or otherwise to the satisfaction of the authority having charge of public ways in the city of Lynn.

SECTION 3. Said chapter three hundred and fifty is hereby further amended by striking out section seven and inserting in place thereof the following: — *Section 7.* The town shall pay not less than one fourth nor more than two thirds of the whole cost of said system or systems of sewerage and sewage disposal, including the fee for entrance into the Lynn outfall sewer. In providing for the payment of the remaining portion of the cost of said system or systems of sewerage and sewage disposal or for the use of said system or systems, the town shall determine by vote which of the methods permitted by general laws it will adopt and shall by vote determine the sewer assessment rates, and the provisions of said general laws relative to the assessment, apportionment, division, reassessment, abatement and collection of sewer assessments, to liens therefor and to interest thereon shall apply to assessments made under this act, except that interest shall be at the rate of six per cent per annum. The collector of taxes of said town shall certify the payment or payments of such assessments or apportionments thereof to the sewer commissioners, or to the selectmen acting as such, who shall preserve a record thereof. *1929, 350, § 7, amended.*

Payment of cost of sewers, how determined.

SECTION 4. Said chapter three hundred and fifty is hereby further amended by striking out section eight and inserting in place thereof the following: — *Section 8.* For the purpose of paying the necessary expenses and liabilities incurred under this act for the construction of a system of main drains and common sewers, with such connections and other works as may be required for a system of sewage disposal as set forth in section one, including the fee for entrance into the Lynn outfall sewer, the town may borrow such sums as may be necessary, not exceeding, in the aggregate, five hundred thousand dollars, and may issue bonds or notes therefor, which shall bear on their face the words, Saugus Sewerage Loan, Act of 1929. Each authorized *1929, 350, § 8, amended.*

Town may borrow money for purposes of act.

issue shall constitute a separate loan. Indebtedness incurred under this act shall be in excess of the statutory limit, but shall, except as provided herein, be subject to chapter forty-four of the General Laws.

1929, 350,
§ 10, amended.

Powers of
board of
sewer com-
missioners.

SECTION 5. Said chapter three hundred and fifty is hereby further amended by striking out section ten and inserting in place thereof the following: — *Section 10.* Said board of sewer commissioners may annually appoint a clerk and may appoint a superintendent of sewers who shall not be a member of the board, and shall define their duties. It may remove the clerk or superintendent at its pleasure. Said board may, in its discretion, prescribe for the users of said systems of sewers and sewage disposal such annual rentals or charges based upon the benefits derived therefrom as it may deem proper, subject however to such rules and regulations as may be fixed by vote of the town. Said town may contract with the city of Lynn for the disposal of sewage through the Lynn outfall sewer as authorized by chapter two hundred and fifty-nine of the acts of nineteen hundred and twenty-nine and amendments thereof.

1929, 350,
§ 13, amended.

Approval of
plans, etc.,
by state
department of
public health.

SECTION 6. Said chapter three hundred and fifty is hereby further amended by striking out section thirteen and inserting in place thereof the following: — *Section 13.* No act shall be done under authority of the preceding sections, except in the making of surveys, plans and other preliminary investigations, until the plans for said system of sewerage and sewage disposal have been approved by the state department of public health. Upon application to said department for its approval, it shall give a hearing, after due notice to the public. At such hearing, plans showing in detail all the work to be done in constructing said system of sewerage and sewage disposal shall be submitted for the approval of said department.

Approved June 10, 1933.

Chap.260 AN ACT SUBMITTING TO THE VOTERS OF SUFFOLK COUNTY THE QUESTION OF MAKING JUNE SEVENTEENTH A LEGAL HOLIDAY IN SAID COUNTY.

Be it enacted, etc., as follows:

At the biennial state election in nineteen hundred and thirty-four, the registered voters of the municipalities in Suffolk county shall be entitled to vote upon the question of making June seventeenth in each year a legal holiday in said county, and such question shall be printed upon the official ballot to be used in said municipalities at said election in the following form: — "Shall June seventeenth be made a legal holiday in Suffolk county?"

The votes upon said question shall be received, sorted, counted and declared, and copies of records thereof transmitted to the state secretary, laid before the governor and council, and by them opened and examined, in accordance with the laws relating to votes for state officers and copies of records thereof, so far as such laws are applicable. The governor shall make known the result by declaring the number of votes in the affirmative and the number in the negative, and shall transmit a statement of such result, in writing, to the general court during the first week of the session in the year nineteen hundred and thirty-five.

Approved June 10, 1933.

An Act authorizing the Pride of Boston Cemetery Association to reconstruct certain walks and other ways in its cemetery in the city of Woburn.

Chap.261

Be it enacted, etc., as follows:

Section 1. The Pride of Boston Cemetery Association, a cemetery corporation organized under general law, is hereby authorized to reconstruct such walks and other ways in its cemetery located in the city of Woburn as it may deem necessary for the protection of persons using said walks or other ways from injury due to any defects that may exist therein. Said corporation, in carrying out the work of such reconstruction, may lower the grade of such part of any grave lot adjoining such walk or way as may be found to be extended beyond its original boundary line and into the area which formerly was a part of such walk or way.

Section 2. This act shall take effect upon its passage; but the authority conferred thereby is hereby declared to be limited to such authority as the general court is competent to grant.   *Approved June 14, 1933.*

An Act authorizing the commissioner of banks to respond to summonses or subpoenas by an employee or other assistant in his department.

Chap.262

Whereas, The deferred operation of this act would tend to defeat its purpose, therefore it is hereby declared to be an emergency law, necessary for the immediate preservation of the public convenience.

Emergency preamble.

Be it enacted, etc., as follows:

Chapter two hundred and thirty-three of the General Laws is hereby amended by inserting after section three, as appearing in the Tercentenary Edition thereof, the following new section: — *Section 3A.* If the commissioner of banks is summoned as a witness in any proceeding involving his official acts, unless the court or tribunal shall otherwise order, it shall be a sufficient compliance if he causes an employee or other assistant in his department having knowledge in the premises to appear.

Approved June 14, 1933.

G. L. (Ter. Ed.), 233, new section after § 3.

Employee of commissioner of banks may respond to summons on commissioner.

Chap.263　　An Act relative to the grading of milk.

Be it enacted, etc., as follows:

G. L. (Ter.
Ed.), 94,
§§ 13, 14, 14A
and 15,
amended.

Milk regula-
tion board.

Rules and
regulations.

'Grade A"
milk.
Standard.

Section 1. Chapter ninety-four of the General Laws is hereby amended by striking out sections thirteen, fourteen, fourteen A and fifteen, as appearing in the Tercentenary Edition thereof, and inserting in place thereof the following six sections: — *Section 13.* The milk regulation board established under section forty-two of chapter six, in this and the following section called the board, after a hearing as provided in the following section and with the approval of the governor and council, shall make rules and regulations establishing grades of milk, one of which shall be termed "Grade A", and regulating, and establishing standards for, the production, processing, labelling and sale of milk of such grades, including bacterial standards and sanitary standards for all grades of milk and fat standards and milk solids standards for grade A milk. The board may also by such rules and regulations establish any food or nutritional standards for special grades of milk and may specify how such special grades of milk shall be tested prior to being sold or delivered, or offered for sale or delivery. The board may from time to time, after like hearing and with like approval, amend any rule or regulation adopted and approved under this section. No standard established by said board shall fall below the Massachusetts legal standard for milk, or any standard hereafter prescribed by law for milk of the same grade to which the standard established by the board relates.

Rules and
regulations to
be approved
by governor
and council.

Publication
and hearing.

Section 13A. The board, before submitting such rules and regulations to the governor and council for approval, shall hold a public hearing thereon and shall give notice thereof by mail, postage prepaid, to all parties known to it to be directly interested. After adopting rules and regulations under section thirteen, the board shall publish the same in a newspaper published in each county in the commonwealth in which such a paper is published, at least fourteen days before submitting them for the approval of the governor and council. Any person objecting to such rules and regulations may within seven days after such publication petition the governor and council for a hearing before approval of the same, and the governor and council shall hear the petitioner, after giving due notice to the board and to all persons appearing at the hearing before the board whose attendance appears of record. The governor and council shall notify the board, within thirty days of such submission or within thirty days of such hearing, of their action on such rules and regulations. The provisions of this section relative to notice and publication shall apply to amendments of such rules and regulations, except that the governor and council may, upon the application of the board, authorize it to dispense with such notice and publication with regard to amendments deemed by the governor and council to be unimportant or of an emergency nature.

Section 13B. Any person selling milk graded as described in the rules and regulations adopted and approved under sections thirteen and thirteen A, or amended from time to time under authority thereof, in addition to such labelling as may be required, may state upon the package in which such milk is contained the state wherein such milk was produced, provided that all the milk contained in such package so labelled was produced exclusively in one state.

Section 13C. Except as otherwise provided in section thirteen D, whoever sells or offers for sale any milk of any grade other than one established under authority of sections thirteen and thirteen A, or labels or sells or offers for sale any milk labelled in imitation of any grade so established, shall be punished by a fine of not more than fifty dollars.

Section 13D. Whoever himself or by his servant or agent sells, offers for sale, exchanges or delivers or has in his custody or possession with intent to sell, offer for sale, exchange or deliver any milk designated as any grade established under authority of sections thirteen and thirteen A, and not conforming to any standard adopted for such grade, or any milk in any city or town, the board of health whereof has adopted under authority of section thirteen E bacterial standards for any grade of milk, and not conforming to such standards, or in any way violates any rule or regulation adopted and approved, or amended, under said sections thirteen and thirteen A, shall be punished by a fine of not more than fifty dollars; provided, that for a subsequent offence within one year thereafter the punishment shall be by a fine of not less than one hundred nor more than two hundred dollars.

Section 13E. Boards of health of cities and towns may adopt bacterial standards for any grade of milk established under sections thirteen and thirteen A by the board, which shall be numerically less but not greater than such standards established by the board for any such grade. The establishment of any grade of milk under authority of said sections thirteen and thirteen A shall not be construed to prevent the exercise by such boards of the powers and duties conferred and imposed upon them ·by sections forty-one and forty-three, nor shall it be construed to prevent the sale of milk the production of which is regulated under authority of sections twenty to twenty-five, inclusive, of chapter one hundred and eighty; but this section shall not be deemed to authorize the sale or delivery of any milk designated as any grade established under said sections thirteen and thirteen A and not conforming to the standard so established for such grade, nor to authorize any violation of any rule or regulation adopted and approved, or amended, under said sections.

G. L. (Ter. Ed.), 94, § 18, amended.
Penalty for selling, etc., milk illegally labelled.

SECTION 2. Said chapter ninety-four is hereby further amended by striking out section eighteen, as so appearing, and inserting in place thereof the following: — *Section 18.* Whoever himself or by his servant or agent sells, exposes for sale, or has in his custody or possession with intent to sell, milk labelled as to its fat content which, upon analysis, is found to contain less milk fat than is stated upon the label, cap or tag, and whoever himself or by his servant or agent sells, exposes for sale or exchange, or delivers milk not wholly produced in the commonwealth in containers bearing, upon a label, cap, tag, or otherwise, words indicating that such milk was produced in the commonwealth, and whoever in any manner represents that milk not wholly produced in the commonwealth was wholly produced therein, shall be punished for the first offence by a fine of not more than fifty dollars, for the second offence by a fine of not less than fifty nor more than one hundred dollars, and for a subsequent offence by a fine of not less than one hundred nor more than two hundred dollars.

Time of taking effect of act.

SECTION 3. This act, so far as it relates to the adoption and approval of rules and regulations, including notice and hearings before the milk regulation board and before the governor and council, shall take effect ninety days after its passage, but it shall not otherwise take effect until such rules and regulations have been adopted and approved; and the rules, regulations and standards adopted under section fourteen A of chapter ninety-four of the General Laws, as appearing in the Tercentenary Edition thereof, shall remain in force until rules and regulations establishing grades and standards as provided in this act have been adopted and approved as hereinbefore provided.

Approved June 14, 1933.

Chap.264 AN ACT TO PROVIDE A DEPARTMENT OF SOLDIERS' RELIEF AND STATE AND MILITARY AID IN THE CITY OF CHELSEA, AND SUBJECTING THE OFFICE OF COMMISSIONER OF SAID DEPARTMENT TO THE CIVIL SERVICE LAWS.

Be it enacted, etc., as follows:

SECTION 1. There is hereby established in the city of Chelsea a department of soldiers' relief and state and military aid, to be under the direction of a commissioner, who shall perform all duties imposed by law relative to the payment and disbursement of state aid, military aid and soldiers' relief. Except as hereinafter provided, the office of said commissioner shall be subject to the civil service laws and rules and regulations. The present incumbent of the office of clerk of the committee on military and state aid in said city, if holding such office upon the effective date of this act, shall thereupon assume the office of commissioner of said department and continue therein without taking a civil service examination, and his term of office shall be unlimited, except that he may be removed in accordance with such laws and rules and regulations.

SECTION 2. This act shall take effect upon its acceptance during the current year by vote of the board of aldermen of said city, subject to the provisions of its charter.   *Approved June 14, 1933.*

AN ACT RELATIVE TO THE PAYMENT OF THE EXPENSE OF PREPARING NECESSARY COPIES AND PAPERS FOR TRANSMISSION TO THE SUPREME JUDICIAL COURT IN APPELLATE CRIMINAL PROCEEDINGS.

*Chap.*265

Be it enacted, etc., as follows:

Section thirty-three of chapter two hundred and seventy-eight of the General Laws, as appearing in the Tercentenary Edition thereof, is hereby amended by striking out, in the fourth line, the word "commonwealth" and inserting in place thereof the word: — county, — so as to read as follows: — *Section 33.* Copies and papers relative to a question of law which arises in a criminal case in the superior court upon appeal, exception, report or otherwise shall be prepared by the clerk of the court at the expense of the county and shall thereupon be transmitted to and entered in the law docket of the supreme judicial court for the commonwealth, or for the proper county, as soon as may be after such question of law has been reserved and duly made matter of record in the superior court. Copies and papers as aforesaid shall be as specified by, and the number of copies to be prepared hereunder and the persons for whose use the same shall be transmitted shall be as provided in, the provisions of section one hundred and thirty-five of chapter two hundred and thirty-one relative to appellate proceedings in civil cases, except as otherwise provided in respect to the transcript of the evidence by sections thirty-three A to thirty-three G, inclusive, and the rules made thereunder, in criminal cases subject to said sections. Entry of a case hereunder shall not transfer the case, but only the question to be determined.

G. L. (Ter. Ed.), 278, § 33, amended.

Transmission of papers in certain actions pending in superior court.

Approved June 14, 1933.

AN ACT RELATIVE TO APPLICATIONS TO ASSESSORS FOR ABATEMENTS OF LOCAL TAXES.

*Chap.*266

Be it enacted, etc., as follows:

SECTION 1. Chapter fifty-nine of the General Laws, as most recently amended in section fifty-nine by section one of chapter one hundred and sixty-five of the acts of the current year, is hereby further amended by striking out said section fifty-nine and inserting in place thereof the following: — *Section 59.* A person aggrieved by the taxes assessed upon him may, within nine months after the date

G. L. (Ter. Ed.), 59, § 59, etc., amended.

Abatements of local taxes.

of the notice required by section three of chapter sixty, apply in writing to the assessors, on a form approved by the commissioner, for an abatement thereof; and if they find him taxed at more than his just proportion, or upon an assessment of any of his property in excess of its fair cash value, they shall make a reasonable abatement. A person aggrieved by a tax assessed upon him under section seventy-five or reassessed upon him under section seventy-seven may apply for such abatement at any time within six months after notice of such assessment or reassessment is sent to him. A tenant of real estate paying rent therefor and under obligation to pay more than one half of the taxes thereon may apply for such abatement. If a person other than the person to whom a tax on real estate is assessed is the owner thereof, or has an interest therein, or is in possession thereof, and pays the tax, he may thereafter prosecute in his own name any application, appeal or action provided by law for the abatement or recovery of such tax, which after the payment thereof shall be deemed for the purposes of such application, appeal or action, to have been assessed to the person so paying the same.

Application of act.

SECTION 2. This act shall apply to the taxes assessed for the current and subsequent years.

Approved June 14, 1933.

*Chap.*267 AN ACT RESTRICTING THE APPOINTMENT OF PERSONS FOR TEMPORARY EMPLOYMENT UNDER THE CIVIL SERVICE LAWS.

Emergency preamble.

Whereas, The deferred operation of this act would in part defeat its purpose, therefore it is hereby declared to be an emergency law, necessary for the immediate preservation of the public convenience.

Be it enacted, etc., as follows:

G. L. (Ter. Ed.), 31, new section after § 15.

Employees of state, counties, cities or towns not to be certified for temporary employment.

Chapter thirty-one of the General Laws is hereby amended by inserting after section fifteen, as appearing in the Tercentenary Edition thereof, the following new section: — *Section 15A.* No person in the employ of the commonwealth or of any county, city or town shall be certified for temporary employment under this chapter.

Approved June 16, 1933.

*Chap.*268 AN ACT INSURING INFORMATION TO PIECE OR JOB WORKERS IN FACTORIES AND WORKSHOPS RELATIVE TO THEIR COMPENSATION.

Be it enacted, etc., as follows:

G. L. (Ter. Ed.), 149, new section after § 157.

Chapter one hundred and forty-nine of the General Laws is hereby amended by inserting after section one hundred and fifty-seven, as appearing in the Tercentenary Edition thereof, the following new section: — *Section*

157A. Every person operating a factory or workshop shall supply to each employee therein who is paid by the piece, either at the time when such employee starts work or before the particular job or unit of work assigned to him is completed, and in any event before the day on which the next pay roll is calculated, a printed or written ticket, stating the basis of remuneration for the particular operation to be performed by such employee, or, in lieu of supplying such ticket, shall post in such factory or workshop within forty-eight hours after any such employee has completed any particular job or unit of work a statement showing the amount of pay earned thereon by such employee in addition to any hourly, daily or weekly rate, or by such other method as may be approved by the department of labor and industries, to which he may be entitled therefor.

Basis of remuneration to be furnished to piece or job workers.

Approved June 16, 1933.

An Act revising the municipal zoning laws.   *Chap.269*

Be it enacted, etc., as follows:

Section 1. Chapter forty of the General Laws is hereby amended by striking out sections twenty-five to thirty A, inclusive, as appearing in the Tercentenary Edition thereof, and inserting in place thereof the following: — *Section 25.* For the purpose of promoting the health, safety, convenience, morals or welfare of its inhabitants, any city, except Boston, and any town, may by ordinance or by-law regulate and restrict the height, number of stories, and size of buildings and structures, the size and width of lots, the percentage of lot that may be occupied, the size of yards, courts and other open spaces, the density of population, and the location and use of buildings, structures and land for trade, industry, residence or other purposes.

G. L. (Ter. Ed.), 40, §§ 25 to 30A, amended.

Limitation of particular classes of buildings, etc.

For any or all of such purposes such an ordinance or by-law may divide the municipality into districts of such number, shape and area as may be deemed best suited to carry out the purposes of sections twenty-five to thirty A, inclusive, and within such districts it may regulate and restrict the erection, construction, reconstruction, alteration or use of buildings and structures, or use of land, and may prohibit noxious trades within the municipality or any specified part thereof. All such regulations and restrictions shall be uniform for each class or kind of buildings, structures or land, and for each class or kind of use, throughout each district, but the regulations and restrictions in one district may differ from those in other districts.

Such regulations and restrictions shall be designed among other purposes to lessen congestion in the streets; to secure safety from fire, panic and other dangers; to provide adequate light and air; to prevent the overcrowding of land; to avoid undue concentration of population; to facilitate the adequate provision of transportation, water, sewerage, schools, parks and other public requirements; and to increase the amenities of the municipality.

Due regard shall be paid to the characteristics of the different parts of the city or town, and the ordinances or by-laws established hereunder in any city or town shall be the same for zones, districts or streets having substantially the same character; and such regulations and restrictions shall be made with a view to conserving the value of buildings and encouraging the most appropriate use of land throughout the city or town.

Ordinance or by-law not to apply to existing structures. Exceptions.

Section 26. Such an ordinance or by-law or any amendment thereof shall not apply to existing buildings or structures, nor to the existing use of any building or structure, or of land to the extent to which it is used at the time of adoption of the ordinance or by-law, but it shall apply to any change of use thereof and to any alteration of a building or structure when the same would amount to reconstruction, extension or structural change, and to any alteration of a building or structure to provide for its use for a purpose or in a manner substantially different from the use to which it was put before alteration, or for its use for the same purpose to a substantially greater extent. Such an ordinance or by-law may regulate non-use of non-conforming buildings and structures so as not to unduly prolong the life of non-conforming uses. A building, structure or land used or to be used by a public service corporation may be exempted from the operation of such an ordinance or by-law if, upon petition of the corporation, the department of public utilities shall, after public notice and hearing, decide that the present or proposed situation of the building, structure or land in question is reasonably necessary for the convenience or welfare of the public.

Modification of by-laws, etc.

Section 27. Such ordinances or by-laws may be adopted and from time to time be changed by amendment, addition or repeal, but only in the manner hereinafter provided. No ordinance or by-law originally establishing the boundaries of the districts or the regulations and restrictions to be enforced therein, and no ordinance or by-law changing the same as aforesaid, shall be adopted until after the planning board, if any, or, in a town having no such board, the board of selectmen, has held a public hearing thereon after due notice given and has submitted a final report with recommendations to the city council or town meeting; provided, that, in case of a proposed ordinance or by-law originally establishing the boundaries of the districts or the regulations and restrictions to be enforced therein, it shall be sufficient if a public hearing is held and a final report with recommendations submitted by a zoning board appointed for the purpose by the city council or selectmen. No such ordinance as proposed to be originally established or changed as aforesaid shall be adopted until after the city council or a committee designated or appointed for the purpose by it has held a public hearing thereon, at which all interested persons shall be given an opportunity to be heard. At least twenty days' notice of the time and place of such hearing before the city council or committee thereof shall be published in an official publication, or a newspaper of general circulation, in the municipality. After such notice, hearings and report a city council or town meeting may adopt, reject, or amend and adopt any such proposed ordinance or by-law. No change of any such ordinance or by-law shall be adopted except by a two thirds vote of all the members of the city council where there is a commission form of government, or a single branch or of each branch where there are two branches, or by a two thirds vote of a town meeting; provided, that in case there is filed with the city clerk prior to the close of the first hearing before the city council or committee thereof a written protest against such change, stating the reasons, duly signed by the owners of twenty per cent or more of the area of the land proposed to be included in such change, or of the area of the land immediately adjacent, extending three hundred feet therefrom, or of the area of other land within two hundred feet of the land proposed to be included in such change, no such change of any such ordinance shall be adopted except by a unanimous vote of all the members of the city council, whatever its form, if it consists of less than nine members or, if it consists of nine or more members, by a three fourths vote of all the members thereof where there is a commission form of government or a single branch, or of each branch where there are two branches.

When such by-laws or any changes therein are submitted to the attorney general for approval as required by section thirty-two, there shall also be furnished to him a statement explaining clearly the by-laws or changes proposed, together with maps or plans, when necessary.

Section 28. No such ordinance or amendment thereof shall affect any permit issued in a city before notice of hearing on the question of adoption is first given, and no such by-law or amendment thereof shall affect any permit issued in any town before notice of hearing on the question of adoption or before expiration of the time for inserting articles in the warrant for the town meeting at which such by-law or amendment is adopted, whichever occurs first; provided, that construction work under such permit is commenced within six months after its issue.

Section 29. The inspector of buildings in a city or town, or the officer or board having supervision of the construction of buildings or the power of enforcing the municipal building laws, or, if in any town there is no such officer or board, the selectmen, shall withhold a permit for the construction or alteration of any building or structure if the building or structure as constructed or altered would be in violation of any such ordinance or by-law or amend-

Ordinances, etc., not to affect certain permits.

Withholding of permits.

ment thereof; and state and municipal officers shall refuse
any permit or license for a new use of a building, structure
or land which use would be in violation of any such ordinance or by-law or amendment thereof.

Section 30. Such ordinances or by-laws shall provide
for a board of appeals which may be the existing board of
appeals under the local building or planning ordinances or
by-laws. Pending provision for a board of appeals, the
city council or selectmen shall act as a board of appeals.
Any new board of appeals established hereunder shall
consist of at least three members, who shall be appointed
by the mayor, subject to the confirmation of the city council, or by the selectmen, for terms of such length and so
arranged that the term of one appointee will expire each
year; and said board shall elect annually a chairman from
its own number. Any board so established may also act
as the board of appeals under the local building or planning
ordinances or by-laws.

Any member may be removed for cause by the appointing authority upon written charges and after a public
hearing. Vacancies shall be filled for unexpired terms in
the same manner as in the case of original appointments.
Such ordinances or by-laws may provide for the appointment in like manner of associate members of the board of
appeals; and in case of a vacancy, inability to act, or
interest on the part of a member of said board, his place
may be taken by an associate member designated by the
mayor or selectmen.

The board shall adopt rules, not inconsistent with the
provisions of any such ordinance or by-law, for conducting
its business and otherwise carrying out the purposes of
sections twenty-five to thirty A, inclusive. Meetings of
the board shall be held at the call of the chairman, and also
when called in such other manner as the board shall determine in its rules. Such chairman, or in his absence the
acting chairman, may administer oaths, summon witnesses
and call for the production of papers. All hearings of the
board shall be open to the public. The board shall cause
to be made a detailed record of its proceedings, showing
the vote of each member upon each question, or, if absent
or failing to vote, indicating such fact, and setting forth
clearly the reason or reasons for its decisions, and of its
other official actions, copies of all of which shall be immediately filed in the office of the city or town clerk and
shall be a public record, and notice of decisions shall be
mailed forthwith to parties in interest as hereinafter
designated.

Such ordinances or by-laws may provide that the board
may, in appropriate cases and subject to appropriate
conditions and safeguards, make special exceptions to the
terms of the ordinances or by-laws in harmony with their
general purpose and intent, and in accordance with general
or specific rules therein contained.

Appeals to the board of appeals may be taken by any person aggrieved by reason of his inability to obtain a permit from any administrative official under the provisions of sections twenty-five to thirty A, inclusive..

Such appeals shall be taken within a reasonable time, as provided by the rules of the board, by filing with the officer from whom the appeal is taken, and with the board of appeals, a notice of appeal specifying the grounds thereof. Such officer shall forthwith transmit to the board all the papers constituting the record upon which the action appealed from was taken.

The board of appeals shall fix a reasonable time for the hearing of the appeal or other matter referred to it, and give public notice thereof in an official publication, or a newspaper of general circulation, in the municipality, and also send notice by mail, postage prepaid, to the petitioner and to the owners of all property deemed by the board to be affected thereby, as they appear on the most recent local tax list, and decide the same within a reasonable time. At the hearing any party may appear in person or by agent or by attorney.

The board of appeals shall have the following powers:

1. To hear and decide appeals where it is alleged by the applicant for a permit that there is error in any order or decision made by an administrative official in the enforcement of sections twenty-five to thirty A, inclusive, or of any ordinance or by-law adopted thereunder.

2. To hear and decide requests for special permits upon which such board is required to pass under such ordinance or by-law.

3. To authorize upon appeal with respect to a particular parcel of land a variance from the terms of such an ordinance or by-law where, owing to conditions especially affecting such parcel but not affecting generally the zoning district in which it is located, a literal enforcement of the provisions of the ordinance or by-law would involve substantial hardship to the appellant, and where desirable relief may be granted without substantial detriment to the public good and without substantially derogating from the intent or purpose of such ordinance or by-law, but not otherwise.

In exercising the above-mentioned powers such board may, in conformity with the provisions of sections twenty-five to thirty A, inclusive, reverse or affirm in whole or in part, or may modify, any order or decision, and may make such order or decision as ought to be made, and to that end shall have all the powers of the officer from whom the appeal is taken and may issue or direct the issue of a permit.

In exercising the powers under paragraph 3 above, the board may impose limitations both of time and of user, and a continuation of the use permitted may be conditioned upon compliance with regulations to be made and amended from time to time thereafter.

Local board of appeals, powers and duties.

The concurring vote of all the members of the board shall be necessary to reverse any order or decision of any such administrative official, or to decide in favor of the applicant on any matter upon which it is required to pass under any such ordinance or by-law, or to effect any variance in the application of any such ordinance or by-law.

Any person aggrieved by a decision of the board of appeals, whether or not previously a party to the proceeding, or any municipal officer or board, may appeal to the superior court sitting in equity for the county in which the land concerned is situated; provided, that such appeal is filed in said court within fifteen days after such decision is recorded. It shall hear all pertinent evidence and determine the facts, and, upon the facts as so determined, annul such decision if found to exceed the authority of such board, or make such other decree as justice and equity may require. The foregoing remedy shall be exclusive, but the parties shall have all rights of appeal and exception as in other equity cases.

Costs shall not be allowed against the board unless it shall appear to the court that the board acted with gross negligence or in bad faith or with malice in making the decision appealed from.

All issues in any proceeding under this section shall have precedence over all other civil actions and proceedings.

Enforcement by injunction.

Section 30A. The superior court shall have jurisdiction in equity to enforce the provisions of sections twenty-five to thirty, inclusive, and any ordinances or by-laws made thereunder, and may restrain by injunction violations thereof.

G. L. (Ter. Ed.), 111, § 143, amended.

SECTION 2. Chapter one hundred and eleven of the General Laws is hereby amended by striking out section one hundred and forty-three, as appearing in the Tercentenary Edition thereof, and inserting in place thereof the following: — *Section 143.* The board of health in a city or town may from time to time assign certain places for the exercise of any trade or employment which is a nuisance or hurtful to the inhabitants, injurious to their estates, dangerous to the public health, or is attended by noisome and injurious odors, subject, however, to the provisions of any ordinance or by-law adopted therein under sections twenty-five to thirty A, inclusive, of chapter forty, or corresponding provisions of earlier laws, and it may prohibit the exercise thereof within the limits of the town or in places not so assigned, in any event. Such assignments shall be entered in the records of the town, and may be revoked when the board shall think proper.

Assignment of places for offensive trades.

G. L. (Ter. Ed.), 233, § 8, amended.

SECTION 3. Section eight of chapter two hundred and thirty-three of the General Laws, as appearing in the Tercentenary Edition thereof, is hereby amended by striking out, in the eleventh and twelfth lines, the word "twenty-seven" and inserting in place thereof the word: — thirty, —

so as to read as follows: — *Section 8.* Witnesses may be summoned to attend and testify and to produce books and papers at a hearing before a city council, or either branch thereof, or before a joint or special committee of the same or of either branch thereof, or before a board of selectmen, a board of police commissioners, a fire commissioner or a board of fire commissioners, a commissioner of public safety, a school board, a licensing board or licensing authorities for the granting of licenses for certain non-intoxicating beverages, as defined in section one of chapter one hundred and thirty-eight, a board of registrars of voters, the police commissioner or election commissioners of Boston, the metropolitan district commission, or a board of appeals designated or appointed under section thirty of chapter forty, as to matters within their authority; and such witnesses shall be summoned in the same manner, be paid the same fees and be subject to the same penalties for default, as witnesses in civil cases before the courts. The presiding officer of such council, or of either branch thereof, or a member of any such committee, board or commission, or any such commissioner, may administer oaths to witnesses who appear before such council, branch thereof, committee, board, commission or commissioner, respectively.

Witnesses before town officers, boards, etc.

SECTION 4. Except in Boston, the provisions of said section thirty, as appearing in section one of this act, shall apply in the consideration of all appeals and other matters referred to any board of zoning appeals after the effective date of this act, and in the case of all court appeals from decisions in zoning matters which are recorded after said date. All ordinances and by-laws adopted under authority granted in whole or in part by sections twenty-five to thirty A, inclusive, of chapter forty of the General Laws, or corresponding provisions of earlier laws, which are in force immediately prior to said date, shall, except in so far as they are inconsistent with the requirements of this act, continue in effect until changed as provided herein. Nothing in this act shall prevent any existing board of zoning appeals from continuing to act.

Application of certain section.
Boston excepted from certain provisions of act.

Approved June 16, 1933.

AN ACT RELATIVE TO RECOUNTS OF VOTES CAST AT ELECTIONS.

Chap.270

Be it enacted, etc., as follows:

Chapter fifty-four of the General Laws is hereby amended by striking out section one hundred and thirty-five, as appearing in the Tercentenary Edition thereof, and inserting in place thereof the following: — *Section 135.* If, on or before five o'clock in the afternoon on the third day following an election in a ward of a city or in a town, ten or more voters of such ward or town, except Boston, and in

G. L. (Ter. Ed.), 54, § 135, etc., amended.
Local or statewide recount of votes, how and by whom conducted,

notice of result, amendment of record. Boston fifty or more voters of a ward, shall sign in person, adding thereto their respective residences on the preceding April first, and cause to be filed with the city or town clerk a statement, bearing a certificate by the registrars of voters of the number of names of subscribers which are names of registered voters in such ward or town, and sworn to by one of the subscribers, that they have reason to believe and do believe that the records, or copies of records, made by the election officers of certain precincts in such ward or town, or in case of a town not voting by precincts, by the election officers of such town, are erroneous, specifying wherein they deem them to be in error and that they believe a recount of the ballots cast in such precincts or town will affect the election of one or more candidates voted for at such election, specifying the candidates, or will affect the decision of a question voted upon at such election, specifying the question, the city or town clerk shall forthwith transmit such statement and the envelope containing the ballots, sealed, to the registrars of voters, who shall, without unnecessary delay, but not before the last hour for filing requests for recounts as aforesaid, open the envelopes, recount the ballots and determine the questions raised; but upon a recount of votes for town officers in a town where the selectmen are members of the board of registrars of voters, the recount shall be made by the moderator, who shall have all the powers and perform all the duties conferred or imposed by this section upon registrars of voters.

Statement in state-wide recount; form of to be approved by state secretary. State-wide recounts in cases of offices to be filled or questions to be voted upon at the state election by all the voters of the commonwealth may be requested as provided in the foregoing provisions of this section so far as applicable, except that any petition therefor shall be on a form approved and furnished by the state secretary, shall be signed in the aggregate by at least one thousand voters, not less than two hundred and fifty to be from each of four different counties, and shall be submitted on or before five o'clock in the afternoon of the tenth day following such election to the registrars of voters of the city or town in which the signers appear to be voters, who shall forthwith certify thereon the number of signatures which are names of registered voters in said city or town, and except that such petitions for recount shall be filed with the state secretary on or before five o'clock in the afternoon of the fifteenth day following such election. He shall hold such petitions for recount until after the official tabulation of votes by the governor and council and if it then appears that the difference in the number of votes cast for the two leading candidates for the office, or in the number of affirmative and negative votes on a question, for which the recount is desired, is more than one per cent of the total number of votes cast for such office or on such question, the petitions for recount shall be void. If such difference in the votes so cast appears to be one per cent or less of the total votes cast for such office or on such question, he shall forthwith order the clerk of each city and town of the commonwealth to transmit forthwith, and said clerk shall so transmit, the envelopes containing the ballots, sealed except in the case of those containing ballots which have already been recounted in respect to said office or question under authority of the preceding paragraph, to the registrars of the city or town who shall, without unnecessary delay, open the envelopes, recount the ballots cast for said office or on said question and determine the questions raised. If a state-wide recount is petitioned for, all ballots cast at a state election shall be held, except as otherwise provided herein, by the city and town clerks until the expiration of sixty days after said election.

The registrars shall, before proceeding to recount the ballots, give not less than three days' written notice to each of the several candidates whose names appear on the ballot for the office in question, or to such person as shall be designated by the petitioners for a recount of ballots cast upon questions submitted to the voters, of the time and place of making the recount, and each such candidate or person representing petitioners as aforesaid shall be allowed to be present and to witness such recount at any table where a recount of the ballots affecting such candidate is being held, either in person, accompanied with counsel if he so desires, or by an agent appointed by him in writing. In the case of a recount of ballots cast for offices which are filled by all the voters of the commonwealth, such notice may be given to the duly organized state political committees. In the case of a recount of the ballots cast upon a question submitted to all the voters as aforesaid, one representative from any committee organized to favor or to oppose the question so submitted shall be permitted to be present and witness the recount. Candidates and persons representing petitioners to be notified, etc.

All recounts shall be upon the questions designated in the statements or petitions filed, and no other count shall be made, or allowed to be made, or other information taken, or allowed to be taken, from the ballots on such recount, except that in the case of a recount of the ballots cast for an office, the votes cast for all of the candidates for such office, including blanks cast, shall be recounted. Recounts to be upon questions designated in statements, etc.

If all of the candidates for an office whose names are printed on the ballot, in respect to which a petition for a recount has been filed, request in writing, filed with the city or town clerk, or, in a state-wide recount, with the state secretary, that the recount be discontinued, the city or town clerk or the state secretary, as the case may be, shall immediately order the recount discontinued whereupon proceedings hereunder shall terminate. Recount may be discontinued, when.

The registrars shall, when the recount is complete, enclose all the ballots in their proper envelopes, seal each envelope with a seal provided therefor, and certify upon Record and notice of result.

each envelope that it has been opened and again sealed in conformity to law; and shall likewise make and sign a statement of their determination of the questions raised. The envelopes, with such statement, shall be returned to the city or town clerk, who shall alter and amend, in accordance with such determination, such records as have been found to be erroneous; and the records so amended shall stand as the true records of the election. Copies of such amended records of votes cast at a state election shall be made and transmitted as required by law in the case of copies of original records; provided, that such copies of amended records shall in case of a state-wide recount be transmitted by the city or town clerk to the state secretary within four days of the completion of such recount. If, in case of a recount of votes for town officers, it shall appear that a person was elected other than the person declared to have been elected, the registrars of voters shall forthwith make and sign a certificate of such fact, stating therein the number of votes cast, as determined by the recount, for each candidate for the office the election to which is disputed, and shall file the same with the town clerk. The town clerk shall record the certificate and shall, within twenty-four hours after such filing, cause a copy of such certificate, attested by him, to be delivered to or left at the residence of the person so declared to have been elected, and to the person who by such certificate appears to be elected.

Clerical assistance.

Registrars of voters may employ such clerical assistance as they deem necessary to enable them to carry out the provisions of this section.   *Approved June 16, 1933.*

Chap.271 AN ACT ESTABLISHING IN THE TOWN OF MILFORD REPRE-
SENTATIVE TOWN GOVERNMENT BY LIMITED TOWN MEET-
INGS.

Be it enacted, etc., as follows:

Representative town government in town of Milford. Districts, establishment of.

SECTION 1. Upon the acceptance of this act by the town of Milford, as hereinafter provided, the selectmen shall forthwith divide the territory thereof into voting precincts, each of which shall be plainly designated and shall contain not less than four hundred registered voters. All precincts shall contain approximately an equal number of registered voters. The precincts shall be so established as to consist of compact and contiguous territory, to be bounded as far as possible, by the center line of known streets and ways or by other well defined limits. Their boundaries shall be reviewed, and, if need be, wholly or partly revised by the selectmen in December, once in five years, or in December of any year when so directed by a vote of a representative town meeting held not later than November twentieth of that year. The selectmen shall, within twenty days after any establishment or revision of the precincts, file a report of their doings with the town clerk, the registrars of voters and the assessors with a map or maps or description of the precincts and the names and residences of the registered voters therein. The selectmen shall also cause to be posted in the town hall a map or maps or description of the precincts as established or revised from time to time, with the names and residences of the registered voters therein. They shall also cause to be posted in at least one public place in each precinct a description of that precinct with the names and residences of the registered voters therein. The division of the town into voting precincts and any revision of such precincts shall take effect upon the date of the filing of the report thereof by the selectmen with the town clerk. Whenever the precincts are established or revised, the town clerk shall forthwith give written notice thereof to the state secretary, stating the number and designation of the precincts. Meetings of the registered voters of the several precincts for elections, for primaries, and for voting upon any question to be submitted to all the registered voters of the town, shall be held on the same day and at the same hour and at such place or places within the town as the selectmen shall in the warrant for such meeting direct. The provisions of the general laws, relating to precinct voting at elections, so far as the same are not inconsistent with this act, shall apply to all elections and primaries in the town upon the establishment of voting precincts as hereinbefore provided.

SECTION 2. Other than the officers designated in section three as town meeting members at large, the representative town meeting membership shall in each precinct consist of the largest number divisible by three which will admit of a representation thereof in the approximate proportion which the number of registered voters therein bears to the total number of registered voters in the town and which will cause the total membership to be as nearly two hundred and forty as may be. Representative town meeting membership, number, etc.

The registered voters in every precinct shall, at the first annual town election held after the establishment of such precincts, and at the first annual town election following any precinct revision, conformably to the laws relative to elections not inconsistent with this act, elect by ballot the number of registered voters in the precinct, other than the officers designated in section three as town meeting members at large, provided in the first sentence of this section, to be town meeting members of the town. The first third, in the order of votes received, of members so elected shall serve three years, the second third in such order shall serve two years, and the remaining third in such order shall serve one year, from the day of the annual town meeting; in case of a tie vote affecting the division into thirds, as aforesaid, the members elected from the precinct shall by ballot determine the same; and thereafter except as is otherwise provided herein, at each annual town election the registered voters of each precinct shall, in like manner, elect one third of the number of elected town meeting members to which that precinct is entitled for the term of three years, and shall at such election fill for the unexpired term or terms any vacancy or vacancies then existing in the number of town meeting members in any such precinct. The terms of office of all elected town meeting members from every precinct revised as aforesaid shall cease upon the election as hereinbefore provided of their successors. The town clerk shall, after every election of town meeting members, forthwith notify each such member by mail of his election.

Town meeting members at large.

SECTION 3. Any representative town meeting held under the provisions of this act, except as otherwise provided herein, shall be limited to the voters elected under section two, together with the following, designated as town meeting members at large; namely, any member of the general court of the commonwealth from the town, the moderator, the town clerk, the selectmen, the town treasurer, the town counsel, the highway surveyor, the chairman of the trustees of the public library, the chairman of the finance committee, the chairman of the school committee, the chairman of the board of assessors, the chairman of the board of health, the chairman of the park commission, the chairman of the board of town cemeteries, the chairman of the registrars of voters, the tax collector, the chairman of the board of public welfare and the town accountant. The town clerk shall notify the town meeting members of the time and place at which representative town meetings are to be held, the notices to be sent by mail at least seven days before the meeting. The town meeting members, as aforesaid, shall be the judges of the election and qualifications of their members. A majority of the town meeting members shall constitute a quorum for doing business; but a less number may organize temporarily and may adjourn from time to time, but no town meeting shall adjourn over the date of an election of town meeting members. All town meetings shall be public. The town meeting members as such shall receive no compensation. Subject to such conditions as may be determined from time to time by the members of the representative town meeting, any registered voter of the town who is not a town meeting member may speak at any representative town meeting, but shall not vote. A town meeting member may resign by filing a written resignation with the town clerk, and such resignation shall take effect upon the date of such filing. A town meeting member who removes from the town shall cease to be a town meeting member and an elected town meeting member who removes from one precinct to another or is so removed by a revision of precincts shall not retain membership after the next annual election.

SECTION 4. Nominations of candidates for town meeting members to be elected under this act shall be made by nomination papers, which shall bear no political designation, shall be signed by not less than thirty voters of the precinct in which the candidate resides, and shall be filed with the town clerk at least ten days before the election; provided, that any town meeting member may become a candidate for re-election by giving written notice thereof to the town clerk at least thirty days before election. No nomination papers shall be valid in respect to any candidate whose written acceptance is not thereon or attached thereto when filed. *Nomination of candidates for town meeting members.*

Proviso.

SECTION 5. The articles in the warrant for every town meeting, so far as they relate to the election of the moderator, town officers and town meeting members, and as herein provided, to referenda, and all matters to be acted upon and determined by ballot, shall be so acted upon and determined by the registered voters of the town in their respective precincts. All other articles in the warrant for any town meeting, beginning with the town meeting at which said town meeting members are first elected, shall be acted upon and determined exclusively by town meeting members at a meeting to be held at such time and place as shall be set forth by the selectmen in the warrant for the meeting, subject to the referendum provided for by section eight. *Warrant articles, how acted upon.*

SECTION 6. A moderator shall be elected by ballot at each annual town meeting, and shall serve as moderator of all town meetings, except as otherwise provided by law, until a successor is elected and qualified. Nominations for and election of a moderator shall be as in the case of other elective town officers, and any vacancy in the office may be filled by the town meeting members at a meeting held for that purpose. If a moderator is absent, a moderator pro tempore may be elected by the town meeting members. *Moderator, election, etc.*

SECTION 7. Any vacancy in the full number of town meeting members from any precinct, whether arising from a failure of the registered voters thereof to elect, or from any other cause, may be filled, until the next annual election, by the remaining members of the precinct from among the registered voters thereof. Upon petition therefor, signed by not less than ten town meeting members from the precinct, notice of any vacancy shall promptly be given by the town clerk to the remaining members from the precinct in which the vacancy or vacancies exist, and he shall call a special meeting of such members for the purpose of filling any vacancy. He shall cause to be mailed to every such member, not less than five days before the time set for the meeting, a notice specifying the object, time and place of the meeting. At the said meeting a majority of the members from such precinct shall constitute a quorum, and they shall elect from their own number a chairman and a clerk. The choice to fill any vacancy shall *Vacancies in town meeting membership, how filled.*

be by ballot, and a majority of the votes cast shall be required for a choice. The chairman and clerk shall count the ballots and shall make a certificate of the choice and forthwith file the same with the town clerk, together with a written acceptance by the member or members so chosen, who shall thereupon be deemed elected and qualified as a town meeting member or members, subject to the right of all the town meeting members to judge of the election and qualifications of the members as set forth in section three.

Votes, when operative. Referendum. Section 8. A vote passed at any representative town meeting authorizing the expenditure of twenty thousand dollars or more as a special appropriation, or establishing a new board or office or abolishing an old or merging two or more boards, or fixing the term of office of town officers, where such term is optional, or increasing or reducing the number of members of a board, or adopting a new by-law, or amending an existing by-law, shall not be operative until after the expiration of five days, exclusive of Sundays and holidays, from the dissolution of the meeting. If, within said five days, a petition, signed by not less than five per cent of the registered voters of the town, containing their names and addresses as they appear on the list of registered voters, is filed with the selectmen asking that the question or questions involved in such a vote be submitted to the registered voters of the town at large, then the selectmen, after the expiration of five days, shall forthwith call a special meeting for the sole purpose of presenting to the registered voters at large the question or questions so involved. The polls shall be opened at two o'clock in the afternoon and shall be closed not earlier than eight o'clock in the evening, and all votes upon any questions so submitted shall be taken by ballot, and the check list shall be used in the several precinct meetings in the same manner as in the election of town officers. The questions so submitted shall be determined by a majority vote of the registered voters of the town voting thereon, but no action of the representative town meeting shall be reversed unless at least twenty-five per cent of the registered voters shall so vote. Each question so submitted shall be in the form of the following question which shall be placed on the official ballot: — "Shall the town vote to approve the action of the representative town meeting whereby it was voted (brief description of the substance of the vote)?" If such petition is not filed within the said period of five days, the vote of the representative town meeting shall become operative upon the expiration of the said period.

Town to act through town meeting members. Section 9. The town of Milford, after the acceptance of this act, shall have the capacity to act through and be bound by its said town meeting members who shall, when convened from time to time as herein provided, constitute representative town meetings; and the representative town meetings shall exercise exclusively, so far as will conform to the provisions of this act, all powers vested in the municipal corporation. Action in conformity with all provisions of law now or hereafter applicable to the transaction of town affairs in town meetings shall, when taken by any representative town meeting in accordance with the provisions of this act, have the same force and effect as if such action had been taken in a town meeting open to all the voters of the town as heretofore organized and conducted.

SECTION 10. The representative town meeting may make such rules consistent with general law as may be considered necessary for conducting its meetings. *Rules.*

SECTION 11. The representative town meeting may appoint such committees of its members for investigation and report as it may consider necessary. *Committees.*

SECTION 12. All by-laws or parts of by-laws of the town inconsistent with the provisions of this act are hereby repealed. *Repeal of certain by-laws.*

SECTION 13. This act shall not abridge the right of the inhabitants of Milford to hold general meetings, as that right is secured to them by the constitution of this commonwealth; nor shall this act confer upon any representative town meeting in Milford the power finally to commit the town to any measure affecting its municipal existence or changing its government, without action thereon by the voters of the town at large, using the ballot and the check list therefor. *Certain rights not abridged, etc.*

SECTION 14. This act shall be submitted to the registered voters of the town of Milford at the annual town election in the year nineteen hundred and thirty-four. The vote shall be taken by ballot in accordance with the provisions of the general laws, so far as the same shall be applicable, in answer to the following question, which shall be placed upon the official ballot to be used for the election of town officers: — "Shall an act passed by the general court in the year nineteen hundred and thirty-three, entitled 'An Act establishing in the town of Milford representative town government by limited town meetings', be accepted by this town?" If accepted by a majority of the voters voting thereon, this act shall take effect for all purposes incidental to the annual town election in said town in the year nineteen hundred and thirty-five and shall take full effect beginning with said election. *Acceptance of act.*

SECTION 15. If this act is rejected by the registered voters of the town of Milford when submitted to said voters under section fourteen, it may again be submitted for acceptance in like manner from time to time to such voters at any annual town meeting in said town not later than the annual town election in the year nineteen hundred and thirty-seven, and, if accepted by a majority of the voters voting thereon at such an election, shall thereupon take effect for all purposes incidental to the next annual town election in said town and shall take full effect beginning with said election. *Resubmission of act after rejection, etc.* *Approved June 16, 1933.*

*Chap.*272 AN ACT RELATIVE TO OBTAINING AND COMMUNICATING IN-
FORMATION AND TO THE USE OF PERSUASION IN THE COURSE
OF CERTAIN TRADE DISPUTES.

Be it enacted, etc., as follows:

G. L. (Ter.
Ed.), 149,
§ 24,
amended.

Section twenty-four of chapter one hundred and forty-nine of the General Laws, as appearing in the Tercentenary Edition thereof, is hereby amended by adding at the end thereof the following:—, nor for attending, in the course of a lawful trade dispute, at any place where such person or persons may lawfully be, for the purpose of peacefully obtaining or communicating information or of so persuading or attempting to persuade, — so as to read as follows:—

Peaceful
persuasion
not penalized
in course of
certain labor
and trade
disputes.

Section 24. No person shall be punished criminally, or held liable or answerable in any action at law or suit in equity, for persuading or attempting to persuade, by printing or otherwise, any other person to do anything, or to pursue any line of conduct not unlawful or actionable or in violation of any marital or other legal duty, unless such persuasion or attempt to persuade is accompanied by injury or threat of injury to the person, property, business or occupation of the person persuaded or attempted to be persuaded, or by disorder or other unlawful conduct on the part of the person persuading or attempting to persuade, or is a part of an unlawful or actionable conspiracy, nor for attending, in the course of a lawful trade dispute, at any place where such person or persons may lawfully be, for the purpose of peacefully obtaining or communicating information or of so persuading or attempting to persuade.

Approved June 16, 1933.

---

*Chap.*273 AN ACT RELATIVE TO THE ENFORCEMENT OF CONSERVATOR-
SHIP PROCEEDINGS IN RESPECT TO TRUST COMPANIES.

Be it enacted, etc., as follows:

G. L. (Ter.
Ed.), 172, new
section after
§ 89.

Chapter one hundred and seventy-two of the General Laws, as amended, is hereby further amended by adding after section eighty-nine, added by section one of chapter eighty-seven of the acts of nineteen hundred and thirty-three, the following new section:— *Section 90.* The supreme judicial court, or any justice thereof, shall have jurisdiction in equity to enforce the provisions of sections eighty-three to eighty-nine, inclusive, and to act upon all applications and in all proceedings thereunder.

Enforcement
of conservator-
ship proceed-
ings.

Approved June 16, 1933.

An Act providing for additional statutory court sessions of the probate court for worcester county. *Chap.274*

Be it enacted, etc., as follows:

Section sixty-two of chapter two hundred and fifteen of the General Laws, as appearing in the Tercentenary Edition thereof, is hereby amended by striking out the paragraph contained in the fifty-sixth and fifty-seventh lines and inserting in place thereof the following: — G. L. (Ter. Ed.), 215, § 62, amended.

Worcester, at Worcester, each Tuesday of every month except the first, second, fourth and fifth Tuesdays of August and each Friday of every month except August. Probate court, additional sessions in Worcester county.

Approved June 16, 1933.

An Act authorizing contributions by the county of barnstable for the construction of sea walls or other forms of shore protection for towns in said county. *Chap.275*

Be it enacted, etc., as follows:

Section 1. The county of Barnstable is hereby authorized to contribute to the cost of constructing sea walls or other works to be built by the department of public works during the years nineteen hundred and thirty-three, nineteen hundred and thirty-four and nineteen hundred and thirty-five under the provisions of section eleven of chapter ninety-one of the General Laws for the protection of the shores of the towns in said county from erosion by the sea, and the treasurer of said county, with the approval of the county commissioners, may pay the county's proportion of such cost from the highway appropriation or, for the purpose of so contributing, may borrow from time to time on the credit of the county such sums as may be necessary, not exceeding, in the aggregate, thirty-four thousand dollars, and may issue bonds or notes of the county therefor, which shall bear on their face the words, Barnstable County Shore Protection Loan, Act of 1933. Each authorized issue shall constitute a separate loan, and such loans shall be payable in not more than five years from their dates. Such bonds or notes shall be signed by the treasurer of the county and countersigned by a majority of the county commissioners. The county may sell such securities at public or private sale upon such terms and conditions as the county commissioners may deem proper, but not for less than their par value. Indebtedness incurred under this act shall, except as herein provided, be subject to chapter thirty-five of the General Laws. Construction of sea walls in Barnstable county.

Section 2. The county treasurer, with the approval of the county commissioners, may issue temporary notes of the county payable in not more than one year from their dates, in anticipation of the issue of serial bonds or notes County may borrow money.

under the preceding section, but the time within which such serial bonds or notes shall become due and payable shall not, by reason of such temporary notes, be extended beyond the time fixed by said section. Any notes issued in anticipation of the serial bonds or notes shall be paid from the proceeds thereof.

SECTION 3. This act shall take effect upon its passage.

Approved June 21, 1933.

---

*Chap.*276 AN ACT PROHIBITING UNAUTHORIZED PERSONS FROM WEARING THE UNIFORM, OR ANY DISTINCTIVE PART THEREOF, OF CERTAIN MILITARY, NAVAL AND VETERANS' ORGANIZATIONS.

Emergency preamble.

Whereas, The deferred operation of this act would tend to defeat its purpose, therefore it is hereby declared to be an emergency law, necessary for the immediate preservation of the public convenience.

Be it enacted, etc., as follows:

G. L. (Ter. Ed.), 264, § 10A, amended.

Exploiting uniform of army, etc., penalized.

Chapter two hundred and sixty-four of the General Laws is hereby amended by striking out section ten A, as appearing in the Tercentenary Edition thereof, and inserting in place thereof the following: — *Section 10A.* Whoever wears the uniform, or any distinctive part thereof, of the United States army, navy, marine corps, revenue cutter service, or coast guard, or of the national guard, or of any organization enumerated in section seventy of chapter two hundred and sixty-six, or wears a hat, cap or other apparel similar to or resembling the hat, cap or other distinctive part of any such uniform, while engaged, for personal profit, in soliciting alms, in selling merchandise or taking orders for the same, in seeking or receiving contributions in support of any cause, enterprise or undertaking or in soliciting or receiving subscriptions to any book, paper or magazine, shall be punished by a fine of not more than one hundred dollars, or by imprisonment for not more than three months; provided, that this section shall not apply to the sale of property or any other act or transaction conducted under authority of the government of the United States, and provided further, that no person shall be subject to prosecution hereunder for wearing the uniform, or any distinctive part thereof, while engaged as aforesaid, of any organization enumerated in said section seventy if he so acted under authority of such organization or any post, camp or other unit thereof.   *Approved June 21, 1933.*

AN ACT AUTHORIZING PAYMENT OF DIVIDENDS FROM CLOSED BANKS TO CERTAIN MINORS AND TO THE NEXT OF KIN OF CERTAIN DECEASED PERSONS.

*Chap.*277

Whereas, The deferred operation of this act would tend to defeat its purpose, therefore it is hereby declared to be an emergency law, necessary for the immediate preservation of the public convenience.

Emergency preamble.

Be it enacted, etc., as follows:

Chapter one hundred and sixty-seven of the General Laws, as appearing in the Tercentenary Edition thereof, is hereby amended by inserting after section thirty-one the following new section: — *Section 31A.* In the case of dividends payable under section thirty-one to a minor, having no known guardian, on a deposit which does not exceed one hundred dollars, the commissioner, in his discretion, may make any dividend payment to such minor or either of his parents, and such payment shall be a valid discharge to the same extent as if made to the legal representative of such minor. In the case of a deposit which does not exceed one hundred dollars standing in the name of a decedent for the allowance of whose will or for the administration of whose estate no petition has been filed within sixty days after his death, the commissioner, in his discretion, may make any dividend payment, payable under said section, on account of such deposit, to the person or persons whom he finds entitled thereto, and such payment shall be a valid discharge to the same extent as if made to the legal representative of the decedent.

G. L. (Ter. Ed.), 167, new section after § 31.

Commissioner of banks may pay dividends from closed banks to certain minors, etc.

Approved June 21, 1933.

AN ACT CONFIRMING AND ESTABLISHING CERTAIN BOUNDARY LINES IN TIDE WATER.

*Chap.*278

Be it enacted, etc., as follows:

SECTION 1. Chapter one of the General Laws is hereby amended by striking out section three, as appearing in the Tercentenary Edition thereof, and inserting in place thereof the following: — *Section 3.* The territorial limits of the commonwealth shall extend one marine league from its sea-shore at extreme low water mark, and the exterior line of the commonwealth as located and defined by the board of harbor and land commissioners under chapter one hundred and ninety-six of the acts of eighteen hundred and eighty-one shall be prima facie the marine boundary of the commonwealth. If an inlet or arm of the sea does not exceed two marine leagues in width between its headlands, a straight line from one headland to the other shall be equivalent to the shore line.

G. L. (Ter. Ed.), 1, § 3, amended.

Marine boundaries of the commonwealth.

SECTION 2. Chapter thirty-four of the General Laws is hereby amended by striking out section one, as so ap-

G. L. (Ter. Ed.), 34, § 1, amended.

pearing, and inserting in place thereof the following: —

Seaward
boundaries of
counties.
Section 1. The seaward boundary of counties bordering on the open sea shall coincide with the marine boundary of the commonwealth. The boundary lines in tide water between adjacent coastal counties shall coincide with and are hereby established to be the boundary lines in tide water between the adjoining coastal municipalities of said counties, as confirmed and established by section one of chapter forty-two. Counties separated by waters within the jurisdiction of the commonwealth shall exercise a concurrent jurisdiction over such waters. Each county shall be a body politic and corporate for the purposes of suit, of buying and holding, for county uses, personal estate and land lying therein, and of contracting and doing other necessary acts relative to its property and affairs.

G. L. (Ter.
Ed.), 42, § 1,
amended.
Seaward
boundaries
of cities and
towns.
SECTION 3. Chapter forty-two of the General Laws is hereby amended by striking out section one, as so appearing, and inserting in place thereof the following: — *Section 1.* The seaward boundary of cities and towns bordering on the open sea shall coincide with the marine boundary of the commonwealth. The boundary lines in tide water between adjacent coastal municipalities, as located and defined by the board of harbor and land commissioners under chapter one hundred and ninety-six of the acts of eighteen hundred and eighty-one, except in so far as the boundary lines so located and defined purported to vary boundary lines in tide water between municipalities theretofore established by the general court, together with such boundary lines theretofore so established, as such boundary lines have been subsequently changed by the general court or defined by decrees of the land court, with such additions to or subtractions from the length thereof as have been made by natural changes in the shore line of the commonwealth, are hereby confirmed and established as the legal boundary lines in tide water between said adjacent municipalities; provided, that such boundary lines shall hereafter be changed from time to time to conform to any change in said shore line.   *Approved June 21, 1933.*

Chap.279 AN ACT TO IMPOUND THE BIRTH RECORDS OF CHILDREN BORN
OUT OF WEDLOCK.

Be it enacted, etc., as follows:

G. L. (Ter.
Ed.), 46, new
section after
§ 2.
Impounding
of certain
birth records.
Chapter forty-six of the General Laws is hereby amended by inserting after section two, as appearing in the Tercentenary Edition thereof, the following new section: — *Section 2A.* Examination of records and returns of illegitimate births, or of copies of such records in the office of the state secretary, shall not be permitted except upon proper judicial order, or upon request of a person seeking his own birth record, or his attorney, parent, guardian or conservator, or of a person whose official duties, in the opinion of the

town clerk or state secretary, entitle him to the information contained therein, nor shall certified copies thereof be furnished except upon such order, or the request of such person.   *Approved June 21, 1933.*

AN ACT RELATIVE TO THE RECORDING OF CERTAIN BIRTHS.   *Chap.*280

Be it enacted, etc., as follows:

SECTION 1. Section one of chapter forty-six of the General Laws, as appearing in the Tercentenary Edition thereof, is hereby amended by striking out the third sentence in the second paragraph and inserting in place thereof the following: — The term "illegitimate" shall not be used in the record of a birth of a child to a single woman, nor in the record of such birth to a married woman unless the illegitimacy has been legally determined or has been admitted by the sworn statement of the woman and her husband, or, if the town clerk is satisfied that both the woman and her husband cannot be located, by the sworn statement of either of them and by evidence beyond all reasonable doubt to substantiate such statement, which statement and evidence have been submitted by the town clerk to a judge of probate or to a justice of a district court, and have been approved by such judge or justice.

SECTION 2. Section thirteen of said chapter forty-six, as so appearing, is hereby amended by adding at the end of the second paragraph thereof the following: — If, however, the birth of such child was recorded as that of a legitimate child of the mother and the man who was her husband at the time of such birth, the record shall not be amended as provided in this section unless the illegitimacy has been legally determined or has been admitted by the sworn statement of the mother and such husband, or, if the town clerk is satisfied that both the mother and such husband cannot be located, by the sworn statement of either of them and by evidence beyond all reasonable doubt to substantiate such statement, which statement and evidence have been submitted by the town clerk to a judge of probate or to a justice of a district court, and have been approved by such judge or justice.

Approved June 21, 1933.

G. L. (Ter. Ed.), 46, § 1, amended.

Use of term "illegitimate" pertaining to birth records, regulated.

G. L. (Ter. Ed.), 46, § 13, amended. Correction of errors in record, amendment of records, regulated.

AN ACT PROVIDING FOR THE CONSTRUCTION BY THE METRO-   *Chap.*281
POLITAN DISTRICT COMMISSION OF AN EXTENSION OF THE NORTH METROPOLITAN SEWERAGE SYSTEM IN ARLINGTON TO A POINT NEAR THE LEXINGTON-ARLINGTON BOUNDARY LINE.

Be it enacted, etc., as follows:

SECTION 1. The metropolitan district commission is hereby authorized to construct and maintain an extension of the main sewer in the valley of Mill or Sucker brook in the town of Arlington, from its present terminus at Park avenue in said town to a point in the town of Lexington near the Lexington-Arlington boundary line, and for this purpose may exercise all the powers conferred upon it under chapter ninety-two of the General Laws relative to the construction, maintenance and operation of systems of sewage disposal.

SECTION 2. The cost of the construction authorized by section one shall be paid out of the unexpended balances remaining from the proceeds of loans issued under authority of chapter one hundred and sixteen of the acts of nineteen hundred and twenty-four, and of chapter one hundred and eighty-four of the acts of nineteen hundred and twenty-seven, as amended by chapter two hundred and eleven of the acts of nineteen hundred and twenty-eight, and as affected by chapter one hundred and eighty-eight of the acts of nineteen hundred and twenty-nine, and not required for the purposes of said chapter one hundred and sixteen, said chapter one hundred and eighty-four, chapter two hundred and thirteen of the acts of nineteen hundred and twenty-six or chapter three hundred and eighty-one of the acts of nineteen hundred and thirty-one.

SECTION 3. This act shall take effect upon its passage.
Approved June 23, 1933.

Chap.282 AN ACT RELATIVE TO THE HOLDING OF MUNICIPAL ELECTIONS IN THE CITY OF SOMERVILLE.

Be it enacted, etc., as follows:

SECTION 1. Section seven of chapter two hundred and eighty-one of the acts of nineteen hundred and thirty-two is hereby amended by inserting after the word "wards" in the second line the words: — and voting precincts, — so as to read as follows: — *Section 7.* The preliminary elections and the regular municipal elections shall be held by wards and voting precincts and the board of aldermen shall designate on or before the eighth Tuesday preceding a regular municipal election or on or before the fourth Tuesday preceding a special municipal election, the polling places where the preliminary elections and the regular municipal elections shall be held. The regularly appointed election officers shall serve at both the preliminary elections and the regular municipal elections.

SECTION 2. This act shall take effect upon its passage.
Approved June 23, 1933.

AN ACT CLARIFYING THE LAW RELATIVE TO TAKING LAND BY
EMINENT DOMAIN FOR HIGHWAY PURPOSES.

Chap.283

Be it enacted, etc., as follows:

SECTION 1. Chapter forty of the General Laws is hereby amended by striking out section fourteen, as appearing in the Tercentenary Edition thereof, and inserting in place thereof the following: — *Section 14.* The aldermen of any city, except Boston, or the selectmen of a town may purchase, or take by eminent domain under chapter seventy-nine, any land, easement or right therein within the city or town not already appropriated to public use, for any municipal purpose for which the purchase or taking of land, easement or right therein is not otherwise authorized or directed by statute; but no land, easement or right therein shall be taken or purchased under this section unless the taking or purchase thereof has previously been authorized by the city council or by vote of the town, nor until an appropriation of money, to be raised by loan or otherwise, has been made for the purpose by a two thirds vote of the city council or by a two thirds vote of the town, and no lot of land shall be purchased for any municipal purpose by any city subject to this section for a price more than twenty-five per cent in excess of its average assessed valuation during the previous three years.

G. L. (Ter. Ed.), 40, § 14, amended.

Taking or purchase of land by cities and towns.

SECTION 2. Section seven of chapter eighty-two of the General Laws, as so appearing, is hereby amended by striking out, in the third to sixth lines, inclusive, the words ", including an easement in land adjoining the location of the highway consisting of a right to have the land of the location protected by having the surface of the adjoining land slope from the boundary of the location", — so as to read as follows: — *Section 7.* If it is necessary, for the purpose of laying out, altering or relocating a highway, or establishing a building line in connection therewith, to acquire land, or an easement or right therein, the commissioners shall, at the same time that the highway is laid out, altered or relocated, take such land, easement or right by eminent domain under chapter seventy-nine. Any person sustaining damage in his property by the laying out, alteration, relocation or discontinuance of a highway, or by specific repairs thereon, or by the establishment or discontinuance of a building line, shall be entitled to recover the same under said chapter. If no entry has been made upon land taken for highway purposes, or if the location has for any other cause become void, or if specific repairs which have been ordered are not made, a person who has suffered loss or been put to expense by the proceedings shall be entitled to recover indemnity therefor under said chapter.

G. L. (Ter. Ed.), 82, § 7, amended.

Takings by eminent domain of easements, etc., in connection with laying out, etc., of highways.

SECTION 3. Said chapter eighty-two, as so appearing, is hereby further amended by inserting after section thirty-

G. L. (Ter. Ed.), 82, new section after § 32A.

Takings for
slope purposes.

two A the following new section: — *Section 32B.* Wherever in this chapter or in any city charter a board of officers is authorized to take land by eminent domain under chapter seventy-nine, in connection with the laying out, widening, altering or relocating of a public way, such board of officers shall be authorized to take an easement in land adjoining the location of the public way consisting of a right to have the land of the location protected by having the surface of such adjoining land slope from the boundary of the location.　　　　　*Approved June 23, 1933.*

Chap.284 AN ACT PROVIDING FOR THE LICENSING OF CLUBS DISPENSING FOOD OR BEVERAGES.

Be it enacted, etc., as follows:

G. L. (Ter.
Ed.), 140,
new heading
and sections
after § 21D.

Chapter one hundred and forty of the General Laws is hereby amended by inserting after section twenty-one D, as appearing in the Tercentenary Edition thereof, the following heading and sections: —

ORGANIZATIONS DISPENSING FOOD OR BEVERAGES TO MEMBERS AND GUESTS.

Club, etc.,
licenses,
issuance of.

Section 21E. Licensing authorities may grant a license to any club, society, association or other organization, whether incorporated or unincorporated, authorizing it to dispense food and beverages to be consumed on its premises, to its stockholders or members and their guests, but to no others; provided, that the licensing authorities are satisfied that such organization is a proper one to which to grant such a license. Such licenses and the granting thereof shall be subject to the provisions of sections two and four, except that compliance with the provisions of law relative to innholders or common victuallers shall not be required as a condition of obtaining such license. If such organization is unincorporated, the names of all the officers and members shall be submitted with the application for the license, and shall be kept available for public inspection. Section two hundred and one shall apply to the premises of any organization subject to this section. If any such organization at any time exercises in an improper manner the authority conferred upon it by such license the licensing authorities, after notice to the licensee and reasonable opportunity for a hearing, may upon satisfactory proof thereof suspend or revoke the license. The provisions of this and the following section shall not apply to literary, benevolent, charitable, scientific or religious corporations or religious organizations or associations whose real or personal property is exempt from taxation, nor to any club so long as it is licensed to sell wines and malt beverages under section four of chapter one hundred and twenty of the acts of nineteen hundred and thirty-three, nor to any recognized veteran or fraternal organization.

Section 21F. Any officer or employee of any such organization who dispenses or causes to be dispensed any food or beverage on its premises, unless such organization is then licensed under section twenty-one E, shall be punished by a fine of not more than one hundred dollars for the first or second offence and by such fine and imprisonment for not more than three months for each subsequent offence. If any officer or employee of any such organization which is incorporated is convicted of any offence under this section, the selectmen, or the aldermen, in the place where such organization is situated, except Boston, and in Boston the police commissioner, shall immediately give notice to the state secretary, who, upon receipt thereof, shall declare the charter of such organization void, and shall publish a notice in at least one newspaper published in the county where such organization is located that such incorporation is void and of no further effect.

Penalty.

Approved June 23, 1933.

AN ACT PROVIDING FOR APPEALS BY PERSONS AGGRIEVED BY FAILURE OF CITIES AND TOWNS TO RENDER OLD AGE ASSISTANCE.

*Chap.*285

Be it enacted, etc., as follows:

Chapter one hundred and eighteen A of the General Laws is hereby amended by inserting after section two, as appearing in the Tercentenary Edition thereof, the following new section: — *Section 2A.* Any person aggrieved by the failure of any town to render assistance under this chapter shall have a right of appeal to a board composed of the superintendent of old age assistance in the department, the director of the division of aid and relief and a member of the advisory board of the department designated by the commissioner of public welfare, which board shall forthwith make a thorough investigation and determine whether or not financial assistance should be rendered, which determination shall be final.

G. L. (Ter. Ed.), 118A, new section after § 2.

Board to hear appeals on refusals to render old age assistance. Powers and duties.

Approved June 23, 1933.

AN ACT PROVIDING FOR THE EXTENSION AND REPAIR OF CERTAIN SEA WALLS AND OTHER SHORE PROTECTION IN THE TOWN OF SCITUATE.

*Chap.*286

Be it enacted, etc., as follows:

SECTION 1. Subject to the conditions herein imposed, the department of public works is hereby authorized and directed to build extensions to certain sea walls and other shore protection and to repair existing sea walls and other shore protection in the town of Scituate for the purpose of protecting the shore in said town from erosion by the sea. No work shall be begun until the town of Scituate has as-

Extension, etc., of sea walls in town of Scituate.

sumed liability, in the manner provided by section twenty-nine of chapter ninety-one of the General Laws, for all damages that may be incurred hereunder, nor until there has been paid into the treasury of the commonwealth by the county of Plymouth the sum of eighteen thousand seven hundred and fifty dollars, and by said town of Scituate the sum of eighteen thousand seven hundred and fifty dollars, which together with such sum, not exceeding thirty-seven thousand five hundred dollars, as may hereafter be appropriated by the commonwealth, shall constitute a fund for the improvements herein authorized; provided, that the total cost of such improvement shall not exceed seventy-five thousand dollars and provided, further, that if any of the aforesaid sum remains after the completion of such improvements one fourth of such remainder shall be repaid to said county and one fourth thereof shall be repaid to said town.

County of Plymouth, authority to borrow money.

SECTION 2. For the purpose of meeting the payments required to be made by the county of Plymouth under this act, the treasurer of said county, with the approval of the county commissioners, may borrow from time to time, on the credit of the county, such sums as may be necessary, not exceeding, in the aggregate, eighteen thousand seven hundred and fifty dollars, and may issue bonds or notes of the county therefor, which shall bear on their face the words, Plymouth County—Scituate Sea Wall Loan, Act of 1933. Each authorized issue shall constitute a separate loan, and such loans shall be payable in not more than five years from their dates. Such bonds or notes shall be signed by the treasurer of the county and countersigned by a majority of the county commissioners. The county may sell the said securities at public or private sale upon such terms and conditions as the county commissioners may deem proper, but not for less than their par value. Indebtedness incurred under this act shall, except as herein provided, be subject to chapter thirty-five of the General Laws.

Temporary notes of county may be issued.

SECTION 3. The county treasurer, with the approval of the county commissioners, may issue temporary notes of the county, payable in not more than one year from their dates, in anticipation of the issue of serial bonds or notes under the preceding section, but the time within which such serial bonds or notes shall become due and payable shall not, by reason of such temporary notes, be extended beyond the time fixed by said section. Any notes issued in anticipation of the serial bonds or notes shall be paid from the proceeds thereof.

Town of Scituate, authority to borrow money.

SECTION 4. For the purpose of meeting the payments required to be made by the town of Scituate under this act, said town may borrow from time to time such sums as may be necessary, not exceeding in the aggregate, eighteen thousand seven hundred and fifty dollars, and may issue notes therefor, which shall bear on their face the words,

Town of Scituate, Sea Wall Loan, Act of 1933. Each authorized issue shall constitute a separate loan, and such loans shall be paid within five years from their dates. Indebtedness incurred by said town under this act shall be in excess of the statutory limit, but shall, except as herein provided, be subject to chapter forty-four of the General Laws.

SECTION 5. This act shall take full effect upon its acceptance during the current year by vote of the county commissioners of Plymouth county and by vote of the town of Scituate in town meeting and the filing in the office of the said department of certified copies of said votes.

Approved June 23, 1933.

Acceptance of act.

AN ACT RELATIVE TO THE ESTABLISHMENT OF AUTOMOBILE PARKING AREAS IN CONNECTION WITH THE PROPOSED STATE RESERVATION AT SALISBURY BEACH.

Chap.287

Be it enacted, etc., as follows:

SECTION 1. Section two of chapter four hundred and forty-two of the acts of nineteen hundred and thirty-one, as amended by chapter sixty-two of the acts of nineteen hundred and thirty-two, is hereby further amended by striking out the paragraphs contained in lines twenty to thirty-six, inclusive, as printed in said section two, and inserting in place thereof the following: —

(c) Unnamed street south of Thirteenth street from easterly location line of state highway to the land described in said paragraph I.

(d) Unnamed street south of Brookline street from easterly location line of state highway to the land described in said paragraph I.

III. As areas for automobile parking: —

A parcel or parcels of land in that part of Salisbury, known as Salisbury beach, bounded on the east by the parcel of land described in paragraph I, on the south by the Merrimack river, on the west by a line one mile west of the shore line of the Atlantic ocean and running parallel with said shore line, and on the north by the Massachusetts-New Hampshire boundary line.

All of the takings described in paragraphs I and II are shown on a plan entitled "Plan of Salisbury Beach and Environs prepared for the Salisbury Beach and Duxbury Beach Reservations Commission by Morse & Dickinson, Engineers, 11 Beacon Street, Boston, Mass. 1928."

SECTION 2. Notwithstanding the provisions of section fourteen of chapter twenty-nine of the General Laws, so much of the appropriation made by section two of said chapter four hundred and forty-two as may be necessary for the purposes of this act shall without further appropriation be available at any time up to and including June tenth, nineteen hundred and thirty-four.

Approved June 23, 1933.

Chap.288 AN ACT RELATIVE TO COSTS AND EXPENSES IN DIVORCE
CASES.

Be it enacted, etc., as follows:

G. L. (Ter.
Ed.), 208,
§ 38, amended.

Chapter two hundred and eight of the General Laws is
hereby amended by striking out section thirty-eight, as
appearing in the Tercentenary Edition thereof, and insert-

Court may
award costs in
divorce
actions.

ing in place thereof the following: — *Section 38.* In any
proceeding under this chapter, whether original or subsidiary, the court may, in its discretion, award costs and expenses, or either, to either party, whether or not the marital
relation has terminated. In any case wherein costs and
expenses, or either, may be awarded hereunder to a party,
they may be awarded to his or her counsel, or may be apportioned between them.　　　*Approved June 23, 1933.*

Chap.289 AN ACT REGULATING THE DISPOSITION OF PASTERS OR
STICKERS, SO-CALLED, IN OR NEAR POLLING PLACES.

Be it enacted, etc., as follows:

G. L. (Ter.
Ed.), 54, § 65,
amended.

SECTION 1. Chapter fifty-four of the General Laws
is hereby amended by striking out section sixty-five, as
appearing in the Tercentenary Edition thereof, and in-

Conduct of
elections.

serting in place thereof the following: — *Section 65.* At
an election of state or city officers, and of town officers in
towns where official ballots are used, the presiding election
officer at each polling place shall, before the opening of the

Posting in-
structions, etc.

polls, post at least three cards of instruction, three cards
containing abstracts of the laws imposing penalties upon
voters, three copies of measures to be submitted to the
people, if any, and at least five specimen ballots within the
polling place outside the guard rail, and the cards of instruction and a copy of each measure to be submitted to the

Other posters
or cards for-
bidden.

people in each marking compartment; and no other poster,
card, handbill, placard, picture or circular intended to
influence the action of the voter shall be posted, exhibited,
circulated or distributed in the polling place, in the building
where the polling place is located, on the walls thereof, on
the premises on which the building stands, on the sidewalk adjoining the premises where such election is being
held, or within one hundred and fifty feet of the entrance
to such polling place. Pasters, commonly called stickers,
shall not be posted in the polling place, in the building where
the polling place is located, on the walls thereof, on the
premises on which the building stands, on the sidewalk
adjoining the premises where such election is being held,
or within one hundred and fifty feet of the entrance to such
polling place, nor shall they be circulated or distributed in
such polling place. Such pasters shall be subject to all the
restrictions imposed by sections forty-one and forty-four
as to names and residences of candidates and the size of the

type in which the names shall be printed; but no political or other designation shall appear on such pasters, and no vote by paster shall be counted if such designation appears. The presiding election officer shall, at the opening of the polls, publicly open the packages containing the ballots and deliver them to the ballot clerks. All specimen ballots not posted shall be kept in the custody of the presiding officer until after the closing of the polls. Opening of ballots, etc.

SECTION 2. Chapter fifty-six of the General Laws is hereby amended by striking out section thirty-nine, as so appearing, and inserting in place thereof the following: — *Section 39.* Whoever posts, exhibits, circulates or distributes any poster, card, handbill, placard, picture or circular, intended to influence the action of a voter, or any paster to be placed upon the official ballot, in violation of section sixty-five of chapter fifty-four shall be punished by a fine of not more than twenty dollars. G. L. (Ter. Ed.), 56, § 39, amended. Distributing cards, etc., in or near polling places. Penalty.

Approved June 23, 1933.

An Act granting to the United States of America the right, title and interest of the commonwealth in and to all great ponds in the Fort Devens Military Reservation and ceding jurisdiction over such ponds and over all lands heretofore or hereafter acquired by the United States of America as part of such reservation. *Chap.*290

Be it enacted, etc., as follows:

SECTION 1. There is hereby granted to the United States of America all the right, title and interest which the commonwealth has the power to convey in and to all great ponds, including the waters and the lands under the same, situated within the Fort (formerly Camp) Devens Military Reservation, as now located. The department of public works is hereby authorized and directed to execute and deliver to the United States a good and sufficient deed of conveyance as evidence of this grant. Certain lands ceded to United States.

SECTION 2. Consent to their acquisition is hereby granted and jurisdiction is hereby ceded and granted to the United States of America over all lands and great ponds the title to which has been, is, or shall be acquired by the said United States of America as part of the Fort (formerly Camp) Devens Military Reservation; but upon the express condition that, as to all lands and great ponds not coming within the previous consent and cession of jurisdiction in chapter four hundred and fifty-six of the acts of nineteen hundred and twenty-one, the jurisdiction hereby ceded and granted shall not vest until the United States of America shall have acquired title to the lands and great ponds last mentioned and shall have filed in the office of the state secretary a description and plan thereof, authenticated by the officer of the United States who is the Jurisdiction.

official custodian of the original documents from which said description and plan were compiled; and upon the further express condition that the commonwealth shall retain concurrent jurisdiction with the United States of America in and over the lands and great ponds last mentioned, in so far that all civil processes and such criminal processes as may issue under the authority of the commonwealth against any person or persons charged with crimes, may be executed thereon in the same manner as though this cession had not been made; provided, that the exclusive jurisdiction shall revert to and revest in the commonwealth whenever the lands and great ponds last mentioned shall cease to be used for purposes of national defense.

Approved June 23, 1933.

*Chap.*291 AN ACT AUTHORIZING THE DEPARTMENT OF AGRICULTURE TO AID IN THE PROMOTION AND DEVELOPMENT OF THE COMMERCIAL FISHING INDUSTRY.

Be it enacted, etc., as follows:

G. L. (Ter. Ed.), 128, § 2, amended.

SECTION 1. Section two of chapter one hundred and twenty-eight of the General Laws, as appearing in the Tercentenary Edition thereof, is hereby amended by inserting after the word "vegetables" in the twenty-fourth line the following new paragraph: —

Powers and duties of department of agriculture relative to the commercial fishing industry.

(g) Aid in the promotion and development of the commercial fishing industry; investigate improved methods of marketing and distributing commercial fish products within the commonwealth; and establish standards and design brands or labels for the identification of commercial fish products processed, prepared or packed for distribution and for retail sales.

G. L. (Ter. Ed.), 128, § 6, amended.

Lectures and publications.

SECTION 2. Section six of said chapter one hundred and twenty-eight, as so appearing, is hereby amended by adding at the end thereof the following: — and commercial fisheries, — so as to read as follows: — *Section 6.* The commissioner may arrange for lectures before the department, and may issue for general distribution such publications as he considers best adapted to promote the interests of agriculture and commercial fisheries.

Approved June 26, 1933.

*Chap.*292 AN ACT PERMITTING CERTAIN PUBLIC OFFICERS TO PARTICIPATE IN CERTAIN BANK REORGANIZATIONS.

Emergency preamble.

Whereas, The present banking emergency requires this act to be effective forthwith, therefore it is hereby declared to be an emergency law, necessary for the immediate preservation of the public safety and convenience.

Be it enacted, etc., as follows:

G. L. (Ter. Ed.), 167, new section after § 20.

Chapter one hundred and sixty-seven of the General Laws is hereby amended by inserting after section twenty, as appearing in the Tercentenary Edition thereof, under the heading "Reorganization", the following new section: — *Section 20A.* Any officer of the commonwealth or of any political subdivision thereof, or of any public or quasi-public body or corporation, receiving public or quasi-public moneys, including trust and sinking funds, who lawfully and in good faith and in the exercise of due care has deposited any of such moneys to the credit of any political subdivision of the commonwealth, or of any department, board, commission or other activity of the commonwealth or of any political subdivision thereof, or of any such body or corporation, as the case may be, in a bank as defined in section one, or in a national banking association doing business within the commonwealth, may, subject to the approval hereinafter required, on behalf of the commonwealth or political subdivision thereof or of the public or quasi-public body or corporation, on behalf of which such moneys were deposited, and without thereby incurring any personal liability for the loss of any such moneys by reason of any reorganization hereinafter referred to, assent to and participate in a plan of reorganization of such bank or national banking association, if such plan shall have previously been approved by the commissioner or by the comptroller of the currency, as the case may be, and may enter into all necessary agreements in connection therewith. The state treasurer, subject to the approval hereinafter required, may act under authority of this section as to any public moneys deposited by himself or any other officer of the commonwealth to the credit of the commonwealth and not specifically to the credit of any department, board, commission or other activity thereof.

Certain public officers may participate in bank reorganizations.

No action shall be taken under authority of this section unless and until approved, in case of action of the state treasurer or any other officer of the commonwealth, by the governor and council; in case of action of any officer of a county, city or town, by the county commissioners, mayor and city council, or board of selectmen, as the case may be; in case of action of any officer of a district, by the prudential committee thereof, or other officer or board exercising similar powers therein; and in case of action of any officer of a public or quasi-public body or corporation, by its board of directors or board of trustees or other officers or board thereof exercising similar powers.

Approval of action of certain officers required.

Approved June 27, 1933.

AN ACT INCREASING THE RATES OF LEGACY AND SUCCESSION TAXES IN CERTAIN INSTANCES.

Chap.293

Whereas, The deferred operation of this act would tend to defeat its purpose, therefore it is hereby declared to be an emergency law, necessary for the immediate preservation of the public convenience.

Emergency preamble.

Be it enacted, etc., as follows:

G. L. (Ter. Ed.), 65, § 1, amended.

Section one of chapter sixty-five of the General Laws, as appearing in the Tercentenary Edition thereof, is hereby amended by striking out the table therein contained and inserting in place thereof the following table: —

Table of rates of certain legacy, etc., taxes.

RELATIONSHIP OF BENEFICIARY TO DECEASED.	RATE PER CENTUM OF TAX ON VALUE OF PROPERTY OR INTEREST.							
	On Value not over $10,000.	On Excess above $10,000, not over $25,000.	On Excess above $25,000, not over $50,000.	On Excess above $50,000, not over $250,000.	On Excess above $250,000, not over $500,000.	On Excess above $500,000, not over $750,000.	On Excess above $750,000, not over $1,000,000.	On Excess above $1,000,000.
CLASS A. Husband, wife, father, mother; child, adopted child, adoptive parent, grandchild, . . .	1%	1%	2%	4%	5%	6%	7%	8%
CLASS B. Lineal ancestor, except father or mother; lineal descendant, except child or grandchild; lineal descendant of adopted child; lineal ancestor of adoptive parent; wife or widow of a son; husband of a daughter, . . .	1%	2%	4%	5%	6%	7%	8%	9%
CLASS C. Brother, sister, half brother, half sister, nephew, niece, step-child or step-parent, .	3%	5%	7%	8%	9%	10%	11%	12%
CLASS D. All others, . . .	5%	6%	7%	8%	9%	10%	11%	12%

Approved June 27, 1933.

---

*Chap.*294 AN ACT AUTHORIZING COMPACTS BETWEEN THE COMMONWEALTH AND CERTAIN OTHER STATES RELATIVE TO THE INTERSTATE TRANSMISSION OF ELECTRICITY AND GAS.

Emergency preamble.

Whereas, The deferred operation of this act would cause unnecessary delay and inconvenience, therefore it is hereby declared to be an emergency law, necessary for the immediate preservation of the public convenience.

Be it enacted, etc., as follows:

Interstate compacts relative to transmission of electricity, etc., authorized.

The commission supervising the department of public utilities is hereby empowered to negotiate and execute, in the name of the commonwealth of Massachusetts, and subject to the constitution and laws of the United States, compacts with the states and commonwealths of New York, Vermont, Connecticut, New Jersey and Pennsylvania, or with any one or more of such states or commonwealths, or with any other state adjoining the commonwealth of

Massachusetts, each acting through such official body thereof as may be thereto authorized by its laws, for the purpose of establishing joint regulation and control of rates and charges for electricity and gas transmitted between such states and commonwealths. The commission shall report the provisions of any such compact to the general court at its annual session next following the consummation and execution of any such compact and shall recommend such legislation, both state and federal, as may be necessary to render such compact effective; provided, that no such compact shall be binding on the part of this commonwealth until in all respects approved by the general court.   *Approved June 27, 1933.*

An Act abolishing the Norfolk, Bristol and Plymouth Union Training School.   *Chap.*295

Be it enacted, etc., as follows:

SECTION 1. Chapter seventy-seven of the General Laws is hereby amended by striking out section one, as appearing in the Tercentenary Edition thereof, and inserting in place thereof the following: — *Section 1.* The county commissioners of each county, except Barnstable, Berkshire, Bristol, Franklin, Hampshire, Dukes, Nantucket, Norfolk, Plymouth and Suffolk, shall maintain either separately or jointly with the commissioners of other counties as hereinafter provided, in a suitable place, remote from a penal institution, a school for the instruction and training of children committed thereto as habitual truants, absentees or school offenders. The commissioners of Barnstable, Berkshire, Bristol, Franklin, Hampshire, Dukes, Nantucket, Norfolk and Plymouth counties shall assign a training school established by law as the place for the instruction and training of children so committed within their respective counties, and shall pay for their support in said school such reasonable sum as the commissioners having control of said school may fix. Commitments from Boston, Chelsea, Revere and Winthrop shall be to the training school for Middlesex county. The town from which an habitual truant, absentee or school offender is committed to a county training school shall pay to the county maintaining it two dollars a week toward his support, and reports of the condition and progress of its pupils in said school shall be sent each month to the superintendent of schools of such town; but Boston, Chelsea, Revere and Winthrop shall pay to Middlesex county, for the support of each child committed to the training school of said county, two dollars and fifty cents a week, and an additional sum for each child sufficient to cover the actual cost of maintenance.

SECTION 2. The chairmen of the commissioners of Norfolk, Bristol and Plymouth counties, having the management and control of the Norfolk, Bristol and Plym-

Marginal notes:

G. L. (Ter. Ed.), 77, § 1, amended.

Certain counties to maintain training schools.

Commitments from and payments by other counties.

Norfolk, Bristol and Plymouth union training school, closing of.

outh union training school shall, on or before the first day of September in the current year, close the said school, and the land, buildings and equipment used by said school shall revert to the county or counties having title thereto and may be sold or leased or used for county purposes by such county or counties.

SECTION 3. This act shall take effect upon its passage.

Approved June 27, 1933.

*Chap.*296 AN ACT MAKING AN APPROPRIATION FOR ADJUSTING THE SALARIES OF CERTAIN EMPLOYEES OF THE COMMONWEALTH.

Be it enacted, etc., as follows:

SECTION 1. The sum of one hundred and fifteen thousand dollars, of which not more than thirty thousand dollars shall be paid from the Highway Fund, not more than eight thousand dollars from the several funds of the metropolitan district commission, and the remainder from the General Fund, is hereby appropriated to meet the additional payments required for paying the salaries of certain employees of the commonwealth to be increased as of June first in the current year as recommended by the governor in a message to the general court dated May twenty-fifth, nineteen hundred and thirty-three. The sum appropriated by this act shall be apportioned by the comptroller of the commonwealth to the proper appropriations made during the current year in such amounts as may be certified by the division of personnel and standardization of the commission on administration and finance to be necessary to carry out the provisions of this act.

SECTION 2. This act shall take effect upon its passage.

Approved June 27, 1933.

*Chap.*297 AN ACT AUTHORIZING THE CONVEYANCE OF A PARCEL OF STATE LAND IN THE TOWN OF MARSHFIELD AND THE REMOVAL FROM ADJOINING STATE LAND OF CERTAIN STRUCTURES.

Be it enacted, etc., as follows:

SECTION 1. The commissioner of conservation is hereby authorized, subject to the approval of the governor and council, to convey, on behalf of the commonwealth, to Lysander B. Sherman, a certain parcel of land owned by the commonwealth and located in the town of Marshfield, bounded and described as follows: —

Beginning on the southerly side of Ocean street at the northeast corner of land of the grantee; thence running in an easterly direction by the southerly line of Ocean street by a curved line, the radius of which is eight hundred and thirty-one feet, a distance of twenty and seventy-one hundredths feet to a concrete bound; thence turning and running south forty-seven minutes west and bounded easterly by land of the commonwealth, seventy-five and fifty-four hundredths feet to a concrete bound; thence turning and running south eighty-five degrees fifty minutes forty seconds west and bounded southerly by land of the commonwealth, a distance of fourteen and twenty hundredths feet to the southeast corner of land of the grantee; thence turning and running north four degrees nine minutes twenty seconds west and bounded westerly by land of the grantee, seventy-five feet to the point of beginning, and containing thirteen hundred and six square feet of land. The said grantee shall, in consideration of said conveyance, pay into the treasury of the commonwealth the sum of twenty-five dollars.

SECTION 2. Said commissioner of conservation is hereby further authorized to permit said Sherman to remove from the land owned by the commonwealth and adjoining the land to be conveyed hereunder any buildings or structures which he has constructed thereon wholly at his own expense; provided, that such buildings or structures shall be removed within thirty days from the effective date of this act without expense to the commonwealth.

SECTION 3. This act shall take effect upon its passage.
Approved June 27, 1933.

AN ACT ANNEXING A PART OF THE TOWN OF SAUGUS TO THE TOWN OF WAKEFIELD.

Chap.298

Be it enacted, etc., as follows:

SECTION 1. All the territory now within the town of Saugus enclosed by the following boundary lines, to wit: — Beginning at a point in the present boundary line between the towns of Saugus and Wakefield north thirty-two degrees, forty-two minutes, seventeen seconds west and four hundred and twenty-three feet distant from the existing corner bound of the city of Melrose and the towns of Saugus and Wakefield, marked by a rough boulder, having a drill hole in the top, situated in woods on the easterly slope of a hill known as Mt. Zion; thence north thirty-two degrees, forty-two minutes, nineteen seconds west three thousand feet to the existing bound known as Saugus-Wakefield five, an angle in the present boundary line between the towns of Saugus and Wakefield, marked by a granite bound, situated at the westerly end of a wall about two hundred feet southeasterly from the junction of High street and Greenwood avenue; thence north sixty-four degrees, fourteen minutes, nineteen seconds east fifteen hundred and twenty-three feet to the existing bound known as Saugus-Wakefield four, an angle in the present boundary line between the towns of Saugus and Wakefield, marked by a granite bound situated on the northerly slope of a wooded hill known as Rattlesnake Rock; thence north seventy-six degrees, fourteen minutes,

Certain territory in town of Saugus annexed to town of Wakefield.

nineteen seconds east seven hundred feet to a point in the present boundary line between the towns of Saugus and Wakefield; thence south seven degrees, nineteen minutes, thirty-three seconds west thirty-three hundred and seventy-nine feet to the point of beginning, — is hereby set off and separated from the town of Saugus and annexed to and made a part of the town of Wakefield, and shall hereafter constitute a part of the county of Middlesex. The inhabitants of said annexed territory shall hereafter be inhabitants of said town of Wakefield and of said county of Middlesex and shall, except as hereinafter provided, enjoy all the rights and privileges and be subject to all the duties and liabilities of the inhabitants of said last mentioned town and county.

Overdue taxes to be paid to town of Saugus.

SECTION 2. The inhabitants of, and the estates within, the territory set off and separated from the town of Saugus and annexed to the town of Wakefield by this act, and the owners of all such estates, shall be holden to pay to the town of Saugus all arrears of taxes which have legally been assessed upon them by said town prior to the effective date hereof and, in addition, until the next state valuation, such proportion of the state and county taxes as may be legally incumbent upon them to pay shall be collected by the tax collector of the town of Saugus and paid to the treasurer of said town.

Poor relief.

SECTION 3. The town of Wakefield shall be liable for the support of all persons now or hereafter needing relief or support whose settlement was gained either by original acquisition or by derivation within the limits of the territory set off and separated from the town of Saugus and annexed to the town of Wakefield by this act.

Transfer of corporate property.

SECTION 4. The corporate property of the town of Saugus within the territory set off and separated from said town and annexed to the town of Wakefield by this act shall be vested in and is hereby declared to be the property of said town of Wakefield.

Listing, etc., of voters in annexed territory.

SECTION 5. The inhabitants of the territory set off and separated from the town of Saugus and annexed to the town of Wakefield by this act shall continue to be a part of the town of Saugus for the purpose of electing members of the executive council, senators and representatives in the general court and presidential electors, until the next apportionment shall be made, and it shall be the duty of the board of registrars of voters of said town of Wakefield to make a true list of the persons on the territory hereby annexed qualified to vote at any such election, and to post the list in said territory, and to correct the same, as required by law, and to deliver the same to the selectmen of said town of Saugus at least seven days before any such election, and the same shall be taken and used by the selectmen of said last mentioned town for any such election in the same manner as if it had been prepared by the board of registrars thereof.

Section 6.   The town clerk of the town of Saugus shall Duties of town clerks.
prepare a list of registered voters in the territory hereby
annexed to the town of Wakefield and forward the same to
the town clerk of said town of Wakefield, and the names
of persons on this list shall be placed on the registers of said
town of Wakefield and shall be added to, and become a
part of, the voting lists of said town of Wakefield.   Unless
otherwise provided by said town of Wakefield, the territory
annexed thereto by this act shall be a part of precinct two
thereof.

Section 7.   The powers and privileges reserved to the Certain contract rights and liabilities.
town of Saugus and the selectmen thereof in any orders,
decrees or contracts made by the selectmen of Saugus in
such territory prior to the effective date of this act shall
inure to and be exercised by the town of Wakefield and the
selectmen thereof, respectively, as fully as if said orders,
decrees or contracts had originally been made by the town
of Wakefield or any authorized officer thereof.

Section 8.   The several courts within the county of Court jurisdiction.
Middlesex, after this act takes effect, shall have the same
jurisdiction over all causes and proceedings in civil causes,
and over all matters in probate and insolvency, which
shall have accrued prior to the effective date of this act
within the territory hereby annexed, which said courts now
have over like proceedings, causes and actions within the
county of Middlesex; provided, that the several courts
within the county of Essex shall have and retain jurisdiction
of all causes, proceedings and matters that shall have right-
fully been begun in said courts prior to such effective date;
and the superior court within the county of Middlesex
and the first district court of eastern Middlesex shall, after
such effective date, have the same jurisdiction of all crimes,
offences and misdemeanors committed within the territory
hereby annexed which they now exercise over crimes,
offences and misdemeanors committed in their respective
jurisdictions.   All suits, actions, proceedings, complaints,
indictments and prosecutions, and all matters of probate
and insolvency, which shall be pending within said territory
before any court or commission, or before the trial justice
in said town of Saugus, upon such effective date shall be
heard and determined as if this act had not taken effect.

Section 9.   This act shall take effect upon its ac- Acceptance of act.
ceptance, during the current year, by vote of the board of
selectmen of each of the towns of Wakefield and Saugus,
and the filing of certified copies thereof in the office of the
state secretary.   *Approved June 27, 1933.*

Chap.299 AN ACT PROVIDING RETIREMENT ALLOWANCES AND DISA-
BILITY AND DEATH BENEFITS BASED ON ANNUITY AND
PENSION CONTRIBUTIONS FOR EMPLOYEES OF THE TOWN
OF BROOKLINE.

Be it enacted, etc., as follows:

PURPOSE OF ACT.

SECTION 1. The purpose of this act is to improve the
efficiency of the public service of the town of Brookline,
hereinafter called the town, by the retirement of disabled
or superannuated employees.

DEFINITIONS.

SECTION 2. The following words and phrases as used
in this act, unless a different meaning is plainly required
by the context, shall have the following meanings: —

(1) "Retirement system", the arrangement provided
in this act for the retirement of, and payment of retirement
allowances to, employees as defined in paragraph (2) of
this section.

(2) "Employee", any person who is regularly employed
in the service of, and whose salary or compensation is paid
by, the town, except employees who hold office by popular
election, who were not members at the time of their election, and teachers in the public schools as defined by section
six of chapter thirty-two of the General Laws.   In all cases
of doubt the retirement board shall decide who is an employee within the meaning of this act.

(3) "Member", any employee included in the retirement
system as provided in section four of this act.

(4) "Retirement board", the board provided in section
fourteen of this act to administer the retirement system.

(5) "Service", service as an employee as described in
paragraph (2) of this section and paid for by the town of
Brookline.

(6) "Prior service", service rendered prior to the date
the retirement system becomes first operative, for which
credit is allowable under the provisions of section five of
this act.

(7) "Membership service", service as an employee rendered since last becoming a member.

(8) "Creditable service", "prior service" plus "membership service", for which credit is allowable as provided in
section five of this act.

(9) "Pensioner", any person in receipt of a pension, an
annuity, a retirement allowance or other benefit as provided
by this act, who has thereby ceased to be a member as
defined in subsection (3) of this section.

(9A) "Beneficiary", any person having an insurable
interest in the life of a member or pensioner and designated by him as the person entitled to receive such benefits
as may be due at the death of such member or pensioner.

(10) "Regular interest", interest at four per centum per annum compounded annually; provided, that if the actual net interest earned on the reserves of the retirement system be less than four per centum, the rate may be reduced to not less than three per centum per annum after the retirement board has given the members ninety days' notice of a proposed reduction in rate; and provided, further, that such a reduction shall not affect any payments or credits made prior to the date of the change in rate.

(11) "Accumulated contributions", the sum of all the amounts deducted from the compensation of a member and standing to his credit in the annuity savings fund, together with regular interest thereon.

(12) "Annuity", annual payments for life derived from the accumulated contributions of a member. "Annuity-certain", annual payments for a definite term independent of life derived from the accumulated contributions of a member. All annuities and annuities-certain shall be paid in monthly instalments, due on the first day of each month. Annuities shall not be apportioned for a fractional part of a month.

(13) "Pension", annual payments for life derived from contributions made by the town. All pensions shall be paid in monthly instalments, due on the first day of the month, and shall not be apportioned for a fractional part of a month.

(14) "Retirement allowance", the sum of the "annuity" or the "annuity-certain" and the "pension".

(15) "Regular compensation", the annual compensation determined by the head of the department for the individual service of each employee in that department and the compensation determined by duly constituted authority for appointed officers of the town, exclusive of bonus or overtime payments.

(16) "Annuity reserve", the present value of all payments to be made on account of any annuity or benefit in lieu of any annuity computed upon the basis of such mortality tables as shall be adopted by the retirement board and regular interest.

(17) "Pension reserve", the present value of all payments to be made on account of any pension or benefit in lieu of any pension computed upon the basis of such mortality tables as shall be adopted by the retirement board and regular interest.

(18) "Actuarial equivalent", a benefit of equal value when computed upon the basis of such mortality tables as shall be approved by the retirement board and regular interest.

NAME AND DATE SYSTEM IS FIRST OPERATIVE.

SECTION 3. A retirement system is hereby established and placed under the management of the retirement board for the purpose of providing retirement allowances under the provisions of this act for employees of, or employees paid by, the town. The retirement system so created shall have the powers and privileges of a corporation and shall be known as the "Brookline Retirement System", and by such name all of its business shall be transacted, all of its funds invested, all warrants for money drawn and payments made, and all of its cash and securities and other property held. The retirement system so created shall begin operation upon the first day of January following the acceptance of this act in accordance with the provisions of section twenty-two.

MEMBERSHIP.

SECTION 4. (1) The membership of the retirement system shall be constituted as follows: —

(a) All persons who become employees and, except as otherwise provided in the last sentence of subsection (2) of section nine, all employees who enter or re-enter the service of the town on or after the day the retirement system becomes operative may become members of the retirement system on their own application, and all such employees who shall complete one year of service thereafter and disability pensioners restored to active service to whom the provisions of subsection (3) of said section nine apply shall become members of the retirement system, and after becoming members as above provided shall receive no pension or retirement allowance from any other pension or retirement system supported wholly or in part by the town, nor shall they be required to make contributions to any other pension or retirement system of the town, anything to the contrary in this or any other special or general law notwithstanding.

(b) All persons who are employees on the date when this retirement system becomes operative and who are not then covered by any other pension or retirement law of the commonwealth shall become members as of the first day this retirement system becomes operative, unless on or before a date not more than sixty days thereafter, to be set by the retirement board, any such employee shall file with the retirement board on a form prescribed by the board a notice of his election not to be covered in the membership of the system and a duly executed waiver of all present and prospective benefits which would otherwise inure to him on account of his participation in the retirement system.

(c) An employee who is covered by any other pension or retirement law of the commonwealth on the date when this retirement system becomes operative shall not be considered to have become a member of this retirement system unless said employee shall then or thereafter make written application to join this system and shall therein waive and renounce all benefits of any other pension or retirement system supported wholly by the town, but no such employee shall receive credit for prior service unless he make such application for membership within one year from the date this retirement system becomes operative.

(2) An employee whose membership in the retirement system is contingent on his own election and who elects not to become a member may thereafter apply for and be admitted to membership; but no such employee shall receive prior service credit unless he becomes a member within one year from the date this retirement system becomes operative.

(3) The retirement board may deny the right to become members to any class of officials appointed for fixed terms, or to any class of part-time employees, or it may, in its discretion, make optional with persons in any such class their individual entrance into membership.

(4) It shall be the duty of the head of each department to submit to the retirement board a statement showing the name, title, compensation, duties, date of birth and length of service of each member of his department, and such information regarding other employees therein as the retirement board may require. The retirement board shall then place each member in one of the following groups: —

Group 1. — General employees, including clerical, administrative and technical workers, laborers, mechanics and all others not otherwise classified;

Group 2. — Members of the police department and the fire department of the town;

Or in any other group of not less than two hundred and fifty persons which may be hereafter recommended by the actuary on the basis of service and mortality experience, and approved by the retirement board, to cover all or part of any group or groups previously created or any additional classes of employees. When the duties of a member so require, the retirement board may reclassify him in and transfer him to another group.

(5) Should any member in any period of six consecutive years after last becoming a member be absent from service more than five years, or should any member withdraw his accumulated contributions or become a pensioner hereunder or die, he shall thereupon cease to be a member.

CREDITABLE SERVICE.

SECTION 5. (1) Under such rules and regulations as the retirement board shall adopt, each member who was an employee on the date this retirement system becomes operative, or during the year prior thereto, who becomes a member on or prior to the expiration of the first year of operation of the retirement system, shall file a detailed statement of all service as an employee rendered by him prior to the day on which the system first became operative for which he claims credit, and of such facts as the retirement board may require for the proper operation of the system.

(2) The retirement board shall fix and determine by

appropriate rules and regulations how much service in any year is equivalent to a year of service, but in no case shall more than one year of service be creditable for all service in one calendar year, nor shall the retirement board allow credit as service for any period of more than one month's duration during which the employee was absent without pay.

(3) Subject to the above restrictions and to such other rules and regulations as the retirement board may adopt, the retirement board shall verify, as soon as practicable after the filing of such statements of service, the service therein claimed, and shall certify as creditable all or such part of the service claimed as may be allowable.

(4) Upon verification of the statements of service the retirement board shall issue prior service certificates certifying to each member entitled to credit for prior service the length of service rendered prior to the date the retirement system first became operative, with which he is credited on the basis of his statement of service. So long as membership continues a prior service certificate shall for retirement purposes be final and conclusive as to such service; provided, that within one year from the date of issuance or modification of such certificate it may, after hearing, be modified or corrected.

When membership ceases, except upon retirement for superannuation or disability, such prior service certificates shall become void. Should the employee again become a member, such employee shall enter the system as an employee not entitled to prior service credit except as provided in subsection (3) of section nine.

(5) Creditable service at retirement shall consist of the membership service rendered by the member since he last became a member and also, if he has a prior service certificate which is in full force and effect, the amount of the service certified on his prior service certificate.

SERVICE RETIREMENT.

Conditions for Allowance.

, SECTION 6. (1) Any member in service who shall have attained age sixty shall, either upon his own written application or that of the head of his department, be retired for superannuation not less than thirty nor more than ninety days after the filing of such application. A member whose retirement is applied for by the head of his department shall be entitled to a notice of such application and to a hearing before the retirement board, provided he requests such hearing in writing within ten days of the receipt of such notice; and unless the retirement board finds, on hearing, that the member is able to properly perform his duties and files a copy of its findings with the head of his department, the retirement shall become effective thirty days from the time of the filing of such finding.

Any member in service classified as a policeman or fireman under group 2 of section four who shall have attained age sixty-five, and any member otherwise classified who shall have attained age seventy, shall be retired for superannuation not less than thirty nor more than ninety days after attaining such respective ages, or after this system becomes operative, if such respective ages were attained prior thereto.

Notwithstanding the preceding provisions of this section, any member who is the head of a department or a member of a board in charge of a department or departments may, if, in the case of the head of the police or fire department, other statutory requirements as to his continued employment after the age of sixty-five years are complied with, be retained in service for periods of one year at a time upon reappointment by the selectmen or other appointing power; or, if his continued employment does not require a reappointment, then he may be retained in service for periods of one year at a time upon the written approval thereof of the board of selectmen.

Amount of Allowance.

(2) Upon retirement for superannuation a member of the retirement system shall receive a retirement allowance consisting of: —

(a) An annuity which shall be the actuarial equivalent of his accumulated contributions at the time of his retirement, and

(b) A pension for membership service equal to the annuity allowable at age sixty, computed on the basis of contributions made prior to the attainment of age sixty, and

(c) If he has a prior service certificate in full force and effect an additional pension which is the actuarial equivalent of twice the pension which would have been payable under paragraph (b) above, on account of the accumulated contributions which would have resulted from contributions made during the period of his creditable prior service had the system then been in operation, and

(d) If the member was over sixty years of age at the time the retirement system was established, an additional pension which is the actuarial equivalent of the accumulation of four per cent contributions from the date the member attained the age of sixty to the date when the system was established but not beyond the age of seventy, with interest to the date of retirement but not beyond the age of seventy.

The total pension of any member payable under the provisions of this section shall not, however, exceed two thousand dollars nor shall it exceed one half his average annual regular compensation during the five fiscal years immediately preceding his retirement, nor shall the total pension of any member who has fifteen or more years of total creditable service be less than the amount which, added to his annuity, shall make his total retirement allowance equal to four hundred and eighty dollars per annum.

ORDINARY DISABILITY RETIREMENT.

Conditions for Allowance.

SECTION 7. (1) Upon the application of a member in service or of the head of his department, any member who has had twenty or more years of creditable service may be retired by the retirement board, not less than thirty and not more than ninety days next following the date of filing such application, on an ordinary disability retirement allowance; provided, that a physician of the retirement board, after a medical examination of such member, shall certify that such member is mentally or physically incapacitated for the further performance of duty, that such incapacity is likely to be permanent, and that such member should be retired.

Amount of Allowance.

(2) Upon retirement for ordinary disability a member shall receive a service retirement allowance if he has attained age sixty; otherwise he shall receive an ordinary disability retirement allowance consisting of: —

(a) An annuity-certain equal to ten per centum per annum of his accumulated contributions at the time of his retirement or to twenty dollars per month, whichever is greater, which shall be payable in equal monthly instalments until such accumulated contributions together with regular interest on the unexpended balance shall be exhausted, and

(b) A pension of ninety per centum of the pension that would have been provided by the town for the member had he remained without further change of compensation in the service of the town until he reached age sixty and then retired.

ACCIDENTAL DISABILITY RETIREMENT.

Conditions for Allowance.

SECTION 8. (1) Upon application of a member in service, or of the head of his department, any member who has been totally and permanently incapacitated for duty as the natural and proximate result of an accident occurring in the performance and within the scope of his duty at some definite time and place, without wilful negligence on his part, shall be retired not less than thirty nor more than ninety days following the date of filing of such application; provided, that a physician of the retirement board, after an examination of such member, shall report that said member is physically or mentally incapacitated for the further performance of duty, that such incapacity is likely to be permanent, and that said member should be retired, and the retirement board shall concur in such report and find that the physical or mental incapacity is the natural and proximate result of such an accident and that such disability is not the result of wilful negligence on the part of said member and that said member should be retired.

Amount of Allowance.

(2) Upon retirement for accidental disability a member shall receive a service retirement allowance if he has attained age sixty; otherwise he shall receive an accidental disability retirement allowance consisting of: —

(a) An annuity-certain equal to ten per centum per annum of his accumulated contributions at the time of his retirement or to twenty dollars per month, whichever is greater, which shall be payable in equal monthly instalments until such accumulated contributions together with regular interest on the unexpended balance shall be exhausted, and

(b) A pension equal to one half of the average rate of his regular annual compensation for the fiscal year immediately preceding the date of the accident.

RE-EXAMINATION OF PENSIONERS RETIRED ON ACCOUNT
OF DISABILITY.

Section 9. (1) Once each year during the first five years following retirement of a member on a disability retirement allowance, and once in every three-year period thereafter, the retirement board may, and upon his application shall, require any disability pensioner who has not yet attained age sixty to undergo a medical examination by a physician or physicians designated by the retirement board and approved by the board of selectmen, such examination to be made at the place of residence of said pensioner or other place mutually agreed upon. Should any disability pensioner who has not yet attained the age of sixty refuse to submit to at least one medical examination in any such period of one or three years, as the case may be, his allowance may be discontinued until his withdrawal of such refusal, and should his refusal continue for a year, all his rights in and to his pension shall be revoked by the retirement board.

(2) Should such physician or physicians report and certify to the retirement board that such disability pensioner is engaged in or is able to engage in a gainful occupation paying more than the difference between his retirement allowance and his final regular compensation, and should the retirement board concur in such report, then the amount of his pension shall be reduced to an amount which, together with his annuity-certain and the amount earnable by him, shall equal the amount of his final regular compensation. Should his earning capacity be later changed, the amount of his pension may be further modified; pro-

vided, that the new pension shall not exceed the amount of the pension originally granted nor shall it exceed an amount which, when added to the amount earnable by the pensioner together with his annuity-certain equals the amount of his final regular compensation. A pensioner restored to active service at a salary less than the final regular compensation upon the basis of which he was retired shall not become a member of the retirement system.

(3) Should a disability pensioner be restored to active service at a compensation not less than his final regular compensation, his retirement allowance shall cease, he shall again become a member of the retirement system, and he shall contribute thereafter at the same rate he paid prior to disability. Any balance of the fund held for the payment of his annuity-certain which has not been expended at the time he is restored to full active service as a member shall be credited to his account in the Annuity Savings Fund. Any prior service certificate on the basis of which his service was computed at the time of his retirement shall be restored to full force and effect, and in addition upon his subsequent retirement he shall be credited with all his service as a member.

(4) Should a disability pensioner die before the annuity-certain has expired, the balance of the fund held for the payment of his annuity-certain which has not been expended at the time of his death shall be paid to his designated beneficiary, if living, otherwise to his legal representative, subject to the proviso contained in subsection (2) of section ten.

RETURN OF ACCUMULATED CONTRIBUTIONS.

SECTION 10. (1) Within sixty days after the filing with the retirement board of a request therefor, any member who shall have ceased to be an employee by resignation or discharge or for any reason other than death or retirement under the provisions of this act shall be paid the amount of his accumulated contributions.

(2) Should a member die while an employee, his accumulated contributions shall be paid to his designated beneficiary, if living, otherwise to his legal representative; provided, that if the sum so due does not exceed three hundred dollars, and there has been no demand therefor by a duly appointed executor or administrator, payment may be made, after the expiration of three months from the date of death of such member, to the persons appearing, in the judgment of the retirement board, to be entitled thereto, and such payment shall be a bar to recovery by any other person.

ACCIDENTAL DEATH BENEFIT.

SECTION 11. If, upon receipt by the retirement board of proper proofs of the death of a member, the retirement board shall decide that such death was the natural and proximate result of an accident occurring at some definite time and place while the member was in the actual performance and within the scope of his duty, and not the result of wilful negligence on his part, and if the deceased member is survived by any of the dependents enumerated below, there shall be paid, in addition to accumulated contributions under subsection (2) of section ten or to any unexpended balance under subsection (4) of section nine, an accidental death benefit consisting of a pension equal to one half the average regular annual compensation received by the deceased member for the fiscal year preceding the date of the accident, said pension to be paid: —

(a) To the dependent husband or wife of the deceased member during life or until remarriage; or

(b) If there be no husband or wife or if the husband or wife dies or remarries before every child of such deceased member shall have attained the age of eighteen years, then to his child or children under such age, divided in such manner as the retirement board in its discretion shall determine, to continue as a joint and survivor pension until every such child dies or attains the age of eighteen years; or

(c) If there be no dependent husband or wife, or child under the age of eighteen years, surviving such deceased member, then to either his dependent father or dependent mother, as the retirement board in its discretion shall determine, to continue for life or until remarriage.

OPTIONAL BENEFITS.

SECTION 12. (1) Subject to the provisions that no optional election shall be effective in case a pensioner dies within thirty days after retirement, and that such a pensioner shall be considered as an active member at the time of death, until the first payment on account of any retirement allowance is made, the member may elect to convert the retirement allowance otherwise provided for in this system into a lesser retirement allowance of equivalent actuarial value payable throughout his or her life with the provision that: —

Option 1. — If the pensioner dies before having received in annuity payments an amount equal to the present value of the annuity at the date of the member's retirement, the balance shall be paid to such surviving beneficiary as the pensioner shall have nominated by written designation duly acknowledged and filed with the retirement board, or, if there be no beneficiary living, then to the legal representative of the pensioner, without change in the amount of the pension; or

Option 2. — Upon the death of the pensioner, the lesser retirement allowance shall be continued throughout the life of and paid to such surviving beneficiary as the pensioner shall have nominated by written designation duly

acknowledged and filed with the retirement board at the
date of the member's retirement; or

Option 3. — Upon the death of the pensioner, one half
of the lesser retirement allowance shall be continued
throughout the life of and paid to such surviving beneficiary
as the pensioner shall have nominated by written designation duly acknowledged and filed with the retirement board
at the date of the member's retirement.

(2) If the member be an incompetent at the date of
retirement, the election of one of the optional benefits
provided in this section may be made by the member's
wife or husband, or if there be no wife or husband, then
by the member's conservator or guardian.

COMPENSATION BENEFITS OFFSET.

SECTION 13. Any amounts paid or payable by the
town under the provisions of the workmen's compensation
law to a member or to the dependents of a member on
account of death or disability shall be offset against and
payable in lieu of any benefits payable out of funds provided
by the town under the provisions of this act on account of
the death or disability of a member. If the value of the
total commuted benefits under the workmen's compensation law is less than the reserve on the pension otherwise
payable under this act, the value of such commuted payments shall be deducted from such pension reserve and such
benefits as may be provided by the pension reserve so
reduced shall be payable under the provisions of this act.

ADMINISTRATION.

SECTION 14. (1) The management of the retirement
system is hereby vested in a retirement board, the membership of which shall be constituted as follows: —

(a) The treasurer of the town,

(b) One person who shall not be a member of the retirement system and who shall be appointed by the board of
selectmen to serve for a term of three years commencing
on the date when the retirement system becomes first
operative and until the qualification of his successor, and

(c) One person who shall be a member of the retirement system and who shall be appointed by the board of
selectmen, to serve for a term of one year, commencing
on the date when the retirement system becomes first
operative and until the qualification of his successor.

(2) As the terms of office of the appointed members
expire, their successors shall be appointed for terms of
three years each and until the qualification of their successors. On a vacancy occurring in the appointed membership of the retirement board, for any cause other than
the expiration of a term of office, a successor to the person
whose place has become vacant shall be appointed for the
unexpired term in the same manner as above provided.

(3) The members of the retirement board shall receive

such compensation as the board of selectmen shall determine and they shall be reimbursed from the expense fund for any expense or loss of salary or wages which they may incur through service on the retirement board.

(4) The retirement board shall elect from its membership a chairman, and shall by a majority vote of all its members appoint a secretary, who may be, but need not be, one of its members. It shall engage such actuarial and other services as shall be required to transact the business of the retirement system. The funds to meet the costs of administering the retirement system shall be derived from appropriations of the town. The retirement board shall submit an estimate of such costs to the board of selectmen not later than January fifteenth of each year. Such amount as shall be required in the first year of operation to defray the expenses of the establishment and maintenance of the retirement system shall be appropriated by the town.

(5) The retirement board shall keep in convenient form such data as shall be necessary for actuarial valuations of the various funds of the retirement system and for checking the experience of the system.

(6) The retirement board shall keep a record of all of its proceedings, which shall be open to public inspection. It shall publish annually a report showing the transactions of the retirement system for the preceding fiscal year, the amount of accumulated cash and securities of the system, and the last balance sheet showing the financial condition of the system by means of actuarial valuation of the assets and liabilities thereof. The board shall submit said report to the board of selectmen and shall furnish copies thereof to the town clerk for distribution.

Legal Adviser.

(7) The town counsel shall be the legal adviser of the retirement board.

Medical Examinations.

(8) The retirement board, subject to the approval of the board of selectmen, shall appoint a physician and fix his compensation, and said physician shall arrange for and pass upon all medical examinations required under the provisions of this act, shall investigate all essential statements and certificates by or in behalf of a member in connection with an application for disability retirement, and shall report in writing to the retirement board his conclusions and recommendations upon all the matters referred to him. If required, other physicians may be employed by the retirement board to report on special cases.

Duties of Actuary.

(9) The retirement board shall designate an actuary who shall be the technical adviser of the retirement board

on matters regarding the operation of the funds created by
the provisions of this act, and shall perform such other
duties as are required in connection therewith.

(10) Immediately after the establishment of the retirement system the actuary shall make such investigation of
the mortality, service and compensation experience of the
members of the system as he shall recommend and the
retirement board shall authorize, and on the basis of such
investigation he shall recommend for adoption by the
retirement board such tables and such rates as are required
by section fifteen. The retirement board shall adopt
tables and certify rates, and as soon as practicable thereafter the actuary shall make a valuation, based on such
tables and rates, of the assets and liabilities of the funds
created by this act.

(11) Three years after the system becomes operative,
and at least once in each five-year period thereafter, the
actuary shall make an actuarial investigation into the
mortality, service and compensation experience of the
members and pensioners of the retirement system, and shall
make a valuation of the assets and liabilities of the funds
thereof, and taking into account the result of such investigation and valuation the retirement board shall —

(a) Adopt for the retirement system such mortality,
service and other tables as shall be deemed necessary; and

(b) Certify the rates of contribution payable by the
town on account of new entrants.

(12) On the basis of such tables as the retirement board
shall from time to time adopt, the actuary shall make an
annual valuation of the assets and liabilities of the reserve
funds of the system created by this act.

METHOD OF FINANCING.

SECTION 15. All of the assets of the retirement system
shall be credited, according to the purpose for which they
are held, to one of the following five funds, namely, the
Annuity Savings Fund, the Annuity Reserve Fund, the
Pension Accumulation Fund, the Pension Reserve Fund
or the Expense Fund.

Annuity Savings Fund.

(1) (a) The Annuity Savings Fund shall be the fund
to which shall be paid the deductions from the compensation of members. The treasurer of the town shall withhold
four per centum of the regular compensation due on each
pay day to all employees who are members of this retirement system. The various amounts so withheld shall be
transferred immediately thereafter to the retirement system
and credited to the accounts of the respective members
so contributing, and shall be paid into and become a part
of said Annuity Savings Fund.

(b) In determining the amount earnable by a member in
a payroll period, the retirement board may consider the

rate of annual compensation payable to such member on
the first day of the payroll period as continuing throughout
such payroll period, and it may omit deduction from compensation for any period less than a full payroll period if an
employee was not a member on the first day of the payroll
period.

(c) The deductions provided for herein shall be made
notwithstanding that the minimum compensation provided
for by law for any member shall be reduced thereby. Every
member shall be deemed to consent and agree to the deductions provided for herein and shall receipt for his full
salary or compensation, and the payment of his full salary
or compensation less the deductions provided for hereunder
shall be considered a full and complete discharge and
acquittance of all claims and demands whatsoever for the
services rendered by such person during the period covered
by such payment, except as to the benefits provided under
this act.

(d) In addition to the contributions deducted from
compensation as hereinbefore provided, subject to the
approval of the retirement board, any member may redeposit in the Annuity Savings Fund by a single payment
or by an increased rate of contribution an amount equal
to the total amount which he previously withdrew therefrom, as provided in this act, or any part thereof; or any
member may deposit therein by a single payment or by
an increased rate of contribution an amount computed to be
sufficient to purchase an additional annuity, which together with his prospective retirement allowance, will
provide for him a total retirement allowance of not more
than one half of his salary at age sixty. Such additional
amounts so deposited shall be treated as a part of his accumulated contributions, except in the event of his retirement, when they shall not be used to increase the pension
payable, and shall be treated as excess contributions returnable to the member in cash or in providing an excess annuity of equivalent actuarial value. The accumulated
contributions of a member withdrawn by him or paid to his
estate or to his designated beneficiary in event of his death
as provided in this act shall be paid from the Annuity
Savings Fund. Upon the retirement of a member his
accumulated contributions shall be transferred from the
Annuity Savings Fund to the Annuity Reserve Fund.

Annuity Reserve Fund.

(2) The Annuity Reserve Fund shall be the fund from
which shall be paid all annuities and all benefits in lieu
of annuities, payable as provided in this act. Should a
pensioner, retired on account of disability, be restored to
active service with a compensation not less than his regular
compensation at the time of his last retirement, any unexpended balance of the fund held for the payment of his
annuity-certain shall be transferred from the Annuity

Reserve Fund to the Annuity Savings Fund, and credited
to his individual account therein.

Pension Accumulation Fund.

(3) (*a*) The Pension Accumulation Fund shall be the
fund into which shall be accumulated all reserves for the
payment of all pensions and other benefits payable from
contributions made by the town, and from which shall be
paid all pensions and other benefits on account of members
with prior service credit. Contributions to and payments
from the Pension Accumulation Fund shall be made as
follows: —

(*b*) On account of each member there shall be paid
annually into the Pension Accumulation Fund by the said
town, for the preceding fiscal year, a certain percentage of
the regular compensation of each member, to be known as
the "normal contribution", and an additional percentage of
his regular compensation to be known as the "accrued
liability contribution". The rates per centum of such
contributions shall be fixed on the basis of the liabilities
of the retirement system as shown by actuarial valuation.
Until the first valuation the normal contribution shall be
three and thirty hundredths per centum, and the accrued
liability contribution shall be five and eighteen hundredths
per centum, of the regular annual compensation of all
members.

(*c*) On the basis of regular interest and of such mortality
and other tables as shall be adopted by the retirement
board, the actuary engaged by the board to make each
valuation required by this act during the period over which
the accrued liability contribution is payable, immediately
after making such valuation, shall determine the uniform
and constant percentage of the regular compensation of
the average new entrant, which if contributed on the basis
of compensation of such new entrant throughout his entire
period of active service is computed to be sufficient to
provide for the payment of any pension payable on his
account. The rate per centum so determined shall be
known as the "normal contribution" rate. After the accrued liability contribution has ceased to be payable, the
normal contribution rate shall be the rate per centum of
the regular compensation of all members obtained by
deducting from the total liabilities of the Pension Accumulation Fund the amount of the funds in hand to the credit of
that fund and dividing the remainder by one per centum
of the present value of the prospective future salaries of
all members as computed on the basis of the mortality and
service tables adopted by the retirement board and regular
interest. The normal rate of contribution shall be determined by the actuary after each valuation.

(*d*) Immediately succeeding the first valuation, the
actuary engaged by the retirement board shall compute

the rate per centum of the total regular compensation of all members which is equivalent to four per centum of the amount of the total pension liability on account of all members and pensioners which is not dischargeable by the aforesaid normal contribution made on account of such members during the remainder of their active service. The rate per centum originally so determined shall be known as the "accrued liability contribution rate".

(e) The total amount payable in each year to the Pension Accumulation Fund shall be not less than the sum of the rates per centum known as the normal contribution rate and the accrued liability contribution rate of the total compensation earnable by all members during the preceding year; provided, that the amount of each annual accrued liability contribution shall be at least three per centum greater than the preceding annual accrued liability payment, and that the aggregate payments of the town shall be sufficient when combined with the amount in the fund to provide the pensions and other benefits payable out of the fund during the year then current.

(f) The accrued liability contribution shall be discontinued as soon as the accumulated reserve in the Pension Accumulation Fund shall equal the present value, as actuarially computed and approved by the retirement board, of the total liability of such fund less the present value, computed on the basis of the normal contribution rate then in force, of the prospective normal contributions to be received on account of persons who are at that time members.

(g) All pensions, and benefits in lieu thereof, with the exception of those payable on account of members who receive no prior service allowance, payable from contributions of the town, shall be paid from the Pension Accumulation Fund.

(h) Upon the retirement of a member not entitled to credit for prior service, an amount equal to his pension reserve shall be transferred from the Pension Accumulation Fund to the Pension Reserve Fund.

Pension Reserve Fund.

(4) The Pension Reserve Fund shall be the fund from which shall be paid the pensions to members not entitled to credit for prior service and benefits in lieu thereof. Should such a pensioner, retired on account of disability, be restored to active service with a compensation not less than his average regular compensation for the year preceding his last retirement, the pension reserve thereon shall be transferred from the Pension Reserve Fund to the Pension Accumulation Fund. Should the pension of a disability pensioner be reduced as a result of an increase in his earning capacity, the amount of the annual reduction in his pension shall be paid annually into the Pension Accumulation Fund during the period of such reduction.

Expense Fund.

(5) The Expense Fund shall be the fund to which shall be credited all money appropriated by the town to pay the administration expenses of the retirement system, and from which shall be paid all the expenses necessary in connection with the administration and operation of the system.

Appropriations.

(6) (a) On or before the fifteenth day of January in each year the retirement board shall certify to the board of selectmen the amount of the appropriations required for the current calendar year to maintain the funds for all the benefits provided under this act and items of appropriation providing for such amounts shall be included in the budget.

(b) To cover the requirements of the system for the period prior to the date when the first regular appropriation is due, as provided by paragraph (a) of this subsection, such amounts as shall be necessary to cover the needs of the system shall be paid into the Pension Accumulation Fund and the Expense Fund by special appropriations to the system.

MANAGEMENT OF FUNDS.

SECTION 16. (1) The retirement board shall invest the funds of the retirement system in such securities as are approved from time to time by the bank commissioner for the investment of the funds of savings banks under the laws of the commonwealth and in deposits in such banks.

(2) The retirement board shall annually allow regular interest on the average balance for the preceding fiscal year to the credit of the various funds from the interest and dividends earned from investments. Any excess earnings over the amount so credited shall be used for reducing the amount of contributions required of the town during the ensuing fiscal year. Any deficiency shall be paid by the town during the ensuing fiscal year.

(3) The treasurer of the town shall be custodian of the several funds. All payments from said funds shall be made by him only upon vouchers signed by one member of the retirement board and approved by the town accountant and the board of selectmen. A duly attested copy of a resolution of the retirement board designating such member and bearing upon its face a specimen signature of such member shall be filed with the treasurer as his authority for making payments upon such vouchers. No voucher shall be drawn unless it shall have been previously authorized by resolution of the retirement board.

(4) For the purpose of meeting disbursements for pensions, annuities and other payments an amount of money, not exceeding ten per centum of the total amount in the several funds of the retirement system, may be kept on deposit in one or more banks or trust companies organized

under the laws of the commonwealth or of the United States; provided, that the sum on deposit in any one bank or trust company shall not exceed ten per centum of the paid-up capital and surplus thereof.

(5) The retirement board may, in its discretion, transfer to or from the Pension Accumulation Fund the amount of any surplus or deficit which may develop in the reserves creditable to the Annuity Reserve Fund or the Pension Reserve Fund, as shown by actuarial valuation.

(6) Except as otherwise provided herein, no member and no employee of the retirement board shall have any direct interest in the gains or profits of any investment made by the retirement board, nor as such receive any pay or emolument for his services. No member or employee of the retirement board shall, directly or indirectly, for himself or as an agent, in any manner use any of the securities or other assets of the retirement board, except to make such current and necessary payments as are authorized by the retirement board; nor shall any member or employee of the retirement board become an endorser or surety or in any manner an obligor for moneys loaned by or borrowed from the retirement system.

(7) The retirement board may at any time in its discretion, with the approval of the commissioner of insurance, elect to have underwritten and guaranteed by an insurance company or companies approved by him any or all of the benefits included in the retirement system. Any payment of premium to an insurance company in consideration of the insurance company's guarantee to fulfill certain obligations assumed shall be deemed not inconsistent with the provisions of the retirement plan relating to management and investment of funds under the retirement system.

(8) Each member of the retirement board, and the treasurer of the town in his capacity as custodian of the several funds shall severally give bond for the faithful performance of his duties in a sum and with sureties or surety approved by the board of selectmen.

EXEMPTION OF FUNDS FROM TAXATION AND EXECUTION.

Section 17. The pensions, annuities and retirement allowances and the accumulated contributions and the cash and securities in the funds created by this act are hereby exempted from any state, county or municipal tax of this commonwealth, and shall not be subject to execution or attachment by trustee process or otherwise, in law or in equity, or under any other process whatsoever, and shall be nonassignable except as specifically provided in this act.

RECEIPT OF BOTH RETIREMENT ALLOWANCE AND SALARY FORBIDDEN.

Section 18. No pensioner of the retirement system shall be paid for any service, except service as a juror and such service as he may be called upon to perform in the police or fire department in a time of public emergency, rendered by him to the town after the date of the first payment of any retirement allowance hereunder, except as provided in section nine of this act, and except as further provided in this section.

Notwithstanding the above provision, a pensioner may be employed, for periods of not exceeding one year at a time, with the approval of the board of selectmen, and may receive compensation from the town for the services so rendered; provided, that the annual rate of compensation paid, together with the retirement allowance received, shall not exceed the regular compensation of the said pensioner at the time of retirement.

RIGHT OF APPEAL.

SECTION 19. The supreme judicial court shall have jurisdiction in equity upon the petition of the retirement board or any interested party or upon the petition of not less than ten taxable inhabitants of the town to compel the observance and restrain any violation of this act and the rules and regulations authorized or established thereunder.

TENURE UNAFFECTED.

SECTION 20. Nothing contained in this act shall affect the right or power of the town or other duly constituted authority in regard to demotion, transfer, suspension or discharge of any employee.

INCONSISTENT ACTS.

SECTION 21. Any of the provisions of sections forty-four, forty-five and seventy-seven of chapter thirty-two of the General Laws which may be inconsistent herewith, and any other act or parts of acts inconsistent herewith, shall, on and after the effective date of this act, apply only to such employees of the town as are, on said effective date, entitled to the benefits thereof. Nothing herein contained shall be construed as affecting the provisions of sections six to nineteen, inclusive, and sections forty-nine to sixty, inclusive, or of section ninety-two, of said chapter thirty-two.

DATE ACT EFFECTIVE.

SECTION 22. This act shall take full effect upon its acceptance by the town of Brookline by a two thirds vote of the town meeting members present and voting thereon at a limited town meeting called for the purpose within two years of the passage of this act, but not otherwise.

Approved June 27, 1933.

AN ACT EXTENDING THE JURISDICTION OF THE SUPREME
JUDICIAL COURT TO PERMIT LATE ENTRY OF APPEALS,
EXCEPTIONS AND REPORTS, AND LIMITING THE RIGHT OF
APPEAL TO SAID COURT FROM CERTAIN ORDERS, AND
RELATIVE TO APPEALS FROM APPELLATE DIVISIONS OF
DISTRICT COURTS.

Chap.300

Be it enacted, etc., as follows:

SECTION 1. Chapter two hundred and eleven of the
General Laws is hereby amended by striking out section
eleven, as appearing in the Tercentenary Edition thereof,
and inserting in place thereof the following: — *Section 11.*
If, by mistake or accident or other sufficient cause, an
appeal from any court to the full court or a bill of exceptions or report which has been allowed by any court is not
duly entered in the full court, that court, upon petition filed
within one year after the appeal, bill of exceptions or report
should have been entered, and upon terms, may allow the
appellant to enter his appeal or the excepting party to
enter his bill of exceptions or the proper party to enter the
report. But no security by bond, attachment or otherwise which has been discharged by the omission to enter
an appeal, bill of exceptions or report shall be revived or
continued in force by the entry thereof.

(margin: G. L. (Ter. Ed.), 211, § 11, amended. Late entry of appeal to full court.)

SECTION 2. Section one hundred and thirty-three of
chapter two hundred and thirty-one of the General Laws,
as so appearing, is hereby amended by inserting after the
word "effect" in the sixteenth line the following new
sentence: — There shall be no right to take an appeal,
exceptions or other proceeding in the nature of an appeal
from such an order dismissing an appeal, overruling
exceptions or discharging a report for any cause above
stated, except by leave of the full court under section
eleven of chapter two hundred and eleven, — so as to read
as follows: — *Section 133.* If, at law, in equity or in
probate proceedings, an appellant or an excepting party,
or, in a case reported after a verdict, finding or decision,
the party at whose request it is reported, or, in a case
reported without decision under section one hundred and
eleven, the plaintiff neglects to enter the appeal, exceptions
or report in the supreme judicial court or to take the necessary measures by ordering proper copies to be prepared or
otherwise for the hearing of the case, or if an appellant or
an excepting party neglects to provide a transcript of the
evidence or of the instructions to the jury within the time
ordered by the justice under section one hundred and
twenty-one, the court in which the appeal was taken or by
which the exceptions were allowed or the case reported
may, upon the application of the adverse party and after
notice to all parties interested, order the appeal dismissed,
the exceptions overruled or the report discharged, and
thereupon, in the case of appeal or exceptions, the decision,

(margin: G. L. (Ter. Ed.), 231, § 133, amended. Affirmance of judgment by court appealed from.)

ruling, order or decree appealed from, or excepted to, shall
Right of appeal limited. be in full force and effect. There shall be no right to take
an appeal, exceptions or other proceeding in the nature of
an appeal from such an order dismissing an appeal, overruling exceptions or discharging a report for any cause
above stated, except by leave of the full court under section
eleven of chapter two hundred and eleven. Whenever
after the entry in the supreme judicial, superior or probate
court of a decree after rescript from the full bench of the
supreme judicial court in a suit in equity or in probate
proceedings, an appeal is claimed from the decree, the
justice by whom or by whose order the decree was entered
may inquire into any reasons assigned for the appeal, and
if he deems that the decree conforms to the terms of the
rescript and the appeal is claimed merely for the purpose of
delay, he may order the appeal dismissed, and such proceedings may forthwith be had and such processes may
forthwith issue as are necessary to carry out the provisions
of the decree. And if a further appeal is claimed from an
order so dismissing an appeal it shall not operate to suspend or supersede the carrying into effect of the terms of
the decree, and the full bench of the supreme judicial
court may order such dismissal of appeal affirmed and the
imposition of reasonable terms and double costs to the
appellee.

G. L. (Ter. Ed.), 231, § 141, etc., amended. SECTION 3. Section one hundred and forty-one of said
chapter two hundred and thirty-one, as most recently
amended by section two of chapter one hundred and thirty
of the acts of nineteen hundred and thirty-two, is hereby
further amended by inserting after the word "thirty-two"
in the twenty-fourth line the words: — , one hundred and
Sections applicable to civil actions before district courts. thirty-three, — so as to read as follows: — *Section 141.*
Sections one, two, three, four, five, six, seven, ten, eleven,
twelve, thirteen, thirteen A,. fourteen, fifteen, sixteen,
seventeen, eighteen, nineteen, twenty, twenty-one, twenty-
two, twenty-three, twenty-five, twenty-six, twenty-seven,
twenty-eight, twenty-nine, thirty, thirty-one, thirty-two,
thirty-three, thirty-four, thirty-five, thirty-six, thirty-
seven, thirty-eight, thirty-nine, forty, forty-one, forty-two,
forty-three, forty-four, forty-five, forty-seven, forty-eight,
forty-nine, fifty, fifty-one, fifty-two, fifty-three, fifty-four,
fifty-six, fifty-seven, fifty-eight, fifty-eight A, fifty-nine B,
sixty-one, sixty-two, sixty-three, sixty-four, sixty-five,
sixty-six, sixty-seven, sixty-eight, sixty-nine, seventy,
seventy-two, seventy-three, seventy-four, seventy-five,
seventy-nine, eighty-five, eighty-five A, eighty-seven,
eighty-eight, eighty-nine, ninety, ninety-one, ninety-two,
ninety-three, ninety-four, ninety-five, ninety-seven, ninety-
eight, ninety-nine, one hundred and one, one hundred and
two, one hundred and three, one hundred and four, one
hundred and five, one hundred and six, one hundred and
seven, one hundred and eight, one hundred and nine, one
hundred and ten, one hundred and twenty-four, one hun-

dred and twenty-five, one hundred and twenty-six, one hundred and thirty-two, one hundred and thirty-three, one hundred and thirty-four and one hundred and thirty-five, one hundred and thirty-six, one hundred and thirty-seven, one hundred and thirty-eight, one hundred and thirty-nine, one hundred and forty, one hundred and forty A and one hundred and forty-seven shall apply to civil actions before district courts, and no other sections of this chapter shall so apply, except to the municipal court of the city of Boston under section one hundred and forty-three.

SECTION 4. This act shall take effect on September thirtieth in the current year. *Approved June 27, 1933.*

Effective date.

AN ACT REGULATING THE DRIVING OR OPERATION OF VEHICLES TRAVELING IN THE SAME DIRECTION.

*Chap.*301

Be it enacted, etc., as follows:

Chapter eighty-nine of the General Laws is hereby amended by striking out section two, as appearing in the Tercentenary Edition thereof, and inserting in place thereof the following: — *Section 2.* The driver of a vehicle passing another vehicle traveling in the same direction shall drive a safe distance to the left of such other vehicle; and, if the way is of sufficient width for the two vehicles to pass, the driver of the leading one shall not unnecessarily obstruct the other. *Approved June 27, 1933.*

G. L. (Ter. Ed.), 89, § 2, amended.

Law of the road. Persons passing in same direction to turn to left.

AN ACT AUTHORIZING THE DESTRUCTION OF CERTAIN BOOKS, RECORDS AND PAPERS RELATING TO CLOSED BANKS.

*Chap.*302

Whereas, The deferred operation of this act would tend to defeat its purpose, therefore it is hereby declared to be an emergency law, necessary for the immediate preservation of the public convenience.

Emergency preamble.

Be it enacted, etc., as follows:

Chapter one hundred and sixty-seven of the General Laws is hereby amended by inserting after section thirty-five, as appearing in the Tercentenary Edition thereof, the following new section: — *Section 35A.* After the expiration of six years from the order for final distribution, the commissioner may, with the approval of the supreme judicial court, cause to be destroyed any or all of the books, records, correspondence and other papers in his possession concerning any such bank and the liquidation thereof.

G. L. (Ter. Ed.), 167, new section after § 35.

Destruction of certain books, etc., of closed banks.

Approved June 28, 1933.

Chap.303 AN ACT CHANGING THE LAWS RELATING TO TAXATION OF
CERTAIN CLASSES OF CORPORATIONS, ESPECIALLY AS THEY
RELATE TO SUBSIDIARY OR CONTROLLED CORPORATIONS.

Be it enacted, etc., as follows:

G. L. (Ter.
Ed.), 63, § 33,
amended.

Minimum tax
of domestic
subsidiary
corporations.

SECTION 1. Chapter sixty-three of the General Laws
is hereby amended by striking out section thirty-three, as
appearing in the Tercentenary Edition thereof, and inserting in place thereof the following: —*Section 33*. The net
income of a domestic business corporation which is a subsidiary of another corporation or closely affiliated therewith
by stock ownership shall be determined by eliminating all
payments to the parent corporation or affiliated corporations in excess of fair value, and by including fair compensation to such domestic business corporation for all commodities sold to or services performed for the parent corporation or affiliated corporations. For the purposes of
determining such net income, the commissioner may, in
the absence of satisfactory evidence to the contrary, presume that an apportionment by reasonable rules of the
consolidated net income of corporations participating in
the filing of a consolidated return of net income to the
federal government fairly reflects the net income taxable
under this chapter, or may otherwise equitably determine
such net income by reasonable rules of apportionment of
the combined income of the subsidiary, its parent and
affiliates or any thereof.

If in the opinion of the commissioner the capital of a
domestic business corporation, which is a subsidiary of
another corporation or closely affiliated therewith by stock
ownership, is inadequate for its business needs apart from
credit extended or indebtedness guaranteed by the parent
or an affiliated corporation, the commissioner shall, in
determining the corporate excess, determine the value of
the capital truly employed by such domestic business
corporation and consider such value the value of its capital
stock disregarding its indebtedness owed to or guaranteed
by the parent or an affiliated corporation, and the corporate
excess thus determined shall in such case constitute the
corporate excess taxable under the provisions of this
chapter.

Such a domestic business corporation shall incorporate
in the tax returns required under section thirty-five such
information as the commissioner may reasonably require
for determination of the excise pursuant to the provisions
of this section, and failure to so incorporate such information shall subject the corporation and its officers to the
penalties provided by sections forty-six, forty-nine and
fifty.

G. L. (Ter.
Ed.), 63,
§ 39A,
amended.

SECTION 2. Said chapter sixty-three is hereby further
amended by striking out section thirty-nine A, as so appearing, and inserting in place thereof the following: —

Section 39A. The net income of a foreign corporation which is a subsidiary of another corporation or closely affiliated therewith by stock ownership shall be determined by eliminating all payments to the parent corporation or affiliated corporations in excess of fair value, and by including fair compensation to such parent corporation for all commodities sold to or services performed for the parent corporation or affiliated corporations. For the purposes of determining such net income, the commissioner may, in the absence of satisfactory evidence to the contrary, presume that an apportionment by reasonable rules of the consolidated net income of corporations participating in the filing of a consolidated return of net income to the federal government fairly reflects the net income taxable under this chapter, or may otherwise equitably determine such net income by reasonable rules of apportionment of the combined income of the subsidiary, its parent and affiliates or any thereof. *Minimum tax of foreign subsidiary corporations.*

If in the opinion of the commissioner the capital of a foreign corporation, which is a subsidiary of another corporation or closely affiliated therewith by stock ownership, is inadequate for its business needs apart from credit extended or indebtedness guaranteed by the parent or an affiliated corporation, the commissioner shall, in determining the corporate excess employed within the commonwealth, determine the value of the capital truly employed by such foreign corporation and consider such value the value of its capital stock disregarding its indebtedness owed to or guaranteed by the parent or an affiliated corporation, and the corporate excess employed within the commonwealth as thus determined shall in such case constitute the corporate excess taxable under the provisions of this chapter.

Such a corporation shall incorporate in its tax return required under section forty such information as the commissioner may reasonably require for determination of the excise pursuant to the provisions of this section, and failure to so incorporate such information shall subject the corporation and its officers to the penalties provided by sections forty-six, forty-nine and fifty.

SECTION 3. This act shall take effect as of January first, nineteen hundred and thirty-three and shall apply to taxes assessed and payable in the year nineteen hundred and thirty-three and thereafter. *Effective date, etc.*

Approved June 28, 1933.

AN ACT REGULATING THE SALE, DISTRIBUTION, STORAGE AND USE OF BENZOL AND ITS COMPOUNDS. *Chap.*304

Be it enacted, etc., as follows:

Chapter one hundred and forty-nine of the General Laws is hereby amended by inserting after section one hundred and forty-two, as appearing in the Tercentenary Edition *G. L. (Ter. Ed.), 149, six new sections after § 142.*

thereof, under the sub-title BENZOL AND MIXTURES CONTAINING BENZOL, the six following new sections:—

Benzol, etc., containers to be marked. *Section 142A.* No person shall keep for sale, sell, transport or store, and no person shall have for use in any manufacturing or mercantile establishment, benzene, represented by the chemical formula C_6H_6, in sections one hundred and forty-two B to one hundred and forty-two F, inclusive, called benzol, in any receptacle other than part of a vehicle used exclusively for outdoor transportation, unless such receptacle is marked with the word "BENZOL" and with the words "BEWARE OF POISONOUS FUMES".

Labels, how marked. *Section 142B.* No person shall keep for sale, sell, transport or store, and no person shall have for use in any manufacturing or mercantile establishment, any material containing benzol, in any receptacle other than part of a vehicle used exclusively for outdoor transportation, unless such receptacle is marked with one of the following combinations of words and figures:

"CONTAINS LESS THAN 20 PER CENT BENZOL",
"CONTAINS 10 TO 60 PER CENT BENZOL",
"CONTAINS MORE THAN 50 PER CENT BENZOL",

truly indicating the proportion of benzol incorporated in the mixture as last compounded, and with the words "BEWARE OF POISONOUS FUMES".

Size of type on label specified. *Section 142C.* The words and figures required by the two preceding sections shall be clear and conspicuous and shall be of such size and be so placed as the commissioner shall by reasonable rules or regulations designate.

Commissioner of labor and industries to make rules, etc. *Section 142D.* The commissioner may, by reasonable rules or regulations, exempt from the provisions of sections one hundred and forty-two A and one hundred and forty-two B, under such restrictions as he may deem advisable, (a) closed receptacles which are in the possession of the manufacturer by whom the contents of such receptacles were made or compounded or of a common carrier, provided in each case that he is satisfied that such contents are to be used only outside the commonwealth; (b) receptacles containing material used exclusively as motor fuel; (c) receptacles containing material which, as last compounded, contained less than one per cent benzol by weight.

Reports of sales, etc. *Section 142E.* The commissioner shall, by reasonable rules or regulations, require such reports of the manufacture, sale, receipt, possession or use of benzol or of materials containing benzol as he may deem advisable for the protection of persons exposed to possible injury by such benzol or materials containing benzol.

Penalty. *Section 142F.* Whoever violates any provision of section one hundred and forty-two A, one hundred and forty-two B or one hundred and forty-two C, or any rule or regulation made under section one hundred and forty-two C, one hundred and forty-two D or one hundred and forty-two E, and whoever, being charged with the duty of marking any receptacle containing benzol or any material in which benzol is included, fails so to mark the same, and whoever wilfully removes or defaces any mark made in accordance with any of said provisions or rules or regulations, shall be punished by a fine of not more than one hundred dollars.   *Approved June 28, 1933.*

An Act to prevent certain fraudulent nominations.   *Chap.*305

Be it enacted, etc., as follows:

Chapter fifty-three of the General Laws is hereby amended by inserting after section twelve, as appearing in the Tercentenary Edition thereof, the following new section: — *Section 12A.* If objection is filed under section eleven by a person duly nominated for any state, city or town office alleging that an apparent nomination for the same office is of a fictitious or non-existing person or that the name under which a person has been apparently nominated for such office is not his true name, the state ballot law commission or the proper board named in section twelve shall summon the apparent nominee to appear before it and submit to examination. If no person appears in response to such summons or if a person representing himself to be the nominee appears and after a hearing the commission or board is satisfied that the allegations contained in such objection are true, the commission or board shall sustain the objection and vacate the nomination.

Approved June 28, 1933.

G. L. (Ter. Ed.), 53, new section after § 12.

Fraudulent nominations, prevention of.

An Act relative to the regulation and limitation of hackney carriages in the city of Boston.   *Chap.*306

Be it enacted, etc., as follows:

Section four of chapter three hundred and ninety-two of the acts of nineteen hundred and thirty is hereby amended by adding at the end thereof the following new sentence: — Said commissioner shall, if public convenience and necessity so require, fix a limit for the number of licenses to be issued under this section, but may from time to time, after a reasonable notice and a hearing, change the limit so fixed. In fixing or changing such limit he shall be guided by the number of hackney carriages actually being operated and not by the number of licenses issued and outstanding. If an applicant is refused a license hereunder by reason of the fact that the maximum number of licenses limited as aforesaid has been issued, the department of public utilities, on petition of such applicant, may after a hearing determine that public convenience and necessity require that a higher limit than that fixed by said police commissioner shall be established, in which case the limit set by said department shall be considered final.   *Approved June 28, 1933.*

Chap.307 AN ACT AUTHORIZING CITIES AND TOWNS TO BORROW ON
ACCOUNT OF PUBLIC WELFARE AND SOLDIERS' BENEFITS
FROM THE COMMONWEALTH AND ELSEWHERE AND AU-
THORIZING THE COMMONWEALTH TO ISSUE BONDS OR
NOTES TO PROVIDE FUNDS THEREFOR.

Emergency preamble.

Whereas, The deferred operation of this act would tend
to defeat its purpose, therefore it is hereby declared to be
an emergency law, necessary for the immediate preservation of the public convenience.

Be it enacted, etc., as follows:

Emergency finance board.

Powers and duties relative to financial relief of cities and towns.

SECTION 1. The emergency finance board, established
under section one of chapter forty-nine of the acts of the
current year, hereinafter referred to as the board, shall, in
addition to the powers and duties conferred or imposed
upon it by said chapter, exercise and perform the powers
and duties hereinafter so conferred or imposed, and, except
as hereinafter provided, the provisions of said section one
shall apply to the board when acting under this act. Each
appointive member of the board, when acting under this
act, shall receive from the commonwealth as compensation,
in addition to any sums so payable for action under said
chapter forty-nine, for each day's attendance at board
meetings during the current fiscal year, the sum of thirty
dollars and, for each day's attendance as aforesaid thereafter, the sum of fifteen dollars; provided, that the total
amount paid hereunder to any member for compensation as
aforesaid shall not exceed twenty-five hundred dollars
during the current fiscal year nor one thousand dollars in
any fiscal year thereafter. Separate records and accounts
shall be kept by the board of its action under this act. The
existence of the board, for the purposes of this act, shall
terminate upon payment in full to the commonwealth of
all amounts due hereunder from the cities and towns, and
nothing in said chapter forty-nine shall be construed to
terminate its existence earlier.

Cities and towns au- thorized to borrow money.

SECTION 2. Any city or town, by a two thirds vote as
defined in section one of chapter forty-four of the General
Laws and with the approval of the mayor or the selectmen
and of the board, may borrow, during the year nineteen
hundred and thirty-three, outside its debt limit as fixed
by section ten of said chapter forty-four for use only as
provided in section four, a sum not exceeding the excess of
the amount expended by such city or town in the year
nineteen hundred and thirty-two over that expended by it
in the year nineteen hundred and twenty-nine for public
welfare including mothers' aid and old age assistance, and
soldiers' benefits including state aid, military aid, soldiers'
burials and soldiers' relief, as determined by the board,
and may issue bonds or notes therefor which shall bear on
their face the words, (name of city or town) Municipal

Relief Loan, Act of 1933. Each authorized issue shall constitute a separate loan, and such loans shall be paid in not more than five years from their dates and, except as herein provided, shall be subject to chapter forty-four of the General Laws. Any expense incurred by the board in passing upon applications for loans by cities and towns from others than the commonwealth shall be charged to such cities and towns and added to their respective quotas of the state tax.

SECTION 3. On petition of the treasurer of any city, with the approval of the mayor, or the treasurer of any town, with the approval of the selectmen, after a loan has been authorized under the preceding section, the board may, if in its judgment the financial affairs of such city or town warrant, approve the loaning of money by the commonwealth to an amount which, together with the amount of bonds and notes issued under section two and sold to others than the commonwealth, will not exceed the limitation provided in said preceding section, from funds provided under section seven of this act, and the state treasurer shall loan said city or town the amount so approved upon receipt of its bonds or notes of equivalent face value. The rate of interest on all loans made to cities and towns by the commonwealth under this act shall be fixed by the state treasurer with the approval of the board at such amount as in his judgment will cover the entire cost to the commonwealth including interest on money borrowed for the purposes of this act, expense of issuing bonds and expenses of the board, its employees and such other expenses as may be necessary for a proper administration of this act, except expenses assessed under the preceding section.

SECTION 4. The proceeds of loans issued under authority of this act by any city or town shall be used only to meet appropriations for public welfare, soldiers' benefits or maturing debt made prior to any application by it for a loan hereunder, or shall be treated by the assessors as an estimated receipt in fixing its tax rate.

SECTION 5. The commissioner of public welfare and the commissioner of state aid and pensions shall, upon request of the board, make investigations and report to it as to the administration of public relief in any city or town seeking approval by the board of any loan under authority of this act, and the board may investigate and make recommendations in writing to officials, boards and commissions of such a city or town concerning said administration or concerning its finances; and no loan shall be approved by the board until its recommendations, if any, have been complied with to its satisfaction. In any city or town which has obtained a loan from the commonwealth in the current year under authority of this act, no subsequent appropriation in said year shall be valid without the written approval of the board. Until all loans made hereunder by the commonwealth to any city or town have been repaid

Board to approve loans.

Use of loans restricted.

Information to board to be furnished by certain state officials.

in full, no appropriation by such city or town in any year subsequent to the current year for a purpose other than one for which an appropriation was made for the current year or for an amount in excess of any appropriations made for said current year for a similar purpose shall be valid without the written approval of the board.

SECTION 6. If a city or town fails to make payment of principal or interest on any bond or note issued to the commonwealth under sections two and three, when due, the state treasurer shall, not later than the issue of his warrant for its share of the state tax in any year, issue his warrant requiring its assessors to assess a tax to the amount necessary to make such payment in full and the amount of such warrant shall be collected and paid to the state treasurer in the same manner and subject to the same penalties as state taxes. The state treasurer shall have authority to withhold, to the extent necessary to make good any failure to make payment of the sums due, any sum due the city or town from the commonwealth and not previously pledged.

SECTION 7. The state treasurer, with the approval of the governor and council, may borrow from time to time such sums as may be necessary to provide funds for loans to municipalities as aforesaid and may issue bonds or notes of the commonwealth to an amount not exceeding thirty million dollars. Such bonds or notes shall be issued for such maximum term of years as the governor may recommend to the general court in accordance with section three of Article LXII of the amendments to the constitution of the commonwealth, shall be payable not later than November thirtieth, nineteen hundred and forty, and shall bear interest at such terms and at such rates as shall be fixed by the state treasurer, with the approval of the governor and council.

The state treasurer may borrow from time to time in anticipation of the serial issue and may issue notes therefor and may renew the same, but the maturity of the temporary loans shall be not later than two years from the date of the first temporary loan and in no event later than the date of the serial loans herein authorized.

SECTION 8. Until payment to the commonwealth of all principal and interest on account of any bonds or notes issued by a city or town hereunder and held by the commonwealth, so much of any moneys received by the commonwealth under the Federal Emergency Relief Act of 1933 as would otherwise be allocated to such city or town shall forthwith be applied by the state treasurer toward the payment of bonds or notes issued hereunder by such city or town and then held by the commonwealth, in the order of their maturities, and thereafter interest shall be payable only on the balance of such bonds or notes remaining unpaid.

SECTION 9. Income received by any inhabitant of the commonwealth during the years nineteen hundred and thirty-three, nineteen hundred and thirty-four and nineteen hundred and thirty-five from dividends on shares in all corporations, joint stock companies and banking associations, organized under the laws of this commonwealth or under the laws of any state or nation, except co-operative banks, building and loan associations and credit unions chartered by the commonwealth, and except savings and loan associations under the supervision of the commissioner of banks, shall be taxed at the rate of six per cent per annum.   Except as otherwise provided in this section, the provisions of chapter sixty-two of the General Laws, as amended, shall apply to the taxation of income received by any such inhabitant during said years.   Subsection (b) of section one of said chapter sixty-two shall not apply to income received during said years.

SECTION 9A.   The credit for dividends paid to inhabitants of this commonwealth by foreign corporations provided by section forty-three of chapter sixty-three of the General Laws in determining the tax leviable on such corporations under paragraph (2) of section thirty-nine of said chapter sixty-three shall not be allowed to foreign corporations or to foreign manufacturing corporations in respect to dividends so paid in the years nineteen hundred and thirty-three, nineteen hundred and thirty-four and nineteen hundred and thirty-five. *Taxes on dividends for certain years.*

SECTION 10.   Every corporation organized under the laws of this commonwealth, and every corporation doing business therein, including every banking association organized under the laws of any state or nation, and every partnership, association or trust the beneficial interest in which is represented by transferable shares, doing business in the commonwealth unless the dividends paid on its shares are exempt from taxation under said section one of said chapter sixty-two shall in nineteen hundred and thirty-four, nineteen hundred and thirty-five and nineteen hundred and thirty-six file with the commissioner of corporations and taxation, hereinafter called the commissioner, in such form as he shall prescribe, a complete list of the names and addresses of its shareholders as of record on December thirty-first next preceding, or on any other date satisfactory to the commissioner, or in its discretion, of such shareholders as are residents of the commonwealth, together with the number and class of shares held by each shareholder, and the rate of dividends paid on each class of stock for said preceding year.   The second paragraph of section thirty-three of said chapter sixty-two shall not apply to returns relative to shareholders receiving dividends in the years nineteen hundred and thirty-three, nineteen hundred and thirty-four and nineteen hundred and thirty-five. *Certain corporations to file lists of stockholders with commissioner of corporations and taxation.*

SECTION 11.   The state treasurer shall, on or before November twentieth, in the years nineteen hundred and thirty-four, nineteen hundred and thirty-five and nineteen *Distribution of taxes.*

hundred and thirty-six, distribute to the several cities and towns, in proportion to the amounts of state tax imposed upon such cities and towns in said years, respectively, the proceeds of the taxes collected by the commonwealth under section nine of this act, after deducting a sum sufficient to reimburse the commonwealth for the expenses incurred in the collection and distribution of said taxes, and for such of said taxes as have been refunded under section twenty-seven of chapter fifty-eight of the General Laws, as appearing in the Tercentenary Edition thereof, during said years, together with any interest or costs paid on account of refunds, which shall be retained by the commonwealth; provided, that the state treasurer may withhold out of the amount to which any city or town would otherwise be entitled as aforesaid so much thereof as is necessary to pay the principal or interest of any bonds or notes issued by such city or town under section two and then held by the commonwealth and remaining unpaid, and thereafter interest shall be payable only on the balance of such bonds or notes remaining unpaid. Any amount payable to a city or town hereunder shall be included by the assessors thereof as an estimated receipt, and be deducted, in accordance with the provisions of section twenty-three of chapter fifty-nine, from the amount required to be raised by taxation to meet appropriations made in such years for public welfare, soldiers' benefits and maturing debts, in that order.   *Approved July 1, 1933.*

---

*Chap.*308 AN ACT RELATIVE TO THE PARTIAL PAYMENT OF LOCAL TAXES.

Emergency preamble.

Whereas, The deferred operation of this act would tend to defeat its purpose, therefore it is hereby declared to be an emergency law, necessary for the immediate preservation of the public convenience.

Be it enacted, etc., as follows:

Section fifty-two of chapter two hundred and fifty-four of the acts of the current year is hereby made effective as of July first, nineteen hundred and thirty-three.
                Approved July 7, 1933.

---

*Chap.*309 AN ACT RELATIVE TO THE LICENSING OF CERTAIN AMUSEMENT ENTERPRISES TO BE HELD ON THE LORD'S DAY AT AMUSEMENT PARKS AND BEACH RESORTS.

Emergency preamble.

Whereas, The deferred operation of this act would tend to defeat its purpose, therefore it is hereby declared to be an emergency law, necessary for the immediate preservation of the public convenience.

Be it enacted, etc., as follows:

G. L. (Ter. Ed.), 136, § 4A, amended.

SECTION 1. Chapter one hundred and thirty-six of the General Laws is hereby amended by striking out section four A, inserted by section two of chapter one hundred and fifty of the acts of the current year, and inserting in place thereof the following: — *Section 4A.* The mayor of a city or the selectmen of a town, upon written application therefor, and upon such terms and conditions as they may prescribe, may grant licenses for the maintenance and operation upon the Lord's day at amusement parks or beach resorts, so called, in such city or town, of any enterprise hereinafter described, for admission to which or for the use of which a payment of money or other valuable consideration may or may not be charged, namely: — Bowling alleys, shooting galleries restricted to the firing therein of rifles, revolvers or pistols using cartridges not larger than twenty-two calibre, photographic galleries or studios in which pictures are made and sold, games, and such amusement devices as may lawfully be operated therein on secular days; provided, that no such license shall be granted to have effect before one o'clock in the afternoon, nor shall it have effect unless the proposed enterprise shall, upon application accompanied by a fee of two dollars, have been approved in writing by the commissioner of public safety as provided in the case of public entertainments under section four. Any licensee hereunder may distribute premiums or prizes in connection with any game or device lawfully maintained and operated by him under authority hereof. Any such license may, after notice and a hearing given by the mayor or selectmen issuing the same, or by said commissioner, be suspended, revoked or annulled by the officer or board giving the hearing.

Licenses for operation on the Lord's day of certain amusements at beach resorts, etc.

SECTION 2. This act shall be operative as of April twenty-eighth of the current year.

When operative.

Approved July 7, 1933.

AN ACT TO IMPROVE THE METHOD OF EXAMINATION OF BANKS.

*Chap.*310

Whereas, The deferred operation of this act would tend to defeat its purpose, therefore it is hereby declared to be an emergency law, necessary for the immediate preservation of the public convenience.

Emergency preamble.

Be it enacted, etc., as follows:

Chapter one hundred and sixty-seven of the General Laws is hereby amended by inserting after section two, as appearing in the Tercentenary Edition thereof, the following new section: — *Section 2A.* Whenever the commissioner deems it expedient he may cause a meeting of the board of directors of a trust company or co-operative bank or the board of trustees of a savings bank to be held in such manner and at such time and place as he may direct. Any report of an examination of the affairs of such a bank under section two, any conclusions drawn therefrom by the commissioner and any directions or recommendations made by

G. L. (Ter. Ed.), 167, new section after § 2.

Report of commissioner of banks to directors thereof, after examination of bank.

him relative thereto and any other matters concerning the operation or condition of such·bank may be presented to such board by the commissioner in person or by such assistant as he may designate, and the person having custody of the records of such bank, hereinafter referred to as the recording officer, shall forthwith incorporate such directions and recommendations in the records of such meeting. Each director or trustee of such bank, who is present at such meeting shall forthwith sign a certificate or other acknowledgment in such form as may be prescribed by the commissioner that he has heard the directions and recommendations of the commissioner or read the records containing the same. The recording officer of such bank shall within seven days after the date of such meeting transmit to the commissioner the said certificates or other forms of acknowledgment signed as aforesaid and also an attested copy of the records of such meeting. The recording officer shall also within such period mail by registered mail an attested copy of the records of such meeting and a blank form for said certificate or other form of acknowledgment to each director or trustee who is absent therefrom, and each such director or trustee, unless excused by the commissioner for physical and mental incapacity or absence from the commonwealth, shall sign and return as soon as may be to the recording officer such certificate or other form of acknowledgment. The commissioner may make rules and regulations relative to the filing of such certificates or other form of acknowledgment by absent directors or trustees and relative to their transmission to him.   *Approved July 7, 1933.*

---

*Chap.*311 AN ACT CHANGING THE LAWS RELATIVE TO THE SALE OF MEAT AND MEAT PRODUCTS CONTAINING CERTAIN PRESERVATIVES.

Emergency preamble.

Whereas, The deferred operation of this act would tend to defeat its purpose, therefore it is hereby declared to be an emergency law, necessary for the immediate preservation of the public convenience.

Be it enacted, etc., as follows:

G. L. (Ter. Ed.), 94, § 153A, amended.

Sale of meat, etc., containing preservatives, regulated.

Chapter ninety-four of the General Laws is hereby amended by striking out section one hundred and fifty-three A, inserted by chapter one hundred and sixteen of the acts of the current year, and inserting in place thereof the following: — *Section 153A.* Whoever himself or by his agent sells or offers for sale any meat or meat product which contains any sulphur dioxide or compound thereof in excess of one tenth of one per cent when calculated as anhydrous sodium sulphite shall be punished by a fine of not less than twenty-five nor more than one hundred dollars; and whoever himself or by his agent sells, offers for sale or delivers any meat or meat product which contains any sulphur dioxide or compound thereof not in excess of one tenth of one per cent when calculated as anhydrous sodium sulphite and fails to cause each package containing such meat or meat product so sold, offered for sale or delivered to be conspicuously labeled or marked upon the outside thereof in not less than eight point type with the following "contains not more than 1/10 of 1% sodium sulphite" shall be punished by a fine of not less than fifteen nor more than one hundred dollars.

Approved July 7, 1933.

AN ACT RELATIVE TO THE RIGHTS AND POWERS OF THE SOUTH EASTON AND EASTONDALE FIRE AND WATER DISTRICT AND OF ITS WATER COMMISSIONERS. *Chap.*312

Be it enacted, etc., as follows:

SECTION 1. The South Easton and Eastondale fire and water district, established by chapter two hundred and thirty-two of the Special Acts of nineteen hundred and fifteen, shall have and exercise all the rights and powers of fire districts under chapter forty-eight of the General Laws, as appearing in the Tercentenary Edition thereof, and the water commissioners of said district shall have and exercise all the rights and powers of prudential committees of fire districts under said chapter forty-eight, as so appearing.

SECTION 2. This act shall take effect on its acceptance by a majority vote of the registered voters of said South Easton and Eastondale fire and water district present and voting at a district meeting duly called in accordance with said chapter two hundred and thirty-two.

Approved July 7, 1933.

AN ACT PROVIDING FOR ABSENT VOTING AT REGULAR CITY ELECTIONS. *Chap.*313

Be it enacted, etc., as follows:

SECTION 1. Chapter fifty-four of the General Laws is hereby amended by inserting after section one hundred and three, as appearing in the Tercentenary Edition thereof, the following new section: — *Section 103A.* Sections eighty-six to one hundred and three, inclusive, of this chapter and sections twenty-seven and thirty-four of chapter fifty-six shall, so far as applicable, apply to regular city elections in any city which accepts this section by vote of its city council, subject to the provisions of its charter. All the rights, powers, duties and obligations conferred and imposed upon the state secretary by said sections shall, with respect to said city elections, be exercised and performed by the city clerk of such city, and, in construing

G. L. (Ter. Ed.), 54, new section after § 103.

Certain sections relative to absent voting to apply in certain cities.

said sections for the purposes of this section, any reference to state elections shall be considered as referring to city elections in such city.

In each such city which holds its regular city election annually, or which holds such election biennially in the even numbered years, and in which the date for such election is fixed by general or special law at a date earlier than the third Tuesday of December, the date of such city election shall be said third Tuesday and not such earlier date.

SECTION 2. Section ten of chapter fifty-three of the General Laws, as so appearing, is hereby amended by striking out the second paragraph and inserting in place thereof the following: — In any city which does not accept section one hundred and three A of chapter fifty-four, certificates of nomination for city offices shall be filed on or before the third Monday, and nomination papers on or before the second Wednesday, preceding the day of the election, except as otherwise provided in any special law affecting such city. In any city which accepts said section one hundred and three A, certificates of nomination and nomination papers for any regular city election shall be filed on or before the Thursday following the fourth Tuesday preceding such city election. In any such city the time for presenting nomination papers for certification to the registrars of voters, and for certifying the same, shall be governed by section seven of this chapter, notwithstanding any contrary provision in any special law.

SECTION 3. Section eleven of said chapter fifty-three, as so appearing, is hereby amended by adding at the end thereof the following: — This section shall be in force in any city which accepts section one hundred and three A of chapter fifty-four, any special provision of law to the contrary notwithstanding.

SECTION 4. Section thirteen of said chapter fifty-three, as so appearing, is hereby amended by adding at the end thereof the following: — This section shall be in force in any city which accepts section one hundred and three A of chapter fifty-four, any special provision of law to the contrary notwithstanding.

SECTION 5. Said chapter fifty-three, as amended in section twenty-eight by section five of chapter three hundred and ten of the acts of nineteen hundred and thirty-two, is hereby further amended by striking out said section twenty-eight and inserting in place thereof the following: — *Section 28.* State primaries shall be held on the seventh Tuesday preceding biennial state elections, city primaries on the third Tuesday preceding regular city elections, town primaries on the second Tuesday preceding town elections, primaries before all special elections on the second Tuesday preceding such elections, and party primaries on the last Tuesday in April; except that city primaries or preliminary elections held under general or special law before regular city elections in cities which accept section one hundred and three A of chapter fifty-four shall be held on the fourth Tuesday preceding such city elections.

Except in Boston, primaries shall be held wholly or partly by wards, precincts or towns, as the aldermen or selectmen may designate.

SECTION 6. Said chapter fifty-three is hereby further amended by inserting after section seventy-two, as so appearing, the following new section: — *Section 72A.* In any city which accepts section one hundred and three A of chapter fifty-four, caucuses before regular city elections shall be held on the fourth Tuesday preceding such city elections, notwithstanding any contrary provision in any general or special law. *G. L. (Ter. Ed.), 53, new section after § 72. Caucuses in cities having absent voting.*

SECTION 7. Section fifteen of chapter forty-three of the General Laws, as appearing in the Tercentenary Edition thereof, is hereby amended by inserting after the word "year" in the seventh line the following new sentence: — If in any city which accepts section one hundred and three A of chapter fifty-four the plan theretofore or thereafter adopted provides for elections to be held annually, all regular municipal elections shall take place on the third Tuesday in December, — and also by inserting after the word "year" in the twelfth line the following: — ; provided, that in any city which adopts or has adopted such a plan and which accepts said section one hundred and three A all regular municipal elections shall take place biennially on the third Tuesday of December in every even numbered year, — so as to read as follows: — *Section 15.* Except as provided in this section, the first city election next succeeding the adoption of any plan provided for by this chapter shall take place on the third Tuesday of December next succeeding such adoption, and thereafter the city election shall take place annually on the Tuesday next following the first Monday of December, and the municipal year shall begin and end at ten o'clock in the morning of the first Monday of January in each year. If in any city which accepts section one hundred and three A of chapter fifty-four the plan theretofore or thereafter adopted provides for elections to be held annually, all regular municipal elections shall take place on the third Tuesday in December. If the plan adopted provides for elections to be held biennially in every even numbered year, then the regular municipal election next succeeding the adoption of such plan shall take place on the third Tuesday of December succeeding such adoption, and thereafter said election shall take place biennially on the Tuesday next following the first Monday of December, in every even numbered year; provided, that in any city which adopts or has adopted such a plan and which accepts said section one hundred and three A all regular municipal elections shall take place biennially on the third Tuesday of December in every even numbered year. *G. L. (Ter. Ed.), 43, § 15, amended. Dates of elections in cities.*

If the plan adopted provides for elections to be held

biennially in every odd numbered year, then the regular municipal election held under the provisions of such plan shall take place on the Tuesday next following the first Monday of December in every odd numbered year.

G. L. (Ter. Ed.), 43, § 44A, amended.

SECTION 8. Section forty-four A of said chapter forty-three, as so appearing, is hereby amended by striking out the second sentence and inserting in place thereof the following: — In such a city which accepts section one hundred and three A of chapter fifty-four, on the fourth Tuesday, and in any other such city, on the third Tuesday, preceding every regular city election, and in all such cities, on the third Tuesday preceding any special election, at which any office mentioned in this chapter is to be filled, there shall be held, except as otherwise provided in section forty-four G, a preliminary election for the purpose of nominating candidates therefor, and section sixteen shall

Preliminary elections in cities. Nominations.

not apply, — so as to read as follows: — *Section 44A.* In every city, governed on September first, nineteen hundred and twenty-two, by any plan provided by this chapter, which accepts sections forty-four A to forty-four G, inclusive, in the manner provided by section forty-four H, and in every city, except Boston, which, after said date adopts any such plan in the manner provided in this chapter, the provisions of sections forty-four A to forty-four G, inclusive, shall apply. In such a city which accepts section one hundred and three A of chapter fifty-four, on the fourth Tuesday, and in any other such city, on the third Tuesday, preceding every regular city election, and in all such cities, on the third Tuesday preceding any special election, at which any office mentioned in this chapter is to be filled, there shall be held, except as otherwise provided in section forty-four G, a preliminary election for the purpose of nominating candidates therefor, and section sixteen shall not apply. The first regular election, if occurring in the year in which sections forty-four A to forty-four G, inclusive, are accepted, shall be held on the third Tuesday of December. At every regular, preliminary and special election, the ballots used shall be governed by the provisions of section forty-nine and the polls shall be open during such hours, in accordance with general law, as the city council may prescribe. No vote of the city council changing such hours shall take effect unless accepted by a majority of the voters of the city voting thereon at a biennial state election, and the state secretary, upon the receipt at least thirty days before such an election of a copy of the vote of the city council proposing such a change, certified by the city clerk, shall cause the question of its acceptance to be placed upon the ballot to be used in said city at such election. *Approved July 7, 1933.*

An Act relative to emergency water supply for *Chap*.314
    certain state institutions.

Be it enacted, etc., as follows:

Chapter forty of the General Laws is hereby amended by G. L. (Ter. striking out section forty, as appearing in the Tercentenary $\substack{\text{Ed.}), 40, § 40,}$ amended. Edition thereof, and inserting in place thereof the following: — *Section 40.* The metropolitan district commission Emergency water supply in cities or towns using the metropolitan water supply, in cities and the city council in other cities, the selectmen or water com- towns. missioners in other towns, water commissioners of water supply and fire and water districts, officers having control of county institutions having water works, heads of state departments having control of state institutions having water works, hereinafter described as officers having control of such an institution, and water companies supplying any communities in the commonwealth, in cases of emergency, may, on behalf of their respective bodies politic or corporate, take by eminent domain under chapter seventy-nine the right to draw water from any stream, pond or reservoir or from ground sources of supply by means of driven, artesian or other wells not already appropriated to uses of a municipal or other public water supply, or may purchase water from any city, town or water company, or county or state institution having water works, for a period of not more than six months in any year in quantities necessary to relieve the emergency; but no such taking or purchase shall be made until after the department of public health has approved the water as a proper source of water supply and unless and until, in the case of towns and water supply and fire and water districts, the selectmen or water commissioners have first been authorized so to take or purchase by a vote of the voters at a town meeting or a district meeting, as the case may be, or, in the case of water companies, said companies have first been so ordered in writing by said department. The proper authority as aforesaid may also take by eminent domain under said chapter seventy-nine the right to use any land for the time necessary to use such water; provided, that, in the case of such a taking by a water company, said department shall first prescribe the limits within which such rights shall be taken. The vote of a city council or of the voters of a town or of a water supply or water and fire district or the action of county or state officers as aforesaid or of the metropolitan district commission or the written order of said department of public health to a water company to make or authorize such taking or purchase as aforesaid shall be conclusive evidence of the existence of the emergency. Any city, town or water company or the aforesaid officers having control of any county or state institution having water works may, for a period of not more than six months in any year, sell to the metropolitan district commission, to any city, town, water supply or fire and water district, or water company, or to any county or state institution having water works, such quantities of water as may be available at the time, and the approval of said department of public health shall be conclusive evidence that such quantities are safely available for sale. In such emergencies the said parties interested may agree to install for the purpose temporary pipes and other works in any city or town; provided, that the installation or repair of such pipes or other works in or along any highway shall be done with the least possible hindrance to public travel, and shall be subject to the direction and approval of the officers or departments having charge of the maintenance of said highways.   *Approved July 7, 1933.*

*Chap.*315 An Act REGULATING WORKMEN'S COMPENSATION PAYMENTS BY THE COMMONWEALTH.

Be it enacted, etc., as follows:

G. L. (Ter. Ed.), 152, new section after § 69.

Payments by commonwealth of workmen's compensation regulated.

Chapter one hundred and fifty-two of the General Laws is hereby amended by inserting after section sixty-nine, as appearing in the Tercentenary Edition thereof, the following new section: — *Section 69A.* No compensation shall be paid by the commonwealth under this chapter without the previous written consent of the attorney general or an order of the department or member thereof, and no such order shall be entered until the attorney general has been given an opportunity to appear and be heard in behalf of the commonwealth. *Approved July 7, 1933.*

*Chap.*316 An Act RELATIVE TO ESTATE TAXES IN THE CASE OF PERSONS DYING WHILE RESIDENTS OF FOREIGN COUNTRIES.

Be it enacted, etc., as follows:

G. L. (Ter. Ed.), 65A, § 1, etc., amended.

Transfer of certain estates. Taxation of estates of persons dying while residents of foreign countries.

SECTION 1. Chapter sixty-five A of the General Laws, as amended in section one by chapter two hundred and eighty-four of the acts of nineteen hundred and thirty-two, is hereby further amended by striking out the second paragraph and inserting in place thereof the following: — A tax is hereby imposed upon the transfer of real property or tangible personal property in the commonwealth of every person who at the time of death was a resident of the United States but not a resident of the commonwealth, and upon the transfer of all property, both real and personal, within the commonwealth of every person who at the time of death was not a resident of the United States, the amount of which shall be a sum equal to such proportion of the amount by which the credit allowable under the applicable federal revenue act for estate, inheritance, legacy and succession taxes actually paid to the several states exceeds the amount actually so paid for such taxes, exclusive of estate taxes based upon the difference between such credit and other estate taxes and inheritance, legacy and succes-

sion taxes, as the value of the property in the commonwealth bears to the value of the entire estate, subject to
estate tax under the applicable federal revenue act.

Section 2. This act shall take effect as of December
first, nineteen hundred and thirty-two.

Approved July 7, 1933.

Effective
date.

An Act providing for the establishment of the
Swansea Fire and Water District.

*Chap.*317

Be it enacted, etc., as follows:

Section 1. The inhabitants of the town of Swansea
residing in that part of the town bounded and described
as follows: beginning at the mouth of Cole's river at a
point in the Massachusetts-Rhode Island state line;
thence running northerly, easterly and northerly again
by the channel of said Cole's river to a point five hundred
feet distant from and northerly of the centre line of Milford
road; thence running easterly always five hundred feet
from and parallel to the centre line of Milford road to
Hortonville road and continuing in the same direction five
hundred feet easterly of the centre line of Hortonville
road; thence running southerly five hundred feet from and
parallel to the centre line of Hortonville road to a point
five hundred feet north of the centre line of Main street;
thence running easterly five hundred feet from and parallel
to the centre line of Main street to a point fifteen hundred
feet east of the centre line of Elm street extended; thence
southerly in a straight line to the Swansea-Somerset town
line at a point measured in said town line five hundred feet
easterly of the centre line of Elm street; thence running
westerly and southerly by the town line between Swansea
and Somerset to a point in the Massachusetts-Rhode Island
state line; and thence running by said state line to the
point of beginning, and comprising the portions of the
town known as Swansea Village, Ocean Grove and South
Swansea; — shall constitute a water district and are hereby
made a body corporate by the name of the Swansea Fire
and Water District, hereinafter called the district, for the
purpose of supplying themselves with water for the extinguishment of fires and for domestic and other purposes,
with power to establish fountains and hydrants and to
relocate and discontinue the same, to regulate the use of
such water and to fix and collect rates to be paid therefor,
and to take by eminent domain under chapter seventy-
nine of the General Laws, or acquire by lease, purchase or
otherwise, and to hold, for the purposes mentioned in
this act, property, lands, rights of way and other easements, and to prosecute and defend all actions relating to
the property and affairs of the district.

Swansea fire
and water
district,
territory
within.

Section 2. For the purposes aforesaid, said district,
acting by and through its board of water commissioners
hereinafter provided for, may contract with the town of

May purchase
water from
town of
Somerset.

Somerset, or any other town or city, acting through its
water department, or with any water company, or with
any water district for whatever water may be required,
authority to furnish the same being hereby granted, and/or
may take under chapter seventy-nine of the General Laws,
or acquire by purchase or otherwise, and hold, the waters,
or any portion thereof, of any pond or stream, or of any
ground sources of supply by means of driven, artesian or
other wells within the town of Swansea, not already used
for public water supply, and the water rights connected
with any such water sources; and for said purposes may
take as aforesaid, or acquire by purchase or otherwise, and
hold, all lands, rights of way and other easements necessary for collecting, storing, holding, purifying and preserving the purity of the water and for conveying the same to
any part of said district; provided, that no source of water
supply or lands necessary for preserving the quality of
the water shall be so taken or used without first obtaining
the advice and approval of the state department of public
health, and that the location of all dams, reservoirs and
wells to be used as sources of water supply under this act

District to
have necessary
powers to
establish
water system.
shall be subject to the approval of said department. Said
district may construct on the lands acquired and held
under this act proper dams, reservoirs, standpipes, tanks,
buildings, fixtures and other structures, and may make
excavations, procure and operate machinery and provide
such other means and appliances, and do such other things
as may be necessary for the establishment and maintenance
of complete and effective water works; and for that purpose may construct wells and reservoirs and establish
pumping works, and may construct, lay and maintain
aqueducts, conduits, pipes and other works under or over
any land, water courses, railroads, railways and public or
other ways, and along such ways, in said town, in such
manner as not unnecessarily to obstruct the same; and for
the purposes of constructing, laying, maintaining, operating and repairing such conduits, pipes and other works, and
for all proper purposes of this act, said district may dig up
or raise and embank any such lands, highways or other
ways in such manner as to cause the least hindrance to
public travel on such ways; provided, that all things done
upon any such way shall be subject to the direction of the
selectmen of the town of Swansea. Said district shall not
enter upon, construct or lay any conduit, pipe or other
works within the location of any railroad corporation
except at such time and in such manner as it may agree
upon with such corporation, or, in case of failure to so
agree, as may be approved by the department of public
utilities.

Right to recover
damages.
SECTION 3. Any person sustaining damages in his
property by any taking under this act or any other thing
done under authority thereof may recover such damages
from said district under said chapter seventy-nine; but

the right to damages for the taking of any water, water right or water source, or for any injury thereto, shall not vest until water is actually withdrawn or diverted under authority of this act.

SECTION 4. For the purpose of paying the necessary expenses and liabilities incurred under the provisions of this act, other than expenses of maintenance and operation, the said district may borrow from time to time such sums as may be necessary, not exceeding, in the aggregate, two hundred thousand dollars, and may issue bonds or notes therefor, which shall bear on their face the words, Swansea Fire and Water District Loan, Act of 1933. Each authorized issue shall constitute a separate loan, and such loans shall be payable in not more than thirty years from their dates. Indebtedness incurred under this act shall be subject to chapter forty-four of the General Laws. *District may borrow money.*

SECTION 5. Said district shall, at the time of authorizing said loan or loans, provide for the payment thereof in accordance with section four of this act; and when a vote to that effect has been passed, a sum which, with the income derived from water rates, will be sufficient to pay the annual expense of operating its water works and the interest as it accrues on the bonds or notes issued as aforesaid by the district, and to make such payments on the principal as may be required under the provisions of this act, shall without further vote be assessed upon said district by the assessors of said town annually thereafter until the debt incurred by said loan or loans is extinguished. *Payment of loan.*

SECTION 6. Any land taken or acquired under this act shall be managed, improved and controlled by the commissioners hereinafter provided for, in such manner as they shall deem for the best interest of the district. *Property to be under control of commissioners.*

SECTION 7. Whenever a tax is duly voted by said district for the purposes of this act, the clerk shall send a certified copy of the vote to the assessors of said town, who shall assess the same upon property in said district in the same manner in all respects in which town taxes are required by law to be assessed. The assessment shall be committed to the town collector, who shall collect said tax in the manner provided by law for the collection of town taxes, and shall deposit the proceeds thereof with the district treasurer for the use and benefit of said district. Said district may collect interest on overdue taxes in the manner in which interest is authorized to be collected on town taxes. *Assessment of taxes.*

SECTION 8. A meeting or meetings of the voters of the territory described in this act shall be called, on petition of ten or more legal voters therein, by a warrant from the selectmen of said town, or from a justice of the peace, directed to one of the petitioners, requiring him to give notice of the meeting by posting copies of the warrant in two or more public places in the district seven days at least before the time of the meeting. Such justice of the *Meeting to accept act.*

peace, or one of the selectmen, shall preside at such meeting
until a clerk is chosen and sworn, and the clerk shall preside
until a moderator is chosen.   After the choice of a moderator for the meeting the question of the acceptance of this
act shall be submitted to the voters, and if it is accepted
by a majority of the voters present and voting thereon,
the meeting may then proceed to act on the other articles
contained in the warrant.

Board of water
commissioners,
election. SECTION 9.   Said district shall elect by ballot, either
at the same meeting at which this act shall have been ac-
cepted or at a later meeting called for the purpose, three
persons to hold office, one until the expiration of three
years, one until the expiration of two years, and one until
the expiration of one year, from the day of the next succeeding annual district meeting, to constitute a board of
water commissioners; and at every annual meeting after
such next succeeding annual district meeting one such
commissioner shall be elected by ballot for the term of
three years.   All the authority granted to said district
by this act, except sections four and five, and not otherwise
specifically provided for, shall be vested in said board of
water commissioners, who shall be subject, however, to
such instructions, rules and regulations as the district may
by vote impose.   Said commissioners shall appoint a
treasurer of said district, who may be one of their number,
who shall give bond to the district in such an amount and
with such surety or sureties as may be approved by the
commissioners.   A majority of the commissioners shall
constitute a quorum for the transaction of business.   Any
vacancy occurring in said board from any cause may be
filled for the remainder of the unexpired term by said
district at any legal meeting called for the purpose.   No
money shall be drawn from the district treasury on account
of the water works except upon a written order of said
commissioners or a majority of them.

Commis-
sioners,
powers and
duties.
Rates, fixing of. SECTION 10.   Said board of commissioners shall fix
just and equitable prices and rates for the use of water,
and shall prescribe the time and manner of payment.   The
income of the water works shall be appropriated to defray
all operating expenses, interest charges and payments on
the principal as they accrue upon any bonds or notes issued
for water supply purposes.   If there should be a net
surplus remaining after providing for the aforesaid charges,
it may be appropriated for such new construction as said
commissioners may recommend, and in case a surplus
should remain after payment for such new construction
the water rates shall be reduced proportionately.   Said
commissioners shall annually, and as often as said district
may require, render a report upon the condition of the
works under their charge, and an account of their doings,
including an account of receipts and expenditures.

By-laws,
rules, etc. SECTION 11.   Said district may adopt by-laws prescribing by whom and how meetings may be called, notified

and conducted; and, upon the application of ten or more legal voters in said district, meetings may also be called by warrant as provided in section eight. Said district may also establish rules and regulations for the management of its water works, not inconsistent with this act or with law, and may choose such other officers not provided for in this act as it may deem necessary or proper.

Section 12. Whoever wilfully or wantonly corrupts, pollutes or diverts any water obtained or supplied under this act, or wilfully or wantonly injures any reservoir, standpipe, aqueduct, pipe or other property owned or used by said district for any of the purposes of this act, shall forfeit and pay to said district three times the amount of damages assessed therefor, to be recovered in an action of tort, and upon conviction of any of the above wilful or wanton acts shall be punished by a fine not exceeding one hundred dollars or by imprisonment in jail for a term not exceeding six months. *Penalty for polluting water, etc.*

Section 13. This act shall take full effect upon its acceptance by a majority vote of the voters of said district present and voting thereon at a district meeting called in accordance with the provisions of section eight. *Acceptance of act.*

Section 14. Upon a petition in writing addressed to said commissioners by any owner of real estate in said town, abutting on said district, setting forth that the petitioner desires to have certain accurately described portions of his real estate included in said district, said commissioners shall cause a duly warned meeting of said district to be called, at which meeting the voters may vote on the question of including said real estate within said district. If a majority of the voters present and voting thereon vote in the affirmative, the district clerk shall within ten days file with the town clerk of said town and with the state secretary an attested copy of said petition and vote, describing precisely the real estate added to said district; and thereupon said real estate shall become and be a part of said district and shall be holden under this act in the same manner and to the same extent as the real estate described in section one.   *Approved July 7, 1933.* *Referendum on extension of district.*

Chap.318

An Act relative to the indemnification of certain public employees for damages sustained through operation of certain publicly owned vehicles, and subjecting employees of certain county and district hospitals to certain provisions of the workmen's compensation laws.

Be it enacted, etc., as follows:

Section 1. Section three B of chapter twelve of the General Laws, as appearing in the Tercentenary Edition thereof, is hereby amended by inserting after the word "motor" in the fifth line the words: — or other, — so as to *G. L. (Ter. Ed.), 12, § 3B, amended.*

Indemnifica-
tion or pro-
tection of
state officers,
etc., in con-
nection with
actions for
personal
injuries arising
out of the
operation of
state-owned
motor or other
vehicles.

read as follows: — *Section 3B.* Upon the filing with the attorney general of a written request of any officer or employee of the commonwealth or of the metropolitan district commission that the attorney general defend him against an action for damages for bodily injuries, including death at any time resulting therefrom, arising out of the operation of a motor or other vehicle owned by the commonwealth, including one under the control of said commission, wherein such officer or employee consents to be bound by any decision that the attorney general may make in connection with the trial or settlement of such action, the attorney general shall, if after investigation it appears to him that such officer or employee was at the time the cause of action arose acting within the scope of his official duties or employment, take over the management and defence of such action. The attorney general may adjust or settle any such action, at any time before, during or after trial, if he finds after investigation that the plaintiff is entitled to damages from such officer or employee, and in such case there shall be paid from the state treasury for settlement in full of such action from such appropriation as may be made by the general court for the purposes of this section such sum, not exceeding five thousand dollars, as the attorney general shall determine to be just and reasonable and as the governor and council shall approve.

If an execution issued on a final judgment in such an action is presented to the state treasurer by an officer qualified to serve civil process and if there is also presented to or on file with said state treasurer a certificate of the attorney general certifying that said execution was issued on a judgment in an action in which he appeared for and defended the defendant in accordance with the provisions of this section, there shall be paid from the state treasury from the appropriation above referred to, the amount of the execution, including costs and interest, up to but not in excess of five thousand dollars.

G. L. (Ter.
Ed.), 35, § 28,
amended.

SECTION 2. Section twenty-eight of chapter thirty-five of the General Laws, as so appearing, is hereby amended by inserting after the word "motor" in the ninth line the

Estimates
of county
expenses.

words: — or other, — so as to read as follows: — *Section 28.* The county commissioners shall annually prepare estimates of county receipts and expenditures for the ensuing year, in the form prescribed by the director of accounts and upon blanks by him furnished, including estimates for construction and repair of county buildings and for effecting insurance providing indemnity for or protection to the officers and employees of the county against loss by reason of their liability to pay damages to others for bodily injuries, including death at any time resulting therefrom, caused by the operation, within the scope of their official duties or employment, of motor or other vehicles owned by the county, to an amount not exceeding five thousand dollars on account of injury to or death of one person, or for providing indemnity or protection as aforesaid without insurance, with a statement of the corresponding appropriations for the preceding year, and expenditures for each of the three preceding years, explaining any difference between the amount of an estimate and the latest appropriation for the same purpose, and citing the laws relating thereto. The clerk of the commissioners shall record the foregoing in a book kept therefor, and, on or before January twentieth, shall send a copy thereof, by him attested and signed by the chairman, to the said director, who shall analyze and classify said estimates, and report the same to the general court not later than February tenth. The director shall upon their request send a copy of said report to the mayor of each city and to the selectmen of each town in the commonwealth.

SECTION 3. Clause (1) of section five of chapter forty of the General Laws, as so appearing, is hereby amended by inserting after the word "motor" in the ninth line of said clause the words: — or other, — so that said clause will read as follows: — (1) To pay a proper charge of an insurance company for acting as surety on the official bond of any town officer, or to pay a proper charge for effecting insurance providing indemnity for or protection to any officer or employee of the town against loss by reason of his liability to pay damages to others for bodily injuries, including death at any time resulting therefrom, caused by the operation, within the scope of his official duties or employment, of motor or other vehicles owned by the town, to an amount not exceeding five thousand dollars on account of injury to or death of one person.

G. L. (Ter. Ed.), 40, § 5, etc., amended.

Cities and towns authorized to carry motor or other vehicle insurance to protect its employees.

SECTION 4. Section one hundred A of chapter forty-one of the General Laws, as so appearing, is hereby amended by inserting after the word "motor" in the seventh line the words: — or other, — so as to read as follows: — *Section 100A.* A city which accepts this section by vote of its city council subject to the provisions of its charter, or a town which accepts the same by vote of its inhabitants at an annual town meeting, may, after an appropriation has been made therefor, indemnify an officer or employee thereof for expenses or damages incurred by him in the defence or settlement of a claim against him for bodily injuries, including death at any time resulting therefrom, arising out of the operation of a motor or other vehicle owned by such city or town, to an amount not exceeding five thousand dollars; provided, that after investigation it shall appear to the mayor or selectmen that such officer or employee was at the time the claim arose acting within the scope of his official duties or employment, and provided, further, that the defence or settlement of such claim shall have been made by the city solicitor or the town counsel, or, if the town has no town counsel, by an attorney employed for the purpose by the selectmen, upon the request

G. L. (Ter. Ed.), 41, § 100A, amended.

Indemnification of officers, etc., of cities and towns for damages, etc., incurred out of the operation of publicly owned motor and other vehicles.

of said officer or employee and at the direction of the mayor or selectmen. This section shall not apply in respect to a claim against an officer or employee which is covered by a policy of insurance effected by the city or town under clause (1) of section five of chapter forty.

G. L. (Ter. Ed.), 260, § 4, amended.

SECTION 5. Section four of chapter two hundred and sixty of the General Laws, as so appearing, is hereby amended by inserting after the word "motor" in the twelfth line the words: — or other, — so as to read as

Limitation of certain actions.

follows: — *Section 4.* Actions for assault and battery, false imprisonment, slander, actions against sheriffs, deputy sheriffs, constables or assignees in insolvency for the taking or conversion of personal property, actions of tort for injuries to the person against counties, cities and towns, and actions of contract or tort for malpractice, error or mistake against physicians, surgeons, dentists, optometrists, hospitals and sanitaria, shall be commenced only within two years next after the cause of action accrues; and actions for libel and actions of tort for bodily injuries or for death the payment of judgments in which is required to be secured by chapter ninety and also such actions against officers and employees of the commonwealth, of the metropolitan district commission, and of any county, city or town, arising out of the operation of motor or other vehicles owned by the commonwealth, including those under the control of said commission, or by any such county, city or town, suits by judgment creditors in such actions of tort under section one hundred and thirteen of chapter one hundred and seventy-five and clause (10) of section three of chapter two hundred and fourteen and suits on motor vehicle liability bonds under section thirty-four G of said chapter ninety shall be commenced only within one year next after the cause of action accrues.

G. L. (Ter. Ed.), 111, new section after § 83.

SECTION 6. Chapter one hundred and eleven of the General Laws, as so appearing, is hereby amended by inserting after section eighty-three the following new section: — *Section 83A.* The county commissioners of any county, acting as trustees of a hospital established therein under sections seventy-eight to ninety, inclusive, may effect insurance providing indemnity for or protection to the officers and employees of such hospital against loss by reason of their liability to pay damages to others for bodily injuries, including death at any time resulting therefrom, caused by the operation, within the scope of their official duties or employment, of motor or other vehicles owned by the district maintaining such hospital, to an amount not exceeding five thousand dollars on account of the injury to or death of one person. The expense of such insurance shall be included as a part of the cost of maintenance of such hospital.

Indemnification, etc., of certain employees of county hospitals.

G. L. (Ter. Ed.), 152, § 69, amended.

SECTION 7. Chapter one hundred and fifty-two of the General Laws, as so appearing, is hereby amended by striking out section sixty-nine and inserting in place thereof the following: — *Section 69.* The commonwealth and any county, city, town or district having the power of taxation which has accepted chapter eight hundred and seven of the acts of nineteen hundred and thirteen, and any county or district maintaining a hospital established under sections seventy-eight to ninety, inclusive, of chapter one hundred and eleven, if the trustees of said hospital accept the provisions of this section, shall pay to laborers, workmen and mechanics employed by it who receive injuries arising out of and in the course of their employment, or, in case of death resulting from such injury, to the persons entitled thereto, the compensation provided by this chapter. Compensation payable under this chapter to an injured employee of the commonwealth who receives full maintenance in addition to his cash salary or wage, and compensation payable thereunder to his dependents in case of his death, shall be based upon his average weekly wages plus the sum of seven dollars per week in lieu of the full maintenance received by him. Sections seventy to seventy-five, inclusive, shall apply to the commonwealth and to any county, city, town or district having the power of taxation which has accepted said chapter eight hundred and seven, and to any county or district maintaining a hospital established under said sections seventy-eight to ninety, inclusive, if the trustees of said hospital accept the provisions of this section. The terms laborers, workmen and mechanics, as used in sections sixty-eight to seventy-five, inclusive, shall include foremen, subforemen and inspectors of the commonwealth or of any such county, city, town or district, to such extent as the commonwealth or such county, city, town or district, acting respectively through the governor and council, county commissioners, city council, the qualified voters in a town or district meeting, or the trustees of such hospital, shall determine, as evidenced by a writing filed with the department.

Workmen's compensation, so-called, paid by commonwealth, etc.

Section 8. Any city or town which, prior to the effective date of this act, had accepted said section one hundred A of chapter forty-one of the General Laws may, if a city, by vote of its city council subject to the provisions of its charter, or, if a town, by vote of its inhabitants at an annual town meeting, accept said section one hundred A as amended by section four of this act, otherwise the provisions of said section as heretofore in effect shall continue to apply therein.

Acceptance of provisions of the act.

Section 9. The provisions of sections one to six, inclusive, shall apply only to causes of action arising after their effective date.   *Approved July 7, 1933.*

Application of certain sections.

Chap.319 An Act providing reciprocal relations in respect to
death taxes upon estates of non-resident decedents.

Be it enacted, etc., as follows:

G. L. (Ter.
Ed.), 65, six
new sections
after § 24.

Chapter sixty-five of the General Laws is hereby amended
by inserting after section twenty-four, as appearing in the
Tercentenary Edition thereof, the six following new sec-
Term "death
tax", etc.,
defined.
tions: — *Section 24A.* The terms "death tax" and "death
taxes", as used in the five following sections, shall include
inheritance, succession, transfer and estate taxes and any
taxes levied against the estate of a decedent upon the
occasion of his death.

Executors,
etc., of non-
resident
decedents to
file proof of
death taxes.
Exception.

Section 24B. At any time before the expiration of
eighteen months after the qualification in any probate court
in this commonwealth of any executor of the will or administrator of the estate of any non-resident decedent,
such executor or administrator shall file with such court
proof that all death taxes, together with interest or penalties
thereon, which are due to the state of domicile of such
decedent, or to any political sub-division thereof, have been
paid or secured, or that no such taxes, interest or penalties are due, as the case may be, unless it appears that
letters testamentary or of administration have been issued
on the estate of such decedent in the state of his domicile,
in the four following sections called the domiciliary state.

Form, etc., of
proof.

Section 24C. The proof required by section twenty-
four B may be in the form of a certificate issued by the
official or body charged with the administration of the
death tax laws of the domiciliary state. If such proof has
not been filed within the time limited in section twenty-
four B, and if within such time it does not appear that
letters testamentary or of administration have been issued
Duties of
register of
probate.
in the domiciliary state, the register of probate shall forthwith upon the expiration of such time notify by mail the
official or body of the domiciliary state charged with the
administration of the death tax laws thereof with respect
to such estate, and shall state in such notice so far as is
known to him (*a*) the name, date of death and last domicile
of such decedent, (*b*) the name and address of each executor
or administrator, (*c*) a summary of the values of the real
estate, tangible personalty, and intangible personalty,
wherever situated, belonging to such decedent at the time of
his death, and (*d*) the fact that such executor or administrator has not filed theretofore the proof required in section
twenty-four B. Such register shall attach to such notice
a plain copy of the will and codicils of such decedent, if
he died testate, or, if he died intestate, a list of his heirs and
next of kin, so far as is known to such register. Within
sixty days after the mailing of such notice the official or
body charged with the administration of the death tax
laws of the domiciliary state may file with such probate

court in this commonwealth a petition for an accounting in such estate, and such official or body of the domiciliary state shall, for the purposes of this section, be a party interested for the purpose of petitioning such probate court for such accounting. If such petition be filed within said period of sixty days, such probate court shall decree such accounting, and upon such accounting being filed and approved shall decree either the payment of any such tax found to be due to the domiciliary state or subdivision thereof or the remission to a fiduciary appointed or to be appointed by the probate court, or other court charged with the administration of estates of decedents, of the domiciliary state, of the balance of the intangible personalty after the payment of creditors and expenses of administration in this commonwealth.

Section 24D. No final account of an executor or administrator of a non-resident decedent shall be allowed unless either (1) proof has been filed as required by section twenty-four B, or (2) notice under section twenty-four C has been given to the official or body charged with the administration of the death tax laws of the domiciliary state, and such official or body has not petitioned for an accounting under said section within sixty days after the mailing of such notice, or (3) an accounting has been had under said section twenty-four C, a decree has been made upon such accounting and it appears that the executor or administrator has paid such sums and remitted such securities, if any, as he was required to pay or remit by such decree, or (4) it appears that letters testamentary or of administration have been issued by the domiciliary state and that no notice has been given under said section twenty-four C. *Restriction on allowance of accounts of executors, etc.*

Section 24E. Sections twenty-four A to twenty-four D, inclusive, shall apply to the estate of a non-resident decedent, only in case the laws of the domiciliary state contain a provision, of any nature or however expressed, whereby this commonwealth is given reasonable assurance, as finally determined by the commissioner, of the collection of its death taxes, interest and penalties from the estates of decedents dying domiciled in this commonwealth, when such estates are administered in whole or in part by a probate court, or other court charged with the administration of estates of decedents, in such other state. *Application of certain sections limited.*

Section 24F. The provisions of sections twenty-four A to twenty-four E, inclusive, shall be liberally construed in order to ensure that the domiciliary state of any non-resident decedent whose estate is administered in this commonwealth shall receive any death taxes, together with interest and penalties thereon, due to it from the estate of such decedent. *Approved July 7, 1933.* *Certain sections to be liberally construed.*

*Chap.*320 AN ACT PROVIDING FOR THE REINSTATEMENT OF CERTAIN MUNICIPAL OFFICERS AND EMPLOYEES.

Emergency preamble.

Whereas, The deferred operation of this act would tend to defeat its purpose, therefore, it is hereby declared to be an emergency law, necessary for the immediate preservation of the public convenience.

Be it enacted, etc., as follows:

G. L. (Ter. Ed.), 31, new section after § 46B.

Reinstatement of certain municipal officers and employees.

Chapter thirty-one of the General Laws is hereby amended by inserting after section forty-six B, as appearing in the Tercentenary Edition thereof, the two following new sections: — *Section 46C.* An officer or employee of a city or town who has become separated from the classified civil service by suspension, discharge or for any other cause except inability to work on account of sickness shall, within thirty days after the filing of a written request by the appointing officer, be entitled to a hearing before the commissioner. Upon good cause shown the commissioner may authorize his reinstatement in the same position or in a position in the same class and grade as that formerly held by him; provided, that the appointing officer shall so reinstate such officer or employee only in case the city council of such city or the board of selectmen of such town so vote and then subject to any terms and conditions contained in such vote.

Proviso.

Reinstatement, etc., where civil service rating has been lost by reason of sickness.

Section 46D. An officer or employee of a city or town who has become separated from the classified civil service by reason of inability to work on account of sickness may be reinstated by the appointing officer, in his discretion, in the same position or in a position in the same class and grade as that formerly held by him.

Approved July 11, 1933.

*Chap.*321 AN ACT TEMPORARILY INCREASING THE MEMBERSHIP OF THE BOARD OF TAX APPEALS AND RELATIVE TO THE PROCEDURE BEFORE SAID BOARD.

Emergency preamble.

Whereas, The deferred operation of this act would in part defeat its purpose, therefore it is hereby declared to be an emergency law, necessary for the immediate preservation of the public convenience.

Be it enacted, etc., as follows:

Temporary increase in membership of board of tax appeals.

SECTION 1. Until December first, nineteen hundred and thirty-seven, the board of tax appeals, established by section one of chapter fifty-eight A of the General Laws, shall consist of five members, and two members, in addition to the three heretofore appointed under said section one, shall be appointed by the governor, with the advice and consent of the council, to serve until said December first.

G. L. (Ter. Ed.), 58A, § 7, amended.

SECTION 2. Chapter fifty-eight A of the General Laws is hereby amended by striking out section seven, as appearing in the Tercentenary Edition thereof, and inserting in place thereof the following: — *Section 7.* Any party taking an appeal to the board from a decision or determination of the commissioner or of a board of assessors, hereinafter referred to as the appellee, shall file a petition with the clerk of the board of tax appeals and serve upon said appellee in the manner provided in section nine a copy thereof. Where two or more parcels of real estate are included in one decision of a board of assessors, the board of tax appeals in its discretion may require that each parcel be the subject of a separate petition. The commissioner shall forthwith furnish a copy of each such petition served upon him to the attorney general. The petition upon such appeal shall set forth specifically the facts upon which the party taking an appeal, hereinafter called the appellant, relies, together with a statement of the contentions of law which the appellant desires to raise. The appellant shall state upon the petition the address at which service of any pleading, motion, order, notice or process in connection with the appeal can be made upon him. Within such time as the board by its rules may prescribe, the appellee shall file with the board an answer stating fully each finding of fact and ruling of law made with respect to the tax or determination in issue and denying or admitting each and every allegation of fact contained in the petition; except that, in an appeal under section sixty-four or sixty-five of chapter fifty-nine, if the appellee desires to raise no issue other than the question whether there has been an overvaluation of the property on which the tax appealed from was assessed, no answer need be filed. If no answer is filed in such a case, the allegation of overvaluation of such property shall be held to be denied and all other material facts alleged in the petition admitted. If an answer is filed a copy shall be served upon the appellant, in the manner provided in section nine. The party taking the appeal shall at the time of filing the petition pay an entry fee of ten dollars for each appeal from a decision of the commissioner or, in the case of an appeal from a decision of a board of assessors, an entry fee equal to ten cents on each one thousand dollars of the assessed value of that portion of the real estate or personal property, or both, the tax on which is sought to be abated, except that the minimum entry fee shall be five dollars. The board shall not consider, unless equity and good conscience so require, any issue of fact or contention of law not specifically set out in the petition upon appeal or raised in the answer. At any time before the decision upon the appeal by the board or by the supreme judicial court on appeal under section thirteen, the appellee may abate the tax appealed from in whole or in part or change his or its determination.

SECTION 3. Said chapter fifty-eight A is hereby further amended by inserting after section seven, as so appearing, the following new section: — *Section 7A.* The board shall establish by rule an alternative procedure, herein-

Rules and
regulations.
Waiver of
appeal.
after referred to as the informal procedure, for the determination of petitions for abatement of any tax upon real estate or tangible personal property, where such procedure is elected by both parties. Such procedure, to the extent that the board may consider practicable, shall eliminate formal rules of pleading, practice and evidence, and, except for the entry fee herein provided, may eliminate any or all fees and costs, or may provide that costs shall be in the discretion of the board. An appellant desiring to be heard under the informal procedure shall pay to the clerk the entry fee provided in section seven and shall file a written waiver of the right of appeal to the supreme judicial court, except upon questions of law raised by the pleadings or by an agreed statement of facts or shown by the report of the board, an election of the informal procedure and a written statement subscribed by him of the facts in the case and of the amount claimed in abatement together with such additional information as the clerk may require. The clerk shall then serve a copy of the statement upon the appellee. No further pleadings shall be required under this procedure if the appellee intends to offer no other defense than that the property was not overvalued; otherwise it shall file with the board within thirty days of the service of the statement an answer similar to that required under the procedure provided by section seven, hereinafter referred to as the formal procedure. The appellee may elect to have the appeal heard under the formal procedure by so notifying the clerk in writing and by paying to him a transfer fee of five dollars, each within ten days of the date of the service of such statement, in which case the said statement shall be considered to be a petition and such service to be service of the petition and the waiver of the right of appeal by the appellant shall be void. If the appellee does not so transfer the case, the informal procedure shall be deemed to have been accepted and all right of appeal waived by the appellee, except upon questions of law raised by the pleadings or by an agreed statement of facts or shown by the report of the board. The chairman shall provide for the speedy hearing of all appeals to be heard under the informal procedure. The chairman shall make every effort to reduce the expense of hearing cases filed under the informal procedure by directing whenever possible that petitions for abatement of taxes assessed upon real estate situated in the same general locality of the same town be heard together, irrespective of the identity of the appellants.

G. L. (Ter.
Ed.), 58A,
§ 8, amended.
Hearings.
SECTION 4. Said chapter fifty-eight A is hereby further amended by striking out section eight, as so appearing, and inserting in place thereof the following: — *Section 8.* A hearing shall be granted if any party to an appeal so requests, and, upon motion of any party to an appeal or by direction of the board, any appeal may be set down for a hearing. Hearings may be held before less than a

majority of the members of the board, and the chairman may assign members to hold hearings. Hearings before the board or before members of the board shall be open to the public and such hearings and all proceedings shall be conducted in accordance with such rules of practice and procedure as the board may make and promulgate. The chairman may direct that two or more petitions for abatement of the taxes assessed upon real estate situated in the same general locality of the same town be heard together, irrespective of the identity of the appellants.

SECTION 5. Said chapter fifty-eight A is hereby further amended by striking out section ten, as so appearing, and inserting in place thereof the following: — *Section 10.* At the request of any party made before any evidence is offered, the board shall order that all proceedings in a pending appeal be officially reported by a stenographer. The board may contract for the reporting of such proceedings at the expense of the commonwealth in the first instance, but shall collect the cost thereof from the persons requesting that the proceedings be reported. In such contract the board may provide that one or more copies of the transcript be supplied to the board without cost to the commonwealth, and may fix the terms and conditions upon which transcripts will be supplied to other persons and agencies by the stenographer. No proceedings shall be reported officially until an amount equal to the cost thereof, as estimated by the clerk, shall have been deposited with him at such times and in such manner as may be provided by the rules of the board. Any excess deposit over the actual cost shall be returned to the depositor by the clerk. If no party requests that the proceedings be reported, all parties shall be deemed to have waived all rights of appeal to the supreme judicial court upon questions as to the admission or exclusion of evidence, or as to whether a finding was warranted by the evidence. The right of appeal upon questions of law raised by the pleadings or by an agreed statement of facts or shown by the report of the board shall not be deemed to be waived. For its own information only, the board shall have stenographic notes of hearings taken and may have transcripts thereof prepared in proceedings which are not officially reported at the request of a party.

SECTION 6. Section twelve of said chapter fifty-eight A, as so appearing, is hereby amended by striking out, in the first and second lines, the words ", together with the entry fee of ten dollars required in section seven," — so as to read as follows: — *Section 12.* Witness fees and expenses of service of process may be taxed as costs against the unsuccessful party to the appeal, in the discretion of the board. In the event that the commonwealth, or any official thereof, is the unsuccessful party to an appeal, the costs shall be paid from the state treasury upon certificate of a member of the board in such form as the board may

Marginal notes:

G. L. (Ter. Ed.), 58A, § 10, amended. Stenographic reports of proceedings. Deposit required.

G. L. (Ter. Ed.), 58A, § 12, amended. Costs.

prescribe by regulation. In the event that a subdivision of the commonwealth, or any official thereof, is the unsuccessful party to an appeal, the costs shall be paid from the treasury of such subdivision by the treasurer thereof upon certificate of a member of the board in such form as the board may prescribe by regulation. In the event that costs are taxed against an unsuccessful taxpayer, a member of the board shall certify the amount of the same and they may be recovered in an action of contract by the state treasurer, in the case of a tax assessed by the commissioner, or by the treasurer of the subdivision of the commonwealth in behalf of which the tax appealed from was assessed.

G. L. (Ter. Ed.), 58A, § 13, etc., amended.

SECTION 7. Said chapter fifty-eight A, as most recently amended in section thirteen by section one of chapter two hundred and eighteen of the acts of nineteen hundred and thirty-one, is hereby further amended by striking out said section thirteen and inserting in place thereof the following: — *Section 13.* The board shall make a decision in each case heard by it and may make findings of fact and report thereon in writing. Except in cases heard under the informal procedure authorized by section seven A, the board shall make such findings and report thereon if so requested by either party within ten days of a decision without findings of fact. Such report may, in the discretion of the board, contain an opinion in writing, in addition to the findings of fact and decision. All reports, findings and opinions of the board and all evidence received by the board, including a transcript of any official report of the proceedings, shall be open to the inspection of the public; except that the originals of books, documents, records, models, diagrams and other exhibits introduced in evidence before the board may be withdrawn from the custody of the board in such manner and upon such terms as the board may in its discretion prescribe. The decision of the board shall be final as to findings of fact. From any decision of the board upon an appeal from a decision or determination of the commissioner, or of a board of assessors, except decisions of the board under sections twenty-five and twenty-six of chapter sixty-five, an appeal as to matters of law may be taken to the supreme judicial court by either party to the proceedings before the board who has not waived such right of appeal. A claim of appeal shall be filed with the clerk of the board within twenty days after the date of the decision of the board, or within twenty days after the date of a report of findings of fact, if such report is made on request of a party after the decision; and within twenty days thereafter, or within such further time as the board may allow, the appealing party shall enter the appeal in said court, in the county where either party lives or has his usual place of business or in Suffolk county, and shall file with the clerk of said court a copy of the record before the board, shall serve by registered mail upon the adverse party a copy of

Findings, decisions and opinions, reports of appeals to supreme judicial court.

the claim of appeal and a notice that he has entered said appeal and shall file an affidavit of such service with said clerk. The record in such an appeal shall include copies of the following: — the tax returns and lists, if any, filed by the taxpayer, so far as material to the controversy, the original assessment or other original determination in issue, so far as material, the application for abatement or other petition filed with the commissioner or with the board of assessors and the decision or determination thereon, the petition upon appeal to the board, the answer to the petition and other pleadings, if any, filed with the board, the report and findings of the board including any opinions filed, all requests for rulings of law and findings of fact and the disposition of each by the board, the claim of appeal to the supreme judicial court and such portion of any official report of the proceedings before the board as may be necessary for the consideration of any question of law raised before the board, which it is alleged that the board has erroneously decided. Each claim of appeal shall set out separately and particularly each error of law asserted to have been made by the board, with precise references to the portions and particulars of the proceedings before the board in which it is alleged that error of law occurred. Upon the entry of the appeal it shall be heard and determined by the full court. Within ten days from the entry of the appeal in the supreme judicial court the appealing party shall give the clerk of said court an order in writing to print the record filed with him and the affidavit of service for transmission to the full court, and, thereupon, in the manner provided in the second paragraph of section one hundred and thirty-five of chapter two hundred and thirty-one for carrying questions of law to the full court, the expense shall be estimated, notified to and paid by the appealing party, said record shall be printed and, together with any original papers, transmitted to the full court, and said appeal shall be entered on the docket of the full court. The court shall not consider any issue of law which does not appear to have been raised in the proceedings before the board. The court upon determination of the appeal may make such order as such determination may require including an order for costs. Upon the entry of such order, with or without an order for costs, a copy thereof shall be transmitted by the clerk of said court to the clerk of said board. If the order grants an abatement of a tax assessed by the commissioner or by the board of assessors of a town and the tax has been paid, the amount abated with interest at the rate of six per cent per annum from the time when the tax was paid, and, if costs are ordered against the commissioner or against a board of assessors, the amount thereof, shall be paid to the taxpayer by the state treasurer or by the town treasurer, as the case may be, and, if unpaid in the latter case, execution therefor may issue against the town as in actions at law. If costs are ordered against a taxpayer execution shall issue therefor. The appeal to the supreme judicial court under this section shall be the exclusive method of reviewing any action of the board, except action under sections twenty-five and twenty-six of chapter sixty-five. For want of prosecution of an appeal in accordance with the provisions of this section the board, or, if the appeal has been entered in the supreme judicial court, a justice of that court, may dismiss the appeal. Upon dismissal of an appeal the decision of the board shall thereupon have full force and effect.

"Informal procedure" to apply to certain pending cases.

SECTION 8. Either party to an appeal pending before said board on the effective date of this act may file a request in writing with its clerk that such appeal be heard under the informal procedure established under section seven A of said chapter fifty-eight A. The clerk shall forthwith serve a copy of such request upon the other party to the appeal in the manner provided in section nine of said chapter fifty-eight A. Unless within ten days such other party files with the clerk a written statement that he objects to the hearing of such appeal under said informal procedure, such appeal shall be so heard and both parties thereto shall be deemed to have waived all rights of appeal to the supreme judicial court, except as provided in section seven A of said chapter fifty-eight A.

Provisions of act not to limit action of board in certain cases.

SECTION 9. Notwithstanding anything contained in this act, the board in considering any appeal brought before it may make such decision as equity may require and may reduce or increase the amount of the assessment appealed from. *Approved July 11, 1933.*

---

*Chap.*322 AN ACT MAKING APPROPRIATIONS FOR MAINTENANCE OF CERTAIN COUNTIES, FOR INTEREST AND DEBT REQUIREMENTS AND FOR CERTAIN PERMANENT IMPROVEMENTS, GRANTING A COUNTY TAX FOR SAID COUNTIES, AND MAKING CERTAIN ADJUSTMENTS RELATIVE TO COMPENSATION AND TRAVEL ALLOWANCES OF CERTAIN COUNTY OFFICIALS AND EMPLOYEES.

Emergency preamble.

Whereas, The deferred operation of this act would cause substantial inconvenience, therefore it is hereby declared to be an emergency law, necessary for the immediate preservation of the public convenience.

Be it enacted, etc., as follows:

Appropriations for maintenance of certain counties, etc.

SECTION 1. The following sums are hereby appropriated for the counties hereinafter specified for the year nineteen hundred and thirty-three. No direct drafts against the account known as the reserve fund shall be made, but transfers from this account to other accounts may be made to meet extraordinary or unforeseen expenditures upon the request of the county commissioners and with the approval of the director of accounts.

Section 2.

Barnstable County.

Item
1 For interest on county debt, a sum not exceeding
   eight thousand twelve dollars and fifty cents   . $8,012 50
2 For reduction of county debt, a sum not exceeding
   fifteen thousand dollars 15,000 00
3 For salaries of county officers and assistants, a sum
   not exceeding nineteen thousand seven hundred
   twenty-five dollars 19,725 00
4 For clerical assistance in county offices, a sum not
   exceeding nine thousand three hundred eighty-
   nine dollars 9,389 00
5 For salaries and expenses of district courts, a sum not
   exceeding eighteen thousand six hundred seventy-
   five dollars 18,675 00
6 For salaries of jailers, masters and assistants, and
   support of prisoners in jails and houses of correction, a sum not exceeding sixteen thousand three
   hundred fifty dollars 16,350 00
7 For criminal costs in the superior court, a sum not
   exceeding eighteen thousand dollars   .   .   .   18,000 00
8 For civil expenses in the supreme judicial, superior,
   probate, and land courts, a sum not exceeding nine
   thousand dollars 9,000 00
10 For transportation expenses of county and associate
   commissioners, a sum not exceeding one thousand
   dollars 1,000 00
11 For medical examiners, inquests, and commitments
   of the insane, a sum not exceeding two thousand
   dollars 2,000 00
12 For auditors, masters and referees, a sum not exceeding two thousand dollars 2,000 00
14 For repairing, furnishing and improving county
   buildings, a sum not exceeding seven thousand
   dollars 7,000 00
15 For care, fuel, lights and supplies in county buildings, other than jails and houses of correction, a
   sum not exceeding twelve thousand nine hundred
   dollars 12,900 00
16 For highways, including state highways, bridges and
   land damages, a sum not exceeding fifty-five thousand dollars 55,000 00
18 For training school, a sum not exceeding one thousand dollars 1,000 00
19 For county aid to agriculture, a sum not exceeding
   eleven thousand seven hundred fifty dollars   .   11,750 00
20 For the sanatorium, a sum not exceeding fifty-one
   thousand dollars 51,000 00
20a For county health service, a sum not exceeding ten
   thousand nine hundred twenty dollars   .   .   10,920 00
23 For miscellaneous and contingent expenses of the
   current year, a sum not exceeding two thousand
   dollars 2,000 00
23a For unpaid bills of previous years, a sum not exceeding one thousand dollars 1,000 00
23b For a state fire patrol, a sum not exceeding one thousand five hundred dollars 1,500 00
24 For a reserve fund, a sum not exceeding ten thousand
   dollars 10,000 00
   And the county commissioners of Barnstable county
   are hereby authorized to levy as the county tax of
   said county for the current year, in the manner
   provided by law, the sum of one hundred ninety-
   six thousand eight hundred thirty-seven dollars

Item

and thirteen cents, to be expended, together with
the cash balance on hand and the receipts from
other sources, for the above purposes . . . $196,837 13

Berkshire County.

1   For interest on county debt, a sum not exceeding
    eight thousand five hundred dollars . . . $8,500 00
2   For reduction of county debt, a sum not exceeding
    seventeen thousand dollars 17,000 00
3   For salaries of county officers and assistants, a sum
    not exceeding twenty-eight thousand seven hun-
    dred dollars 28,700 00
4   For clerical assistance in county offices, a sum not
    exceeding ten thousand three hundred dollars . 10,300 00
5   For salaries and expenses of district courts, a sum
    not exceeding forty-one thousand fifty dollars . 41,050 00
6   For salaries of jailers, masters and assistants, and
    support of prisoners in jails and houses of correc-
    tion, a sum not exceeding thirty-two thousand
    seven hundred dollars 32,700 00
7   For criminal costs in the superior court, a sum not
    exceeding eight thousand dollars . . . 8,000 00
8   For civil expenses in the supreme judicial, superior,
    probate, and land courts, a sum not exceeding
    fifteen thousand dollars 15,000 00
10 For transportation expenses of county and associate
    commissioners, a sum not exceeding one thousand
    five hundred dollars 1,500 00
11 For medical examiners, inquests, and commitments
    of the insane, a sum not exceeding five thousand
    dollars 5,000 00
12 For auditors, masters and referees, a sum not ex-
    ceeding three thousand dollars 3,000 00
14 For repairing, furnishing and improving county
    buildings, a sum not exceeding thirteen thousand
    five hundred dollars 13,500 00
15 For care, fuel, lights and supplies in county build-
    ings, other than jails and houses of correction, a
    sum not exceeding nineteen thousand seven hun-
    dred and fifty dollars 19,750 00
16 For highways, including state highways, bridges
    and land damages, a sum not exceeding one hun-
    dred fifty thousand dollars 150,000 00
16a For examination of dams, a sum not exceeding one
    thousand dollars 1,000 00
17 For law libraries, a sum not exceeding one thousand
    dollars 1,000 00
18 For training school, a sum not exceeding one thou-
    sand dollars 1,000 00
19 For county aid to agriculture, a sum not exceeding
    ten thousand nine hundred and fifty dollars . 10,950 00
20 For the sanatorium (Hampshire county), a sum not
    exceeding eight thousand one hundred sixty-four
    dollars and twenty-nine cents 8,164 29
21 For the care and maintenance of Greylock state
    reservation, a sum not exceeding four thousand
    dollars 4,000 00
21a For the care and maintenance of Mount Everett
    state reservation, a sum not exceeding one thou-
    sand dollars 1,000 00
22 For pensions, a sum not exceeding eight hundred
    five dollars 805 00
23 For miscellaneous and contingent expenses of the
    current year, a sum not exceeding three thousand
    five hundred dollars 3,500 00

Item
23a For unpaid bills of previous years, a sum not exceeding five hundred dollars $500 00
24 For a reserve fund, a sum not exceeding eight thousand dollars 8,000 00
And the county commissioners of Berkshire county are hereby authorized to levy as the county tax of said county for the current year, in the manner provided by law, the sum of three hundred sixty-four thousand, one hundred forty-nine dollars and forty-eight cents, to be expended, together with the cash balance on hand and the receipts from other sources, for the above purposes . . . $364,149 48

Bristol County.

1 For interest on county debt, a sum not exceeding thirty-three thousand dollars $33,000 00
2 For reduction of county debt, a sum not exceeding fifty-four thousand dollars 54,000 00
3 For salaries of county officers and assistants, a sum not exceeding forty-five thousand nine hundred fifty dollars 45,950 00
4 For clerical assistance in county offices, a sum not exceeding thirty-three thousand two hundred fifty dollars 33,250 00
5 For salaries and expenses of district courts, a sum not exceeding one hundred five thousand four hundred dollars 105,400 00
6 For salaries of jailers, masters and assistants, and support of prisoners in jails and houses of correction, a sum not exceeding seventy-two thousand dollars 72,000 00
7 For criminal costs in the superior court, a sum not exceeding fifty-nine thousand six hundred dollars 59,600 00
8 For civil expenses in the supreme judicial, superior, probate, and land courts, a sum not exceeding forty-nine thousand eight hundred dollars . . 49,800 00
10 For transportation expenses of county and associate commissioners, a sum not exceeding one thousand five hundred dollars 1,500 00
11 For medical examiners, inquests, and commitments of the insane, a sum not exceeding sixteen thousand five hundred dollars 16,500 00
12 For auditors, masters and referees, a sum not exceeding nine thousand dollars . . . 9,000 00
14 For repairing, furnishing and improving county buildings, a sum not exceeding fourteen thousand dollars 14,000 00
15 For care, fuel, lights and supplies in county buildings, other than jails and houses of correction, a sum not exceeding forty-one thousand eight hundred fifty dollars 41,850 00
16 For highways, including state highways, bridges and land damages, a sum not exceeding forty-three thousand dollars 43,000 00
17 For law libraries, a sum not exceeding eight thousand dollars 8,000 00
18 For training school, a sum not exceeding nine thousand five hundred dollars 9,500 00
19 For the agricultural school, a sum not exceeding fifty thousand four hundred twenty-nine dollars and fifty cents 50,429 50
22 For pensions, a sum not exceeding nine thousand three hundred fifty dollars 9,350 00

Item
23　For miscellaneous and contingent expenses of the current year, a sum not exceeding one thousand dollars　.　.　.　.　.　.　.　$1,000 00
23a　For unpaid bills of previous years, a sum not exceeding four thousand dollars　.　.　.　4,000 00
24　For a reserve fund, a sum not exceeding ten thousand dollars　.　.　.　.　10,000 00
　　And the county commissioners of Bristol county are hereby authorized to levy as the county tax of said county for the current year, in the manner provided by law, the sum of five hundred forty-six thousand five hundred dollars, to be expended, together with the cash balance on hand and the receipts from other sources, for the above purposes $546,500 00

County of Dukes County.

1　For interest on county debt, a sum not exceeding two thousand two hundred dollars　.　.　.　$2,200 00
2　For reduction of county debt, a sum not exceeding thirteen thousand two hundred sixty-eight dollars and nineteen cents　.　.　.　.　.　13,268 19
3　For salaries of county officers and assistants, a sum not exceeding five thousand six hundred fifty dollars　.　.　.　.　.　.　.　5,650 00
4　For clerical assistance in county offices, a sum not exceeding one thousand three hundred forty dollars　.　.　.　.　.　.　.　1,340 00
5　For salaries and expenses of district courts, a sum not exceeding three thousand nine hundred dollars　.　3,900 00
6　For salaries of jailers, masters and assistants, and support of prisoners in jails and houses of correction, a sum not exceeding two thousand dollars　.　2,000 00
7　For criminal costs in the superior court, a sum not exceeding one thousand five hundred dollars　.　1,500 00
8　For civil expenses in the supreme judicial, superior, probate, and land courts, a sum not exceeding one thousand five hundred dollars　.　.　.　.　1,500 00
10　For transportation expenses of county and associate commissioners, a sum not exceeding two hundred fifty dollars　.　.　.　.　.　250 00
11　For medical examiners, inquests, and commitments of the insane, a sum not exceeding three hundred dollars　.　.　.　.　.　.　.　300 00
12　For auditors, masters and referees, a sum not exceeding three hundred fifty dollars　.　.　.　350 00
14　For repairing, furnishing and improving county buildings, a sum not exceeding one thousand dollars　.　.　.　.　.　.　.　.　1,000 00
15　For care, fuel, lights and supplies in county buildings, other than jails and houses of correction, a sum not exceeding two thousand five hundred dollars　.　.　.　.　.　.　.　.　2,500 00
16　For highways, including state highways, bridges and land damages, a sum not exceeding six thousand dollars　.　.　.　.　.　.　.　6,000 00
17　For law libraries, a sum not exceeding one hundred fifty dollars　.　.　.　.　.　.　150 00
18　For training school, a sum not exceeding two hundred fifty dollars　.　.　.　.　.　250 00
19　For county aid to agriculture, a sum not exceeding four hundred dollars　.　.　.　.　.　400 00
20　For the sanatorium (Barnstable county), a sum not exceeding five thousand five hundred dollars　5,500 00
21　For the Gay Head reservation, a sum not exceeding two hundred dollars　.　.　.　.　.　200 00

Item

23 For miscellaneous and contingent expenses of the
current year, a sum not exceeding two hundred
fifty dollars $250 00
24 For a reserve fund, a sum not exceeding five hundred dollars 500 00
And the county commissioners of the county of
Dukes County are hereby authorized to levy as
the county tax of said county for the current year,
in the manner provided by law, the sum of thirty-
nine thousand eight hundred twelve dollars and
eighty-four cents, to be expended, together with
the cash balance on hand and the receipts from
other sources, for the above purposes . . . $39,812 84

Essex County.

1 For interest on county debt, a sum not exceeding
fifteen thousand dollars $15,000 00
2 For reduction of county debt, a sum not exceeding
forty-five thousand dollars 45,000 00
3 For salaries of county officers and assistants, a sum
not exceeding fifty-four thousand dollars . .   54,000 00
4 For clerical assistance in county offices, a sum not
exceeding ninety-six thousand four hundred dollars   96,400 00
5 For salaries and expenses of district courts, a sum
not exceeding one hundred eighty-one thousand
eight hundred dollars 181,800 00
6 For salaries of jailers, masters and assistants, and
support of prisoners in jails and houses of correction, a sum not exceeding eighty-seven thousand
nine hundred dollars 87,900 00
7 For criminal costs in the superior court, a sum not
exceeding ninety-five thousand dollars . .   95,000 00
8 For civil expenses in the supreme judicial, superior,
probate, and land courts, a sum not exceeding
seventy thousand five hundred dollars . . .   70,500 00
9 For trial justices, a sum not exceeding four thousand
six hundred fifty dollars 4,650 00
10 For transportation expenses of county and associate commissioners, a sum not exceeding one
thousand eight hundred dollars 1,800 00
11 For medical examiners, inquests, and commitments
of the insane, a sum not exceeding fifteen thousand dollars 15,000 00
12 For auditors, masters and referees, a sum not exceeding thirty-six thousand dollars 36,000 00
14 For repairing, furnishing and improving county
buildings, a sum not exceeding twenty-two thousand four hundred dollars 22,400 00
15 For care, fuel, lights and supplies in county buildings,
other than jails and houses of correction, a sum not
exceeding sixty-four thousand dollars . . .   64,000 00
16 For highways, including state highways, bridges and
land damages, a sum not exceeding one hundred
fourteen thousand two hundred fifty dollars .   114,250 00
17 For law libraries, a sum not exceeding eight thousand
eight hundred dollars 8,800 00
18 For training school, a sum not exceeding forty-eight
thousand nine hundred fifty dollars . . .   48,950 00
19 For maintenance of the independent agricultural
school, a sum not exceeding one hundred fifty-four
thousand eighty dollars 154,080 00
19a For the independent agricultural school equipment
and buildings, a sum not exceeding four thousand
six hundred fifty dollars 4,650 00

Item
22 For pensions, a sum not exceeding three thousand
    three hundred seventy-five dollars   .   .   . $3,375 00
23 For miscellaneous and contingent expenses of the
    current year, a sum not exceeding five thousand
    dollars 5,000 00
23a For unpaid bills of previous years, a sum not exceed-
    ing five thousand dollars 5,000 00
24 For a reserve fund, a sum not exceeding twenty
    thousand dollars 20,000 00
    And the county commissioners of Essex county are
    hereby authorized to levy as the county tax of
    said county for the current year, in the manner
    provided by law, the sum of eight hundred thirty-
    one thousand nine hundred twenty-five dollars, to
    be expended, together with the cash balance on
    hand and the receipts from other sources, for the
    above purposes $831,925 00

Franklin County.

1   For interest on county debt, a sum not exceeding
    twenty thousand three hundred sixty-one dollars
    and eighty-eight cents $20,361 88
2   For reduction of county debt, a sum not exceeding
    thirty-three thousand dollars   .   .   .   33,000 00
3   For salaries of county officers and assistants, a sum
    not exceeding eighteen thousand four hundred
    seventy dollars 18,470 00
4   For clerical assistance in county offices, a sum not
    exceeding six thousand nine hundred ten dollars .   6,910 00
5   For salaries and expenses of district courts, a sum not
    exceeding fourteen thousand four hundred dollars   14,400 00
6   For salaries of jailers, masters and assistants, and
    support of prisoners in jails and houses of cor-
    rection, a sum not exceeding twenty-four thousand
    five hundred dollars 24,500 00
7   For criminal costs in the superior court, a sum not
    exceeding seven thousand dollars   .   .   .   7,000 00
8   For civil expenses in the supreme judicial, superior,
    probate, and land courts, a sum not exceeding
    thirteen thousand dollars 13,000 00
10 For transportation expenses of county and associate
    commissioners, a sum not exceeding six hundred
    dollars 600 00
11 For medical examiners, inquests, and commitments
    of the insane, a sum not exceeding two thousand
    dollars 2,000 00
12 For auditors, masters and referees, a sum not ex-
    ceeding two thousand dollars 2,000 00
14 For repairing, furnishing and improving county
    buildings, a sum not exceeding one thousand dollars   1,000 00
15 For care, fuel, lights and supplies in county buildings,
    other than jails and houses of correction, a sum not
    exceeding fifteen thousand dollars   .   .   .   15,000 00
16 For highways, including state highways, bridges and
    land damages, a sum not exceeding forty-seven
    thousand seven hundred eighty-seven dollars   .   47,787 00
16a For examination of dams, a sum not exceeding five
    hundred dollars 500 00
17 For law libraries, a sum not exceeding two thousand
    dollars 2,000 00
19 For county aid to agriculture, a sum not exceeding
    nine thousand seven hundred thirty-seven dollars   9,737 00
20 For the sanatorium (Hampshire county), a sum not
    exceeding ten thousand two hundred five dollars
    and thirty-six cents 10,205 36

Item
20a For Greenfield health camp (chapter 354, Acts of
1928), a sum not exceeding two thousand dollars . $2,000 00
21 For Mount Sugar Loaf state reservation, a sum not
exceeding one thousand eight hundred dollars . 1,800 00
22 For pensions, a sum not exceeding eight hundred
fifty dollars 850 00
23 For miscellaneous and contingent expenses of the
current year, a sum not exceeding one thousand
six hundred dollars 1,600 00
23a For unpaid bills of previous years, a sum not exceeding five hundred dollars 500 00
24 For a reserve fund, a sum not exceeding five thousand
dollars 5,000 00
And the county commissioners of Franklin county
are hereby authorized to levy as the county tax of
said county for the current year, in the manner
provided by law, the sum of two hundred three
thousand nine hundred ninety-seven dollars, to be
expended, together with the cash balance on hand
and the receipts from other sources, for the above
purposes $203,997 00

Hampden County.

1 For interest on county debt, a sum not exceeding
seventy-four thousand dollars $74,000 00
2 For reduction of county debt, a sum not exceeding
one hundred thirty-one thousand dollars . 131,000 00
3 For salaries of county officers and assistants, a sum
not exceeding forty-four thousand nine hundred
dollars 44,900 00
4 For clerical assistance in county offices, a sum not
exceeding fifty-four thousand dollars . . 54,000 00
5 For salaries and expenses of district courts, a sum not
exceeding one hundred ten thousand five hundred
dollars 110,500 00
6 For salaries of jailers, masters and assistants, and
support of prisoners in jails and houses of correction, a sum not exceeding eighty-six thousand dollars 86,000 00
7 For criminal costs in the superior court, a sum not
exceeding forty-one thousand eight hundred dollars 41,800 00
8 For civil expenses in the supreme judicial, superior,
probate, and land courts, a sum not exceeding
forty-nine thousand seven hundred dollars . 49,700 00
9 For trial justices, a sum not exceeding two thousand
five hundred dollars 2,500 00
10 For transportation expenses of county and associate
commissioners, a sum not exceeding one thousand
dollars 1,000 00
11 For medical examiners, inquests, and commitments of
the insane, a sum not exceeding twelve thousand
dollars 12,000 00
12 For auditors, masters and referees, a sum not exceeding eighteen thousand dollars . . . 18,000 00
14 For repairing, furnishing and improving county
buildings, a sum not exceeding twelve thousand
dollars 12,000 00
15 For care, fuel, lights and supplies in county buildings,
other than jails and houses of correction, a sum not
exceeding sixty-three thousand eight hundred
dollars 63,800 00
16 For highways, including state highways, bridges and
land damages, a sum not exceeding one hundred
fifty thousand dollars 150,000 00
17 For law libraries, a sum not exceeding eight thousand
seven hundred dollars 8,700 00

Item

18	For training school, a sum not exceeding thirty-four thousand six hundred dollars	$34,600 00
19	For county aid to agriculture, a sum not exceeding forty-five thousand dollars	45,000 00
20	For the sanatorium (Hampshire county), a sum not exceeding sixteen thousand three hundred twenty-eight dollars and fifty-eight cents	16,328 58
20a	For the preventorium, a sum not exceeding three thousand dollars	3,000 00
21	For Mount Tom state reservation, a sum not exceeding ten thousand five hundred sixty-three dollars and sixty-seven cents	10,563 67
22	For pensions, a sum not exceeding five thousand dollars	5,000 00
23	For miscellaneous and contingent expenses of the current year, a sum not exceeding five thousand sixteen dollars and sixty-four cents	5,016 64
23a	For unpaid bills of previous years, a sum not exceeding two thousand dollars	2,000 00
24	For a reserve fund, a sum not exceeding ten thousand dollars	10,000 00
	And the county commissioners of Hampden county are hereby authorized to levy as the county tax of said county for the current year, in the manner provided by law, the sum of eight hundred thirty-two thousand dollars, to be expended, together with the cash balance on hand and the receipts from other sources, for the above purposes	$832,000 00

Hampshire County.

1	For interest on county debt, a sum not exceeding ten thousand five hundred dollars	$10,500 00
2	For reduction of county debt, a sum not exceeding twenty-one thousand five hundred dollars	21,500 00
3	For salaries of county officers and assistants, a sum not exceeding nineteen thousand seven hundred fifty dollars	19,750 00
4	For clerical assistance in county offices, a sum not exceeding ten thousand six hundred fifty dollars	10,650 00
5	For salaries and expenses of district courts, a sum not exceeding twenty-five thousand dollars	25,000 00
6	For salaries of jailers, masters and assistants, and support of prisoners in jails and houses of correction, a sum not exceeding twenty-four thousand six hundred dollars	24,600 00
7	For criminal costs in the superior court, a sum not exceeding twenty-one thousand dollars	21,000 00
8	For civil expenses in the supreme judicial, superior, probate, and land courts, a sum not exceeding fourteen thousand dollars	14,000 00
10	For transportation expenses of county and associate commissioners, a sum not exceeding one thousand dollars	1,000 00
11	For medical examiners, inquests, and commitments of the insane, a sum not exceeding three thousand dollars	3,000 00
12	For auditors, masters and referees, a sum not exceeding four thousand dollars	4,000 00
14	For repairing, furnishing and improving county buildings, a sum not exceeding three thousand dollars	3,000 00
15	For care, fuel, lights and supplies in county buildings, other than jails and houses of correction, a sum not exceeding thirteen thousand seven hundred fifty dollars	13,750 00

Item
16 For highways, including state highways, bridges and land damages, a sum not exceeding fifty-nine thousand six hundred eighty-eight dollars and seventy-five cents $59,688 75
17 For law libraries, a sum not exceeding one thousand two hundred dollars 1,200 00
19 For county aid to agriculture, a sum not exceeding ten thousand five hundred fifty dollars . . 10,550 00
20 For the sanatorium, a sum not exceeding seven thousand five hundred dollars 7,500 00
20a For the preventorium, a sum not exceeding one thousand five hundred dollars 1,500 00
21 For Mount Tom state reservation, a sum not exceeding one thousand four hundred fifty dollars . 1,450 00
22 For pensions, a sum not exceeding two thousand five hundred dollars 2,500 00
23 For miscellaneous and contingent expenses of the current year, a sum not exceeding six thousand dollars 6,000 00
23a For unpaid bills of previous years, a sum not exceeding five hundred fifty-eight dollars and fifty-three cents 558 53
24 For a reserve fund, a sum not exceeding eight thousand five hundred dollars 8,500 00
And the county commissioners of Hampshire county are hereby authorized to levy as the county tax of said county for the current year, in the manner provided by law, the sum of two hundred nineteen thousand five hundred sixteen dollars and thirty-nine cents, to be expended, together with the cash balance on hand and the receipts from other sources, for the above purposes $219,516 39

Middlesex County.

1 For interest on county debt, a sum not exceeding eighty-seven thousand five hundred dollars . $87,500 00
2 For reduction of county debt, a sum not exceeding two hundred forty-two thousand one hundred dollars 242,100 00
3 For salaries of county officers and assistants, a sum not exceeding seventy-five thousand four hundred dollars 75,400 00
4 For clerical assistance in county offices, a sum not exceeding two hundred twenty-two thousand five hundred dollars 222,500 00
5 For salaries and expenses of district courts, a sum not exceeding three hundred twenty-eight thousand dollars 328,000 00
6 For salaries of jailers, masters and assistants, and support of prisoners in jails and houses of correction, a sum not exceeding two hundred thirty-seven thousand dollars 237,000 00
7 For criminal costs in the superior court, a sum not exceeding two hundred seventeen thousand dollars 217,000 00
8 For civil expenses in the supreme judicial, superior, probate, and land courts, a sum not exceeding one hundred twenty-eight thousand three hundred and fifty dollars 128,350 00
9 For trial justices, a sum not exceeding one thousand dollars 1,000 00
10 For transportation expenses of county and associate commissioners, a sum not exceeding two thousand five hundred dollars 2,500 00
11 For medical examiners, inquests, and commitments of the insane, a sum not exceeding thirty thousand dollars 30,000 00

Item
12 For auditors, masters and referees, a sum not exceeding thirty-four thousand dollars . . . $34,000 00
14 For repairing, furnishing and improving county buildings, a sum not exceeding sixty thousand dollars 60,000 00
15 For care, fuel, lights and supplies in county buildings, other than jails and houses of correction, a sum not exceeding one hundred twenty-three thousand five hundred dollars 123,500 00
16 For highways, including state highways, bridges and land damages, a sum not exceeding one hundred ninety-eight thousand eight hundred dollars . 198,800 00
17 For law libraries, a sum not exceeding ten thousand seven hundred and fifty dollars 10,750 00
18 For training school, a sum not exceeding fifty-four thousand nine hundred dollars 54,900 00
19 For county aid to agriculture, a sum not exceeding thirty-eight thousand six hundred dollars . . 38,600 00
21 For Walden Pond state reservation, a sum not exceeding thirteen thousand nine hundred dollars . 13,900 00
22 For pensions, a sum not exceeding thirty thousand dollars 30,000 00
23 For miscellaneous and contingent expenses of the current year, a sum not exceeding five thousand dollars 5,000 00
23a For unpaid bills of previous years, a sum not exceeding four thousand dollars 4,000 00
24 For a reserve fund, a sum not exceeding ten thousand dollars 10,000 00
And the county commissioners of Middlesex county are hereby authorized to levy as the county tax of said county for the current year, in the manner provided by law, the sum of one million eight hundred twelve thousand six hundred forty-six dollars and twenty-nine cents, to be expended, together with the cash balance on hand and the receipts from other sources, for the above purposes . . $1,812,646 29

Norfolk County.

1 For interest on county debt, a sum not exceeding seven thousand dollars $7,000 00
2 For reduction of county debt, a sum not exceeding two thousand forty-four dollars and twelve cents . 2,044 12
3 For salaries of county officers and assistants, a sum not exceeding thirty-two thousand nine hundred and fifty dollars 32,950 00
4 For clerical assistance in county offices, a sum not exceeding eighty-one thousand three hundred dollars 81,300 00
5 For salaries and expenses of district and municipal courts, a sum not exceeding one hundred fifteen thousand four hundred and fifty dollars . . 115,450 00
6 For salaries of jailers, masters and assistants, and support of prisoners in jails and houses of correction, a sum not exceeding sixty thousand seven hundred and fifty dollars 60,750 00
7 For criminal costs in the superior court, a sum not exceeding sixty-two thousand three hundred and fifty dollars 62,350 00
8 For civil expenses in the supreme judicial, superior, probate, and land courts, a sum not exceeding thirty-four thousand eight hundred dollars . 34,800 00
10 For transportation expenses of county and associate commissioners, a sum not exceeding one thousand dollars 1,000 00

Item

11 For medical examiners, inquests, and commitments of the insane, a sum not exceeding eleven thousand five hundred dollars $11,500 00
12 For auditors, masters and referees, a sum not exceeding fifteen thousand dollars . . . 15,000 00
14 For repairing, furnishing and improving county buildings, a sum not exceeding twenty-seven thousand dollars 27,000 00
15 For care, fuel, lights and supplies in county buildings, other than jails and houses of correction, a sum not exceeding fifty-nine thousand two hundred and fifty dollars 59,250 00
16 For highways, including state highways, bridges and land damages, a sum not exceeding forty-nine thousand and fifty dollars 49,050 00
17 For law libraries, a sum not exceeding one thousand five hundred dollars 1,500 00
18 For training school, a sum not exceeding four thousand eight hundred and fifty dollars . . . 4,850 00
19 For the agricultural school, a sum not exceeding sixty-eight thousand six hundred dollars . . 68,600 00
22 For pensions, a sum not exceeding eight thousand dollars 8,000 00
23 For miscellaneous and contingent expenses of the current year, a sum not exceeding three thousand two hundred fifty-one dollars and sixteen cents . 3,251 16
23a For unpaid bills of previous years, a sum not exceeding two thousand dollars 2,000 00
24 For a reserve fund, a sum not exceeding seven thousand five hundred dollars 7,500 00
    And the county commissioners of Norfolk county are hereby authorized to levy as the county tax of said county for the current year, in the manner provided by law, the sum of four hundred sixty-four thousand eight hundred fifty-four dollars, to be expended, together with the cash balance on hand and the receipts from other sources, for the above purposes $464,854 00

Plymouth County.

1 For interest on county debt, a sum not exceeding twenty thousand dollars $20,000 00
2 For reduction of county debt, a sum not exceeding fifty-six thousand seven hundred fifty dollars . 56,750 00
3 For salaries of county officers and assistants, a sum not exceeding twenty-nine thousand fifty dollars . 29,050 00
4 For clerical assistance in county offices, a sum not exceeding nineteen thousand seven hundred fifty dollars 19,750 00
5 For salaries and expenses of district courts, a sum not exceeding fifty-eight thousand six hundred dollars 58,600 00
6 For salaries of jailers, masters and assistants, and support of prisoners in jails and houses of correction, a sum not exceeding ninety-four thousand nine hundred dollars 94,900 00
7 For criminal costs in the superior court, a sum not exceeding fifty-three thousand seven hundred dollars 53,700 00
8 For civil expenses in the supreme judicial, superior, probate, and land, courts, a sum not exceeding twenty-seven thousand five hundred dollars . 27,500 00
10 For transportation expenses of county and associate commissioners, a sum not exceeding two thousand dollars 2,000 00

Item
11 For medical examiners, inquests and commitments
      of the insane, a sum not exceeding five thousand
      five hundred dollars $5,500 00
12 For auditors, masters and referees, a sum not ex-
      ceeding ten thousand dollars 10,000 00
13 For building county buildings, a sum not exceed-
      ing five thousand dollars 5,000 00
14 For repairing, furnishing and improving county
      buildings, a sum not exceeding twelve thousand
      dollars 12,000 00
15 For care, fuel, lights and supplies in county build-
      ings, other than jails and houses of correction, a
      sum not exceeding twenty-five thousand nine hun-
      dred fifteen dollars 25,915 00
16 For highways, including state highways, bridges and
      land damages, a sum not exceeding sixty thousand
      dollars 60,000 00
16a For shore protection, a sum not exceeding four thou-
      sand dollars 4,000 00
17 For law libraries, a sum not exceeding three thou-
      sand dollars 3,000 00
18 For training school, a sum not exceeding four thou-
      sand dollars 4,000 00
19 For county aid to agriculture, a sum not exceed-
      ing sixteen thousand six hundred fifty dollars   .   16,650 00
22 For pensions, a sum not exceeding two hundred forty
      dollars 240 00
23 For miscellaneous and contingent expenses of the
      current year, a sum not exceeding three thousand
      ninety-one dollars and two cents   .   .   .   3,091 02
23a For unpaid bills of previous years, a sum not exceed-
      ing one thousand two hundred dollars   .   .   1,200 00
24 For a reserve fund, a sum not exceeding ten thou-
      sand dollars 10,000 00
      And the county commissioners of Plymouth county
      are hereby authorized to levy as the county tax of
      said county for the current year, in the manner
      provided by law, the sum of four hundred forty
      thousand eight hundred dollars, to be expended,
      together with the cash balance on hand and the
      receipts from other sources, for the above purposes $440,800 00

Worcester County.

1 For interest on county debt, a sum not exceeding
      fourteen thousand five hundred dollars   .   . $14,500 00
3 For salaries of county officers and assistants, a sum
      not exceeding fifty-five thousand dollars   .   .   55,000 00
4 For clerical assistance in county offices, a sum not
      exceeding seventy thousand dollars   .   .   .   70,000 00
5 For salaries and expenses of district courts, a sum
      not exceeding one hundred fifty-three thousand
      five hundred fifty dollars 153,550 00
6 For salaries of jailers, masters and assistants, and
      support of prisoners in jails and houses of correc-
      tion, a sum not exceeding one hundred thousand
      dollars   .   .   .   .   100,000 00 .
7 For criminal costs in the superior court, a sum not
      exceeding seventy-three thousand seven hundred
      fifty dollars 73,750 00
8 For civil expenses in the supreme judicial, superior,
      probate, and land courts, a sum not exceeding
      seventy-two thousand seven hundred dollars   .   72,700 00
9 For trial justices, a sum not exceeding one thousand
      dollars 1,000 00

Item
10 For transportation expenses of county and associate commissioners, a sum not exceeding three thousand seven hundred fifty dollars . . . $3,750 00
11 For medical examiners, inquests, and commitments of the insane, a sum not exceeding eighteen thousand dollars 18,000 00
12 For auditors, masters and referees, a sum not exceeding thirty thousand dollars 30,000 00
14 For repairing, furnishing and improving county buildings, a sum not exceeding eighteen thousand five hundred dollars 18,500 00
15 For care, fuel, lights and supplies in county buildings, other than jails and houses of correction, a sum not exceeding fifty-seven thousand one hundred dollars 57,100 00
16 For highways, including existing contracts, state highways, bridges and land damages, a sum not exceeding three hundred eighty-one thousand two hundred fifty dollars 381,250 00
17 For law libraries, a sum not exceeding eight thousand five hundred fifty dollars . . . 8,550 00
18 For training school, a sum not exceeding nineteen thousand four hundred fifty dollars . . 19,450 00
19 For county aid to agriculture, a sum not exceeding forty-one thousand four hundred dollars . . 41,400 00
20a For the preventorium, a sum not exceeding three thousand dollars 3,000 00
21 For state reservations, a sum not exceeding twenty-two thousand eight hundred fifty dollars . 22,850 00
22 For pensions, a sum not exceeding fifteen thousand dollars 15,000 00
23 For miscellaneous and contingent expenses of the current year, a sum not exceeding four thousand six hundred dollars 4,600 00
23a For unpaid bills of previous years, a sum not exceeding two thousand five hundred dollars . . 2,500 00
24 For a reserve fund, a sum not exceeding ten thousand dollars 10,000 00
    And the county commissioners of Worcester county are hereby authorized to levy as the county tax of said county for the current year, in the manner provided by law, the sum of nine hundred eighty-one thousand four hundred ninety-eight dollars, to be expended, together with the cash balance on hand and the receipts from other sources, for the above purposes $981,498 00

SECTION 3. The county commissioners of the several counties, with the approval of the county personnel board, shall make adjustments in the compensation of every official and employee which was reduced more than ten per cent by the provisions of chapter one hundred and eighty-six of the current year, or where in the judgment of the county commissioners and the county personnel board the reduction imposed thereby is inequitable; provided, that such adjustments shall be made only where the compensation received is less than three thousand dollars. *Certain salary adjustments authorized.*

SECTION 4. Travel allowances for officials and employees using their own cars on county business shall be at the rate of six cents per mile for small cars and eight cents per mile for large cars unless otherwise specifically provided by law. *Approved July 12, 1933.* *Rate per mile for use of automobiles.*

*Chap.*323 AN ACT PROVIDING FOR THE ENFORCEMENT OF THE PAY-
MENT OF SOLDIERS' RELIEF BY CITIES AND TOWNS IN
CERTAIN CASES.

Emergency
preamble.

Whereas, The deferred operation of this act would in
part defeat its purpose, therefore it is hereby declared to
be an emergency law, necessary for the immediate preservation of the public convenience.

Be it enacted, etc., as follows:

G. L. (Ter.
Ed.), 115,
§ 18, etc.,
amended.

Soldiers' relief.
Supreme court
may compel
granting of.

Section eighteen of chapter one hundred and fifteen of
the General Laws, as amended by chapter two hundred
and seventy of the acts of nineteen hundred and thirty-two,
is hereby further amended by adding at the end of the
first paragraph the following new sentence: — The supreme
judicial court, by mandamus, upon petition of the attorney
general at the relation of the commissioner, may compel
the proper city or town officer to give the amount of relief
determined by the commissioner.

Approved July 12, 1933.

*Chap.*324 AN ACT RELATIVE TO THE INDEMNIFICATION BY THE CITY
OF BOSTON OF MEMBERS OF ITS POLICE AND FIRE FORCES
AND OTHERS FOR CERTAIN EXPENSES OR DAMAGES
INCURRED BY THEM.

Be it enacted, etc., as follows:

Indemnifica-
tion of police
and firemen of
city of Boston
for damages
incurred in
course of duty.

SECTION 1. The city of Boston may indemnify a member of its police or fire force, or a person required to assist
a member of its police force in the discharge of his duties,
to an amount not more than that recommended by its
police commissioner or fire commissioner, as the case may
be, for expenses or damages sustained while acting as
such member or as such assistant and such damages may
include loss of pay by reason of absence from duty on the
part of such member because of temporary incapacity
caused by injury suffered through no fault of his own
while in the actual performance of duty. Said city may
also indemnify such member for expenses or damages
incurred by him in the defence or settlement of a claim
against him for acts done by him while acting as such
member; provided, that the defence or settlement of such
claim shall have been made by the corporation counsel of
said city. If such member or such assistant be dead, such
expenses or damages shall be payable to his widow, or, if
he leaves no widow, then to his next of kin who, at the
time of his death, were dependent upon his wages for
support.

SECTION 2. This act shall be construed to authorize
the city of Boston to pay compensation, in the manner
herein provided, for damages for personal injuries, whether
or not death results; and for property damage, sustained

by a person while assisting a member of its police force in the discharge of his duty upon his requirement.

Section 3. Section one hundred of chapter forty-one of the General Laws, as appearing in the Tercentenary Edition thereof, is hereby amended by adding thereto the following: — This section shall not apply to the city of Boston.

G. L. (Ter. Ed.), 41, § 100, amended.

Section not to apply to Boston.

Section 4. This act shall take effect upon its passage.

Approved July 12, 1933.

An Act relative to collection of taxes on real estate by sale or taking and to redemption of tax titles and making certain minor adjustments in the laws relating to such taxes.

Chap.325

Whereas, The deferred operation of this act would tend to defeat its purpose, which is in part to provide for the performance of certain official acts on September first of the current year, therefore it is hereby declared to be an emergency law, necessary for the immediate preservation of the public convenience.

Emergency preamble.

Be it enacted, etc., as follows:

Section 1. Section thirty-seven of chapter sixty of the General Laws, as appearing in the Tercentenary Edition thereof, is hereby amended by striking out, in the fourth line, the word "Such" and inserting in place thereof the words: — Except as provided in section sixty-one, such, — and by striking out, in the ninth line, the word "thirty" and inserting in place thereof the word: — sixty, — so as to read as follows: — *Section 37.* Taxes assessed upon land, including those assessed under sections twelve, thirteen and fourteen of chapter fifty-nine, shall with all incidental charges and fees be a lien thereon from April first in the year of assessment. Except as provided in section sixty-one, such lien shall terminate at the expiration of two years from October first in said year, if the estate has in the meantime been alienated and the instrument alienating the same has been recorded, otherwise it shall continue until a recorded alienation thereof; but if while such lien is in force a tax sale or taking has been made, and the deed or instrument of taking has been duly recorded within sixty days, but the sale or taking is invalid by reason of any error or irregularity in the proceedings subsequent to the assessment, the lien shall continue for ninety days after a release, notice or disclaimer, under sections eighty-two to eighty-four, inclusive, has been duly recorded, or for ninety days after the sale or taking has been finally adjudged invalid by a court of competent jurisdiction. There shall be no lien for taxes reassessed if the property is alienated before the reassessment. Said taxes, if unpaid for fourteen days after demand therefor, may, with said charges and fees, be levied by sale of the real estate, if the

G. L. (Ter. Ed.), 60, § 37, etc., amended.

Lien of tax upon real estate, levy by sale, validity of title.

lien thereon has not terminated. No tax title shall be held to be invalid by reason of any errors or irregularities in the proceedings of the collector which are neither substantial nor misleading.

SECTION 2. Section thirty-eight of said chapter sixty, as so appearing, is hereby amended by striking out, in the second line, the word "September" and inserting in place thereof the word: — July, — so as to read as follows: —

Section 38. If a mortgagee of land situated in the place of his residence, before July first of the year in which the tax is assessed, gives written notice to the collector that he holds a mortgage on land, with a description of the land, the demand for payment shall be made on the mortgagee instead of the mortgagor.

SECTION 3. Section thirty-nine of said chapter sixty, as so appearing, is hereby amended by striking out, in the sixth line, the word ", summons", — so as to read as

follows: — *Section 39.* If a mortgagee or an owner of land causes a notice, designating a place in the town where such land lies at which all papers relative to taxes on such land which are to be served on him may be left, to be recorded in January of any year in the office of the clerk of such town and, during said month, to be delivered to the collector thereof, the collector shall serve at such place any notice, demand for payment or other paper relating to the taxes on such land which is to be served by him. The collector shall not advertise the sale of such land for two months after the time of a demand so made.

SECTION 4. Section forty-five of said chapter sixty, as so appearing, is hereby amended by striking out, in the fifteenth line, the word "thirty" and inserting in place thereof the word: — sixty, — so as to read as follows: —

Section 45. The collector shall execute and deliver to the purchaser a deed of the land, stating the cause of sale, the price for which the land was sold, the name of the person on whom the demand for the tax was made, the places where the notices were posted, the name of the newspaper in which the advertisement of the sale was published, and the residence of the grantee, and shall contain a warranty that the sale has in all particulars been conducted according to law. The deed shall convey the land to the purchaser, subject to the right of redemption. The title thus conveyed shall, until redemption or until the right of redemption is foreclosed as hereinafter provided, be held as security for the repayment of the purchase price, with all intervening costs, terms imposed for redemption and charges, with interest thereon, and the premises conveyed shall also be subject to and have the benefit of all easements and restrictions lawfully existing in, upon or over said land or appurtenant thereto when so taken. Such deed shall not be valid unless recorded within sixty days after the sale. If so recorded it shall be prima facie evidence of all facts essential to the validity of the title thereby conveyed, whether the deed was executed on or before as well as since July first, nineteen hundred and fifteen. No sale hereafter made shall give to the purchaser any right to possession of the land until the expiration of two years after the date of the sale.

SECTION 5. Section forty-eight of said chapter sixty, as so appearing, is hereby amended by striking out, in the tenth line, the word "thirty" and inserting in place thereof the word: — sixty, — so as to read as follows: — *Section 48.* If at the time and place of sale no person bids for the land offered for sale an amount equal to the tax and charges, and if the sale has been adjourned one or more times, the collector shall then and there make public declaration of the fact; and, if no bid equal to the tax and charges is then made, he shall give public notice that he purchases for the town by which the tax is assessed said land as offered for sale at the amount of the tax and the charges and expenses of the levy and sale. Said amount, together with the cost of recording the deed of purchase, shall be allowed him in his settlement with such town, provided he has caused the deed to be duly recorded within sixty days after the purchase and to be delivered to the town treasurer.

G. L. (Ter. Ed.), 60, § 48, amended.

Collector to purchase for city or town if bid insufficient.

SECTION 6. Said chapter sixty is hereby further amended by striking out section fifty, as so appearing, and inserting in place thereof the following: — *Section 50.* If the town becomes the purchaser, the deed to it, in addition to the statements required by section forty-five, shall set forth the fact that no sufficient bid was made at the sale or that the purchaser failed to pay the amount bid, as the case may be, and shall confer upon such town the rights and duties of an individual purchaser. Every such deed and every instrument of taking described in section fifty-four shall be in the custody of the town treasurer, and there shall be set up on the books of the town, whether kept by the treasurer or otherwise, a separate account of each parcel of land covered by any such deed or instrument, to which shall be charged the amount stated in the deed or instrument, the cost of recording the same, and, upon certification in accordance with section sixty-one, all uncollected taxes assessed to such parcel for any year subsequent to that for the taxes for which such parcel was purchased or taken, with all legal costs and charges, until redemption or foreclosure. The town treasurer shall institute proceedings for foreclosure as soon as such proceedings are authorized by sections sixty-two and sixty-five. The commissioner may at his discretion institute proceedings in the name of the treasurer in the event that such proceedings are not instituted by the treasurer. Any expense incurred by the commissioner hereunder shall be assessed against the city or town and collected in the same manner as expenses for auditing municipal accounts under the provisions of section forty-one of chapter forty-four.

G. L. (Ter. Ed.), 60, § 50, amended.

Deed to city or town. Contents, custody, proceedings for foreclosure.

G. L. (Ter. Ed.), 60, § 54, amended.

SECTION 7. Section fifty-four of said chapter sixty, as so appearing, is hereby amended by striking out, in the seventh line, the word "thirty" and inserting in place thereof the word: — sixty, — so as to read as follows: —

Instrument of taking, form, contents, effect.

Section 54. The instrument of taking shall be under the hand and seal of the collector and shall contain a statement of the cause of taking, a substantially accurate description of each parcel of land taken, the name of the person to whom the same was assessed, the amount of the tax thereon, and the incidental expenses and costs to the date of taking. Such an instrument of taking shall not be valid unless recorded within sixty days of the date of taking. If so recorded it shall be prima facie evidence of all facts essential to the validity of the title so taken, whether the taking was made on or before as well as since July first, nineteen hundred and fifteen. Title to the land so taken shall thereupon vest in the town, subject to the right of redemption. Such title shall, until redemption or until the right of redemption is foreclosed as hereinafter provided, be held as security for the repayment of said taxes with all intervening costs, terms of redemption and charges, with interest thereon.

G. L. (Ter. Ed.), 60, § 55, amended.

SECTION 8. Section fifty-five of said chapter sixty, as so appearing, is hereby amended by striking out, in the fourth line, the word "thirty" and inserting in place thereof the word: — sixty, — so as to read as follows: — *Section*

Fees for taking.

55. If land has been so taken there shall be allowed to the collector and added to the tax the charges and fees fixed by section fifteen, and also the cost of recording the instrument of taking, provided he has caused such instrument to be duly recorded within sixty days after the taking and to be delivered to the town treasurer.

G. L. (Ter. Ed.), 60, § 61, amended.
Lien for subsequent taxes to continue after sale or taking.
Payment on foreclosure, etc.

SECTION 9. Said chapter sixty is hereby further amended by striking out section sixty-one, as so appearing, and inserting in place thereof the following: — *Section 61.* Whenever a town shall have purchased or taken real estate for payment of taxes the lien of the town on such real estate for all taxes assessed subsequently to the assessment for payment of which the estate was purchased or taken shall continue, and it shall be unnecessary for the town to take or sell said real estate for non-payment of said subsequent taxes, costs and interest; and on redemption from such taking or purchase, said subsequent taxes, costs and interest shall be paid to the town, and the payment shall be made a part of the terms of redemption, except that if any of the said subsequent taxes have not been certified by the collector to the treasurer to be added to the tax title account, then redemption may be made by payment only of the amount of the tax for which the estate was purchased or taken and of such subsequent taxes as shall have been so certified, together with costs and interest. The collector shall certify to the treasurer on September first of the year following that of their assessment all subsequent taxes which become part of the terms of redemption and the treasurer shall give him a certificate stating that the amount or amounts have been added to the tax title account or accounts and the collector shall be credited as if the tax had been paid in money.

SECTION 10. Said chapter sixty is hereby further amended by striking out section sixty-two, as so appearing, and inserting in place thereof the following: — *Section 62.* Any person having an interest in land taken or sold for non-payment of taxes, including those assessed under sections twelve, thirteen and fourteen of chapter fifty-nine, or his heirs or assigns, at any time prior to the filing of a petition for foreclosure under section sixty-five, if the estate has been taken or purchased by the town, may redeem the same by paying or tendering to the treasurer the amount of the tax and all intervening taxes, with all costs, charges and fees, and interest at eight per cent per annum on the whole, or may pay or tender to the treasurer not less than fifty per cent of the tax for the non-payment of which the estate was taken or purchased, together with all costs, charges and fees, and interest as aforesaid on the whole amount of the tax title account then due, which payment shall be received, receipted for, and applied toward the redemption of the estate so taken or purchased. From time to time thereafter prior to the filing of such petition for foreclosure, such person may likewise pay or tender, successively in the order of their date, the balance of the tax of which partial payment was made and a first instalment of not less than fifty per cent and a second instalment of the balance, if any, of each year's tax which at the time of payment or tender of such instalment has been added to the tax title account under sections fifty and sixty-one, until all taxes upon the property which have been added to the tax title account are paid or tendered in full, whereupon such estate shall be redeemed. Each payment or tender hereunder shall include, in addition to the tax or part of a tax paid, all intervening costs, charges, fees and interest which at the time of such payment or tender have become part of the tax title account. The treasurer upon accepting any payment hereunder may extend the time during which proceedings for the foreclosure of all rights of redemption may not be instituted, for a period not exceeding one year beyond the time provided by section sixty-five; but not more than one such extension shall be granted. An extension granted hereunder shall be entered upon the tax title account, and a written statement thereof shall be given to the person who made the payment.

Any such person may so redeem by paying or tendering to the purchaser, his legal representatives or assigns, at any time prior to the filing of such petition for foreclosure, if the purchaser is other than the town, the original sum and intervening taxes and costs paid by him and interest on the whole at said rate. In each case he shall also pay

G. L. (Ter. Ed.), 60, § 62, amended.

Redemption of land taken or sold for taxes.

or tender, for examination of title and a deed of release, not more than three dollars in the aggregate, and in addition thereto the actual cost of recording the tax deed or evidence of taking. He may redeem the land by paying or tendering to the collector the sum which he would be required to pay to the purchaser, with one dollar additional. If land taken by or sold to a city or town for non-payment of taxes is redeemed, the city treasurer or acting city treasurer, notwithstanding the provisions of the charter of his city, or the town treasurer, as the case may be, shall sign, execute and deliver on behalf of the city or town a release of all the right, title and interest, which it acquired by such taking or purchase, in and to the land so redeemed. No person shall knowingly collect or attempt to collect for the redemption of any such land a sum of money greater than that authorized by this section.

Nothing in this section nor in sections sixty-five to seventy-five, inclusive, shall be construed to prevent the title of a person or a city or town purchasing land at a sale under section seventy-nine or eighty from becoming absolute without any foreclosure proceedings under said sections sixty-five to seventy-five, inclusive.

G. L. (Ter. Ed.), 60, § 63, amended.

SECTION 11. Section sixty-three of said chapter sixty, as so appearing, is hereby amended by striking out, in the eighth line, the words "on demand" and inserting in place thereof the word: — forthwith, — so as to read as follows:

Person paying collector to receive certificate which releases tax title, etc.

— *Section 63.* The collector shall receive any money paid to him instead of the purchaser and give to the person paying it a certificate specifying the amount paid, the name of the person to whom and the real estate on which the tax was originally assessed, and the registry of deeds and the book and page of the records therein where the collector's deed is recorded; and the recording of the certificate in said registry shall extinguish all right and title acquired under the collector's deed. The collector shall forthwith pay over all money so paid, to the person entitled thereto as determined by him, except that he shall retain one dollar for the use of the town and shall account to it therefor. If the amount so paid is less than the purchaser was entitled to, the balance with interest at eight per cent per annum may after demand therefor be recovered in contract by the purchaser against the person paying such amount, if the action is commenced within three months after such payment to the collector.

G. L. (Ter. Ed.), 60, § 65, amended.

SECTION 12. Section sixty-five of said chapter sixty, as so appearing, is hereby amended by inserting after the word "taxes" in the first line the words: — , except as provided in section sixty-two, — so as to read as follows: —

Petition for foreclosure of rights of redemption under tax title.

Section 65. After two years from a sale or taking of land for taxes, except as provided in section sixty-two, whoever then holds the title thereby acquired may bring a petition in the land court for the foreclosure of all rights of redemption thereunder. Such petition shall be made in the form to be prescribed by said court and shall set forth a description of the land to which it applies, with its assessed valuation, the petitioner's source of title, giving a reference to the place, book and page of record, and such other facts as may be necessary for the information of the court. Two or more parcels of land may be included in any petition brought by a town, whether under a taking or as purchaser of such title or titles.

SECTION 13. Section seventy-eight of said chapter sixty, as so appearing, is hereby amended by striking out the last sentence and inserting in place thereof the following: — In case of foreclosure, any such taxes, or balances due on taxes paid in part, remaining unpaid, shall be credited to the collector as if collected by him, unless already so credited, — so as to read as follows: — *Section 78.* Before foreclosure or redemption, taxes on land taken or purchased by a town shall be assessed to the person to whom they would be assessed if the land had not been so taken or purchased. In case of a sale under the following section, such taxes shall be deducted from the proceeds thereof, before any surplus is disposed of as therein provided. In case of foreclosure, any such taxes, or balances due on taxes paid in part, remaining unpaid, shall be credited to the collector as if collected by him, unless already so credited.

G. L. (Ter. Ed.), 60, § 78, amended.

Assessment of taxes on land taken or purchased by city or town.

SECTION 14. Section seventy-nine of said chapter sixty, as so appearing, is hereby amended by striking out, in the twenty-second line, the word "thirty" and inserting in place thereof the word: — sixty, — so that. the second paragraph will read as follows: —

G. L. (Ter. Ed.), 60, § 79, amended.

Upon the recording thereof the treasurer may sell all the parcels included therein, severally or together, at public auction to the highest bidder, first giving notice of the time and place of sale by posting a notice of the sale in some convenient and public place in the town fourteen days at least before the sale. If the sale under this section shall not be made within four years from said taking or purchase, it shall be made by the treasurer for the time being when he deems best, or at once upon service on him of a written demand by any person interested therein. The treasurer shall execute and deliver to the highest bidder a deed, without covenant except that the sale has in all particulars been conducted according to law. Title taken pursuant to a sale under this section shall be absolute upon the recording of the deed of the treasurer in the proper registry of deeds within sixty days of its date.

Sale without foreclosure of lands taken or purchased by city or town in certain cases.

SECTION 15. Section eighty of said chapter sixty, as so appearing, is hereby amended by striking out, in the thirteenth line, the word "thirty" and inserting in place thereof the word: — sixty, — so as to read as follows: — *Section 80.* If no person bids at such a sale and if the sale has been adjourned one or more times, the treasurer shall then and there make public declaration of the fact, and if

G. L. (Ter. Ed.), 60, § 80, amended.

Proceedings upon lack of bids, etc., at sale.

no bid is then made he shall give public notice that he purchases for the town by which the tax is assessed; or if the person to whom the land is sold does not within ten days pay to the treasurer the sum bid by him the sale shall be void and the town shall be deemed to be the purchaser of the land. If the town becomes the purchaser hereunder, the treasurer shall execute to it a deed which shall set forth the fact that no bid was made at the sale or that the purchaser failed to pay the amount bid, as the case may be. The title of the town to land conveyed by deed of the treasurer under this section shall be absolute upon the recording of said deed in the proper registry of deeds within sixty days of its date.

G. L. (Ter. Ed.), 60, § 84A, amended.

Refunds to holders of tax titles judicially adjudged invalid.

SECTION 16. Said chapter sixty is hereby further amended by striking out section eighty-four A, as so appearing, and inserting in place thereof the following: — *Section 84A.* If a tax title is for any reason adjudged invalid by a court of competent jurisdiction, said court may order the treasurer of the city or town where the land affected is situated, upon receipt of a release by the holder of said title of all the interest which he may have under his tax deed, to refund to such holder the amount paid therefor but not exceeding the amount received by the city or town, with interest at the rate of ten per cent per annum from the date of the tax sale, together with three dollars for an examination of the title. Said order shall specify the cause of the invalidity of the said title. The treasurer shall forthwith record said release in the proper registry of deeds, and thereupon, if the said invalidity was caused by an error, omission or informality in the assessment of the tax, the treasurer shall notify the board by which the tax or assessment was laid, which shall forthwith reassess it as provided in section seventy-seven of chapter fifty-nine; and if such invalidity was caused by an error, omission or informality in the proceedings of the collector, the treasurer shall thereupon notify the collector who shall forthwith collect the unpaid tax or assessment in conformity to law.

G. L. (Ter. Ed.), 60, § 95, amended.

Credits and payments to collector.

SECTION 17. Said chapter sixty is hereby amended by striking out section ninety-five, as so appearing, and inserting in place thereof the following: — *Section 95.* The collector shall be credited with all sums abated; with the amount of taxes assessed upon any person committed to jail for non-payment of his tax within two years from the receipt of the tax list by the collector, and who has not paid his tax; with any sums which the town may see fit to abate to him, due from persons committed after the expiration of two years; with all sums withheld by the treasurer of a town under section ninety-three; subject to the provisions of sections forty-eight and fifty-five, with the amount of the taxes and costs, charges and fees where land has been purchased or taken by the town for non-payment of taxes; upon certification in accordance with section sixty-one, with the amount of subsequent taxes which have become part of the terms of redemption in any tax title held by the town; and with the amount of any other taxes for which he is entitled to credit under section seventy-eight. When a collector is credited with the amount of taxes assessed upon any person committed to jail for the non-payment of his tax, who has not paid his tax, said collector shall also be paid and credited with the fees and charges which have become a part of said taxes and to which he or the officer acting under his warrant is entitled.

SECTION 18. Chapter fifty-nine of the General Laws is hereby amended by striking out section sixty-five A, as inserted by section one of chapter two hundred and eighteen of the acts of nineteen hundred and thirty-two, and inserting in place thereof the following: — *Section 65A.* No sale or taking of real property for non-payment of taxes shall affect the hearing of any application for abatement of such taxes duly made under any provision of this chapter prior to the institution of proceedings for such sale or taking, or the institution, hearing or disposition of any proceeding arising from such application, nor shall the addition of any subsequent taxes to a tax title account affect the hearing of any application for abatement of such subsequent taxes duly made under any provision of this chapter prior to such addition being made, or the institution, hearing or disposition of any proceeding arising from such application. If a final finding be made that the person aggrieved by the assessment of such taxes is entitled to an abatement, he shall be granted such reasonable abatement as justice may require. In case the purchaser of the property is other than the town, the person so aggrieved shall be entitled to relief in the same manner and in the same amount, including interest and charges, as if the payment made to the town for the purchase of the property had been made as a direct payment of the taxes, interest and charges for the non-payment of which the property was sold. In case the property is taken or purchased by the town, the person so aggrieved shall be entitled to have the amount to be paid or tendered in redemption under the provisions of section sixty-two of chapter sixty reduced to the amount which would have been required to have been so paid or tendered if the abatement or abatements had become effective before the taking or purchase or addition to the tax title account.

SECTION 19. Chapter two hundred and eighteen of the acts of nineteen hundred and thirty-two is hereby amended by striking out section two and inserting in place thereof the following: — *Section 2.* This act shall apply to all applications for abatement of taxes on real property filed subsequently to the first day of October, nineteen hundred and twenty-nine, whether any such application be made before or after the effective date of this act, and shall apply to all proceedings arising from any such application.

Marginal notes:

G. L. (Ter. Ed.), 59, § 65A, etc., amended.

Sale or taking not to affect hearings on abatement of tax.

1932, 218, § 2, amended.

Application of act.

Collector to
certify taxes
subsequently
assessed, etc.

SECTION 20. The collector of each city or town shall certify to the treasurer thereof on or before September first, nineteen hundred and thirty-three, all taxes assessed subsequently to the assessment for which any real estate was purchased or taken by such city or town under section forty-eight or section fifty-three of chapter sixty of the General Laws, which were assessed at too early a date to be certified under section sixty-one of said chapter sixty, as amended by section nine of this act, on September first of the year following their assessment. Thereupon the treasurer shall give to the collector a certificate stating that the amounts of all such subsequent taxes have been added to the respective tax title accounts and the collector shall be credited as if such taxes had been paid in money. No taxes so credited shall again be credited to the collector under section seventy-eight of said chapter sixty, as amended by section thirteen of this act.

Effective
date of act.

SECTION 21. Section two of this act shall take effect on December thirty-first, nineteen hundred and thirty-three. In all other respects this act shall take effect upon its passage.   *Approved July 12, 1933.*

---

*Chap.*326 AN ACT RELATIVE TO ALTERATIONS OF CROSSINGS OF STATE HIGHWAYS AND RAILROADS.

Be it enacted, etc., as follows:

G. L. (Ter.
Ed.), 159,
§ 59, amended.

Alteration of
certain grade
crossings.

SECTION 1. Chapter one hundred and fifty-nine of the General Laws is hereby amended by striking out section fifty-nine, as appearing in the Tercentenary Edition thereof, and inserting in place thereof the following: — *Section 59.* If a public way and a railroad cross each other, and the board of aldermen of the city or the selectmen of the town where the crossing is situated, or the department of public works, if the crossing and its approaches are in direct continuation of a state highway, or the directors of the railroad corporation, or the directors of a railway company having tracks on said way, deem it necessary for the security or convenience of the public that an alteration not involving the abolition of a crossing at grade should be made in the crossing, the approaches thereto, the location of the railroad or way, or in a bridge at the crossing, they shall apply to the board of county commissioners, or, if the crossing is situated, in whole or in part, in Boston, to the department of public utilities, which shall, after public notice, hear all parties interested, and, if it decides that such alteration is necessary, shall prescribe the manner and limits within which it shall be made, and shall forthwith certify its decision to the parties and to said department of public utilities. If a state highway and a railroad cross each other and the department of public works, after public notice and a hearing of all parties interested, decides that it is necessary for the security or convenience of the public that an alteration as aforesaid should be made in the crossing, the approaches thereto, the location of the railroad or way, or in a bridge at the crossing, and if no application under the foregoing provisions of this section relative to said crossing is then pending, said department of public works may order such alteration, prescribing in such order the manner and limits within which such alteration shall be made, and shall forthwith certify its decision to the parties and to said department of public utilities; provided, that a party aggrieved by a decision or order of said department of public works hereunder may appeal to the department of public utilities in the same manner as in the case of an appeal under section one hundred and eleven of chapter one hundred and sixty by a person aggrieved by a decision or order of the county commissioners, and the provisions of sections one hundred and eleven to one hundred and thirteen, inclusive, of said chapter shall apply to appeals hereunder except that for the purposes of this section, reference in said sections one hundred and eleven to one hundred and thirteen, inclusive, to the county commissioners shall refer to the department of public works.

Hearings by the department of public works shall be held in the county where such crossing is situated and a copy of its decision and of the plan of said alteration shall be filed by it in the office of the county commissioners of the said county. This proceeding may include any case where there is need of the rebuilding of a highway bridge or any structural change or renewal in order to strengthen or improve it. If any railway company is authorized to lay and use tracks upon the said way, the said company shall bear such part of the expense of building, rebuilding, changing, renewing, repairing or improving a bridge forming a part of said way, or of altering or improving the approaches thereto, as the commission provided for in sections sixty-one and sixty-two deem just. *Hearings.*

SECTION 2. Section sixty of said chapter one hundred and fifty-nine, as so appearing, is hereby amended by inserting after the word "corporation" in the third line the following: — , the commonwealth, — so as to read as follows: — *Section 60.* If it is decided that the location of the railroad or of the way shall be changed, land or other property may be taken therefor by eminent domain on behalf of the railroad corporation, the commonwealth or the town, as the case may be, under chapter seventy-nine, and damages may be recovered therefor under said chapter. *G. L. (Ter. Ed.), 159, § 60, amended.* *Land may be taken and damages assessed.*

SECTION 3. Section sixty-one of said chapter one hundred and fifty-nine, as so appearing, is hereby amended by inserting after the word "continuation" in the twelfth line the words: — or a part, — so as to read as follows: — *Section 61.* A commission of three disinterested persons, appointed as provided in the following section, shall determine which party shall carry such decision into effect and *G. L. (Ter. Ed.), 159, § 61, amended.* *Award to be made by commission.*

which party shall pay the charges and expenses of making such alteration and the future charges for keeping such bridge or crossing and the approaches thereto in repair, as well as the costs of the application to the county commissioners, or the department, and of the hearing before said commission; and it may apportion all such charges, expenses and costs between the railroad corporation, the railway company having tracks on said way, and the counties, cities or towns where said crossing is situated and other cities and towns which may be specially benefited; and if the crossing and its approaches are in direct continuation or a part of a state highway, the commonwealth may be included in such apportionment and its share shall be paid from the annual appropriation for maintenance and repair of state highways. If a railway company is authorized to lay and use tracks upon any bridge in a highway built, repaired or altered as above provided for, or the approaches to which are altered or improved as above provided for, the said commission shall determine what part of the charges and expenses of making such changes or improvements, or of keeping such bridge or crossing and approaches in good condition, shall be paid by said railway company.

G. L. (Ter. Ed.), 159, § 62, amended.

Commission, appointment, award.

SECTION 4. Section sixty-two of said chapter one hundred and fifty-nine, as so appearing, is hereby amended by striking out, in the second line, the words "the division of highways of", — so as to read as follows: — *Section 62.* Upon application of the county commissioners, the department, the department of public works, the board of aldermen, the selectmen or the directors of the railroad corporation or of the railway company for the appointment of such commission, the superior court shall cause notice thereof to be given to the other parties interested fourteen days at least before the time fixed for the hearing; and thereupon, after hearing, shall appoint such commission, one member of which shall be a member of and designated by the department. The commission shall meet as soon as may be after its appointment, and, after notice to and a hearing of the parties, shall make a written award and return it to said court.   *Approved July 12, 1933.*

Chap.327

AN ACT RELATIVE TO TAXATION OF BANKS, TRUST COMPANIES AND CERTAIN OTHER CORPORATIONS, ESPECIALLY WITH RESPECT TO THE DEFINITION OF NET INCOME.

Emergency preamble.

Whereas, The deferred operation of this act would tend to defeat its purpose, therefore it is hereby declared to be an emergency law, necessary for the immediate preservation of the public convenience.

Be it enacted, etc., as follows:

G.L. (Ter. Ed.), 63, § 1, amended.

SECTION 1. Section one of chapter sixty-three of the General Laws, as appearing in the Tercentenary Edition thereof, is hereby amended by striking out the paragraph defining "Net income" and inserting in place thereof the following: —

"Net income", the gross income from all sources, without exclusion, for the taxable year, less the deductions, other than losses sustained by the bank in other fiscal or calendar years and other than dividends, allowable by the federal revenue act applicable for said taxable year. Banks, etc., taxation of. "Net income" defined.

SECTION 2. Section two of said chapter sixty-three, as so appearing, is hereby amended by adding at the end of the first sentence the words: —; and, provided, further, that such rate shall not be higher than six per cent, — so as to read as follows: — *Section 2*. Every bank shall pay annually a tax measured by its net income, as defined in section one, at the rate assessed upon other financial corporations; provided, that such rate shall not be higher than the highest of the rates assessed under this chapter upon mercantile and business corporations doing business in the commonwealth; and, provided, further, that such rate shall not be higher than six per cent. The commissioner shall determine the rate on or before July first of each year after giving a hearing thereon, and at or prior to such hearing he shall make available to all banks requesting the same a statement showing the aggregates of the income returnable during the preceding calendar year and taxable under this chapter and the aggregates of the taxes under this chapter of such year, with respect to the following classes of corporations: (1) domestic financial corporations, (2) foreign financial corporations, (3) domestic manufacturing corporations as defined in section thirty-eight C, (4) foreign manufacturing corporations as defined in section forty-two B, (5) domestic business corporations as defined in section thirty, (6) foreign corporations as defined in said section thirty. The commissioner shall seasonably notify the banks of his determination. Appeal by a bank from the determination of the commissioner may be taken to the board of tax appeals within ten days after the giving of such notice. G. L. (Ter. Ed.), 63, § 2, amended. Annual tax of banks, trust companies, etc. Rate, how determined. Appeals.

SECTION 3. Section thirty of said chapter sixty-three, as amended by sections three and four of chapter fifty-eight of the acts of the current year, is hereby further amended by striking out the paragraph numbered 5 and inserting in place thereof the following: — G. L. (Ter. Ed.), 63, § 30, etc., amended.

5. "Net income", the gross income from all sources, without exclusion, for the taxable year, less the deductions, other than losses sustained by the corporation in other fiscal or calendar years and other than dividends, allowable by the federal revenue act applicable for said taxable year. Business corporations. "Net income" defined

SECTION 4. Section thirty-four of said chapter sixty-three, as so appearing, is hereby amended by striking out all after the first sentence, — so as to read as follows: — *Section 34*. If two or more domestic business corporations participated in the filing of a consolidated return of income to the federal government, the tax under paragraph (2) of G. L. (Ter. Ed.), 63, § 34, amended. Net income where federal return consolidated.

section thirty-two may, at their option, be assessed upon their combined net income, which tax shall be assessed to all said corporations and collected from any one or more of them.

G. L. (Ter. Ed.), 63, § 36, amended.
Correction of return.
Additional tax.

SECTION 5. Said chapter sixty-three is hereby further amended by striking out section thirty-six, as so appearing, and inserting in place thereof the following:—*Section 36.* Any final determination of the federal net income made pursuant to the provisions of federal law under which such net income is found to differ from the net income originally reported to the federal government shall be reported by the corporation to the commissioner within seventy days of receipt by it of notice of such final determination, with a statement of the reasons for the difference, in such detail as the commissioner may require. If from such report or upon investigation it shall appear that the tax with respect to income imposed by this chapter has not been fully assessed, the commissioner shall within six months of the receipt of such report or within six months of discovery of such a determination, if unreported, assess the deficiency, with interest at the rate of six per cent per annum from October twentieth of the year in which the original return of income of the corporation was due to be filed, and the tax so assessed shall be payable thirty days from the date of notice to the corporation of such assessment. If, upon investigation of the facts so reported, it appears that a less tax with respect to income was due the commonwealth than was paid, the commissioner shall abate the excess upon written application therefor by the corporation, filed with the commissioner within sixty days of the filing of said report with him. The commissioner shall certify the amount of such abatement to the state treasurer, who shall repay the amount so certified with interest at the rate of six per cent per annum from the date of overpayment, without further appropriation therefor.

G. L. (Ter. Ed.), 63, § 39, amended.
Excise on foreign corporations.

SECTION 6. The last paragraph of section thirty-nine of said chapter sixty-three, as so appearing, is hereby amended by striking out the last sentence,—so that said paragraph will read as follows:—

If two or more foreign corporations doing business in this commonwealth participated in the filing of a consolidated return of income to the federal government, the tax under paragraph (2) above may, at their option, be assessed upon their combined net income, in which case the tax shall be assessed to all said corporations and collected from any one or more of them.

Application of act.

SECTION 7. This act shall apply to taxes assessed in the year nineteen hundred and thirty-three and thereafter.

Approved July 17, 1933.

An Act further regulating the granting of old age assistance.

*Chap.*328

Whereas, The deferred operation of this act would tend to defeat its purpose, therefore it is hereby declared to be an emergency law, necessary for the immediate preservation of the public convenience.

Emergency preamble.

Be it enacted, etc., as follows:

Chapter one hundred and eighteen A of the General Laws, as most recently amended in section one by chapter two hundred and nineteen of the acts of the current year, is hereby further amended by striking out said section one and inserting in place thereof the following: — *Section 1.* Adequate assistance to deserving citizens in need of relief and support seventy years of age or over who shall have resided in the commonwealth not less than twenty years immediately preceding the date of application for such assistance, subject to such reasonable exceptions as to continuity of residence as the department of public welfare, in this chapter called the department, may determine by rules hereinafter authorized, shall be granted under the supervision of the department. Financial assistance granted hereunder shall be given from the date of application therefor, but in no event before the applicant reaches the age of seventy, and in determining the amount of assistance to be given for any period preceding the date on which the application was favorably passed upon, consideration shall be given to the amount of welfare relief, if any, given to such applicant during said period under any other provision of law. Such assistance shall, wherever practicable, be given to the aged person in his own home or in lodgings or in a boarding home, and it shall be sufficient to provide such suitable and dignified care. No person receiving assistance hereunder shall be deemed to be a pauper by reason thereof. *Approved July 17, 1933.*

G. L. (Ter. Ed.), 118A, § 1, etc., amended.

State department of public welfare to supervise rendering of assistance to aged persons.

An Act making certain changes in the general laws relating to inland fish, birds and mammals, and revising the general laws relating to marine fish and fisheries, including shellfish.

*Chap.*329

Be it enacted, etc., as follows:

Section 1. The General Laws are hereby amended by inserting after chapter one hundred and twenty-nine the following new chapter with the following title: —

G. L. (Ter. Ed.), new chapter 129A, added.

CHAPTER 129A.

MARINE FISH AND FISHERIES, INLAND FISH AND FISHERIES,
BIRDS AND MAMMALS.   GENERAL PROVISIONS.

Definitions and Rules of Construction.

Definitions.

Section 1.   In this chapter, and in chapters one hundred
and thirty and one hundred and thirty-one, unless hereinafter or therein otherwise stated, the following words
shall have the following meanings and the following rules
of construction shall apply:

"Angling", fishing with hand line or rod, with naturally
or artificially baited hook, except that not more than three
flies may be used on a single leader.

"Birds", wild or undomesticated birds.

"Close season", the time during which fish, birds or
mammals cannot lawfully be taken.

"Coastal warden", a coastal warden appointed under
section seven of chapter twenty-one.

"Coastal waters" shall include all waters of the commonwealth within the rise and fall of the tide, but not
within or above any fishway or dam, also all such waters
between the rise and fall of the tide and the marine limits
of the jurisdiction of the commonwealth.

"Commissioner", the commissioner of conservation.

"Dealer", in chapter one hundred and thirty, any person
who commercially handles fish.

"Department", the department of conservation.

"Deputy", in this chapter, any deputy warden appointed
under section seven of chapter twenty-one; in chapter one
hundred and thirty, a deputy coastal warden, and, in
chapter one hundred and thirty-one, a deputy inland fish
and game warden, so appointed.

"Deputy coastal warden", in chapter one hundred and
thirty, a deputy coastal warden appointed under said section seven.

"Director", the director of the division of fisheries and
game.

"Division", the division of fisheries and game.

"Fish", in chapter one hundred and thirty, any crusta-
cean or marine fish, whether free swimming or free moving,
and any shellfish or sea worms, whether or not embedded
in the soil.   All provisions of said chapter relative to fish
shall, so far as apt, apply also to lobster meat and crab
meat after the same has been taken from the shell.

The verb "To fish", in all of its moods and tenses, to
take or to attempt to take fish by any method or means,
whether or not such method or means results in their
capture; and, in chapter one hundred and thirty-one, said
verb also includes every attempt to take and every act of
assistance to any other person in taking or attempting to
take fish, except operating a boat or assisting a person
licensed under said chapter one hundred and thirty-one
by cutting holes in the ice for ice fishing.

"Game", in chapter one hundred and thirty-one, any wild bird or mammal commonly hunted for food or sport.

"Great pond", a natural pond the area of which is twenty acres or more.

"Hook", any lure or device capable of taking not more than one fish at a time.

The verb "To hunt", in all of its moods and tenses, in chapter one hundred and thirty-one, includes pursuing, shooting, killing and capturing mammals and birds, and all lesser acts such as disturbing, harrying or worrying, or placing, setting, drawing or using any device commonly used to take mammals and birds, whether or not they result in taking; and includes every attempt to take and every act of assistance to any other person in taking or attempting to take mammals and birds.

"Inland waters" shall include all waters within the commonwealth other than those herein defined as coastal waters.

"Mammals", wild or undomesticated mammals.

"Marine fisheries", all fisheries in coastal waters.

"Open season", the time during which fish, birds and mammals may lawfully be taken.

"Supervisor", the state supervisor of marine fisheries appointed under section eight A of chapter twenty-one.

"Truckman", in chapter one hundred and thirty, any person, other than a common carrier, using a truck or other vehicle in distributing fish.

"Warden", in this chapter, any warden appointed under section seven of chapter twenty-one; in chapter one hundred and thirty, a coastal warden, and in chapter one hundred and thirty-one, a fish and game warden, so appointed.

A person who knowingly counsels, aids or assists in a violation of any provision of this chapter or of chapter one hundred and thirty or of chapter one hundred and thirty-one, or knowingly shares in any of the proceeds of said violation by receiving or possessing either fish, birds or mammals, shall be deemed to have incurred the penalties imposed thereby upon the person guilty of such violation.

Whenever the taking of fish, birds or mammals is allowed by law, reference is had to taking by lawful means and in lawful manner.

Unless the context otherwise requires, any reference to the taking or having in possession of a fish, bird or mammal shall include the taking or having in possession of any part or portion thereof.

In construing this chapter and chapters one hundred and thirty and one hundred and thirty-one, the provisions thereof forbidding possession of various species of fish, birds and mammals during certain periods of the year shall not be held to prohibit a resident of the commonwealth who has legally taken, killed or come into possession of such fish, birds or mammals from having the dead bodies or carcasses thereof in possession, for his own personal use and not for sale, unless prohibited by federal legislation or regulation so to do; but the burden shall be on him to prove that such possession was lawful in its origin. Also, in construing said chapters, such provisions forbidding possession shall not be held to prohibit a person from bringing into this commonwealth, for his own personal use and not for sale, the dead bodies or carcasses of fish, birds or mammals which were lawfully taken or killed in another state, province or country, or from having such fish, birds or mammals in possession for the aforesaid purpose after the arrival thereof in this commonwealth, unless prohibited by federal legislation or regulation so to do, if before any such fish, birds or mammals are so imported they are tagged or marked in accordance with the laws of such other state, province or country and with the federal laws relative to interstate commerce, and if no more such fish, birds or mammals are imported at one time than is permitted by the laws of such other state, province or country to be exported therefrom; but the burden shall be on him to prove that such possession was lawful in its origin.

General Provisions.

Revocation, etc., of licenses or permits.

Section 2. Licenses or permits issued by the director or supervisor under chapter one hundred and thirty or chapter one hundred and thirty-one may be suspended or revoked for cause by the officer issuing them.

Town clerk's fee for issuing license.

Section 3. Any town clerk issuing any license under authority of chapter one hundred and thirty or chapter one hundred and thirty-one may, except as otherwise provided by law, retain for his own use twenty-five cents from the fee for each such license.

Duplicate license. Fee.

Section 4. Whoever loses or by mistake or accident destroys his license may, upon application to the director or to the town clerk of the town issuing the same, and upon payment of a fee of fifty cents, receive a duplicate license; provided, that such application is accompanied by an affidavit setting forth the circumstances of said loss and also, if application is made to the director, in any case where he did not issue the original license, by a statement from the person who issued the original license or his successor in office, which statement shall contain the number and form of the license, the date of its issue and a personal description of the licensee.

Record of licenses issued.

Section 5. The director, the supervisor and the clerk of every town shall make a record, in books kept therefor, of all licenses issued by them, respectively, and shall date each license as of the date of issue; and no other date shall be placed on such license. Such books shall be supplied by the division, shall be the property of the commonwealth, shall be open to public inspection during the usual office hours of the town clerk, the director or the supervisor, as the case may be, and shall be subject at all times to audit and inspection by the director, by the state auditor or by the comptroller or by their respective agents. Every town clerk shall, on the first Monday of every month, pay to the division all moneys received by him for licenses issued during the month preceding, except the fees retained under section three. All such remittances shall be by check, United States post office money order, express money order, or in lawful money of the United States. Every town clerk shall, within thirty days next succeeding January first in each year, return to the division all license books received during the year preceding, including all stubs and void and unused licenses. Any town clerk vio- *Penalty.* lating any provision of this section shall be punished by a fine of not less than fifty nor more than five hundred dollars, or by imprisonment for not less than one month nor more than one year, or both.

Section 6. Unless otherwise specifically provided by *Licenses* law, every license issued under chapter one hundred and *void upon conviction* thirty-one held by any person found guilty of a violation *of offence* of any provision of said chapter shall be void, and shall *under fish and game laws.* immediately be surrendered to the officer securing such finding. The officer shall forthwith forward such void licenses to the director. No person shall be given a license under authority of said chapter during the period of one year from the date of his being found guilty as aforesaid, and any such license so issued shall be void and shall be surrendered on demand of any officer authorized to enforce said chapter. No fee received for a license made void under this section shall be refunded to the holder of such license. Whoever violates any provision of this section, or is in any way a party to such violation, shall be punished by a fine of not less than ten nor more than fifty dollars, or by imprisonment for not more than one month, or both.

Miscellaneous Powers and Duties of Director, Supervisor, Wardens, etc.

Section 7. The director, supervisor, wardens, deputies *Enforcement* and members of the state police shall enforce the laws relat- *of laws.* ing to fish, birds and mammals. Each warden, when on *Badges.* duty, shall wear and display a metallic badge bearing the seal of the commonwealth and the words "fish and game warden" or "coastal warden", as the case may be, and each deputy, when on duty, shall wear and display a metallic badge bearing the seal of the commonwealth and the words "deputy fish and game warden" or "deputy coastal warden", as the case may be, together with a number to be assigned by the director. The director, with the approval of the governor, may in writing authorize any warden to have in his possession and carry a revolver, club, billy, handcuffs, twisters, or any other weapon or article required in the performance of his official duty.

Section 8. Whoever, not being a warden or deputy, *Penalty for impersonating* possesses or wears any badge described in the preceding *warden, etc.*

section or in any way impersonates a warden or deputy shall be punished by a fine of not less than ten nor more than fifty dollars.

Director, etc., may enter lands in performance of duties.

Section 9. The director, supervisor, wardens and deputies may, in the performance of their duties, enter upon and pass through or over private lands, whether or not covered by water.

Director, etc., to have powers of police officers, etc.

Section 10. The director, supervisor, wardens and deputies shall have and exercise throughout the commonwealth, for the enforcement of the laws relating to fish, birds and mammals, including dogs, all the powers of constables, except the service of civil process, of shellfish constables and of police officers.

Power of director, etc., to arrest without warrant.

Section 11. The director, supervisor, wardens and deputies, members of the state police and all other officers qualified to serve criminal process may arrest without a warrant any person found violating any provision of this chapter or chapter one hundred and thirty or chapter one hundred and thirty-one, or of any ordinance, rule or regulation made under authority thereof, and detain him until a warrant for his arrest for such violation is procured or is refused; and may seize any boat, vessel, motor vehicle, as defined in section one of chapter ninety, or other vehicle and its tackle, apparel, furniture and implements and any other personal property, used in such violation, and any fish illegally taken or held, which shall be forfeited.

Search warrants.

Section 12. A court or official authorized to issue warrants in criminal cases shall, upon a sworn complaint that the complainant believes that any fish, birds or mammals unlawfully taken or possessed are concealed in any boat, vehicle, car, box, locker, crate, package, building or other particular place, other than a dwelling house, if satisfied that there is reasonable cause for such belief, issue a warrant to search therefor. The warrant shall designate and describe the place to be searched and the articles for which search is to be made and, if possible, the person by whom the articles are believed to be owned, kept or possessed, and shall be directed to any officer named in the following section commanding him to search the place where the fish, birds or mammals for which he is required to search are believed to be concealed, and to seize such fish, birds or mammals.

Search and seizure of fish, birds and mammals illegally taken.

Section 13. The director, supervisor, any warden or deputy or any member of the state police to whom a warrant issued under the preceding section is committed shall search the place described in the warrant and seize the fish, birds or mammals therein described, and such fish, birds or mammals, if unlawfully taken or held, shall be forfeited; provided, that this and the following section shall not apply to fish, birds or mammals passing through the commonwealth under authority of the laws of the United States. Fish, birds or mammals so seized may be libelled under chapter two hundred and fifty-seven, or, at the discretion of the officer, be sold at private sale or by public auction, and the net proceeds of such sale may be so libelled, in the same manner and with the same effect as if such proceeds were the property itself, unless the person named in the warrant or some person in his behalf shall before the commencement of such libel or sale request that the fish, birds or mammals be preserved until final action is had thereon.

Section 14. The director, supervisor, a warden or deputy, or any member of the state police may request any person whom he reasonably believes to be engaged in unlawfully hunting, fishing, trapping or to be unlawfully in possession of fish, birds or mammals, or to be in possession of fish, birds or mammals unlawfully taken, to forthwith display for inspection all fish, birds and mammals then in his possession, and may arrest without a warrant a person refusing or failing to comply with such request. *Display of fish, etc., upon demand.*

Section 15. Any person violating any of the provisions of the preceding section shall be punished by a fine of not less than ten nor more than twenty-five dollars. *Penalty.*

Section 16. The director may destroy from time to time license books, stubs, licenses and license blanks, after the same have been properly audited by the state auditor, and such other documents as the director deems advisable, after the same have been noted on the official records. *Destruction of certain old documents.*

Section 17. The director, or the supervisor, or his or their agents when so authorized by him or them, may take fish, birds or mammals at any time or in any manner for purposes connected with propagation or scientific observation. *Director, etc., may take fish, etc., for certain purposes.*

Section 18. The director may investigate questions relating to fish, birds or mammals, and may, personally or by assistants, institute and conduct inquiries pertaining to such questions. *Investigation as to fish, etc.*

Section 19. The director may establish and maintain properties at such places within the commonwealth as he may select for the purpose of propagating and rearing fish, birds and mammals. *Establishment of properties for propagation of fish, etc.*

Section 19A. The director may occupy and control Mill pond, otherwise known as Gun Rock pond, at Weir Village, in Yarmouth, for the purpose of cultivating food fish for distribution within the commonwealth. Whoever, without the written consent of the director, fishes in said pond in any other manner than by angling, shall fór a first offence be punished by a fine of not less than fifty nor more than two hundred dollars, and for a subsequent offence by a fine of not less than one hundred nor more than two hundred dollars. *Control of Mill pond in town of Yarmouth.*

Section 20. Whoever without right enters in or upon any building or other structure or any area of land, flats or water, set apart and used by or under authority of the director or supervisor for conducting scientific experiments *Penalty for illegally entering buildings, etc., used in scientific investigation or for propagation.*

or investigations or for propagation, after the director or supervisor has caused printed notices of such occupation and use and the purposes thereof to be placed in a conspicuous position upon any such building or other structure or adjacent to any such area of land, flats or water, and whoever injures or defaces any such building or other structure or any notice posted as aforesaid, or injures or destroys any property used in such experiments or investigations or for such purposes, or otherwise interferes therewith, shall be punished by a fine of not less than fifty nor more than two hundred dollars or by imprisonment for not more than six months.

Discharge of
waste material
into certain
waters regu-
lated.

Section 21. If the director determines that the fisheries of any inland waters of the commonwealth, or if the commissioner and supervisor determine that any marine fisheries of the commonwealth, are of sufficient value to warrant the prohibition or regulation of the discharge or escape of sawdust, shavings, garbage, ashes, acids, oil, sewage, dyestuffs, or other waste material from any sawmill, manufacturing or mechanical plant, or dwelling house, stable or other building, which may, directly or indirectly, materially injure such fisheries, said director or commissioner and supervisor, as the case may be, shall by a written order sent by mail to or served upon the owner or tenant thereof prohibit or regulate the discharge or escape therefrom of any or all such injurious substances into such inland or coastal waters, as the case may be. Such order shall take effect in ten days after its date and may be revoked or modified by the officer or officers making it at any time. Before any such order is made such officer or officers shall, after reasonable notice to all parties in interest, give a public hearing in the county where the sawmill, manufacturing or mechanical plant, dwelling house, stable or other building to be affected by the order is located, at which hearing any person shall be heard. Upon petition of any party aggrieved by such order, filed within six months after its date, the superior court may, in equity, after such notice as it deems sufficient, hear all interested parties, and annul, alter or affirm the order. If such petition is filed by the party aggrieved within ten days after the date of said order, said order shall not take effect, unless such petition shall be dismissed, until altered or affirmed as aforesaid. Whoever, in violation of any order of the director, or of the commissioner and supervisor, of which he has had due notice hereunder and which has taken effect, or in violation of any order of said court made hereunder, discharges from such plant or building under his control any of the aforesaid materials, the discharge of which therefrom is forbidden by such order, or suffers or permits the same to be discharged or to escape from such plant or building, into any inland or coastal waters of the commonwealth, shall be punished by a fine of not less than fifty nor more than two hundred dollars.

Penalty.

Section 22. Except in case of emergency imperilling life or property or of unavoidable accident, whoever from any sources other than those designated in the preceding section puts, throws, discharges or suffers or permits to be discharged or to escape into any inland or coastal waters of the commonwealth, any oil, or any poisonous or other substance, whether simple, mixed or compound, which may directly or indirectly materially injure the fish, fish spawn or seed therein, or takes any such fish by such means, or whoever kills or destroys fish in such waters by the use of dynamite or other explosives, or takes any such fish by such means, or explodes dynamite or other explosive in such waters, shall be punished by a fine of not less than fifty nor more than five hundred dollars or by imprisonment for not more than one year. This section shall not apply to operations of the United States, or of the commonwealth or a political subdivision thereof, nor to operations authorized or permitted thereby, nor to the use of explosives for raising the body of a drowned person.

Penalty for poisoning, etc., fish.

Exceptions.

Section 23. Whoever, contrary to the provisions of either of the two preceding sections, himself, or by his agent or servant, does, or allows or suffers to be done, any act causing damage to the fisheries therein named shall be liable in tort, in twice the amount of damage thereby done, to the town where such damage occurs on account of any injury to the public fisheries within its limits, and to any person having fishery rights therein on account of any injury to his private fishery rights.

Action in tort for damage to fisheries.

Section 23A. The director, supervisor, wardens, deputies and members of the state police may seize and remove, summarily if need be, at the expense of the owner using and maintaining the same, all illegal obstructions, except dams, mills or machinery, to the passage of salt water fish coming into fresh water to spawn. The director may examine all dams or obstructions upon brooks, rivers and streams where the law requires fish ways to be maintained, or where in his judgment fish ways are needed, and he shall determine whether the fish ways, if any, are suitable and sufficient for the passage of such fish in such brooks, rivers and streams or whether a fish way is needed for the passage of such fish over such dam or obstruction; and shall prescribe by written order what changes or repairs, if any, shall be made therein, and where, how and when a new fish way shall be built, and at what times the same shall be kept open, and shall serve a copy of such order upon the owner of the dam or obstruction. A certificate of the director that service has been so made shall be sufficient proof thereof. The supreme judicial or superior court shall, on petition of the director, have jurisdiction in equity or otherwise to enforce any such order and to restrain any violation thereof.

Authority to remove illegal obstructions.

Section 23B. Any owner of such a dam or obstruction who refuses or neglects to keep open or maintain a fish

Penalty for refusal, etc., to keep open fish way.

way at the times prescribed by the director shall forfeit fifty dollars for each day of such refusal or neglect.

Director may at expense of owner, construct or repair a fish way.

Section 23C. If the director deems that a passage for fish should be provided or if he finds that there is no fish way or an insufficient fish way in or around a dam where a fish way is required by law to be maintained, he may enter with workmen and materials upon the premises of the person required to maintain a fish way there and may, at the expense of the commonwealth, if in his opinion the person required by law to construct or maintain such fish way is unable to afford such expense, otherwise at the expense of the owner of such dam, improve an existing fish way, or cause one to be constructed if none exists, and may, if necessary, take the land of any other person who is not obliged by law to maintain said fish way; and if a fish way has been constructed in accordance with this section, he shall not require the owner of the dam to alter such fish way within five years after its completion.

Damages for taking land, liability of commonwealth.

Section 23D. All damages caused by taking land under the preceding section shall, upon the application of either party, be recovered from the commonwealth under chapter seventy-nine. The amount so recovered shall be a charge against the person required by law to construct and maintain such fish way and shall be recovered in contract in the name of the commonwealth, with costs and with interest at the rate of twelve per cent per annum.

Rights of Riparian Proprietors.

Riparian proprietor, control of fisheries.

Section 24. A riparian proprietor of a non-navigable stream may, within the limits of his own premises, enclose the waters thereof for the artificial propagation, cultivation and maintenance of fish if he furnishes a suitable passage for migratory salt water fish naturally frequenting such waters to spawn.

Ownership of fish artificially propagated.

Section 25. Fish artificially propagated, cultivated or maintained, while within the waters enclosed as provided in the preceding section, shall be the property of the person so propagating, cultivating or maintaining them. Any person legally engaged in their propagation, culture and maintenance may take them in his own waters at pleasure, and may have them in his possession for purposes properly connected with said culture and maintenance, and may at all times sell them for these purposes, but shall not sell them for food if of a size, or at a season, prohibited by law or by any rule, regulation or by-law applicable thereto, nor shall he sell them for any other purpose so prohibited.

Penalty for fishing where fish are artificially propagated.

Section 26. Whoever, not being the employee or agent of, and engaged in the business of, the riparian proprietor of a non-navigable brook or stream, the waters of which are enclosed for the artificial propagation, cultivation and maintenance of fish under the provisions of section twenty-four, fishes in such waters so enclosed, without the written consent of such riparian proprietor, shall, in addition to the penalty provided in section eighty-seven of chapter one hundred and thirty, be punished by a fine of not less than ten nor more than twenty-five dollars for each fish, or each provision, rule or regulation, in respect to which such violation occurs.

Section 27. The riparian proprietor on a non-navigable tidal stream, enclosed or unenclosed, in which fish are lawfully propagated, cultivated or maintained, shall have the control of the fishery thereof within his own premises and opposite thereto to the middle of the stream, and a riparian proprietor at the mouth of such stream shall also have control of the fishery thereof beyond and around the mouth of the stream so far as the tide ebbs, if it does not ebb more than eighty rods; and whoever fishes within such limits without permission of the owner shall be punished as provided in section twenty-six. No such proprietor shall obstruct, or permit the obstruction of, a suitable passage for salt water migratory fish through so much of such stream as is within his control. *Owners of certain streams to control fisheries. Obstruction of passage for salt water fish prohibited.*

Section 28. For the purposes of this chapter and of chapters one hundred and thirty and one hundred and thirty-one, no tidal stream shall be considered navigable above the point where, on the average throughout the year, it has a channel less than forty feet wide and four feet deep during the three hours nearest the hour of high tide. *Navigable stream defined.*

Section 29. Upon the application of any party in interest, of the aldermen of a city, of the selectmen of a town or of the supervisor, the department of public works may from time to time, for the purposes of this chapter and said chapters one hundred and thirty and one hundred and thirty-one, arbitrarily fix and define the tidal bounds and mouths of streams and ordinary or mean high water mark and mean and extreme low water marks, and alter or amend the same, and thereupon said department shall file a plan, showing the location of the same, with the registry of deeds for the county or registry district, and with the clerk of the city or town, in which the land lies. *Department of public works to define tidal bounds, etc., of streams.*

Miscellaneous Provisions.

Section 30. Actions and prosecutions under the laws relative to fish, birds and mammals shall, unless otherwise expressly provided, be commenced within one year after the time when the cause of action accrued or the offence was committed. *Limitation of actions.*

Section 31. All fines, penalties and forfeitures recovered in prosecutions under the laws relative to birds, fish and mammals, as defined in section one, shall be equally divided between the county where such prosecution is made and the town where the offence is committed; provided, that if the prosecuting officer is a warden or state police officer receiving compensation from the commonwealth, such fines, penalties and forfeitures shall be paid to the commonwealth. *Disposition of fines and penalties.*

Section 32. All birds, fish and mammals, as so defined, which are unlawfully taken, held, possessed or dealt with contrary to this chapter or chapters one hundred and thirty or one hundred and thirty-one, may, in addition to any or all of the penalties contained therein be seized, libelled in accordance with the provisions of chapter two hundred and fifty-seven, and forfeited to the commonwealth.

Whenever seizure and confiscation or forfeiture is provided by any section, unless another procedure is therein indicated, such confiscation or forfeiture shall be according to the provisions of said chapter two hundred and fifty-seven, the net proceeds thereof to be divided as is provided in the preceding section.

Section 33. This chapter and chapters one hundred and thirty and one hundred and thirty-one shall not be deemed to affect any provisions or penalties contained, or any privileges granted, in any special statute relating to fisheries in any particular place.

Section 34. Any occupation under this chapter or chapter one hundred and thirty or chapter one hundred and thirty-one of tide waters, or great ponds containing ten acres or more, or any work done therein, shall be subject to the approval of the department of public works under chapter ninety-one, and to the provisions of that chapter.

SECTION 2. Chapter one hundred and thirty of the General Laws, as amended, is hereby further amended by striking out said chapter and inserting in place thereof the following: —

CHAPTER 130.

MARINE FISH AND FISHERIES, INCLUDING CRUSTACEA AND SHELLFISH.

General Provisions.

Section 1. The mayor of a city or the selectmen of a town may designate as shellfish constables one or more constables in his or their city or town, however elected or appointed, for the detection and prosecution of violations of the laws of the commonwealth, or local ordinances, rules or regulations, relative to shellfish or shell fisheries.

Section 2. The director, supervisor, any coastal warden or deputy, or any shellfish constable may, without a warrant, search any boat, vessel, car, motor vehicle as defined in section one of chapter ninety, or other vehicle in which he has reasonable cause to believe and does believe that fish frequenting the coastal waters taken, held, kept, possessed, transported or held for transportation or sale in violation of law may be found, and seize any such fish there found, and seize and confiscate the said vehicle and all devices employed in committing the illegal act or acts and hold the same for forfeiture according to law. Any fish so seized may be libelled, or sold and the net proceeds libelled, in accordance with section thirty-two of chapter one hundred and twenty-nine A.

Section 3. The supervisor shall devise a system of statistical information useful to the marine fish industries of the commonwealth and shall compile information obtained thereunder. Upon the request of the supervisor the commissioner may require for such purposes the attendance of witnesses and the production of books and documents, and the commissioner may examine witnesses on oath; and such witnesses shall be examined in the same manner and paid the same fees as in civil actions in the superior court. The supervisor shall prepare from time to time and distribute bulletins and reports embodying statistical and other information relative to marine fisheries and the state secretary shall cause to be printed for distribution to such industries such numbers of such bulletins and reports as the commission on administration and finance may approve. The supervisor may also conduct certain biological research for the purpose of conserving and increasing the supply of fish in the coastal waters. He shall also assist and co-operate with local authorities in the promulgation of rules and regulations for the purpose of better control and conservation of such fish. *Statistical information relative to marine fish, collection of.*

Duties of supervisor. Reports.

Section 4. The director may occupy, use and control not exceeding six ponds, other than great ponds, and estuaries, creeks or other arms of the sea, within the commonwealth, and the necessary land thereto adjoining, for the scientific investigation of the habits, propagation and distribution of fish frequenting the coastal waters, if such occupation and use do not impair the private rights of any person or materially obstruct any navigable waters. Notice of such occupation and use and the purpose thereof shall be conspicuously posted by the director at the nearest points to said ponds and estuaries, creeks or other arms of the sea, and shall be recorded in the registry of deeds in the county or district where they are situated. *Control of certain ponds, etc., for scientific investigation.*

Whoever, after the posting and recording of such notice, takes any fish from any pond or estuary, creek or other arm of the sea occupied as aforesaid shall be punished by a fine of not less than ten nor more than one hundred dollars, or by imprisonment for not less than one nor more than three months. *Penalty.*

Section 5. The entrance or discharge into or on any of the tidal waters or flats of the commonwealth, or the tributaries of such waters, of sewage or any other substance which might be injurious to the public health or might tend to contaminate any shellfish areas or shellfish therein, which may be determined by the supervisor and the commissioner of public health to be of commercial value, where no such entrance or discharge existed on July first, nineteen hundred and thirty-three, is hereby prohibited; *Pollution of tide waters or flats prohibited.*

provided, that this section shall not be deemed to interfere with the exercise of any right of drainage existing on
said date, or with any drainage thereafter approved by
the department of public health.

Enforcement
of preceding
section.

Section 5A. The supreme judicial court or any justice
thereof, and the superior court or any justice thereof,
shall have jurisdiction in equity to enforce the preceding
section. Proceedings to enforce the same may be instituted and prosecuted by the attorney general at the request of the commissioner of public health or of the commissioner of conservation.

Penalty
for polluting
certain waters.

Section 5B. Whoever, contrary to section five, permits
the entrance or discharge into or on any part of said waters
or flats, or the tributaries of such waters, of sewage or any
other substance injurious to the public health or tending
to contaminate any shellfish area or shellfish therein shall
be punished by a fine of not more than five hundred dollars
and shall be liable in tort, in twice the amount of damage
thereby done, to the city or town where such damage
occurs on account of any injury to the public fisheries
within its limits, and to the owners or lessees of any private
rights therein on account of any injury to their private
fishery rights.

Penalty for
taking fish
without the
common-
wealth.

Section 6. Whoever, other than a common carrier,
carries out of the commonwealth in any vessel or smack
owned without the commonwealth any fish, except oysters,
taken within the coastal waters, and whoever in any such
vessel or smack takes any fish within the coastal waters for
the purpose of carrying them out of the commonwealth,
shall be punished by a fine of fifty dollars, and all fish so
taken or carried shall be forfeited to the commonwealth.

Selectmen,
etc., duty to
enforce certain
sections.

Section 6A. Aldermen, selectmen, police officers and
constables shall cause the provisions of sections thirteen,
fourteen and twenty-five to be enforced in their respective
cities and towns.

Pollock and Mackerel.

Seining of
pollock and
spike
mackerel.

Penalty.

Section 7. No person shall seine in the harbors and
rivers of the commonwealth pollock weighing less than
three quarters of a pound, or spike mackerel weighing less
than one quarter of a pound. Violation of any provision
of this section shall be punished by a fine of not less than
twenty-five nor more than fifty dollars, or by imprisonment for not less than one nor more than two months,
or both.

Herring, Alewives and Shad.

Towns may
open ditches,
etc., to create
herring
fisheries.

Section 8. A town may open ditches, sluiceways or
canals into any pond within its limits for the introduction
and propagation in such pond or in any part thereof of
herring, alewives or other swimming marine food fish, and
for the creation of fisheries for the same; and may take
by eminent domain under chapter seventy-nine such land,

waters and easements within its limits as may be necessary for such ditches, sluiceways and canals and for the construction and proper operation and use of such fishery and approaches thereto.

Section 9. A town creating such fishery shall own it, may make regulations concerning it, and may lease it for terms of not more than five years, on conditions agreed upon. A town may lease for like periods, and on like conditions, any such fishery owned by it or any public fishery of swimming marine food fish regulated and controlled by it. _{Towns shall own such fisheries.}

Section 10. Whoever takes, kills or hauls on shore any herring, alewives or other swimming marine food fish in a fishery created by a town, without its permission or that of its lessees, or in a fishery created by a corporation, without the permission of such corporation, or in a public fishery regulated and controlled by a town, contrary to its regulations, shall be punished by a fine of not less than five nor more than fifty dollars. Prosecutions under this section shall be commenced within thirty days after the commission of the offence.

Section 11. The three preceding sections shall not impair the rights of any person under any law passed before April twenty-fifth, eighteen hundred and sixty-six, or under any contract existing on said date, or authorize a town to enter upon or build canals or sluiceways into a pond which is private property.

Section 12. Whoever on Sunday, Tuesday or Thursday takes shad or alewives, except in the Connecticut, Taunton Great, Nemasket and Merrimack rivers and their tributaries, in any other manner than by angling, and whoever between June fifteenth and March first takes shad, except in the Connecticut and Merrimack rivers, or alewives, shall, in addition to the penalty provided in section eighty-seven, forfeit for each shad so taken five dollars, and for each alewife so taken twenty-five cents.

Smelt.

Section 13. Whoever sells or offers or exposes for sale or has in his possession a smelt taken in the commonwealth between March fifteenth and June first shall forfeit one dollar for every such smelt; and the possession of a smelt between said dates shall be prima facie evidence of violation of this section.

Section 14. Except as provided in section eighteen and in chapter three hundred and six of the acts of nineteen hundred and eleven, whoever takes a smelt in any other manner than by angling shall, in addition to the penalty provided in section eighty-seven, forfeit one dollar for each smelt so taken.

Section 15. Sections thirteen and fourteen shall not apply in the counties of Bristol, Barnstable, Nantucket and Dukes county to smelt taken in a seine or net during the time and in the manner in which fishing is allowed for perch, herring or alewives, nor to smelt lawfully taken under said chapter three hundred and six.

Use of net, seine, etc., for catching smelts in Boston harbor, etc., prohibited.

Section 16. Except as provided in said chapter three hundred and six, no person shall set, draw, use or attempt to set, draw or use any net, seine, trap or device for catching smelt, other than a naturally or artificially baited hook, in the waters of Boston harbor, Hingham harbor, Weir river, Weymouth Fore river, Weymouth Back river, Neponset river, Charles river, Mystic river, or in any cove, bay, inlet or tributary thereof; but this section shall not prohibit the use of traps for catching lobsters.

Possession of net, etc., prima facie evidence.

Section 17. Possession of any net, seine, trap or device for catching fish, other than a naturally or artificially baited hook, in or upon the harbors, rivers or tributaries referred to in the preceding section, or on the banks of the same, if adapted to and apparently intended for the present catching of smelt, shall be prima facie evidence of a violation of the provisions of said section, and the possession in or upon said harbors, rivers or tributaries, or on the banks of the same, of any fresh smelt, between sunset and sunrise, or under other circumstances reasonably indicating the catching of the same otherwise than by a naturally or artificially baited hook, shall be prima facie evidence that said smelt were caught contrary to such provisions by the person in whose possession they are found.

Penalties.

Section 18. Whoever violates any provision of section sixteen, or buys, receives or transports smelt, knowing or having reasonable cause to believe that the same have been taken contrary to any provision of said section, shall, in addition to the penalty provided in section eighty-seven, be punished for a first offence, by a fine of not less than fifty nor more than two hundred dollars or by imprisonment for not less than six nor more than twelve months, or both, and for a subsequent offence by both said fine and imprisonment.

Searches, seizure and libelling of property.

Section 19. The director, supervisor, any coastal warden or deputy, any member of the state police, any sheriff, deputy sheriff, or any police officer or constable within his jurisdiction, may search for and seize, without a warrant, any smelt which he has reason to suspect were taken contrary to any provision of section sixteen, and the net, seine, trap or other device, and the vessel, boat, vehicle, craft, and its tackle, apparel, furniture and implements, or other apparatus used in connection with such receiving, buying, transporting or other violation of said section, and the cask, barrel or other vessel or wrapper containing said smelts, which property shall be forfeited.

Regulation of Fish Weirs, Nets, Seines, Trawls and Traps.

Town officers may authorize fish weirs, etc.

Section 20. The aldermen of a city or the selectmen of a town lying upon tide water may, in writing, authorize any person to construct weirs, pound nets or fish traps in tide water in locations where no harbor lines exist and also in locations beyond established harbor lines, within the limits of such city or town, for a term not exceeding five years, upon such conditions and subject to such regulations as the aldermen or the selectmen may, in their discretion, impose; but no authority or license so given shall be valid unless approved in writing by the department of public works, upon such terms and subject to such conditions as it may, in its discretion, impose.

Section 21. Whoever wilfully destroys or injures any such weir, pound net or fish trap, or takes fish therefrom without the consent of the owner, shall forfeit not more than twenty dollars to the use of the owner. Such forfeiture shall be in addition to any civil liability for damages. Penalty for injuring such fish weirs.

Section 22. Whoever constructs or maintains a weir, pound net or fish trap in tide water, without the authority mentioned in section twenty and, if from an island in tide water, without such authority from the aldermen of every city and the selectmen of every town which is distant not over two miles from said island, shall forfeit ten dollars for each day he maintains such weir, pound net or fish trap; and he may be enjoined therefrom. Penalty for constructing unauthorized fish weirs.

Section 23. Whoever takes any fish or lobster from a trap, trawl or seine set for catching fish or lobsters, without the consent of the owner thereof, and whoever wilfully molests or interferes with such trap, trawl or seine, shall be punished by a fine of not less than twenty nor more than fifty dollars or by imprisonment for two months, or both. Penalty for taking fish, etc., from traps, etc.

Annual Reports of Catches.

Section 24. The owner of every pound net, weir, fyke net or similar contrivance, fishing pier, seine, drag or gill net, lobster pot or trap used in any of the coastal waters for fishing purposes, and every licensee under section thirty-three, shall annually, on or before October twentieth, make a written report, on oath, to the supervisor, of the number of pounds and the value of each kind of edible fish, other than lobsters, caught by his pound net, weir, fyke net or similar contrivance, pier, seine, drag or gill net, and the number and value of lobsters taken by him in pots or traps, or the number and value of lobsters and crabs, or crabs, caught or taken by him from certain waters, as the case may be, during the year last preceding the date of said report, and the number and value of the devices, if any, used in such catching or taking, and the number of persons, if any, employed therein; and for such purpose the supervisor shall annually, on or before March fifteenth, provide him, upon his application, with suitable blank forms for such reports, so arranged that each month's catch may be separately recorded thereon; and, in filling out such reports, such owner shall give the results of each month's fishing, so far as practicable. Such owner shall Annual reports of catches.

apply to the supervisor for such blank forms. The owner of any cars or other contrivances used for keeping lobsters shall have his name and residence legibly marked thereon. Any licensee under said section thirty-three refusing, or knowingly or wilfully neglecting, to make the report required hereby shall not receive a new license until such report is made. Whoever knowingly and wilfully violates any provision of this section shall be punished by a fine of not less than ten nor more than one hundred dollars.

Lobsters and Crabs.

Penalty for taking female lobsters.

Section 25. Whoever takes, sells or has in possession any female lobster bearing eggs shall be punished by a fine of not less than ten nor more than one hundred dollars, or by imprisonment for not less than one nor more than three months; but a person who takes any such lobster and immediately returns it alive to the waters from which it was taken shall not be subject to such penalty. This section shall not apply to lobsters spawning in lobster cars or pounds if they are immediately liberated alive in the coastal waters, nor to the taking, sale or possession of lobsters as provided in the following section.

Supervisor to purchase lobsters with eggs attached, caught along shores of commonwealth.

Section 26. The supervisor shall, except as hereinafter provided, purchase to the extent of the money provided therefor, and at a rate not above the wholesale market price of other lobsters, lobsters with eggs attached taken along the shores of the commonwealth. Whoever takes or handles any such lobsters with eggs attached which are not marked as hereinafter provided may safely store the same in lobster cars or sections of cars used for such purpose only, and shall keep them separate from other lobsters until such time as the supervisor or his agents gather and pay for the same. The supervisor or his agents shall mark each lobster purchased hereunder by punching a hole in any except the middle flipper of its tail, and shall liberate said lobster in the vicinity of the place of purchase. The commissioner in his annual budget estimates, filed pursuant to section three of chapter twenty-nine, shall include a statement of appropriation or appropriations recommended by him for the purpose of carrying out the provisions of this section.

Certain marked lobsters not to be taken.

Penalty.

Section 27. Any lobster marked by a hole in any flipper of its tail shall be immediately returned alive to the waters from which it was taken and shall not be sold or purchased by any person. Any person having in possession any lobster so marked, except for the purposes of this or the preceding section, or any lobster mutilated in such manner as to hide or obliterate the said mark, shall be punished by a fine of not less than fifty nor more than two hundred dollars.

Penalty for sale of un-cooked and dead lobsters.

Section 28. Whoever cooks, buys, sells, offers or exposes for sale, gives away, or knowingly delivers, transports, ships, or receives for food purposes any lobster, or any part thereof, which is uncooked and dead, shall be punished by a fine of not less than fifty nor more than two hundred dollars, or by imprisonment for not less than ten nor more than sixty days, or both.

Section 29. No person shall buy, sell, expose for sale, give away, deliver, transport, ship, carry or have in his possession any lobster meat after the same has been taken from the shell, except as hereinafter provided. The foregoing shall not apply to lobster meat in the possession of a common carrier for transportation and which is marked as provided in section thirty-seven, or of which it has no notice; nor to canned lobster meat from lobsters of the length required by section thirty-one, when certified to the satisfaction of the supervisor to be such, and when certified, to the satisfaction of the department of public health, by the board of health of the city or town where canned, to have been in suitable condition for human consumption when canned, and to have been canned under healthful conditions, and so as to insure the continuance, until use, of such condition; nor to such meat sold for food by a licensed victualler; nor to such meat removed from the shell on the premises where it is to be eaten; nor to such meat removed from the shell by a wholesale or retail dealer in lobsters at his regular place of business therefor; provided, that said dealer has a written permit from the supervisor for the sale and delivery of such lobster meat; and provided, further, that such lobster meat is so removed or sold under such conditions and regulations as the supervisor may prescribe, and that the premises where the meat is so removed or sold are at all reasonable times open to the inspection of the director, supervisor, wardens and deputies. Such a permit may be granted for any period not exceeding one year upon written application to the supervisor and the payment of a fee of ten dollars, and may be revoked by the supervisor for the violation by the holder thereof of any provision of chapter one hundred and twenty-nine A or of this chapter or of sections sixty-six to eighty-eight A, inclusive, of chapter ninety-four.

Section 30. Any lobster meat unlawfully sold, given away, shipped, bought or transported shall be liable to seizure and may be confiscated.

Section 31. Whoever sells or offers for sale, or has in possession for a period longer than is necessary for measuring or for any other purpose than legally disposing of the same, a lobster measuring less than three and one sixteenth inches in length, alive or dead, cooked or uncooked, measured from the rear of the eye socket along a line parallel to the center line of the body shell to the rear end of the body shell, shall be punished by a fine of not less than five nor more than ten dollars for every such lobster, and such lobster shall be seized and forfeited, and shall be disposed of by the supervisor to the best interest of the commonwealth; and in all prosecutions under this section any

Sale of lobster meat regulated.

Lobster meat unlawfully sold, etc., may be confiscated.

Penalty for selling, etc., small lobsters.

mutilation of any lobster which affects its measurement as
aforesaid shall be ˚prima facie evidence that the lobster
was or is less than the required length.   This section shall
not apply to common carriers having lobsters in possession
for the purpose of transportation.   The commissioner of
public safety, upon written request of the commissioner,
may detail one or more of the state police to enforce this
section.

Protection of
lobster
industry.

Section 32.   No person, either as principal, agent or
employee, shall at any time catch lobsters in, or take them
from, any waters within the jurisdiction of the commonwealth, or place, set, keep, maintain, supervise, lift, raise
or draw in or from the said waters, or cause to be placed,
set, kept, maintained, supervised, lifted, raised or drawn in
or from the said waters, any pot, trap or other contrivance
designed for, or adapted to, the taking of lobsters, unless
licensed so to do as provided in the following section.   In
Dukes county no such lobster pot, trap or other contrivance
shall be set, kept or maintained on a trawl or runner or
otherwise than separately and plainly buoyed.

Licenses.

Section 33.   The clerk of any town in the county of
Essex, Middlesex, Suffolk, Norfolk, Plymouth, Barnstable,
Bristol, Dukes or Nantucket, situated on the shores of the
commonwealth, shall grant licenses in the form prescribed
by the supervisor, and upon a blank furnished, by him, to
catch or take both lobsters and crabs, or to catch or take
crabs only, from the coastal waters within the county
where the town lies; provided, that any such license granted
by the clerk of any town in Plymouth or Norfolk county
shall authorize such catching or taking from the coastal
waters within both of said counties.   Except as hereinafter
provided, such licenses to catch or take both lobsters and
crabs shall be granted only to individuals who are citizens
of the commonwealth and who have resided therein for at
least one year next preceding the date of the same.   The
clerk of any such town may grant such a license to catch or
take both lobsters and crabs to any individual who is an
alien and who resides in the county where the town lies;
provided, that such alien has resided in said county, and
has been actually engaged in lobster fishing in the coastal
waters within any of the aforesaid counties, for five years
next preceding December first, nineteen hundred and
twenty; and may grant such a license to catch or take
crabs only to any citizen of the commonwealth, or to any
alien residing in the commonwealth who, prior to June first,
nineteen hundred and thirty, has filed his declaration of
intention to become a citizen of the United States; provided, that if any such alien shall not become a citizen of
the United States within the term of five years and ninety
days next subsequent to such filing he shall not thereafter
be entitled to receive or act under a license issued hereunder.   A non-resident citizen of the United States temporarily residing in any town granting licenses hereunder

may, during June, July, August and September in each
year, upon payment of the fee required by this section,
procure from the clerk of such town a license to take lobsters for consumption by the licensee and his family only,
which such clerk is hereby authorized to issue. Licenses
hereunder, except those granted to non-residents, shall expire on December thirty-first next succeeding the granting
of the same unless sooner made void as provided in the
following section. The town clerk granting a license hereunder shall collect therefor a fee of five dollars, which, less
twenty-five cents to be retained by him, shall be forwarded
to the supervisor on the first Monday of the following
month, together with a description of the licensee and of
his buoys, if any, and such other information as may be
required by the supervisor. Such descriptions and information shall be given upon coupons to be provided by the
supervisor therefor. All books of forms furnished to town
clerks under this section shall be returned to the supervisor on January first of each year. Each applicant for a
license shall state the color scheme or other special markings
of the buoys, if any, to be used by him, which shall be set
forth in his license, and all buoys used by him shall be
marked accordingly, and all buoys, pots and traps used by
him shall be marked with the licensee's initials or name,
which shall be branded or cut into the surface thereof. A
licensee under this section shall at all times, while acting
in pursuance of his license, exhibit it upon the demand of
any officer qualified to serve criminal process, and upon
failure so to do shall be punished by a fine of five dollars.

Section 33A. The supervisor shall state in his annual
report the number of licenses granted under the preceding
section. *Report of supervisor.*

Section 34. Every license issued under section thirty-
three held by any person convicted of a violation of any
provision of sections twenty-five to forty-one, inclusive,
of this chapter or of sections sixty-six to eighty-eight A,
inclusive, of chapter ninety-four, or of similar provisions of
earlier laws, shall be void, if such person has within three
years prior to such conviction been convicted of a violation of the same or any other provision of this chapter or
of said sections sixty-six to eighty-eight A, inclusive, or of
similar provisions of earlier laws, and shall immediately be
surrendered to the officer securing such conviction, or to
any other officer authorized to enforce any of the provisions
of this chapter or of said sections sixty-six to eighty-eight A,
inclusive, who shall forthwith forward such license to the
supervisor. No license under the preceding section shall
be issued to any person within the period of one year immediately following the date of his second or subsequent
conviction as aforesaid, and any license so issued shall be
void and shall be surrendered upon demand of any officer
authorized to enforce this chapter or said sections sixty-six
to eighty-eight A, inclusive; provided, that a conviction *Revocation of license.*

of having short lobsters in possession shall not be counted as such second or subsequent conviction under this section if less than five per cent in count of the lobsters in possession were short lobsters.

Hours of drawing lobster pots. *Section 35.* No person shall tend, lift, raise or draw a lobster or crab pot or trap, or take lobsters or crabs from such a pot or trap, except during the period from one half hour before sunrise until one half hour after sunset, except that traps may be taken up by the owner or by his employee or agent, if licensed under section thirty-three, at any time when they are endangered by storms, and except that the supervisor, a coastal warden or deputy may at any time lift, raise or draw such pot or trap and its contents.

Penalty. *Section 36.* Violation of any provision of section thirty-two or section thirty-five shall be punished by a fine of not less than twenty-five nor more than one hundred dollars.

Transportation of lobsters regulated. *Section 37.* All barrels, boxes or other containers containing lobsters, or lobster meat after the same has been taken from the shell, shall, before being delivered to any carrier, be marked by the shipper in a plain and legible manner on the outside thereof "LOBSTERS", or "LOBSTER MEAT", as the case may be, in capital letters at least one inch in length, together with the full name and address of the shipper, and, in the case of such lobster meat, also with the words "removed under permit No.   ", followed by the number of the permit under which the same was taken from the shell; and, unless in barrels, boxes or other containers so marked, no lobster or lobster meat shall be transported. Any such barrels, boxes or other containers delivered to or transported by any carrier without being marked as above required, and the lobsters or lobster meat therein, shall be seized and forfeited. Violation of any provision of this section shall be punished by a fine of not less than ten nor more than fifty dollars. This section and section thirty-nine shall not apply to lobsters or lobster meat passing through the commonwealth under authority of the laws of the United States.

Disposition of lobster meat, etc., seized. *Section 38.* In case of seizure by any duly authorized officer of any lobsters or lobster meat contained in any barrel, box or other container which is not marked as provided in the preceding section, or of any lobster measuring less than the length prescribed by section thirty-one, such lobsters as are alive and measure less than such prescribed length shall be liberated, and all other such lobsters and all such lobster meat found in such barrel, box or other container shall be held and disposed of as provided in section forty.

Penalty for transporting illegally taken lobsters, etc. *Section 39.* Any carrier who knowingly receives or carries from place to place any lobster or lobster meat in barrels, boxes or other containers not marked as provided in section thirty-seven shall be punished by a fine of not more than fifty dollars.

Forfeiture of lobsters, etc., illegally taken. *Section 40.* When any lobster or lobster meat is seized for the violation of any provision of section thirty-seven, the officer making the seizure shall immediately notify the shipper thereof, if known, and shall proceed to enforce, in accordance with chapter two hundred and fifty-seven, the forfeiture of such lobsters as he is not required to liberate, or of such lobster meat. He shall cause the appraisal required by section thirteen of said chapter to be made within twenty-four hours after the time of such seizure, and after said appraisal may sell the said lobsters or lobster meat at such time and in such manner as he deems proper. He shall pay the proceeds thereof into the court before which the libel for forfeiture is pending, and the court may decree a forfeiture of said proceeds, or payment thereof to a claimant, or other appropriate disposition thereof.

Section 41. No person, either as principal, agent or employee, shall at any time catch crabs in, or take them from, the coastal waters, or place, set, keep, maintain, supervise, lift, raise or draw in or from the said waters, or cause to be placed, set, kept, maintained, supervised, lifted, raised or drawn in or from the said waters, any pot, trap or other contrivance designed for, or adapted to, the taking of crabs, unless licensed so to do as provided in section thirty-three. Violation of any provision of this section shall be punished by a fine of not less than ten nor more than twenty-five dollars. Nothing in this section or said section thirty-three shall be construed to prohibit or regulate the taking of crabs solely for bait purposes, or for family use.

Taking of crabs regulated.

Certain Shellfish and Eels.

Section 42. No person shall take from the flats or coastal waters of the commonwealth scallops other than adult scallops, or sell or offer for sale or have in possession such scallops so taken. For the purposes of this section an adult scallop shall be a scallop with a well-defined raised annual growth line. Scallops taken from the tide waters of the commonwealth shall be culled when taken, and all scallops other than adult scallops shall immediately be returned alive to tide water which is at least three feet deep at mean low water; but it shall not be unlawful to sell or have in possession scallops other than adult scallops unavoidably left in the catch after it has been culled, to the amount of not more than five per cent of the total catch remaining. All scallops taken in accordance with this section shall be taken ashore in the shell. This and the following section shall not apply to seed and adult scallops carried by storm and tide from the natural beds and deposited on beaches and flats where, in the opinion of the supervisor, they cannot survive, but the taking and sale of the said seed and adult scallops may be authorized by him at any season of the year, subject to sections forty-seven, forty-eight, fifty-one, fifty-three to fifty-five, inclusive, fifty-seven and sixty-three. The supervisor shall prescribe rules and regulations governing the taking and

Taking of scallops regulated.

sale of said seed and adult scallops by special permits or otherwise, to prevent the sale of seed scallops at any time, or the sale of adult scallops between April first and October first, except as authorized herein.

Close season for taking scallops.

Section 43. Except as provided in sections forty-two and forty-five, no person shall take scallops between April first and October first from the flats or coastal waters of the commonwealth, or buy or sell or have in possession scallops so taken; but this section shall not apply to the taking of adult scallops for bait in the coastal waters adjacent to the town of Nantucket from April first to May fifteenth, inclusive.

Number of scallops to be taken, regulated.

Section 44. Except as provided in section forty-two, no person shall take more than ten bushels of scallops, including shells, in one day.

Supervisor may modify close season.

Section 45. The provisions of the two preceding sections in respect to the open and close season, and in respect to the number of scallops that may be taken, may be temporarily modified if, on petition of the aldermen or selectmen to the supervisor, the supervisor, after investigation, determines that, owing to unusual circumstances, such modification is expedient. In that case, in his discretion, he may authorize, for a prescribed period, the aldermen or selectmen to issue permits to inhabitants of their respective cities or towns to take scallops in such quantities and at such times as he deems expedient.

Penalty.

Section 46. Whoever violates any provision of the four preceding sections shall be punished by a fine of not more than twenty-five dollars. Possession of scallops, other than adult scallops, except as otherwise provided in section forty-two, shall be prima facie evidence that such scallops were unlawfully taken.

Dredging; limit on scallops to be taken.

Section 47. No person shall take by dredging scallops exceeding in quantity one and one half bushels, including shells, in any one week from the coastal waters adjoining any city or town, without first obtaining a written permit specifically authorizing the same from the aldermen or selectmen thereof.

Taking of eels and shellfish regulated.

Section 48. Except as provided in sections forty-two to forty-six, inclusive, and except in the case of shellfish on private grants licensed under section fifty-seven, or shellfish on areas closed for municipal cultivation under section fifty-five, and except that the private rights of any person shall not be impaired thereby, the aldermen or the selectmen, if so instructed by their respective cities or towns, in addition to any action authorized by section fifty-one, in their discretion may from time to time control, regulate or prohibit the taking of eels and any or all kinds of shellfish and seaworms within such cities and towns. For the purpose of such control, regulation or prohibition the aldermen or the selectmen may, from time to time, without other or special authority therefor, make any regulations not contrary to law in regard to said fisheries that they deem ex-

Local regulations.

pedient, including the times, places, methods, purposes, uses, sizes, quantities or any other particulars of such taking, and may grant permits, subject to the exceptions hereinabove mentioned and subject also to any such regulations, then or thereafter in force, for the taking of eels and such shellfish and seaworms within such cities and towns. Any such instructions hereunder shall continue in force until subsequent action of such city or town shall alter, amend, rescind or repeal the same. Any regulations made under any such instruction shall continue in force, as far as such instruction shall continue to authorize the same, until the aldermen or selectmen of said city or town shall alter, amend, rescind or repeal the same.

Any regulations made hereunder shall state when the *Publication of* same shall take effect, and shall be published by posting a *regulations,* copy of the same in the office of the aldermen or selectmen *etc.* making the same, and in the office of the city or town clerk, and in three or more public places in said city or town, or by publishing the same once in a newspaper, if any, published in said city or town, twenty-four hours at least before the time set for the same to take effect. The records of the aldermen or selectmen, as to the contents of the regulations, and the method and time of publication thereof, or a copy thereof attested by their secretary, shall be prima facie evidence of such facts therein stated. The records of the city or town as to the instructions to the aldermen or selectmen, or a copy thereof attested by the city or town clerk, shall be prima facie evidence of such instructions.

Section 49. All permits issued under section forty- *Permits.* eight or section fifty-one shall be issued in the name of the body authorizing the issuing of the same; but, under a vote of such body, any such permit shall be valid if issued bearing the signature of any one member thereof, or of the city or town clerk. A record of the name, residence and address of all persons to whom such permits are issued, with any special details relating to such permits, shall be entered by the officers issuing the same in a book kept in their office for that purpose.

Section 50. Any inhabitant of the commonwealth who *Holders of* holds a permit issued under section forty-eight by the alder- *permits,* men or selectmen of the city or town from the waters of *limit of catch* which the fish therein referred to are to be taken, and any *etc.* native Indian without a permit, may, subject to the exceptions mentioned in said section forty-eight and to any regulations made under said section, and to all other provisions of law, take for his own family use, from the waters of any city or town, eels, soft-shelled clams, quahaugs, razor fish, and, from October first to the following April first, both dates inclusive, adult scallops, but not exceeding one half bushel of quahaugs and of soft-shelled clams, including shells, in any one day, or one bushel of each, including shells, in any one week, and not exceeding one and one half bushels of adult scallops, including shells, in any one week, and, for bait, from the waters of his own city or town any of such shellfish, but as to scallops only from October first to April first; provided, that nothing in this section shall be construed to allow the taking of any shellfish of a size prohibited by law, or from an area used for municipal cultivation under section fifty-five during the period of such use or within two years thereafter.

Penalty for illegal taking of shellfish, etc. *Section 51.* Whoever takes any shellfish or seaworms from their beds, or destroys them or wilfully obstructs their growth therein, except upon a private grant by authority of the licensee or transferee thereof, and except as is otherwise provided by law, or whoever takes shellfish from or disturbs them in areas closed under section fifty-five, shall be punished by a fine of not less than five nor more than twenty dollars for every bushel of such shellfish, including the shells, or for every hundred seaworms; but the aldermen of a city or the selectmen of a town may, in addition to any action authorized by section forty-eight, but subject to the exceptions set forth therein, at any time give a written permit to any person to take such shellfish and seaworms from their beds in such city or town, prescribing the times, places, methods, purposes, sizes, quantities, kinds or any other particulars of such taking; provided, that nothing in this section shall be construed to authorize any taking otherwise prohibited by law. Every inhabitant of such city or town may, without such permit, take from the waters, flats or creeks therein for the use of his family oysters not exceeding in any week one bushel, including the shells.

Penalty for illegal taking of eels. Whoever takes any eels without a permit issued as provided in this chapter, or except as is otherwise provided by law, shall be punished by a fine of not less than ten nor more than fifty dollars. This paragraph shall not affect section one of chapter two hundred and fifty-five of the acts of eighteen hundred and ninety-three.

Taking of small quahaugs or soft-shelled clams prohibited. *Section 52.* Whoever takes or has in possession quahaugs or soft-shelled clams less than two inches in longest diameter to the amount of more than five per cent of any batch shall be punished by a fine of not less than three nor more than fifty dollars; provided, that it shall not be unlawful to take such quahaugs or soft-shelled clams or have the same in possession under authority of a permit therefor, which the supervisor is hereby authorized to grant, for replanting for seed purposes in waters or flats within the commonwealth.

Permits for taking shellfish not to be issued to aliens. *Section 53.* No permit for the taking of shellfish for commercial purposes shall be issued to an unnaturalized foreign born person unless he has been a resident of the county wherein the city or town to the officials of which he applies for a permit is situated for at least five years next preceding the date of his application therefor, or has taken shellfish as an article of commerce for such period. Exception. This section shall not prohibit any such person from taking for his own family use the shellfish allowed for such use to all inhabitants of the commonwealth under and in accordance with section fifty.

Section 54.   Whenever two or more municipalities have joint property in, or the right of joint control of, any marine fisheries, the aldermen of the cities and the selectmen of the towns which share in such joint property or control may exercise jointly the powers conferred upon such officers by any provisions of chapter one hundred and twenty-nine A, and of this chapter, including sections forty-eight and fifty-five, respectively, only if separately instructed by their respective cities and towns thereunder.   Such joint exercise of such powers shall be by a joint board composed of aldermen or selectmen, or both, as hereinafter provided, in a meeting called by such officers representing the oldest of such municipalities, or, in default thereof for twenty-four hours after receiving from any of such officers of any of such municipalities a request therefor, by such officers representing any one of such municipalities, by a notice in writing stating the time, place and purpose of such meeting, served upon such officers of all such municipalities, in the same manner that a summons to a witness in a civil action is served, forty-eight hours at least before the time appointed for such meeting.   Any of the officers calling such meeting, if appointed thereby for that purpose, may preside thereat until the meeting regularly organizes.   At any meeting of such joint board each city and each town shall be entitled to one vote for each member of its municipal board represented thereon; provided, that no such city or town shall be entitled to more votes than there are members of the smallest municipal board so represented. Such meeting may act by a majority of the votes of the members present thereat.   Any regulation, notice of regulations, permit, license or other instrument authorized to be issued by such joint board shall be valid if issued by a majority of the votes of the members of such joint board present at such meeting.   Upon a vote authorizing the same, any such permit issued bearing the signature of any one member of such joint board shall be valid.

Section 55.   Cities by a two thirds vote of the board of aldermen, and towns by a two thirds vote at a town meeting, may appropriate money for the cultivation, propagation and protection of shellfish.   The aldermen or selectmen, when so authorized by their respective cities or towns, may from time to time declare a close season for any or all kinds of shellfish for not more than three years in such waters, flats or creeks, not then the subject of a private grant, within the limits of their respective cities and towns, as they deem proper, and may plant, grow and protect shellfish in such waters, flats or creeks; provided, that no private rights are impaired; and provided, further, that when any close season, declared as aforesaid, shall have ended, such flats, waters or creeks shall not within two

Marginal notes:

Joint control of fisheries by cities or towns.

Appropriation by cities and towns for propagation.

Close season for taking shellfish in certain areas.

years thereafter be licensed for the private cultivation of shellfish.

Certain towns may lease, etc., certain lands for propagation.

Section 56. For the purpose of securing and promoting the proper conservation, development, utilization and control of the natural resources of the commonwealth, any town bordering upon the coastal waters may acquire by gift, purchase or lease the exclusive right to plant and cultivate, and dig, dredge or otherwise gather and remove, and dispose of, one or more species of shellfish in, on or from any land on tidal waters therein in private ownership and below the line of mean high water. Section fourteen of chapter forty, so far as applicable, shall apply to the acquisition of rights under this section.

City or town officers may regulate the taking, etc., of certain fish, etc. Licenses.

Section 57. The aldermen of any city or the selectmen of any town, when so instructed by their respective cities or towns, may, upon written application therefor and after public notice and hearing thereon as hereinafter provided, grant to any inhabitant of such city or town, to a firm composed of inhabitants thereof, or to a corporation the entire capital stock of which is owned by inhabitants thereof, a license for a period not exceeding fifteen years to plant, grow, dig and take shellfish and to plant shells for the purpose of catching shellfish seed, in such city or town at all times of the year and within the limits specified in the license, except on areas then or within two years prior thereto closed for municipal cultivation under the provisions of section fifty-five; provided, that scallops shall not be taken between April first and October first upon, in or from any waters, flats or creeks below mean high water mark within such city or town at any place where the aldermen or selectmen shall determine that there is no substantial natural shellfish bed. Licenses under this section shall be issued upon such terms and conditions as the aldermen or selectmen issuing the same deem proper, but not so as to impair the private rights of any person or to materially obstruct navigable waters, and they shall describe by metes and bounds the waters, flats or creeks covered thereby.

Transfer and renewal of license.

Section 58. Any such license may be transferred to any person to whom it might originally have been granted, and, whether or not so transferred, may, within two years before the expiration of its term, be renewed for a further term of not exceeding fifteen years from the expiration of the original term. The provisions of this chapter applicable to the original issuance of such license shall, so far as apt, apply to a transfer or a renewal thereof hereunder.

Applications for licenses.

Section 59. Any inhabitant, firm or corporation qualified as provided in section fifty-seven and desiring to obtain a license thereunder shall present to the aldermen or selectmen a written application setting forth the name and residence of the applicant, a reasonably definite description of the desired territory, and a request that the territory be surveyed and a plan thereof made, if the same has not already been done, and that such license be granted to the applicant.

Section 60. No license referred to in section fifty-seven shall be granted, transferred or renewed until after a public hearing, due notice of which has been posted in three or more public places, and published in a newspaper, if any, published in the city or town where the territory described in the application is situated, at least ten days before the time fixed for the hearing, stating the name and residence of the applicant or transferee, as the case may be, the date of the filing of the application for such license, transfer or renewal, and the location, area and description of the said territory.

Section 61. Before granting any such license the alder- men or selectmen shall cause to be made a survey and plan of the territory within which such licenses are to be granted, and, upon granting any such license, shall without charge locate and mark upon the ground the corners of the licensed premises and shall cause to be marked upon a copy of such plan to be kept in the office of the city or town clerk the territory covered by such license. The licensee upon receiving his license shall cause the territory covered thereby to be plainly marked out by monuments, marks or ranges and by stakes or buoys, with the number of his license painted in figures at least two inches in height in a conspicuous place on each of said stakes or buoys or on flags attached thereto, which shall be maintained by him or his transferee during the term of the license or of any renewal thereof. Failure to place or reasonably to maintain the same shall be sufficient cause for revocation of the license.

Section 62. The aldermen or selectmen shall keep in their offices plans showing all such licensed areas, and, in a book devoted to that purpose only, a record of each license granted and of all transfers or renewals thereof, which shall include the name and residence of the licensee or transferee, the dates of issue, transfer, renewal and expiration thereof, and a copy of the description of the licensed area as the same appears in the license. Each license, and all transfers or renewals thereof, shall forthwith after the granting or approval thereof be transmitted by the board so granting or approving the same to the city or town clerk, who shall record the same in a book kept especially therefor in his office. The licensee or transferee shall within thirty days after such issue or approval pay to the said clerk for each license or renewal issued or transfer approved one dollar for such recording, and for each license issued shall also pay four dollars as reimbursement of said city or town for the cost incurred in making such survey and plan and in granting said license, a record of which payment shall forthwith be entered upon said record by said clerk, and such license, transfer or renewal shall not take effect until said fees are paid and entry thereof made as aforesaid. Said records shall be open to public inspection at all reasonable times. Forms for such licenses and for the transfer or renewal of the same shall be provided by the aldermen or selectmen at the expense of their city or town.

Licensee to have exclusive use of flats, etc.

Section 63. The licensee or transferee, or his legal representatives, shall, for the purposes aforesaid, have during the term of the license or of any renewal thereof the exclusive use of the waters, flats or creeks described in the license, and the exclusive right to take all shellfish therefrom during the time therein specified, notwithstanding any regulations made by the aldermen or selectmen of the city or town; provided, that this section shall not be construed to authorize any taking prohibited by law. The licensee or transferee, or his legal representatives, may in tort recover treble damages of any person who without his or their consent, unless otherwise authorized by law or by lawful regulation so to do, digs or takes shellfish of any kind, or shells, from such waters, flats or creeks, or disturbs the same thereon, during the continuance of the license or of any renewal thereof.

Annual fee.

Section 64. Every such licensee or transferee shall pay to the city or town, on or before a date to be fixed by the aldermen or selectmen, an annual fee of not less than one nor more than five dollars per acre, such fee to be fixed for terms of five years according to a just and equitable valuation of the licensed area by the authorities granting such license. If said fee is not paid within six months after it becomes due the license shall thereupon be forfeited. Money received from such annual fees may be expended, so far as may be necessary, for the survey of the licensed areas and the protection of the shell fisheries thereon and for the protection of shell fisheries which remain public and the propagation of shellfish thereon.

Report by licensee of quantity of shellfish planted.

Section 65. Every licensee or transferee of a license referred to in section fifty-seven shall submit on oath on or before October twentieth in each year to the aldermen or selectmen of the city or town wherein the territory covered by the license is situated a report of the total number of bushels of each kind of shellfish planted, produced or marketed during the preceding year upon or from such territory, and an estimate of the total number of bushels of each kind of shellfish at that time planted or growing thereon; and if the total amount then thereon falls below the market value of twenty-five dollars per acre within the first two years of the term of said license, or below the market value of fifty dollars per acre per year for any three consecutive years thereafter, said value to be determined by the aldermen or selectmen by such reasonable method as they deem best, they may declare the license to be forfeited; whereupon the licensed premises, with all shellfish then thereon, shall revert to the city or town wherein situated.

Penalty for injuring boundary marks, etc.

Section 66. Whoever wilfully injures, defaces, destroys or removes any mark or bound used to define the extent of any shellfish license or grant, or places any unauthorized mark thereon, or ties or fastens any boat or vessel thereto, shall be punished by a fine of not less than three nor more than twenty dollars, and shall be liable in tort for double damages and costs to the licensee or transferee injured by such act.

Section 67. Whoever works a dredge, oyster tongs or rakes, or any other implement for the taking of shellfish of any description upon any shellfish grounds or beds covered by a license granted under section fifty-seven, or in any way disturbs the growth of the shellfish thereon, or discharges any substance which may directly or indirectly injure the shellfish thereon, without the consent of the licensee, transferee, lessee or owner thereof, or whoever, while upon or sailing over any such grounds or beds, casts, hauls, or has overboard any such dredge, tongs, rake or other implement for the taking of shellfish of any description, under any pretence or for any purpose whatever, without the consent of the licensee, transferee, lessee or owner, shall for the first offence be punished by a fine of not more than twenty dollars or by imprisonment for not more than one month, and for a subsequent offence by a fine of not more than fifty dollars or by imprisonment for not more than six months. *Penalty for injuring shellfish areas.*

Section 68. No person shall dig, take or carry away any shellfish or shells between one hour after sunset and one hour before sunrise, by any method whatever, from any waters, flats or creeks as to which a license has been granted under section fifty-seven. A licensee or transferee of such a license violating this section shall, in addition to all other penalties provided, forfeit his license and the shellfish remaining on the licensed premises. *Hours within which shellfish may be taken from licensed areas, etc.*

Section 69. Whoever violates the preceding section, or whoever, without the consent of the licensee or transferee, digs or takes any shellfish or shells from any waters, flats or creeks described in any license granted under section fifty-seven during the continuance of such license, or of any renewal thereof, shall be punished by a fine of not more than one hundred dollars or by imprisonment for not less than one nor more than six months, or both. *Penalty.*

Section 70. The department of public health shall examine from time to time, or upon the request of the supervisor, the tidal waters and flats in the commonwealth and samples of the shellfish therein or thereon in order to determine what areas thereof are so contaminated that shellfish obtained therefrom are unfit for food or dangerous to the public health. The department shall determine and promulgate definite bounds of areas found to be contaminated as aforesaid and shall publish in a newspaper published in the town in which or adjacent to which any such contaminated area is situated, and shall file in the office of the clerk of such town, the results of its examination in relation thereto, and shall cause to be posted at points on *Department of public health to determine contaminated areas.*

or near any such area a description thereof specifying said bounds, and a statement that such area is contaminated. The department shall also forthwith notify the supervisor of its determination as aforesaid. The record of a bacteriological count made in any examination hereunder shall be subject to inspection upon request. When such determination ceases to be in force, notice thereof shall be published and posted and the supervisor forthwith notified in the manner hereinbefore provided.

Shellfish taken from contaminated areas, purification of. Permits.

Section 71. The supervisor may grant, and may revoke, written permits for the digging or taking of shellfish from an area determined under section seventy or corresponding provisions of earlier laws to be contaminated, such permits to be upon the express condition, which shall be set forth therein, that all shellfish dug or taken from the area covered by such permit by the holder thereof shall, before being used or disposed of for consumption as food, be purified at a plant approved in writing by the commissioner of public health as to the location, construction and operation thereof. Said commissioner shall not so approve any such plant unless requested in writing so to do by the city council of the city or the selectmen of the town wherein said plant is located, and he may revoke such approval at any time upon receipt of evidence satisfactory to him of violation of any condition upon which such approval is based or of any rule or regulation promulgated by the department of public health under this section. Upon request of any party in interest, a hearing shall be given by said commissioner or by some person designated by him before such revocation shall be final and, pending the hearing, the revocation of the approval of the plant shall be in effect. Said department may from time to time promulgate rules and regulations to carry out the provisions of this section. Violation of any condition contained in a permit granted by the supervisor hereunder shall render the holder thereof liable to the penalties set forth in section seventy-two and forfeiture of the permit.

Penalty for taking shellfish from contaminated areas.

Section 72. No person, without a permit from the supervisor under the preceding section, shall dig or take shellfish for any purpose from any area determined under section seventy or under corresponding provisions of earlier laws to be contaminated, while such determination is in force; nor shall any person knowingly transport or cause to be transported or have in possession shellfish so dug or taken, or make use of a certificate issued under section seventy-three after its revocation or cancellation as therein provided, or wilfully fail to surrender the same at the request of said supervisor. Violation of any of the foregoing provisions of this section shall be punished by a fine of not less than twenty nor more than one hundred dollars or by imprisonment for not more than thirty days, or both. The superior court shall have jurisdiction in equity to enforce this section and section seventy-three and the rules and regulations of the supervisor made under said section seventy-three, and to restrain the violation thereof. In any prosecution for a violation of so much of this section as prohibits the digging or taking, without the permit therein referred to, of shellfish from areas determined to be contaminated, possession, except by a common carrier, of shellfish apparently so dug or taken shall be prima facie evidence of a violation thereof.

Section 73. Except as provided in sections seventy-one and seventy-two, no person shall, for commercial use, dig or take shellfish in the commonwealth without a bed certificate, stating that the tidal waters and flats from which said shellfish are or are to be dug or taken, and the shellfish therein and thereon, are free from contamination, and no firm, corporation or other person shall engage in the distribution of shellfish commercially in the commonwealth without a dealer's certificate. Such bed certificates and dealers' certificates shall be issued by the supervisor under rules and regulations as hereinafter provided. The supervisor, upon the request of and the payment of a fee of ten dollars by a person who buys, or maintains an establishment for packing, shellfish, except scallops, and desires to ship the same outside the commonwealth, and, upon the request of and the payment of a fee of two dollars by a person who digs or takes such shellfish and desires to ship the same outside the commonwealth, may annually issue certificates relative to the condition of the establishment or equipment of such person. The supervisor shall promulgate rules and regulations relative to the form, contents and use of all certificates issued by him under this section, in such manner as will most effectively safeguard the public health and meet the provisions of the laws, rules, regulations or requirements of the United States as to interstate commerce in shellfish and of other states in relation to the importation, inspection and consumption of shellfish within their respective limits. Said rules and regulations shall be subject to the approval of the department of public health in so far as sanitary requirements are concerned. At the request of the commissioner of public health, or of his own motion, the supervisor shall revoke and cancel and require the surrender of any certificate issued by him under this section, if, in his opinion, after a hearing by him or some person designated by him, the holder thereof is guilty of violating any such rule or regulation, or any provision of this or the preceding section, or upon a change in the facts and conditions set forth in such certificate. Pending the hearing the certificate shall be deemed to be suspended. The provisions of this section and of the rules and regulations made hereunder shall be enforced, and any violation thereof shall be punished or restrained, as provided in the preceding section.

Bed certificates, issuance of.

Rules and regulations of department of public health.

Penalty.

Transportation of shellfish taken without the commonwealth.

Section 74. No person shall transport, or cause to be transported, into this commonwealth for consumption as food any shellfish taken or dug from grounds outside the commonwealth, or sell, cause to be sold, or keep, offer or expose for sale for consumption as aforesaid any shellfish so taken or dug, unless there is on file in the department of public health a certificate, approved by said department, in which the state board or department of health or other board or officer having like powers of the state, country or province where such grounds are situated states that such grounds are free from contamination, and also a certificate, approved as aforesaid, in which such state board or department of health or other board or officer having like powers states that the establishment and equipment of the person shipping said shellfish into the commonwealth are in good, sanitary condition, nor unless the container of such shellfish shall at all times, while in such transportation, bear a label or tag legibly marked with the name and address of the producer and of the shipper thereof and the numbers of such certificates, and the name of the place where and the date when taken, and absence of such label or tag so marked or failure to allow such inspection shall be prima facie evidence of violation of this section; provided, that the foregoing provisions relative to transportation shall not apply to common carriers, their servants or agents. No such certificate shall be approved by the department of public health which does not meet the provisions of the laws, rules, regulations and requirements of the United States as to interstate commerce in shellfish. A list of certificates shall be filed with the supervisor. Whoever violates any provision of this section shall be punished by a fine of not less than twenty nor more than fifty dollars, or by imprisonment for not more than thirty days, or both. The provisions of this section shall be enforced by the department of public health, local boards of health and all officers qualified to serve criminal process.

Certificate.

Penalty.

Establishment of purification plants in certain cities and towns, petition for.

Section 75. The aldermen of a city or the selectmen of a town wherein lies any area determined and declared by the department of public health, in accordance with section seventy, to be contaminated, or ten per cent of the registered voters in any such city or town, may file a petition with the supervisor, stating that the petitioners deem that the shell fisheries in such area are of sufficient commercial value to warrant the construction and maintenance of a new purification plant, or the maintenance of an existing purification plant, as described in section seventy-one.

Hearing on petition.

Section 76. Upon the filing of a petition under the preceding section, the supervisor shall forthwith, after public notice and a hearing, determine whether the shellfish in such area, or in such area and in such similar areas as might reasonably be served by the same purification plant, are of sufficient commercial value to warrant the construction and maintenance of a new purification plant, or the maintenance of an existing purification plant, as described in section seventy-one. If such determination is in the affirmative, he shall, subject to the approval of the commissioner of public health, prescribe the location and plan of such plant and the limits of the areas to be served thereby, or, as to any such purification plant already in existence, he may, subject to like approval, approve the location, plan and limits thereof, in whole or in part, or prescribe such changes therein as he may deem suitable, and shall request the department of public health to make a determination as is provided in the following section. Such city or town may thereupon construct or change such plant as prescribed and approved and may appropriate such sum or sums as may be reasonably necessary therefor.

Section 77. Upon receipt of the request provided for by the preceding section, the department of public health shall, as soon as may be and in such manner as it may deem proper, determine the sources of pollution of the contaminated area or areas referred to therein, and the proportions in which cities and towns within the commonwealth are causing or contributing to the cause of such pollution; and shall forthwith report such determination to the commissioner of conservation, who shall thereupon make application to the supreme judicial court for the relief provided for in the following section. *Department of public health to determine sources of pollution.*

Section 78. The supreme judicial court, on application under the preceding section and after notice to each of the cities and towns named in the report of the department of public health as causing or contributing to the contamination of the area or areas in question, appoint three commissioners, herein referred to as apportionment commissioners, who shall not be residents of any of said cities or towns. Such commissioners shall, after due notice and hearing, and in such manner as they shall deem just and equitable, determine the proportion which each of said cities and towns shall bear of the cost of such purification plant as is prescribed or approved under section seventy-six, the compensation and expenses of the apportionment commissioners, and the expenses of maintaining such plant thereafter, and shall report their findings to said court as soon as may be. When said report shall have been accepted by the court it shall be conclusive as to all matters referred to said commissioners and shall be binding upon all parties, who shall thereupon pay the costs in accordance with the order of the court. The court shall have jurisdiction in equity to enforce sections seventy-five to eighty, inclusive, and shall fix and determine the compensation of said apportionment commissioners and shall allow such expenses incurred by them in carrying out the provisions of said sections as it shall approve. *Application to court to determine proportion of cost of purification plant to be assessed on cities and towns.*

Section 79. After the completion of the construction of a purification plant prescribed by the supervisor with the approval of the commissioner of public health under section *Maintenance of purification plant.*

seventy-six, or after their approval of such an existing plant, the same shall be maintained by the city or town in which it is located until such time as the supervisor may determine that the shellfish in the area or areas served by it are not of sufficient commercial value to warrant its continuance. On or before January fifteenth of each year such city or town shall submit to the supervisor an itemized statement certified by its treasurer, showing all sums expended by it during the preceding year on account of any such plant. The supervisor shall approve such sums as he finds to be correct and proper charges. Such proportions of the total amount thereof as have been determined by the apportionment commissioners to be allocable to cities and towns he shall apportion thereto in the proportions fixed by said apportionment commissioners in their report, as accepted by the supreme judicial court, and shall forthwith notify each such city or town of the amounts so apportioned, which shall thereupon be due and payable to the city or town in which said plant is located. Should such last mentioned city or town fail to maintain such purification plant in good condition, or to operate the same, the supreme judicial court shall have jurisdiction, upon application of ten registered voters in any one or more of the cities and towns contributing to the expense of such plant, to compel it to put the plant in good condition and to operate the same.

Purification of shellfish.

Section 80. Such purification plant shall accept and treat for purification, free of charge, all shellfish dug or taken from the area or areas for which such plant is established.

Application of certain sections.

Section 81. Sections seventy-five to eighty, inclusive, shall not be deemed to affect section twelve A of chapter forty or section seventy-one of this chapter.

Receptacles containing shellfish to be marked, etc.

Section 82. No wholesale dealer in shellfish shall receive any receptacle containing shellfish unless such receptacle bears a label or tag legibly marked with the source of supply, the date when taken, and either the certificate or permit number or the name and address of the producer or shipper. He shall for sixty days after receipt of such receptacle keep in his place of business a record of the markings on such tag or label, which record shall at all reasonable times be open to inspection by any representative of the department of public health or of the state inspector of fish.

No retail dealer in shellfish shall receive any receptacle containing shellfish unless such receptacle bears the label or tag marked as required by the preceding paragraph, or a duplicate thereof. He shall for sixty days after receipt of such receptacle keep in his place of business the tag or a copy of the label, which shall at all reasonable times be open to inspection as provided in the preceding paragraph.

Propagation of fish, etc., by proprietors of lands, etc.

Section 83. The proprietors of lands, meadows or flats, upon which a pond or part of a pond is created and maintained by excavating or by enclosing the same, or both, and by the artificial flowing of the same with coastal waters, for the purpose of cultivating and maintaining fish thereon, shall have the exclusive right to cultivate, and the exclusive ownership and control of, all fish thereon, whether artificially or naturally propagated, and may take the same therefrom and dispose of the same without any permit or license therefor; provided, that no fish determined by the supervisor to be injurious may be cultivated or maintained thereon, and that no fish may be taken therefrom of a size, at a season, or for a purpose, prohibited by law or by any rule, regulation or by-law applicable thereto; and provided, further, that so much thereof as may be below mean high water line before any excavation therefor may not be used for such cultivation or maintenance of fish, unless the aldermen or the selectmen, jointly with the supervisor, determine and certify that no substantial natural shellfish bed exists thereon.

No such pond shall include lands, meadows or flats of the commonwealth, a county, city or town, without the consent of the department of public works, the county commissioners, the aldermen or the selectmen, as the case may be.

Section 84. An artificial pond created and maintained in the manner and for the purpose provided in the preceding section, bounded in part by land belonging to the commonwealth or to a county, city or town, shall become the exclusive property of the riparian proprietors of the other lands bounding the same as to the fisheries therein only in the manner provided by section forty-six of chapter one hundred and thirty-one. Section forty-seven of said chapter shall apply to the taking of fish from such a pond. *Rights of certain riparian owners.*

Miscellaneous Provisions.

Section 85. A bounty of five dollars shall be paid to every person killing a seal in the commonwealth; provided, that within ten days after such killing he exhibits to any town treasurer the whole skin of the seal, with the nose in the same condition as at the time of the killing, and signs and makes oath to a certificate stating the date and place of killing, that he killed the seal and that it was killed in this commonwealth. The treasurer shall thereupon cause to be cut off and burned the nose of the seal, wholly destroying it, and shall pay the said bounty, taking the claimant's receipt therefor, and shall then forward to the state treasurer the said certificate with a statement that he has paid the said bounty in accordance herewith, and that the claimant personally appeared before him and made oath as aforesaid. The state treasurer shall then pay to the town treasurer the sum of five dollars and fifty cents, of which sum fifty cents shall be retained by the town treasurer as a fee for his services hereunder. Whoever obtains the bounty herein provided for by a false repre- *Bounty on seals.* *Certificate.* *Penalty.*

seutation, or whoever brings into the commonwealth a seal, whether alive or dead, which was not taken or killed in this commonwealth or in the waters thereof, for the purpose of obtaining the said bounty, shall be punished by a fine of not less than fifty nor more than five hundred dollars.

Taking of kelp, etc., regulated. *Section 86.* Any person may take and carry away kelp or other seaweed between high and low water mark while it is actually adrift in tide waters; but for such purpose no person shall enter on upland or on lawfully enclosed flats without the consent of the owner or lawful occupant thereof. This section shall not apply to any town where the subject matter thereof is regulated by special law.

Penalty for violations of certain sections. *Section 87.* Whoever takes any fish in violation of any provision of section twelve or fourteen of this chapter, or of section twenty-six of chapter one hundred and twenty-nine A, or whoever violates any provision of section eighteen of this chapter or of section twenty-seven of chapter one hundred and twenty-nine A, shall, in addition to the penalties therein provided, forfeit the boat and apparatus used.

General penalty. *Section 88.* Unless the context otherwise requires, a violation of any provision of this chapter, or of any rule or regulation made under authority thereof, for which no other penalty is provided, shall be punished by a fine of not less than ten nor more than fifty dollars.

Reports of convictions. *Section 89.* A final conviction of a violation of any provision of this chapter or of sections seventy-four to eighty-eight A, inclusive, of chapter ninety-four shall be reported forthwith by the court or magistrate to the commissioner. The supervisor shall forthwith report to the clerks of all cities and towns bordering upon coastal waters the names, offences and periods of ineligibility of every person becoming ineligible to hold any license under this chapter by reason of violation of law, or of any suspension or revocation of a license under section two of chapter one hundred and twenty-nine A.

G. L. (Ter. Ed.), 21, § 7, amended. SECTION 3. Chapter twenty-one of the General Laws is hereby amended by striking out section seven, as appearing in the Tercentenary Edition thereof, and inserting in place thereof the following: — *Section 7.* Except as provided in section eight, the director may, subject to the approval of the commissioner, appoint and remove such experts, fish and game wardens, coastal wardens, deputy coastal wardens, and clerical and other assistants as the work of the division may require, and their compensation shall be paid by the commonwealth. On written application of the city council of a city or the selectmen of a town, the director may, subject to like approval, appoint in such city or town, from a list of names to be submitted to him by such city council or selectmen, a fish and game warden, or a deputy coastal warden, as the case may be, who shall act under his authority and instructions and have the same powers and duties as a fish and game warden, or a coastal

Experts, fish and game wardens, and other assistants.

warden, as the case may be, appointed as above provided; the annual compensation of every such fish and game warden, or deputy coastal warden, as such, not exceeding two hundred dollars, shall be determined and paid by the city or town in which he is appointed. The director may also, subject to like approval, appoint deputy fish and game wardens and deputy coastal wardens, who shall serve without compensation.

Fish and game wardens and deputy fish and game wardens may be authorized by the director, subject to like approval, to exercise the powers and duties of coastal wardens and deputy coastal wardens, and coastal wardens and deputy coastal wardens may be so authorized, subject to like approval, to exercise the powers and duties of fish and game wardens and deputy fish and game wardens.

SECTION 4. Said chapter twenty-one is hereby further amended by striking out section eight A, as so appearing, and inserting in place thereof the following: — *Section 8A.* There shall be a state supervisor of marine fisheries serving in the division, who shall be appointed for terms of three years by the governor with the advice and consent of the council. The salary of said supervisor shall be fixed by the commissioner, subject to the approval of the governor and council. The supervisor shall have charge of the enforcement of the provisions of chapter one hundred and thirty and of all other provisions of law relative to marine fish and fisheries, including shellfish, except as contained in sections seventy-four to eighty-eight A, inclusive, of chapter ninety-four, and shall have general direction of the coastal wardens and deputy coastal wardens appointed under section seven engaged in the enforcement of said provisions; provided, that in carrying out all powers and duties conferred upon him the supervisor shall act with the approval of the director. G. L. (Ter. Ed.), 21, § 8A, amended. State supervisor of marine fisheries.

SECTION 5. Chapter ninety-four of the General Laws is hereby amended by striking out section seventy-four, as so appearing, and inserting in place thereof the following: — *Section 74.* All fresh food fish before being offered for sale, placed in cold storage, salted or smoked shall be graded as follows: — G. L. (Ter. Ed.), 94, § 74, amended. Fish to be graded. Grades established.

"Prime", fish in extra fine condition.

"Superior", fish in suitable condition to stand shipment outside the commonwealth for human consumption as fresh fish.

"Standard", fish in suitable condition for immediate human consumption as fresh fish.

All other fish shall be classified as refuse, shall be deemed unsuitable for human consumption, and may be used only for fish meal, fertilizer or other non-food purposes.

No person shall represent, sell, offer for sale or advertise fresh, frozen, salted or smoked fish of any grade under any misleading or other than the truthful and correct name and grade or corresponding term for such fish.

The word "fish" as used in this section shall be taken to mean all swimming fish.

G. L. (Ter. Ed.), 94, new section 74A, added.
Word "fish" defined.

SECTION 6. Said chapter ninety-four is hereby amended by inserting after section seventy-four, as so appearing, the following new section: — *Section 74A.* The word "fish" as used in sections seventy-seven to eighty-two, inclusive, shall include all swimming fish, all crustacea, and all shellfish.

Repeals.

SECTION 7. Sections seventy-five, seventy-six and seventy-nine of said chapter ninety-four, as so appearing, are hereby repealed.

G. L. (Ter. Ed.), 94, § 77, amended.

SECTION 8. Section seventy-seven of said chapter ninety-four, as so appearing, is hereby amended by striking out the first sentence.

G. L. (Ter. Ed.), 94, § 78, amended.
Restrictions on sale of frozen fish.

SECTION 9. Said chapter ninety-four is hereby further amended by striking out section seventy-eight, as so appearing, and inserting in place thereof the following: — *Section 78.* No person shall sell, or represent for the purpose of sale, otherwise than as frozen, fish which have been frozen.

G. L. (Ter. Ed.), 94, new section 78A, added.
Sale of native lobsters regulated.

SECTION 10. Said chapter ninety-four is hereby further amended by inserting after section seventy-eight, as so appearing, the following new section: — *Section 78A.* No person shall sell, or represent for the purpose of sale, any lobster as a native lobster unless the same shall have been originally caught or taken along the shores of the commonwealth.

G. L. (Ter. Ed.), 94, § 81, amended.
Certain duties of state inspector of fish.

SECTION 11. Said chapter ninety-four is hereby further amended by striking out section eighty-one, as so appearing, and inserting in place thereof the following: — *Section 81.* The state inspector of fish or his deputy shall enforce sections seventy-four to eighty-three, inclusive, and section eighty-eight A, and may inspect all fish offered or exposed for sale or kept with intent to sell, and for such purpose may enter any place where fish is stored, kept, offered or exposed for sale. If on inspection it is found that such fish is tainted, diseased, corrupted, decayed, unwholesome or unfit for food from any cause, the inspector or his deputy shall seize and cause the same to be destroyed forthwith or disposed of otherwise than for food. All money received by the inspector or his deputy for fish disposed of as aforesaid, after deducting the expense of said seizure and disposal, shall be paid to the owner of such fish. The director of the division of fisheries and game of the department of conservation shall from time to time make rules and regulations necessary for the enforcement of sections seventy-four to eighty-three, inclusive, and section eighty-eight A.

G. L. (Ter. Ed.), 94, § 83, amended.
Sale of fish at wholesale regulated.
Penalty.

SECTION 12. Said chapter ninety-four is hereby further amended by striking out section eighty-three, as so appearing, and inserting in place thereof the following: — *Section 83.* All food fish sold at wholesale shall be sold by weight at the time of delivery. Whoever violates this section shall be punished by a fine of not less than twenty-five nor more than one hundred dollars. The word "fish" as used in this section shall be taken to mean all swimming fish, and all crustacea.

SECTION 13. Said chapter ninety-four is hereby further amended by striking out section eighty-eight A, as so appearing, and inserting in place thereof the following: — *Section 88A.* No person shall sell, exchange, transport or deliver, or offer or expose for sale, exchange or delivery, or have in his custody or possession with intent to sell, exchange, transport or deliver, any scallops which have been soaked, or any scallops not in the shell unless such scallops are in a box, carton, tray or other container plainly and conspicuously stamped, labeled or marked with (*a*) the word "Massachusetts", followed by the name of the town or of the locality where taken, if taken from waters or flats within the commonwealth; or (*b*) the name of the state, country or province where taken, if taken from waters or flats outside the commonwealth; or (*c*) the words "SEA SCALLOPS", if of the species commonly so known.

G. L. (Ter. Ed.), 94, § 88A, amended.

Scallops. Marking of containers, etc., regulated.

Whoever fails to comply with any provision of this section, or whoever falsely stamps, labels or marks such a box, carton, tray or other container, shall be punished by a fine of not less than ten nor more than fifty dollars.

Penalty.

This section shall not apply to common carriers having scallops in possession for the purpose of transportation.

SECTION 14. Chapter one hundred and thirty-one of the General Laws is hereby amended by striking out from its title, as appearing in the Tercentenary Edition thereof, the words "POWERS AND DUTIES OF THE DIVISION OF FISHERIES AND GAME" so that the title of said chapter will read as follows: — GAME AND INLAND FISHERIES.

G. L. (Ter. Ed.), 131, title amended.

SECTION 15. Said chapter one hundred and thirty-one is hereby further amended by striking out section thirteen, as so appearing, and inserting in place thereof the following: — *Section 13.* Whoever violates any provision of sections five to twelve, inclusive, for which no specific penalty is provided or is in any way directly or indirectly a party to any such violation, shall be punished by a fine of not less than ten nor more than fifty dollars or by imprisonment for not more than one month or both.

G. L. (Ter. Ed.), 131, § 13, amended.

Penalties for violation of certain sections.

SECTION 16. Said chapter one hundred and thirty-one is hereby further amended by striking out section forty-four, as so appearing, and inserting in place thereof the following: — *Section 44.* Except as provided in the following section and in section fifty-one, and except as otherwise provided in section eighty-three of chapter one hundred and thirty, the riparian proprietors of any pond, other than a great pond, and the proprietors of any pond or parts of a pond created by artificial flowing, shall have exclusive control of the fisheries therein.

G. L. (Ter. Ed.), 131, § 44, amended.

Exclusive fishery of riparian owners.

SECTION 17. Section forty-nine of said chapter one hundred and thirty-one, as so appearing, is hereby further

G. L. (Ter. Ed.), 131, § 49, amended.

amended by striking out, in the second line, the words
"which at any season frequent fresh water" and inserting
in place thereof the words: — in inland waters, — so as to
read as follows: — *Section 49.* Whoever, except as otherwise permitted by law, takes any fish in inland waters, in
any other manner than by angling, shall be punished by a
fine of not less than twenty nor more than fifty dollars; but
towns may permit the use of nets and seines for taking
herring and alewives or of pots for the taking of eels. This
section shall not prohibit spearing eels, carp or those species
of fish commonly known as "suckers". The possession by
any person in or upon inland waters or upon the banks of
the same, except as allowed by law, of any net, trap, trawl,
or other device adapted for taking fish shall be prima facie
evidence of a violation of this section. This section shall
not apply to ponds or waters now or hereafter held under
lease from the department.

SECTION 18. Said chapter one hundred and thirty-one
is hereby further amended by inserting after section sixty-
one, as so appearing, the following new section: — *Section
61A.* The director may permit the taking of smelt in
great ponds of the commonwealth, subject to rules and
regulations made by him and approved by the governor
and council. Violation of any such rule or regulation shall
be punished by a fine of not less than five nor more than
fifty dollars.

SECTION 19. Said chapter one hundred and thirty-one,
as so appearing, is hereby further amended by adding at
the end thereof the following new section: — *Section 137.*
The director shall, during April, May and June, for the
better protection of salmon fry in the Merrimack river,
cause wire screens to be erected and maintained at the
entrance of the canals in Lowell and Lawrence at the expense of the companies owning and operating said canals.

SECTION 20. Sections one to four, inclusive, nine to
eleven, inclusive, fourteen to twenty-four, inclusive, twenty-
seven to thirty-four, inclusive, forty-two, and fifty-two to
fifty-five, inclusive, of said chapter one hundred and thirty-
one, as so appearing, are hereby repealed.

Approved July 17, 1933.

Marginal notes (left column):

Restrictions on taking of fish frequenting inland waters.

Penalty.

G. L. (Ter. Ed.), 131, new section 61A, added.
Taking of smelts in great ponds.

G. L. (Ter. Ed.), 131, new section 137, added.
Protection of salmon fry in Merrimack river.

Repeals.

Chap.330 AN ACT PROVIDING FOR THE PLACING OF RIPRAP FOR THE
PROTECTION OF THE SHORE AT STONY BEACH IN THE
TOWN OF HULL.

Be it enacted, etc., as follows:

SECTION 1. Subject to the conditions herein imposed,
the department of public works is hereby authorized and
directed to place riprap for the purpose of protecting the
shore at Stony Beach in the town of Hull from erosion by
the sea. No work shall be begun until the town of Hull
has assumed liability, in the manner provided by section

twenty-nine of chapter ninety-one of the General Laws, for all damages that may be incurred hereunder, nor until there has been paid into the treasury of the commonwealth by the county of Plymouth the sum of four thousand dollars, and by said town of Hull the sum of four thousand dollars, which together with such sum, not exceeding eight thousand dollars, as may hereafter be appropriated by the commonwealth, shall constitute a fund for the improvement herein authorized; provided, that the total cost of such improvement shall not exceed sixteen thousand dollars; and provided, further, that if any of the aforesaid sum remains after the completion of such improvement one fourth of such remainder shall be repaid to said county and one fourth of such remainder shall be repaid to said town.

Section 2. This act shall take full effect upon its acceptance during the current year by vote of the county commissioners of Plymouth county and by vote of the town of Hull in town meeting, and the filing in the office of the said department of certified copies of said votes.

Approved July 17, 1933.

An Act providing for the settlement of certain claims of the commonwealth against the middlesex tuberculosis hospital district for the care and treatment of certain tubercular patients. *Chap.331*

Be it enacted, etc., as follows:

Section 1. The county commissioners of Middlesex county, on behalf of the Middlesex tuberculosis hospital district, may pay, and the commonwealth shall receive, in full settlement of all claims of the commonwealth against said district or county arising out of the care and treatment of tubercular patients under sections seventy-eight to ninety-one, inclusive, of chapter one hundred and eleven of the General Laws, such sums as may be approved by the attorney general and the commission on administration and finance.

Section 2. The said county commissioners are hereby authorized and empowered to apportion and assess the cost of such settlement, including legal fees and other expenses necessarily incurred in connection therewith, upon the cities and towns in the Middlesex tuberculosis hospital district, in proportion to their valuation, as established as the basis for state and county taxes, in the same manner as the care, maintenance and repair of hospitals is apportioned and assessed under section eighty-five of chapter one hundred and eleven of the General Laws, and shall have the right to borrow on the credit of the county such sum or sums as may be necessary for the purposes hereof, in accordance with the provisions of section eighty-two of said chapter one hundred and eleven.

Approved July 17, 1933.

*Chap.*332 AN ACT RELATIVE TO THE USE OF CERTAIN TRAILERS ON THE
WAYS OF THE COMMONWEALTH AND TO THE FEES FOR
THE REGISTRATION OF CERTAIN MOTOR VEHICLES AND
TRAILERS.

Be it enacted, etc., as follows:

G. L. (Ter.
Ed.), 90, § 1,
etc., amended.

SECTION 1. Section one of chapter ninety of the
General Laws, as most recently amended by section one
of chapter two hundred and seventy-one of the acts of
nineteen hundred and thirty-two, is hereby further
amended by inserting after the word "vehicles" in the
forty-sixth line, as appearing in the Tercentenary Edition
of said Laws, the two following new paragraphs: —

Definitions.
"Semi-trailer".

"Semi-trailer", a trailer so designed and used in combination with a tractor that some part of the weight of
such trailer and that of its load rests upon, and is carried
by, the tractor.

"Semi-trailer
unit".

"Semi-trailer unit", a motor unit composed of a tractor
and a semi-trailer.

G. L. (Ter.
Ed.), 90, § 1,
etc., further
amended.

SECTION 2. Said section one, as amended as aforesaid,
is hereby further amended by striking out the definition of
"Trailer" as contained in the fifty-second to the fifty-sixth
lines, inclusive, as so appearing, and inserting in place
thereof the two following definitions: —

Definitions.
"Tractor".

"Tractor", a motor vehicle having no carrying capacity
of its own, but which is designed and used for drawing
another vehicle or for industrial or agricultural purposes.

"Trailer".

"Trailer", a vehicle used for carrying passengers or
personal property and having no motive power of its own,
but which is drawn by, or used in combination with, a
motor vehicle. It shall not include a pole dolly or pole
dickey, so called, nor a pair of wheels commonly used as an
implement for other purposes than transportation.

G. L. (Ter.
Ed.), 90, § 19,
amended.

SECTION 3. Section nineteen of said chapter ninety, as
appearing in the said Tercentenary Edition, is hereby
amended by striking out the last sentence and inserting in

Dimensions
of motor
trucks and
trailers.

place thereof the following: — No trailer having a carrying
capacity of more than one thousand pounds, other than a
semi-trailer, or a heavy duty platform trailer used for
purposes other than the transportation of goods, wares
and merchandise, shall be operated or drawn on the ways
of the commonwealth; and no motor vehicle shall be operated on any way to draw more than one trailer or other
vehicle.

G. L. (Ter.
Ed.), 90, § 33,
etc., amended.

SECTION 4. Section thirty-three of said chapter ninety,
as most recently amended by section one of chapter one
hundred and eighty-three of the acts of the current year,
is hereby further amended by striking out the paragraph
amended by section twelve of chapter one hundred and
eighty of the acts of nineteen hundred and thirty-two and
inserting in place thereof the two following paragraphs: —

Fees.

(1) For the registration of every non-gasoline driven

automobile used for the transportation of goods, wares or merchandise except an electric motor truck or an electric commercial automobile, fifty cents, or, in the case of an electric motor truck or an electric commercial automobile so used, twenty-five cents, and of every gasoline driven automobile so used, fifteen cents, for every hundred pounds of the weight of such vehicle and of its maximum carrying capacity, but in no event less than twenty dollars in the case of a non-gasoline driven automobile so used or six dollars in the case of a gasoline driven automobile so used; provided, that for the registration of every automobile of the semi-passenger type of a carrying capacity not exceeding one thousand pounds used for the transportation of tools, utensils, goods, wares or merchandise, the fee shall be fifteen dollars when non-gasoline driven and four dollars and fifty cents when gasoline driven. (2) For the registration of every trailer of a carrying capacity exceeding one thousand pounds used for the transportation of goods, wares or merchandise, fifteen cents for every hundred pounds of the weight of such vehicle and of its maximum carrying capacity, but in no event less than six dollars. (3) For the registration of every trailer of a carrying capacity not exceeding one thousand pounds used for the transportation of goods, wares or merchandise, four dollars and fifty cents, and when not so used, one dollar. The provisions of this paragraph shall not apply to any vehicle the fee for the registration of which is provided for in the second preceding paragraph. The aforesaid weight shall mean the weight of such vehicle when fully equipped for the road. The commissioner of public works may establish rules for determining the weight of such vehicle and its maximum carrying capacity, and he may in his discretion use the maker's weight with due allowance for extras.

For the registration of every tractor, six dollars.

SECTION 5. This act shall take effect on the first day of January, nineteen hundred and thirty-six.

Approved July 17, 1933.

Effective date.

AN ACT PROVIDING FOR THE DISPOSAL OF THE SEWAGE FROM THE MASSACHUSETTS HOSPITAL SCHOOL THROUGH THE SEWERAGE SYSTEM OF THE TOWN OF CANTON.

*Chap.*333

Be it enacted, etc., as follows:

SECTION 1. The trustees of the Massachusetts hospital school are hereby authorized to discharge the sewage from said school into the sewerage system of the town of Canton as hereinafter provided.

Massachusetts hospital school sewage may be discharged into town of Canton sewerage system.

SECTION 2. Said town of Canton is hereby authorized to construct and maintain a sewer from the present terminus of the town's fifteen inch sewer northeasterly of the New York, New Haven and Hartford railroad at land of Foley;

Canton, authority to construct certain sewer.

thence on private lands to Sherman street; thence crossing
said street and on private lands to a point on Pleasant
street opposite the northwesterly corner of Reservoir
pond; thence crossing said Pleasant street and on private
lands to the existing eight inch outlet sewer of said school,
a total distance of about eight thousand three hundred and
sixty feet, to consist of fifteen inch, twelve inch and ten
inch pipes, with usual manholes and appurtenances,
according to plans filed in the office of the town clerk of
said town, entitled "Plans and profiles of proposed sewer
at Canton, Mass. connecting the Massachusetts Hospital
School with the Town of Canton Sewerage System, January, 1933", copies of which are filed with the department
of public health and the trustees of said school.

Takings by eminent domain.   SECTION 3.   The sewer commissioners of said town,
acting for and in behalf of said town, may take by eminent
domain under chapter seventy-nine of the General Laws,
or acquire by purchase or otherwise, any lands, water
rights, rights of way or easements, public or private,
necessary for the construction and maintenance of the
above mentioned sewer.

Any person injured in his property by any action of the
said sewer commissioners under this act may recover damages from said town under said chapter seventy-nine.

Distribution of cost of sewer.   SECTION 4.   Fifty per cent of the cost of constructing
the sewer hereunder, including interest on any temporary
loan made as hereinafter provided, shall be paid by said
town of Canton and fifty per cent by the commonwealth.
In the course of the progress of the work, as sections or
portions of it are completed, the selectmen of said town
shall certify to the state department of public welfare and
to the state treasurer the cost of such section or portion.
Fifty per cent of the amount so certified shall be paid by
the commonwealth from time to time as promptly as
possible after such certifications are received, the said
payments to be from the appropriation made therefor.
For the purpose of providing the necessary funds to meet
the portion of the cost to be ultimately paid by the commonwealth hereunder, the treasurer of said town may,
with the approval of the selectmen, incur debt outside the
debt limit and issue notes therefor for a period not exceeding one year from their dates; and the proceeds of such
reimbursement shall be applied to the discharge of the loan.
The proceeds of any such loan shall be available for the
purpose aforesaid without any appropriation.

Duties of sewer com-missioners.   SECTION 5.   The sewer commissioners of said town
shall do and perform all acts and things proper or necessary
for the purposes of this act and shall complete the construction of said sewer on or before March first, nineteen
hundred and thirty-four.   All contracts made by said
commissioners shall be made in the name of the town of
Canton and be signed by said commissioners and shall be
subject to the approval of the trustees of said hospital

school; but no contracts shall be made or obligations incurred by said commissioners for any purpose in excess of the amount of money appropriated by the town therefor and the amount to be ultimately borne by the commonwealth as provided in the preceding section.

SECTION 6. There shall further be paid by the commonwealth to said town of Canton as full compensation for the right to dispose of the sewage from said hospital school through the sewerage system of said town in each year for five years, beginning with the year in which said sewage shall first be discharged into said sewerage system, a sum equal to six cents per one hundred cubic feet of water used in said year at said school for culinary and other domestic purposes. Thereafter the annual payments shall be in such amount as shall be mutually agreed upon by the trustees of said school and the selectmen of said town; and if said town and said trustees shall be unable to agree then the amount to be paid annually shall be determined by three commissioners to be appointed by the supreme judicial court, upon the application of either party in interest and after notice to the other. The award of said commissioners, when accepted by said court, shall be binding upon said town and the commonwealth. When the amount of any annual payment is determined by agreement or award as aforesaid, it shall be certified to the commissioner of public welfare and to the state treasurer by a certificate signed by the selectmen of said town and by said trustees in case of an agreement, or by a certificate of the clerk of said court in the case of an award, and such amount shall continue to be paid annually by the commonwealth as aforesaid until changed by a new agreement or a new award made upon application of either said town or said trustees and duly certified in the manner above provided, but no such change shall be made oftener than once in five years. All amounts payable by the commonwealth hereunder shall be paid annually out of the appropriation for maintenance of the said hospital school.

Commonwealth to pay to town of Canton for right to dispose of certain sewage.

SECTION 7. This act shall take effect upon its acceptance by a majority vote of the voters of the town of Canton present and voting thereon at a town meeting to be held within sixty days after its passage.

Acceptance of act.

Approved July 17, 1933.

AN ACT MAKING CERTAIN CORRECTIONS AND CHANGES IN THE LAWS RELATING TO SAVINGS BANKS AND SAVINGS DEPARTMENTS OF TRUST COMPANIES.

*Chap.*334

Be it enacted, etc., as follows:

SECTION 1. Chapter one hundred and sixty-seven of the General Laws is hereby amended by striking out section fourteen, as appearing in the Tercentenary Edition thereof, and inserting in place thereof the following: —

G. L. (Ter. Ed.), 167, § 14, amended.

Section 14.   Deposits may be received by any bank in the names of two persons, payable to either, or to either or the survivor.   Such deposits or any part thereof, or any dividends thereon, may be paid to either of such persons or his assignee, whether the other be living or not, provided they are not then attached at law or in equity in a suit against either person, and the bank then has no notice in writing of any assignment of the account by either to any person other than an assignee to whom payment is being made hereunder.   All such payments shall be valid.

SECTION 2.   Section seventeen of said chapter one hundred and sixty-seven, as so appearing, is hereby repealed.

SECTION 3.   Section one of chapter one hundred and sixty-eight of the General Laws, as so appearing, is hereby amended by adding at the end thereof the following new paragraphs: —

"Deposit book", "depositor's book", "pass book", the book issued to the depositor by such bank as evidence of his deposit.

"Savings bank', a savings bank or institution for savings incorporated as such in this commonwealth.

SECTION 4.   Said chapter one hundred and sixty-eight is hereby amended by striking out section two, as so appearing, and inserting in place thereof the following: — *Section 2.*   Savings banks shall have all the powers and privileges specified in this chapter and shall be subject thereto so far as is consistent with the provisions of their respective charters; and any such corporation may, by vote at its annual meeting or at a meeting called for the purpose, accept any provision of this chapter which is inconsistent with its charter.

SECTION 5.   Section eleven of said chapter one hundred and sixty-eight, as so appearing, is hereby amended by inserting after the word "corporation" in the fourth line the following new sentence: — In the absence or inability of the clerk to serve, the president or a vice president may give the notice or notices required by this section, — and by adding at the end thereof the following new sentence: — The annual meeting, and meetings of the trustees or board of investment, of such corporation may be held at any place in the town where the banking house is located, — so as to
read as follows: — *Section 11.*   The annual meeting of such corporation shall be held at such time as the by-laws direct.   Special meetings may be held by order of its trustees; and its clerk shall give notice of special meetings upon written request of ten members of the corporation. In the absence or inability of the clerk to serve, the president or a vice president may give the notice or notices required by this section.   Notice of all meetings shall be given by advertisement in a newspaper published in the county where the corporation is located, and by mailing to each incorporator at least seven days before such meeting

a written or printed notice thereof. The names of those present at meetings shall be entered in the records of the corporation. The annual meeting, and meetings of the trustees or board of investment, of such corporation may be held at any place in the town where the banking house is located.

SECTION 6. Section thirteen of said chapter one hundred and sixty-eight, as so appearing, is hereby amended by inserting after the word "clerk" in the fourth line the words: —, who shall be clerk of the corporation and board of trustees, — so as to read as follows: — *Section 13.* The officers of such corporation shall be a president, one or more vice presidents, a board of investment of not less than three, a board of not less than eleven trustees from which the officers hereinbefore mentioned shall be chosen, a treasurer, a clerk, who shall be clerk of the corporation and board of trustees, and such other officers as it may find necessary for the management of its affairs. All officers shall be sworn, and shall hold their several offices until others are elected, and qualified in their stead; and a record of every such qualification shall be filed and preserved by the clerk of the corporation. The trustees shall be elected from the incorporators, and no person shall hold an office in two such corporations at the same time. Only one of the persons holding the offices of president, treasurer or clerk shall at the same time be a member of the board of investment. The treasurer, vice treasurer or assistant treasurer shall not be clerk either of the corporation or of the trustees. Not more than three fifths of the members of any such corporation shall be officers thereof at any one time.

G. L. (Ter. Ed.), 168, § 13, amended.

Officers.

SECTION 7. Said chapter one hundred and sixty-eight is hereby further amended by striking out section seventeen, as so appearing, and inserting in place thereof the following: — *Section 17.* At the first meeting after their election, the trustees shall elect an auditing committee of not less than three trustees, of which committee neither the treasurer nor more than one member of the board of investment shall be members, who shall at least once during the twelve months following their election, and oftener if required by the commissioner, cause to be made at such time and in such form and manner as the commissioner may determine, by a certified public accountant not connected with said bank, a thorough examination and audit of the books, securities, cash, assets, liabilities, income and expenditures of the corporation, including an accurate trial balance of the depositors' ledger, for the period elapsed since the preceding examination and audit, or for such other period as the commissioner may prescribe. Said certified public accountant shall be chosen by the auditing committee, subject to the approval of the commissioner, within thirty days after their election. Said accountant shall personally direct and supervise the making of said examination and audit, except that, with the consent of

G. L. (Ter. Ed.), 168, § 17, amended.

Auditing committee.

the commissioner, he may verify a trial balance of the depositors' ledger made by the bank within six months, and, with the consent of the commissioner, such assistance as shall be necessary may be furnished by the bank. Said accountant shall report to the auditing committee the result of his examination and audit, and at the next meeting of the trustees thereafter the committee shall render a report, which shall be read, stating in detail the nature, extent and result of the examination and audit, and their report and the accountant's report shall be filed and preserved with the records of the corporation. The committee shall file with the commissioner a copy of the report of the accountant within ten days after its completion. Said accountant and the auditing committee shall certify and make oath that the reports made by them under this section are correct according to their best knowledge and belief. If the committee fails to cause to be made an examination and audit, including an accurate trial balance of the depositors' ledger as herein provided, the commissioner shall cause them to be made by a certified public accountant in such form and manner as he may prescribe, and the expense thereof shall be paid by the bank.

G. L. (Ter. Ed.), 168, § 25, amended, new section 25A, added.
Where business may be transacted.

SECTION 8. Said chapter one hundred and sixty-eight is hereby further amended by striking out section twenty-five, as so appearing, and inserting in place thereof the following two sections: — *Section 25.* Such corporation shall carry on its usual business at its banking house only, and a deposit shall not be received or payment on account of deposits be made by the corporation or by a person on its behalf in any other place than at its banking house, which shall be in the town where the corporation is established; except that the corporation may, with the written permission of and under regulations approved by the commissioner, maintain and establish one or more branch offices or depots in the town where its banking house is located, or in towns not more than fifteen miles distant therefrom where there is no savings bank at the time when such permission is given.

Encouragement of savings among school children.

Section 25A. In order to encourage saving among school children, the corporation may, with the written consent of and under regulations approved by the commissioner, and, in the case of public schools, by the commissioner and the school committee in the town where the school is situated, arrange for the collection of savings from the school children by the principal or teachers of such schools or by collectors.

G. L. (Ter. Ed.), 168, § 26, amended.

Annual report to commissioner.

SECTION 9. Said chapter one hundred and sixty-eight is hereby further amended by striking out section twenty-six, as so appearing, and inserting in place thereof the following: — *Section 26.* The treasurer of such corporation shall, annually within twenty days after the last business day of October, make a report to the commissioner in such form as he may prescribe, showing accurately the condition of such corporation at close of business on that day, specifying the following particulars: name of corporation and names of incorporators and officers; place where located; amount of deposits; amount of each item of other liabilities; each particular kind of investment, stating the par value, estimated market value and amount invested in each; loans to counties, cities, towns or districts; loans on mortgages of real estate; loans on personal security, stating amount of each class separately; estimated value of real estate, and amount invested therein; cash on deposit in banks and trust companies, with the names of such banks and trust companies and the amount deposited in each; cash on hand; the whole amount of interest or profits received, and the rate and amount of each semi-annual and extra dividend for the previous year; the times for the dividends fixed by the by-laws; the rates of interest received on loans; the total amount of loans bearing each specified rate of interest; the number of outstanding loans of an amount not exceeding three thousand dollars each, and the aggregate amount of the same; the number of open accounts; the number and amount of deposits received; the number and amount of withdrawals; the number of accounts opened and the number of accounts closed, severally, during the previous year; and the annual expenses of the corporation, together with such other information as the commissioner may require. The president, or in his absence from the commonwealth, or disability, a vice president, the treasurer, or in his absence from the commonwealth, or disability, an assistant treasurer, and a majority of the auditing committee shall certify on oath that such reports are correct according to their best knowledge and belief.

SECTION 10. Section twenty-seven of said chapter one hundred and sixty-eight, as so appearing, is hereby amended by striking out, in the eleventh line, the word "and" and inserting in place thereof the word: — or, — so as to read as follows: — *Section 27.* The treasurer of such corporation shall, within twenty days after the last business day of October in the year nineteen hundred and twenty-two and in every fifth year thereafter, return to the commissioner a sworn statement of the name, the amount standing to his credit, the last known residence or post office address, and the fact of death, if known to him, of each depositor who shall not have made a deposit therein or withdrawn therefrom any part of his deposit, or any part of the interest thereon, during the twenty years last preceding such last business day of October; he shall also give notice of such deposits in one or more newspapers published in or nearest to the town where such corporation is located, or in one or more newspapers published in or nearest to the town where the depositor was last known to reside, at least once in each of three successive weeks; but this section shall not apply to a deposit made by or in the

G. L. (Ter. Ed), 168, § 27, amended.

Return of unclaimed deposits.

name of a person known to an officer of the corporation to be living, to a deposit the deposit book of which has during such period been brought into the bank to be verified or to have interest added, or to a deposit which, with the accumulations thereon, shall be less than twenty-five dollars. The treasurer of a savings bank who neglects or refuses to make the sworn return required by this section shall be punished by a fine of one hundred dollars. The commissioner shall incorporate in his annual report, or in a supplementary report, each return made to him as provided in this section.

G. L. (Ter. Ed.), 168, § 28, amended.

Books of deposit to be verified.

SECTION 11. Said chapter one hundred and sixty-eight is hereby further amended by striking out section twenty-eight, as so appearing, and inserting in place thereof the following: — *Section 28.* During the first six months of the year nineteen hundred and thirty-four, and of each third year thereafter, such corporations shall call in the deposit books of their depositors for verification, under rules to be prescribed by the commissioner.

G. L. (Ter. Ed.), 168, § 29, amended.

No officer, etc., to borrow funds of corporation or become surety.

SECTION 12. Section twenty-nine of said chapter one hundred and sixty-eight, as so appearing, is hereby amended by inserting after the word "assigned" in the eleventh line the following new sentence: — No such corporation shall make a loan to any of its employees, — and by adding at the end thereof the following: — , or to loans on deposit books made under section fifty-one A, — so as to read as follows: — *Section 29.* No president, treasurer, member of a board of investment, or officer of such corporation charged with the duty of investing its funds, shall borrow or use any portion thereof, be surety for loans to others or, directly or indirectly, whether acting individually or as trustee holding property in trust for another person, be an obligor for money borrowed of the corporation; and if such member or officer, either individually or as trustee holding property in trust for another person, becomes the owner of real estate upon which a mortgage is held by the corporation, his office shall become vacant at the expiration of sixty days thereafter unless he has ceased to be the owner of the real estate or has caused said mortgage to be discharged or assigned. No such corporation shall make a loan to any of its employees. This section shall not apply to loans held by such corporation on June eighth, nineteen hundred and eight, or to renewals thereof, or to the deposit of money, as provided in section fifty-four, in banks or trust companies of which one or more trustees or officers of such corporation are directors, or to loans on deposit books made under section fifty-one A.

G. L. (Ter. Ed.), 168, § 33A, amended.

Sale of travelers' checks, etc.

SECTION 13. Said chapter one hundred and sixty-eight is hereby further amended by striking out section thirty-three A, as so appearing, and inserting in place thereof the following: — *Section 33A.* Savings banks may, under regulations made by the commissioner, receive money for the purpose of transmitting the same, or equivalents thereof, by means of letters of credit, bills of exchange, drafts, or travelers' checks, to another state or country.

SECTION 14. Said chapter one hundred and sixty-eight is hereby further amended by striking out section thirty-four, as so appearing, and inserting in place thereof the following: — *Section 34.* If a deposit is made with such corporation by one person in trust for another, the name and residence of the person for whom it is made shall be disclosed, and it shall be credited to the depositor as trustee for such person. Payments may be made to the trustee; and if no other notice of the existence and terms of a trust has been given in writing to the corporation, in case of the death of the trustee the amount then on deposit, with the dividends thereon, may be paid to the person for whom such deposit was made, or to his legal representative, or, if such deposit does not exceed two hundred dollars, it may be paid to a minor or to either of the parents of such minor. All payments made in accordance with this section shall be valid payments.

G. L. (Ter. Ed.), 168, § 34, amended.

Deposits made in trust, name, etc., of beneficiary to be disclosed.

SECTION 15. Said chapter one hundred and sixty-eight is hereby further amended by striking out section thirty-five, as so appearing, and inserting in place thereof the following: — *Section 35.* A person indebted to such a corporation may, when proceeded against for the collection of such indebtedness or for the enforcement of any security therefor, set off or recoup the amount of a deposit held and owned by him at the time of the commencement of such proceeding, provided, that if a proceeding in equity has been commenced to restrain the corporation from doing its actual business or if the commissioner has taken possession of such corporation as provided in section twenty-two of chapter one hundred and sixty-seven, no deposit shall so be set off or recouped by any such person unless held and owned by him on the date of the commencement of such proceeding or of possession so taken, and that the right of set-off or recoupment shall be determined as of such date whether the indebtedness of the depositor, or the deposit, is then due or payable or becomes due or payable at a later date. Any indebtedness against which a deposit is permitted to be set off or recouped as aforesaid may be secured or unsecured. Section three of chapter two hundred and thirty-two shall not apply to a set-off hereunder. Notwithstanding the foregoing, a judgment shall not be rendered against such corporation in favor of the defendant for any balance found due from it if a proceeding in equity has been commenced against the corporation or the commissioner has taken possession thereof, as aforesaid. The word "deposit", as used in this section, shall include interest due thereon.

G. L. (Ter. Ed.), 168, § 35, amended.

Depositor allowed to set off his deposits in certain proceedings.

SECTION 16. Section forty-five of said chapter one hundred and sixty-eight, as so appearing, is hereby amended by striking out, in the second line, the words "net profits" and inserting in place thereof the word: — income, — by

G. L. (Ter. Ed.), 168, § 45, amended.

striking out in the third line the word "have" and inserting
in place thereof the word: — has, — and by striking
out, in the fifth, sixth and ninth lines, the word "five"
and inserting in place thereof, in each instance, the
words: — seven and one half, — so as to read as follows: —

Guaranty fund.

Section 45. The trustees shall, immediately before making each semi-annual dividend, set apart as a guaranty
fund from the income which has accumulated during the
six months last preceding not less than one eighth nor more
than one fourth of one per cent of the whole amount of
deposits, until such fund amounts to seven and one half per
cent thereof, and no additions shall be made to it when it
amounts to seven and one half per cent, or more, thereof.
Such fund shall thereafter be held to meet contingencies or
losses in its business from depreciation of its securities,
or otherwise. When such fund amounts to less than seven
and one half per cent of the whole amount of deposits, no
losses shall be met therefrom except upon written approval
of the commissioner.

G. L. (Ter. Ed.), 168, § 47, amended.

SECTION 17. Said chapter one hundred and sixty-eight
is hereby further amended by striking out section forty-
seven, as so appearing, and inserting in place thereof the

Manner of division of income.

following: — *Section 47.* The income of such corporation,
after deducting the reasonable expenses incurred in the
management thereof, the taxes paid, and the amounts set
apart for the guaranty fund, shall be divided among its
depositors or their legal representatives, at periods of not
less than three months nor more than six months as determined by its by-laws, in the manner set forth in this
section and in section fifty. An ordinary dividend shall
be declared at least every six months from income which
has been earned, and which has been collected during the
six months next preceding the date of the dividend, except
that there may be added to such income, from the earnings
remaining undivided after declaration of the preceding
semi-annual dividend, an amount sufficient to enable the
corporation to declare an ordinary dividend at a rate not
in excess of the rate of such preceding dividend; but the
total ordinary dividends declared during any twelve
months shall not exceed the net income of the corporation
actually collected during such period, except upon written
approval of the commissioner. If ordinary dividends are
declared oftener than every six months they shall be declared from income which has been earned, and which has
been collected during the next preceding six months, after
deducting therefrom previous ordinary dividends paid,
the reasonable expenses incurred, the taxes paid and the
amount to be set apart for the guaranty fund. Dividends
shall be treated as deposits, and if not withdrawn shall be
considered, in computing the dividend next following, as
having been on deposit for the preceding interest period.
Ordinary dividends shall be at such rate, not exceeding five
per cent a year, as the trustees shall determine. No divi-

dend shall be paid in excess of the rate of four per cent a year unless the maximum semi-annual amount of one fourth of one per cent of the whole amount of deposits, as required by section forty-five, has been set apart for the guaranty fund. Any excess of income remaining after the payment of any dividend shall be credited to a profit and loss account. No ordinary dividends shall be declared or paid except as above provided, nor upon a deposit of less than three months' standing; but, if the by-laws of the corporation so provide, ordinary dividends may be declared and paid upon deposits of one, two, four or five months' standing. In the computation of such dividends, when the day on which deposits begin to draw interest, as provided in the by-laws or regulations, falls on a Sunday or legal holiday, deposits made on the next succeeding business day, and remaining on deposit through the balance of the monthly period, may be construed as having been on deposit one full month, within the meaning of this section. The corporation may, by its by-laws, provide that a dividend shall not be declared or paid on deposits less than three dollars, or that fractional parts of a dollar shall not be included in principal in computing dividends.

SECTION 18. Section forty-nine of said chapter one hundred and sixty-eight, as so appearing, is hereby amended by striking out, in the sixth line. the words "of the profits", — so as to read as follows: — *Section 49.* If, at the time provided by the by-laws for making ordinary dividends, the net income for the interest period last preceding, over and above the amount to be set apart for the guaranty fund, does not amount to one and one half per cent of the deposits, if said period is six months, or a proportional percentage thereof, if the period is less than six months, no dividend shall be declared or paid, except such as shall be approved in writing by the commissioner. G. L. (Ter. Ed.), 168, § 49, amended. When dividend is not to be paid.

SECTION 19. Said chapter one hundred and sixty-eight is hereby further amended by striking out section fifty, as so appearing, and inserting in place thereof the following: — *Section 50.* Whenever the guaranty fund and profit and loss account together amount to fifteen and one quarter per cent of the deposits after an ordinary dividend is declared, an extra dividend at a rate of not less than one quarter of one per cent shall be declared, to be computed in the same manner as such ordinary dividend, and such extra dividend shall be paid on the day on which the ordinary dividend is paid; but in no case shall the payment of an extra dividend as herein provided reduce the guaranty fund and profit and loss account together to less than fifteen per cent of the deposits. G. L. (Ter. Ed.), 168, § 50, amended. When extra dividends shall be paid.

SECTION 20. Said chapter one hundred and sixty-eight is hereby amended by striking out section fifty-one A, as so appearing, and inserting in place thereof the following: — *Section 51A.* Such corporation shall, upon application by a depositor or by either of two joint depositors under sec- G. L. (Ter. Ed.), 168, § 51A, amended. Loans to depositors.

tion fourteen of chapter one hundred and sixty-seven, make a loan to him, secured by his deposit book up to the amount of said deposit account, for a time not extending beyond the end of the dividend period in which the loan was made. Said corporation may charge the depositor interest for, or may collect discount in advance upon, the loan at a rate not exceeding one per cent more than the combined rates of the next preceding dividend distribution of such corporation. The corporation shall keep posted in its banking room a notice containing the substance of this section and section fifty-one in such form as the commissioner may prescribe.

G. L. (Ter. Ed.), 168, § 53, amended.

SECTION 21. Said chapter one hundred and sixty-eight is hereby amended by striking out section fifty-three, as so appearing, and inserting in place thereof the following: —

Payments to minors.

Section 53. Money deposited in the name of a minor may, at the discretion of the treasurer, be paid to such minor or to the person making the original deposit; and the same shall be a valid payment.

G. L. (Ter. Ed.), 168, § 54, amended.

SECTION 22. Section fifty-four of said chapter one hundred and sixty-eight, as so appearing, is hereby amended by striking out the first two paragraphs of clause First and inserting in place thereof the following: —

Investments authorized.

In first mortgages of real estate located in the commonwealth not exceeding sixty per cent of the value of such real estate; but not more than seventy per cent of the whole amount of deposits shall be so invested. If a loan is made on unimproved and unproductive real estate the amount loaned thereon shall not exceed forty per cent of the value of such real estate. No loan on mortgage shall be made except upon written application showing the date, name of applicant, amount asked for and security offered, nor except upon the report of not less than two members of the board of investment who shall certify on said application, according to their best judgment, the value of the premises to be mortgaged; and such application shall be filed and preserved with the records of the corporation. No loan on mortgage shall be made for a period extending beyond three years from the date of the note.

Not later than three years after the date of such loan not less than two members of the board of investment shall certify in writing, according to their best judgment, the value of the premises mortgaged; and the premises shall be revalued in the same manner at intervals of not more than three years so long as they are mortgaged to such corporation. Such report shall be filed and preserved with the records of the corporation. If such loan is made on demand or for a shorter period than three years, a revaluation in the manner above prescribed shall be made of the premises mortgaged not later than three years after the date of such loan and at least every third year thereafter. If at the time a revaluation is made the amount loaned is in excess of sixty per cent, or, in the case of unimproved and unproductive real estate, in excess of forty per cent, of the value of the premises mortgaged, a sufficient reduction in the amount of the loan shall be required, as promptly as may be practicable, to bring the loan within sixty per cent, or, in the case of unimproved and unproductive real estate, within forty per cent of the value of said premises.

SECTION 23. Clause Second of said section fifty-four, as so appearing, is hereby amended by striking out subdivisions (a), (e) and (f) and inserting in place thereof the following subdivisions: — G. L. (Ter. Ed). 168, § 54, etc., further amended.

(a) In the public funds of the United States or of this commonwealth, or in the legally authorized bonds or notes of any other state of the United States, but not including a territory or dependency thereof, which has not within the twenty years prior to the making of such investment defaulted in the payment of any part of either principal or interest of any legal debt; provided, that the full faith and credit of such state is pledged for the payment of such bonds or notes. Investments. Public funds.

(e) In the legally authorized bonds for municipal purposes, or in refunding bonds issued to take up at maturity bonds which have been issued for other than municipal purposes, of any city of any state of the United States, other than a territory or dependency thereof, which was incorporated as such at least twenty-five years prior to the date of such investment, which has at such date not less than thirty thousand nor more than one hundred thousand inhabitants, as established by the last national or state census, or city census certified to by the city clerk or treasurer of said city and taken in the same manner as a national or state census, preceding such date, and whose net indebtedness does not exceed five per cent of the valuation of the taxable property therein, to be ascertained by the last preceding valuation of property therein for the assessment of taxes. Municipal bonds.

(f) In the legally authorized bonds for municipal purposes, or in refunding bonds issued to take up at maturity bonds which have been issued for other than municipal purposes, of any city of any state of the United States, other than a territory or dependency thereof, which was incorporated as such at least twenty-five years prior to the date of such investment, which has at such date more than one hundred thousand inhabitants, established in the same manner as is provided in subdivision (e) of this clause, and whose net indebtedness does not exceed seven per cent of the valuation of the taxable property therein, to be ascertained as provided in said subdivision (e).

SECTION 24. Said clause Second, as so appearing, is hereby further amended by adding at the end thereof the following new subdivision: — G. L. (Ter. Ed.), 168, § 54, etc., further amended.

(h) The provisions of subdivisions (d), (e) and (f) of this clause shall not authorize the investment of funds in the bonds or notes of any county, city, town or district Investment of funds in certain municipal, etc., bonds, limited.

which has been in default for more than one hundred and twenty days in the payment of any of its indebtedness or interest thereon within ten years next preceding the making of such investment. A county, city, town or district shall be considered to be in default within the meaning of this subdivision while any unpaid and overdue obligation, either principal or interest, shall remain outstanding.

G. L. (Ter. Ed.), 168, § 54, etc., further amended.

SECTION 25. Said section fifty-four, as so appearing, is hereby further amended by striking out paragraph (2) of subdivision (c) of clause Ninth.

G. L. (Ter. Ed.), 168, § 54, etc., further amended.

SECTION 26. Subdivision (e) of said clause Ninth is hereby amended by striking out paragraphs (2), (3) and (5) and inserting in place thereof the following new paragraphs: —

Investments further regulated.

(2) Bonds or notes authorized for investment by clause Second, Third, Fourth, Fifth, Sixth, Sixth A, or Seventeenth at no more than ninety per cent of the market value thereof, at any time while such note is held by such corporation; or

(3) Deposit books of depositors, or of one of two joint depositors under section fourteen of chapter one hundred and sixty-seven, in savings banks and in savings departments of trust companies incorporated in this commonwealth, up to the amount of said deposit accounts, and unpledged shares of co-operative banks so incorporated at not more than ninety per cent of their withdrawal value; or

(5) Such other bonds, notes or shares of corporations or associations at no more than eighty per cent of the market value thereof, at any time while such note is held by such corporation; provided, that, if the commissioner shall disapprove any such bonds, notes or shares, he may make such written recommendations to the board of investment of such corporation as the case may require, and may in his discretion include in his annual report a statement of the facts in each case in which such board of investment has not complied with his recommendations in a manner satisfactory to him; or

G. L. (Ter. Ed.), 168, § 55, amended.

SECTION 27. Section fifty-five of said chapter one hundred and sixty-eight, as so appearing, is hereby amended by adding at the end thereof the following new paragraph: —

Liquidation or merger of savings banks.

The office or offices of any savings bank merged with another may, with the permission of and under regulations approved by the commissioner, be maintained as a branch office or branch offices of the continuing bank.

G. L. (Ter. Ed.), 168, new section 57 added.

SECTION 28. Said chapter one hundred and sixty-eight is hereby further amended by adding after section fifty-six, inserted by section one of chapter forty-one of the acts of the current year, the following new section: —

May become member of protective association.

Section 57. Any such corporation, by vote of its board of investment, and with the approval of the commissioner, may become a member of an association or associations organized for the purpose of protecting and promoting the interests of savings banks, and, subject to like approval, may pay to such association or associations its proportionate share of the expenses thereof, if in the opinion of the board of investment of such corporation such expenses are reasonable and necessary.

SECTION 29.   Section sixty-seven of chapter one hundred and seventy-two of the General Laws, as appearing in the Tercentenary Edition thereof, is hereby amended by adding at the end thereof the following paragraph: —

G. L. (Ter. Ed.), 172, § 67, amended.

Interest on deposits in such savings departments may be declared and paid for periods of not less than one month nor more than six months, as determined by the by-laws of such corporations, from income which has been earned and which has been collected during the next preceding six months, and which is available after deducting previous dividends paid, the reasonable expenses incurred in the management thereof, the taxes paid, and the amounts required to be set apart for the guaranty fund.   In the computation of such interest, when the day on which deposits in the savings department of any such corporation begin to draw interest, as provided in its by-laws or regulations, falls on a Sunday or legal holiday, deposits made on the next succeeding business day, and remaining on deposit through the balance of the monthly period, may be construed as having been on deposit one full month, within the meaning of this section.   *Approved July 17, 1933.*

Interest on deposits in savings departments of trust companies.

AN ACT RELATIVE TO THE INCLUSION OF CERTAIN ITEMS IN COMPUTING SEWER ASSESSMENTS IN THE TOWN OF DANVERS.

*Chap.*335

Be it enacted, etc., as follows:

SECTION 1.   Chapter two hundred and twenty-six of the acts of the current year is hereby amended by striking out section one and inserting in place thereof the following: — *Section 1.*   The whole share of the cost of construction of the system of sewage disposal of the South Essex Sewerage District chargeable to the town of Danvers under chapter three hundred and thirty-nine of the acts of nineteen hundred and twenty-five, as amended, including amounts hereafter payable as well as amounts already paid by said town on account of said share, shall be included by said town as an item in determining the total cost of the system of sewerage and sewage disposal in said town constructed under chapter two hundred and twenty-nine of the Special Acts of nineteen hundred and sixteen, for the purpose of assessing estates benefited thereby under authority of said chapter two hundred and twenty-nine.

SECTION 2.   This act shall take effect upon its passage.
        Approved July 18, 1933.

Chap.336 AN ACT PROVIDING FOR THE PERMANENT MAINTENANCE BY THE COMMONWEALTH OF THE MOUNT GREYLOCK WAR MEMORIAL UNDER THE GREYLOCK RESERVATION COMMISSION, AND PLACING SAID COMMISSION UNDER THE GOVERNOR AND COUNCIL.

Be it enacted, etc., as follows:

G. L. (Ter. Ed.), 6, § 17, etc., amended.

SECTION 1. Section seventeen of chapter six of the General Laws, as most recently amended by section one of chapter one hundred and twenty of the acts of the current year, is hereby further amended by striking out the word "and" in the eighth line and inserting in place thereof a comma, and by inserting after the word "library" in the same line the words: — and the Greylock reservation

Officers, etc., serving under governor and council.

commission, — so as to read as follows: — *Section 17.* The armory commissioners, the art commission, the commission on administration and finance, the commissioner of state aid and pensions, the commissioners on uniform state laws, the public bequest commission, the state ballot law commission, the board of trustees of the Soldiers' Home in Massachusetts, the milk regulation board, the alcoholic beverages control commission, the trustees of the state library and the Greylock reservation commission shall serve under the governor and council, and shall be subject to such supervision as the governor and council deem necessary or proper.

G. L. (Ter. Ed.), 6, new sections 46 and 47, added.

SECTION 2. Said chapter six is hereby amended by adding after section forty-five, inserted therein by section two of said chapter one hundred and twenty, the following two new sections, under the heading, GREYLOCK RESER-

Greylock reservation commission.

VATION COMMISSION: — *Section 46.* The Greylock reservation commission, established by chapter five hundred and forty-three of the acts of eighteen hundred and ninety-eight, in this and the following section called the commission, shall continue to serve as an unpaid commission, consisting of three persons, all of whom shall be residents of the county of Berkshire. As the term of a member expires, the governor shall, with the advice and consent of the council, appoint his successor for a term of six years.

Powers and duties respecting Mount Greylock War Memorial, etc.

Section 47. In addition to the powers and duties vested in the commission by said chapter five hundred and forty-three, it shall have full authority, subject to the approval of the governor and council, permanently to care for, protect and maintain, on behalf of the commonwealth, the Mount Greylock War Memorial, constructed by the Mount Greylock War Memorial Commission under the provisions of chapter four hundred and eleven of the acts of nineteen hundred and thirty. The cost of maintenance of said memorial, together with its adjacent grounds, comprising a radius of two hundred and eighty feet, of which the memorial structure is the centre point, shall be borne by the commonwealth. The necessary expense for the care and maintenance of the remainder of the Greylock state reservation shall continue to be borne by the county of Berkshire as provided in said chapter five hundred and forty-three.

SECTION 3. Nothing herein shall affect the tenure of the members of said commission as constituted on the effective date of this act, which shall take effect as of June first in the current year.   *Approved July 18, 1933.*

Application of act to existing commission.

AN ACT PROVIDING FOR THE REMOVAL AND PUNISHMENT OF BANK OFFICERS WHO PERSIST IN IMPROPER PRACTICES.

*Chap.*337

Be it enacted, etc., as follows:

Chapter one hundred and sixty-seven of the General Laws is hereby amended by striking out section five, as appearing in the Tercentenary Edition thereof, and inserting in place thereof the following: — *Section 5.* If, in the opinion of the commissioner, any officer of any bank, including a director or trustee thereof, shall have continued to violate any law relating to such bank or shall have continued unsafe or unsound practices in conducting the business of such bank or shall have used his official position in a manner contrary to the interests of such bank or its depositors or shall have been negligent in the performance of his duties, after having been warned in writing by the commissioner to discontinue any such delinquency, the commissioner shall certify the facts to a board composed of the state treasurer, the attorney general and the commissioner of corporations and taxation. In such event the board shall cause notice to be served on such officer, director or trustee to appear before such board, to show cause why he should not be removed from office. A copy of such notice shall be sent by registered mail to each officer, director or trustee of the bank affected. If, after granting the officer, director or trustee so summoned a reasonable opportunity to be heard, the said board finds that he has continued to be guilty of any such delinquency, the said board in its discretion, may order that such officer, director or trustee be removed from office and from all participation in the management of such bank. Copies of such order shall be served upon the delinquent officer and upon such bank, whereupon such officer shall cease to be an officer of such bank and shall no longer participate in any way in the management thereof; provided, that such order and the findings of fact upon which it is based shall not be made public or disclosed to any one except the delinquent officer and the other officers, directors and trustees of such bank, otherwise than in the course of any judicial proceeding under this section. The board shall thereupon transmit to the attorney general a transcript of the evidence and findings, and the attorney general shall, on behalf of the commonwealth, institute such proceedings as he may deem

G. L. (Ter. Ed.), 167, § 5, amended.
Commissioner of banks may prosecute violations of banking laws by officers of banks.

necessary. Any person removed from office as herein provided who thereafter participates in any manner in the management of any bank in this commonwealth shall be punished by imprisonment in the state prison for not more than five years or by a fine of not more than five thousand dollars, or both.

Within twenty days after the service of an order of removal under this section upon the person removed thereby, he may file a petition in the supreme judicial court for the county of Suffolk for a review of the removal; but, pending such review, the order shall remain in full force and effect. The court shall have jurisdiction in equity to annul, reverse or affirm such order, shall review all questions of fact and of law involved and may make any appropriate order or decree. The decision of the court shall be final and conclusive. *Approved July 18, 1933.*

---

*Chap.*338 AN ACT REQUIRING DEALERS IN MILK OR CREAM TO BE LICENSED AND BONDED.

Be it enacted, etc., as follows:

G. L. (Ter. Ed.), 94, § 1, etc., amended.

SECTION 1. Section one of chapter ninety-four of the General Laws, as amended by chapter one hundred and fifty-eight of the acts of nineteen hundred and thirty-two and by sections one to five, inclusive, of chapter sixty-seven of the acts of nineteen hundred and thirty-three, is hereby further amended by adding at the end thereof the following: —

"Milk plant", etc., defined.

"Milk plant" and "manufactory" shall include, respectively, a place where milk or cream is received or purchased from producers for sale or resale and a place where it is so received or purchased for manufacture into other products, with or without facilities or equipment for its preparation for market or for its manufacture, as the case may be, and with or without physical facilities, at the place where the milk or cream is purchased, for the receiving or physical handling thereof.

G. L. (Ter. Ed.), 94, § 42A, amended, and sections 42B to 42K added. Licenses to operate milk plants, etc., form of.

SECTION 2. Said chapter ninety-four is hereby further amended by striking out section forty-two A, as so appearing, and inserting in place thereof the following eleven sections: — *Section 42A.* No person buying milk or cream from producers shall operate any milk plant or manufactory unless licensed to operate such plants and manufactories by the commissioner of agriculture, in this section and in sections forty-two B to forty-two K, inclusive, called the commissioner. Application for such license shall be made on or before January first in each year, for the license year beginning March first following, or at any time later than January first in any year for the balance of the license year after the date of issue of the license, which date shall be at least two months subsequent to the filing of the application. Such application shall be made upon a form prescribed by the commissioner, and shall contain a statement of such information as he may require to aid him in fixing the amount of the bond hereinafter required. Such statement shall be made under the penalties of perjury by the applicant, if an individual, and, if the applicant is a corporation, by its president and treasurer. A license shall not be issued unless the applicant shall execute and file at the time of filing the application, or within such further time as the commissioner may allow, a bond or other security satisfactory to the commissioner or shall be relieved therefrom as provided in section forty-two E. The commissioner, if satisfied with the financial responsibility and good faith of the applicant and with the bond or other security filed with him, shall issue to such applicant, upon payment of a fee of five dollars, a license entitling the applicant to operate milk plants and manufactories within the commonwealth for the license year or balance thereof, as the case may be.

Section 42B. The bond required by the preceding section shall be payable to the commissioner and shall be in a sum fixed by him. Said sum shall be substantially equivalent to the total purchase price, as determined by the commissioner, of milk and cream purchased by the applicant from Massachusetts producers in the average period between payments by him to producers during the three months immediately preceding the date of application for a license, plus ten per cent of such total purchase price, or, if the applicant is not then operating any milk plant or manufactory, shall be substantially equivalent to the total purchase price, as estimated by the commissioner, of milk and cream to be so purchased in the estimated average period between payments by the applicant to producers during the period for which the license is to issue, plus ten per cent thereof. Such bond shall be in a form prescribed by the commissioner and shall be executed by the applicant for a license and by a surety company authorized to do business in this commonwealth. It shall be upon the condition that the applicant, if granted a license, shall faithfully comply with the provisions of this chapter applicable to milk plants and manufactories, shall not give any cause for the revocation of his license under section forty-two H and shall promptly pay all amounts due to producers for milk or cream sold by them to him during the license period for which the application is made. In lieu of such bond, the commissioner may accept a note of like amount payable to him, secured by a mortgage of real estate or personal property, or both, or by a deposit of cash or collateral with him. Any such mortgage, or note secured by cash or collateral, shall be upon the same condition as is herein provided for a bond. Any cash or collateral deposited under this section or under section forty-two D shall be deposited by the commissioner with the state treasurer, who shall hold the same subject to section forty-two C.

Bond.

Amount of bond to be fixed by commissioner.

Default of
conditions of
bond, etc.

Claims against
licensee,
filing of.

Section 42C. Upon default by the licensee in any of
the conditions of his bond, mortgage or note secured by
cash or collateral, if there is reason to believe that the
licensee owes for purchases of milk or cream from producers,
the commissioner shall give reasonable notice to all producers, whom he has reason to believe the licensee so owes,
to file verified claims with him, and may, if he deems it
advisable, fix a limit of time within which such claims shall
be filed. The commissioner or his duly authorized assistant shall examine claims so filed and shall certify the
amounts determined by him to be due thereon. Upon
such default, he or his duly authorized assistant may
bring an action upon any bond given under the two preceding sections, may foreclose any mortgage given thereunder and sell the mortgaged property, and may sell any
collateral deposited with him thereunder. He may apply
the sum recovered in any such action, or the proceeds of
the sale of any such mortgaged property or deposited collateral, or any cash deposited as security, toward the payment of any claims of producers filed and certified under
this section, and, if the amount thereof is more than sufficient to pay all such claims, shall pay any balance remaining,
after deducting all expenses, to the licensee or his legal
representatives or surety or other person entitled thereto.
In any action upon such bond the certificate of the commissioner in determining the amounts due shall be prima
facie evidence of the facts therein stated.

Licensee to
file statement
of assets, etc.

Section 42D. The licensee shall from time to time, when
required by the commissioner, file with the commissioner a
statement of his assets, liabilities and disbursements covering a period to be prescribed by the commissioner, containing the names of the producers from whom the licensee
has purchased milk or cream and the amount due to each
such producer. Such statement shall be made under the
penalties of perjury by the applicant, if an individual, or,
if the applicant is a corporation, by its president and treasurer. If it appears from such statement, or from facts
otherwise ascertained by the commissioner, that the
security afforded by bond, mortgage or otherwise to producers selling milk or cream to such licensee does not
adequately protect such producers, the commissioner may
require such licensee to give, immediately or within such
time as the commissioner may fix, additional security in
such sum as he shall determine; but the total amount of
security given by such licensee shall not thereby be made
to exceed by more than twenty-five per cent the total
purchase price of the maximum amount of milk and cream
purchased by him from producers in any period in the
preceding three months equal in length to the average
period between payments by him to producers during said
three months.

Certain
licensees not
required to
file bond.

Section 42E. If an applicant for a license under section
forty-two A is a producer of milk or cream, or both, and, in

addition to that produced by him, purchases per day from other producers not more than one hundred quarts of milk or its equivalent in cream or in milk and cream, as determined by the commissioner, and if the commissioner is satisfied from an investigation of the financial condition of the applicant that he is solvent and possessed of sufficient assets to reasonably assure compensation to his present and future creditors, the commissioner may, by an order filed in the department of agriculture, relieve such applicant from filing a bond or other security.

Section 42F. Every operator of a milk plant or manufactory shall keep, in such form as the commissioner may prescribe, a record of all transactions concerning purchases of milk and of cream by him. Records to be kept.

Section 42G. The commissioner or his duly authorized assistant may investigate the financial standing and past conduct of any person`applying for or holding a license under section forty-two A, or any transaction by him in connection with the operation of a milk plant or manufactory, and in such investigation may examine the books of account or other documents or records of any applicant or licensee, and may take testimony therein under oath; but information relating to the general business of any applicant or licensee disclosed by such investigation and not relating to the purposes of sections forty-two A to forty-two J, inclusive, shall be treated by the commissioner as confidential. Investigation of financial standing, etc., of applicants for licenses.

Section 42H. The commissioner may refuse to grant a license under section forty-two A, or may revoke such a license already granted, when he is satisfied of the existence of any of the following causes: Revocation, etc., of licenses.

1. That a judgment has been obtained against the applicant or licensee by any producer of milk or cream and remains unsatisfied of record.

2. That there has been a failure to make prompt settlements with producers from whom the applicant or licensee buys milk or cream.

3. That there has been a continued course of dealing of such nature as to satisfy the commissioner of the inability or unwillingness of the applicant or licensee to conduct business properly or of an intent to deceive or defraud producers.

4. That there has been a continued failure by the applicant or licensee to keep records required by the commissioner or by law.

The commissioner may also revoke a license if the licensee has been duly required to give additional security under section forty-two D and has failed so to do.

Section 42I. The commissioner, before determining to revoke any license issued under section forty-two A, shall give the licensee ten days' notice, by delivery in hand or by mail, of the time and place of a hearing to determine whether or not such license shall be revoked. At such hearing, the Hearings.

commissioner or his duly authorized assistant shall receive evidence and give the licensee an opportunity to be heard, and shall thereafter file an order either dismissing the proceeding or revoking such license.

Penalty.

Section 42J. Whoever, without having a license under section forty-two A in full force and effect, operates a milk plant or a manufactory shall be punished by a fine of not more than fifty dollars for each consecutive period of twenty-four hours during which such unlicensed operation continues.

Appeal from decision of commissioner on revocation, etc., of license.

Section 42K. Any person aggrieved by a decision of the commissioner refusing to issue a license, or revoking a license, shall have the right of appeal to a board consisting of the attorney general, the commissioner of public welfare and the commissioner of corporations and taxation, or assistants appointed by them, which board shall grant the person appealing and the commissioner a prompt hearing and sustain or reverse the decision of the commissioner. The determination of said board shall be final.

Approved July 18, 1933.

*Chap.*339 AN ACT ESTABLISHING THE EAST CHELMSFORD WATER DISTRICT OF CHELMSFORD.

Be it enacted, etc., as follows:

East Chelmsford Water District of Chelmsford established.

SECTION 1. The inhabitants of the town of Chelmsford liable to taxation in that town and residing within the territory known as East Chelmsford comprised within the following boundary lines, to wit: — Beginning at a point in the Concord river in the boundary line between the town of Chelmsford and the city of Lowell; thence running westerly along said boundary line to a point in the easterly boundary line of the Chelmsford water district; thence running southeasterly along said easterly boundary line in the former location of the old Middlesex canal, so called, to River Meadow brook; thence running southwesterly along said brook and along said easterly boundary line to a point two hundred yards southerly of Billerica road; thence running southeasterly parallel with said Billerica road and two hundred yards southerly thereof to a point in the boundary line between the towns of Billerica and Chelmsford; thence running northeasterly along the said last-mentioned boundary line to a point in the Concord river; thence running northerly in said river along said last-mentioned boundary line and the boundary line between the town of Chelmsford and the city of Lowell to the point of beginning, — shall constitute a water district, and are hereby made a body corporate by the name of the East Chelmsford Water District of Chelmsford, hereinafter called the district, for the purpose of supplying themselves with water for the extinguishment of fires and for domestic and other purposes, with power to establish fountains and hydrants and to relocate and discontinue the same, to regulate the use of such water and to fix and collect rates to be paid therefor, and to take by eminent domain under chapter seventy-nine of the General Laws, or acquire by lease, purchase or otherwise, and to hold for the purposes mentioned in this act, property, lands, rights of way and other easements, and to prosecute and defend all actions relating to the property and affairs of the district.

SECTION 2. For the purposes aforesaid, said district, acting by and through its board of water commissioners hereinafter provided for, may contract with the Chelmsford Water District or the city of Lowell, or any other town or city, acting through its water department, or with any water company, or with any other water district, for whatever water may be required, authority to furnish the same being hereby granted, and/or may take under chapter seventy-nine of the General Laws, or acquire by purchase or otherwise, and hold, the waters, or any portion thereof, of any pond or stream, or of any ground sources of supply by means of driven, artesian or other wells within the town of Chelmsford not already appropriated for the purposes of a public water supply, and the water rights connected with any such water sources; and for such purposes may take as aforesaid, or acquire by purchase or otherwise, and hold, all lands, rights of way and other easements necessary for collecting, storing, holding, purifying and preserving the purity of the water and for conveying the same to any part of said district created hereby; provided, that no source of water supply or lands necessary for preserving the quality of the water shall be so taken or used without first obtaining the advice and approval of the state department of public health, and that the location of all dams, reservoirs and wells to be used as sources of water supply under this act shall be subject to the approval of said department. Said district may construct on the lands acquired and held under this act proper dams, reservoirs, standpipes, tanks, buildings, fixtures and other structures, and may make excavations, procure and operate machinery and provide such other means and appliances and do such other things as may be necessary for the establishment and maintenance of complete and effective water works; and for that purpose may construct pipe lines, wells and reservoirs and establish pumping works, and may construct, lay and maintain aqueducts, conduits, pipes and other works under or over any land, water courses, railroads, railways and public or other ways, and along such ways, in said town, in such manner as not unnecessarily to obstruct the same; and for the purposes of constructing, laying, maintaining, operating and repairing such conduits, pipes and other works, and for all proper purposes of this act, said district may dig up or raise and embank any such lands, highways or other ways in such manner as to cause the least hindrance to public travel on such ways; provided,

(margin note: May contract with city of Lowell, etc.)

(margin note: Takings by eminent domain.)

that all things done upon any such way shall be subject to the direction of the selectmen of the town of Chelmsford. Said district shall not enter upon, construct or lay any conduit, pipe or other works within the location of any railroad corporation except at such time and in such manner as it may agree upon with such corporation, or in case of failure so to agree, as may be approved by the department of public utilities.

Damages, recovery of.

SECTION 3. Any person sustaining damages in his property by any taking under this act or any other thing done under authority thereof may recover such damages from said district under said chapter seventy-nine; but the right to damages for the taking of any water, water right or water source, or for any injury thereto, shall not vest until water is actually withdrawn or diverted under authority of this act.

District may borrow money, etc.

SECTION 4. For the purpose of paying the necessary expenses and liabilities incurred for the system of water supply under the provisions of this act, other than expenses of maintenance and operation, the said district may borrow from time to time such sums as may be necessary, not exceeding, in the aggregate, one hundred thousand dollars, and may issue bonds or notes therefor, which shall bear on their face the words, East Chelmsford Water District Loan, Act of 1933. Each authorized issue shall constitute a separate loan, and such loans shall be payable in not more than thirty years from their dates. Indebtedness incurred under this act shall be subject to chapter forty-four of the General Laws.

Payment of loans, etc.

SECTION 5. Said district shall, at the time of authorizing said loan or loans, provide for the payment thereof in accordance with section four of this act; and when a vote to that effect has been passed, a sum which, with the income derived from water rates, will be sufficient to pay the annual expense of operating its water works and the interest as it accrues on the bonds or notes issued as aforesaid by the district, and to make such payments on the principal as may be required under the provisions of this act, shall without further vote be assessed upon said district by the assessors of said town of Chelmsford annually thereafter until the debt incurred by said loan or loans is extinguished.

Land taken to be controlled, etc., by commissioners.

SECTION 6. Any land taken or acquired under this act shall be managed, improved and controlled by the commissioners hereinafter provided for, in such manner as they shall deem for the best interest of the district.

Assessment of taxes.

SECTION 7. Whenever a tax is duly voted by said district for the purposes of this act, the clerk shall send a certified copy of the vote to the assessors of said town, who shall assess the same in the same manner in all respects in which town taxes are required by law to be assessed; provided, that no estate shall be subject to any tax assessed on account of the system of water supply under this act if, in the judgment of the board of water commissioners hereinafter provided for, after a hearing, such estate is so situated that it can receive no aid in the extinguishment of fire from the said system of water supply, or if such estate is so situated that the buildings thereon, or the buildings that might be constructed thereon, in any ordinary or reasonable manner could not be supplied with water from the said system; but all other estates in said district shall be deemed to be benefited and shall be subject to the tax. A certified list of the estates exempt from taxation under the provisions of this section shall annually be sent by the board of water commissioners to the assessors, at the same time at which the clerk shall send a certified copy of the vote as aforesaid. The assessment shall be committed to the town collector, who shall collect said tax in the manner provided by law for the collection of town taxes, and shall deposit the proceeds thereof with the district treasurer for the use and benefit of said district. Said district may collect interest on overdue taxes in the manner in which interest is authorized to be collected on town taxes.

SECTION 8. The first meeting of said district shall be called, within four years after the passage of this act, on petition of ten or more legal voters therein, by a warrant from the selectmen of said town, or from a justice of the peace, directed to one of the petitioners, requiring him to give notice of the meeting by posting copies of the warrant in two or more public places in the district seven days at least before the time of the meeting. Such justice of the peace, or one of the selectmen, shall preside at such meeting until a clerk is chosen and sworn, and the clerk shall preside until a moderator is chosen. After the choice of a moderator for the meeting the question of the acceptance of this act shall be submitted to the voters, and if it is accepted by two thirds of the voters present and voting thereon it shall take effect, and the meeting may then proceed to act on the other articles in the warrant. *District meeting, how called.*

SECTION 9. Said district shall, after the acceptance of this act as aforesaid, elect by ballot, either at the same meeting at which this act is accepted or at a special meeting thereafter called for the purpose, three persons to hold office, one until the expiration of three years, one until the expiration of two years, and one until the expiration of one year from the day of the next succeeding annual district meeting, to constitute a board of water commissioners; and at every annual meeting following such next succeeding annual district meeting one such commissioner shall be elected by ballot for the term of three years. All the authority granted to said district by this act, and not otherwise specifically provided for, shall be vested in said board of water commissioners, who shall be subject, however, to such instructions, rules and regulations as the district may by vote impose. Said commissioners shall appoint a treasurer of said district, who may be one of their number, *Board of water commissioners, election, terms, powers.*

who shall give bond to said district in such an amount as
may be approved by the commissioners. A majority of
the commissioners shall constitute a quorum for the transaction of business. Any vacancy occurring in said board
from any cause may be filled for the remainder of the unexpired term by said district at any legal meeting called for
the purpose. No money shall be drawn from the treasury
of said district on account of the water works except upon
a written order of said commissioners or a majority of them.

Water rates,
fixing of. SECTION 10. Said commissioners shall fix just and
equitable prices and rates for the use of water, and shall
prescribe the time and manner of payment. The income
of the water works shall be appropriated to defray all
operating expenses, interest charges and payments on the
principal as they shall accrue upon any bonds or notes
issued under authority of this act. If there should be a
net surplus remaining after providing for the aforesaid
charges, it may be appropriated for such new construction
as said commissioners may recommend, and in case a
surplus should remain after payment for such new construction the water rates shall be reduced proportionately.
Said commissioners shall annually, and as often as said
district may require, render a report upon the condition of
the works under their charge, and an account of their
doings, including an account of receipts and expenditures.

By-laws, rules
and regulations. SECTION 11. Said district may adopt by-laws prescribing by whom and how meetings may be called, noti-
fied and conducted; and, upon the application of ten or
more legal voters in said district meetings may also be
called by warrant as provided in section eight. Said
district may also establish rules and regulations for the
management of its water works, not inconsistent with this
act or with law, and may choose such other officers not
provided for in this act as it may deem necessary or proper.

Penalty for
polluting
water. SECTION 12. Whoever wilfully or wantonly corrupts,
pollutes or diverts any water obtained or supplied under
this act, or wilfully or wantonly injures any reservoir,
standpipe, aqueduct, pipe or other property owned or used
by said district for any of the purposes of this act shall
forfeit and pay to said district three times the amount of
damages assessed therefor, to be recovered in an action of
tort, and upon conviction of any of the above acts shall be
punished by a fine not more than one hundred dollars or by
imprisonment in jail for not more than twelve months.

Acceptance
of act. SECTION 13. This act shall take full effect upon its
acceptance by a two thirds vote of the voters of said district present and voting thereon at a district meeting called,
in accordance with the provisions of section eight, within
four years after its passage; but it shall become void unless
said district shall begin to distribute water to consumers
within two years after its acceptance as aforesaid.

Additions to
territory of
district. SECTION 14. Upon a petition in writing addressed to
said commissioners by any owner of real estate in said

town, abutting on said district, setting forth that the petitioner desires to have certain accurately described portions of his real estate included in said district, said commissioners shall cause a duly warned meeting of said district to be called at which meeting the voters may vote on the question of including said real estate within said district. If a majority of the voters present and voting thereon vote in the affirmative, the district clerk shall within ten days file with the town clerk of said town and with the state secretary an attested copy of said petition and vote, describing precisely the real estate added to said district; and thereupon said real estate shall become and be a part of said district and shall be holden under this act in the same manner and to the same extent as the real estate described in section one.

Approved July 18, 1933.

An Act relative to the payment of annuities to dependents of policemen, firemen or investigators or examiners of the registry of motor vehicles killed or dying from injuries received in the performance of duty.

Chap.340

Be it enacted, etc., as follows:

Section 1. Section eighty-nine of chapter thirty-two of the General Laws, as most recently amended by chapter two hundred and seventy-six of the acts of nineteen hundred and thirty-two, is hereby further amended by striking out, in the sixth line, the words "within one year", — and by striking out, in the twentieth and twenty-first lines, the words "the attending physician or medical examiner" and inserting in place thereof the words: — all members of a board consisting of two physicians designated by the mayor and city council, the selectmen, the commissioner of public safety or the commissioner of public works, as the case may be, and one physician to be designated by the commissioner of public health, — and by striking out, in the sixty-sixth line, the word "of", — so as to read as follows: — *Section 89.* If a member of the police or fire force of a city or town, or a member of the department of public safety doing police duty, or an investigator or examiner of the registry of motor vehicles in the department of public works doing police duty, is killed, or dies from injuries received, while in the performance of his duty as a member of such force or as such a member of said department of public safety or as such an investigator or examiner of said registry, as the case may be, and it shall be proved to the satisfaction of the mayor and city council or selectmen, or of the commissioner of public safety subject to the approval of the governor and council, or of the commissioner of public works, subject to like approval, as the case may be, that such death was the natural and proximate result of an

G. L. (Ter. Ed.), 32, § 89, etc., amended.

Annuities to dependents of policemen, firemen, or investigators or examiners of registry of motor vehicles killed, etc., in performance of duty.

accident occurring during the performance and within the
scope of his duty as a member of such force or as such a
member of said department of public safety or as such an
investigator or examiner of said registry, as the case may
be, and all members of a board consisting of two physicians
designated by the mayor and city council, the selectmen,
the commissioner of public safety or the commissioner of
public works, as the case may be, and one physician to be
designated by the commissioner of public health shall
certify to the city, town or state treasurer, as the case may
be, that the death was the direct result of the said injury,
there shall be paid except as hereinafter provided, out of the
city, town or state treasury, as the case may be, to the
following dependents of such deceased person the following annuities: To the widow, so long as she remains unmarried, an annuity not exceeding one thousand dollars a
year, increased by not exceeding two hundred dollars for
each child of such deceased person during such time as
such child is under the age of eighteen or over said age and
physically or mentally incapacitated from earning; and,
if there is any such child and no widow or the widow later
dies, such an annuity as would have been payable to the
widow had there been one or had she lived, to or for the
benefit of such child, or of such children in equal shares,
during the time aforesaid; and, if there is any such child
and the widow remarries, in lieu of the aforesaid annuity
to her, an annuity not exceeding two hundred and sixty
dollars to or for the benefit of each such child during the
time aforesaid; and, if there is no widow and no such child,
an annuity not exceeding one thousand dollars to or for the
benefit of the father or mother of the deceased if dependent
upon him for support at the time of his death, during such
time as such beneficiary is unable to support himself or
herself and does not remarry. The total amount of all
such annuities shall not exceed the annual rate of compensation received by such deceased person at the date of
his death, except that if such deceased person was a reserve
or special policeman or a reserve or call fireman of a city
or town and, at the time he was killed or at the time he
received the injuries resulting in his death, was performing
duty to which he was assigned or called as such policeman
or fireman and for the performance of which he was entitled to compensation from said city or town, the total
amount of all such annuities shall not exceed the annual
rate of compensation payable to a regular or permanent
member of the police or fire force thereof, as the case may
be, for the first year of service therein, and if there are no
regular or permanent members of the police or fire force
thereof, as the case may be, said total amount shall not
exceed the sum of one thousand dollars. The amount of
any such annuity shall from time to time be determined
within the limits aforesaid by the mayor and city council,
the selectmen, or the commissioner of public safety subject

to the approval of the governor and council, or the commissioner of public works, subject to like approval, as the case may be.

In case the deceased was a member of a contributory retirement system for public employees, the benefits provided under this section shall be in the alternative for the benefits, if any, provided by such retirement system for dependent widows and children or for dependent fathers or mothers; and the widow, or if there is no widow, the legal representative of the children entitled thereto, if any, otherwise the father or mother in the order named, shall elect which benefits shall be granted. Such election shall be made in writing and shall be filed with the retirement board in charge of the system of which the deceased was a member and shall not be subject to change or revocation after the first payment of any benefit thereunder.

SECTION 2.   This act shall apply to the deaths of police- Application men and firemen resulting from injuries received on or after $\substack{\text{of act to certain cases.}}$ tain cases. January first, nineteen hundred and thirty, but shall not affect any annuity granted under said section eighty-nine prior to the effective date hereof.

(*This bill, returned by the governor to the House of Representatives, the branch in which it originated, with his objections thereto, was passed by the House of Representatives, July 17, 1933, and, in concurrence, by the Senate, July 19 (P.M.), 1933, the objections of the governor notwithstanding, in the manner prescribed by the constitution; and thereby has "the force of a law".*)

AN ACT ESTABLISHING A MUNICIPAL FINANCE COMMISSION *Chap.*341
FOR THE TOWN OF MILLVILLE.

Whereas, The deferred operation of this act would tend Emergency to defeat its purpose, therefore it is hereby declared to be an preamble. emergency law, necessary for the immediate preservation of the public convenience.

Be it enacted, etc., as follows:

SECTION 1.   There is hereby established a commission, Millville Municipal to be known as the Millville Municipal Finance Commis- $\substack{\text{cipal Finance Commission}}$ sion, hereinafter called the commission, to consist of three established. members, designated by the governor, with the advice and consent of the council, each of whom shall, at the time of designation, be regularly employed in the service of the commonwealth, and such members shall serve for a period terminating on April twentieth, nineteen hundred and thirty-six. The governor, with like advice and consent, shall, from time to time, designate one of the members as chairman, may remove any member and shall fill any vacancy in the commission for the unexpired term. The action of any two of the members shall constitute the action of the commission; and whenever any action by the commission is required to be in writing, such writing shall be sufficient when signed by any two of the members. Such members shall receive no additional compensation for acting hereunder, but shall be paid by the town their necessary traveling and other expenses incurred in the performance of their duties hereunder.

Powers and duties of commission.

Section 2. Until April twentieth, nineteen hundred and thirty-six, the town of Millville shall have the capacity to act through and to be bound by the commission and not otherwise, except as hereinafter provided, and the commission shall have and exercise exclusively, so far as will conform to the provisions of this act, all rights, powers and duties now or hereafter conferred or imposed upon the inhabitants of said town and its officers, notwithstanding the common law or any provision of statutory law to the contrary. The commission may exercise and perform such rights, powers and duties through one or more existing boards or officers or newly appointed boards, officers or agents as it may designate; provided, that upon the qualification of the members of the commission the board of selectmen, the board of public welfare and the school committee of said town shall cease to exist, except that the members of the board of selectmen as at present constituted shall have the power to submit to the commission recommendations as to its appointments and shall perform all duties imposed upon selectmen relative to jurors. The commission, on behalf of the town, may issue bonds or notes of the town, but only with the approval of the governor and council. The commission shall have the power of appointment of all officers hereunder and shall fix their compensation and assign to them such of the powers and duties of the commission as it shall specify; may purchase supplies; may employ persons to do work for the town; and, except as herein provided, may remove any person now or hereafter holding office or position in or under the town government. Except as otherwise provided herein, every person holding any office or position as aforesaid shall continue to serve until his office or position is abolished or until his removal or resignation.

Apportionment of certain assessments.

Section 3. The commission may file with the county commissioners of Worcester county a request that the outstanding assessment on account of the Worcester County Tuberculosis hospital be apportioned over a period not to exceed fifteen years and the county commissioners may borrow on the credit of the county to fund the temporary loan now outstanding, as provided in chapter one hundred and eleven of the acts of nineteen hundred and thirty-two. Such request, if filed with said county commissioners on or before August fifteenth in the current year, shall have the same effect as a like vote of the town under section two of said chapter one hundred and eleven would have had if filed with said county commissioners within the time limited therein.

Assessments for taxes.

Section 4. The assessors, or the board, officer or

agent appointed or designated by the commission to perform the duties of assessors, shall assess all property within said town, as far as may be, at its fair cash value at a rate not more than twenty per cent in excess of the average rate of tax of all cities and towns of the commonwealth for the preceding year, and any amount necessary to meet expenditures over and above the amount to be raised from taxes and estimated to be received from other sources shall be advanced temporarily by the commonwealth upon receipt of notes of the town payable in not more than three years from their dates. *Excess.*

SECTION 5. The said town, acting through the commission, may also borrow a sum not exceeding ten thousand dollars for the purpose of paying temporary loans or other obligations unpaid on January first of the current year, and may issue notes therefor, which shall bear on their face the words, Millville Funding Loan, Act of 1933, and such notes shall be paid in not more than five years from June thirtieth, nineteen hundred and thirty-three; and may also borrow for said purposes from time to time, for periods not extending beyond July first, nineteen hundred and thirty-five, sums not exceeding, in the aggregate, thirty thousand dollars, in anticipation of the collection of unpaid taxes and other accounts receivable as appearing on the books of said town as of December thirty-first, nineteen hundred and thirty-two, and may issue notes therefor, which shall bear on their face the words, Millville Temporary Funding Loan, Act of 1933. Upon tender to the state treasurer of any notes issued by the town under this section or issued by it in anticipation of revenue, they shall forthwith be purchased by the commonwealth at the face value thereof. Such notes, if issued for purposes of sale to the commonwealth, shall bear such rates of interest as in the judgment of the state treasurer and the commission will cover the entire cost to the commonwealth incurred on account of loans to the town hereunder, including interest on money borrowed by the commonwealth under the following section and all expenses in connection with the issue of its notes thereunder. None of the receipts from the collection of taxes assessed by said town for the year nineteen hundred and thirty-two or for any year prior thereto shall be appropriated for any purposes other than the payment of liabilities of said town outstanding on January first of the current year, so long as any portion of said temporary funding loan remains unpaid. If any portion of said temporary funding loan remains unpaid on July first, nineteen hundred and thirty-five, such portion shall be included in the tax levy of that year. *Temporary loans.*

SECTION 6. The state treasurer, with the approval of the governor and council, may borrow from time to time, on the credit of the commonwealth, such sums as may be necessary to provide funds for loans to the town of Millville as provided in this act, but not exceeding, in the aggregate, *Commonwealth may borrow money to assist town.*

one hundred and fifty thousand dollars, and may issue and renew notes of the commonwealth therefor, bearing interest payable at such times and at such rate as shall be fixed by the state treasurer, with the approval of the governor and council. Such notes shall be issued for such maximum term of years as the governor may recommend to the general court in accordance with section three of Article LXII of the amendments to the constitution of the commonwealth, but such notes, whether original or renewal, shall be payable not later than November thirtieth, nineteen hundred and thirty-nine. All notes issued under this section shall be signed by the state treasurer, approved by the governor and countersigned by the comptroller.

Authority of commission terminated, when.

SECTION 7. In the month of March in the year nineteen hundred and thirty-six, the commission shall call a town meeting for the purpose of filling all offices heretofore provided to be filled by vote of the inhabitants, and the persons elected at such meeting shall, on April twentieth of said year, or as soon thereafter as they qualify for their offices, take over the affairs of said town of Millville.

Extension of time within which town may pay loans.

SECTION 8. If, on April twentieth, nineteen hundred and thirty-six, the principal and interest on all notes issued by said town hereunder and purchased by the commonwealth have not been paid in full, the state treasurer shall have authority not later than the issue of his warrant for the town's share of the state tax, to issue his warrant requiring its assessors to include in its next annual tax levy the amount necessary to pay in full the portion thereof remaining due or to include in that and any succeeding levy the amount necessary to pay any instalment thereof as determined and certified to him by the commission as hereinafter provided. If, in the opinion of the commission, the financial affairs of said town warrant, the commission may direct the assessment of the amount remaining due, in such number of annual instalments, not exceeding three, as may seem advisable; provided, that the amount of any instalment payable in any year shall not be less than the amount of any instalment payable in any subsequent year. Prior to April twentieth, nineteen hundred and thirty-six, the commission shall determine and certify to the state treasurer the amount of each instalment required to be assessed upon the said town in the several years. The amount included under authority hereof in the state treasurer's warrant to the assessors of the said town shall be collected and paid to him in the same manner and subject to the same penalties as state taxes, and if such amount is not duly paid as aforesaid by the said town, the state treasurer shall have authority to withhold, from any sum due from the commonwealth to it and not previously pledged, the amount necessary to pay in full the amount remaining due to the commonwealth on April twentieth, nineteen hundred and thirty-six.   *Approved July 22, 1933.*

AN ACT AMENDING THE LAWS RELATIVE TO THE TAXATION *Chap.*342
OF BUSINESS AND MANUFACTURING CORPORATIONS.

Whereas, The deferred operation of this act would tend Emergency
to defeat its purpose, therefore it is hereby declared to be preamble.
an emergency law, necessary for the immediate preservation of the public convenience.

Be it enacted, etc., as follows:

SECTION 1. Chapter sixty-three of the General Laws G. L. (Ter.
is hereby amended by striking out section thirty-two, as Ed.), 63, § 32,
appearing in the Tercentenary Edition thereof, and in- amended.
serting in place thereof the following: — *Section 32.* Ex- Excise on
cept as otherwise provided in sections thirty-four and domestic
business
thirty-eight B, every domestic business corporation shall corporations.
pay annually an excise equal to the sum of the following,
provided, that every such corporation shall pay annually
a total excise not less in amount than one twentieth of one
per cent of the fair value of its capital stock on the day fixed
for determination of the value of its corporate excess: —
    (1) An amount equal to five dollars per thousand upon
the value of its corporate excess.
    (2) An amount equal to two and one half per cent of its
net income determined to be taxable in accordance with the
provisions of this chapter.
    Liability for such excise shall be incurred by corporate
existence at any time within the taxable year, or, in case
the corporation has not established a taxable year, upon
April first of the year in which the excise is to be assessed.
    SECTION 2. Section thirty-two A of said chapter sixty- G. L. (Ter.
three, as so appearing, is hereby amended by striking out, Ed.), 63,
§ 32A,
in the third and fourth lines, the words ", with respect to amended.
the carrying on or doing of business by it," — so as to read
as follows: — *Section 32A.* Every domestic business cor- Excise on
poration deriving its profits principally from the ownership, such corporations princi-
sale, rental or use of real estate or tangible personal prop- pally dealing
erty shall pay annually a total excise under this chapter in real estate
or tangible
not less in amount than one twentieth of one per cent of personal
said corporation's gross receipts from business assignable property.
to this commonwealth as defined in clause six of section
thirty-eight.
    SECTION 3. Section thirty-eight of said chapter sixty- G. L. (Ter.
three, as so appearing, is hereby amended by adding at Ed.), 63,
§ 38, amended.
the end thereof the following new paragraph: —
    10. A domestic corporation shall be deemed to carry on Allocation of
business outside this commonwealth within the meaning remainder of
net income.
of this section only when its activities in another state or
country give such state or country jurisdiction to tax the
corporation in respect to such activities.
    SECTION 4. Section thirty-nine of said chapter sixty- G. L. (Ter.
three, as so appearing, and as amended by section six of Ed.), 63, § 39,
etc., amended.
chapter three hundred and twenty-seven of the acts of the

current year, is hereby further amended by adding at the end thereof the following new paragraph: —

Excise on foreign corporations. Liability for such excise shall be incurred by corporate activity within the commonwealth at any time within the taxable year, or, in case the corporation has not established a taxable year, upon April first of the year in which the excise is to be assessed.

G. L. (Ter. Ed.), 63, § 42, etc., amended. SECTION 5. Said chapter sixty-three, as amended in section forty-two by section eleven of chapter one hundred and eighty of the acts of nineteen hundred and thirty-two, is hereby further amended by striking out said section forty-two and inserting in place thereof the following: —

Determination of net income of foreign corporations from business in the commonwealth. *Section 42.* Upon application by a foreign corporation carrying on part of its business outside the commonwealth, on or before the time when its return under this chapter is due to be filed, the commissioner shall determine its income derived from business carried on within the commonwealth by a method other than that set forth in the preceding section, provided it shall appear that the method so set forth is not reasonably adapted to approximate, in the case of the applying corporation, the income so derived. A foreign corporation which so applies, and every such corporation which is foreign to the United States and which is required to return to the federal government only income from sources within the United States, shall on or before May tenth file with the commissioner, under oath of its treasurer, a statement in such detail as the commissioner shall require, showing the amount of its annual net income derived from business carried on within the commonwealth and such other information as the commissioner may require with reference thereto, and the commissioner shall by reasonable methods determine the amount of the net income received from business carried on within the commonwealth. The amount thus determined shall be the net income taxable under this chapter and the foregoing determination shall be in lieu of the determination required by the preceding section. If a foreign corporation in any year applies to the commissioner to have its income derived from business carried on within the commonwealth determined by a method other than that set forth in the preceding section and the commissioner makes such determination, the commissioner may, in his discretion, with respect to any year during the two year period following the year for which such application was made, require similar information from such corporation if it shall appear that the allocating method set forth in the preceding section is not reasonably adapted to approximate for the pertinent year the income derived from business carried on within the commonwealth and may, by reasonable methods, determine such income in the same manner as if the corporation had applied to have its income so determined.

A corporation aggrieved by any action or refusal to act

of the commissioner in respect to any matters arising under this section shall have the same right of appeal as is provided in section seventy-one.

SECTION 6. This act shall take effect as of January first, nineteen hundred and thirty-three, and shall apply to taxes assessed in the year nineteen hundred and thirty-three and thereafter; provided, that the provisions of section five shall not become operative until January first, nineteen hundred and thirty-four. Effective date of act.

Approved July 22, 1933.

AN ACT TO AUTHORIZE BANKS AND CREDIT UNIONS TO CO-OPERATE IN ACTION UNDER THE FEDERAL HOME OWNERS' LOAN ACT OF 1933. *Chap.343*

Whereas, The deferred operation of this act would tend to defeat its purpose, therefore it is hereby declared to be an emergency law, necessary for the immediate preservation of the public convenience. Emergency preamble.

Be it enacted, etc., as follows:

In connection with assistance being given during the period limited by the act of congress, known as the Home Owners' Loan Act of 1933, to any home owner by the Home Owners' Loan Corporation created by said act, under subsection (g) or subsection (d) of section four thereof, and notwithstanding any other provision of law, any savings bank, co-operative bank, credit union or trust company, with the approval of its officers, board, committee or majority thereof, authorized by law to approve loans secured by mortgage of real estate, and subject to such terms and conditions as such officers, board, committee or majority may require in each case, may accept in exchange for any real estate, as defined in said subsection (d), held or owned by it as the result of the foreclosure of a mortgage thereon, or in exchange for, or in consideration of the discharge of, any home mortgage, as defined in subsection (c) of section two of said act, or other obligation secured by real estate and eligible for acquisition by said Home Owners' Loan Corporation under said subsection (d), in addition to any other lawful consideration, bonds of said Home Owners' Loan Corporation, and may compound any loan secured by such home mortgage or other obligation eligible for such acquisition and receive such bonds as the consideration, in whole or in part, for such compounding. All savings banks, co-operative banks, credit unions and trust companies are hereby authorized to exercise any powers and to do any and all things incidental or necessary to give effect to any such transaction. Banks, etc., authorized to co-operate under Federal Home Owners' Loan Act of 1933.

Approved July 22, 1933.

*Chap.*344 AN ACT RELATIVE TO THE RECEIPT AND DISPOSITION OF FUNDS RECEIVED BY THE COMMONWEALTH UNDER THE FEDERAL EMERGENCY RELIEF ACT OF 1933.

Emergency preamble.

Whereas, The deferred operation of this act would tend to defeat its purpose, therefore it is hereby declared to be an emergency law, necessary for the immediate preservation of the public convenience.

Be it enacted, etc., as follows:

Distribution of federal funds by emergency finance board.

SECTION 1. The emergency finance board created under chapter forty-nine of the acts of the current year is hereby authorized and directed to distribute to the cities and towns of the commonwealth in such amounts and under such conditions as it may determine and conformably to such rules, regulations and instructions as the federal government may issue, all moneys received by the commonwealth as a grant or grants under the Federal Emergency Relief Act of 1933. The state treasurer shall receive all moneys so granted, and all disbursements thereof shall be upon the certification of said board.

Federal grants to be considered in fixing local tax rates.

SECTION 2. From such information as he may receive from said board, the commissioner of corporations and taxation shall determine and certify to any city or town seasonably before the fixing of its tax rate for the current year the amount received or anticipated to be received by such city or town from such grant or grants during the current year, which said assessors shall treat as an estimated receipt in fixing said rate.

1933, 307, § 2, amended.

SECTION 3. Section two of chapter three hundred and seven of the acts of the current year is hereby amended by adding at the end thereof the following new sentence: —

Determination of amount of loan to cities and towns.

In determining whether or not the financial affairs of any such city or town justify the board in approving a loan under this or the following section, the board shall take into consideration the amount which such city or town has received or may receive from any grant or grants made under the Federal Emergency Relief Act of 1933.

1933, 307, § 8, repealed.

SECTION 4. Section eight of said chapter three hundred and seven is hereby repealed. *Approved July 22, 1933.*

*Chap.*345 AN ACT TO ENABLE THE ASSISTANT SUPERINTENDENT OF THE STATE INFIRMARY TO APPROVE ACCOUNTS IN CERTAIN CASES.

Emergency preamble.

Whereas, The deferred operation of this act would tend to defeat its purpose, therefore it is hereby declared to be an emergency law, necessary for the immediate preservation of the public convenience.

Be it enacted, etc., as follows:

G. L. (Ter. Ed.), 122, § 6, amended.

Section six of chapter one hundred and twenty-two of the General Laws, as appearing in the Tercentenary Edition thereof, is hereby amended by inserting after the

word "superintendent" in the third line the words: — , by the assistant superintendent, — so as to read as follows: --
Section 6. All accounts for the maintenance of the state infirmary shall be approved by the trustees thereof, or, if the trustees so vote, by the superintendent, by the assistant superintendent or by the chairman or some other member designated by him, and shall be filed with the comptroller and paid by the commonwealth.

Approved July 22, 1933.

Accounts of state infirmary.

An Act making certain adjustments in the laws regulating the manufacture, transportation and sale of wines and malt beverages.

*Chap.*346

Whereas, The deferred operation of this act would tend to defeat its purpose, therefore it is hereby declared to be an emergency law, necessary for the immediate preservation of the public convenience.

Emergency preamble.

Be it enacted, etc., as follows:

SECTION 1. Section six of chapter one hundred and twenty of the acts of the current year, as amended by chapter two hundred and sixteen of the acts of said year, is hereby further amended by inserting after the word "containers" in the fifth line the words: — , and in quantities not exceeding eight gallons in any single transaction, — so that the first sentence will read as follows: — The local licensing authorities in any city or town wherein the granting of such licenses is authorized under this act may grant a license to any suitable applicant, approved by the commission, to sell at retail, in bottles or other containers, and in quantities not exceeding eight gallons in any single transaction, wines and malt beverages not to be drunk on the premises.

1933, 120, § 6, etc., amended.

License to sell at retail wines, etc.

SECTION 2. Section seven of said chapter one hundred and twenty is hereby amended by adding at the end thereof the following new paragraph: —
Nothing contained in this act shall disqualify the holder of a license under this section or under section nine or nine A from also holding a license under section six.

1933, 120, § 7, amended.

Limitation of certain provisions.

SECTION 3. Said chapter one hundred and twenty is hereby further amended by inserting after section seven the following new section: — *Section 7A.* The holder of a license under section seven, eight, nine or nine A may sell wines and malt beverages to incorporated hospitals whose real or personal property is exempt from taxation under the laws of the commonwealth, in such quantities and subject to such restrictions as the commission may by regulation prescribe.

1933, 120, new section 7A, added.

Sales to hospitals regulated.

SECTION 4. Section eight of said chapter one hundred and twenty is hereby amended by inserting after the word "licenses" in the thirtieth line the words: — and, in such

1933, 120, § 8, amended.

amount as the commission may by its regulations prescribe, in kegs of a capacity not exceeding eight gallons, to
holders of retail licenses, — so that the second paragraph
will read as follows: — Manufacturers of wines or malt
beverages may sell the same to any licensee holding a valid
license granted by the licensing authorities for the sale
within the commonwealth in accordance with the provisions of this act, and may also sell wines or malt beverages
for export from this commonwealth into any state where
the sale of the same is not by law prohibited, and into any
foreign country.   All wines and malt beverages sold by any
manufacturer thereof shall be sold and delivered only in
bottles filled and sealed by such manufacturer upon his own
premises, and in such manner, and under such conditions,
and with such labels or other marks to identify the manufacturer, as the commission shall from time to time prescribe by regulations; provided, that sales of wines and
malt beverages may be made in kegs, casks or barrels to
holders of wholesale licenses and, in such amount as the
commission may by its regulations prescribe, in kegs of a
capacity not exceeding eight gallons, to holders of retail
licenses; and provided, further, that sales of wines and malt
beverages may be made in kegs, casks or barrels by any
manufacturer or holder of a wholesale license to any common victualer, innholder or club, licensed by the local
licensing authorities to sell wines and malt beverages to be
drunk on the premises, if the nature and extent of the
restaurant, hotel or club business of such licensee is, in the
judgment of the commission, such as to justify the sale by
such licensee of wines and malt beverages by draft under
such conditions as the commission may from time to time
by regulation prescribe.

1933, 120, § 9, amended.

SECTION 4A.   Section nine of said chapter one hundred
and twenty is hereby amended by inserting after the word
"section", in the twenty-seventh line, the words: — and
section nine A, — so that the last sentence will read as
follows: — In order to ensure the necessary control of
traffic in wines and malt beverages for the preservation of
the public peace and order, the shipment of such wines and
malt beverages into the commonwealth, except as provided
in this section and section nine A, is hereby prohibited.

Shipment of wines, etc., regulated.

1933, 120, new section 9A, added.

SECTION 5.   Said chapter one hundred and twenty
is hereby further amended by inserting after section nine
the following new section: — *Section 9A*.   The commission
may grant to any suitable applicant a general importer's
license which shall authorize the holder thereof to import
into the commonwealth from other states and foreign countries wines and malt beverages in the same manner and
subject to the same restrictions as a holder of a foreign
manufacturer's agency license under section nine, except
that the holder of a general importer's license shall not be
restricted to dealing in the goods of any specified manufacturer.   Except as herein provided, the provisions of

General importer's license.

said section nine shall apply to licenses granted under this section and to the business authorized thereby.

SECTION 6. Said chapter one hundred and twenty is hereby further amended by striking out section ten, as amended by section one of chapter two hundred and thirty-four of the acts of the current year, and inserting in place thereof the following: — *Section 10.* Every manufacturer of wines or malt beverages and every holder of a foreign manufacturer's agency license or a general importer's license for the sale thereof shall, in addition to the license fees elsewhere provided in this act, be liable for and pay to the commonwealth as an excise, for the privilege enjoyed by him as such manufacturer, foreign manufacturer's agency or general importer, the sum of one dollar for each and every barrel of thirty-one gallons of wine or malt beverages sold within the commonwealth by such manufacturer, foreign manufacturer's agency or general importer, respectively, or a proportionate amount where any other form of container is used. Every person subject to this section shall keep a true and accurate account of all wines and malt beverages sold by him and shall make a return thereof to the commissioner of corporations and taxation, hereinafter called the commissioner, within ten days after the last day of each month, covering his sales during such month, and shall at the time of such return make payment to the commissioner of the amount due under this section for such sales in such month. The commissioner is hereby authorized to prescribe rules and regulations governing the method of keeping accounts, making returns and paying the excise provided for in this section. Such rules and regulations may provide for the waiver of payment of the excise in respect to any wines or malt beverages if it appears that an excise has already been paid under the provisions of this section in respect thereto.

Sums due to the commonwealth under this section may be recovered by the attorney general in an action brought in the name of the commissioner. The commission may suspend the license of a person subject to this section, at the suggestion of the commissioner, for failure to pay such sums when due. The commissioner shall have the same powers and remedies with respect to the collection of said sums as he has with respect to the collection of income taxes under chapter sixty-two of the General Laws.

SECTION 7. Said chapter one hundred and twenty is hereby further amended by striking out section fifteen and inserting in place thereof the following: — *Section 15.* It shall be unlawful for any person licensed to sell wines or malt beverages not to be drunk on the premises, or any proprietor of a restaurant or of a hotel or any club duly licensed to sell wines or malt beverages to be drunk on the premises, to lend or borrow money, or receive credit, directly or indirectly, to or from any manufacturer of wines or malt beverages, or to or from any member of the family

1933, 120, § 10, amended.

Excise.

1933, 120, § 15, amended.

Loaning money to licensees by manufacturers, etc., prohibited.

of such a manufacturer, or to or from any stockholder in a corporation manufacturing such wines and malt beverages, and for any such manufacturer, or any member of the family of such manufacturer, or any stockholder in a corporation manufacturing such wines or malt beverages, to lend money or otherwise extend credit, except in the usual course of business and for a period not exceeding sixty days, directly or indirectly, to any such licensee, or to acquire, retain or own, directly or indirectly, any interest in the business of any such licensee or in the premises occupied by any such licensee in the conduct of the licensed business, or in any equipment, property or furnishings used on such premises, or, except as otherwise provided in this act, for any person, firm, corporation or association to acquire, own or retain, directly or indirectly, any such interest while such person, firm, corporation or association also owns or holds or controls a majority interest, as partner, stockholder, trustee, or in any other manner or capacity, in the business or plant of any manufacturer, wholesaler of wines or malt beverages or the holder of a foreign manufacturer's agency or general importer's license. The violation of any of the above provisions of this section shall be sufficient cause for the revocation of the licenses of all licensees involved in such violation.

1933, 120, § 49, amended.

Transportation of wines, etc., regulated.

SECTION 8. Said chapter one hundred and twenty is hereby further amended by striking out section forty-nine and inserting in place thereof the following: — *Section 49.* No person shall manufacture, sell, or expose, or keep for sale, or transport, wines or malt beverages, except as authorized in this act; provided, that sheriffs, deputy sheriffs, constables, trustees in bankruptcy, and public officers acting under judicial process, and executors, administrators, receivers and trustees duly authorized by proper judicial order or decree, and assignees under voluntary assignments for the benefit of creditors if such assignees are authorized by special permit issued by the commission, may sell and transport wines and malt beverages, subject to such conditions and restrictions as the commission may prescribe.

1933, 97, § 3, repealed.

SECTION 9. Section three of chapter ninety-seven of the acts of the current year is hereby repealed.

Approved July 22, 1933.

An Act authorizing the commissioner of labor and *Chap.*347
industries to suspend the six o'clock law, so
called, relating to the hours of employment of
women in the textile and leather industries during the operation of the respective codes for the
regulation of the textile and leather industries
under authority of the national industrial recovery act.

Whereas, The deferred operation of this act would in Emergency
part defeat its purpose, therefore it is hereby declared to preamble.
be an emergency law, necessary for the immediate preservation of the public health, safety and convenience.

Be it enacted, etc., as follows:

Section 1. The commissioner of labor and industries Suspension
is hereby authorized, in conformity with Article XX of law.
Part the First of the Constitution of the Commonwealth, Textiles, etc.
to suspend, for and during such time as any code for the
regulation of any of the textile industries, approved by the
President of the United States under the provisions of the
National Industrial Recovery Act, is in effect, and subject
to such restrictions and conditions as the said commissioner may prescribe, so much of section fifty-nine of
chapter one hundred and forty-nine of the General Laws,
as amended by section one of chapter one hundred and
ninety-three of the acts of the current year, as prohibits the
employment of women in the manufacture of textile goods
after six o'clock in the evening; and, during such time,
those parts of said section fifty-nine which are so suspended
shall be inoperative and of no effect.

Section 2. The said commissioner is hereby author- Same subject.
ized, in conformity with said Article XX, to suspend, for Leather manu-
and during such time as any code for the regulation of the facture.
leather industry, approved by the President of the United
States under the provisions of the said National Industrial
Recovery Act, is in effect, and subject to such restrictions
and conditions as the said commissioner may prescribe,
so much of said section fifty-nine, as so amended, as prohibits the employment of women in the manufacture of
leather after six o'clock in the evening; and, during such
time, those parts of said section fifty-nine which are so
suspended shall be inoperative and of no effect.

Approved July 22, 1933.

An Act authorizing the construction of a new high *Chap.*348
level bridge over the weymouth fore river to re-
place the fore river bridge, so-called, and for its
maintenance as a state highway.

Whereas, The deferred operation of this act would de- Emergency
feat its purpose, not only to provide for the safety of the preamble.
travelling public but also to afford relief in the present

unemployment emergency, therefore it is hereby declared to be an emergency law, necessary for the immediate preservation of the public safety and convenience.

Be it enacted, etc., as follows:

Weymouth
Fore River
bridge.

SECTION 1. The department of public works, hereinafter called the department, is hereby authorized and directed to construct a new high level bridge, with suitable approaches and with a draw, over the Weymouth Fore river between that part of the city of Quincy known as Quincy Point and the town of Weymouth in replacement of the existing Fore River bridge, so-called, together with a temporary way and a temporary bridge and approaches thereto, to make necessary alterations to street railway and railroad tracks and in connecting ways and to construct any necessary drainage outlets.

Takings.

SECTION 2. The department may, on behalf of the commonwealth, take by eminent domain, under chapter seventy-nine of the General Laws, or acquire by purchase or otherwise, such public or private lands, public parks or reservations, or parts thereof or rights therein, and/or public ways, as it may deem necessary for carrying out the provisions of section one; provided, that no damages shall be paid for public lands, parks or reservations so taken.

Cost, etc.

SECTION 3. The cost of constructing said bridge and land takings for the same, including any damages awarded or paid on account of any taking of land or property therefor, or any injury to the same, any sums paid for lands or rights purchased, and all other expenses incurred in carrying out the provisions of section one, shall not exceed, in the aggregate, two million two hundred thousand dollars. The department may make a contract or contracts for said construction involving the expenditure of funds not exceeding the amount herein authorized to be expended, upon receipt of assurance from the proper federal authorities that the federal government will furnish by grant or

Federal funds.

loan, or both, under the National Industrial Recovery Act, the funds necessary to meet the cost of said construction, notwithstanding the provisions of section twenty-seven of chapter twenty-nine of the General Laws, as appearing in the Tercentenary Edition thereof. To meet expenses incurred, in anticipation of the securing of funds under said act, in carrying out said construction, expenditures may be made from the appropriation made by item five hundred and seventy-nine of chapter one hundred and seventy-four of the acts of the current year.

Bridge to
become state
highway.

SECTION 4. When the work authorized herein shall have been completed, any new location of the Fore River Railroad Corporation established hereunder shall be conveyed to it by the commonwealth, and the permanent bridge referred to in section one, with its abutments and draw, shall become and be maintained as a state highway, except that so much of the cost of maintenance of said bridge as represents the compensation paid to persons employed in operating the draw shall be paid by the city of Quincy and the towns of Braintree and Weymouth in such proportions as shall be determined by the department. Assessments for compensation paid as aforesaid shall be made and collected by the state treasurer as a part of the annual state tax. *Approved July 22, 1933.*

---

*Chap.*349

An Act providing for immediate construction of the proposed bridge over the Saugus river between the city of Lynn and the point of pines in the city of Revere.

Whereas, The deferred operation of this act would defeat its purpose, not only to provide for the safety of the travelling public but also to afford relief in the present unemployment emergency, therefore it is hereby declared to be an emergency law, necessary for the immediate preservation of the public safety and convenience.

Emergency preamble.

Be it enacted, etc., as follows:

The department of public works is hereby authorized and directed to proceed with the construction of the new bridge over the Saugus river between the cities of Lynn and Revere, as provided by chapter two hundred and forty-one of the acts of nineteen hundred and thirty-two, and may make a contract or contracts for said construction involving the expenditure of funds not exceeding the amount authorized to be expended by section three of said chapter two hundred and forty-one, upon receipt of assurance from the proper federal authorities that the federal government will furnish by grant or loan, or both, under the National Industrial Recovery Act, the funds necessary to meet the cost of said construction, notwithstanding the provisions of section twenty-seven of chapter twenty-nine of the General Laws, as appearing in the Tercentenary Edition thereof. To meet expenses incurred, in anticipation of the securing of funds under said act, in carrying out said construction, expenditures may be made from the appropriation made by item five hundred and seventy-nine of chapter one hundred and seventy-four of the acts of the current year. *Approved July 22, 1933.*

Saugus river bridge, construction, etc.

---

*Chap.*350

An Act providing for the payment and distribution of income taxes in two instalments, regulating the assessment and refunding of interest thereon, and fixing the date when certain late assessments thereof are payable.

Be it enacted, etc., as follows:

Section 1. Chapter sixty-two of the General Laws is hereby amended by striking out section thirty-seven, as appearing in the Tercentenary Edition thereof, and insert-

G. L. (Ter. Ed.), 62, § 37, amended.

ing in place thereof the following: — *Section 37.* If the commissioner finds from the verification of a return, or otherwise, that the income of any person subject to taxation under this chapter, or any portion thereof, has not been assessed, he may, at any time within two years after September first of the year in which such assessment should have been made, assess the same, first giving notice to the person so to be assessed of his intention, and such person shall thereupon have an opportunity within ten days after such notification to confer with the commissioner in person or by counsel or other representative as to the proposed assessment. After the expiration of ten days from such notification the commissioner shall assess the income of such person subject to taxation, or any portion thereof, which he believes has not theretofore been assessed, and he shall thereupon give notice as provided in section thirty-nine to the person so assessed. The provisions of this chapter in respect to the abatement and collection of taxes shall apply to a tax so assessed. Whenever, in the course of a verification of the returns of a taxpayer under section thirty, the commissioner finds that an overpayment of the total amount of taxes due from such taxpayer has been made on any year's return subject to verification, the amount of such overpayment shall be deducted from the amount of any additional tax found to be due on any other year's return so verified, and only the net amount thus determined to be due, with interest as provided in section thirty-seven A, shall be assessed additionally.

SECTION 2. Said chapter sixty-two is hereby further amended by inserting after section thirty-seven the following new section: — *Section 37A.* Except as otherwise provided in section twenty-five in the case of a person removing from the commonwealth or a fiduciary making final distribution, one half of the tax imposed by this chapter shall be due and payable in advance of assessment at the time when the tax return is required to be filed, and the remaining half on October first following. So much of each half of said tax as is not paid at its due date shall bear interest from said date at the rate of one half of one per cent per month, or major fraction thereof, until it is paid, if paid prior to assessment, otherwise until the tax as assessed is required to be paid. Taxes assessed under sections thirty-five, thirty-six and thirty-seven shall include interest as provided in this section to the date when the tax so assessed, or any unpaid balance thereof, is required to be paid, which shall be the thirtieth day following the date of the notice of the assessment, if such notice issues after September first of the year in which the tax return is required to be filed, or on October first next following the date of issue if such notice issues on or before said September first.

SECTION 3. Section thirty-nine of said chapter sixty-two, as so appearing, is hereby amended by striking out the first sentence and inserting in place thereof the following: — The commissioner shall, as soon as may be, give Notice of date tax is due. written notice to every person assessed under this chapter of the amount of the tax assessed and of the time when the same, or any unpaid balance thereof, is required to be paid.

SECTION 4. Said chapter sixty-two is hereby further G. L. (Ter. Ed.), 62, § 41, etc., amended. amended by striking out section forty-one, as amended by chapter one hundred and fifty-two of the acts of nineteen hundred and thirty-two, and inserting in place thereof the following: — *Section 41.* Assessed taxes remaining unpaid Interest. after the date upon which the same are required to be paid Remedies of commissioner. shall bear interest at the rate of six per cent per annum, which shall be added to and become part of the tax. The commissioner shall have for the collection of taxes assessed under this chapter all the remedies provided by chapter sixty for the collection of taxes on personal estate by collectors of taxes of towns, except that any warrant for the collection of a tax assessed under this chapter may be issued to any sheriff, deputy sheriff or constable and he shall have authority to proceed thereunder anywhere within the commonwealth. The officer to whom a warrant for the collection of such a tax is given shall collect said tax and interest as herein provided and may collect and receive for his fees the sum which an officer would be entitled by law to receive upon an execution for a like amount. Any action of contract brought to recover any such tax shall be brought in the name of the commonwealth.

SECTION 5. Section forty-three of said chapter sixty- G. L. (Ter. Ed.), 62, § 43, amended. two, as appearing in the Tercentenary Edition of the General Laws, is hereby amended by inserting after the word "paid" in the eleventh line the words: — , but not from a time earlier than October first of the year in which the return of income subject to said tax was required to be filed, — so as to read as follows: — *Section 43.* Any person Abatement by commissioner. aggrieved by the assessment of a tax under this chapter may apply to the commissioner for an abatement thereof at any time within six months after the date of the notice of the assessment, or, if he dies during said six months his executor or administrator may apply for such abatement within one month after his appointment; and if, after a hearing, the commissioner finds that the tax is excessive in amount or that the person assessed is not subject thereto, he shall abate it in whole or in part accordingly. If the tax has been paid, the state treasurer shall repay to the person assessed the amount of such abatement, with interest thereon at the rate of six per cent per annum from the time when it was paid, but not from a time earlier than October first of the year in which the return of income subject to said tax was required to be filed. The commissioner shall notify the petitioner by registered letter of his decision upon the petition.

SECTION 6. Said chapter sixty-two is hereby further G. L. (Ter. Ed.), 62, § 46, amended. amended by striking out section forty-six, as so appearing, and inserting in place thereof the following: — *Section 46.* If the tax abated has been paid, the state treasurer, upon presentation to him of the notice of the decision of the board, shall repay to the petitioner the amount of the abatement and interest at the rate of six per cent per annum from the time of payment, but not from a time earlier than October first of the year in which the return of income subject to said tax was required to be filed.

SECTION 7. Chapter fifty-eight of the General Laws is hereby amended by striking out section eighteen, as so appearing, and inserting in place thereof the following: — *Section 18.* The state treasurer shall, on or before April fifteenth in each year, distribute the amounts of taxes on incomes under chapter sixty-two theretofore collected by the commonwealth to the several cities and towns in proportion to the amounts of the last preceding state tax imposed upon them, and shall, on or before November twentieth in the same year, distribute to such cities and towns in the same proportion the balance of such taxes collected after said April fifteenth, after deducting a sum sufficient to reimburse the commonwealth for the expenses incurred in the collection and distribution of said income taxes and for such of said taxes as have been refunded under said chapter sixty-two or section twenty-seven of this chapter during said year, together with any interest or costs paid on account of refunds, which shall be retained by the commonwealth, and after deducting also a sufficient sum to be distributed under Part I of chapter seventy.

SECTION 8. Section thirteen of chapter fifty-eight A of the General Laws, as most recently amended by section seven of chapter three hundred and twenty-one of the acts of the current year, is hereby further amended by striking out the sentence included in lines sixty to sixty-seven, inclusive, as printed in the Tercentenary Edition thereof,
and inserting in place thereof the following: — If the order grants an abatement of a tax assessed by the commissioner or by the board of assessors of a town and the tax has been paid, the amount abated with interest at the rate of six per cent per annum from the time when the tax was paid but, in case of a tax assessed under chapter sixty-two, not from a time earlier than October first of the year in which the return of income subject to said tax was required to be filed, and, if costs are ordered against the commissioner or against a board of assessors, the amount thereof, shall be paid to the taxpayer by the state treasurer or by the town treasurer, as the case may be, and, if unpaid in the latter case, execution therefor may issue against the town as in actions at law.

SECTION 9. This act shall not apply in the case of taxes upon income received during the calendar year nineteen hundred and thirty-two.   *Approved July 22, 1933.*

An Act relative to the judicial enforcement of *Chap.351*
certain contracts relative to membership in labor
or employers' organizations.

Be it enacted, etc., as follows:

SECTION 1. Chapter one hundred and forty-nine of G. L. (Ter.
the General Laws is hereby amended by inserting after Ed.), 149, new
section twenty, as appearing in the Tercentenary Edition added.
thereof, the following new section: — *Section 20A.* No Judicial en-
contract, whether written or oral, between any employee forcement of
or prospective employee and his employer, prospective contracts.
employer or any other person, whereby either party thereto
undertakes or promises not to join or not to remain a
member of some specified labor organization or any labor
organization, or of some specified employer organization or
any employer organization, and/or to withdraw from an
employment relation in the event that he joins or remains a
member of some specified labor organization or any labor
organization, or of some specified employer organization or
any employer organization or organizations, shall afford
any basis for the granting of legal or equitable relief by any
court against a party to such undertaking or promise.

SECTION 2. This act shall take effect on the first day of Effective date.
November in the current year, and shall apply only to
contracts made after its effective date.

Approved July 22, 1933.

An Act establishing the West Boylston water dis- *Chap.352*
trict of West Boylston.

Be it enacted, etc., as follows:

SECTION 1. The inhabitants of the town of West West Boylston
Boylston liable to taxation in that town and residing within of West
the territory not included within the Pinecroft Water Boylston
District of said town as at present constituted shall consti- established.
tute a water district, and are hereby made a body corporate
by the name of the West Boylston Water District of West
Boylston, hereinafter called the district, for the purpose
of supplying themselves with water for the extinguishment
of fires and for domestic and other purposes, with power to
establish fountains and hydrants and to relocate and discontinue the same, to regulate the use of such water and to
fix and collect rates to be paid therefor, and to take by
eminent domain under chapter seventy-nine of the General
Laws except as limited by this act, or acquire by lease,
purchase or otherwise, and to hold for the purposes mentioned in this act, property, lands, rights of way and other
easements, and to prosecute and defend all actions relating
to the property and affairs of the district.

SECTION 2. For the purposes aforesaid, said district, May take
acting by and through its board of water commissioners water from
hereinafter provided for, may take under section twenty- reservoir.

two of chapter four hundred and eighty-eight of the acts
of eighteen hundred and ninety-five, as amended by
chapter four hundred and fifty-six of the acts of eighteen
hundred and ninety-seven, not more than two million gallons of water per day from the Wachusett reservoir above
the dam at Clinton, may contract with the city of Worcester, or any town or other city, acting through its water
department, or with any water company, or with any water
district, for whatever water may be required, authority to
furnish the same being hereby granted, and/or may take
under chapter seventy-nine of the General Laws, or acquire
by purchase or otherwise, and hold, the waters, or any
portion thereof, of any pond or stream, or of any ground
sources of supply by means of driven, artesian or other
wells within the town of West Boylston, and the water
rights connected with any such water sources; and for
said purposes may take as aforesaid, or acquire by purchase
or otherwise, and hold, all lands, rights of way and other
easements necessary for collecting, storing, holding, purifying and preserving the purity of the water and for conveying the same to any part of said district; provided, that
no source of water supply or lands necessary for preserving
the quality of the water shall be so taken or used without
first obtaining the advice and approval of the state department of public health, and that the location of all dams,
reservoirs and wells to be used as sources of water supply
under this act shall be subject to the approval of said department; and provided, further, that no such source of
water supply or lands shall be so taken within that portion
of said town of West Boylston included within said Pinecroft Water District. Said West Boylston water district
may construct on the lands acquired and held under this
act proper dams, reservoirs, standpipes, tanks, buildings,
fixtures and other structures, and may make excavations,
procure and operate machinery and provide such other
means and appliances and do such other things as may be
necessary for the establishment and maintenance of complete and effective water works; and for that purpose may
construct pipe lines, wells and reservoirs and establish
pumping works on lands of the metropolitan district commission subject to the approval of said commission and
shall maintain and operate the same in a manner satisfactory to said commission, and may construct, lay and
maintain aqueducts, conduits, pipes and other works under
or over any land, water courses, railroads, railways and
public or other ways, and along such ways, within its own
limits, in such manner as not unnecessarily to obstruct the
same; and for the purposes of constructing, laying, maintaining, operating and repairing such conduits, pipes and
other works, and for all proper purposes of this act, said
district may dig up or raise and embank any such lands,
highways or other ways in such manner as to cause the
least hindrance to public travel on such ways; provided,

May construct
dams, etc.

that all things done upon any such way shall be subject to the direction of the selectmen of the town of West Boylston. Said district shall not enter upon, construct or lay any conduit, pipe or other works within the location of any railroad corporation except at such time and in such manner as it may agree upon with such corporation, or in case of failure so to agree, as may be approved by the department of public utilities.

SECTION 3. Any person sustaining damages in his property by any taking under this act or any other thing done under authority thereof may recover such damages from said district under said chapter seventy-nine; but the right to damages for the taking of any water, water right or water source, or for any injury thereto, shall not vest until water is actually withdrawn or diverted under authority of this act. *Damages for takings.*

SECTION 4. For the purpose of paying the necessary expenses and liabilities incurred for the system of water supply under the provisions of this act, other than expenses of maintenance and operation, the said district may borrow from time to time such sums as may be necessary, not exceeding, in the aggregate, one hundred and thirty-five thousand dollars, and may issue bonds or notes therefor, which shall bear on their face the words, West Boylston Water District Loan, Act of 1933. Each authorized issue shall constitute a separate loan, and such loans shall be payable in not more than thirty years from their dates. Indebtedness incurred under this act shall be subject to chapter forty-four of the General Laws. *District may borrow money, etc.*

SECTION 5. Said district shall, at the time of authorizing said loan or loans, provide for the payment thereof in accordance with section four of this act; and when a vote to that effect has been passed, a sum which, with the income derived from water rates, will be sufficient to pay the annual expense of operating its water works and the interest as it accrues on the bonds or notes issued as aforesaid by the district, and to make such payments on the principal as may be required under the provisions of this act, shall without further vote be assessed upon said district by the assessors of said town of West Boylston annually thereafter until the debt incurred by said loan or loans is extinguished. *Payment of loans.*

SECTION 6. Any land taken or acquired under this act shall be managed, improved and controlled by the commissioners hereinafter provided for, in such manner as they shall deem for the best interest of the district. *Board of water commissioners to control land, etc.*

SECTION 7. Whenever a tax is duly voted by said district for the purposes of this act, the clerk shall send a certified copy of the vote to the assessors of said town, who shall assess the same in the same manner in all respects in which town taxes are required by law to be assessed; provided, that no estate shall be subject to any tax assessed on account of the system of water supply under this act *Assessment of taxes.*

if, in the judgment of the board of water commissioners hereinafter provided for, after a hearing, such estate is so situated that it can receive no aid in the extinguishment of fire from the said system of water supply, or if such estate is so situated that the buildings thereon, or the buildings that might be constructed thereon, in any ordinary or reasonable manner could not be supplied with water from the said system; but all other estates in said district shall be deemed to be benefited and shall be subject to the tax. The assessment shall be committed to the town collector, who shall collect said tax in the manner provided by law for the collection of town taxes, and shall deposit the proceeds thereof with the district treasurer for the use and benefit of said district. Said district may collect interest on overdue taxes in the manner in which interest is authorized to be collected on town taxes.

District meeting.

SECTION 8. The first meeting of said district shall be called, within four years after the passage of this act, on petition of ten or more legal voters therein, by a warrant from the selectmen of said town, or from a justice of the peace, directed to one of the petitioners, requiring him to give notice of the meeting by posting copies of the warrant in two or more public places in the district seven days at least before the time of the meeting. Such justice of the peace, or one of the selectmen, shall preside at such meeting until a clerk is chosen and sworn, and the clerk shall preside until a moderator is chosen. After the choice of a moderator for the meeting the question of the acceptance of this act shall be submitted to the voters, and if it is accepted by two thirds of the voters present and voting thereon it shall take effect, and the meeting may then proceed to act on the other articles in the warrant.

Board of water commissioners, election, term, powers and duties.

SECTION 9. Said district shall, after the acceptance of this act as aforesaid, elect by ballot, either at the same meeting at which this act is accepted or at a special meeting thereafter called for the purpose, three persons to hold office, one until the expiration of three years, one until the expiration of two years, and one until the expiration of one year from the day of the next succeeding annual district meeting, to constitute a board of water commissioners; and at every annual meeting subsequent to such next succeeding annual district meeting one such commissioner shall be elected by ballot for the term of three years. All the authority granted to said district by this act, and not otherwise specifically provided for, shall be vested in said board of water commissioners, who shall be subject, however, to such instructions, rules and regulations as the district may by vote impose. Said commissioners shall appoint a treasurer of said district, who may be one of their number, who shall give bond to said district in such an amount as may be approved by the commissioners. A majority of the commissioners shall constitute a quorum for the transaction of business. Any vacancy occurring in said board from any cause may be filled for the remainder of the unexpired term by said district at any legal meeting called for the purpose. No money shall be drawn from the treasury of said district on account of the water works except upon a written order of said commissioners or a majority of them.

SECTION 10. Said commissioners shall fix just and equitable prices and rates for the use of water, and shall prescribe the time and manner of payment. The income of the water works shall be appropriated to defray all operating expenses, interest charges and payments on the principal as they shall accrue upon any bonds or notes issued under authority of this act. If there should be a net surplus remaining after providing for the aforesaid charges, it may be appropriated for such new construction as said commissioners may recommend, and in case a surplus should remain after payment for such new construction the water rates shall be reduced proportionately. Said commissioners shall annually, and as often as said district may require, render a report upon the condition of the works under their charge, and an account of their doings, including an account of receipts and expenditures. *Water rates, how fixed.*

SECTION 11. Said district may adopt by-laws prescribing by whom and how meetings may be called, notified and conducted; and, upon the application of ten or more legal voters in said district meetings may also be called by warrant as provided in section eight. Said district may also establish rules and regulations for the management of its water works, not inconsistent with this act or with law, and may choose such other officers not provided for in this act as it may deem necessary or proper. *By-laws.*

SECTION 12. Whoever wilfully or wantonly corrupts, pollutes or diverts any water obtained or supplied under this act, or wilfully or wantonly injures any reservoir, standpipe, aqueduct, pipe or other property owned or used by said district for any of the purposes of this act shall forfeit and pay to said district three times the amount of damages assessed therefor, to be recovered in an action of tort, and upon conviction of any of the above acts shall be punished by a fine not exceeding one hundred dollars or by imprisonment in jail for not more than six months. *Penalty for polluting water.*

SECTION 13. This act shall take full effect upon its acceptance by a two thirds vote of the voters of said district present and voting thereon at a district meeting called, in accordance with the provisions of section eight, within four years after its passage; but it shall become void unless said district shall begin to distribute water to consumers within two years after its acceptance as aforesaid. *Acceptance of act.*

Approved July 22, 1933.

Chap.353 AN ACT FURTHER PREFERRING DOMESTIC PRODUCTS IN
PURCHASES FOR STATE DEPARTMENTS AND INSTITUTIONS
AND BY CERTAIN CONTRACTORS ON STATE WORK.

Be it enacted, etc., as follows:

G. L. (Ter.
Ed.), 7, § 22,
amended.

SECTION 1. Section twenty-two of chapter seven of the
General Laws, as appearing in the Tercentenary Edition
thereof, is hereby further amended by striking out clause
(17) and inserting in place thereof the following: —

Purchase of
supplies, etc.,
preference for
domestic
products.

(17) A preference in the purchase of supplies and
materials, other considerations being equal, in favor, first,
of supplies and materials manufactured and sold within
the commonwealth, and, second, of supplies and materials
manufactured and sold elsewhere within the United States.

G. L. (Ter.
Ed.), 7, new
section 23A,
added.
Rules and
regulations of
commission
on administra-
tion and
finance relative
to purchase
of domestic
products.

SECTION 2. Said chapter seven is hereby further
amended by inserting after section twenty-three, as so appearing, the following new section: — *Section 23A.* Rules,
regulations and orders adopted under clause (17) of section twenty-two shall, so far as may be approved by the
governor and council, apply to the purchase by contractors
of supplies and materials in the execution of any contract
to which the commonwealth is a party for the construction,
reconstruction or repair of any public work; and there
shall be inserted in any such contract a stipulation to such
effect. Any appointed officer or agent of the commonwealth entering into such a contract in its behalf who fails
to insert such a stipulation in such a contract as required
by such a rule, regulation or order may, after a hearing
before the governor and council, be removed by them.

Approved July 22, 1933.

Chap.354 AN ACT RELATIVE TO EMERGENCY BORROWINGS BY THE
CITY OF WORCESTER.

Be it enacted, etc., as follows:

SECTION 1. The provisions of chapter two hundred
and eleven of the Special Acts of nineteen hundred and
sixteen and any acts in amendment thereof shall not apply
to loans of the city of Worcester authorized or to be authorized under the provisions of chapter three hundred and
seven of the acts of the current year, or under the National
Industrial Recovery Act, so called, or any legislation of the
commonwealth complementary thereto.

SECTION 2. This act shall take effect upon its passage.

Approved July 22, 1933.

AN ACT AUTHORIZING THE CITY OF LEOMINSTER TO CON- *Chap.*355
STRUCT AND OPERATE A SYSTEM OR SYSTEMS OF SEWERS
AND OF SEWAGE DISPOSAL.

Be it enacted, etc., as follows:

SECTION 1. The city of Leominster, for the purpose of City of
providing better surface or other drainage, guarding against Leominster
                                                             may operate
pollution of water, and otherwise protecting the public sewer system.
health, is hereby authorized to lay out, construct, maintain and operate a system or systems of main drains and
common sewers for a part or the whole of its territory, and
also a system of sewage disposal for said city; and, for the
purposes aforesaid, the city may take by eminent domain
under chapter seventy-nine of the General Laws, or acquire
by purchase or otherwise, any lands, water rights, water
privileges, rights of way or easements in said city necessary for the establishment of such system or systems, and
may dig out, deepen, widen, clear of obstructions, clean,
pave, wall and enclose any river, brook, stream or water
course, and may straighten or alter the channels or divert
the waters thereof, and may lay, make and maintain sub-
drains, and discharge the waters into any brook, stream or
water course within said city.

SECTION 2. The mayor, as soon as may be after the Board of sewer
effective date of this act, shall appoint, subject to confirma- commissioners.
tion by the city council, three legal voters of said city who,
with the mayor and the president of the city council for
the time being, ex-officiis, shall constitute a board of
sewage commissioners, hereinafter called the board, one of
the members of which shall be designated as chairman in
the original appointment. The board, subject to the
approval of the city council, shall have full and sole charge
of the construction of the system or systems of sewerage
and sewage disposal authorized and provided for by this
act or by any amendment, substitution or extension thereof,
and of the sewers and drains necessary to be constructed
incidental thereto, and shall continue to hold office until
the completion of said system or systems, but not longer in
any event than seven years. The board shall organize as
soon as may be after the qualification of its appointed
members. Any appointed member may be removed at
any time for cause, and his successor may be appointed in
like manner to serve for the unexpired term. Removal
from the city of any member shall constitute a vacation of
his office. Any vacancy in the office of chairman shall be
filled by designation of the mayor as in the case of the
original appointment.

SECTION 3. The members of the board shall serve Compensation
without compensation, but shall be allowed such actual of members.
expenses as are incurred by them in the performance of
their duties hereunder.

SECTION 4. The board, subject to the approval of the Board may
                                                        employ
                                                        engineers, etc.

city council, may employ such supervising and consulting engineers as it deems the interests of the city require, may employ such other assistants as it deems necessary and proper, and may delegate and apportion its various powers and duties to and among sub-departments or sub-divisions to be created by it, each of which may be in charge of a superintendent or foreman. Any such superintendent or foreman may be removed at any time by the board. No contract in excess of three hundred dollars for labor or material for the work hereby authorized shall be made by said board without the approval of the city council, and all bills for work done or material furnished under any such contract shall be audited by the city auditor.

Approval of state department of health.

SECTION 5. Nothing shall be done under authority of this act, except in the making of surveys and other preliminary investigations, until the plans for said system or systems have been approved by the state department of public health. Upon application to said department for such approval, it shall give a hearing, after due notice to the public. At such hearing plans showing all the work to be done in constructing said system or systems shall be submitted for its approval.

Repeal of certain special acts.

SECTION 6. So much of chapter three hundred and nine of the acts of nineteen hundred and four, and chapter three hundred and sixty of the Special Acts of nineteen hundred and seventeen, and of any acts in addition to or in amendment thereof, as may be inconsistent with this act are hereby repealed.

SECTION 7. This act shall take effect upon its passage.

Approved July 22, 1933.

---

*Chap.*356 AN ACT PROVIDING FOR THE ACQUISITION OF ADDITIONAL LAND FOR THE CONSTRUCTION OF A STATE HIGHWAY IN THE TOWN OF MILTON AND THE HYDE PARK DISTRICT OF THE CITY OF BOSTON.

Emergency preamble.

Whereas, The deferred operation of this act would tend to defeat its purpose, therefore it is hereby declared to be an emergency law, necessary for the immediate preservation of the public convenience.

Be it enacted, etc., as follows:

The department of public works is hereby directed to complete the acquisition of land as authorized by, and for the purpose set forth in, section three of chapter four hundred and twenty of the acts of nineteen hundred and thirty. The cost of acquiring land hereunder shall not exceed forty thousand dollars and shall be paid, subject to appropriation, from the Highway Fund.

Approved July 22, 1933.

An Act temporarily discontinuing the income tax exemption as to dividends of certain foreign corporations.

*Chap.*357

Whereas, The deferred operation of this act would tend to defeat its purpose, therefore it is hereby declared to be an emergency law, necessary for the immediate preservation of the public convenience.

Emergency preamble.

Be it enacted, etc., as follows:

Section 1. Pending the taxation of dividends under section nine of chapter three hundred and seven of the acts of the current year, dividends, other than stock dividends paid in new stock of the company issuing the same, on shares in all corporations and joint stock companies organized under the laws of any state or nation other than this commonwealth, except banks which are subject to taxation under section two of chapter sixty-three of the General Laws, received from October first to December thirty-first, nineteen hundred and thirty-two, inclusive, shall be taxed at the same rate, in the same manner and to the same persons as dividends now taxable under chapter sixty-two of the General Laws, and the provisions of said chapter shall apply to the taxation of all dividends taxable hereunder, except that subsection (*b*) of section one of said chapter sixty-two shall not so apply unless this act is held invalid by a final judgment, order or decree of the supreme judicial court or of the supreme court of the United States, in which case said subsection shall apply to all income taxable thereunder received during the period covered by this act, and so much of every assessment made hereunder as is warranted by said subsection (*b*) shall remain in full force and effect.

Income tax on dividends heretofore exempt.

Section 2. No fiduciary shall be compelled to pay a tax under this act upon any income which was not taxable when received and which was distributed by him prior to the effective date of this act, except to the extent to which he shall have, after said effective date and prior to September first, nineteen hundred and thirty-five, funds of said trust or estate due to the beneficiary to whom said income was distributed.

Not to apply to income received by certain fiduciaries.

Section 3. The commissioner of corporations and taxation may require any corporation which paid to residents of this commonwealth from October first to December thirty-first, nineteen hundred and thirty-two, inclusive, dividends made taxable by this act and not heretofore taxable under said chapter sixty-two, to file with him at such time in the current year as he may deem advisable a complete list of the names and addresses of its shareholders as of record on any date in the year nineteen hundred and thirty-two subsequent to September fifteenth satisfactory to the commissioner, or, in its discretion, of such share-

Commissioner of corporations and taxation may require list of shareholders, etc.

holders as are residents of the commonwealth, in each case, together with the number of shares held by each.

SECTION 4. Section eighteen of chapter fifty-eight of the General Laws shall not apply to any taxes upon dividends made taxable by this act and not heretofore taxable under said chapter sixty-two, which taxes shall be retained by the commonwealth; but said section eighteen shall continue to apply to taxes upon dividends taxable under this act which have heretofore been taxable under said chapter sixty-two. Notwithstanding the provisions of section eleven of chapter three hundred and seven of the acts of the current year, the proceeds of all taxes collected by the commonwealth under section nine of said chapter on dividends on shares in all corporations and joint stock companies organized under the laws of any state or nation other than this commonwealth, except banks which are subject to taxation under section two of chapter sixty-three of the General Laws, which dividends were made taxable by said section nine and were not taxable prior to the effective date of said chapter three hundred and seven, shall be retained by the commonwealth.

Approved July 22, 1933.

---

*Chap.*358 AN ACT PROVIDING FOR THE REPAIR OF THE SLADE'S FERRY BRIDGE, SO CALLED, OVER THE TAUNTON RIVER BETWEEN THE CITY OF FALL RIVER AND THE TOWN OF SOMERSET.

Emergency
preamble.
Whereas, The deferred operation of this act would cause substantial inconvenience, therefore it is hereby declared to be an emergency law, necessary for the immediate preservation of the public convenience.

Be it enacted, etc., as follows:

Repair of
Slade's Ferry
bridge.
SECTION 1. The department of public works, hereinafter called the department, is hereby authorized and directed to repair and render safe and adequate for public travel and use for highway purposes the bridge over the Taunton river between the city of Fall River and the town of Somerset, commonly called the Slade's Ferry bridge; provided, that the New York, New Haven and Hartford Railroad contributes and pays into the state treasury toward the cost of said work the sum of thirty thousand dollars. The draw in said bridge, if altered hereunder, shall be in such location and of such width and construction as the department may determine, subject to the approval of the proper federal authorities.

Distribution
of cost.
SECTION 2. The cost of the work hereunder shall not exceed one hundred and fifty thousand dollars. Fifty per cent of said cost shall be paid by the commonwealth from item five hundred and seventy-six of chapter one hundred and seventy-four of the acts of the current year. Of the balance of said cost over and above the amounts payable by the commonwealth and by said railroad as aforesaid,

seventy-four per cent shall be assessed upon the city of Fall River, fifteen per cent upon the town of Somerset and eleven per cent upon the town of Swansea. One half of the amount of said assessments shall be made and collected by the state treasurer as a part of the annual state tax in each of the years nineteen hundred and thirty-three and nineteen hundred and thirty-four.

SECTION 3. This act shall take full effect only upon its acceptance, within sixty days after its passage, by the mayor and city council of the city of Fall River and by the selectmen of the towns of Swansea and Somerset. *Acceptance of act.*

Approved July 22, 1933.

AN ACT PROVIDING FOR ENLARGING THE SWANSEA FIRE AND WATER DISTRICT. *Chap.359*

Be it enacted, etc., as follows:

SECTION 1. The inhabitants of the town of Swansea residing in that part of said town bounded and described as follows: — beginning at the Massachusetts–Rhode Island state line where such line is intersected by a line parallel to and five hundred feet west of the center line of Seaview avenue; thence running northerly in said line parallel to and five hundred feet west of the center line of Seaview avenue to a point five hundred feet south of the center line of Davis street; thence running westerly in a line parallel with and five hundred feet south of the center line of Davis street extended and continuing in the same direction to a point five hundred feet west of the center line of Touisset avenue; thence running northerly in a line parallel with and five hundred feet west of the center line of Touisset avenue to the highway known under the contemplated name of Barton avenue; thence running to a point on the right of way of the New York, New Haven & Hartford Railroad Company, lessee, five hundred feet west of the center line of River road where it is crossed by said railroad; thence in a line parallel with and five hundred feet distant from the center line of said River road to a point five hundred feet west of the center line of Pearse road; thence running northerly in a line five hundred feet distant from and parallel with the center line of Pearse road to a point one thousand feet north of Wilbur avenue; thence running easterly in a line one thousand feet distant from and parallel with the center line of Wilbur avenue to the channel of Cole's river; thence generally southerly by the channel of Cole's river to the Massachusetts–Rhode Island state line; thence in a westerly direction to the point of beginning, — are hereby added to and included in and shall constitute a part of the Swansea fire and water district, established by chapter three hundred and seventeen of the acts of the current year.

SECTION 2. This act shall take effect upon its acceptance by a majority vote of the voters of said district present and voting thereon at a duly called district meeting.

Approved July 22, 1933.

---

*Chap.*360 AN ACT EXTENDING THE APPLICATION OF CERTAIN PROVISIONS OF THE DIVORCE LAW TO SEPARATE SUPPORT CASES.

Be it enacted, etc., as follows:

G. L. (Ter. Ed.), 209, § 33, amended.

Attachment of husband's property in certain actions of separate support.

Chapter two hundred and nine of the General Laws, as appearing in the Tercentenary Edition thereof, is hereby amended by striking out section thirty-three and inserting in place thereof the following: — *Section 33.* Upon such petition, an attachment of the husband's property may be made as upon a libel for divorce; and sections seventeen, thirty-three, thirty-five and thirty-eight of chapter two hundred and eight shall apply to proceedings upon such petition and to all subsidiary proceedings arising thereunder, so far as appropriate. *Approved July 22, 1933.*

---

*Chap.*361 AN ACT PROVIDING FOR CERTAIN FINANCIAL RE-ADJUSTMENTS IN THE CITY OF REVERE.

Be it enacted, etc., as follows:

City of Revere, refunding certain loans.

SECTION 1. The city of Revere is hereby authorized to refund or extend from time to time temporary loans issued in anticipation of the revenue of nineteen hundred and thirty-two, to an amount not exceeding three hundred thousand dollars, for a period or periods not extending beyond one year and six months from the effective date of this act, such borrowing to be outside its statutory limit of indebtedness, and for such purpose may issue bonds or notes of the city. None of the receipts from the collection of taxes assessed by said city for the year nineteen hundred and thirty-two and prior years shall be appropriated for any purpose other than the payment of liabilities of said city outstanding on January first, nineteen hundred and thirty-three or of loans refunded or extended as hereinbefore authorized.

Loans, issuance of.

SECTION 2. For the purpose of paying in part the temporary loans issued in anticipation of the revenue of nineteen hundred and thirty-two, said city is also authorized to borrow, prior to the fixing of its tax rate in the current year, a sum not exceeding two hundred thousand dollars and may issue from time to time bonds or notes of the city, which shall bear on their face the words, City of Revere Funding Loan, Act of 1933. Each authorized issue shall constitute a separate loan, and such loans shall be paid in not more than five years from their dates. Indebtedness incurred hereunder shall be in excess of the statutory limit, but shall, except as herein provided, be subject to chapter forty-four of the General Laws, exclusive of the limitation contained in the first paragraph of section seven of said chapter. Until payment in full of the principal and interest on the bonds or notes issued under this section, no appropriation by such city in any year subsequent to the current year for a purpose other than one for which an appropriation has been made for the current year, or for an amount in excess of any appropriations made for said current year for a similar purpose, shall be valid without the written approval of the Emergency Finance Board, established under section one of chapter forty-nine of the acts of the current year, and any contract or other obligation entered into by any officer or department of said city whereby the appropriation for such officer or department is exceeded shall be void and unenforceable.

SECTION 3. In the event that any borrowing is authorized by said city under section two, said city shall appropriate prior to the fixing of its tax rate for the current year, a sum not less than four hundred eighty-nine thousand three hundred and fifty dollars toward the payment of temporary loans issued in anticipation of the revenue of nineteen hundred and thirty-two, and shall include such sum in said tax levy, in addition to all amounts otherwise required by law to be raised by taxation in the current year.

Appropriations in anticipation of revenue.

SECTION 4. This act shall take effect upon its passage.
Approved July 22, 1933.

An Act relative to the protection of the public in the event of a food or fuel emergency.

Chap.362

Whereas, The deferred operation of this act would defeat its purpose, therefore it is hereby declared to be an emergency law, necessary for the immediate preservation of the public health, safety and convenience.

Emergency preamble.

Be it enacted, etc., as follows:

Chapter twenty-three of the General Laws is hereby amended by striking out section nine H, as appearing in the Tercentenary Edition thereof, and inserting in place thereof the following: — *Section 9H.* Whenever the governor shall determine that an emergency exists in respect to food or fuel, or both, he may, with the approval of the council, by a writing signed by him, designate the director of the division on the necessaries of life to act as an emergency food or fuel administrator, or both, and thereupon the director shall have, with respect to food or fuel, or both, as the case may be, all the powers and authority granted by the Commonwealth Defense Act of nineteen hundred and seventeen, being chapter three hundred and forty-two of the General Acts of nineteen hundred and seventeen, to persons designated or appointed by the governor under section twelve of said chapter three hundred

G. L. (Ter. Ed.), 23, § 9H, amended.

Director of division of necessaries of life to act as emergency fuel administrator.

and forty-two; and the governor may revoke such written authority at any time. During such an emergency, the governor, with the approval of the council, may make and promulgate rules and regulations, effective forthwith, for the carrying out of the purposes of this section and for the performance by the commonwealth and the cities and towns thereof of any function affecting food or fuel authorized under Article XLVII of the amendments to the constitution. Violation of any such rule or regulation shall be punished by a fine of not more than five hundred dollars or by imprisonment for not more than six months, or by both. The provisions of said chapter three hundred and forty-two are hereby made operative to such extent as the provisions of this section may from time to time require.

Approved July 22, 1933.

Chap.363 AN ACT MAKING CERTAIN MASSACHUSETTS VETERANS RE-
CEIVING HOSPITAL TREATMENT OUTSIDE THE COMMON-
WEALTH ELIGIBLE TO RECEIVE MILITARY AID.

Emergency
preamble.

Whereas, The deferred operation of this act would tend to defeat its purpose, therefore it is hereby declared to be an emergency law, necessary for the immediate preservation of the public convenience.

Be it enacted, etc., as follows:

G. L. (Ter.
Ed.), 115, new
section 12A,
added.

Veterans re-
ceiving hospital
treatment out-
side the com-
monwealth
eligible to
receive military
aid.

Chapter one hundred and fifteen of the General Laws is hereby amended by inserting after section twelve, as appearing in the Tercentenary Edition thereof, the following new section: — *Section 12A.* No veteran, who is or shall be otherwise entitled to military aid, shall lose his right thereto by reason of his absence from the commonwealth while receiving hospital treatment, under order of the United States veterans' bureau, at any hospital located outside the commonwealth. *Approved July 22, 1933.*

Chap.364 AN ACT ESTABLISHING IN THE DEPARTMENT OF PUBLIC
WELFARE A STATE BOARD OF HOUSING AND DEFINING ITS
POWERS AND DUTIES, AND RELATIVE TO CERTAIN LIMITED
DIVIDEND CORPORATIONS UNDER THE CONTROL OF SAID
BOARD.

Emergency
preamble.

Whereas, The deferred operation of this act would tend to defeat its purpose, therefore it is hereby declared to be an emergency law, necessary for the immediate preservation of the public health, safety and convenience.

Be it enacted, etc., as follows:

G. L. (Ter.
Ed.), 18, two
new sections
17 and 18,
added.

SECTION 1. Chapter eighteen of the General Laws, as appearing in the Tercentenary Edition thereof, is hereby amended by adding at the end thereof, under the caption, STATE BOARD OF HOUSING, the following two new sections: —

Section 17. There shall be in the department an unpaid state board of housing, in this and the following section referred to as the housing board, consisting of five members appointed by the governor, with the advice and consent of the council, who shall be designated in their initial appointments to serve respectively for one, two, three, four and five years from December first in the year of appointment. The housing board shall annually elect one of its members as chairman. Upon the expiration of the term of office of a member, his successor shall be appointed in the manner aforesaid for five years. The majority of the members of the housing board shall constitute a quorum for the transaction of its business. A vacancy therein shall not impair its powers nor affect its duties. It shall have a seal which shall be judicially noticed, and shall make an annual report to the general court and such additional reports to the general court and the governor as it or he shall deem necessary or advisable. The principal office of the housing board shall be in Boston but it may sit at any place within the commonwealth. The time and place of its meetings shall be prescribed by the chairman. Adequate offices in the state house or elsewhere in said city shall be provided for the housing board, and the proper county commissioners shall provide it with suitable rooms in courthouses or other buildings when necessary for hearings outside said city.

State housing board, members, appointment, etc.

Section 18. The housing board may, subject to the approval of the governor and council, appoint and fix the compensation of such employees, including a clerk, and make such expenditures, as may be necessary in order to execute effectively the functions vested in it. The members and employees of the housing board shall receive their necessary traveling expenses and, except as otherwise provided by law, their expenses actually incurred for subsistence while traveling outside the city of Boston in the performance of their duties. The necessary administrative and other expenses of the housing board shall be paid from such appropriations as may be made for the purpose. All moneys received by the housing board as fees or otherwise shall be paid at least monthly to the state treasurer.

Board may appoint clerks, etc.

SECTION 2. The heading before section twenty-three of chapter one hundred and twenty-one of the General Laws, as so appearing, is hereby amended so as to read as follows: — STATE BOARD OF HOUSING AND CERTAIN LIMITED DIVIDEND CORPORATIONS; and said section twenty-three is hereby amended by striking out, in the first line, the words "commissioner and board" and inserting in place thereof the words: — state board of housing, in this and the eleven following sections called the housing board, — and by adding at the end thereof the following: — , and shall supervise and control, as hereinafter provided, the operations of corporations formed under authority of section

G. L. (Ter. Ed.), 121, § 23, amended.

twenty-six E, — so as to read as follows: — *Section 23.*
The state board of housing, in this and the eleven following
sections called the housing board, shall investigate defective
housing, the evils resulting therefrom and the work being
done in the commonwealth and elsewhere to remedy them,
study the operation of building laws and laws relating to
tenement houses, encourage the creation of local planning
boards, gather information relating to town planning for
the use of such boards, and promote the formation of organizations intended to increase the number of wholesome
homes for the people, and shall supervise and control, as
hereinafter provided, the operations of corporations formed
under authority of section twenty-six E.

SECTION 3. Section twenty-four of said chapter one
hundred and twenty-one, as so appearing, is hereby
amended by striking out, in the first line, the words "commissioner and" and inserting in place thereof the word: —
housing, — and by striking out, in the ninth line, the word
"they" and inserting in place thereof the word: — it, —

so as to read as follows: — *Section 24.* The housing board
may, with the consent of the governor and council, take
by eminent domain or purchase in behalf of and in the
name of the commonwealth tracts of land for the purpose
of relieving congestion of population and providing homesteads or small houses and plots of ground for mechanics,
laborers, wage earners of any kind, or others, citizens of
the commonwealth; and may hold, improve, subdivide,
build upon, sell, repurchase, manage and care for such
land and the buildings constructed thereon, in accordance
with such terms and conditions as it may determine.

SECTION 4. Said chapter one hundred and twenty-one
is hereby further amended by striking out section twenty-
five, as so appearing, and inserting in place thereof the

following: — *Section 25.* The housing board may sell
such land or any parts thereof, with or without buildings
thereon, for cash or upon such instalments, terms and
contracts and subject to such restrictions and conditions as
it may determine, and may take mortgages upon said
land, with or without buildings thereon, for such portion
of the purchase price and upon such terms as it deems
advisable, but no tract of land shall be sold for less than its
cost, including the cost of any buildings thereon. All
proceeds from the sale of land and buildings or from other
sources shall be paid to the commonwealth.

SECTION 5. Section twenty-six of said chapter one
hundred and twenty-one, as so appearing, is hereby
amended by striking out, in the first line, the words "commissioner and" and inserting in place thereof the word: —

housing, — so as to read as follows: — *Section 26.* The
housing board shall call the attention of mayors and city
councils and selectmen in towns having planning boards, to
the provisions of sections seventy to seventy-two, inclusive, of chapter forty-one; and it shall furnish information

and suggestions from time to time to city governments, selectmen and planning boards, which may tend to promote the purposes of said sections and of section twenty-three of this chapter.

Section 6. Said chapter one hundred and twenty-one is hereby further amended by inserting after section twenty-six the eight following new sections: — *Section 26A.* Whenever the housing board is requested by a corporation formed under authority of section twenty-six E to approve one or more areas within or adjacent to a locality within the commonwealth in which it is alleged that there exist bad housing conditions which are not being remedied through the ordinary operation of private enterprise, the housing board, if it first determines that such conditions exist therein, may approve one or more such areas for the provision thereon of such buildings, structures or facilities by one or more of such corporations as the board may consider best suited to remedy such conditions. No such project shall be approved unless it shall appear practicable to rent the accommodations to be provided at monthly rentals approved by the housing board as proper for the location. No such project shall be approved which is in contravention of any zoning, housing or building ordinances in effect in the locality in which any such approved area is located, or which conflicts with the plans of the local planning board, if any.

Section 26B. Subject to the approval of the governor and council, the housing board may make, and may from time to time alter or amend, rules and regulations relative to any or all of its functions, powers and duties, and specifically relative to (1) the formation, management, control and dissolution of corporations formed under authority of section twenty-six E; (2) regulation and control, including rental or other charges thereof or in connection therewith, of all property, real and personal, owned or controlled by any such corporation in connection with any project carried on by it under sections twenty-three to twenty-six H, inclusive; (3) reports by any such corporation; (4) reorganization of any such corporation.

Any act done, or instrument of lease or otherwise executed, by any such corporation in violation of any such rule or regulation shall be null and void, and the housing board, whenever it shall be of the opinion that such corporation is failing or omitting, or about to fail or omit, to do anything required of it by law or by rule or regulation of the housing board or is doing or about to do anything, or permitting or about to permit anything to be done, which is in violation of law or of any such rule or regulation, or which is improvident or prejudicial to the interests of the public or of the creditors or stockholders of such corporation, may commence and prosecute an action or proceeding in equity for the purpose of stopping or preventing, or requiring, as

Marginal notes: G. L. (Ter. Ed.), 121, new sections 26A to 26H, added. Approval of areas for development. Rules and regulations respecting housing corporations. Actions for breach of rules and regulations.

the case may be, by injunction or otherwise, any such act or failure or omission to act.

Section 26C. No building, construction or reconditioning shall be undertaken by any such corporation without the written approval of the housing board, nor unless approval of the area or areas in question has previously been obtained from the housing board under section twenty-six A.

Section 26D. The housing board may charge and collect for an approved project from such a corporation reasonable fees, in accordance with rates established by rules and regulations of the housing board, for the examination of plans and specifications and the supervision of construction, in an amount not to exceed one fifth of one per cent of the cost of the project, nor more than five thousand dollars for any one project; for the holding of a public hearing upon application of such a corporation the housing board shall receive therefrom an amount sufficient to meet the reasonable cost of advertising the notice of such hearing and of the transcript of testimony taken thereat; and for any examination or investigation made upon application of such a corporation, the housing board shall receive therefrom an amount reasonably calculated to meet the expenses of the housing board incurred in connection therewith. The board may authorize such a corporation to include such fees as part of the cost of a project, or as part of any other charges which said corporation may be authorized by the rules and regulations of the housing board to make.

Section 26E. Three or more persons may associate themselves by written agreement of association, in a form furnished or approved by the commissioner of corporations and taxation, with the intention of forming a limited dividend corporation for the purpose of carrying out one or more projects authorized and approved, or to be authorized and approved, by the housing board. The agreement of association shall not be presented for filing to the state secretary, nor shall he file it, unless it is accompanied by a certificate of the housing board that it approves the project or projects for the carrying out of which the corporation is formed and that it consents to the formation of such corporation. The laws relative to business corporations, so far as consistent with the provisions of sections twenty-three to twenty-six H, inclusive, and rules and regulations made under authority thereof, shall apply to corporations so formed; provided, that one director of every such corporation shall at all times be a person designated by the housing board and need not be a stockholder in such corporation; and corporations so formed are hereby declared to be instrumentalities of the commonwealth.

Section 26F. Any such corporation may acquire land by gift or purchase, or, with the approval of the housing board if so authorized hereunder, may take land by eminent domain for the purposes set forth in section twenty-four or for projects approved under section twenty-six A; and, subject to rules and regulations of the housing board, may hold, improve, subdivide, build upon, sell, repurchase, manage and care for such land and any buildings thereon.

With the authorization of the governor and council, the housing board may from time to time approve the taking of property by eminent domain for such purposes by any such corporation.

Section 26G. Every such corporation shall be deemed to have been organized to serve a public purpose, and shall remain at all times subject to the supervision and control of the housing board. All real estate acquired by any such corporation and all structures erected by it shall be deemed to be acquired or erected for the purpose of promoting the public health, safety and welfare and subject to sections twenty-three to twenty-six H, inclusive. The stockholders of every such corporation shall be deemed, when they subscribe to and receive the stock thereof, to have agreed that they shall at no time receive or accept from the corporation, in repayment of their investment in its stock, any sums in excess of the par value of the stock, together with cumulative dividends at the rate of six per centum per annum, and that any surplus earnings in excess of such amount, if and when said corporation shall be dissolved, shall revert to the commonwealth. No stockholder in any such corporation shall receive any dividend in any one year in excess of six per centum per annum, except that when in any preceding year dividends in the amount authorized to be paid by such corporation shall not have been paid in full on the said stock, the stockholders shall be entitled to the payment of any deficiency, without interest, out of any surplus earned in any succeeding year.

Section 26H. Should the gross receipts of any such corporation from the operation of any project undertaken by it to provide housing for families of low income, under authority of sections twenty-three to twenty-six H, inclusive, exceed (*a*) operating and management expenses; (*b*) taxes; (*c*) interest on mortgages and income debenture certificates; (*d*) dividends; (*e*) authorized transfer to surplus; and (*f*) amortization; the balance may, in the discretion of the housing board, be applied in whole or in part as a rebate on rentals due during the fiscal year of such corporation in which the balance was earned; provided, that the amount available for this purpose shall be entirely so applied within one year after it becomes available. The charges for operation and maintenance may include insurance and reserves essential to the management of the property or necessary to meet requirements for depreciation and amortization of bonded indebtedness, but the amount set aside therefor shall be subject to the approval of the housing board. Nothing in sections twenty-three to twenty-six H, inclusive, shall be construed to obligate the

Corporations subject to control of housing board.

Control of board over receipts of corporation.

commonwealth, or to pledge its credit, to any payment whatsoever to any such corporation or to any stockholder, bondholder or creditor thereof, nor shall anything herein contained be construed as granting to any such corporation any exemption from taxation.

G. L. (Ter. Ed.), 121, § 27, repealed.

SECTION 7. Section twenty-seven of said chapter one hundred and twenty-one, as so appearing, is hereby repealed.

Corporation may contract with federal authority.

SECTION 8. Any corporation formed under authority of section twenty-six E of chapter one hundred and twenty-one of the General Laws may enter into any contract with the federal emergency administrator of public works authorized by the act of congress approved June sixteenth, nineteen hundred and thirty-three, and known as the National Industrial Recovery Act, or with the reconstruction finance corporation, with respect to the construction, reconstruction, alteration or repair under public regulation or control of low-cost housing and slum clearance or similar projects, and may accept and receive aid from him or it in the construction or financing of such projects and may purchase or lease from such federal emergency administrator property acquired by him in connection with the construction of any such project; provided, that such corporation shall at all times remain subject to sections twenty-three to twenty-six H, inclusive, of said chapter one hundred and twenty-one, and nothing in said sections or in this act shall render the commonwealth liable for any indebtedness or liability incurred, acts done (including any taking by eminent domain), or omissions or failures to act of any such corporation. *Approved July 22, 1933.*

Chap.365 AN ACT ENABLING THE COMMONWEALTH TO SECURE CERTAIN BENEFITS PROVIDED BY THE NATIONAL INDUSTRIAL RECOVERY ACT.

Whereas, It is the conviction of the general court

(1) That the commonwealth should effectively co-operate with the federal government in its policy of stimulating employment by the undertaking of an extensive program of public works;

(2) That such a program should anticipate the normal needs of the near future and should furnish a maximum of employment while involving a minimum of maintenance costs;

(3) That loans made to the states by the federal government in furtherance of such co-operation should be repaid and that therefore, without waiving any right on the part of the commonwealth to receive as favorable consideration as any other state in the event of any postponement, reduction or cancellation of payments of principal or interest upon such loans, provision should be made for such payment by the allocation thereto of a portion of certain existing

revenues, with the understanding that such revenues will
be released, as soon as may be, by resort to new revenues
derived from such portion of the taxes and fees accruing
to the commonwealth from the manufacture and sale of
wines, beers and liquors following ratification of the twenty-
first amendment, as is not required to meet the commonwealth's share of the cost of financing old age assistance;
and

Whereas, The deferred operation of this act would tend Emergency
to defeat its purpose to alleviate promptly conditions of preamble.
widespread unemployment, therefore it is hereby declared
to be an emergency law, necessary for the immediate preservation of the public convenience.

Be it enacted, etc., as follows:

SECTION 1. There shall be in the department of the Emergency
state treasurer, but in no manner subject to his control, an public works
emergency public works commission, hereinafter called the organization,
commission, consisting of the chairman of the commission members,
on administration and finance, ex officio, one resident of term, etc.
the commonwealth appointed by the president of the senate,
one such resident appointed by the speaker of the house of
representatives, and two such residents appointed by the
governor; and the commission shall continue in office
until and including June thirtieth, nineteen hundred and
thirty-five, but no longer. The commission shall elect
from its own number a chairman. Any vacancy in the
appointive membership of the commission shall be filled
for the unexpired term in the same manner as original
appointments. The action of a majority of the members
shall constitute action of the commission; and whenever
any action by the commission is required to be in writing,
such writing shall be sufficient when signed by a majority
of its members.

Each appointive member of the commission shall receive Compensation
from the commonwealth as compensation for each day's of members.
attendance at meetings of the commission, the sum of
thirty dollars; provided, that the total amount paid hereunder to any such member shall not exceed three thousand
dollars in any period of twelve months. Members of the
commission shall receive their traveling and other necessary
expenses incurred in the performance of their duties. The
commission may employ, subject to the approval of the
governor and council, a secretary and such additional
expert and clerical assistants as it may require. The commission may call upon any officer, department, board or
commission of the commonwealth for such information and
assistance as may be needed in carrying out the provisions
of this act.

The commission shall be furnished with quarters in the
state house or elsewhere in the city of Boston. On or
before December first of each year of its existence, the
commission shall make a report of its doings to the general

court, and at any time upon request of the governor shall make such a report to him.

Commonwealth may engage in public works projects. SECTION 2. The commonwealth may engage in any public works project included in any "comprehensive program of public works" prepared under section two hundred and two of Title II of the National Industrial Recovery Act, but only in case such project is approved, as hereinafter provided, by the commission and by the governor and in case the proper federal authorities have obligated the federal government to make a grant therefor of federal money under section two hundred and three of said title; provided, that such approval shall not be granted for any project which will cause the aggregate expenditure hereunder to be in excess of twenty-two million dollars, and provided further that out of such sum not more than ten million dollars shall be expended for the construction, reconstruction and resurfacing of roads and for projects similar to those enumerated in section two hundred and four of said act. All projects for the construction, reconstruction or resurfacing of roads and the construction of sewers shall be done by human labor, except in so far as machinery is, in the opinion of the state or federal officer or department having charge of the project, reasonably necessary, and the wages for such labor shall not be less than the prevailing rate of wages as established by the federal government. Nothing contained in this act shall be construed to prevent the commonwealth from engaging hereunder in any project for which funds have already been appropriated in whole or in part, if such project shall be approved as herein required. Such projects, so approved, shall be carried out in all respects subject to the provisions of said Title II and to such terms, conditions, rules and regulations, not inconsistent with applicable federal laws and regulations, as the commission may establish, with the approval of the governor, to ensure the proper execution of such projects. The commonwealth may accept and use for carrying out any projects so approved any grant or loan of federal funds under section two hundred and three of said Title II, and, for the purpose only of carrying out such projects, may from time to time borrow from the United States of America on the credit of the commonwealth such sums, not exceeding in the aggregate seventeen million dollars, as may be required, and may issue bonds, notes or other forms of written acknowledgment of debt, carrying such rates of interest as the state treasurer may fix, with the approval of the governor and the proper federal authorities. Such bonds, notes or other forms of written acknowledgment of debt shall be issued for such terms as the governor may recommend to the general court in accordance with section three of Article LXII of the amendments to the constitution of the commonwealth, but in no event for a shorter term than the maximum term permitted by the federal government for that particular issue. Until other provision is made by the general court, all interest payments and payments on account of principal for money borrowed under this act shall be paid from the Highway Fund, without appropriation.

Section 3. The several officers, departments, boards and commissions of the commonwealth, or ten citizens of the commonwealth, may submit to the commission any such proposed public works project, in such form as the commission may by rule or regulation require, accompanied by preliminary studies and general specifications sufficient for a careful estimate by a competent contractor. If, in the opinion of the commission after a public hearing and careful investigation, any such project is in the public interest and otherwise meets the requirements of the policy set forth in the preamble of this act, it shall approve the same and thereafter such project may be submitted to the governor for his approval. A list of such approved projects shall, as soon as may be, be submitted to the proper federal authorities under the National Industrial Recovery Act, for their approval. *State departments, etc., to submit proposed projects to commission for approval.*

Section 4. No payment shall be made or obligation incurred for the carrying out of any project which has been approved by the commission and the governor and approved for federal aid by the proper federal authorities, until plans and specifications therefor have been approved by the commission, unless otherwise provided by such rules or regulations as the commission may make. *Approval of plans, etc., required.*

Section 5. The state treasurer shall receive all moneys granted or loaned to the commonwealth under section two hundred and three of said Title II. Payment from the state treasury for expenditures incurred under this act shall be made upon vouchers filed with the comptroller in accordance with the procedure prescribed under section eighteen of chapter twenty-nine of the General Laws, and all other provisions of said chapter twenty-nine shall apply in the case of any project undertaken under this act or any expenditure necessary for carrying out the purposes hereof, except in so far as such provisions of law may be in conflict with applicable federal laws and regulations. *Duties of state treasurer.*

Section 6. Any state officer, board, commission or department charged with the duty of carrying out any project so approved shall have, in addition to any powers expressly given by statute, such powers as may be determined and certified by the commission to be proper and reasonably necessary to carry out such project, including the power to take property by eminent domain on behalf of the commonwealth; provided, that if such officer, board, department or commission is aggrieved by such action, he or it may within ten days after notice thereof appeal to the governor, whose decision shall be final. The commission is hereby authorized to make all necessary orders, rules and regulations and perform all necessary actions under this act; and none of such orders, rules, regulations *Extraordinary powers granted to state officers, etc.*

and actions shall be declared inoperative, illegal or void for
any omission of a technical nature in respect thereto.

Governor to
secure benefits
under National
Industrial
Recovery Act.

SECTION 7. The governor of the commonwealth is
hereby authorized to take any and all steps necessary from
time to time to enable this commonwealth to secure any
benefits to which it may be entitled under the National
Industrial Recovery Act, and the commission is hereby
directed to co-operate and assist him in every way possible.
The governor may give the consent of the commonwealth
that any state officer and employee may act as agent of
the federal government as provided in said act.

Approved July 22, 1933.

*Chap.*366 AN ACT ENABLING CITIES AND TOWNS AND FIRE, WATER,
LIGHT AND IMPROVEMENT DISTRICTS TO SECURE THE
BENEFITS PROVIDED BY THE NATIONAL INDUSTRIAL
RECOVERY ACT.

Emergency
preamble.

Whereas, The deferred operation of this act would tend
to defeat its purpose to alleviate promptly conditions of
widespread unemployment, therefore it is hereby declared
to be an emergency law, necessary for the immediate preservation of the public convenience.

Be it enacted, etc., as follows:

PART I.

Emergency
finance board,
additional
powers.

SECTION 1. The Emergency Finance Board, established
under section one of chapter forty-nine of the acts of the
current year, in this act referred to as the board, shall, in
addition to the powers and duties otherwise conferred
or imposed upon it, exercise and perform the powers and
duties hereinafter conferred or imposed upon it, and the
provisions of said section one relative to action by the
board shall apply in the case of action under this act.
Each appointive member of the board, when acting under
this act, shall receive from the commonwealth as compensation, in addition to any sums otherwise so payable, for
each day's attendance at board meetings, the sum of
thirty dollars; provided, that the total amount paid hereunder to any member for compensation as aforesaid shall
not exceed three thousand dollars in any period of twelve
months.

Additional
compensation
for certain
state officers
serving on
board.

The director of the division of accounts, and an assistant in said division designated by him, and the state
treasurer shall, for each day's services rendered in connection with the work of the board under this act and chapter
three hundred and seven of the acts of the current year,
be paid thirty dollars in addition to his regular compensation; provided, that the total amount paid hereunder to
said director or to said assistant or to said treasurer for
compensation as aforesaid shall not exceed two thousand
dollars in any period of twelve months.

Separate records and accounts shall be kept by the board of its action under this act.

At the request of the board, in so far as is practicable, the attorney general, the commissioner of public works, the commissioner of corporations and taxation and the commission on administration and finance shall assign for temporary service for the board, such employees in their respective departments as the board may require in carrying out the provisions of this act, and any expense incurred by any such department by reason of such assignment shall be deemed an expense of the board. The board may also employ, subject to the approval of the governor and council, such additional expert and clerical assistance as it may require, but the cost thereof in no event shall exceed twenty thousand dollars for the balance of the fiscal year ending November thirtieth, nineteen hundred and thirty-three. _{Certain state employees assigned to board.}

SECTION 2. Any city or town, including Boston, by a two thirds vote as defined in section one of chapter forty-four of the General Laws, with the approval of the mayor of such a city, may engage in any public works project included in any "comprehensive program of public works" prepared under section two hundred and two of Title II of the National Industrial Recovery Act, but only in case such project is approved, as hereinafter provided, by the board and by the governor and in case the proper federal authorities have obligated the federal government to make a grant therefor of federal money under section two hundred and three of said title. Such projects, so approved, shall be carried out in all respects subject to the provisions of said Title II and to such terms, conditions, rules and regulations, not inconsistent with applicable federal laws and regulations, as the board may establish, with the approval of the governor, to ensure the proper execution of such projects. Any such city or town may accept and use for carrying out any project so approved any grant or loan of federal funds under section two hundred and three of said Title II; and, for the purpose only of carrying out such project, may borrow from the United States of America for such project such sums as may be fixed by the board as hereinafter provided, and may issue bonds, notes or other forms of written acknowledgment of debt for such terms and carrying such rates of interest as may be fixed by the board as hereinafter provided. The aggregate amount that may be borrowed hereunder by any city or town for projects for which borrowings are authorized under section seven of said chapter forty-four shall not exceed its limit of indebtedness, as determined in accordance with section ten of said chapter, by more than one per cent on the average of the assessors' valuations of its taxable property for the three preceding years, such valuations to be reduced and otherwise determined as provided in said section ten; and the amount that may be borrowed hereunder by any _{Cities and towns may engage in program of public works, etc.} _{May borrow money.}

city or town for any project for which borrowings are
authorized by section eight of said chapter shall not exceed
the limit provided in said section eight for such projects
by more than one per cent of the last preceding assessed
valuation of such city or town. For the purposes of the
foregoing sentence, the limit of indebtedness of the city
of Boston shall be computed in accordance with the provisions of section ten of said chapter forty-four as provided
in section two of chapter two hundred and twenty-five of
the acts of nineteen hundred and thirty-one. In fixing
the amounts that may be borrowed hereunder for projects
for which borrowings are not authorized by said chapter
forty-four, the board shall be guided by the above limitations as applied to the provisions of said chapter applicable
to like projects. The board shall fix the terms of and
rates of interest on the bonds, notes or other forms of
written acknowledgment of debt issued hereunder in
accordance with the applicable federal laws and regulations
and subject to the approval of the proper federal authorities, but such terms shall in no event be for a shorter time
than the maximum term permitted by the federal government for that particular issue. All the provisions of said
chapter forty-four, exclusive of the limitation contained
in the first paragraph of section seven thereof, shall apply
to any borrowing hereunder by any city or town, including
Boston and Worcester, except as hereinbefore provided
and except in so far as such provisions of law may be in
conflict with applicable federal laws and regulations. Each
city or town seeking the approval of any project by the
board shall submit to it all information required with
respect to the financial condition of such city or town, its
outstanding indebtedness within and without its limit of
indebtedness, the estimated cost of the project, the alleged
necessity therefor and the proposed method of financing
the same. In granting or withholding its approval, the
board shall take into consideration, among other things,
the necessity of the proposed project, the ability of such
city or town to finance the same, the extent to which the
carrying out of the project will tend to relieve unemployment and the extent to which the maintenance of the
project when completed will tend to increase or decrease
the annual expenditures of such city or town and to increase
or decrease the tax burden upon its inhabitants.

Work to be done by human labor.
Exceptions.

SECTION 2A. All projects for the construction, reconstruction or resurfacing of roads and the construction of
sewers shall be done by human labor, except in so far as
machinery is, in the opinion of the federal, city or town
officer or department having charge of the project, reasonably necessary, and the wages for such labor shall not be
less than the prevailing rate of wages as established by the
federal government.

Board to approve local projects.

SECTION 3. Any officer or department of a city or
town charged with the duty of carrying out any project

so approved shall have, in addition to any powers expressly given by statute, such powers as may be determined and certified by the board to be proper and reasonably necessary to carry out such project, including the power to take property by eminent domain on behalf of such city or town provided that no source of water supply and no works for the disposal of sewage shall be installed without first having the approval of the state department of public health. If such officer or department is aggrieved by *Appeal.* such action, he or it may, within ten days after notice thereof, appeal to the governor, whose decision shall be final. The board is hereby authorized to make all necessary orders, rules and regulations and perform all necessary actions under this act; and none of such orders, rules, regulations and actions shall be declared inoperative, illegal or void for any omission of a technical nature in respect thereto. Nothing in this act shall require any action in contravention of applicable federal laws and rules and regulations nor preclude action in conformity therewith.

SECTION 4. The governor of the commonwealth is *Governor to* hereby authorized to take any and all steps necessary *out projects.* from time to time to enable the cities and towns of this commonwealth to secure any benefits to which they may be entitled under the National Industrial Recovery Act, and the board is hereby directed to co-operate and assist him in every way possible.

SECTION 5. Unless inconsistent with the provisions of *Contracts* Title II of the National Industrial Recovery Act, all con- *to be awarded* tracts awarded under the provisions of this act shall only be awarded to citizens of the United States of America or to corporations a majority of whose officers and directors are citizens of the United States of America.

SECTION 6. The provisions of Part I of this act shall, *Certain provi-* so far as applicable, apply to any fire, water, light or im- *to fire, etc.,* provement district. *districts.*

PART II.

CONSTRUCTION OF A SUBWAY IN THE CITY OF BOSTON.

SECTION 1. The following words as used in Part II *Definitions.* of this act shall, unless the context otherwise requires, have the following meanings: —

"City" shall mean the city of Boston.

"Company" shall mean the Boston Elevated Railway Company, its successors and assigns.

"Department" shall mean the transit department of the city of Boston, or such board or officers as may succeed to its rights and duties.

"Premises" shall mean the property authorized to be acquired or constructed by the department under the provisions of section two of Part II of this act, except equipment.

"Equipment" shall mean the property which the department is authorized to provide and furnish under the provisions of section three of Part II of this act.

Whenever any act is required or authorized to be done or performed by the department under Part II of this act, such action shall be in the name of and on behalf of the city of Boston, and whenever any action is required or permitted to be taken by the city under Part II of this act, such act shall be performed by the department, unless otherwise expressly provided by Part II of this act.

Subway in Boston.

SECTION 2. Provided the board and the governor approve the public works project as hereinafter authorized, and the conditions hereinafter set forth are complied with, the department may construct within the limits of the city a subway connecting with or being an extension of any existing subway; provided such project as so approved is also approved by the proper federal authorities and a substantial part of the cost of construction of said extension can be obtained under the provisions of the National Industrial Recovery Act. Such project so approved shall be carried out in all respects subject to the provisions of Title II of the National Industrial Recovery Act, subject to the terms and conditions imposed by the board and to the rules and regulations promulgated pursuant to section two of Part I of this act, and the city may accept and use for the carrying out of such project any grant or loan of federal funds under said Title II.

Transit department of Boston, duties under act.

SECTION 3. The department shall provide, equip and furnish the subway or extension authorized by virtue of section two of Part II and the stations and approaches thereof and thereto to the same extent and manner as provided in section three of chapter four hundred and eighty of the acts of nineteen hundred and twenty-three, with respect to the railway authorized by said act.

Transit department to have necessary powers.

SECTION 4. For the purposes of Part II of this act the department shall have all the powers conferred upon the Boston transit commission by chapter five hundred and forty-eight of the acts of eighteen hundred and ninety-four and by chapter seven hundred and forty-one of the acts of nineteen hundred and eleven and amendments thereof, either generally or in connection with the construction or operation of any tunnel or subway authorized by said chapters, and like powers as conferred by chapter four hundred and eighty of the acts of nineteen hundred and twenty-three with respect to the works authorized thereunder, and by all other acts conferring authority upon the Boston transit commission or the department.

The premises and equipment may be constructed upon, under or over public or private ways or lands including lands devoted to the public use and property belonging to a railroad company.

For the purpose of constructing the work authorized by Part II of this act the department may enter upon and use the land of others. Any person injured in his property

by such entry or use of his land by the department may
recover his damages under chapter seventy-nine of the
General Laws.

SECTION 5. To meet the cost of the premises and equip- Board may
ment, the city, with the approval of the emergency finance issue bonds.
board, may issue bonds which shall be designated on their
face Subway Bonds, Acts of 1933, in the same manner as
bonds issued under section eleven of said chapter four hundred and eighty of the acts of nineteen hundred and twenty-
three and the provisions of said section shall apply to the
premises and equipment and all action taken under authority of this section, provided, however, that the city shall
obtain as large a sum as is possible under the provisions
of the National Industrial Recovery Act.

SECTION 6. All rentals or other payments received by Rentals, etc.,
the city under Part II of this act shall be used so far as to be applied
necessary for the payment of interest on the obligations etc., on bonds,
incurred hereunder and the balance shall be used for the etc.
payment of the principal thereof or the accumulation of
a sinking fund therefor. All indebtedness incurred under
Part II of this act shall be outside of the statutory limit of
indebtedness of the city, but within the limitations set
forth in Part I.

SECTION 7. No construction work shall be done under Plans to be
Part II of this act, however, unless and until a plan therefor approved by
shall be approved by the commission of the department of ment of public
public utilities and the mayor of the city and unless and utilities.
until a contract between the city and the company shall
have been executed for the sole and exclusive use by the
company of the premises and equipment for a term beginning with the use thereof and ending upon the termination
of the lease or contract for use as at present extended of
the Boylston street subway. Any plan so approved may
be altered at any time by a new plan approved in like
manner except that after the execution of said contract
for use no such alteration shall be made without the consent thereto of the company in writing nor at any time
except with the approval of said emergency finance board,
the governor and such approvals as may be required under
the provisions of the National Industrial Recovery Act
or regulations made thereunder. The contract shall be
in the same general form as that authorized by said chapter
four hundred and eighty, except in so far as any other
provision may be agreed upon by the department and the
company as specially applicable to the demised premises.
The net cost of the premises and equipment shall be determined in the manner provided in said chapter four hundred
and eighty, except that there shall be deducted from the
amount so determined all amounts received by the city as
direct grants, or by remission of bonds or other obligations,
or in any manner or form whatsoever amounting in substance directly or indirectly to a contribution to the cost
of the premises and equipment under the National Indus-

trial Recovery Act. The rental shall be payable annually
on the twenty-fifth day of July in each year. Such contract for use shall provide that the company shall pay to
the city for each full year ending with the last day of June,
and ratably for any portion of the year, an annual rental
which shall be sufficient to provide an amount equal to one
half of one per cent of the net cost of the premises and
equipment in addition to the annual amount of interest on
bonds issued to pay for said net cost, but not less than four
and one half per cent of said net cost in any event; provided, however, that said annual rental shall be payable
by the company in any year only if and to the extent that
the reserve fund provided for by section five of chapter one
hundred and fifty-nine of the Special Acts of nineteen
hundred and eighteen exceeds on the last day·of June the
amount originally established; provided, however, that
such excess shall be determined and the obligation to pay
the rental shall accrue only after deducting from said reserve
fund the full amount of the rental payable under any contracts executed under the authority of chapter three hundred and forty-one of the acts of nineteen hundred and
twenty-five as amended and after fully reimbursing the
commonwealth as provided in sections eleven and thirteen
of said chapter one hundred and fifty-nine. If by virtue
of the foregoing provisos the company is not required to
make the full rental payment as above provided for the
premises and equipment authorized by this act, the city
shall place any amounts so unpaid in its next ensuing tax
levy.

Provisions of certain special acts not to apply.

SECTION 8. The provisions of chapter five hundred and
fifty of the acts of nineteen hundred and seven as amended,
and of sections one hundred and ten and one hundred and
eleven of chapter forty-one of the General Laws as appearing in the Tercentenary Edition thereof shall not apply
to the work authorized by virtue of Part II of this act.

Acceptance by city of Boston. Preliminary investigations.

SECTION 9. Upon acceptance of Part II of this act by
vote of the city council of the city, approved by the mayor,
the department may immediately make such preliminary
investigations, surveys and plans as it may deem expedient, and to that end may enter upon any lands and place
and maintain marks therein and may make excavations
and borings and do all other acts necessary for such investigations and surveys. The department may expend such
sums not in excess of ten thousand dollars as it deems
necessary therefor. The expenses incurred in making such
preliminary investigations, surveys and plans shall be paid
from the loans authorized by chapter seven hundred and
forty-one of the acts of nineteen hundred and eleven, but
if and when the construction is begun hereunder, the amount
so expended shall be transferred and charged to the.cost
of the premises.

Contracts to comply with requirements

SECTION 10. The department may make contracts for
work authorized by virtue of Part II of this act but all

contracts subject thereto shall comply with all requirements of the National Industrial Recovery Act and shall be subject to the rules and regulations promulgated pursuant to section two of Part I of this act, and all contracts involving two thousand dollars or more in amount shall be in writing and signed by a majority of the department. No such written contract shall be altered except by an instrument in writing, signed by the contractor and a majority of the department, and also by the sureties on any bond given by the contractor for the completion of the original contract. No such contract and no alteration of any such contract shall be valid or binding on the city unless executed in the manner aforesaid. *of National Industrial Recovery Act.*

SECTION 11. Notwithstanding anything in Part II of this act contained, the department with the approval of the emergency finance board is hereby authorized to construct and equip the premises in accordance with any requirements of the National Industrial Recovery Act or rules and regulations made thereunder and to take any action in its judgment necessary in order to procure as nearly as it deems practicable the maximum amount obtainable under said act as a direct grant and the maximum amount which may be borrowed under the provisions of said act. *Modification of provisions of Part II of act.*

SECTION 12. Said contract for use shall not in any respect impair any right which the commonwealth or any political subdivision thereof may at any time have to take the railway properties and rights of the company or any right which the commonwealth or any political subdivision thereof may have under section sixteen of chapter one hundred and fifty-nine of the Special Acts of nineteen hundred and eighteen or under section seventeen of chapter three hundred and thirty-three of the acts of nineteen hundred and thirty-one. In the event of such taking the compensation to be paid to the company shall not be enhanced by reason of such contract nor shall it be diminished because of the fact that without it properties might be cut off. *Contracts not to impair rights of commonwealth, etc.*

SECTION 13. The provisions of Part I of this act, so far as inconsistent with Part II, shall not apply to Part II, nor preclude action thereunder. The inclusion of Part II in this act shall not be construed as in any way indicating any intent on the part of the general court to prefer the project authorized under said Part II over any other project which may be submitted to the board by the city of Boston. *Provisions of Part I not to apply to Part II of act.*

SECTION 14. Part II of this act shall take full effect only upon its acceptance both by vote of the city council of the city of Boston, approved by the mayor, and by the Boston Elevated Railway Company by vote of its board of directors, and upon the filing of certificates of such acceptances with the state secretary, provided that such acceptances, approval and filing occur during the current year, except that section nine shall take effect as provided therein. *Acceptance of Part II of act.*

PART III.

RAPID TRANSIT EXTENSIONS OUTSIDE THE CITY OF BOSTON.

Definitions.

SECTION 1. The following words as used in Part III of this act shall, unless the context otherwise requires, have the following meanings: —

"Company" shall mean the Boston Elevated Railway Company, its successors and assigns.

"Department" shall mean the transit department of the city of Boston, or such board or officers as may succeed to its rights and duties.

"District" shall mean the Boston metropolitan district established by section one of chapter three hundred and eighty-three of the acts of nineteen hundred and twenty-nine.

"Premises" shall mean the property authorized to be acquired or constructed by the department under the provisions of Part III, except equipment.

"Equipment" shall mean the property which the department is authorized to provide and furnish under the provisions of the second paragraph of section eight of Part III of this act.

"Trustees" shall mean the board of trustees of the Boston metropolitan district established by section two of said chapter three hundred and eighty-three.

Rapid transit extensions outside of city of Boston.

SECTION 2. Provided the board and the governor approve the public works project as hereinafter authorized, and the conditions hereinafter set forth are complied with, the trustees, in the name and on behalf of the district, may construct a rapid transit extension or extensions outside the city of Boston connecting with existing lines of the company, by means of subways, tunnels, ramps, viaducts, reserved spaces, private rights of way, surface tracks with cuts or fill, bridges or other forms of construction; provided such project as so approved is also approved by the proper federal authorities and a substantial part of the cost of the construction and equipment of each such extension can be obtained under the provisions of the National Industrial Recovery Act. Such project so approved shall be carried out in all respects subject to the provisions of Title II of the National Industrial Recovery Act and to the terms and conditions imposed by the board and to the rules and regulations promulgated pursuant to section two of Part I of this act, and the district may accept and use for the carrying out of such project any grant or loan of federal funds under said Title II.

Trustees of Boston metropolitan district to prepare plans, etc.

SECTION 3. The trustees shall immediately cause to be prepared by the department preliminary plans together with all preliminary investigations, surveys, borings and estimates of the cost for the construction and equipment of such an extension provided not more than the sum of twenty-five thousand dollars shall be expended therefor and upon approval of the project as required in the preceding section or prior thereto if the same are required as a condition of any such approval shall cause final and detailed plans to be prepared by the department for the construction and equipment of any such extension.

SECTION 4. No work of construction shall be done under Part III of this act (a) until the trustees have caused to be prepared plans showing the proposed location of any such extension, the general form and method of construction, the location and equipment of proposed tracks and the alignment and grade thereof, and the proposed stations and approaches and other structures, which plans shall be submitted to the metropolitan transit council and the company, for examination; nor (b) until the trustees, after public hearing notice of which shall be published at least one week prior thereto in at least two newspapers published in the city of Boston, shall formally approve and sign the same; nor (c) until a contract for the exclusive use of the same by the company has been executed as hereinafter provided. Any such plan so approved and signed may be altered at any time before the execution of the contract for use of the extension included therein and its equipment, by a new plan prepared, submitted and approved in like manner; but after execution of the contract for use no changes shall be made in the plan for the premises without the consent of the company thereto in writing nor at any time except with the approval of the board, the governor, and such approvals as may be required under the provisions of the National Industrial Recovery Act or regulations made thereunder. If and when the aforesaid conditions have been complied with, the department in behalf of the district shall construct and equip the same. *Construction work not to commence, until, etc.*

SECTION 5. For the purposes of Part III of this act the department shall have all the powers conferred upon the Boston transit commission by chapter five hundred and forty-eight of the acts of eighteen hundred and ninety-four and by chapter seven hundred and forty-one of the acts of nineteen hundred and eleven and amendments thereof, either generally or in connection with the construction or operation of any tunnel or subway authorized by said chapters, and like powers as conferred by chapter four hundred and eighty of the acts of nineteen hundred and twenty-three with respect to the works authorized thereunder, and by all other acts conferring authority upon the Boston transit commission or the department; provided, that whenever any act or action is authorized, required or permitted by said statutes to be done by, or in the name or in behalf of the city of Boston, the department shall have like power and authority to act in the name and in behalf of the district. *Powers of department, etc.*

SECTION 6. For the purposes of constructing the works authorized by Part III of this act, the department may *Damages to property.*

enter upon and use the land of others. Any person injured in his property by such entry or use of his land by the department may recover his damages from the district under chapter seventy-nine of the General Laws.

SECTION 7. Any such extension may be constructed upon, under or over public or private ways or public lands or lands devoted to the public use including, with its consent, any property belonging to a railroad or a terminal company, but such consent shall not be required to crossings above or below grade or to taking of property outside the location of a railroad.

SECTION 8. The department, in connection with the construction of any such extension, shall lay out and construct therefor, terminals, stations, shelters, transfer areas, inclosed or otherwise, yards and other structures necessary or convenient in connection with the operation thereof or their use by the public, including connections with any existing tracks of the company.

The department shall also provide, equip and furnish any such extension, and the property and structures provided for by the preceding paragraph to the same extent and manner as provided in section three of chapter four hundred and eighty of the acts of nineteen hundred and twenty-three, with respect to the railway authorized by said chapter.

SECTION 9. In the employment of laborers, workmen, mechanics, engineers and all employees engaged in carrying out the provisions of Part III of this act, the department shall, in so far as may be consistent with the provisions of the National Industrial Recovery Act and of this act, and the rules and regulations made thereunder or promulgated by the board employ persons resident in the several cities and towns composing the district in as nearly as may be practicable the same ratio as the current expenses of the district are apportioned under section twelve of said chapter three hundred and eighty-three of the acts of nineteen hundred and twenty-nine.

SECTION 10. To meet the cost of carrying out the provisions of Part III of this act the trustees in behalf of the district shall obtain as large a sum as is possible under the provisions of the National Industrial Recovery Act and so far as necessary in their judgment to provide funds required to carry out the provisions of Part III of this act, shall from time to time, with the approval of the board, issue and sell bonds of the district in the manner and subject to the provisions of section ten of chapter three hundred and eighty-three of the acts of nineteen hundred and twenty-nine and section two of chapter one hundred and forty-seven of the acts of nineteen hundred and thirty-two, and the provisions of said sections shall apply thereto in the same manner and to the same extent as if such notes or bonds of the district were specifically authorized in said chapter three hundred and eighty-three.

SECTION 11.   When plans have been approved as afore- said and the approvals required by section two of Part III of this act have been given, the trustees in the name and behalf of the district may execute a contract with the company, upon the terms and conditions herein prescribed for the sole and exclusive use of the premises and equipment thereof for the running of trains and/or cars therein and thereon and for such other uses as the trustees and the company may agree upon for a term which shall extend from the beginning of the use of the premises to the first day of July, nineteen hundred and eighty-one, at a rental as hereinafter provided.   Such contract for use shall continue in force after the expiration of the definite term specified upon the same terms and conditions until the same is terminated by notice from the district or from the company as hereinafter provided.   The district may ter- minate said contract on the first day of July, nineteen hundred and eighty-one or on the first day of July of any year thereafter by giving at least two years' prior notice in writing, and the company may likewise terminate said contract on the first day of July, nineteen hundred and eighty-one or on the first day of any year thereafter by giving to the trustees at least two years' prior notice in writing; but no notice on the part of either the district or the company shall be given more than three years prior to the date therein fixed for termination.   Such contract for use shall provide that the company shall pay to the district for each full year ending with the last day of June and ratably for any portion of a year, an annual rental which shall be sufficient to provide an amount equal to one half of one per cent of the net cost of the premises and equipment in addition to the annual amount of interest on bonds issued to pay for said net cost, but not less than four and one half per cent of said net cost in any event; provided, however, that said annual rental shall be payable by the company in any year only if and to the extent that the reserve fund provided for by section five of chapter one hundred and fifty-nine of the Special Acts of nineteen hundred and eighteen exceeds on the last day of June the amount originally established; provided, however, that such excess shall be determined and the obligation to pay rental shall accrue only after deducting from said reserve fund the full amount of the rental payable under any contracts executed under the authority of the Governor Square Act, so-called, being chapter three hundred and forty-one of the acts of nineteen hundred and twenty-five, as amended, and after deducting the full amount of the rental payable under any contract for use of any subway extension made under Part II of this act and after fully reimbursing the commonwealth as provided in sections eleven and thirteen of said chapter one hundred and fifty-nine.   If by reason of the foregoing provisos the company does not make the full rental payment as above

provided for the premises and equipment authorized by
Part III of this act, any amount so unpaid shall annually
be raised by taxation in the manner and as provided in
section twelve of said chapter three hundred and eighty-
three. Rental shall be payable annually on the twenty-
fifth day of July in each year.

The use of the whole or any part of the premises and
equipment by the company and the accrual of rental
therefor shall begin upon certification by the commission
of the department of public utilities that the premises and
equipment or any part of said premises and equipment
are in safe and proper condition for operation, and as to
any part that the operation of such part prior to the completion of the whole premises is in the public interest.

The net cost shall be deemed to include, except as otherwise provided herein, all expenditures incurred in acquisition and construction of the premises and equipment,
including damages, expenses, such proportion of the salaries and expenses of the department as may in its opinion
be properly chargeable thereto, and interest on the debt
incurred for the acquisition and construction of the premises and equipment prior to the beginning of the use thereof;
and in determining the same there shall be deducted the
premiums realized from the sale of bonds included in
determining the rental and any interest received by the
district upon the proceeds of such bonds prior to the
expenditure of such proceeds and the proceeds from the
sale of any property acquired in connection with the construction of the premises and later sold, provided that
there shall be deducted from the amount so determined
all amounts received by the district as direct grants, or
by remission of bonds or other obligation, or in any manner or form whatsoever amounting in substance, directly
or indirectly, to a contribution to the cost of the premises
and equipment under the National Industrial Recovery
Act.

Such contract for use shall provide that all equipment
furnished by the district shall be maintained and kept by
the company in proper repair and condition, and shall
contain such provisions for depreciation, obsolescence and
losses with respect to such equipment as may be agreed
upon. Such contract shall also contain such other provisions and conditions not affecting the term or the rental
nor inconsistent with the provisions of this act as the
trustees and the company may agree upon.

SECTION 12. Every person sustaining damage by reason
of property or rights in property taken under authority
of Part III of this act or in carrying out its provisions,
except public ways or lands, shall be entitled to recover
the same from the district under chapter seventy-nine of
the General Laws. Neither the members of the department nor the trustees shall be liable personally for any
such damage.

Section 13. The department may make contracts in the name of the district for the work authorized by Part III of this act but all contracts subject thereto shall comply with all requirements of the National Industrial Recovery Act and shall be subject to the rules and regulations promulgated pursuant to section two of Part I of this act, and all contracts involving two thousand dollars or more in amount shall be in writing and signed by a majority of the department and shall not be binding until approved by vote of the trustees. No such contract shall be altered except by an instrument in writing, signed by the contractor and a majority of the department, and also by the sureties on any bond given by the contractor for the completion of the original contract, and approved by vote of the trustees. No such contract and no alteration of any such contract shall be valid or binding on the district unless executed in the manner aforesaid. *Contracts to comply with requirements of National Industrial Recovery Act.*

Section 14. Notwithstanding anything in Part III of this act contained, but subject to the approval of the board and the governor, the trustees and the department are hereby authorized to construct and equip said premises in accordance with any requirements of the National Industrial Recovery Act or rules and regulations made thereunder and to take any action in their judgment necessary in order to procure as nearly as they deem practicable the maximum amount obtainable under said act as a direct grant and the maximum amount which may be borrowed under the provisions of said act. *All necessary action to be taken to secure federal funds.*

Section 15. The provisions of Part I of this act, so far as inconsistent with Part III, shall not apply to Part III, nor preclude action thereunder. The inclusion of Part III in this act shall not be construed as in any way indicating any intent on the part of the general court to prefer the project authorized under said Part III over any other project which may be submitted to the board. *Certain provisions of Part I not to apply to Part III of act.*

Section 16. Said contract for use shall not in any respect impair any right which the commonwealth or any political subdivision thereof may at any time have to take the railway properties and rights of the company or any right which the commonwealth or any political subdivision thereof may have under section sixteen of chapter one hundred and fifty-nine of the Special Acts of nineteen hundred and eighteen or under section seventeen of chapter three hundred and thirty-three of the acts of nineteen hundred and thirty-one. In the event of such taking the compensation to be paid to the company shall not be enhanced by reason of such contract nor shall it be diminished because of the fact that without it properties might be cut off. *Contracts for use of extensions, etc., not to impair rights of commonwealth, etc.*

Section 17. Part III of this act shall take full effect only upon its acceptance both by the district acting by the metropolitan transit council and by the Boston Elevated Railway Company by vote of its board of directors and *Acceptance of Part III.*

upon the filing of certificates of such acceptances with the state secretary, provided, that such acceptances, approval and filing occur during the current year.

PART IV.

Removal of elevated structures in city of Boston authorized.

SECTION 1. Provided the board and the governor approve the project as hereinafter authorized, and the conditions hereinafter set forth are complied with, the transit department of the city of Boston, or such board or officers as may succeed to its rights and duties, may remove existing elevated structures of the Boston Elevated Railway Company in said city; provided, any such project as so approved is also approved by the proper federal authorities and a substantial part of the cost of said removal can be obtained under the provisions of the National Industrial Recovery Act. Such project so approved shall be carried out in all respects subject to the provisions of Title II of the National Industrial Recovery Act, subject to the terms and conditions imposed by the board and to the rules and regulations promulgated by said board.

Acceptance of Part IV of act.

SECTION 2. Part IV of this act shall take full effect only upon its acceptance both by vote of the city council of the city of Boston, approved by the mayor, and by the Boston Elevated Railway Company by vote of its board of directors, and upon the filing of certificates of such acceptances with the state secretary, provided that such acceptances, approval and filing occur during the current year.

Approved July 22, 1933.

Chap.367 AN ACT RELATIVE TO THE TERMS OF CERTAIN BONDS AND NOTES TO BE ISSUED BY THE COMMONWEALTH.

Be it enacted, etc., as follows:

SECTION 1. The bonds or notes which the state treasurer is authorized to issue under chapter three hundred and seven of the acts of the current year, authorizing cities and towns to borrow on account of public welfare and soldiers' benefits from the commonwealth and elsewhere and authorizing the commonwealth to issue bonds or notes to provide funds therefor, shall be for maximum terms of years to expire not later than November thirtieth, nineteen hundred and forty, as recommended by the governor in a message to the general court dated July twenty-second, nineteen hundred and thirty-three, in pursuance of section three of Article LXII of the amendments to the constitution.

SECTION 2. The notes which the state treasurer is authorized to issue under chapter three hundred and forty-one of the acts of the current year, establishing a municipal finance commission for the town of Millville, shall be issued for maximum terms of years to expire not later than November thirtieth, nineteen hundred and thirty-nine, as recommended by the governor in a message to the general court dated July twenty-second, nineteen hundred and thirty-three, in pursuance of section three of Article LXII of the amendments to the constitution.

Approved July 22, 1933.

AN ACT RELATIVE TO THE TERMS OF CERTAIN BONDS, NOTES OR OTHER FORMS OF WRITTEN ACKNOWLEDGMENT OF DEBT TO BE ISSUED BY THE COMMONWEALTH.

*Chap.*368

Be it enacted, etc., as follows:

The terms of the bonds, notes and other forms of written acknowledgment of debt which the state treasurer is authorized to issue under chapter three hundred and sixty-five of the acts of the current year, authorizing the commonwealth from time to time to borrow from the United States of America such sums as may be required for carrying out the purposes of said chapter, shall be the maximum terms permitted by the federal government for the respective issues.   *Approved July 22, 1933.*

AN ACT TO APPORTION AND ASSESS A STATE TAX OF NINE MILLION DOLLARS.

*Chap.*369

Whereas, A delay in the taking effect of this act would cause great inconvenience in the collection of the state tax, therefore it is hereby declared to be an emergency law, necessary for the immediate preservation of the public convenience.

Emergency preamble.

Be it enacted, etc., as follows:

SECTION 1. Each city and town in the commonwealth shall be assessed and pay the sum with which it stands charged in the following schedule, that is to say: —

State tax apportioned and assessed.

Abington, eighty-three hundred seventy dollars	$8,370 00
Acton, fifty-one hundred thirty dollars	5,130 00
Acushnet, forty-seven hundred seventy dollars	4,770 00
Adams, seventeen thousand one hundred ninety dollars	17,190 00
Agawam, twelve thousand three hundred thirty dollars	12,330 00
Alford, three hundred sixty dollars	360 00
Amesbury, fifteen thousand three hundred dollars	15,300 00
Amherst, twelve thousand one hundred fifty dollars	12,150 00
Andover, twenty-three thousand four hundred ninety dollars	23,490 00
Arlington, seventy-eight thousand five hundred seventy dollars	78,570 00
Ashburnham, twenty-six hundred ten dollars	2,610 00
Ashby, thirteen hundred fifty dollars	1,350 00
Ashfield, fifteen hundred thirty dollars	1,530 00
Ashland, thirty-eight hundred seventy dollars	3,870 00
Athol, fifteen thousand six hundred sixty dollars	15,660 00
Attleboro, thirty-four thousand eight hundred thirty dollars	34,830 00
Auburn, eighty-three hundred seventy dollars	8,370 00
Avon, three thousand and sixty dollars	3,060 00
Ayer, forty-nine hundred fifty dollars	4,950 00
Barnstable, twenty-seven thousand eight hundred ten dollars	27,810 00

Barre, forty-five hundred dollars	$4,500 00
Becket, eleven hundred seventy dollars . .	1,170 00
Bedford, thirty-six hundred ninety dollars . .	3,690 00
Belchertown, twenty-one hundred sixty dollars . .	2,160 00
Bellingham, thirty-six hundred dollars . . .	3,600 00
Belmont, fifty-seven thousand and sixty dollars . .	57,060 00
Berkley, eleven hundred seventy dollars . .	1,170 00
Berlin, fourteen hundred forty dollars . . .	1,440 00
Bernardston, twelve hundred sixty dollars . .	1,260 00
Beverly, sixty thousand eight hundred forty dollars .	60,840 00
Billerica, eleven thousand eight hundred eighty dollars .	11,880 00
Blackstone, thirty-six hundred dollars . . .	3,600 00
Blandford, nine hundred ninety dollars . . .	990 00
Bolton, fifteen hundred thirty dollars . . .	1,530 00
Boston, two million three hundred twenty-two thousand seven hundred twenty dollars	2,322,720 00
Bourne, eleven thousand two hundred fifty dollars .	11,250 00
Boxborough, five hundred forty dollars . . .	540 00
Boxford, fourteen hundred forty dollars . . .	1,440 00
Boylston, twelve hundred sixty dollars . . .	1,260 00
Braintree, thirty-two thousand five hundred eighty dollars	32,580 00
Brewster, twenty-four hundred thirty dollars . .	2,430 00
Bridgewater, eighty-four hundred sixty dollars . .	8,460 00
Brimfield, fifteen hundred thirty dollars . . .	1,530 00
Brockton, one hundred seven thousand and ten dollars .	107,010 00
Brookfield, eighteen hundred ninety dollars . .	1,890 00
Brookline, two hundred one thousand six hundred ninety dollars	201,690 00
Buckland, thirty-five hundred ten dollars . .	3,510 00
Burlington, thirty-three hundred thirty dollars . .	3,330 00
Cambridge, two hundred fifty-two thousand two hundred seventy dollars	252,270 00
Canton, eleven thousand nine hundred seventy dollars .	11,970 00
Carlisle, thirteen hundred fifty dollars . . .	1,350 00
Carver, thirty-six hundred ninety dollars . .	3,690 00
Charlemont, fourteen hundred forty dollars . .	1,440 00
Charlton, twenty-four hundred thirty dollars . .	2,430 00
Chatham, sixty-eight hundred forty dollars . .	6,840 00
Chelmsford, eighty-five hundred fifty dollars .	8,550 00
Chelsea, seventy-one thousand two hundred eighty dollars	71,280 00
Cheshire, twenty-one hundred sixty dollars . .	2,160 00
Chester, two thousand and seventy dollars . .	2,070 00
Chesterfield, eight hundred ten dollars . . .	810 00
Chicopee, fifty-nine thousand five hundred eighty dollars	59,580 00
Chilmark, eight hundred ten dollars . . .	810 00
Clarksburg, eleven hundred seventy dollars . .	1,170 00
Clinton, eighteen thousand six hundred thirty dollars .	18,630 00
Cohasset, twelve thousand six hundred ninety dollars .	12,690 00
Colrain, two thousand and seventy dollars . .	2,070 00
Concord, twelve thousand five hundred ten dollars .	12,510 00
Conway, thirteen hundred fifty dollars . . .	1,350 00
Cummington, seven hundred twenty dollars . .	720 00
Dalton, eighty-three hundred seventy dollars . .	8,370 00
Dana, eight hundred ten dollars . . .	810 00
Danvers, seventeen thousand one hundred dollars . .	17,100 00
Dartmouth, fifteen thousand and thirty dollars . .	15,030 00
Dedham, thirty-one thousand five hundred ninety dollars	31,590 00
Deerfield, fifty-four hundred dollars . . .	5,400 00
Dennis, forty-two hundred thirty dollars . .	4,230 00
Dighton, fifty-five hundred eighty dollars . .	5,580 00
Douglas, twenty-six hundred ten dollars . .	2,610 00
Dover, forty-six hundred eighty dollars . . .	4,680 00
Dracut, fifty-nine hundred forty dollars . . .	5,940 00
Dudley, forty-eight hundred sixty dollars . .	4,860 00
Dunstable, six hundred thirty dollars . . .	630 00

Duxbury, eighty-five hundred fifty dollars . . .	$8,550 00	State tax ap-
East Bridgewater, seven thousand and twenty dollars .	7,020 00	portioned
East Brookfield, fourteen hundred forty dollars . .	1,440 00	and assessed.
East Longmeadow, fifty-two hundred twenty dollars .	5,220 00	
Eastham, fifteen hundred thirty dollars . . .	1,530 00	
Easthampton, thirteen thousand one hundred forty dollars	13,140 00	
Easton, seventy-nine hundred twenty dollars . .	7,920 00	
Edgartown, fifty-seven hundred sixty dollars . .	5,760 00	
Egremont, eleven hundred seventy dollars . . .	1,170 00	
Enfield, eight hundred ten dollars	810 00	
Erving, twenty-nine hundred seventy dollars. . .	2,970 00	
Essex, twenty-one hundred sixty dollars . . .	2,160 00	
Everett, ninety-three thousand three hundred thirty dollars	93,330 00	
Fairhaven, sixteen thousand two hundred ninety dollars	16,290 00	
Fall River, one hundred sixty-two thousand four hundred fifty dollars	162,450 00	
Falmouth, twenty-five thousand two hundred ninety dollars	25,290 00	
Fitchburg, seventy-four thousand three hundred forty dollars	74,340 00	
Florida, sixteen hundred twenty dollars . . .	1,620 00	
Foxborough, eight thousand and ten dollars . . .	8,010 00	
Framingham, forty-five thousand two hundred seventy dollars	45,270 00	
Franklin, twelve thousand three hundred thirty dollars	12,330 00	
Freetown, twenty-two hundred fifty dollars . . .	2,250 00	
Gardner, thirty-one thousand six hundred eighty dollars	31,680 00	
Gay Head, one hundred eighty dollars	180 00	
Georgetown, twenty-six hundred ten dollars . . .	2,610 00	
Gill, twelve hundred sixty dollars	1,260 00	
Gloucester, fifty thousand eight hundred fifty dollars .	50,850 00	
Goshen, four hundred fifty dollars	450 00	
Gosnold, fifteen hundred thirty dollars . . .	1,530 00	
Grafton, sixty-two hundred ten dollars . . .	6,210 00	
Granby, fourteen hundred forty dollars . . .	1,440 00	
Granville, twenty-three hundred forty dollars . .	2,340 00	
Great Barrington, twelve thousand five hundred ten dollars	12,510 00	
Greenfield, thirty-five thousand one hundred dollars .	35,100 00	
Greenwich, eight hundred ten dollars	810 00	
Groton, fifty-eight hundred fifty dollars . . .	5,850 00	
Groveland, twenty-one hundred sixty dollars . .	2,160 00	
Hadley, thirty-eight hundred seventy dollars. . .	3,870 00	
Halifax, eighteen hundred ninety dollars . . .	1,890 00	
Hamilton, sixty-eight hundred forty dollars . . .	6,840 00	
Hampden, nine hundred dollars	900 00	
Hancock, five hundred forty dollars	540 00	
Hanover, fifty-one hundred thirty dollars . . .	5,130 00	
Hanson, thirty-seven hundred eighty dollars . .	3,780 00	
Hardwick, thirty-eight hundred seventy dollars . .	3,870 00	
Harvard, twenty-seven hundred ninety dollars . .	2,790 00	
Harwich, seven thousand and twenty dollars . .	7,020 00	
Hatfield, thirty-six hundred ninety dollars . . .	3,690 00	
Haverhill, seventy-eight thousand eight hundred forty dollars	78,840 00	
Hawley, three hundred sixty dollars	360 00	
Heath, five hundred forty dollars	540 00	
Hingham, eighteen thousand seven hundred twenty dollars	18,720 00	
Hinsdale, thirteen hundred fifty dollars . . .	1,350 00	
Holbrook, forty-eight hundred sixty dollars . . .	4,860 00	
Holden, forty-six hundred eighty dollars . . .	4,680 00	
Holland, two hundred seventy dollars	270 00	
Holliston, forty-nine hundred fifty dollars . . .	4,950 00	

Holyoke, one hundred thirty-four thousand seven hundred thirty dollars	$134,730 00
Hopedale, sixty-eight hundred forty dollars . . .	6,840 00
Hopkinton, forty-one hundred forty dollars . . .	4,140 00
Hubbardston, twelve hundred sixty dollars . . .	1,260 00
Hudson, ten thousand and eighty dollars . . .	10,080 00
Hull, twenty thousand four hundred thirty dollars .	20,430 00
Huntington, fourteen hundred forty dollars . . .	1,440 00
Ipswich, ninety-six hundred thirty dollars . . .	9,630 00
Kingston, fifty-six hundred seventy dollars . . .	5,670 00
Lakeville, eighteen hundred ninety dollars . . .	1,890 00
Lancaster, forty-one hundred forty dollars . . .	4,140 00
Lanesborough, seventeen hundred ten dollars . .	1,710 00
Lawrence, one hundred forty-eight thousand nine hundred fifty dollars	148,950 00
Lee, sixty-eight hundred forty dollars	6,840 00
Leicester, fifty-one hundred thirty dollars . . .	5,130 00
Lenox, seventy-eight hundred thirty dollars . . .	7,830 00
Leominster, thirty-two thousand eight hundred fifty dollars	32,850 00
Leverett, seven hundred twenty dollars . . .	720 00
Lexington, twenty-six thousand one hundred dollars .	26,100 00
Leyden, four hundred fifty dollars	450 00
Lincoln, thirty-six hundred ninety dollars . . .	3,690 00
Littleton, thirty-two hundred forty dollars . . .	3,240 00
Longmeadow, fourteen thousand five hundred eighty dollars	14,580 00
Lowell, one hundred fifty-four thousand and eighty dollars	154,080 00
Ludlow, eleven thousand four hundred thirty dollars .	11,430 00
Lunenburg, twenty-nine hundred seventy dollars .	2,970 00
Lynn, one hundred eighty-five thousand five hundred eighty dollars	185,580 00
Lynnfield, forty-three hundred twenty dollars .	4,320 00
Malden, ninety-five thousand and forty dollars .	95,040 00
Manchester, fourteen thousand eight hundred fifty dollars	14,850 00
Mansfield, ten thousand one hundred seventy dollars .	10,170 00
Marblehead, twenty-four thousand five hundred seventy dollars	24,570 00
Marion, sixty-one hundred twenty dollars . . .	6,120 00
Marlborough, twenty-one thousand seven hundred eighty dollars	21,780 00
Marshfield, eighty-seven hundred thirty dollars . .	8,730 00
Mashpee, nine hundred ninety dollars . . .	990 00
Mattapoisett, forty-six hundred eighty dollars . .	4,680 00
Maynard, ninety-one hundred eighty dollars . .	9,180 00
Medfield, thirty-eight hundred seventy dollars . .	3,870 00
Medford, one hundred five thousand one hundred twenty dollars	105,120 00
Medway, forty-five hundred ninety dollars . . .	4,590 00
Melrose, forty-six thousand eight hundred ninety dollars	46,890 00
Mendon, eighteen hundred dollars	1,800 00
Merrimac, twenty-eight hundred eighty dollars . .	2,880 00
Methuen, twenty-seven thousand one hundred eighty dollars	27,180 00
Middleborough, twelve thousand one hundred fifty dollars	12,150 00
Middlefield, four hundred fifty dollars	450 00
Middleton, twenty-four hundred thirty dollars . .	2,430 00
Milford, twenty thousand seven hundred ninety dollars .	20,790 00
Millbury, eighty-six hundred forty dollars . . .	8,640 00
Millis, thirty-nine hundred sixty dollars . . .	3,960 00
Millville, nineteen hundred eighty dollars . . .	1,980 00
Milton, forty-four thousand nine hundred ten dollars .	44,910 00
Monroe, eleven hundred seventy dollars . . .	1,170 00
Monson, forty-nine hundred fifty dollars . . .	4,950 00
Montague, fifteen thousand seven hundred fifty dollars .	15,750 00
Monterey, nine hundred ninety dollars . . .	990 00

Montgomery, three hundred sixty dollars . .	$360 00	State tax ap-
Mount Washington, two hundred seventy dollars . .	270 00	portioned
Nahant, seven thousand and twenty dollars . . .	7,020 00	and assessed.
Nantucket, fourteen thousand seven hundred sixty dollars	14,760 00	
Natick, twenty-five thousand four hundred seventy dollars	25,470 00	
Needham, twenty-nine thousand and seventy dollars .	29,070 00	
New Ashford, one hundred eighty dollars	180 00	
New Bedford, one hundred ninety-seven thousand nine hundred ten dollars	197,910 00	
New Braintree, seven hundred twenty dollars . .	720 00	
New Marlborough, seventeen hundred ten dollars .	1,710 00	
New Salem, six hundred thirty dollars . . .	630 00	
Newbury, twenty-eight hundred eighty dollars .	2,880 00	
Newburyport, eighteen thousand nine hundred dollars .	18,900 00	
Newton, one hundred ninety-five thousand three hundred dollars	195,300 00	
Norfolk, twenty-two hundred fifty dollars . .	2,250 00	
North Adams, thirty-one thousand eight hundred sixty dollars	31,860 00	
North Andover, eleven thousand seven hundred dollars .	11,700 00	
North Attleborough, fourteen thousand three hundred ten dollars	14,310 00	
North Brookfield, thirty-six hundred dollars . .	3,600 00	
North Reading, three thousand and sixty dollars .	3,060 00	
Northampton, thirty-six thousand three hundred sixty dollars	36,360 00	
Northborough, twenty-eight hundred eighty dollars	2,880 00	
Northbridge, thirteen thousand five hundred ninety dollars	13,590 00	
Northfield, twenty-six hundred ten dollars . .	2,610 00	
Norton, thirty-four hundred twenty dollars . .	3,420 00	
Norwell, twenty-seven hundred dollars	2,700 00	
Norwood, thirty-four thousand nine hundred twenty dollars	34,920 00	
Oak Bluffs, sixty-one hundred twenty dollars .	6,120 00	
Oakham, six hundred thirty dollars . . .	630 00	
Orange, seventy-six hundred fifty dollars . .	7,650 00	
Orleans, forty-seven hundred seventy dollars .	4,770 00	
Otis, seven hundred twenty dollars . . .	720 00	
Oxford, forty-five hundred ninety dollars . .	4,590 00	
Palmer, fourteen thousand one hundred thirty dollars .	14,130 00	
Paxton, twelve hundred sixty dollars . . .	1,260 00	
Peabody, thirty-four thousand two hundred ninety dollars	34,290 00	
Pelham, eight hundred ten dollars . . .	810 00	
Pembroke, thirty-six hundred dollars . . .	3,600 00	
Pepperell, forty-two hundred thirty dollars . .	4,230 00	
Peru, three hundred sixty dollars . . .	360 00	
Petersham, nineteen hundred eighty dollars . .	1,980 00	
Phillipston, five hundred forty dollars . . .	540 00	
Pittsfield, eighty-three thousand four hundred thirty dollars	83,430 00	
Plainfield, four hundred fifty dollars . . .	450 00	
Plainville, twenty-two hundred fifty dollars . .	2,250 00	
Plymouth, thirty-three thousand nine hundred thirty dollars	33,930 00	
Plympton, nine hundred dollars	900 00	
Prescott, ninety dollars	90 00	
Princeton, sixteen hundred twenty dollars . .	1,620 00	
Provincetown, fifty-eight hundred fifty dollars .	5,850 00	
Quincy, one hundred sixty-two thousand two hundred seventy dollars	162,270 00	
Randolph, seventy-nine hundred twenty dollars .	7,920 00	
Raynham, twenty-five hundred twenty dollars . .	2,520 00	
Reading, twenty thousand and seventy dollars .	20,070 00	
Rehoboth, three thousand and sixty dollars . .	3,060 00	

Revere, fifty-two thousand five hundred sixty dollars	.	$52,560 00
Richmond, nine hundred ninety dollars	. .	990 00
Rochester, eighteen hundred dollars	. .	1,800 00
Rockland, eleven thousand two hundred fifty dollars	.	11,250 00
Rockport, seventy-three hundred eighty dollars	. .	7,380 00
Rowe, nine hundred dollars	. . .	900 00
Rowley, eighteen hundred ninety dollars	. .	1,890 00
Royalston, eleven hundred seventy dollars	. .	1,170 00
Russell, fifty-six hundred seventy dollars	. .	5,670 00
Rutland, nineteen hundred eighty dollars	. .	1,980 00
Salem, seventy-five thousand eight hundred seventy dollars	. . . . .	75,870 00
Salisbury, thirty-nine hundred sixty dollars	. .	3,960 00
Sandisfield, nine hundred dollars	. . .	900 00
Sandwich, thirty-four hundred twenty dollars	.	3,420 00
Saugus, nineteen thousand six hundred twenty dollars	.	19,620 00
Savoy, three hundred sixty dollars	. . .	360 00
Scituate, fifteen thousand five hundred seventy dollars	.	15,570 00
Seekonk, sixty-three hundred ninety dollars	. .	6,390 00
Sharon, eighty-one hundred dollars	. .	8,100 00
Sheffield, two thousand and seventy dollars	. .	2,070 00
Shelburne, thirty-six hundred ninety dollars	.	3,690 00
Sherborn, twenty-four hundred thirty dollars	.	2,430 00
Shirley, twenty-eight hundred eighty dollars	.	2,880 00
Shrewsbury, eleven thousand seven hundred dollars	.	11,700 00
Shutesbury, five hundred forty dollars	. .	540 00
Somerset, fifteen thousand eight hundred forty dollars	.	15,840 00
Somerville, one hundred sixty-three thousand four hundred forty dollars	. . . . .	163,440 00
South Hadley, ten thousand five hundred thirty dollars		10,530 00
Southampton, eleven hundred seventy dollars	.	1,170 00
Southborough, forty-seven hundred seventy dollars	.	4,770 00
Southbridge, seventeen thousand one hundred dollars	.	17,100 00
Southwick, twenty-five hundred twenty dollars	.	2,520 00
Spencer, sixty-eight hundred forty dollars	.	6,840 00
Springfield, three hundred seventy-five thousand eight hundred forty dollars	. . .	375,840 00
Sterling, twenty-four hundred thirty dollars	. .	2,430 00
Stockbridge, sixty-six hundred sixty dollars	.	6,660 00
Stoneham, nineteen thousand five hundred thirty dollars		19,530 00
Stoughton, twelve thousand four hundred twenty dollars		12,420 00
Stow, nineteen hundred eighty dollars	. .	1,980 00
Sturbridge, two thousand and seventy dollars	.	2,070 00
Sudbury, thirty-one hundred fifty dollars	. .	3,150 00
Sunderland, sixteen hundred twenty dollars	. .	1,620 00
Sutton, twenty-two hundred fifty dollars	. .	2,250 00
Swampscott, thirty-one thousand six hundred eighty dollars	. . . . . .	31,680 00
Swansea, fifty-eight hundred fifty dollars	.	5,850 00
Taunton, fifty-one thousand six hundred sixty dollars	.	51,660 00
Templeton, forty-six hundred eighty dollars	.	4,680 00
Tewksbury, five thousand and forty dollars	.	5,040 00
Tisbury, seventy-two hundred dollars	. .	7,200 00
Tolland, four hundred fifty dollars	. .	450 00
Topsfield, thirty-six hundred dollars	. .	3,600 00
Townsend, thirty-three hundred thirty dollars	.	3,330 00
Truro, eighteen hundred ninety dollars	. .	1,890 00
Tyngsborough, sixteen hundred twenty dollars	.	1,620 00
Tyringham, five hundred forty dollars	. .	540 00
Upton, two thousand and seventy dollars	. .	2,070 00
Uxbridge, ten thousand and eighty dollars	. .	10,080 00
Wakefield, twenty-nine thousand three hundred forty dollars	. . . . .	29,340 00
Wales, five hundred forty dollars	. . .	540 00
Walpole, twenty-one thousand one hundred fifty dollars		21,150 00

Waltham, seventy-four thousand three hundred forty dollars	$74,340 00	State tax apportioned and assessed.
Ware, nine thousand and ninety dollars . .	9,090 00	
Wareham, fifteen thousand eight hundred forty dollars .	15,840 00	
Warren, forty-five hundred dollars	4,500 00	
Warwick, five hundred forty dollars . . .	540 00	
Washington, two hundred seventy dollars . .	270 00	
Watertown, seventy thousand two hundred ninety dollars	70,290 00	
Wayland, seven thousand and twenty dollars . .	7,020 00	
Webster, fifteen thousand three hundred ninety dollars .	15,390 00	
Wellesley, forty-three thousand seven hundred forty dollars	43,740 00	
Wellfleet, twenty-five hundred twenty dollars . .	2,520 00	
Wendell, fourteen hundred forty dollars . .	1,440 00	
Wenham, forty-five hundred dollars . .	4,500 00	
West Boylston, twenty-nine hundred seventy dollars .	2,970 00	
West Bridgewater, forty-three hundred twenty dollars .	4,320 00	
West Brookfield, eighteen hundred dollars . .	1,800 00	
West Newbury, fifteen hundred thirty dollars . .	1,530 00	
West Springfield, thirty-six thousand six hundred thirty dollars	36,630 00	
West Stockbridge, sixteen hundred twenty dollars .	1,620 00	
West Tisbury, one thousand and eighty dollars .	1,080 00	
Westborough, sixty-one hundred twenty dollars .	6,120 00	
Westfield, twenty-seven thousand six hundred thirty dollars	27,630 00	
Westford, fifty-five hundred eighty dollars . .	5,580 00	
Westhampton, five hundred forty dollars . .	540 00	
Westminster, eighteen hundred ninety dollars . .	1,890 00	
Weston, eleven thousand two hundred fifty dollars .	11,250 00	
Westport, seventy-five hundred sixty dollars .	7,560 00	
Westwood, sixty-one hundred twenty dollars . .	6,120 00	
Weymouth, fifty-eight thousand seven hundred seventy dollars	58,770 00	
Whately, fifteen hundred thirty dollars . .	1,530 00	
Whitman, eleven thousand nine hundred seventy dollars	11,970 00	
Wilbraham, four thousand and fifty dollars . .	4,050 00	
Williamsburg, eighteen hundred dollars . .	1,800 00	
Williamstown, nine thousand and ninety dollars .	9,090 00	
Wilmington, fifty-five hundred eighty dollars .	5,580 00	
Winchendon, eighty-one hundred ninety dollars .	8,190 00	
Winchester, thirty-nine thousand and sixty dollars .	39,060 00	
Windsor, six hundred thirty dollars . . .	630 00	
Winthrop, thirty-two thousand four hundred dollars .	32,400 00	
Woburn, thirty thousand eight hundred seventy dollars	30,870 00	
Worcester, four hundred thirty-two thousand four hundred fifty dollars	432,450 00	
Worthington, eight hundred ten dollars . .	810 00	
Wrentham, forty-eight hundred sixty dollars . .	4,860 00	
Yarmouth, fifty-eight hundred fifty dollars . .	5,850 00	

$9,000,000 00

SECTION 2. The state treasurer shall forthwith send his warrant, according to the provisions of section twenty of chapter fifty-nine of the General Laws to the selectmen or assessors of each city and town taxed as aforesaid, requiring them respectively to assess the sum so charged, and to add the amount of such tax to the amount of city, town and county taxes to be assessed by them respectively on each city and town.

SECTION 3. The state treasurer in his warrant shall require the selectmen or assessors to pay, or issue severally their warrant or warrants requiring the treasurers of their several cities and towns to pay to the state treasurer, on or before November twentieth in the year nineteen hundred and thirty-three, the sums set against said cities and towns in the schedule aforesaid; and the selectmen or assessors, respectively, shall return a certificate of the names of the treasurers of their several cities and towns, with the sum which each may be required to collect, to the state treasurer at some time before September first in the year nineteen hundred and thirty-three.

Notice to treasurers of delinquent cities and towns. SECTION 4. If the amount due from any city or town, as provided in this act, is not paid to the state treasurer within the time specified, then the state treasurer shall notify the treasurer of such delinquent city or town, who shall pay into the treasury of the commonwealth, in addition to the tax, such further sum as would be equal to one per cent per month during the delinquency from and after November twentieth in the year nineteen hundred and thirty-three; and if the same remains unpaid after December first in the year nineteen hundred and thirty-three, an information may be filed by the state treasurer in the supreme judicial court, or before any justice thereof, against such delinquent city or town; and upon notice to such city or town, and a summary hearing thereon, a warrant of distress may issue against such city or town to enforce the payment of said taxes under such penalties as the court, or the justice thereof before whom the hearing is had, shall order. Nothing herein contained shall be construed to prevent the state treasurer from deducting at any time, from any moneys which may be due from the commonwealth to the delinquent city or town, the whole or any part of said tax, with the interest accrued thereon, which shall remain unpaid. *Approved July 22, 1933.*

*Chap.*370 AN ACT TRANSFERRING A PORTION OF THE PROCEEDS OF THE GASOLINE TAX FROM THE HIGHWAY FUND TO THE GENERAL FUND.

Emergency preamble. *Whereas,* The deferred operation of this act would tend to defeat its purpose, therefore it is hereby declared to be an emergency law, necessary for the immediate preservation of the public convenience.

Be it enacted, etc., as follows:

Transfer of sum of money to General Fund. The state treasurer is hereby authorized and directed to transfer the sum of eight million, twenty-eight thousand, three hundred and twenty dollars from the Highway Fund to the General Fund. *Approved July 22, 1933.*

AN ACT IN ADDITION TO THE GENERAL APPROPRIATION ACT
MAKING APPROPRIATIONS TO SUPPLEMENT CERTAIN ITEMS
CONTAINED THEREIN, AND FOR CERTAIN NEW ACTIVITIES
AND PROJECTS.

Chap.371

Be it enacted, etc., as follows:

SECTION 1. To provide for supplementing certain items
in the general appropriation act, and for certain new
activities and projects, the sums set forth in section two,
for the particular purposes and subject to the conditions
stated therein, are hereby appropriated from the general
fund or ordinary revenue of the commonwealth, unless
some other source of revenue is expressed, subject to the
provisions of law regulating the disbursement of public
funds and the approval thereof.

Appropriations
to supplement
certain items
contained
in general
appropriation
act, and for
certain new
activities and
projects.

SECTION 2.

Service of the Legislative Department.

Item		
4	For the compensation for travel of representatives, a sum not exceeding three hundred and forty-five dollars, the same to be in addition to any amount heretofore appropriated for the purpose	$345 00
7	For such additional clerical assistance to, and with the approval of, the clerk of the house of representatives, as may be necessary for the proper despatch of public business, a sum not exceeding four hundred and five dollars, the same to be in addition to any amount heretofore appropriated for the purpose	405 00
11	For the compensation for travel of doorkeepers, assistant doorkeepers, general court officers, pages, and other employees of the sergeant-at-arms, authorized by law to receive the same, a sum not exceeding two hundred and fifty-two dollars, the same to be in addition to any amount heretofore appropriated for the purpose .	252 00
22	For traveling and such other expenses of the committees of the present general court as may be authorized by order of either branch of the general court, a sum not exceeding five hundred dollars, the same to be in addition to any amount heretofore appropriated for the purpose	500 00
22a	For expenses of the committee on judiciary in matters relating to the case of Judge Stone, a sum not exceeding eight thousand dollars .	8,000 00
24	For printing, binding and paper ordered by the senate and house of representatives, or by concurrent order of the two branches, with the approval of the clerks of the respective branches, a sum not exceeding eleven thousand dollars, the same to be in addition to any amount heretofore appropriated for the purpose .	11,000 00
26	For expenses in connection with the publication of the bulletin of committee hearings and of the daily list, and for the expense of printing a cumulative index to the acts and resolves of the current year, with the approval of the joint committee on rules, a sum not exceeding three thousand dollars, the same to be in addition to any amount heretofore appropriated for the purpose	$3,000 00

Item
33   For contingent expenses of the senate and house
of representatives, and necessary expenses in
and about the state house, with the approval
of the sergeant-at-arms, a sum not exceeding
twenty-five hundred dollars, the same to be in
addition to any amount heretofore appropriated
for the purpose $2,500 00

Total $26,002 00

Service of Legislative Investigations.

34d   For expenses of a study relative to changes in the
charter of the city of Boston, as authorized by
chapter twenty-three of the resolves of the current
year, a sum not exceeding five thousand dollars,
the same to be assessed in accordance with the
provisions of said resolve   .   .   . $5,000 00

34e   For expenses of an investigation by a special commission of the advisability of licensing contractors and builders, as authorized by chapter
thirty-three of the resolves of the current year,
a sum not exceeding one hundred dollars .   .   100 00

34f   For expenses of an investigation by a special commission relative to a proposed bridge over the
Mystic river, as authorized by chapter thirty-
six of the resolves of the current year, a sum not
exceeding five thousand dollars, the same to be
assessed in accordance with the provisions of
said resolve 5,000 00

34g   For expenses of an investigation and study by a
special commission of the banking structure of
the commonwealth, as authorized by chapter
thirty-five of the resolves of the current year, a
sum not exceeding twenty-five hundred dollars   2,500 00

34h   For expenses of an investigation by a special commission of the laws relative to primaries and
elections, as authorized by chapter thirty-nine
of the resolves of the current year, a sum not
exceeding one thousand dollars   .   .   1,000 00

34i   For expenses of an investigation by a special commission of certain questions relating to the
granite and foundry industries and of the problem of industrial disease compensation generally,
as authorized by chapter forty-three of the resolves of the current year, a sum not exceeding
nine thousand dollars   .   .   .   9,000 00

34j   For expenses of a commission on interstate compacts affecting labor and industries, as authorized by chapter forty-four of the resolves of the
current year, a sum not exceeding two thousand dollars 2,000 00

34k   For certain expenses in connection with the interstate legislative assembly and the commission
on conflicting taxation, as authorized by chapter
forty-five of the resolves of the current year,
a sum not exceeding one thousand dollars   .   1,000 00

34l   For expenses of an investigation by a joint special
committee of the general court of certain questions relating to the Boston Elevated Railway
Company, as authorized by chapter forty-nine
of the resolves of the current year, a sum not
exceeding twenty-five hundred dollars, the
same to be assessed in accordance with the provisions of said resolve 2,500 00

Item
34m For expenses of the special commission on stabilization of employment, as authorized by chapter fifty of the resolves of the current year, a sum not exceeding nineteen hundred dollars, the same to be in addition to any amount heretofore appropriated for the purpose $1,900 00

34o For the expenses of the committee on public welfare authorized to travel during the recess of the general court, for the purpose of visiting the various state institutions, a sum not exceeding fifteen hundred dollars 1,500 00

34p For expenses of investigation by a special commission relative to the prevalence of crime and means for the suppression thereof, a sum not exceeding ten thousand dollars . . . 10,000 00

Total $41,500 00

Service of the Land Court.

87 For engineering, clerical and other personal services, a sum not exceeding twenty-eight dollars, the same to be in addition to any amount heretofore appropriated for the purpose . . $28 00

Service of the Militia.

110 For certain allowances for national guard officers, as authorized by paragraph (d) of section one hundred and forty-five of chapter thirty-three of the General Laws, as appearing in the Tercentenary Edition thereof, a sum not exceeding two hundred dollars, the same to be in addition to any amount heretofore appropriated for the purpose $200 00

121 For compensation for accidents and injuries sustained in the performance of military duty, a sum not exceeding three thousand dollars, the same to be in addition to any amount heretofore appropriated for the purpose 3,000 00

Total $3,200 00

Service of Special Military Expenses.

129a For reimbursement of taxes for the year nineteen hundred and thirty-three on certain property in the town of Natick purchased by the commonwealth for military purposes, a sum not exceeding six thousand dollars $6,000 00

For Expenses on Account of Wars.

157a For maintenance of headquarters in the state house of the Grand Army of the Republic, Department of Massachusetts, as authorized by chapter thirteen of the resolves of the current year, a sum not exceeding twenty-five hundred dollars, the same to be in addition to any amount heretofore appropriated for the purpose . . $2,500 00

Service of the Alcoholic Beverages Control Commission.

160a For the administrative expenses of the alcoholic beverages control commission, including salaries of the commissioners and their employees, and for all contingent expenses required for the administration of chapter one hundred and twenty of the acts of the current year, including rent of offices, travel, and office and incidental expenses,

Item

a sum not exceeding twenty-five thousand dollars, the same to be in addition to any amount heretofore appropriated for the purpose, and to be payable from fees collected under said chapter one hundred and twenty . . . $25,000 00

For Exhibition of Fishing Schooner "Gertrude L. Thebaud".

160b   For expenses of an exhibition of the fishing schooner "Gertrude L. Thebaud" at the exposition in Chicago, as authorized by chapter forty-one of the resolves of the current year, a sum not exceeding fifteen thousand dollars . . $15,000 00

For the Maintenance of the Mount Greylock War Memorial.

160c   For expenses of maintenance of the Mount Greylock war memorial, as authorized by chapter three hundred and thirty-six of the acts of the current year, a sum not exceeding twenty-five hundred dollars $2,500 00

Service of the Superintendent of Buildings.

169   For other personal services incidental to the care and maintenance of the state house, a sum not exceeding two thousand dollars, the same to be in addition to any amount heretofore appropriated for the purpose $2,000 00

170   For personal services of the central mailing room, a sum not exceeding four hundred dollars, the same to be in addition to any amount heretofore appropriated for the purpose 400 00

171   For contingent, office and other expenses of the superintendent, a sum not exceeding fifty dollars, the same to be in addition to any amount heretofore appropriated for the purpose . . 50 00

Total $2,450 00

Service of the Secretary of the Commonwealth.

180   For services other than personal, traveling expenses, office supplies and equipment, for the arrangement and preservation of state records and papers, and for advertising the purpose of sections twenty-eight A to twenty-eight D of chapter six of the General Laws, as appearing in the Tercentenary Edition thereof, a sum not exceeding three hundred dollars, the same to be in addition to any. amount heretofore appropriated for the purpose $300 00

Service of the State Board of Retirement.

206   For requirements of annuity funds and pensions for employees retired from the state service under authority of law, a sum not exceeding five thousand dollars, the same to be in addition to any amount heretofore appropriated for the purpose $5,000 00

Service of the Board of Tax Appeals.

207   For personal services of the members of the board and employees, a sum not exceeding seven thousand dollars, the same to be in addition to any amount heretofore appropriated for the purpose $7,000 00

Item		
208	For services other than personal, traveling expenses, office supplies and equipment, and rent, a sum not exceeding four thousand dollars, the same to be in addition to any amount heretofore appropriated for the purpose	$4,000 00
	Total	$11,000 00

Service of the Department of Agriculture.

Division of Markets:

232	For personal services, a sum not exceeding fifteen hundred dollars, the same to be in addition to any amount heretofore appropriated for the purpose	$1,500 00
233	For other expenses, a sum not exceeding fifteen hundred dollars, the same to be in addition to any amount heretofore appropriated for the purpose	1,500 00
	Total	$3,000 00

Service of State Reclamation Board.

241	For expenses of the board, a sum not exceeding two thousand dollars, the same to be in addition to any amount heretofore appropriated for the purpose	$2,000 00
B 1933, c. 89	For carrying out mosquito control projects in accordance with the provisions of chapter one hundred and twelve of the acts of nineteen hundred and thirty-one, except that no expenditures from the funds hereby appropriated shall be made in any city or town unless a petition from the mayor of the city or the selectmen of the town for the said work is received and approved by the state reclamation board, a sum not exceeding twenty-five thousand dollars, the same to be in addition to any amount heretofore appropriated for the purpose	25,000 00
	Total	$27,000 00

Service of the Department of Conservation.

Administration:

244	For traveling expenses of the commissioner, a sum not exceeding five hundred dollars, the same to be in addition to any amount heretofore appropriated for the purpose	$500 00

Division of Forestry:

247	For personal services of office assistants, a sum not exceeding sixteen hundred and twenty dollars, the same to be in addition to any amount heretofore appropriated for the purpose. The amount herein appropriated is hereby made available for the salary of a confidential secretary, subject to approval by the governor and council and beginning June twelfth of the current year	1,620 00
248	For services other than personal, including printing the annual report, and for traveling expenses, necessary office supplies and equipment, and rent, a sum not exceeding fifteen hundred dollars, the same to be in addition to any amount heretofore appropriated for the purpose	1,500 00

ACTS, 1933. — CHAP. 371.

Item
255 In addition to the sum heretofore appropriated by
this item there may be expended, for taking
options and for searching titles of additional
land, not to exceed twenty thousand acres, a
sum not exceeding ten thousand dollars . . $10,000 00

Salisbury Beach Reservation:
261a For the maintenance of Salisbury beach reservation, a sum not exceeding forty-two hundred
dollars, the same to be assessed upon the cities
and towns of the commonwealth, exclusive of
those comprising the metropolitan parks district but including Cohasset, in the manner provided in section four of chapter one hundred
and thirty-two A of the General Laws, as appearing in the Tercentenary Edition thereof.
This appropriation is to cover such necessary
expenses as may be incurred beginning June
nineteenth of the current year . . . 4,200 00

Propagation of game birds, etc.:
270 For the maintenance of game farms and fish
hatcheries, and for the propagation of game
birds and animals and food fish, a sum not exceeding fifteen thousand four hundred twenty
dollars and sixty cents, the same to be in addition to any amount heretofore appropriated for
the purpose 15,420 60

State Supervisor of Marine Fisheries:
279 For office and other expenses of the state supervisor of marine fisheries, a sum not exceeding
five hundred dollars, the same to be in addition
to any amount heretofore appropriated for the
purpose 500 00

Enforcement of shellfish and other marine fishery laws:
282a For the extermination of starfish in the waters
of Buzzards Bay, Vineyard Sound and Nantucket Sound, as authorized by chapter one
hundred and seventy-two of the acts of the current year, a sum not exceeding fifteen thousand
dollars, the same to be in addition to any
amount heretofore appropriated for the purpose 15,000 00

Total $48,740 60

Mount Everett State Reservation.

291a For the purchase of land for the Mount Everett
state reservation, as authorized by chapter two
hundred and thirty of the acts of the current
year, a sum not exceeding twelve hundred
dollars $1,200 00

Service of the Department of Banking and Insurance.

Division of Banks:
293 For services of deputy, directors, examiners and
assistants, clerks, stenographers and experts, a
sum not exceeding fifty-four hundred dollars,
the same to be in addition to any amount heretofore appropriated for the purpose . . $5,400 00

Item
294 For services other than personal, printing the
     annual report, traveling expenses, office supplies
     and equipment, a sum not exceeding five thou-
     sand dollars, the same to be in addition to any
     amount heretofore appropriated for the purpose $5,000 00

     Supervisor of Loan Agencies:
296 For services other than personal, printing the
     annual report, office supplies and equipment, a
     sum not exceeding one hundred and seventy
     dollars, the same to be in addition to any amount
     heretofore appropriated for the purpose .   .   170 00

          Total $10,570 00

Service of the Department of Corporations and Taxation.

     Income Tax Division (the following appropria-
     tion is to be made from the receipts from the
     income tax):
310 For services other than personal, and for traveling
     expenses, office supplies and equipment, a sum
     not exceeding five thousand dollars, the same to
     be in addition to any amount heretofore appro-
     priated for the purpose. Beginning December
     first of the current year, the department may
     anticipate an increased appropriation to cover
     such necessary expenses as are required by the
     provisions of chapter three hundred and seven
     of the acts of the current year, as amended   . $5,000 00

Service of the Department of Education.

331 For aid to certain pupils in state teachers' colleges,
     under the direction of the department of edu-
     cation, a sum not exceeding two thousand dol-
     lars, the same to be in addition to any amount
     heretofore appropriated for the purpose .   . $2,000 00

     English-speaking Classes for Adults:
334 For personal services of administration, a sum not
     exceeding one hundred and fifty dollars, the
     same to be in addition to any amount heretofore
     appropriated for the purpose 150 00

     Division of Immigration and Americanization:
339 For personal services, a sum not exceeding twenty-
     six hundred and three dollars, the same to be in
     addition to any amount heretofore appro-
     priated for the purpose 2,603 00

     Teachers' Retirement Board:
352 For payment of pensions to retired teachers, a
     sum not exceeding twenty-two thousand dol-
     lars, the same to be in addition to any amount
     heretofore appropriated for the purpose .   .   22,000 00

     Massachusetts State College:
378 For maintenance and current expenses of the
     Massachusetts state college, with the approval
     of the trustees, a sum not exceeding five hundred
     dollars, the same to be in addition to any
     amount heretofore appropriated for the pur-
     pose 500 00
378a (This item omitted.)

          Total $27,253 00

Service of the Department of Civil Service and Registration.

Item

Board of Registration of Barbers:
412 For travel and other necessary expenses, a sum
     not exceeding fifteen hundred dollars, the same
     to be in addition to any amount heretofore ap-
     propriated for the purpose $1,500 00

Service of the Department of Labor and Industries.

420 For personal services for the inspectional service
     and for traveling expenses of the commissioner,
     assistant commissioners, associate commissioners
     and inspectors of labor, and for services other
     than personal, printing the annual report, rent of
     district offices, and office supplies and equip-
     ment for the inspectional service, a sum not ex-
     ceeding three thousand dollars, the same to be in
     addition to any amount heretofore appropriated
     for the purpose $3,000 00
423 For personal services for the division on necessaries
     of life, a sum not exceeding fifty-eight hundred
     dollars, the same to be in addition to any amount
     heretofore appropriated for the purpose . .   5,800 00
424 For clerical and other assistance for the board of
     conciliation and arbitration, a sum not exceed-
     ing five thousand dollars, the same to be in addi-
     tion to any amount heretofore appropriated for
     the purpose 5,000 00
426 For compensation and expenses of wage boards, a
     sum not exceeding one thousand dollars, the same
     to be in addition to any amount heretofore ap-
     propriated for the purpose 1,000 00
431 For services other than personal, traveling ex-
     penses, office supplies and equipment for the
     division on necessaries of life, a sum not ex-
     ceeding nine hundred and fifty dollars, the same
     to be in addition to any amount heretofore ap-
     propriated for the purpose 950 00
433 For services other than personal, printing, travel-
     ing expenses and office supplies and equipment
     for minimum wage service, a sum not exceeding
     one thousand dollars, the same to be in addi-
     tion to any amount heretofore appropriated for
     the purpose 1,000 00

     Total $16,750 00

Service of the Department of Mental Diseases.

     For the maintenance of and for certain improve-
     ments at the following institutions under the
     control of the Department of Mental Diseases:
446a (This item omitted.)
451 Grafton state hospital, a sum not exceeding fifteen
     hundred dollars, the same to be in addition to
     any amount heretofore appropriated for the
     purpose $1,500 00
453a For furnishings and equipment for the medical
     and surgical building at the Metropolitan.state
     hospital, a sum not exceeding twenty-five thou-
     sand dollars 25,000 00
453b For furnishings for the superintendent's house at
     the Metropolitan state hospital, a sum not ex-
     ceeding three thousand dollars . . .   3,000 00
454 Northampton state hospital, a sum not exceeding
     five thousand dollars, the same to be in addition

Item

	to any amount heretofore appropriated for the purpose	$5,000 00
455	Taunton state hospital, a sum not exceeding one thousand dollars, the same to be in addition to any amount heretofore appropriated for the purpose	1,000 00
456	Westborough state hospital, a sum not exceeding one thousand dollars, the same to be in addition to any amount heretofore appropriated for the purpose	1,000 00
458a	For emergency repairs to roofs damaged by fire and for certain fire protection at the Worcester state hospital, a sum not exceeding forty-one thousand dollars	41,000 00
458b	(This item combined with Item 458a.)	
461	Walter E. Fernald state school, a sum not exceeding two hundred and fifty dollars, the same to be in addition to any amount heretofore appropriated for the purpose	250 00
	Total	$77,750 00

Service of the Department of Correction.

464	For personal services of deputies, members of the board of parole and advisory board of pardons, agents, clerks and stenographers, a sum not exceeding fifteen hundred dollars, the same to be in addition to any amount heretofore appropriated for the purpose	$1,500 00
	For the maintenance of and for certain improvements at the following institutions under the control of the Department of Correction:	
475	State prison, a sum not exceeding forty-seven hundred and fifty dollars, the same to be in addition to any amount heretofore appropriated for the purpose	4,750 00
476	Massachusetts reformatory, a sum not exceeding thirty-nine hundred dollars, the same to be in addition to any amount heretofore appropriated for the purpose	3,900 00
478	Reformatory for women, a sum not exceeding twenty-six hundred dollars, the same to be in addition to any amount heretofore appropriated for the purpose	2,600 00
480	State prison colony, a sum not exceeding seventy-nine hundred dollars, the same to be in addition to any amount heretofore appropriated for the purpose	7,900 00
481a	For the establishment of industries at the state prison colony in the town of Norfolk, a sum not exceeding thirty-five thousand dollars, to be paid from the state prison industries fund . .	35,000 00
	Total	$55,650 00

Service of the Department of Public Welfare.

Girls' Parole:

504	For traveling expenses of said agents for girls paroled, for board, medical and other care of girls, and for services other than personal, office supplies and equipment, a sum not exceeding five hundred dollars, the same to be in addition to any amount heretofore appropriated for the purpose	$500 00

Item

For the maintenance of and for certain improvements at the institutions under the control of the trustees of the Massachusetts training schools, with the approval of said trustees, as follows:

506　Industrial school for boys, a sum not exceeding fifteen hundred dollars, the same to be in addition to any amount heretofore appropriated for the purpose $1,500 00

508　Lyman school for boys, a sum not exceeding eighteen hundred dollars, the same to be in addition to any amount heretofore appropriated for the purpose 1,800 00

Massachusetts Hospital School:

509　For the maintenance of the Massachusetts hospital school, to be expended with the approval of the trustees thereof, a sum not exceeding nine hundred dollars, the same to be in addition to any amount heretofore appropriated for the purpose 900 00

Total $4,700 00

Service of the Department of Public Health.

Water Supply and Disposal of Sewage, Engineering Division:

533　For personal services of the director, engineers, clerks and other assistants, a sum not exceeding twenty-five hundred dollars, the same to be in addition to any amount heretofore appropriated for the purpose $2,500 00

534　For other services, including traveling expenses, supplies, materials and equipment, a sum not exceeding thirteen hundred dollars, the same to be in addition to any amount heretofore appropriated for the purpose 1,300 00

For the maintenance of and for certain improvements at the sanatoria, as follows:

544　Rutland state sanatorium, to provide for the payment of a certain deficit, a sum not exceeding six hundred seventy-one dollars and twenty-five cents, the same to be in addition to any amount heretofore appropriated for the purpose . . 671 25

Pondville Cancer Hospital:

546　For maintenance of the Pondville cancer hospital, including care of radium, a sum not exceeding one thousand dollars, the same to be in addition to any amount heretofore appropriated for the purpose 1,000 00

Total $5,471 25

Service of the Department of Public Works.

Functions of the department relating to highways:

578b　For completing the public works office building and for the settlement of certain claims in connection with the construction of said building, a sum not exceeding eighty-five thousand dollars, the same to be in addition to any amount heretofore appropriated for the purposes and to be paid from the Highway Fund. Any sums awarded by the department of public works on account of said claims shall be subject to the approval of the attorney general . . . $85,000 00

Item
579 In addition to the sum heretofore appropriated by
Item 579 of chapter one hundred and seventy-
four of the acts of the current year, there is
hereby added the further sum of one million
eight hundred and thirty thousand dollars, to
be paid from the Highway Fund, which, together with the appropriation made by Item 585
of said chapter one hundred and seventy-four,
may be used by the department of public works
in supplementing and expediting the receiving
of the benefits provided by the National Industrial Recovery Act or of any other federal
money available for the construction of any
highway projects, including bridges, authorized
by special legislation, or otherwise, and of certain highway improvements in the city of
Revere as provided in said Item 585 as the department may find necessary $1,830,000 00
573a For personal services of the superintendent, elevator operators, watchmen, mechanical handy-
men and porters employed at the new public
works building, a sum not exceeding five thousand dollars, the same to be in addition to any
amount heretofore appropriated for the purpose,
and to be paid from the Highway Fund . . 5,000 00
580 For administering the law relative to advertising
signs near highways, a sum not exceeding sixty-
five hundred dollars, to be paid from the General
Fund and to be in addition to any amount heretofore appropriated for the purpose . . 6,500 00
585 (This item combined with Item 579.)
585a For expenses of certain highway improvements, as
authorized by chapter three hundred and fifty-
six of the acts of the current year, a sum not
exceeding forty thousand dollars, to be paid
from the Highway Fund and to be in addition
to any amount heretofore appropriated for the
purpose 40,000 00

Functions of the department relating to waterways and public lands:
591a For certain shore protection in the town of Nahant,
a sum not exceeding fifteen thousand dollars,
which sum is hereby made available at such
time as the town of Nahant pays into the treasury of the commonwealth an equal sum of
fifteen thousand dollars 15,000 00
591b For the improvement of the dike across the mouth
of the Herring river in the town of Wellfleet, as
authorized by chapter two hundred and seventeen of the acts of the current year, a sum not
exceeding ten thousand dollars . . . 10,000 00
591c For the extension of certain sea walls in the town
of Scituate, as authorized by chapter two hundred and eighty-six of the acts of the current
year, a sum not exceeding thirty-seven thousand
five hundred dollars 37,500 00
591d For placing riprap for the protection of the shore
at Stony Beach in the town of Hull, as authorized by chapter three hundred and thirty of the
acts of the current year, a sum not exceeding
eight thousand dollars 8,000 00

Item

Functions of the department relating to Port of Boston (the following items are to be paid from the Port of Boston receipts):

602   For dredging channels and filling flats, a sum not exceeding twenty-five thousand dollars, the same to be in addition to any amount heretofore appropriated for the purpose $25,000 00

C 1933, ch. 89   For removing abandoned hulks or wrecks lying along the waterfront of Boston harbor, a sum not exceeding twenty-five thousand dollars, the same to be in addition to any amount heretofore appropriated for the purpose 25,000 00

Total $2,087,000 00

Service of the Department of Public Utilities.

The following item is to be assessed upon the gas and electric companies:

614   For other services, printing the annual report, for rent of offices and for necessary office supplies and equipment, a sum not exceeding five hundred dollars, the same to be in addition to any amount heretofore appropriated for the purpose $500 00

Division of Smoke Inspection (the following items are to be assessed upon the cities and towns comprising the district defined by chapter six hundred and fifty-one of the acts of nineteen hundred and ten, and acts in amendment thereof or in addition thereto):

617   For personal services of the division for the period ending May thirty-first of the current year, upon which date all functions of this division shall cease, a sum not exceeding one hundred and seventy-five dollars, the same to be in addition to any amount heretofore appropriated for the purpose 175 00

618   For other services, printing the annual report, rent of offices, travel, and necessary office supplies and equipment, a sum not exceeding eleven hundred and seventy-five dollars, the same to be in addition to any amount heretofore appropriated for the purpose 1,175 00

618a   (This item combined with Item 618.)

Sale of Securities:

620   In addition to the sum heretofore appropriated by this item there may be expended for the settlement of counsel fees incurred by certain employees of the division in matters of criminal action in the superior court, said employees having been indicted, a sum not exceeding two thousand and twenty-five dollars . . . 2,025 00

Total $3,875 00

Miscellaneous.

The following item is to be paid from the Highway Fund, with the approval of the Metropolitan District Commission:

623   For resurfacing of boulevards and parkways, a sum not exceeding fifty thousand dollars, the same to be in addition to any amount heretofore appropriated for the purpose, provided that human labor be used as far as may be possible . $50,000 00

Unclassified Accounts and Claims.

Item
626   For the compensation of any veteran who may be retired by the governor under the provisions of sections fifty-six to fifty-nine, inclusive, of chapter thirty-two of the General Laws, as appearing in the Tercentenary Edition thereof, a sum not exceeding four thousand dollars, the same to be in addition to any amount heretofore appropriated for the purpose $4,000 00

627   For the compensation of certain prison officers and instructors formerly in the service of the commonwealth, now retired, a sum not exceeding sixteen hundred dollars, the same to be in addition to any amount heretofore appropriated for the purpose 1,600 00

628   For the compensation of state police officers formerly in the service of the commonwealth, and now retired, a sum not exceeding one thousand dollars, the same to be in addition to any amount heretofore appropriated for the purpose 1,000 00

For certain other aid:

631   For the payment of certain annuities and pensions of soldiers and others under the provisions of certain acts and resolves, a sum not exceeding eight hundred and fifty dollars, the same to be in addition to any amount heretofore appropriated for the purpose 850 00

Claims:

636a   For the payment of claims authorized by certain resolves of the current year, a sum not exceeding fifty-six thousand eight hundred eleven dollars and eighteen cents, of which sum one hundred sixty dollars and forty-one cents shall be charged to the Highway Fund. Said payments shall be certified by the comptroller of the commonwealth only upon the filing of satisfactory releases or other evidence that the payments are accepted in full compensation on the part of the commonwealth in respect thereto . 56,811 18

Total $64,261 18

Other Appropriations.

34n   For expenses of such special recess committee as may be appointed to investigate relative to public expenditures, a sum not exceeding four thousand dollars $4,000 00

160d   For expenses of such board as may be appointed to formulate projects or perform any act necessary to enable the commonwealth to receive certain benefits provided by the National Industrial Recovery Act, a sum not exceeding seventeen thousand seven hundred and fifty dollars 17,750 00

208b   For expenses of the emergency finance board relative to enabling cities and towns to secure the benefits provided by the National Industrial Recovery Act, a sum not exceeding seventeen thousand seven hundred and fifty dollars . 17,750 00

19   For personal services of the counsel to the house of representatives and assistants, a sum not exceeding twenty-five hundred seventy dollars and seventeen cents, the same to be in addition to any amount heretofore appropriated for the purpose 2,570 17

Item
32   For office expenses of the counsel to the house of representatives, a sum not exceeding thirty dollars, the same to be in addition to any amount heretofore appropriated for the purpose .   . $30 00

22   For traveling and such other expenses of the committees of the present general court as may be authorized by order of either branch of the general court, a sum not exceeding five thousand seventy dollars and seventy-two cents, the same to be in addition to any amount heretofore appropriated for the purpose .   .   .   5,070 72

136 For the maintenance of armories of the first class, including the purchase of certain furniture, a sum not exceeding eight thousand dollars, the same to be in addition to any amount heretofore appropriated for the purpose 8,000 00

Total $55,170 89

DEFICIENCIES.

For deficiencies in certain appropriations of previous years, in certain items, as follows:

Judicial Department.

Probate and Insolvency Courts:
For the compensation of judges of probate when acting outside their own counties for other judges of probate, the sum of one hundred and twenty-five dollars $125 00

Department of Public Works.

For the maintenance and repair of state highways, including care of snow on highways, expenses of traffic signs and lights, and payment of damages caused by defects in state highways, with the approval of the attorney general; for care and repair of road-building machinery; and for the purchase and improvement of a nursery for roadside planting, the sum of three hundred forty-seven dollars and eighty-four cents, to be paid from the Highway Fund   .   ..   347 84

Metropolitan District Commission.

For maintenance of park reservations, the sum of ten dollars 10 00

Total $482 84

Metropolitan District Commission.

638a For additional summer police officers in the metropolitan district, a sum not exceeding three thousand dollars $3,000 00

The following item is to be assessed upon the several districts in accordance with the methods fixed by law, unless otherwise provided, and to be expended under the direction and with the approval of the metropolitan district commission:

640 For services and expenses of the division of metropolitan planning, as authorized by chapter three hundred and ninety-nine of the acts of nineteen hundred and twenty-three, a sum not exceeding

Item

ten thousand dollars, the same to be in addition
to any amount heretofore appropriated for the
purpose	.	.	.	.	.	.	.	$10,000 00

General and Highway Funds	.	.	.	.$2,685,844 76
Metropolitan District Commission	.	.	.	$13,010 00

Section 3. The following amendments and transfers
are hereby authorized in appropriations previously made:

State Quartermaster.

Item 138 of chapter one hundred and seventy-four of the acts
of the present year is hereby amended by adding at the end
thereof the following: — "provided, that in consideration of
caretakers paid from federal funds being located at the
armory stations of batteries of field artillery the adjutant
general is hereby authorized to apportion between the field
artillery regiments and the stations of the transport facilities
and services of the field artillery at the commonwealth depot
and motor park at Natick the funds of the commonwealth
appropriated for field artillery mechanics, or the balance of
same unexpended on July first of the present year".

Department of Conservation.

The appropriations authorized by Items 272 and 273 of chapter
one hundred and seventy-four of the acts of the present year
are hereby made effective as of June tenth of the present year,
notwithstanding the effective date of said chapter one hundred
and seventy-four.

A transfer in the sum of fifteen hundred dollars is hereby made
from Item 281 of chapter one hundred and seventy-four of
the acts of the present year, which sum shall be apportioned
and added to certain other appropriations, made under authority of said chapter one hundred and seventy-four, as follows:
Item 278, four hundred dollars.
Item 279, four hundred dollars.
Item 280, seven hundred dollars.

Division of Animal Industry:
The division is hereby authorized to pay certain claims arising
from cattle killed during the fiscal year nineteen hundred
and thirty-one, in the sum of two hundred thirty-three dollars
and two cents from the appropriation made by Item 290
of chapter one hundred and seventy-four of the acts of the
present year.

Department of Labor and Industries.

A transfer in the sum of nine hundred dollars is hereby made
from Item 422 of chapter one hundred and seventy-four of
the acts of the present year, and said sum is hereby added to
Item 430 of said chapter one hundred and seventy-four.

Department of Mental Diseases.

Wrentham State School:
The sum of ten thousand seven hundred dollars is hereby transferred from the unexpended balance of Item 4821 of chapter
two hundred and sixty-eight of the acts of nineteen hundred
and thirty-one, and is hereby made available for the construction of a new roof for the boiler building.

Department of Correction.

In consideration of the transfer of prisoners from the Prison
Camp and Hospital in the town of Rutland to the State
Prison Colony in the town of Norfolk, the comptroller is
hereby authorized to approve the transfer of such property,
including that used in the maintenance of industries, as may

be properly utilized for the maintenance of said State Prison Colony or in the operation of any industries which may be established at said colony.

The commissioner of correction may, for the purposes of chapters three hundred and seventy-five of nineteen hundred and twenty-six and three hundred and twenty-one of nineteen hundred and twenty-seven, and for the protection of the Ware River water supply, transfer the land and buildings comprising the prison camp and hospital located in the town of Rutland to the metropolitan district water supply commission and its successors, for such sum of money as may be agreed upon by said commissioner and said commission, and thereafter said prison camp and hospital shall no longer be used for prison camp, hospital or other institutional purposes.

Department of Public Safety.

The following transfers are hereby made between appropriation items of this department authorized by chapter one hundred and seventy-four of the acts of the present year:

From Item 569, the sum of twenty-five hundred dollars, the same to be added to Item 549.

From Item 556, the sum of seven hundred dollars, the same to be added to Item 562.

From Item 550, the sum of twenty-eight hundred dollars, the same to be added to Item 551.

From Item 550, the sum of nine hundred dollars, the same to be added to Item 552.

From Item 550, the sum of three hundred and seventy-five dollars, the same to be added to Item 565.

Department of Public Works.

Item 579 of chapter one hundred and seventy-four of the acts of the present year is hereby amended by striking out the word "twenty-five" in line six.

Item 585 of chapter one hundred and seventy-four of the acts of the present year is hereby amended by striking out the word "thirty-three" in lines eleven and twelve and inserting in place thereof the word "thirty-four".

Metropolitan District Commission.

The unexpended balances of appropriations heretofore made under authority of chapter three hundred and seventy-one of the acts of nineteen hundred and twenty-nine, as amended, are hereby reappropriated and made available for the purposes of said chapter three hundred and seventy-one, as amended.

Department of Mental Diseases.

Belchertown State School:

The appropriation made by Item 469 of chapter one hundred and seventy of the acts of nineteen hundred and thirty-two is hereby amended by inserting after the word "equipment", in the first and second lines, the words: —and the alteration to the laundry building.

Wrentham State School:

The unexpended balance of the appropriation made by Item 482g of chapter two hundred and forty-five of the acts of nineteen hundred and thirty-one is hereby made available for "additional wells and changes in standpipe and water supply".

Department of Agriculture.

The department of agriculture is hereby authorized, beginning December first of the current year, to anticipate an appropriation to cover necessary expenses for the administration of chapter three hundred and thirty-eight of the acts of the current year requiring dealers in milk or cream to be licensed and bonded.

Department of Public Works.

The treasurer and receiver-general is hereby directed to assess upon the municipalities of the metropolitan parks district, including the city of Revere, in proportion to the respective taxable valuations of the property of said municipalities as defined by section fifty-nine of chapter ninety-two of the General Laws, from time to time as certified by the department of public works, such sums as represent that portion of the cost of certain work authorized by section one of chapter four hundred and forty-five of the acts of nineteen hundred and thirty-one, as amended by chapter two hundred and fifty-eight of the acts of nineteen hundred and thirty-two, which, under section six of said chapter four hundred and forty-five, as so amended, are to be paid by said municipalities, and such sums as in the aggregate amount to one third of the cost of the work authorized by section three of said chapter four hundred and forty-five, as amended.

Section 4.   This act shall take effect upon its passage

372

Chapter 372, Acts of 1933.

Referendum petition filed August 2, 1933.

See page 729.

r.
A,
ged,

1. , Carriers of Passengers by Motor Vehicle   are hereby inserted before section one of said chapter.

Section 2.   Said chapter one hundred and fifty-nine A is hereby further amended by adding after section sixteen, as so appearing, the following new sections under the headings

"PART II.",

"CARRIERS OF PROPERTY BY MOTOR VEHICLE".

G. L. (Ter. Ed.), 159A, new sections 17 to 30, added.

Section 17.   The term "common carrier" as used in this section means any person engaged in the common carriage of property for hire by motor vehicle over regular routes between points within this commonwealth. The words "regular routes" as herein used mean routes over which any person is usually or ordinarily operating any motor vehicle, even though there may be departures, periodic or irregular, from said routes.

Term "common carrier" defined.

Words "regular routes" defined.

No person or railroad, street railway or other transportation company shall operate any motor vehicle not running on rails or tracks upon any public way within the com-

Licensing of certain motor carriers of property.

be properly utilized for the maintenance of said State Prison Colony or in the operation of any industries which may be established at said colony.

The commissioner of correction may, for the purposes of chapters three hundred and seventy-five of nineteen hundred and twenty-six and three hundred and twenty-one of nineteen hundred and twenty-seven, and for the protection of the Ware River water supply, transfer the land and buildings comprising the prison camp and hospital located in the town of Rutland to the metropolitan district water supply commission and its successors, for such sum of money as may be agreed upon by said commissioner and said commission, and thereafter said prison camp and hospital shall no longer be used for prison camp, hospital or other institutional purposes.

Department of Public Safety.

The following transfers are hereby made between appropriation items of this department authorized by chapter one hundred and seventy-four of the acts of the present year:

From Item 569, the sum of twenty-five hundred dollars, the same to be added to Item 549.

From Item 556, the sum of seven hundred dollars, the same

The unexpended balances of appropriations heretofore made under authority of chapter three hundred and seventy-one of the acts of nineteen hundred and twenty-nine, as amended, are hereby reappropriated and made available for the purposes of said chapter three hundred and seventy-one, as amended.

Department of Mental Diseases.

Belchertown State School:

The appropriation made by Item 469 of chapter one hundred and seventy of the acts of nineteen hundred and thirty-two is hereby amended by inserting after the word "equipment", in the first and second lines, the words: —and the alteration to the laundry building.

Wrentham State School:

The unexpended balance of the appropriation made by Item 482g of chapter two hundred and forty-five of the acts of nineteen hundred and thirty-one is hereby made available for "additional wells and changes in standpipe and water supply".

Department of Agriculture.

The department of agriculture is hereby authorized, beginning December first of the current year, to anticipate an appropriation to cover necessary expenses for the administration of chapter three hundred and thirty-eight of the acts of the current year requiring dealers in milk or cream to be licensed and bonded.

Department of Public Works.

The treasurer and receiver-general is hereby directed to assess upon the municipalities of the metropolitan parks district, including the city of Revere, in proportion to the respective taxable valuations of the property of said municipalities as defined by section fifty-nine of chapter ninety-two of the General Laws, from time to time as certified by the department of public works, such sums as represent that portion of the cost of certain work authorized by section one of chapter four hundred and forty-five of the acts of nineteen hundred and thirty-one, as amended by chapter two hundred and fifty-eight of the acts of nineteen hundred and thirty-two, which, under section six of said chapter four hundred and forty-five, as so amended, are to be paid by said municipalities, and such sums as in the aggregate amount to one third of the cost of the work authorized by section three of said chapter four hundred and forty-five, as amended.

SECTION 4.   This act shall take effect upon its passage.
                                    Approved July 22, 1933.

AN ACT PROVIDING FOR THE SAFETY AND REGULATION OF THE USE OF THE HIGHWAYS BY MOTOR VEHICLES TRANSPORTING PROPERTY FOR HIRE IN THE COMMONWEALTH, AND FOR THE SUPERVISION AND CONTROL OF SUCH MOTOR VEHICLES AND SUCH TRANSPORTATION.

Chap.372

Be it enacted, etc., as follows:

SECTION 1.   The title of chapter one hundred and fifty-nine A of the General Laws, as appearing in the Tercentenary Edition thereof, is hereby changed to "CARRIERS BY MOTOR VEHICLE", and the headings "PART I.", "CARRIERS OF PASSENGERS BY MOTOR VEHICLE" are hereby inserted before section one of said chapter.

G. L. (Ter. Ed.), 159A, title changed, etc.

SECTION 2.   Said chapter one hundred and fifty-nine A is hereby further amended by adding after section sixteen, as so appearing, the following new sections under the headings

G. L. (Ter. Ed.), 159A, new sections 17 to 30, added.

"PART II.",

"CARRIERS OF PROPERTY BY MOTOR VEHICLE".

Section 17.   The term "common carrier" as used in this section means any person engaged in the common carriage of property for hire by motor vehicle over regular routes between points within this commonwealth. The words "regular routes" as herein used mean routes over which any person is usually or ordinarily operating any motor vehicle, even though there may be departures, periodic or irregular, from said routes.

Term "common carrier" defined.

Words "regular routes" defined.

No person or railroad, street railway or other transportation company shall operate any motor vehicle not running on rails or tracks upon any public way within the com-

Licensing of certain motor carriers of property.

Fees.
Certificate.

monwealth in the business of transporting property for hire as a common carrier without a certificate obtained as hereinafter provided from the department of public utilities, hereinafter called the department. Whether or not any motor vehicle is being operated as a common carrier within the meaning of this section shall be a question of fact to be determined by the department. The department shall have authority and jurisdiction to determine applications for such certificates. Every application for a certificate shall be made in writing in such form as the department may prescribe, shall be verified by oath or written declaration that it is made under the penalties of perjury, and shall contain such information as the department may require. Upon the filing of any such application and the payment of the fee hereinafter prescribed, the department shall within a reasonable time fix the time and place for a hearing thereon. A written notice of such hearing shall be mailed by the department at least ten days before the date fixed therefor to all common carriers, including steam and electric railway companies, serving any part of the route proposed to be served by the applicant, to the commissioner of public works and to any other person who may, in the opinion of the department, be interested in or affected by the issuance of such certificate. Any person having an interest in the subject matter shall have the right, in accordance with the rules and regulations prescribed therefor by the department, to make representations and to introduce evidence in favor of or in opposition to the issuance of such certificate in whole or in part. After such hearing the department may issue to the applicant a certificate in a form to be prescribed by the department, or may refuse to issue the same, or may issue it for the partial exercise only of the privilege sought, and may attach to the exercise of the rights granted by such certificate such limitations as to the number of motor vehicles covered by such certificate and such terms and conditions as in its judgment public interest may require; provided, that if no protest to the granting of the certificate be filed with the department prior to the time fixed for the hearing and if the department is satisfied that the certificate sought by the applicant should be granted, the certificate may be granted without a public hearing. In determining whether or not such a certificate shall be granted, the department shall take into consideration the existing transportation facilities and the effect upon them of granting such certificate, the public need for the service the applicant proposes to render, the financial responsibility of the applicant, the ability of the applicant efficiently to perform the service for which authority is requested, conditions of and effect upon the public ways involved, and the safety of the public using such ways. No such certificate shall be issued unless and until it is established to the satisfaction of the department that there exists a public need for such additional service. No such certificate shall be denied solely on the ground that there is an existing rail service. A certificate shall be granted as a matter of right if it appears to the satisfaction of the department, after a hearing, that responsible service is being rendered by the applicant over the route or routes covered by the application, and that the applicant has been operating substantial service over said route or routes from February first, nineteen hundred and thirty-three, and in such case the operation thereof may lawfully be continued pending the issue of such certificate; provided, that application therefor is made within sixty days from the effective date of this section.

Section 18. Any person required to procure a certificate under the provisions of the preceding section shall be subject to all the provisions of Part II of this chapter so far as applicable, and to such orders, rules and regulations as shall be adopted and promulgated by the department under the authority of said Part II, after public hearing, and such person and the service rendered or furnished shall be included under the general supervision and regulation of the department and shall be subject to its jurisdiction and control in the same manner and to the same extent as service performed by other persons engaged in the transportation of property as common carriers for hire. *Application of certain sections.*

Section 19. Every person required to procure a certificate under section seventeen shall file with the department a schedule or schedules showing the rates or charges for service rendered or furnished or to be rendered or furnished within the commonwealth. Such rates shall be just and reasonable. No such person shall charge, demand, exact, receive or collect for any service rendered an amount greater or less than the rate specified in such schedule or schedules, nor shall any such carrier refund or remit in any manner by any device any portion of the rate so specified, nor make or give any unreasonable preference or advantage to any person, nor subject any person to any unreasonable prejudice or discrimination; provided, that if in any instance the department is convinced that the absence of regulation of rates applicable to competing interstate traffic or traffic within adjacent states will operate to the detriment of the interests of motor carriers within the commonwealth or of other interests within the commonwealth, the department shall so modify this requirement as to assure no undue prejudice. The department may, on complaint by any interested party, after notice and hearing, allow or disallow, alter or prescribe such rates. *Schedules of rates, etc., to be filed.*

Section 20. The term "contract carrier" as hereinafter used is intended to include every person engaged in transporting property for hire by motor vehicle, other than a common carrier as defined in section seventeen, except that the term shall not be construed to include any person who does not engage regularly in the transportation business but on occasional trips transports the property of others *Term "contract carrier" defined.*

for hire. Whether or not any person is engaging regularly in the transportation business within the meaning of this paragraph shall be a question of fact to be determined by the department.

It is hereby declared that the business of contract carriers is affected with the public interest and that the safety and welfare of the public upon the public ways within the commonwealth, the preservation and maintenance of such ways and the proper regulation of common carriers using such ways require the regulation of contract carriers to the extent hereinafter provided.

Permits.

Section 21. No contract carrier shall operate any motor vehicle for the transportation of property for hire on any public way within the commonwealth unless there is in force with respect to such carrier a permit, issued by the department, authorizing such operation; provided, that any contract carrier who has been regularly engaged in such business from February first, nineteen hundred and thirty-three, may continue such operation pending the issue of such permit, if the application therefor is made within sixty days from the effective date of this section.

Applications for permits.

Section 22. Applications for such permits shall be made to the department in writing, verified by oath or written declaration that it is made under the penalties of perjury, and shall contain such information as the department may require.

Permits, issuance of.

Section 23. Such a permit shall be issued to any qualified applicant if it shall appear that the applicant is fit, willing and able properly to perform the service of contract carrier, and to conform to the provisions of Part II of this chapter and the lawful requirements, rules and regulations of the department made thereunder and that the proposed operation is not inconsistent with the public interest. The department shall specify in the permit the operations covered thereby and shall attach to it at the time of issuance, and from time to time thereafter, such terms and conditions not inconsistent with the character of the holder as a contract carrier as the public interest may require.

Department of public utilities to make rules, etc.

Section 24. The department of its own motion may, and on petition of any interested party after a public hearing shall, prescribe rules and regulations covering the operation of contract carriers in competition with common carriers over the public ways within the commonwealth, and prescribe minimum rates and charges of contract carriers in competition with common carriers to be collected by such contract carriers, which rates and charges in general shall not be less than those charged by such common carriers for substantially the same or similar service. Nothing in this section shall apply to the transportation of property by motor vehicle for any common carrier when the rate charged the public for transportation of such property is already published and filed with the department.

Section 25. In order that there may be proper supervision and control of the use of the public ways within the commonwealth, every common carrier and every contract carrier regularly engaged in transporting property between points within and points without the commonwealth or across or through the commonwealth is hereby required to obtain a permit for such operation from the department, and all persons making two or more such trips in any thirty-day period shall be deemed to be so regularly engaged. Whether or not any person is so regularly engaged shall be a question of fact to be determined by the department. Application for such permits shall be made in the manner and form to be prescribed by the department in its regulations, and such permits shall issue as a matter of right upon compliance with such regulations and payment of fees herein required, unless the department shall find that the condition of the public ways to be used is such that the operation proposed would be unsafe, or the safety of other users thereof would be endangered thereby.

Regulation of carriers transporting property without the commonwealth.

Section 26. Each application for such a certificate or such a permit shall be accompanied by a fee of two dollars. Distinguishing plates shall be prescribed and furnished by the department for, and shall be displayed at all times on, each motor vehicle operated under any of the provisions of Part II of this chapter. Transfer of such plates from one vehicle to another is prohibited except upon authority and consent of the department. The charge for each set of plates shall be two dollars. Any such certificate or any such permit issued as aforesaid may be assigned and transferred, with the approval and consent of the department, by the holder, or by the holder's personal representative to whom the rights and privileges under said certificate or permit shall pass at the death of said holder. The department is authorized to prescribe the conditions precedent to such transfer and make any necessary rules and regulations pertaining thereto. No certificate or permit granted under said Part II shall be effective after the first day of January following its issue. Renewals shall be issued upon application made in accordance with the requirements of the department upon the payment of the fees prescribed in the case of original applications; provided, that the department shall have power to refuse to renew any existing permit or certificate or to cancel any such permit or certificate only when there is wilful or continued violations of the provisions of said Part II or the regulations of the department made under authority thereof and after a hearing, at least ten days' notice of which shall be given to the holder of the permit or certificate; and, provided, further, that no order of the department refusing to renew any existing permit or certificate shall be effective until ten days after such order has been issued and a copy

Fees.

thereof mailed to the holder of such permit or certificate.

Penalty.

Section 27. It shall be unlawful for any driver to operate, or for the owner of the vehicle to require or permit any driver to operate, any motor vehicle for the transportation of property for hire on the public ways within the commonwealth, when the driver has been continuously on duty for more than twelve hours, and after a driver has been continuously on duty for twelve hours it shall be unlawful for him to operate, or for the owner of the vehicle to permit him to operate, any such motor vehicle on said public ways until he shall have had at least eight consecutive hours off duty.

It shall be unlawful for any driver to operate, or for the owner of the vehicle to require or permit any driver to operate, any motor vehicle for the transportation of property for hire on said public ways when the driver has been on duty more than sixteen hours in the aggregate in any twenty-four hour period, and when a driver has been on duty sixteen hours in any twenty-four hour period, it shall be unlawful for him to operate, or for the owner of the vehicle to require or permit him to operate, a motor vehicle on the public ways within the commonwealth until he shall have had at least ten consecutive hours off duty. Periods of release from duty herein required shall be given at such place and under such circumstances that rest and relaxation from the strain of the duties of the employment may be obtained. No period off duty shall be deemed to break the continuity of service unless it be for at least three consecutive hours at a place where there is opportunity for a rest. In case of an unforeseen emergency the driver may complete his run or tour of duty if such run or tour of duty, except for the delay caused by such emergency, would reasonably have been completed without a violation of this section.

The department shall have authority to make such rules and regulations as it deems necessary or advisable to insure proper enforcement of the provisions of this section.

Exemptions.

Section 28. There shall be exempted from the provisions of Part II of this chapter, (1) motor vehicles operated exclusively within the limits of a single city or town, or within twenty miles of the limits thereof; (2) motor vehicles while engaged exclusively in work for any branch of the government of the United States or for any department of the commonwealth, or for any county, city, town or district; (3) motor vehicles while engaged exclusively in the delivery of the United States mail. Nothing contained in said Part II shall apply to owners or operators of motor vehicles carrying their own property solely.

General penalty.

Section 29. The provisions of section fifteen shall apply to violations of any provision of said Part II.

Validity of certain sections not affected if other sections

Section 30. If any part, subdivision or section of said Part II shall be declared unconstitutional, the validity of its remaining provisions shall not be affected thereby.

It is hereby declared to be the legislative intent that said Part II would have been enacted had such void or ineffective part, subdivision or section not been included therein.

SECTION 3. Section one A of chapter ninety of the General Laws, as appearing in the Tercentenary Edition thereof, is hereby amended by striking out, in the fifth line, the word "or" and inserting in place thereof the words: — other than one subject thereto solely under Part II of said chapter one hundred and fifty-nine A, or one owned, — so as to read as follows: — *Section 1A.* No motor vehicle or trailer, except one owned by a person, firm or corporation, for the operation of which security is required to be furnished under section six of chapter one hundred and fifty-nine A, or one owned by any other corporation subject to the supervision and control of the department of public utilities other than one subject thereto solely under Part II of said chapter one hundred and fifty-nine A, or one owned by a street railway company under public control, or by the commonwealth or any political subdivision thereof, shall be registered under sections two to five, inclusive, unless the application therefor is accompanied by a certificate as defined in section thirty-four A. Ambulances, fire engines and apparatus, police patrol wagons and other vehicles used by the police department of any city or town or park board solely for the official business of such department or board (whether or not owned as aforesaid) shall not be subject to the requirements of this section.   *Approved July 22, 1933.*

For Chapters 373 to 377, inclusive,
passed at the Extra Session,
see pages 735 to 781.

RESOLVES.

RESOLVE VALIDATING THE ACTS OF ANTONIO C. VIEIRA OF NEW BEDFORD AS A NOTARY PUBLIC. *Chap.* 1

Resolved, That the acts of Antonio C. Vieira of New Bedford as a notary public, between January fifteenth, nineteen hundred and twenty-seven, and October twenty-fifth, nineteen hundred and thirty-two, both dates inclusive, are hereby confirmed and made valid to the same extent as if during said time he had been qualified to discharge the duties of said office.

Approved February 9, 1933.

RESOLVE VALIDATING ACTION OF THE LIEUTENANT GOVERNOR, ACTING GOVERNOR, IN PROCLAIMING CERTAIN BANK HOLIDAYS, SO-CALLED, LEGALIZING ALL ACTS AND OMISSIONS OF BANKING INSTITUTIONS IN OBSERVING THE SAME, AND AUTHORIZING THE GOVERNOR TO PROCLAIM ADDITIONAL BANK HOLIDAYS. *Chap.* 2

Resolved, That the action of the lieutenant governor of the commonwealth, acting governor, on March fourth of the current year, in proclaiming and setting apart March fourth and March sixth of said year as legal holidays on which all banking institutions in the commonwealth should be closed, is hereby validated and confirmed, and all acts and omissions of all such institutions in reliance upon such action are hereby declared to be lawful, to the same extent as though authority for such action had been previously granted by the general court; and be it further

Resolved, That the governor may from time to time proclaim such additional bank holidays as in his judgment the emergency may require. *Approved March 6, 1933.*

RESOLVE TO VALIDATE THE ACTS OF JOSEPH A. BIANCO OF MEDFORD AS A JUSTICE OF THE PEACE. *Chap.* 3

Resolved, That the acts of Joseph A. Bianco of Medford as a justice of the peace, between September twenty-seventh, nineteen hundred and twenty-three and October twentieth, nineteen hundred and thirty-two, both dates inclusive, are hereby confirmed and made valid to the same extent as if during said time he had been qualified to discharge the duties of said office. *Approved March 17, 1933.*

Chap. 4 RESOLVE VALIDATING THE ACTS OF GEORGE T. STORRS OF
WARE AS A NOTARY PUBLIC.

Resolved, That the acts of George T. Storrs of Ware as
a notary public, between November twenty-fifth, nineteen
hundred and thirty-one and February twenty-eighth,
nineteen hundred and thirty-three, both dates inclusive,
are hereby confirmed and made valid to the same extent
as if during said time he had been qualified to discharge
the duties of said office.   *Approved April 3, 1933.*

Chap. 5 RESOLVE DIRECTING THE ART COMMISSION TO CONSIDER THE
MATTER OF A SUITABLE MEMORIAL TO THE LATE CALVIN
COOLIDGE.

Resolved, That the art commission for the commonwealth is hereby directed to consider the matter of a
suitable and fitting memorial to commemorate the notable
career and public service of the late Calvin Coolidge.
Said commission shall recommend the type and location
of the memorial and prepare estimates of the approximate
cost thereof. It shall report to the general court its
findings and recommendations, together with drafts of
legislation necessary to carry its recommendations into
effect by filing the same with the clerk of the house of
representatives not later than the first Wednesday of
December of the current year.   *Approved April 5, 1933.*

Chap. 6   RESOLVE IN FAVOR OF THE TOWN OF IPSWICH.

Resolved, That the department of education is hereby
authorized to approve the payment to the town of Ipswich,
out of that part of the proceeds of the tax on incomes
available for educational purposes under chapter seventy
of the General Laws, the sum of eleven thousand, six
hundred and five dollars, being the amount, in addition
to the sums already received, which the town would have
received in nineteen hundred and thirty-one and nineteen
hundred and thirty-two under authority of said chapter
seventy, except for errors in the claims for reimbursement filed with said department.
                              Approved April 6, 1933.

Chap. 7 RESOLVE PROVIDING FOR AN INVESTIGATION RELATIVE TO
STATE ASSISTANCE TO VETERANS IN ACQUIRING FARMS AND
HOMES.

Resolved, That an unpaid special commission, to consist
of the attorney general, the commissioner of agriculture,
the commissioner of labor and industries, the commissioner
of corporations and taxation, with power in each of said
officials to designate and appoint to said commission in his

stead a member of his department, and the commissioner of state aid and pensions, is hereby established for the purpose of investigating the subject matter of current house bill numbered five hundred and fifty-two, providing state assistance to veterans in acquiring farms and homes. The commission may hold public hearings and shall be entitled to receive the co-operation and assistance of all public officials, boards and commissions. The commission shall report the results of its investigations to the general court by filing its recommendations, together with drafts of legislation to carry such recommendations into effect, with the clerk of the senate on or before the first Wednesday of December in the current year.

Approved April 26, 1933.

RESOLVE TO VALIDATE THE ACTS OF KATHARINE L. PEARL OF BOXFORD AS A NOTARY PUBLIC. *Chap.* 8

Resolved, That the acts of Katharine L. Pearl of Boxford as a notary public, between October twenty-first, nineteen hundred and thirty-two, and January sixth, nineteen hundred and thirty-three, both dates inclusive, are hereby confirmed and made valid to the same extent as if during said time she had been qualified to discharge the duties of said office. *Approved April 26, 1933.*

RESOLVE PROVIDING FOR A STUDY BY THE ART COMMISSION RELATIVE TO THE ERECTION BY THE COMMONWEALTH OF A MEMORIAL TO THE WOMEN OF MASSACHUSETTS WHO SERVED IN THE WORLD WAR. *Chap.* 9

Resolved, That the art commission of the commonwealth is hereby directed to consider and study the matter of the erection within the state house of a memorial tablet to commemorate the services and sacrifices of the women of Massachusetts who served in the world war. Said commission shall report to the general court the results of its study and its recommendations, together with drafts of such legislation as may be necessary to carry the same into effect, by filing the same with the clerk of the house of representatives on or before the first Wednesday of December in the current year. *Approved April 26, 1933.*

RESOLVE PROVIDING FOR AN INVESTIGATION AND STUDY BY A SPECIAL COMMISSION RELATIVE TO THE USE OF CERTAIN LANDS AND WATERS IN THE COMMONWEALTH FOR RECREATIONAL PURPOSES. *Chap.* 10

Resolved, That a special commission, to consist of the commissioner of conservation, the commissioner of public health and the chairman of the metropolitan district commission, shall make an investigation and study of the lands

and waters which are under the control of the commonwealth or any political subdivision thereof, including those
within the watersheds of the sources of water supply of the
metropolitan water district, with a view to determining
whether or not any of such lands or waters may be used for
the purpose of providing the citizens of the commonwealth
with further facilities for boating, bathing, fishing and other
recreational activities. Any such officer, if he so elects,
may designate an officer or employee in his department who
shall serve in his place on said commission. Said commission shall hold hearings and may call upon other state
officers and officers of the several counties and municipalities for such information as may be needed in the course
of its work. Said commission shall report to the general
court the results of its investigation and study and its recommendations, if any, together with drafts of legislation to
carry the same into effect, by filing the same with the clerk
of the house of representatives on or before the first Wednesday of December of the current year.

Approved May 5, 1933.

Chap. 11 RESOLVE PROVIDING FOR AN INVESTIGATION RELATIVE TO
THE TAXATION OF CERTAIN PROPERTY OWNED BY THE CITY
OF SPRINGFIELD IN THE TOWN OF RUSSELL AND USED BOTH
FOR WATER SUPPLY AND FOR THE GENERATION OF ELEC-
TRICITY IN CONNECTION WITH THE COBBLE MOUNTAIN
DEVELOPMENT, SO CALLED.

Resolved, That the commissioner of corporations and
taxation, the chairman of the commission supervising the
department of public utilities, and the chief engineer in the
department of public works, are hereby constituted a
special commission, without additional compensation, and
are authorized and directed to investigate and report relative to the taxation by the town of Russell of the dam and
other structures of the Cobble mountain development, so
called, owned by the city of Springfield in said town, and
particularly to inquire into the subject matter of current
senate document seventy-three and current house document five hundred and thirty-nine, relative to such taxation.
The special commission shall inquire into all phases of the
use of said dam and other structures both for water supply
and for power purposes, including their size and extent in
respect to the development of a water supply, and shall
collect all available information concerning the question of
such taxation. The special commission shall hold hearings
at which all parties interested may appear, may require by
summons the attendance and testimony of witnesses and
the production of books and papers, and shall report to the
general court the results of its investigations and its recommendations, if any, together with drafts of legislation necessary to carry its recommendations into effect, by filing

the same with the clerk of the senate on or before the first
Wednesday in December in the current year.

Approved May 5, 1933.

RESOLVE PROVIDING FOR AN INVESTIGATION BY THE METRO- *Chap.* 12
POLITAN DISTRICT COMMISSION OF THE ADVISABILITY OF
ESTABLISHING AN ADEQUATE AUXILIARY WATER SUPPLY
FOR COMMUNITIES SUPPLIED WITH WATER FROM THE SPOT
POND RESERVOIR.

Resolved, That the metropolitan district commission is
hereby authorized and directed to investigate the advisability and probable cost of establishing and maintaining an
adequate auxiliary water supply for supplying water, in
cases of emergency, to communities now supplied with
water from the Spot Pond reservoir.   Said commission shall
report to the general court the results of its investigation
and its recommendations, if any, together with drafts of
legislation necessary to carry said recommendations into effect by filing the same with the clerk of the house
of representatives on or before the first Wednesday of
December in the current year.   *Approved May 5, 1933.*

RESOLVE IN AID OF THE GRAND ARMY OF THE REPUBLIC, *Chap.* 13
DEPARTMENT OF MASSACHUSETTS.

Resolved, That, subject to appropriation, there be allowed and paid from the treasury of the commonwealth a
sum not exceeding twenty-five hundred dollars to aid in
defraying the expenses of maintaining in the state house the
headquarters of the Grand Army of the Republic, Department of Massachusetts.   Payments for such aid shall be
made upon the presentation to the comptroller of vouchers
therefor, approved by the assistant adjutant general and
the commander of said department.

Approved May 5, 1933.

RESOLVE PROVIDING FOR AN INVESTIGATION BY THE DEPART- *Chap.* 14
MENT OF PUBLIC WORKS AS TO THE COST AND DETAILED
ROUTES OF TWO PROPOSED STATE HIGHWAYS IN OR NEAR
THE CITY OF FITCHBURG, AND OF CERTAIN PROPOSED
EXTENSIONS OF ONE OF SAID HIGHWAYS.

Resolved, That the department of public works is hereby
authorized and directed to investigate the cost, and the
most satisfactory route, of a state highway commencing at
a point in the existing state highway in the town of Harvard,
thence through the town of Lancaster and the city of
Leominster to a point in the existing state highway in the
town of Westminster, together with such extensions of said
proposed state highway to a point in the town of Box-
borough and to a point in the city of Fitchburg as the said
department may deem necessary, in order to provide a

suitable through route running in a general easterly and westerly direction south of said city of Fitchburg, and also of the proposed state highway referred to in section one of current senate document numbered one hundred and nine. Said department shall report to the general court the results of its investigations, and its recommendations, if any, together with drafts of legislation necessary to carry such recommendations into effect, by filing the same with the clerk of the senate on or before the first Wednesday of December in the current year, and shall file at the same time a copy thereof with the budget commissioner.

Approved May 9, 1933.

Chap. 15 RESOLVE PROVIDING FOR AN INVESTIGATION RELATIVE TO SPOT POND BROOK IN THE TOWN OF STONEHAM AND CITIES OF MELROSE AND MALDEN.

Resolved, That the department of public health and the metropolitan district commission, acting as a joint board, are hereby authorized and directed to investigate the matter of improving Spot Pond brook, so called, in the town of Stoneham, city of Melrose and city of Malden, from its source at Doleful pond, in the Middlesex Fells reservation in the said town of Stoneham to the Malden river in the said city of Malden. In connection with said investigation, said board shall consult with the appropriate officials of said cities and town and shall consider the reports relative to said brook submitted to the general court under the provisions of chapter one hundred of the resolves of nineteen hundred and thirteen and chapter fifty of the resolves of nineteen hundred and fourteen, and all plans and data compiled by the officials who submitted said reports. Said board shall report to the general court its findings and its recommendations, if any, together with drafts of legislation necessary to carry its recommendations into effect and estimates of the probable cost of any improvements recommended by it, by filing the same with the clerk of the house of representatives on or before the first Wednesday of December in the current year.

Approved May 9, 1933.

Chap. 16 RESOLVE PROVIDING FOR AN INVESTIGATION BY THE DEPARTMENT OF PUBLIC WORKS RELATIVE TO THE CONSTRUCTION OF A HIGHWAY IN THE CITY OF QUINCY AND TOWN OF MILTON.

Resolved, That the department of public works is hereby directed to consider the advisability, feasibility and probable cost of improving highway conditions by the construction of a highway along the following route: Beginning at the westerly approach of the proposed new Fore River bridge at Washington street in the city of Quincy; thence over public and private lands and public and private ways, in a general westerly direction, to the easterly end of Water street in said city; thence northwesterly along said Water street over the proposed new bridge over the tracks of the New York, New Haven and Hartford railroad at Quincy Adams; thence along said Water street to Copeland street; thence along said Copeland street to Miller street; thence along said Miller street and over private lands to the Willard street crossing of the Granite branch of said railroad; thence crossing said railroad at said point and paralleling said railroad on the southwesterly side in a general northwesterly direction across property of the Granite Railway Company; thence continuing along the valley to the foot of steep grade on Grove street; thence in a general westerly direction to a point at or about the Shawmut spring, so called; and thence continuing in same direction to a point at Quarry lane and Pleasant street, opposite Reedsdale road, in the town of Milton.

Said department shall report the results of its investigation, and its recommendations, if any, together with drafts of legislation necessary for carrying such recommendations into effect, by filing the same with the clerk of the house of representatives on or before the first Wednesday of December in the current year.   *Approved May 9, 1933.*

RESOLVE PROVIDING FOR AN INVESTIGATION BY THE DEPARTMENT OF PUBLIC UTILITIES RELATIVE TO THE ERECTION AND MAINTENANCE OF PROTECTIVE DEVICES AT RAILROAD CROSSINGS, DRAWBRIDGES AND OTHER LOCATIONS.   *Chap.* 17

Resolved, That the department of public utilities is hereby authorized and directed to investigate the subject matter of current house document number three hundred and eighty-six relative to the erection and maintenance of protective devices at railroad crossings, drawbridges and other locations. Said department shall report to the general court the results of its investigations, and its recommendations, if any, together with drafts of legislation necessary to carry the same into effect by filing the same with the clerk of the house of representatives on or before the first Wednesday of December in the current year.
Approved May 9, 1933.

RESOLVE IN FAVOR OF THE TOWN OF LUDLOW.   *Chap.* 18

Resolved, That the department of education is hereby authorized to approve the payment to the town of Ludlow, out of that part of the proceeds of the tax on incomes available for educational purposes under chapter seventy of the General Laws, of the sum of eighteen thousand five hundred and fifty-seven dollars, being the aggregate amount, in addition to the sums already received, which the town would have received in nineteen hundred and thirty-one and nineteen hundred and thirty-two under authority of said chapter seventy, except for errors in the claims for reimbursement filed with said department.

Approved May 9, 1933.

Chap. 19 RESOLVE PROVIDING FOR THE DISTRIBUTION OF THE TERCEN-TENARY EDITION OF THE GENERAL LAWS TO CERTAIN MEMBERS OF THE PRESENT GENERAL COURT.

Resolved, That the state secretary, in distributing the Tercentenary Edition of the General Laws to members of the general court in accordance with chapter fifty-three of the resolves of nineteen hundred and thirty-two, shall also distribute, upon written request, one copy thereof, and of the index thereto, to each member of the present general court who was not a member of the general court of the years nineteen hundred and thirty-one and nineteen hundred and thirty-two.   *Approved May 9, 1933.*

Chap. 20 RESOLVE PROVIDING FOR AN INVESTIGATION BY THE METRO-POLITAN DISTRICT COMMISSION RELATIVE TO THE ADVISA-BILITY OF CONSTRUCTING A BEACH ON THE MALDEN RIVER IN THE CITY OF EVERETT AND OF CONSTRUCTING AND MAINTAINING A BATHHOUSE THEREAT.

Resolved, That the metropolitan district commission is hereby authorized and directed to investigate the advisa-bility of constructing a beach on the Malden river in the city of Everett near the Revere beach parkway and of constructing and maintaining a public bathhouse at said beach. Said commission shall report to the general court the results of its investigation, and its recommendations, if any, together with drafts of legislation necessary for carrying the same into effect, by filing the same with the clerk of the house of representatives on or before the first Wednesday of December in the current year.

Approved May 12, 1933.

Chap. 21 RESOLVE PROVIDING FOR AN INVESTIGATION BY THE DEPART-MENT OF PUBLIC WORKS RELATIVE TO TRAFFIC CONDI-TIONS ON OR NEAR THE NEWBURYPORT TURNPIKE, SO CALLED, AND AS TO THE ABOLITION OF THE RAILROAD GRADE CROSSING AT STATE STREET IN THE TOWN OF NEWBURY.

Resolved, That the department of public works is hereby directed to study and investigate as to (1) traffic conditions on the state highway known as the Newburyport turnpike, with a view to determining the most effective and feasible means and methods of relieving the existing inconvenient and dangerous conditions thereon, and in that connection to comply, so far as feasible, with the provisions of senate document numbered two hundred and thirty-five, both as to methods of procedure to be followed and as to results to be accomplished; (2) traffic routes in and to the north of the city of Newburyport, substantially as set forth in current senate document numbered two hundred and thirty-four; (3) the advisability of extending to the Merrimack river a certain state highway in the town of Salisbury, substantially as set forth in current house document numbered six hundred and one; and (4) the advisability and feasibility of the abolition of the crossing at grade, in the town of Newbury, of that portion of the so-called Newburyport turnpike in said town known as State street, and the tracks of the Boston and Maine Railroad, in substantial compliance with the provisions of current senate document numbered two hundred and sixty-eight. The department is also directed to prepare estimates of the expense of such projects to accomplish, in whole or in part, the purposes of the several senate and house documents hereinbefore referred to as are deemed by it feasible, and to report to the general court by filing its recommendations and estimates, and drafts of legislation necessary to effect the same, with the clerk of the senate on or before the first Wednesday of December in the current year, and at the same time to file a copy thereof with the budget commissioner.

Approved May 16, 1933.

RESOLVE IN FAVOR OF THE TOWN OF SHIRLEY.   *Chap.* 22

Resolved, That the department of education is hereby authorized to approve the payment to the town of Shirley, out of that part of the proceeds of the tax on incomes available for educational purposes under chapter seventy of the General Laws, of the sum of five hundred and fifty dollars, being the amount, in addition to the sums already received, which the town would have received in nineteen hundred and thirty-two under authority of said chapter seventy, except for errors in the claims for reimbursement filed with said department.   *Approved May 16, 1933.*

RESOLVE PROVIDING FOR A STUDY RELATIVE TO CHANGES IN THE CHARTER OF THE CITY OF BOSTON AND IN THE LAWS RELATING TO THE ADMINISTRATION OF THE AFFAIRS OF SAID CITY.   *Chap.* 23

Resolved, That a special unpaid commission to consist of two members of the senate to be designated by the president thereof, five members of the house of representatives to be designated by the speaker thereof, and two persons to be appointed by the governor, with the advice and consent of the council, is hereby established for the purpose of inquiring into the desirability of making changes in the charter of the city of Boston and in the general and special laws and municipal ordinances and regulations relating to the administration of the affairs of said city. The commission shall organize by the choice of a chairman and a

clerk forthwith upon the designation and appointment of
its members. The commission shall be provided with
quarters in the state house or elsewhere and may expend
in the aggregate for expert, legal and clerical assistance and
other expenses the sum of five thousand dollars and such
additional sums not exceeding such amount as the governor
and council may approve and as may hereafter be appropriated. Any and all money expended under the provisions
of this resolve shall be repaid to the commonwealth by said
city by the inclusion of the amount thereof in the state tax
to be assessed on said city for the year nineteen hundred and
thirty-four. The said commission shall report to the general court the results of its study and its recommendations,
together with drafts of legislation necessary to carry its
recommendations into effect, by filing the same with the
clerk of the house of representatives not later than the first
Wednesday of December in the current year.

Approved May 16, 1933.

Chap. 24 RESOLVE PROVIDING FOR AN INVESTIGATION BY THE DEPART-
MENT OF PUBLIC WORKS RELATIVE TO CERTAIN PROPOSED
TRAFFIC ROUTES.

Resolved, That the department of public works is hereby
authorized and directed to consider and investigate the
location, construction cost and desirability of the following
proposed through routes in the metropolitan district:

(a) The completion of the ten mile circumferential
highway from its present northern terminus at Worcester
street in the town of Wellesley near the Charles river
northerly and easterly through the metropolitan district
to connect with the main state highways leading to the
north;

(b) A route beginning at or near Watertown square and
extending along California street and along the banks of
the Charles river and westerly to a connection with Weston
street and Main street in the western part of Waltham.

Said department shall report to the general court its
findings and recommendations, together with drafts of
legislation necessary to carry such recommendations into
effect, by filing the same with the clerk of the house of
representatives not later than the first Wednesday of
December in the current year, and shall at the same time
file a copy thereof with the budget commissioner.

Approved May 18, 1933.

Chap. 25 RESOLVE PROVIDING FOR THE WIDENING OF BOYLSTON
STREET IN THE TOWN OF CLINTON FOR THE PURPOSE OF
ESTABLISHING A PARKING AREA NEAR THE WACHUSETT
DAM.

Resolved, That department of public works is hereby
authorized and directed to widen, to a width of not less than
forty feet, Boylston street in the town of Clinton for a dis-

tance of about eight hundred feet extending from the foot of the ramp northerly of the Wachusett dam to the foot of Wilson street, to adjust the grade of said Boylston street to the present setting of the grounds at the entrance to said dam and to construct suitable curbing and sidewalks along that portion of said Boylston street widened as aforesaid. For said purposes said department may expend not exceeding ten thousand dollars from item number five hundred and seventy-six of the general appropriation act of the current year.   *Approved May 18, 1933.*

RESOLVE IN FAVOR OF PERSONS WHO SUSTAINED PERSONAL INJURIES OR PROPERTY DAMAGE RESULTING FROM THE BOMBING OF THE HOME OF THE LATE HONORABLE WEBSTER THAYER IN THE CITY OF WORCESTER.

Chap. 26

Resolved, That, for the purpose of promoting the public good, and after an appropriation has been made, there be allowed and paid out of the treasury of the commonwealth to each of the persons determined by the attorney general to be entitled to compensation for personal injuries or property damage resulting from the bombing of the home of the late Honorable Webster Thayer in the city of Worcester, such sum as the attorney general shall determine to be just and reasonable and as the governor and council shall approve, but not exceeding, in the aggregate, fifteen thousand dollars.

Approved June 6, 1933.

RESOLVE IN FAVOR OF THE WIDOW OF THE LATE HONORABLE WEBSTER THAYER.

Chap. 27

Whereas, The death of the Honorable Webster Thayer, an associate justice of the superior court of the commonwealth, was attributable to his enfeebled health, caused by mental and physical distress directly due to persistent and constant threats of murderous violence by avowed or secret enemies of our institutions of government; and

Whereas, The assaults threatened against him were, in truth, in defiance of the commonwealth, and of its authority; and

Whereas, A state ought, in honor, and by its own inherent power, to defend, at any cost, its judges in the fearless performance of their lawful duties in life, and should likewise protect their estates and their dependents against loss sustained through extraordinary and unprecedented perils courageously met by them; and

Whereas, In consummation of the atrocious purpose of the threatened assaults upon the life of Judge Thayer, on the night of September twenty-seventh of the year last past, his home was destroyed by a bomb and he and his wife sustained serious injury and had forever taken away from them the security and happiness of their own dwelling; and

Whereas, Although his lamented death precludes the granting of an honorarium, or recompense to him, the commonwealth should nevertheless, in its maintenance of the inviolable authority of the law thereof, make recognition of, and in some measure provide reimbursement for, losses sustained and for sacrifices never before demanded of, or imposed upon, any other one of the honored judiciary of Massachusetts; now, therefore, be it

Resolved, That, after an appropriation has been made, there be allowed and paid out of the treasury of the commonwealth to the widow of the late Honorable Webster Thayer the sum of twenty-five thousand dollars.

Approved June 6, 1933.

Chap. 28 RESOLVE PROVIDING FOR AN UNPAID COMMISSION TO CONSIDER THE NEED OF EXTENDING RELIEF BECAUSE OF LOSS OF TAXES IN CERTAIN COMMUNITIES DUE TO THE CONSTRUCTION OF CERTAIN ADDITIONS TO THE METROPOLITAN WATER SYSTEM.

Resolved, That a special unpaid commission, to consist of one member of the senate to be designated by the president thereof, three members of the house of representatives to be designated by the speaker thereof, and three additional members to be appointed by the governor, with the advice and consent of the council, is hereby established for the purpose of considering what action should be taken by way of legislation or otherwise in respect to the loss of property and taxes by certain towns due to the construction of certain additions to the metropolitan water system, being more particularly described as the towns of Barre, Belchertown, Dana, Hardwick, Hubbardston, New Salem, Oakham, Petersham, Pelham, Phillipston, Princeton, Rutland, Ware and Westminster. The commission shall be provided with quarters in the state house, may hold hearings, and may expend for expert, clerical and other services a sum not exceeding five hundred dollars, to be paid from item six hundred and forty-five of chapter one hundred and seventy-four of the acts of the current year. The commission shall report to the general court the result of its study and investigations and its recommendations, with drafts of legislation necessary to give effect to the same, by filing its report with the clerk of the house of representatives not later than the first Wednesday in December in the current year.   *Approved June 16, 1933.*

Chap. 29 RESOLVE IN FAVOR OF JOHN F. TIERNAN OF BROOKLINE.

Resolved, That, for the purpose of discharging the moral obligation of the commonwealth and after an appropriation has been made therefor, there be paid out of the treasury of the commonwealth to John F. Tiernan of Brookline the sum of four hundred dollars, being the amount paid for hospital and medical expenses on account of an injury received during the course of his employment by the commonwealth at Commonwealth pier on November twenty-eight, nineteen hundred and thirty-one.·

(This resolve, returned by the governor to the House of Representatives, the branch in which it originated, with his objections thereto, was passed by the House of Representatives, June 19, 1933, and, in concurrence, by the Senate, June 20, 1933, the objections of the governor notwithstanding, in the manner prescribed by the constitution; and thereby has "the force of a law".)

RESOLVE IN FAVOR OF THOMAS W. KINGDON OF HOLDEN. *Chap.* 30

Resolved, That there shall be paid out of the treasury of the commonwealth to Thomas W. Kingdon of Holden three hundred and seven dollars to reimburse him for expenses of medical and hospital care incurred by him on account of injuries received while in the employ of the metropolitan district water supply commission. Said amount shall be paid from the funds provided for metropolitan water supply purposes by chapter three hundred and seventy-five of the acts of nineteen hundred and twenty-six and chapters one hundred and eleven and three hundred and twenty-one of the acts of nineteen hundred and twenty-seven, and any additions thereto or amendments thereof.

(This resolve, returned by the governor to the House of Representatives, the branch in which it originated, with his objections thereto, was passed by the House of Representatives, June 19, 1933, and, in concurrence, by the Senate, June 20, 1933, the objections of the governor notwithstanding, in the manner prescribed by the constitution; and thereby has "the force of a law".)

RESOLVE PROVIDING FOR AN INVESTIGATION BY THE DEPART- *Chap.* 31
MENT OF PUBLIC WORKS RELATIVE TO THE CONSTRUCTION
OF A NEW STATE HIGHWAY IN THE TOWNS OF HOPKINTON,
UPTON, NORTHBRIDGE, SUTTON, DOUGLAS AND WEBSTER.

Resolved, That the department of public works is hereby authorized and directed to investigate the subject matter of current house documents numbered three hundred and sixty-four and six hundred, relative to the construction of a new state highway in the towns of Hopkinton, Upton, Northbridge, Sutton, Douglas and Webster. Said department shall report to the general court the results of its investigation and its recommendations, if any, together with drafts of legislation necessary for carrying such recommendations into effect, by filing the same with the clerk of the house of representatives on or before the first Wednesday of December in the current year.

Approved June 23, 1933.

Chap. 32   Resolve in favor of the town of South Hadley.

Resolved, That the department of education is hereby authorized to approve the payment to the town of South Hadley, out of that part of the proceeds of the tax on incomes available for educational purposes under chapter seventy of the General Laws, of the sum of sixty-seven hundred and eighty-four dollars, being the amount, in addition to the sums already received, which the town would have received in nineteen hundred and thirty-two under authority of said chapter seventy, except for errors in the claims for reimbursement filed with said department.

Approved June 23, 1933.

Chap. 33   Resolve providing for an investigation by a special commission of the advisability of licensing contractors and builders and relative to certain matters relating to contracts for and the employment of persons on public works.

Resolved, That a special commission, to consist of the attorney general, the commissioner of labor and industries, the commissioner of public safety and the commissioner of public works and three persons to be appointed by the governor, of whom one shall be a contractor, one an architect and one a representative of labor, is hereby established to investigate the subject matter of current senate documents numbered two hundred and sixty-four and two hundred and ninety-four and current house documents numbered one hundred and ninety-nine and nine hundred and thirty-three, relative to the licensing of contractors and builders and relative to certain matters relating to contracts for and the employment of persons on public works. Any such member other than an appointive member, if he so elects, may designate an officer or employee in his department to serve in his place on said commission. Said commission shall be provided with quarters in the state house, shall hold hearings and may expend for clerical and other expenses, from such amount, not exceeding one hundred dollars, as may be appropriated by the general court, such sums as the governor and council may approve. The commission shall report to the general court the results of its investigation, and its recommendations, if any, together with drafts of legislation necessary to carry said recommendations into effect, by filing the same with the clerk of the house of representatives on or before the first Wednesday of December in the current year.   *Approved June 26, 1933.*

RESOLVE IN FAVOR OF WILLIAM E. DAVIS OF SPRINGFIELD. *Chap.* 34

Resolved, That, for the purpose of discharging the moral obligation of the commonwealth in the premises and after an appropriation has been made therefor, there be paid from the treasury thereof, in monthly instalments beginning as of April first in the current year, the sum of nine hundred dollars per year for a period of five years to William E. Davis of Springfield, who became disabled by reason of injuries received at Camp Devens, July sixteenth, nineteen hundred and twenty-two, in attempting to save state property while serving in the military forces of the commonwealth.   *Approved June 27, 1933.*

RESOLVE PROVIDING FOR AN INVESTIGATION AND STUDY BY *Chap.* 35
A SPECIAL COMMISSION OF THE BANKING STRUCTURE OF
THE COMMONWEALTH.

Resolved, That a special unpaid commission is hereby established, to consist of one senator to be designated by the president of the senate, three representatives to be designated by the speaker of the house of representatives, and three members to be appointed by the governor, with the advice and consent of the council, for the purpose of investigating and studying the entire structure of the banking institutions subject to the supervision of the commissioner of banks, with a view to making such changes therein as will strengthen said institutions and promote their usefulness to the public. The commission shall devote especial attention to the devising of means and methods of insuring greater security to the funds entrusted to said institutions, of preventing the possibility of the use of said funds for other than legitimate banking purposes, and of restricting the activities of said institutions to the field of legitimate banking. The subject matter of the following legislative documents of the current year shall also be considered by the commission, to wit: — Senate documents numbered thirty-four, fifty-three, seventy-one, ninety-seven, ninety-eight, one hundred, one hundred and twenty-two, two hundred and seventy-four, four hundred and nineteen and four hundred and twenty; House documents numbered four hundred and ninety-one, five hundred and seventy-three, eight hundred and seventeen, nine hundred and fifty-two, nine hundred and fifty-three, ten hundred and sixty-nine and ten hundred and seventy-one; and so much of public document numbered twelve as relates to (1) segregation of thrift accounts in trust companies and other commercial banks, (2) prohibiting officers of banking institutions from participating in any business consisting in whole or in part of the sale of securities, (3) prohibiting banking institutions from engaging in the sale of securities, (4) prohibiting banking institutions from engaging in any business other than the receiving of deposits of money and the making of loans on proper collateral and credits, and (5) requiring brokers and salesmen to furnish bonds as a condition precedent to licensing them to sell securities.

The commission shall elect its chairman, shall be provided with quarters in the state house, shall hold hearings, may require by summons the attendance and testimony of witnesses and the production of books and papers, and may expend for clerical, expert and other expenses such sums, not exceeding in the aggregate twenty-five hundred dollars, as may be appropriated. The commission shall report to the general court the results of its investigation and its recommendations, together with drafts of legislation necessary to carry its recommendations into effect, by filing the same with the clerk of the senate not later than the first Wednesday of December in the current year.

Approved June 28, 1933.

Chap. 36 RESOLVE PROVIDING FOR AN INVESTIGATION BY A SPECIAL COMMISSION RELATIVE TO A PROPOSED BRIDGE OVER THE MYSTIC RIVER BETWEEN THE CITIES OF BOSTON AND CHELSEA.

Resolved, That an unpaid special commission, to consist of the commissioner and associate commissioners of public works and one official of each of the cities of Boston, Chelsea and Revere to be designated by the mayor thereof, is hereby established to investigate the matter of constructing a new bridge, with or without draws, over the Mystic river from a point at or near City square in the Charlestown district of the city of Boston to a point at or near Chelsea square in the city of Chelsea. Said commission shall also consider whether it is feasible so to reconstruct the present bridge over said river between said Charlestown district and said city of Chelsea as to make it adequate for traffic requirements. Said commission shall report its conclusions to the general court by filing the same with the clerk of the house of representatives on or before December first in the current year. It shall also inquire as to whether the newly constructed or reconstructed bridge, in view of the fact that it will serve as part of a main route of travel, should be taken over and maintained by the commonwealth. It shall include in its report sketches and plans of any bridge recommended by it hereunder and if it finds that reconstruction of the present bridge is feasible, shall also submit plans for such reconstruction, and shall include in its report an estimate of the cost of any work recommended by it and also an equitable allotment of said cost among the different units of government concerned. To carry out the purposes of this resolve, said commission may expend such sum, not exceeding five thousand dollars, as may hereafter be appropriated therefor by the general court. The commonwealth shall be reimbursed for all expenditures hereunder as follows: — seventy-five per cent by the city of Boston, fifteen per cent by the city of Chelsea and ten per cent by the city of Revere. The amounts to be paid as aforesaid by said cities shall be assessed and collected by the state treasurer in the same manner and at the same time as state taxes.

Approved June 28, 1933.

RESOLVE IN FAVOR OF THE HEIRS OF CATHERINE PARK, ALSO KNOWN AS KATIE BARR. *Chap.* 37

Resolved, That, subject to appropriation, there be allowed and paid from the treasury of the commonwealth, under the direction of the attorney general, to the heirs at law or next of kin of Catherine Park, also known as Katie Barr, who died in the city of Cambridge in the year nineteen hundred and eleven, or to their lawful representatives, such sum as may be found by the attorney general to have been paid into said treasury as the balance of the assets belonging to the estate of said Catherine Park, also known as Katie Barr, under the provisions of section ten of chapter one hundred and ninety-four of the General Laws, or corresponding provisions of earlier laws, notwithstanding the expiration of the time limited by said section for the recovery of such sum.   *Approved June 28, 1933.*

RESOLVE IN FAVOR OF HAROLD A. CADY OF DALTON.   *Chap.* 38

Resolved, That, for the purpose of discharging the moral obligation of the commonwealth in the premises and after an appropriation has been made therefor, there be paid out of the treasury of the commonwealth to Harold A. Cady of Dalton a sum not exceeding one hundred sixty dollars and forty-one cents to reimburse him for money expended in settlement of a claim against him on account of damage to the automobile of another sustained in a collision in March of nineteen hundred and thirty-two in Dalton between said automobile and an automobile owned by the commonwealth and operated by said Cady in the performance of his official duties as a highway maintenance foreman in the department of public works.

(This resolve, returned by the governor to the House of Representatives, the branch in which it originated, with his objections thereto, was passed by the House of Representatives, June 29, 1933, and, in concurrence, by the Senate, July 5, 1933, the objections of the governor notwithstanding, in the manner prescribed by the constitution; and thereby has "the force of a law".)

Chap. 39 RESOLVE PROVIDING FOR AN INVESTIGATION BY A SPECIAL COMMISSION OF THE LAWS RELATING TO PRIMARIES AND ELECTIONS WITH A VIEW TO THEIR REVISION AND IMPROVEMENT.

Resolved, That a special unpaid commission to consist of one member of the senate to be designated by the president thereof, three members of the house of representatives to be designated by the speaker thereof, and three persons to be appointed by the governor, with the advice and consent of the council, is hereby established for the purpose of inquiring into the laws relating to primaries and elections, with a view to revising and perfecting the same. The commission shall be provided with quarters in the state house, may hold hearings therein and elsewhere, shall be entitled to receive the assistance of the state secretary and all other public officers, and may expend for the employment of clerical and other assistance and to meet such expenditures as the performance of its duties may require, such sums, not exceeding one thousand dollars, as may be appropriated. Said commission shall report to the general court the results of its inquiry and its recommendations, together with drafts of legislation necessary to carry its recommendations into effect, by filing the same with the clerk of the senate not later than the first Wednesday in December in the current year.

Approved July 7, 1933.

Chap. 40 RESOLVE PROVIDING FOR AN INVESTIGATION BY THE JUDICIAL COUNCIL AS TO CERTAIN MATTERS RELATING TO FEES AND ALLOWANCES OF SHERIFFS AND THEIR DEPUTIES, CONSTABLES AND OTHER PUBLIC OFFICERS, AND AS TO CERTAIN WITNESS FEES.

Resolved, That the judicial council be requested to investigate the subject matter of current senate document numbered five, being the special report of the director of accounts under chapter twenty-six of the resolves of nineteen hundred and thirty-two, relative to fees and allowances in connection with service of writs, executions, warrants, summonses, subpoenas, notices, precepts and like processes, to the attendance of public officers and others as witnesses, and to proper allowances to public officers for expenses in transporting prisoners and in other official travel; and also the subject matter of current house document numbered two hundred and seventy-four, relative to establishing the fees of witnesses before certain tribunals, and of current house document numbered five hundred and thirty-one, relative to further regulation of witness fees of certain police officers; and to include its conclusions and recommendations in relation thereto, with

drafts of such legislation as may be necessary to give effect
to the same, in its annual report for the current year.

Approved July 7, 1933.

RESOLVE PROVIDING FOR EXHIBITION OF THE FISHING *Chap.* 41
SCHOONER GERTRUDE L. THEBAUD AT THE EXPOSITION
IN CHICAGO IN THE CURRENT YEAR, FOR THE PURPOSE OF
PROMOTING THE INTERESTS OF THE FISHING INDUSTRY
OF MASSACHUSETTS, AND MAKING AN APPROPRIATION
THEREFOR.

Resolved, That an unpaid special commission, to consist of
three persons to be appointed by the governor, is hereby
established to contract and arrange for the exhibition,
under its supervision and control, of the fishing schooner
Gertrude L. Thebaud at the world's fair, entitled, "A
Century of Progress", international exposition, to be held
at Chicago, Illinois, in the current year, as symbolizing the
Massachusetts fishing industry, a basic and historic industry in the development of the commonwealth, and in
furtherance of the interests of such industry, at a cost to the
commonwealth not exceeding fifteen thousand dollars.
Said commission in making any such contract or arrangement shall provide proper safeguards for the interests of
the commonwealth with respect to the advertising or distribution of Massachusetts products in connection with
such exhibit. For the purposes hereof, there is hereby
appropriated from the general fund or revenue of the
commonwealth, subject to the provisions of law regulating
the disbursement of public funds and the approval thereof,
the sum of fifteen thousand dollars.

Approved July 7, 1933.

RESOLVE IN FAVOR OF WILLIAM J. GROVES OF GLOUCESTER. *Chap.* 42

Resolved, That, for the purpose of promoting the public
good, and after an appropriation has been made therefor,
there be allowed and paid out of the treasury of the commonwealth to William J. Groves of Gloucester, the sum of
fifteen hundred dollars, in quarterly instalments of one
hundred and twenty-five dollars each, on account of injuries sustained by him while in the performance of military
duty with company M, fifteenth infantry, Massachusetts
state guard.

*(The foregoing was laid before the governor on the fifth day
of July, 1933, and after five days it had "the force of a law",
as prescribed by the constitution, as it was not returned by
him with his objections thereto within that time.)*

Chap. 43 RESOLVE PROVIDING FOR AN INVESTIGATION BY A SPECIAL COMMISSION OF CERTAIN QUESTIONS RELATIVE TO THE GRANITE AND FOUNDRY INDUSTRIES AND OF THE PROBLEM OF INDUSTRIAL DISEASE COMPENSATION GENERALLY.

Resolved, That a special commission, to consist of the commissioner of labor and industries, the commissioner of public health, the chairman of the department of industrial accidents, the commissioner of insurance and the attorney general, is hereby established to investigate and study the problem of diseases caused by dust in the granite and foundry industries, of protection from said diseases, and of compensation insurance in said industries and the problem of industrial disease compensation generally. Any member of said commission may, if he so elects, designate an officer or employee in his department who shall serve in his place on said commission. Said commission shall be provided with quarters in the state house, may employ such clerical and other assistance as it deems necessary, and may expend for the purposes of this resolve such sums, not exceeding, in the aggregate, nine thousand dollars, as may hereafter be appropriated therefor. Said commission shall report to the general court the results of its investigation and study, and its recommendations, if any, together with drafts of legislation necessary to carry said recommendations into effect, by filing the same with the clerk of the house of representatives on or before December first in the current year. *Approved July 12, 1933.*

Chap. 44 RESOLVE CREATING A COMMISSION ON INTERSTATE COMPACTS AFFECTING LABOR AND INDUSTRIES.

WHEREAS, The industrial depression has brought about an acute competitive situation in the great manufacturing states of the United States, whereby the wages and conditions of employment of the workers are subject to grave impairment; and

WHEREAS, The wise and humane laws of the commonwealth of Massachusetts enacted for the purpose of bettering the conditions of employment are jeopardized by this competitive situation; and

WHEREAS, It is in the interest of the workers in the commonwealth that uniform standards should be adopted and should conform to the more enlightened statutes in effect among the several states; and

WHEREAS, The constitution of the United States in Article I, section ten, permits of securing such uniform standards by interstate compacts entered into by the several states with the consent of the congress of the United States; now, therefore, be it

RESOLVED

(1) that there be hereby established an unpaid commission, to be known as the Commission on Interstate Compacts affecting Labor and Industry, to consist of seven members, of whom one shall be a member of the senate, to be designated by the president thereof, three shall be members of the house of representatives, to be designated by the speaker thereof, and three shall be appointed by the governor. The commission is hereby authorized, on the part of Massachusetts, to meet with like commissions appointed with like authority on the part of the states of New York, Rhode Island, Connecticut, Vermont, New Hampshire, Maine, Pennsylvania and New Jersey, or any of them, for the purpose of negotiating or agreeing upon a joint report. Said report shall recommend to the legislatures of the participating states a policy to be pursued by such states with reference to the establishment of uniform wages, hours of labor and conditions and standards of employment by the enactment of such legislation by such states as will constitute an interstate compact. The commission is hereby requested to report to the general court on December first of each year of its existence and also as soon as it determines on a policy.

(2) that the members of the commission appointed as aforesaid shall serve without compensation, but shall be paid their necessary expenses in the performance of their duties. They shall select one of their number as chairman and may employ a secretary and such other assistants as are needed in the performance of their duties. For the purposes of this resolve, said commission may expend such sums, not exceeding, in the aggregate, two thousand dollars, as may hereafter be appropriated therefor.

(3) that the state secretary shall forthwith communicate the text of this resolve to the like official of each of the states mentioned herein with the respectful request that such states in their discretion establish commissions with like powers to treat with the commission appointed hereunder.   *Approved July 12, 1933.*

RESOLVE RELATIVE TO CERTAIN EXPENSES IN CONNECTION WITH THE INTERSTATE LEGISLATIVE ASSEMBLY AND THE COMMISSION ON CONFLICTING TAXATION. *Chap.* 45

Resolved, That, subject to appropriation, there may be paid out of the state treasury a sum not exceeding one thousand dollars for defraying the expenses of delegates representing the general court in attendance upon sessions of the Interstate Legislative Assembly held during the current year and for promoting the purposes of the Commission on Conflicting Taxation authorized and created by the Interstate Legislative Assembly held at Washington, District of Columbia, on February third and fourth

of the current year.   Delegates to future meetings shall not
exceed three in number and shall represent both political
parties.   *Approved July 12, 1933.*

Chap. 46 RESOLVE PROVIDING FOR AN INVESTIGATION LOOKING TO
THE IMPROVEMENT AND EXPANSION OF BUSINESS AND
RESIDENTIAL CONDITIONS IN THOSE SECTIONS OF BOSTON
KNOWN AS ROXBURY, JAMAICA PLAIN AND FOREST HILLS,
BY THE REMOVAL OF THE ELEVATED RAILWAY STRUCTURE
IN SAID SECTIONS.

Resolved, That the metropolitan planning division of
the metropolitan district commission and the transit department of the city of Boston, acting jointly, are hereby
authorized and directed to investigate as to the desirability,
feasibility and probable cost of the removal of the existing
elevated railway structure of the Boston Elevated Railway
Company in the city of Boston, between the southerly
entrance of the Washington Street tunnel and Forest Hills
station; and as to the desirability, route and probable cost
of a tunnel, subway or such other means of rapid transit
as would be an adequate substitute for said elevated structure.   Said metropolitan planning division and said transit
department, acting jointly, shall report to the general court
the results of their investigation and their recommendations, if any, together with drafts of legislation necessary
to carry said recommendations into effect, by filing the
same with the clerk of the house of representatives not
later than the fifteenth day of December, nineteen hundred
and thirty-four.   *Approved July 12, 1933.*

Chap. 47 RESOLVE AUTHORIZING THE ALCOHOLIC BEVERAGES CON-
TROL COMMISSION TO ORDER THE REFUNDING OF CERTAIN
LICENSE AND PERMIT FEES.

Resolved, That the alcoholic beverages control commission may order refunded to any person who applied, not
later than the first day of July in the current year, for a
license or permit from said commission under chapter one
hundred and twenty of the acts of said year, as amended,
the fee paid by him for such a license or permit, in case he
has withdrawn or shall withdraw his application prior to
the issue of any license or permit in pursuance thereof or
surrenders a license or permit so issued if the said commission is satisfied that no right, power or privilege has been
exercised thereunder.   Any sums ordered refunded as
aforesaid may be paid from monies on hand received by
the said commission under said chapter one hundred and
twenty, or, without appropriation, from the state treasury,
from monies paid thereinto under section seventeen of said
chapter, upon order of the said commission certified by the
comptroller.   *Approved July 12, 1933.*

Resolve in favor of John A. Carroll of Waltham. *Chap.* 48

Resolved, That, for the purpose of discharging the moral obligation of the commonwealth in the premises, and after an appropriation has been made therefor, there shall be allowed and paid out of the treasury of the commonwealth to John A. Carroll of Waltham, the sum of sixteen hundred and forty-three dollars and twenty-four cents to reimburse him for money paid for expenses of defense of, and in satisfaction of an execution issued in, an action brought against him, as an individual, in the superior court for the county of Suffolk, to recover damages for a certain act done in the performance of his duties as a state police officer.

(*This resolve, returned by the governor to the House of Representatives, the branch in which it originated, with his objections thereto, was passed by the House of Representatives July 11, 1933, and, in concurrence, by the Senate, July 12, 1933, the objections of the governor notwithstanding, in the manner prescribed by the constitution; and thereby has "the force of a law".*)

Resolve providing for an investigation by a joint special committee of the general court of certain questions relating to the Boston Elevated Railway Company. *Chap.* 49

Resolved, That a joint special committee, consisting of two members of the senate to be designated by the president thereof and five members of the house of representatives to be designated by the speaker thereof, is hereby authorized to sit during the recess of the general court to investigate questions relating to the ownership, management and operation of the Boston Elevated Railway Company as follows: —

(*a*) Whether the existing method of assessing deficits in the operation of said company is impractical and unfair to the cities and towns assessed, and if so, what other method or methods of making such assessments would be practical and on a basis that would be fair and just with respect to said cities and towns;

(*b*) What additional provisions, if any, or what changes, if any, in existing provisions relating to the refunding of maturing obligations of said company should be made;

(*c*) What financial obligations might devolve upon the commonwealth or the Boston metropolitan district in the event of the acquisition of the properties of said company either by eminent domain or under the option granted by section seventeen of chapter three hundred and thirty-three of the acts of nineteen hundred and thirty-one;

(*d*) What form of continuous and unhampered management of the properties of said company without legislative interference, in the event of their acquisition as aforesaid, would be constitutional;

(e) Whether the sale of the power plants and appurtenant properties of said company is desirable;

(f) Whether the sale of power by said company to the Eastern Massachusetts Street Railway Company or other public utilities is desirable.

Said committee may expend for expenses and clerical and other assistance such sums, not exceeding, in the aggregate, twenty-five hundred dollars, as may hereafter be appropriated, the same to be assessed upon the several cities and towns included in the Boston metropolitan district in the manner provided in section twelve of chapter three hundred and eighty-three of the acts of nineteen hundred and twenty-nine for the assessment of the expenses of said district. Said committee shall report to the general court its findings and its recommendations, if any, together with drafts of legislation necessary for carrying said recommendations into effect, by filing the same with the clerk of the house of representatives on or before the first Wednesday of December in the current year.

Approved July 13, 1933.

Chap. 50 RESOLVE REVIVING AND CONTINUING THE SPECIAL COMMISSION ON STABILIZATION OF EMPLOYMENT.

Resolved, That the unpaid special commission, established by chapter sixty-four of the resolves of nineteen hundred and thirty-one and known as the special commission on the stabilization of employment, is hereby revived and continued for the period ending March thirty-first, nineteen hundred and thirty-four, for the purposes specified in said chapter sixty-four, and particularly to investigate further the subject of unemployment benefits, insurance and reserves. In the course of its investigation the commission shall consider the subject matter of current house documents numbered eight hundred and twenty-one and nine hundred and five and of that portion of current house document numbered twelve hundred contained in pages one hundred and ninety-two to two hundred and thirty-six, inclusive, thereof. The commission shall make a supplementary report to the general court of the results of its investigation hereunder and its recommendations, if any, together with drafts of legislation necessary to carry said recommendations into effect, and file said report with the clerk of the house of representatives on or before the first Wednesday in December of the current year. For the purposes of this resolve, said commission may expend such sum, not exceeding nineteen hundred dollars, as may be hereafter appropriated therefor, in addition to the unexpended balance of the amount appropriated by item one hundred and seventy-nine b of chapter four hundred and sixty of the acts of nineteen hundred and thirty-one.

Approved July 17, 1933.

RESOLVE IN FAVOR OF THE HEIRS OF THOMAS BURKE. *Chap.* 51

Resolved, That, subject to appropriation, there be allowed and paid from the treasury of the commonwealth, under the direction of the attorney general, to the heirs at law or next of kin of Thomas Burke, who died in the city of Fall River in the year nineteen hundred and twenty-two, or to their lawful representatives, such sum as may be found by the attorney general to have been paid into said treasury as the balance of the assets belonging to the estate of said Thomas Burke, under the provisions of section ten of chapter one hundred and ninety-four of the General Laws, notwithstanding the expiration of the time limited by said section for the recovery of such sum.

Approved July 17, 1933.

RESOLVE ACCEPTING THE PROVISIONS OF AN ACT OF CONGRESS ESTABLISHING A NATIONAL EMPLOYMENT SYSTEM AND PROVIDING FOR COOPERATION BETWEEN THE NATIONAL GOVERNMENT AND THE STATES IN THE PROMOTION OF SUCH A SYSTEM. *Chap.* 52

Resolved, That the commonwealth hereby accepts the provisions of the act of Congress, approved June sixth, nineteen hundred and thirty-three, entitled "An Act to provide for the establishment of a national employment system and for cooperation with the states in the promotion of such system, and for other purposes," conformably to the provisions of section four thereof, and designates the department of labor and industries as the state agency to cooperate with the United States Employment Service under said act, and vests said department with all powers necessary thereto. The state treasurer is hereby authorized to receive, on behalf of the commonwealth, all funds granted to the commonwealth under authority of said act.

Approved July 22, 1933.

RESOLVE IN FAVOR OF THE HEIRS OR NEXT OF KIN OF THE LATE JOSEPH A. LOGAN. *Chap.* 53

Resolved, That, for the purpose of promoting the public good and in consideration of his long and meritorious service in the general court of this commonwealth, there be allowed and paid out of the treasury of the commonwealth to the heirs or next of kin of the late Joseph A. Logan, who died while a member of the present house of representatives, the balance of the salary to which he would have been entitled had he lived and served until the end of the current session. *Approved July 22, 1933.*

Chap. 54 RESOLVE PROVIDING FOR AN INVESTIGATION BY A SPECIAL
UNPAID COMMISSION RELATIVE TO THE PREVALENCE OF
CRIME AND MEANS FOR THE SUPPRESSION THEREOF.

Resolved, That an unpaid special commission, consisting
of three persons to be appointed by the governor, is hereby
established to make a thorough investigation into the
practice and procedure followed throughout the commonwealth in the apprehension, conviction and punishment of
gangs, gangsters, racketeers and other persistent violators
of the law, persons engaged in the operation of pools and
lotteries, slot machines, clubs dispensing intoxicating
liquors, so-called speakeasies, and other illegal practices,
and persons who have been frequently and repeatedly
brought before the courts of the commonwealth and not
punished, in order to determine the causes for failure to
punish; to place the responsibility for the existing evils in
these connections; to devise measures for improving the
law in regard to such matters; to improve the respect for
law and to eradicate the existing evils in the present system
of criminal practice and procedure; and to consider other
related matters contained in the message of the governor
dated July thirteenth of the current year, printed as current
house document numbered fifteen hundred and seventy-
eight. Said commission may hold hearings, shall be provided with quarters in the state house or elsewhere, may
require by summons the attendance and testimony of
witnesses, may administer oaths, may require the production of books and papers pertaining to any matter
under investigation, and may expend for clerical and other
assistance and expenses such sums, subject to appropriation, not exceeding, in the aggregate ten thousand dollars,
as may be approved by the governor and council. The
commission shall report to the general court its findings
and its recommendations, together with drafts of legislation necessary to carry such recommendations into effect,
by filing the same with the clerk of the senate on or before
the first Wednesday in December of the current year, and
at the same time shall file a copy thereof with the governor.
Approved July 22, 1933.

Chap. 55 RESOLVE PROVIDING FOR AN INVESTIGATION AND STUDY BY
A SPECIAL COMMISSION OF THE GENERAL SUBJECT OF
PUBLIC EXPENDITURES.

Resolved, That a special commission, consisting of four
members of the senate to be designated by the president thereof, twelve members of the house of representatives to be designated by the speaker thereof and five
members to be appointed by the governor, is hereby
authorized to sit during the recess of the general court
to investigate and study the general subject of public

expenditures, including, in addition to expenditures by the commonwealth, such expenditures by counties, cities, towns and districts as are required or encouraged by the commonwealth, to consider ways and means for curtailing, limiting and reducing such expenditures, to consider the advisability of repealing or modifying any existing legislation which necessitates or encourages the making of public expenditures unwisely or beyond the reasonable means of the public in view of existing conditions, and generally to investigate and study the entire problem of public expenditures with a view to alleviating the burden thereof. It shall particularly investigate the subject matter of current senate documents twenty-nine, four hundred and eight and four hundred and thirty-six, and current house documents seven hundred and two and fourteen hundred and seventy-five. Said commission shall also investigate and report relative to the advisability of enacting legislation requiring justices of district courts to give their entire time to the discharge of their judicial duties and forbidding such justices to engage in the general practice of law. Said commission may hold hearings and may call upon the commissioner of corporations and taxation and other departments, commissions, officers, committees, and agents of the commonwealth and of the several counties, municipalities and districts for such information as may be needed in the course of its investigation and study. Said commission shall be provided with quarters in the state house or elsewhere, and may expend for expert, clerical and other services and expenses such sums, not exceeding, in the aggregate, four thousand dollars, as may hereafter be appropriated. Said commission shall report to the general court the results of its investigation and study, and its recommendations, together with drafts of legislation necessary to carry its recommendations into effect, by filing the same with the clerk of the senate not later than December thirty-first in the current year.

Approved July 22, 1933.

THE COMMONWEALTH OF MASSACHUSETTS

OFFICE OF THE SECRETARY,
BOSTON, August 15, 1933.

Petition filed
requesting
referendum on
chapter 203,
Acts of 1933.

Pursuant to the provisions of Article XLVIII of the Amendments to the Constitution, "The Referendum. III. Referendum Petitions. Section 3", (Article 97 of the Rearrangement of the Constitution), a petition was filed in this office June 6, 1933, by the required number of qualified voters, asking for a referendum on Chapter 203, Acts of 1933, entitled, "An Act relative to the use, setting and maintenance of certain traps or other devices for the capture of fur-bearing animals", approved May 16, 1933, and requesting that the operation of said law be suspended.

Operation of
law suspended.

Said petition was completed by the filing in this office August 14, 1933, of more than a sufficient number (21,168) of subsequent signatures of qualified voters of the Commonwealth and the operation of the law was suspended thereby. Said law will be submitted to the people at the state election November 6, 1934, for their approval or disapproval.

FREDERIC W. COOK,
Secretary of the Commonwealth.

THE COMMONWEALTH OF MASSACHUSETTS

OFFICE OF THE SECRETARY,
BOSTON, October 21, 1933.

Pursuant to the provisions of Article XLVIII of the Amendments to the Constitution, "The Referendum. III. Referendum Petitions. Section 3", (Article 97 of the Rearrangement of the Constitution), a petition was filed in this office August 2, 1933, by the required number of qualified voters, asking for a referendum on Chapter 372, Acts of 1933, entitled, "An Act providing for the safety and regulation of the use of the highways by motor vehicles transporting property for hire in the commonwealth, and for the supervision and control of such motor vehicles and such transportation", approved July 22, 1933, and requesting that the operation of said law be suspended. *Petition filed requesting referendum on chapter 372, Acts of 1933.*

Said petition was completed by the filing in this office October 20, 1933, of more than a sufficient number (17,188) of subsequent signatures of qualified voters of the Commonwealth and the operation of the law was suspended thereby. Said law will be submitted to the people at the state election November 6, 1934, for their approval or disapproval. *Operation of law suspended.*

FREDERIC W. COOK,
Secretary of the Commonwealth.

NUMBER OF ACTS AND RESOLVES APPROVED, APPROVAL
WITHHELD, LIST OF ACTS VETOED BY THE GOVERNOR
AND PASSED OVER HIS VETO AND ACT DECLARED EMER-
GENCY LAW BY THE GOVERNOR UNDER AUTHORITY OF
THE CONSTITUTION.

The general court, during its first annual session held
in 1933, passed 369 Acts and 50 Resolves which received
executive approval and 1 Resolve from which executive
approval was withheld but has become law by virtue of
chapter 1, section 1, Article 2 of the Constitution of the
Commonwealth.

The governor returned 15 Acts and 5 Resolves with his
objections thereto in writing. Upon 12 of said Acts and
1 of said Resolves his objections were sustained.

One (1) Resolve entitled "Resolve in favor of William
J. Groves of Gloucester" (Chapter 42) was passed, but
failed to receive executive approval; as, however, it was
not returned, with objections thereto, within five days
after it had been received in the executive department,
the general court not having been prorogued in the meantime, said resolve has the force of law, under the provisions
of the Constitution governing such cases, and has been so
certified.

Twelve (12) Acts entitled, respectively, "An Act authorizing the town of Marblehead to pay an annuity to the
widow of George P. Kelley"; "An Act removing the
disqualification of members of school committees in certain cities to hold elective public office during their term of
office"; "An Act relative to the powers of certain special
police officers in towns"; "An Act exempting veterans of
the Spanish War, the Philippine Insurrection or the Chinese
Relief Expedition from certain requirements of the civil
service laws"; "An Act further regulating the marking and
use of motor vehicles purchased by the commonwealth";
"An Act establishing a temporary banking advisory
board"; "An Act authorizing the county of Plymouth to
pay a certain sum of money to the widow of Jere B.
Howard"; "An Act to regulate the placing of swordfish in
cold storage"; "An Act relative to sterilizing and disin-
fecting previously used material intended for use in filling
mattresses and certain other articles"; "An Act eliminating
educational requirements as a prerequisite to the taking of
civil service examinations"; "An Act authorizing cities and
towns to regulate and license the business of dry cleaning
and renovating clothing, wearing apparel and household
furnishings"; "An Act amending the definition of 'Temporary or Transient Business' in the laws relative to
transient vendors, and requiring certain transient vendors
to make deposits of money or give bonds for certain purposes"; and one (1) Resolve entitled "Resolve in favor of
Harry A. Pattison of Cohasset" were passed and laid be-

fore the governor for his approval; were returned by him with his objections thereto, to the branch in which they respectively originated; were reconsidered, and the vote being taken on their passage, the objections of the governor thereto notwithstanding, they were rejected, and said acts and resolve thereby became void.

Three (3) Acts entitled, respectively, "An Act changing the time of holding city primaries in the city of Medford" (Chapter 88); "An Act providing for the establishment of a right of way for public access to Lake Marguerite, also known as Simon Pond, in the town of Sandisfield" (Chapter 180); "An Act relative to the payment of annuities to dependents of policemen, firemen or investigators or examiners of the registry of motor vehicles killed or dying from injuries received in the performance of duty" (Chapter 340); and four (4) Resolves entitled, respectively, "Resolve in favor of John F. Tiernan of Brookline" (Chapter 29); "Resolve in favor of Thomas W. Kingdon of Holden" (Chapter 30); "Resolve in favor of Harold A. Cady of Dalton" (Chapter 38); and "Resolve in favor of John A. Carroll of Waltham" (Chapter 48) were passed and laid before the governor for his approval; were returned by him with his objections thereto, to the branch in which they respectively originated; were reconsidered, agreeably to the provisions of the constitution, and the vote being taken on their passage, the objections of the governor thereto notwithstanding, they were passed, and said acts and resolves have thereby the force of law.

One (1) Act passed by the general court at its first annual session held in 1933, entitled "An Act relative to proceedings for the sale or taking of property for non-payment of taxes and related proceedings" (Chapter 164) was declared to be an emergency law by the governor in accordance with the provisions of the forty-eighth amendment to the Constitution "The Referendum. II. Emergency Measures". Said Chapter 164 thereby took effect at three o'clock P.M. on May 17, 1933.

The general court was prorogued on Saturday, July 22, 1933, at fifty-seven minutes past eleven o'clock P.M., the session having occupied 200 days.

ACTS

PASSED BY THE

General Court of Massachusetts

AT AN

EXTRA SESSION, 1933

CONVENED ON WEDNESDAY, THE EIGHTH DAY OF
NOVEMBER, AND ADJOURNED ON MONDAY, THE
FOURTH DAY OF DECEMBER, 1933.

AN ACT PROVIDING FOR THE EXERCISE OF LOCAL OPTION RELATIVE TO THE LICENSING OF SALES OF ALCOHOLIC BEVERAGES AND CONFERRING CERTAIN POWERS ON LICENSING AUTHORITIES IN ANTICIPATION OF THE ENACTMENT OF FURTHER LEGISLATION REGULATING SUCH LICENSING AND SALES.

*Chap.*373

Whereas, The deferred operation of this act would defeat its purpose, therefore it is hereby declared to be an emergency law, necessary for the immediate preservation of the public convenience.

Emergency preamble.

Be it enacted by the Senate and House of Representatives in General Court assembled, and by the authority of the same, as follows:

SECTION 1. If the mayor of a city which holds its annual or biennial municipal election at any time hereafter in the current year so orders, there shall be placed on the official ballot to be used at such election the following questions: —

Form of questions to be placed on official ballot in certain cities during the current year.

1. Shall licenses be granted in this city for the sale therein of all alcoholic beverages (whisky, rum, gin, malt beverages, wines and all other alcoholic beverages)?

YES.	
NO.	

2. Shall licenses be granted in this city for the sale therein of wines and malt beverages (wines and beer, ale and all other malt beverages)?

YES.	
NO.	

The following directions shall also be placed on said ballot immediately above the foregoing questions: —

Directions.

To obtain a full expression of opinion, voters should vote on both of the following questions:

(a) If a voter desires to permit the sale of any and all alcoholic beverages in this city, he will vote "YES" on both questions.

(b) If he desires to permit the sale of wines and malt beverages only herein, he will vote "NO" on question 1 and "YES" on question 2.

(c) If he desires to prohibit the sale of any and all alcoholic beverages herein, he will vote "NO·" on both questions.

If a majority of the votes cast in such city in answer to question one are in the affirmative, such city shall be taken to have authorized the sale therein of all alcoholic beverages for such period of time, prior to the first day of January, nineteen hundred and thirty-five, as such sale may be legal under such provisions of law as may hereafter be enacted, and in all respects subject to such provisions.

If a majority of the votes cast in such city in answer to question one are not in the affirmative, but a majority thereof in answer to question two are in the affirmative, such city shall be taken to have authorized the sale therein of wines and malt beverages only, for such period of time, prior to the first day of January, nineteen hundred and thirty-five, as such sale may be legal under such provisions of law as may hereafter be enacted, and in all respects subject to such provisions.

Mayor and selectmen may authorize granting of licenses pending vote, etc.

SECTION 2. Prior to January first, nineteen hundred and thirty-five, and pending the taking, in any manner herein or hereafter authorized, of a vote in any city or town, on the question of granting licenses for the sale therein of alcoholic beverages, the granting of such licenses and the sale of such beverages shall be authorized therein, subject to all applicable provisions of law hereafter enacted, upon the filing with the city or town clerk of an order by the mayor of such city or the selectmen of such town authorizing the granting of such licenses and the making of such sales in such city or town; provided, that such order may limit the granting of such licenses and sales thereunder to licenses and sales of wines and malt beverages only.

Form of questions to be placed on official ballots at special elections, etc.

SECTION 3. The city council of any city which has not voted under the provisions of section one and the selectmen of any town may, and except as hereinafter provided, shall upon petition signed by the registered voters in such city or town equal in number to at least one per cent of the whole number of registered voters therein, and conforming to the provisions of section thirty-eight of chapter forty-three of the General Laws with respect to initiative petitions, call a special election therein for the purpose of submitting to the voters the following questions, which shall be printed on the ballot to be used at such election: —

> 1. Shall licenses be granted in this city (or town) for the sale therein of all alcoholic beverages (whisky, rum, gin, malt beverages, wines and all other alcoholic beverages)?

YES.	
NO.	

> 2. Shall licenses be granted in this city (or town) for the sale therein of wines and malt beverages (wines and beer, ale and all other malt beverages)?

YES.	
NO.	

Directions.

The following directions shall also be placed on said ballot immediately above the foregoing questions: —

To obtain a full expression of opinion, voters should vote on both of the following questions.

(a)   If a voter desires to permit the sale of any and all alcoholic beverages in this city (or town), he will vote "YES" on both questions.

(b)   If he desires to permit the sale of wines and malt beverages only herein, he will vote "NO" on question 1 and "YES" on question 2.

(c)   If he desires to prohibit the sale of any and all alcoholic beverages herein, he will vote "NO" on both questions.

If a majority of the votes cast at such special election in such city or town in answer to question one are in the affirmative, such city or town shall be taken to have authorized the sale therein of all alcoholic beverages for such period of time, prior to the first day of January, nineteen hundred and thirty-five, as such sale may be legal under such provisions of law as may hereafter be enacted, and in all respects subject to such provisions.

If a majority of the votes cast at such special election in such city or town in answer to question one are not in the affirmative, but a majority thereof in answer to question two are in the affirmative, such city or town shall be taken to have authorized the sale therein of wines and malt beverages only, for such period of time, prior to the first day of January, nineteen hundred and thirty-five, as such sale may be legal under such provisions of law as may hereafter be enacted, and in all respects subject to such provisions.

If such a petition is filed in a town using official ballots in the election of town officers not more than thirty days preceding its annual town election, a special election shall not be held in such town but said questions shall be placed upon the ballot to be used at such annual town election and voted upon with the same effect as if submitted as aforesaid at a special election in said town. *Vote may be taken at annual town meeting in certain cases.*

Section 4.   The licensing authorities in the several cities and towns, as defined in section three of chapter one hundred and twenty of the acts of the current year, are hereby authorized to receive applications for local licenses for the sale therein of alcoholic beverages and to investigate as to such applicants and the premises wherein the licensed business is to be conducted, in anticipation of the enactment of laws regulating such sale. *Licensing authorities may receive applications for licenses, etc., pending further legislation.*

Section 5.   The alcoholic beverages control commission, established under section forty-three of chapter six of the General Laws, inserted by section two of said chapter one hundred and twenty, is hereby authorized to receive applications for licenses to manufacture, sell at wholesale and to import alcoholic beverages and for permits to transport such beverages and to make all investigations necessary for acting on such applications, in anticipation of the enactment of laws regulating the manufacture, sale at wholesale, importation and transportation of such beverages. *Alcoholic beverages control commission may receive applications for licenses, etc., pending further legislation.*

Approved November 24, 1933.

*Chap.*374 AN ACT AUTHORIZING THE MANUFACTURE AND PREPARATION
OF ALCOHOLIC BEVERAGES IN ANTICIPATION OF LEGISLA-
TION AUTHORIZING THE RETAIL SALE THEREOF.

Emergency
preamble.

Whereas, The sole and exclusive purpose of this act is to
authorize the manufacture, preparation for sale and accumulation within the commonwealth of a supply of alcoholic
beverages in anticipation of the passage of legislation making the retail sale of such beverages lawful; and

Whereas, The deferred operation of this act would defeat
its purpose, therefore it is hereby declared to be an emergency law, necessary for the immediate preservation of the
public convenience.

Be it enacted, etc., as follows:

Words "wines
and malt bev-
erages"
defined.

SECTION 1. For the purposes of this act, the words
"wines and malt beverages", as used in section forty-four
of chapter six of the General Laws, added by section two of
chapter one hundred and twenty of the acts of the current
year, shall include alcoholic beverages as defined in section
two of this act.

Certain
terms
defined.

SECTION 2. The following words as used in this act,
unless the context otherwise requires, shall have the following meanings: —

"Commission", the alcoholic beverages control commission established under section forty-three of said
chapter six.

"Alcoholic beverages", any liquid intended for human
consumption as a beverage and containing one half of one
per cent or more of alcohol by volume at sixty degrees
Fahrenheit.

"Wines", all fermented alcoholic beverages made from
fruits, flowers, herbs or vegetables, other than cider made
from apples, and containing not more than twenty-four
per cent of alcohol by volume at sixty degrees Fahrenheit.

"Malt beverages", all alcoholic beverages manufactured
or produced by the process of brewing or fermentation of
malt, with or without cereal grains or fermentable sugars,
or of hops, and containing not more than twelve per cent of
alcohol by weight.

Manufacture,
etc., of alco-
holic bever-
ages.

SECTION 3. No person shall manufacture with intent
to sell, sell or expose or keep for sale, transport, import or
export alcoholic beverages, except as authorized by chapter
one hundred and thirty-eight of the General Laws, by chapter one hundred and twenty of the acts of the current year,
or by this act. Violation of this section shall be punished,
except as provided in section nine, by a fine of not less than
one hundred nor more than one thousand dollars, or by
imprisonment for not more than one year, or both.

Provisions of
act not to
apply to
alcoholic bev-

SECTION 4. This act shall not apply to the manufacture
of alcoholic beverages by a person for his own private use
or to sales of cider at wholesale by the original makers

thereof, or to sales of cider by farmers, not to be drunk on the premises, in quantities not exceeding in the aggregate the product of apples raised by them in the season of, or next preceding, such sales, or to sales of cider in any quantity by such farmers not to be drunk on the premises if such cider does not contain more than three per cent of alcohol by weight at sixty degrees Fahrenheit; nor shall this act apply to sales of cider by the original makers thereof other than such makers and farmers selling not to be drunk on the premises as aforesaid, if the cider does not contain more than three per cent alcohol as aforesaid, not to be drunk on the premises as aforesaid. *erages manufactured for personal use nor to the manufacture or sale of cider in certain cases.*

Section 5. The commission may issue to individuals, and to partnerships composed solely of individuals, who are both citizens of the United States and residents of the commonwealth, and to corporations organized under the laws of the commonwealth whereof all the directors are citizens of the United States and a majority residents of the commonwealth, temporary licenses as wholesalers and importers (1) to sell for resale to other licensees duly licensed under the laws of the commonwealth to be enacted for regulating the manufacture, transportation and sale of such beverages, alcoholic beverages manufactured by any manufacturer licensed under the provisions of section six, and to import such beverages into the commonwealth from other states and foreign countries for sale to such licensees, or (2) to sell for resale wines and malt beverages so manufactured to such licensees, and to import as aforesaid wines and malt beverages for sale to such licensees. Licenses may be granted under this section authorizing the holders (a) to sell wines to be used for sacramental purposes only, to any registered, regularly ordained priest, minister or rabbi, or to any church or religious society, (b) to sell alcoholic beverages to registered pharmacists holding certificates of fitness under section twenty-seven of said chapter one hundred and thirty-eight, or (c) to sell alcohol for use in the manufacture or preparation of articles mentioned in section thirty-five of chapter one hundred and twelve of the General Laws, or to sell alcoholic beverages for any or all the purposes specified in this section. Importations of beverages by any licensee under this section may be in casks, barrels, kegs or other containers, as well as in bottles, in either case bearing such seals, or other evidences of the identity and origin of the contents, as the commission may prescribe. Subject to such regulations as may be prescribed by the commission, licensees under this section may bottle, and may rectify or blend, any alcoholic beverages purchased by them in bulk, but such bottling, including the sealing and labelling of the bottles, and such rectifying and blending, shall be done only upon such premises and under such conditions as the commission shall approve. For the purposes of use in such rectifying or blending, licensees may purchase from authorized dealers therein *Commission may issue temporary licenses to wholesalers and importers.*

ethyl alcohol in such quantities and under such conditions as the commission shall approve. No person, firm, corporation, association or other combination of persons, directly or indirectly, or through any agent, employee, stockholder, officer or other person, or any subsidiary whatsoever, shall be granted more than one license throughout the commonwealth under this section. The license fee for a license issued under this section to sell and import all alcoholic beverages shall be at an annual rate of not less than two thousand nor more than five thousand dollars. The license fee for a license issued under this section to sell and import wines and malt beverages only shall be at an annual rate of not less than one thousand nor more than twenty-five hundred dollars. The license fee for a license issued under this section to sell wines for sacramental use only shall be at an annual rate of not less than two hundred and fifty nor more than one thousand dollars. The holder of a wholesaler's and importer's license may sell such alcoholic beverages as he is licensed to sell hereunder, for export from this commonwealth into any state where the sale of the same is not by law prohibited and into any foreign country.

Shipments of alcoholic beverages regulated. In order to ensure the necessary control of traffic in alcoholic beverages for the preservation of the public peace and order, the shipment of such beverages into the commonwealth, except as provided in this section and in said chapter one hundred and twenty, is hereby prohibited.

Temporary license to manufacture alcoholic beverages. SECTION 6. The commission may issue to individuals, and to partnerships composed solely of individuals, who are both citizens of the United States and residents of the commonwealth, and to corporations organized under the laws of this commonwealth or of any other state of the United States admitted to do business in this commonwealth, temporary licenses to manufacture alcoholic beverages in the commonwealth. Manufacturers of such beverages may sell the same to any licensee under section five and to any licensee holding a valid license granted for the sale within the commonwealth in accordance with laws to be enacted regulating the manufacture, transportation and sale of such beverages, and may also sell such beverages for export from this commonwealth into any state where the sale of the same is not by law prohibited, and into any foreign country. Licensees under this section may also sell such beverages to any registered pharmacist holding a certificate of fitness under section twenty-seven of said chapter one hundred and thirty-eight. Subject to such regulations as may be prescribed by the commission, licensees under this section may rectify or blend, but only upon such premises and under such conditions as the commission shall approve, alcoholic beverages manufactured by them. All alcoholic beverages sold by any manufacturer thereof shall be sold and delivered in such manner, and under such conditions, and with such labels or other marks to identify the manufacturer, as the commission shall from time to time prescribe by regulations; provided, that sales of such beverages may be made in kegs, casks, barrels or bottles, to holders of wholesalers' and importers' licenses under section five.

Every licensee under this section shall keep such records in such detail and affording such information as the commission may from time to time prescribe, and shall file with the commission, whenever and as often as it may require, duplicates of copies of such records; and the commission shall at all times, through its designated officers or agents, have access to all books, records and other documents of every licensed manufacturer relating to the business which he is licensed hereunder to conduct. *Licensee to keep records*

The license fee for each manufacturer of alcoholic beverages, in respect of each plant, shall be such sum, computed at an annual rate of not less than two thousand nor more than five thousand dollars, as under the circumstances of the licensee's probable volume of sales under this section, the capacity of his plant and the location thereof, the commission shall deem just and proper. *Fee.*

SECTION 7. The commission may grant to any holder of a manufacturer's or wholesaler's and importer's license under this act a temporary permit to store alcoholic beverages in any city or town; provided, that there shall not be granted to such manufacturer or wholesaler and importer, in the aggregate, more than three such permits in the commonwealth nor more than one such permit in any city or town. A permit so granted to the holder of such a license shall authorize him to transport such beverages between any premises covered by such license and any place of storage for which he has such a permit and also between one such place of storage and another. The commission may make and enforce rules and regulations governing the storage and transportation of beverages under such permits and establish fees therefor at an annual rate of not exceeding five hundred dollars for any one permit. *Temporary permits to store alcoholic beverages.* *Rules, etc.*

SECTION 8. Every manufacturer of alcoholic beverages and every holder of a wholesaler's and importer's license for the sale thereof shall, in addition to the license fees elsewhere provided in this act, be liable for and pay to the commonwealth, for the privilege enjoyed by him as such manufacturer or wholesaler and importer under this act, such excises or taxes as may hereafter be imposed. *Excise.*

SECTION 9. Licensees under section five or six may, for the purposes of this act only, transport and deliver anywhere in the commonwealth alcoholic beverages lawfully bought by or lawfully sold by them, in vehicles operated under the control of themselves or of their employees; provided, that the owner of every such vehicle shall have obtained for such vehicle from the commission a vehicle permit for the transportation of alcoholic bever- *Transportation permits.*

ages. The fee for each vehicle permit shall be one dollar for each vehicle. Copies of such permits shall be furnished by the commission for one dollar each. All permits issued under this section shall expire on the thirty-first day of December, nineteen hundred and thirty-four, unless earlier suspended or revoked by the commission. Every person operating such a vehicle when engaged in such transportation or delivery shall carry the vehicle permit or a copy thereof for each vehicle operated by him and shall, upon demand of any constable, policeman, member of the state police, or any inspector of the commission or of the registry of motor vehicles, produce such permit or copy for inspection; and failure to produce such permit or copy shall constitute prima facie evidence of unlawful transportation and shall in the discretion of the commission be sufficient cause for the suspension or revocation of such permit. Except as herein provided, alcoholic beverages may be transported within the commonwealth only by a railroad or steamboat corporation, or an individual or corporation regularly and lawfully conducting a general express or trucking business, and in each case holding a transportation permit in full force and effect issued by the commission and valid for one year unless earlier suspended or revoked. The fee for each such transportation permit shall be five dollars, and each vehicle used in the transportation of alcoholic beverages under such transportation permit shall carry a certified copy thereof. Each certified copy shall be issued by the commission for a fee of one dollar; provided, that the transportation fee payable by a railroad or steamship company covering all the cars or vessels thereof, shall be one hundred dollars. Whoever knowingly transports within the commonwealth any alcoholic beverages except as authorized by this section or by section eleven or twelve of said chapter one hundred and twenty shall be punished by a fine not exceeding two hundred dollars or by imprisonment for not more than six months, or both.

SECTION 10. Holders of transportation permits which were issued by the commission under the provisions of said chapter one hundred and twenty may, under such a permit, but only for a period of sixty days from the effective date of this act, transport alcoholic beverages.

SECTION 11. No license shall be granted under this act unless the license fee has been paid to the commission nor unless the applicant shall have filed with the commission a bond running to the commission in such penal sum and form approved by the commission signed by the applicant and with a surety company authorized to do business in the commonwealth as surety, conditioned upon performance by the licensee of all the conditions of the license and observance of all the provisions of this act. Permits issued under section seven shall be deemed licenses for the purposes of this section.

Section 12. All moneys received by the commission and by the commissioner of corporations and taxation under this act shall be paid into the treasury of the commonwealth and, after the expenses of the commission have been paid, used so far as necessary, for reimbursing cities and towns for assistance given by them to aged citizens under the provisions of chapter one hundred and eighteen A of the General Laws, in the manner provided by section three of said chapter, and any balance remaining shall be used to reimburse the cities and towns for assistance to said aged persons and be distributed on the same basis.

Fees to be used for assistance of aged persons.

Approved December 1, 1933.

An Act establishing the salaries of the members of the alcoholic beverages control commission.

Chap.375

Be it enacted, etc., as follows:

Section 1. Section forty-three of chapter six of the General Laws, inserted by section two of chapter one hundred and twenty of the acts of the current year, is hereby amended by striking out, in the twelfth line, the words "five thousand" and inserting in place thereof the words: — seventy-five hundred, — and by striking out, in the thirteenth line, the word "four" and inserting in place thereof the word: — seven, — so as to read as follows: — *Section 43.* There shall be a commission to be known as the alcoholic beverages control commission, to consist of three members, to be appointed by the governor, with the advice and consent of the council. Not more than two of such members shall be members of the same political party. Said members shall be designated in their initial appointments to serve for one, two and three years, respectively. The governor shall designate one of the members as chairman. Upon the expiration of the term of office of a member, his successor shall be appointed in the manner aforesaid for three years. The chairman shall receive a salary not to exceed seventy-five hundred dollars and each other member shall receive a salary not to exceed seven thousand dollars. The governor may, with like advice and consent, remove any such member and fill any vacancy for the remainder of the unexpired term.

G. L. (Ter. Ed.) 6, § 43, amended.

Alcoholic beverages control commission, appointment, term and salary of members.

Section 2. Salaries established by this act shall be subject to chapter one hundred and five of the acts of the current year.

Salaries subject to 1933, 105.

Section 3. This act shall not take effect until an appropriation has been made sufficient to cover the same and then as of January first in the year nineteen hundred and thirty-four.

When effective.

Approved December 4, 1933.

*Chap.*376 AN ACT AUTHORIZING AND REGULATING THE MANUFACTURE, TRANSPORTATION, SALE, IMPORTATION AND EXPORTATION OF ALCOHOL AND ALCOHOLIC BEVERAGES.

Emergency preamble.

Whereas, The deferred operation of this act would in part defeat its purpose to enable the people of the commonwealth to take immediate advantage of the repeal of the eighteenth amendment to the constitution of the United States, therefore this act is hereby declared to be an emergency law, necessary for the immediate preservation of the public health, safety and convenience.

Be it enacted, etc., as follows:

G. L. (Ter. Ed.), 6, § 44, amended.

Alcoholic beverages control commission, duties.

SECTION 1. Section forty-four of chapter six of the General Laws, added by section two of chapter one hundred and twenty of the acts of the current year, is hereby amended by striking out the first paragraph and inserting in place thereof the following: — The commission shall have general supervision of the conduct of the business of manufacturing, importing, exporting, storing, transporting and selling alcoholic beverages as defined in section one of chapter one hundred and thirty-eight and also of the quality, purity and alcoholic content thereof.

G. L. (Ter. Ed.), 138, amended.

SECTION 2. The General Laws are hereby amended by striking out chapter one hundred and thirty-eight and inserting in place thereof the following new chapter, under the title:

ALCOHOLIC LIQUORS.

Definitions.

Section 1. The following words as used in this chapter, unless the context otherwise requires, shall have the following meanings: —

"Commission", the alcoholic beverages control commission established under section forty-three of chapter six.

"Alcoholic beverages", any liquid intended for human consumption as a beverage and containing one half of one per cent or more of alcohol by volume at sixty degrees Fahrenheit.

"Wines", all fermented alcoholic beverages made from fruits, flowers, herbs or vegetables, other than cider made from apples, and containing not more than twenty-four per cent of alcohol by volume at sixty degrees Fahrenheit.

"Malt beverages", all alcoholic beverages manufactured or produced by the process of brewing or fermentation of malt, with or without cereal grains or fermentable sugars, or of hops, and containing not more than twelve per cent of alcohol by weight.

"Hotel", a building or part of a building owned or leased and operated by a person holding a duly issued and valid license as an innholder, under the provisions of chapter one hundred and forty and provided with adequate and sanitary kitchen and dining room equipment and capacity for preparing, cooking and serving suitable food for its guests, including travelers and strangers and its other patrons and customers, and in addition meeting and complying with all the requirements imposed upon innholders under said chapter one hundred and forty.

"Restaurant", space, in a suitable building, leased or rented or owned by a person holding a duly issued and valid license as a common victualler under the provisions of said chapter one hundred and forty, and provided with adequate and sanitary kitchen and dining room equipment and capacity for preparing, cooking and serving suitable food for strangers, travelers and other patrons and customers, and in addition meeting and complying with all the requirements imposed upon common victuallers under said chapter one hundred and forty.

"Club", a corporation chartered for any purpose described in section two of chapter one hundred and eighty, whether under federal or state law, including any body or association lawfully operating under a charter granted by a parent body so chartered, and including also any organization or unit mentioned in clause twelfth of section five of chapter forty, owning, hiring, or leasing a building, or space in a building, of such extent and character as may be suitable and adequate for the reasonable and comfortable use and accommodation of its members; provided, that such club files with the local licensing authorities and the commission annually within the first ten days of February in each year a list of the names and residences of its officers; and provided, further, that its affairs and management are conducted by a board of directors, executive committee, or similar body chosen by the members at its annual meeting, and that no member or any officer, agent or employee of the club is paid, or directly or indirectly receives in the form of salary or other compensation, any profits from the disposition or sale of alcoholic beverages to the members of the club or its guests introduced by members beyond the amount of such salary as may be fixed and voted annually within two months after January first in each year by the members or by its directors or other governing body and as reported by the club to the local licensing authorities and the commission within three months after such January first, and as shall in the judgment of the local licensing authorities and the commission be reasonable and proper compensation for the services of such member, officer, agent or employee.

"Local licensing authorities", the licensing boards and commissions established in any city or town under special statute or city charter or under section four or corresponding provisions of earlier laws, or, in a city having no such board or commission or having a board rendered inactive under section eight, the aldermen, or, in a town having no such board or commission, the selectmen.

"Licensing authorities", the commission or the local licensing authorities, or both, as the case may be.

Definitions.

"Tavern", an establishment where alcoholic beverages may be sold, as authorized by this chapter, with or without food, to be served to and drunk by patrons sitting at tables in plain view of other patrons, all entrances to which shall open directly from a public way. No woman shall be allowed as patron in a tavern. The business conducted therein shall be open to public view from the sidewalk level and the establishment shall be properly lighted. No window facing a public way shall be obstructed by any screen or other object extending more than five feet above the level of the sidewalk on which the establishment abuts, but in no event shall any screen or obstruction prevent a clear view of the interior of said tavern. Said windows shall contain no advertising matter other than the name of the proprietor, followed by the word "Tavern" or "Tavern-Keeper".

Regulation of sale and manufacture of alcoholic beverages, etc.

Section 2. No person shall manufacture, with intent to sell, sell or expose or keep for sale, transport, import or export alcoholic beverages or alcohol, except as authorized in this chapter; provided, that sheriffs, deputy sheriffs, constables, state police officers, trustees in bankruptcy, and public officers acting under judicial process, and executors, administrators, receivers and trustees duly authorized by proper judicial order or decree, and assignees under voluntary assignments for the benefit of creditors if such assignees are authorized by special permit issued by the commission, and insurers and their agents in disposing of such beverages damaged by fire or other casualty if authorized by such a permit, may sell and transport alcoholic beverages, subject to such conditions and restrictions as the commission may prescribe. Violation of this section shall be punished except as provided in section twenty-two by a fine of not less than one hundred nor more than one thousand dollars or by imprisonment for not more than one year, or both.

Provisions of chapter not to apply to manufacture for personal use.

Section 3. This chapter shall not apply to the manufacture of alcoholic beverages by a person for his own private use or to sales of cider at wholesale by the original makers thereof, or to sales of cider by farmers, not to be drunk on the premises, in quantities not exceeding in the aggregate the product of apples raised by them in the season of, or next preceding, such sales, or to sales of cider in any quantity by such farmers not to be drunk on the premises if such cider does not contain more than three per cent of alcohol by weight at sixty degrees Fahrenheit; nor shall this chapter apply to sales of cider by the original makers thereof other than such makers and farmers selling not to be drunk on the premises as aforesaid, if the cider does not contain more than three per cent alcohol as aforesaid, not to be drunk on the premises as aforesaid.

LICENSING BOARDS.

Section 4. In each city which is not exempt by the provisions of section ten there shall be a licensing board appointed by the mayor, consisting of three persons, who shall not be engaged, directly or indirectly, in the manufacture or sale of alcoholic beverages, who have been residents of the city in which they are appointed for at least two years immediately preceding their appointment, and who shall not hold any other public office except that of notary public and justice of the peace. One member shall be appointed from each of the two leading political parties and the third member may also be appointed from one of said parties. If any member of said board engages directly or indirectly in such manufacture or sale, his office shall immediately become vacant.

Licensing boards, appointment, etc.

Section 5. The terms of office of the members first appointed shall commence at the date of their appointment, and shall be so arranged as to expire at the end of two, four or six years from the first Monday in June in the year of their appointment, the date of expiration to be specified in their respective commissions; and thereafter a member shall be appointed for a term of six years from the first Monday in June of the year in which the previous term expires. All members shall hold office until their respective successors are qualified. They may be removed by the mayor for cause, after charges preferred, reasonable notice thereof, and a hearing thereon; and the mayor shall, in the order of removal, state his reasons therefor. Any member of said board may, within seven days after notice of his removal, apply to the superior court for a review of the charges, of the evidence submitted thereunder, and of the findings thereon by the mayor. Notice of the entry of such application shall be given to the mayor by serving upon him an attested copy thereof. The entry fee, costs, and all proceedings upon such application shall be according to the rules regulating the trial of civil causes. The court, after a hearing, shall affirm or revoke the order of the mayor removing such member, and there shall be no appeal from the decision.

Terms, removal.

If any member of said board who has been removed from office shall apply to the superior court for the review provided for in this section, he shall be entitled to a speedy hearing, and in no event shall the removal take effect until the court shall have affirmed the order removing the member; and until such order is affirmed the member shall continue to exercise the powers and perform the duties of his office.

Section 6. The mayor shall designate one member as chairman, who shall also act as secretary. Two members shall be a quorum for the transaction of business. If a member ceases to be a resident of the city for which he is appointed or becomes unable to perform his official duties, there shall be a vacancy in the board. All vacancies shall

Chairman, secretary, vacancies, how filled.

be filled by the mayor for the remainder of the unexpired term in the manner provided for an original appointment.

Board to be provided with offices. *Section 7.* Each city which has such a board shall provide it with suitable rooms, properly furnished, heated and lighted, shall pay such salaries as the city council, subject to the approval of the mayor, may from time to time establish, and shall also pay all expenses incurred by said board for blank books, printing and other necessary expenses approved by said board.

Limitation of preceding section. *Section 8.* If, at any biennial state election, a city in which such board has been appointed shall not vote to authorize the granting of licenses for the sale of any alcoholic beverages, all obligations imposed upon said city by the preceding section shall cease from and after the thirty-first day of December next following such vote and, from and after said date, the powers and duties granted to and imposed upon said board in respect to such licenses as it is authorized to grant under this chapter irrespective of any vote under section eleven and licenses of innholders and common victuallers shall vest in the aldermen of said city. If said city shall, at a subsequent biennial state election again vote to authorize the granting of licenses for the sale of such beverages, the obligations imposed by the preceding section shall be revived and shall attach to said city from and after January first next following such vote and, from and after said date, the powers and duties of the aldermen relative to such licenses shall revest in the licensing board appointed in said city. This section shall not apply to a city wherein by a special statute such a board is vested with all the powers and duties in respect to the granting of licenses of innholders and common victuallers notwithstanding any vote under this chapter.

Record and report. *Section 9.* Each board shall keep a record of its doings and hearings and shall make a quarterly report of its doings to the mayor. It may prescribe the forms of applications for licenses, may require any statement which may be made before it and papers which may be filed with it relative to applications for licenses to be sworn to, and for such purpose any member may administer oaths.

Certain cities exempt from certain sections. *Section 10.* The following cities shall be exempt from the operation of the six preceding sections: First, cities having a licensing board or commission created by special statute or under the provisions of a charter. Second, other cities not having a board appointed under the earlier provisions of law antecedent to and corresponding with the provisions of section four, under section three of chapter one hundred and twenty of the acts of nineteen hundred and thirty-three, but if any such city hereafter, at a biennial state election, votes to authorize the granting of licenses for the sale of any alcoholic beverage the board shall, thereupon, not later than the thirty-first day of December following said election, be appointed for such city as above provided, and the provisions of the six preceding sections shall thereafter apply to said city; provided, that if such city is authorized by vote of the people or otherwise prior to the biennial state election of nineteen hundred and thirty-four to grant such licenses the board shall be appointed as aforesaid within thirty days after such authorization and the provisions of said sections shall thereafter apply to said city.

Section 10A. The local licensing authority in each city and town in which the granting of licenses for the sale of any alcoholic beverage is authorized shall file with the commission during the month of December of each year in which such licenses are granted a full report of its action during the preceding twelve months, with the number of licenses of each class granted, and the revenue therefrom, together with the established schedule of fees for all classes of licenses. *Licensing authorities to report annually to commission.*

Section 11. The state secretary shall cause to be placed on the official ballot used in the cities and towns at each biennial state election the following questions: — *Form of questions to be placed on official ballot at biennial state election.*

1. Shall licenses be granted in this city (or town) for the sale therein of all alcoholic beverages (whisky, rum, gin, malt beverages, wines and all other alcoholic beverages)?

| YES. | |
| NO. | |

2. Shall licenses be granted in this city (or town) for the sale therein of wines and malt beverages (wines and beer, ale and all other malt beverages)?

| YES. | |
| NO. | |

The following directions shall also be placed on said ballot immediately above the foregoing questions: — *Directions.*

To obtain a full expression of opinion, voters should vote on both of the following questions. (a) If a voter desires to permit the sale of any and all alcoholic beverages in this city (or town) he will vote "YES" on both questions.

(b) If he desires to permit the sale of wines and malt beverages only herein, he will vote "NO" on question 1 and "YES" on question 2.

(c) If he desires to prohibit the sale of any and all alcoholic beverages herein, he will vote "NO" on both questions.

If a majority of the votes cast in a city or town in answer to question one are in the affirmative, such city or town shall be taken to have authorized, for the two calendar years next succeeding, the sale in such city or town of all alcoholic beverages, subject to the provisions of this chapter.

If a majority of the votes cast in a city or town in answer to question one are not in the affirmative, but a majority thereof in answer to question two are in the affirmative, such city or town shall be taken to have authorized, for said calendar years, the sale therein of wines and malt beverages only, subject to the provisions of this chapter.

Submission of question at municipal elections.

Section 11A. The provisions of section three of chapter three hundred and seventy-three of the acts of the current year shall be held to authorize the submission of the questions specified in said section at a regular municipal election in a city or town upon petition of one per cent of the whole number of registered voters therein in like manner as provided in said section or by vote of the city council or selectmen thereof, with the same effect as if submitted at a special election called under said section. If there is filed with the clerk of any city or town under the provisions of said section three, as affected by this section, a petition requesting that the questions specified in said section three be submitted to the voters thereof at a regular or special municipal election to be held prior to April fifteenth, nineteen hundred and thirty-four, or if the city council or selectmen thereof vote to submit the same thereat and if there is filed with the clerk of such city or town, a petition conforming to the requirements of said section three, requesting that the question of licensing the sale in such city or town of alcoholic beverages in taverns be at the same time submitted to the voters thereof or if both such requests are contained in one petition, there shall be printed on the ballot to be used at such election, in addition to the questions set forth in said section three, the following question:

Petition.

Taverns.

"Shall licenses be granted in this city (or town) for the sale therein of alcoholic beverages in taverns?"

YES.	
NO.	

If a majority of the votes cast in such city or town in answer to the question hereinbefore set forth are in the affirmative, but not otherwise, such city or town shall be taken to have authorized the sale therein in taverns of such alcoholic beverages, if any, as are from time to time lawfully authorized to be sold in such city or town, subject in all respects to the provisions of this chapter.

SALE OF ALCOHOLIC BEVERAGES OR WINES AND MALT BEVERAGES TO BE DRUNK ON THE PREMISES.

Granting of licenses.

Section 12. A common victualler duly licensed under chapter one hundred and forty to conduct a restaurant, an innholder duly licensed under said chapter to conduct a hotel and a keeper of a tavern as defined by this chapter, in any city or town wherein the granting of licenses to sell all alcoholic beverages or only wines and malt beverages, as the case may be, is authorized by this chapter, subject however, in the case of a tavern, to the provisions of section eleven A, may be licensed by the local licensing authorities, subject to the prior approval of the commission after investigation except as provided in section twenty-three, to sell to travelers, strangers and other patrons and customers not under twenty-one years of age, such beverages to be served and drunk, in case of a hotel or restaurant licensee, only in the dining room or dining rooms and in such other public rooms or areas of a hotel as the local licensing authorities may deem reasonable and proper, and approve in writing, and, in the case of a hotel, restaurant or tavern licensee, only served to and drunk by patrons sitting at tables or at counters equipped with stools; and provided, further, that no alcoholic beverage shall be served to or drunk by a woman in a tavern; and provided, further, that no tavern license shall be granted to the holder of a hotel license hereunder. Such sales may also be made by licensed innholders to registered guests occupying private rooms in their hotels. During such time as the sale of such alcoholic beverages is authorized in any city or town under this chapter, the authority to grant licenses to innholders and common victuallers therein under chapter one hundred and forty shall be vested in the local licensing authorities.

Any club in any city or town wherein the granting of licenses to sell alcoholic beverages, or only wines and malt beverages, as the case may be, is authorized under this chapter may be licensed by the local licensing authorities, subject to the approval of the commission after investigation, to sell such beverages to its members only, and also, subject to regulations made by the local licensing authorities, to guests introduced by members, and to no others, and provided further that such beverages shall be served to and drunk by members or guests only sitting at tables. *Club licenses.*

The local licensing authorities may determine in the first instance, when originally issuing and upon each annual renewal of licenses under this section, the amount of the license fee, in no case less than two hundred and fifty nor more than twenty-five hundred dollars for the sale of all alcoholic beverages, and in no case less than one hundred nor more than one thousand dollars for the sale of wines and malt beverages only, except as hereinafter provided, to be paid by each licensee respectively; provided, that the minimum license fee in the case of a club license for the sale of all alcoholic beverages shall be one hundred dollars. Before issuing a license to any applicant therefor under this section, or before a renewal of such license, the local licensing authorities shall cause an examination to be made of the premises of the applicant to · determine that such premises comply in all respects with the appropriate definition of section one and that the applicant is not less than twenty-one years of age and a person of good character in the city or town in which he seeks a license hereunder. Whenever in the opinion of the local licensing authorities any applicant fails to establish to their satisfaction his compliance with the above requirements, or any other reasonable requirements which they may from time to time make with respect to licenses under this section or the conduct of his business by any licensee *Fees.*

hereunder, or fails to maintain such compliance, the local licensing authorities may refuse to issue or to renew or, if already issued, may, after hearing or opportunity therefor suspend, revoke or cancel any license to such applicant. In case of suspension, revocation or cancellation of a license, no abatement or refund of any part of the fee paid therefor shall be made.

Hours during which licensed premises may be kept open.

The hours during which sales of such alcoholic beverages may be made by any licensee as aforesaid shall be fixed by the local licensing authorities either generally or specially for each licensee; provided, that no such sale shall be made on any day between the hours of two and eight o'clock ante meridian and, except as provided in section thirty-three, no such licensee shall be barred from making such sales on any day after eleven o'clock ante meridian and before eleven o'clock post meridian, and that no tavern shall be kept open on any day after eleven o'clock post meridian.

No person, firm, corporation, association or other combination of persons, directly or indirectly, or through any agent, employee, stockholder, officer or other person, or any subsidiary whatsoever, licensed under the provisions of section fifteen, eighteen or nineteen shall be granted a license under this section.

No licensee under this section, or any employee of such licensee, shall serve any alcoholic beverage to any customer or other person in the licensed premises without charge.

In cities and towns which vote to authorize under section eleven the granting of licenses for the sale of all alcoholic beverages, specific licenses may nevertheless be granted under this section for the sale of wines or malt beverages only, or both. The licensing authorities may refuse to grant licenses under this section in certain geographical areas of their respective cities or towns, where the character of the neighborhood may warrant such refusal.

All malt beverages sold by a licensee under this section on the premises containing not more than three and two tenths per cent of alcohol by volume at sixty degrees Fahrenheit shall be expressly sold as such.

License to railroad corporation, etc.

Section 13. A railroad or car corporation operating any line of railroad or cars within the commonwealth may sell, in any dining car or club car, buffet car or lounge car of a train after leaving and before reaching the terminal stops of such train or car, alcoholic beverages to be drunk in such cars, if the commission sees fit to issue a license to

Fee.

such railroad or car corporation, the license fee for which shall be one hundred dollars and one dollar for each certified copy thereof. The commission may also issue licenses to sell alcoholic beverages to the owner or operator of any vessel or shipping company carrying passengers and operating out of any port of the commonwealth, under such regulations as the commission may prescribe as to the portions of the vessel in which the same may be sold to be drunk while the vessel is under way. The annual license fee for each vessel shall be one hundred dollars. No other license shall be required for the sales hereinbefore in this section authorized. Whenever in the opinion of the commission any applicant fails to establish to its satisfaction his compliance with the above requirements, or any other reasonable requirements which it may from time to time make with respect to licenses under this section or the conduct of his business by any licensee hereunder, or fails to maintain such compliance, it may refuse to issue or to renew or, if already issued, may after hearing or opportunity therefor suspend, revoke or cancel any license to such applicant. In case of suspension, revocation or cancellation of a license, no abatement or refund of any part of the fee paid therefor shall be made.

Section 14. In a city or town wherein the granting of licenses to sell all alcoholic beverages or wines and malt beverages only is authorized under this chapter, special licenses for the sale of malt beverages only may be issued by the local licensing authorities, to the responsible manager of any indoor or outdoor activity or enterprise. Special licenses for the dispensing of malt beverages in dining halls maintained by incorporated educational institutions authorized to grant degrees may be granted by the local licensing authorities in such a city or town to such institutions; provided, that such beverages shall be served only at tables reserved for persons over twenty-one years of age. The fees for licenses granted under this section shall be fixed from time to time by the local licensing authorities and need not be uniform. Special licenses.

SALE OF ALCOHOLIC BEVERAGES NOT TO BE DRUNK ON THE PREMISES.

Section 15. The local licensing authorities in any city or town which votes to authorize the granting of licenses for the sale of all alcoholic beverages, and such authorities in any city or town which votes to authorize the granting of licenses for the sale of wines and malt beverages only, may grant licenses for the sale at retail of such alcoholic beverages or wines and malt beverages, as the case may be, not to be drunk on the premises, to applicants therefor who are citizens and residents of the commonwealth, or partnerships composed solely of such citizens and residents or to corporations organized under the laws of the commonwealth and whereof all directors shall be citizens of the United States and a majority residents of the commonwealth. No person, firm, corporation, association, or other combination of persons, directly or indirectly, or through any agent, employee, stockholder, officer or other person or any subsidiary whatsoever, shall be granted, in the aggregate, more than three such licenses in the commonwealth, or be granted more than one such license Licenses for sale, etc., not to be drunk on the premises.

in a town or two in a city. No such license shall be granted except to an applicant approved by the commission after investigation except as provided in section twenty-three. Each license shall describe the premises to which it applies. Not more than one location shall be included in any such license, nor shall any location or premises for which a license has been granted under section twelve be included therein or connected therewith. Every licensee hereunder shall keep conspicuously posted in such room a price list of the beverages sold therein. Sales by such licensees shall be only in the original manufacturer's, or wholesaler's and importer's package, which shall be labelled as to price. All malt beverages containing not more than three and two tenths per cent of alcohol by volume at sixty degrees Fahrenheit shall be so labelled.

Fee.

Any sale of such beverages shall be conclusively presumed to have been made in the store wherein the order was received from the customer. The fee for such a license shall not be less than seventy-five nor, except as hereinafter provided, more than one thousand dollars in case the license is for the sale of wines and malt beverages only, nor less than one hundred nor, except as hereinafter provided, more than two thousand dollars in case the license is for the sale of all alcoholic beverages. The local licensing authorities shall fix the amount of the license fee within the aforesaid limits, for the shop or other place of business designated in the license, such amount being subject to change from year to year by said authorities as they shall deem just and proper in view of the location of the licensee's place of business, his probable volume of sales, or of his actual volume of sales in the previous year. The local licensing authorities may prescribe the hours within which the sale of alcoholic beverages may be made by licensees under this section. Sales of alcoholic beverages by licensees hereunder shall be made only between the hours of nine o'clock ante meridian and eleven o'clock post meridian.

Penalty for adulteration of alcoholic beverages.

Section 16. Any person holding a license under section twelve, thirteen, fourteen or fifteen to sell alcoholic beverages, who shall allow any adulteration of said beverages so as to change their alcoholic content, shall be punished by a fine of not less than two hundred nor more than five hundred dollars, and such license shall be suspended for a period of not less than six months.

Limitation of licenses to be granted.

Section 16A. If in any city or town eighty per cent of the total number of licenses permitted to be granted under section seventeen to any class of licensee has been granted and there are applications for licenses pending before the local licensing authorities or if there are pending before the commission appeals from refusals of the local licensing authorities of such city or town to grant licenses in such class, every such applicant and every such appellant shall, for the purposes of said section, be deemed to have been granted a license until his application or appeal has been dismissed.

Section 16B. After June first, nineteen hundred and thirty-four, applications for licenses or permits to be granted by the commission shall be granted or dismissed not later than thirty days after the filing of the same, and, except as provided in section sixteen A, applications for licenses to be granted by the local licensing authorities shall be acted upon within a like period and if favorably acted upon by the said authorities shall be submitted for approval by the commission not later than three days following such favorable action. A license so approved shall be issued by said authorities not later than three days following receipt of notice of approval by the commission.

Time within which applications for licenses, etc., shall be granted, etc.

NUMBER OF LICENSES GRANTED BY LOCAL LICENSING AUTHORITIES LIMITED.

Section 17. Except as otherwise provided in this chapter, the number of licenses granted by the local licensing authorities in any city or town under sections twelve and fifteen shall not exceed in the aggregate one for each population unit of one thousand or fraction thereof; provided, that the total number of licenses granted under section fifteen in any city or town shall not exceed one for each population unit of five thousand or fraction thereof; and provided, further, that the licensing authorities in any town may grant two licenses under section fifteen, irrespective of population, and provided, further, that, in the city of Boston licenses under section twelve may be granted up to a total not exceeding one thousand and licenses under section fifteen up to a total not exceeding three hundred and fifty, and provided, further, that in any city or town which has an increased resident population during the summer months, the local licensing authorities may make an estimate prior to April first in any year of such temporary resident population as of July tenth following, and one additional license, under section twelve to be effective from April first to October thirty-first, only, may be granted for each unit of one thousand, or additional fraction thereof, of such population as so estimated, and one additional license under section fifteen to be effective from April first to October thirty-first, only, may be granted for each population unit of five thousand or additional fraction thereof, of such population as so estimated; and provided, further, that said authorities may grant in addition seasonal licenses under section twelve to duly incorporated clubs in any city or town if deemed by them to be in the public interest. Any license issued under section twelve or fifteen for the sale of wines or malt beverages only or both shall not be included in the number of licenses that may be granted in any city or town as provided in this section.

Number of licenses.

Seasonal licenses.

Said local licensing authorities shall not grant a license

to any person or corporation under more than one section of this chapter unless expressly authorized therein. Any license issued under section twelve to a legally chartered club in any city or town shall not be included in the number of licenses that may be granted in any city or town as provided in this section.

Number of licenses to be issued, restricted pending issuance of tavern licenses.

In order that there may be an adequate number of taverns during the current year where authorized, not more than seventy-five per cent of the maximum number of licenses under sections twelve and fifteen prescribed for any city or town, except Boston, and not more than seventy per cent of the maximum number of licenses under section twelve prescribed for the city of Boston, shall be granted prior to May first, nineteen hundred and thirty-four, or, in any city or town which votes under section eleven A in favor of granting tavern licenses, prior to the expiration of thirty days from the date on which said vote is so taken. The foregoing restrictions shall not apply to towns having a population of one thousand or less.

WHOLESALERS' AND IMPORTERS' LICENSES.

Wholesalers' and importers' licenses.

Section 18. The commission may issue to individuals and to partnerships composed solely of individuals, who are both citizens and residents of the commonwealth, and to corporations organized under the laws of the commonwealth whereof all the directors are citizens of the United States and a majority thereof residents of the commonwealth, licenses as wholesalers and importers (1) to sell for resale to other licensees under this chapter alcoholic beverages manufactured by any manufacturer licensed under the provisions of section nineteen and to import alcoholic beverages into the commonwealth from other states and foreign countries for sale to such licensees, or (2) to sell for resale wines and malt beverages so manufactured to such licensees and to import as aforesaid wines and malt beverages for sale to such licensees. Licenses may be granted under this section authorizing the holders (a) to sell wines to be used for sacramental purposes only, to any registered, regularly ordained priest, minister or rabbi, or to any church or religious society, (b) to sell alcoholic beverages to registered pharmacists holding certificates of fitness under section thirty, (c) to sell alcoholic beverages as authorized by section twenty-eight, or (d) to sell alcohol for use in the manufacture or preparation of articles mentioned in section thirty-five of chapter one hundred and twelve, or to sell alcoholic beverages for any or all the purposes specified in this section. Importations of beverages by any licensee under this section may be in casks, barrels, kegs or other containers, as well as in bottles, in either case bearing such seals, or other evidences of the identity and origin of the contents, as the commission may prescribe. Subject to such regulations as may be prescribed by the commission, licensees under this section may bottle, and may rectify or blend, any alcoholic beverages purchased by them in bulk, but such bottling, including the sealing and labelling of the bottles, and such rectifying and blending, shall be done only upon such premises and under such conditions as the commission shall approve. No person, firm, corporation, association or other combination of persons, directly or indirectly, or through any agent, employee, stockholder, officer or other person, or any subsidiary whatsoever, shall be granted more than one license throughout the commonwealth under this section. The license fee for a license issued under this sec- Fee. tion to sell and import all alcoholic beverages shall be not less than two thousand nor more than five thousand dollars. The license fee for a license issued under this section to sell and import wines and malt beverages only shall be not less than five hundred nor more than twenty-five hundred dollars; provided that the license fee for a license issued under this section to sell wines for sacramental use only shall not be less than two hundred and fifty nor more than one thousand dollars.

Nothing contained in this section shall prevent the holder of a wholesaler's and importer's license from selling such alcoholic beverages as he is licensed to sell hereunder, for export from this commonwealth into any state where the sale of the same is not by law prohibited and into any foreign country. Such a holder may also hold licenses under section fifteen, notwithstanding the provisions of section twenty-five.

In order to ensure the necessary control of traffic in alcoholic beverages for the preservation of the public peace and order, the shipment of such beverages into the commonwealth, except as provided in this section, is hereby prohibited.

MANUFACTURE OF ALCOHOLIC BEVERAGES.

Section 19. The commission may issue to individuals, Licenses to manufacture. and to partnerships composed solely of individuals, who are both citizens and residents of the commonwealth, and to corporations organized under the laws of this commonwealth or of any other state of the United States admitted to do business in this commonwealth, licenses to manufacture alcoholic beverages. Manufacturers of such beverages may sell the same to any licensee holding a valid license granted by the licensing authorities for the sale within the commonwealth in accordance with the provisions of this chapter, and may also sell such beverages for export from this commonwealth into any state where the sale of the same is not by law prohibited, and into any foreign country; and manufacturers of such beverages may sell the same to any registered pharmacist holding a certificate of fitness under section thirty and also as authorized by section twenty-eight.

Licensees
may rectify,
etc., alcoholic
beverages.

Subject to such regulations as may be prescribed by the commission, licensees under this section may rectify or blend, but only upon such premises and under such conditions as the commission shall approve, alcoholic beverages manufactured by them. All alcoholic beverages sold by any manufacturer thereof shall be sold and delivered in such manner, and under such conditions, and with such labels or other marks to identify the manufacturer, as the commission shall from time to time prescribe by regulations; provided, that sales of such beverages may be made in kegs, casks, barrels or bottles, to holders of wholesalers' and importers' licenses; and provided, further, that sale of wines and malt beverages may be made in kegs, casks or barrels by any manufacturer or holder of a wholesaler's and importer's license to any common victualler, innholder, club, tavern, railroad, car corporation or the owner or operator of any vessel or shipping company carrying passengers, licensed by the local licensing authorities or commission to sell all alcoholic beverages or wines and malt beverages only to be drunk on the premises, if the nature and extent of the licensed business of the restaurant, hotel, club, tavern, railroad, car corporation, vessel or shipping company is, in respect to the sale of such beverages, in the judgment of the commission, such as to justify the sale by such licensee of wines and malt beverages by draft under such conditions as the commission may from time to time by regulation prescribe.

Licensees to
keep records.

Every licensed manufacturer of alcoholic beverages shall keep such records in such detail and affording such information as the commission may from time to time prescribe, and shall file with the commission, whenever and as often as it may require, duplicates of copies of such records; and the commission shall at all times, through its designated officers or agents, have access to all books, records and other documents of every licensed manufacturer relating to the business which he is licensed hereunder to conduct.

Fee.

The license fee for each manufacturer of alcoholic beverages, in respect of each plant, shall be such sum, not less than two thousand nor more than five thousand dollars, as under the circumstances of the licensee's probable volume of sales under this section, the capacity of his plant and the location thereof, the commission shall deem just and proper.

STORAGE PERMITS FOR MANUFACTURERS, WHOLESALERS AND IMPORTERS.

Storage
permits.

Section 20. The commission may grant to any holder of a manufacturer's or wholesaler's and importer's license under this chapter a permit to store alcoholic beverages in any city or town; provided, that there shall not be granted to such manufacturer or wholesaler and importer, in the aggregate, more than three such permits in the commonwealth nor more than one such permit in any city or town. A permit so granted to the holder of such a license shall authorize him to transport such beverages between any premises covered by such license and any place of storage for which he has such a permit and also between one such place of storage and another. The commission may make and enforce rules and regulations governing the storage and transportation of beverages under such permits and establish annual fees therefor not to exceed five hundred dollars for any one permit.

Commission to make rules, etc.

ADDITIONAL EXCISE FOR PRIVILEGE OF MANUFACTURING AND SELLING, OR IMPORTING AND SELLING, ALCOHOLIC BEVERAGES.

Section 21. Every licensed manufacturer of alcoholic beverages and every holder of a wholesaler's and importer's license for the sale thereof shall, in addition to the license fees elsewhere provided in this chapter, be liable for and pay to the commonwealth as an excise, for the privilege enjoyed by him as such manufacturer or wholesaler and importer, the sum of forty cents for each proof gallon of all alcoholic beverages containing in excess of twenty-four per cent of alcohol by volume, the sum of ten cents for each gallon of wine, including vermouth, and the sum of one dollar for each barrel of thirty-one gallons of malt beverages, sold within the commonwealth, or a proportionate amount when any other form of container is used. Every person subject to this section shall keep a true and accurate account of all alcoholic beverages sold by him and shall make a return thereof to the commissioner of corporations and taxation, hereinafter called the commissioner, within ten days after the last day of each month, covering his sales during such month, and shall at the time of such return make payment to the commissioner of the amount due under this section for such sales in such month. The commissioner is hereby authorized to prescribe rules and regulations governing the method of keeping accounts, making returns and paying the excise provided for in this section. Such rules and regulations shall provide for the waiver of payment of the excise in respect to any alcoholic beverages if it appears. that an excise has already been paid under the provisions of this section in respect thereto; provided, however, that alcoholic beverages manufactured within or imported into the commonwealth and exported therefrom shall be exempt from such excise tax.

Excise.

Returns to be made by licensees.

Rules, etc.

Sums due to the commonwealth under this section may be recovered by the attorney general in an action brought in the name of the commissioner. The commission may suspend the license of a person subject to this section, at the suggestion of the commissioner, for failure to pay such sums when due. The commissioner shall have the same powers and remedies with respect to the collection of said

sums as he has with respect to the collection of income
taxes under chapter sixty-two.

TRANSPORTATION.

Transporta-
tion permits.
Exceptions.

Section 22. Any person may, but only for his own use
and that of his family and guests, transport in packages as
purchased alcoholic beverages, without any license or permit, but not exceeding in amount, at any one time, one
gallon of alcoholic beverages other than wines or malt
beverages, three gallons of wines and eight gallons of malt
beverages, or their measured equivalents; provided, that
any person may, without any license or permit, transport
from his place of residence to a new place of residence
established by him, wines manufactured by him for his
own private use. Licensees for the sale of alcoholic beverages may transport and deliver anywhere in the commonwealth alcoholic beverages lawfully bought by or lawfully
sold by them, in vehicles operated under the control of themselves or of their employees; provided, that the owner of
every such vehicle shall have obtained for such vehicle
from the commission a vehicle permit for the transportation

Fee.

of alcoholic beverages. The fee for each vehicle permit
shall be one dollar for each vehicle. Copies of such permits shall be furnished by the commission for one dollar
each. All permits issued under this section shall expire
on the thirty-first day of December of the year of issue
unless earlier suspended or revoked by the commission.
Every person operating such a vehicle when engaged in
such transportation or delivery shall carry the vehicle permit or a copy thereof for each vehicle operated by him and
shall, upon demand of any constable, policeman, member
of the state police, or any inspector of the commission or
of the registry of motor vehicles, produce such permit or
copy for inspection; and failure to produce such permit or
copy shall constitute prima facie evidence of unlawful
transportation and shall in the discretion of the commission
be sufficient cause for the suspension or revocation of such
permit. Except as herein provided, alcoholic beverages
may be transported within the commonwealth only by a
railroad or steamboat corporation, or an individual or
corporation regularly and lawfully conducting a general
express or trucking business, and in each case holding a
transportation permit in full force and effect issued by the
commission and valid for one year unless earlier suspended
or revoked. The fee for each such transportation permit
shall be five dollars, and each vehicle other than a railroad
car, used in the transportation of alcoholic beverages under
such transportation permit shall carry a certified copy
thereof. Each certified copy shall be issued by the commission for a fee of one dollar; provided, that the transportation fee payable by a railroad or steamship company
covering all the cars or vessels thereof, shall be one hun-

Penalty.

dred dollars. Whoever knowingly transports within the

commonwealth any alcoholic beverages except as authorized by this section shall be punished by a fine not exceeding two hundred dollars or by imprisonment for not more than six months, or both.

GENERAL PROVISIONS AS TO LICENSES AND PERMITS.

Section 23. The terms licenses and permits, wherever employed as substantives in this chapter, are used in their technical sense of a license or permit revocable at pleasure and without any assignment of reasons therefor by the licensor, the commonwealth, acting through the same officers or agents and under the same delegated authority, as authorized the issue of such licenses. The provisions for the issue of licenses and permits hereunder imply no intention to create rights generally for persons to engage or continue in the transaction of the business authorized by the licenses or permits respectively, but are enacted with a view only to meet the reasonable demand of the public for pure alcoholic beverages and, to that end, to provide, in the opinion of the local licensing authorities, an adequate number of places at which the public may obtain, in the manner and for the kind of use indicated, the different sorts of beverages for the sale of which provision is made. *Terms licenses and permits.*

No holder of such a license or permit hereunder shall have any property right in any document or paper evidencing the granting of such license or permit and issued by the licensing authorities, and said authorities, upon the expiration, suspension, revocation, cancellation or forfeiture of such a license or permit shall be entitled to the immediate possession thereof. The superior court shall have jurisdiction in equity, on petition of the licensing authorities, to enforce this provision.

No such licensee or permittee shall have any vested or monetary right in the continuance of his license or permit. Whenever it appears by sale of premises in connection with which a license has been issued, by probate or bankruptcy proceedings, or otherwise, that such license has acquired any monetary value in excess of the license fee, the licensing authorities may increase the amount of the license fee correspondingly, notwithstanding any maximum limitation herein upon fees for that class of licenses, or may take other action deemed by them appropriate to divest the license of such monetary value or to make such value inure to the benefit of the city or town instead of the licensee or his estate or his assigns.

Whenever it shall appear to the local licensing authorities that the nature of the business, or of the equipment of and service of any hotel, restaurant, club or tavern no longer satisfies the definition thereof contained in this chapter, or that alcoholic beverages are being or have been sold and served therein over, and drunk by customers standing at, a bar or counter, instead of being drunk sitting at tables or at counters equipped with stools in dining or *Cancellation of licenses, etc.*

other rooms or quarters as contemplated by or authorized under the provisions of this chapter, it shall be the duty of the local licensing authorities forthwith to cancel the license of such hotel, restaurant, club or tavern. All licenses and permits granted under this chapter, unless otherwise provided therein, shall expire on the thirty-first day of December of the year of issue, subject, however, to cancellation or revocation within such term; provided, that the licensing authorities may, when first issuing licenses under this chapter, provide that they shall be temporary only for such less period than the period ending the thirty-first day of December in the year nineteen hundred and thirty-four as the licensing authorities may determine in order to enable said authorities to make such further and more complete investigation of the fitness of applicants to whom such temporary licenses are issued, as to the premises in which the licensee's business is to be conducted, and for any other purposes deemed by the licensing authorities material.

Licenses, etc., to expire, when.

Temporary licenses.

The provisions of sections twelve and fifteen requiring the prior approval of the commission to the granting of licenses thereunder shall not apply to licenses first granted under said sections; but no such license not approved by the commission on or before the first day of June, nineteen hundred and thirty-four, shall be valid after said date until so approved, and if disapproved by the commission prior to said date shall thereupon become void. The fee for licenses first granted under said sections, if for the entire calendar year nineteen hundred and thirty-four and for any additional period prior to January first of said year, shall not be increased by reason of said additional period.

REGULATIONS.

Commission to make regulations.

Section 24. The commission shall, with the approval of the governor and council, make regulations not inconsistent with the provisions of this chapter for clarifying, carrying out, enforcing and preventing violation of, all and any of its provisions, for inspection of the premises and method of carrying on the business of any licensee, for insuring the purity, and penalizing the adulteration, or in any way changing the quality or content, of any alcoholic beverage, for the proper and orderly conduct of the licensed business, for establishing maximum prices chargeable by licensees under this chapter, and regulating all advertising of alcoholic beverages. Every such regulation, when so approved, shall be printed in full in one issue of some newspaper of general circulation published on the same day in each of the cities of Boston, New Bedford, Lowell, Worcester, Springfield and Pittsfield and copies of such regulations shall be furnished to each licensee. Fourteen days from and after the date of such publication, any such regulation made and approved as aforesaid shall have the force and

Regulations to be published.

effect of law unless and until amended or annulled by the commission with the approval of the governor and council.

The commission shall, at least annually on or before December thirty-first of each year, publish in a convenient pamphlet form all regulations then in force, and shall furnish copies of such pamphlets to every licensee authorized under the provisions of this chapter to sell alcoholic beverages.

Section 25. It shall be unlawful for any licensee under section twelve or fifteen to lend or borrow money or receive credit, directly or indirectly, to or from any manufacturer, wholesaler or importer of alcoholic beverages, and for any such manufacturer, wholesaler or importer to lend money or otherwise extend credit except in the usual course of business and for a period not exceeding ninety days, directly or indirectly, to any such licensee, or to acquire, retain or own, directly or indirectly, any interest in the business of any such licensee. The commission may revoke the license of any licensee who in its opinion is violating this section or participating in such a violation. _{*Lending, etc., money by licensees restricted.*}

Nothing in this chapter shall prevent a person holding any interest in a business licensed under section nineteen from holding at the same time any interest in not more than one business licensed under section eighteen.

ALIENS.

Section 26. No license for the sale of alcoholic beverages and no vehicle permit for the transportation thereof shall be issued to any person who is not, at the time of his application therefor, a citizen of the United States, or to any agent of any such person, or to any corporation a majority of whose directors are in fact aliens, and no person not such a citizen shall be appointed as manager or other principal representative of any licensee. _{*Licenses, etc., not to be issued to aliens.*}

No corporation, organized under the laws of the commonwealth or of any other state or foreign country, shall be given a license to sell in any manner any alcoholic beverages unless such corporation shall have first appointed, in such manner as the licensing authorities by regulation prescribe, as manager or other principal representative, a citizen of the United States, and shall have vested in him by properly authorized and executed written delegation as full authority and control of the premises, described in the license of such corporation, and of the conduct of all business therein relative to alcoholic beverages as the licensee itself could in any way have and exercise if it were a natural person resident in the commonwealth, nor unless such manager or representative is, with respect to his character, satisfactory to the licensing authorities. _{*Foreign corporations to appoint local representative.*}

No provision of this chapter shall impair any right growing out of any treaty to which the United States is a party.

Certain receipts from licenses, etc., to be used for assistance to certain aged persons.

Section 27. All moneys received by the commission and by the commissioner of corporations and taxation under this chapter shall be paid into the treasury of the commonwealth and, after the expenses of the commission have been paid, used so far as necessary, for reimbursing cities and towns for assistance given by them to aged citizens under the provisions of chapter one hundred and eighteen A, in the manner provided by section three of said chapter, and all moneys so received by local licensing authorities shall be paid monthly into the treasuries of their respective cities and towns.

Sales to certain religious, etc., societies authorized.

Section 28. The holder of a license under section eighteen or nineteen may sell alcoholic beverages to churches and religious societies, educational institutions licensed under section fourteen, incorporated hospitals and homes for aged people whose real or personal property is exempt from taxation under the laws of the commonwealth, in such quantities and subject to such restrictions as the commission may by regulation prescribe. The holder of such a license may also sell and deliver such beverages to any person on any federal or state military or naval reservation authorized by the commanding officer thereof to purchase and receive the same.

DRUGGISTS.

Sales by druggists authorized.

Section 29. A registered pharmacist in a city or town who holds a certificate of fitness under the following section, having complied with all provisions of law relative to the practice of pharmacy, irrespective of the vote of the city or town under section eleven, may use alcohol for the manufacture of United States pharmacopœia or national formulary preparations and all medicinal preparations unfit for beverage purposes, and may sell alcohol, and, upon the prescription of a registered physician, (1) alcoholic liquors other than wines and malt beverages, (2) malt beverages, and (3) wines. Each of the three foregoing classes shall be sold only on separate prescriptions and in quantity not exceeding one quart of such alcoholic liquors, one gallon of wines and one gallon of malt beverages. Every such prescription shall be dated and signed by the physician and shall contain the name of the person prescribed for.

All such prescriptions shall be retained and kept on file in a separate book by the pharmacist selling the same and shall not be refilled. Such prescription book shall be open at all times to inspection of the board of registration in pharmacy, local licensing authorities and police officers. Nothing in this chapter shall disqualify a registered pharmacist from being licensed under section fifteen, provided that he sells no cooked food to be consumed on the premises; but a license issued to a druggist under said section shall not be included in computing the number of licenses that may be granted in any city or town as provided in sec-

tion seventeen. The words "alcoholic liquor" and "alcoholic liquors", as used in this and the eight following
sections, are hereby defined to mean any liquor intended for
human consumption and containing one half of one per cent
or more of alcohol by volume at sixty degrees Fahrenheit.

All alcoholic liquors sold under authority of this section
shall be sold in the original sealed packages only.

Section 30. The board of registration in pharmacy may,
upon the payment of a fee of not more than five dollars
by a registered pharmacist who desires. to exercise the
authority conferred by section twenty-nine, issue to him a
certificate of fitness, which shall not be valid after one year
from its date, stating that in the judgment of said board he
is a proper person to be intrusted with such authority and
that the public good will be promoted by the granting
thereof. The board and the local licensing authorities
may, after giving a hearing to the parties interested, revoke or suspend such certificate for any cause which they
may deem proper, and such revocation or suspension shall
revoke or suspend all authority conferred by section
twenty-nine.

Section 30A. A registered pharmacist in a city or town
wherein the granting of licenses to sell all alcoholic beverages is authorized may be licensed by local licensing authorities to sell alcoholic liquors for medicinal, mechanical or
chemical purposes without a physician's prescription, except
on Sundays or legal holidays or on any day on which a
state or municipal election, caucus or primary is held in
the city or town in which such pharmacist is licensed, the
said sales to be recorded in the manner prescribed in section
thirty E. The fee for such license shall be not less than fifty
dollars nor more than three hundred dollars.

Section 30B. No license for the sale of alcoholic liquors,
except as provided in the preceding section or as permitted
in section twenty-nine, shall be granted to retail druggists.
One or more licenses may be granted annually under the
provisions of section thirty A by the licensing authorities
of a city or town to retail druggists who are registered
pharmacists actively engaged in business on their own
account, or on the account of the widow, executor or administrator of a deceased registered pharmacist, or of the
wife of one who has become incapacitated, upon presentation to said authorities of the certificate prescribed by section thirty, if it appears that the applicant is a proper
person to receive such license. A registered pharmacist
who owns stock of the actual value of at least five hundred
dollars in a corporation which has been incorporated for
the purpose of carrying on the drug business, and who
conducts in person the business of a store of such corporation, shall be considered as actively engaged in business on
his own account and as qualified to receive a license for
such store. The licensing authorities may refuse to grant
any and all such licenses.

Termination
of license.

Section 30C. A license issued under section thirty A shall become null and void without any process or decree, if the registered pharmacist to whom it has been granted ceases to conduct his business in person and on his own account, or upon the revocation of his certificate of registration as a pharmacist, unless the registered pharmacist has been unable to so conduct his business or has died, and his business is continued by his wife, widow, executor or administrator under another registered pharmacist.

Sales for
certain
purposes
restricted.

Section 30D. Retail pharmacists licensed under section thirty A shall not sell alcoholic liquor of any kind for medicinal, mechanical or chemical purposes except upon the certificate of the purchaser, which shall state the use for which it is wanted, and which shall be immediately cancelled at the time of sale in such manner as to show the date of cancellation.

Record book
for sales of
alcoholic
beverages.

Section 30E. Every retail pharmacist licensed under section thirty A shall keep a book in which he shall enter, at the time of every such sale, the date thereof, the name of the purchaser, the kind, quantity and price of said liquor, the purpose for which it was sold, and the residence by street and number, if any, of said purchaser. If such sale is made upon the prescription of a physician, the book shall also contain the name of the physician and shall state the use for which said liquor is prescribed and the quantity to be used for such purpose, and the prescription shall be cancelled in the manner provided in the preceding section with reference to certificates. Said book shall be in form substantially as follows:

Date.	Name of Purchaser.	Residence.	Kind and Quantity.	Purpose of Use.	Price.	Name of Physician.

Certificate.

The certificate mentioned in the preceding section shall be a part of said book and shall not be detached therefrom, and shall be in form substantially as follows:

Certificate.

I wish to purchase   and I certify that I am not a minor and that the same is to be used for *Mechanical *Chemical *Medicinal purposes.

(* Draw a line through the words which do not indicate the purpose of the purchase.)

Signature

Cancelled

Books, etc.,
to be open
for in-
spection.

Section 30F. The book, certificates and prescriptions provided for in the two preceding sections shall at all times be open to the inspection of the board of registration in pharmacy, the local licensing authorities, to the inspection of the aldermen, selectmen, board of public welfare, sheriffs, constables, police officers and justices of the peace.

Section 30G. A person, not a registered pharmacist, who procures a license for the sale of alcoholic liquors under section thirty A in the name of a registered pharmacist who is dead, or in the name of a registered pharmacist by borrowing, hiring or purchasing the use of his certificate, and, being himself the owner or manager of the place, personally or by his servants sells alcoholic liquors, shall be punished by a fine of not less than fifty nor more than five hundred dollars and by imprisonment for not less than one nor more than six months. Section eleven of chapter two hundred and seventy-nine shall not apply to a conviction under this section. *Penalty for illegal sale of alcoholic beverages in name of pharmacist.*

Section 31. No person, except a citizen of the United States, shall be employed to sell, serve or deliver any alcoholic beverage. Violation of any provision of this section shall be punished by a fine of not less than twenty-five dollars, and shall be sufficient cause for the revocation or suspension of the license of any licensee under this chapter contributing to or aiding or abetting such violation. *Employment of aliens by licensees prohibited.*

Section 32. No holder of a license or permit under this chapter shall himself or through an agent or employee go from town to town or from place to place in the same town selling, bartering, hawking or peddling, or exposing or carrying for sale, barter, hawking or peddling, any alcoholic beverages from a vehicle. All sales of such beverages under section fifteen of this chapter, where transportation and delivery are required, shall be made only upon orders actually received at the licensed place of business prior to the shipment thereof. Violation of this section shall be punished by a fine not exceeding two hundred dollars or by imprisonment for not more than six months, or both. *Peddling, etc., of alcoholic beverages prohibited.* *Penalty.*

Section 33. No licensee for the sale of alcoholic beverages not to be drunk on the premises shall sell or deliver any such beverages on Sundays or legal holidays, nor shall such licensee sell or deliver any such beverages in any city or town on any day on which a state or municipal election, caucus or primary is held, nor shall there be sold in a tavern any such beverages on Sunday or during polling hours on any day on which such an election, caucus or primary is held in the city or town in which such tavern is conducted. *Sales on Sundays regulated.*

Section 34. No person shall receive a license or permit under this chapter who is under twenty-one years of age. Whoever being licensed under this chapter employs any person under twenty-one years of age in the direct handling or selling of alcoholic beverages or whoever makes a sale of any such beverages to any person under twenty-one years of age shall be punished by a fine of not more than two hundred dollars or by imprisonment for not more than six months, or both. *Employment of minors prohibited.*

Section 35. No rule or regulation made by the metropolitan district commission for the government and use *Certain rules, etc., not to apply to*

licensed
premises.

of the reservations or boulevards under its care shall prohibit or restrict the sale of alcoholic beverages in any building or place outside the limits of said reservations or
boulevards if a license for such sale has been granted
hereunder.

Analysis of
alcoholic
beverages by
department of
public health.

Section 36. The analyst or assistant analyst of the department of public health shall upon request make, free of
charge, an analysis of all alcoholic beverages sent to it by
the licensing authorities or by police officers or other officers
authorized by law to make seizures of alcoholic beverages,
if the department is satisfied that the analysis requested
is to be used in connection with the enforcement of the
laws of the commonwealth. The said department shall
return to such police or other officers, as soon as may be,
a certificate, signed by the analyst or assistant analyst
making such analysis, of the percentage of alcohol which
such samples of beverages contain. Such certificate shall
be prima facie evidence of the composition and quality
of the alcoholic beverages to which it relates, and the
court may take judicial notice of the signature of the
analyst or the assistant analyst, and of the fact that he
is such.

Certificate to
accompany
sample.

Section 37. A certificate shall accompany each sample
of beverages sent for analysis by an officer to the department of public health stating by whom the beverages were
seized, the date of the seizure and the name and residence
of the officer who seized said beverages. Said department
shall note upon said certificate the date of the receipt and
the analysis of said alcoholic beverages and the percentage
of the alcohol, as required by the preceding section. Said
certificate shall be in the following form:

ss.   CITY OF (OR TOWN OF)   19
To the Department of Public Health.

SIRS: — I send you herewith a sample of
taken from alcoholic beverages seized by me
                    (date)   19   .
Ascertain the percentage of alcohol it contains, and
return to me a certificate herewith upon the annexed form.

Constable of
Police Officer of
COMMONWEALTH OF MASSACHUSETTS.
DEPARTMENT OF PUBLIC HEALTH,
BOSTON,   19   .

This is to certify that the   received by this de-
partment with the above statement and analyzed by me
contains   per cent of alcohol.
Received   19   .
Analysis made   19   .
DEPARTMENT OF PUBLIC HEALTH,
By.......................
Analyst.

Section 38. The state secretary shall provide and cause officers to be supplied with a suitable number of the forms prescribed by the preceding section. The certificate of the department of public health, given substantially in the form hereinbefore set forth, shall be admitted as evidence on trials for the forfeiture of alcoholic beverages as to the composition and quality of the beverages to which it relates. *State secretary to provide certain forms.*

Section 39. No person shall tamper with samples of alcoholic beverages taken as provided in section sixty-three or alter the statements made upon the forms or certificates aforesaid. *Tampering with samples forbidden.*

Section 40. Any court or trial justice may cause alcoholic beverages which have been seized under this chapter to be analyzed by a competent chemist, and the reasonable expense thereof, including a fee of not more than five dollars for each analysis, shall be taxed, allowed and paid like other expenses in criminal cases. *Court may order analysis.*

Section 41. The delivery of alcoholic beverages in or from a building, booth, stand or other place, except a private dwelling house, or in or from a private dwelling house if any part thereof or its dependencies is used as an inn, eating house or shop of any kind, or other place of common resort, such delivery in either case being to a person not a resident therein, shall be prima facie evidence that such delivery is a sale. *Delivery of alcoholic beverages prima facie evidence of sale, when.*

Section 42. If two persons of full age make complaint to a district court or trial justice or justice of the peace authorized to issue warrants in criminal cases that they have reason to believe and do believe that alcoholic beverages, described in the complaint, are kept or deposited by a person named therein in a store, shop, warehouse, building, vehicle, steamboat, vessel or place, and are intended for sale contrary to law, such court or justice, if it appears that there is probable cause to believe said complaint to be true, shall issue a search warrant to a sheriff, deputy sheriff, city marshal, chief of police, deputy chief of police, deputy marshal, police officer, including a state police officer, or constable, commanding him to search the premises in which it is alleged that such alcoholic beverages are deposited, and to seize such beverages, the vessels in which they are contained and all implements of sale and furniture used or kept and provided to be used in the illegal keeping or sale of such beverages, and securely keep the same until final action thereon, and return the warrant with his doings thereon, as soon as may be, to a district court or trial justice having jurisdiction in the place in which such beverages are alleged to be kept or deposited. *Search warrant.*

Section 43. A warrant shall not be issued for the search of a dwelling house, if no inn, tavern, store, grocery, eating house or place of common resort is kept therein, unless one of the complainants makes oath that he has evidence that such alcoholic beverages have been sold therein or taken *Search of dwelling house.*

therefrom for the purpose of being sold by the occupant, or by his consent, or permission, contrary to law, within one month next before making such complaint, and are then kept therein for sale contrary to law by the person complained against. Such complainant shall state the facts and circumstances which constitute such evidence, and such allegations shall be recited in the complaint and warrant.

Section 44. The complaint shall particularly designate the building, structure and place to be searched, the alcoholic beverages to be seized, the person by whom they are owned, kept or possessed and intended for sale, and shall allege the intent of such person to sell the same contrary to law. The warrant shall allege that probable cause has been shown for the issuing thereof; and the place to be searched, the alcoholic beverages to be seized, and the person believed to be the owner, possessor, or keeper of such beverages, intending to sell the same contrary to law, shall be designated therein with the same particularity as in the complaint and the complaints shall be summoned to appear as witnesses.

Search of premises and seizure of alcoholic beverages.

Section 45. The officer to whom the warrant is committed shall search the premises and seize the alcoholic beverages described in the warrant, the casks or other vessels in which the same are contained, and all implements of sale and furniture used or kept and provided to be used in the illegal keeping or sale of such beverages, if they are found in or upon said premises, and shall convey the same to some place of security, where he shall keep the beverages and vessels until final action is had thereon.

Penalty for search or seizure without a warrant.

Section 46. A sheriff, deputy sheriff, city marshal, chief of police, deputy chief of police, deputy or assistant marshal, police officer, including a state police officer, or constable who, without a search warrant duly committed to him, searches for or seizes alcoholic beverages in a dwelling shall be punished by a fine of not less than five nor more than one hundred dollars.

Notice to keeper of alcoholic beverages seized.

Section 47. The court or trial justice before whom the warrant is returned shall, within twenty-four hours after the seizure thereunder of the alcoholic beverages and the vessels containing them, issue a notice, under seal, and signed by the justice or the clerk of said court, or by the trial justice, commanding the person complained against as the keeper of the beverages seized and all other persons who claim any interest therein or in the casks or vessels containing the same to appear before said court or trial justice, at a time and place therein named, to answer to said complaint and show cause why such beverages and the vessels containing them should not be forfeited.

Form and service of notice.

Section 48. The notice shall contain a description of the number and kind of vessels, the quantity and kind of alcoholic beverages seized, as nearly as may be, and shall state when and where they were seized. It shall, not less than fourteen days before the time appointed for the trial, be served by a sheriff, deputy sheriff, constable or police officer upon the person charged with being the keeper thereof by leaving an attested copy thereof with him personally or at his usual place of abode, if he is an inhabitant of the commonwealth, and by posting an attested copy on the building in which the beverages were seized, if they were found in a building; otherwise in a public place in the city or town in which the beverages were seized.

Section 49. If, at the time appointed for trial, said notice has not been duly served, or other sufficient cause appears, the trial may be postponed to some other day and place, and such further notice issued as shall supply any defect in the previous notice; and time and opportunity for trial and defence shall be given to persons interested. _{Postponement of trial.}

Section 50. At the time and place designated in the notice, the person complained against, or any person claiming an interest in the alcoholic beverages and vessel seized, or any part thereof, may appear and make his claim verbally or in writing, and a record of his appearance and claim shall be made, and he shall be admitted as a party to the trial. Whether a claim as aforesaid is made or not, the court or trial justice shall proceed to try, hear and determine the allegations of such complaint, and whether said beverages and vessels, or any part thereof, are forfeited. If it appears that the beverages, or any part thereof, were at the time of making the complaint owned or kept by the person alleged therein for the purpose of being sold in violation of law, the court or trial justice shall render judgment that such and so much of the beverages so seized as were so unlawfully kept, and the vessels in which they are contained, shall, except as hereinafter provided, be forfeited to the commonwealth. If a motor vehicle is seized under the provisions of this chapter and is held to be a container or implement of sale of alcoholic beverages contrary to law, the court or trial justice shall, unless good cause to the contrary is shown, order a sale of such motor vehicle by public auction and the officer making the sale, after deducting the expense of keeping the motor vehicle, the fee for the seizure and the cost of the sale, shall pay all liens, according to their priorities, which are established, by intervention or otherwise, at said trial or in other proceedings brought for said purpose, as being bona fide and as having been created without the lienor having any notice that such motor vehicle was being used or was to be used as a container or implement of sale of alcoholic beverages contrary to law. The balance, if any, of the proceeds of the sale shall be forfeited to the commonwealth and shall be paid by said officer into its treasury. All liens against any motor vehicle sold under the provisions of this section shall be transferred from said motor vehicle to the proceeds of its sale. _{Claimant of alcoholic beverages may be admitted as a party.}

Section 51. Any beverages and vessels so forfeited shall, by authority of the written order of the court or trial _{Disposition of forfeited alcoholic beverages, etc.}

justice, be forwarded to the commissioner of public safety, who upon receipt of the same shall notify said court or justice thereof. If, in the judgment of the commissioner, it is for the best interests of the commonwealth that such beverages and vessels be destroyed, he shall destroy or cause the destruction of such beverages and vessels, but if in his judgment it is for the best interests of the commonwealth to sell the same, he shall cause the same to be sold, or he may deliver such alcoholic beverages to any department or agency of the commonwealth for medical, mechanical or scientific uses. The proceeds of such sales shall be paid into the treasury of the commonwealth. The officer who serves said order of the court or justice shall be allowed therefor fifty cents, but shall not be entitled to receive any traveling fees or mileage on account of the service thereof.

Alcoholic beverages not forfeited to be returned.

Section 52. If it is not proved on the trial that all or part of the beverages seized was kept or deposited for sale contrary to law, the court or trial justice shall issue a written order to the officer having the same in custody to return so much thereof as was not proved to be so kept or deposited and the vessels in which it is contained, to the place as nearly as may be from which it was taken, or to deliver it to the person entitled to receive it. After executing such order, the officer shall return it to the court or trial justice with his doings endorsed thereon.

Forfeiture of furniture, etc.

Section 53. All implements of sale and furniture seized under sections forty-two and forty-five shall be forfeited and disposed of in the manner provided for the forfeiture and disposition of alcoholic beverages; but the court or trial justice may, if it is deemed to be for the interest of the commonwealth, order the destruction or sale of said property by any officer qualified to serve criminal process and the proceeds of a sale thereof shall be paid over to the county; and said officer shall make return of the order for such destruction or sale and his doings thereon to the court or justice issuing the same. The provisions of this section shall not apply to a motor vehicle if seized and held to be an implement of sale as aforesaid, but the disposition of such a motor vehicle shall be governed by the provisions of section fifty.

Section 54. If no person appears and is admitted as a party as aforesaid, or if judgment is rendered in favor of all the claimants who appear, the cost of the proceedings shall be paid as in other criminal cases. If only one party appearing fails to sustain his claim, he shall pay all the costs except the expense of seizing and keeping the beverages, and an execution shall be issued against him therefor. If judgment is rendered against two or more claimants of distinct interest in the beverages, the cost shall, according to the discretion of the court or trial justice, be apportioned among such parties, and executions shall be issued against them severally. If such execution is not forthwith paid, the defendant therein named shall be committed to jail, and shall not be discharged therefrom until he has paid the same and the costs of commitment, or until he has been imprisoned thirty days.

Section 55. A claimant whose claim is not allowed as aforesaid, and the person complained against, shall each have the same right of appeal to the superior court as if he had been convicted of crime; but before his appeal is allowed he shall recognize to the commonwealth in the sum of two hundred dollars, with sufficient surety or sureties, to prosecute his appeal to the superior court and to abide the sentence of the court thereon. Upon such appeal, any question of fact shall be tried by a jury. On the judgment of the court after verdict, whether a forfeiture of the whole or any part of the alcoholic beverages and vessels seized, or otherwise, similar proceedings shall be had as are directed in the five preceding sections. *Appeal.*

Section 56. A deputy sheriff, chief of police, deputy chief of police, city marshal, deputy or assistant marshal, police officer, including a state police officer, or constable, or, in the county of Dukes or Nantucket, the sheriff anywhere within his county, or any inspector of the commission, may without a warrant arrest any person whom he finds in the act of illegally transporting or delivering alcoholic beverages, and seize the said beverages, vessels and implements of sale in the possession of such person, and detain them until warrants can be procured against such person, and for the seizure of said beverages, vessels and implements, under this chapter. Such officers shall enforce or cause to be enforced the penalties provided by law against every person who is guilty of a violation of any law relative to the sale of alcoholic beverages of which they can obtain reasonable proof. *Arrest without warrant in certain cases.*

Section 57. Upon the conviction of a holder of a license or permit under this chapter of the violation of any law relative to the business he is licensed or permitted to pursue, the court in which he has been convicted shall send to the authorities which issued the license or permit a certificate under seal, showing the time and place of such conviction. *Licensing authorities to be notified of conviction.*

Section 58. Upon the conviction of a person of the illegal keeping or sale of alcoholic beverages, the court wherein he has been convicted shall issue and cause to be served upon the owner of the building, or agent of such owner in charge of the building, used for such illegal keeping or sale, if he resides within the commonwealth and is not the person so convicted, a written notice that the tenant of said building has been convicted as aforesaid; and a return thereof shall be made to the court or magistrate issuing it. Such notice, so served, shall be deemed to be due and sufficient notice under section twenty of chapter one hundred and thirty-nine.

Section 59. The forms heretofore in use may continue to be used in prosecutions under this chapter, and if sub- *Forms for prosecution.*

stantially followed shall be deemed sufficient to fully and plainly, substantially and formally describe the several offences in each of them set forth, and to authorize the lawful doings of the officers acting by virtue of the warrants issued in substantial conformity therewith; but this section shall not exclude the use of other suitable forms.

Section 60. All alcoholic beverages which are kept for sale contrary to law and the implements and vessels actually used in selling and keeping the same are declared to be common nuisances.

Section 61. All buildings or places used by clubs for the purpose of selling, distributing or dispensing alcoholic beverages to their members or others shall be deemed common nuisances unless duly licensed under this chapter. Whoever keeps or maintains, or assists in keeping or maintaining, such a common nuisance shall be punished by a fine of not less than fifty nor more than five hundred dollars or by imprisonment for not less than three months nor more than one year, or both.

Section 62. A violation by any person of any provision of this chapter for which a specific penalty is not provided or a violation by a licensee of any provision of his license or of any regulation made under authority of this chapter shall be punished by a fine of not less than fifty nor more than five hundred dollars or by imprisonment for not less than one month nor more than one year, or both.

Section 63. The licensing authorities or their agents may at any time enter upon the premises of a person who is licensed by them under this chapter to ascertain the manner in which such person conducts his business. Such licensing authorities or their agents may at any time take samples for analysis from any beverages kept on such premises, and the vessel or vessels containing such samples shall be sealed on the premises by the seal of the vendor, and shall remain so sealed until presented to the state department of public health for analysis and duplicate samples shall be left with the dealer.

Section 63A. Any person who hinders or delays any authorized inspector in the performance of his duties, or who refuses to admit to or locks out any such inspector from any place which such inspector is authorized to inspect, or who refuses to give to such inspector such information as may be required for the proper enforcement of this chapter, shall be punished by a fine of not less than fifty nor more than two hundred dollars or by imprisonment for not more than two months, or both.

Section 64. The local licensing authorities after notice to the licensee and reasonable opportunity for him to be heard by them, may declare his license forfeited, or may suspend his license for such period of time as they may deem proper, upon satisfactory proof that he has violated or permitted a violation of any condition thereof, or any law of the commonwealth. If the license is declared to have been forfeited, the licensee shall be disqualified to receive a license for one year after the expiration of the term of the license so forfeited, and if he is the owner of the premises described in such forfeited license, no license shall be issued to be exercised on said premises for the residue of the term thereof.

Section 65. Upon revocation, forfeiture or suspension by the licensing authorities of a license or permit granted under this chapter, the holder thereof shall forthwith deliver the same to such authorities. Refusal so to deliver, or failure so to do for seven days following a request therefor by such authorities, shall be punished by a fine of not more than one hundred dollars or by imprisonment for not more than three months, or both. *Licensee to deliver license upon revocation, etc.* *Penalty.*

Section 66. In respect to their constitutionality, all the provisions of this chapter are hereby declared to be separable. *Constitutionality.*

Section 67. Any applicant for a license who is aggrieved by the action of the local licensing authorities in refusing to grant the same or by their failure to act within the period of thirty days limited by section sixteen B, or any one who is aggrieved by the action of such authorities in suspending, cancelling, revoking or declaring forfeited the same, may appeal therefrom to the commission within five days following notice of such action or the expiration of said period, and the decision of the commission shall be final; but pending a decision on the appeal, the action of the local licensing authorities shall have the same force and effect as if the appeal had not been taken. Upon the petition of twenty-five persons who are taxpayers of the city or town in which a license has been granted by such authorities or registered voters in the voting precinct or district wherein the licensed premises are situated, or upon its own initiative, the commission may investigate the granting of such license and may, after a hearing, revoke or modify such license if, in its opinion, circumstances warrant. *Appeal on refusals, etc., to grant license.*

If the local licensing authorities fail to grant a license or to perform any other act when lawfully ordered so to do by the commission upon appeal or otherwise, within such time as it may prescribe, the commission may itself issue such license or perform such act, with the same force and effect as if granted or performed by the local licensing authorities.

SALES TO BE PROHIBITED IN TIMES OF RIOT.

Section 68. The mayor of a city and the selectmen of a town may, in cases of riot or great public excitement, order licensees under this chapter not to sell, give away or deliver any alcoholic beverages on the licensed premises for a period not exceeding three days at any one time. Whoever, himself or by his agents or servants, sells, gives away *Regulation of sales in times of riot, etc.*

or delivers any such beverages in violation of an order given under the provisions of this section shall be punished by a fine of two hundred dollars, and upon conviction, his license shall be revoked by the licensing authority.

Sales to drunkards, etc., prohibited.

Section 69. No alcoholic beverage shall be sold or delivered on any premises licensed under this chapter to a person who is known to be a drunkard, to an intoxicated person, or to a person who is known to have been intoxicated within the six months last preceding, or to a person known to be supported in whole or in part by public charity.

License not to be issued until fee is paid.

Section 70. No license, except special licenses issued under section fourteen, shall be granted under this chapter unless the license fee has been paid to the licensing authorities nor unless the applicant shall have filed with such authorities a bond running to the commonwealth or the city or town, as the case may be, in a penal sum and form approved by the commission signed by the applicant and with a surety company authorized to do business in the commonwealth as surety, conditioned upon performance by the licensee of all the conditions of the license and observance of all the provisions of this chapter. Permits issued under section twenty shall be deemed licenses for the purpose of this section.

Rules, etc., to take effect, when.

Section 71. All rules and regulations made under the provisions of this chapter by the commission or by the commissioner of corporations and taxation shall not take effect until approved by the governor and council.

License to sell, etc., methyl, etc., alcohol.

Section 72. The board of health of a city or town may annually grant to persons who apply therefor licenses for the sale or dealing therein, within such city or town, of methyl alcohol or wood alcohol, so called, or denatured alcohol, or any preparation used for manufacturing or commercial purposes which contains more than three per cent of any of the said alcohols, and is intended for use other than as a beverage. The fee for such a license shall be one dollar. A registered pharmacist may make such sales without such a license. The state department of public health may annually grant to persons who apply therefor licenses for the manufacture, sale or dealing therein, within the commonwealth, and for the importation into and exportation from the commonwealth, of any of such alcohols or preparations, the fee for which shall be one hundred dollars. Licenses shall be granted under this section only if it appears that the applicant is a proper person to receive the same.

Form of label on containers of wood alcohol, etc.

Section 73. Every barrel or keg containing methyl alcohol or wood alcohol, so called, or denatured alcohol containing methyl alcohol, or any drug or medicine intended for external use containing methyl alcohol, shall bear in capital letters not less than three fourths nor more than one and one half inches in height, stencilled thereon or printed upon a label affixed thereto, the words "POISON, NOT

FOR INTERNAL USE". Every other container of any such alcohol, drug or medicine shall bear a label of white paper on which shall be printed in red capital letters not less than one fourth of an inch in height, the words "DEADLY POISON", the name and place of business of the vendor, and the statement that he is a registered pharmacist or the holder of a license under the preceding section, together with number of his license, and, in legible type, the words "NOT FOR INTERNAL USE, CAUSES BLINDNESS. KEEP FROM THE EYES'. Whoever, *Penalty.* himself or by his servant or agent, sells, exchanges or delivers any such alcohol, drug or medicine in any container not conforming to this section shall be punished by a fine of not less than fifty nor more than two hundred dollars.

Section 74. The sale of methyl alcohol, wood alcohol, *Offence of unlawful sale of wood alcohol, etc.* so called, denatured alcohol, or any preparation containing alcohol as described in section seventy-two by a person not a registered pharmacist or not licensed under said section or by a licensee or registered pharmacist to a person under sixteen years of age or to any person without reasonable investigation and inquiry to determine that the same is not to be used for drinking purposes, shall constitute the offence of unlawful sale of alcohol and may be described as such in any complaint or indictment without more; but a person so charged shall be entitled to a bill of particulars in accordance with section forty of chapter two hundred and seventy-seven.

Section 75. Except as otherwise provided in section *Penalty for violation of certain sections.* seventy-three, violation of any provision of sections seventy-two to seventy-four, inclusive, shall be punished by a fine of not more than one hundred dollars or by imprisonment for not more than six months, or both.

Section 76. The licensing authorities of a city or town *Licenses to dealers in paints, etc.* may annually grant licenses to retail dealers in paints or chemicals for the sale of alcohol, other than alcohol described in section seventy-two, for mechanical, manufacturing or chemical purposes only, the fee for which shall be one dollar. The commission may annually grant licenses for the manufacture, transportation, importation, exportation and sale of alcohol, other than alcohol described in section seventy-two, for mechanical, manufacturing or chemical purposes only, or for sale to any person holding a license under section eighteen or nineteen or to any registered pharmacist holding a certificate of fitness, or to any hospital or educational or scientific institution for use other than for beverage purposes. Licenses shall be granted under this section only if it appears that the applicant therefor is a proper person to receive such a license. The fee for such a license shall be one hundred dollars.

Section 77. A license granted under the preceding section shall become null and void without any process or *Termination of license in certain cases.* decree if the licensee ceases to carry on the licensed business.

Section 78. Every person to whom such a license is granted shall keep a book in which he shall enter, at the time of every sale of alcohol, the date thereof, the name and residence of the purchaser, his residence by street and number, if any, the quantity and price of the alcohol sold, and the purpose for which it is to be used. Said book shall be in form substantially as follows:

Date.	Name of Purchaser.	Residence, giving Street and Number, if Any.	Quantity.	Price.	Purpose of Use.

G. L. (Ter. Ed.), 233, § 8, etc., amended.

SECTION 3. Section eight of chapter two hundred and thirty-three of the General Laws, as most recently amended by section three of chapter two hundred and sixty-nine of the acts of nineteen hundred and thirty-three, is hereby further amended by inserting after the word "board" the first time it occurs in the eighth line, the words: —, the alcoholic beverages control commission established by section forty-three of chapter six, — and by striking out the words "for the granting of licenses for certain non-intoxicating beverages" in the ninth and tenth lines, — so as to read as follows: — *Section 8.* Witnesses may be summoned to attend and testify and to produce books and papers at a hearing before a city council, or either branch thereof, or before a joint or special committee of the same or of either branch thereof, or before a board of selectmen, a board of police commissioners, a fire commissioner or a board of fire commissioners, a commissioner of public safety, a school board, the alcoholic beverages control commission established by section forty-three of chapter six, a licensing board or licensing authorities, as defined in section one of chapter one hundred and thirty-eight, a board of registrars of voters, the police commissioner or election commissioners of Boston, the metropolitan district commission, or a board of appeals designated or appointed under section thirty of chapter forty, as to matters within their authority; and such witnesses shall be summoned in the same manner, be paid the same fees and be subject to the same penalties for default, as witnesses in civil cases before the courts. The presiding officer of such council, or of either branch thereof, or a member of any such committee, board or commission, or any such commissioner, may administer oaths to witnesses who appear before such council, branch thereof, committee, board, commission or commissioner, respectively.

Witnesses before town officers, commissions, etc.

G. L. (Ter. Ed.), 272, § 25, amended.

SECTION 4. Chapter two hundred and seventy-two of the General Laws, as appearing in the Tercentenary Edition thereof, is hereby amended by striking out section twenty-five and inserting in place thereof the following: — *Section 25.* Any person owning, managing or controlling a restaurant, tavern or other place in any town, where food or drink is sold to the public to be consumed upon the premises or required to be licensed under chapter one hundred and thirty-eight, and any employee of such person, who

Use of certain enclosures in restaurants, etc., prohibited.

provides, maintains, uses or permits the use of a booth, stall or enclosure of any description whatever which is so closed by curtains, screens or other devices that the persons within cannot at any time plainly be seen by other persons in such restaurant, tavern or other place, or in any division thereof, unless the enclosure is approved by the licensing authorities, and any person conducting such an establishment who maintains barred or barricaded entrances or exits thereto or other devices or appliances designed to impede access thereto by police officers, official inspectors and other officers entitled to enter the same, shall be punished by a fine of not less than fifty nor more than five hundred dollars or by imprisonment for not more than six months, or both.

SECTION 5. All licenses heretofore issued under authority of chapter one hundred and thirty-eight of the General Laws, and in effect immediately prior to the taking effect of this act, shall continue to have full force and effect for the term for which issued, unless sooner revoked by the authority issuing the same. *Certain licenses to continue, etc.*

SECTION 6. Section twenty-one of chapter one hundred and thirty-eight of the General Laws, as revised by section two of this act, shall apply to alcoholic beverages manufactured and sold under authority of chapter three hundred and seventy-four of the acts of the current year. *Application of certain excise provisions.*

REPEAL OF CHAPTER ONE HUNDRED AND TWENTY OF NINE-
    TEEN HUNDRED AND THIRTY-THREE, AND SAVING
    CLAUSE.

SECTION 7. Sections three to fifty-five, inclusive, of chapter one hundred and twenty of the acts of nineteen hundred and thirty-three, as amended by chapters two hundred and sixteen, two hundred and thirty-four and three hundred and forty-six of the acts of said year, are hereby repealed; but notwithstanding such repeal, all licenses and permits issued under said chapter one hundred and twenty and in force when this act takes effect shall continue in force until the same have expired as therein provided, and all acts performed thereunder shall be lawful and valid to the same extent as if said sections had not been repealed; and provided, further, that all authority and jurisdiction conferred upon the alcoholic beverages control commission and the local licensing authorities by said chapter one hundred and twenty in respect to such licenses and permits and to all acts performed thereunder shall continue in force until the expiration of such licenses and permits. The holder of such a license granted under the provisions of section four or six of said chapter one hundred and twenty may at his option surrender the same, whereupon he shall be entitled to a rebate of a proportionate part of the fee paid therefor or to a credit thereof in case he receives from the same licensing authority a new license under chapter one hundred and thirty-eight of the *Repeal.*

General Laws, as revised by this act. Cities and towns may raise and appropriate such funds as may be necessary to make such rebates.

TIME OF TAKING EFFECT.

Effective
date.

SECTION 8. This act shall take effect upon the ratification of the twenty-first amendment to the constitution of the United States, repealing the eighteenth amendment thereto.   *Approved December 4, 1933.*

Chap.377 AN ACT MAKING APPROPRIATIONS INCIDENT TO THE EXTRA SESSION OF THE GENERAL COURT AND FOR OTHER PURPOSES.

Be it enacted, etc., as follows:

Appropriations
incident to
extra session
of the general
court, etc.

SECTION 1. To provide for certain expenditures authorized at the extra session of the general court, the sums set forth in section two, for the particular purposes and subject to the conditions stated therein, are hereby appropriated from the general fund or revenue of the commonwealth, for the fiscal year ending November thirtieth, nineteen hundred and thirty-four, subject to the provisions of law regulating the disbursements of public funds and the approval thereof.

SECTION 2.

Service of the Legislative Department.

For additional compensation of senators for their services during the present extra session of the general court, to wit, of one hundred and fifty dollars for each senator, a sum not exceeding six thousand dollars . . .	$6,000 00
For compensation for travel of senators for the present extra session, a sum not exceeding fourteen hundred and fifty dollars	1,450 00
For additional compensation of representatives for their services during the present extra session of the general court, to wit, of one hundred and fifty dollars for each representative, a sum not exceeding thirty-six thousand dollars	36,000 00
For compensation for travel of representatives in connection with the present extra session, a sum not exceeding ninety-one hundred and sixty-two dollars . . .	9,162 00
For compensation of the pages employed by the sergeant-at-arms for the present extra session, a sum not exceeding eleven hundred and seventy-five dollars . . .	1,175 00
For compensation of the sergeant-at-arms and other employees of his department for the present extra session, a sum not exceeding eighteen hundred and fifty dollars .	1,850 00
For compensation for travel of the sergeant-at-arms and other employees of his department for the present extra session, a sum not exceeding fifteen hundred and seventy-five dollars . . .	1,575 00
For additional compensation of the clerks and assistant clerks of the senate and house of representatives for their services during the present extra session, a sum not exceeding seven hundred dollars	700 00
For additional compensation of the chaplains of the senate and house of representatives for their services during the present extra session, to wit, fifty dollars each, a sum not exceeding one hundred dollars	100 00

For additional clerical assistance in the office of the clerk of
the house of representatives during the present extra
session, a sum not exceeding three hundred and ninety
dollars $390 00
For personal services of the secretary to the counsel to the
senate during the present extra session, a sum not exceeding one hundred and fifty dollars 150 00
For personal services of assistants in the office of the counsel
to the house of representatives during the present extra
session, a sum not exceeding two hundred and seventy-
five dollars 275 00
For personal services of assistants to the president of the
senate and the speaker of the house of representatives
during the present extra session, a sum not exceeding two
hundred and fifty dollars 250 00
For certain contingent expenses of the senate and house of
representatives during the present extra session, a sum
not exceeding fourteen hundred and fifty dollars   .   .   1,450 00
For additional compensation of the counsels to the senate
and house of representatives for their services during the
present extra session, a sum not exceeding four hundred
dollars 400 00

Service of the Alcoholic Beverages Control Commission.

The alcoholic beverages control commission is hereby
authorized, beginning December first of the current year,
to anticipate an appropriation for the fiscal year nineteen
hundred and thirty-four on the basis of monthly expenditures of not exceeding eighty-nine hundred and fifty
dollars.

Service of the Division of Civil Service.

For expenses incurred by the civil service commission in
connection with an examination held on Saturday, November twenty-fifth, nineteen hundred and thirty-three, a
sum not exceeding twenty-five hundred dollars   .   . $2,500 00

Total $63,427 00

Section 3.   This act shall take effect upon its passage.
                                       Approved December 4, 1933.

NOTE.

The general court of 1933 during its extra session passed
5 Acts, which received executive approval.

The general court was prorogued on Monday, December 4, 1933, at nineteen minutes before eleven o'clock P.M.,
the session having occupied 27 days.

The Commonwealth of Massachusetts

In the Year One Thousand Nine Hundred and Thirty-Three.

RESOLUTIONS RATIFYING THE PROPOSED AMENDMENT TO THE CONSTITUTION OF THE UNITED STATES FIXING THE COMMENCEMENT OF THE TERMS OF PRESIDENT AND VICE PRESIDENT AND MEMBERS OF CONGRESS AND FIXING THE TIME OF THE ASSEMBLING OF CONGRESS.

Whereas, The seventy-second Congress by both houses passed the following proposed amendment to the Constitution of the United States by a constitutional majority of two thirds thereof, to wit,

Joint Resolution proposing an amendment to the Constitution of the United States fixing the commencement of the terms of President and Vice President and Members of Congress and fixing the time of the assembling of Congress.

ARTICLE —

SECTION 1. The terms of the President and Vice President shall end at noon on the 20th day of January, and the terms of Senators and Representatives at noon on the 3d day of January, of the years in which such terms would have ended if this article had not been ratified; and the terms of their successors shall then begin.

SEC. 2. The Congress shall assemble at least once in every year, and such meeting shall begin at noon on the 3d day of January, unless they shall by law appoint a different day.

SEC. 3. If, at the time fixed for the beginning of the term of the President, the President elect shall have died, the Vice President elect shall become President. If a President shall not have been chosen before the time fixed for the beginning of his term, or if the President elect shall have failed to qualify, then the Vice President elect shall act as President until a President shall have qualified; and the Congress may by law provide for the case wherein neither a President elect nor a Vice President elect shall have qualified, declaring who shall then act as President, or the manner in which one who is to act shall be selected, and such person shall act accordingly until a President or Vice President shall have qualified.

SEC. 4. The Congress may by law provide for the case of the death of any of the persons from whom the House of Representatives may choose a President whenever the right of choice shall have devolved upon them, and for the case of the death of any of the persons from whom the Senate may choose a Vice President whenever the right of choice shall have devolved upon them.

Amendment to United States Constitution

Sec. 5. Sections 1 and 2 shall take effect on the 15th day of October following the ratification of this article.

Sec. 6. This article shall be inoperative unless it shall have been ratified as an amendment to the Constitution by the legislatures of three-fourths of the several States within seven years from the date of its submission.

Resolved, That the said proposed amendment is hereby ratified by the Legislature of the Commonwealth of Massachusetts.

Resolved, That a certified copy of the foregoing preamble and resolution be forwarded by the Governor to the Secretary of State of the United States, in accordance with section two hundred and five of the Revised Statutes of the United States.

Adopted in the Senate (30 Yeas—0 Nays) January 18, 1933, and, in concurrence, in the House of Representatives (217 Yeas—1 Nay), January 24, 1933.

The foregoing Amendment to the Constitution of the United States was submitted under the provisions of General Laws, Chapter 53, Section 18, to the voters of the Commonwealth at the State Election held November 8, 1932. The total number of votes cast in the affirmative and in the negative for said amendment was as follows:—

Yes.	No.	Blanks.	Total Ballots.
784,821	134,786	689,941	1,609,548

Votes on Question No. 2—"Law Proposed by Initiative Petition."

Returns of Votes upon the Question—"Shall the proposed law which provides for an additional method of nominating candidates for nomination, at the state primaries in September, by members of political parties, for those offices to be filled by all the voters of the Commonwealth at a state election.

It provides that the state conventions of the political parties, in each state election year, shall be held before and not after the state primaries, as now, namely, not later than June 15. In order to elect delegates to such party conventions, party primaries are established to be held on the last Tuesday in April. Among other things, these state conventions may endorse candidates for offices to be filled by all the voters and to be voted upon at the state primaries. Such endorsement places a candidate in nomination, at such state primaries, without the necessity of filing nomination papers. The name of the endorsed candidate is to be placed first on the ballot and against his name is to be placed the words "Endorsed by (the name of political party) convention" in addition to the eight-word statement now authorized by law. Candidates endorsed by a party convention may accept said endorsement within ten days, and having so accepted may not withdraw.

It also provides for the election of district members of state committees and members of ward and town committees at the proposed party primaries in April, as well as delegates to the state party conventions, instead of at the state primaries in September, as now.

It also provides for the election of delegates to national conventions (to nominate candidates for President) at the proposed party primaries instead of at the primaries, now specially held for that purpose, and which existing law requires to be held on the last Tuesday in April (the same day proposed for the proposed party primaries).

It also provides for certain other new provisions of law and certain changes in existing laws, relating to holding state conventions and party primaries, the number and election of delegates to state conventions, the number of members at large of a state committee, and other matters, which in more detail chiefly are as follows:

State conventions are to be composed solely of delegates elected at the party primaries, and the number is to be one from each ward and town and one additional for every fifteen hundred votes or major fraction thereof above the first fifteen hundred votes cast at the preceding state election in such ward or town for the political party candidate for Governor, instead of a number now fixed by the state committee of each party (not less than one from each ward or town) and certain members designated by existing law.

The time, for notice to the State Secretary by aldermen or selectmen of their determination to hold primaries by wards, precincts or groups of precincts, to be March 1, instead of August 1, as now.

The names of candidates for election for delegates to a state convention and for district members of a state committee to be arranged individually by alphabet instead of in groups arranged by lot, as now.

Vacancies in the office of delegate to a state or national convention not to be filled except in case of a tie vote, and then by delegates from the same district, within ten days, and if no other delegate or if not so filled, then by a state committee, rather than solely by the

*remaining members of the delegation; and statement of filling of
such vacancy to be filed with the State Secretary.*

*Seating of delegates at state conventions to be in groups by senatorial
districts, and order of business at said conventions defined.*

*Voting on candidates, by a convention, to be by roll call, if more
than one candidate for the office, or by groups of delegates unless
any member of such group objects.*

*The number of members at large of a state committee of a political
party to be fixed by the state convention of a party instead of by
the state committee, as now.*

*The existing provisions as to preparation and filing of nomination
papers, objections to nominations, preparation, number, substance, arrangement and form of ballots, hours during which
polls shall be open, opening of ballot boxes, canvass and return of
votes, return and certification of votes, now applicable to state
primaries to be applicable to the proposed party primaries.*

*The power of a state committee to fix the number of district delegates
to a national convention to be continued, but the date, of giving
notice to the State Secretary, of such fixation to be March 1 instead
of on or before the third Wednesday in March, as now.*

*The power of city and town committees to fix the number of members
of ward and town committees to be continued, but the date, of giving
notice to the State Secretary, of such fixation to be March 1, instead
of August 1, as now,* which was approved in the Senate by a
vote of 21 in the affirmative and 17 in the negative and was disapproved in the House of Representatives by a vote of 62 in the
affirmative and 138 in the negative, *be approved?"* submitted
under the provisions of Article XLVIII of the Amendments to the
Constitution to the Voters of the Commonwealth at the State
Election held November 8, 1932.

County of Barnstable.

Cities and Towns.	Yes.	No.	Blanks.	Total Ballots.
Barnstable	853	476	1,632	2,961
Bourne	277	189	699	1,165
Brewster	95	45	244	384
Chatham	212	127	529	868
Dennis	197	137	560	894
Eastham	46	39	201	286
Falmouth	538	313	1,181	2,032
Harwich	221	154	542	917
Mashpee	25	15	98	138
Orleans	202	75	394	671
Provincetown	140	134	1,071	1,345
Sandwich	207	79	405	691
Truro	44	38	145	227
Wellfleet	117	54	310	481
Yarmouth	214	145	413	772
Totals	3,388	2,020	8,424	13,832

County of Berkshire.

Cities and Towns.	Yes.	No.	Blanks.	Total Ballots.
Adams	1,143	836	2,628	4,607
Alford	13	15	71	99
Becket	59	63	198	320
Cheshire	194	117	374	685
Clarksburg	94	72	339	505
Dalton	572	296	1,224	2,092
Egremont	48	51	148	247
Florida	51	18	90	159
Great Barrington	610	375	1,554	2,539
Hancock	25	19	128	172
Hinsdale	116	78	338	532
Lanesborough	152	68	289	509
Lee	417	212	1,018	1,647
Lenox	299	183	872	1,354
Monterey	32	27	83	142

County of Berkshire.—Concluded.

Cities and Towns.	Yes.	No.	Blanks.	Total Ballots.
Mount Washington	11	6	22	39
New Ashford	6	0	27	33
New Marlborough	83	48	241	372
NORTH ADAMS	2,341	1,066	5,499	8,906
Otis	14	39	92	145
Peru	16	6	42	64
PITTSFIELD	5,997	3,722	9,851	19,570
Richmond	76	49	143	268
Sandisfield	24	19	85	128
Savoy	15	32	55	102
Sheffield	184	88	302	574
Stockbridge	213	137	465	815
Tyringham	35	20	80	135
Washington	17	18	58	93
West Stockbridge	105	174	187	466
Williamstown	520	279	1,111	1,910
Windsor	26	27	106	159
Totals	13,508	8,160	27,720	49,388

County of Bristol.

Cities and Towns.	Yes.	No.	Blanks.	Total Ballots.
Acushnet	293	222	676	1,191
ATTLEBORO	2,463	1,501	4,615	8,579
Berkley	77	61	241	379
Dartmouth	542	465	1,391	2,398
Dighton	190	158	597	945
Easton	686	439	1,371	2,496
Fairhaven	909	701	1,981	3,591
FALL RIVER	7,577	7,337	21,807	36,721
Freetown	117	99	338	554
Mansfield	762	455	1,341	2,558
NEW BEDFORD	8,769	6,278	17,730	32,777
North Attleborough	1,021	632	2,867	4,520
Norton	299	163	581	1,043
Raynham	163	124	488	775
Rehoboth	173	139	473	785
Seekonk	418	275	662	1,355
Somerset	391	371	1,213	1,975
Swansea	326	314	849	1,489
TAUNTON	3,274	2,056	8,610	13,940
Westport	190	223	919	1,332
Totals	28,640	22,013	68,750	119,403

County of Dukes County.

Cities and Towns.	Yes.	No.	Blanks.	Total Ballots.
Chilmark	14	38	73	125
Edgartown	89	45	314	448
Gay Head	4	7	42	53
Gosnold	12	20	16	48
Oak Bluffs	123	79	371	573
Tisbury	154	105	343	602
West Tisbury	37	22	69	128
Totals	433	316	1,228	1,977

County of Essex.

Cities and Towns.	Yes.	No.	Blanks.	Total Ballots.
Amesbury	1,334	607	2,389	4,330
Andover	1,694	654	2,435	4,783
BEVERLY	3,471	1,922	5,502	10,895
Boxford	137	71	130	338
Danvers	1,618	764	2,604	4,986
Essex	213	78	417	708
Georgetown	224	153	554	931
GLOUCESTER	2,353	1,375	4,982	8,710
Groveland	283	162	622	1,067
Hamilton	415	134	477	1,026
HAVERHILL	5,185	3,100	10,061	18,346
Ipswich	698	232	1,265	2,195
LAWRENCE	7,080	4,338	18,481	29,899
LYNN	12,223	8,069	16,891	37,183
Lynnfield	324	161	477	962
Manchester	589	140	601	1,330
Marblehead	1,975	858	2,308	5,141
Merrimac	357	146	647	1,150
Methuen	2,118	1,103	5,509	8,730
Middleton	189	107	351	647
Nahant	369	135	480	984
Newbury	222	128	460	810
NEWBURYPORT	1,751	863	3,910	6,524
North Andover	853	464	2,192	3,509
PEABODY	2,190	1,124	4,215	7,529
Rockport	441	241	998	1,680
Rowley	147	119	429	695
SALEM	5,691	2,356	9,343	17,390
Salisbury	215	100	680	995

County of Essex.—Concluded.

Cities and Towns.	Yes.	No.	Blanks.	Total Ballots.
Saugus	1,785	1,224	2,967	5,976
Swampscott	2,185	920	1,954	5,059
Topsfield	217	75	252	544
Wenham	241	117	225	583
West Newbury	148	115	376	639
Totals	58,935	32,155	105,184	196,274

County of Franklin.

	Yes.	No.	Blanks.	Total Ballots.
Ashfield	59	67	225	351
Bernardston	83	62	206	351
Buckland	126	96	502	724
Charlemont	85	71	195	351
Colrain	88	95	362	545
Conway	64	51	235	350
Deerfield	284	123	525	932
Erving	129	59	267	455
Gill	77	70	214	361
Greenfield	2,106	1,032	3,751	6,889
Hawley	34	14	52	100
Heath	17	24	76	117
Leverett	24	31	124	179
Leyden	27	25	60	112
Monroe	26	17	42	85
Montague	704	330	1,947	2,981
New Salem	41	32	93	166
Northfield	240	184	417	841
Orange	739	272	1,267	2,278
Rowe	15	18	71	104
Shelburne	219	116	479	814
Shutesbury	19	6	30	55
Sunderland	101	49	152	302
Warwick	38	51	78	167
Wendell	50	14	65	129
Whately	60	39	243	342
Totals	5,455	2,948	11,678	20,081

County of Hampden.

	Yes.	No.	Blanks.	Total Ballots.
Agawam	601	380	1,497	2,478
Blandford	33	27	134	194
Brimfield	71	58	211	340
Chester	108	57	359	524
CHICOPEE	3,575	1,768	9,338	14,681
East Longmeadow	409	251	738	1,398
Granville	36	54	241	331
Hampden	94	54	214	362
Holland	16	15	44	75
HOLYOKE	6,016	3,078	14,443	23,537
Longmeadow	982	442	1,014	2,438
Ludlow	636	305	1,391	2,332
Monson	392	196	1,090	1,678
Montgomery	10	6	59	75
Palmer	841	407	2,102	3,350
Russell	118	77	323	518
Southwick	114	41	292	447
SPRINGFIELD	18,002	8,721	30,070	56,793
Tolland	6	7	49	62
Wales	41	35	103	179
West Springfield	2,019	1,000	3,640	6,659
WESTFIELD	1,820	1,091	3,992	6,903
Wilbraham	250	157	473	880
Totals	36,190	18,227	71,817	126,234

County of Hampshire.

	Yes.	No.	Blanks.	Total Ballots.
Amherst	826	471	1,272	2,569
Belchertown	185	117	572	874
Chesterfield	14	71	148	233
Cummington	57	44	179	280
Easthampton	816	489	2,384	3,689
Enfield	56	35	105	196
Goshen	26	25	71	122
Granby	91	61	220	372
Greenwich	21	22	55	98
Hadley	163	134	393	690
Hatfield	159	78	450	687
Huntington	115	78	425	618
Middlefield	11	15	66	92
NORTHAMPTON	2,776	1,439	5,107	9,322
Pelham	32	37	128	197
Plainfield	32	16	78	126
Prescott	2	5	7	14
South Hadley	897	470	1,502	2,869
Southampton	65	47	246	358
Ware	638	220	1,976	2,834

County of Hampshire.—Concluded.

Cities and Towns.	Yes.	No.	Blanks.	Total Ballots.
Westhampton	32	51	77	160
Williamsburg	176	134	524	834
Worthington	34	39	123	196
Totals	7,224	4,098	16,108	27,430

County of Middlesex.

Cities and Towns.	Yes.	No.	Blanks.	Total Ballots.
Acton	467	222	548	1,237
Arlington	7,657	3,121	6,273	17,051
Ashby	103	47	181	331
Ashland	337	136	575	1,048
Ayer	462	207	681	1,350
Bedford	326	158	357	841
Belmont	5,542	1,609	3,763	10,914
Billerica	887	478	1,170	2,535
Boxborough	56	30	69	155
Burlington	220	125	350	695
CAMBRIDGE	15,216	6,820	18,358	40,394
Carlisle	97	50	144	291
Chelmsford	1,036	486	1,397	2,919
Concord	1,283	424	1,305	3,012
Dracut	538	326	1,172	2,036
Dunstable	46	19	111	176
EVERETT	5,319	2,611	7,841	15,771
Framingham	3,056	1,242	4,174	8,472
Groton	421	177	624	1,222
Holliston	484	187	756	1,427
Hopkinton	469	164	629	1,262
Hudson	1,119	329	1,549	2,997
Lexington	2,089	768	1,742	4,599
Lincoln	304	84	301	689
Littleton	268	96	295	659
LOWELL	12,392	6,348	18,042	36,782
MALDEN	7,598	3,469	10,095	21,162
MARLBOROUGH	2,281	927	3,659	6,867
Maynard	808	350	1,342	2,500
MEDFORD	9,652	4,437	10,270	24,359
MELROSE	5,572	2,200	4,249	12,021
Natick	2,685	897	2,841	6,423
NEWTON	18,306	3,954	7,932	30,192
North Reading	240	137	392	769
Pepperell	430	194	717	1,341
Reading	2,069	932	1,843	4,844
Sherborn	167	59	240	466
Shirley	267	76	375	718
SOMERVILLE	13,876	7,062	16,728	37,666
Stoneham	1,673	800	2,182	4,655
Stow	201	79	216	496
Sudbury	215	108	284	607
Tewksbury	352	148	521	1,021
Townsend	250	90	479	819
Tyngsborough	136	76	298	510
Wakefield	2,332	986	3,455	6,773
WALTHAM	5,864	2,466	6,692	15,022
Watertown	5,849	2,368	5,502	13,719
Wayland	539	192	598	1,329
Westford	327	165	725	1,217
Weston	824	247	476	1,547
Wilmington	510	217	709	1,436
Winchester	3,379	831	1,939	6,149
WOBURN	3,163	1,327	3,550	8,040
Totals	149,759	61,058	160,716	371,533

County of Nantucket.

Cities and Towns.	Yes.	No.	Blanks.	Total Ballots.
Nantucket	290	160	967	1,417

County of Norfolk.

Cities and Towns.	Yes.	No.	Blanks.	Total Ballots.
Avon	308	175	578	1,061
Bellingham	255	131	653	1,039
Braintree	2,776	1,585	3,306	7,667
Brookline	10,768	2,749	7,502	21,019
Canton	1,018	326	1,205	2,549
Cohasset	613	190	766	1,569
Dedham	2,455	907	2,865	6,227
Dover	253	77	173	503
Foxborough	648	307	1,001	1,956
Franklin	860	347	1,542	2,749
Holbrook	391	275	894	1,560
Medfield	318	190	496	1,004
Medway	375	218	756	1,349
Millis	242	124	480	846
Milton	4,312	1,298	3,117	8,727
Needham	2,295	744	2,104	5,143

County of Norfolk.—Concluded.

Cities and Towns.	Yes.	No.	Blanks.	Total Ballots.
Norfolk	184	99	233	516
Norwood	1,966	938	2,805	5,709
Plainville	200	116	399	715
QUINCY	11,742	5,816	12,731	30,289
Randolph	877	480	1,610	2,967
Sharon	685	297	662	1,644
Stoughton	1,035	483	1,673	3,191
Walpole	984	492	1,279	2,755
Wellesley	2,857	763	1,704	5,324
Westwood	436	162	493	1,091
Weymouth	3,170	1,419	4,263	8,852
Wrentham	297	174	473	944
Totals	52,320	20,882	55,763	128,965

County of Plymouth.

	Yes.	No.	Blanks.	Total Ballots.
Abington	798	420	1,446	2,664
Bridgewater	703	385	1,209	2,297
BROCKTON	7,259	5,521	13,625	26,405
Carver	84	31	244	359
Duxbury	361	139	478	978
East Bridgewater	373	293	810	1,476
Halifax	111	52	141	304
Hanover	357	152	568	1,077
Hanson	248	174	536	958
Hingham	1,432	462	1,217	3,111
Hull	528	176	584	1,288
Kingston	293	107	557	957
Lakeville	112	85	267	464
Marion	183	123	391	697
Marshfield	379	136	535	1,050
Mattapoisett	161	98	445	704
Middleborough	843	528	1,891	3,262
Norwell	258	127	389	774
Pembroke	199	107	308	614
Plymouth	1,342	516	2,605	4,463
Plympton	58	34	125	217
Rochester	73	63	168	304
Rockland	961	533	2,179	3,673
Scituate	705	254	886	1,845
Wareham	585	278	1,231	2,094
West Bridgewater	370	256	678	1,304
Whitman	885	528	2,177	3,590
Totals	19,661	11,578	35,690	66,929

County of Suffolk.

	Yes.	No.	Blanks.	Total Ballots.
BOSTON	102,978	48,186	118,985	270,149
CHELSEA	3,228	1,581	7,428	12,237
REVERE	3,400	2,100	6,319	11,819
Winthrop	3,762	1,068	2,917	7,747
Totals	113,368	52,935	135,649	301,952

County of Worcester.

	Yes.	No.	Blanks.	Total Ballots.
Ashburnham	207	64	437	708
Athol	1,116	513	2,227	3,856
Auburn	895	383	1,268	2,546
Barre	362	134	580	1,076
Berlin	149	84	244	477
Blackstone	323	548	631	1,502
Bolton	102	82	129	313
Boylston	146	62	259	467
Brookfield	196	83	309	588
Charlton	241	90	498	829
Clinton	1,432	803	3,273	5,508
Dana	41	24	126	191
Douglas	229	325	284	838
Dudley	447	137	791	1,375
East Brookfield	122	49	188	359
FITCHBURG	5,837	2,111	6,817	14,765
GARDNER	2,020	815	3,542	6,377
Grafton	787	298	1,265	2,350
Hardwick	211	92	545	848
Harvard	197	85	233	515
Holden	580	201	694	1,475
Hopedale	570	237	563	1,370
Hubbardston	123	45	189	357
Lancaster	346	150	508	1,004
Leicester	631	201	1,023	1,855
LEOMINSTER	3,112	935	4,051	8,098
Lunenburg	314	74	369	757
Mendon	166	69	256	491
Milford	1,614	603	3,493	5,710
Millbury	882	285	1,593	2,760

County of Worcester.—Concluded.

Cities and Towns.	Yes.	No.	Blanks.	Total Ballots.
Millville	176	98	519	793
New Braintree	43	11	59	113
North Brookfield	467	104	691	1,262
Northborough	328	108	475	911
Northbridge	1,528	560	1,578	3,666
Oakham	44	20	96	160
Oxford	507	187	939	1,633
Paxton	96	42	144	282
Petersham	122	61	183	366
Phillipston	48	26	82	156
Princeton	123	34	133	290
Royalston	59	43	139	241
Rutland	233	78	274	585
Shrewsbury	1,007	315	1,093	2,415
Southborough	406	127	469	1,002
Southbridge	1,578	807	3,285	5,670
Spencer	807	252	1,721	2,780
Sterling	233	100	364	697
Sturbridge	187	75	452	714
Sutton	238	148	395	781
Templeton	393	169	828	1,390
Upton	330	113	508	951
Uxbridge	752	337	1,299	2,388
Warren	375	148	798	1,321
Webster	1,862	511	2,664	5,037
West Boylston	343	106	451	900
West Brookfield	211	67	312	590
Westborough	832	300	1,021	2,153
Westminster	215	63	295	573
Winchendon	707	250	1,309	2,266
WORCESTER	27,003	11,556	34,123	72,682
Totals	64,651	26,398	93,084	184,133

Aggregate of Votes.

Counties.	Yes.	No.	Blanks.	Total Ballots.
BARNSTABLE	3,388	2,020	8,424	13,832
BERKSHIRE	13,508	8,160	27,720	49,388
BRISTOL	28,640	22,013	68,750	119,403
DUKES COUNTY	433	316	1,228	1,977
ESSEX	58,935	32,155	105,184	196,274
FRANKLIN	5,455	2,948	11,678	20,081
HAMPDEN	36,190	18,227	71,817	126,234
HAMPSHIRE	7,224	4,098	16,108	27,430
MIDDLESEX	149,759	61,058	160,716	371,533
NANTUCKET	290	160	967	1,417
NORFOLK	52,320	20,882	55,763	128,965
PLYMOUTH	19,661	11,578	35,690	66,929
SUFFOLK	113,368	52,935	135,649	301,952
WORCESTER	64,651	26,398	93,084	184,133
Totals	553,822	262,948	792,778	1,609,548

APPENDIX

The following table and the index to the Acts and Resolves of the current year have been prepared by WILLIAM E. DORMAN, Esq., and HENRY D. WIGGIN, Esq., counsel, respectively, to the Senate and House of Representatives, in accordance with section fifty-one of chapter three of the General Laws.

TABLE

TO WHAT EXTENT THE GENERAL LAWS OF THE COMMONWEALTH, AS APPEARING IN THE TERCENTENARY EDITION, HAVE BEEN AFFECTED BY LEGISLATION ENACTED BY THE GENERAL COURT SINCE JANUARY FIRST, NINETEEN HUNDRED AND THIRTY-TWO.*

Chapter 1. — Jurisdiction of the Commonwealth and of the United States.

Act granting to United States all rights of the Commonwealth in and to great ponds within Fort Devens Military Reservation, and ceding jurisdiction over such ponds and certain other lands, 1933, 290.
Sect. 3 revised, 1933, 278 § 1.

Chapter 3. — The General Court.

Sects. 12 and 13. For legislation establishing the salaries of the present clerk and assistant clerk of the senate, see 1932, 181.

Chapter 4. — Statutes.

Sect. 7, clause Eighteenth. [See 1933, 260 (submitting to the voters of Suffolk county the question of making June 17th a legal holiday in said county).]

Chapter 5. — Printing and Distribution of Laws and Public Documents.

As to the distribution of the Tercentenary Edition of the General Laws, see 1932, Resolve 53; 1933, Resolve 19.
Sect. 1, last paragraph revised, 1932, 254.
Sect. 9 amended, 1933, 245 § 1.

Chapter 6. — The Governor, Lieutenant Governor and Council, Certain Officers under the Governor and Council, and State Library.

For temporary legislation establishing an emergency finance board, and defining its powers and duties, see 1933, 49, 104.
For temporary legislation establishing the emergency public works commission, and defining its powers and duties, see 1933, 365, as affected by 1933, 368.
Sect. 12B added, 1932, 14 (relative to the observance of the anniversary of the death of Brigadier General Casimir Pulaski).
Sect. 12C added, 1932, 153 (relative to the observance of the anniversary of the battle of Bunker Hill). (See 1933, 260.)

* For table showing changes in legislation made during the years 1921 to 1931, inclusive, see Table of Changes contained in pages 485-597 of the Acts and Resolves of 1932.

SECT. 12D added, 1932, 242 (relative to the observance of the anniversary of the Boston Massacre, etc.).

SECT. 17 amended, 1932, 305 § 1; 1933, 120 § 1; 336 § 1. (See 1933, 336 § 3.)

SECT. 42 added, under caption "MILK REGULATION BOARD", 1932, 305 § 2.

SECTS. 43–45 added, 1933, 120 § 2 (relative to the alcoholic beverages control commission).

SECT. 43 amended, 1933, 375 § 1.

SECT. 44, first paragraph revised, 1933, 376 §1.

SECTS. 46 and 47 added, 1933, 336 § 2 (relative to the Greylock reservation commission). (See 1933, 336 § 3.)

Chapter 7. — Commission on Administration and Finance.

SECT. 22, clause (17) revised, 1933, 353 § 1.

SECT. 23A added, 1933, 353 § 2 (providing a preference in the purchase of supplies and materials by contractors for certain state work in favor of domestic supplies and materials).

Chapter 8. — Superintendent of Buildings, and State House.

SECT. 10A revised, 1933, 170.

SECT. 17 amended, 1932, 188 § 1; 1933, 199 § 1.

SECT. 18 amended, 1932, 188 § 2; 1933, 199 § 2.

Chapter 10. — Department of the State Treasurer.

For temporary legislation establishing an emergency finance board, and defining its powers and duties, see 1933, 49, 104.

For temporary legislation establishing the emergency public works commission, and defining its powers and duties, see 1933, 365, as affected by 1933, 368.

SECT. 8 amended, 1932, 180 § 1.

Chapter 12. — Department of the Attorney General, and the District Attorneys.

SECT. 3, last sentence amended, 1932, 180 § 2.

SECT. 3B amended, 1933, 318 § 1. (See 1933, 318 § 9.)

Chapter 13. — Department of Civil Service and Registration.

SECT. 3 amended, 1932, 180 § 3.

SECT. 10 amended, 1932, 8.

SECT. 40 amended, 1933, 149 § 1.

Chapter 18. — Department of Public Welfare.

SECTS. 17 and 18 added, under caption "STATE BOARD OF HOUSING", 1933, 364 § 1 (establishing within the department a state board of housing).

Chapter 19. — Department of Mental Diseases.

Division of examination of prisoners abolished, 1933, 77 § 4.

Chapter 20. — Department of Agriculture.

SECT. 4 amended, 1933, 74 § 1.

Chapter 21. — Department of Conservation.

SECT. 3 revised, 1933, 75 § 1.
SECTS. 3A and 3B repealed, 1932, 180 § 4.
SECT. 7 revised, 1933, 329 § 3.
SECT. 8A revised, 1933, 329 § 4.
SECT. 11 revised, 1933, 75 § 2.
SECT. 12 revised, 1933, 75 § 3.

Chapter 22. — Department of Public Safety.

SECT. 9C added, 1933, 239 (relative to the uniform of members of the state police).

Chapter 23. — Department of Labor and Industries.

Caption before SECTS. 9A–9C changed to "THE MASSACHUSETTS INDUSTRIAL AND DEVELOPMENT COMMISSION", 1932, 99.
SECT. 9A revised, 1932, 99; repealed, 1933, 73.
SECT. 9B repealed, 1933, 73.
SECT. 9C revised, 1932, 187; repealed, 1933, 73.
SECT. 9H revised, 1933, 362.

Chapter 25. — Department of Public Utilities.

SECT. 9A added, 1933, 76 § 2 (providing for certain employees serving directly under the commission of the department to perform its duties relative to smoke abatement in Boston and vicinity).
SECT. 10 amended, 1933, 76 § 3.
SECT. 10A added, 1933, 76 § 4 (providing for the apportionment of expenses incurred by the department in the performance of its duties relative to smoke abatement in Boston and vicinity).
SECT. 12B revised, 1932, 290 § 2.
SECTS. 12C–12F repealed, 1933, 76 § 1.

Chapter 29. — State Finance.

For temporary legislation as to emergency state financing, see 1933, 49, 104, 307, 341, 365, 367, 368.
SECT. 31, last sentence amended, 1932, 127 § 2.

Chapter 30. — General Provisions Relative to State Departments, Commissions, Officers and Employees.

For temporary act reducing the salary or other compensation of state officers and employees, see 1933, 105, as affected by 1933, 296.
Provisions relative to expenses incurred for midday meals by state employees, 1933, 174 § 8.

Chapter 31. — Civil Service.

For act, extending to May 15th, 1933, the existing preference in the classified labor service to persons with dependents, see 1932, 183. [For prior legislation, see 1930, 111; 1931, 316.]
SECT. 4, sixth paragraph revised, 1932, 282 § 1. (See 1932, 282 § 4.)
SECT. 6, sentence added at end, 1932, 260.

SECT. 15A added, 1933, 267 (restricting the appointment of persons for temporary employment under the civil service laws).

SECT. 19A added, 1932, 146 (relative to appointments to the regular fire forces in certain cities having reserve fire forces).

SECT. 21 amended, 1932, 89; revised, 1933, 137.

SECT. 46 amended, 1932, 282 § 2.

SECTS. 46C and 46D added, 1933, 320 (providing for the reinstatement of certain municipal officers and employees).

Chapter 32. — Retirement Systems and Pensions.

SECT. 3, paragraph (4) revised, 1932, 268.

SECT. 7, paragraph (4) amended, 1932, 127 § 18.

SECT. 10, paragraph (2) revised, 1932, 255.

SECT. 52 amended, 1932, 114 § 1.

SECT. 53 amended, 1932, 114 § 2.

SECT. 81 amended, 1933, 103.

SECT. 85B added, 1932, 253 (regulating the retirement and pensioning of certain members of the police forces of park boards of cities and towns).

SECT. 89 revised, 1932, 276; amended, 1933, 340 § 1. (See 1933, 340 § 2.)

Chapter 33. — Militia.

SECT. 6 revised, 1933, 254 § 1. (See 1933, 254 § 66.)

SECT. 18 amended, 1932, 15.

SECT. 48, subsection (a) revised, 1932, 161; same subsection amended, 1933, 166.

SECT. 60 amended, 1933, 153 § 1.

SECT. 90, last sentence of paragraph (k) revised, 1933, 17.

SECT. 98, sentence added at end, 1933, 6.

Chapter 34. — Counties and County Commissioners.

SECT. 1 revised, 1933, 278 § 2.

SECT. 17 revised, 1932, 74.

SECT. 23 added, 1932, 297 (authorizing counties to receive certain gifts).

Chapter 35. — County Treasurers, State Supervision of County Accounts, and County Finances.

For temporary legislation relative to salary reductions in the several counties, see 1933, 121, 186. (See also 1933, 322 § 3.)

Provisions relative to travel allowance of county officials and employees using their own cars on official business, 1933, 322 § 4.

SECT. 3 revised, 1932, 56.

SECT. 25 amended, 1933, 175 § 1.

SECT. 27 amended, 1933, 175 § 2.

SECT. 28 amended, 1933, 318 § 2. (See 1933, 318 § 9.)

SECT. 37 amended, 1933, 28.

SECT. 37A amended, 1933, 29.

Chapter 37. — Sheriffs.

SECT. 22 amended, 1932, 180 § 5.

Chapter 38. — Medical Examiners.

Sect. 8 revised, 1932, 118 § 1.

Chapter 40. — Powers and Duties of Cities and Towns.

Sect. 4, third paragraph revised, 1932, 271 § 6. (See 1932, 271 § 7.)

Sect. 5, clause (1) amended, 1933, 318 § 3 (see 1933, 318 § 9); clause (12) amended, 1932, 114 § 3; 1933, 153 § 2; 245 § 2.

Sect. 9 amended, 1933, 245 § 3.

Sect. 14 revised, 1933, 283 § 1.

Sect. 17 amended, 1933, 254 § 2. (See 1933, 254 § 66.)

Sects. 25–33. See 1932, 143; 1933, 204; for special zoning provisions for Boston.

Sects. 25–30A stricken out, and new sections 25–30A (municipal zoning laws) inserted, 1933, 269 § 1. (See 1933, 269 § 4.)

Sect. 32 revised, 1933, 185 § 1. (See 1933, 185 § 2.)

Sect. 40 revised, 1933, 314.

Sect. 42A revised, 1932, 197 § 2. (See 1932, 197 § 3.)

Sect. 42E, last sentence amended, 1932, 180 § 6.

Chapter 41. — Officers and Employees of Cities, Towns and Districts.

For temporary legislation relative to salary reductions in Boston, see 1933, 121.

Sect. 13A added, 1932, 289 § 5 (provisions relative to bonds of city clerks). [For prior legislation, see G. L. chapter 140 § 148, repealed by 1932, 289 § 6.]

Sect. 19A added, 1933, 70 § 1 (requiring the filing with the state secretary of certificates of appointment or election of clerks or assistant or temporary clerks of cities or towns, and granting authority to said secretary to authenticate attestations of any such officer). (See 1933, 70 § 2.)

Sect. 37 revised, 1933, 82 § 2.

Sect. 91B added, 1933, 128 (further regulating the appointment of constables).

Sect. 99 amended, 1932, 124.

Sect. 100, sentence added at end, 1933, 324 § 3.

Sect. 100A amended, 1933, 318 § 4. (See 1933, 318 §§ 8, 9.)

Sect. 111 revised, 1932, 109.

Chapter 42. — Boundaries of Cities and Towns.

Boundary line between Saugus and Wakefield (portion) established, 1933, 298.

Sect. 1 revised, 1933, 278 § 3.

Chapter 43. — City Charters.

Sect. 15 amended, 1933, 313 § 7.

Sect. 44A amended, 1933, 313 § 8.

Sect. 44H amended, 1932, 180 § 7.

Chapter 43A. — Standard Form of Representative Town Meeting Government.

Act relative to Wellesley, 1932, 202; to Needham, 1932, 279; to Webster, 1933, 13; to South Hadley, 1933, 45; to Easthampton, 1933, 178; to Milford, 1933, 271.

Chapter 44. — Municipal Finance.

For temporary legislation ˙establishing an emergency finance board in the department of the state treasurer, and providing for the borrowing of money by cities and towns against certain tax titles, see 1933, 49, 104.

For temporary act authorizing cities and towns to borrow on account of public welfare and soldiers' benefits from the commonwealth and elsewhere, and authorizing the commonwealth to issue bonds or notes to provide funds therefor, see 1933, 307 (as changed by 1933, 344 §§ 3, 4, and as affected by 1933, 367 § 1).

For temporary act relative to funds granted under the federal emergency relief act of 1933, see 1933, 344.

For emergency legislation incident to the National Recovery Act, see 1933, 366.

For temporary legislation in aid of the town of Millville, see 1933, 341.

SECT. 29. As to tax limit of Boston, see 1932, 125; 1933, 159.

SECT. 46A added, 1932, 155 (making permanent certain provisions of law relative to investigations of municipal accounts and financial transactions by the director of accounts). [For prior temporary legislation, see 1926, 210; 1929, 335.]

SECT. 54 amended, 1933, 200.

Chapter 46. — Return and Registry of Births, Marriages and Deaths.

SECT. 1, third sentence of second paragraph revised, 1933, 280 § 1.

SECT. 2A added, 1933, 279 (regulating the impounding of birth records of children born out of wedlock).

SECT. 13, second paragraph amended, 1933, 280 § 2.˙

SECT. 17 revised, 1932, 12.

Chapter 48. — Fires, Fire Departments and Fire Districts.

For temporary act to enable districts, etc., to secure the benefits provided by the National Industrial Recovery Act, see 1933, 366 Part I § 6.

SECT. 15 amended, 1932, 180 § 8.

Chapter 50. — General Provisions relative to Primaries, Caucuses and Elections.

SECT. 2 amended, 1932, 141 § 1.

Chapter 51. — Voters.

SECT. 1, paragraph added at end, 1932, 206.
SECT. 2 amended, 1933, 254 § 3.   (See 1933, 254 § 66.)
SECT. 3 amended, 1933, 254 § 4.   (See 1933, 254 § 66.)
SECT. 4 amended, 1933, 254 § 5.   (See 1933, 254 §§ 65, 66.)

Sect. 7 amended, 1933, 254 § 6.   (See 1933, 254 §§ 65, 66.)
Sect. 8 amended, 1933, 254 § 7.   (See 1933, 254 § 66.)
Sect. 9 amended, 1933, 254 § 8.   (See 1933, 254 § 66.)
Sect. 14B added, 1933, 254 § 9 (amending special acts relative to the listing of voters in certain municipalities so as to conform to the change in taxing date from April 1 to January 1).   (See 1933, 254 §§ 65, 66.)
Sect. 26 amended, 1932, 48 § 1.
Sect. 27 revised, 1932, 48 § 2.
Sect. 32 amended, 1933, 254 § 10.   (See 1933, 254 § 66.)
Sect. 34 amended, 1933, 254 § 11.   (See 1933, 254 § 66.)
Sect. 36 amended, 1933, 254 § 12.   (See 1933, 254 § 66.)
Sect. 37 amended, 1933, 254 § 13.   (See 1933, 254 § 66.)
Sect. 43 amended, 1933, 254 § 14.   (See 1933, 254 § 66.)
Sect. 55 amended, 1933, 254 § 15.   (See 1933, 254 § 66.)

Chapter 52. — Political Committees.

Sect. 1 amended, 1932, 310 § 1.
Sect. 2 amended, 1932, 310 § 2.
Sect. 9 amended, 1932, 310 § 3.

Chapter 53. — Nominations, Questions to be submitted to the Voters, Primaries and Caucuses.

Sect. 2 amended, 1932, 310 § 4..
Sect. 7 amended, 1933, 254 § 16.   (See 1933, 254 § 66.)
Sect. 8, first paragraph amended, 1932, 135 § 4; section amended, 1933, 35 § 1.
Sect. 10, second paragraph revised, 1933, 313 § 2.
Sect. 11, sentence added at end, 1933, 313 § 3.
Sect. 12A added, 1933, 305 (to prevent certain fraudulent nominations).
Sect. 13, sentence added at end, 1933, 313 § 4.
Sect. 22A amended, 1932, 80.
Sect. 28 amended, 1932, 310 § 5; revised, 1933, 313 § 5.
Sect. 32 amended, 1932, 310 § 6.
Sect. 34 revised, 1932, 310 § 7.
Sect. 35 amended, 1932, 310 § 8.
Sect. 40 revised, 1932, 30.
Sect. 41 revised, 1932, 310 § 9.
Sect. 42 amended, 1932, 310 § 10.
Sect. 43 amended, 1932, 310 § 11.
Sect. 44 revised, 1932, 310 § 12.
Sect. 45 amended, 1932, 310 § 13.
Sect. 47 amended, 1932, 310 § 14.
Sect. 48 amended, 1932, 310 § 15.
Sect. 49 revised, 1932, 310 § 16.
Sect. 51 amended, 1932, 310 § 17.
Sect. 52 amended, 1932, 310 § 18.
Sect. 53 revised, 1932, 310 § 19.
Sect. 53A amended, 1932, 310 § 20.
Sect. 54 revised, 1932, 310 § 21.
Sects. 54A and 54B added, 1932, 310 § 22 (relative to proceedings

at pre-primary conventions, to the form of certificates of nomination of candidates thereat, and to the acceptance of such nominations).

SECTS. 65 to 70 (and caption) repealed, 1932, 310 §.23.

SECT. 72A added, 1933, 313 § 6 (relative to caucuses before regular city elections in cities having absent voting).

SECT. 117 amended, 1932, 141 § 2.

SECT. 121 added, 1932, 141 § 3 (authorizing the nomination by caucuses other than those of political or municipal parties of two candidates for each town office).

Chapter 54. — Elections.

SECT. 11 amended, 1932, 76 § 1.

SECT. 11A added, 1932, 76 § 2 (dispensing with the appointment of deputy election officers in certain cities).

SECT. 41, third paragraph amended, 1933, 35 § 2.

SECT. 42 amended, 1932, 135 § 5.

SECT. 43 revised, 1932, 135 § 1.

SECT. 65 revised, 1933, 289 § 1.

SECT. 78 revised, 1932, 135 § 2.

SECT. 103A added, 1933, 313 § 1 (providing for absent voting at regular city elections).

SECT. 132 amended, 1932, 33.

SECT. 135, first paragraph amended, 1933, 254 § 17; section revised, 1933, 270. (See 1933, 254 § 66.)

SECT. 151 amended, 1932, 135 § 3.

Chapter 56. — Violations of Election Laws.

SECT. 39 revised, 1933, 289 § 2.

Chapter 58. — General Provisions relative to Taxation.

SECT. 1, fifth sentence amended, 1932, 180 § 9.

SECT. 2 amended, 1933, 254 § 18. (See 1933, 254 § 66.)

SECT. 3 amended, 1933, 254 § 19. (See 1933, 254 § 66.)

SECT. 13 amended, 1933, 254 § 20. (See 1933, 254 § 66.)

SECT. 15 amended, 1933, 254 § 21. (See 1933, 254 § 66.)

SECT. 18 revised, 1933, 350 § 7; affected, 1933, 357 § 4. (See 1933, 307 § 11; 350 § 9.)

SECT. 21 amended, 1933, 254 § 22. (See 1933, 254 § 66.)

SECT. 24 amended, 1933, 254 § 23. (See 1933, 254 § 66.)

SECT. 26 amended, 1933, 254 § 24. (See 1933, 254 § 66.)

Chapter 58A. — Board of Tax Appeals.

For legislation temporarily increasing the membership of the board of tax appeals, see 1933, 321 § 1.

SECT. 6 amended, 1932, 180 § 10; revised, 1933, 167 § 4. (See 1933, 167 § 5.)

SECT. 7 revised, 1933, 321 § 2. (See 1933, 321 § 9.)

SECT. 7A added, 1933, 321 § 3 (providing for the establishment of informal procedure before the board of tax appeals). (See 1933, 321 §§ 8, 9.)

SECT. 8 revised, 1933, 321 § 4. (See 1933, 321 § 9.)

SECT. 10 revised, 1933, 321 § 5. (See 1933, 321 § 9.)

SECT. 12 amended, 1933, 321 § 6. (See 1933, 321 § 9.)
SECT. 13 revised, 1933, 321 § 7; one sentence revised, 1933, 350 § 8.
(See 1933, 321 § 9; 350 § 9.)

Chapter 59. — Assessment of Local Taxes.

For temporary provisions relative to old age assistance taxes and
state reimbursement of cities and towns for old age assistance given
by them, see 1932, 259 §§ 1, 2. (For prior legislation, see 1931, 398.)
As to Boston, see 1932, 125; 1933, 159.
SECT. 5, clause Third, subsection (c) amended, 1933, 198 § 1. (See
1933, 198 § 2); clause Twenty-third amended, 1932, 114 § 4.
SECT. 6 amended, 1933, 254 § 25. (See 1933, 254 § 66.)
SECT. 8 amended, 1933, 80; 254 § 26. (See 1933, 254 § 66.)
SECT. 9 amended, 1933, 254 § 27. (See 1933, 254 § 66.)
SECT. 10 amended, 1933, 254 § 28. (See 1933, 254 § 66.)
SECT. 11 amended, 1933, 254 § 29. (See 1933, 254 § 66.)
SECT. 18, opening paragraph and paragraphs First and Second
amended, 1933, 254 § 30. (See 1933, 254 § 66.)
SECT. 19 amended, 1933, 254 § 31. (See 1933, 254 § 66.)
SECT. 20 revised, 1933, 254 § 32. (See 1933, 254 § 66.)
SECT. 21 revised, 1933, 254 § 33. (See 1933, 254 § 66.)
SECT. 29, last three sentences revised, 1933, 254 § 34. (See 1933,
254 § 66.)
SECT. 33 amended, 1933, 254 § 35. (See 1933, 254 § 66.)
SECT. 39 amended, 1933, 254 § 36. (See 1933, 254 § 66.)
SECT. 41 amended, 1933, 254 § 37. (See 1933, 254 § 66.)
SECT. 45 amended, 1933, 254 § 38; form appended to section
amended, 1933, 254 § 39. (See 1933, 254 § 66.)
SECT. 47 amended, 1933, 254 § 40. (See 1933, 254 § 66.)
SECT. 49 amended, 1933, 254 § 41. (See 1933, 254 § 66.)
SECT. 57 amended, 1933, 151 § 1; revised, 1933, 254 § 42. (See
1933, 151 § 2; 254 § 66.)
SECT. 59, sentence added at end, 1933, 165 § 1; revised, 1933, 254
§ 43; 266 § 1. (See 1933, 254 § 66; 266 § 2.)
SECT. 61, last sentence revised, 1933, 165 § 2.
SECT. 64, first paragraph amended, 1933, 130 § 1.
SECT. 65 amended, 1933, 130 § 2; 167 § 1.
SECT. 65A added, 1932, 218 § 1 (providing that the sale or taking of
real property for payment of unpaid taxes thereon shall not prejudice
proceedings for the abatement of such taxes); revised, 1933, 325
§ 18. (See 1932, 218 § 2; 1933, 325 § 19.)
SECT. 73 amended, 1933, 254 § 44. (See 1933, 254 § 66.)
SECT. 74 amended, 1933, 254 § 45. (See 1933, 254 § 66.)
SECT. 83 amended, 1933, 254 § 46. (See 1933, 254 § 66.)
SECT. 84 amended, 1933, 254 § 47. (See 1933, 254 § 66.)
SECT. 85 amended, 1933, 254 § 48. (See 1933, 254 § 66.)
SECT. 86 amended, 1933, 254 § 49. (See 1933, 254 § 66.)

Chapter 60. — Collection of Local Taxes.

Temporary acts providing for advance payments on account of
taxes (for 1932, 1933 and 1934) in certain cities and towns, 1932, 94;
1933, 99.

SECT. 1, third paragraph revised, 1933, 164 § 1.
SECT. 3 revised, 1933, 254 § 50. (See 1933, 254 § 66.)
SECT. 5 revised, 1933, 168 § 2.
SECT. 16 revised, 1933, 168 § 1; amended, 1933, 254 § 51. (See 1933, 168 § 4; 254 § 66.)
SECT. 18 repealed, 1932, 54 § 1.
SECT. 22 revised, 1933, 254 § 52; affected, 1933, 308. (See 1933, 254 § 66.)
SECT. 23 revised, 1932, 197 § 1.
SECT. 37 amended, 1933, 254 § 53; 325 § 1. (See 1933, 254 § 66.)
SECT. 38 amended, 1933, 254 § 54; 325 § 2. (See 1933, 254 § 66; 325 § 21.)
SECT. 39 amended, 1933, 325 § 3.
SECT. 42 revised, 1933, 164 § 2.
SECT. 43, last sentence revised, 1932, 54 § 2.
SECT. 45 amended, 1933, 325 § 4.
SECT. 48 amended, 1933, 325 § 5. (See 1933, 325 § 20.)
SECT. 50 revised, 1933, 325 § 6.
SECT. 51 amended, 1933, 254 § 55. (See 1933, 254 § 66.)
SECT. 53 revised, 1933, 164 § 3. (See 1933, 325 § 20.)
SECT. 54 amended, 1933, 325 § 7.
SECT. 55 amended, 1933, 325 § 8.
SECT. 58 revised, 1932, 2.
SECT. 59 amended, 1933, 254 § 56. (See 1933, 254 § 66.)
SECT. 61 revised, 1933, 325 § 9. (See 1933, 325 § 20.)
SECT. 62 revised, 1933, 325 § 10.
SECT. 63 amended, 1933, 325 § 11.
SECT. 65 amended, 1933, 325 § 12.
SECT. 78 amended, 1933, 325 § 13. (See 1933, 325 § 20.)
SECT. 79, second paragraph amended, 1933, 325 § 14.
SECT. 80 amended, 1933, 325 § 15.
SECT. 84A revised, 1933, 325 § 16.
SECT. 92 revised, 1933, 82 § 1.
SECT. 95 revised, 1933, 325 § 17.
SECT. 105 revised, 1933, 168 § 3.
Form 2 in schedule at end of chapter repealed, 1932, 54 § 1; schedule of forms at end of chapter stricken out, 1933, 168 § 3.

Chapter 61. — Taxation of Forest Products and Classification and Taxation of Forest Lands.

SECT. 3 amended, 1933, 254 § 57. (See 1933, 254 § 66.)

Chapter 62. — Taxation of Incomes.

For temporary legislation, discontinuing the income tax exemption as to dividends of certain corporations, see 1933, 307, 357.
SECT. 33, paragraph added, 1932, 186.
SECT. 36 amended, 1933, 167 § 2.
SECT. 37 revised, 1933, 350 § 1. (See 1933, 350 § 9.)
SECT. 37A added, 1933, 350 § 2 (providing for the payment of income taxes in two installments). (See 1933, 350 § 9.)
SECT. 39, first sentence revised, 1933, 350 § 3. (See 1933, 350 § 9.)

Sect. 41 revised, 1932, 152; 1933, 350 § 4. (See 1933, 350 § 9.)
Sect. 43 amended, 1933, 350 § 5. (See 1933, 350 § 9.)
Sect. 46 revised, 1933, 350 § 6. (See 1933, 350 § 9.)

Chapter 63. — Taxation of Corporations.

Sect. 1, paragraph defining "Net income" revised, 1933, 327 § 1. (See 1933, 327 § 7.)
Sect. 2 amended, 1933, 327 § 2. (See 1933, 327 § 7.)
Sect. 3 amended, 1933, 254 § 58. (See 1933, 254 § 66.)
Sect. 5 amended, 1933, 254 § 59. (See 1933, 254 § 66.)
Sect. 30, paragraph contained in lines 48–51 amended, 1933, 58 § 3; paragraph contained in lines 70–74 amended, 1933, 58 § 4; paragraph 5 revised, 1933, 327 § 3. (See 1933, 58 § 5; 327 § 7.)
Sect. 32 revised, 1933, 342 § 1. (See 1933, 342 § 6.)
Sect. 32A amended, 1933, 342 § 2. (See 1933, 342 § 6.)
Sect. 33 revised, 1933, 303 § 1. (See 1933, 303 § 3.)
Sect. 34 amended, 1933, 327 § 4. (See 1933, 327 § 7.)
Sect. 35 revised, 1933, 58 § 1.
Sect. 36 revised, 1933, 327 § 5. (See 1933, 327 § 7.)
Sect. 38, paragraph 10 added at end, 1933, 342 § 3. (See 1933, 342 § 6.)
Sect. 39, last paragraph amended, 1933, 327 § 6; new paragraph added at end, 1933, 342 § 4. (See 1933, 327 § 7; 342 § 6.)
Sect. 39A revised, 1933, 303 § 2. (See 1933, 303 § 3.)
Sect. 40 revised, 1933, 58 § 2.
Sect. 42, last sentence amended, 1932, 180 § 11; section revised, 1933, 342 § 5. (See 1933, 342 § 6.)
Sect. 43. See 1933, 307 § 9A.
Sect. 45 amended, 1933, 195 § 1. (See 1933, 195 § 2.)
Sect. 53, first paragraph amended, 1933, 254 § 60. (See 1933, 254 § 66.)
Sect. 54, paragraph in lines 9—17 amended, 1933, 254 § 61. (See 1933, 254 § 66.)
Sect. 71 amended, 1933, 167 § 3.

Chapter 64A. — Taxation of Sales of Gasoline and Certain Other Motor Vehicle Fuel.

Chapter affected, 1932, 248.

Chapter 65. — Taxation of Legacies and Successions.

Sect. 1, table revised, 1933, 293.
Sects. 24A–24F added, 1933, 319 (providing reciprocal relations in respect to death taxes upon estates of non-resident decedents).

Chapter 65A. — Taxation of Transfers of Certain Estates.

Sect. 1, paragraph added at end, 1932, 284; second paragraph revised, 1933, 316 § 1. (See 1933, 316 § 2.)

Chapter 69. — Powers and Duties of the Department of Education.

Sect. 6 amended, 1932, 127 § 3.
Sect. 8 amended, 1932, 127 § 4.

Chapter 70. — School Funds and Other State Aid for Public Schools.

SECT. 2 amended, 1932, 127 § 5.
SECT. 6 amended, 1932, 127 § 6.
SECT. 18 amended, 1932, 127 § 7.

Chapter 71. — Public Schools.

SECT. 46A amended, 1932, 159.
SECT. 52 amended, 1932, 90.
SECT. 58 amended, 1932, 127 § 8.

Chapter 73. — State Teachers Colleges (former title, State Normal Schools).

Title changed, 1932, 127 § 9.
SECT. 1 amended, 1932, 127 § 10.
SECT. 2 amended, 1932, 127 § 11.
SECT. 3 amended, 1932, 127 § 12.
SECT. 4 amended, 1932, 127 § 13.
SECT. 4A amended, 1932, 127 § 14.
SECT. 5 amended, 1932, 127 § 15.
SECT. 6 amended, 1932, 127 § 16.
SECT. 7 amended, 1932, 127 § 17.

Chapter 74. — Vocational Education.

SECT. 11 amended, 1933, 102 § 2.   (See 1933, 102 § 4.)
SECT. 23 repealed, 1933, 102 § 3.   (See 1933, 102 § 4.)

Chapter 77. — School Offenders and County Training Schools.

For legislation requiring the closing of the Norfolk, Bristol and Plymouth union training school, see 1933, 295 § 2.
SECT. 1 revised, 1933, 295 § 1.

Chapter 80. — Betterments.

SECT. 1 amended, 1933, 254 § 62.   (See 1933, 254 § 66.)
SECT. 4 revised, 1933, 63 § 1.
SECT. 5 amended, 1933, 157 § 2.   (See 1933, 157 § 3.)
SECT. 10 revised, 1933, 147.
SECT. 10A added, 1933, 157 § 1 (providing that failure of a board of officers to take action upon a petition for abatement of a betterment assessment shall, for the purposes of appeal, be equivalent to refusal to abate the assessment).   (See 1933, 157 § 3.)
SECT. 13 amended, 1933, 63 § 2; 254 § 63.   (See 1933, 254 § 66.)

Chapter 81. — State Highways.

SECT. 19, last four sentences stricken out, 1933, 187 § 1.   (See 1933, 187 § 2.)

Chapter 82. — The Laying Out, Alteration, Relocation and Discontinuance of Public Ways, and Specific Repairs Thereon.

SECT. 7 amended, 1933, 283 § 2.
SECT. 32B added, 1933, 283 § 3 (authorizing the taking of easements of slope, so called, by county, city or town officers in connection with the laying out, widening, altering or relocating of public ways).

Chapter 84. — Repair of Ways and Bridges.

Sect. 18 revised, 1933, 114 § 1.
SECT. 19 amended, 1933, 114 § 2.
SECT. 20 revised, 1933, 114 § 3.

Chapter 85. — Regulations and By-Laws relative to Ways and Bridges.

SECT. 17B added, 1933, 43 (prohibiting riding upon the rear or on the side of street railway cars or motor buses without the consent of the persons in charge thereof).

Chapter 89. — Law of the Road.

SECT. 2 revised, 1933, 301.

Chapter 90. — Motor Vehicles and Aircraft.

SECT. 1, paragraph defining "motor vehicles" amended, 1932, 182; paragraph (defining "school bus") added, 1932, 271 § 1; two paragraphs (defining "semi-trailer" and "semi-trailer unit") added, 1933, 332 § 1; paragraph in lines 52–56 stricken out, and two paragraphs (defining "tractor" and "trailer") inserted, 1933, 332 § 2. (See 1932, 271 § 7; 1933, 332 § 5.)

SECT. 1A amended, 1933, 372 § 3.

SECT. 2, fourth paragraph revised, 1932, 5; last paragraph revised, 1933, 54.

SECT. 3, first sentence revised, 1933, 188.

SECT. 7 amended, 1932, 123 § 1; 1933, 51; second sentence amended, 1933, 109. (See 1932, 123 § 2.)

SECT. 7A revised, 1932, 41, 271 § 2. (See 1932, 271 § 7.)

SECT. 7B added, 1932, 271 § 3 (prerequisites to operation of school bus). (See 1932, 271 § 7.)

SECT. 9A revised, 1932, 168 § 1. (See 1932, 168 §§ 2, 3.)

SECT. 15 amended, 1932, 271 § 5; 1933, 26 § 1. (See 1932, 271 § 7.)

SECT. 17, sentence added at end, 1932, 271 § 4. (See 1932, 271 § 7.)

SECT. 19, last sentence revised, 1933, 332 § 3. (See 1933, 332 § 5.)

SECT. 22, two paragraphs added at end, 1933, 191.

SECT. 22A added, 1932, 304 § 1 (requiring the suspension of licenses to operate motor vehicles issued to persons who do not satisfy judgments in motor vehicle accident cases involving property damage). (See 1932, 304 § 2.)

SECT. 23, new paragraph added at end, 1933, 69.

SECT. 24 amended, 1932, 26 § 1.

SECT. 29, last sentence amended, 1932, 26 § 2.

SECT. 33, paragraph in lines 21–41 amended, 1932, 180 § 12; same paragraph stricken out, and two paragraphs inserted, 1933, 332 § 4; first three paragraphs stricken out, and five new paragraphs inserted, 1932, 249 § 1; fourth paragraph (as appearing in 1932, 249 § 1) amended, 1933, 183 § 1. (See 1932, 249 § 2; 1933, 183 § 2; 332 § 5.)

SECT. 34 amended, 1933, 197 § 3.

SECT. 34B, second paragraph revised, 1933, 83 § 1; fourth paragraph revised, 1933, 83 § 2. (See 1933, 83 § 3.)

SECT. 34C amended, 1932, 180 § 13.

Sect. 34H, first paragraph amended, 1933, 119 § 4; new paragraph inserted, 1933, 119 § 5. (See 1933, 119 § 6.)
Sect. 53, last sentence amended, 1932, 180 § 14.

Chapter 92. — Metropolitan Sewers, Water and Parks.
Sect. 56 revised, 1933, 197 § 1.
Sect. 57 amended, 1933, 197 § 2.

Chapter 94. — Inspection and Sale of Food, Drugs and Various Articles.
Sect. 1, paragraph in lines 128–132 (defining "pasteurized milk") revised, 1932, 158; section amended in part, 1933, 67 §§ 1–5; paragraph (defining "milk plant" and "manufactory") added, 1933, 338 § 1.
Sects. 13, 14, 14A and 15 stricken out, and new sections 13–13E (relative to the grading of milk) inserted, 1933, 263 § 1. (See 1933, 263 § 3.)
Sect. 16 stricken out and sections 16–16I (regulating the production, sale and distribution of milk) inserted, 1932, 305 § 3. (See 1932, 305 § § 5, 6.)
Sect. 17A amended, 1933, 124.
Sect. 18 revised, 1933, 263 § 2. (See 1933, 263 § 3.)
Sect. 29A revised, 1933, 253.
Sect. 30 revised, 1933, 253.
Sect. 31 revised, 1933, 253.
Sect. 42A stricken out, and new sections 42A–42K (requiring dealers in milk or cream to be licensed and bonded) inserted, 1933, 338 § 2.
Sect. 43 revised, 1932, 305 § 4. (See 1932, 305 §§ 5, 6.)
Sect. 74 revised, 1933, 329 § 5.
Sect. 74A added, 1933, 329 § 6 (definition of "fish").
Sects. 75 and 76 repealed, 1933, 329 § 7.
Sect. 77, first sentence stricken out, 1933, 329 § 8.
Sect. 78 revised, 1933, 329 § 9.
Sect. 78A added, 1933, 329 § 10 (prohibiting certain misrepresentations in the sale of lobsters).
Sect. 79 repealed, 1933, 329 § 7.
Sect. 81 revised, 1933, 329 § 11.
Sect. 83 revised, 1933, 329 § 12.
Sect. 88A revised, 1933, 329 § 13.
Sect. 123 amended, 1932, 180 § 15.
Sect. 153A added, 1933, 116 (relative to the sale of meat and meat products containing certain preservatives); revised, 1933, 311.
Sect. 245 revised, 1933, 94 § 2.
Sect. 249G added, under caption "material for road construction", 1933, 94 § 1 (authorizing certain officers to direct the weighing of material for road construction).
Sect. 250 revised, 1933, 67 § 6.
Sect. 252 amended, 1933, 67 § 7.
Sect. 254 amended, 1933, 67 § 8.
Sect. 255 amended, 1933, 67 § 9.
Sect. 256 revised, 1933, 67 § 10.
Sect. 257 revised, 1933, 67 § 11.

SECT. 258 revised, 1933, 67 § 12.

SECT. 295A added, under heading "PETROLEUM PRODUCTS", 1933, 228 (relative to prevention of fraud and misrepresentation in the sale of gasoline, lubricating oils and other motor fuels, and to prevention of the adulteration thereof).

Chapter 100. — Auctioneers.

SECT. 5 amended, 1932, 156 § 1.
SECT. 14 revised, 1932, 156 § 2.
SECT. 16 revised, 1932, 156 § 3.

Chapter 101. — Transient Vendors, Hawkers and Pedlers.

SECT. 5 amended, 1933, 254 § 64.   (See 1933, 254 § 66.)

Chapter 102. — Shipping and Seamen, Harbors and Harbor Masters.

SECT. 15 revised, 1932, 232 § 1,
SECT. 15A added, 1932, 232 § 2 (penalty for improper operation of motor and other boats).
SECT. 17 revised, 1932, 57.

Chapter 108A. — Partnerships.

SECT. 34, first paragraph amended, 1932, 180 § 16.

Chapter 110A. — Promotion and Sale of Securities.

C a er repealed and superseded by 1932, 290 § 1.   (See 1932, 290 §§ 3ᵇ 4ᵖⱡ)

Chapter 111. — Public Health.

SECT. 27A revised, 1932, 209.
SECT. 83A added, 1933, 318 § 6 (relative to the indemnification or protection of officers and employees of tuberculosis hospital districts in connection with actions for personal injuries arising out of the operation of vehicles owned by such districts).   (See 1933, 318 § 9.)
SECT. 85A revised, 1932, 65.
SECT. 110, second sentence amended, 1932, 180 § 17.
SECT. 118 amended, 1933, 44.
SECT. 143 revised, 1933, 269 § 2.

Chapter 112. — Registration of Certain Professions and Occupations.

SECT. 2, second sentence revised, 1933, 171 § 1.   (See 1933, 171 § 2.)
SECT. 9 revised, 1933, 152.
SECT. 24 amended, 1932, 227; 1933, 126.
SECT. 45, second sentence amended, 1932, 180 § 18.
SECT. 87O amended, 1933, 149 § 2.   (See 1933, 149 § 3.)

Chapter 115. — State and Military Aid, Soldiers' Relief, etc.

SECT. 2A added, 1932, 113 (requiring the furnishing of information to the commissioner of state aid and pensions by certain banks and other depositories relative to certain deposits therein).

SECT. 12A added, 1933, 363 (making certain Massachusetts veterans receiving hospital treatment outside the commonwealth eligible to receive military aid).

SECT. 15 amended, 1932, 106.

SECT. 17, paragraph added, 1932, 63.

SECT. 18, sentence added at end of first paragraph, 1933, 323; paragraph added at end, 1932, 270.

SECT. 19 amended, 1932, 250.

SECT. 20 amended, 1932, 251.

Chapter 116. — Settlement.

SECT. 2 revised, 1933, 213.

Chapter 117. — Support by Cities and Towns.

SECT. 2A added, 1933, 181 (authorizing local boards of public welfare to aid needy persons in the cultivation of vegetable gardens).

SECT. 35 amended, 1932, 180 § 19.·

Chapter 118A. — Adequate Assistance to Certain Aged Citizens.

For temporary provisions relative to old age assistance taxes and state reimbursement of cities and towns for old age assistance given by them, see 1932, 259 §§ 1, 2. (For prior legislation, see 1931, 398.)

For legislation authorizing collectors of taxes to include, in demands issued under G. L., ch. 60 § 16 statements of old age assistance taxes, see 1933, 168 § 4.

For legislation providing for the use of certain money received as fees under the beer bill, so called, for reimbursing the cities and towns of the commonwealth on account of assistance rendered under this chapter, see 1933, 120 § 17, as revised by 1933, 234 § 2.

SECT. 1 amended, 1933, 219; revised, 1933, 328.

SECT. 2A added, 1933, 285 (providing for appeals by persons aggrieved by failure of cities and towns to render old age assistance).

SECT. 3 revised, 1932, 259 § 3.

Chapter 119. — Protection and Care of Children, and Proceedings against Them.

SECT. 12 revised, 1932, 180 § 20.

SECT. 63 revised, 1932, 95 § 1.

SECT. 65 amended, 1932, 95 § 2.

SECT. 74 amended, 1933, 196 § 1.

SECT. 75 amended, 1933, 196 § 2.

Chapter 120. — Massachusetts Training Schools.

SECT. 21, first sentence amended, 1932, 180 § 21.

Chapter 121. — Powers and Duties of the Department of Public Welfare, and the Massachusetts Hospital School.

SECT. 23 (and caption) amended, 1933, 364 § 2. (See 1933, 364 § 8.)

SECT. 24 amended, 1933, 364 § 3. (See 1933, 364 § 8.)

SECT. 25 revised, 1933, 364 § 4. (See 1933, 364 § 8.)

SECT. 26 amended, 1933, 364 § 5. (See 1933, 364 § 8.)

SECTS. 26A–26H added, 1933, 364 § 6 (relative to the powers and duties of the state board of housing, and to limited dividend corporations under its control). (See 1933, 364 § 8.)
SECT. 27 repealed, 1933, 364 § 7.
SECT. 42 amended, 1932, 180 § 22.

Chapter 122. — State Infirmary.

SECT. 6 amended, 1933, 345.

Chapter 123. — Commitment and Care of the Insane and Other Mental Defectives.

SECT. 32 revised, 1933, 115.
SECT. 39B added, 1932, 204 (relative to the disposition of unclaimed belongings at certain state hospitals, known as "patients' valuables").
SECT. 39C added, 1933, 256 (relative to the disposition of moneys represented by certain bank books belonging to former patients of certain state hospitals).
SECT. 52 amended, 1932, 85.
SECT. 90, first sentence amended, 1932, 180 § 23.

Chapter 125. — Penal and Reformatory Institutions of the Commonwealth.

SECT. 4 amended, 1932, 282 § 3.
SECT. 30 amended, 1932, 180 § 24.

Chapter 127. — Officers and Inmates of Penal and Reformatory Institutions, Paroles and Pardons.

SECT. 16, last sentence stricken out, 1933, 77 § 1.
SECT. 17 revised, 1933, 77 § 2.
SECT. 18 amended, 1933, 77 § 3.
SECT. 67A added, 1932, 252 § 1 (regulating the sale of prison made goods). (See 1932, 252 § 2.)
SECT. 111A added, 1933, 169 (relative to transfers of defective delinquents and drug addicts from one institution to another under the department of correction).
SECT. 133 revised, 1933, 134 § 1. (See 1933, 134 § 2.)
SECT. 146 revised, 1932, 221 § 1.
SECT. 151, last sentence amended, 1932, 180 § 25.

Chapter 128. — Agriculture.

SECT. 2, paragraph (g) added, 1933, 291 § 1.
SECT. 6 amended, 1933, 291 § 2.
SECT. 39 repealed, 1933, 74 § 2.
SECT. 42 revised, 1932, 166.

Chapter 129A. — Marine Fish and Fisheries, Inland Fish and Fisheries, Birds and Mammals. General Provisions.

Chapter added, 1933, 329 § 1.

Chapter 130. — Marine Fish and Fisheries, including Crustacea and Shellfish (former title, Powers and Duties of the Division of Fisheries and Game. Fisheries).

Entire chapter repealed, and new chapter 130 (with new title) inserted, 1933, 329 § 2.
The following reference is to the original chapter 130:

SECT. 48A added, 1933, 118 (prohibiting the taking of certain herring or alewives from the waters of Plymouth harbor, Kingston bay, Duxbury bay and certain waters of Plymouth bay).

Chapter 131. — Game and Inland Fisheries (former title, Powers and Duties of the Division of Fisheries and Game.   Game and Inland Fisheries).

Title amended, 1933, 329 § 14.
SECTS. 1–4 repealed, 1933, 329 § 20.
SECT. 5 amended, 1932, 272 § 1; 1933, 214 § 1.
SECT. 6 revised, 1932, 272 § 2.
SECT. 7 revised, 1932, 272 § 3.
SECT. 8 revised, 1932, 272 § 4.
SECT. 8A added, 1933, 214 § 2 (establishing special fox hunting licenses for non-resident members and guests of clubs or associations conducting fox hunts).
SECTS. 9–11 repealed, 1933, 329 § 20.
SECT. 12 amended, 1932, 272 § 5; revised, 1933, 214 § 3.
SECT. 13 revised, 1933, 329 § 15.
SECTS. 14–24 repealed, 1933, 329 § 20.
SECT. 24A added, 1932, 78 (relative to the establishment in certain brooks and streams of breeding areas for fish).
SECTS. 27–34 repealed, 1933, 329 § 20.
SECT. 42 repealed, 1933, 329 § 20.
SECT. 44 revised, 1933, 329 § 16.
SECT. 45, sentence added at end, 1932, 77.
SECT. 49 amended, 1933, 329 § 17.
SECTS. 52–55 repealed, 1933, 329 § 20.
SECT. 61A added, 1933, 329 § 18 (regulating the taking of smelt in great ponds).
SECT. 74 revised, 1932, 272 § 6.
SECT. 77 revised, 1933, 154.
SECT. 85 amended, 1932, 28.
SECT. 86A added, 1932, 60 (authorizing the director of fisheries and game to suspend or modify the open season or bag limit as to ruffed grouse and quail).
SECT. 87A added, 1933, 122 (relative to the taking or killing of waterfowl and other migratory birds in certain cases).
SECT. 92 amended, 1932, 52.
SECT. 99 amended, 1932, 180 § 26.
SECT. 100A added, 1932, 82 (prohibiting the hunting of beavers).
SECT. 104 revised, 1933, 192 § 1.
SECT. 105A revised, 1933, 203.
SECT. 109 revised, 1932, 264; 1933, 192 § 2.
SECT. 112 revised, 1933, 192 § 3.
SECT. 135 revised, 1932, 81; 272 § 7.
SECT. 137 added, 1933, 329 § 19 (relative to the protection of salmon fry in the Merrimack river).

Chapter 132. — Forestry.

SECT. 5 repealed, 1932, 180 § 27.

Chapter 132A. — State Parks and Reservations Outside of the Metropolitan Parks District.

SECT. 9 amended, 1933, 75 § 4.

Chapter 136. — Observance of the Lord's Day.

SECT. 2 amended, 1933, 150 § 1.

SECT. 4A added, 1933, 150 § 2 (relative to the licensing of certain enterprises to be held on the Lord's day at amusement parks and beach resorts); revised, 1933, 309 § 1. (See 1933, 309 § 2.)

SECT. 6, fourth paragraph amended, 1932, 96; paragraph added at end, 1933, 150 § 3.

SECT. 13 amended, 1932, 105.

SECT. 17, sentence added at end, 1933, 150 § 4.

SECT. 22. See 1933, 136.

Chapter 138. — Alcoholic Liquors (old title, Intoxicating Liquors and Certain Non-Intoxicating Beverages).

Beer bill, so called, 1933, 120 (amended by 1933, 216; 234; 346). (See also 1933, Res. 47.)

Act providing for a convention to act upon a proposed amendment to the constitution of the United States relative to the repeal of the eighteenth amendment, 1933, 132.

SECT. 1, paragraph in lines 4–7 amended, 1933, 97 § 1. (See 1933, 97 § 3; 346 § 9.)

SECT. 2 affected, 1933, 120 § 53.

SECT. 3 amended, 1933, 97 § 2. (See 1933, 97 § 3; 346 § 9.)

Chapter stricken out, and new chapter 138 inserted, 1933, 376 § 2.

Chapter 140. — Licenses.

SECT. 12 revised, 1932, 86; 1933, 92.

SECTS. 21E and 21F added, under caption "ORGANIZATIONS DISPENSING FOOD OR BEVERAGES TO MEMBERS AND GUESTS", 1933, 284 (providing for the regulation of such organizations).

SECT. 51 amended, 1932, 275.

SECT. 137 amended, 1932, 289 § 1.

SECT. 145 amended, 1932, 289 § 2.

SECT. 145A added, 1932, 289 § 3 (relative to the furnishing of anti-rabic vaccine).

SECT. 147 revised, 1932, 289 § 4.

SECT. 148 repealed, 1932, 289 § 6. (See G. L. chapter 41 § 13A, inserted by 1932, 289 § 5.)

SECT. 161, first two sentences amended, 1932, 289 § 7.

. SECT. 172 revised, 1932, 289 § 8.

SECT. 175 revised, 1932, 289 § 9.

Chapter 146. — Inspection of Boilers, Air Tanks, etc., Licenses of Engineers, Firemen, and Operators of Hoisting Machinery.

SECT. 16 revised, 1932, 180 § 28.

Chapter 147. — State and Other Police, and Certain Powers and Duties of the Department of Public Safety.

SECT. 36 revised, 1932, 79.

Chapter 148. — Fire Prevention.

SECT. 1, definition of "local licensing authority" amended, 1932, 102.

SECT. 10A added, 1932, 75 (relative to the granting of certain permits and the making of certain inspections by municipal officers designated by the state fire marshal).

SECT. 13, first paragraph amended, 1932, 22 § 1. (See 1932, 22 § 2.)

SECT. 27A added, 1932, 283 (relative to the protection of life and property from fire hazards incident to the present industrial emergency).

Chapter 149. — Labor and Industries.

For legislation relative to interstate compacts affecting labor and industry, see 1933, Res. 44.

SECT. 20A added, 1933, 351 § 1 (relative to the judicial enforcement of certain contracts relative to membership in labor or employers' organizations). (See 1933, 351 § 2.)

SECT. 24 amended, 1933, 272.

SECT. 50 revised, 1933, 225.

SECT. 56 amended, 1932, 110 § 1.

SECT. 57 amended, 1932, 110 § 2.

SECT. 59 amended, 1933, 193 § 1. (For temporary act, authorizing the commissioner of labor and industries to suspend certain provisions relative to the hours of employment of women in the textile and leather industries, see 1933, 347.)

SECT. 66 amended, 1933, 193 § 2.

SECT. 84 amended, 1932, 180 § 29.

SECT. 104 amended, 1932, 27.

SECT. 135 amended, 1933, 64.

SECTS. 142A–142F added, under caption "BENZOL AND MIXTURES CONTAINING BENZOL", 1933, 304 (regulating the sale, distribution, storage and use of benzol and its compounds).

SECT. 147A added, 1932, 234 (requiring the furnishing of certain information to the department of labor and industries with respect to the performance of certain industrial work in tenements and dwelling houses).

SECT. 148, last sentence amended, 1932, 101 § 1.

SECT. 150, sentence added at end, 1932, 101 § 2.

SECT. 157A added, 1933, 268 (insuring to piece or job workers in factories and workshops information relative to their compensation).

SECT. 178A added, 1932, 175 (authorizing the payment of small amounts of wages or salary of intestate employees to certain next of kin without administration).

Chapter 151. — The Minimum Wage.

SECT. 8 amended, 1933, 110.

SECTS. 11A–11D added, 1933, 220 § 1 (relative to the more effective enforcement of decrees of the minimum wage commission). (See 1933, 220 § 2.)

Chapter 152. — Workmen's Compensation.

SECT. 11 amended, 1932, 129 § 1.

SECT. 12, last paragraph amended, 1932, 117 § 1.   (See 1932, 117 § 2.)

SECT. 13, sentence added at end, 1933, 68.

SECT. 36, paragraph (*j*) revised, 1933, 257.

SECT. 69 revised, 1933, 318 § 7.

SECT. 69A added, 1933, 315 (regulating workmen's compensation payments by the Commonwealth).

SECT. 75 revised, 1932, 19.

Chapter 154. — Assignment of Wages.

SECT. 8 added, 1933, 96 (exempting orders for payment of labor or trade union or craft dues or obligations from the operation of the laws regulating assignments of wages).

Chapter 155. — General Provisions relative to Corporations.

SECT. 10 amended, 1933, 11.

SECT. 50 amended, 1933, 66.

Chapter 156. — Business Corporations.

SECT. 12, form of certificate revised, 1932, 67.

SECT. 41 revised, 1932, 136.

SECT. 54 amended, 1932, 180 § 30.

Chapter 157. — Co-operative Corporations.

SECT. 16, last sentence amended, 1932, 180 § 31.

Chapter 159. — Common Carriers.

SECT. 59 revised, 1933, 326 § 1.

SECT. 60 amended, 1933, 326 § 2.

SECT. 61 amended, 1933, 326 § 3.

SECT. 62 amended, 1933, 326 § 4.

SECT. 103 amended, 1933, 10.

Chapter 159A. — Carriers by Motor Vehicle (former title, Common Carriers of Passengers by Motor Vehicle).

Title amended, and headings, "PART I.", "CARRIERS OF PASSENGERS BY MOTOR VEHICLE", inserted before Section 1, 1933, 372 § 1.

SECTS. 17–30 added, under headings, "PART II.", "CARRIERS OF PROPERTY BY MOTOR VEHICLE", 1933, 372 § 2 (regulating carriers of property by motor vehicle).

Chapter 160. — Railroads.

SECT. 70 amended, 1932, 238.

SECT. 70A revised, 1932, 236.

SECT. 104 revised, 1933, 176.

Chapter 161. — Street Railways.

Name of metropolitan transit district changed to Boston Metropolitan District, and authority to issue notes and bonds defined, 1932, 147.

Temporary act, extending to January 15th, 1939, the period of public control and management of the Eastern Massachusetts Street Railway Company, 1933, 108.

Temporary act relative to the purchase of bonds of the Boston Elevated Railway Company by the Boston Metropolitan District for the purpose of refinancing certain maturing obligations of said Company, 1933, 235.

Chapter 163. — Trackless Trolley Companies.

SECT. 12 added, 1932, 185 (requiring trackless trolley companies to furnish security for civil liability on account of personal injuries or property damage caused by their vehicles).

Chapter 164. — Manufacture and Sale of Gas and Electricity.

For legislation authorizing compacts relative to the interstate transmission of electricity and gas, see 1933, 294.

SECT. 17A added, 1932, 132 (regulating the lending of money by gas and electric companies).

SECT. 33 amended, 1932, 180 § 32.

SECT. 85A added, 1933, 202 § 1 (requiring the filing with the department of public utilities of certain contracts of gas and electric companies with affiliated companies).

SECT. 105A added, 1932, 119 (regulating the storage, transportation and distribution of gas).

Chapter 165. — Water and Aqueduct Companies.

SECT. 4A added, 1933, 202 § 2 (requiring the filing with the department of public utilities of certain contracts of water companies with affiliated companies).

Chapter 166. — Telephone and Telegraph Companies, and Lines for the Transmission of Electricity.

SECT. 22, second paragraph amended, 1932, 36.

SECT. 22A added, 1932, 266 (relative to the placing underground of certain wires); revised, 1933, 251.

Chapter 167. — Banks and Banking.

For temporary act, authorizing the commissioner of banks to borrow within two years from March 30th, 1932, funds for the payment of dividends in liquidation of certain closed banks, see 1932, 122.

For temporary act, operative until January 1st, 1938, authorizing savings banks and savings departments of trust companies to grant loans on proofs of claim of depositors in closed savings banks and in savings departments of closed trust companies, see 1932, 217.

For temporary act, authorizing the governor to proclaim the existence of a banking emergency, and providing for the further protection of depositors in banks and the maintenance of the banking structure of the commonwealth, see 1933, 59. (See also 1933, Res. 2.)

For temporary act, facilitating the reorganization of certain trust companies, and empowering certain holders of deposits in certain national banking associations to take in substitution therefor preferred stock in such associations, see 1933, 112.

For temporary act, authorizing banks and credit unions to cooperate in action under the Federal Home Owners' Loan Act of 1933, see 1933, 343.

Sect. 2A added, 1933, 310 (improving the method of examination of banks).

Sect. 5 revised, 1933, 337.

Sect. 14 revised, 1933, 334 § 1.

Sect. 17 repealed, 1933, 334 § 2.

Sect. 20 amended, 1933, 190.

Sect. 20A added, 1933, 292 (permitting certain public officers to participate in certain bank reorganizations)..

Sect. 22.   See 1933, 59 § 5; 112 § 7.

Sect. 23.   See 1933, 112 § 6.

Sect. 24 amended, 1932, 294; 1933, 41 § 4.

Sect. 31A added, 1933, 277 (authorizing payment of dividends on small deposits in closed banks to certain minors and to the next of kin of certain deceased persons without probate proceedings).

Sect. 35A added, 1933, 302 (authorizing the destruction of certain books, records and papers relating to closed banks).

Chapter 168. — Savings Banks.

For temporary act, establishing the Mutual Savings Central Fund, Inc., for the term of five years, see 1932, 44.

For temporary act, operative until January 1st, 1938, authorizing savings banks and savings departments of trust companies to grant loans on proofs of claim of depositors in closed savings banks and in savings departments of closed trust companies, see 1932, 217.

For temporary act, authorizing the governor to proclaim the existence of a banking emergency, and providing for the further protection of depositors in banks and the maintenance of the banking structure of the commonwealth, see 1933, 59. (See also 1933, Res. 2.)

For temporary act, authorizing banks and credit unions to cooperate in action under the Federal Home Owners' Loan Act of 1933, see 1933, 343.

Sect. 1, two paragraphs (defining "deposit book [etc.]" and "savings bank") added at end, 1933, 334 § 3.

Sect. 2 revised, 1933, 334 § 4.

Sect. 2A added, 1933, 46 § 1 (authorizing savings banks to become members of the Federal Home Loan Bank established for the district of New England).

Sect. 11 amended, 1933, 334 § 5.

Sect. 13 amended, 1933, 334 § 6.   (See 1933, 41 § 1.)

Sect. 17 revised, 1933, 334 § 7.

Sect. 25 revised, 1933, 334 § 8.

Sect. 25A added, 1933, 334 § 8 (authorizing the collection of savings from school children through principals, teachers, etc.).

Sect. 26 revised, 1933, 334 § 9.

Sect. 27 amended, 1933, 334 § 10.

SECT. 28 revised, 1933, 334 § 11.
SECT. 29 amended, 1933, 334 § 12.
SECT. 33A revised, 1933, 334 § 13.
SECT. 34 revised, 1933, 334 § 14.
SECT. 35 revised, 1933, 334 § 15.
SECT. 45 amended, 1933, 334 § 16.
SECT. 47 revised, 1933, 334 § 17.
SECT. 49 amended, 1933, 334 § 18.
SECT. 50 revised, 1933, 334 § 19.
SECT. 51 revised, 1932, 245 § 1.
SECT. 51A revised, 1933, 334 § 20.
SECT. 53 revised, 1933, 334 § 21.

SECT. 54, clause First, first two paragraphs revised, 1933, 334 § 22;
clause Second, subdivisions (a), (e) and (f) revised, 1933, 334 § 23;
subdivision (h) added, 1933, 334 § 24 (forbidding investment of funds
in bonds or notes of county, etc., in default, and defining term "in
default"); clause Third affected, 1933, 111; clause Fourth amended,
1932, 112; clause Seventh, second paragraph revised, 1932, 220; clause
Ninth, subdivision (c), paragraph (2) stricken out, 1933, 334 § 25;
subdivision (e), paragraphs (2), (3) and (5) revised, 1933, 334 § 26;
clause Sixteenth affected, 1933, 111.

SECT. 55, paragraph added at end, 1933, 334 § 27 (authorizing the
continuing of the offices of a merged savings bank as branch offices of
the continuing bank).

SECT. 56 added, 1933, 41 § 1 (authorizing savings banks to purchase, loan upon or participate in loans upon the assets of certain
closed and other banks).

SECT. 57 added, 1933, 334 § 28 (authorizing savings banks to become members of savings bank associations).

Chapter 169. — Deposits with Others than Banks.

For temporary act, authorizing the governor to proclaim the
existence of a banking emergency, and providing for the further protection of depositors in banks and the maintenance of the banking
structure of the commonwealth, see 1933, 59.   (See also 1933, Res. 2.)

Chapter 170. — Co-operative Banks.

For temporary act, establishing the Co-operative Central Bank, for
the term of five years, see 1932, 45.

For temporary act, authorizing the governor to proclaim the
existence of a banking emergency, and providing for the further protection of depositors in banks and the maintenance of the banking
structure of the commonwealth, see 1933, 59.   (See also 1933,
Res. 2.)

For temporary act, authorizing banks and credit unions to co-
operate in action under the Federal Home Owners' Loan Act of 1933,
see 1933, 343.

SECT. 16 revised, 1932, 292 § 1.
SECT. 19 amended, 1932, 292 § 2.
SECT. 20A added, 1932, 292 § 3 (authorizing payment to spouse or
next of kin without administration in case value of shares does not
exceed two hundred dollars).

Sect. 36A added, 1932, 292 § 4 (authorizing and regulating borrowings to meet withdrawals and to loan against shares).

Sect. 40, paragraph added at end, 1932, 233 § 1.

Sect. 41 amended, 1932, 233 § 2.

Sect. 42 amended, 1932, 233 § 3.

Sect. 45A added, 1933, 46 § 2 (authorizing co-operative banks to become members of the Federal Home Loan Bank established for the district of New England).

Sect. 50 added, 1932, 201 (authorizing co-operative banks to become members of certain leagues).

Chapter stricken out and new chapter inserted, 1933, 144.

Chapter 171. — Credit Unions.

For temporary act, establishing the Central Credit Union Fund, Inc., for the term of five years, see 1932, 216.

For temporary act, authorizing the governor to proclaim the existence of a banking emergency, and providing for the further protection of depositors in banks and the maintenance of the banking structure of the commonwealth, see 1933, 59. (See also 1933, Res. 2.)

For temporary act, authorizing banks and credit unions to co-operate inaction under the Federal Home Owners' Loan Act of 1933, see 1933, 343.

Sect. 15, last sentence stricken out, and paragraph added at end, 1933, 163 § 1.

Sect. 21 amended, 1933, 163 § 2.

Sect. 24, paragraph added at end of subdivision (A), 1933, 163 § 3.

Chapter 172. — Trust Companies.

For temporary act, operative until January 1st, 1938, authorizing savings banks and savings departments of trust companies to grant loans on proofs of claim of depositors in closed savings banks and in savings departments of closed trust companies, see 1932, 217.

For temporary act, authorizing the governor to proclaim the existence of a banking emergency, and providing for the further protection of depositors in banks and the maintenance of the banking structure of the commonwealth, see 1933, 59. (See also 1933, Res. 2.)

For temporary act, facilitating the reorganization of certain trust companies, and empowering certain holders of deposits in certain national banking associations to take in substitution therefor preferred stock in such associations, see 1933, 112.

For temporary act, authorizing banks and credit unions to co-operate in action under the Federal Home Owners' Loan Act of 1933, see 1933, 343.

Sect. 44A added, 1933, 41 § 2 (authorizing trust companies to purchase, loan upon or participate in loans upon the assets of certain closed and other banks.)

Sect. 61 amended, 1933, 41 § 3.

Sect. 66 revised, 1932, 245 § 2.

Sect. 67, paragraph added at end, 1933, 334 § 29 (regulating the declaration and payment of interest on deposits in savings departments of trust companies).

SECT. 82 added, under caption "SET-OFF OR RECOUPMENT OF DEPOSITS", 1932, 295 § 1.   (See 1932, 295 § 2.)
SECTS. 83–89 added, under caption "CONSERVATORSHIP", 1933, 87 § 1.
SECTS. 83, 88.   See 1933, 112 §§ 6, 9.
SECT. 90 added, 1933, 273 (relative to the enforcement of conservatorship proceedings in respect to trust companies).

Chapter 175. — Insurance.

For temporary act, relative to the support and regulation of the business of insurance companies during the present emergency, see 1933, 65.
SECT. 5 amended, 1933, 107 § 2.
SECT. 6, first paragraph amended, 1933, 107 § 3.
SECT. 11, third paragraph amended, 1933, 5.
SECT. 50, third sentence amended, 1932, 180 § 33.
SECT. 54A added, 1932, 165 (permitting certain insurance companies to make outside the commonwealth contracts insuring personal property against all risks or hazards).
SECT 79 revised, 1933, 23 § 1.
SECT. 90B revised, 1933, 23 § 2.
SECT. 94, first two paragraphs stricken out, and new paragraph inserted, 1933, 81.
SECT. 97 amended, 1933, 31.
SECT. 102 amended, 1932, 174 § 1.   (See 1932, 174 § 2.)
SECT. 106 revised, 1932, 150 § 1.   (See 1932, 150 § 4.)
SECT. 113A, provision (2) amended, 1933, 119 § 1; revised, 1933, 145 § 1; provision (2A) added, 1933, 145 § 2.   (See 1933, 145 § 3.)
SECT. 113D, first paragraph revised, 1933, 119 § 2; paragraph added at end, 1933, 119 § 3; fourth paragraph revised, 1933, 146 § 1; sixth paragraph revised, 1933, 146 § 2.   (See 1933, 119 § 6; 146 § 3.)
SECT. 114 amended, 1932, 180 § 34.
SECT. 116A amended, 1932, 180 § 35.
SECTS. 125, 126.   See 1933, 42.
SECT. 132, first paragraph revised, 1933, 101 § 1.
SECT. 140, third paragraph amended, 1933, 101 § 2.
SECT. 144, last paragraph revised, 1933, 101 § 3.
SECT. 151, clause Second amended, 1933, 107 § 1.
SECT. 155, clause First revised, 1932, 150 § 2.   (See 1932, 150 § 4.)
SECT. 156A amended, 1933, 30.
SECT. 160A added, 1933, 25 § 1 (prohibiting the printing or publication of certain advertisements for or on behalf of unlicensed insurance companies).
SECT. 185, second paragraph revised, 1932, 150 § 3.

Chapter 176. — Fraternal Benefit Societies.

For temporary act, relative to the support and regulation of the business of insurance companies during the present emergency, see 1933, 65.
SECT. 5 amended, 1933, 25 § 2.
SECT. 23 amended, 1932, 46.
SECT. 40, first two sentences amended, 1932, 180 § 36.

Sect. 45, second paragraph amended, 1932, 104.

Sect. 46B added, 1932, 47 § 1 (authorizing certain fraternal benefit societies to acquire, hold, manage and dispose of real property, and confirming title to such property heretofore acquired by certain of such societies).

Chapter 178. — Savings Bank Life Insurance.

For temporary act, relative to the support and regulation of the business of insurance companies during the present emergency, see 1933, 65.

Sect. 26 revised, 1932, 103.

Chapter 180. — Corporations for Charitable and Certain Other Purposes.

Sect. 10 amended, 1932, 180 § 37.

Sect. 26A added, 1933, 236 § 1 (requiring the filing of annual returns by certain incorporated clubs and other corporations). (See 1933, 236 § 2.)

Chapter 185. — The Land Court and Registration of Title to Land.

Sect. 25A added, 1933, 55 (relative to the power of the land court to enforce its orders and decrees, and relative to service of its processes).

Chapter 194. — Public Administrators.

Sect. 7 revised, 1933, 100.

Sect. 9, last sentence amended, 1932, 180 § 38; section affected, 1932, 180 § 45.

Chapter 195. — General Provisions relative to Executors and Administrators.

Sects. 1–4 repealed, 1933, 221 § 1. (See 1933, 221 § 8.)

Sect. 8 amended, 1933, 221 § 2. (See 1933, 221 § 8.)

Chapter 196. — Allowances to Widows and Children, and Advancements.

Sect. 2 amended, 1933, 36.

Chapter 197. — Payment of Debts, Legacies and Distributive Shares.

Sect. 2 amended, 1933, 221 § 3. (See 1933, 221 § 8.)

Sect. 9 amended, 1933, 221 § 4. (See 1933, 221 § 8.)

Chapter 202. — Sales, Mortgages and Leases of Real Estate by Executors, Administrators, Guardians and Conservators.

Sect. 4A added, 1933, 129 (relative to the use and management of real estate of a decedent by his executor or administrator for the purpose of the payment of debts from the rents thereof).

Sect. 20 revised, 1933, 221 § 5. (See 1933, 221 § 8.)

Chapter 203. — Trusts.

Sect. 17A added, 1932, 50 (relative to the sale of real estate by foreign testamentary trustees).

Chapter 204. — General Provisions relative to Sales, Mortgages, Releases, Compromises, etc., by Executors, etc.
SECT. 26 amended, 1933, 221 § 6.   (See 1933, 221 § 8.)

Chapter 207. — Marriage.
SECT. 20 amended, 1933, 127.
SECT. 38 revised, 1932, 162.

Chapter 208. — Divorce.
SECT. 19 revised, 1932, 3.
SECT. 38 revised, 1933, 288.

Chapter 209. — Husband and Wife.
SECT. 33 revised, 1933, 360.

Chapter 211. — The Supreme Judicial Court.
For provision for the publication and sale of advance sheets of the opinions and decisions of the supreme judicial court, see 1932, Res. 2.
SECT. 11 revised, 1933, 300 § 1.   (See 1933, 300 § 4.)

Chapter 212. — The Superior Court.
For act further extending to January 1st, 1936, the operation of certain provisions of law relative to the more prompt disposition of criminal cases in the superior court, see 1932, 157.
For act relative to sittings and sessions of the superior court, see 1932, 144.   (For prior temporary legislation, see 1927, 306; 1928, 228.)
SECT. 14 revised, 1932, 144 § 1.   (For prior temporary legislation, see 1927, 306; 1928, 228.)
SECT. 14A added, 1932, 144 § 2 (regulating the establishing of sessions and sittings of the superior court).   [For prior temporary legislation, see 1927, 306; 1928, 228.]
SECTS. 15–18 repealed, 1932, 144 § 3.
SECT. 25 amended, 1932, 144 § 4.

Chapter 213. — Provisions Common to the Supreme Judicial and Superior Courts.
SECT. 6 amended, 1932, 144 § 5.

Chapter 215. — Probate Courts.
SECT. 6 amended, 1933, 237 § 1.
SECT. 62, fifth paragraph revised, 1932, 107; paragraph in lines 56 and 57 revised, 1933, 274.

Chapter 218. — District Courts.
For act further extending to January 1st, 1936, the operation of certain provisions of law authorizing certain justices of district courts to sit in criminal cases in the superior court, see 1932, 157.
SECT. 1, first paragraph under caption "Franklin" revised, 1932, 87 § 1.

SECT. 10 amended, 1932, 160 § 1.
SECT. 29 amended, 1932, 55.
SECT. 62 amended,* 1932, 235 § 1; revised,* 1932, 247 § 1.
SECT. 76 amended, 1932, 269 § 1.

Chapter 220. — Courts and Naturalization.

SECTS. 16 and 17 repealed, 1932, 144 § 3.
SECT. 19 repealed, 1932, 16.

Chapter 221. — Clerks,. Attorneys and Other Officers of Judicial Courts.

SECT. 5 amended, 1932, 51.
SECT. 58 amended, 1932, 40 § 1.
SECT. 60 repealed, 1932, 40 § 2.
SECT. 94, first sentence amended, 1932, 180 § 39.

Chapter 228. — Survival of Actions and Death and Disabilities of Parties.

.SECT. 5 amended, 1933, 221 § 7.   (See 1933, 221 § 8.)

Chapter 231. — Pleading and Practice.

SECT. 63 amended, 1932, 84 § 1.
SECT. 69 amended, 1932, 177 § 1.   (See 1932, 177 § 2.)
SECT. 73 repealed, 1932, 180 § 40.
SECT. 78 repealed, 1932, 180 § 40.
SECT. 84A added, 1933, 247 § 1 (relative to the joint trial in the superior court of actions involving the same subject matter). (See 1933, 247 § 2.)
SECT. 108, second sentence of third paragraph revised, 1933, 255 § 1.   (See 1933, 255 § 2.)
SECT. 133 amended, 1933, 300 § 2.   (See 1933, 300 § 4.)
SECT. 140A added, 1932, 130 § 1 (relative to the effect of a settlement by agreement of an action of tort growing out of a motor vehicle accident upon the right of a defendant in such action to maintain a cross action).
SECT. 141 amended, 1932, 130 § 2; 1933, 300 § 3. (See 1933, 300 § 4.)

Chapter 233. — Witnesses and Evidence.

SECT. 3A added, 1933, 262 (authorizing the commissioner of banks to respond to summonses or subpoenas by an employee or other assistant in his department.)
SECT. 8 amended, 1933, 269 § 3; 376 § 3.
SECT. 22 amended, 1932, 97 § 1.
SECT. 26 amended, 1932, 71 § 1.
SECT. 29 amended, 1932, 71 § 2.   ·
SECT. 30 amended, 1932, 71 § 3.
SECT. 32 amended, 1932, 71 § 4.
SECT. 33 amended, 1932, 71 § 5.
SECT. 34 amended, 1932, 71 § 6.
SECT. 45 amended, 1932, 71 § 7.
SECT. 46 amended, 1932, 71 § 8.

* Void for non-acceptance.

SECT. 47 amended, 1932, 71 § 9.
SECT. 48 amended, 1932, 71 § 10.
SECT. 49 amended, 1932, 71 § 11.

Chapter 250. — Writs of Errors, Vacating Judgment, Writs of Review.
SECT. 16 amended, 1933, 244 § 1.   (See 1933, 244 § 2.)

Chapter 255. — Mortgages, Conditional Sales and Pledges of Personal Property, and Liens thereon.
SECT. 1.   See 1933, 142 (recording of federal crop loans to farmers)

Chapter 258. — Claims against the Commonwealth.
SECT. 3 revised, 1932, 180 § 41.

Chapter 260. — Limitation of Actions.
SECT. 4 amended, 1933, 318 § 5.   (See 1933, 318 § 9.)

Chapter 262. — Fees of Certain Officers.
SECT. 5 amended, 1933, 201.
SECT. 25 amended, 1933, 162.
SECT. 34 amended, 1933, 21.

Chapter 263. — Rights of Persons Accused of Crime.
SECT. 6 amended, 1933, 246 § 1.   (See 1933, 246 § 2.)

Chapter 264. — Crimes against Governments.
SECT. 5 revised, 1932, 298; amended, 1933, 153 § 3.
SECT. 10A revised, 1933, 276.

Chapter 265. — Crimes against the Person.
SECT. 25 revised, 1932, 211.

Chapter 266. — Crimes against Property.
SECT. 1 revised, 1932, 192 § 1.
SECT. 2 revised, 1932, 192 § 2.
SECTS. 3 and 4 repealed, 1932, 192 § 3.
SECT. 5 revised, 1932, 192 § 4.
SECT. 5A added, 1932, 192 § 5 (defining and providing penalties for attempts to commit arson).
SECT. 6 repealed, 1932, 192 § 3.
SECT. 8 revised, 1932, 192 § 6.
SECT. 10 revised, 1932, 192 § 7.
SECT. 54.   See 1933, 59 § 3.
SECT. 70 amended, 1933, 245 § 4.
SECTS. 75A and 75B added, 1932, 11 (penalizing the fraudulent operation of slot machines, coin-box telephones and other coin receptacles, and the manufacture and sale of devices intended to be used in such operation).

**Chapter 272. — Crimes against Chastity, Morality, Decency and Good
Order.**

Sect. 25 revised, 1933, 376 § 4.

Sect. 92A added, 1933, 117 (preventing advertisements tending to
discriminate against persons of any religious sect, creed, class, denomination or nationality by places of public accommodation, resort
or amusement).

Chapter 273. — Desertion, Non-Support and Illegitimacy.

Sect. 2 amended, 1933, 224.

Chapter 275. — Proceedings to prevent Crimes.

Sect. 15 repealed, 1932, 180 § 42.

**Chapter 276. — Search Warrants, Rewards, Fugitives from Justice, Arrest,
Examination, Commitment and Bail. Probation Officers and Commission on Probation.**

Sect. 37A added, 1932, 180 § 43 (relative to the assignment of
counsel to appear, on behalf of a person accused of a capital crime, at
his preliminary examination). [For prior legislation, see G. L. chapter
277 §§ 48, 49, repealed by 1932, 180 § 44.]

Sect. 98 amended, 1932, 145.

Chapter 277. — Indictments and Proceedings before Trial.

Sect. 2 amended, 1932, 144 § 6.

Sects. 48 and 49 repealed, 1932, 180 § 44.   (See G. L. chapter 276
§ 37A, inserted by 1932, 180 § 43.)

Chapter 278. — Trials and Proceedings before Judgment.

Sect. 33 amended, 1933, 265.

Chapter 279. — Judgment and Execution.

Sect. 9 amended, 1932, 221 § 2.

The Commonwealth of Massachusetts

OFFICE OF THE SECRETARY, BOSTON, December 15, 1933.

I certify that the acts and resolves contained in this volume are true copies of the originals on file in this department.

I further certify that the table of changes in general laws has been prepared, and is printed as an appendix to this edition of the laws, by direction of the Joint Committee on Rules of the General Court, in accordance with the provisions of General Laws, Tercentenary Edition, chapter 3, section 51.

FREDERIC W. COOK,
Secretary of the Commonwealth.

INDEX.

A.

B.

DEPARTMENTS, STATE:
    See Commonwealth, departments, boards, commissions, etc., of;
        also specific titles as follows:—
    Agriculture, Department of.
    Attorney General.
    Auditor, State.
    Banking and Insurance, Department of.
    Civil Service and Registration, Department of.
    Conservation, Department of.
    Corporations and Taxation, Department of.
    Correction, Department of.
    Education, Department of.
    Industrial Accidents, Department of.
    Labor and Industries, Department of.
    Mental Diseases, Department of.
    Metropolitan District Commission.
    Public Health, Department of.
    Public Safety, Department of.
    Public Utilities, Department of.
    Public Welfare, Department of.
    Public Works, Department of.
    Secretary, State.
    Treasurer, State.

F.

H.

J.

N.

O.

P.

910　INDEX.

Q.

T.

U.

V.

W.

*Under this title there are indexed the provisions of law relating to wines and malt beverages containing not more than 3.2 per cent of alcohol by weight. Of said provisions, sections 3 to 55, inclusive, of chapter 120 of the acts of 1933 and chapters 216, 234 and 346 of the acts of said year, referred to under this title, were repealed by section 7 of chapter 376 of the acts of said year. For superseding provisions of law relating to wines and malt beverages in general, see Alcoholic beverages.

Lightning Source UK Ltd.
Milton Keynes UK
UKHW022152171218
334172UK00011B/348/P